Annual Review of
Psychology

Annual Review of Psychology

Volume 64, 2013

Susan T. Fiske, *Editor*

Princeton University

Daniel L. Schacter, *Associate Editor*

Harvard University

Shelley E. Taylor, *Associate Editor*

University of California, Los Angeles

www.annualreviews.org • science@annualreviews.org • 650-493-4400

Annual Reviews

4139 El Camino Way • P.O. Box 10139 • Palo Alto, California 94303-0139

Annual Reviews
Palo Alto, California, USA

International Standard Serial Number: 0066-4308
International Standard Book Number: 978-0-8243-0264-1
Library of Congress Catalog Card Number: 50-13143

All Annual Reviews and publication titles are registered trademarks of Annual Reviews.

⊗ The paper used in this publication meets the minimum requirements of American National Standards for Information Sciences—Permanence of Paper for Printed Library Materials, ANSI Z39.48-1992.

Annual Reviews and the Editors of its publications assume no responsibility for the statements expressed by the contributors to this *Annual Review*.

TYPESET BY APTARA
PRINTED AND BOUND BY EDWARDS BROTHERS MALLOY, ANN ARBOR, MICHIGAN

Preface

The *Annual Review of Psychology* contains multitudes. Dating back more than 60 years to 1950, it contains scores of classic and cutting-edge reviews. But our topic here is the topics. In our master-plan outline of psychology, which guides our rotation of review topics, we have 24 major categories (and dozens of subcategories), ranging from biological bases of behavior, through cognitive processes, social psychology, education, health, research methods, to timely topics. This last is especially useful, as it allows the editorial committee to capitalize on breaking news that does not yet fit into our traditional outline.

Over the years, some areas have expanded beyond what one series can manage, so we are proud to share psychological science with our successful spin-offs. In 1978, the *Annual Review of Neuroscience* began to cover "molecular and cellular neuroscience, neurogenetics, development, plasticity and repair, systems neuroscience, cognitive neuroscience, behavior, and neurobiology of disease" (description from the webpage, http://www.annualreviews.org/journal/neuro). It rests securely among the top two impact factors in neuroscience journals.

Since 2005, the *Annual Review of Clinical Psychology* has applied psychological principles to recognized mental disorders, catapulting its impact factor to first-rank in clinical psychology (social science) and third-rank in overall psychology (science). It has become a critical resource for both scientists and practitioners who keep up with the science.

This year marks the inaugural editorial committee meeting to found the *Annual Review of Organizational Psychology and Organizational Behavior*, which aims to capture the "micro" management domain: human resource management and organizational behavior. It aims to integrate psychology and management, a much-needed role. Within a few years, we expect success equal to its predecessor Annual Review series.

As part of the psychology family, the *Annual Review of Psychology* impact factor still ranks first in overall psychology, within both science and social science. And it still contains multitudes.

Susan T. Fiske, Princeton, New Jersey

Daniel L. Schacter, Cambridge, Massachusetts

Shelley E. Taylor, Los Angeles, California

Annual Review of
Psychology

Volume 64, 2013

Contents

Indexes

Errata

An online log of corrections to *Annual Review of Psychology* articles may be found at
http://psych.AnnualReviews.org/errata.shtml

Related Articles

From the *Annual Review of Clinical Psychology*, Volume 9 (2013)

Worry and Generalized Anxiety Disorder: A Review and Synthesis of Research on Its Nature, Etiology, and Treatment
Michelle G. Newman, Sandra J. Llera, Thane M. Erickson, Amy Przeworski, and Louis Castonguay

From the *Annual Review of Law and Social Science*, Volume 8 (2012)

From the *Annual Review of Neuroscience*, Volume 35 (2012)

From the *Annual Review of Public Health*, Volume 33 (2012)

From the *Annual Review of Sociology*, Volume 38 (2012)

Shifting Gears: Seeking New Approaches for Mind/Brain Mechanisms

Michael S. Gazzaniga

The Sage Center, University of California, Santa Barbara, California 93106-9660;
email: m.gazzaniga@psych.ucsb.edu

Annu. Rev. Psychol. 2013. 64:1–20

First published online as a Review in Advance on
September 17, 2012

The *Annual Review of Psychology* is online at
psych.annualreviews.org

This article's doi:
10.1146/annurev-psych-113011-143817

Keywords

split brain, corpus callosum, modular, self-cueing, eye-hand
coordination, emotion, dynamical systems

Abstract

Using an autobiographical approach, I review several animal and human split-brain studies that have led me to change my long-term view
on how best to understand mind/brain interactions. Overall, the view
is consistent with the idea that complex neural systems, like other complex information processing systems, are highly modular. At the same
time, how the modules come to interact and produce unitary goals is
unknown. Here, I review the importance of self-cueing in that process
of producing unitary goals from disparate functions. The role of self-
cueing is demonstrably evident in the human neurologic patient and
especially in patients with hemispheric disconnection. When viewed in
the context of modularity, it may provide insights into how a highly
parallel and distributed brain locally coordinates its activities to produce an apparent unitary output. Capturing and understanding how this
is achieved will require shifting gears away from standard linear models
and adopting a more dynamical systems view of brain function.

Contents

INTRODUCTION

With all we know about memory and its failings, any kind of retrospective should be suspect. How many times have we called up past experiences that seem key to our lives, rolled them around, and then let current times tag them before putting them back to sleep? Over time, how can our memories possibly resemble the way things truly were?

There is something about the personalities we have known, however, that sticks and seems as true to us in the present as it was the day we formed our opinion about the stuff of certain people. Class reunions are a telling moment. Harry, 50 years later, is still an ass, while Bob is still cool. Even though we have not laid eyes on them since graduation night, the 50 intervening years have done nothing to change our views. On the other hand, and somewhat paradoxically, our ideas on how to understand mechanisms of nature do seem to change. These stubborn realities are fair warning about what follows. In short, my views on the flow of events and ideas that have captured my interests are undoubtedly influenced by all these intangibles.

When I began my intellectual journey of the past 50 years or so, the world and its challenges were to be understood in straightforward ways, with simple models of structure/function relationships being the dominant reality. In animal research, make a lesion, see what happens. Make another lesion, see what happens. In human research, study all patients who happen to have lesions in different places or study surgical patients who have particular kinds of disconnections. Or, in both animal and human physiology, eavesdrop on neurons and see if the neural code that directs behavior can be figured out.

The straightforward thrusts of youth in a scientific field that was itself young are telling and important. Yet what is more important to realize is that scientific progress, as it unfolds in spurts of insight arriving in a field of hard, mundane work, is commonly disorderly and mostly nonlinear. Stuff happens along the way. One influences others and at the same time is massively influenced by others. One of the beautiful things about science is that how one looks at a body of work after it is completed might well pose questions that are different from those that one originally imagined. While this shifting perspective is going on, the experiments conducted sit there, unmistakable and sure-footed. Their ultimate richness, or possible banality, fluctuates as surrounding knowledge and theory accrue to our human culture.

In my case, one overarching truth, which emerges from split-brain research as well as the study of neurological disorders and functional imaging studies, is that the human brain is not an all-purpose centralized computing device. Instead, it is organized in modular fashion, consisting of distributed, specialized circuits that have been sculpted by evolution and development to perform specific subfunctions while somehow preserving substantial plasticity (Gazzaniga 2011).

In the past, when experimental results were consistent with this perspective, it was enough to stop there. Clearly, however, such a formulation begs the question: How does a distributed mechanical process give rise to unitary, functional output? Over the years, many experiences and new hunches have made me realize that if any deeper understanding of mind-brain relationships is to come about, it would necessitate shifting to a more dynamical systems approach. My animal work, my work on patients, and my endless discussions with students, friends, and colleagues led me to this conclusion. My goal in this essay is to capture this journey of discovery and to illuminate how this view came to be.

THE EARLY YEARS

For me, it all started with a feeling—a feeling about the need to know "What's it all about?" I can trace it back to my teenage years and often thought it was promoted by being the fourth out of five children of Dante and Alice Gazzaniga. For many years, I was the youngest and was less differentiated than my older brothers and sister. It fell to me to keep the peace in a vigorous family. When my younger sister came along, my role changed as my older siblings shipped out to college and I was left behind to help raise Becky with my parents. Everybody loved Becky, so it was more like the three of us were competing to take care of her.

This is all to say that there are always plenty of social forces around us shaping and modifying our natural dispositions. My disposition was "contrarian." If somebody said this is the way things are, I was always thinking about the alternatives. In part, this also relates to my many inadequacies at advanced quantification, so I always tried to frame whatever issue was being discussed in more accessible terms. Sometimes it worked wonderfully; sometimes it was a total bust. So, quantitative skills do not come naturally to me. To the extent that I possess any, they were hard to acquire and were never "felt." When I was a graduate student at Caltech, and for some reason or another I had to learn how to derive the laws of thermodynamics, I did it totally by rote and got through it. After I was done, I can remember complaining to Seymour Benzer that I simply didn't get it, didn't feel the laws. Benzer said, "That's all right, most physicists don't either." Benzer was a very gentle man.

This is all presented in the spirit of full disclosure. I am not quantitative, period. And yet for 50 years I have enjoyed a rich intellectual life with scientists who are exceptionally gifted in mathematics. What's up with that? I once heard Duncan Luce say that statistics should not be taught to psychologists. He felt the newly trained students would come to think that statistics was the important part, not the question being examined. Often we hear specialists talk endlessly about the quantitative details of their research, whereas they are seemingly blasé about the net idea that comes out of all the work. This is the danger Luce was talking about, and I think we all see this happening far too frequently.

More fundamentally, the feeling of being interested in the question of what life is all about is a wonderful center for the mind. Whatever crazy, mindless activity one might be engaged in during the day, whether it be learning historical facts, a foreign language, or how to play football, coming home mentally each night to that question has been a wonderful tonic. One's mind really is an exclusive island that one can retreat to frequently, if not daily, where no one can bug you, and where one's own interpretations of the world are continually revised and updated.

Somehow all of this was working on me early in life and found me trotting off to Dartmouth College, where my older brilliant brother Alan was already a star football player and a man about town, soon to enter medical school. His tales of life in Hanover captivated me, and I dearly hoped I would get in. It all worked out, and from the moment I hit the Hanover plain I was in love with it all. The freshman beanie was placed on my head, and for a week I schlepped furniture up and down dorm steps for the upperclassmen. Somehow, it was exciting and refreshing.

Then I discovered Baker Library with its famous Tower Room. One could grab a book, sit in a carrel, and read away the afternoon. I discovered *Crime and Punishment* there and became mesmerized by my new life. To this day, I think of that experience with a fondness that

I am sure is disproportionate. Nonetheless, the world of ideas was upon me.

THE CALTECH YEARS
WITH ROGER SPERRY

It wasn't until my junior year that I began to hit my pace. I took a seminar from an experimental psychologist, William M. Smith, and soon found myself working in his laboratory. There is nothing like coming of age, discovering you cannot only read about science, you can also do science. Bill Smith started me on the lifelong process of learning how to do things—how to build gadgets to test ideas. He was a technologist and, in those days, that meant building contraptions. One of these contraptions held the head while other devices measured eye movements. Visual displays were constructed in such a way as to have specified delays in their signal. I suppose this version of "shop" broke the ice and set the stage for the thought that You Too Can Be a Scientist. I also noted that it was hard work.

I lived off campus rather than in my fraternity, a place that became the much-fabled Animal House. It was a zoo, and Saturday night was usually enough for me, so the off-campus arrangement was not only a necessity but also a relief. It was there that one night I found myself reading Roger Sperry's work on nerve growth. Nobody can read his work without being amazed and overwhelmed by its cleverness and power. Sperry was at Caltech in Pasadena, and my family lived in Glendale, only a few miles away. More importantly, my girlfriend lived in nearby San Marino. Bingo, I said to myself. I will work for him in the summer and that will also give me the chance to see my girlfriend. I wrote Sperry a letter, and to my utter amazement, he answered and invited me to have a summer NSF fellowship. Life was good.

The field I was about to enter was then called psychobiology. Trying to find a definition of this term is challenging, as it was made up to describe those interested in the biological underpinnings of behavior, perception, memory, consumption, and motivation.

In later years, it was recast as the biological study of mental processes. Sperry was one of its early practitioners. Indeed, he was the Hixon Professor of Psychobiology at Caltech.

Actually meeting Sperry in his Kerckhoff Hall office was the first of my many meetings with "the man." His scientific reputation was exceptional, and deservedly so. From neurodevelopment to animal psychobiology, he was the intellectual leader of his time. I wondered what was he going to be like. Would he quiz me about what I knew? Was he going to direct me to do something? Was he even going to be there? This neophyte was nervous. In fact, Sperry was a soft-spoken and sober guy who was not rattled by much. A few weeks before, a monkey had gotten loose from the animal room and hopped into his office and up on his desk. He looked up and said to his guest, "Maybe we should go next door. It might be quieter over there."

What I have learned over the years is that people have two realities—the everyday person and the "metro" person. Put differently, one is the personal self and the other the public self, which is constructed by the public for the public: It is your job, your reputation, the model the world builds about you. It is usually not you. The metro self idea explains why millions believed John Lennon never died. The metro self lived on in their heads and, of course, that was very alive.

What happens in life is that we can come to live to feed the metro self and to have the metro self tell us what to do as well. It is this thing that isn't the real you running your life, making demands on you and vice versa. Meanwhile, the real you is trying to see your friends, have a drink, and talk about whatever. In my life, 20 years of lunches with Leon Festinger demonstrated that someone who had a large metro self could also be exceptionally personal and not let the metro self intrude (Gazzaniga 2006). Actually, as I think about it, I know lots of people who pull this off.

At any rate, I came to my life in science with a disposition that was and remains insatiable. I did not arrive on the scene with deep theory or sophisticated knowledge. From the start, it

Figure 2

In this simple bedside test, a split-brain patient can easily carry out a spoken command to make a particular kind of gesture with the right hand. The left hand can subsequently make the same gesture as long as the eyes are open. However, if the examiner's first request is to make a particular gesture with the left hand, the patient fails to do so. See text for an explanation of the cueing involved.

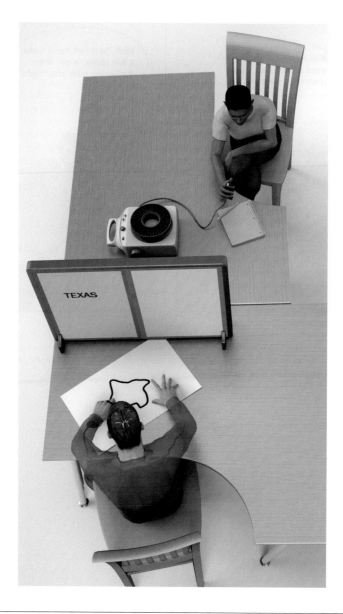

Figure 3

The word "Texas" is presented to a patient's left visual field, which solely projects to the right hemisphere. The left dominant speech hemisphere says it didn't see anything. Nonetheless, the left hand, which gets its major motor control from the right hemisphere, is able to draw a picture of Texas in any orientation. The patient explains, "I don't see the word, then I start drawing something and then it starts bringing what the word was. It's almost like the left hand was telling me what the word was when I am startin' to draw.... It's almost like I got this left side telling me what the word is after I put it in motion, which sounds stupid... 'cause I don't think I see it and then I start going here and something clicks and says what it was."

Figure 4

A split-up command is presented to a patient. He is simply told to draw what he sees. In this task he has to integrate "1928" solely projected to the right hemisphere with "car" solely presented to the left hemisphere. He fails in judging whether the two commands are the same, but using his left hand he is able to draw a car of the correct vintage.

Figure 5

Split-brain monkeys were examined to discover how one disconnected hemisphere could successfully guide the ipsilateral arm/hand toward a discrete object in space. The studies revealed that the seeing hemisphere first oriented the whole body toward the object, which cued the nonseeing hemisphere the X and Y coordinates of the object. Subsequently, the appropriate ipsilateral hand posture was formed only when the hand touched the object, thereby cueing the nonseeing hemisphere via touch information.

Figure 6

A special testing apparatus and cage were built to test for cross-cueing in the monkey. The animal viewed a visual discrimination task on a panel, and the entire area was illuminated in either red or green light. The animal viewed the task through a half-silvered mirror device that allowed another object to be presented intermittently, with the aim of determining whether such events would interfere with the animal's behavior.

Figure 7

In this test, a simple match to sample task was presented to each hemisphere (Gazzaniga & LeDoux 1978). The patient was asked to find the matching stimulus from a group of four pictures. After the patient responded, he was asked, "Why did you do that?" The discovery of the "interpreter" modules resulted from this kind of study.

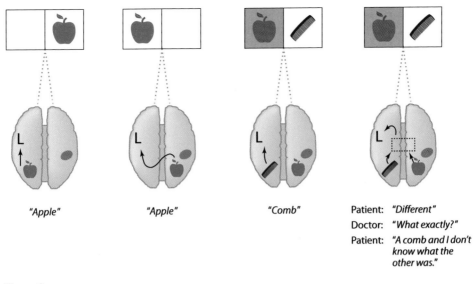

"Apple"   "Apple"   "Comb"   Patient: *"Different"*
                                                  Doctor: *"What exactly?"*
                                                  Patient: *"A comb and I don't
                                                  know what the
                                                  other was."*

Figure 8

This composite picture represents each of the experimental paradigms. The two pictures on the left describe the typical left and right single visual field naming trials. The two pictures on the right describe a typical response during the simultaneous bilateral visual field trials in the same/different paradigm.

was all about seeing a problem that appeared sensible to me and then starting the process of thinking on your feet, that is to say, trying to solve the problem in front of you. It is the act of solving problems in front of us that eventually leads to larger theories about the way things work. And nowhere does one have to think on his feet more than when studying split-brain patients.

I have always been amused by my colleagues who claim they knew Roger Sperry. I can say with a fair degree of confidence that nobody knew him like I knew him, both the good and the difficult. For five years I spent several hours per week in his office, one on one. We talked about everything—life, politics, science, gossip, you name it. On most of these occasions I would be reporting on the results of my road-trip testing sessions with split-brain patients or the special Saturday sessions we had at Caltech. After we were totally into the research, he would join me at the sessions. He always took copious notes of our exchanges and always asked probing and enlightening questions. It was the best time of my life.

UNCOVERING BRAIN MECHANISMS: THE ROLE OF SELF-CUEING

In studies of the neurologically disrupted patient, certain general principles emerge. For example, patients strive to complete a goal that has been set by the patient's examiner. One might think and hope they are solving a task one way when in fact they are solving it another. The challenge is to identify *the way* they are solving it. Once that identification is made, underlying mechanisms are revealed that are frequently surprising. Overall, investigations reveal one primary constant of evolved mechanisms that emanate from modular systems: self-cueing out in the periphery of the information processing system that automatically occurs outside of central design and control. Let me give an example from a simple bedside test.

Case D.R. is a split-brain patient from the Dartmouth series of cases. After her surgery,

she showed all the standard disconnection phenomena. Visual information did not transfer between the hemispheres, nor did tactile information. Her left hemisphere was dominant for language and speech while her right functioned at a lower cognitive level, being able to recognize pictures but unable to read.

We wanted to examine her motor control capacity. I asked her to hold out her two hands, fists closed; that was the starting position for each subsequent command. Next I asked her to make the hitchhiker gesture with her right hand. She did so instantly. I then asked her to do the same thing with her left hand. She also did that quickly. I asked her to make the A-ok gesture with her right hand. Again, she did so quickly, and when asked to do it with her left hand, she complied with no problem.

Here is where learning begins when testing neurologic patients. One has to make sure that the task a patient is trying to complete for you is being done the way you imagined it would be done. In this case I knew the patient had undergone split-brain surgery. I knew there was tremendous variation on how well a disconnected hemisphere could control the ipsilateral hand. There never was a problem in controlling the contralateral hand because both the sensory and motor systems needed for such activity were all together in the same hemisphere (Gazzaniga et al. 1967). But controlling the ipsilateral hand was a different story. How did the dominant left hemisphere get the motor messages to systems that control the left hand? After all, those systems were mainly managed by the disconnected right hemisphere.

The first patient I had studied at Caltech 30 years earlier was Case J.W. (**Figure 1**). He was remarkably unable to control an ipsilateral arm and hand while having little problem controlling the contralateral arm and hand from a particular hemisphere. This is quite a dramatic situation, and many of the original split-brain stories about two minds instead of one being in our skulls came from that clear behavior. But as more patients were added to the study pool, many began to show good control over the ipsilateral arm as well as the contralateral arm

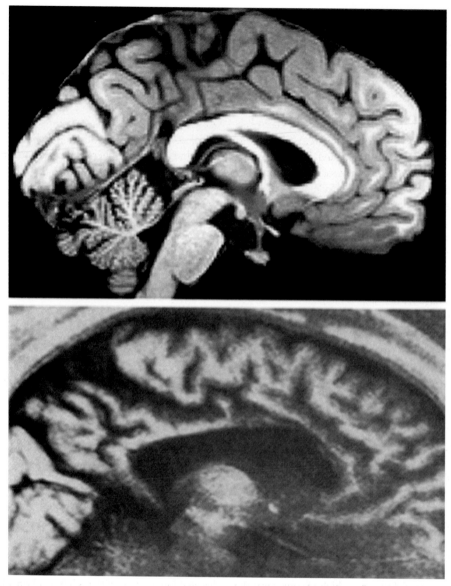

Figure 1

Magnetic resonance imaging of both a normal brain and a split-brain patient (J.W.). The normal brain clearly shows the intact corpus callosum, whereas the scan for a split-brain patient such as J.W. shows its complete absence. J.W. does show the intact anterior commissure, whereas in the first patient, W.J., it had been sectioned as well.

(Gazzaniga et al. 1962, 1967). Yet even when there was good control of the ipsilateral arm, good control over the ipsilateral hand seemed to elude the patients. How did all of this work?

I had intensively studied related issues in split-brain monkeys and determined the underlying mechanisms to explain this variation (Gazzaniga 1964). All of this was on my mind when Case D.R. was making her hand gestures with both hands. So, knowing that the patient had undergone split-brain surgery and that her dominant language hemisphere was disconnected from the motor systems of her right hemisphere, I was eager to learn how she was completing the task of controlling her ipsilateral hand so easily. What do you do? Armed with this knowledge, I changed the exam ever so slightly, and bingo, out came the answer.

Instead of asking D.R. to make a hitchhiker gesture first with her right hand, I asked her to make it first with her left hand. She couldn't do it. After she failed, I then asked her to make it with her right hand, which she did instantly. It was the same story with the A-ok sign. If the instruction was for the left hand to do it first, there was no ability to do so (**Figure 2**, see color insert).

Obviously what was going on was that when the right hand went first, it set up a model and an image for the right hemisphere to see and to copy, which it easily did when the left hemisphere's turn to respond came around. The patient had cross-cued the information from one hemisphere to the other outside of the callosal disconnection. If this were true, then what would happen if the patient was asked to do the task with her eyes closed? With bedside testing like this, that is easily done. The exam continued.

I asked the patient to close her eyes and to make a hitchhiker sign with her right hand, which she instantly carried out. Now with her eyes still closed, I asked her to make it with her left hand. Amazingly, she could not do it. The patient's right hemisphere could not understand the spoken command, and with her eyes closed she could not cue herself by looking at a model to copy, which of course was the right hand. As a consequence, the left hand sat there frozen with inaction.

This one simple bedside test reveals so much. It not only reveals the dramatic disconnection effects of the surgery but also a basic truth about living organisms. We are all about singular, unitary goals, about obtaining the desired behavior as framed in a command to action in the niche that is challenging us. We somehow achieve this unitary output from a highly modularized brain with multiple decision centers, not just one (Gazzaniga 1985, 2011). How does that all work?

In human patients, where neuronal pathways are disrupted, the goal is achieved through alternate mechanisms and strategies. In this instance, it was clear that the right hemisphere—the hemisphere that has major contralateral control over the left hand—could not follow a verbal command because it was disconnected from the left hemisphere. The explanation might have been, however, that the left hemisphere could have governed the ipsilateral left hand through ipsilateral corticospinal pathways that we know exist (Gazzaniga et al. 1967). Yet we know that that explanation could not be true because the verbal command could not be followed both when the eyes were closed and when the left hand was directed to respond before the right hand. What was going on?

Clearly the right hemisphere could execute the command only when it visually saw a model of the posture being requested. Thus it could follow a nonverbal command and get to the goal in question. The overall system with all of its separate modules had cued itself into completing the goal. This cueing is ubiquitous.

Examples of self-cueing come at almost every level of study: Cueing is how disconnected modules solve the puzzle of coordinating their separate skills to complete a goal. Another example comes from watching Case J.W. carry out a command given to his disconnected and silent right hemisphere (although it was able to read some words). I flashed the word "Texas" and asked him what he saw. The left speech hemisphere replied, "Nothing." When I then directed him to draw with his left hand what he had seen upside down, I was stunned to see that without hesitation he picked up a pen and drew an outline of the state of Texas, upside down! (**Figure 3**, see color insert).

On another test, J.W. was asked to draw with his left hand what he saw. In this test I flashed the word "car" to the left hemisphere and "1928" to the right hemisphere. In this fashion neither hemisphere knew what the other had seen. Could he possibly draw an old-fashioned car? J.W. was a model car enthusiast, and he knew a lot about cars of all kinds. Yet the hemisphere privy to the command "car" did not know what vintage. The hemisphere privy to vintage did not know whether it was a car or a truck or something else he was to draw. How could he possibly complete the task?

J.W. quickly picked up the pen once again and drew an old coupe (**Figure 4**, see color insert)! Somehow each hemisphere was contributing to the task, not by synthesizing and integrating the information in the brain, but rather by using the piece of paper. The integration of modular-specific information was being coordinated, perhaps not unlike two people dancing, where one takes the lead. It is true that each hemisphere could initiate and/or stop a movement. With each being able to watch the picture of the car unfold, as one side initiated a command to move the pen in one direction, the other could jump in and override the initial command with the command to stop the movement.

This striking result, which reveals the idea and importance of self-cueing and of independently controlled systems, found its origins in much earlier and unrelated work. During the original split-brain work at Caltech, I carried out an extensive program of subhuman primate research as well. Again, the overall puzzle was why animals that had their brains divided, sometimes far more extensively than ever disconnected in humans, always seemed like they were behaving in an integrated way when it came to carrying out goal-directed behavior. How, for example, was the left hemisphere of a rhesus monkey with a deeply split-brain—a hemisphere disconnection that extended down into the pons—able to control its ipsilateral left hand? We were so committed to the idea that all information came from a central command center, which had to directly connect to particular peripheral muscles, that what we observed at first made no sense to us. Dozens of studies finally revealed one major finding: The animals were engaged in self-cueing. One hemisphere was reading the cues set up by the other (Gazzaniga 1964). Here is how we discovered it worked.

We took high-speed films of split-brain monkeys reaching for objects such as grapes with one eye closed. In animals the optic chiasm was also divided, which means information presented to one eye went only to the ipsilateral hemisphere. So, if we occluded the right eye (and I did this by various means including a specially designed contact lens), only the left hemisphere could see. Then, when one eye was occluded, say the right eye, we filmed how well the two hands retrieved grapes presented to the animal at the end of a wand. With visual information now restricted to the left hemisphere, the right hand was quick and deliberate in retrieving the much-desired grapes. As the hand moved to grasp the grape, the posture of the hand properly formed in anticipation of retrieving the morsel of food.

At the same time, however, when the animal tried to use the left hand, a different strategy was evident (**Figure 5**, see color insert). Cueing was active at many levels. First, the monkey would orient the entire body toward the general direction of the object. The left, seeing hemisphere had control over gross body posture and orientation and could easily position the entire body in the correct orientation toward the desired point in space occupied by the grapes. As a consequence, the right hemisphere knew, in a general sort of way through proprioceptive feedback mechanisms, where the object was located. Then the left arm would reach out in the direction of the object. The left hemisphere can initiate arm movements and/or signal the right hemisphere to "go." As a result, the right hemisphere commanded the left hand to start off in the appropriate direction, which it knew because of the proprioceptive feedback (Gazzaniga 1966b, 1969). In short, the right hemisphere knew roughly where the object was on an X/Y grid, but it did not know the Z dimension. Here was the fascinating part: The left hand remained ill formed and nonanticipatory in getting ready to grasp the object. The right hemisphere couldn't actually see it, and the left could not control the distal digits of the left hand. As a result, the hand always looked ill posed for actually grasping the grape—until the magic happened. Eventually the hand bumped into the grape! At that moment, the somatosensory/motor system of the right hemisphere was cued, and it clicked in. The right hand snapped to, formed the correct posture, and grasped the grape, much as we do when we stick our hand into a dark drawer to pull something out—as soon as we feel it, we know how to grab it.

Back-and-forth cueing is going on at all levels and by systems more or less independent of one another. Yet somehow the system stumbles forward to complete the action. Although it now looks like dynamic feedback, in those days we called it cross-cueing, and in fact I did some other experiments related to this idea in the realm of emotions.

COGNITIVE AND EMOTIONAL CUEING

Emotions color our cognitive states almost moment to moment. Older, more subcortical parts of the brain are heavily involved in the management of emotions, and many of the structures have interhemispheric connections (Gazzaniga 1966a). Could emotions experienced by one hemisphere be detected by or have influence on the opposite hemisphere?

The first experiments were carried out using monkeys. In brief, monkeys were outfitted with goggles that were equipped with a green lens and a red lens, one color for each eye. Thus, if an animal was experiencing the world in a green-lit room, only one hemisphere could see—the eye and hemisphere viewing the world through a green lens. If a red light was on, only the opposite hemisphere could see, and the hemisphere with a green light saw nothing. In my experiments, the animals viewed a visual task through a specially designed chamber that contained a half-silvered mirror. If the monkey looked straight ahead and only the red light was on, one hemisphere saw a geometric visual discrimination task and the other hemisphere saw nothing. Since the viewing chamber was also equipped with a half-silvered mirror that was invisible, a separate visual image could be projected to the opposite hemisphere if a green light flashed on. We wanted to know what would happen to the work pattern of one hemisphere if the other were suddenly exposed to an emotionally laden stimulus, such as a snake. Would the emotionally provoked brain half dominate or subcortically influence the brain half that was engaged in the simple and emotionally neutral task of visual learning (**Figure 6**, see color insert)?

The answer was clear. The animals jumped back, and the hemisphere that had experienced the emotion cued the rest of the animal by its action. Something was wrong, the discrimination task ceased, and the animal was agitated: cross-system cueing once again.

Cross-cueing also was evident in the cognitive domain, and the work on our patients solidified the idea. Modular or separate systems, cueing each other in order to appear unified, purposeful, and integrated, seemed to be everywhere. As I note, we detected this early on in split-brain animal and human work at Caltech and saw it occur time and again when testing our patients over the next 40 years. We moved quickly from animal studies to human studies and then back to animal studies. In one of the first observations, I was in the process of seeing if simple colored lights could be named in both visual fields in patients who spoke only out of the left hemisphere. In the early days there was always concern regarding whether information of a low level could transfer over from the right hemisphere and be described by the left hemisphere.

During one such study, patient N.G. demonstrated our newly discovered strategy. The test was as follows: If a colored light (say red or green) came on in the right visual field, which projected to the left brain, there was no hesitation, and it was quickly named correctly. When a light came on in the left field, however, matters changed. If N.G. said "green," which meant that the left hemisphere had uttered "green" and it was "green," the patient said nothing else, and we got ready for the next trial. With that kind of overall response, either the stimulus had transferred or the right hemisphere was speaking. At this point we didn't know the answer.

The telltale trials were when the right hemisphere saw a particular color, for example, red, and the left hemisphere guessed the wrong color, for example, green. After a few flat-out mistakes, the patient learned a strategy to make it appear she could do such a task. As the left hemisphere would start to guess and say "gree," it would stop and then guess correctly by saying "red." What was happening was that the disconnected right hemisphere heard the "gree" being uttered by the left hemisphere and stopped the speech process, or it nodded the head, shrugged the shoulders, or gave some kind of cue to stop the speech emanating from the left brain. That then cued the left hemisphere to change its response and conclude that it must be the other color! The left hemisphere quickly then restated the answer and said the correct color. All of this happened in the blink of an eye.

Steven Hillyard, another person I came to know at Caltech, took an interest in split-brain patients early on, even as an undergraduate at Caltech. Hillyard is by far one of the best scientists I know. He lets the data do the talking and is a stickler for details. He and I were collaborating on a study years after we both had left Caltech and were trying to figure out the language capacity of a patient, L.B. We set up an easy test for the patient. All he had to do was to name numbers (1 to 9), which were flashed to either the left or the right visual field. Normally, we would expect right visual field stimuli to be correctly and quickly named. Thus if a "1" or a "4" or a "7" flashed up in random order, the patient's left speaking hemisphere would respond correctly. It did, and the reaction time for each stimulus was about the same.

What initially surprised us, however, was that the right hemisphere seemed to be naming all the numbers too. What was going on? Was this our first patient to show transfer of information between the hemispheres? Was this a right hemisphere that could speak? This possibility is always there and must always be checked out.

Hillyard plotted the reaction times for each response, and the strategy L.B. was using became apparent. All stimuli flashed to the left hemisphere, which is to say any number from 1 to 9, yielded the same reaction time. However, when the same list of numbers was presented to the right hemisphere randomly, 1 was reacted to more quickly than 2, which was reacted to more quickly than 3, which in turn was reacted to more quickly than 4, and so on all the way up to 9. Another cross-cueing strategy revealed! The left speaking hemisphere started counting using some somatic cueing systems such as a slight head bob, and when the number of bobs hit the number that was presented to the right hemisphere, the right hemisphere sent a stop signal, at which point the left knew that must be the number flashed. The left hemisphere said it, not the right (Gazzaniga & Hillyard 1971)! Unbelievable. When we then ran another series of trials where the patient had to respond immediately, the left hemisphere continued to respond correctly and quickly, whereas the score for the right hemisphere dropped to chance.

The constant shifting of strategies and mechanisms to carry out a goal reminds me of the story that Daniel Dennett often tells about great magicians. There are several ways to do every trick, each calling upon a different routine or technique. Ralph Hall was a master at this. Just when someone thought he had identified the way Hall did a particular trick, Hall would change the strategy, thereby dumbfounding his challenger, and carry on with his tricks. The brain does the same thing.

I am not at all sure how conscious I might have been about my continued interest in this sort of constant shifting of strategies of both animals and humans to complete goals no matter how one interrupted the normal mechanisms of neural function were. I was certainly well trained and versed in its many occurrences, which could explain why I continued to be drawn to related phenomena. After a short stint in Pisa, I found myself starting my second academic career at the University of California, Santa Barbara (UCSB) and became captivated and strongly influenced by David Premack. Up to that point, I really didn't know much about experimental psychology as a science and an approach to understanding the mind. As I relate below, the idea of cueing and different strategies came up again in a totally different context that was driven, in part, by what I learned from Premack.

THE INTERMEDIATE YEARS

My perspectives on mental mechanisms all changed as I spent most of my subsequent professional life surrounded by the top psychologists of our time: David Premack, Leon Festinger, and George Miller. It was a feast, each so utterly different in nature and style, yet all so incredibly close in intellect, drive, and savvy. You could not spend time with any of them without coming away the better. The one skill they all had was to let the other guy's mind wander (mine, for example) and then, after whatever was on your mind had been said, to go to work on showing it was either hilariously wrong or contained kernels of possible insight. Both experiences were enlightening, to say the least.

I have written about Festinger (Gazzaniga 2006) and Miller (Gazzaniga 1986) elsewhere, so I focus here on Premack, who started me down this trail of friendships. Sperry had always told me that it was psychologists who thought deeply about the mental, not biologists. Now I was seeing it firsthand.

It is difficult to think of a living psychologist more influential than David Premack. When we consider our origins, our history, and our uniqueness as humans, it is Premack who has been our best guide in the understanding of who we are. As I write this, I can tell you that he is still at it, and with more gusto than ever.

Before his pioneering work on the cognitive and the "possible" language capacities of the chimpanzee, Premack untangled the very simple but (at the time) incorrect picture of the nature of motivation. Behaviorists had developed the view that animals were motivated by external contingencies, failing to consider that animals might have internal states and preferences (Premack 1959). Premack turned the entire view of the nature of reinforcement on its ear by looking beyond what was easily

observable. Using the methods of science, he unearthed the underlying principles of what motivates living creatures to act.

He employed these skills in squaring off with chimps, in particular a chimp named Sarah who lived down the hall from me for years when our time overlapped at UCSB. I don't care for chimps. I have always found them too aggressive and bestial, and quite frankly, I would walk in the other direction when Sarah approached with her trainer or with David.

Sarah was no ordinary chimp. She was exceptionally smart and engaging. She was also volatile. Premack perfectly managed her by being even more unpredictable and clever than she had ever seen a human be. This was one *homo sapiens* that always beat her at her own game. Premack established a social relationship with her and then began to use it to explore exactly what was, and was not, in and on Sarah's mind. At that time, Premack was beginning to clarify the intellectual limits of our closest living relative, and in doing so, he began to unearth the factors that make humans unique.

In time I left for New York University and began to study neurologic patients with disorders such as global aphasia. Along with my graduate student, Andrea Velletri-Glass, I began to wonder if a severely disabled human, who evidenced no language or communicative skill, could learn the protolanguage system in which Premack had successfully trained Sarah (Velletri-Glass et al. 1973). With air travel, phone calls, faxes, and later email and the Internet, we began a collaboration with David. We intensely studied several patients and discovered that patients with focal left hemisphere lesions were rendered severely aphasic but could, nonetheless, learn the protolanguage to varying degrees. In other words, their spared right hemisphere could communicate at the level of a clever chimpanzee, but not much more.

Premack's work did not go unnoticed by the University of Pennsylvania. Before we knew it, David and his wife Ann were on a plane with Sarah, headed to Honey Brook, Pennsylvania, where a chimp facility had been specially built in Amish country. It was there, with Sarah and a small group of young chimps, that Premack gave birth to the idea of "theory of mind" (Premack & Woodruff 1978). We may have a theory about a chimp, about our dog, about an old sweater, but does a chimp have a theory about us? Does the chimp have a theory about other chimps? Does it have some primitive understanding of the mental states of others? As in all breakthroughs, the ingenious way that a question is asked makes the impact. This is another Premack specialty. Premack has the rare ability to turn an issue on its ear, and the idea of whether an animal could have a theory about humans (or anything else) did exactly that. He changed our perspective and opened up a wealth of ideas in the psychological community about our nature and our origins.

The Amish chimp facility was cleverly designed, allowing for a wide range of tests and observations. A torrent of research soon originated, serving as the basis for the landmark book *The Mind of an Ape* (Premack & Premack 1983). One startling observation Premack made was that chimps do not engage in pedagogy. The flip side of the observation is that humans are the only primates that teach their young.

Although a great deal of Premack's work was rooted in what animals could or could not do, it became obvious to him that babies and infants were a great source of information about our psychological nature. When do babies understand sociality? When do they understand that some social acts are positive and others negative, and do they recognize the preconditions for morality? How could that be tested? Does social intelligence develop as the result of experience? Or is it there from infancy? Premack and his constant companion in every aspect of life, his wife, Ann, pursued these questions and developed a psychology of the affect and emotion of the newborn. Of course, others had studied infants, but these questions were tested in a novel way, which is captured in their book, *Original Intelligence: Unlocking the Mystery of Who We Are* (Premack & Premack 2003). David Premack is an example of this truth: We don't all have to be smart—just a few can make a difference. His ideas and research are singular.

We are all influenced by others, and these influences pop out in many ways. While I was spending a lot of time stewing about cueing, I obviously was also listening. In what later became known as the Premack Principle, he showed that what served as a reinforcer was reversible and could be predicted by the preference structure of an animal. Thus, a rat deprived of running would drink water, if that gave it the opportunity to run. Conversely, if a rat was deprived of water, it would run in order to have the opportunity to drink. This was a powerful idea and it stuck with me. When I moved to New York University, Premack gave me one of his unique testing systems to take along to investigate an idea I had. Would an adipsic rat (a rat that will not drink as the result of a lateral hypothalamic lesion) drink if given the opportunity to run? If the answer was yes, it would urge a more dynamic view of brain function and caution against the ever-growing tendency to see static models relating structure to function. In fact, we learned adipsic rats gladly drank if that was what they had to do in order to run (Gazzaniga et al. 1974).

There it was again—a different strategy allowed a dynamical system, the brain, to accomplish a goal. In this case, the observer was creating new contingencies that evoked the different strategy, but this investigation also revealed it was a dangerous proposal to say that one had discovered any particular brain network underlying the motivation to drink water. It was a striking finding and, I might add, largely ignored!

Once I was hooked on the idea, I tried all kinds of experiments to further the demonstration that these are inherently dynamical systems. In one wild experiment, I tested monkeys who had undergone inferior temporal lobe lesions that rendered them unable to learn visual discriminations for a food reward. I wondered if they would learn the new discriminations if they were given the opportunity to run in a large monkey wheel I had specially built for them. What I discovered was that monkeys hate to run in a wheel. Instead, they would engage the game of visual learning in order to lock the wheel so it wouldn't move (Gazzaniga 1978)! Capitalizing on that preference, I saw some evidence of learning. Same point, different species.

THE INTERPRETER

It struck me a few years back that it took 25 years for us to ask the right question in one of the perceptual/cognitive settings of our patient testing program. In the early phase of split-brain testing, we were constantly testing to see if visual information of any kind was cross-communicated from one hemisphere to the other. We were also looking into possible extinction phenomena such that the failure to report left field stimuli in split-brain patients might be related to that well-known clinical symptomatology. Accordingly, after flashing information to either visual field or to both simultaneously, we would ask split-brain patients, "What did you see?" The patients would dutifully respond and describe information that was solely projected to their right visual field. No surprise, and all was copacetic.

Finally, Joseph LeDoux and I stumbled across the right question to ask. First we changed how we asked the patients to respond. We gave each hand a multiple-choice option. The left hand was free to choose one of four pictures that best matched the left visual field stimulus. The right hand was free to choose one of another four options to match stimuli presented in the right visual field. With the task set up in this fashion, we could change our question. Instead of asking what the patient had seen, we would let each hand respond and then ask, "Why did you do that?"

The disconnection story, with its huge effects evident even at the bedside, was well known and established. We were not ready for the huge insight this slight manipulation of the standard test would yield. We felt we were simply fishing around to discover why each patient seemed so utterly normal in everyday life, so integrated. Each patient managed his life with singular purpose, drove to work in some instances, raised children, and enjoyed the this-and-that's of everyday life. We couldn't

figure out why their disconnected state wasn't more disruptive. The answer came one day in a snowy trailer park in Burlington, Vermont, when we tested patient P.S.

P.S. was one of the first patients from the Dartmouth series of cases that we studied in detail. We had a chance to work him up both pre- and postoperatively, first in Hanover and then at his home, after surgery. He was a major case, as he was one of the first patients in the East Coast series to show all of the lateralized phenomena we had demonstrated to exist in the Caltech series. Speech and language were lateralized to his left hemisphere, and visual-motor skills, such as being able to draw three-dimensional objects, were possible only from his right hemisphere. In many ways he was an exciting confirmation of all the earlier work, and he had been operated on by a different surgeon.

One could have stopped there and declared success. Each side of the brain could work on its own problem without getting confused with the other problem. It could organize the correct response and carry it out. In short, there was no blanking out by one hemisphere when the other was working. But as I just reviewed, we would have missed the boat if we had stopped there. One of us had the good sense to ask P.S. the question, "Why did you do that—why did you point to those pictures?"

It was his answer, which we knew came from his left brain, that gave rise to the concept of the interpreter. There appears to be a special module in the left hemisphere that makes up an explanation for why all the modules do what they do. It is the mechanism for generating our narratives; it is the thing that keeps a storyline going in all of us and that tries to make sense out of the many independent functions we have going on at any one time. In this instance, Case P.S. had seen a chicken claw with his left brain, and his right hand chose a picture of a chicken. His right brain had seen a picture of a snow scene, and his left hand picked up a picture of a shovel. When asked why he had done all of this, he said from his left hemisphere, "The chicken claw goes with the chicken, and you need a shovel to clean out the chicken shed" (**Figure 7**, see color insert).

There it was. It took 25 years to ask the right question, and in doing so, perhaps the most important finding from all of split-brain research was revealed. One of our seemingly infinite modules generates the storyline as to why we do the things we do, feel the things we feel, and see the patterns in our behavior that contribute to our theory about ourselves. Once you see it at work in this simple experiment, you see it everywhere. The responses from discrete modules pour out of all of us, and evolution invented a module to make it all seem like it pours forth from a "self."

My students and I have seen this time and again over the past 25 years, and each of us has our favorite examples. In digging through old videotapes of our experiments, I came across one. Case J.W. was flashed the word "smile" to the right hemisphere and the word "face" to the left hemisphere. He was simply asked to draw what he sees. His right hand drew a smiling face. "Why did you do that?" I asked. He said, "What do you want, a sad face? Who wants a sad face around?"

In a very recent test on Case V.P., my colleague Michael Miller was examining the unlikely proposition that the hemispheres of the brain may manage different dimensions of moral decisions. Prior brain imaging work on neurologically normal subjects suggested that the right temporal-parietal junction was involved in tracking the beliefs of others while the left hemisphere managed one's own beliefs (Saxe & Kanwisher 2003). This would suggest that someone with a lesion in the right hemisphere temporal-parietal junction might not consider the beliefs of others when making a moral decision and thereby would be more prone to utilitarian beliefs, beliefs that had meaning only for one's self. There is such evidence. It also would predict that a split-brain patient, when talking about his choices on tests that probe such moral values, might be more utilitarian in his outlook than would normal controls. After all, and because of their callosal disconnection, the area of the brain managing the beliefs of others was now disconnected from the part of the brain considering a moral dilemma from the perspective of the personal self (Miller et al. 2010). Incredibly, that is exactly what was found. But Miller and his colleagues didn't stop there. They asked the patients why their answers reflected a lack of concern for the other person's well-being. Each time one could hear the interpreter jump in and spin the story.

In one example, J.W. was read a scenario in which a waitress intended harm toward a customer by serving him some sesame seeds, believing the customer was highly allergic to them. As it turned out, the customer was not allergic to the sesame seeds, and he was fine. However, when J.W. was asked whether the waitress's action was permissible or forbidden, J.W. responded on the basis of the outcome and not the belief, i.e., he said it was permissible. Moments later, though, as if that didn't seem right to his verbal left hemisphere, he spontaneously offered that "sesame seeds are tiny little things, they don't hurt nobody" (Miller et al. 2010). This rationalization offered by J.W.'s left hemisphere seemed to defend his immediate response, which was based solely on the outcome.

THE GIFFORD LECTURES AND MOVING FORWARD

Psychologists all feel the tug—an insatiable desire—to carry on the quest to know more about the situation in which we humans find ourselves. Thinking about these things is what the Lord Gifford lecture series in Scotland is all about, and I was invited to give Gifford lectures in 2009. Though submitting my own perspective in that forum was as scary as it was heady, it did give me the opportunity to step back and look at the flow of my own life and to examine how my thinking on mind/brain issues has evolved. It also focused me on what I would like to do moving forward. In a word, it was a time to abandon the car-mechanic view of mechanism that most of us possess and move on to thinking about dynamical systems.

The fields of psychology and neuroscience have been dead set on an overall model of how things work. In a phrase, we want a beginning, middle, and end. Things start at A, progress to B, with an outcome of C. In psychological terms, things start with sensation and perception, progress to associative mechanisms, and then to motor systems. In neuroscience, information arrives in sensory centers, becomes integrated into a percept, and then is fed to various associative cortices and finally to a motor neuron system for execution and movement. The model, by its utter reasonableness, is ingrained in us as to how things must work and how anyone must approach understanding anything. A beginning, a middle, and an end.

Beginning five or more years ago, a stirring among many scientists began to pick up in speed. In the study of action, in particular, an idea that has held up until relatively recently is that cortical motor neurons direct a lower motor system in some way to carry out a task. On top of the commanding neurons is the "will" to make those commands: One is free to decide what to do. This idea has given way to a much more dynamic model of action in which the entire system is running 24/7, with its purpose to do something: to act. It is full of Bayesian priors and internal complexity, and its ultimate goal is achieved by integrating the sensory information available to it. It is automatic, just like another machine, and it is relentless. Alas, there is no more beginning/middle/end model of the world.

Leibniz saw this years ago with his mill analogy. In his 1714 *La Monadologie*, he asked his readers to imagine an enlarged view of the workings of a mill so that all the individual parts could be seen such that one could walk between them. All you find are mechanical components that push against each other, and there is little if any trace of the function of the mill as a whole (Bassett & Gazzaniga 2011). When this analogy is applied to the modern problem of mind/brain research, one realizes that the physical parts of the brain are decomposable, but the mental parts are indivisible. They are realized at another level of organization, where the parts

interact to produce another coarse-grained system or layer. There is limited value in studying the parts alone. There is a deep need to capture how the elements interact in the whole schema of a functioning system (Doyle & Csete 2011). It is like trying to grab hold of mercury. It is a much harder problem than the one most of us were raised on, but it must be recognized that it is the problem.

During the past 50 years, of course, huge advances have been made throughout biology, neuroscience, and cognitive science. Scientists are beginning to consider whether there is what one could call a universal architecture for information-processing systems of any kind, studied at any level. One of the catchall phrases that runs through this kind of thinking is that all information systems are highly "modular." In neuroscience, this has specific meaning, with more locality and local circuits being discovered all over the brain. It is as if as the brain became more engaged with the environment and acquired more adaptations, it needed more local command centers with low-energy and short connections to handle the routine responses to the increasing needs of a more adaptive system. That, I think, is a fairly well-established truth.

At a totally different level, large corporations adopt a modular model. Coca Cola, for example, has some 300 bottling plants around the world. Because it becomes unwieldy to command such a diverse set of operations from a central source, in this case, from corporate headquarters in Atlanta, local control and operation are used.

The need for modularity in cognitive models is well known, and it is now commonplace to recognize this overall structure. From my perspective, this sort of framework makes total sense. The entire corpus of split-brain work is full of observations revealing the modularity of brain organization. The various lateralized specializations of the left and right hemispheres started everyone thinking about the overall issue. This view of the overall brain architecture was consistent with studies at every level of examination, from visual-motor control, to perceptual skills, and up to language skills and social moral adjustments. The underpinnings of our mental life were happening throughout the workings of a vastly parallel and distributed system.

One of the most dramatic demonstrations of brain modularity comes from our studies of Case P.S., who began to be able to speak out of the right hemisphere as well as the left hemisphere. This ability increased over time but started out simply enough. We always ran simple naming tasks, tests where each visual field was probed with pictures and words. Normally, a split-brain patient names the right visual field stimuli with speed and accuracy. The left visual field stimuli go unnamed because they were solely projected to the right hemisphere. Starting a year or two after surgery, P.S. began to name visual stimuli in both fields (Gazzaniga et al. 1979). We determined it was not visual transfer by showing that he could not say whether two objects that were presented, one to each visual field, were the same or different. Somehow the right hemisphere was now speaking.

In a sense we were not confronted with two systems, each housing untold numbers of modules, but rather we were simply looking at two super modules, each trying to say what is on its mind in a coordinated and sequenced way, sort of like an old couple who have been living together far too long.

In a free-form conversation with Case P.S., it would be virtually impossible to detect at least two large modular systems interacting to produce a coherent, articulate story line that seemed utterly normal in every regard. But as we discovered, that dazzling unitary speech behavior is the product of discrete modules that are massively self-cued to appear coherent despite being of isolated and rather independent modules. An understanding of this situation would provide insight into how the entire system might work. Experiments were needed.

A second patient, Case V.P., began to speak from the right hemisphere as well. We began to focus on this development and started our explorations by asking V.P. to say compound words that were quickly flashed and presented visually across the visual midline. My favorite example is when we presented the word breakfast across the midline such that "break" appeared in the left visual field and "fast" was presented to the right visual field. This meant, of course, that the right hemisphere saw the word "break," and since it didn't know whether another word fragment was projected at the same time, started to say "bre" as in "brake." Almost instantly, V.P. stopped saying it that way and corrected herself, saying "breck" because her left hemisphere (which has to finish the word) knows its fragment is "fast" and thus knows the first phonemes must sound like "breck' instead of "brake." Independent modular systems were cueing the other, so the desired goal was achieved. It is sort of a brain version of a "don't ask, don't tell" policy. Everything remains independent but it all cooperates toward a final goal.

Needless to say, a highly modular view of the brain begs more than one question. Why is it that we feel so much psychological unity in our everyday lives? Why do we feel so strongly that a unified self calls the shots, experiences life in particular ways, and is indeed us? We all have a narrative about ourselves, yet we are learning increasingly more about how utterly distributed the processing systems are throughout our brain and that they work rather independently. How can all of this come together?

The radical truth to emerge from split-brain research, the study of neurological disorders, and functional imaging studies is that the human brain is not an all-purpose, centralized computing device but rather is organized in a modular fashion, consisting of distributed, specialized circuits that have been sculpted by evolution and development to perform specific subfunctions while preserving substantial plasticity (Gazzaniga 1985, 2011). The question is how a distributed mechanical process gives rise to unitary, functional output. A debate in cognitive science has been whether a dynamical system or traditional computational framework is more appropriate for describing this process. Within the complex systems community, it is recognized that these two perspectives are not at odds. What is needed is a compelling computational description of how unitary output can arise from noisy, fast dynamics in many-body systems, and what role competition, operating at multiple spatial and temporal scales, comes to play in this process (Bassett & Gazzaniga 2011, Gazzaniga et al. 2009).

My scientific goal over the coming years is to try to provide an empirically grounded account of how functional states of mind arise from the collective mechanical states of the brain. It is one of the most intriguing problems solved by nervous systems—how cells coordinate their behavior using multiple spatial and temporal scales to generate adaptive behavior. This goal needs all the help it can get.

INTERACTING MODULES: THE VAST UNCONSCIOUS

Characterizing our overall architecture as being modular in nature, and further that the modules interact in purposeful ways outside our conscious awareness, is almost a truism. Any reflection on how our brain accomplishes all the things we consciously enjoy makes it clear that the heavy lifting for our human mental life goes on automatically and beyond conscious control and can even involve our somatic system (Valero-Cuevas et al. 2007). This reality, nonetheless, needs experimental support and revelation. Split-brain research has had more than its share of studies that manifest this truth.

In the contemporary experimental psychology literature, a number of studies have focused on how subliminal stimuli can facilitate or inhibit subsequent perceptual or semantic judgments, although, in general, the results of such efforts have been limited to small changes in response latencies. In contrast, in the neurologic patient, the impact of nonconscious processes on behavior can be much more striking. For example, it has been widely reported that patients with lesions of the visual cortex are able to direct their eyes or point to visual stimuli that they deny having "seen." Additional findings in the neurologic literature include the ability of amnesic patients to

acquire motor and problem-solving skills with little or no recollection of the training session, and the capacity of patients with parietal lobe lesions to use visual information in an "extinguished" hemifield for cognitive judgments (Volpe et al. 1979) (**Figure 8**, see color insert).

Probably the most direct evidence of nonconscious processing comes from the human split-brain literature. In previous split-brain studies, it has been shown that behaviors can be elicited from a mute right hemisphere in spite of the fact that they originate outside of the conscious awareness of the dominant left hemisphere. Moreover, in patients with partial posterior callosal section, information presented to the right hemisphere can be transmitted through remaining anterior fibers in a fragmented form. Ultimately, the unstimulated left hemisphere can infer what was presented to the right hemisphere (Sidtis et al. 1981).

In one dramatic study on Case J.W., we showed that nonconscious processes can control overt behavior by demonstrating that information presented to the right hemisphere can influence a left hemisphere–specific response, even though the left hemisphere is completely unaware that it possesses the information for the correct response (Gazzaniga et al. 1987). In this experiment, either the number 1 or 2 was flashed to the left or right visual field. Case J.W. was required to name it or write it out. He was able to correctly name the numbers in either visual field. Through several control experiments, it became evident that J.W. had not developed right hemisphere speech. Nonetheless, somehow the right hemisphere was communicating which of the two options to report from the left hemisphere. What was so striking, however, is that even though the left hemisphere was calling upon this information for its correct verbal and written response, it could not use the information in making a simple, conscious, match-to-sample judgment. Modules were interacting and working at one level, but they were using mechanisms not accessible by conscious processes.

It should be noted that it was not clear how the information presented to the right hemisphere was transmitted to the left hemisphere. Simple cross-cueing strategies seen in our other tests did not appear to be active in J.W. If cross-cueing, which had been traditionally viewed as a conscious process, were active, the left hemisphere would be aware of the nature of the information and would be able to respond in the between-hemisphere comparison tasks.

It remains possible that a new kind of cross-cueing strategy was active, one that worked totally outside the realm of conscious awareness. Overall, given the pattern of the results, it would appear that the transfer of information was neural in nature. Consistent with this view were the findings of other studies done with J.W., where it was shown that early responses in the visual evoked potential were different for the 1 as opposed to the 2 when flashed in the left visual field but not the right. That finding suggests visual information was being encoded in a different way and that information was transmitted to the left hemisphere. Also, given the callosal disconnection, it would appear that the information was communicated via subcortical structures, although the possible role of the intact anterior commissure cannot be ruled out. It seems that the nature of the communicated information is noncognitive and establishes some kind of simple response readiness in the left brain for one of two possible responses already known to the left hemisphere.

Taken together, observations like the foregoing reveal that the modules that make up our conscious thought interact and process information commonly and automatically. Although psychologists are committed to the chore of ascertaining what we take to be the cognitive variables in decision making and the like, the successful interaction of peripheral modules may well be where the larger problem lies in identifying how mind/brain layers interact.

A FINAL WORD

Early in my life, I did start with some mighty lofty questions, like what are these beliefs we humans carry around by the bucketful, and how are they formed? Beliefs are what make human life special and worth living. Each of us has them, and each of us sees many of them turn into values. We kill each other, rescue each other, love each other, and hate each other because of beliefs.

We know a lot about beliefs. We can get outside of them and learn how they are formed and indeed some of the brain parts that construct them. We also know how our brains are built and organized, with each brain possessing thousands if not millions of discrete processing centers, commonly referred to as modules or instincts. Most of these modules work outside of our conscious awareness, and most of them secrete their influence on us by biasing our responses to our daily challenges. As Mark Twain said, "Any emotion, if it is sincere, is involuntary."

As those churning, unconscious systems react to our experiences, making us feel one way or another about something, they produce powerful mental experiences. One of our other brain modules, the interpreter module, notes the cacophony of reactions of all of the modules and constructs theories and beliefs as to why we act and feel the way we do. It is this system that gives each of us our own personal narrative—our story.

Many people are resistant to this model of human existence. Although no one has a problem with the idea that things like clocks work automatically and human cells work automatically, people do not like the idea that the brain works automatically. If that were true, it sort of suggests that we would be forced to believe we are simply along for the ride—that the real work for mental life is being done automatically by the brain. Where are we in that framework? There seems to be no room for the phenomenal self and the entity in charge of our actions.

That is the wrong way to think about it. We are what we do, what we experience, what we learn. We humans build stories and theories about it all, and we live within those stories, those interpretations of all of these constantly impinging experiences. That is what we are and that it is how it works. Full stop.

So, we humans are built in certain ways and indeed have certain moral rules that are there in newborn babies and aging adults. What is different about us is that we all cook up different beliefs about why we respond the way we do. Our variation comes from that interpreter giving each person his own spin and story—because each of us draws on different experiences.

Many times the stories of others seem preposterous. It can be their religious story, their political story, or their philosophy of life. They can annoy and irritate and leave one trembling with the sense of superiority, the sense that the other person is uninformed while one alone has it right. Yet, as the great physicist Max Born said, "The belief that there is only one truth, and that oneself is in possession of it, is the root of all evil in the world." Take a step back when you feel this way. Think about it a minute and appreciate that after all everything is a story—yours as well as the other guy's.

This overall view of life and mind didn't just appear from life. It was derived, at least to a large extent, by my professional work, by trying to understand mind/brain relationships. It comes from seeing how a very special group of human beings, the wonderful patients I have studied for 50 years, have revealed great secrets about how the brain does construct our mental lives, and by knowing those secrets, what it means for us all. There are, of course, always differing interpretations of studies in the area of brain and mind. That reality reminds me of the story about two members of a rabbi's congregation coming to him to resolve two conflicting statements, and after each finishes with his version, the rabbi says, "That's true." They then ask, "But Rabbi, if I what I say is true and what he says is true, how can they both be true?" And the rabbi says, "That is true too." What is so exciting about science, of course, is that science is always both true and valid for all. The interpretation we give a datum can be dead wrong, but the underlying observations, if done properly, are rock solid. I know that one of the beauties of split-brain research is that the underlying observations are rock solid.

DISCLOSURE STATEMENT

The author is not aware of any affiliations, memberships, funding, or financial holdings that might be perceived as affecting the objectivity of this review.

ACKNOWLEDGMENTS

A lifetime of being surrounding by great and talented people, from family to colleagues to third-party reviewers, has made my career a joy to experience. In the end, my wife Charlotte and my six children kept the engine running. For this effort, special thanks to Danielle Bassett, Steve Hillyard, Rebecca Gazzaniga, Gary Lewis, Michael B. Miller, David Premack, and many more. Supported by the Sage Center and by the Institute for Collaborative Biotechnologies through contract no. W911NF-09-D-0001 from the U.S. Army Research Office.

LITERATURE CITED

Bassett DH, Gazzaniga MS. 2011. Understanding complexity in the human brain. *Trends Cogn. Sci.* 15(5):200–9

Doyle JC, Csete ME. 2011. Architecture, constraints, and behavior. *Proc. Natl. Acad. Sci. USA* 108(Suppl. 3)15624–30

Gazzaniga MS. 1964. Cerebral mechanisms involved in ipsilateral eye-hand use in split-brain monkeys. *Exp. Neurol.* 10:148–55

Gazzaniga MS. 1966a. Interhemispheric cueing systems remaining after section of neocortical commissures in monkeys. *Exp. Neurol.* 16:28–35

Gazzaniga MS. 1966b. Visuomotor integration in split-brain monkeys with other cerebral lesions. *Exp. Neurol.* 16:289–98

Gazzaniga MS. 1969. Cross-cueing mechanisms and ipsilateral eye-hand control in split-brain monkeys. *Exp. Neurol.* 23:11–17

Gazzaniga MS. 1974. Determinants of cerebral recovery. In *Plasticity and Recovery of Function in the Central Nervous System*, ed. DG Stein, JJ Rosen, N Butters, pp. 203–15. New York: Academic

Gazzaniga MS. 1978. Is seeing believing: notes on clinical recovery. In *Recovery from Brain Damage: Research and Theory*, ed. S Finger, pp. 409–14. New York: Plenum

Gazzaniga MS. 1985. *The Social Brain.* New York: Basic Books

Gazzaniga MS. 1986. George Miller and the birth of cognitive neuroscience. In *Mind and Brain: Dialogues in Cognitive Neuroscience*, ed. JE LeDoux, W Hirst. New York: Cambridge Univ. Press

Gazzaniga MS. 2006. Lunch with Leon. *Perspect. Psychol. Sci.* 1(1):88–94

Gazzaniga MS. 2011. *Who's in Charge? Free Will and the Science of the Brain.* New York: HarperCollins

Gazzaniga MS, Bogen JE, Sperry RW. 1962. Some functional effects of sectioning the cerebral commissures in man. *Proc. Natl. Acad. Sci. USA* 48:1765–69

Gazzaniga MS, Bogen JE, Sperry RW. 1967. Dyspraxia following division of the cerebral commissures. *Arch. Neurol.* 16:606–12

Gazzaniga MS, Doron KW, Funk CM. 2009. Looking toward the future: perspectives on examining the architecture and function of the human brain as a complex system. In *The Cognitive Neurosciences*, ed. MS Gazzaniga, pp. 1247–54. Cambridge, MA: MIT Press. 4th ed.

Gazzaniga MS, Hillyard SA. 1971. Language and speech capacity of the right hemisphere. *Neuropsychologia* 9:273–80

Gazzaniga MS, Holtzman JD, Smylie CS. 1987. Speech without conscious awareness. *Neurology* 37:682–85

Gazzaniga MS, LeDoux JE. 1978. *The Integrated Mind.* New York: Plenum

Gazzaniga MS, LeDoux JE, Smylie CS, Volpe BT. 1979. Plasticity in speech organization following commissurotomy. *Brain* 102:805–15

Gazzaniga MS, Szer IS, Crane AM. 1974. Modification of drinking behavior in the adipsic rat. *Exp. Neurol.* 42:483–89

Miller MB, Sinnott-Armstrong WA, Young L, King D, Paggi A, et al. 2010. Abnormal moral reasoning in complete and partial callosotomy patients. *Neuropsychologia* 48(7):2215–20

Premack D. 1959. Toward empirical behavior laws: I. Positive reinforcement. *Psychol. Rev.* 66:219–33

Premack DG, Premack AJ. 1983. *The Mind of an Ape.* New York: Norton

Premack DG, Premack AJ. 2003. *Original Intelligence: Unlocking the Mystery of Who We Are.* New York: McGraw-Hill

Premack DG, Woodruff G. 1978. Does the chimpanzee have a theory of mind? *Behav. Brain Sci.* 1:515–26

Saxe R, Kanwisher N. 2003. People thinking about thinking people: the role of the temporo-parietal junction in "theory of mind." *NeuroImage* 19:1835–42

Sidtis JJ, Volpe BT, Holtzman JD, Wilson DH, Gazzaniga MS. 1981. Cognitive interaction after staged callosal section: evidence for a transfer of semantic activation. *Science* 212:344–46

Valero-Cuevas FJ, Yi JW, Brown D, McNamara RV 3rd, Paul C, Lipson H. 2007. The tendon network of the fingers performs anatomical computation at a macroscopic scale. *IEEE Trans. Biomed. Eng.* 54:1161–66

Velletri Glass A, Gazzaniga MS, Premack D. 1973. Artificial language training in global aphasics. *Neuropsychologia* 11:95–103

Volpe BT, LeDoux JE, Gazzaniga MS. 1979. Information processing of visual stimuli in an extinguished field. *Nature* 282:722–24

The Endocannabinoid System and the Brain

Raphael Mechoulam[1] and Linda A. Parker[2]

[1]Institute for Drug Research, Hebrew University, Medical Faculty, Jerusalem 91120, Israel; email: mechou@cc.huji.ac.il

[2]Department of Psychology and Collaborative Neuroscience Program, University of Guelph, Guelph, Ontario N1G 2W1, Canada; email: parkerl@uoguelph.ca

Annu. Rev. Psychol. 2013. 64:21–47

First published online as a Review in Advance on July 12, 2012

The *Annual Review of Psychology* is online at psych.annualreviews.org

This article's doi: 10.1146/annurev-psych-113011-143739

Keywords

Δ^9-tetrahydrocannabinol (THC), anandamide, anxiety, 2-arachidonoyl glycerol (2-AG), cannabidiol, cannabinoid receptors, cognition, depression, memory, neurogenesis, reward

Abstract

The psychoactive constituent in cannabis, Δ^9-tetrahydrocannabinol (THC), was isolated in the mid-1960s, but the cannabinoid receptors, CB1 and CB2, and the major endogenous cannabinoids (anandamide and 2-arachidonoyl glycerol) were identified only 20 to 25 years later. The cannabinoid system affects both central nervous system (CNS) and peripheral processes. In this review, we have tried to summarize research—with an emphasis on recent publications—on the actions of the endocannabinoid system on anxiety, depression, neurogenesis, reward, cognition, learning, and memory. The effects are at times biphasic—lower doses causing effects opposite to those seen at high doses. Recently, numerous endocannabinoid-like compounds have been identified in the brain. Only a few have been investigated for their CNS activity, and future investigations on their action may throw light on a wide spectrum of brain functions.

Contents

INTRODUCTION: CANNABIS AND THE BRAIN

Cannabis Use Over Millennia: A Bird's-Eye View

The Assyrians (about second millennium BC to sixth century BC) used cannabis for its psychoactive, mind-altering effects as well as for its medical properties. It was named either *ganzi-gun-nu* ("the drug that takes away the mind") or *azzalu*, which was apparently a drug for "depression of spirits," for a female ailment (possibly amenorrhea), or even for annulment of witchcraft (Campbell Thomson 1949). The importance of cannabis intoxication seems to have been central in early Zoroastrian shamanic ecstasy (Mechoulam 1986). Its wide use in the Middle East has continued ever since. Indeed, it was a central theme in Arab poetry of the Middle Ages (Rosenthal 1971). In China and India it was known for the dual nature of its effects. In the Chinese classic medical pharmacopeia Ben Ts'ao, originally compiled around the first century AD, cannabis was recommended for numerous maladies, "but when taken in excess it could cause seeing devils" (Mechoulam 1986, p. 9).

In Europe, cannabis was introduced by the Napoleonic soldiers returning from Egypt and by British physicians returning from India. Industrial hemp, which contains negligible amounts of psychoactive material, was of course grown previously, but the psychoactive variety was unknown. The psychological effects caused by cannabis preparations—presumably North African hashish—became known in Europe mostly through the writings of members of the Parisian *Le Club des Hachichins* in the mid-nineteenth century, particularly Baudelaire, Gautier, and Moreau (Mechoulam 1986). Baudelaire, a major literary figure at the time, emphasized the "groundless gaiety" and "the distortion of sounds and colours" following cannabis use. Moreau, a psychiatrist, in his 1845 book, *Hashish and Mental Illness* (Moreau 1973), described in detail numerous psychological phenomenon noted in experimental subjects: feeling of happiness, excitement and dissociation of ideas, errors of time and space, enhancement of the sense of hearing, delusions, fluctuations of emotions, irresistible impulses, and illusions and hallucinations. This diversity of actions—some of them opposite to each other—has confounded cannabis research ever since. Indeed, Moreau reported that some of his volunteers experienced "…occurrences of delirium or of actual madness". He concluded, "There is not a single, elementary manifestation of mental illness that cannot be found in the mental changes caused by hashish…" (Moreau 1973, p. 18). But today few marijuana users will reach a state of "delirium or of actual madness." In most cases, they will report an increase in relaxation and euphoria and possibly enhancement of their senses, but an impairment of memory. These striking differences are probably due to the well-known biphasic activity of Δ^9-tetrahydrocannabinol (THC)—the psychoactive constituent—whose effects at low doses may be opposite to those produced by high doses. Moreau's volunteers presumably orally consumed large amounts of hashish, whereas today North Americans and Europeans usually smoke cannabis, and most users adjust their dose to achieve the desired effects.

Surprisingly, research on cannabis advanced slowly. A major reason for the neglect was the lack of knowledge of its basic chemistry. Modern research—namely research over the past 150 years—is based on quantitative data. Unlike morphine and cocaine, which had been isolated and made available in the nineteenth century and thus could be quantitatively investigated in vitro, in animals, and in humans, the psychoactive constituent(s) of cannabis were not isolated and their structures were not elucidated until the 1960s; hence quantitative research was not possible before then.

It is conceivable that the material reaching Europe in the past varied widely in its contents; thus its medical use also was not reliable, and research with it was of little value. Indeed, around the beginning of the twentieth century cannabis almost disappeared, both as a medicinal agent and for recreational purposes in Europe and in North America. In addition, the anti-cannabis laws made research on it, particularly in academic institutions, very difficult. Indeed, from the early 1940s until the mid-1960s, research on cannabis was limited to a few scattered groups. This paucity of early research has now been more than compensated for by the avalanche of papers on the plant cannabinoids and on the endogenous cannabinoids. Not surprisingly, the burst of recreational marijuana use, in the mid-1960s in the United States and later in Europe, coincided with the new wave of research on cannabis.

Δ^9-Tetrahydrocannabinol and Cannabidiol

Over nearly a century, numerous attempts were made to isolate in pure form the active marijuana constituent(s) and to elucidate its (or their) structure(s), but these attempts were unsuccessful (Mechoulam & Hanus 2000). Now we can understand the reason for this lack of success. There are more than 60 cannabis constituents, with closely related structures and physical properties, making their separation difficult. With the advance of modern separation techniques, the isolation and the structure elucidation of the active principle, THC, was finally achieved in 1964 (Gaoni & Mechoulam 1964). Shortly thereafter, THC was synthesized (Mechoulam et al. 1967). Thus, THC became widely available for research, and several thousand papers have been published on it. Surprisingly, although most of the plant cannabinoids have now been identified—and their structures are related chemically—the only major mood-altering constituent is THC.

Another major plant cannabinoid is cannabidiol (CBD), which was isolated during the late 1930s, but its structure was elucidated only in 1963 (Mechoulam & Shvo 1963). As it does not parallel THC in its central nervous system (CNS) effects, initially only a limited amount of research was focused on it. However, over the past two decades CBD was found to be a potent anti-inflammatory agent, to attenuate the memory-impairing effects produced by THC, and to cause a plethora of other effects. Hundreds of publications have addressed its various actions (for a review, see Mechoulam et al. 2009). Both THC and CBD are present in the plant mainly as their nonpsychoactive carboxylic precursors (THC-acid and CBD-acid), which slowly lose their acidic function (decarboxylate) in the

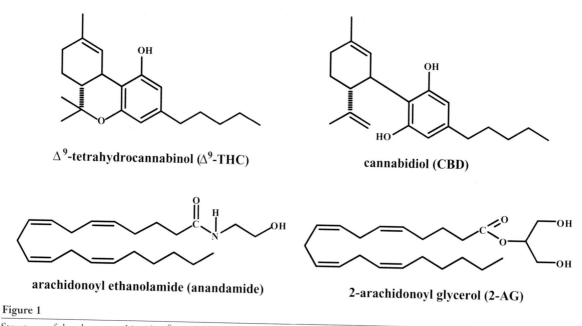

Δ^9-tetrahydrocannabinol (Δ^9-THC)

cannabidiol (CBD)

arachidonoyl ethanolamide (anandamide)

2-arachidonoyl glycerol (2-AG)

Figure 1

Structures of the plant cannabinoids Δ^9-tetrahydrocannabinol and cannabidiol and of the endogenous cannabinoids anandamide and 2-arachidonoyl glycerol.

plant on heating. The structures of THC and CBD are presented in **Figure 1**.

The cannabis plant varieties differ tremendously in their contents. In industrial hemp the concentration of THC is less than 0.3%, in hashish in the 1960s it was about 5%, whereas in marijuana it was about 2% to 3%, but nowadays strains have been developed—mostly for illegal use—that contain up to 25%.

The Endocannabinoid Receptors

Originally it was assumed that cannabinoids act through a nonspecific membrane-associated mechanism; however, the very high stereospecificity of the action of some synthetic cannabinoids pointed to a more specific mechanism (Mechoulam et al. 1988). The first data indicating that cannabinoids may act through receptors were published by Howlett, who showed that cannabinoids inhibit adenylate cyclase formation, and the potency of the cannabinoids examined paralleled the level of their pharmacological action (Howlett et al. 1986). The same group shortly thereafter indeed

reported the existence of binding sites in the brain (Devane et al. 1988). Their distribution was found to be consistent with the pharmacological properties of psychotropic cannabinoids (Herkenham et al. 1990), and the receptor was cloned (Matsuda et al. 1990). A second, peripheral receptor, CB2, was later identified in the spleen (Munro et al. 1993). Both CB1 and CB2 receptors belong to the superfamily of G protein–coupled receptors (GPCRs). The two cannabinoid receptors exhibit 48% amino acid sequence identity. Both receptor types are coupled through G proteins to adenylyl cyclase and mitogen-activated protein kinase (for a detailed review on the pharmacology of cannabinoids, see Howlett et al. 2002).

The CB1 Receptor

It was originally believed that the CB1 receptor was expressed mainly in the CNS, and hence it was considered a brain cannabinoid receptor. We are now aware that it is present in numerous peripheral organs, although in some of them the receptor levels are low. CB1 receptors are among the most abundant GPCRs in the brain. The highest densities of CB1 receptors, in the rodent brain, are noted in the basal ganglia, substantia nigra, globus pallidus, cerebellum, and hippocampus, but not in the brainstem. The high CB1 levels in the sensory and motor regions are consistent with the important role of CB1 receptors in motivation and cognition. CB1 receptors appear to be involved in γ-aminobutyric acid (GABA) and glutamate neurotransmission, as they are found on GABAergic and glutamatergic neurons (Howlett et al. 2002). The CB1 receptor is present and active from the earliest phases of ontogenetic development, including during the embryonal stages, which indicates that it is of importance in neuronal development and newborn suckling (Fride et al. 2009). Surprisingly the CB1 receptor levels in rats are increased on transition from adolescence [postnatal days (PND) 35–37] to adulthood (PND 70–72), a pattern that is opposite to that of other neuroreceptor systems (Verdurand et al. 2012). Also, unexpectedly, ligands that interact similarly with CB1 receptors may have significantly different pharmacological profiles. This may be due to the ability of CB1 receptors to form heteromeric complexes with other GPCRs (Pertwee et al. 2010).

The distribution of CB1 receptors differs in neonatal brain and adult brain. It is abundant in white matter areas at the early age but is much less abundant later (Romero et al. 1997). It is of interest to determine whether this difference has anything to do with the behavioral landmarks associated with different ages.

The CB1 receptors are found primarily on central and peripheral neurons in the presynapse. These locations facilitate their inhibition of neurotransmitter release, which is one of the major functions of the endocannabinoid system. Activation of CB1 receptors leads to a decrease in cyclic adenosine monophosphate (cAMP) accumulation and hence to inhibition of cAMP-dependent protein kinase (PKA). CB1 receptor activation leads to stimulation of mitogen-activated protein (MAP) kinase activity, which is a mechanism by which cannabinoids affect synaptic plasticity, cell migration, and possibly neuronal growth (Howlett et al. 2002). CB1 receptors are also coupled, again through G proteins, to several types of calcium and potassium channels.

Several types of CB1 receptor gene knockout mice are available and are widely used (Zimmer et al. 1999). CB1 receptor gene polymorphisms have been observed, and their importance is yet unknown, although susceptibility to addiction and neuropsychiatric conditions has been suggested (Zhang et al. 2004).

The CB2 Receptor

It was originally assumed that CB2 receptors were present only in cells of the immune system; however, they have now been identified throughout the CNS (Ashton et al. 2006, Onaivi et al. 2008a, van Sickle et al. 2005), particularly in microglial cells (Nunez et al. 2004, Stella 2004), though at lower levels than those of the CB1 receptors. Under some pathological conditions, CB2 receptor expression is enhanced in the CNS as well as in other tissues. It seems possible that the CB2 receptor is part of a general protective system (for a review, see Pacher & Mechoulam 2011). In that review, we speculated that "The mammalian body has a highly developed immune system which guards against continuous invading protein attacks and aims at preventing, attenuating or repairing the inflicted damage. It is conceivable that through evolution analogous biological protective systems have evolved against nonprotein attacks. There is emerging evidence that lipid endocannabinoid signaling through CB2 receptors may represent an example/part of such a protective system" (Pacher & Mechoulam 2011, p. 194). In view of the various protective effects associated with the CB2 receptor, several synthetic CB2-specific receptor agonists, which do not bind to the CB1 receptor, have been synthesized. HU-308 was one of the first such compounds reported (Hanus et al. 1999); however, numerous additional ones are now known, and since they do not cause the psychoactive effects associated with CB1 agonists, several pharmaceutical firms are presently active in the field.

CB2 receptor agonists might be expected to become drugs in various fields, including neuropsychiatric, cardiovascular, and liver disease.

Endogenous Cannabinoid Agonists

The discovery of the cannabinoid receptors suggested that endogenous molecules, which may stimulate (or inhibit) the receptors, are presumably present in the mammalian body. The plant constituent THC, which, apparently by a quirk of nature, binds to these receptors, is a lipid compound; hence it was assumed that any possible endogenous cannabinoid molecules (endocannabinoids) would also be lipids. Indeed, we were able to isolate and identify two compounds, one from brain—which we named anandamide, based on the Sanskrit word *ananda* ("supreme joy")—and a second one [2-arachidonoyl glycerol (2-AG)] from peripheral tissues (Devane et al. 1992, Mechoulam et al. 1995). Their structures are presented in **Figure 1**. These two endogenous cannabinoids have been investigated in great detail (for a review, see Howlett et al. 2002). Additional endogenous molecules that bind to the cannabinoid receptors have been identified, but some of them may be artifacts, and interest in them is negligible.

Unlike most neurotransmitters (e.g., acetylcholine, dopamine, and serotonin), anandamide and 2-AG are not stored in vesicles but rather are synthesized when and where they are needed. Again, unlike most neurotransmitters, their action is not postsynaptic but rather mostly presynaptic, i.e., they serve as fast retrograde synaptic messengers (Howlett et al. 2002). However, whether both endocannabinoids, or only 2-AG, serve as fast retrograde synaptic messengers remains to be established. Thus 2-AG, after its postsynaptic synthesis, crosses the synapse and activates the cannabinoid presynaptic receptor, which makes possible the inhibition of various neurotransmitter systems that are present there. This is a primary activity of the endocannabinoids.

Contrary to THC, which is metabolized over several hours and excreted (or stored as one of its metabolites), endocannabinoids are rapidly removed by a membrane transport process yet to be fully characterized (Fu et al. 2011). In the cell, anandamide is hydrolyzed to arachidonic acid and ethanolamine by fatty acid amide hydrolase (FAAH). 2-AG is also hydrolyzed enzymatically, both by FAAH and by monoacyl hydrolases. Suppression of these enzymes prolongs the activity of the endocannabinoids (Gaetani et al. 2009).

Although there is solid evidence that the activation of presynaptic CB1 receptors can lead to inhibition of the release of a number of different excitatory or inhibitory neurotransmitters both in the brain and in the peripheral nervous system, there is also in vivo evidence that CB1 receptor agonists can stimulate dopamine (DA) release in the nucleus accumbens (Gardner 2005). This effect apparently stems from a cannabinoid receptor-mediated inhibition of glutamate release. Indeed, many of the actions of cannabinoid receptor agonists (including endocannabinoids) are dose-dependently biphasic (Sulcova et al. 1998). Endocannabinoids also exhibit an "entourage effect"—namely enhancement of their activity by structurally related, biologically inactive, endogenous constituents (Ben-Shabat et al. 1988). The multiple functions of endocannabinoid signaling in the brain have recently been very well reviewed (Katona & Freund 2012).

In the following review of the effects of brain endocannabinoids and related fatty acid amides of amino acids (FAAAs) and closely related compounds on emotions and cognition, we summarize the large number of published observations. It seems that many of the FAAAs in the CNS that have been investigated—and most have not been investigated yet—have significant effects. If we assume that the dozens of compounds of this type present in the brain are not biosynthesized by mistake but rather play some physiological role, it is tempting to speculate that their levels and their interactions may be of importance in the profile of emotions and possibly of individual personalities. This topic is further discussed in the Conclusions section of this review.

THE CANNABINOID SYSTEM IN ANXIETY AND DEPRESSION

Freud considered the problem of anxiety a "nodal point, linking up all kinds of most important questions; a riddle, of which the solution must cast a flood of light upon our whole mental life" (Freud 1920). We have made some progress since Freud's time, but according to the National Institute of Mental Health, anxiety disorders still affect about 40 million people in the United States alone, and antianxiety drugs are among the top prescription drugs.

Cannabis has been used for millennia as a medicinal agent (Mechoulam 1986). In India, bangue (the local name for cannabis at the time) was believed to help the user to be "delivered from all worries and care" (Da Orta 1563), and its extensive present-day use throughout the world is presumably due, in part at least, to the same effects. For recent reviews on cannabis and anxiety, see Gaetani et al. (2009), Moreira & Wotjak (2010), Parolaro et al. (2010), and Zanettini et al. (2012). For general reviews on the endocannabinoid system, including detailed data on anxiety and depression and emerging pharmacotherapy, see Pacher et al. (2006) and Pertwee (2009).

A few years ago the major pharmaceutical firm Sanofi-Aventis developed and initiated marketing for an antagonist (or more precisely an inverse agonist) of the CB1 receptor. Because CB1 agonists enhance appetite, such a drug could become a major weapon against obesity. Many other companies had related compounds in various stages of development. The Sanofi compound, named rimonabant, indeed affected obesity and even blocked the psychoactive effects of THC, including short-term memory and lowered cocaine-seeking responses to suitable cues (in animals). However, although psychiatric disorders were indicated as exclusion criteria, rimonabant-treated patients had enhanced anxiety problems and suicidal tendencies (Christensen et al. 2007), and the drug had to be withdrawn from the market. This rather expensive proof is a further addition to previous evidence, indicating the importance of the CB1 cannabinoid system in anxiety. Interestingly, Lazary et al. (2011) have recently suggested that as some variants of the CB1 receptor gene contribute more significantly than others to the development of anxiety and depression, by genomic screening—possibly in combination with the gene of the serotonin transporter—high-risk individuals could be identified and excluded from the treatment population and thus CB1 antagonists could still be useful. Such screening and treatment would represent a model for modern personalized medicine.

As mentioned previously, many of the psychological effects of cannabis, as well as of THC, are biphasic, depending principally on the dose level and to a certain extent upon the personality of the user. In normal subjects, THC may cause either euphoria and relaxation or dysphoria and anxiety (D'Souza et al. 2004, Wade et al. 2003). Pure THC may not entirely mimic the effects of cannabis, which contains additional cannabinoid constituents, such as CBD, that modulate the effect of THC. Besides, CB1 receptors rapidly desensitize following the administration of agonists, further diminishing the effect of agonists.

Cannabidiol, which does not bind to either CB1 or CB2, possesses anxiolytic and antipsychotic properties (Mechoulam et al. 2002) both in animals and in humans. It shows anxiolytic-like effects with mice in the elevated plus maze and in the Vogel conflict test (Guimarães et al. 1990, Moreira et al. 2006). In humans it was found to lower anxiety in stressful situations (Bergamaschi et al. 2011). The mode of action of CBD as an anxiolytic molecule is not well understood. Most probably it involves action as a serotonin receptor 1A (5-HT$_{1A}$) agonist (Campos & Guimaraes 2008), enhancement of adenosine signaling through inhibition of uptake (Carrier et al. 2006), or inhibition of the GPR55 receptor (Sharir & Abood 2010).

Endocannabinoids and Anxiety

There are no direct experimental data on the role of endocannabinoids on anxiety in humans. To our knowledge neither anandamide nor 2-AG has ever been administered to human subjects. This is an absurd situation, presumably a result of regulatory limitations. By contrast, when insulin was discovered in the 1920s, it became an available drug within a year. We can only assume that, because many of the physiological systems are regulated through checks and balances by a variety of endogenous molecules, the endocannabinoids, which affect neurotransmitter release, apparently exert such an action on anxiety, which is a normal human reaction to a variety of stressful conditions.

Considerable data exist on the direct effects of endocannabinoids on anxiety in animals. Rubino et al. (2008) have shown that methanandamide (a stable analog of anandamide) injected into the prefrontal cortex of rats leads to an anxiolytic response. However, large increases of the dose administered led to an anxiogenic response due to TRPV1 stimulation.

An indirect pathway for enhancement of endocannabinoid levels is by blocking their enzymatic hydrolysis. The Piomelli group (Kathuria et al. 2003) reported a novel class of potent, selective, and systemically active carbamate-based inhibitors of FAAH, the enzyme responsible for the degradation of anandamide. The best inhibitors in this series (URB532 and URB597) had anxiolytic properties in rats in the elevated zero-maze test and suppressed isolation-induced vocalizations due to augmented brain levels of anandamide. These effects could be prevented by blockage of the CB1 receptor. These results indirectly confirmed that anandamide has antianxiety properties. The rationale behind this approach is based on the mechanism of anandamide formation and release, which is known to take place when and where needed. As mentioned above, contrary to the classical neurotransmitters, anandamide is not stored in synaptic vesicles but rather is synthesized and released in the synaptic cleft following neuronal activation. Presumably its levels and those of FAAH in anxiety and depression will be highest in the brain areas involved in the regulation of mood and emotions. Therefore, inhibition of anandamide

metabolism would enhance CB1 activation mainly where anandamide levels are highest. Following the same experimental rationale, Moise et al. (2008) confirmed that URB597 inhibited FAAH activity and led to elevated levels of additional fatty acid amides (N-palmitoyl ethanolamine and N-oleoyl ethanolamine), but not of anandamide itself, in hamster brain. However, Cippitelli et al. (2008) have reported an elevation of anandamide levels in rats with URB597, which was found to reduce anxiety associated with alcohol withdrawal. Blockade of the CB1 receptor with rimonabant induced anxiogenic-like behavior in the elevated plus maze; URB597 induced anxiolytic-like effects in this assay. URB597 did not alter unconditioned or conditioned social defeat or rotarod performance.

Enhancement of 2-AG levels produces similar effects. Sciolino et al. (2011) have shown that enhancement of endocannabinoid signaling with JZL184, an inhibitor of the 2-AG-hydrolyzing enzyme monoacylglycerol lipase (MGL), produces anxiolytic effects under conditions of high environmental aversiveness in rats.

Recently, two parallel publications indicated that the CB2 receptor is also involved in endogenous antianxiolytic activity. García-Gutiérrez & Manzanares (2011) reported that mice overexpressing the CB2 receptor showed lower anxiety-like behaviors in the open field, the light-dark box, and the elevated plus maze tests, indicating that increased expression of the CB2 receptor significantly modifies the response to stress in these tests. Busquets-Garcia et al. (2011), using doses of URB597 and JZL184 that selectively modulated the concentrations of anandamide and 2-AG, respectively, recorded similar anxiolytic-like effects in two behavioral paradigms. However, whereas the anxiolytic-like effects of URB597 were mediated through a CB1-dependent mechanism, the anxiolytic-like effects of JZL184 were CB1 independent. The anxiolytic-like effects of JZL184 were absent in CB2 knockout mice and were prevented by pretreatment with selective CB2 antagonists. These two publications indicate the crucial role of the CB2 receptor on the modulation of anxiety. As activation of the CB2 receptor does not lead to undesirable psychoactivity, these observations may be of significant clinical importance, and therefore the CB2 receptor represents a novel target to modulate anxiety-like responses. The protective effect of the CB2 receptor is in line with our previous suggestion that this receptor is part of a general protective mechanism (Pacher & Mechoulam 2011).

The molecular mechanism of the effect of endocannabinoids on anxiety is still to be fully clarified. Andó et al. (2012) have confirmed considerable involvement of CB1 receptors in the effect of exo- and endocannabinoids on GABA efflux. However, they also found that CB2-like receptors are likely involved. Hofmann et al. (2011) have described a new form of cannabinoid-mediated modulation of synaptic transmission, so far in the dentate gyrus only. They report that anandamide action under certain conditions is not mediated by CB1 receptors, CB2 receptors, or vanilloid type I receptors, and is still present in CB1$^{-/-}$ animals. It would be of interest to determine whether this new pathway (through a receptor?) is involved in anxiety and depression.

The endocannabinoid system plays a gatekeeper role with regard to activation of the hormonal hypothalamic-pituitary-adrenal (HPA) axis. Tonic endocannabinoid signaling constrains HPA axis activity, ultimately habituating the stress response and restoring homeostasis. Specifically, glucocorticoids produced in response to stress recruit endocannabinoids to increase the excitability of principal neurons in the prelimbic region of the medial prefrontal cortex; the principal neurons initiate inhibitory relays terminating HPA axis activation (Hill et al. 2011). However, following chronic stress, endocannabinoid signaling downregulation is implicated in the overload of hormonal signaling that can result in anxiety and depression in humans. For an excellent review of this literature, see Riebe & Wotjak (2011).

The Endocannabinoid System, Neurogenesis, and Depression

Hill et al. (2008) have summarized the results of the experimental work done on the endocannabinoid system and depression and have concluded that research so far supports the assumption that hypofunctional endocannabinoid signaling contributes to depressive illness and that enhanced endocannabinoid signaling is associated with antidepressant efficacy. However, a hyperfunctional endocannabinoid system contributes to depression. This discrepancy was explained by showing that in the animal model of depression that was used, endocannabinoid signaling was differentially altered in various brain areas. The antidepressive drug imipramine affected some, though not all, of these changes.

In view of the excellent existing summary by Hill et al. (2008), in the present review we discuss mainly the relation between cannabinoids, their two known receptors, and neurogenesis. A leading current hypothesis of depression is that is it is linked with neurogenesis. This hypothesis is based on the downregulation of neurogenesis in depressive-like behaviors in animals and on its upregulation by antidepressant treatments.

Over the past few years, considerable data have indicated that the endocannabinoid system plays a central role in neurogenesis (for reviews, see Galve-Roperh et al. 2009, Oudin et al. 2011). It is established that CB1 mRNA is expressed in many regions of the developing brain (Buckley et al. 1998), activation of CB1 is required for the axonal growth response (Williams et al. 2003), the endocannabinoid system drives neural progenitor cell proliferation (Aguado et al. 2006), and cannabinoids actually promote neurogenesis (Berghuis et al. 2007). Reductions in adult neurogenesis were noted in CB1- and CB2-knockout mice (Aguado et al. 2006, Palazuelos et al. 2006). Jin et al. (2004) have reported that both CB1 and VR1 receptors are involved in adult neurogenesis.

Endocannabinoids, particularly 2-AG and diacylglycerol lipases (DAGLs), which are involved in 2-AG synthesis, play a major role in axonal growth and guidance during development (Oudin et al. 2011). Harkany and colleagues (Keimpema et al. 2010) have shown that the synthesizing enzymes (the DAGLs) alone are not sufficient to account for the growth effect of 2-AG, but both the DAGLs and the degradation enzyme, MGL, play a role. However, MGL is temporally and spatially restricted from the neurite tip, thus enhancing 2-AG activity during axonal growth. The CB2 receptor has recently been shown to promote neural progenitor cell proliferation via mTORC1 signaling (Palazuelos et al. 2012).

Because depression decreases neurogenesis, the findings summarized above are particularly exciting, as they not only help us understand the role of endocannabinoids as endogenous antidepressants but also suggest that synthetic endocannabinoid-like compounds may be developed as a novel type of antidepressive drug.

Onaivi et al. (2008a) and van Sickle et al. (2005) have reported that, contrary to previous reports, CB2 receptors are present in the brain. This unexpected discovery led several groups to investigate the relevance of this receptor in various brain pathological states. Thus, transgenic mice overexpressing the CB2 receptor showed decreased depressive-like behaviors in several relevant assays. Also, contrary to wild-type mice, these transgenic mice showed no changes in BDNF gene and protein expression under stress (García-Gutiérrez et al. 2010). The Onaivi group reported that in Japanese depressed subjects there is high incidence of a certain polymorphism in the CB2 gene (Onaivi et al. 2008b). Hu et al. (2009) compared the antidepressant action of the CB2 agonist GW405833 with the action of desipramine in two antidepressive rodent assays—the time of immobility and a swimming assay. Although both desipramine and GW405833 significantly reduced immobility, contrary to desipramine, GW405833 had no effect in the swimming test. These results indicate that desipramine and cannabinoid drugs have different mechanisms in their antidepressive action.

These results together indicate that as increased CB2 receptor expression reduces depressive-related behaviors, apparently via a mechanism that differs from the mode of action of most antidepressants used at present, the CB2 receptor could be a novel therapeutic target for depression. It will be of interest to establish whether the activity of the CB2 receptor in depression is related to neurogenesis.

CANNABINOIDS AND REWARD SYSTEMS

Although the conditions under which cannabinoid drugs have rewarding effects are more restricted than with other drugs of abuse (such as cocaine and heroin), when they produce reward-related behavior, similar brain structures are involved (for an excellent recent review, see Serrano & Parsons 2011).

Rewarding/Aversive Effects of Cannabinoids

In humans, marijuana produces euphoria, but dysphoria, dizziness, and anxiety are also reported, probably the result of the previously mentioned biphasic effects of THC. Following administration of THC to humans, some studies have shown increased dopamine transmission (Bossong et al. 2009) but others have shown no change in dopamine transmission (Barkus et al. 2011) as measured by positron emission tomography. The endocannabinoid system may play a specific role in appreciation of rewards, as THC pretreatment attenuated the brain response to feedback of monetary rewards as measured by functional magnetic resonance imaging (fMRI) (van Hell et al. 2012).

In animal models, early research suggested that THC was not rewarding to monkeys (Harris et al. 1974) when assessed in the drug self-administration paradigm. In rodents, some investigators have reported that THC (as well as other abused drugs such as cocaine) reduces the threshold for electrical brain stimulation reward (Gardner et al. 1988), but other investigators report that it increases the threshold (Vlachou et al. 2007). Unlike the self-administration paradigm, the conditioned place preference (CPP) paradigm can be used to assess both the rewarding and the aversive effects of drugs. Conflicting findings were reported in studies using the CPP paradigm with rodents. Early reports revealed that THC produced CPPs (Lepore et al. 1995), but other reports showed conditioned place aversions (e.g., Mallet & Beninger 1998a, Parker & Gillies 1995) due to differing CPP procedures. Indeed, unlike other rewarding drugs, such as cocaine or heroin, low-dose pre-exposure to the effects of THC is necessary to establish a CPP in rodents (Valjent & Maldonado 2000).

More recently, Tanda et al. (2000) have developed a very sensitive and reliable method of establishing self-administration in monkeys, which relies on the use of very low doses of THC but does not require pre-exposure to the drug. In addition, both anandamide (Justinova et al. 2005) and 2-AG (Justinova et al. 2011) are self-administered by monkeys with or without a cannabinoid self-administration history, and both effects are prevented by pretreatment with rimonabant, indicating that the rewarding effect is CB1 receptor mediated. Treatment with the FAAH inhibitor, URB597, shifts the anandamide self-administration dose-response curve to the left, such that anandamide has rewarding effects at lower doses (Justinova et al. 2008). However, URB597 is not self-administered by monkeys (Justinova et al. 2008) and does not produce a CPP in rats (Gobbi et al. 2005), possibly because it neither causes THC-like effects nor increases extracellular mesolimbic DA levels in rats (Justinova et al. 2008, Solinas et al. 2007). In contrast, DA is known to be released in the striatum by THC (Bossong et al. 2009). Cues associated with marijuana use also activate the reward neurocircuitry associated with addiction in humans (Filbey et al. 2009). Indeed, microinjections of THC into the posterior ventral tegmental area (VTA) and into the posterior shell of the nucleus accumbens (NAcc) serve as rewards for both self-administration and CPP in rats (Zangen et al. 2006).

Cannabinoids and Relapse

Treatment of addiction is often hindered by the high rate of relapse following abstinence from the addicting drug. Multiple factors such as exposure to drug-associated stimuli, drug priming, and stress can precipitate drug craving and relapse in humans. In humans, alterations in the CB1 receptor gene and in the FAAH gene have been shown to enhance fMRI activity in reward-related areas of the brain during exposure to marijuana cues (Filbey et al. 2010).

Considerable recent research suggests that CB1 receptor antagonism (or inverse agonism) interferes with drug- and cue-induced relapse in animal models. Relapse is characterized by drug-seeking behavior in extinction triggered by renewed exposure to drug-associated cues or a priming dose of a drug itself (Everitt & Robbins 2005). Such drug-seeking behavior contrasts with actual drug-taking behavior during the self-administration session. Rimonabant prevents drug-associated cues from producing relapse following extinction training in rats and mice (De Vries & Schoffelmeer 2005). Recent evidence suggests that rimonabant is relatively more effective in interfering with drug-seeking behavior than drug-taking behavior (De Vries & Schoffelmeer 2005). In an early report, the CB1 receptor agonist, HU-210, was shown to reinstate cocaine seeking following long-term extinction of cocaine self-administration (De Vries et al. 2001), an effect that was prevented by rimonabant. Of most therapeutic importance, however, was that rimonabant alone blocked drug seeking evoked by the cocaine-paired cues and by a priming injection of cocaine, as well as seeking of heroin (De Vries et al. 2005, Fattore et al. 2003), methamphetamine (Anggadiredja et al. 2004), and nicotine (De Vries et al. 2005) evoked by drug-associated cues and by a priming injection of the drug itself. Therefore, blockade (or inverse agonism) of the CB1 receptor interferes generally with drug-seeking behavior.

Drug-seeking behavior represents the incentive motivational effects of addictive drugs under control of the mesolimbic DA system.

The regulation of the primary rewarding effects of drugs of abuse may be in part controlled by endocannabinoid release in the VTA, which produces inhibition of the release of GABA, thus removing the inhibitory effect of GABA on dopaminergic neurons (Maldonado et al. 2006). In the NAcc, released endocannabinoids act on CB1 receptors on axon terminals of glutamatergic neurons. The resulting reduction in the release of glutamate on GABA neurons that project to the VTA results in disinhibition of the VTA dopamine neurons. Blockade of CB1 receptors attenuates the release of DA in the NAcc in response to rewarding medial forebrain bundle electrical stimulation (Trujillo-Pisanty et al. 2011). The prefrontal cortex and NAcc appear to play a primary role in the prevention of cue-induced reinstatement of heroin (Alvarez-Jaimes et al. 2008) and cocaine (Xi et al. 2006) seeking by CB1 antagonism.

Although blockade of CB1 receptors affects cue- and drug-induced relapse, it does not appear to affect cocaine seeking that is reinstated by exposure to mild footshock stress (De Vries et al. 2001). Indeed, stress-induced relapse to heroin or cocaine seeking is much more sensitive to manipulations of the corticotrophin-releasing factor and noradrenaline systems than the DA system (Shaham et al. 2000). For instance, infusion of noradrenergic antagonists into the bed nucleus of the stria terminalis or the central nucleus of the amygdala prevents footshock-induced but not cocaine-induced reinstatement of cocaine seeking (Leri et al. 2002).

Rimonabant showed great promise as an antirelapse treatment; however, as mentioned above, it was removed from the European market as a treatment for obesity because of the undesirable side effects of anxiety. The generality of the effects of cannabinoids on motivational processes may explain these undesirable side effects. Given that rimonabant not only acts as a CB1 antagonist but is also a CB1 inverse agonist, the relapse-preventing properties, and potentially the adverse side effects, may also be mediated by its inverse cannabimimetic effects that are opposite in direction from those produced by cannabinoid receptor agonists (Pertwee 2005). Recent evidence suggests that at least some adverse side effects of CB1 receptor antagonists/inverse agonists seen in clinical trials (e.g., nausea) may reflect their inverse agonist properties (Bergman et al. 2008). It will be of interest to evaluate the potential of more newly developed CB1 receptor neutral antagonists, such as AM4113 (Sink et al. 2008), to prevent drug-seeking behavior.

Recently, selective CB2 receptor agonists were shown to inhibit intravenous cocaine self-administration, cocaine-enhanced locomotion, and cocaine-enhanced accumbens extracellular dopamine in wild-type and CB1 receptor knockout mice but not in CB2 knockout mice. This effect was blocked by a selective CB2 receptor antagonist. These findings suggest that brain CB2 receptors also modulate cocaine's effects (Xi et al. 2011). Again, as mentioned above, the CB2 receptor seems to have general protective properties (Pacher & Mechoulam 2011).

Although considerable evidence indicates that antagonism of the CB1 receptor interferes with cue- and drug-induced relapse, there is a growing literature suggesting that FAAH inhibition and cannabidiol also prevent relapse to drug seeking. FAAH inhibition has been selectively evaluated for prevention of nicotine seeking (Forget et al. 2009, Scherma et al. 2008). However, it is not clear if these effects are mediated by the action of anandamide or other fatty acids [oleoylethanalamide (OEA) and palmitoylethanalamide (PEA)], which act on peroxisome proliferator-activated receptor-α (PPAR-α) receptors, because Mascia and colleagues (2011) recently showed that selective PPAR-α agonists also counteract the reinstatement of nicotine seeking in rats and monkeys. Thus, elevations in fatty acids produced by blockade of FAAH may have potential in treating relapse. Most recently, Cippitelli et al. (2011) found that FAAH inhibition reduced anxiety produced by nicotine withdrawal. Cannabidiol, the nonpsychoactive compound in marijuana, also attenuated cue-induced reinstatement of heroin seeking as well as restored disturbances of glutamatergic and endocannabinoid systems in the accumbens produced by heroin seeking (Ren et al. 2009). Apparently, in addition to the many other ailments that cannabidiol improves (Mechoulam et al. 2002), it may also be a potential treatment for heroin craving and relapse.

CANNABINOIDS AND COGNITION

Cognition involves the ability to acquire, store, and later retrieve new information. Several recent reviews are available on the effects of cannabis on cognition in humans and other animals (Akirav 2011, Marsicano & Lafenetre 2009, Ranganathan & D'Souza 2006, Riedel & Davies 2005). Clearly, the chief psychoactive component in cannabis, THC, produces acute cognitive disturbances in humans and animals, more profoundly affecting short-term than long-term memory.

Effects of Cannabis on Cognition in Humans

When under the influence of THC, humans demonstrate transient impairment in short-term episodic and working memory and consolidation of these short-term memories into long-term memory, but no impairment in retrieval of information once it has been previously encoded into long-term storage (Ranganathan & D'Souza 2006). However, a recent naturalistic study revealed that cannabidiol prevented the memory-impairing effects of acute THC in humans (Morgan et al. 2010). Therefore, the relative THC/cannabidiol ratio in cannabis will profoundly modify the effects of cannabis on memory in human marijuana smokers.

The effect of chronic cannabis exposure on cognitive abilities of abstinent individuals is, however, controversial and fraught with contradictions in the literature. Polydrug abuse and pre-existing cognitive and emotional differences between cannabis users and nonusers make interpretation of the human literature problematic. In a review of the literature, Solowij & Battisti (2008) conclude that chronic exposure to marijuana is associated with dose-related cognitive impairments, most consistently in attention and working memory functions—not dissimilar to those observed under acute intoxication. On the other hand, several reports indicate that few, if any, cognitive impairments are produced by heavy cannabis use over several years (e.g., Dregan & Gulliford 2012, Lyketsos et al. 1999). More recently, a thorough review of the specific versus generalized effects of drugs of abuse on cognition (Fernandez-Serrano et al. 2011) reported that there has been only one study (Fried et al. 2005) of "pure" cannabis users. Fried et al. (2005) conducted a longitudinal examination of young adults using neurocognitive tests that had been administered prior to the first experience with marijuana smoke. Individuals were defined (by urination samples and self-reports) as light (fewer than five times a week) or heavy (greater than five times a week) current or former (abstinent for at least three months) users. Current heavy users performed worse than nonusers in overall IQ, processing speed, and immediate and delayed memory tests. In contrast, former heavy marijuana smokers did not show any cognitive impairment. Fernandez-Serrano et al. (2011) conclude that the acute effects of cannabis on prospective memory are attenuated in long-term abstinence (at least three months).

Drawing conclusions from the human literature is challenging (Ranganathan & D'Souza 2006) because of widely differing methodologies, including different tasks, lack of sufficient controls, participant selection strategies (only experienced cannabis users included in samples), different routes of administration, different doses administered, often small sample sizes, tolerance of and dependence on cannabinoids, and the timing of the test (given the long half-life of THC). In addition, factors such as a predisposition to substance use in general may confer greater vulnerability to cannabis-related cognitive effects. Therefore, experimental investigation of the effects of cannabinoids on various processes involved in learning and memory rely heavily upon animal models. These models provide insights into the critical role of the endocannabinoid system in the physiology of learning and memory.

Effects of CB1 Agonists on Learning and Memory in Nonhumans

Consistent with the human literature, most reports using animal models suggest that acute administration of CB1 agonists selectively disrupts aspects of short-term or working memory while leaving retrieval of previously learned memory (long-term or reference memory) largely intact. A common behavioral paradigm designed to evaluate these different aspects of memory is the delayed matching (or nonmatching) to sample (DMS) task. Once the animal has learned to perform this operant task (reference memory), it must then indicate (usually by pressing a bar) which test sample matches (or does not match) the original sample stimulus presented several seconds earlier (working memory). CB1 agonists (THC and WIN-55,212) disrupt accuracy of such performance in a delay-dependent manner, consistent with a selective disruption of working memory (Heyser et al. 1993). These effects are blocked by the CB_1 antagonist rimonabant. It is important to note that these effects occur at doses that do not interfere with the acquisition of the original reference memory of the task. A simpler variant of the DMS procedure used in rodents, the spontaneous object recognition task, does not rely upon prior operant training, but instead relies upon a rodent's natural preference to explore novel objects. In this task, a rat or mouse is allowed to spontaneously explore two identical objects, then after a delay is given a choice to explore a novel object or the previously presented sample object. In this measure of short-term memory, CB1 agonists (WIN-55,212 and CP55,940) produced a delay-dependent deficit in discrimination between the novel and familiar objects in the choice task (O'Shea et al. 2004, Schneider & Koch 2002), with the disruptive effect enhanced 21 days after chronic pretreatment in adolescents but not adults (O'Shea et al. 2004).

Spatial memory tasks also rely upon accurate working memory. A demanding spatial memory task is the 8-arm radial maze, which requires rats to first learn which arms contain food rewards (reference memory) and then to remember which arms have already been visited in a test session (working memory) after an imposed delay. THC increases the number of working memory errors (re-entries) at low doses, and these effects are blocked by rimonabant (Lichtman & Martin 1996). The impairment of working memory by THC (5 mg/kg) in adult rats is enhanced following chronic exposure (once a day for 90 days), but disappears following 30 days of abstinence from the drug (Nakamura et al. 1991). On the other hand, adolescent rats treated with very high escalating doses of THC (2.5–10 mg/kg) chronically for 10 days and left undisturbed for 30 days until their adulthood exhibited greater impairment in spatial working memory on the radial arm maze than did vehicle controls. The working memory deficit was also accompanied by a decrease in hippocampal dendritic spine density and length (Rubino et al. 2009).

The commonly employed spatial memory task, the Morris water maze, requires animals to navigate in a pool of water to locate a hidden platform by learning its location relative to salient visual cues. The water maze task can be used to evaluate the effect of cannabinoid agonists on reference memory (location of the platform remaining fixed across days and on trials within a day) and working memory (location of platform is changed each day, but remains constant across trials within a day). In the water maze task, THC disrupts working memory at much lower doses than those that disrupt reference memory; in fact, doses sufficient to disrupt working memory are below those that produce other effects characteristic of CB1 agonism, including antinociception, hypothermia, catalepsy, or hypomotility (Varvel et al. 2001). Vaporized marijuana smoke produces a similar effect (Niyuhire et al. 2007a).

Although exogenous CB1 agonists consistently suppress working memory in these models, manipulations that elevate endogenous cannabinoids do not consistently produce such an impairment. On the one hand, elevation of anandamide (by FAAH inhibition), but not 2-AG (by MGL inhibition), interfered with the consolidation of contextual conditioned fear and object recognition memory (Busquets-Garcia et al. 2001); on the other hand, several other studies have reported facilitation of working memory by FAAH inhibition (Campolongo et al. 2009a, Mazzola et al. 2009, Varvel et al. 2007). Likewise, FAAH-deficient mice (with tenfold increases in brain levels of anandamide) also showed improved rather than impaired performance in this task. Therefore, the effects of exogenously administered CB1 agonists are not always consistent with the effects of manipulations that elevate the natural ligands for the receptors. However, FAAH inhibition also elevates several other fatty acids, including OEA and PEA, which are ligands for PPAR-α. Mazzola et al. (2009) recently found that the enhanced acquisition of a passive avoidance task by the FAAH inhibitor, URB597, was not only reversed by a CB1 antagonist, but also by a PPAR-α antagonist (MK 886). The PPAR-α agonist (WAY1463) also enhanced passive avoidance performance, and this effect was blocked by a PPAR-α antagonist (Campolongo et al. 2009a). Therefore, FAAH inhibition may enhance memory not only by increasing anandamide, but also by elevating OEA and PEA. Most recently, Pan et al. (2011) reported that MGL knockout mice, with elevated levels of 2-AG, show improved learning in an object recognition and water maze task. Thus, there is evidence that both anandamide and 2-AG enhance learning and memory under some conditions.

Effects of CB1 Antagonists on Learning and Memory in Nonhumans

The findings that CB1 agonists produce working memory deficits suggest that inhibition of these receptors may lead to enhancement of short-term memory. However, the literature is replete with mixed findings. CB1 antagonist administration produces memory enhancement in mice in an olfactory recognition task (Terranova et al. 1996) and a spatial memory task in an 8-arm radial maze (Lichtman 2000).

In addition, CB1-/- mice are able to retain memory in an object recognition test for at least 48 hours after the first trial, whereas wild-type controls lose their capacity to retain memory after 24 hours (Reibaud et al. 1999). In contrast, studies using other paradigms, such as the DMS, have shown no benefits of rimonabant on learning or memory (e.g., Hampson & Deadwyler 2000, Mallet & Beninger 1998b). One explanation (Varvel et al. 2009) for the mixed findings is that the temporal requirements of the task predict the potential of CB1 antagonism to facilitate or not facilitate performance. Studies showing enhancement of memory generally require memory processes lasting minutes or hours, whereas studies showing that rimonabant is ineffective generally require retention of information lasting for only seconds, suggesting that blockade of CB1 receptors may prolong the duration of a memory rather than facilitate learning. If this is the case, then rimonabant may facilitate retention of memories tested after long intervals but may have no benefits in tasks such as DMS and repeated acquisition that require rapid relearning of new information (for review, see Varvel et al. 2009).

Role of Endocannabinoids in the Hippocampus in Learning and Memory

The decrement in working memory by cannabinoids appears to involve their action at the hippocampus. The hippocampus is one of the areas of the brain with the highest density of CB1 receptors, and large amounts of anandamide are found in the rodent hippocampus. Interestingly, the selective detrimental effect of CB1 agonists on working memory (but not reference memory) resembles the effects of hippocampal lesions on these two forms of memory (Hampson & Deadwyler 2000, Heyser et al. 1993). Furthermore, THC-induced deficits in the DMS paradigm are associated with specific decreases in firing of individual hippocampal neurons during the sample but not the match part of the experiment (Heyser et al. 1993). Intracranial administration of the CB1 agonists directly into the hippocampus also disrupts working memory performance in an 8-arm radial maze (Lichtman et al. 1995, Wegener et al. 2008), water maze spatial learning (Abush & Akirav 2010), and object recognition memory (Clarke et al. 2008). In contrast, intrahippocampal AM251 also has been shown to disrupt memory consolidation of an inhibitory avoidance task (de Oliveira et al. 2005). Recent work suggests that the cannabinoid and the cholinergic systems in the hippocampus interact during performance of a short-term memory task in the rat (Goonawardena et al. 2010). These effects may be mediated by cannabinoid-induced decreases in acetylcholine release in the hippocampus. Acetylcholine is also implicated in the pathophysiology of Alzheimer's disease and other disorders associated with declined cognitive function.

Overall, the literature implicates changes in hippocampal functioning as the source of working memory deficits produced by THC, although other brain regions are currently being investigated as well (Marsicano & Lafenetre 2009). Cannabinoid receptors localized to different brain regions modulate distinct learning and memory processes, such that the role of endocannabinoids in other regions may be different than their role in the hippocampus. In fact, Campolongo et al. (2009b) showed that infusion of CB1 agonist WIN 55,212,2 into the basolateral amygdala actually enhanced consolidation of inhibitory avoidance learning by enhancing the action of glucocorticoids in this region. Consistently, Tan et al. (2011) found that delivery of a CB1 antagonist to this region interferes with olfactory fear conditioning. The differential effects of CB1 agonists on different brain regions may account for different findings reported between systemic and localized administration of cannabinoid agonists.

Long-term changes in synaptic strength are believed to underlie associative memory formation in the hippocampus and amygdala. The impairments in working memory produced by CB1 agonists may be the result of the suppression of glutamate release in the hippocampus, which is responsible for the establishment of long-term potentiation, a putative mechanism for synaptic plasticity (Abush & Akirav 2010, Shen et al. 1996). Retrograde signaling by endocannabinoids results in suppression of neurotransmitter release at both excitatory (glutamatergic) and inhibitory (GABAergic) synapses in the hippocampus in a short- and a long-term manner. Endocannabinoid-induced long-term depression (LTD) is one of the best examples of presynaptic forms of long-term plasticity. Recent evidence indicates that presynaptic activity coincident with CB1 receptor activation and NMDA receptor activation is required for some forms of endocannabinoid LTD. The long-lasting effects of LTD appear to be mediated by a CB1 receptor–induced reduction of cAMP/PKA activity in the hippocampus (Heifets & Castillo 2009).

Endocannabinoid Modulation of Extinction of Aversive Memory

Avoidance of aversive stimuli is crucial for survival of all animals and is highly resistant to extinction. Considerable evidence indicates that the endogenous cannabinoid system is specifically involved in extinction learning of aversively motivated learned behaviors (Marsicano et al. 2002, Varvel & Lichtman 2002). A seminal paper by Marsicano et al. (2002) reported that CB1 knockout mice and wild-type mice administered the CB1 antagonist rimonabant showed impaired extinction in classical auditory fear-conditioning tests, with unaffected memory acquisition and consolidation. This effect appeared to be mediated by blockade of elevated anandamide in the basolateral amygdala during extinction (Marsicano et al. 2002). Using the Morris water maze task, Varvel & Lichtman (2002) reported that CB1 knockout mice and wild-type mice exhibited identical acquisition rates in learning to swim to a fixed platform; however, the CB1-deficient mice demonstrated impaired extinction of the originally learned task when the location of the hidden platform was moved to the opposite side of the tank. Because animals deficient in CB1 receptor activity show impairments in suppressing previously learned behaviors, CB1 agonists would be expected to facilitate extinction of learned behaviors in nondeficient animals. Indeed, WIN-55,212 facilitated extinction of contextual fear memory and spatial memory in rats (Pamplona et al. 2006).

The effect of enhancing the endogenous levels of anandamide by blocking its reuptake or by inhibiting FAAH during extinction learning has also recently been investigated. Chhatwal et al. (2005) reported that the reuptake blocker (and FAAH inhibitor) AM404 selectively facilitated extinction of fear-potentiated startle in rats, an effect that was reversed by rimonabant pretreatment. Varvel et al. (2007) reported that mice deficient in FAAH, either by genetic deletion (FAAH$^{-/-}$) or by pharmacological inhibition, displayed both faster acquisition and extinction of spatial memory tested in the Morris water maze; rimonabant reversed the effect of FAAH inhibition during both task phases. These effects appear to be specific to extinction of aversively motivated behavior, because neither CB1-deficient mice (Holter et al. 2005) nor wild-type mice treated with rimonabant (Niyuhire et al. 2007b) displayed a deficit in extinction of operant responding reinforced with food. Most recently, Manwell et al. (2009) found that the FAAH inhibitor URB597 promoted extinction of a conditioned place aversion produced by naloxone-precipitated morphine withdrawal but did not promote extinction of a morphine-induced or amphetamine-induced CPP.

It has been well established that extinction is not unlearning, but instead is new inhibitory learning that interferes with the originally learned response (Bouton 2002). The new learning responsible for extinction of aversive learning appears to be facilitated by activation of the endocannabinoid system and prevented by inhibition of the endocannabinoid system. More recent work has suggested that the apparent effects of manipulation of the endocannabinoids on extinction may actually reflect its effects on reconsolidation of the memory that requires reactivation (Lin et al. 2006, Suzuki et al. 2008). That is, every time a consolidated memory is recalled it switches to a labile state and is subject to being disrupted. Depending upon the conditions of retrieval and the strength of the original trace, these reactivated memories can undergo two opposing processes: reconsolidation, when the conditions favor the permanence of the trace, or extinction, when the conditions indicate that the memory has no reason to persist. Suzuki et al. (2008) have proposed that the endocannabinoid system is important for the destabilization of reactivated contextual fear memories; that is, reconsolidation or extinction relies on a molecular cascade (protein synthesis and cAMP response element-binding-dependent transcription) that is impeded by prior blockade of the CB1 receptors. Fear memory cannot be altered during restabilization if it was not previously destabilized via activation of the CB1 receptor. Whatever the actual mechanism for facilitated extinction of aversive memories with activation of the endocannabinoid system and inhibited extinction with inhibition of the endocannabinoid system, these results have considerable implications for the treatment of posttraumatic stress disorder. Progress in enhancing endocannabinoid signaling will be of great benefit in the treatment of this distressing disorder.

CONCLUSIONS

Cannabinoid research was originally initiated with the limited aim of understanding the action of an illicit drug. After the chemistry of the plant and the pharmacological and psychological actions of THC were elucidated—or actually only assumed to be elucidated—in the 1960s and early 1970s, research in the field waned. However, over a decade starting from the mid-1980s, two specific receptors and their ligands—the bases of the endocannabinoid system—were found to be involved in a wide spectrum of biological processes. This endocannabinoid system has opened new vistas in the life sciences, particularly in aspects associated with the CNS.

One of the main results of activation of the presynaptic CB1 receptor is inhibition of neurotransmitter release. By this mechanism the endocannabinoids reduce excitability of presynaptic neurons. CB1 receptors are responsible for the well-known marijuana effects as well as for effects on cognition, reward, and anxiety. In contrast, a major consequence of CB2 receptor activation is immunosuppression, which limits inflammation and associated tissue injury. Enhancement of CB2 receptor expression and/or of endocannabinoid levels has been noted in numerous diseases, including CNS-related ones. Thus, a main result of CB2 receptor activation seems to be a protective effect in a large number of physiological systems.

In the present review we have summarized evidence that cannabinoids modulate anxiety, brain reward function, and cognition by acting at CB1 (and possibly CB2) receptors in distinct brain regions. The effects of cannabis on anxiety appear to relate to the dose of THC and are modulated by the anxiolytic action of cannabidiol (if present in the plant material). A major function of the endocannabinoid system is the homeostatic regulation of the HPA axis in response to stressors. Although THC does not appear to be as rewarding as other drugs of abuse (cocaine, heroin, amphetamine) in animal models of drug abuse, recent work suggests that under optimal conditions, animals do self-administer THC. The rewarding effects of THC are mediated by elevation of DA in the mesolimbic DA system. Blockade of CB1 receptors in this system interferes with the potential of drugs or drug-related cues (but not stress) to produce relapse in animal models.

Both the animal and human literatures suggest that CB1 agonists interfere with short-term working memory and may interfere with consolidation of these memories into long-term memories while leaving previously learned long-term reference memory intact. In cannabis, these effects of THC may be prevented by a sufficiently high dose of cannabidiol. In addition, the memory-impairing effects of THC are usually limited to the acute effects of the drug itself. Recent literature suggests that the endocannabinoid system may play an especially important role in the extinction of aversively motivated learning. Treatments

that amplify the action of endocannabinoids may play a critical role in treating posttraumatic stress disorder in the future. Memory decline in aging may also be protected by the action of the endocannabinoid system. Mice lacking CB1 receptors showed accelerated age-dependent deficits in spatial learning as well as a loss of principal neurons in the hippocampus, which was accomplished by neuroinflammation (Albayram et al. 2011). These exciting findings suggest that CB1 receptors on hippocampal GABAergic neurons protect against age-dependent cognitive declines. In addition, interesting recent work suggests that cannabidiol reduces microglial activity after β-amyloid administration in mice and prevents the subsequent spatial learning impairment (Martin-Moreno et al. 2011), suggesting that this nonpsychoactive compound in marijuana may be useful in treating Alzheimer's disease. Cannabidiol has also been shown to recover memory loss in iron-deficient mice, a model of neurogenerative disorders (Fagherazzi et al. 2012).

A very large number of anandamide-like compounds, namely FAAAs or chemically related entities, have been found in the brain (Tan et al. 2010). The action of very few of them has been evaluated. However, those that have been investigated show a variety of effects. Arachidonoyl serine has vasodilator activity— an important protective property in some brain diseases—and lowers the damage caused by head injury (Cohen-Yeshurun et al. 2011). Surprisingly, this effect is blocked by CB2 antagonists, although this compound does not bind to the CB2 receptor. Apparently, its action is indirectly CB2 related. Oleoyl serine, which is antiosteoporotic, is also found in the brain (Smoum et al. 2010); oleoylethanolamide regulates feeding and body weight (Fu et al. 2005); stearoylethanolamide shows apoptotic activity (Maccarrone et al. 2002); the anti-inflammatory palmitoylethanolamide may also be protective in human stroke (Naccarato et al. 2010); arachidonoyl glycine is antinociceptive (Bradshaw et al. 2009); and arachidonoyl dopamine affects synaptic transmission in dopaminergic neurons by activating both cannabinoid and vanilloid receptors (Marinelli et al. 2007). Presumably, the additional many dozens of related endogenous molecules found in the brain will also exhibit a wide spectrum of activities. Why does the brain invest so much synthetic endeavor (and energy) to prepare such a large cluster of related molecules rather than just a few of them?

If subtle chemical disparity is one of the causes for the variability in personality—an area in psychology that is yet to be fully understood—we may have to look for a large catalog of compounds in the brain with distinct CNS effects. Is it possible that the above-described large cluster of chemically related anandamide-type compounds in the brain is related to the chemistry of the human personality and the individual temperamental differences? It is tempting to assume that the huge possible variability of the levels and ratios of substances in such a cluster of compounds may allow an infinite number of individual differences, the raw substance which of course is sculpted by experience. The known variants of CB1 and FAAH genes (Filbey et al. 2010, Lazary et al. 2010) may also play a role in these differences. If this intellectual speculation is shown to have some factual basis, it may lead to major advances in molecular psychology.

DISCLOSURE STATEMENT

The authors are not aware of any affiliations, memberships, funding, or financial holdings that might be perceived as affecting the objectivity of this review.

ACKNOWLEDGMENTS

The authors would like to thank Erin Rock for editorial help. The authors were supported by a grant from the National Institute of Drug Abuse (U.S.) to R.M. (DA-9789) and from the Natural Sciences and Engineering Research Council of Canada (92057) to L.A.P.

LITERATURE CITED

Abush H, Akirav I. 2010. Cannabinoids modulate hippocampal memory and plasticity. *Hippocampus* 20:1126–38

Aguado T, Palazuelos J, Monory K, Stella N, Cravatt B, et al. 2006. The endocannabinoid system promotes astroglial differentiation by acting on neural progenitor cells. *J. Neurosci.* 26:1551–61

Akirav I. 2011. The role of cannabinoids in modulating emotional and non-emotional memory processes in the hippocampus. *Front. Behav. Neurosci.* 5:34

Albayram O, Alferink J, Pitsch J, Piyanova A, Neitzert K, et al. 2011. Role of CB1 cannabinoid receptors on GABAergic neurons in brain aging. *Proc. Natl. Acad. Sci. USA* 108:11256–61

Alvarez-Jaimes L, Polis I, Parsons LH. 2008. Attenuation of cue-induced heroin-seeking behavior by cannabinoid CB1 antagonist infusions into the nucleus accumbens core and prefrontal cortex, but not basolateral amygdala. *Neuropsychopharmacology* 33:2483–93

Andó RD, Bíró J, Csölle C, Ledent C, Sperlágh B. 2012. The inhibitory action of exo- and endocannabinoids on [(3)H]GABA release are mediated by both CB1 and CB2 receptors in the mouse hippocampus. *Neurochem. Int.* 60:145–52

Anggadiredja K, Nakamichi M, Hiranita T, Tanaka H, Shoyama Y, et al. 2004. Endocannabinoid system modulates relapse to methamphetamine seeking: possible mediation by the arachidonic acid cascade. *Neuropsychopharmacology* 29:1470–78

Ashton JC, Friberg D, Darlington CL, Smith PF. 2006. Expression of the cannabinoid CB2 receptor in the rat cerebellum: an immunohistochemical study. *Neurosci. Lett.* 396:113–16

Barkus E, Morrison PD, Vuletic D, Dickson JC, Ell PJ, et al. 2011. Does intravenous Δ9-tetrahydrocannabinol increase dopamine release? A SPET study. *J. Psychopharmacol.* 25:1462–28

Ben-Shabat S, Fride E, Sheskin T, Tamiri T, Rhee MH, et al. 1988. An entourage effect: Inactive endogenous fatty acid glycerol esters enhance 2-arachidonoyl-glycerol cannabinoid activity. *Eur. J. Pharmacol.* 353:23–31

Bergamaschi MM, Queiroz RH, Chagas MH, de Oliveira DC, De Martinis BS, et al. 2011. Cannabidiol reduces the anxiety induced by simulated public speaking in treatment-naïve social phobia patients. *Neuropsychopharmacology* 36:1219–26

Berghuis P, Rajnicek AM, Morozov YM, Ross R, Mulder J. 2007. Hardwiring the brain: Endocannabinoids shape neuronal connectivity. *Science* 316:1212–16

Bergman J, Delatte MS, Paronis CA, Vemuri K, Thakur GA, Makriyannis A. 2008. Some effects of CB1 antagonists with inverse agonist and neutral biochemical properties. *Physiol. Behav.* 93:666–70

Bossong MG, van Berckel BN, Boellaard R, Zuurman L, Schuit RC, et al. 2009. Delta 9-tetrahydrocannabinol induces dopamine release in the human striatum. *Neuropsychopharmacology* 34:759–66

Bouton ME. 2002. Context, ambiguity, and unlearning: sources of relapse after behavioral extinction. *Biol. Psychiatry* 52:976–86

Bradshaw HB, Rimmerman N, Hu SS, Burstein S, Walker JM. 2009. Novel endogenous N-acyl glycines: identification and characterization. *Vitam. Horm.* 81:191–205

Buckley NE, Hansson S, Harta G, Mezey E. 1998. Expression of the CB1 and CB2 receptor messenger RNAs during embryonic development in the rat. *Neuroscience* 82:1131–49

Busquets-Garcia A, Puighermanal E, Pastor A, de la Torre R, Maldonado R, et al. 2011. Differential role of anandamide and 2-arachidonoylglycerol in memory and anxiety-like responses. *Biol. Psychiatry* 70:479–86

Campbell Thomson R. 1949. *A Dictionary of Assyrian Botany*. London: British Acad.

Campolongo P, Roozendaal B, Trezza V, Cuomo V, Astarita G, et al. 2009a. Fat-induced satiety factor oleoylethanolamide enhances memory consolidation. *Proc. Natl. Acad. Sci. USA* 106:8027–31

Campolongo P, Roozendaal B, Trezza V, Hauer D, Schelling G, et al. 2009b. Endocannabinoids in the rat basolateral amygdala enhance memory consolidation and enable glucocorticoid modulation of memory. *Proc. Natl. Acad. Sci. USA* 106:4888–93

Campos AC, Guimaraes FS. 2008. Involvement of 5HT1A receptors in the anxiolytic-like effects of cannabidiol injected into the dorsolateral periaqueductal gray of rats. *Psychopharmacology (Berl.)* 199:223–30

Carrier EJ, Auchampach JA, Hillard CJ. 2006. Inhibition of an equilibrative nucleoside transporter by cannabidiol: a mechanism of cannabinoid immunosuppression. *Proc. Natl. Acad. Sci. USA* 103:7895–900

Chhatwal JP, Davis M, Maguschak KA, Ressler KJ. 2005. Enhancing cannabinoid neurotransmission augments the extinction of conditioned fear. *Neuropsychopharmacology* 30:516–24

Christensen R, Kristensen PK, Bartels EM, Bliddal H, Astrup A. 2007. Efficacy and safety of the weight-loss drug rimonabant: a meta-analysis of randomised trials. *Lancet* 370:1706–13

Cippitelli A, Astarita G, Duranti A, Caprioli G, Ubaldi M, et al. 2011. Endocannabinoid regulation of acute and protracted nicotine withdrawal: effect of FAAH inhibition. *PLoS ONE* 6:e28142

Cippitelli A, Cannella N, Braconi S, Duranti A, Tontini A, et al. 2008. Increase of brain endocannabinoid anandamide levels by FAAH inhibition and alcohol abuse behaviours in the rat. *Psychopharmacology (Berl.)* 198:449–60

Clarke JR, Rossato JI, Monteiro S, Bevilaqua LR, Izquierdo I, Cammarota M. 2008. Posttraining activation of CB1 cannabinoid receptors in the CA1 region of the dorsal hippocampus impairs object recognition long-term memory. *Neurobiol. Learn. Mem.* 90:374–81

Cohen-Yeshurun A, Trembovler V, Alexandrovich A, Ryberg E, Greasley PJ, et al. 2011. N-arachidonoyl-L-serine is neuroprotective after traumatic brain injury by reducing apoptosis. *J. Cereb. Blood Flow Metab.* 31:1768–77

Da Orta G. 1563. *Coloquios dos Simples e Drogas e Cousas Medicinais da India*. Goa, India: G Da Orta. Reproduced in 1872 by Academia das Cientias de Lisboa, Portugal; cited from Booth M. 2003. *Cannabis: A History.* New York: St. Martin's

De Oliveira AL, de Oliveira LF, Camboim C, Diehl F, Genro BP, et al. 2005. Amnestic effect of intrahippocampal AM251, a CB1-selective blocker, in the inhibitory avoidance, but not in the open field habituation task, in rats. *Neurobiol. Learn Mem.* 83:119–24

Devane WA, Dysarz FA 3rd, Johnson MR, Melvin LS, Howlett AC. 1988. Determination and characterization of a cannabinoid receptor in rat brain. *Mol. Pharmacol.* 34:605–13

Devane WA, Hanus L, Breuer A, Pertwee RG, Stevenson LA, et al. 1992. Isolation and structure of a brain constituent that binds to the cannabinoid receptor. *Science* 258:1946–49

De Vries TJ, de Vries W, Janssen MC, Schoffelmeer AN. 2005. Suppression of conditioned nicotine and sucrose seeking by the cannabinoid-1 receptor antagonist SR141716A. *Behav. Brain Res.* 161:164–68

De Vries TJ, Schoffelmeer AN. 2005. Cannabinoid CB1 receptors control conditioned drug seeking. *Trends Pharmacol. Sci.* 26:420–26

De Vries TJ, Shaham Y, Homberg JR, Crombag H, Schuurman K, et al. 2001. A cannabinoid mechanism in relapse to cocaine seeking. *Nat. Med.* 7:1151–54

Dregan A, Gulliford MC. 2012. Is illicit drug use harmful to cognitive functioning in the mid-adult years? A cohort-based investigation. *Am. J. Epidemiol.* 175:218–27

D'Souza DC, Perry E, MacDougall L, Ammerman Y, Cooper T. 2004. The psychotomimetic effects of intravenous delta-9-tetrahydrocannabinol in healthy individuals: implications for psychosis. *Neuropsychopharmacology* 29:1558–72

Everitt BJ, Robbins TW. 2005. Neural systems of reinforcement for drug addiction: from actions to habits to compulsion. *Nat. Neurosci.* 8:1481–89

Fagherazzi EV, Garcia VA, Maurmann N, Bervanger T, Halenslager LH, et al. 2012. Memory-rescuing effects of cannabidiol in an animal model of cognitive impairment relevant to neurodegenerative disorders. *Psychopharmacology (Berl.)* 219:1133–40

Fattore L, Spano MS, Cossu G, Deiana S, Fratta W. 2003. Cannabinoid mechanism in reinstatement of heroin-seeking after a long period of abstinence in rats. *Eur. J. Neurosci.* 17:1723–26

Fernandez-Serrano MJ, Perez-Garcia M, Verdejo-Garcia A. 2011. What are the specific versus generalized effects of drugs of abuse on neuropsychological performance? *Neurosci. Biobehav. Rev.* 35:377–406

Filbey FM, Schacht JP, Myers US, Chavez RS, Hutchison KE. 2009. Marijuana craving in the brain. *Proc. Natl. Acad. Sci. USA* 106:13016–21

Filbey FM, Schacht JP, Myers US, Chavez RS, Hutchison KE. 2010. Individual and additive effects of the CNR1 and FAAH genes on brain response to marijuana cues. *Neuropsychopharmacology* 35:967–75

Forget B, Coen KM, LeFoll B. 2009. Inhibition of fatty acid amide hydrolase reduces reinstatement of nicotine seeking but not break point for nicotine self-administration—comparison with CB(1) receptor blockade. *Psychopharmacology (Berl.)* 205:613–24

Freud S. 1920/1953. *A General Introduction to Psychoanalysis.* New York: Permabooks

Fride E, Gobshtis N, Dahan H, Weller A, Giuffrida A, et al. 2009. The endocannabinoid system during development: emphasis on perinatal events and delayed effects. *Vitam. Horm.* 81:139–58

Fried PA, Watkinson B, Gray R. 2005. Neurocognitive consequences of marihuana—a comparison with pre-drug performance. *Neurotoxicol. Teratol.* 27:231–39

Fu J, Bottegoni G, Sasso O, Bertorelli R, Rocchia W. 2011. A catalytically silent FAAH-1 variant drives anandamide transport in neurons. *Nat. Neurosci.* 15:64–69

Fu J, Oveisi F, Gaetani S, Lin E, Piomelli D. 2005. Oleoylethanolamide, an endogenous PPAR-alpha agonist, lowers body weight and hyperlipidemia in obese rats. *Neuropharmacology* 48:1147–53

Gaetani S, Dipasquale P, Romano A, Righetti L, Cassano T, et al. 2009. The endocannabinoid system as a target for novel anxiolytic and antidepressant drugs. *Int. Rev. Neurobiol.* 85:57–72

Galve-Roperh I, Palazuelos J, Aguado T, Guzman M. 2009. The endocannabinoid system and the regulation of neural development: potential implications in psychiatric disorders. *Eur. Arch. Psychiatry Clin. Neurosci.* 259:371–82

Gaoni Y, Mechoulam R. 1964. Isolation, structure and partial synthesis of an active constituent of hashish. *J. Am. Chem. Soc.* 86:1646–47

García-Gutiérrez MA, Manzanares J. 2011. Overexpression of CB2 cannabinoid receptors decreased vulnerability to anxiety and impaired anxiolytic action of alprazolam in mice. *J. Psychopharmacol.* 25:111–20

García-Gutiérrez MS, Pérez-Ortiz JM, Gutiérrez-Adán A, Manzanares J. 2010. Depression-resistant endophenotype in mice overexpressing cannabinoid CB(2) receptors. *Br. J. Pharmacol.* 160:1773–84

Gardner EL. 2005. Endocannabinoid signaling system and brain reward: emphasis on dopamine. *Pharmacol. Biochem. Behav.* 8:263–84

Gardner EL, Paredes W, Smith D, Donner A, Milling C, et al. 1988. Facilitation of brain stimulation reward by delta 9-tetrahydrocannabinol. *Psychopharmacology (Berl.)* 96:142–44

Gobbi G, Bambico FR, Mangieri R, Bortolato M, Campolongo P, et al. 2005. Antidepressant-like activity and modulation of brain monoaminergic transmission by blockade of anandamide hydrolysis. *Proc. Natl. Acad. Sci. USA* 102:18620–25

Goonawardena AV, Robinson L, Hampson RE, Riedel G. 2010. Cannabinoid and cholinergic systems interact during performance of a short-term memory task in the rat. *Learn. Mem.* 17:502–11

Guimarães FS, Chiaretti TM, Graeff FG, Zuardi AW. 1990. Antianxiety effect of cannabidiol in the elevated plus-maze. *Psychopharmacology (Berl.)* 100:558–59

Hampson RE, Deadwyler SA. 2000. Cannabinoids reveal the necessity of hippocampal neural encoding for short-term memory in rats. *J. Neurosci.* 20:8932–42

Hanus L, Breuer A, Tchilibon S, Shiloah S, Goldenberg D, et al. 1999. HU-308: a specific agonist for CB_2, a peripheral cannabinoid receptor. *Proc. Natl. Acad. Sci. USA* 96:14228–33

Harris RT, Waters W, McLendon D. 1974. Evaluation of reinforcing capability of delta-9-tetrahydrocannabinol in rhesus monkeys. *Psychopharmacologia* 37:23–29

Heifets BD, Castillo PE. 2009. Endocannabinoid signaling and long-term synaptic plasticity. *Annu. Rev. Physiol.* 71:283–306

Herkenham M, Lynn AB, Little MD, Johnson MR, Melvin LS. 1990. Cannabinoid receptor localization in brain. *Proc. Natl. Acad. Sci. USA* 87:1932–36

Heyser CJ, Hampson RE, Deadwyler SA. 1993. Effects of delta-9-tetrahydrocannabinol on delayed match to sample performance in rats: alterations in short-term memory associated with changes in task specific firing of hippocampal cells. *J. Pharmacol. Exp. Ther.* 264:294–307

Hill MN, Carrier EJ, McLaughlin RJ, Morrish AC, Meier SE, et al. 2008. Regional alterations in the endocannabinoid system in an animal model of depression: effects of concurrent antidepressant treatment. *J. Neurochem.* 106:2322–36

Hill MN, McLaughlin RJ, Pan B, Fitzgerald ML, Roberts CJ, et al. 2011. Recruitment of prefrontal cortical endocannabinoid signaling by glucocorticoids contributes to termination of the stress response. *J. Neurosci.* 31:10506–15

Hofmann ME, Bhatia C, Frazier CJ. 2011. Cannabinoid receptor agonists potentiate action potential-independent release of GABA in the dentate gyrus through a CB1 receptor-independent mechanism. *J. Physiol.* 589:3801–21

Holter SM, Kallnik M, Wurst W, Marsicano G, Lutz B, Wotjak CT. 2005. Cannabinoid CB1 receptor is dispensable for memory extinction in an appetitively-motivated learning task. *Eur. J. Pharmacol.* 510:69–74

Howlett AC, Barth F, Bonner TI, Cabral G, Casellas P, et al. 2002. Classification of cannabinoid receptors. *Pharmacol. Rev.* 54:161–202

Howlett AC, Qualy JM, Khachatrian LL. 1986. Involvement of Gi in the inhibition of adenylate cyclase by cannabimimetic drugs. *Mol. Pharmacol.* 29:307–13

Hu B, Doods H, Treede RD, Ceci A. 2009. Depression-like behaviour in rats with mononeuropathy is reduced by the CB2-selective agonist GW405833. *Pain* 143:206–12

Jin K, Xie L, Kim SH, Parmentier-Batteur S, Sun Y, et al. 2004. Defective adult neurogenesis in CB1 receptor knockout mice. *Mol. Pharmacol.* 66:204–8

Justinova Z, Mangieri RA, Bortolato M, Chefer SI, Mukhin AG, et al. 2008. Fatty acid amide hydrolase inhibition heightens anandamide signaling without producing reinforcing effects in primates. *Biol. Psychiatry* 64:930–37

Justinova Z, Solinas M, Tanda G, Redhi GH, Goldberg SR. 2005. The endogenous cannabinoid anandamide and its synthetic analog R(+)-methanandamide are intravenously self-administered by squirrel monkeys. *J. Neurosci.* 25:5645–50

Justinova Z, Yasar S, Redhi GH, Goldberg SR. 2011. The endogenous cannabinoid 2-arachidonoylglycerol is intravenously self-administered by squirrel monkeys. *J. Neurosci.* 31:7043–48

Katona I, Freund TF. 2012. The multiple functions of endocannabinoid signaling in the brain. *Annu. Rev. Neurosci.* 35:529–58

Kathuria S, Gaetani S, Fegley D, Valiño F, Duranti A, et al. 2003. Modulation of anxiety through blockade of anandamide hydrolysis. *Nat. Med.* 9:76–81

Keimpema E, Barabas K, Morozov YM, Tortoriello G, Torii M, et al. 2010. Differential subcellular recruitment of monoacylglycerol lipase generates spatial specificity of 2-arachidonoyl glycerol signaling during axonal pathfinding. *J. Neurosci.* 30:13992–4007

Lazary J, Juhasz G, Hunyady L, Bagdy G. 2011. Personalized medicine can pave the way for the safe use of CB1 receptor antagonists. *Trends Pharmacol. Sci.* 32:270–80

Lepore M, Vorel SR, Lowinson J, Gardner EL. 1995. Conditioned place preference induced by delta 9-tetrahydrocannabinol: comparison with cocaine, morphine, and food reward. *Life Sci.* 56:2073–80

Leri F, Flores J, Rodaros D, Stewart J. 2002. Blockade of stress-induced but not cocaine-induced reinstatement by infusion of noradrenergic antagonists into the bed nucleus of the stria terminalis or the central nucleus of the amygdala. *J. Neurosci.* 22:5713–18

Lichtman AH. 2000. SR 141716A enhances spatial memory as assessed in a radial-arm maze task in rats. *Eur. J. Pharmacol.* 404:175–79

Lichtman AH, Dimen KR, Martin BR. 1995. Systemic or intrahippocampal cannabinoid administration impairs spatial memory in rats. *Psychopharmacology (Berl.)* 119:282–90

Lichtman AH, Martin BR. 1996. Delta 9-tetrahydrocannabinol impairs spatial memory through a cannabinoid receptor mechanism. *Psychopharmacology (Berl.)* 126:125–31

Lin HC, Mao SC, Gean PW. 2006. Effects of intra-amygdala infusion of CB1 receptor agonists on the reconsolidation of fear-potentiated startle. *Learn. Mem.* 13:316–21

Lyketsos CG, Garrett E, Liang KY, Anthony JC. 1999. Cannabis use and cognitive decline in persons under 65 years of age. *Am. J. Epidemiol.* 149:794–800

Maccarone M, Pauselli R, Di Rienzo M, Finazzi-Agrò A. 2002. Binding, degradation and apoptotic activity of stearoylethanolamide in rat C6 glioma cells. *Biochem. J.* 366(Pt. 1):137–44

Maldonado R, Valverde O, Berrendero F. 2006. Involvement of the endocannabinoid system in drug addiction. *Trends Neurosci.* 29:225–32

Mallet PE, Beninger RJ. 1998a. Delta-9-tetrahydrocannabinol, but not the endogenous cannabinoid receptor ligand anandamide, produces conditioned place avoidance. *Life Sci.* 62:2431–39

Mallet PE, Beninger RJ. 1998b. The cannabinoid CB1 receptor antagonist SR141716A attenuates the memory impairment produced by delta-9-tetrahydrocannabinol or anandamide. *Psychopharmacology (Berl.)* 140:11–19

Manwell LA, Satvat E, Lang ST, Allen CP, Leri F, Parker LA. 2009. FAAH inhibitor, URB-597, promotes extinction and CB(1) antagonist, SR141716, inhibits extinction of conditioned aversion produced by naloxone-precipitated morphine withdrawal, but not extinction of conditioned preference produced by morphine in rats. *Pharmacol. Biochem. Behav.* 94:154–62

Marinelli S, Di Marzo V, Florenzano F, Fezza F, Viscomi MT, et al. 2007. N-arachidonoyl-dopamine tunes synaptic transmission onto dopaminergic neurons by activating both cannabinoid and vanilloid receptors. *Neuropsychopharmacology* 32:298–308

Marsicano G, Lafenetre P. 2009. Roles of the endocannabinoid system in learning and memory. *Curr. Top. Behav. Neurosci.* 1:201–30

Marsicano G, Wotjak CT, Azad SC, Bisogno T, Rammes G, et al. 2002. The endogenous cannabinoid system controls extinction of aversive memories. *Nature* 418:530–34

Martin-Moreno AM, Reigada D, Ramirez BG, Mechoulam R, Innamorato N, et al. 2011. Cannabidiol and other cannabinoids reduce microglial activation in vitro and in vivo: relevance to Alzheimer's disease. *Mol. Pharmacol.* 79:964–73

Mascia P, Pistis M, Justinova Z, Panililo LV, Luchicchi A, et al. 2011. Blockade of nicotine reward and reinstatement by activation of alpha-type peroxisome proliferator-activated receptors. *Biol. Psychiatry* 69:633–41

Matsuda LA, Lolait SJ, Brownstein MJ, Young AC, Bonner TI. 1990. Structure of a cannabinoid receptor and functional expression of the cloned cDNA. *Nature* 346:561–64

Mazzola C, Medalie J, Scherma M, Panlilio LV, Solinas M, et al. 2009. Fatty acid amide hydrolase (FAAH) inhibition enhances memory acquisition through activation of PPAR-alpha nuclear receptors. *Learn. Mem.* 16:332–37

Mechoulam R. 1986. The pharmacohistory of *Cannabis sativa*. In *Cannabinoids as Therapeutic Agents*, ed. R Mechoulam, pp. 1–19. Boca Raton, FL: CRC Press

Mechoulam R, Ben-Shabat S, Hanus L, Ligumsky M, Kaminiski NE, et al. 1995. Identification of an endogenous 2-monoglyceride, present in canine gut, that binds to cannabinoid receptors. *Biochem. Pharmacol.* 50:83–90

Mechoulam R, Braun P, Gaoni Y. 1967. A stereospecific synthesis of (−)-Δ^1 and (−)-Δ^6-tetrahydrocannabinols. *J. Am. Chem. Soc.* 89:4552–54

Mechoulam R, Feigenbaum JJ, Lander N, Segal M, Jarbe TUC, et al. 1988. Enantiomeric cannabinoids: stereospecificity of psychotropic activity. *Experientia* 44:762–64

Mechoulam R, Hanus L. 2000. A historical overview of chemical research on cannabinoids. *Chem. Phys. Lipids* 108:1–13

Mechoulam R, Parker LA, Gallily R. 2002. Cannabidiol: an overview of some pharmacological aspects. *J. Clin. Pharmacol.* 42:11–19S

Mechoulam R, Peters M, Murillo-Rodriguez E, Hanus LO. 2009. Cannabidiol—recent advances. In *Cannabinoids in Nature and Medicine*, ed. DM Lambert, pp. 83–101. New York: Wiley-VCH

Mechoulam R, Shvo Y. 1963. The structure of cannabidiol. *Tetrahedron* 19:2073–78

Moise AM, Eisenstein SA, Astarita G, Piomelli D, Hohmann AG. 2008. An endocannabinoid signaling system modulates anxiety-like behavior in male Syrian hamsters. *Psychopharmacology (Berl.)* 200:333–46

Moreau JJ. 1973/1845. *Hashish and Mental Illness*. New York: Raven (From French)

Morgan CJ, Schafer G, Freeman TP, Curran HV. 2010. Impact of cannabidiol on the acute memory and psychotomimetic effects of smoked cannabis: naturalistic study. *Br. J. Psychiatry* 197:285–90

Moreira FA, Aguiar DC, Guimarães FS. 2006. Anxiolytic-like effect of cannabidiol in the rat Vogel conflict test. *Prog. Neuropsychopharmacol. Biol. Psychiatry* 30:1466–71

Moreira FA, Wotjak CT. 2010. Cannabinoids and anxiety. *Curr. Top. Behav. Neurosci.* 2:429–50

Munro S, Thomas KL, Abu-Shaar M. 1993. Molecular characterization of a peripheral receptor for cannabinoids. *Nature* 365:61–65

Naccarato M, Pizzuti D, Petrosino S, Simonetto M, Ferigo L, et al. 2010. Possible anandamide and palmitoylethanolamide involvement in human stroke. *Lipids Health Dis.* 9:47

Nakamura EM, da Silva EA, Concilio GV, Wilkinson DA, Masur J. 1991. Reversible effects of acute and long-term administration of delta-9-tetrahydrocannabinol (THC) on memory in the rat. *Drug Alcohol. Depend.* 28:167–75

Niyuhire F, Varvel SA, Martin BR, Lichtman AH. 2007a. Exposure to marijuana smoke impairs memory retrieval in mice. *J. Pharmacol. Exp. Ther.* 322:1067–75

Niyuhire F, Varvel SA, Thorpe AJ, Stokes RJ, Wiley JL, Lichtman AH. 2007b. The disruptive effects of the CB1 receptor antagonist rimonabant on extinction learning in mice are task-specific. *Psychopharmacology (Berl.)* 191:223–31

Nunez E, Benito C, Pazos MR, Barbachano A, Fajardo O, et al. 2004. Cannabinoid CB2 receptors are expressed by perivascular microglial cells in the human brain: an immunohistochemical study. *Synapse* 53:208–13

Onaivi ES, Ishiguro H, Gong JP, Patel S, Meozzi PA, et al. 2008a. Functional expression of brain neuronal CB2 cannabinoid receptors are involved in the effects of drugs of abuse and in depression. *Ann. N. Y. Acad. Sci. USA* 1139:434–49

Onaivi ES, Ishiguro H, Gong JP, Patel S, Meozzi PA, et al. 2008b. Brain neuronal CB2 cannabinoid receptors in drug abuse and depression: from mice to human subjects. *PLoS ONE* 3:e1640

O'Shea M, Singh ME, McGregor IS, Mallet PE. 2004. Chronic cannabinoid exposure produces lasting memory impairment and increased anxiety in adolescent but not adult rats. *J. Psychopharmacol.* 18:502–8

Oudin MJ, Hobbs C, Doherty P. 2011. DAGL-dependent endocannabinoid signalling: roles in axonal pathfinding, synaptic plasticity and adult neurogenesis. *Eur. J. Neurosci.* 34:1634–46

Pacher P, Batkai S, Kunos G. 2006. The endocannabinoid system as an emerging target of pharmacotherapy. *Pharmacol. Rev.* 58:389–462

Pacher P, Mechoulam R. 2011. Is lipid signaling through cannabinoid 2 receptors part of a protective system? *Prog. Lipid Res.* 50:193–211

Palazuelos J, Aguado T, Egia A, Mechoulam R, Guzman M. 2006. Non-psychoactive CB2 cannabinoid agonists stimulate neural progenitor proliferation. *FASEB J.* 20:2405–7

Palazuelos J, Ortega Z, Díaz-Alonso J, Guzmán M, Galve-Roperh I. 2012. CB2 cannabinoid receptors promote neural progenitor cell proliferation via mTORC1 signaling. *J. Biol. Chem.* 287:1198–209

Pamplona FA, Prediger RD, Pandolfo P, Takahashi RN. 2006. The cannabinoid receptor agonist WIN 55,212-2 facilitates the extinction of contextual fear memory and spatial memory in rats. *Psychopharmacology (Berl.)* 188:641–49

Pan B, Wang W, Zhong P, Blankman JK, Cravatt BF, Liu Q. 2011. Alterations of endocannabinoid signaling, synaptic plasticity, learning, and memory in monoacylglycerol lipase knock-out mice. *J. Neurosci.* 31:13420–30

Parolaro D, Realini N, Vigano D, Guidali C, Rubino T. 2010. The endocannabinoid system and psychiatric disorders. *Exp. Neurol.* 24:3–14

Parker LA, Gillies T. 1995. THC-induced place and taste aversions in Lewis and Sprague-Dawley rats. *Behav. Neurosci.* 109:71–78

Pertwee RG. 2005. Inverse agonism and neutral antagonism at cannabinoid CB1 receptors. *Life Sci.* 76:1307–24

Pertwee RG. 2009. Emerging strategies for exploiting cannabinoid receptor agonists as medicines. *Br. J. Pharmacol.* 156:397–411

Pertwee RG, Howlett AC, Abood ME, Alexander SP, Di Marzo V, et al. 2010. Cannabinoid receptors and their ligands: beyond CB1 and CB2. *Pharmacol. Rev.* 62:588–631

Ranganathan M, D'Souza DC. 2006. The acute effects of cannabinoids on memory in humans: a review. *Psychopharmacology (Berl.)* 188:425–44

Reibaud M, Obinu MC, Ledent C, Parmentier M, Bohme GA, Imperato A. 1999. Enhancement of memory in cannabinoid CB1 receptor knock-out mice. *Eur. J. Pharmacol.* 379:R1–2

Ren Y, Whittard J, Higuera-Matas A, Morris CV, Hurd YL. 2009. Cannabidiol, a non-psychotropic component of cannabis, inhibits cue-induced heroin seeking and normalizes discrete mesolimbic neuronal disturbances. *J. Neurosci.* 29:14764–69

Riebe CJ, Wotjak CT. 2011. Endocannabinoids and stress. *Stress* 14:384–97

Riedel G, Davies SN. 2005. Cannabinoid function in learning, memory and plasticity. *Handb. Exp. Pharmacol.* 168:445–77

Romero J, Garcia-Palomero E, Berrendero F, Garcia-Gil L, Hernandez ML, et al. 1997. Atypical location of cannabinoid receptors in white matter areas during rat brain development. *Synapse* 26:317–23

Rosenthal F. 1971. *The Herb: Hashish Versus Medieval Muslim Society*. Leiden: Brill

Rubino T, Realini N, Braida D, Guidi S, Capurro V, et al. 2009. Changes in hippocampal morphology and neuroplasticity induced by adolescent THC treatment are associated with cognitive impairment in adulthood. *Hippocampus* 19:763–72

Rubino T, Realini N, Castiglioni C, Guidali C, Viganó D, et al. 2008. Role in anxiety behavior of the endocannabinoid system in the prefrontal cortex. *Cereb. Cortex* 18:1292–301

Scherma M, Panlilio LV, Fadda P, Fattore L, Gamaleddin I, et al. 2008. Inhibition of anandamide hydrolysis by cyclohexyl carbamic acid 3'-carbamoyl-3-yl ester (URB597) reverses abuse-related behavioral and neurochemical effects of nicotine in rats. *J. Pharmacol. Exp. Ther.* 327:482–90

Schneider M, Koch M. 2002. The cannabinoid agonist WIN 55,212-2 reduces sensorimotor gating and recognition memory in rats. *Behav. Pharmacol.* 13:29–37

Sciolino NR, Zhou W, Hohmann AG. 2011. Enhancement of endocannabinoid signaling with JZL184, an inhibitor of the 2-arachidonoylglycerol hydrolyzing enzyme monoacylglycerol lipase, produces anxiolytic effects under conditions of high environmental aversiveness in rats. *Pharmacol. Res.* 64:226–34

Serrano A, Parsons LH. 2011. Endocannabinoid influence in drug reinforcement, dependence and addiction-related behaviors. *Pharmacol. Therapeut.* 132:215–41

Shaham Y, Erb S, Stewart J. 2000. Stress-induced relapse to heroin and cocaine seeking in rats: a review. *Brain Res. Brain Res. Rev.* 33:13–33

Sharir H, Abood ME. 2010. Pharmacological characterization of GPR55, a putative cannabinoid receptor. *Pharmacol. Ther.* 126:301–13

Shen M, Piser TM, Seybold VS, Thayer SA. 1996. Cannabinoid receptor agonists inhibit glutamatergic synaptic transmission in rat hippocampal cultures. *J. Neurosci.* 16:4322–34

Sink KS, McLaughlin PJ, Wood JA, Brown C, Fan P, et al. 2008. The novel cannabinoid CB1 receptor neutral antagonist AM4113 suppresses food intake and food-reinforced behavior but does not induce signs of nausea in rats. *Neuropsychopharmacology* 33:946–55

Smoum R, Bar A, Tan B, Milman G, Attar-Namdar M, et al. 2010. Oleoyl serine, an endogenous N-acyl amide, modulates bone remodeling and mass. *Proc. Natl. Acad. Sci. USA* 107:17710–15

Solinas M, Yasar S, Goldberg SR. 2007. Endocannabinoid system involvement in brain reward processes related to drug abuse. *Pharmacol. Res.* 56:393–405

Solowij N, Battisti R. 2008. The chronic effects of cannabis on memory in humans: a review. *Curr. Drug Abuse Rev.* 1:81–98

Stella N. 2004. Cannabinoid signaling in glial cells. *Glia* 48:267–77

Sulcova E, Mechoulam R, Fride E. 1998. Biphasic effects of anandamide. *Pharmacol. Biochem. Behav.* 59:347–52

Suzuki A, Mukawa T, Tsukagoshi A, Frankland PW, Kida S. 2008. Activation of LVGCCs and CB1 receptors required for destabilization of reactivated contextual fear memories. *Learn. Mem.* 15:426–33

Tan B, O'Dell DK, Yu YW, Monn MF, Hughes HV, et al. 2010. Identification of endogenous acyl amino acids based on a targeted lipidomics approach. *J. Lipid Res.* 51:112–19

Tan H, Lauzon NM, Bishop SF, Chi N, Bechard M, Laviolette SR. 2011. Cannabinoid transmission in the basolateral amygdala modulates fear memory formation via functional inputs to the prelimbic cortex. *J. Neurosci.* 31:5300–12

Tanda G, Munzar P, Goldberg SR. 2000. Self-administration behavior is maintained by the psychoactive ingredient of marijuana in squirrel monkeys. *Nat. Neurosci.* 3:1073–74

Terranova JP, Storme JJ, Lafon N, Perio A, Rinaldi-Carmona M, et al. 1996. Improvement of memory in rodents by the selective CB1 cannabinoid receptor antagonist, SR 141716. *Psychopharmacology (Berl.)* 126:165–72

Trujillo-Pisanty I, Hernandez G, Moreau-Debord I, Cossette M, Conover D, et al. 2011. Cannabinoid receptor blockade reduces the opportunity cost at which rats maintain operant performance for rewarding brain stimulation. *J. Neurosci.* 31:5426–35

Valjent E, Maldonado R. 2000. A behavioural model to reveal place preference to delta 9-tetrahydrocannabinol in mice. *Psychopharmacology (Berl.)* 147:436–38

van Hell HH, Jager G, Bossong MS, Brouwer A, Jansma JM, et al. 2012. Involvement of the endocannabinoid system in reward processing in the brain. *Psychopharmcology (Berl.)* 219:981–90

Van Sickle MD, Duncan M, Kingsley PJ, Mouihate A, Urbani P, et al. 2005. Identification and functional characterization of brainstem cannabinoid CB2 receptors. *Science* 310:329–32

Varvel SA, Hamm RJ, Martin BR, Lichtman AH. 2001. Differential effects of delta 9-THC on spatial reference and working memory in mice. *Psychopharmacology (Berl.)* 157:142–50

Varvel SA, Lichtman AH. 2002. Evaluation of CB1 receptor knockout mice in the Morris water maze. *J. Pharmacol. Exp. Ther.* 301:915–24

Varvel SA, Wise LE, Lichtman AH. 2009. Are CB(1) receptor antagonists nootropic or cognitive impairing agents? *Drug Dev. Res.* 70:555–65

Varvel SA, Wise LE, Niyuhire F, Cravatt BF, Lichtman AH. 2007. Inhibition of fatty-acid amide hydrolase accelerates acquisition and extinction rates in a spatial memory task. *Neuropsychopharmacology* 32:1032–41

Verdurand M, Nguyen V, Stark D, Zahra D, Gregoire MC, et al. 2012. Comparison of cannabinoid CB(1) receptor binding in adolescent and adult rats: a positron emission tomography study using [F]MK-9470. *Int. J. Mol. Imag.* In press

Vlachou S, Nomikos GG, Stephens DN, Panagis G. 2007. Lack of evidence for appetitive effects of delta 9-tetrahydrocannabinol in the intracranial self-stimulation and conditioned place preference procedures in rodents. *Behav. Pharmacol.* 18:311–19

Wade DT, Robson P, House H, Makela P, Aram J. 2003. A preliminary controlled study to determine whether whole-plant cannabis extracts can improve intractable neurogenic symptoms. *Clin. Rehabil.* 17:21–29

Wegener N, Kuhnert S, Thuns A, Roese R, Koch M. 2008. Effects of acute systemic and intra-cerebral stimulation of cannabinoid receptors on sensorimotor gating, locomotion and spatial memory in rats. *Psychopharmacology (Berl.)* 198:375–85

Williams EJ, Walsh FS, Doherty P. 2003. The FGF receptor uses the endocannabinoid signaling system to couple to an axonal growth response. *J. Cell Biol.* 160:481–86

Xi ZX, Gilbert JG, Peng XQ, Pak AC, Li X, Gardner EL. 2006. Cannabinoid CB1 receptor antagonist AM251 inhibits cocaine-primed relapse in rats: role of glutamate in the nucleus accumbens. *J. Neurosci.* 26:8531–36

Xi ZX, Peng XQ, Li X, Song R, Zhang HY, et al. 2011. Brain cannabinoid CB2 receptors modulate cocaine's actions in mice. *Nat. Neurosci.* 14:1160–66

Zanettini C, Panlilio LV, Alicki M, Goldberg SR, Haller J, et al. 2012. Effects of endocannabinoid system modulation on cognitive and emotional behavior. *Front. Behav. Neurosci.* 5:57

Zangen A, Solinas M, Ikemoto S, Goldberg SR, Wise RA. 2006. Two brain sites for cannabinoid reward. *J. Neurosci.* 26:4901–7

Zhang PW, Ishiguro H, Ohtsuki T, Hess J, Carillo F. 2004. Human cannabinoid receptor 1: 5' exons, candidate regulatory regions, polymorphisms, haplotypes and association with polysubstance abuse. *Mol. Psychiatry* 9:916–23

Zimmer A, Zimmer AM, Hohmann AG, Herkenham M, Bonner TI. 1999. Increased mortality, hypoactivity and hypoalgesia in cannabinoid CB1 receptor knockout mice. *Proc. Natl. Acad. Sci. USA* 96:5780–85

Synesthesia

Jamie Ward[1,2]

[1]School of Psychology and [2]Sackler Center for Consciousness Science, University of Sussex, Brighton, BN1 9QH United Kingdom; email: jamiew@sussex.ac.uk

Annu. Rev. Psychol. 2013. 64:49–75

First published online as a Review in Advance on June 29, 2012

The *Annual Review of Psychology* is online at psych.annualreviews.org

This article's doi: 10.1146/annurev-psych-113011-143840

Keywords

color, synaesthesia, imagery, connectivity, multisensory, spatial

Abstract

Although synesthesia has been known about for 200 years, it is only in the past decade or so that substantial progress has been made in studying it empirically and in understanding the mechanisms that give rise to it. The first part of the review considers the characteristics of synesthesia: its elicited nature, automaticity, prevalence, and consistency, and its perceptual and spatial phenomenology. The second part considers the causes of synesthesia both in terms of candidate neural mechanisms and the distal influences that shape this: genetic differences in developmental synesthesia and plasticity following sensory loss in acquired synesthesia. The final part considers developmental synesthesia as an individual difference in cognition and summarizes evidence of its influence on perception, imagery, memory, art/creativity, and numeracy.

Contents

INTRODUCTION

Synesthesia is a remarkable way of perceiving the world. One attribute of a stimulus (e.g., its sound, shape, or meaning) may inevitably lead to the conscious experience of an additional attribute. For example, the word "Phillip" may taste of sour oranges, the letter A may be luminous red, and a C# note on the violin may be a brown fuzzy line extending from left to right in the lower left part of space. The attributes do not always lie in different senses (e.g., a visually presented letter may trigger a color).

In fact, the trigger itself may be an internal representation that is not physically presented. A sum such as 5 + 2 may be sufficient to trigger the color associated with 7 (Dixon et al. 2000), and synesthetic experiences of taste can occur even if the inducing word is inaccessible, as in a tip-of-the-tongue state (Simner & Ward 2006). Of course to those who do have synesthesia, it seems equally remarkable that these kinds of experiences aren't shared by everyone.

A precise definition of what synesthesia is (and what it isn't) remains a matter of some debate. An uncontroversial starting point would be to say that synesthesia is elicited. Grossenbacher & Lovelace (2001) introduced the term "inducer" to describe the stimulus that elicits the synesthesia and the term "concurrent" to denote the experience itself. Thus, every type of synesthesia can be minimally described as an inducer-concurrent pairing. For instance, music-taste and grapheme-color denote types of synesthesia in which music elicits taste, and graphemes (units of written language) elicit colors. It is important to note that the inducer is not substituted by the concurrent, so music-taste synesthetes continue to hear music as well as tasting it (Beeli et al. 2005). This starting position enables us to distinguish synesthesia from seemingly similar phenomena such as illusions (in which the inducer is, in some sense, misperceived) and hallucinations (a concurrent without an inducer). A further generally agreed defining property is the notion of automaticity, by which it is generally meant that the concurrent is a (virtually) inevitable consequence of encountering the inducer. Synesthetes have very little control over the onset or content of their experiences. It is in this sense, among others, that we can say that synesthesia is more akin to perception than mental imagery. For those without synesthesia (nonsynesthetes), if we *see* a green 5 then we can neither switch the green off nor change it to pink; but if we *imagine* a 5 it could take any color or none at all. For those with synesthesia, their experiences resemble the former more than the latter. However, in other important respects synesthetic experiences resemble mental images more than percepts;

for instance, synesthetic visual responses to music aren't affected by shutting or moving the eyes.

One of the things that a theory of synesthesia must explain is the pattern of inducers and concurrents that are found. The most common synesthetic inducers are linguistic in nature: letters, digits, and words—particularly words that form part of a series (Simner et al. 2006). The most common synesthetic concurrents are visual in nature. This includes color and colored textures. It also includes spatial forms in which sequences such as numbers or years are visualized as linear or convoluted landscapes (Sagiv et al. 2006). These are also called number forms, calendar forms, etc., or number-space, time-space synesthesia, etc. However, the range of possible inducers and concurrents is very large, with new combinations still being discovered. This also leads to a puzzle as to what combinations of inducer and concurrent could reasonably be labeled as synesthesia. With a very broad definition, any automatic association could potentially meet the criteria for being classed as synesthesia.

A common solution to this problem is to restrict the definition of synesthesia to percept-like concurrent experiences. Another solution would be to go beyond the superficial characteristics and consider the underlying causes (Simner 2012). The assumption of most contemporary researchers is that there will be a set of underlying causal mechanisms that give rise to synesthesia, and these will probably differ from those causal mechanisms that lead some people to have, say, vivid visual imagery (although the mechanisms could also overlap in interesting ways). There could also be multiple causal pathways that give rise to synesthesia. Synesthesia exists as both a developmental condition (i.e., existing throughout the lifespan with no known precipitating event) and as an acquired condition (i.e., as the result of a precipitating event such as acquired sensory loss). It remains a matter of debate as to whether these two different distal causes have anything in common in terms of the underlying neural mechanisms or whether two completely separate accounts

are needed. More controversially, it has been suggested that synesthesia-like experiences can be induced by hypnosis (Kadosh et al. 2009) or by expertise with sensory substitution devices in the blind (Ward & Meijer 2010). Again, the main controversy here is whether this relates in any way to the same causal mechanisms that underpin conventional forms of synesthesia.

One of the reasons why synesthesia is of interest to psychology in general is the assumption that it could inform "normal" models of perception and cognition. Synesthesia should be explicable in terms of modifications to models of sensory and cognitive development and brain function just like other acquired and developmental conditions. At the very least, the existence of synesthesia invites psychologists to reconsider their notions of what "normal" is. Synesthesia could be regarded as an example of an individual difference in cognition: It is not only associated with unusual experiences but also impacts on many aspects of functioning (memory, numeracy, perception, personality) (see sidebar Famous Synesthetes).

This review starts by considering the history of scientific enquiry into synesthesia. The remainder of the review is divided into three main sections. First, the characteristics of synesthesia are considered such as its prevalence,

FAMOUS SYNESTHETES

Some famous synesthetes include the philosopher Ludwig Wittgenstein (1889–1951; "the vowel e is yellow," etc.; see ter Hark 2009); the composer Olivier Messiaen (1908–1992; his compositions were influenced by the color of musical keys; see Bernard 1986); the actor Geoffrey Rush (born 1951; colored numbers and days; see Astle 2007); the psychiatrist Eugen Bleuler (1857–1939; he published an influential book on synesthesia before turning to his more famous work on schizophrenia; see Bleuler & Lehmann 1881); the physicist Richard Feynman (1918–1988; he saw his formulae in color and wondered what they looked like to his students; see Feynman 1988); and the author Vladimir Nabokov (1899–1977; who described the letters kzspygv as creating the spectrum from red to violet; see Nabokov 1967).

automaticity, consistency, and its similarity to veridical perception. The main focus of this part of the review is on developmental synesthesia. However, the second section, which considers the causes of synesthesia, discusses how both acquired and developmental synesthesia may arise. The final section considers how developmental synesthesia is related to other aspects of cognitive functioning. For instance, I consider how it could be linked to enhanced memory and, in some cases, impaired numeracy.

HISTORICAL PERSPECTIVES ON SYNESTHESIA

The first documented case of synesthesia, that is generally accepted as such, dates back to 1812. Georg Sachs was an Austrian doctor who, for his medical dissertation, submitted an account of himself and his sister on the topic of albinism—a condition that affected both of them. It is within this thesis that he describes his own synesthesia, giving detailed examples of colors for numbers and letters and other series (for an English translation, see Jewanski et al. 2009).

Although we know of no earlier documented case, the idea that color may not solely be derived from light/vision was treated with open-mindedness in the intellectual circles of the Enlightenment period. The scientist Robert Boyle (1627–1691) mentions the case of a congenital blind man who could tell the color of cloth by touch (see Larner 2006). Although unlikely to be a true case of touch-color synesthesia (Jewanski et al. 2009), the case illustrates the fact that eminent figures were willing to entertain such ideas. Isaac Newton (1642–1727) himself believed that there was a law of physics that connected the colors of the spectrum with seven tonal intervals of the musical octave (Pesic 2006).

By the nineteenth century, color associations were recognized as a phenomenon of biology rather than physics. However, one early debate centered on whether synesthesia originated from the eyes or brain. Cornaz (1848) rediscovered the Sachs case, interpreted it as

the opposite of Daltonism (or color blindness), and gave synesthesia its first name, hyperchromatopsia. Although not explicitly articulated as such, we could regard this as implying additional forms of color receptors in the eye. Cornaz sparked the first significant interest in synesthesia, leading to new cases being reported (Jewanski et al. 2011). However, his eye-based explanation never gained widespread credence. Evidence against his account included observations in new cases that colors can be triggered by the *idea* of a letter alone (Chabalier 1864) and that synesthetic colors coexist with the real text color and therefore resemble an associated perception rather than a misperception/illusion (Perroud 1863). The term pseudochromesthesia was coined to reflect this new understanding (Chabalier 1864), and more detailed neuroscientific accounts were proposed during the 1870s. One suggestion was that two different sensory nerves might stimulate each other if they cross or are near each other (Nussbaumer 1873), or, in more phrenological terms, that the cerebral "organs" of music, color, and language lie next to each other and may interconnect (Lusanna 1873). Another interesting account is that the sensory specialization of the nerves is not present from birth but is learned via experience, and synesthetes may fail to make this developmental differentiation of the senses (Ranke 1875).

During the mid-nineteenth century there was general acceptance that synesthesia was not pathological despite consensus that it reflected an alteration in underlying biology (Jewanski et al. 2011). Although not considered dysfunctional, nor was it typically considered functional. Perhaps the first systematic attempt to describe synesthesia as a functional entity came from the British polymath, Francis Galton (1822–1911). In 1878, Galton read an obituary by the son of a famous calculating prodigy and engineer, George Bidder (1806–1878), in which both father and son were described as seeing "mental pictures of figures and diagrams" when dealing with numbers. Bidder Jr. provided Galton with a drawing

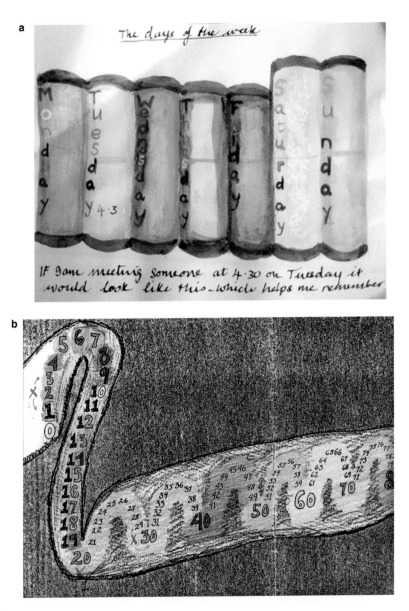

Figure 1

Spatial forms for numbers and time may either be colored or not. The days of the week were produced by Tessa Verrecchia (with permission). The number form is taken from Richard E. Cytowic, from Cytowic & Eagleman (2009), *Wednesday is Indigo Blue: Discovering the Brain of Synesthesia*, Cambridge, MA: MIT Press. (Permission is granted to copy, distribute, and/or modify this document under the terms of the GNU Free Documentation License.)

of his own number form, sparking Galton's interest in mental imagery and its possible role in intellectual ability (Burbridge 1994). For Galton, phenomena such as number forms and color associations were regarded as an individual difference in mental imagery, and he did not seek to attach a special name to it. While he asserted its biological and hereditary nature, he also acknowledged that number forms are in some sense constructed during childhood (he likens it to nest building in animals) and only retained into adulthood if they are useful to the user (Galton 1883). Examples of spatial forms are shown in **Figure 1** (see color insert).

In the last two decades of the nineteenth century, there was a rapid growth in the number of different varieties of synesthesia and the number of new cases that were reported. For instance, Bleuler & Lehmann (1881) document 76 synesthetes, including the first examples of pain-color, taste-color, and smell-color. Nor were the reports limited to color as the concurrent, and nor were the concurrent experiences necessarily percept-like in nature. For instance, personifications (associating genders and personalities to, say, graphemes) were typically grouped alongside color associations (Galton 1883). As such, it was clear that the most popular terminology of the day, namely "colored hearing," did not do justice to what was being documented. The term "sunaisthesis" (from which synesthesia derives) had been used since antiquity. For instance, Aristotle used it to refer to rather different phenomena such as shared feelings—similar to modern notions of empathy (Flakne 2005). It had also been used in medical contexts to denote things such as referred sensations, the photic sneeze, and bodily sensations from hearing nails scratching a blackboard (e.g., Vulpian 1866), and it was from this context that the word synesthesia was coined as an umbrella term to accommodate the recent proliferation of cases that had been reported (e.g., Calkins 1895). The 1890s notion of synesthesia is broadly similar to that used today, although the links to referred sensations (and so on) have been largely dropped.

The twentieth century took synesthesia on a rather different journey away from its earlier medical heritage. The notion of synesthesia became incorporated in cultural movements of the time in the visual arts (e.g., the work of Kandinsky), literature, music, and spirituality (see Dann 1998). As such, synesthesia began to coexist as both a biological entity and as a cultural metaphor for the expression of intersensory correspondence. Moreover, synesthesia was not an area of research that fitted well with the new psychological movement of the time, namely behaviorism. In the behaviorist tradition, synesthesia was little more than a learned association (e.g., Howells 1944), and so by the mid-twentieth century synesthesia had stopped being a puzzle for many psychologists and had become trivial. It would take several more decades to reclaim some scientific credibility.

THE CHARACTERISTICS OF SYNESTHESIA

Although the general characteristics of synesthesia were described well over 100 years ago, there has been a strong emphasis in the contemporary literature on developing testable criteria that might distinguish synesthesia from phenomena such as imagery or cross-sensory metaphor (such as "sharp cheese"). The sections below consider the prevalence of synesthesia, its internal consistency and automaticity, and its perceptual and spatial characteristics.

Internal Consistency of Associations

Efforts in the 1980s to study synesthesia objectively, rather than just as case descriptions, concentrated on measures of test-retest consistency (e.g., Baron-Cohen et al. 1987). In a typical test, synesthetes would be given a list of inducers and asked to generate their concurrent experience, whereas controls would be asked to freely associate a concurrent. This procedure is then repeated, often weeks or months later, and test-retest consistency is calculated. Using this method, grapheme-color synesthetes are often found to be around 80% to 100% consistent and controls around 30% to 50% consistent (e.g., Mattingley et al. 2001). The method can be adapted for other concurrent experiences such as taste/flavor (Ward & Simner 2003). In recent years, there has been a shift away from using verbal descriptions of color concurrents to using visual color pickers and having the test and retest occurring within the same session (Eagleman et al. 2007).

Although measures of consistency have been extremely influential, it goes without saying that having a very high consistency isn't necessarily uniquely diagnostic, and some element of first-person report of synesthesia is used in conjunction with this measure. In line with this, controls trained to have highly consistent word-color associations do not activate color-sensitive regions of the brain (area V4) as much as synesthetes in response to those same words (Nunn et al. 2002).

The Prevalence of Synesthesia

One method of assessing prevalence has been to place an advertisement in a newspaper or magazine and divide the number of respondents who both report synesthesia and pass an internal consistency measure by the circulation figure. These studies have tended to find a prevalence of around 1 in 2,000, with a preponderance of female synesthetes as high as 5:1 (Barnett et al. 2008a, Baron-Cohen et al. 1996, Rich et al. 2005). However, this should be construed as a very conservative prevalence rate given that one can't draw firm conclusions about people who fail to respond to the advertisement. A more reliable method is to screen a large sample of the population for reports of synesthesia and supplement this with an objective measure (typically internal consistency). **Table 1** shows the prevalence of various types of synesthesia obtained using this method. This method produced higher prevalence rates and a female:male ratio close to 1:1. Most of these synesthetes have multiple types of synesthesia, suggesting that different

Table 1 Current estimates of the prevalence of different types of synesthesia

Type of synesthesia	Prevalence (%)
Spatial forms (e.g., calendar→space)[a,b]	2.2–20.0
Days→color[c]	2.8
Vision→touch (mirror touch)[d]	1.6
Grapheme (letter + number)→color[c]	1.4
Month→color[c]	1.0
People→color[c]	0.4
Music→color[c]	0.2
Taste→shape[c]	0.2

[a]Brang et al. (2010), [b]Sagiv et al. (2006), [c]Banissy et al. (2009a), [d]Simner et al. (2006).

types of developmental synesthesia have a common cause. For instance, spatial forms are five times more prevalent in grapheme-color synesthetes than in those lacking color concurrents, suggesting that these types of synesthesia are not independent (Sagiv et al. 2006). The most prevalent type of nonvisual synesthesia appears to be so-called mirror touch or vision-touch synesthesia, in which observing touch to another person triggers tactile sensations on the body of the perceiver (Banissy et al. 2009a).

The Automaticity of Synesthesia

Aside from consistency, the most common way of establishing the authenticity of synesthesia has been to use a synesthetic version of the Stroop test. The original version of this test uses color names printed in congruent or incongruent colors (e.g., RED printed in either red or green ink; see MacLeod 1991). In synesthetic versions, color names are replaced by the inducer. If a synesthete perceives the letter "A" as red, then he/she will be faster at naming the printed color of a grapheme if it is congruent with the synesthesia ("A" printed in red) relative to when it is incongruent with it ("A" printed in green; Mattingley et al. 2001). The effect is found for other types of synesthesia, such as music-taste (Beeli et al. 2005) and music-color (Ward et al. 2006a). Related tasks have also been used for spatial forms by showing a slower response time when the spatial arrangement of externally presented stimuli (such as months, numbers) is incompatible with the spatial arrangement of the form (e.g., Sagiv et al. 2006, Smilek et al. 2006). The synesthetic Stroop effect does not prove that synesthetic colors are truly seen rather than just known (as an overlearned association). Indeed, controls can be trained to show comparable interference effects, but trained controls still differ from synesthetes on measures such as functional magnetic resonance imaging (fMRI) (Elias et al. 2003) and conditioned physiological responses to color (Meier & Rothen 2009).

When attention to the grapheme is reduced, the synesthetic Stroop effect is also reduced (Mattingley et al. 2006), and the Stroop effect is abolished if the grapheme is presented subliminally followed by a supraliminal color patch (Mattingley et al. 2001). This suggests that the degree of automaticity of synesthesia is a function of attention to (and awareness of) the inducer. This issue is returned to in the next section.

The Perceptual Reality of Synesthesia

Synesthesia can be construed as a conscious experience in the absence of the normal preconscious sensory stimulation and therefore has the potential to inform theories about conscious perception. Psychophysical and functional imaging studies have attempted to establish which perceptual processes are involved in the synesthetic experience. Most of the evidence here has come from grapheme-color synesthesia. It should be noted at the outset that the experiences of synesthetes are heterogeneous. For some grapheme-color synesthetes, the colors are seen on the surface of the grapheme itself, and these individuals have been referred to as projectors (Dixon et al. 2004). Other grapheme-color synesthetes claim to see the colors elsewhere (e.g., on an external or internal screen) or just to know the colors, and Dixon et al. (2004) have referred to

this larger group as associators. As such, it is possible that different types of synesthetes may make somewhat different demands on the perception/attention network, and there is some evidence to support this idea.

In terms of psychophysical studies, synesthetic and real colors interact under binocular rivalry and can bias the direction of apparent motion (Kim et al. 2006). Thus, synesthetic colors can affect other aspects of perception (which suggests that they are not just verbal associations). Another line of evidence has come from visual search tasks. In normal perception, the time taken to detect a target is fast, and independent of the number of items to search, if the target can be discriminated from distractors on the basis of color—a phenomenon known as pop-out (e.g., Treisman 1988). Would the same hold true for a color that is not physically present, such as synesthetically induced colors? Some case reports have suggested that this might be so (e.g., Palmeri et al. 2002, Smilek et al. 2001), but this is not replicated at the group level (e.g., Edquist et al. 2006). In those cases that did report an effect, it was qualitatively different from pop-out: for instance, by being dependent on the number of distractors (Palmeri et al. 2002) or dependent on initial fixation location (Laeng et al. 2004). This is consistent with the view that attention to a grapheme is needed to elicit a synesthetic color, whereas veridical colors can guide visual search preattentively.

A task conceptually related to visual search is the embedded figures task of Ramachandran & Hubbard (2001). They presented synesthetes with visual arrays of graphemes (for one second) in which some graphemes could be grouped together into shapes (e.g., a triangle). The task was to report the shape from four alternatives, and their two synesthetes outperformed controls on this task. Hubbard et al. (2005a) and Ward et al. (2010) replicated the finding but noted that the effect was variable across synesthetes and fell short of true pop-out levels based on performance with real color. Importantly, Ward et al. (2010) obtained trial-by-trial phenomenological reports and were able to link these to performance. For these briefly presented stimuli, many synesthetes reported no color at all. For synesthetes who did report colors (and these were more likely to be projectors), only some of the letters were perceived as colored, and the more letters that were colored, the better they performed. Thus, synesthetic colors may facilitate perceptual grouping, but not independently of attention and varying according to the spatial location of the colors.

A more comprehensive account of the neural basis of synesthesia is given below in the context of the causes of synesthesia. However, in light of the present discussion, it is worthwhile considering activity in one particular region, namely the color-sensitive region in the fusiform cortex (V4), and its possible link to concurrent color experiences. Typically, studies that have investigated this have attempted to locate the region functionally by comparing veridical colors against grey-scale equivalents with fMRI and then assessing whether the same region responds during the presence of an achromatic inducer that elicits synesthetic color. Area V4 has been shown to be activated by synesthetic color when the inducer consists of speech (Nunn et al. 2002) or an achromatic grapheme (e.g., Hubbard et al. 2005a). However, not all studies have reported this (e.g., Hupé et al. 2012). Areas more anterior to V4 have been shown by various studies to be more active during synesthetic experiences of color, and this has been linked to other aspects of processing such as color retrieval or cascaded feedback (for a review, see Rouw et al. 2011). Van Leeuwen et al. (2011) provide evidence that different patterns of functional connectivity between these more anterior regions and V4 may discriminate between projectors and associators.

In summary, with regard to the perceptual reality of the synesthetic concurrent, most of the evidence has come from experiences of color. The empirical evidence suggests that synesthetic colors are not just like real colors in terms of either behavior or neural basis, although the evidence shows that synesthetes do indeed differ from controls on a number of measures (i.e., the existence of synesthesia is not undermined by this research). With regard to the visual ventral stream, it would be reasonable to conclude that color concurrents involve higher regions (V4 and beyond), with little evidence behaviorally (Hong & Blake 2008) or neurally (Rouw et al. 2011) that lower regions such as V1 are implicated in the color experience itself (although they could still be implicated in synesthesia in other ways; Barnett et al. 2008b). In other modalities, there is functional imaging evidence that concurrent experiences of synesthetic touch are linked to activity within somatosensory cortices (Beauchamp & Ro 2008, Blakemore et al. 2005). The evidence that synesthetic flavor experiences are linked to gustatory cortex is more equivocal (Jones et al. 2011).

Extension in Space

In veridical perception, linking spatial information from different senses requires a series of computations that take into account information about the orientation of the sensory receptors in space (e.g., Morgan 2003). For example, in order to decide whether a seen object is located to the left, front, or right of space, one cannot simply read off the location of the object on the retina. One would also need to take into account whether the eyes (and the head) are themselves oriented to the front, the left, or the right. This suggests a hierarchy of spatial processes starting from the sensory receptors themselves and progressing ultimately to a spatial representation of the external world that is independent of the observer.

Synesthetic concurrents tap into these same spatial maps. Consider this quote from Galton (1883): "The diagram of the numerals has roughly the shape of a horseshoe, lying on a slightly inclined plane with the open end towards me; zero is in front of my left eye. When I move my eyes without moving my head, the diagram remains fixed in space and does not follow the movement of my eye. When I move the head, the diagram unconsciously follows the movement." What Galton's participant is describing is a number form that lies in a head-centered spatial reference frame. Not all spatial forms are like this: Some are fixed relative to the body rather than head, and still others are reported to lie only on an "inner screen" or "mind's eye" that is not defined by egocentric coordinates (Smilek et al. 2006). Some synesthetes can vary the perspective from which the form is viewed (Jarick et al. 2009). With respect to spatial forms, one can say that there are two levels of spatial relationship: an internal structure that determines the spatial relationship of the elements (e.g., numbers) to each other, and a second level that specifies the spatial relationship(s) between the form itself and the observer. In terms of neural mechanisms, Eagleman (2009) speculates that the former may be part of the (right-lateralized) ventral visual stream of object perception; the latter may involve regions around the intraparietal sulcus known to be involved in coding egocentric space (Tang et al. 2008).

These kinds of differences are by no means limited to spatial forms. Consider grapheme-color synesthesia. So-called projectors can be understood in terms of the concurrent experience lying in an object-centered frame of reference (the object, in this case, is the printed word). Other grapheme-color synesthetes describe seeing the colors on a body-centered frame of reference (e.g., the colors are seen on a screen that is a fixed location relative to the body, sometimes even inside the body itself), and still others see it on a nonegocentric imagined screen (Ward et al. 2007). These differences are not well captured by the umbrella term "associator," and there is evidence that these finer spatial distinctions manifest themselves in terms of both behavior (Ward et al. 2007) and neural substrates (van Leeuwen et al. 2010).

At least five different spatial reference frames can be observed across the range of synesthesias: object centered, head centered, body centered, imaginal centered (or nonegocentric), and eye centered. All of these are known to exist in normal cognition from single-cell recordings (Morgan 2003) or spatial impairments such as neglect (Halligan et al. 2003), and the use

of spatial reference frames provides one example of how characteristics of synesthesia can be understood in terms of differences within a normative model of perception. Other object-centered examples include projecting colored auras onto faces or projecting colors onto the fingers when counting (see Ward 2008). Body- and head-centered reference frames would include seeing colors inside the mouth when eating (Downey 1911) or projecting synesthetic tastes into the mouth (Ward & Simner 2003). Some sound-vision synesthetes experience the vision as emanating from the sound source (object centered), others in front of their body (body centered), and still others on an inner screen (Goller et al. 2009). When touch is the concurrent (e.g., mirror-touch synesthesia), then it is necessarily experienced on the body, but even here there are two spatial subtypes (Banissy et al. 2009a). For some synesthetes, seeing touch to a left cheek may elicit touch on their left cheek (an anatomical spatial relationship), whereas for others it may be felt on the right cheek (a reflected or specular spatial relationship).

In acquired synesthesia, Armel & Ramachandran (1999) report a case of touch-vision synesthesia arising after blindness. Synesthetic visual sensations were projected onto the spatial location of the touched body part (e.g., hands) irrespective of where the body part was located in space. They measured the intensity of tactile stimulation required to induce visual photisms and noted that they were easier to induce (i.e., lower threshold) when the hand was in front of the person rather than behind the head. This suggests a body-based spatial reference frame that additionally incorporates information about gaze and/or head orientation. Acquired audio-visual synesthesia arising from partial loss of vision due to optic nerve injury is linked to photisms that appear in the blind scotoma of the synesthete's visual field, that is, an eye-centered spatial reference frame (Jacobs et al. 1981). There are no known examples of an eye-centered frame of reference in developmental synesthesia consistent with this primarily involving higher visual processes.

Finally, there are some synesthetes who claim to know the color (or other concurrent) but deny perceiving it. These individuals could be classed as having a nonspatial (and indeed a nonperceptual) form of synesthesia. The distinction between knowing and perceiving has parallels with Block's (e.g., 2005) notion of access versus phenomenal consciousness (briefly, the former is reportable and the latter experiential). It could also reflect a resolved synesthesia in which the perceptual components have faded over time but associative components are retained.

THE CAUSES OF SYNESTHESIA

When considering the causes of synesthesia, it can be helpful to make a distinction between proximal and distal (or ultimate) causes. For instance, in developmental synesthesia we can say that the unusual experiences are caused by functional and structural differences within the brain. This is the proximal cause. The distal cause, in this instance, would be the role of genetic (and environmental?) differences in creating these brain-level differences.[1] The challenge for research in this area is to join up these different levels of explanation: from genes, to brain structure/function, to cognition and unusual conscious experiences. This section begins by considering the neural basis of synesthesia. It then examines the distal causes of both developmental and acquired synesthesia. Finally, it considers the origins of the particular associations themselves.

Proximal Causes: The Neural Mechanisms of Synesthesia

Candidate neural mechanisms of synesthesia all have something in common insofar as they are believed to reflect differences in connectivity relative to the neurotypical brain. Moreover,

these differences are typically assumed to lie at the cortical level, reflecting the complex nature of the inducer/concurrent. Beyond this starting position, there is far less agreement as to how these differences in connectivity might be realized. Bargary & Mitchell (2008) provide a useful taxonomy of candidate neural mechanisms in terms of a 2 × 2 space of theories. One factor is whether the inducer and concurrent are connected directly or indirectly. This is reminiscent of the debate in the multisensory processing literature as to whether unimodal sensory regions influence each other directly (feedforward only) or indirectly by converging (feedforward) onto some common hub that then influences the input regions via feedback activity. Both types of direct and indirect mechanism are known to exist in the normal brain during multisensory processing, and the dominance of one type of mechanism over the other may reflect the timing, the task, or the nature of the stimuli (e.g., Driver & Noesselt 2008). The second orthogonal factor is the nature of the connectivity differences themselves: structural or functional. Structural differences are assumed to reflect extra connections in synesthetes relative to controls, whereas functional differences are assumed to reflect pathways that are common to synesthetes and nonsynesthetes alike but such that these routes are normally inhibited in the typical brain yet are active (i.e., disinhibited) in synesthetes.

Structural differences are found in the brains of people with developmental synesthesia. Diffusion tensor imaging shows greater white matter organization in synesthetes relative to controls in several brain regions (Rouw & Scholte 2007). There are also differences in gray matter density (both cortical thickening and thinning) in synesthetes relative to controls (Banissy et al. 2012, Weiss & Fink 2009). One current challenge for researchers is to link these differences to the actual characteristics of synesthesia because many of the structural changes are not in the regions that process the inducer and/or concurrent (the affected regions are considered in more detail below). As such, these studies have not struck a definitive blow against functional

---

[1]One could even push the levels of explanation further back to the evolutionary origins of these genetic differences (see Brang & Ramachandran 2011).

accounts. The functional versus structural dichotomy can also be construed as two extreme end points, and it is possible that both are involved to different degrees. Faster-acting functional changes (e.g., disinhibition) may initiate structural changes, as has been documented in the neuroplastic changes following blindness (Pascual-Leone et al. 2005). Functional accounts also offer a way of explaining both developmental and acquired synesthesia within a single mechanism (Grossenbacher & Lovelace 2001). But there is no necessary reason why developmental and acquired synesthesia should be explicable by the same neural mechanism.

With regard to the issue of whether inducer-concurrent connectivity is direct or indirect, Bargary & Mitchell (2008) argue that the unidirectional nature of synesthesia (graphemes trigger colors but not vice versa) favors the direct, feedforward-only models. However, there is evidence of some implicit bidirectionality; for instance, judging the size of colored lines is biased by the presence of number-color associations, suggesting that the color can activate numerical representations (e.g., Cohen Kadosh et al. 2007). It is also conceivable that the directness of the mapping varies according to the type of synesthesia or even between individuals with putatively the same type of synesthesia. In mirror-touch synesthesia, there is a rather complex spatial transformation between the inducer (seeing a body part touched) and concurrent (feeling touch) that is suggestive of an indirect inducer-to-concurrent route (Banissy et al. 2009a). Grapheme-color synesthesia would be a stronger candidate for a direct route, given that they are anatomically adjacent (Ramachandran & Hubbard 2001). But there is also some evidence that this could be variable between synesthetes depending on the spatial reference frame, which may depend on indirect connectivity via parietal regions (van Leeuwen et al. 2011).

It has been shown that dense connectivity between adjacent and nearby regions (with sparser long-distance connectivity) is an optimal configuration for information transfer and minimizing wiring (Sporns et al. 2004), and this may bias the pairing of inducers and concurrents in synesthesia. Ramachandran & Hubbard (2001) proposed that grapheme-color synesthesia may be particularly prevalent because regions involved in color perception (V4) and letter/digit recognition lie adjacent to each other in the fusiform cortex (and this affords opportunities for connectivity). This basic idea has been extended to other types of synesthesia (for a review, see Hubbard et al. 2011). Consider the difference between grapheme-color synesthesia and lexical-gustatory synesthesia (Ward et al. 2005). When grapheme-color synesthetes see (or hear) a word, the color depends on its spelling: A word such as PHOTO may be colored by the first letter (P), or sometimes the vowel (O), or, less frequently, as a sequence of five colors. (Even in Chinese, the colors of words depend on their constituent characters and radicals; Simner et al. 2011.) But when a word is experienced as a taste/flavor, the taste is unrelated to the spelling; rather, similar sounding words tend to taste the same (Ward et al. 2005). There is no cognitive reason why the color of words should depend on written language but the taste of words should depend on spoken language. These differences do make sense when one considers the neural architecture of the brain.

The parietal lobes are involved in number processing (and possibly other ordinal sequences) and spatial processing, and it has been suggested that differences in connectivity here may underpin the spatial form of synesthesia (Hubbard et al. 2005b). Not all types of synesthesia can be readily accounted for by adjacency between inducer and concurrent, but nor is adjacency the sole mode of connectivity. A more serious limitation of the adjacency principle is that it offers no account as to why spatial forms should be more prevalent than grapheme-color synesthesia, or why grapheme-color synesthesia should be more prevalent than lexical-gustatory synesthesia. One needs to make further assumptions to account for this: for instance, by relating to regional difference in gene expression or by assuming there are other differences in visual/spatial perception

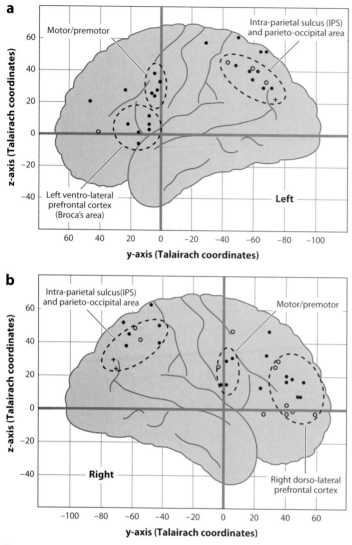

a

Motor/premotor

Intra-parietal sulcus (IPS) and parieto-occipital area

Left ventro-lateral prefrontal cortex (Broca's area)

Left

z-axis (Talairach coordinates)

60 40 20 0 −20 −40

y-axis (Talairach coordinates)

60 40 20 0 −20 −40 −60 −80 −100

b

Intra-parietal sulcus (IPS) and parieto-occipital area

Motor/premotor

Right

Right dorso-lateral prefrontal cortex

z-axis (Talairach coordinates)

60 40 20 0 −20 −40

y-axis (Talairach coordinates)

−100 −80 −60 −40 −20 0 20 40 60

Figure 2

(*a,b*) The filled circles (•) show loci of maximal activity from nine functional magnetic resonance imaging (fMRI) studies reviewed by Rouw et al. (2011) on the lateral frontal and parietal cortex (activity elsewhere, including the ventral visual stream, is not shown here but is discussed in the text). All studies involved color as the concurrent and linguistic inducers (letters, numbers, words) presented either visually or as speech. The open circles (o) are from an fMRI study of number forms (Tang et al. 2008). All contrasts compare synesthetes against a nonsynesthetic baseline (either control participants and/or stimuli that do not induce synesthesia). The "+" indicates locations in which grapheme-color synesthesia has been shown to be disrupted by transcranial magnetic stimulation (Esterman et al. 2006, Muggleton et al. 2007, Rothen et al. 2010). All coordinates are based on the Talairach system [converted from the Montreal Neurological Institute (MNI) system if necessary], and the locations of the sulci are only approximate.

that lead to vision being more prevalent as a concurrent (for which there is some evidence).

Finally, it was noted above that many of the structural and functional brain differences between synesthetes and controls do not lie in regions implicated in the processing of the inducer or concurrent. In particular, regions in the frontal and parietal lobes have been consistently implicated. Activation maxima on the lateral surface of the frontal and parietal lobes are depicted in **Figure 2a,b**. Within the parietal lobes, two areas have been highlighted: the intraparietal sulcus (IPS) on the lateral surface and the precuneus/retrosplenial region on the medial surface (these regions themselves can be subdivided, but possible subdivisions aren't considered here). The IPS region is associated with increased gray matter in grapheme-color synesthesia (Weiss & Fink 2009) and is activated in fMRI (relative to control participants) when graphemes are presented (Weiss et al. 2005). Transcranial magnetic stimulation over a nearby region disrupts the synesthetic Stroop effect (Esterman et al. 2006, Muggleton et al. 2007). The functional role of this region in synesthesia is assumed to be in binding, that is, in linking the grapheme and color into a spatially localized perceptual whole. It may also be implicated in attentional aspects of synesthesia. The functional role of the precuneus/retrosplenial region in synesthesia is unclear, although the region itself is implicated in imagery across a variety of sensory domains as well as self-directed and internal thought more generally (Cavanna & Trimble 2006). Increased white matter in this region has been found in grapheme-color synesthesia (e.g., Hupé et al. 2012), and functional activity in this region (relative to controls) has been found in a diverse range of types of synesthesia, including lexical-gustatory (contrasting synesthetes against controls when presented with inducers; Jones et al. 2011) and associating genders to graphemes (contrasting inducing versus noninducing stimuli; Amin et al. 2011) in addition to color (contrasting inducing versus noninducing stimuli; Nunn et al. 2002). Finally, regions in the lateral frontal cortex (ventral, dorsal, and motor) have been found to be activated by synesthetes relative to controls (Rouw et al. 2011), but this may reflect differences in task demands for synesthetes relative to controls (who have an "extra" dimension to process). There is little evidence of structural changes in prefrontal regions (Rouw et al. 2011), consistent with this suggestion.

Distal Causes of Developmental Synesthesia

Developmental synesthesia has long been known to run in families (Jewanski et al. 2011). However, the particular associations do not run in families. Family members don't agree on the colors of graphemes any more than do unrelated synesthetes (Barnett et al. 2008a). Nor do the patterns of inducers and concurrent appear to be strongly familial. For instance, synesthetes with lexical-gustatory synesthesia (a rare type) tend to have relatives with the more common color-based synesthesia (Ward et al. 2005). Genetic differences appear to convey a susceptibility to synesthesia but don't specify the presence/absence of synesthesia in a deterministic way. One early suggested genetic mechanism was X-linked dominant inheritance (Baron-Cohen et al. 1996). However, this has not been supported by further research on inheritance patterns and genetic linkage studies (Asher et al. 2009, Tomson et al. 2011). These studies confirm genetic differences between affected and unaffected members of the same families, and the current evidence suggests the involvement of multiple genes, but with no candidates on the X chromosome.

Bargary & Mitchell (2008) discuss three possible kinds of molecular mechanisms that could mediate between gene level and connectivity levels of explanation. First, there are genes involved in axon guidance. Genetic polymorphisms in molecules mediating axon guidance could result in different patterns of connectivity. Second, there might be disruption of border formation. Borders are regions of the brain in which activity is not propagated between adjacent regions due to either inhibition or the absence of axons between the regions. Borders are determined developmentally by differences in gene expression, and a breakdown in border formation could be one explanation of synesthesia. Finally, there may be a failure to prune synaptic connections between regions that are transiently connected in early development. This mechanism may be partly under genetic control. Further progress in this important area will depend on isolating candidate genes in synesthetes and then exploring the normal role of these genes in mouse models of brain development.

Failure to prune normally transient synaptic connections has been a particularly influential idea in the synesthesia literature. This derives from the suggestion that synesthesia is a normal phase of early development that, in most people, drops out during childhood (e.g., Maurer & Mondloch 2006). Infants are born with about 150% the level of adult synapses, and synaptic elimination is a normal part of learning and development (Huttenlocher & Dabholkar 1997). In animal studies, for instance, there are transient connections from auditory to visual areas that diminish developmentally (e.g., Innocenti et al. 1988), but one possibility is that such pathways may be retained in synesthesia. Infants show far less evidence of functional specialization and show somewhat different patterns of multisensory influence relative to older children (e.g., Maurer & Mondloch 2006). Moreover, many of the same associations found in adult synesthetes are found in infants (see discussion below). However, so far there is no direct evidence that links early differences in multisensory processing with later development of synesthesia, and virtually nothing is known about the characteristics of synesthesia itself prior to the age of 6 years. Given that synesthesia runs in families, future research could compare the infants/children of synesthetes against those lacking a familial susceptibility.

Considering children ages 6 years and up, grapheme-color synesthesia appears to be no more prevalent in the early school years than in adulthood (Simner et al. 2006, 2009a). However, there is evidence of developmental changes during this time. Child synesthetes are far less consistent in their grapheme-color associations than are adult synesthetes—fewer than half of the letters and numbers are consistently colored (Simner et al. 2009a). (Note: This level of consistency is still significantly higher than that of the average child asked to freely associate colors for graphemes.) But when tested a year later, the number of consistent associations in the child synesthetes (but not the controls) increased. This suggests that synesthesia is not just a residual form of infantile perception, but rather continues to develop during childhood. However, it is unclear what is developing (the concurrent experiences themselves or the stability of the inducer-concurrent associations), and it is unclear what precedes it developmentally. Even in adulthood, new synesthetic associations can be formed. For instance, if a synesthete learns musical notation (Ward et al. 2006b) or learns a second written language that uses different printed characters (e.g., Witthoft & Winawer 2006), the new associations are derived from old ones (e.g., on the basis of having similar shape, meaning, or phonology). Needless to say, this also points to an important role for the environment in synesthesia insofar as exposure to literacy is culturally dependent. We know nothing about how synesthesia is manifested in illiterate cultures.

Distal Causes of Acquired Synesthesia

Synesthesia can be acquired in two general ways: by sensory loss (e.g., blindness) or pharmacologically [e.g., lysergic acid diethylamide (LSD)]. Superficially, acquired synesthesia has different characteristics from developmental forms of synesthesia. The inducers tend to be simple sensory stimuli rather than learned and meaningful stimuli (e.g., graphemes, days of the week). This could reflect the participation of different brain regions or pathways in acquired versus developmental synesthesia, and it could also be related to the different times of onset that afford different opportunities for reorganization.

Acquired loss of sensory input can sometimes lead to symptoms of synesthesia. In all the examples considered below there is a clear pattern, namely, that the impaired modality acts as the synesthetic concurrent. Induced visual experiences following blindness are the most frequently documented, particularly acquired auditory-visual synesthesia (see Afra et al. 2009), although the prevalence of these experiences is unknown. Acquired touch-vision synesthesia following blindness has also been documented (Armel & Ramachandran 1999). Loss of somatosensory input through amputation or paralysis is also commonly associated with phantom pain, and acquired synesthetic sensations of touch may be induced through visual observation of touch in the location of the phantom limb (e.g., Ramachandran et al. 1995) or even by observing touch on another person (e.g., Goller et al. 2011). In the case of hearing and deafness, tinnitus (phantom sounds) can arise after damage to the peripheral auditory system, and it has been suggested that tinnitus is evoked by somatosensory inputs (Cacace et al. 1999), that is, acquired somatosensory-auditory synesthesia. After having cochlear implants fitted, prelingually deaf people report tactile experiences to sounds (McFeely et al. 1998), that is, acquired auditory-somatosensory synesthesia. In addition to sensory loss following damage to the sensory organs and peripheral nerves, acquired synesthesia has been reported after damage to the thalamus (e.g., Ro et al. 2007). Ro et al. (2007) document a patient with left-sided somatosensory weakness following a thalamic lesion who developed auditory-somatosensory synesthesia.

In terms of a general mechanism for acquired synesthesia arising from sensory loss, the sensory cortex associated with the concurrent experience remains functional but is denied its previous primary inputs. It may therefore come to rely more on existing multisensory inputs (cortico-cortical or from subcortical projections), which then take on the role of the inducer. The onset of synesthesia can be as soon as days or as long as one to two years (see Afra et al. 2009). This suggests the operation of two different kinds of neural plasticity (Pascual-Leone et al. 2005): fast-acting removal of inhibition from existing pathways and slower-acting formation of new connections. One thing that needs to be accounted for in acquired synesthesia is why some patients with sensory loss experience it, but most (apparently) do not. This raises the possibility of individual differences in reorganization or differences in the way that transient phenomena (e.g., spontaneous hallucinations) stabilize into synesthesia. It would be interesting to know whether there is any relationship between the genes that give rise to developmental synesthesia and the tendency for some (but not others) to acquire synesthesia following a coincidental sensory loss.

Finally, the temporary induction of synesthetic experiences following consumption of hallucinogenic drugs (LSD, mescaline, psilocybin) offers the clearest example of a fast-acting mechanism (minutes to hours; e.g., Hartman & Hollister 1963) that presumably arises via unmasking of pre-existing pathways. Marek & Aghajanian (1998) propose a neurobiological mechanism of disinhibition leading to synesthesia based on LSD's known action on serotonergic receptors on inhibitory interneurons in the cortex.

Where Do the Specific Associations Originate?

Most synesthetes have little or no insight into where their particular associations originate. They don't tend to come from alphabet books (Rich et al. 2005), although a few cases are known to have been biased by these (e.g., Witthoft & Winawer 2006). If the associations reflected chance contingencies in the environment (e.g., having a friend named Anne who likes to wear red), then one would expect minimal agreement among synesthetes. But synesthetic associations are not chance occurrences. The subsections below consider evidence from various types of synesthesia that the associations are nonrandom. It is claimed, instead, that synesthetic associations have their

origins in cross-sensory correspondences that are found in typical (i.e., nonsynesthetic) brains.

Audio-visual associations. Despite a significant amount of individual difference in the precise way in which music and other sounds are "seen" by synesthetes, there are some common underlying principles. High-pitch sounds, relative to low-pitch sounds, are perceived by synesthetes as being brighter, smaller, and higher in space (e.g., Fernay et al. 2012, Ward et al. 2006a). Temporal aspects of music and sounds tend to be mapped on to visual space such that, at least in Western synesthetes, music is seen to progress from left to right (Ward et al. 2008a). Changes in timbre (for a given pitch) tend to affect saturation more than lightness (Ward et al. 2006a).

Studies with the general population show cross-modal biases in speed of responding to one dimension while ignoring an irrelevant dimension in the other modality (for a review, see Marks 2004). This has been reported for pitch and lightness (high is lighter), pitch and size (high is smaller), and pitch and vertical position (high pitch is spatially higher). Similar results have been found in infants and young children (Walker et al. 2010), and luminance-pitch associations are also found in chimpanzees (Ludwig et al. 2011).

Letter-color associations. Synesthetes tend to agree on letter-color associations more than would be expected by chance; thus A tends to be red, B tends to be blue, C tends be yellow, O tends to be white, and so on (Barnett et al. 2008a, Rich et al. 2005, Simner et al. 2005). There does not appear to be a single factor that determines this, but rather at least three constraining factors: grapheme frequency, color names, and letter shape. With regard to the linguistic frequency of the grapheme, Simner et al. (2005) considered color categories and found a correlation between grapheme frequency and color term frequency (i.e., common letters tend to have common colors such as red and yellow, whereas uncommon letters have colors such as purple or brown). Beeli et al. (2007) considered

RGB space (rather than color categories) and found inverse correlations between grapheme frequency and saturation and lightness (i.e., uncommon graphemes are darker and less saturated). With regard to color names, it is found that R = red, Y = yellow, B = blue, and G = green more than would be expected by chance (e.g., Simner et al. 2005). Finally, it has been noted that similarly shaped graphemes (as determined by letter confusability matrix) tend to evoke similar colors (Brang et al. 2011a).

When nonsynesthetes are asked to freely associate color terms to graphemes, they don't show an effect of grapheme frequency, but they are biased by color names such that G = green, etc. (Simner et al. 2005). There are also shape-based influences. Spector & Maurer (2011) asked children of different ages to associate colors to letters. In one condition they were shown a Perspex shape (e.g., O) and asked which colored box they would open to find another one (given two choices such as white/black or green/red). In another condition they were told the letter name (e.g., O) and asked which box it might be in. Preliterate children (ages 3 to 4) chose nonrandomly when given a shape (e.g., O = white, X = black, C = yellow) but randomly when given a letter name. More recently, it has been shown that infants have nonrandom shape-color associations (Wagner & Dobkins 2011).

Number-color associations. For number-color synesthetes, single-digit numbers tend to progress from light to dark and saturated to unsaturated as the number increases in magnitude (Beeli et al. 2007).[2] Associations between hue and specific numbers have not been noted. Beyond 10, numbers tend to be colored by the constituent digits (so 12 would be some combination of the colors for 1 and 2). The association between magnitude and luminance is also found in adult nonsynesthetes.

If asked to decide which of two numbers is larger (e.g., 3 or 6), performance is facilitated if the smaller number is lighter and the larger number is darker than when it is vice versa (Cohen Kadosh & Henik 2006), and these number-luminance associations are mediated by the parietal lobes (Kadosh et al. 2008).

Spatial forms. Spatial forms, at least from synesthetes in the West, tend to run in a left-to-right direction (e.g., Eagleman 2009, Jonas et al. 2011, Sagiv et al. 2006). This is assumed to reflect a cultural bias from reading direction. Associations between space and number are found in nonsynesthetes too, with a general left-to-right association with magnitude on response time measures (Fias & Fischer 2005).

In addition to direction, the shape of spatial forms reflects the internal structure of the sequence. Number forms often bend or break at decade boundaries—10, 20, etc. (Sagiv et al. 2006). Months are more likely to be represented in a circular arrangement than numbers, reflecting their cyclical nature (Brang et al. 2010). Handedness may further influence the direction of rotation, with left-handers arranging the months counterclockwise and right-handers clockwise (Brang et al. 2011b). Spatial forms involving the alphabet tend to bend/break around phrases in the alphabet song (Jonas et al. 2011).

Makioka (2009) provides a computational model of number forms that could also be extended to other sequences. Variations in an input layer (corresponding to number size) are mapped onto a two-dimensional output layer (corresponding to space) using a self-organizing map. Similarities in the inputs (e.g., the number 5 is more similar to 6 than it is 8) give rise to its sequential structure (i.e., 5 is spatially nearer to 6 than 8 in the output layer). Bends/breaks in the form reflect a combination of noise in the model and a decomposition of the input layer into separate representations of tens and units. Circular arrangements of months are predicted by this model if the input representation of January and December are similar to each other (despite being at opposite ends of the verbal sequence).

In summary, synesthetic associations are not random, and nor are they likely to be based on chance occurrences within the environment. Instead they have a rich structure that is based on the multisensory correspondences found in the typically developing brain from a young age. Different causal mechanisms, discussed above, would then act on these associations so that for individuals with synesthesia they are consciously perceived (internally stable, etc.), whereas in most others they exert indirect effects.

THE CONSEQUENCES OF SYNESTHESIA

What are the consequences of having synesthesia for other aspects of cognition such as memory, creativity, or numeracy? The answer to this question is of general interest to psychologists for a number of reasons. First, the question has obvious relevance to those with an interest in individual differences. Second, the question is relevant for the broader theoretical issue as to how perception interfaces with (or underpins) other aspects of cognition.

In thinking about how synesthesia may be linked to other cognitive differences (both weaknesses and strengths), one could entertain a number of possibilities. These are summarized in **Figure 3**. The first possibility is that synesthesia exerts a direct influence on cognition. That is, the synesthetic associations themselves (e.g., 5 = red, 6 = salty) participate in other cognitive domains and affect cognitive performance in those domains. The second possibility is that changes in cognitive performance are an outcome of the more general structural/functional differences known to exist in the brains of synesthetes. For example, this position is advocated by Ramachandran & Hubbard (2003, p. 58) with respect to creativity: "[S]ynesthesia causes excess communication among brain maps. Depending on where and how widely in the brain the trait was expressed, it could lead to

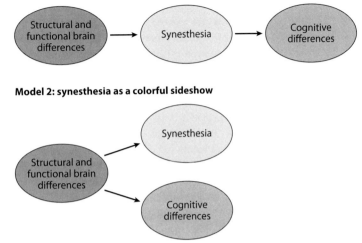

Model 1: synesthesia as directly causal

Structural and functional brain differences → Synesthesia → Cognitive differences

Model 2: synesthesia as a colorful sideshow

Structural and functional brain differences → Synesthesia

Structural and functional brain differences → Cognitive differences

Figure 3

How might synesthesia be related to individual differences in cognition? Two different models are outlined here, in which synesthesia either has a direct role or is a co-occurring symptom linked to a mediating variable (such as structural/functional brain differences).

both synesthesia and to a propensity towards linking seemingly unrelated concepts and ideas—in short, creativity. This would explain why the apparently useless synesthesia gene has survived in the population." Disentangling these two scenarios is not straightforward because the chain of causality is not amenable to experimental manipulation. However, one prediction is that if synesthesia is directly involved, then the affected domain should be relatively circumscribed to synesthesia-related material.

Perception

Synesthetes with grapheme-color synesthesia perform better on tests of color perception relative to controls (Banissy et al. 2009b, Yaro & Ward 2007). Moreover, there does appear to be a relationship between the modality of the synesthetic concurrent and the modality in which perception is enhanced. Thus, mirror-touch synesthetes have enhanced tactile acuity (but normal color perception), whereas grapheme-color synesthetes show the opposite profile (Banissy et al. 2009b). This suggests a direct relationship between synesthesia and differences in perceptual ability: It is not simply the case that synesthetes are better perceivers in some general sense. However, it is unclear from these data whether we can conclude that the differences in perception are a consequence or a cause. Barnett et al. (2008b) speculate that the differences in perception may predate the emergence of synesthesia because differences are found in early visual pathways (early in terms of developmental maturity and in terms of visual hierarchy). From electroencephalogram recordings, they suggest that grapheme-color synesthetes may have a perceptual enhancement of the parvocellular system (sensitive to color, high contrast, high spatial frequency) relative to magnocellular system (sensitive to motion, low contrast, low spatial frequency). Interestingly, synesthetes show both increased cortical thickness in a color-related region (V4) and reduced cortical thickness in a region related to motion perception (V5/MT) (Banissy et al. 2012). As such, the existing evidence suggests that perceptual changes in visual synesthesia aren't limited to the concurrent (color), nor are they as broad as the sense itself (vision), but rather may affect an intermediate systems level.

Imagery

People with grapheme-color synesthesia report more vivid visual imagery than matched controls (Barnett & Newell 2007). Synesthetes with spatial forms also report greater use and vividness of visual imagery, but not spatial imagery (Price 2009). The latter may imply that forms are more like visual objects than maps (as suggested by Eagleman 2009). There is also evidence that grapheme-color synesthetes are faster at visual imagery, at least when it involves letters (Spiller & Jansari 2008). It is possible that enhancements in imagery closely parallel enhancements in perception, given the close relationship between perception, imagery, and visual memory (e.g., Slotnick et al. 2012). Consistent with this, Seron et al. (1992) report a greater imbalance between visualizing and

verbalizing strategies in daily life in synesthetes with number forms (verbalizing weaker) relative to controls.

Memory

Some notable cases of exceptional memory abilities have been linked to synesthesia. Luria (1968) describes the case of S (now known to be Solomon Shereshevskii), who performed feats of extraordinary memory to entertain public audiences. S also reported having multiple forms of synesthesia in which, for instance, a voice may elicit colors, textures, and tastes. Daniel Tammet (2006) gives an autobiographical account of both his synesthesia and his prodigious memory. For instance, he was able to memorize pi to over 20,000 decimal places and reported doing so by using his synesthesia: Each digit had a characteristic color, shape, and texture that, when placed together as a sequence, created an undulating landscape that he could read off from his mind's eye. In formal testing, Tammet appeared to rely less on conventional ways of chunking stimuli that were found to benefit controls (Bor et al. 2007). This suggests that he relies on his own strategies for encoding material mnemonically (e.g., based on his synesthesia). Tammet also has Asperger's syndrome, and one suggestion is that the (presumably coincidental) co-occurrence of synesthesia and Asperger's leads to a particularly beneficial synergy for memorizing.

Both Tammet and S came to the attention of researchers because of their abilities, but is synesthesia associated with enhanced memory in unselected cases? The answer to this question is yes, but not all aspects of memory are affected equally (e.g., Rothen & Meier 2010a, Yaro & Ward 2007). In grapheme-color synesthesia, one of the most consistent findings is that long-term memory for verbal material (such as free recall of word lists) is better than for matched controls (e.g., Radvansky et al. 2011, Yaro & Ward 2007). This may be expected on the basis that, for these individuals, words are encoded visually (e.g., as a pattern of colors) in addition to verbally/semantically.

Indeed, Radvansky et al. (2011) showed that synesthetes were less influenced by semantic factors than were controls in free recall, suggesting that they may rely more on perceptual encoding. Synesthetes with calendar forms (i.e., experiencing months and years spatially) are better at retrieving autobiographical events from date cues, and they are more accurate at dating news events (Simner et al. 2009b). This suggests that they can use their internal synesthetic representations to give an organized structure to certain memoranda.

The evidence above suggests a close link between the nature of the synesthesia and the nature of memory enhancement. However, the evidence is not quite as clear-cut as this. First, not all verbal memory tasks show an enhancement. Grapheme-color synesthetes do not show enhanced performance on digit span (e.g., Rothen & Meier 2010a) or on remembering the position of digits in a matrix (e.g., Yaro & Ward 2007). This suggests that it is not just the material (and whether it triggers synesthesia) but how one has to process it mnestically. Associating an item to a position (in a sequence or matrix) requires forming a specific contextual association, whereas free recall can be done at the item level itself. Thus, spatial and sequential memory may not be enhanced in grapheme-color synesthesia even if the participating stimuli induce synesthesia. Second, the memory enhancement is also found for some visual material. Synesthetes have better memory for colors (Yaro & Ward 2007) and do particularly well on tasks such as learning to pair colors with abstract shapes (Rothen & Meier 2010a). Gaining a better understanding of precisely which type of visual stimuli do and do not give rise to enhanced memory is an important challenge for future research. It is possible that the changes in perceptual ability (described above) also affect the ability to encode certain types of material into memory.

Art and Creativity

It has been observed that both the hobbies and occupations of synesthetes are skewed toward the creative industries, relative to national estimates of numbers employed in that sector, in both Australia (Rich et al. 2005) and the United Kingdom (Ward et al. 2008b). Moreover, the prevalence of grapheme-color synesthesia is higher in arts students compared to those from other subjects (Rothen & Meier 2010b), and synesthetes (as a mixed group) are more likely to be engaged in visual arts as a hobby (Rich et al. 2005, Ward et al. 2008b). This is particularly true of auditory-visual synesthetes, for whom music and other sounds trigger a very rich experience of colors, shapes, texture, and movement. These individuals are far more likely than other synesthetes to play musical instruments and be engaged in visual art, and Ward et al. (2008b) suggest that the synesthesia provides a particularly vivid source of artistic inspiration for these individuals (i.e., Model 1 in **Figure 3**). In addition, an enhanced color sense could lead to a more general interest in the visual arts in synesthetes with color as the concurrent.

Artistic engagement is only one way in which creativity can be expressed. Creativity as a cognitive ability can be assessed by tests that tap an ability to form novel and adaptive (i.e., useful/meaningful) associations. Ramachandran & Hubbard (2003) suggest that the kinds of brain changes that give rise to synesthesia may also give rise to creativity as a cognitive ability. Ward et al. (2008b) gave two tests of creativity to a group of synesthetes and controls: a test of divergent thinking (generating alternative uses for objects) and a test of convergent thinking (finding a conceptual link between three words). The synesthetes did outperform the controls, but only on the test of convergent thinking (even after entering education as a regressor). This provides some support for Ramachandran & Hubbard's (2003) suggestion, but not complete support (as their theory predicts that all aspects of creativity are enhanced). It would be important to extend and replicate the result using other tests and measures (including in the nonverbal domain) and taking into account other potential confounds (e.g., vocabulary level).

Numeracy

Rich et al. (2005) asked a large sample of synesthetes ($n = 192$) to report their strengths and weaknesses in an open-ended way and then compared this to a control group. The list of strengths included memory, languages, written and verbal communications, and art. The list of weaknesses included sense of direction and coordination/balance. Interestingly, mathematics was described both more often as a strength and more often as a weakness (relative to controls). Daniel Tammet (2006), described above, would be an example of a synesthete who is able to use his synesthesia to perform extraordinary calculations (e.g., 37^5). As with his general memorizing ability, he may use his synesthesia to store a large number of numerical facts to aid in calculation.

In what ways could synesthesia also be disadvantageous to numerical cognition? There is some evidence of numerical difficulties in synesthetes with number forms (although not necessarily in grapheme-color synesthesia). Specifically, this group is significantly slower with single-digit multiplication but performed normally on subtraction (Ward et al. 2009). Different arithmetical operations rely on different cognitive mechanisms, with multiplication normally relying more on retrieval of verbal facts (e.g., $5 \times 5 = 25$) and subtraction relying on online calculation (e.g., Dehaene et al. 2003). Ward et al. (2009) argued that synesthetes with number forms might tend to be biased toward a slower visuo-spatial strategy (rather than faster verbal retrieval) and that this impacts multiplication most because the strategy is less suited to that operation. Other studies have shown that synesthetes with number forms have worse performance on numerical tasks when the numbers are spatially incompatible with their internal representation (e.g., Gertner et al. 2009, Sagiv et al. 2006). Although spatial processes have a role to play in nonsynesthetic numerical cognition, the presence of a number form may impair the ability to represent numbers in a flexible manner according to task demands (Gertner et al. 2009).

Summary

At the start of this section, I outlined two broad ways in which synesthesia could be linked to individual differences in cognition. Synesthesia could be directly related to individual differences in cognition, or the relationship may be more indirect (e.g., both synesthesia and individual differences in cognition coemerge from a common mediating factor). One way in which to explore this is to determine how specific or general the profile of differences is. In the domain of perception and imagery there is evidence of enhanced abilities, and the benefits are found to be relatively specific to domains related to the synesthesia (e.g., to color perception and visual imagery in grapheme-color synesthesia) but are not limited to stimuli that act as inducers/concurrents. For memory, it is undoubtedly the case that synesthetic associations (to words, etc.) can be used to directly develop mnemonics and may bias the way that information is encoded. However, there is also evidence of a broader influence (e.g., grapheme-color synesthetes have enhanced visual memory for certain achromatic stimuli; Rothen & Meier 2010a). For psychometric measures of creativity, further evidence is needed to determine how and when synesthesia affects performance on these tests. However, the evidence that synesthesia (in general) is linked to artistic inclinations is more robust and may be even more common in those who have very rich synesthetic experiences (such as those linked to visualized music; i.e., a direct link between synesthesia and artistic tendencies). Although cognitive difficulties have been self-reported in synesthesia, these have been under-researched. So far, the clearest evidence comes from a link between number forms and some difficulty on certain tests of numerical cognition (i.e., a direct link between synesthetic phenomenology and cognitive outcome).

CONCLUDING REMARKS

Research into synesthesia is at a crossroads. The onus is no longer on researchers to establish its existence—this is beyond doubt. However, the nature of synesthesia remains harder to pin down. I suggest that it straddles perception, imagery, and memory, and this is broadly consistent with contemporary theories that acknowledge shared mechanisms across these domains. A greater challenge for researchers is to place synesthesia within the bigger picture. Are we studying synesthesia in order to understand synesthesia itself? This is not an unreasonable research agenda given how many people are estimated to have it. However, I have argued in this review that we can use synesthesia as a tool to understand cognition more generally. Synesthesia provides a window into, among other things, how conscious experiences are created; how genetic differences affect brain development and cognition; and how different ways of perceiving the world may impact upon memory, numeracy, artistic inclinations, and so on. It is likely to be on these fronts that the value of synesthesia research will be realized.

SUMMARY POINTS

1. Empirical research into synesthesia shows it to be a genuine phenomenon that cannot be reduced to associative learning, vivid imagination, or metaphorical thinking. It can be thought of as an alternative mode of perceiving (and conceptualizing) the world.

2. Synesthetic experiences are elicited (i.e., triggered by a stimulus) and automatic (at least when the inducer is attended), and many definitions also incorporate the notion that they are percept-like in nature. They tend to be internally consistent (at least in adults) and spatially extended (utilizing various spatial reference frames).

3. It is generally believed that the patterns of inducer-concurrent pairings found in synesthesia are derived from the same principles that determine cortical connectivity in general; for instance, favoring connectivity between adjacent regions.

4. There is evidence of structural differences in the brains of developmental forms of synesthesia (both in white matter and gray matter), but these differences are by no means limited to regions of the brain that process the inducer or concurrent.

5. Acquired synesthesia may occur as a result of sensory loss (such that the lost modality acts as the synesthetic concurrent), and this may reflect both disinhibition of existing pathways and slower-acting structural changes in connectivity.

6. The particular associations themselves are not random but structured. They may reflect a universal tendency to associate certain attributes together (e.g., pitch with luminance, shape with color) that is present from a very early age. This suggests a link between synesthesia and normal modes of multisensory processing, but whereas synesthetes directly experience these associations (e.g., 3 is bright yellow), they tend to exist as declarative knowledge or implicit rules in other adults (e.g., as revealed in response time measures).

7. Synesthesia conveys various cognitive benefits in perception, imagery, and memory. These benefits tend to be relatively circumscribed (e.g., not all aspects of perception are improved) and bear some relation to the type of synesthesia experienced. They also lead to possible difficulties (e.g., in numeracy), although these are less explored.

FUTURE ISSUES

1. How does synesthesia manifest itself in cultures that are very different from our own? To what extent is synesthesia culturally situated despite having a biological basis?

2. What is the role of the hypothetical synesthesia genes in normal brain development, and how is their action altered in people with synesthesia?

3. Why is it that only some individuals with sensory loss (blindness, deafness, amputation) go on to acquire synesthesia? What is different about their brains or their environment?

4. What insights can synesthesia give us into consciousness—its function, its neural basis, or the hard problem of why things feel the way they do?

5. What specific cognitive problems are associated with synesthesia, and in what ways are they directly related to the presence of synesthesia itself?

DISCLOSURE STATEMENT

The author is not aware of any affiliations, memberships, funding, or financial holdings that might be perceived as affecting the objectivity of this review.

LITERATURE CITED

Afra M, Funke M, Matsuo F. 2009. Acquired auditory-visual synesthesia: a window to early cross-modal sensory interactions. *Psychol. Res. Behav. Manag.* 2:31–37

Amin M, Olu-Lafe O, Claessen LE, Sobczak-Edmans M, Ward J, et al. 2011. Understanding grapheme personification: a social synaesthesia? *J. Neuropsychol.* 5:255–82

Armel KC, Ramachandran VS. 1999. Acquired synaesthesia in retinitis pigmentosa. *Neurocase* 5:293–96

Asher JE, Lamb JA, Brocklebank D, Cazier JB, Maestrini E, et al. 2009. A whole-genome scan and fine-mapping linkage study of auditory-visual synesthesia reveals evidence of linkage to chromosomes 2q24, 5q33, 6p12, and 12p12. *Am. J. Hum. Genet.* 84:279–85

Astle D. 2007. Geoffrey Rush: a man for all seasons. *Sun Herald*, May 20. **http://www.grippers.com.au/grippers-articles/2007/5/20/geoffrey-rush-a-man-for-all-seasons/**

Banissy MJ, Kadosh RC, Maus GW, Walsh V, Ward J. 2009a. Prevalence, characteristics and a neurocognitive model of mirror-touch synaesthesia. *Exp. Brain Res.* 198:261–72

Banissy MJ, Stewart L, Muggleton NG, Griffiths T, Walsh V, et al. 2012. Grapheme-colour and tone-colour synaesthesia is associated with structural brain differences in visual regions implicated in colour, form and motion. *Cogn. Neurosci.* 3:29–35

Banissy MJ, Walsh V, Ward J. 2009b. Enhanced sensory perception in synaesthesia. *Exp. Brain Res.* 196:565–71

Bargary G, Mitchell KJ. 2008. Synaesthesia and cortical connectivity. *Trends Neurosci.* 31:335–42

Barnett KJ, Finucane C, Asher JE, Bargary G, Corvin AP, et al. 2008a. Familial patterns and the origins of individual differences in synaesthesia. *Cognition* 106:871–93

Barnett KJ, Foxe JJ, Malholm S, Kelly SP, Shalgi S, et al. 2008b. Differences in early sensory-perceptual processing in synesthesia: a visual evoked potential study. *NeuroImage* 15:605–13

Barnett KJ, Newell FN. 2007. Synaesthesia is associated with enhanced, self-rated visual imagery. *Conscious. Cogn.* 17:1032–39

Baron-Cohen S, Burt L, Smith-Laittan F, Harrison J, Bolton P. 1996. Synaesthesia: prevalence and familiality. *Perception* 25:1073–79

Baron-Cohen S, Wyke MA, Binnie C. 1987. Hearing words and seeing colours: an experimental investigation of a case of synaesthesia. *Perception* 16:761–67

Beauchamp MS, Ro T. 2008. Neural substrates of sound-touch synesthesia after a thalamic lesion. *J. Neurosci.* 28:13696–702

Beeli G, Esslen M, Jäncke L. 2005. Synaesthesia: when coloured sounds taste sweet. *Nature* 434:38

Beeli G, Esslen M, Jäncke L. 2007. Frequency correlates in grapheme-color synaesthesia. *Psychol. Sci.* 18:788–92

Bernard JW. 1986. Messiaen's synaesthesia: the correspondence between color and sound structure in his music. *Music Percept.* 4:41–68

Blakemore S-J, Bristow D, Bird G, Frith C, Ward J. 2005. Somatosensory activations during the observation of touch and a case of vision-touch synesthesia. *Brain* 128:1571–83

Bleuler E, Lehmann K. 1881. *Zwangsmaessige Lichtempfindungen durch Scall und verwandte Erscheinungen auf dem Gebiete der anderen Sinnesempfindungen.* Leipzig: Fues's Verlag

Block N. 2005. Two neural correlates of consciousness. *Trends Cogn. Sci.* 9:46–52

Bor D, Billington J, Baron-Cohen S. 2007. Savant memory for digits in a case of synaesthesia and Asperger syndrome is related to hyperactivity in the lateral prefrontal cortex. *Neurocase* 13:311–19

Brang D, Ramachandran VS. 2011. Survival of the synesthesia gene: Why do people hear colors and taste words? *PLoS Biol.* 9:e1001205

Brang D, Rouw R, Ramachandran VS, Coulson S. 2011a. Similarly shaped letters evoke similar colors in grapheme-color synesthesia. *Neuropsychologia* 49:1355–58

Brang D, Teuscher U, Miller LE, Ramachandran VS, Coulson S. 2011b. Handedness and calendar orientations in time-space synaesthesia. *J. Neuropsychol.* 5:323–32

Brang D, Teuscher U, Ramachandran VS, Coulson S. 2010. Temporal sequences, synesthetic mappings, and cultural biases: the geography of time. *Conscious. Cogn.* 19:311–20

Burbridge D. 1994. Galton's 100: an exploration of Francis Galton's imagery studies. *Br. J. Hist. Sci.* 27:443–63

Cacace AT, Cousins JP, Parnes SM, Semenoff D, Holmes T, et al. 1999. Cutaneous-evoked tinnitus. I. Phenomenology, psychophysics and functional imaging. *Audiol. Neurootol.* 4:247–57

Calkins MW. 1895. Synaesthesia. *Am. J. Psychol.* 7:90–107

Cavanna AE, Trimble MR. 2006. The precuneus: a review of its functional anatomy and behavioural correlates. *Brain* 129:564–83

Chabalier. 1864. De la pseudochromesthesie. *J. Med. Lyon* 1:92–102

Cohen Kadosh R, Cohen Kadosh K, Henik A. 2007. The neuronal correlates of bi-directional synaesthesia: a combined ERP and fMRI study. *J. Cogn. Neurosci.* 19:2050–59

Cohen Kadosh R, Henik A. 2006. A common representation for semantic and physical properties. *Exp. Psychol.* 53:87–94

Cornaz CAE. 1848. *Des abnormalities congenitales de jeux et de leurs annexes.* Lausanne: Bridel

Dann KT. 1998. *Bright Colors Falsely Seen.* London: Yale Univ. Press

Dehaene S, Piazza M, Pinel P, Cohen L. 2003. Three parietal circuits for number processing. *Cogn. Neuropsychol.* 20:487–506

Dixon MJ, Smilek D, Cudahy C, Merikle PM. 2000. Five plus two equals yellow. *Nature* 406:365

Dixon MJ, Smilek D, Merikle PM. 2004. Not all synaesthetes are created equal: projector versus associator synaesthetes. *Cogn. Affect. Behav. Neurosci.* 4:335–43

Downey JE. 1911. A case of colored gustation. *Am. J. Psychol.* 22:528–39

Driver J, Noesselt T. 2008. Multisensory interplay reveals crossmodal influences on "sensory-specific" brain regions, neural responses, and judgments. *Neuron* 57:11–23

Eagleman DM. 2009. The objectification of overlearned sequences: a new view of spatial sequence synesthesia. *Cortex* 45:1266–77

Eagleman DM, Kagan AD, Nelson SS, Sagaram D, Sarma AK. 2007. A standardized test battery for the study of synesthesia. *J. Neurosci. Methods* 159:139–45

Edquist J, Rich AN, Brinkman C, Mattingley JB. 2006. Do synaesthetic colours act as unique features in visual search? *Cortex* 42:222–31

Elias LJ, Saucier DM, Hardie C, Sart GE. 2003. Dissociating semantic and perceptual components of synaesthesia: behavioural and functional neuroanatomical investigations. *Cogn. Brain Res.* 16:232–37

Esterman M, Verstynen T, Ivry RB, Robertson LC. 2006. Coming unbound: disrupting automatic integration of synesthetic color and graphemes by TMS of the right parietal lobe. *J. Cogn. Neurosci.* 18:1570–76

Fernay L, Reby D, Ward J. 2012. Visualized voices: a case study of audio-visual synesthesia. *Neurocase* 18:50–56

Feynman RP. 1988. *What Do You Care What Other People Think?* London: Unwin

Fias W, Fischer MH. 2005. Spatial representation of number. In *Handbook of Mathematical Cognition*, ed. JID Campbell, pp. 43–54. Hove, UK: Psychol. Press

Flakne A. 2005. Embodied and embedded: friendship and the sunaisthetic self. *Epoche* 10:37–63

Galton F. 1883. *Inquiries into Human Faculty and Its Development*. New York: AMS Press

Gertner L, Henik A, Kadosh RC. 2009. When 9 is not on the right: implications from number-form synesthesia. *Conscious. Cogn.* 18:366–74

Goller AI, Nowak S, Richard K, Ward J. 2011. Mirror-touch synaesthesia in the phantom limb of amputees. *Cortex*. doi: 10.1016/j.cortex.2011.05.002. In press

Goller AI, Otten LJ, Ward J. 2009. Seeing sounds and hearing colors: an event-related potential study of auditory-visual synesthesia. *J. Cogn. Neurosci.* 21:1869–81

Grossenbacher PG, Lovelace CT. 2001. Mechanisms of synaesthesia: cognitive and physiological constraints. *Trends Cogn. Sci.* 5:36–41

Halligan PW, Fink GR, Marshall JC, Vallar G. 2003. Spatial cognition: evidence from visual neglect. *Trends Cogn. Sci.* 7:125–33

Hartman AM, Hollister LE. 1963. Effect of mescaline, lysergic acid diethylamide and psilocybin on color perception. *Psychopharmacologia* 4:441–51

Hong SW, Blake R. 2008. Early visual mechanisms do not contribute to synesthetic color experience. *Vision Res.* 48:1018–26

Howells TH. 1944. The experimental development of color-tone synesthesia. *J. Exp. Psychol.* 34:87–103

Hubbard EM, Arman AC, Ramachandran VS, Boynton GM. 2005a. Individual differences among grapheme-colour synaesthetes: brain-behavior correlations. *Neuron* 45:975–85

Hubbard EM, Brang D, Ramachandran VS. 2011. The cross-activation theory at 10. *J. Neuropsychol.* 5:152–77

Hubbard EM, Piazza M, Pinel P, Dehaene S. 2005b. Interactions between numbers and space in parietal cortex. *Nat. Rev. Neurosci.* 6:435–48

Hupé JM, Bordier C, Dojat M. 2012. The neural bases of grapheme-color synesthesia are not localized in real color-sensitive areas. *Cereb. Cortex*. In press

Huttenlocher PR, Dabholkar AS. 1997. Regional differences in synaptogenesis in human cerebral cortex. *J. Comp. Neurol.* 387:167–78

Innocenti GM, Berbel P, Clarke S. 1988. Development of projections from auditory to visual areas in the cat. *J. Comp. Neurol.* 272:242–59

Jacobs L, Karpik A, Bozian D, Gothgen S. 1981. Auditory-visual synesthesia: sound-induced photisms. *Arch. Neurol.* 38:211–16

Jarick M, Dixon MJ, Stewart MT, Maxwell EC, Smilek D. 2009. A different outlook on time: Visual and auditory month names elicit different mental vantage points for a time-space synaesthete. *Cortex* 45:1217–28

Jewanski J, Day SA, Simner J, Ward J. 2011. The development of a scientific understanding of synesthesia during the mid-nineteenth century (1849–1873). *J. Hist. Neurosci.* 20:284–305

Jewanski J, Day SA, Ward J. 2009. A colorful albino: the first documented case of synaesthesia, by Georg Tobias Ludwig Sachs in 1812. *J. Hist. Neurosci.* 18:293–303

Jonas CN, Taylor AJG, Hutton S, Weiss PH, Ward J. 2011. Visuo-spatial representations of the alphabet in synaesthetes and non-synaesthetes. *J. Neuropsychol.* 5:302–22

Jones C, Gray MA, Minati L, Simner J, Critchley HD, Ward J. 2011. The neural basis of illusory gustatory sensations: two rare cases of lexical-gustatory synaesthesia. *J. Neuropsychol.* 5:243–54

Kadosh RC, Henik A, Catena A, Walsh V, Fuentes LJ. 2009. Induced cross-modal synaesthetic experience without abnormal neuronal connections. *Psychol. Sci.* 20:258–65

Kadosh RC, Kadosh KC, Henik A. 2008. When brightness counts: the neuronal correlate of numerical-luminance interference. *Cereb. Cortex* 18:337–43

Kim C-Y, Blake R, Palmeri TJ. 2006. Perceptual interaction between real and synesthetic colors. *Cortex* 42:195–203

Laeng B, Svartdal F, Oelmann H. 2004. Does colour synesthesia pose a paradox for early-selection theories of attention? *Psychol. Sci.* 15:277–81

Larner AJ. 2006. A possible account of synaesthesia dating from the seventeenth century. *J. Hist. Neurosci.* 15:245–49

Ludwig VU, Adachi I, Matsuzawa T. 2011. Visuoauditory mappings between high luminance and high pitch are shared by chimpanzees (*Pan troglodytes*) and humans. *Proc. Natl. Acad. Sci. USA* 108:20661–65

Luria A. 1968. *The Mind of a Mnemonist*. New York: Basic Books

Lusanna F. 1873. *Fisiolgia der Colori*. Padone, Italy: F. Sacchetto

MacLeod CM. 1991. Half a century of research on the Stroop effect: an integrative review. *Psychol. Bull.* 109:163–203

Makioka S. 2009. A self-organizing learning account of number-form synaesthesia. *Cognition* 112:397–414

Marek GJ, Aghajanian GK. 1998. Indoleamine and the phenethylamine hallucinogens: mechanisms of psychotomimetic action. *Drug Alcohol. Dep.* 51:189–98

Marks LE. 2004. Cross-modal interactions in speeded classification. In *The Handbook of Multisensory Processes*, ed. G Calvert, C Spence, BE Stein, pp. 85–104. Cambridge, MA: MIT Press

Mattingley JB, Payne J, Rich AN. 2006. Attentional load attenuates synaesthetic priming effects in grapheme-colour synaesthesia. *Cortex* 42:213–21

Mattingley JB, Rich AN, Bradshaw JL. 2001. Unconscious priming eliminates automatic binding of colour and alphanumeric form in synaesthesia. *Nature* 410:580–82

Maurer D, Mondloch CJ. 2006. The infant as synesthete? *Attention Perform.* XXI:449–71

McFeely WJ, Antonelli PJ, Rodriguez FJ, Holmes AE. 1998. Somatosensory phenomena after multichannel cochlear implantation in prelingually deaf adults. *Am. J. Otol.* 19:467–71

Meier B, Rothen N. 2009. Training grapheme-colour associations produces a synaesthetic Stroop effect, but not a conditioned synaesthetic response. *Neuropsychologia* 47:1208–11

Morgan M. 2003. *The Space Between Our Ears: How the Brain Represents Visual Space*. London: Oxford Univ. Press

Muggleton N, Tsakanikos E, Walsh V, Ward J. 2007. Disruption of the synaesthetic Stroop effect following right posterior parietal TMS. *Neuropsychologia* 45:1582–85

Nabokov V. 1967. *Speak, Memory: An Autobiography Revisited*. New York: Vintage Books

Nunn JA, Gregory LJ, Brammer M, Williams SCR, Parslow DM, et al. 2002. Functional magnetic resonance imaging of synesthesia: activation of V4/V8 by spoken words. *Nat. Neurosci.* 5:371–75

Nussbaumer FA. 1873. Uber subjective Farben-Empfindungen, die durch objektive Gehorempfindungen erzeugt werdeb. *Wiener Med. Wochenschr.* 1:4–7

Palmeri TJ, Blake R, Marois R, Flanery MA, Whetsell W. 2002. The perceptual reality of synesthetic colors. *Proc. Natl. Acad. Sci. USA* 99:4127–31

Pascual-Leone A, Amedi A, Fregni F, Merabet LB. 2005. The plastic human brain cortex. *Annu. Rev. Neurosci.* 28:377–401

Perroud M. 1863. De l'hyperchromatopsie. *Mem. Soc. Sci. Med. Lyon* 2:37–41

Pesic P. 2006. Issac Newton and the mystery of the major sixth: a transcription of his manuscript "Of Musick" with commentary. *Interdisc. Sci. Rev.* 31:291–306

Price MC. 2009. Spatial forms and mental imagery. *Cortex* 45:1229–45

Radvansky GA, Gibson BS, McNerney MW. 2011. Synesthesia and memory: color congruency, von Restorff, and false memory effects. *J. Exp. Psychol.: Learn. Mem. Cogn.* 37:219–29

Ramachandran VS, Hubbard EM. 2001. Psychophysical investigations into the neural basis of synaesthesia. *Proc. R. Soc. Lond. B* 268:979–83

Ramachandran VS, Hubbard EM. 2003. Hearing colors, tasting shapes. *Sci. Am.* 288:52–99

Ramachandran VS, Rogers-Ramachandran D, Cobb S. 1995. Touching the phantom limb. *Nature* 377:489–90

Ranke J. 1875. Contributions to a doctrine of crossing-sense organs. *J. Sci. Zool.* 25:143–62

Rich AN, Bradshaw JL, Mattingley JB. 2005. A systematic, large-scale study of synaesthesia: implications for the role of early experience in lexical-colour associations. *Cognition* 98:53–84

Ro T, Farnè A, Johnson RM, Wedeen V, Chu Z, et al. 2007. Feeling sounds after a thalamic lesion. *Ann. Neurol.* 62:433–41

Rothen N, Meier B. 2010a. Grapheme-colour synaesthesia yields an ordinary rather than extraordinary memory advantage: evidence from a group study. *Memory* 18:258–64

Rothen N, Meier B. 2010b. Higher prevalence of synaesthesia in art students. *Perception* 39:718–20

Rothen N, Nyffeler T, von Wartburg R, Muri R, Meier B. 2010. Parieto-occipital suppression eliminates implicit bidirectionality in grapheme-colour synaesthesia. *Neuropsychologia* 48:3482–87

Rouw R, Scholte HS. 2007. Increased structural connectivity in grapheme-color synesthesia. *Nat. Neurosci.* 10:792–97

Rouw R, Scholte HS, Colizoli O. 2011. Brain areas involved in synaesthesia: a review. *J. Neuropsychol.* 5:214–42

Sagiv N, Simner J, Collins J, Butterworth B, Ward J. 2006. What is the relationship between synaesthesia and visuo-spatial number forms? *Cognition* 101:114–28

Seron X, Pesenti M, Noel M-P, Deloche G, Cornet JA. 1992. Images of numbers, or "when 98 is upper left and 6 sky blue." *Cognition* 44:159–96

Simner J. 2012. Defining synaesthesia. *Br. J. Psychol.* 103:1–15

Simner J, Harrold J, Creed H, Monro L, Foulkes L. 2009a. Early detection markers for synaesthesia in childhood populations. *Brain* 132:57–64

Simner J, Hung W-Y, Shillcock R. 2011. Synaesthesia in a logographic language: the colouring of Chinese characters and Pinyin/Bopomo spellings. *Conscious. Cogn.* 20:1376–92

Simner J, Lanz M, Jansari A, Noonan K, Glover L, et al. 2005. Non-random associations of graphemes to colours in synaesthetic and normal populations. *Cogn. Neuropsychol.* 22:1069–85

Simner J, Mayo N, Spiller M-J. 2009b. A foundation for savantism? Visuo-spatial synaesthetes present with cognitive benefits. *Cortex* 45:1246–60

Simner J, Mulvenna C, Sagiv N, Tsakanikos E, Witherby SA, et al. 2006. Synaesthesia: the prevalence of atypical cross-modal experiences. *Perception* 35:1024–33

Simner J, Ward J. 2006. Synaesthesia: the taste of words on the tip of the tongue. *Nature* 444:438

Slotnick SD, Thompson W, Kosslyn SM. 2012. Visual memory and visual mental imagery recruit common control and sensory regions of the brain. *Cogn. Neurosci.* 3:14–20

Smilek D, Callejas A, Merikle P, Dixon M. 2006. Ovals of time: space-time synesthesia. *Conscious. Cogn.* 16:507–19

Smilek D, Dixon MJ, Cudahy C, Merikle PM. 2001. Synaesthetic photisms influence visual perception. *J. Cogn. Neurosci.* 13:930–36

Spector F, Maurer D. 2011. The colors of the alphabet: naturally-biased associations between shape and color. *J. Exp. Psychol.: Hum. Percept. Perform.* 37:484–95

Spiller MJ, Jansari AS. 2008. Mental imagery and synaesthesia: Is synaesthesia from internally-generated stimuli possible? *Cognition* 109:143–51

Sporns O, Chialvo DR, Kaiser M, Hilgetag CC. 2004. Organization, development and function of complex brain networks. *Trends Cogn. Sci.* 8:418–25

Tammet D. 2006. *Born on a Blue Day*. London: Hodder & Stoughton

Tang J, Ward J, Butterworth B. 2008. Number forms in the brain. *J. Cogn. Neurosci.* 20:1547–56

ter Hark M. 2009. Coloured vowels: Wittgenstein on synaesthesia and secondary meaning. *Philosophia* 37:589–604

Tomson SN, Avidan N, Lee K, Sarma AK, Tushe R, et al. 2011. The genetics of colored sequence synesthesia: suggestive evidence of linkage to 16q and genetic heterogeneity for the condition. *Behav. Brain Res.* 223:48–52

Treisman A. 1988. Features and objects: the fourteenth Bartlett Memorial Lecture. *Q. J. Exp. Psychol.* 40A:201–37

van Leeuwen TM, den Ouden HEM, Hagoort P. 2011. Effective connectivity determines the nature of subjective experience in grapheme-color synesthesia. *J. Neurosci.* 31:9879–84

van Leeuwen TM, Petersson KM, Hagoort P. 2010. Synaesthetic colour in the brain: beyond colour areas. A functional magnetic resonance imaging study of synaesthetes and matched controls. *PLoS ONE* 5:e12074

Vulpian A. 1866. *Leçons sur la physiologie générale et comparée du système nerveux, faites en 1864 au Muséum d'histoire naturelle*. Paris: Gerner-Baillière

Wagner K, Dobkins KR. 2011. Synaesthetic associations decrease during infancy. *Psychol. Sci.* 22:1067–72

Walker P, Bremner JG, Mason U, Spring J, Mattock K, et al. 2010. Preverbal infants' sensitivity to synaesthetic cross-modality correspondences. *Psychol. Sci.* 21:21–25

Ward J. 2008. *The Frog Who Croaked Blue: Synesthesia and the Mixing of the Senses.* London: Routledge

Ward J, Huckstep B, Tsakanikos E. 2006a. Sound-colour synaesthesia: To what extent does it use cross-modal mechanisms common to us all? *Cortex* 42:264–80

Ward J, Jonas C, Dienes Z, Seth A. 2010. Grapheme-colour synaesthesia improves detection of embedded shapes, but without pre-attentive "pop-out" of synaesthetic colour. *Proc. R. Soc. London B Biol. Sci.* 277:1021–26

Ward J, Meijer P. 2010. Visual experiences in the blind induced by an auditory sensory substitution device. *Conscious. Cogn.* 19:492–500

Ward J, Moore S, Thompson-Lake D, Salih S, Beck B. 2008a. The aesthetic appeal of auditory-visual synaesthetic perceptions in people without synaesthesia. *Perception* 37:1285–96

Ward J, Sagiv N, Butterworth B. 2009. The impact of visuo-spatial number forms on simple arithmetic. *Cortex* 45:1261–65

Ward J, Salih S, Li R, Sagiv N. 2007. Varieties of grapheme-colour synaesthesia: a new theory of phenomenological and behavioural differences. *Conscious. Cogn.* 16:913–31

Ward J, Simner J. 2003. Lexical-gustatory synaesthesia: linguistic and conceptual factors. *Cognition* 89:237–61

Ward J, Simner J, Auyeung V. 2005. A comparison of lexical-gustatory and grapheme-colour synaesthesia. *Cogn. Neuropsychol.* 22:28–41

Ward J, Thompson-Lake D, Ely R, Kaminski F. 2008b. Synaesthesia, creativity and art: What is the link? *Br. J. Psychol.* 99:127–41

Ward J, Tsakanikos E, Bray A. 2006b. Synaesthesia for reading and playing musical notes. *Neurocase* 12:27–34

Weiss PH, Fink GR. 2009. Grapheme-colour synaesthetes show increased grey matter volumes of parietal and fusiform cortex. *Brain* 132:65–70

Weiss PH, Zilles K, Fink GR. 2005. When visual perception causes feeling: enhanced cross-modal processing in grapheme-color synesthesia. *NeuroImage* 28:859–68

Witthoft N, Winawer J. 2006. Synesthetic colors determined by having colored refrigerator magnets in childhood. *Cortex* 42:175–83

Yaro C, Ward J. 2007. Searching for Shereshevskii: What is superior about the memory of synaesthetes? *Q. J. Exp. Psychol.* 60:682–96

RELATED RESOURCES

- The author's webpage is located at **http://www.sussex.ac.uk/synaesthesia**.
- The Synesthesia Battery is an online resource for synesthetes to test themselves and for researchers to obtain color consistency measures (**http://www.synesthete.org**).
- The U.K. Synaesthesia Association (**http://www.uksynaesthesia.com**) and the American Synesthesia Association (**http://www.synesthesia.info**) organize annual meetings for researchers, synesthetes, and others with a personal or professional interest.
- An email discussion list (the Synesthesia List) is moderated by Sean Day of Trident Technical College (Charleston, South Carolina). Details can be found at **http://www.daysyn.com/ Synesthesia-List.html**

Visual Aesthetics and Human Preference

Stephen E. Palmer, Karen B. Schloss,
and Jonathan Sammartino

Department of Psychology, University of California, Berkeley, California 94720;
email: sepalmer@gmail.com, kschloss@berkeley.edu, jonathansammartino@gmail.com

Annu. Rev. Psychol. 2013. 64:77–107

First published online as a Review in Advance on
September 27, 2012

The *Annual Review of Psychology* is online at
psych.annualreviews.org

This article's doi:
10.1146/annurev-psych-120710-100504

Keywords

visual perception, color, harmony, shape, spatial composition, art

Abstract

Human aesthetic preference in the visual domain is reviewed from
definitional, methodological, empirical, and theoretical perspectives.
Aesthetic science is distinguished from the perception of art and from
philosophical treatments of aesthetics. The strengths and weaknesses of
important behavioral techniques are presented and discussed, including
two-alternative forced-choice, rank order, subjective rating, produc-
tion/adjustment, indirect, and other tasks. Major findings are reviewed
about preferences for colors (single colors, color combinations, and
color harmony), spatial structure (low-level spatial properties, shape
properties, and spatial composition within a frame), and individual differences in both color and spatial structure. Major theoretical accounts
of aesthetic response are outlined and evaluated, including explanations
in terms of mere exposure effects, arousal dynamics, categorical prototypes, ecological factors, perceptual and conceptual fluency, and the
interaction of multiple components. The results of the review support
the conclusion that aesthetic response can be studied rigorously and
meaningfully within the framework of scientific psychology.

Contents

1. INTRODUCTION

We make judgments and decisions every day based on our internal aesthetic responses to aspects of the world around us. We decide to wear this sweater rather than that one because we prefer its color, we buy this poster rather than that one because we like its graphic composition, or we simply choose to sit facing this direction rather than that one in the park because we find the view more pleasurable. Such mundane but ubiquitous aesthetic considerations are so deeply woven into the fabric of our mental lives that we seldom reflect on what our preferences are or why we have them, but these are questions of scientific interest and import. Wearing this or that sweater, buying this or that poster, or facing this or that direction in the park may not seem to have much impact on our material lives, and yet, if we consider the alternative—a world in which we have no such preferences or could make no such choices—what a drab, dull, wearisome world it would be!

Given the pervasive influence of aesthetic responses on our mental lives, it is surprising how little is known about them. The study of aesthetic preference is actually one of the oldest topics in psychology, having been pioneered by Gustav Fechner (1876), one of the founders of modern scientific psychology. Interest in aesthetics has waxed and waned greatly since then, but a revival is now in progress as part of a movement to create an interdisciplinary aesthetic science (Shimamura & Palmer 2012). Our goal in this article is to review recent contributions to this field. Because there are so many, we have concentrated on behavioral research about aesthetic preferences in the visual domain. There is thus no coverage of many important topics in empirical aesthetics, including studies of nonvisual modalities (e.g., music cognition), facial attractiveness (Rhodes 2006), neuroaesthetics (Chatterjee 2011), or aesthetic processes in the creator (Turner 2006), all of which are active fields of current research.

2. FOUNDATIONAL ISSUES

2.1. Aesthetics Versus Art

Because art is so closely associated with visual aesthetics in most people's minds, many readers are likely to assume that the present article reviews the psychological study of visual art. It does not. To understand why, we begin by making a principled distinction between art and aesthetics, which are often taken to be essentially equivalent.

Perhaps the most straightforward difference is that significant aesthetic experiences can (and do) occur anywhere in response to seeing any sort of object, scene, or event, whereas art is limited to the subset of human artifacts intended to be viewed as art, whether in a museum, a gallery, or one's own living room. Who among us has not experienced the ineffable delight produced by the sight of a delicate dew-kissed rose, a majestic snow-capped mountain, a lone seagull gliding silently over a sunset sea, or some other scene of comparable natural beauty? These objects and scenes are not construed as art—unless and until someone paints or photographs them—and yet who can deny that seeing them produces aesthetic experiences?

A second difference is that art has traditionally been identified with positive aesthetic experiences, whereas aesthetic response, in general, spans the range from very positive experiences (consider again viewing the rose, mountain, and seagull described above) to very negative ones (consider instead the sight of a decaying carcass oozing with maggots or a bloody, festering wound). Thus, although art can and (sometimes) does produce significant positive aesthetic experiences in beholders, there is much more to aesthetic experience than just people's reactions to art. By the same token, however, there is much more to art than just the aesthetic responses it evokes in viewers. Art is a social, cultural, institutional, and commercial enterprise of enormous proportions, involving museums, galleries, curators, auctions, critics, collectors, historians, books, royalties, reproductions, and a host of other aspects whose relation to personal aesthetic response to works of art is often tangential, at best. Although aesthetics and art are indeed related, they are conceptually distinct and should be treated as such. The present article reviews the psychology of visual aesthetics, not the psychology of art.

2.2. Defining Aesthetics

Ideally, we would now provide a proper, closed-form definition of aesthetics, something like "The study of human minds and emotions in relation to the sense of beauty." This seems helpful because it identifies minds and emotions as central concepts, but its problem lies in presupposing that the reader already knows what "the sense of beauty" is. For those who do not, this kind of definition is either disturbingly vacuous or implicitly circular. For present purposes, we take aesthetics to be the study of those mental processes that underlie disinterested evaluative experiences that are anchored at the positive end by feelings that would accompany verbal expressions such as "Oh wow! That's wonderful! I love it!" and at the negative end by "Oh yuck! That's awful! I hate it!" Such a definition is nakedly and unapologetically subjective, yet grounded scientifically in certain kinds of behaviors, much like defining pain as that dimension of human experience that leads one to say "Ouch!" and to hold or rub the injured body part. This definition will do nothing to explain the nature of aesthetic experiences to someone who has never had any, but for those who have, it allows them to be identified within our mental lives.

One might try to anchor such a definition objectively in the physical environment by proposing prototypical exemplars that would tie aesthetic experiences to external objects that regularly and reliably elicit them. In dealing with more objective experiential dimensions, such as "red," prototypes are indeed useful: "Red" is that visual experience common to the appearance of ripe strawberries, fresh blood, classic fire engines, etc., when viewed under standard daylight conditions. Unfortunately, this strategy is not available for aesthetics simply because people so seldom agree. If one were to claim that aesthetic response refers to the kind of positive experiences elicited by viewing, say, Van Gogh's *Starry Night*, Michelangelo's *David*, Frank Lloyd Wright's *Fallingwater*, and Ansel Adams's *Moon Over Half Dome*, at least two important problems arise.

One problem is that different people's aesthetic responses differ so greatly that there may be some individuals who have strongly negative aesthetic experiences to all of the supposedly positive prototypes. This potential lack of agreement about aesthetic response even to such prototypes effectively derails the prototype strategy. The other problem is that aesthetic response, at least in our view, does not refer just to positive experiences or even just to extreme experiences. We assume that virtually everyone has some aesthetic response to virtually everything they see (e.g., Palmer et al. 2012b, Reber 2012). In most cases it may linger only fleetingly, if at all, in the "fringe" of human consciousness but it can come into focal awareness under appropriate circumstances, such as when the aesthetic response is extreme (seeing something so wonderful or so awful that the aesthetic response spontaneously bursts into consciousness), when one's attention is directed to aesthetic response by context (in viewing paintings in a museum or gallery or even in shopping for home furnishings), or when one is given explicit instructions to do so (in a laboratory experiment). The fact that aesthetic responses are not always conscious, however, does not mean that people don't have them all the time.

Another possible strategy for defining aesthetic response objectively is to "neurologize" it, as advocated in the emerging field of neuroaesthetics (e.g., Ramachandran & Hirstein 1999, Zeki 1999). The substantive claim is that aesthetics can be defined by some specified type(s) of activity in some specified set(s) of neurons in some specified area(s) of the brain. The hope is to identify the neural activity that actually produces aesthetic experiences, whatever that might be. Mary may love Van Gogh's *Starry Night* and hate Da Vinci's *Mona Lisa*, whereas Bill may have the opposite reactions, but if positive (and negative) aesthetic experiences arise from correlated amounts and/or types of neural activity in the same or functionally similar brain areas, perhaps aesthetic response can be objectively identified with that neural activity. The difficulty is that such neurological criteria cannot logically supplant the

behavioral manifestations of subjective, experiential criteria within individuals. The reason is that, even though neural activity may be ontologically prior to subjective experience (i.e., the specified brain activity causes the aesthetic experience), it is epistemologically secondary and derivative. The logic of this claim is that, to find the kind of brain activity that causes people's aesthetic responses, one must first identify behavioral manifestations of the target subjective aesthetic experiences and then determine what brain activity is correlated with those kinds of behavioral events. Without the behavioral measures, the neural correlates project can never get off the ground.

2.3. Philosophical Foundations

There is a long history of philosophical inquiry into aesthetics that predates all of the psychological studies we review below. As with many philosophical issues, its history begins in antiquity with treatments by Plato and Aristotle, and it continues, largely unresolved, to the present day. We do not attempt to review this extensive literature in any detail, as it has been reviewed elsewhere (e.g., Dickie 1997). We do want to comment, however, on a few central issues that are specifically relevant to the content of this review.

Much of the philosophical literature on aesthetics is explicitly concerned with art. Plato and Aristotle actually took quite different views on this subject. Plato denounced art as mere imitation that imparts no true knowledge of reality and even damages the soul. Aristotle extolled it precisely because people are indeed able to learn from (and even delight in) imitation. They agreed, however, on the importance of unity, harmony, and integration—see Plato's discussion of a good argument in the *Phaedrus* and Aristotle's analysis of tragic plot structure in the *Poetics*—a theme that was elaborated by later writers, including Kant and Dewey.

Kant's (1892/1951) views on philosophical aesthetics in his *Critique of Judgment* have been particularly influential. His approach was decidedly psychological because he identified beauty explicitly with the viewer's mental experiences rather than the object's physical properties. Aesthetic judgments, he claimed, were characterized by three key features: their subjectivity, their disinterested nature, and their claim of universality. Aesthetic judgments are subjective because they rest on personal experiences (e.g., liking/disliking), which have no objective empirical content with respect to the object itself, but only with respect to the relation between the object and the viewer. Unlike many other such liking/disliking judgments, however, aesthetic judgments are "disinterested" in the sense that they do not involve desire. Preferring a larger to a smaller piece of cake would not count as an aesthetic judgment in Kant's framework, because such a judgment is (presumably) about one's desire to consume the larger one.

Kant argued further that aesthetic judgments "claim universal validity." This assertion can be confusing. Clearly, aesthetic judgments are not universally valid because not everyone agrees about them. Nevertheless, Kant claims that when someone makes an aesthetic judgment, he or she believes that others ought to share that judgment, as if beauty were an objective property of things rather than of our experiences on viewing them. Kant thus argued that aesthetic judgments involve more complex cognitive investments than judgments of "mere agreeability" or "individual preference," which are merely matters of taste for which there appears to be no basis for discussion. Here Kant refers to the importance of the "harmonious free play of the imagination" in aesthetic judgments. Although it may not be entirely clear what this phrase means, it is evident that it refers to some relatively complex mental processes that are likely absent in the appreciation of "mere preferences."

We agree with Kant that aesthetic judgments are subjective and disinterested, but not that they necessarily involve claims of universal validity and/or free play of the imagination. Although the latter may be a hallmark of many people's views about works of art, they are hardly required in characterizing people's preferences for colors, either singly or in combination (see section 4) or in their preferences for the shapes of rectangles or the spatial composition of simple pictures (see section 5). Rather, we see the aesthetic preferences reviewed below to be basic aspects of what become quite complex aesthetic responses that people have to artworks or scenes of natural splendor. Our belief is that eventually enough will be understood about how such simple preferences combine and interact with cognitive and emotional factors to explain more complex evaluative aesthetic claims that are often couched in universal terms and rely on Kantian free play of the imagination. We freely admit that whether this belief is true and how this understanding might unfold in an aesthetic science are as yet unclear.

2.4. On the Possibility of a Science of Aesthetics

Although many writers and researchers find it obvious that aesthetic experiences can be studied scientifically (e.g., Arnheim 1974, Berlyne 1971, Fechner 1876, Jacobson 2006, Shimamura & Palmer 2012), others do not (e.g., Dickie 1962). Indeed, some would surely claim that a science of aesthetics is not only impossible, but also oxymoronic (because science is objective and lawful, whereas aesthetic response is subjective and whimsical). Aesthetic responses are surely subjective (see above), but just as surely, that does not preclude their being studied objectively through behavioral methods (see below). For example, people's experiences of color are not only subjective, but also can differ substantially over individuals owing to color blindness and/or color weakness, and yet there is nevertheless a well-established and technically sophisticated science of color vision (e.g., Kaiser & Boynton 1996, Koenderink 2010). There is no logical certainty that a scientific approach to aesthetics will succeed in identifying regularities in people's aesthetic responses to visual displays, but this is clearly an empirical issue that can only be settled by trying. Below we summarize numerous results that provide significant insight into aesthetic preferences using rigorous scientific methods, providing strong empirical support for the viability of a science of visual aesthetics.

It is important to note that the factual basis of a science of aesthetics is not to settle whether some image or object is "objectively beautiful"—we agree with Kant that this is impossible—but rather to determine whether (or to what degree) some representative set of individuals judge or experience it as beautiful (or ugly). A science of aesthetics thus concerns accurately describing people's aesthetic judgments and discovering the causes and/or reasons for those judgments. We now turn to the question of how one might do so.

3. METHODOLOGICAL ISSUES

Typically, the goal of a descriptive science of visual aesthetics is to determine average relative aesthetic preferences for some set of visual displays among a particular population, given a specific task to judge some aesthetic quality or qualities. The population, the displays, the task, and the aesthetic qualities of interest must all be specified prior to collecting data. The displays can be virtually any visible object, event, or image. The task is typically for the observer to attend to his/her experience of the designated aesthetic quality of the displays (e.g., their color or shape or overall attractiveness) and to indicate his/her evaluation. A variety of behavioral responses are possible—ratings, rankings, descriptions of likes or dislikes—but whatever they are, they must be measured behaviorally. Additional physiological measurements can also be made, such as galvanic skin response, functional magnetic resonance imaging, or event-related electrical potentials. Our review focuses on behavioral measures of aesthetic experiences, however.

Many of the methodological choices will be dictated by the specific hypothesis being tested: e.g., that American observers (the population) will tend to prefer color combinations of similar hue (the aesthetic quality) for a smaller square within a larger square (the displays). The sample of observers is important because people in different cultures, economic groups, and social groups may have systematically different aesthetic experiences to the same visual displays. The large interobserver variability in aesthetic preferences within such groups dictates using larger rather than smaller samples of randomly selected individuals.

If the goal is direct measurement (i.e., scaling) of average preferences among a full set of N visual displays, there are three primary behavioral tasks: two-alternative forced choice (2AFC), rank ordering, and preference ratings. Other methods can provide useful information but suffer from problems that limit their utility.

3.1. Two-Alternative Forced Choice

In most respects the optimal task is 2AFC, in which observers indicate which of two simultaneously presented visual displays they "like better" (prefer aesthetically) for all possible pairs. The average probability of choosing each display over all others is then taken as a global measure of its relative preference. 2AFC paradigms have the advantages of simple responses to indicate choice, trials containing only two displays, essentially no memory load, and minimal response bias effects. Its primary drawback is requiring $N(N-1) = N^2-N$ trials to measure preferences for N stimuli (e.g., 90 trials for 10 stimuli, but 9,900 trials for 100 stimuli). A more efficient alternative that has recently been developed is a Markov Chain Monte Carlo procedure that can be used when the display set is embedded within a dimensional space (Sanborn et al. 2010).

3.2. Rank Ordering

At the other end of the methodological spectrum is a rank-ordering task in which all displays of interest are presented simultaneously, and the observer is required to order them from most to least preferred. The average rank order for each display is then taken as a measure of relative preference. Although individual rank orders are, by definition, merely ordinal, the average rank over observers provides more quantitative information. The primary advantage is that rank ordering requires only a single trial. Its disadvantages derive from the fact that this one trial can be inordinately complex, requiring simultaneous presentation of all N displays (difficult or impossible on a computer screen if the displays are large and/or spatially complex) and a potentially long and complex series of judgments to arrive at the required single, coherent ordering.

3.3. Rating

Ratings of aesthetic preference are an attractive alternative paradigm, especially when the number of displays to be measured (N) is large and/or the visual displays require significant space. The ratings can be made on discrete response scales of a given resolution (e.g., a seven-point Likert scale) or continuous scales (e.g., a line-mark rating), where the latter are often better if memory for specific prior ratings is a concern. Observers are shown a single display on each trial and asked to rate how much they like it. Average ratings for displays are taken as relative preference measurements. The responses are relatively simple, and only N trials are required to measure preferences for N displays. Because it can be difficult for observers to make consistent ratings across trials, especially at the beginning, it is useful to display the entire set (or a representative sample) of displays together with instructions to indicate the most and least liked alternatives to anchor the response scale before the experimental trials begin.

3.4. Production and Adjustment Tasks

Perhaps the most important alternative tasks for assessing aesthetic response are production and adjustment tasks, in which observers are required to produce the most aesthetically preferred possibility given various constraints. Such tasks are particularly useful when the experimental requirements imply a combinatorial explosion of possible displays. For example, suppose that one wanted to study aesthetic preference for all color pairs using a set of 100 possible colors. Because there are 100 * 99 distinct permutations of the two colors, 9,900 trials would be required for a single observation per display, even using an efficient rating task. An adjustment task, such as fixing one color on each trial and asking the observer to adjust the second color to produce the most aesthetically pleasing combination, would be a much more efficient procedure, requiring only 100 trials. The dependent variable would be the probability of each adjusted color being chosen for each fixed color. This efficiency comes at the considerable cost of producing only a very complex and incomplete partial ordering, with many ties for the many combinations that are seldom, if ever, produced.

3.5. Indirect Measures

Various physiological measurements (e.g., galvanic skin response, functional magnetic resonance imaging, event-related electrical potentials) can theoretically be taken as covert aesthetic responses. For example, observers can be instructed simply to look at each display without requiring any behavioral response, with the average magnitude of the physiological measurement(s) of interest being used to create a scaling of the displays as if they were behavioral ratings. Obviously, such methods will be valid only to the extent that the physiological measurements have been validated by comparing direct behavioral measures (e.g., 2AFC probabilities or aesthetic ratings) with the given covert physiological measure(s).

One can also study indirect behavioral measures, such as the probability of looking first at one of two presented displays or the total time spent fixating each of them. Like physiological measures, they must be validated against direct behavioral measures of preference, which are logically primary. When this is not possible—such as with infants or animals—indirect measures are the only alternative. When combined with direct measures, indirect measures can often reveal nonconscious processes at work that are difficult or impossible to study with direct measures.

3.6. Other Measures

All of the above methods rely to some degree on direct, quantifiable, behavioral measures of aesthetic response in which observers are required to evaluate or create images in terms of their aesthetic reactions to them. There are other kinds of measurements that may prove relevant to understanding aesthetic response within the framework of some theory or hypothesis. For example, one might believe that the aspect ratio of an image's rectangular shape or the power function of its spatial frequency spectrum contribute to its aesthetic success (see below). Such physical measurements can be combined (e.g., by correlation) with concurrent behavioral measurements, as described above. The behavioral measures are sometimes neglected, however, because an alternative index is taken as a proxy for aesthetic success, such as the fact that images hang in museums, are included in art books, or are included in some other collection of high repute.

There are several pitfalls to this strategy. One is the implicit assumption that images included in high-profile collections are aesthetically superior to other images for the studied population. This might be true, but it should not be taken for granted. A second more serious caveat is that correlation does not imply causation. Even if it were true, say, that people aesthetically prefer pictures that are wider than they are tall to those that are taller than they are wide, it is not necessarily true that the cause of this preference is their aspect ratios. People might actually prefer landscapes to portraits, for example, where landscapes tend to be wider and portraits taller.

The third problem is perhaps the most serious of all: the frequent failure of art theorists and critics to analyze appropriate contrast sets of images. If an author attributes the success of some acknowledged masterpiece to, say, the upward-pointing triangular composition of the principal elements, one should not take the claim as conclusive unless corresponding samples of other paintings with such upward-triangle compositions are judged aesthetically

and contrasted with similar judgments of paintings with, say, "downward-triangle" or "quadrilateral" compositions. Few art theorists or critics consider such contrast sets, however.

4. COLOR PREFERENCE

4.1. Preference for Single Colors

Early researchers claimed that adult preferences for single colors were not systematic enough to warrant further investigation (e.g., Allesch 1924, Chandler 1928, Cohn 1884). Eysenck (1941) rejected this conclusion, arguing that previous failures arose from unstandardized colors and inadequate statistical analyses. He found reliable effects in analyses of both his own data and von Allesch's previously reported "chaotic" data. Modern studies using standardized colors and sophisticated statistical techniques have clearly established that, despite large individual differences, group color preferences show systematic and reliable patterns as a function of the three primary dimensions of color: hue (basic color), saturation (vividness, purity, or chroma), and lightness (brightness or value) (e.g., Granger 1955b, Guilford & Smith 1959, Hurlbert & Ling 2007, McManus et al. 1981, Ou et al. 2004, Palmer & Schloss 2010).

Hue. Hue preferences among American and British adults follow a relatively smooth curvilinear function in which cool colors (green, cyan, blue) are generally preferred to warm colors (red, orange, yellow), with a maximum at blue and a minimum around yellow to yellow-green (see **Figure 1**). The majority of the variance is due to differences along the violet to yellow-green axis of cone-contrast color space [i.e., S−(L+M), where S, M, and L refer to the output of the short-, medium-, and long-wavelength cones] and/or the blue-yellow dimension of higher-level color-appearance space, with only minor differences along the red to blue-green dimension of cone-contrast (L-M) and/or the red-green dimension of color appearance (Hurlbert & Ling 2007, Ling & Hurlbert 2009, Palmer & Schloss 2010).

Saturation. Western adults generally prefer colors of higher saturation to those of lower saturation for context-free patches of color (McManus et al. 1981, Ou et al. 2004, Palmer & Schloss 2010). Some findings suggest that preferences decrease for colors of very high saturation, which were reportedly "too vivid" (Granger 1955b). Preference for high-saturation colors varies as a function of gender, culture, and object-context, however (see below).

Lightness. Western adults tend to prefer colors of increasing lightness, at least to some point (Guilford & Smith 1959, McManus et al. 1981), although this effect is not always evident (Palmer & Schloss 2010) (see **Figure 1**). Lightness is confounded with saturation across hues, however, and because people generally prefer highly saturated colors, different hues have their peak preference at different lightness levels: e.g., yellow at high lightness levels, red and green at medium lightness levels, and blue and purple at low lightness levels (Guilford & Smith 1959).

Hue x lightness interactions. Of considerable theoretical importance is the frequent finding that dark colors show a different hue preference function than light and medium-lightness colors of equal chroma, at least for warm colors (see **Figure 1**). In particular, dark shades of orange (browns) and yellow (olives) are strongly disliked relative to lighter, equally saturated oranges and yellows and relative to dark red (Guilford & Smith 1959, Palmer & Schloss 2010). Such effects are theoretically important because they are difficult to explain within classic psychophysical models of color appearance. They are consistent with ecological explanations of color preference, however (see below). The overall pattern of preferences for single colors is thus complex, but there are clear and repeatable regularities. For additional reviews of previous work on single color preferences, see Ball (1965) and Whitfield & Wiltshire (1990).

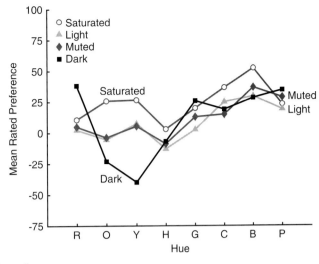

Figure 1

Average color preference ratings from Palmer & Schloss (2010) for the Berkeley Color Project 32 chromatic colors. The 32 chromatic colors include eight hues (R, red; O, orange; Y, yellow; H, chartreuse; G, green; C, cyan; B, blue; and P, purple) at each of four different saturation/lightness levels: saturated (*circles*; the highest chroma colors available on the display), light (*triangles*; the colors roughly midway between the saturated colors and white), muted (*diamonds*; the colors roughly midway between the saturated colors and neutral gray), and dark (*squares*; the colors roughly midway between the saturated colors and black).

4.1.1. Theories of single color preference. The foregoing discussion specifies which colors people like, but not why they like the ones they do or even why they have color preferences at all. Several types of explanations have been suggested, including physiological, psychophysical, emotional, and ecological hypotheses. Because all of these models have been fit to the results shown in **Figure 1** (see Palmer & Schloss 2010), we use them as a benchmark.

The most physiologically based theory suggests that people like colors to an extent that depends on a weighted average of cone contrasts relative to the background color, as computed very early in visual processing: L-M and S-(L+M), where S, M, and L represent the outputs of short-, medium-, and long-wavelength cones, respectively (Hurlbert & Ling 2007). This model fits Hurlbert & Ling's (2007) own data well, but even an augmented model with two additional psychophysical variables—luminance and saturation (Ling & Hurlbert

2009)—accounted for only 37% of the variance in the data of **Figure 1**, presumably because their color sample did not include the highly saturated and easily named colors of Palmer & Schloss's (2010) sample.

A similar, but purely psychophysical, hypothesis is that color preferences are based on conscious color appearances. Palmer & Schloss (2010) tested this possibility using a weighted average of observer-rated redness-greenness, blueness-yellowness, saturation, and lightness of each color, roughly analogous to their coordinates in Natural Color System color space (Hård & Sivik 1981). This model accounted for 60% of the variance in **Figure 1**. The fact that this is considerably better than the cone-contrast model suggests that later, conscious representations of color predict color preferences better than earlier, nonconscious ones.

A third explanation can be constructed in terms of the emotional associations of colors. Perhaps people like colors to the extent that they like the emotions that are evoked by or associated with those colors. Ou et al. (2004) measured color-emotions through subjective ratings and used those ratings to predict color preferences. Their results showed that three factor-analytic dimensions predicted color preferences: active-passive, light-heavy, and cool-warm, with active, light, and cool colors being preferred to passive, heavy, and warm ones. Palmer & Schloss (2010) fit observers' subjective ratings of those three dimensions to the data in **Figure 1** and found that it accounted for 55% of the variance. Ou et al. (2004) did not discuss how color-emotions arise or why some color-emotions predict preferences better than others. It is surprising, for example, that happy-sad was not included because it is such an important evaluative dimension. The difficulty is that the more desirable emotion (happy) is associated with less preferred hues (yellow), whereas the less desirable emotion (sad) is associated more desirable hues (blue) (Terwogt & Hoeksma 1995).

An ecological explanation, called the "ecological valence theory" (EVT), was formulated and tested by Palmer & Schloss (2010). They proposed that people like/dislike a specific color to the degree that they like/dislike all of the environmental objects that are associated with that color. The ecological rationale is that it will be adaptive for organisms to approach objects whose colors they like and avoid objects whose colors they dislike to the extent that their color preferences are correlated with objects that are beneficial versus harmful to them (cf. Humphrey 1976). Palmer & Schloss (2010) reported strong support for the EVT through empirical measurements of what they call weighted affective valence estimates (WAVEs) for the 32 chromatic colors in **Figure 1**. The WAVE for each color measures the extent to which people like the set of objects that are associated with that color. For example, they like blues and cyans, at least in part, because they like clear sky and clean water, and they dislike browns and olive-colors, at least in part, because they dislike feces and rotting food. Average valence (liking/disliking) ratings were measured for all objects named as associates of each color, with each object valence rating being weighted by the similarity between the given object's color and the color with which it was associated. The weighted average valence over all associates for each color explained 80% of the variance in the data shown in **Figure 1** with no estimated parameters.

Several further predictions of the EVT have since been confirmed. One is that if preferences for colored objects causally influence preferences for corresponding colors, then color preferences could be changed by exposure to affectively biased samples of colored objects. Strauss and colleagues (2012) found that when one group saw positive red images (e.g., strawberries and cherries) and negative green images (e.g., mold and snot) and another group saw positive green images (e.g., kiwi fruit and leafy trees) and negative red images (e.g., blood and lesions), the two groups showed the predicted cross-over interaction in preference changes for the corresponding colors from ratings made before versus after seeing the affectively biased colored images. Seeing positive red images selectively increased preference for red, for example, and seeing positive green things selectively increased preference for green.

The EVT also predicts changes in color preference for people who have highly positive (or negative) emotional investments in a social institution that has strong color associations, such as athletic teams, gangs, religious orders, and universities. People should come to like the colors associated with the institution correspondingly more or less, depending on whether their feelings about it are positive or negative. Indeed, students at two rival universities—the University of California, Berkeley and Stanford University—preferred their own university's colors more than their rival's colors, and the magnitude of these differences was correlated with their self-reports of school spirit for their own university (Schloss et al. 2011). These results support the EVT's claim that color preference is influenced by preferences for the institution because it is highly unlikely that people choose their university and cultivate their level of school spirit based on pre-existing color preferences.

4.1.2. Infant color preferences.
Infant color preferences are studied by measuring infants' looking biases when presented with side-by-side color pairs. Longer (e.g., Bornstein 1975) and/or earlier fixations (Teller 1979) are taken as indices of relative preference. Infant color preference tends to be investigated from around 3–4 months, by which time infants' color vision is fully trichromatic (e.g., Knoblauch et al. 2001, Teller 1998).

When infant looking biases are measured for highly saturated colors, the hue preference function tends to have the same general shape as the corresponding adult hue preference function (**Figure 1**, open circles), with a maximum around blue and a minimum around yellow or yellow-green (Bornstein 1975, Franklin et al. 2008, Teller et al. 2004, Zemach et al. 2007). Other patterns have sometimes been reported (Adams 1987), perhaps due to differences in luminance and/or saturation. The similarity of the infant and adult hue preference functions for saturated colors has

led to the general view that color preference might be innate. More recent findings undercut this possibility, however. Franklin et al. (2009) measured looking biases in 4- to 6-month-old infants using the same colors Hurlbert & Ling (2007) used for adults and found that, unlike those of adults (see above), infant preferences varied primarily on a red to blue-green dimension (L-M cone contrast), with redder colors being more preferred, and were not strongly related to the violet to yellow-green dimension [S−(L+M) cone contrast]. More recently, Taylor et al. (2012b) have discovered that 4- to 6-month-old infants exhibit a hue x lightness interaction that is clearly different from the corresponding interaction in adults. Indeed, babies show a bias toward looking at dark-yellow and light-red and a bias against looking at light-blue and dark-green, nearly the opposite of corresponding looking biases in adults ($r = -0.46$). These findings clearly demonstrate that color preferences change dramatically during an individual's lifetime.

4.1.3. Gender differences.
Gender differences have been reported among Western adults in their relative preferences for saturated versus desaturated colors. In particular, men tend to prefer saturated colors more than women do, and these differences are strongly correlated ($r = +0.73$) with observers' judgments of how active/passive colors are, with males generally preferring more active colors and females more passive ones (Palmer & Schloss 2011). Gender differences in saturation develop with age, being absent for young children (~6–9 years), beginning to appear during adolescence (12–13 years), and being clearly apparent by adulthood (17–18 years) (Child et al. 1968). Gender differences have also been reported in hue preference at certain ages. Specifically, girls ages 3–12 tend to prefer pink and purple, whereas boys of that age tend to prefer red and blue (Chiu et al. 2006, Iijima et al. 2001, Picariello et al. 1990). Such gender differences in color preference may develop from exposure to gender-specific toys that are stereotypically colored: pink and purple for girls' toys and red,

blue, and black for boys' toys (Jadva et al. 2010, LoBue & DeLoache 2011, Pennell 1994). This explanation fits well with an ecological theory (Palmer & Schloss 2010), according to which color preferences are determined by preferences for correspondingly colored objects.

Further evidence about ecological effects in gender differences has come from fitting WAVE data (see section 4.1.1) collected separately for adult males and females in England. Taylor & Franklin (2012) found a pattern consistent with EVT predictions: male WAVEs predicted male preferences ($r = 0.86$) better than they predicted female preferences ($r = 0.58$), whereas female WAVEs showed the opposite trend (female-female $r = 0.67$; female-male $r = 0.58$).

4.1.4. Cross-cultural differences.

Although some writers have claimed that color preferences are universal across cultures (e.g., Birren 1961, Eysenck 1941), modern empirical research reveals that both similarities and differences exist. The strongest case for a universal preference is for bluish colors (Adams & Osgood 1973, Hurlbert & Ling 2007, Ou et al. 2004, Saito 1996). There are exceptions, however, such as blue being ranked among the least preferred colors in Kuwait (Choungourian 1968). Blue was apparently also disliked in Ancient Rome, as evidenced by its relative disuse in historical artifacts (Pastoureau 2001), which may have been due to ecological factors. Because blue was greatly liked by Rome's archenemies, the Celts, the Romans may have disliked blue by the same logic as Berkeley students dislike of Stanford's colors and vice versa (see section 4.1.1). A second contender for universality is the robust dislike of dark-yellow (olive), which has been reported for Chinese, British (Ou et al. 2004), Japanese (Yokosawa et al. 2012), and American (Palmer & Schloss 2010) observers. Note that even if such universal color preferences exist, they may reflect universal features of human ecology rather than innate preferences: e.g., clear sky and clean water are universally blue, whereas biological wastes and rotting food are universally dark yellow.

According to the ecological valence theory, WAVEs for a given culture should predict that culture's color preferences better than another culture's color preferences, and vice versa. This prediction is based on the idea that different cultures frequently have different color-object associations and/or different valences for the same objects, both of which can affect color preferences. Preliminary results support this prediction for American versus Japanese cultures (see Palmer & Schloss 2010). Japanese WAVEs accounted for Japanese preferences ($r = 0.66$) better than for American preferences ($r = 0.55$), whereas American WAVEs accounted for American preferences ($r = 0.89$) better than for Japanese preferences ($r = 0.74$).

It must be noted, however, that a radically different pattern of preferences emerged in the nonindustrial Himba people of rural Namibia, who greatly preferred highly saturated colors, largely independent of hue (Taylor et al. 2012a). This large saturation effect is most consistent with a psychophysical account of color preference because saturation is a potent variable in high-level models of color appearance. It may also be due to novelty, as the Himba's chromatic environment is considerably more natural than that of industrialized societies, with far fewer instances of highly saturated colors.

Many researchers have appealed to color symbolism to explain cultural differences. For example, there appears to be a stronger preference for white and whitish colors in Japan, Korea, and Taiwan than in other countries (e.g., the United States, Germany, Australia, Papua New Guinea, and South Africa), perhaps because white symbolizes cleanliness, purity, and the sun, which are more highly valued in these Asian cultures than in the other cultures studied (Saito 1996). Similarly, Chinese observers preferred red more than British participants did, perhaps due to its role as a symbol of good luck in China (Hurlbert & Ling 2007). The idea that color symbolism influences color preferences is conceptually consistent with ecological accounts of color preference (Palmer & Schloss 2010), according to which color preferences are determined by people's preferences for the "things" that are associated with those colors, provided that the "things" include abstractions such as purity and good luck as well as concrete objects and social institutions. Solid empirical evidence for the role of color symbolism in color preference is largely lacking, however.

4.1.5. Object-based differences. A question of considerable applied interest is whether preferences for context-free colored patches (see above) generalize to preferences for colored objects. The answer depends importantly on the degree to which the objects in question have prototypical or characteristic colors. It is highly improbable, for example, that even a resolute blue-lover and yellow-hater would prefer blue bananas to yellow ones. The more sensible question is whether context-free color preferences generalize to artifacts that could conceivably be any color.

Schloss et al. (2012) studied adult preferences for visually presented colors of many such artifacts: interior room walls, room trim, couches, throw pillows, dress shirts/blouses, ties/scarves, and T-shirts. The overall pattern of hue preferences was similar to that for context-free colored squares (**Figure 1**), with cool hues (especially blues) being liked better than warm ones. The primary exception was that people tended not to like large things (such as walls and couches) to be red. In contrast, the pattern of preferences for different lightness levels were markedly different across objects, often depending on practical considerations, such as liking lighter wall colors to make rooms appear brighter and/or larger. Interestingly, context-free squares were the only case in which highly saturated colors were preferred to less saturated ones (Saito 1983, Schloss et al. 2012).

Object color preferences are most likely to deviate from context-free color preferences when there are color conventions for that type of object (Taft 1997). Such conventionality effects can be present even within a basic-level object category, such as luxury sedans being most preferred in achromatic colors (black, grays, or white), consistent with their conventional

formality as serious, sophisticated cars, whereas a VW "Bugs" were preferred in brighter, more saturated colors, including yellow, consistent with their conventional informality as fun, sporty cars (Schloss et al. 2012). These effects may be considered weaker cases of the prototypical banana example described above, but ones in which sociocultural conventions, rather than naturalness, drive color preferences.

4.2. Preference for Color Combinations

Historically, theories about the aesthetics of color combinations have been predicated on several untested assumptions that have led to a confusing literature. For example, the terms "preference" and "harmony" are often used interchangeably, and preference for a combination as a whole is frequently confused with preference for a figural color against a background color (e.g., Chevreul 1839; Granger 1955a,c; Itten 1973). Schloss & Palmer (2011) used a clearer empirical framework for assessing the aesthetics of color combinations by distinguishing among three types of judgments for figure-ground color pairs: (*a*) pair preference (how much the two colors are liked together), (*b*) pair harmony (how well the colors go together, regardless of preference), and (*c*) figural preference (how much the foreground color is liked when viewed against a colored background). They explain the distinction between preference and harmony in terms of a musical analogy: Nearly everyone would agree that Mozart's music is more harmonious than Stravinsky's, and yet some people prefer Stravinsky's music to Mozart's whereas others prefer Mozart's to Stravinsky's (see also Albers 1971, Ou et al. 2004, Whitfield & Wiltshire 1990). Although figural preference involves a judgment about a single color, it is relevant to color combinations because the same color can look strikingly different on different background colors due to the classic perceptual phenomenon of simultaneous color contrast (Chevreul 1839, da Vinci 1942/1956, Helmholtz 1866/1925, Walraven 1976).

4.2.1. Theories of pair preference and/or harmony.

Chevreul (1839) presented one of the most influential theories of color harmony and preference, terms that he used interchangeably. He proposed two distinct types of harmony: harmony of analogous colors and harmony of contrast. Other theories include Itten's (1973) claim that any combination of colors is harmonious if the colors produce neutral gray when mixed together as paints, Munsell's (1921) and Ostwald's (1932) theories that colors are harmonious when they have certain relations in color space (e.g., constant in hue and saturation but varying in lightness), and other theories proposed by Goethe (1810/1970), and Moon & Spencer (1944a,b). Note that none of these theories were formulated on the basis of aesthetic measurements, although some have since been tested empirically. (For a more thorough review, see Westland et al. 2007.)

4.2.2. Empirical research on pair preference and/or harmony.

Studies of aesthetic preferences for color combinations have produced conflicting claims, often because researchers have not distinguished among the three types of judgments described above. For example, Granger (1955a,b) reported that harmony and preference (he also used the terms interchangeably) increased with hue contrast, but several subsequent studies show that both harmony and preference decrease with hue contrast (Ou et al. 2004, Ou & Luo 2006, Schloss & Palmer 2011, Szabó et al. 2010). Granger's finding that preference increases with hue contrast is consistent, however, with subsequent findings on figural color preferences, which increase with hue contrast (Helson & Lansford 1970, Schloss & Palmer 2011).

Schloss & Palmer (2011) measured both pair preference and pair harmony for the same figure-ground color pairs (a small square within a larger square) with the same observers given different instructions (see above). Both measures increased with hue similarity (cf. Chuang & Ou 2001, Ou & Luo 2006, Ou et al. 2011, Szabó et al. 2010), consistent with Chevreul's

harmony of analogous colors. The two measures differed in relation to lightness, however, in that pair preference increased with lightness contrast, whereas pair harmony did not. Harmony also tends to be greater for lighter pairs and for pairs that are more similar in saturation (Ou & Luo 2006, Schloss & Palmer 2011, Szabó et al. 2010). Nevertheless, the overall correlation between ratings of pair preference and pair harmony is highly positive ($r = +0.79$) in Schloss & Palmer (2011). This fact explains why these concepts have so often been equated: people tend, on average, to like harmonious color combinations (see also Ou et al. 2004). Observers agreed more about their ratings of pair harmony (average between-observer $r = +0.51$) than about their ratings of pair preference (average between-observer $r = +0.36$), primarily because pair harmony ratings were almost completely independent of pair preferences for the two component colors. Strikingly, more than 80% of the variance in people's pair preference ratings can be explained by a linear combination of the pair's harmony rating, the preference ratings for the two colors alone, and the lightness difference between figure and ground colors (multiple-$r = 0.89$).

Ratings of figural preference for colors against colored backgrounds are measurably different from both pair preference and pair harmony ratings (Schloss & Palmer 2011). Average figural preferences are highly correlated with preference for the corresponding single figural color against a neutral background ($r = 0.87$) and also with average preference for pairs of colors containing the figural color as figure ($r = 0.74$). After the influences of these two preference factors were removed, however, preferences for hue contrast and lightness contrast were evident (cf. Helson & Lansford 1970). It is likely that these effects are responsible for Chevreul's claims about harmonies of contrast. Indeed, given the general preference for saturated colors (see **Figure 1**), it is not surprising that observers would prefer figural colors against highly contrastive background hues; simultaneous color contrast effects would tend to increase the perceived saturation of the figural color.

5. PREFERENCE FOR SPATIAL STRUCTURE

Virtually every two-dimensional visual display—from painted portraits to photographed landscapes to abstract graphic designs—is composed of elements arranged in space, usually within a rectangular frame. It is therefore important to consider how the spatial properties and arrangements of those elements influence people's aesthetic responses to such displays (e.g., Arnheim 1988).

5.1. Aesthetics of Low-Level Visual Properties

A common theme in aesthetic judgments of low-level visual properties is that images are preferred when their structure mirrors that of natural scenes. Such findings suggest that people prefer images that have the statistical structure to which the human visual system has adapted, whether evolutionarily or ontogenetically.

5.1.1. Spatial frequency. By the time visual information reaches the cortex in area V1, spatial analysis is dominated by local spatial frequency filters that perform something like a piecewise Fourier analysis of the input (cf. De Valois & De Valois 1990). Spectral analyses of paintings and natural scenes reveal that they have similar amplitude spectra, being highest for low spatial frequencies and decreasing approximately linearly with the logarithm of spatial frequency in the classic spectrum of 1/F noise (Graham & Field 2007, Graham & Redies 2010). Not only do more "natural"-looking paintings have the same 1/F power spectrum, but increases within two octaves of three cycles/degree are correlated with viewers' feelings of visual discomfort (Fernandez & Wilkins 2008). It is not clear, however, whether 1/F power spectra are either necessary or sufficient

for producing positive aesthetic responses to images.

5.1.2. Line orientation. Viewers generally prefer horizontal and vertical lines to oblique ones in Mondrian-like images (e.g., Latto et al. 2000), and, generally speaking, more paintings contain horizontal and vertical lines than oblique ones (Latto & Russell-Duff 2002). Given that the visual stimulation to which people are exposed also tends to have more horizontal and vertical lines than oblique lines, at least at higher spatial frequencies (Switkes et al. 1978), these results provide further evidence that people prefer images that mirror the statistical properties of low-level spatial structure in their seen environment.

5.2. Aesthetics of Object Shape

5.2.1. The golden ratio. One of the oldest and most frequently studied questions about the aesthetics of shape concerns the so-called golden ratio or golden section. It is obtained by dividing a line into two parts such that the proportion of the entire line to the longer segment is equal to the proportion of the longer segment to the shorter segment, a ratio of approximately 1.6:1. If the golden ratio characterizes the length-to-width ratio, or aspect ratio, of a rectangle, it defines a shape that has been claimed from antiquity to be particularly pleasing aesthetically (e.g., Green 1995). The golden ratio appears frequently, both in nature (e.g., a person's height relative to his/her arm span) and in aesthetically acclaimed human artifacts (e.g., the base-to-height ratio of the Great Pyramids and the facial dimensions of Da Vinci's *Mona Lisa*) (e.g., Atalay 2004, Konecni 2003, Konecni & Cline 2002, Livio 2002).

Early empirical studies showed that so-called golden rectangles are most preferred, with preference diminishing in both directions as the length-to-width proportions deviate from 1.6:1 (Fechner 1871, 1876). Such claims remain controversial (e.g., Boselie 1984, Green 1995), with some successful replications (e.g., Lalo 1908, Thorndike 1917) but many failures (e.g., Angier 1903, Haines & Davies 1904, Thorndike 1917). Interestingly, preferred aspect ratios of rectangles differ for different semantic categories of objects. People preferred invitation cards for "serious" events (e.g., a classical piano recital) to have aspect ratios close to the golden ratio (peaking at 1.4:1), but the preference functions of those for more casual "fun" events (e.g., a child's birthday party) were virtually flat from 1:1 to 1.5:1 (Raghubir & Greenleaf 2006). A reasonable summary of this field of research is that although many people prefer shapes whose dimensions are in the general neighborhood of the golden ratio, such preferences can and do vary relatively widely across both observers and contexts (McManus 1980).

5.2.2. Complexity and symmetry. In an influential theory of preference for abstract polygon shapes, Birkhoff (1933) proposed that aesthetic preference (M) should vary directly with the number of elements (O) and inversely with the complexity (C, expressed as the number of noncollinear sides) according to the equation $M = O/C$. Experimental tests of this claim have yielded disappointingly low correlations, however, with various other authors giving their own formulations (e.g., Boselie & Leeuwenberg 1985, Eysenck 1941, Eysenck & Castle 1971). One problem with this equation is that it predicts monotonic increases in preference with complexity. In contrast, intermediate complexity of about 10 sides is generally preferred by both adults (Martindale et al. 1988, Munsinger & Kessen 1964b) and children (Munsinger & Kessen 1964a). These results are consistent with Berlyne's (1971) arousal theory of aesthetics (see below). Interestingly, preference effects of complexity show strong contrast effects with massive amounts of familiarization: People familiarized with simple stimuli later tended to prefer more complex stimuli, whereas those familiarized with complex stimuli tended later to prefer simpler stimuli (Tonio & Leder 2009).

More recent research on shape preferences has focused on symmetry structure while holding the number of elements constant, following prior results showing that more symmetrical dot configurations were more easily processed perceptually and better remembered (Garner & Clement 1963). In general, people tend to prefer shapes that are more symmetrical, although there are large and relatively stable individual differences in such effects (Jacobson & Höfel 2002, Palmer & Griscom 2012), as is discussed below.

5.2.3. Contour curvature. A recently discovered phenomenon of shape preference is that people tend to like objects with curved contours more than similar objects with sharp contours (Bar & Neta 2006). Further research has shown this to be true for abstract shapes as well as recognizable objects (Silvia & Barona 2009) and that the preference for curved objects holds for objects with neutral or positive valences, but not for ones with negative valences (Leder et al. 2011). These findings have been interpreted to mean that sharp contours are more threatening than curved ones, given the tendency for objects with sharp contours to be harmful.

5.2.4. Categorical Prototypes. People also tend to prefer object shapes to the extent that they conform to categorical prototypes (Rosch 1975). There is a large, well-known literature on facial attractiveness, showing that people tend to like symmetrical, average faces (for a review, see Rhodes 2006). We do not count this as an aesthetic preference because it is not indifferent in the Kantian sense, presumably being driven by sexual attraction. Nevertheless, the idea that people tend to like prototypical exemplars has found support in other domains, such as color (Martindale & Moore 1988), furniture (Whitfield & Slatter 1979), surrealist paintings (Farkas 2002), and exemplars of other semantic categories (Martindale et al. 1988).

5.3. Aesthetics of Spatial Composition

Whatever the shape of the objects within an image, an important further aspect of aesthetic consideration is spatial composition: the way in which the objects are positioned relative to each other and to the surrounding frame. A primary focus of studies of spatial composition is the balance of the image in terms of how the elements are distributed around the frame's center. Arnheim (1988) and Alexander (2002) both view the understanding and analysis of centers as indispensible aspects of art and design. They typically provide many illustrations of their ideas, but no experimental evidence to justify them. Below we review some of the scientific findings related to frame structure, balance, and centers, as well as more complex aspects of spatial composition.

5.3.1. The structure of a rectangular frame.
Many of the factors related to spatial composition depend critically on the relation between the elements and their surrounding rectangular frame.[1] Arnheim (1974) speculated that a frame has a "structural skeleton" defined by dynamic forces propagated from its sides. Recent empirical measurements have supported Arnheim's intuitions remarkably well (Palmer 1991, Palmer & Griscom 2012, Palmer & Guidi 2011). When observers rated the "goodness of fit" for the placement of a single probe circle at 35 locations within a rectangular frame, the center of the frame always had the highest average goodness rating, which decreased monotonically with distance from the center. The next highest ratings were along the vertical and horizontal axes of symmetry, with smaller increases along the angle bisectors at each corner of the frame, but notably not along the diagonal that runs through the center. Indeed, the central axis of many shapes holds a special salience for other perceptual measures, such as contrast sensitivity (Kovacs & Julesz 1994). Subsequent research revealed that people generally prefer images in which the dot "fits well" within the frame, with average preference ratings being very highly correlated with

average goodness-of-fit ratings ($r = 0.95$), although large individual differences were evident (Palmer & Griscom 2012) (see section 6).

5.3.2. Balance and centers.
Some of the earliest empirical studies of balance investigated images containing a fixed line of some particular length, width, and color plus a test line of some particular length, width, and color. Observers were asked to adjust the position of the test line to make the entire display appear balanced (Pierce 1894, Puffer 1903). All else being equal, test lines were placed farther from the center than the fixed line if they were shorter and/or thinner than the fixed line, but they were placed closer to the center if they were longer and/or thicker. Although these results are consistent with physical concepts of balance, darker colors were treated as if they were heavier (Bullough 1907), thus defying explanation by a purely mechanical analogy, since colors have no physical weight.

Other studies have evaluated perceived balance for works of art and compositions of abstract shapes. When asked to place a fulcrum below the balance point of an artwork image, observers generally indicated pictures were balanced near the center of the frame, with more images being balanced slightly left of center (McManus et al. 1985). For abstract displays of one or two colored squares (red, green, or blue), position strongly influenced perceived balance, but there were also significant interactions with color, with red affecting balance most and blue least. Locher et al. (2005) found similar effects of color when comparing perceived balance in Piet Mondrian's original abstract paintings versus variants with interchanged colors. Observers judged the originals to be balanced near the center and to be more balanced than the color variants. Based on judgments of "balance center," the perceived weight of a region varied as a function of its size and color, with red being perceived as heaviest, blue intermediate, and yellow lightest. In another study, when artwork was modified in ways that influenced balance and composition (e.g., by deleting elements), observers perceived compositionally

---

[1] By "frame" we mean to include cases in which there is no actual frame around the image, but simply the rectangular borders of the image.

balanced images to be more visually "right" (Locher 2003). Finally, when participants arranged paper cutout shapes in an empty frame to produce displays that were "both interesting and pleasant," about half of the designs displayed symmetry at some point in the creation process, and the physical weight was equally distributed around the center in the majority of final designs (Locher et al. 1998).

A quite different claim for the aesthetic importance of centers comes from Tyler's (1998) finding that one of the two eyes in nonprofile portraits of human faces almost always lies at or very near the frame's vertical midline. This strong center bias was much more pronounced for the eye than for the face as a whole, the mouth, or even the single eye in profile portraits. McManus & Thomas (2007) challenged Tyler's claim, finding that people showed no preference for portraits in which one eye was centered compared with otherwise identical images in which neither eye was centered. Controversy continues over reasons for the centered-eye phenomenon, with McManus & Thomas (2007) claiming that it arises from geometric constraints on positioning a single head within a pictorial frame, and Tyler (2007) rebutting their objections.

5.3.3. Compositional biases in pictures of meaningful objects.
Palmer, Gardner/Sammartino, and colleagues have attempted to understand aesthetic preferences for spatial composition of pictures containing just one or two meaningful objects within a rectangular frame. Using several different measures, Palmer and colleagues (2008) found strong, systematic tendencies for symmetrical objects that faced forward to be preferred at the center of the frame (the center bias) and for objects that faced rightward or leftward to be located off-center to the left or right of center, respectively (the inward bias). An inward bias is also evident in artists' paintings and drawings of animals (Bertamini et al. 2011).

Sammartino & Palmer (2012a) found similar biases in preferences for vertical position of single object pictures. For example, when

the image of an object was symmetrical about a horizontal axis (e.g., an eagle seen from directly above or below), they found a center bias. When objects "faced" upward (e.g., a bowl) or downward (e.g., a light fixture), they found an inward bias: People preferred the bowl below the frame's center and the light fixture above it. Ecological biases were also evident, in that people preferred the position of the object within the frame to be consistent with its typical location relative to the observer: Eagles were preferred higher in the frame, whereas stingrays were preferred lower. Complex patterns of preferences arose from the combined influences of these different biases.

Other ecological effects are also evident in people's aesthetic responses to the depicted perspective and size of a focal object in an image. Previous research on canonical perspective had demonstrated that people can recognize everyday objects better from the perspectives from which they are more likely to be seen (e.g., Palmer et al. 1981). Preferences for different perspective views follow a similar pattern (Palmer et al. 1981, Sammartino & Palmer 2012b). Analogously, there is a canonical size effect in aesthetic judgments. People tend to prefer small objects (such as a butterfly) to be smaller within the frame and for larger objects (such as an elephant) to be larger within the frame (Konkle & Oliva 2011), even if each observer sees only different-sized pictures of a single object (Linsen et al. 2011).

Further studies have examined semantic effects in the composition of pictures containing two objects that were either closely related in everyday use (e.g., a champagne bottle and a cake or a liquid detergent bottle and a sponge) or quite distantly related (e.g., a champagne bottle and a sponge or a liquid detergent bottle and a cake) (Leyssen et al. 2012). The results consistently showed that people prefer related objects to be much closer together and unrelated objects to be much farther apart within the frame, even if placing two related objects nearby produced an unbalanced composition. Indeed, when 2AFC comparisons were performed to look explicitly for balance versus semantic relatedness effects, the semantic bias was clearly evident, but there was no bias toward balance. Although this finding appears to contradict previous research on balance (see above), prior research has almost exclusively used abstract geometrical shapes that do not have meaningful ecological relations to one another.

McManus et al. (2011) recently explored various factors that affect the way in which different complex photographic images were cropped within a fixed-size rectangular frame. Participants adjusted the position of the rectangular frame within a larger image so that they achieved the most aesthetically pleasing image that contained a specified location. Some low-level, image-based features, such as color, had little effect on cropping choices, whereas others, such as detail, had more substantial effects, but higher-level, meaning-based features seemed to dominate.

The bulk of these results on spatial composition of pictures of meaningful objects support a general conclusion that prior knowledge plays a crucial role. Even the inward bias depends on observers knowing which side is an object's front, and all the other forms of ecological bias rest on observers knowing the ecological statistics of meaningful objects: the perspective from which they are seen (canonical perspective), how big they are (canonical size), and where they tend to be positioned vertically relative to eye level (which might be termed "canonical elevation"). Although it has never been demonstrated in aesthetic judgments, it seems clear that there would also be large aesthetic differences due to an object's orientation relative to the frame (canonical orientation). All of these effects are consistent with perceptual fluency theories of aesthetic preference (see below): People like pictures of objects to the degree that they are easily perceived (Reber et al. 2004, Winkielman et al. 2006).

5.3.4. Higher-level spatial composition: Effects of meaning, titles, and context.
Higher-level factors, such as meaning, emotion, and/or the interpretation of images in different contexts, are often thought to be important in

aesthetic preference, especially in philosophical discussions, such as Kant's (1892/1951) writings about the importance of "free play of the imagination." Only recently have such factors been investigated experimentally.

Millis (2001) explored the effect of different kinds of titles for illustrations and photographs on four qualities of the aesthetic experience: interest, thoughts, emotions, and aesthetic appreciation. Metaphorical titles, which gave additional information not immediately evident from the image itself (e.g., titling an image of a woman picking flowers *One Day at a Time*) increased aesthetic appreciation over purely descriptive titles (e.g., *Woman Picking Flowers*) or no titles at all. Russell (2003) examined the effects of providing viewers with the artist's names and actual titles and/or brief descriptions of abstract or semi-abstract images on both the viewers' judgments of "meaningfulness" and their aesthetic judgments. He expected meaningfulness to increase aesthetic appeal, but found this to be true only in a within-subjects design. Leder et al. (2006) extended this kind of investigation to both abstract and representational artworks and examined the effects of exposure duration. Titles did not influence liking or content understanding overall, but they did interact with durations. Descriptive titles were more effective at brief 1-second exposures, and elaborative titles were more effective at longer 10-second exposures.

Extending their prior research on biases in object placement within a frame (Palmer et al. 2008), Sammartino & Palmer (2012b) studied systematic effects of different titles on preference for the horizontal placement and perspective views of objects. When the title was purely descriptive (e.g., *Racehorse* and *Man Walking*), they replicated their previous results, with observers preferring the object near the center of the frame and facing inward. When the title elaborated the context in a way that implied unseen objects or portions of an event (e.g., *Front Runner* versus *Dead Last* for the running horse or *Journey's End* versus *Starting Out* for the man walking), they found that the most preferred composition was dramatically different: Compositions that were least preferred with neutral titles were most preferred with elaborative titles that fit the composition. They found analogous effects of elaborative titles on different perspective views of objects.

6. INDIVIDUAL DIFFERENCES

It is widely acknowledged that people differ enormously in their aesthetic preferences for all kinds of different modalities and domains (e.g., McManus 1980, McManus et al. 1981). This fact, more than any other, underlies the well-known adages, "Beauty is in the mind of the beholder" and "There is no accounting for taste." In spatial composition, for example, McManus & Weatherby (1997) found that average positional preferences were close to the golden section value in horizontal placement, but individuals differences (IDs) were so large that few, if any, participants showed preference functions that looked much like the group averages.

In color preferences, Ling & Hurlbert (2009) used their extended, four-parameter cone contrast model (see section 4.1.1) to fit individuals' preference data. It accounted well for IDs (average multiple-$r = 0.71$), indicating that observers differ in the polarity and importance of these four dimensions for single colors. From an ecological perspective, Palmer et al. (2012a) found that, as predicted by the EVT, WAVE measurements for individual observers were more highly correlated with their own color preferences (average $r = +0.55$) than with those of other observers (average $r = +0.40$).

In preferences for two-color combinations, Schloss & Palmer (2011) found that even though average preference ratings correlated very strongly with average harmony ratings ($+0.79$; see above), the same correlations for individuals ranged widely from about zero to $+0.75$. Furthermore, these IDs varied with the amount of formal color training participants had completed, following an inverted-U function, with a maximum for intermediate amounts of training and lower correlations for both

untrained and highly trained individuals. This pattern is consistent with Berlyne's inverted-U prediction (see below).

Eysenck (1940) studied people's aesthetic rankings of sets of spatial images of 18 different types (including portraits, landscapes, and photographs of medieval clocks) as well as to colors, odors, and polygons. After correlating the rankings and performing a factor analysis, he identified a single "general objective factor of aesthetic appreciation" (which he called "t" for "good taste") that varied with the extent to which an individual's rankings agreed with the average rankings of the entire group. It turned out to be relatively constant for individuals across domains. Although Eysenck's interpretation of the t-factor as an objective measure of good taste seems misguided (see section 2.3), this measure might be an important variable in characterizing systematic IDs in aesthetic preferences.

Palmer & Griscom (2012) have recently proposed that "preference for harmony" may be the primary aesthetic ID that underlies Eysenck's t-factor. Following Schloss & Palmer's (2011) findings of IDs in preference for color pairs (see above), they studied the extent to which people's judgments of aesthetic preference among stimuli in different domains (color pairs, configural shapes, spatial compositions, and music) correlated with their own judgments for the same stimuli in their degree of harmony, where harmony is a dimension characterized by simplicity, regularity, and parts that fit well together, regardless of preference. They found that the correlations between average preference and average harmony ratings over all individuals were quite high in all domains (ranging from $+0.97$ for music to $+0.47$ for configural shape) but that the same correlations for individuals were extremely variable: Some people like harmonious stimuli and others dislike them, with IDs in preference for harmony in music ranging from -0.73 to $+0.97$. Most importantly, the correlations between a difference-score measure of preference for harmony were systematically above chance for all pairs of different domains, ranging from

+0.60 for color pairs and music to +0.32 for spatial composition and music. Preference for harmony can explain Eysenck's t-factor because the preference judgments of individuals who prefer harmonious stimuli will necessarily be more highly correlated with average preferences to the degree that people generally prefer harmonious stimuli in that domain, as it was for all four of Palmer and Griscom's domains. Furthermore, they found that specific training in an aesthetic domain (art or music) systematically lowered people's preference for harmony in that domain, consistent with Berlyne's (1971) analysis of the effects of experience.

7. THEORIES OF AESTHETIC RESPONSE

The foregoing review summarizes many of the most important findings about human aesthetic preference in visual domains as indexed by behavioral responses. Although the preferences discussed are fairly basic, the hope is that they constitute a foundation on which a better understanding of more complex aesthetic responses can be built, perhaps eventually including people's powerful aesthetic reactions to works of art. It is by no means obvious that this can be accomplished, and some writers have explicitly claimed that it cannot (Markovic 2010). We now turn to ask why people like the things they do. Several accounts have been suggested.

7.1. Mere Exposure

One possible explanation of why people like some things more than others is the "mere exposure" effect: People tend to like objects and images more as the frequency of seeing them increases (Zajonc 1968). One might try to explain aesthetic preference for, say, photographs of inward-facing objects over outward-facing objects (Palmer et al. 2008) by appealing to the fact that people simply see more pictures of inward-facing objects. The problem is that one must also explain the latter fact. It is tempting to say that it is because photographers like inward-facing pictures more, but then one still needs to

explain this preference in some way other than invoking the mere exposure effect again—i.e., that photographers have seen more pictures of inward-facing objects. The root problem is thus that explanations based purely on exposure frequency lead to infinite regress.

We do not deny that exposure frequency influences people's aesthetic judgments; certainly it does. Cutting, for example, has provided a compelling historical analysis of its influence on aesthetic judgments of certain paintings that are included in the Impressionist canon (Cutting 2003, 2006). The ultimate explanation of their inclusion does not come from mere exposure, however, but rather from differences in the availability of certain paintings at an important historical juncture when the canon was defined: The pictures that were available to the public were included rather than those only available to private owners. The important conclusion for present purposes is that, although mere exposure can explain the perpetuation and even the amplification of a bias across time, it cannot satisfactorily explain its ultimate cause.

7.2. Arousal Dynamics

Daniel Berlyne developed a complex and influential theory of aesthetic response based on a psychobiological conception that pleasure is a matter of the viewer's degree of arousal while viewing an image (Berlyne 1957, 1960, 1971). Arousal, in turn, was proposed to depend on a complex psychobiological response to three types of variables—collative, psychophysical, and ecological—each of which produced responses in a primary reward system and a primary aversion system. The combined effect of these two systems was claimed to produce an inverted-U function of the underlying variable, with aesthetic pleasure first increasing as a function of arousal and then decreasing as arousal became too great. Collative variables are those related to the viewer's expectations (e.g., novelty, complexity, uncertainty, conflict, surprisingness, unfamiliarity), psychophysical variables are those related to sensory dimensions of the stimulus (e.g., intensity, pitch, brightness), and ecological variables are those related to meaningfulness and associations to environmental objects. According to Berlyne's theory, as a relevant variable increases (e.g., complexity), a primary reward system becomes increasingly active and generates positive affect. As complexity continues to increase, however, an aversion system becomes active and generates negative affect. The reward system saturates before the aversion system does, leading to the classic inverted-U curve so closely associated with Berlyne's theorizing. Berlyne claimed that collative variables were the most important, and the bulk of his empirical work was directed at understanding them. We will not attempt a full review of the theory or the evidence relevant to its evaluation. Suffice it to say that although Berlyne amassed much evidence in support of his ideas (e.g., Berlyne 1971, 1974), some of its key predictions have not been supported empirically (Martindale et al. 1990).

7.3. Prototype Theory

Rosch's (1975) transformative research on prototype effects in categorization suggested a different avenue to explaining visual preferences that was developed primarily by Martindale and Whitfield. Simply put, people may prefer prototypical examples of categories to nonprototypical ones. Preferences for prototypes have been demonstrated for colors (Martindale & Moore 1988), furniture (Whitfield & Slatter 1979), faces (Light et al. 1981), exemplars of semantic categories (Martindale et al. 1988), and surrealist paintings (Farkas 2002).

This work can be viewed as an elaboration of the effects of certain ecological variables within Berlyne's framework, with the caveat that many of the effects appear to show monotonic increases with prototypicality rather than the inverted-U-shaped function that Berlyne's theorizing implies. The more recent ecological effects described above for preference effects due to canonical position in the world (Sammartino & Palmer 2012a), canonical perspective (Palmer et al. 1981, Sammartino & Palmer 2012b), and canonical size (Konkle

& Oliva 2011, Linsen et al. 2011) can all be interpreted as supporting the importance of prototypes, albeit with respect to viewpoint-based features of images of objects relative to viewers rather than to category membership. Nevertheless, even preferences for both prototypical examples and canonical features seem too limited to be taken as a general theory of aesthetic response. They are more like ubiquitous factors that influence aesthetic preference. Moreover, prototype theory, by itself, does not clarify why prototypes should be preferred.

7.4. Fluency Theory

An interesting answer to the "why" question is provided by fluency theory, which is perhaps the single most general explanation of aesthetic preference (e.g., Reber 2012; Reber et al. 1998, 2004). Fluency theory posits that people prefer visual displays to the extent that they are processed more easily (or fluently). It does a good job of predicting aesthetic effects due to many low-level features (for a review, see Oppenheimer & Frank 2008), such as preferences for larger (Silvera et al. 2002), more symmetrical (Jacobson & Höfel 2002), more highly contrastive displays (Reber et al. 1998). It can also explain categorical prototype effects (see above) because prototypes are well known to be more easily and quickly processed than nonprototypical examples (e.g., Rosch 1975). The kinds of spatial composition effects described above for untitled, single-object pictures— namely, the fact that people tend to prefer the focal object to be at or near the center of the frame, to face inward both horizontally and vertically, and to be depicted at a height, perspective, and size within the frame that reflect their characteristic height, perspective, and size relative to a standard observer (Palmer et al. 2012b; Sammartino & Palmer 2012a,b)—are also consistent with perceptual fluency. The reason is that these compositional choices tend to make the object most recognizable as the kind of object it is (cf. Estes et al. 2008, Palmer et al. 1981) and therefore lead to the easiest (most fluent) processing for the purpose of object identification. These compositional choices amount to selecting the most likely (or "default") settings of the spatial variables associated with the representational schema for that kind of object (cf. Palmer 1975, Palmer et al. 2012b). Finally, fluency theory even provides a plausible causal explanation of mere exposure effects: The more often a given image is seen, the more easily and fluently it will be processed, and, by hypothesis, increased fluency leads to increased preference.

One problem with fluency theory is that it does not square well with Berlyne's inverted-U results for preference as a function of complexity. More complex stimuli presumably always require more processing than simpler ones, so it seems that fluency theory should predict a monotonic decrease in preference as a function of complexity. The typical result, however, is an initial increase in preference with greater complexity, until some optimum level is reached, after which a decrease with additional complexity is found (see Berlyne 1971 for a review). It is also unclear how fluency would account for preferences for single colors, especially in light of the strong evidence of links to preferences for ecological objects (Palmer & Schloss 2010).

A deeper challenge to fluency theory as a complete account of aesthetic response is that its basic premise—that the most easily processed image will be the most aesthetically pleasing one—seems to contradict a central tenet of art theory: namely, that the aesthetic (or perhaps the artistic) impact of an image is increased by intentionally violating the viewer's expectations. Indeed, the most fluent image of an object would seem to be the most boring image of it—analogous, perhaps, to the formulaic paintings created by Komar and Melamid as the most pleasing pictures for people in different cultures (Wypijewski 1997)—whereas aesthetically pleasing images are expected to be more interesting. Indeed, much of the recent history of art, from Impressionism onward, can be understood as a continual process of violating the rules and conventions of prior art practice. It is presently unclear how one should view the relation between art history and aesthetics, however. Perhaps art has simply become increasingly dominated by novelty and the quest to conceptually stretch the boundaries of art to the detriment of the aesthetic response such art evokes in many or most viewers.

An equally troubling, and possibly related, problem is that fluency theory seems to leave out a crucial variable in aesthetic judgment: namely, the meaning or message of the image as intended by the artist and/or as inferred by the viewer (which assuredly may not be the same). It is perhaps such semantic considerations that lie, in part, behind Kant's suggestion that aesthetic judgments necessarily involve "free play of the imagination" in the beholder, and it is disturbing that such considerations seem to be either irrelevant or possibly even contradicted by perceptual fluency accounts. More recently, fluency theory has been extended to conceptual (rather than perceptual) fluency in an attempt to account for effects of such higher-level semantic variables (Reber et al. 2004, Whittlesea 1993). The common principle is that fluent (easy) processing is aesthetically valued in both perceptual and conceptual domains.

Sammartino & Palmer (2012b) have proposed an alternative to fluency theories of aesthetic response to pictures of objects and scenes based on their concept of representational fit. The suggestion is that people prefer images to the extent that their spatial composition optimally conveys an intended or inferred meaning of the image, thus including a semantic variable that is missing from fluency theory. Interestingly, it also makes the same predictions as fluency when the message intended or inferred for the image is simply the default one: to depict the focal object(s) or event(s), as it typically is in stock photography. Under such circumstances, the best horizontal and vertical position, size, and perspective of the object(s) will be those that make it optimally recognizable. When the intended or inferred meaning is different, however, as it is with the elaborated titles in the studies described above, the otherwise non-preferred compositional choices of position, perspective, and size that are most compatible with the message can produce the highest aesthetic response in viewers (Sammartino & Palmer 2012b). Fluency and representational fit may also be viewed as compatible accounts, however, differing primarily in emphasis, with fluency theory focused on the ease of processing and representational fit theory focused on the reasons that processing is easy.

7.5. Multicomponent Theories of Aesthetic Response to Art

Although the focus of this review has intentionally not been on aesthetic responses to viewing art objects, it is useful to see how the kind of work reviewed above fits within theoretical frameworks designed to account for the aesthetic appreciation of art. Shimamura (2012), for example, has recently presented a very general approach to understanding people's aesthetic responses to art. To the extent that part of people's appreciation of art concerns aesthetic dimensions of their experiences, it is presumably relevant. Shimamura's framework is summarized by its acronym, I-SKE, which stands for the intention (I) behind the artwork in relation to the viewer's sensory (S), knowledge-based (K), and emotional (E) responses. I-SKE is thus a very general framework that seems to encompass much of what matters in people's aesthetic responses to art objects.

The research reviewed in this article generally concerns the aesthetic effect of sensory-perceptual information and its relation to knowledge-based components. Most of the biases identified in preferences for spatial composition, for example, are knowledge based. Surprisingly, knowledge is relevant even for simple color preferences, because they turn out to depend strongly on people's stored knowledge of their affective responses to the objects that are characteristically associated with those colors (Palmer & Schloss 2010).

Leder and colleagues (2004) have formulated a detailed information-processing model that attempts to analyze and synthesize these many diverse aspects of people's appreciation of art, and especially of modern art. It consists of a series of five processes, each of which is influenced by many factors. The five processes are proposed to occur in the following order: (*a*) perception, which responds to stimulus factors, such as complexity, symmetry, color, contrast, and organization; (*b*) implicit classification, which involves integrating this perceptual information into related information stored in memory concerning familiarity, prototypes, and conventions; (*c*) explicit classification of the artwork in terms of its style and content; (*d*) cognitive "mastering" of its style and content by interpreting them within one's knowledge about related art and with respect to the viewer's self; and finally (*e*) evaluation of satisfaction in terms of both the work's cognitive aspects (e.g., understanding of meaning and ambiguity) and the cumulative influence of all the stages of processing on the viewer's affective state. Of the stages, the first two are deemed to be automatic, the last two to be deliberate, with explicit categorization being a mixture of both. In addition to these processes, however, there are many contextual considerations that influence the outcome of the processing, including the situation in which the viewer finds the artwork (museum, gallery, psychology experiment, etc.), what previous experiences the viewer has had with similar artworks, what social and linguistic information the viewer has surrounding the current experience, and what his/her affective state is coming into the current viewing experience.

Comparatively less attention has been paid to emotional components of aesthetic response. However, Silvia's recently proposed "appraisal theory" of aesthetic response is based primarily on analyzing the diverse emotional responses a viewer might have to art objects (e.g., Silvia 2005a,b, 2006, 2012). He divides emotions into several kinds—positive emotions (happiness, enjoyment, pleasure),[2]

---

[2] Silvia does not mention negative emotions (sadness, misery, pain) as a category, but perhaps he intends them to be implied by virtue of being the inverses of the positive emotions.

knowledge emotions (surprise, interest, confusion), hostile emotions (anger, disgust, contempt), and self-conscious emotions (pride, shame, guilt, embarrassment)—and argues that all are relevant to understanding aesthetic responses to art. Positive emotions are classically emphasized in most aesthetic research (see section 2.1), but Silvia argues that the other classes of emotions are indeed relevant to people's reactions to art. This is especially true for modern art, where many artists clearly intend their works to elicit surprise, interest, anger, disgust, shame, and/or guilt rather than pleasure.

8. CONCLUSIONS AND ISSUES FOR FUTURE RESEARCH

We have attempted to summarize, critique, and synthesize the emerging scientific literature concerning human aesthetic response to and preferences for visual stimulation using behavioral methods. We began with the claim that this body of research exemplifies a branch of aesthetic science from a psychological perspective. We submit that the results we have described constitute clear advances in the understanding of this domain. We hope to have convinced the reader that meaningful research in this field is not only possible, but also interesting, important, and fun.

Nevertheless, many critical issues need to be addressed in future research. One is how to connect this body of work with the ongoing literature on behavioral studies of the perception of art. As we said at the outset, aesthetic response and perception of art are conceptually distinct, but overlapping, domains. Can aesthetic preferences for simple features such as individual colors, color combinations, form, texture, and spatial composition somehow be combined to understand the far more complex appreciation of fine art, or do these features form truly emergent wholes (Gestalts) that transcend understanding in terms of their simpler components? Needless to say, this is a daunting task, but there are some bodies of artwork that lend themselves well to beginning to answer the question, such as Piet Mondrian's "grid" paintings in red, yellow, and blue and Josef Albers's *Homage to the Square* series.

A second critical issue is how to extend the present body of research more fully into the burgeoning topics of emotion and cognitive meaning. Much of the research described above concerns what most would call purely formal characteristics of aesthetic appreciation. Indeed, this is why the art of Mondrian and Albers is closer to the reviewed research than that of, say, Monet, Picasso, or Duchamps. Formal aspects are clearly important, but they are just one part of what one wants to know about aesthetic response. Although some inroads have been made recently in this direction both theoretically and empirically, the field is wide open for more systematic research that builds on the increasingly sophisticated understanding of both topics that has arisen in psychology.

A third critical issue, not unrelated to the first two, is how to connect behavioral research on aesthetic preferences with the emerging field of neuroaesthetics. As we also said at the outset, understanding the neural correlates of aesthetic response depends fundamentally on the development of behavioral methods and results. As this behavioral foundation becomes firmer, more precise and detailed studies of the brain regions that produce aesthetic responses can be undertaken with considerable prospects of success. We expect that eventually there will be a synergy between behavioral and neural studies of aesthetics that will help both enterprises reach the common goal of understanding visual aesthetics and human preference.

DISCLOSURE STATEMENT

The authors are not aware of any affiliations, memberships, funding, or financial holdings that might be perceived as affecting the objectivity of this review.

ACKNOWLEDGMENTS

The preparation of this article was supported in part by the National Science Foundation under grants #0745820 and #1059088 and a Google Gift to S.E.P. Any opinions, findings, conclusions, and/or recommendations expressed in this article are those of the authors and do not necessarily reflect the views of the National Science Foundation or Google.

LITERATURE CITED

Adams FM, Osgood CE. 1973. A cross-cultural study of the affective meanings of color. *J. Cross Cult. Psychol.* 4:135–56

Adams RJ. 1987. An evaluation of color preference in early infancy. *Infant Behav. Dev.* 10:143–50

Albers J. 1971. *Interaction of Color.* New Haven, CT: Yale Univ. Press

Alexander C. 2002. *The Nature of Order: An Essay on the Art of Building and the Nature of the Universe.* Berkeley, CA: Cent. Environ. Struct.

Allesch GJv. 1924. Die aesthetische Erscheinungsweise der Farben. *Psychol. Forsch.* 6:1–91

Angier RP. 1903. The aesthetics of unequal division. *Psychol. Rev. Monogr. Suppl.* 4:541–61

Arnheim R. 1974. *Art and Visual Perception: A Psychology of the Creative Eye.* Berkeley: Univ. Calif. Press

Arnheim R. 1988. *The Power of the Center.* Berkeley: Univ. Calif. Press

Atalay B. 2004. *Math and the Mona Lisa: The Art and Science of Leonardo da Vinci.* Washington, DC: Smithsonian Books

Ball VK. 1965. The aesthetics of color: a review of fifty years of experimentation. *J Aes. Art. Crit.* 23:441–52

Bar M, Neta M. 2006. Humans prefer curved visual objects. *Psychol. Sci.* 17:645–48

Berlyne DE. 1957. Uncertainty and conflict: a point of contact between information-theory and behavior-theory concepts. *Psychol. Rev.* 64:329–39

Berlyne DE. 1960. *Conflict, Arousal, and Curiosity.* New York: McGraw–Hill

Berlyne DE. 1971. *Aesthetics and Psychobiology.* New York: Appleton-Century-Crofts

Berlyne DE. 1974. *Studies in the New Experimental Aesthetics: Steps Toward an Objective Psychology of Aesthetic Appreciation.* Oxford, UK: Hemisphere

Bertamini M, Bennet KM, Bode C. 2011. The anterior bias in visual art: the case of images of animals. *Laterality* 16:673–89

Birkhoff GD. 1933. *Aesthetic Measure.* Cambridge, MA: Harvard Univ. Press

Birren F. 1961. *Color Psychology and Color Therapy.* New York: Univ. Books

Bornstein MH. 1975. Qualities of color vision in infancy. *J. Exp. Child. Psychol.* 19:401–19

Boselie F. 1984. The aesthetic attractivity of the golden section. *Psychol. Res.* 45:367–75

Boselie F, Leeuwenberg E. 1985. Birkhoff revisited: beauty as a function of effect and means. *Am. J. Psychol.* 98:1–39

Bullough E. 1907. On the apparent heaviness of colours. *Brit. J. Psychol.* 2:111–52

Chandler AR. 1928. Recent experiments on visual aesthetics. *Psychol. Bull.* 25:720–32

Chatterjee A. 2011. Neuroaesthetics: a coming of age story. *J. Cogn. Neurosci.* 23:53–62

Chevreul ME, ed. 1839. *The Principles of Harmony and Contrast of Colors.* New York: Van Nostrand Reinhold

Child IL, Hansen JA, Hornbeck FW. 1968. Age and sex differences in children's color preferences. *Child Dev.* 39:237–47

Chiu SW, Gervan S, Fairbrother C, Johnson LL, Owen-Anderson AFH, et al. 2006. Sex-dimorphic color preference in children with gender identity disorder: a comparison to clinical and community controls. *Sex Roles* 55:385–95

Choungourian A. 1968. Color preference and cultural variation. *Percept. Mot. Skills* 26:1203–6

Chuang MC, Ou LC. 2001. Influence of a holistic color interval on color harmony. *Color Res. Appl.* 26:29–39

Cohn J. 1884. Experimentelle Untersuchungen über die Gefühlsbetonung der Farben, Helligkeiten und ihrer Combinationen. *Philos. Stud.* 10:562–602

Cutting JE. 2003. Gustave Caillebotte, French Impressionism, and mere exposure. *Psychon. Bull. Rev.* 10:319–43

Cutting JE. 2006. The mere exposure effect and aesthetic preference. In *New Directions in Aesthetics, Creativity, and the Psychology of Art*, ed. P Locher, C Martindale, L Dorfman, pp. 33–46. Amityville, NY: Baywood Publ.

da Vinci L. 1942/1956. *Treatise on Painting*. Princeton, NJ: Princeton Univ. Press

De Valois RL, De Valois KK. 1990. *Spatial Vision*. New York: Oxford Univ. Press

Dickie G. 1962. Is psychology relevant to aesthetics? *Phil. Rev.* 71:285–302

Dickie G. 1997. *Introduction to Aesthetics: An Analytic Approach*. Oxford, UK: Oxford Univ. Press

Estes Z, Verges M, Barsalou LW. 2008. Head up, foot down: Object words orient attention to the objects' typical location. *Psychol. Sci.* 19:93–97

Eysenck HJ. 1940. The general factor in aesthetic judgments. *Brit. J. Psychol. Gen.-Sect.* 31:94–102

Eysenck HJ. 1941. A critical and experimental study of color preference. *Am. J. Psychol.* 54:385–91

Eysenck HJ, Castle MJ. 1971. Comparative study of artists and nonartists on the Maitland Graves Design Judgment Test. *J. Appl. Psychol.* 55:389–92

Farkas A. 2002. Prototypicality-effect in surrealist paintings. *Empir. Stud. Arts* 20:127–36

Fechner GT. 1871. *Zur experimentalen Aesthetik*. Leipzig, Germany: Hirzel

Fechner GT. 1876. *Vorschule der Aesthetik*. Leipzig, Germany: Breitkopf & Härtel

Fernandez D, Wilkins AJ. 2008. Uncomfortable images in art and nature. *Perception* 37:1098–113

Franklin A, Bevis L, Ling Y, Hurlbert A. 2009. Biological components of colour preference in infancy. *Dev. Sci.* 13:346–54

Franklin A, Pitchford N, Hart L, Davies IRL, Clausse S, Jennings S. 2008. Salience of primary and secondary colours in infancy. *Brit. J. Dev. Psychol.* 26:471–83

Garner WR, Clement DE. 1963. Goodness of pattern and pattern uncertainty. *J. Verb. Learn. Verb. Behav.* 2:446–52

Goethe JW. 1810/1970. *Theory of Colours*. Cambridge, MA: MIT Press

Graham DJ, Field DJ. 2007. Statistical regularities of art images and natural scenes: spectra, sparseness and nonlinearities. *Spat. Vis.* 21:149–64

Graham DJ, Redies C. 2010. Statistical regularities in art: relations with visual coding and perception. *Vision Res.* 50:1503–9

Granger GW. 1955a. An experimental study of colour harmony. *J. Gen. Psychol.* 52:21–35

Granger GW. 1955b. An experimental study of colour preferences. *J. Gen. Psychol.* 52:3–20

Granger GW. 1955c. The prediction of preference for color combinations. *J. Gen. Psychol.* 52:213–22

Green CD. 1995. All that glitters: a review of psychological research on the aesthetics of the golden section. *Perception* 24:937–68

Guilford JP, Smith PC. 1959. A system of color-preferences. *Am. J. Psychol.* 72:487–502

Haines TH, Davies SE. 1904. Psychology of aesthetic reaction to rectangular forms. *Psychol. Rev.* 11:249–51

Hård A, Sivik L. 1981. NCS—Natural Color System: a Swedish standard for color notation. *Color Res. Appl.* 6:129–38

Helmholtz HV. 1866/1925. *Physiological Optics*. Rochester, NY: Optical Soc. Am.

Helson H, Lansford T. 1970. The role of spectral energy of source and background color in the pleasantness of object colors. *Appl. Opt.* 9:1513–62

Humphrey N. 1976. The colour currency of nature. In *Colour for Architecture*, ed. T Porter, B Mikellides, pp. 95–98. London: Studio-Vista

Hurlbert AC, Ling Y. 2007. Biological components of sex differences in color preference. *Curr. Biol.* 17:623–25

Iijima M, Arisaka O, Minamoto F, Arai Y. 2001. Sex differences in children's free drawings: a study on girls with congenital adrenal hyperplasia. *Horm. Behav.* 40:99–104

Itten J. 1973. *The Art of Color*. New York: Van Nostrand-Reinhold

Jacobson T. 2006. Bridging the arts and sciences: a framework for the psychology of aesthetics. *Leonardo* 39:155–62

Jacobson T, Höfel LA. 2002. Aesthetic judgments of novel graphic patterns: analyses of individual judgments. *Percept. Mot. Skills* 95:755–66

Jadva V, Hines M, Golombok S. 2010. Infants' preferences for toys, colors, and shapes: sex differences and similarities. *Arch. Sex. Behav.* 39:1261–73

Kaiser PK, Boynton RM. 1996. *Human Color Vision*. Washington, DC: Opt. Soc. Am.

Kant I. 1892/1951. *Critique of Judgment*. New York: Haffner

Knoblauch K, Vital-Durand F, Barbur JL. 2001. Variation of chromatic sensitivity across the life span. *Vision Res.* 41:23–36

Koenderink JJ. 2010. *Color for the Sciences*. Cambridge, MA: MIT Press

Konecni VJ. 2003. The golden section: elusive, but detectable. *Creativity Res. J.* 15:267–75

Konecni VJ, Cline LE. 2002. The "Golden Woman:" an exploratory study of women's proportions in paintings. *Visual Arts Res.* 27:69–78

Konkle T, Oliva A. 2011. Canonical visual size for real-world objects. *J. Exp. Psychol.: Hum. Percept. Perform.* 37:23–37

Kovacs I, Julesz B. 1994. Perceptual sensitivity maps within globally defined visual shapes. *Nature* 370:644–46

Lalo C. 1908. *L'esthétique Expérimentale Contemporaine*. Paris: Alcan

Latto R, Brian D, Kelly B. 2000. An oblique effect in aesthetics: homage to Mondrian (1872–1944). *Perception* 29:981–87

Latto R, Russell-Duff K. 2002. An oblique effect in the selection of line orientation by twentieth century painters. *Empir. Stud. Arts* 20:49–60

Leder H, Belkel B, Oeberst A, Augustin D. 2004. A model of aesthetic appreciation and aesthetic judgments. *Brit. J. Psychol.* 95:489–508

Leder H, Carbon C, Ripsas A. 2006. Entitling art: influence of title information on understanding and appreciation of paintings. *Acta Psychol.* 121:176–98

Leder H, Tinio PP, Bar M. 2011. Emotional valence modulates the preference for curved objects. *Perception* 40:649–65

Leyssen MHR, Linsen S, Sammartino J, Palmer SE. 2012. Aesthetic preference for spatial composition in multiobject pictures. *i-Perception* 3:25–49

Light LL, Hollander S, Kayra-Stuart F. 1981. Why attractive people are harder to remember. *Pers. Soc. Psychol. B* 7:269–76

Ling YL, Hurlbert AC. 2009. A new model for color preference: universality and individuality, *15th Color Imaging Conf. Final Program Proc.*, pp. 8–11

Linsen S, Leyssen MHR, Sammartino J, Palmer SE. 2011. Aesthetic preferences in the size of images of real-world objects. *Perception* 40:291–98

Livio M. 2002. *The Golden Ratio: The Story of Phi, the World's Most Astonishing Number*. New York: Broadway Books

LoBue V, DeLoache JS. 2011. Pretty in pink: the early development of gender-stereotyped colour preferences. *Brit. J. Dev. Psychol.* 29:656–67

Locher P, Overbeeke K, Stappers PJ. 2005. Spatial balance of color triads in the abstract art of Piet Mondrian. *Perception* 34:169–89

Locher PJ. 2003. An empirical investigation of the visual rightness theory of picture perception. *Acta Psychol.* 114:147–64

Locher PJ, Jan Stappers P, Overbeeke K. 1998. The role of balance as an organizing design principle underlying adults' compositional strategies for creating visual displays. *Acta Psychol.* 99:141–61

Markovic S. 2010. Aesthetic experience and the emotional content of paintings. *Psihologija* 43:47–64

Martindale C, Moore K. 1988. Priming, prototypicality, and preference. *J. Exp. Psychol.: Hum. Percept. Perform.* 14:661–70

Martindale C, Moore K, Borkum J. 1990. Aesthetic preference: anomalous findings for Berlyne's psychobiological model. *Am. J. Psychol.* 103:53–80

Martindale C, Moore K, West A. 1988. Relationship of preference judgments to typicality, novelty, and mere exposure. *Empir. Stud. Arts* 6:79–96

McManus IC. 1980. The aesthetics of simple figures. *Brit. J. Psychol.* 71:502–24

McManus IC, Edmondson D, Rodger J. 1985. Balance in pictures. *Brit. J. Psychol.* 76:311–24

McManus IC, Jones AL, Cottrell J. 1981. The aesthetics of colour. *Perception* 10:651–66

McManus IC, Thomas P. 2007. Eye centering in portraits: a theoretical and empirical evaluation. *Perception* 36:167–82

McManus IC, Weatherby P. 1997. The golden section and the aesthetics of form and composition: a cognitive model. *Empir. Stud. Arts* 15:209–32

McManus IC, Zhou FA, l'Anson S, Waterfield L, Stover K, Cook R. 2011. The psychometrics of photographic cropping: the influence of colour, meaning, and expertise. *Perception* 40:332–57

Millis K. 2001. Making meaning brings pleasure: the influence of titles on aesthetic experiences. *Emotion* 1:320–29

Moon P, Spencer DE. 1944a. Aesthetic measure applied to color harmony. *J. Exp. Psychol.* 34:234–42

Moon P, Spencer DE. 1944b. Geometric formulation of classical color harmony. *J. Opt. Soc. Am.* 34:46–59

Munsell AH. 1921. *A Grammar of Color*. New York: Van Nostrand-Reinhold

Munsinger H, Kessen W. 1964a. Age and uncertainty: developmental variation in preference for variability. *J. Exp. Child. Psychol.* 1:1–15

Munsinger H, Kessen W. 1964b. Uncertainty, structure, and preference. *Psychol. Monogr.: Gen. A* 78:1–24

Oppenheimer DM, Frank MC. 2008. A rose in any other font would not smell as sweet: effects of perceptual fluency on categorization. *Cognition* 106:1178–94

Ostwald W. 1932. *Color Science*. London: Windsor Newton

Ou L-C, Luo MR. 2006. A colour harmony model for two-colour combinations. *Color Res. Appl.* 31:191–204

Ou L-C, Luo MR, Sun PL, Hu NC, Chen HS, et al. 2011. A cross-cultural comparison of colour emotion for two-colour combinations. *Color Res. Appl.* 37:23–43

Ou L-C, Luo MR, Woodcock A, Wright A. 2004. A study of colour emotion and colour preference. Part III: colour preference modeling. *Color Res. Appl.* 29:381–89

Palmer SE. 1975. Visual perception and world knowledge: notes on a model of sensory-cognitive interaction. In *Explorations in Cognition*, ed. DA Norman, DE Rumelhart, pp. 279–307. San Francisco: Freeman

Palmer SE. 1991. Goodness, Gestalt, groups, and Garner: local symmetry subgroups as a theory of figural goodness. In *The Perception of Structure: Essays in Honor of Wendell G. Garner*, ed. G Lockhead, J Pomerantz, pp. 23–39. Washington, DC: Am. Psychol. Assoc.

Palmer SE, Gardner JS, Wickens TD. 2008. Aesthetic issues in spatial composition: effects of position and direction on framing single objects. *Spat. Vis.* 21:421–49

Palmer SE, Griscom W. 2012. Accounting for taste: individual differences in preference for harmony. *Psychon. Bull. Rev.* In press

Palmer SE, Guidi S. 2011. Mapping the perceptual structure of rectangles through goodness-of-fit ratings. *Perception* 40:1428–46

Palmer SE, Rosch E, Chase P. 1981. Canonical perspective and the perception of objects. In *Attention and Performance IX*, ed. J Long, A Baddeley, pp. 135–51. Hillsdale: Erlbaum

Palmer SE, Schloss KB. 2010. An ecological valence theory of human color preference. *Proc. Natl. Acad. Sci. USA* 107:8877–82

Palmer SE, Schloss KB. 2011. Ecological valence and human color preference. In *New Directions in Colour Studies*, ed. CP Biggam, CA Hough, CJ Kay, DR Simmons, pp. 361–76. Amsterdam: Benjamins

Palmer SE, Schloss KB, Hawthorne D. 2012a. Ecological influences on individual differences in color preference. Manuscript submitted

Palmer SE, Schloss KB, Sammartino J. 2012b. Hidden knowledge in aesthetic judgments: preference for color and spatial composition. See Shimamura & Palmer 2012, pp. 189–222

Pastoureau M. 2001. *Blue: The History of a Color*. Princeton, NJ: Princeton Univ. Press

Pennell GE. 1994. Babes in toyland: learning an ideology of gender. *Adv. Consumer Res.* 21:359–64

Picariello ML, Greenberg DN, Pillemer DB. 1990. Children's sex related stereotyping of colors. *Child Dev.* 61:1453–60

Pierce E. 1894. Aesthetics of simple forms I: symmetry. *Psychol. Rev.* 1:483–95

Puffer ED. 1903. Studies in symmetry. *Psychol. Rev. Monogr. Suppl.* 4:467–539

Raghubir P, Greenleaf EA. 2006. Ratios in proportion: what should the shape of the package be? *J. Mark.* 70:95–107

Ramachandran VS, Hirstein W. 1999. The science of art: a neurological theory of aesthetic experience. *J. Consciousness Stud.* 6:15–51

Reber R. 2012. Processing fluency, aesthetic pleasure, and culturally shared taste. See Shimamura & Palmer 2012, pp. 223–49

Reber R, Schwarz N, Winkielman P. 2004. Processing fluency and aesthetic pleasure: Is beauty in the perceiver's processing experience? *Pers. Soc. Psychol. Rev.* 8:364–82

Reber R, Winkielman P, Schwarz N. 1998. Effects of perceptual fluency on affective judgments. *Psychol. Sci.* 9:45–48

Rhodes G. 2006. The evolutionary psychology of facial beauty. *Annu. Rev. Psychol.* 57:199–226

Rosch E. 1975. Cognitive representations of semantic categories. *J. Exp. Psychol.: Gen.* 192–233

Russell PA. 2003. Effort after meaning and the hedonic value of paintings. *Brit. J. Psychol.* 94:99–110

Saito M. 1996. A comparative study of color preferences in Japan, China and Indonesia, with emphasis on the preference for white. *Percept. Mot. Skills* 83:115–28

Saito T. 1983. Latent spaces of color preference with and without a context: using the shape of an automobile as the context. *Color Res. Appl.* 8:101–13

Sammartino J, Palmer SE. 2012a. Aesthetic issues in spatial composition: effects of vertical position on framing single objects. *J. Exp. Psychol.: Hum. Percept. Perform.* In press

Sammartino J, Palmer SE. 2012b. Aesthetic issues in spatial composition: representational fit and the role of semantic context. *Perception.* In press

Sanborn AN, Griffiths TL, Shiffrin R. 2010. Uncovering mental representations with Markov chain Monte Carlo. *Cognit. Psychol.* 60:63–106

Schloss KB, Palmer SE. 2011. Aesthetic response to color combinations: preference, harmony, and similarity. *Atten. Percept. Psychol.* 73:551–71

Schloss KB, Poggesi RM, Palmer SE. 2011. Effects of university affiliation and "school spirit" on color preferences: Berkeley versus Stanford. *Psychon. Bull. Rev.* 18:498–504

Schloss KB, Strauss ED, Palmer SE. 2012. Object color preferences. *Color Res. Appl.* In press

Shimamura AP. 2012. *Experiencing Art: Explorations in Aesthetics, Mind, and Brain.* New York: Oxford Univ. Press. In press

Shimamura AP, Palmer SE, eds. 2012. *Aesthetic Science: Connecting Minds, Brains, and Experience.* Oxford, UK: Oxford Univ. Press

Silvera DH, Josephs RA, Giesler RB. 2002. Bigger is better: the influence of physical size on aesthetic preference judgments. *J. Behav. Decis. Making* 15:189–202

Silvia PJ. 2005a. Cognitive appraisals and interest in visual art: exploring an appraisal theory of aesthetic emotions. *Empir. Stud. Arts* 23:119–33

Silvia PJ. 2005b. Emotional responses to art: from collation and arousal to cognition and emotion. *Rev. Gen. Psychol.* 9:342–57

Silvia PJ. 2006. *Exploring the Psychology of Interest.* New York: Oxford Univ. Press

Silvia PJ. 2012. Human emotions and aesthetic experience. See Shimamura & Palmer 2012, pp. 250–75

Silvia PJ, Barona CM. 2009. Do people prefer curved objects? Angularity, expertise, and aesthetic preference. *Empir. Stud. Arts* 27:25–42

Strauss ED, Schloss KB, Palmer SE. 2012. Exposure to colored objects influences color preferences. Manuscript submitted

Switkes E, Mayer MJ, Sloan JA. 1978. Spatial frequency analysis of the visual environment: anisotropy and the carpentered environment hypothesis. *Vision Res.* 18:1393–99

Szabó F, Bodrogi P, Schanda J. 2010. Experimental modeling of colour harmony. *Color Res. Appl.* 35:34–49

Taft C. 1997. Color meaning and context: comparisons of semantic ratings of colors on samples and objects. *Color Res. Appl.* 22:40–50

Taylor C, Clifford A, Franklin A. 2012a. Color preferences are not universal. Manuscript submitted

Taylor C, Franklin A. 2012. The relationship between color–object associations and color preference: further investigation of ecological valence theory. *Psychon. Bull. Rev.* 19:190–97

Taylor C, Schloss KB, Palmer SE, Franklin A. 2012b. Adult color preferences are not evident in infants' responses to color. Manuscript submitted

Teller DY. 1979. The forced-choice preferential looking procedure: a psychophysical technique for use with human infants. *Infant Behav. Dev.* 2:135–53

Teller DY. 1998. Spatial and temporal aspects of infant color vision. *Vision Res.* 38:3275–82

Teller DY, Civan A, Bronson-Castain K. 2004. Infants' spontaneous color preferences are not due to adult-like brightness variations. *Vis. Neurosci.* 21:397–402

Terwogt MM, Hoeksma JB. 1995. Colors and emotions: preferences and combinations. *J. Gen. Psychol.* 122:5–17

Thorndike EL. 1917. Individual differences in judgments of the beauty of simple forms. *Psychol. Rev.* 24:147–53

Tonio PL, Leder H. 2009. Just how stable are stable aesthetic features? Symmetry, complexity, and the jaws of massive familiarization. *Acta Psychol.* 130:241–50

Turner M, ed. 2006. *The Artful Mind: Cognitive Science and the Riddle of Human Creativity.* New York: Oxford Univ. Press

Tyler CW. 1998. Painters centre one eye in portraits. *Nature* 392:877

Tyler CW. 2007. Eye-centering in portraits: reply to McManus and Thomas. *Perception* 36:183–88

Walraven J. 1976. Discounting the background—the missing link in the explanation of chromatic induction. *Vision Res.* 16:289–95

Westland S, Laycock K, Cheung V, Henry P, Mahyar F. 2007. Colour harmony. *Colour: Des. Creativity* 1:1–15

Whitfield T, Slatter P. 1979. The effects of categorization and prototypicality on aesthetic choice in a furniture selection task. *Brit. J. Psychol.* 70:65–75

Whitfield T, Wiltshire T. 1990. Color psychology: a critical review. *Genet. Soc. Gen. Psychol. Monogr.* 116:387–411

Whittlesea BWA. 1993. Illusions of familiarity. *J. Exp. Psychol.: Learn. Mem. Cogn.* 19(6):1235–53

Winkielman P, Halberstadt J, Fazendeiro T, Catty S. 2006. Prototypes are attractive because they are easy on the mind. *Psychol. Sci.* 17:799–806

Wypijewski J, ed. 1997. *Painting by Numbers: Komar and Melamid's Scientific Guide to Art.* New York: Farrar, Straus & Giroux

Yokosawa K, Schloss KB, Asano M, Palmer SE. 2012. Cross-cultural studies of color preferences: US and Japan. Manuscript submitted

Zajonc RB. 1968. Attitudinal effects of mere exposure. *J. Pers. Soc. Psychol.* 9:1–27

Zeki S. 1999. Art and the brain. *J. Consciousness Stud.* 6:76–96

Zemach I, Chang S, Teller DY. 2007. Infant color vision: prediction of infants' spontaneous color preferences. *Vision Res.* 47:1368–81

Detecting Consciousness: A Unique Role for Neuroimaging

Adrian M. Owen

The Brain and Mind Institute, Department of Psychology, The University of Western Ontario, London, Ontario N6A 5B7, Canada; email: adrian.owen@uwo.ca

Annu. Rev. Psychol. 2013. 64:109–33

First published online as a Review in Advance on October 2, 2012

The *Annual Review of Psychology* is online at psych.annualreviews.org

This article's doi:
10.1146/annurev-psych-113011-143729

Keywords

awareness, wakefulness, vegetative state, minimally conscious state, fMRI, EEG

Abstract

How can we ever know, unequivocally, that another person is conscious and aware? Putting aside deeper philosophical considerations about the nature of consciousness itself, historically, the only reliable method for detecting awareness in others has been through a predicted behavioral response to an external prompt or command. The answer may take the form of spoken words or a nonverbal signal such as a hand movement or the blink of an eye, but it is this answer, and only this answer, that allows us to infer awareness. In recent years, rapid technological developments in the field of neuroimaging have provided new methods for revealing thoughts, actions, and intentions based solely on the pattern of activity that is observed in the brain. In specialized centers, these methods are now being employed routinely to detect consciousness in behaviorally nonresponsive patients when all existing clinical techniques have failed to provide that information. In this review, I compare those circumstances in which neuroimaging data can be used to infer consciousness in the absence of a behavioral response with those circumstances in which it cannot. This distinction is fundamental for understanding and interpreting patterns of brain activity following acute brain injury and has profound implications for clinical care, diagnosis, prognosis, and medical-legal decision-making (relating to the prolongation, or otherwise, of life after severe brain injury). It also sheds light on more basic scientific questions about the nature of consciousness and the neural representation of our own thoughts and intentions.

Contents

INTRODUCTION

For most of us, consciousness comes in two flavors, wakefulness and awareness. For example, think about what happens when you undergo a general anesthetic in the context of major surgery—you close your eyes and start to fall asleep (i.e., you lose wakefulness), and you stop having any sense of where you are, who you are, and the predicament that you are in (i.e., you lose awareness). Wakefulness and awareness are two separate components of consciousness that are, at least partially, dissociable. The wakefulness component of consciousness is relatively easy to assess using purely behavioral methods: If a person's eyes are open, then they are awake. For those who would like to be more empirical about it, then techniques such as electroencephalography (EEG) can be used to identify the pattern of electrical signals that characterize the normal waking state in an entirely objective manner. Assessing the awareness component of consciousness is much more difficult. Thus, we cannot just look at a person and know, unequivocally, that they are aware (in this context, I use "awareness" in the commonly understood lay sense; that is, awareness of who we are, where we are in time and space, what we did yesterday, and what our plans may be for tomorrow). In this instance, EEG is also rather limited because there is no standard pattern of resting state EEG signals that will reliably differentiate a state of awareness from a state of unawareness.

So how might we assess awareness in another person? The answer is, we can't, unless the subject of our enquiry is both willing and able to tell us that (s)he is aware. The response may involve verbal affirmation (e.g., "Yes, I am aware"), or an agreed physical signal that is matched to a given stimulus (e.g., the squeezing of a hand in response to the request, "Please squeeze my hand if you are aware"), but some sort of response is always required in order for us to reliably infer that awareness is present. Thus, although the wakefulness component of consciousness can be measured and monitored behaviorally or by using techniques such as EEG, the awareness component of consciousness is an internal state of being that can only be "measured" via some form of self-report.

In a clinical context, this self-report is often referred to as command following. Thus, if a patient is reliably able to squeeze the doctor's hand when requested to do so, (s)he is said to have followed the command and is therefore known to be aware. This is not a new idea: In their seminal text *Diagnosis of Stupor and Coma*, Plum & Posner (1983, p. 3) stated, "The limits of consciousness are hard to define satisfactorily and quantitatively and we can only infer the self-awareness of others by their appearance and by their acts." Again, the inference here is that a distinct action is required in response to a specific command in order for us to unequivocally determine that another person is aware. Although this link between command following and awareness may appear to be rather obvious, it is understandable that some—philosophers, in particular—may find fault in the logic. They might argue, for example, that we can manufacture machines that can "follow commands" by squeezing an arm in response to a request to do so (indeed, we can manufacture machines that can do a whole lot more than that), but such arguments dodge my original question. I did not ask whether we can make a machine that can give the impression that it is aware (we certainly can), but rather, whether a human being who can respond to command by, say, raising an arm or squeezing a hand when asked to do so, is necessarily aware? In this review, I argue that this is most certainly the case and, further, that it is the key to unlocking signs of covert consciousness in situations where all forms of physical response have been rendered unavailable.

WAKEFULNESS WITH (AND WITHOUT) AWARENESS

Following the logic above, our ability to detect awareness in others is limited not by whether they are aware or not, but rather by their ability to communicate that fact through a recognized behavioral response. In recent years, improvements in intensive care have led to an increase in the number of patients who survive severe brain injury. Although some of these patients go on to make a good recovery, many do not, and some of these individuals progress to a condition known as the vegetative state. Central to the description of this complex condition is the concept of wakefulness without awareness, according to which vegetative patients are assumed to be entirely unaware, despite showing clear signs of wakefulness (Jennett & Plum 1972) (see sidebar On the Nature of Consciousness).

ON THE NATURE OF CONSCIOUSNESS

Any discussion about disorders of consciousness such as the vegetative state is problematic because it suggests disruption of an underlying well-understood and clearly defined system known as consciousness. This, of course, is not the case; there is, as yet, no universally agreed definition of consciousness (Laureys et al. 2007). Widely accepted definitions often refer to awareness of the self and the environment (Plum & Posner 1983), and accordingly, patients with disorders of consciousness (e.g., the vegetative state) are often described as lacking "awareness of self or environment." Such descriptions inevitably provoke further questions, including what constitutes awareness and what level of awareness is sufficient for a patient to be described as consciously aware. On the other hand, Koch (2007) has recently stated that the distinction between consciousness and awareness is largely one of social convention, with no clear difference between them. I suggest that the central problem in the assessment of the vegetative state and other disorders of consciousness is not in understanding the nature of consciousness itself, but rather in defining where the transition point lies between what most people would agree is an unconscious or unaware state and what most would agree is a conscious or aware state. This transition point is not always easily recognized in people with severe brain damage, particularly in patients whose neurological course (improvement or deterioration) is evolving slowly.

Thus, such patients often exhibit sleeping and waking cycles, will spontaneously open their eyes (hence, they are "awake"), and may even appear to "look" around a room, although they never fixate on anything, or anyone, and never follow (or track) an object or a person, whether asked to do so or not. The assessment of these patients is extremely difficult and relies heavily on subjective interpretation of observed behavior at rest and in response to stimulation (see sidebar Assessing Awareness Behaviorally). A diagnosis is made after repeated examinations have yielded no evidence of sustained, reproducible, purposeful, or voluntary behavioral response to visual, auditory, tactile, or noxious stimuli. Unfortunately, this means that a positive diagnosis (of vegetative state) is ultimately dependent on a negative finding (no signs of awareness) and is, therefore, inherently

ASSESSING AWARENESS BEHAVIORALLY

Any assessment of awareness that is based on exhibited behavior after brain injury will be prone to error for a number of reasons. First, an inability to move and speak is a frequent outcome of chronic brain injury and does not necessarily imply a lack of awareness. Second, the behavioral assessment is highly subjective: Behaviors such as smiling and crying are typically reflexive and automatic, but in certain contexts they may be the only means of communication available to a patient and therefore reflect a willful, volitional act of intention. These difficulties, coupled with inadequate experience and knowledge engendered through the relative rarity of these complex conditions, contribute to an alarmingly high rate of misdiagnosis (up to 43%) in the vegetative state (Andrews et al. 1996; Childs et al. 1993; Schnakers et al. 2006, 2009).

vulnerable to a Type II error or a false negative result. Indeed, internationally agreed diagnostic criteria for the vegetative state repeatedly emphasize the notion of "no evidence of awareness of environment or self"—in this instance, absence of evidence is widely accepted as adequate evidence of absence.

But imagine a clinical condition in which a brain-injured patient was left entirely conscious (awake and aware), but was nevertheless completely incapable of generating any sort of physical response, be it the blink of an eye, the movement of a hand, or a spoken word—indeed, imagine that the ability to make any behavioral response whatsoever was lost completely, yet conscious awareness remains. Following the arguments above, in such a case (where absolutely every opportunity for command following has been lost), it would be logically impossible to determine whether any level of awareness remains. Irrespective of how aware the patient was, or how skilled the observer was, awareness could not (and typically would not) be inferred because of the complete lack of any responses to external stimulation. Of course, cases of locked-in syndrome following acute brain injury or disease have been reported for many years, but where such cases are unexpectedly discovered it is always through the (sometimes

chance) detection of a minor residual motor response. In the absence of such a response, how could awareness ever be detected? Against this background, it is an unfortunate, but inevitable, fact that a population of patients must exist who retain at least some level of residual conscious awareness yet remain entirely unable to convey that fact to those around them.

ASSESSING COGNITION IN THE ABSENCE OF BEHAVIOR

Recent advances in neuroscience may provide a solution to this problem. If measurable brain responses could be marshaled and used as a proxy for a behavioral response (a thought response, perhaps), then we might find such patients by asking them to signal awareness by generating a pattern of brain activity that is indicative of a specific thought or intention. In the past few years, positron emission tomography (PET), functional magnetic resonance imaging (fMRI), and electroencephalography (EEG) have all been brought to bear on this problem, with varying degrees of success (Cruse and Owen 2010). Such approaches are fraught with problems, not least because in the absence of any corroborative behavior, they often depend, by definition, on a reverse inference (Poldrack 2006, Christoff & Owen 2006); that is to say, the engagement of a given cognitive process has to be inferred solely on the basis of the observed activation in a particular brain region.

PET and fMRI Studies in Nonresponsive Patients

In the first study of its kind, de Jong et al. (1997) measured regional cerebral blood flow in a post-traumatic vegetative patient during an auditorily presented story told by his mother. Compared to nonword sounds, activation was observed in the anterior cingulate and temporal cortices, possibly reflecting emotional processing of the contents, or tone, of the mother's speech. A year later, PET was used in another patient diagnosed as vegetative to study visual processing in response to familiar faces (Menon et al. 1998). Robust activity was observed in the right fusiform gyrus, the so-called human face area (or FFA). In both of these early cases, normal brain activation was observed in the absence of any behavioral responses to the external sensory stimulation.

Normal brain activity in response to complex external stimulation, however, has generally been the exception rather than the rule in studies of vegetative patients. For example, in one study of 15 patients, high-intensity noxious electrical stimulation activated midbrain, contralateral thalamus, and primary somatosensory cortex in every patient (Laureys et al. 2002). However, unlike control participants, the patients did not show the activation in secondary somatosensory, insular, posterior parietal, or anterior cingulate cortices that would be consistent with higher-level cognitive processing.

Di et al. (2007) used event-related fMRI to measure brain activity in seven vegetative patients and four minimally conscious patients (see sidebar Disorders of Consciousness) in response to the patient's own name spoken by a familiar voice. Two of the vegetative patients exhibited no significant activity at all, three patients exhibited activation in primary auditory areas, and two vegetative patients and four minimally conscious patients exhibited activity in higher-order associative temporal lobe areas. Although this result was encouraging (particularly because the two vegetative patients who showed the most widespread activation subsequently improved to minimally conscious state in the following months), like many of these early studies, it lacked cognitive specificity; that is to say, responses to the patient's own name spoken by a familiar voice were compared only to responses to the attenuated noise of the MRI scanner. Therefore, the activation observed may have reflected a specific response to each patient's own name, but it is equally possible that it reflected a low-level orienting response to speech in general, an emotional response to the speaker (see Bekinschtein et al. 2004), or any one of a number of possible cognitive processes relating to the imperfectly matched auditory stimuli.

DISORDERS OF CONSCIOUSNESS

The term "disorders of consciousness" is typically used to refer to three conditions: (a) coma, (b) vegetative state, and (c) minimally conscious state (Giacino et al. 2002, Plum & Posner 1983, Roy. Coll. Phys. 1996/2003). These conditions arise as a result of either a traumatic (e.g., a blow to the head) or a nontraumatic (e.g., a stroke) brain injury and may include damage to areas of the brainstem that mediate wakefulness and/or to cortico-cortical axonal connections that mediate cognitive function and awareness. Although particular patterns of pathology are commonly linked to each of these conditions, they are exclusively defined according to the behaviors exhibited by the patient rather than pathology. The key criteria are: (a) Coma describes an acute condition, typically lasting two to four weeks after brain injury. Comatose patients do not open their eyes and exhibit only reflex responses to stimulation. Unlike vegetative state, therefore, the wakefulness component of consciousness is typically lost. (b) In contrast, the vegetative state describes a condition in which patients open their eyes and demonstrate sleep-wake cycles. Like comatose patients, they do not exhibit purposeful behavior, retaining reflex responses only. (c) The minimally conscious state differs from these conditions through the presence of inconsistent but reproducible evidence of awareness. In contrast to the comatose and vegetative states, minimally conscious patients demonstrate inconsistent but purposeful responses to command and/or sensory stimulation.

Two related conditions that are often confused with coma, the vegetative state, or the minimally conscious state are the locked-in syndrome and brain death. The locked-in syndrome is not a disorder of consciousness but is critically important in the differential diagnosis. Locked-in syndrome patients are awake and fully conscious but have no means of producing speech, limb, or facial movements (Plum & Posner 1983). Brain death, or more accurately brainstem death, is a clinical term that refers to a complete and irreversible loss of brainstem function (Roy. Coll. Phys. 1998), resulting in the inevitable cessation of life. The diagnostic criteria for brain death require the loss of all brainstem reflexes. Vegetative patients typically retain such reflexes and rarely require a life-support system to regulate cardiac and respiratory functions. For an excellent review of death and the brain, see Laureys (2005).

Staffen et al. (2006) used event-related fMRI to compare sentences containing the patient's own name (e.g., "James, hello James"), spoken by a variety of unfamiliar voices, with sentences containing another first name, in a patient who had been vegetative for ten months at the time of the scan. In this case, because identical speech stimuli were used that differed only with respect to the name itself, activations can be confidently attributed to cognitive processing that is specifically related to the patient's own name. Differential cortical processing was observed to the patient's own name in a region of the medial prefrontal cortex, similar to that observed in three healthy volunteers. Selective cortical processing of one's own name (when it is compared directly with another name) requires the ability to perceive and access the meaning of words and may imply some level of comprehension on the part of this patient. However, as the authors point out (Staffen et al. 2006), a response to one's own name is one of the most basic forms of language, is elicited automatically (you can not choose to not attend to your own name), and may not depend on the higher-level linguistic processes that are assumed to underpin comprehension.

In the largest study to date, 41 patients with disorders of consciousness were graded according to their brain activation on a hierarchical series of language paradigms (Coleman et al. 2009). The tasks increased in complexity systematically from basic acoustic processing (a nonspecific response to sound) to more complex aspects of language comprehension and semantics. At the highest level, responses to sentences containing semantically ambiguous words (e.g., "the *creak/creek* came from a *beam* in the *ceiling/sealing*") were compared to sentences containing no ambiguous words (e.g., "her secrets were written in her diary") in order to reveal brain activity associated with spoken language comprehension (Coleman et al. 2007, 2009; Owen et al. 2005a,b; Rodd et al. 2005). Nineteen of the patients (approximately 50%), who had been diagnosed as either vegetative or minimally conscious, showed normal or near-normal temporal-lobe responses in the low-level auditory contrast (sound responses) and in the mid-level speech perception contrast (a specific response to speech over and above the more general response to sounds). Four patients, including two who had been

diagnosed as behaviorally vegetative, were also shown to exhibit normal fMRI activity during the highest-level speech comprehension task, suggesting that the neural processes involved in understanding speech were also intact (Coleman et al. 2009). These results provide compelling evidence for intact high-level residual linguistic processing in some patients who behaviorally meet the clinical criteria for vegetative and minimally conscious states.

EEG Studies in Nonresponsive Patients

Performing fMRI in severely brain-injured patients is enormously challenging; in addition to considerations of cost and scanner availability, the physical stress incurred by patients as they are transferred to a suitably equipped fMRI facility is significant. Movement artefacts often occur in imaging datasets from patients who are unable to remain still; metal implants, including the plates and pins that are common in many traumatically injured populations, may rule out fMRI altogether. EEG measures the activity of groups of cortical neurons from scalp electrodes and is far less expensive than fMRI, both in terms of initial cost and maintenance. EEG recordings are unaffected by any resident metallic implants and, perhaps most importantly, can be used at the bedside (Vaughan et al. 2006). In brain-injured patients, EEG recordings are typically made in the acute period and allow for broad assessments of cortical damage including the occurrence of brain death (see sidebar Disorders of Consciousness). However, uncertainty about the causes of abnormal raw EEG patterns (i.e., damage to the cortex itself or to subcortical structures that influence cortical activity) provides challenges for its use as a more precise tool for the assessment of awareness (Kulkarni et al. 2007). As well as concentrating on aspects of the resting EEG, a number of studies have investigated whether cognitive event-related potentials (ERPs)—averages of segments of EEG locked to the presentation of a stimulus—can be used to assess residual cognitive function in patients with disorders of consciousness. For example, recently it was shown that violations of prosody in nonlinguistic emotional exclamations elicited a reliable N300 component in 6 out of 27 vegetative or minimally conscious patients, suggesting a level of processing of auditory stimuli in these patients beyond their most basic features (Kotchoubey et al. 2009; also see Kotchoubey et al. 2003a, 2005). As is the case for fMRI, one popular stimulus, employed in these cognitive tasks due to its high level of saliency, is the patient's own name. When presented infrequently among tones and other names, a reliable mismatch negativity has been observed in some coma, vegetative state, and minimally conscious state patients, demonstrating some selectivity of those patients' neural responses to hearing their own name (Qin et al. 2008).

BRAIN ACTIVITY AND AWARENESS

But does the presence of normal brain activation, whether acquired through PET, fMRI, or EEG, in behaviorally nonresponsive patients indicate awareness? In most of the cases discussed above and elsewhere in the literature, the answer is probably no. Many types of stimuli, including faces, speech, and pain, will elicit relatively automatic responses from the brain; that is to say, they will occur without the need for active (i.e., conscious) intervention on the part of the participant (e.g., you can not choose to not recognize a face or to not understand speech that is presented clearly in your native language). In addition, a wealth of data in healthy volunteers, from studies of implicit learning (learning of information in an incidental manner, without awareness of what has been learned) and the effects of priming (where unconscious exposure to a stimulus influences a response to a later stimulus; for review, see Schacter 1994) to studies of learning and speech perception during anesthesia (e.g., Bonebakker et al. 1996, Davis et al. 2007), have demonstrated that many aspects of human cognition can go on in the absence of awareness.

Even the semantic content of information that is masked from conscious perception (e.g., by being presented very rapidly) can affect subsequent behavior without the explicit knowledge of the participant, suggesting that some aspects of semantic processing may occur without conscious awareness (Dehaene et al. 1998). By the same argument, "normal" neural responses in patients who are diagnosed as vegetative or minimally conscious do not necessarily indicate that these patients have any conscious experience associated with processing those same types of stimuli.

Anesthetic Studies

To investigate this issue directly, Davis et al. (2007) recently used fMRI in sedated healthy volunteers and exposed them to exactly the same speech stimuli (Rodd et al. 2005) that have been shown to elicit normal patterns of brain activity in some vegetative and minimally conscious patients (Coleman et al. 2007, 2009; Owen et al. 2005a,b). During three scanning sessions, the participants were nonsedated (awake), lightly sedated (a slowed response to conversation), and deeply sedated (no conversational response, rousable by loud command). In each session, they were exposed to sentences containing ambiguous words, matched sentences without ambiguous words, and signal-correlated noise. Equivalent temporal-lobe responses for normal speech sentences compared to signal-correlated noise were observed, bilaterally, at all three levels of sedation, suggesting that a normal brain response to speech sounds is not a reliable correlate of awareness. This result suggests that extreme caution needs to be exercised when interpreting normal responses to speech in patients who are diagnosed as vegetative, a problem of interpretation that applies to many of the activation studies described above. However, when Davis et al. (2007) examined the effects of anesthesia on ambiguous sentences, the frontal lobe and posterior temporal lobe activity that occurs in the awake individual (and is assumed to be a neural marker for semantic processing) was markedly absent, even during light sedation. This finding suggests that vegetative state patients who show this specific pattern of neural activity during the presentation of ambiguous semantic material may be consciously aware (e.g., Coleman et al. 2007, 2009; Owen et al. 2005a,b). However, as tantalizing as such conclusions might be, they are entirely speculative; the fact that awareness is associated with the activity changes that are thought to reflect sentence comprehension does not mean that it is necessary for them to occur (by simple analogy, the fact that amygdala activity is often observed during fMRI studies of fear does not mean that in all studies that have reported amygdala activity, the participants were fearful).

DECODING CONSCIOUS RESPONSES BASED ON BRAIN ACTIVITY

The studies described above confirm that many of the brain responses that have been observed to date using fMRI in brain-damaged patients could have occurred automatically; that is, they could have occurred in the absence of any awareness of self (or others) on the part of the patient. But let us now consider an entirely different type of brain-imaging experiment in which the responses observed cannot occur in the absence of awareness, because they are necessarily guided by a conscious choice, or decision, on the part of the participant.

fMRI Studies in Healthy Participants

Many such experiments have been conducted in healthy participants in recent years, for example, to decode mental decisions or thoughts (e.g., Cerf et al. 2010, Haynes et al. 2007), to demonstrate that fMRI can be deployed as a brain-computer interface (Weiskopf et al. 2004), or simply to examine the neural correlates of various types of mental imagery (Aguirre et al. 1996, Jeannerod & Frak 1999). In one study, healthy volunteers were asked to freely decide which of two tasks to perform

(add or subtract two numbers) and to covertly hold onto that decision during a delay (Haynes et al. 2007). A classifier was trained to recognize the characteristic fMRI signatures associated with the two mental states and in 80% of trials was able to decode which of the two tasks the volunteers were intending to perform before they actually performed it. The principle employed was that certain types of thought are associated with a unique brain activation pattern that can be used as a signature for that specific thought. If a classifier is trained to recognize these characteristic signatures, a volunteer's thoughts can be ascertained (within the constraints of the experimental design) using her/his brain activity alone. More recently, pattern classification of fMRI signals was also used to decode movement intentions moments before their initiation (Gallivan et al. 2011).

Genuine thought-translation devices or brain-computer interfaces as they are widely known, have been developed for fMRI, although to achieve acceptable levels of accuracy they typically rely on mental imagery as a proxy for the physical response being decoded. For example, in one early study, four non-naïve participants learned, with the aid of feedback, to willfully regulate their fMRI signal using self-chosen visual imagery strategies (e.g., pictures of buildings, spatial navigation, clenching, dancing) (Weiskopf et al. 2004). In a more sophisticated design, information derived from both the timing (onset and offset) and the source location of the hemodynamic response was used to decode which of four possible answers was being given to questions (Sorger et al. 2009). To indicate their choice (or thought), participants imagined one of two tasks, beginning at one of four times and continuing for different prespecified durations. An automated decoding procedure deciphered the answer by analyzing the single-trial blood-oxygen-level-dependent responses in real time with a mean accuracy of 94.9%.

Crucially, these paradigms differ from all of the passive fMRI tasks described above (e.g., speech or face perception) that have been used in nonresponsive patients because the fMRI activity observed depends on the participant making a conscious choice to exert a specific willful, or voluntary, response.

This contrast between the responses observed in passive fMRI tasks that are (or at least could be) elicited automatically by an external stimulus and active tasks in which the response itself represents a conscious choice (and is therefore, by definition, a measure of conscious awareness) is absolutely central to the debate about the use of functional neuroimaging in any nonresponsive population, including those with disorders of consciousness. A significant recent addition to this field, therefore, has been the development of fMRI paradigms that render awareness reportable in the absence of an overt behavioral (e.g., motor or speech) response in patients who are entirely behaviorally nonresponsive (Boly et al. 2007, Owen et al. 2006). The most successful of these techniques make use of the general principle observed in studies of healthy participants that imagining performing a particular task generates a robust and reliable pattern of brain activity in the fMRI scanner that is similar to actually performing the activity itself. For example, imagining moving or squeezing the hands will generate activity in the motor and premotor cortices (Jeannerod & Frak 1999), while imagining navigating from one location to another will activate the same regions of the parahippocampal gyrus and the posterior parietal cortex that have been widely implicated in map reading and other so-called spatial navigation tasks (Aguirre et al. 1996).

In one study (Boly et al. 2007), healthy volunteers were asked to imagine hitting a tennis ball back and forth to an imaginary coach when they heard the word tennis (thereby eliciting vigorous imaginary arm movements) and to imagine walking from room to room in their house when they heard the word house (thereby eliciting imaginary spatial navigation). Imagining playing tennis was associated with robust activity in the supplementary motor area in each and every one of the participants scanned (**Figure 1**, see color insert). In contrast, imagining moving from room to room

in a house activated the parahippocampal cortices, the posterior parietal lobe, and the lateral premotor cortices; all of these regions have been shown to contribute to imaginary, or real, spatial navigation (Aguirre et al. 1996, Boly et al. 2007).

The robustness and reliability of these fMRI responses across individuals means that activity in these regions can be used as a neural proxy for behavior, confirming that the participant retains the ability to understand instructions and to carry out different mental tasks in response to those instructions, and therefore is able to exhibit willed, voluntary behavior in the absence of any overt action. Thus, like any other form of action that requires response selection, these brain responses require awareness of the various contingencies that govern the relationship between any given stimulus (in this case, the cue word for one of two possible imagery tasks) and a response (in this case, imagining the task). Put simply, fMRI responses of this sort can be used to measure awareness because awareness is necessary for them to occur.

fMRI Studies in Nonresponsive Patients

Owen et al. (2006, 2007) used this same logic to demonstrate that a young woman who fulfilled all internationally agreed criteria for the vegetative state was, in fact, consciously aware and able to make responses of this sort using her brain activity. The patient, who was involved in a complex road traffic accident and had sustained very severe traumatic brain injuries, had remained entirely unresponsive for a period of six months prior to the fMRI scan. During the scanning session, the patient was instructed to perform the two mental imagery tasks described above. When she was asked to imagine playing tennis (**Figure 1**, patient 5), significant activity was observed repeatedly in the supplementary motor area (Owen et al. 2006) that was indistinguishable from that observed in the healthy volunteers scanned by Boly et al. (2007). Moreover, when she was asked to imagine walking through her home, significant activity was observed in the parahippocampal gyrus, the posterior parietal cortex, and the lateral premotor cortex, which was again indistinguishable from that observed in healthy volunteers (Owen et al. 2006, 2007). On this basis, it was concluded that, despite fulfilling all of the clinical criteria for a diagnosis of vegetative state, this patient retained the ability to understand spoken commands and to respond to them through her brain activity, rather than through speech or movement, confirming beyond any doubt that she was consciously aware of herself and her surroundings. In a follow-up study of 23 patients who were behaviorally diagnosed as vegetative, Monti et al. (2010) showed that 4 (17%) were able to generate reliable responses of this sort in the fMRI scanner (**Figure 1**, patients 1–4).

After a severe brain injury, when the request to move a hand or a finger is followed by an appropriate motor response, the diagnosis can change from vegetative state (no evidence of awareness) to minimally conscious state (some evidence of awareness). By analogy then, if the request to activate, say, the supplementary motor area of the brain by imagining moving the hand is followed by an appropriate brain response, shouldn't we give that response the very same weight? Skeptics may argue that brain responses are somehow less physical, reliable, or immediate than motor responses, but as is the case with motor responses, all of these arguments can be dispelled with careful measurement, replication, and objective verification. For example, if a patient who was assumed to be unaware raised his/her hand in response to command on just one occasion, there would remain some doubt about the presence of awareness given the possibility that this movement was a chance occurrence, coincident with the instruction. However, if that same patient were able to repeat this response to command on 10 occasions, there would remain little doubt that the patient was aware. By the same token, if that patient was able to activate his/her supplementary motor area in response to command (e.g., by being told to imagine playing tennis), and was able to do this on every one of 10 trials, would we not

have to accept that this patient was consciously aware? Like most neuroimaging investigations, replication of this sort was inherent in both of the studies described above (Monti et al. 2010, Owen et al. 2006) because the statistically significant results depended on multiple, similar responses being exhibited across repeated trials.

It has also been suggested that fMRI responses of this sort could reflect an "implicit preconscious neural response" to the key words that were used in those studies (Greenberg 2007, Nachev & Husain 2007). Although no empirical evidence exists to support this possibility, it is nevertheless important to consider its theoretical plausibility. In the volunteers studied by Boly et al. (2007) and in the patients reported by Owen et al. (2006) and Monti et al. (2010), the observed activity was not transient, but rather persisted for the full 30 seconds of each imagery task, i.e., far longer than would be expected, even given the hemodynamics of the fMRI response. In fact, these task-specific changes persisted until the volunteers and the patients were cued with another stimulus indicating that they should switch tasks. No evidence exists to show that single-word stimuli (such as "tennis," "house," or "rest") can unconsciously elicit sustained (i.e., 30 seconds) hemodynamic responses in the supplementary motor area, the parahippocampal gyrus, the posterior parietal cortex, or the lateral premotor cortex, yet considerable data exist to suggest that they cannot. For example, although it is well documented that some words can, under certain circumstances, elicit wholly automatic neural responses, such responses are typically transient and last for just a few seconds. In addition, the activation patterns observed in the studies by Boly et al. (2007), Owen et al. (2006), and Monti et al. (2010) were entirely predicted and were not in brain regions that are known to be involved in word processing, but rather in regions that are known to be involved in the two imagery tasks (also see Weiskopf et al. 2004). In short, temporally sustained fMRI responses in these regions of the brain are impossible to explain in terms of automatic responses to either single key words or to short sentences containing those words. In fact, non-instructive sentences containing the same key words (e.g., "The man enjoyed playing tennis") have been shown to produce no sustained activity in any of these brain regions in healthy volunteers, nor is activity seen when the words tennis and house are presented to naïve participants who have not been previously instructed to perform the imagery tasks (Owen et al. 2007). Finally, the recent evidence of Davis and associates (2007), which shows that even mildly sedated healthy volunteers cannot perform the basic semantic processes that are necessary for speech comprehension, provides additional evidence that words such as tennis and house cannot produce sustained automatic responses in distinct neural regions; producing word-specific neural responses requires, at the very least, comprehension of those words, be it conscious or unconscious.

Another approach to detecting covert awareness after brain injury is to target processes that require the willful adoption of mind-sets in carefully matched (perceptually identical) experimental and control conditions. For example, Monti et al. (2009) presented healthy volunteers with a series of neutral words and alternatively instructed them to just listen, or to count, the number of times a given word was repeated. As predicted, the counting task revealed the frontoparietal network that has been previously associated with target detection and working memory. When tested on this same procedure, a severely brain-injured patient produced a very similar pattern of activity, confirming that he could willfully adopt differential mind-sets as a function of the task conditions and could actively maintain these mind-sets across time; covert abilities that were entirely absent from his documented behavioral repertoire. As in the tennis/spatial navigation examples described above, because the external stimuli (a series of words) were identical in the two conditions, any difference in brain activity observed cannot reflect an automatic brain response (i.e., one that can occur in the absence of consciousness). Rather, the activity must reflect the fact that the patient

has performed a particular action (albeit a brain action) in response to the stimuli on one (but not the other) presentation; in this sense, the brain response is entirely analogous to a (motor) response to command and should carry the same weight as evidence of awareness.

Following similar logic, Monti et al. (2012) used an entirely different type of approach to demonstrate that a patient who was unable to exhibit any signs of command following during standard behavioral testing could nevertheless demonstrate reliable and robust responses in predefined brain regions by willfully modulating his brain activity. The stimuli used were superimposed pictures of faces and houses. When healthy volunteers are requested, following a cue tone, to shift their attentional focus from a face to a house (or vice versa), a distinct shift in fMRI activity from the fusiform gyrus (the FFA) to the parahippocampal gyrus (the parahippocampal place area) is observed (or vice versa) (Monti et al. 2012). With continuous, repeated cues, this effect manifests as a time-locked alternation of activity between these two functionally distinct brain regions, despite the fact that the stimulus remains unchanged throughout. Thus, this change is driven not by the external stimulus per se but rather by the will or the intention of the participant to focus on one or the other aspect of the stimulus and is therefore a reliable indicator of conscious intent (consider, for example, that the participant is not obliged to shift attention—although it would not be in keeping with the experimental instructions, the participant is entirely free to choose not to follow those instructions). When asked to perform the same task, the activity observed in the patient closely resembled the activity observed in the healthy volunteers and, as such, provided the only conclusive evidence that he could indeed follow commands (Monti et al. 2012).

These types of approach all illustrate a paradigmatic shift away from passive (e.g., perceptual) fMRI tasks to more active (e.g., willful) tasks in the assessment of covert awareness after serious brain injury. What sets such tasks apart is that the neural responses required are not produced automatically by the eliciting stimulus, but rather depend on time-dependent and sustained responses generated by the participants themselves. Such behavior (albeit neural behavior) provides a proxy for a motor action and is, therefore, an appropriate vehicle for reportable awareness (Zeman 2009).

EEG Studies in Nonresponsive Patients

Schnakers and associates (2008b) very elegantly extended the passive "own name" paradigm described above to include a volitional aspect whereby in half of the blocks, patients were instructed to count the number of instances of their own name, in contrast to passively listening to identical stimuli in the remaining blocks. Like healthy controls, a group of minimally conscious patients demonstrated reliably larger P3 components, linked to target detection, during the active counting task. Because the only aspect of the task that differed between the two conditions was the patient's intention (to count or to listen), as guided by the prior instruction, it was possible to unequivocally infer that these patients could follow commands and, therefore, that they were aware. In contrast, overt (motor) forms of command following were, at best, inconsistent when the patients were tested behaviorally.

Motor imagery also produces clearly distinguishable modulation of EEG sensorimotor rhythms (Cincotti et al. 2003, Wolpaw et al. 1991) similar to those seen during motor execution, and this has been the basis of several recent attempts to detect conscious awareness after severe brain injury. For example, in one early study, Kotchoubey and colleagues (2003b) described a completely locked-in patient whose slow EEG activity differed significantly between trials when he was asked to "try" to move the left, as compared to the right, hand. In the EEG record, imagined movements (motor imagery) are evident in the form of reductions of power—or event-related desynchronizations (ERDs)—of the mu (~7–13Hz) and/or beta (~13–30Hz) bands over the topographically

appropriate regions of the motor cortex, for example, over the lateral premotor cortex for hand movements and over more medial premotor cortex for toe movements (Pfurtscheller & Neuper 1997). In some individuals, these ERDs may also be accompanied by event-related synchronizations (relative increases in power) over motor areas contralateral to, or surrounding, the ERD (Pfurtscheller et al. 2006, 2008). Using classification techniques, it is now possible, on the basis of these EEG responses alone, to determine with a high degree of accuracy the form of motor imagery being performed by a conscious individual (Guger et al. 2003). For example, Cruse et al. (2011) recently reported a new EEG-based classification technique in which two mental imagery responses (squeezing the right hand or squeezing the toes) were successfully decoded offline in 9 out of 12 healthy individuals, with accuracy rates varying between 60% and 91%. The same approach was then used to attempt to detect evidence of command following in the absence of any overt behavior, in a group of 16 patients who met the internationally agreed criteria for a diagnosis of vegetative state. Three of these patients (19%) were repeatedly and reliably able to generate appropriate EEG responses to the two distinct commands ("squeeze your right hand" or "squeeze your toes"), despite being behaviorally entirely unresponsive, indicating that they were aware and following the task instructions (**Figure 2**, see color insert). In two cases, this was also verified with fMRI. Indeed, on the basis of such data, far broader conclusions about residual cognition can be drawn. For example, performance of this complex task makes multiple demands on many cognitive functions, including sustained attention (over 90-second blocks), response selection (between the two imagery tasks), language comprehension (of the task instructions), and working memory (to remember which task to perform across multiple trials within each block)—all aspects of top-down cognitive control that are usually associated with, and indeed could be said to characterize, normal conscious awareness (Naccache 2006).

Is it possible that appropriate patterns of activity could be elicited in these patients in the absence of awareness? Could they somehow reflect an automatic response to aspects of the task instructions, such as the words right-hand and toes, and not a conscious and overt action on the part of the patient? This is extremely unlikely for a number of reasons. First, the task instructions were delivered once at the beginning of each block of 15 tones that signaled the time to begin each imagery trial. Any automatic response to the previously presented verbal instruction would then have to abate and recur in synchrony with these tones; cues that carried no information in and of themselves about the task to be performed. Indeed, 75% of the healthy control participants tested in that study returned positive EEG outcomes when completing this motor imagery task. However, when these same individuals were instructed *not* to follow the commands—i.e., not to engage in motor imagery—not one participant returned a positive EEG outcome. Evidently, any automatic brain responses generated by listening to the instructions are not sufficient for significant task performance; rather, an act of consistently timed, volitional command following is required. In this context then, it is clear that successful performance of these EEG tasks represents a significant cognitive feat, not only for those patients who were presumed to be vegetative but also for healthy control participants. That is to say, to be deemed successful, each respondent must have consistently generated the requested mental states to command for a prolonged period of time within each trial and must have consistently done so across numerous trials. Indeed, one behaviorally vegetative patient was able to produce EEG responses that were classified with a success rate of 78%. In other words, consistently appropriate EEG responses were generated across approximately 100 trials. Conversely, when assessed behaviorally using accepted, standard clinical measures that were administered by experienced, specialist teams, none of these patients exhibited any signs of awareness, including visual fixation, visual pursuit, or localization to pain.

These results demonstrate that consistent responses to command—a reliable and universally accepted indicator that a patient is not vegetative—need not be expressed behaviorally at all but rather can be determined accurately on the basis of EEG responses.

In a follow-up study (Cruse et al. 2012), 23 minimally conscious state patients (15 with traumatic brain injury and eight with nontraumatic brain injury) completed the same motor imagery EEG task (**Figure 2**). Consistent and robust responses to command were observed in the EEG of 22% of the minimally conscious state patients (5/23). Etiology had a significant impact on the ability to successfully complete this task, with 33% of traumatic patients (5/15) returning positive EEG outcomes compared with none of the nontraumatic patients (0/8). The results suggest that the overt behavioral signs of awareness exhibited by nontraumatic minimally conscious patients appear to be an accurate reflection of their covert cognitive abilities measured using this novel EEG technique. In stark contrast, they demonstrated that one-third of a group of traumatically injured patients in the minimally conscious state possess a range of high-level cognitive faculties that are not evident from their overt behavior.

As a result of the strains of rapid acceleration and deceleration on the brain, the most common neuropathological changes following traumatic brain injury are diffuse axonal injury (Adams et al. 1982, Gennarelli et al. 1982) that predominantly affects both hemispheres, the corpus callosum, brainstem, and cerebellum in the vegetative state and minimally conscious state (Adams et al. 1999, Kinney et al. 1994, Jennett et al. 2001). On the other hand, when these conditions are caused by a nontraumatic injury, such as hypoxic-ischemic encephalopathy, a selective and widespread damage to the neocortex and thalamus is observed, possibly due to the differences in the oxygen requirements of these structures (Adams et al. 2000, Adams & Duchen 1992, Kinney et al. 1994). In the broadest sense then, what is known about the neuropathological mechanisms underlying traumatic brain injury and nontraumatic brain injury, particularly in relation to the relative preservation of the cortex following traumatic brain injury, is reflected here in the differential degree of functional deficit observed across the two groups.

These data also reemphasize the disparity between behavioral signs of awareness and those that may be detected with functional neuroimaging. Thirty-eight percent of those eight minimally conscious state patients who were incapable of following commands with their behavior—i.e., those producing only low-level, nonreflexive behaviors such as visual pursuit—were nevertheless capable of following commands with this EEG paradigm. Indeed, 75% (3/4) of traumatically brain-injured minimally conscious state patients who could not follow commands behaviorally were capable of returning a positive EEG outcome compared with none of the nontraumatically injured minimally conscious state patients. This result adds to the significant body of evidence that an apparent inability to follow commands with external responses does not necessarily reflect the true absence of the cognitive capability to do so (Cruse et al. 2011, Monti et al. 2010, Owen et al. 2006, Schnakers et al. 2008b). Rather, a significant proportion of behaviorally nonresponsive patients retains a range of high-level cognitive capacities beyond those indicated by their behavior.

Anesthetic Studies

In a recent study (Adapa et al. 2011), fMRI was used in healthy volunteers who were asked to imagine playing a game of tennis while sedated using the same task design that has been used to detect covert consciousness in some vegetative and minimally conscious patients (Monti et al. 2010, Owen et al. 2006). During three scanning sessions, the participants were nonsedated (awake), lightly sedated, and deeply sedated and were asked to imagine playing tennis following a prompt. Task-related activity in the premotor cortex was markedly attenuated even at light levels of sedation and was completely absent when the participants were deeply sedated. Following the cessation of propofol and recovery of

awareness, robust activity was again observed in the premotor cortex following the instruction to resume the imagery tasks. This result confirms that healthy volunteers who are measurably nonaware (i.e., unconscious) are not able to generate the characteristic pattern of brain activity that is associated with imagining playing tennis, suggesting that awareness is likely to be necessary for this response to occur in patients.

COMMUNICATION BASED ON BRAIN ACTIVITY

fMRI Studies in Nonresponsive Patients

Owen & Coleman (2008b) extended the general principles discussed above, by which active mental rehearsal is used to signify awareness, to show that communication of "yes" and "no" responses was possible using the same approach. Thus, a healthy volunteer was able to reliably convey a "yes" response by imagining playing tennis and a "no" response by imaging moving around a house, thereby using only their brain activity to provide the answers to simple questions posed by the experimenters. This technique was further refined by Monti et al. (2010), who successfully decoded three "yes" and "no" responses from each of 16 healthy participants with 100% accuracy using only their real-time changes in the supplementary motor area (during tennis imagery) and the parahippocampal place area (during spatial navigation). Moreover, in one traumatic brain injury patient, who had been repeatedly diagnosed as vegetative over a five-year period, similar questions were posed and successfully decoded using the same approach (Monti et al. 2010) (**Figure 3**, see color insert). Thus, this patient was able to convey biographical information that was not known to the experimenters at the time (but was verified as factually correct), such as his father's name and the last place that he had visited on vacation before his accident five years earlier. In contrast, and despite a reclassification to minimally conscious state following the fMRI scan, it remained impossible to establish any form of communication with this patient at the bedside.

Of course, skeptics may argue that fMRI activity alone cannot prove that a person is consciously aware, nor able to communicate, even when a behaviorally nonresponsive patient has been able to provide factually correct answers to five biographical questions about himself using only his brain activity to do so (Monti et al. 2010). However, such skeptics would likely remain unsatisfied after 500 questions, even if 500 correct answers had been decoded. The important point is that by using spatially and temporally reliable fMRI changes as willed responses, we are simply adopting exactly the same behavioral criteria that any of us would accept as reasonable evidence that another person was conscious and aware. For example, it is difficult to imagine a situation in which someone asked another person five questions (drawn from an almost limitless pool of possible questions), received five factually correct answers, and then concluded that the subject of the interrogation was not consciously aware. Returning to a point made in the introduction, this is not to say that we can't make machines that can achieve this same feat, nor that such machines are in any sense "aware," but my argument is that for humans to accomplish this, they must necessarily be aware. (Philosophically, of course, it is possible to imagine that a person could exist who is wholly unaware yet able to respond to an infinite number of questions with factually correct answers, but in the absence of any data to suggest that such a person does or can exist, I do not consider this possibility any further.)

EEG Studies

As discussed above, Kotchoubey and colleagues (2003b) described a completely locked-in patient whose slow EEG activity differed significantly between trials in which he was asked to "try" to move the left or right hands, which in the most basic sense reflects a form of communication. Similarly, Kübler and colleagues (2005) showed that locked-in patients with ALS could learn to modulate their sensorimotor rhythms with more than 70% accuracy, but they did not test any patients diagnosed with a disorder of consciousness (e.g., vegetative state) with this paradigm.

A method for using the P300 modulation paradigm, originally proposed by Farwell & Donchin (1988), also holds promise as an EEG-based communication device. Participants are presented with a screen displaying a matrix of letters, A to Z, and are asked to fixate on the letter that they are trying to communicate (e.g., in order to spell a word). Columns and rows in the matrix flash in a pseudorandomized order, and it is possible to deduce which letter is being attended to by identifying which column and row flashes immediately prior to an evoked P300 component. This technique has proved to be very effective for severely paralyzed and locked-in patients (Kleih et al. 2011, Nijboer et al. 2008), although because it requires visual fixation, it is likely to be of limited use in the vegetative and minimally conscious states. A possible solution to this problem was provided by Sellers & Donchin (2006), who introduced a simpler version of this general paradigm that comprised both visual and auditory versions. The participants were presented with only four visual or auditory stimuli, namely, yes, no, pass, and end. Locked-in patients with ALS could use this system to communicate (Kübler et al. 2009), although classification accuracies were lower in the auditory than in the visual domain.

Building on much of this earlier work, the success of recent EEG techniques for detecting awareness in nonresponsive patients (Cruse et al. 2011, 2012) paves the way for the development of a true brain-computer interface (Birbaumer 2006)—or simple, reliable communication devices—in this patient group. It seems likely that such devices will provide a form of external control and communication based on mappings of distinct mental states—for example, imagining right-hand movements to communicate yes and toe movements to communicate no. Indeed, the degrees of freedom provided by EEG have the potential to take this beyond the sorts of binary responses that have worked well using fMRI (Monti et al.

2010) to allow methods of communication that are far more functionally expressive, based on multiple forms of mental state classification (Farwell & Donchin 1988, Sellers & Donchin 2006, Wolpaw et al. 2002). The development of techniques for the real-time classification of these forms of mental imagery (e.g., Cruse et al. 2011, 2012) will open the door for routine two-way communication with some of these patients, ultimately allowing them to share information about their inner worlds, experiences, and needs.

IMPLICATIONS

Diagnosis

An obvious clinical consequence of the emergence of novel neuroimaging techniques that permit the identification of covert awareness and communication in the absence of any behavioral response is the possibility of improved diagnosis after severe brain injury. Unfortunately, at present, although several of the neuroimaging approaches discussed in this review hold great promise for improving diagnostic accuracy in behaviorally nonresponsive patients, the accepted assessment procedure continues to be a careful neurological exam by a trained examiner that focuses on a set of standard behavioral tests (see sidebar Assessing Awareness Behaviorally). However, in an increasing number of cases, neuroimaging findings have been reported that are entirely inconsistent with the formal clinical diagnosis. For example, the patient described by Owen et al. (2006) was clearly able to produce voluntary responses to command (albeit neural responses) yet was unable to match this with any form of motor response at the bedside. Paradoxically, therefore, this patient's (motor) behavior was consistent with a diagnosis of vegetative state (an absence of evidence of awareness or purposeful response), yet her brain imaging data confirmed that the alternative hypothesis was correct; i.e., that she was entirely aware during the scanning procedure. Clearly the clinical diagnosis of vegetative state

based on behavioral assessment was inaccurate in the sense that it did not accurately reflect her internal state of awareness. On the other hand, she was not misdiagnosed, because the accepted diagnostic standard is based on behavior, and no behavioral marker of awareness was missed. Likewise, the patient described by Monti et al. (2010) was clearly not vegetative because he could generate "yes" and "no" responses in real time by willfully modulating his brain activity. In fact, these consistent responses to command, which allowed him to functionally communicate, suggest a level of residual cognitive function that would actually place this patient beyond the minimally conscious state and (at least) into the severely disabled category. Finally, in the recent study by Cruse et al. (2011), three patients who were clinically defined as vegetative state were able to produce up to 100 responses to command that were detectable only with EEG. Similarly, in the follow-up study (Cruse et al. 2012), a significant minority of minimally conscious patients was able to generate EEG responses that were entirely inconsistent with their formal diagnoses (no evidence of consistent command following). These findings suggest an urgent need for a re-evaluation of the existing diagnostic guidelines for behaviorally nonresponsive patients (including the vegetative state and related disorders of consciousness) and for the development and formal inclusion of validated, standardized neuroimaging procedures into those guidelines.

Prognosis

A related issue concerns the implications that emerging neuroimaging approaches may have for prognosis in this patient group. It is of interest that in the case described by Owen et al. (2006), the patient began to emerge from her vegetative state to demonstrate diagnostically relevant behavioral markers before the prognostically important (for a diagnosis of permanent vegetative state) 12-month threshold was reached, suggesting that early evidence of awareness acquired with functional

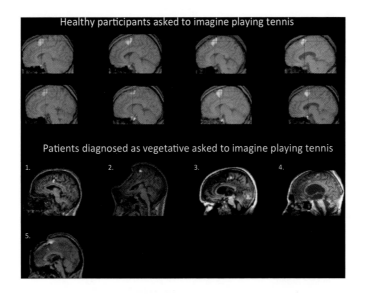

Figure 1

When eight healthy participants were asked to imagine playing tennis, significant activity was observed in the premotor cortex (*top*) in every single case, indicating that they had understood the instruction and were responding by carrying out the appropriate type of mental imagery; that is, following a command. When patients who were behaviorally entirely nonresponsive and were diagnosed as being vegetative were asked to carry out the same mental imagery task, a formally identical pattern of activity was observed in approximately 17% of cases studied. This result confirms that, in spite of an inability to respond physically, these patients can still demonstrate command following by modulating their cortical fMRI activity. Adapted from Boly et al. 2007 (healthy participants), Owen et al. 2006 (Patient 5) and Monti et al. 2010 (Patients 1–4).

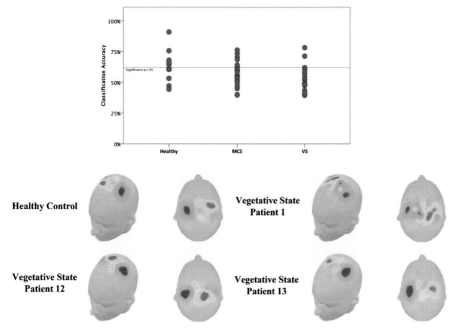

Figure 2

Three of 16 (19%) patients who had been diagnosed as vegetative were repeatedly and reliably able to generate appropriate electroencephalography (EEG) responses to two distinct commands ("squeeze your right hand" or "squeeze your toes") despite being behaviorally entirely unresponsive. Thus, when the scalp distributions of data from a classification procedure are plotted (*bottom*), it is evident that the neurophysiological basis of the positive EEG outcome—with clear foci over the hand and toe motor areas—are formally identical when compared between a healthy control participant and the three patients (maps show the scalp distribution of the single feature—time-point x frequency-band—with the highest absolute coefficient value from one training run of the cross-validation procedure. Red colors indicate coefficient values greater than zero; blues indicate values less than zero). These data confirmed that these patients were, in fact, aware and able to follow task instructions, which, in two cases, was independently verified using fMRI. A similar procedure in a group of minimally conscious patients revealed that 22% were able to reliably and repeatedly follow commands by modulating their EEG responses (*top*). Adapted from Cruse et al. (2011, 2012).

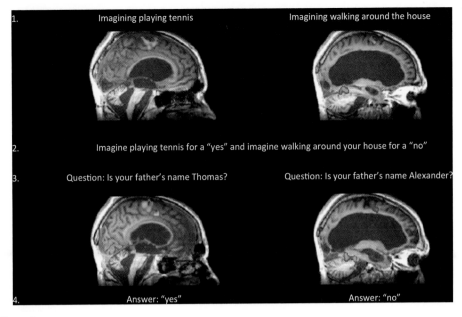

Figure 3

When 16 healthy participants were asked to imagine playing tennis to convey one response ("yes" or "no") and to imagine moving around the rooms of their home to convey the alternative response ("yes" or "no"), their answers to three questions each were decoded with 100% accuracy (Monti et al. 2010). The same procedure was then used with a patient who had been repeatedly diagnosed as vegetative over a five-year period following a road traffic accident. The patient was first asked to imagine playing tennis and then to imagine moving around the rooms of his home in order to generate anatomical localizers in the premotor cortex and parahippocampal gyrus, respectively (*1*). In a subsequent series of scans (*2*), he was asked to imagine playing tennis to convey one response ("yes" or "no") and to imagine moving around the rooms of his home to convey the alternative response ("yes" or "no"). When asked, "Is your father's name Thomas?" the pattern of activity observed was almost identical to the pattern that had previously been associated with him imagining playing tennis—a "yes" response (*3*). When asked, "Is your father's name Alexander?" the pattern of activity observed was almost identical to the pattern that had previously been associated with him imagining moving from room to room in his house—a "no" response (*3*). The patient answered five "yes" or "no" questions in a row correctly (*4*), confirming that he was conscious and able to recall biographical detail about his life. Adapted from Monti et al. 2010.

neuroimaging may have important prognostic value. Indeed, with a marked increase in the number of studies using neuroimaging techniques in patients with disorders of consciousness, a consistent pattern is beginning to emerge. In an excellent review of the available literature, Di et al. (2008) considered 15 separate $H_2{}^{15}O$ PET and fMRI studies involving 48 published cases that were classified as absent cortical activity, typical activity (activity in low-level primary sensory cortices only), and atypical activity (activity in higher-level associative cortices). The results suggest that atypical activity patterns appear to predict recovery from vegetative state with 93% specificity and 69% sensitivity. That is to say, 9 out of 11 patients exhibiting atypical activity patterns recovered consciousness, whereas 21 out of 25 patients with typical primary cortical activity patterns and 4 out of 4 patients with absent activity failed to recover. This important review strongly suggests that functional neuroimaging data can provide important prognostic information beyond that available from bedside examination alone. Similarly, in the large recent study of 41 patients by Coleman et al. (2009), direct evidence of prognostically important information from the neuroimaging data was reported that was at odds with the behavioral assessment at the time of scanning. Thus, contrary to the clinical impression of a specialist team using behavioral assessment tools, two patients who had been referred to the study with a diagnosis of vegetative state did in fact demonstrate clear signs of speech comprehension when assessed using fMRI. More importantly, however, across the whole group of patients, the fMRI data were found to have no association with the behavioral presentation at the time of the investigation, but correlated significantly with subsequent behavioral recovery, six months after the scan. In this case, the fMRI data predicted subsequent recovery in a way that a specialist behavioral assessment could not.

Recently, an effort has also been made to quantify those particular aspects of the raw EEG signal that may be associated with subsequent outcome in patients after serious brain injury. For example, it has been observed (Babiloni et al. 2009) that occipital source power in the alpha band (8–13 Hz) of resting EEG, as calculated with low-resolution electromagnetic tomography, is correlated with recovery outcome at three-month follow-up in a group of vegetative state patients; those who made a behavioral recovery had higher resting alpha band power than those who did not make a significant recovery. The prognostic value of resting EEG has also been demonstrated by Schnakers and colleagues (2008a), who calculated the bispectral indices, a composite measure of the frequency content of the EEG, in a mixed group of vegetative state and minimally conscious state patients. The bispectral indices were positively correlated with behavioral scores of awareness at the time of testing and associated with outcome at one-year post trauma.

End-of-Life Decision-Making

The possibility of using fMRI or EEG for the detection of awareness in behaviorally nonresponsive patients (Cruse et al. 2011, Owen et al. 2006) raises a number of issues for legal decision-making relating to the prolongation, or otherwise, of life after severe brain injury. Foremost is the concern that diagnostic and prognostic accuracy is assured, as treatment decisions often include the possibility of withdrawal of life support. At present, in most civilized jurisdictions, decisions concerning life support (nutrition and hydration) are only made once a diagnosis of permanent vegetative state has been made. In cases in which the critical threshold for a diagnosis of permanent vegetative state has passed, the medical team formally reviews the evidence and discusses this with those closest to the patient. In England and Wales, for example, the courts require that a decision to withdraw nutrition and hydration should be referred to them before any action is taken (Roy. Coll. Phys. 1996). On the other hand, decisions not to use resuscitation in the case of cardiac arrest, or not to use antibiotics or dialysis, can be taken by the doctor in the best interests of the patient after full discussion with all those concerned. Interestingly, according to the same working party, "one cannot ever be certain that a patient in the vegetative state is wholly unaware... in view of this small but undeniable element of uncertainty, it is reasonable to administer sedation when hydration and nutrition are withdrawn to eliminate the possibility of suffering, however remote" (Roy. Coll. Phys. 1996). With the emergence of novel neuroimaging techniques that permit the identification of covert awareness in the absence of any behavioral response (Cruse et al. 2011, Owen et al. 2006), the wording of this statement acquires renewed resonance. In the case described by Owen et al. (2006), and in most of the similar cases that have appeared in the subsequent literature (e.g., Owen & Coleman 2008a), the scans that revealed awareness were acquired before the time at which the decision-making process governing withdrawal of life support is legally permitted to begin (i.e., the patients had not yet reached the point where a diagnosis of permanent vegetative state could be made). Therefore, even if the neuroimaging evidence had been admissible as part of the formal diagnostic and prognostic evaluation, in those particular cases, it was too early for the process governing end-of-life decisions to be made and therefore the situation did not arise. The same is not true of the patient described recently by Monti et al. (2010) who was able to communicate using his fMRI responses despite being repeatedly diagnosed as vegetative over a five-year period. In that case, the scan that revealed awareness was acquired and, indeed, the ability to functionally communicate was demonstrated, several years after the critical point for a diagnosis of permanent vegetative state had been reached. Even so, it is likely to be a number of years before such evidence could ever be used in the context of end-of-life decision-making, and significant legal, ethical, and technical hurdles will need to be overcome beforehand. For example, in principle it would be possible to ask the patient described by Monti et al. (2010) whether he wanted to continue living in his current situation (subject to an appropriate ethical framework being put into place), but would a "yes" or a "no" response be sufficient to be sure that the patient retained the necessary cognitive and emotional capacity to make such a complex decision? Clearly, much more work would need to be done and many more questions asked of the patient (involving considerable time in the scanner) before one could be sure that this was the case, and even then, new ethical and legal frameworks will need to be introduced to determine exactly how such situations are to be managed and by whom. In the short term, it is more likely that this approach will be used to address less ethically challenging issues such as whether or not any patients who are in this situation are experiencing any pain. For example, using this technique, patients who are aware, but cannot move or speak, could be asked if they are feeling any pain, guiding the administration of analgesics where appropriate. Given the portability, relatively low cost, and apparent reliability of new EEG-based techniques, which may allow such questions to be asked very quickly and efficiently at the bedside (e.g., Cruse et al. 2011, 2012), such procedures could soon be used by some patients to express their thoughts, control their environment, and increase their quality of life.

On the other hand, it is important to point out that neuroimaging of covert awareness is unlikely to influence legal proceedings where negative findings have been acquired. False-negative findings in functional neuroimaging studies are common, even in healthy volunteers, and they present particular difficulties in this patient population. For example, a patient may fall asleep during the scan or may not have properly heard or understood the task instructions, leading to an erroneous negative result. Indeed, in the recent study by Monti et al. (2010), no willful fMRI responses were observed in 19 of 23 patients—whether these are true negative findings (i.e., those 19 patients were indeed vegetative) or false-negative findings (i.e., some of those patients were conscious, but this was not detected on the day of the scan) cannot be determined. Accordingly, negative fMRI and EEG findings in patients should never be used as evidence for impaired cognitive function or lack of awareness.

CONCLUSIONS AND FUTURE DIRECTIONS

In the past few years, neuroimaging methods—most notably fMRI and EEG—have been brought to bear on one of the most complex and challenging questions in clinical medicine, that of detecting conscious awareness in patients who are entirely incapable of any physical behavior. The results have exposed an important limitation in our understanding of consciousness and how it is measured—that is, our absolute dependence on a behavioral response for determining whether another human being is conscious or not—and, as such, they have changed the way that many of us think about behavior itself. Thus, an "act" in the sense that Plum and Posner meant it in *Diagnosis of Stupor and Coma* (1983) need no longer be a physical act in the traditional sense (e.g., the blink of an eye or the squeezing of a hand) but, with the aid of modern neuroimaging methods, can now be an act that occurs entirely within the brain itself—a "brain act," perhaps. The recent use of reproducible and robust task-dependent fMRI responses as a form of communication in patients who are assumed to be vegetative (e.g., Monti et al. 2010) represents an important milestone in this process. Thus, information was communicated using only a brain act—information that could not have been known by the experimenters at the time yet could be independently verified later (using more traditional methods of communication with the family) as being factually correct and true. More recently, the use of EEG—a more portable and cost-effective method that can be used at the bedside—to detect consciousness in patients who appeared to be entirely vegetative (Cruse et al. 2011) again reveals our overdependence on traditional forms of behavior for inferring consciousness. Thus, in one of those cases, the

patient was able to perform approximately 100 measurable responses to command that were detected and correctly classified in his EEG record, yet he remained entirely incapable of generating a single physical response despite intense and prolonged clinical examination.

Indeed, the fact that responses like this occur at all allows us to infer not only that the instigator of the response is aware, but also that multiple cognitive processes that are typically associated with conscious awareness are also intact and working normally. For example, an intact long-term memory is required to access the appropriate imagery response (squeeze the hand or squeeze the toes), short-term (or working) memory is required to maintain attention following the stimulus (a simple beep) and to guide the search for the appropriate response at any given point in the task, attentional switching is required (to switch between the various mental states that code for the two imagery tasks), sustained attention is required to maintain the appropriate mental state, and, of course, response selection is required to make the final decision about which brain act to initiate. In short, because brain acts represent a neural proxy for motor behavior, they also confirm that the participant retains the ability to understand instructions and to carry out different mental tasks in response to those instructions, and therefore is able to exhibit willed, voluntary behavior in the absence of any overt action. On this basis, brain acts permit the identification of awareness at the single-subject level, without the need for a motor response.

Although these studies suggest that in the near future, some patients who are entirely behaviorally unresponsive may be able to routinely communicate their thoughts to those around them by simply modulating their neural activity, the use of both fMRI and EEG in this context will continue to present innumerable logistic, computational, and theoretical problems (Owen & Coleman 2007). In some ways, so-called functional near-infrared spectroscopy (fNIRS) combines the advantages of both fMRI and EEG. fNIRS exploits the penetrability of biological tissue by light in the near-infrared spectrum (700–1,000 nm) to infer neural activity. The amount of near-infrared light that is absorbed by blood vessels depends on the concentration of oxygenated and deoxygenated hemoglobin (Villringer & Chanceb 1997). fNIRS is portable, virtually noiseless, considerably cheaper, and less susceptible to movement artefacts than fMRI and has better spatial resolution than EEG. Although the technique allows reliable measurement of hemodynamic responses only in cortical tissue close to the head surface (up to ≈3 cm depth), this would be perfectly acceptable (and likely to be considerably better than EEG) for monitoring the sorts of imagery-related responses that have been detected over premotor regions in recent studies (Cruse et al. 2011, 2012; Monti et al. 2010; Owen et al. 2006). Although in its infancy, some early applications have demonstrated the potential of fNIRS as an efficient brain-computer interface in nonresponsive patients. For example, Haida et al. (2000) were able to detect appropriate brain activation within the motor cortex during a motor imagery task and within language regions during a speech-related task in a completely locked-in ALS patient. Similarly, Naito et al. (2007) mapped two mental imagery tasks, calculation and singing, to "yes" and "no" responses, and were able to detect responses with fNIRS in 40% of 17 completely locked-in patients with 74% accuracy. It remains to be seen whether this technique will prove to be effective in identifying and/or communicating with any patients who have been clinically diagnosed as being in a vegetative state.

In summary, imaging the brain's responses using fMRI, EEG, or less mature techniques such as fNIRS has provided a truly unique role for neuroimaging in the detection of consciousness and has, to some extent, redefined the limits of what we mean by "behavior." In several cases, conscious patients have been "found" by fMRI or EEG, and their behavior (albeit brain behavior) has allowed them to communicate with the outside world in the absence of any physical responses. Of course, just because some of these patients can answer "yes" and "no" questions by modulating their brain activity does not yet mean that we understand everything about their internal mental world. Are they depressed? Are they in pain? Do they want to live or die? We cannot presume to know the answers to these questions. But as long as a question can be answered with a "yes" or a "no" response, then recent developments in brain imaging have provided a means for them to be asked. Indeed, there is no reason why such patients could not be asked the most difficult question of all—"Are you conscious?"

SUMMARY POINTS

1. The only reliable method for detecting awareness in others is through a predicted behavioral response to an external prompt or command—in clinical contexts, this kind of response is often referred to as command following.

2. Following serious brain injury, some patients who are assumed to be entirely unaware, and therefore vegetative, may actually be aware yet simply unable to signal that fact through any recognized behavioral response.

3. Normal brain responses to various forms of passive external stimulation (e.g., faces, speech) have been widely reported in patients with disorders of consciousness, including the vegetative state. However, similar activity has been reported in anesthetized (i.e., unconscious) healthy individuals, suggesting that such responses in patients may be automatic and not indicative of covert awareness.

4. A significant recent addition to this field has been the development of fMRI and EEG paradigms that render awareness reportable in the absence of any overt behavioral response (e.g., motor or speech). These paradigms involve command following in the sense that participants must activate specific brain regions in response to commands—the tasks can be used to measure awareness because awareness is necessary for them to occur.

5. Using fMRI, 17% of patients who had been diagnosed as entirely vegetative on the basis of repeated clinical (behavioral) assessment were able to reliably modulate their brain activity to command, indicating that they were, in fact, conscious and aware.

6. Using EEG at the bedside, a similar approach has been used with comparable levels of success. Of patients diagnosed as entirely vegetative, 19% were able to indicate covert awareness by modulating their EEG responses to command. (EEG is portable and more cost-effective than fMRI.)

7. These techniques have recently been extended to demonstrate that two-way communication ("yes" and "no" questions) with entirely nonresponsive patients is achievable in a limited number of cases, paving the way for true brain-computer interfaces—or simple, reliable communication devices—in this group.

8. These findings have profound implications for clinical care, diagnosis, prognosis, and end-of-life decision-making, but they also shed light on more basic scientific questions about the nature of conscious behavior and the neural representation of our own thoughts and intentions.

DISCLOSURE STATEMENT

The author is not aware of any affiliations, memberships, funding, or financial holdings that might be perceived as affecting the objectivity of this review.

ACKNOWLEDGMENTS

I would like to thank the Canada Excellence Research Chair (CERC) program (Canada), the Medical Research Council (U.K.), and the James S. McDonnell Foundation (U.S.) for their generous funding of my research program.

LITERATURE CITED

Adams JH, Duchen LW. 1992. *Greenfield's Neuropathology*. New York: Oxford Univ. Press. 5th ed.

Adams JH, Graham DI, Jennett B. 2000. The neuropathology of the vegetative state after an acute brain insult. *Brain* 123(Pt. 7):1327–38

Adams JH, Graham DI, Murray LS, Scott G. 1982. Diffuse axonal injury due to nonmissile head injury in humans: an analysis of 45 cases. *Ann. Neurol.* 12(6):557–63

Adams JH, Jennett B, McLellan DR, Murray LS, Graham DI. 1999. The neuropathology of the vegetative state after head injury. *J. Clin. Pathol.* 52(11):804–6

Adapa R, Owen AM, Menon DK, Absalom AR. 2011. *Calibrating consciousness: using graded sedation to test paradigms for the vegetative state*. Poster presented at 17th annu. meet. Org. Hum. Brain Mapp. (OHBM), Quebec City

Adapa R. 2011. *Exploring neural correlates of higher cognition with sedation*. PhD thesis. Univ. Cambridge, UK

Aguirre GK, Detre JA, Alsop DC, D'Esposito M. 1996. The parahippocampus subserves topographical learning in man. *Cereb. Cortex* 6:823–29

Andrews K, Murphy L, Munday R, Littlewood C. 1996. Misdiagnosis of the vegetative state: retrospective study in a rehabilitation unit. *BMJ* 313:13–16

Babiloni C, Sarà M, Vecchio F, Pistola F, Sebastiano F, et al. 2009. Cortical sources of resting-state alpha rhythms are abnormal in persistent vegetative state patients. *Clin. Neurophysiol.* 120(4):719–29

Bekinschtein T, Niklison J, Sigman L, Manes F, Leiguarda R, et al. 2004. Emotional processing in the minimally conscious state. *J. Neurosurg. Neurol. Psychiatry* 75:788

Birbaumer N. 2006. Breaking the silence: brain-computer interfaces (BCI) for communication and motor control. *Psychophysiology* 43:517–32

Boly M, Coleman MR, Davis MH, Hampshire A, Bor D, et al. 2007. When thoughts become action: an fMRI paradigm to study volitional brain activity in non-communicative brain injured patients. *Neuroimage* 36:979–92

Bonebakker A, Bonke B, Klein J, Wolters G, Stijnen T, et al. 1996. Information processing during general anaesthesia: evidence for unconscious memory. In *Memory and Awareness in Anaesthesia*, ed. B Bonke, JGW Bovill, N Moerman, pp. 101–9. Lisse, Netherlands: Swets & Zeitlinger

Cerf M, Thiruvengadam N, Mormann F, Kraskov A, Quiroga RQ, et al. 2010. Online, voluntary control of human temporal lobe neurons. *Nature* 467:1104–8

Childs NL, Mercer WN, Childs HW. 1993. Accuracy of diagnosis of persistent vegetative state. *Neurology* 43:1465–67

Christoff K, Owen AM. 2006. Improving reverse neuroimaging inference: cognitive domain versus cognitive complexity. *Trends Cogn. Sci.* 10(8):352–53

Cincotti F, Mattia D, Babiloni C, Carducci F, Salinari S, et al. 2003. The use of EEG modifications due to motor imagery for brain-computer interfaces. *IEEE Trans. Neural Syst. Rehabil. Eng.* 11(2):131–33

Coleman MR, Davis MH, Rodd JM, Robson T, Ali A, et al. 2009. Towards the routine use of brain imaging to aid the clinical diagnosis of disorders of consciousness. *Brain* 132:2541–52

Coleman MR, Rodd JM, Davis MH, Johnsrude IS, Menon DK, et al. 2007. Do vegetative patients retain aspects of language? Evidence from fMRI. *Brain* 130:2494–507

Cruse D, Chennu S, Chatelle C, Bekinschtein TA, Fernandez-Espejo D, et al. 2011. Bedside detection of awareness in the vegetative state. *Lancet* 378(9809):2088–94

Cruse D, Chennu S, Chatelle C, Fernández-Espejo D, Bekinschtein TA, et al. 2012. The relationship between aetiology and covert cognition in the minimally conscious state. *Neurology* 78:816–22

Cruse D, Owen AM. 2010. Consciousness revealed: new insights into the vegetative and minimally conscious states. *Curr. Opin. Neurol.* 23(6):656–60

Davis MH, Coleman MR, Absalom AR, Rodd JM, Johnsrude IS, et al. 2007. Dissociating speech perception and comprehension at reduced levels of awareness. *Proc. Natl. Acad. Sci. USA* 104(41):16032–37

Dehaene S, Naccache L, Le Clec'H G, Koechlin E, Mueller M, et al. 1998. Imaging unconscious semantic priming. *Nature* 395:597–600

de Jong B, Willemsen AT, Paans AM. 1997. Regional cerebral blood flow changes related to affective speech presentation in persistent vegetative state. *Clin. Neurol. Neurosurg.* 99(3):213–16

Di H, Boly M, Weng X, Ledoux D, Laureys S. 2008. Neuroimaging activation studies in the vegetative state: predictors of recovery? *Clin. Med.* 8:502–7

Di HB, Yu SM, Weng XC, Laureys S, Yu D, et al. 2007. Cerebral response to patient's own name in the vegetative and minimally conscious states. *Neurology* 68:895–99

Farwell LA, Donchin E. 1988. Talking off the top of your head: toward a mental prosthesis utilizing event-related brain potentials. *Electroencephalogr. Clin. Neurophysiol.* 70:510–23

Gallivan JP, McLean DA, Valyear KF, Pettypiece CE, Culham JC. 2011. Decoding action intentions from preparatory brain activity in human parieto-frontal networks. *J. Neurosci.* 31(26):9599–610

Gennarelli TA, Thibault LE, Adams JH, Graham DI, Thompson CJ, Marcincin RP. 1982. Diffuse axonal injury and traumatic coma in the primate. *Ann. Neurol.* 12(6):564–74

Giacino JT, Ashwal S, Childs N, Cranford R, Jennett B, et al. 2002. The minimally conscious state: definition and diagnostic criteria. *Neurology* 58:349–53

Greenberg DL. 2007. Comment on "Detecting awareness in the vegetative state." *Science* 313(5792):1402

Guger C, Edlinger G, Harkam W, Niedermayer I, Pfurtscheller G. 2003. How many people are able to operate an EEG-based brain-computer interface (BCI)? *IEEE Trans. Neural Syst. Rehabil. Eng.* 11:145–47

Haida M, Shinohara Y, Ito Y, Yamamoto T, Kawaguchi F, Koizumi H. 2000. Brain function of an ALS patient in complete locked-in state by using optical topography. In *The Frontier of Mind-Brain Science and Its Practical Applications II*, ed. H Koizumi, pp. 95–97. Tokyo: Hitachi

Haynes JD, Sakai K, Rees G, Gilbert S, Frith C, et al. 2007. Reading hidden intentions in the human brain. *Curr. Biol.* 17(4):323–28

Jeannerod M, Frak V. 1999. Mental imaging of motor activity in humans. *Curr. Opin. Neurobiol.* 9:735–39

Jennett B, Adams JH, Murray LS, Graham DI. 2001. Neuropathology in vegetative and severely disabled patients after head injury. *Neurology* 56(4):486–90

Jennett B, Plum F. 1972. Persistent vegetative state after brain damage. *Lancet* 1:734–37

Kinney HC, Korein J, Panigrahy A, Dikkes P, Goode R. 1994. Neuropathological findings in the brain of Karen Ann Quinlan—the role of the thalamus in the persistent vegetative state. *N. Engl. J. Med.* 330(21):1469–75

Kleih SC, Kaufmann T, Zickler C, Halder S, Leotta F, et al. 2011. Out of the frying pan into the fire—the P300-based BCI faces real-world challenges. *Prog. Brain Res.* 194:27–46

Koch C. 2007. *The Quest for Consciousness: A Neurobiological Approach*. Greenwood Village, CO: Roberts

Kotchoubey B, Kaiser J, Bostanov V, Lutzenberger W, Birbaumer N. 2009. Recognition of affective prosody in brain-damaged patients and healthy controls: a neurophysiological study using EEG and whole-head MEG. *Cogn. Affect. Behav. Neurosci.* 9(2):153–67

Kotchoubey B, Lang S, Herb E, Maurer P, Schmalohr D, et al. 2003a. Stimulus complexity enhances auditory discrimination in patients with extremely severe brain injuries. *Neurosci. Lett.* 352(2):129–32

Kotchoubey B, Lang S, Mezger G, Schmalohr D, Schneck M, et al. 2005. Information processing in severe disorders of consciousness: vegetative state and minimally conscious state. *Clin. Neurophysiol.: Off. J. Int. Fed. Clin. Neurophysiol.* 116(10):2441–53

Kotchoubey B, Lang S, Winter S, Birbaumer N. 2003b. Cognitive processing in completely paralyzed patients with amyotrophic lateral sclerosis. *Eur. J. Neurol.* 10:551–58

Kübler A, Furdea A, Halder S, Hammer EM, Nijboer F, et al. 2009. A brain-computer interface controlled auditory event-related potential (P300) spelling system for locked-in patients. *Ann. N. Y. Acad. Sci.* 1157:90–100

Kübler A, Nijboer F, Mellinger J, Vaughan TM, Pawelzik H, et al. 2005. Patients with ALS can use sensori-motor rhythms to operate a brain-computer interface. *Neurology* 64(10):1775–77

Kulkarni VP, Lin K, Bendabis SR. 2007. EEG findings in the persistent vegetative state. *J. Clin. Neurophysiol.* 24(6):433–37

Laureys S. 2005. Science and society: death, unconsciousness and the brain. *Nat. Rev. Neurosci.* 6(11):899–909

Laureys S, Faymonville ME, Peigneux P, Damas P, Lambermont B. 2002. Cortical processing of noxious somatosensory stimuli in the persistent vegetative state. *Neuroimage* 17(2):732–41

Laureys S, Perrion F, Bredart S. 2007. Self-consciousness in non-communicative patients. *Conscious. Cogn.* 16(3):722–41

Menon DK, Owen AM, Williams EJ, Minhas PS, Allen CMC, et al. 1998. Cortical processing in persistent vegetative state. *Lancet* 352(9123):200

Monti MM, Coleman MR, Owen AM. 2009. Executive functions in the absence of behavior: functional imaging of the minimally conscious state. *Prog. Brain Res.* 249–60

Monti MM, Pickard JD, Owen AM. 2012. Visual cognition in disorders of consciousness: from V1 to top-down attention. *Hum. Brain Mapp.* doi: 10.1002/hbm.21507

Monti MM, Vanhaudenhuyse A, Coleman MR, Boly M, Pickard JD, et al. 2010. Willful modulation of brain activity in disorders of consciousness. *N. Engl. J. Med.* 362(7):579–89

Naccache L. 2006. Psychology. Is she conscious? *Science* 313:1395–96

Nachev P, Husain M. 2007. Comment on "Detecting awareness in the vegetative state." *Science* 315(5816):1221

Naito M, Michioka Y, Ozawa K, Ito Y, Kiguchi M, Kanazawa T. 2007. Communication means for totally locked-in ALS patients based on changes in cerebral blood volume measured with near-infrared light. *IEICE Trans. Inform. Syst.* 90 1028–37

Nijboer F, Furdea A, Gunst I, Mellinger J, McFarland DJ, et al. 2008. An auditory brain-computer interface (BCI). *J. Neurosci. Methods* 167(1):43–50

Owen AM, Coleman MR. 2007. Functional MRI in disorders of consciousness: advantages and limitations. *Curr. Opin. Neurol.* 20(6):632–37

Owen AM, Coleman M. 2008a. Functional imaging in the vegetative state. *Nat. Rev. Neurosci.* 9:235–43

Owen AM, Coleman MR. 2008b. Detecting awareness in the vegetative state. *Ann. N. Y. Acad. Sci.* 1129:130–38

Owen AM, Coleman MR, Davis MH, Boly M, Laureys S, et al. 2007. Response to comments on "Detecting awareness in the vegetative state." *Science* 315:1221c

Owen AM, Coleman MR, Davis MH, Boly M, Laureys S, Pickard JD. 2006. Detecting awareness in the vegetative state. *Science* 313:1402

Owen AM, Coleman MR, Menon DK, Berry EL, Johnsrude IS, et al. 2005a. Using a hierarchical approach to investigate residual auditory cognition in persistent vegetative state. *Prog. Brain Res.* 150:461–76

Owen AM, Coleman MR, Menon DK, Johnsrude IS, Rodd JM, et al. 2005b. Residual auditory function in persistent vegetative state: a combined PET and fMRI study. *Neuropsychol. Rehabil.* 15(3–4):290–306

Pfurtscheller G, Brunner C, Schlogl A, Lopes da Silva FH. 2006. Mu rhythm (de)synchronization and EEG single-trial classification of different motor imagery tasks. *Neuroimage* 31:153–59

Pfurtscheller G, Neuper C. 1997. Motor imagery activates primary sensorimotor area in humans. *Neurosci. Lett.* 239:65–68

Pfurtscheller G, Scherer R, Muller-Putz GR, Lopes da Silva FH. 2008. Short-lived brain state after cued motor imagery in naive subjects. *Eur. J. Neurosci.* 28:1419–26

Plum F, Posner JB. 1983. *The Diagnosis of Stupor and Coma.* New York: Wiley. 3rd ed.

Poldrack RA. 2006. Can cognitive processes be inferred from neuroimaging data? *Trends Cogn. Sci.* 10:59–63

Qin P, Di H, Yan X, Yu S, Yu D, et al. 2008. Mismatch negativity to the patient's own name in chronic disorders of consciousness. *Neurosci. Lett.* 448(1):24–28

Rodd JM, Davis MH, Johnsrude IS. 2005. The neural mechanisms of speech comprehension: fMRI studies of semantic ambiguity. *Cereb. Cortex* 15:1261–69

Roy. Coll. Phys. Work. Group. 1996. The permanent vegetative state. *J. Roy. Coll. Phys. Lond.* 30:119–21

Roy. Coll. Phys. Work. Group. 1996/2003. *The Vegetative State: Guidance on Diagnosis and Management.* London: Roy. Coll. Phys.

Roy. Coll. Phys. 1998. *A Code of Practice for the Diagnosis of Brainstem Death.* London: Roy. Coll. Phys.

Schacter DL. 1994. Priming and multiple memory systems: perceptual mechanisms of implicit memory. In *Memory Systems*, ed. DL Schacter, E Tulving, pp. 233–68. Cambridge, MA: MIT Press

Schnakers C, Giacino J, Kalmar K, Piret S, Lopez E, et al. 2006. Does the FOUR score correctly diagnose the vegetative and minimally conscious states? *Ann. Neurol.* 60:744–45

Schnakers C, Ledoux D, Majerus S, Damas P, Damas F, et al. 2008a. Diagnostic and prognostic use of bispectral index in coma, vegetative state and related disorders. *Brain Inj.* 22(12):926–31

Schnakers C, Perrin F, Schabus M, Majerus S, Ledoux D, et al. 2008b. Voluntary brain processing in disorders of consciousness. *Neurology* 71(20):1614–20

Schnakers C, Vanhaudenhuyse A, Giacino J, Ventura M, Boly M, et al. 2009. Diagnostic accuracy of the vegetative and minimally conscious state: clinical consensus versus standardized neurobehavioral assessment. *BMC Neurol.* 9:35

Sellers EW, Donchin E. 2006. A P300-based brain-computer interface: initial tests by ALS patients. *Clin. Neurophysiol.* 117:538–48

Sorger B, Dahmen B, Reithler J, Gosseries O, Maudoux A, et al. 2009. Another kind of "BOLD response": answering multiple-choice questions via online decoded single-trial brain signals. *Prog. Brain Res.* 177:275–92

Staffen W, Kronbichler M, Aichhorn M, Mair A, Ladurner G. 2006. Selective brain activity in response to one's own name in the persistent vegetative state. *J. Neurol. Neurosurg. Psychiatry* 77:1383–84

Vaughan TM, McFarland DJ, Schalk G, Sarnacki WA, Krusienski DJ, et al. 2006. The Wadsworth BCI research and development program: at home with BCI. *IEEE Trans. Neural Syst. Rehabil. Eng.* 14(2):229–33

Villringer A, Chanceb B. 1997. Non-invasive optical spectroscopy and imaging of human brain function. *Trends Neurosci.* 20(10):435–42

Weiskopf N, Mathiak K, Bock SW, Scharnowski F, Veit R, et al. 2004. Principles of a brain-computer interface (BCI) based on real-time functional magnetic resonance imaging (fMRI). *IEEE Trans. Biomed. Eng.* 51:966–70

Wolpaw JR, Birbaumer N, McFarland DJ, Pfurtscheller G, Vaughan TM. 2002. Brain-computer interfaces for communication and control. *Clin. Neurophysiol.* 113:767–91

Wolpaw JR, McFarland DJ, Neat GW, Forneris CA. 1991. An EEG-based brain-computer interface for cursor control. *Electroencephalogr. Clin. Neurophysiol.* 78(3):252–59

Zeman A. 2009. The problem of unreportable awareness. *Prog. Brain Res.* 177:1–9

Executive Functions

Adele Diamond

Department of Psychiatry, University of British Columbia and BC Children's Hospital, Vancouver, BC V6T 2A1 Canada; email: adele.diamond@ubc.ca

Annu. Rev. Psychol. 2013. 64:135–68

First published online as a Review in Advance on September 27, 2012

The *Annual Review of Psychology* is online at psych.annualreviews.org

This article's doi: 10.1146/annurev-psych-113011-143750

Keywords

cognitive control, self-regulation, creativity, attention, reasoning, working memory, fluid intelligence, inhibitory control, task switching, mental flexibility

Abstract

Executive functions (EFs) make possible mentally playing with ideas; taking the time to think before acting; meeting novel, unanticipated challenges; resisting temptations; and staying focused. Core EFs are inhibition [response inhibition (self-control—resisting temptations and resisting acting impulsively) and interference control (selective attention and cognitive inhibition)], working memory, and cognitive flexibility (including creatively thinking "outside the box," seeing anything from different perspectives, and quickly and flexibly adapting to changed circumstances). The developmental progression and representative measures of each are discussed. Controversies are addressed (e.g., the relation between EFs and fluid intelligence, self-regulation, executive attention, and effortful control, and the relation between working memory and inhibition and attention). The importance of social, emotional, and physical health for cognitive health is discussed because stress, lack of sleep, loneliness, or lack of exercise each impair EFs. That EFs are trainable and can be improved with practice is addressed, including diverse methods tried thus far.

Contents

Executive functions (EFs): a collection of top-down control processes used when going on automatic or relying on instinct or intuition would be ill-advised, insufficient, or impossible

Inhibition (inhibitory control): controlling one's attention, behavior, thoughts, and/or emotions to override a strong internal predisposition or external lure

INTRODUCTION

Executive functions (EFs; also called executive control or cognitive control) refer to a family of top-down mental processes needed when you have to concentrate and pay attention, when going on automatic or relying on instinct or intuition would be ill-advised, insufficient, or impossible (Burgess & Simons 2005, Espy 2004, Miller & Cohen 2001). Using EFs is effortful; it is easier to continue doing what you have been doing than to change, it is easier to give into temptation than to resist it, and it is easier to go on "automatic pilot" than to consider what to do next. There is general agreement that there are three core EFs (e.g., Lehto et al. 2003, Miyake et al. 2000): inhibition [inhibitory control, including self-control (behavioral inhibition) and interference control (selective attention and cognitive inhibition)], working memory (WM), and cognitive flexibility (also called set shifting, mental flexibility, or mental set shifting and closely linked to creativity). From these, higher-order EFs are built such as reasoning, problem solving, and planning (Collins & Koechlin 2012, Lunt et al. 2012). EFs are skills essential for mental and physical health; success in school and in life; and cognitive, social, and psychological development (see **Table 1**).

Table 1 Executive functions (EFs) are important to just about every aspect of life

Aspects of life	The ways in which EFs are relevant to that aspect of life	References
Mental health	EFs are impaired in many mental disorders, including:	
	- Addictions	Baler & Volkow 2006
	- Attention deficit hyperactivity (ADHD)	Diamond 2005, Lui & Tannock 2007
	- Conduct disorder	Fairchild et al. 2009
	- Depression	Taylor-Tavares et al. 2007
	- Obsessive compulsive disorder (OCD)	Penadés et al. 2007
	- Schizophrenia	Barch 2005
Physical health	Poorer EFs are associated with obesity, overeating, substance abuse, and poor treatment adherence	Crescioni et al. 2011, Miller et al. 2011, Riggs et al. 2010
Quality of life	People with better EFs enjoy a better quality of life	Brown & Landgraf 2010, Davis et al. 2010
School readiness	EFs are more important for school readiness than are IQ or entry-level reading or math	Blair & Razza 2007, Morrison et al. 2010
School success	EFs predict both math and reading competence throughout the school years	Borella et al. 2010, Duncan et al. 2007, Gathercole et al. 2004
Job success	Poor EFs lead to poor productivity and difficulty finding and keeping a job	Bailey 2007
Marital harmony	A partner with poor EFs can be more difficult to get along with, less dependable, and/or more likely to act on impulse	Eakin et al. 2004
Public safety	Poor EFs lead to social problems (including crime, reckless behavior, violence, and emotional outbursts)	Broidy et al. 2003, Denson et al. 2011

INHIBITORY CONTROL

Inhibitory control (one of the core EFs) involves being able to control one's attention, behavior, thoughts, and/or emotions to override a strong internal predisposition or external lure, and instead do what's more appropriate or needed. Without inhibitory control we would be at the mercy of impulses, old habits of thought or action (conditioned responses), and/or stimuli in the environment that pull us this way or that. Thus, inhibitory control makes it possible for us to change and for us to choose how we react and how we behave rather than being unthinking creatures of habit. It doesn't make it easy. Indeed, we usually are creatures of habit and our behavior is under the control of environmental stimuli far more than we usually realize, but having the ability to exercise inhibitory control creates the possibility of change and choice. It can also save us from making fools of ourselves.

Inhibitory control of attention (interference control at the level of perception) enables us to selectively attend, focusing on what we choose and suppressing attention to other stimuli. We need such selective attention at a cocktail party when we want to screen out all but one voice. A salient stimulus such as visual motion or a loud noise attracts our attention whether we want it to or not. That is called exogenous, bottom-up, automatic, stimulus-driven, or involuntary attention and is driven by properties of stimuli themselves (Posner & DiGirolamo 1998, Theeuwes 1991). We can also choose voluntarily to ignore (or inhibit attention to) particular stimuli and attend to others based on our goal or intention. Besides being called selective or focused attention, this has been termed attentional control or attentional inhibition, endogenous, top-down, active, goal-driven, voluntary, volitional, or executive attention (Posner & DiGirolamo 1998, Theeuwes 2010).

Another aspect of interference control is suppressing prepotent mental representations (cognitive inhibition). This involves resisting extraneous or unwanted thoughts or memories, including intentional forgetting (Anderson &

Self-control: the aspect of inhibitory control that involves resisting temptations and not acting impulsively or prematurely

Working memory (WM): holding information in mind and mentally working with it (e.g., relating one thing to another, using information to solve a problem)

Cognitive flexibility: changing perspectives or approaches to a problem, flexibly adjusting to new demands, rules, or priorities (as in switching between tasks)

Levy 2009), resisting proactive interference from information acquired earlier (Postle et al. 2004), and resisting retroactive interference from items presented later. Cognitive inhibition is usually in the service of aiding WM and is discussed in the section Inhibitory Control Supports Working Memory. It tends to cohere more with WM measures than with measures of other types of inhibition.

Self-control is the aspect of inhibitory control that involves control over one's behavior and control over one's emotions in the service of controlling one's behavior. Self-control is about resisting temptations and not acting impulsively. The temptation resisted might be to indulge in pleasures when one should not (e.g., to indulge in a romantic fling if you are married or to eat sweets if you are trying to lose weight), to overindulge, or to stray from the straight and narrow (e.g., to cheat or steal). Or the temptation might be to impulsively react (e.g., reflexively striking back at someone who has hurt your feelings) or to do or take what you want without regard for social norms (e.g., butting in line or grabbing another child's toy).

Another aspect of self-control is having the discipline to stay on task despite distractions and completing a task despite temptations to give up, to move on to more interesting work, or to have a good time instead. This involves making yourself do something or keep at something though you would rather be doing something else. It is related to the final aspect of self-control—delaying gratification (Mischel et al. 1989)—making yourself forgo an immediate pleasure for a greater reward later (often termed delay discounting by neuroscientists and learning theorists; Louie & Glimcher 2010, Rachlin et al. 1991). Without the discipline to complete what one started and delay gratification, no one would ever complete a long, time-consuming task such as writing a dissertation, running a marathon, or starting a new business.

Although the above examples typically involve a tug-of-war between a part of you that wants to do x and another part of you that wants to do y (Hofmann et al. 2009), self-control can be needed where there are not competing desires. It is needed, for example, to not blurt out what first comes to mind (which might be hurtful to others or embarrassing to you), to not jump to a conclusion before getting all the facts, or to not give the first answer that occurs to you when if you took more time you could give a better, wiser response.

Errors of impulsivity are errors of not being able to wait. If someone can be helped to wait such errors can often be avoided. Many of us have had the experience of pressing the "send" button for an email only to wish we had not. Many of us have also had the experience of our first interpretation of the intention behind someone's words or actions being incorrect, and we have either been grateful we exercised the self-control to wait until we acquired more information or regretted that we acted precipitously without waiting. On laboratory tasks, young children often rush to respond and thus make errors by giving the prepotent response when a different response is required. Helping young children wait improves their performance. This has been shown using a variety of inhibitory control tasks such as go/no-go (Jones et al. 2003), theory of mind (Heberle et al. 1999), day-night (Diamond et al. 2002), and a Piagetian search task (Riviere & Lecuyer 2003). The subthalamic nucleus appears to play a critical role in preventing such impulsive or premature responding (Frank 2006).

Diamond and colleagues (2002) hypothesized that more time helps in such situations because young children need time to compute the answer. Simpson & Riggs (2007) hypothesized that more time helps because it allows the prepotent response (which is triggered automatically by a stimulus) to race to the response threshold and then fade, enabling the correct answer to compete more successfully [to do something other than your prepotent response requires mental effort and reaches the response threshold more slowly (**Figure 1**; see Band et al. 2003)]. Diamond, Simpson, and Riggs (Simpson et al. 2012) teamed up to test between their hypotheses. The results clearly support Simpson and Riggs's passive-dissipation hypothesis. In a distraction-during-delay condition, preschoolers were able to resist opening boxes on no-go trials. They performed well on such trials despite not being able to compute anything during the delay because they were occupied with a guessing game.

When an incorrect prepotent response is elicited by the sight of a stimulus, individuals can be helped to perform correctly by shielding the stimulus from view, thus reducing or eliminating the need for inhibitory control. For example, in Piaget's famous test of conservation of liquid volume (Piaget 1952/1941), the same amount of liquid is poured into a short, fat beaker and a tall, thin beaker. Of course the water level is much higher in the tall, thin beaker, creating a perceptual pull to think there is more water there. Children of 4 to 5 years, who have just certified that the amount of liquid is the same in two identical short beakers, fall prey to this perceptual pull. Though they see the liquid poured from one of the short beakers into the taller, thinner beaker, upon seeing the higher level of liquid in the tall beaker, they assert there must be more liquid there. However, if they are shielded from seeing the two different levels of liquid and are simply asked which beaker has more liquid, children of 4 to 5 years give the correct answer (Bruner et al. 1966).

Similarly, infants have a prepotent tendency to reach directly for a visible reward. If a transparent barrier is between them and the reward, infants of 6 to 11 months have great difficulty inhibiting the perceptual pull to keep trying to reach straight for the reward despite repeatedly being thwarted by the clear barrier. If the barrier is opaque, thus removing the perceptual pull, more infants at each age succeed in detouring around the barrier and succeed in less time (Diamond 1990, 1991). Many adults use a related strategy by eliminating fattening foods from view when they are trying to diet, thus reducing the degree of self-control needed.

Representative Psychological Tasks Used to Assess Inhibitory Control

Examples of other psychological measures of inhibitory control include the Stroop

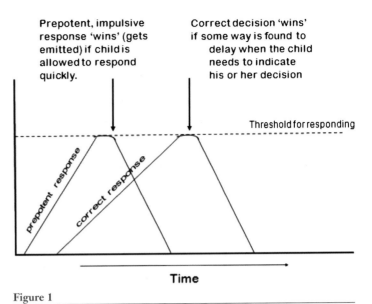

Figure 1

Passive-dissipation model showing how delay can improve performance on inhibitory tasks (from Simpson et al. 2011).

task (MacLeod 1991), Simon task (Hommel 2011), Flanker task (Eriksen & Eriksen 1974, Mullane et al. 2009), antisaccade tasks (Luna 2009, Munoz & Everling 2004), delay-of-gratification tasks (Kochanska et al. 2001, Sethi et al. 2000), go/no-go tasks (Cragg & Nation 2008), and stop-signal tasks (Verbruggen & Logan 2008). One of the many hotly debated aspects of EFs is which component(s) of EFs a task requires. Not everyone agrees that these tasks require inhibitory control [see, for example, MacLeod et al. (2003) on the Stroop task and Roberts & Pennington (1996) on the antisaccade task].

We are trained to read for meaning and to largely ignore superficial characteristics of words such as font style or color of the ink. Incongruent trials on the Stroop task present color words (such as "green") written in the color of another ink ("red"). When required to ignore the meaning of the word (i.e., inhibit our prepotent response to words) and instead attend to and report the color of the ink, people are slower and make more errors.

Simon tasks present two very simple rules: for Stimulus A press on the left; for Stimulus B press on the right. Only one stimulus appears at a time; either stimulus can appear on the right or the left. Although location of the stimulus is irrelevant, people respond more slowly when the stimulus appears on the side opposite its associated response (termed the Simon effect, spatial incompatibility, or stimulus-response compatibility), indicating that we have a pre-potent tendency to respond on the same side as a stimulus (Hommel 2011, Lu & Proctor 1995). That tendency must be inhibited when the lo-cations of stimulus and response are opposite (incompatible). Indeed, when monkeys are to point away from a stimulus, the neuronal pop-ulation vector in primary motor cortex (cod-ing the direction of planned movement) initially points toward the stimulus and only then shifts to the required direction (showing a prepotent tendency at the neuronal level to respond to-ward a stimulus; to do otherwise requires that that impulse be inhibited; Georgopoulos et al. 1989). For comparable results in humans see Valle-Inclán (1996).

The Spatial Stroop task is similar to a Simon task but minimizes memory demands because the stimulus shows you where to respond. You are to press in the direction the arrow is point-ing. Sometimes the arrow appears on the side it is pointing toward (congruent, compatible trials), but sometimes the arrow appears on the other side (incongruent, incompatible trials). The arrow's location is irrelevant, but subjects still have a tendency to press on the side the arrow appears, which must be inhibited when the arrow is pointing in the opposite direction. A version of the Spatial Stroop task appears in the Cambridge Neuropsychological Test Automated Battery (CANTAB; Sahakian et al. 1988).

The Flanker task requires selective at-tention; you are to attend to the centrally presented stimulus and ignore the flanking stimuli surrounding it. When the flanking stimuli are mapped to the opposite response from the center stimulus (incompatible trials), subjects respond more slowly because of the need to exercise top-down control (Eriksen & Eriksen 1974).

Our natural tendency is to look toward a salient stimulus when it appears (i.e., to make a prosaccade). On trials where we are instructed to inhibit that tendency and instead do the opposite (i.e., to look away from the stimu-lus, to make an antisaccade), we are slower and more prone to err (Munoz & Everling 2004). This task is sensitive to developmental improvements throughout late childhood and adolescence (Luna 2009, Luna et al. 2004).

Delay-of-gratification tasks involve placing a delicious snack before young children and ask-ing that they wait before taking it. Children can have more of the treat if they wait, or less if they can't wait. Each child is tested individu-ally. Retesting is difficult because it is critical that the child not know how long the wait will be. This task seems to predict children's EFs and academic performance at much later ages (Eigsti et al. 2006).

Two widely used measures of response inhibition—the go/no-go and stop-signal tasks—are different from other measures in that participants do not inhibit one response to make another; they simply inhibit a response to do nothing. Go/no-go tasks require that you usually press a button when a stimulus appears, but when a certain stimulus appears you should not press. On the stop-signal task, the go signal is presented on all trials; on a minority of trials after the go signal and just as the subject is about to respond, a stop signal appears (usually a sound), indicating that one should not press the button on that trial. Real-world analogies of checking an action that was just on the verge of being made would be when a situation, or your evaluation of it, suddenly changes such as when you are about to cross the street and the light suddenly changes or a batter checks a swing. The go/no-go and stop-signal tasks are not identical in their inhibitory require-ments (Verbruggen & Logan 2008) and differ from many real-world instances of inhibitory control (Aron 2011). Rather than being paradigmatic examples of when inhibitory control is needed, they appear to be unusual cases.

Commonalities and Differences Among Diverse Forms of Inhibitory Control

Are the different aspects of inhibitory control dissociable from one another? Is the same neural system required to resist internal and external distractions? Is the neural system that subserves cognitive inhibition the same as that subserving inhibition of attention and/or action? Is the neural system that subserves inhibition in attention (interference control/selective attention) the same neural system that subserves inhibition in action (inhibiting a prepotent response tendency)? Certainly the forms of inhibition seem quite disparate (Nigg 2000). Yet evidence indicates that diverse types of inhibitory control of attention and action appear to share substantially similar neural bases (Bunge et al. 2002, Cohen et al. 2012). Cognitive inhibition, however, appears to be dissociable (Engelhardt et al. 2008, Friedman & Miyake 2004). There is some emerging evidence that delay of gratification might be dissociable as well (Diamond & Lee 2011).

Factor analyses have found that inhibition of attention (resisting distractor interference) and inhibition of action (inhibiting a prepotent response) are strongly correlated and fall along a single factor (Friedman & Miyake 2004). It is consistently found that when required to exert one type of self-control (e.g., resisting sweets), and then immediately after a second type of self-control in a superficially completely unrelated domain (e.g., the stop-signal task), people are more impaired on the second task than if they did a different difficult task first that did not require self-control (e.g., math calculations; Muraven 2010, Muraven & Baumeister 2000).

Is the neural system required to inhibit an action and not act at all (e.g., on no-go trials) the same as the system required to inhibit one action to do another? Petrides (1986) and de Jong et al. (1995) suggest it is not. Is the neural system that underlies the ability to inhibit an unwanted action the same as the system underlying the ability to check a desired action (e.g., as in not swinging at a poorly pitched ball or as on

the stop-signal task)? Do all of these forms of inhibition develop concurrently, and are they equally susceptible to disruption because of a particular genetic abnormality or environmental insult during development? If they are separable, how are we to divide them into components (Casey 2001, Nigg 2000)? Certainly automatic inhibition (such as that seen in the attentional blink or negative priming) is dissociable from the volitional, effortful inhibitory control discussed here (Carr et al. 2006, Nigg et al. 2002), and although effortful inhibition declines with aging, it is unclear whether automatic inhibition does (Gamboz et al. 2002).

Development of Inhibitory Control

Inhibitory control is disproportionately difficult for young children. For example, the difference in both the speed and accuracy of children's performance at all ages from 4 to 9 between (*a*) always responding on the same side as a stimulus and (*b*) inhibiting that prepotent tendency and always responding on the side opposite a stimulus is greater than the difference in their speed or accuracy for (*a*) holding two stimulus-response associations in mind versus (*b*) holding six stimulus-response associations in mind (Davidson et al. 2006; see **Figure 2**). That's true whether the same-side trials come before or after the opposite-side ones (Wright & Diamond 2012). The reverse is true for adults. It is far harder for us to hold six associations in mind than only two, but it is no harder for us to always respond on the side opposite a stimulus than to always respond on the same side as a stimulus (our speed and accuracy for each are equivalent; Davidson et al. 2006, Lu & Proctor 1995). Inhibitory control continues to mature during adolescence (Luna 2009, Luna et al. 2004).

Inhibitory control early in life appears to be quite predictive of outcomes throughout life, including in adulthood. When 1,000 children born in the same city in the same year were followed for 32 years with a 96% retention rate, Moffitt et al. (2011) found that children who at ages 3 to 11 had better inhibitory control (e.g., were better at waiting their turn, less

Dots Task: Accuracy

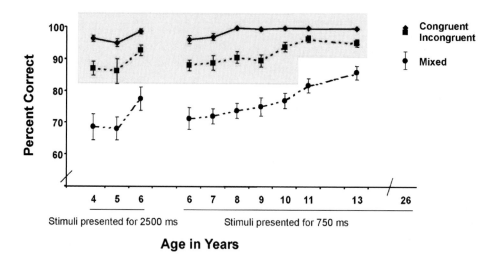

Figure 2

At every age studied, children were slower and less accurate on the congruent block than on the incongruent block. That effect is completely absent in adults, who are as fast and as accurate on the incongruent block as on the congruent one. The memory demands of those two blocks were the same; they differ only in that the incongruent block requires inhibitory control and the congruent block does not (based on Davidson et al. 2006; this is now called Hearts and Flowers.).

easily distracted, more persistent, and less impulsive) were more likely as teenagers to still be in school and were less likely to make risky choices or to be smoking or taking drugs. They grew up to have better physical and mental health (e.g., were less likely to be overweight or to have high blood pressure or substance abuse problems), earn more, and be more law-abiding as adults 30 years later than were those with worse inhibitory control as children, controlling for IQ, gender, social class, and their home lives and family circumstances growing up. They were also happier as adults (Moffitt 2012).

Inhibitory control declines noticeably during normal aging, however (Hasher & Zacks 1988, Hasher et al. 1991). For example, older adults are poor at inhibiting visual distractions (Darowski et al. 2008, Gazzaley et al. 2005) and auditory distractions (Alain & Woods 1999, Barr & Giambra 1990). Older adults show normal enhancement of the to-be-attended stimuli, but less or even no suppression of the stim-

uli to be ignored (Gazzaley et al. 2005), providing rather strong evidence of an inhibitory-control deficit in aging. No matter whether participants are prepared for distraction or not, and regardless of how long the period between the forewarning and stimuli or how long the interval between trials, older adults are substantially worse than younger adults in suppressing irrelevant information (Zanto et al. 2010). Older adults' inhibitory-control problems are also evident on the antisaccade task (Peltsch et al. 2011, Sweeney et al. 2001).

WORKING MEMORY

Another core EF is working memory (WM), which involves holding information in mind and mentally working with it (or said differently, working with information no longer perceptually present; Baddeley & Hitch 1994, Smith & Jonides 1999). The two types of WM are distinguished by content—verbal WM and nonverbal (visual-spatial) WM. WM is critical for making sense of anything that unfolds over time, for that always requires holding in mind what happened earlier and relating that to what comes later. Thus it is necessary for making sense of written or spoken language whether it is a sentence, a paragraph, or longer. Doing any math in your head requires WM, as does mentally reordering items (such as reorganizing a to-do list), translating instructions into action plans, incorporating new information into your thinking or action plans (updating), considering alternatives, and mentally relating information to derive a general principle or to see relations between items or ideas. Reasoning would not be possible without WM. WM is critical to our ability to see connections between seemingly unrelated things and to pull apart elements from an integrated whole, and hence to creativity because creativity involves disassembling and recombining elements in new ways. WM also enables us to bring conceptual knowledge and not just perceptual input to bear on our decisions, and to consider our remembered past and future hopes in making plans and decisions.

Working Memory Versus Short-Term Memory

WM (holding information in mind and manipulating it) is distinct from short-term memory (just holding information in mind). They cluster onto separate factors in factor analyses of children, adolescents, and adults (Alloway et al. 2004, Gathercole et al. 2004). They are linked to different neural subsystems. WM relies more on dorsolateral prefrontal cortex, whereas maintaining information in mind but not manipulating it [as long as the number of items is not huge (suprathreshold)] does not need involvement of dorsolateral prefrontal cortex (D'Esposito et al. 1999, Eldreth et al. 2006, Smith & Jonides 1999). Imaging studies show frontal activation only in ventrolateral prefrontal cortex for memory maintenance that is not suprathreshold.

WM and short-term memory also show different developmental progressions; the latter develops earlier and faster. A Simon task (described above) requires that subjects remember two rules (for Stimulus 1 press on the right; for Stimulus 2 press on the left). A superficially similar task, originally called the Dots task and later renamed the Hearts and Flowers task, also requires that subjects remember two rules (for Stimulus 1 press on the same side as the stimulus; for Stimulus 2 press on the side opposite the stimulus; Davidson et al. 2006, Diamond et al. 2007). Whereas the memory component of the Simon task requires only holding information in mind, note that WM is required for the Dots task because the instruction to use the hand on the same or opposite side as the stimulus must be translated into whether to use the right or left hand. The rules must not only be held in mind but also mentally translated or transformed. Comparing performance on the Simon and Dots tasks across age provides a clear view of the additional toll that WM versus short-term memory exacts for children at least through ages 4 to 13 and for adults (see **Figure 3**; Davidson et al. 2006).

Relations Between Working Memory and Inhibitory Control

They generally need one another and co-occur. One prototypical instance of when EFs are needed is the class of situations where you are to act counter to your initial tendency on the basis of information held in mind. WM and inhibitory control support one another and rarely, if ever, is one needed but not the other.

Working memory supports inhibitory control. You must hold your goal in mind to know what is relevant or appropriate and what to inhibit. By concentrating especially hard on the information you are holding in mind, you increase the likelihood that that information will guide your behavior, and you decrease the likelihood of an inhibitory error (mistakenly emitting the default, or normally prepotent, response when it should have been inhibited).

Using visual cues to help young children remember what they were just told can markedly improve their inhibitory control performance.

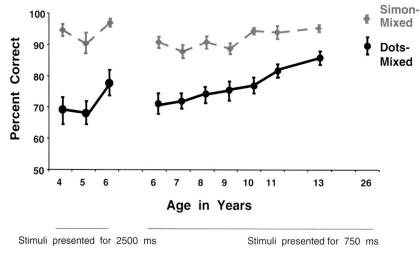

Figure 3

Comparison of the mixed conditions of the Dots (now called Hearts and Flowers) and Simon tasks in percentage of correct responses (based on Davidson et al. 2006).

For example, a school program for 4- to 5-year-olds called Tools of the Mind uses visual aids in an activity called Buddy Reading (Bodrova & Leong 2007). Each child chooses a picture book, pairs up with another child, and they are to take turns telling the story that goes with their book. With each child eager to tell his or her story, no one wants to listen. To help children succeed at inhibitory control, teachers use a visual memory aid, handing one child in each pair a drawing of an ear, explaining, "Ears don't talk; ears listen." With that concrete reminder, the child with the ear inhibits talking and listens. Without it, the child would not be able to do that. After a few months, the picture is no longer needed; the child has internalized the reminder.

Inhibitory control supports working memory. To relate multiple ideas or facts together you must be able to resist focusing exclusively on just one thing, and to recombine ideas and facts in new, creative ways you need to be able to resist repeating old thought patterns. To keep your mind focused on what you want to focus on you must inhibit internal and external distractions. When such inhibition

fails, your mind may wander. Many of us are familiar with suddenly realizing that we don't know what was in the passage we supposedly just read because our mind was elsewhere (it had wandered). Several studies have explored such mind-wandering (e.g., Kane et al. 2007, Mason et al. 2007, Smallwood & Schooler 2009). Meditation is reported to reduce mind-wandering by disciplining the mind in the art of staying focused (Hölzel et al. 2011, Zeidan et al. 2010). Inhibitory control can also aid WM by helping to keep our mental workspace from becoming too cluttered by suppressing extraneous thoughts (i.e., gating out irrelevant information from the WM workspace), resisting proactive interference by deleting no-longer-relevant information from that limited-capacity workspace (Hasher & Zacks 1988, Zacks & Hasher 2006). Hasher and Zacks group cognitive inhibition under WM. As noted above, they may be right that inhibition in the service of protecting the mental workspace for WM is intrinsically allied with WM.

An excellent example of not cluttering one's WM space unnecessarily can be seen with an interesting test developed by Duncan et al. (2008). One group of subjects is instructed on two tasks (a letter task and a number task) and then told they can ignore the number task for the time being because they will only be doing the letter task now. Another group is instructed only on the letter task. The stimuli are presented in two columns. Subjects are instructed that when they see a plus sign they should attend to the column on the right, while a minus sign means attend to the column on the left. When asked before or after testing, all subjects correctly recall what they should do for a plus or minus sign. Everyone obeys those rules perfectly when instructed on only one task. However, when instructed on two tasks, individuals with worse EFs often fail to switch columns when they should. Almost all participants who scored >1 standard deviation below the population mean on a reasoning measure of EFs neglected to observe the plus- and minus-sign rules. Almost no one scoring above the mean on the EF measure did so.

Why would persons with poorer EFs obey the plus- and minus-sign rules when instructed on only one task but ignore them when performing exactly the same task after initially being instructed on a second task they are told to ignore? Presumably it is because they failed to clear the irrelevant task from their mental workspace (they failed to inhibit or suppress it), and so it was cluttering up their limited-capacity WM. In neither condition do they fail to remember the plus- and minus-sign rules; it is simply that in the more-complete instruction condition they fail to act according to those rules.

If the source of their problem is, as we suspect, trying to hold more in WM than is necessary, it is reminiscent of problems young children have. By 10 to 12 months, infants can successfully retrieve an object they see hidden first at Place A and then at Place B even after a five-second delay between hiding and retrieval (A-not-B task; Diamond 1985). Not until a year and a half later do toddlers reliably retrieve an object when they see it placed inside a container and then see that container hidden at Place A and then at Place B with a five-second delay between hiding and retrieval (A-not-B with invisible displacement; Diamond et al. 1997).

For adults the two tasks are comparable—remember whether the reward was hidden at A or B on this trial. It appears that infants try to hold too much in mind when faced with invisible displacement (i.e., that the toy is in the container, and the container was hidden at A or B).

Performance of adults with poorer EFs on the Duncan et al. task is also reminiscent of 3-year-olds on the Dimensional Change Card Sort task (Zelazo et al. 1996). Children of 3 years can sort flawlessly by either color or shape, but when instructed to switch the dimension they are sorting by, they continue to sort by the first dimension. Yet, if you ask them, they can tell you that the second dimension is now relevant, what it is, and how to sort by it (Cepeda & Munakata 2007, Zelazo et al. 1996). It is not that they have forgotten which dimension is relevant or how to sort by it (just as adults with poorer EFs have not forgotten the plus- and minus-sign rules). It is simply that members of neither group use that information to guide their behavior.

Disentangling working memory and inhibitory control. If WM and inhibitory control are so intertwined, is it never possible to ask research questions specific to one or the other? No, it is possible. The influence of either WM or inhibitory control can be minimized or controlled for. For example, on the Hearts and Flowers (previously known as the Dots) task, the congruent and incongruent blocks both involve holding one rule in mind. They differ only in the inhibitory demand present in the incongruent block. Counterbalancing order of presentation of the two blocks (to control for possible order or switching effects), poorer performance on the incongruent block provides an indication of the cost of having to inhibit the prepotent tendency to respond on the same side as the stimulus, controlling for memory demands. A Spatial Stroop task places minimal demands on memory because the stimuli themselves tell you where to respond (eyes looking left or right, or arrows pointing left or right), so performance costs in the incongruent condition of a Spatial Stroop task should primarily be due to difficulty inhibiting the prepotent tendency to respond on the same side as the stimulus.

Conversely, reordering items one has heard according to a rule (e.g., alphabetical or numerical order, size, or distance from a point) requires little attentional or response inhibition and so is a relatively pure measure of WM (plus cognitive inhibition). Comparing performance on the Hearts and Flowers task with a control version ("When the eyes look straight down, press on the same side as the stimulus"; "When the eyes look diagonally to the opposite side, press on the opposite side as the stimulus") enables one to determine the performance cost of having to use WM versus just looking at the stimulus to see where to respond.

Is successful inhibitory control but a result of good working memory? There is disagreement among EF researchers over whether inhibition is separate from WM or whether inhibition is a behavioral product of exercising WM, not a separate cognitive skill. A third view is that WM and inhibition depend on the same limited-capacity system so that increasing the demand on either affects one's ability to do the other (e.g., Engle & Kane 2004, Wais & Gazzaley 2011). The view that WM is primary and inhibitory control derivative has a number of supporters (e.g., Egner & Hirsch 2005, Hanania & Smith 2010, Nieuwenhuis & Yeung 2005). That view is held universally among those who do computational modeling (Miller & Cohen 2001, Munakata et al. 2011). Activation alone is seen as sufficient; there is no need to posit suppression or inhibition. If you are holding your goal firmly enough in mind, you will act appropriately. Representation of one's goal can be more or less robust in WM; when it is weak or fuzzy, one's prepotent behavioral inclination might win out in competition with it (e.g., Munakata et al. 2011).

Other researchers find empirically that suppression (inhibitory control) and enhancement (activation of goals in WM) are indeed dissociable (e.g., Davidson et al. 2006, Gernsbacher & Faust 1991, Zanto et al. 2011). For example, when one stimulus is superimposed on another, and subjects are instructed to attend to stimuli in the outer layer, ignoring the background stimuli, older adults show normal enhancement of the to-be-attended stimuli but little or no suppression of the to-be-ignored stimuli, leading Zanto et al. (2011) to conclude that enhancement and suppression rely on distinct mechanisms, that "suppression is not simply lack of enhancement" (p. 660). The debate continues.

One type of failure of EFs is action slips, where we intend to do one thing but do something else instead (the usual, habitual, or most easily elicited action). On such occasions it is as if we let ourselves run on automatic when we should have been paying attention (when we should have been exercising our EFs). Examples would be (*a*) dialing a friend's old phone number when you know your friend has a new number and probably even reminded yourself when you sat down to call or (*b*) wanting to diverge from your normal route home to do an errand but find that you have driven past the turning point and are headed straight for home.

A large proportion of absent-minded errors actually take the form of intact, well-organized segments of skilled action that are suitable for the environmental context most of the time, but not when changed circumstances require some alteration of normal practice (Reason & Mycielska 1982, pp. 39–40).

Such slips appear to be due to not attending to the goal you are holding in mind. You know perfectly well what you meant to do. If asked, you can immediately state the goal. For a few moments or longer, however, your attention wondered, and without any top-down instructions to do otherwise, you simply did the usual.

The cause of such action errors seems fundamentally different from other instances when people appear to act counter to their intent. One example might be eating luscious chocolate cake when you want to lose weight. When I've done this, there was no temporary lapse in attending to the goal of losing weight; I had that clearly in mind. However, there were two competing goals, and chocolate-now won out over weight-loss-later. A different type of example might be impulsively reacting so quickly that your words or actions come out before top-down control can inhibit them and generate a more considered response (see **Figure 1** above). These types of action errors do not seem to arise from a WM lapse or deficit.

Theories of working memory that incorporate aspects of inhibitory control under what is called working memory. Although EF researchers refer to WM as a subcomponent of EFs, many working-memory researchers use the term WM far more broadly so that it becomes roughly synonymous with EFs. For example, Engle and Kane define WM as the ability to (*a*) maintain selected information in an active, easily retrievable state while (*b*) inhibiting (blocking) distractors and interference (i.e., short-term memory + interference control at the attentional and cognitive levels; Conway & Engle 1994; Kane & Engle 2000, 2002). Functions of the central executive in Baddeley's working-memory model (Baddeley & Hitch 1994) include inhibitory control and cognitive flexibility: (*a*) multitasking, (*b*) shifting between tasks or retrieval strategies, and (*c*) the capacity to attend and inhibit in a selective manner. My own preference would be to reserve the term WM to mean only holding information in mind and working with it (working with information not perceptually present).

Working Memory and Selective, Focused Attention

Focusing on information held in mind for several seconds might as easily be called keeping your attention focused on those mental contents for several seconds. WM and selective, focused attention appear to be similar in many ways, including neural basis. The prefrontal-parietal system that supports WM, enabling us to selectively remain focused on information held in mind, tuning out irrelevant thoughts, overlaps substantially with the prefrontal-parietal system that helps us selectively attend to stimuli in our environment, tuning out irrelevant stimuli (e.g., Awh et al. 2000, Awh & Jonides 2001, Gazzaley & Nobre 2012, Ikkai & Curtis 2011, LaBar et al. 1999, Nobre & Stokes 2011). Simulations have demonstrated that developmental improvements in WM can support developmental improvements in selective attention (Stedron et al. 2005). People are quicker to notice, and respond to, stimuli in a location they are holding in WM, and if forced to orient their attention away from a location they are trying to hold in WM, their memory accuracy suffers (Awh & Jonides 2001, Kuo et al. 2012, Wais et al. 2010).

Representative Psychological Tasks Used to Assess Working Memory

Forward-digit span tasks (repeat back items in the order in which you heard them) are a measure of short-term memory, not WM, as they only require holding information in mind. Backward-digit span (say the items back in reverse order) comes closer to being a WM task unless a person can see in his or her mind the items that were said and simply read them off from last to first. Asking subjects to reorder the items they have heard is an excellent WM measure. It might be repeating the numbers they have just heard (perhaps 6, 9, 4, 7) in numerical order (4, 6, 7, 9), repeating items back reordered by size (e.g., reordering cat, elephant, ant, tiger into the order ant, cat, tiger, elephant), or reordered by distance from points A and B to make the most efficient route. Here, A might be work and B might be home, and the items might be grocers, cleaners, gas station, and post office.

A widely used measure of visual-spatial WM is the Corsi Block test (Lezak 1983). A subject watches the tester touch a series of blocks, then the subject is to touch the blocks in the same order. A computerized version of this and of backward digit span appears in the Automated Working Memory Assessment (AWMA) battery (Alloway 2007, Alloway et al. 2009). It has been standardized on 1,470 children ages 5 to 6 years and 1,719 children ages 8 to 9 years (Alloway et al. 2009), and it has excellent construct validity. Another computerized variant of the Corsi Block task appears as part of the CANTAB battery, normed for children through adults (Luciana & Nelson 2002, Robbins et al. 1998). This does not really require mental manipulation. Bialystok's lab has developed a version that requires reordering (hence manipulation; Feng et al. 2007).

In the Self-Ordered Pointing task devised by Petrides (Petrides et al. 1993, Petrides & Milner 1982), subjects see from 3 to 12 items (which might be line drawings, abstract designs, or boxes containing rewards) and are asked to touch one item at a time, in any order, without repeating a choice, making sure to touch all. When rewards are hidden, subjects get feedback after each choice because after having found the reward in a box once, the box will be empty for the rest of that trial. Remembering which items you have touched by their identity is tested by items that are each different from one another, their locations randomly scrambled after each reach (computerized by Diamond et al. 2004). Remembering which items you have touched by their spatial location is tested by using identical items that remain stationary (e.g., Diamond et al. 1997, Wiebe et al. 2010). The CANTAB battery offers a computerized version of the spatial-identity version. Although this task undoubtedly depends on dorsolateral prefrontal cortex [as studies with lesioned monkeys (Petrides 1995), brain-damaged human adults (Owen et al. 1996), and functional neuroimaging in healthy adults (Petrides et al. 1993) have clearly shown], it is not sensitive to the level of dopamine in dorsolateral prefrontal cortex (Collins et al. 1998; Diamond et al. 1997, 2004), although other EF tasks that depend on dorsolateral prefrontal cortex are sensitive to that.

To study WM, researchers often use complex span tasks, also called WM span tasks, such as counting span or reading span (Barrouillet et al. 2009, Case 1995, Conway et al. 2005, Daneman & Carpenter 1980), but since these tasks often require more subcomponents of EFs

than just holding information in mind and manipulating it, they are really EF measures rather than measures of the working-memory subcomponent alone. N-back tasks (also called AX Continuous Performance Tasks, or AX-CPTs) are also often used to assess WM (Owen et al. 2005, Verhaeghen & Basak 2005), although they too require high levels of selective and sustained attention. It would probably cause less confusion if all of these measures were called EF tasks.

Development of Working Memory

The ability to hold information in mind develops very early; even infants and young children can hold one or two things in mind for quite a long time (Diamond 1995, Nelson et al. 2012). Infants of only 9 to 12 months can update the contents of their WM, as seen on tasks such as A-not-B (Bell & Cuevas 2012, Diamond 1985). However, being able to hold many things in mind or do any kind of mental manipulation (e.g., reordering mental representations of objects by size) is far slower to develop and shows a prolonged developmental progression (Cowan et al. 2002, 2011; Crone et al. 2006; Davidson et al. 2006; Luciana et al. 2005).

WM declines during aging (e.g., Fiore et al. 2012, Fournet et al. 2012). Much of that appears to be due to declining inhibitory control making older adults more vulnerable to proactive and retroactive interference (Hedden & Park 2001, Solesio-Jofre et al. 2012) and to distraction (Rutman et al. 2010, Zanto & Gazzaley 2009). Remember that young children, too, are disproportionately challenged by inhibition compared to young adults (Davidson et al. 2006). Improved ability to inhibit interference appears critical to age-related improvements in WM in children (Hale et al. 1997), just as impaired ability to inhibit interference may underlie WM decline in older adults.

Decline in WM with aging and improvement in WM during development are also highly correlated with decline in speed of processing with aging and its improvement during early development (older adults: Rozas et al.

2008, Salthouse 1992, Zimprich & Kurtz 2012; children: Case et al. 1982, Fry & Hale 2000). How to understand the relation between speed of processing and EFs is controversial; the direction of causality might go either way, or a third factor might be causal for both and hence their correlation (Diamond 2002).

COGNITIVE FLEXIBILITY

Cognitive flexibility (the third core EF) builds on the other two and comes in much later in development (Davidson et al. 2006, Garon et al. 2008). One aspect of cognitive flexibility is being able to change perspectives spatially (e.g., "What would this look like if I viewed it from a different direction?") or interpersonally (e.g., "Let me see if I can see this from your point of view"). To change perspectives, we need to inhibit (or deactivate) our previous perspective and load into WM (or activate) a different perspective. It is in this sense that cognitive flexibility requires and builds on inhibitory control and WM. Another aspect of cognitive flexibility involves changing how we think about something (thinking outside the box). For example, if one way of solving a problem isn't working, can we come up with a new way of attacking this or conceiving of this that hadn't been considered before?

Cognitive flexibility also involves being flexible enough to adjust to changed demands or priorities, to admit you were wrong, and to take advantage of sudden, unexpected opportunities. Suppose you were planning to do X, but an amazing opportunity arose to do Y: Do you have the flexibility to take advantage of serendipity?

When a student isn't grasping a concept, we often blame the student: "If only the student were brighter, he or she would have grasped what I'm trying to teach." We could be flexible and consider a different perspective: "What might I, the teacher, do differently? How can I present the material differently, or word the question differently, so this student can succeed?"

There is much overlap between cognitive flexibility and creativity, task switching, and set shifting. Cognitive flexibility is the opposite of rigidity.

Representative Psychological Tasks Used to Assess Cognitive Flexibility

A family of tasks that taps cognitive flexibility includes design fluency (also called the unusual uses task), verbal fluency, and category (or semantic) fluency. You might be asked, for example, how many uses you can think of for a table or how many words you can think of that begin with the letter F, or you might be asked to alternate between the names of animals and the names of foods (Baldo et al. 2001, Baldo & Shimamura 1997, Chi et al. 2012, Van der Elst et al. 2011). First the most common answers come to mind, such as you can eat or write on a table, but then more flexibly minded or creative people can come up with other uses such as dancing on a table, getting under it to stay dry, standing it on its side and using it as shield, chopping it up for firewood, or using it as a percussion instrument.

Cognitive flexibility is often investigated using any of a wide array of task-switching and set-shifting tasks. The oldest of these is probably the Wisconsin Card Sorting Task (Milner 1964, Stuss et al. 2000), one of the classic tests of prefrontal cortex function. Each card in this test can be sorted by color, shape, or number. The task for the participant is to deduce the correct sorting criterion on the basis of feedback and to flexibly switch sorting rules whenever the experimenter gives feedback that the sorting criterion has changed.

Most task-switching paradigms involve two tasks. Those tasks might be indicating whether (a) a letter is a vowel or consonant, (b) a number is even or odd (e.g., Monsell 2003), (c) a stimulus is on the left or right or in the upper or lower quadrant (e.g., Meiran 1996), or (d) a stimulus is one color or another or one shape or another (e.g., Allport & Wylie 2000). Most task-switching tasks involve pressing a key on the right or left, with each key mapped to one feature of each task (e.g., left might be for a consonant or an even number and right for a vowel or an odd number). The stimuli in most task-switching tasks are bivalent, that is, they have a feature relevant to each of the two tasks, and the correct response for one task is incorrect for the other (e.g., for the stimulus "A2," the correct response for the letter task would be to press right because A is a vowel, whereas the correct response for the number task would be to press left because 2 is an even number).

Zelazo and colleagues developed perhaps the simplest possible test of task switching (Zelazo et al. 1996, 2003). The stimuli are bivalent, and the correct response for one task is incorrect for the other, but only one switch occurs during the entire test [called the Dimensional Change Card Sort Test (DCCS)]. First, one is to sort all six cards by one dimension (color or shape), and then one is to sort all the cards according to the other dimension. Memory demands are intentionally minimized by an illustration at each response location of the features mapped to that response and by the experimenter reminding the child of the current sorting criterion on each trial. Children of 3 years can flawlessly sort by either color or shape, but fail to switch even though they know the other dimension is now relevant and they know the rules for sorting by it. Errors seem to occur because of difficulty in inhibiting or overcoming what might be termed "attentional inertia," the tendency to continue to focus attention on what had previously been relevant (Kirkham et al. 2003, Kloo & Perner 2005; recently modeled by Chatham et al. 2012). Once a child of 3 has focused on the "redness" of a red truck, it's difficult for the child to switch mindsets and focus on its "truckness." The child gets stuck in the previous way of thinking about the stimuli. Indeed, in young children, activation in dorsolateral prefrontal cortex is first driven by the previous trial's rule (Wendelken et al. 2012), much as noted above for the neuronal population vector in motor cortex (Georgopoulos et al. 1989), requiring that the prepotent tendency be inhibited.

That inertial tendency never completely disappears. Traces of it can be seen in the heightened reaction times of healthy, young adults when required to switch and respond on the basis of another dimension (e.g., Diamond & Kirkham 2005, Monsell & Driver 2000). No matter how much warning adults are given about which dimension will be relevant on the upcoming trial, how long the period between the forewarning and when the stimulus appears, or how long the period between trials, adults are slower to respond on trials where the relevant dimension switches than on nonswitch trials (Allport & Wylie 2000, Meiran 1996, Rogers & Monsell 1995). What drives this difference on switch and nonswitch trials is the subset of switch trials where the rule changes (which aspect of the stimulus is relevant changes) but where you should respond does not change. We seem to like everything to stay the same (rule and response site) or everything to change (if the rule changes, we're faster if the response site also changes; Crone et al. 2006, Diamond 2009).

Many other tasks tap similar inertial tendencies such as ambiguous figures where, depending on how you look at a line drawing, you might see a vase or the profiles of two faces, for example. Even when informed of the alternatives in an ambiguous figure, 3-year-olds remain stuck in their initial way of perceiving it; they cannot switch perspectives, just as they cannot switch sorting dimensions (Gopnik & Rosati 2001). By age 4 1/2 to 5 years, most children can see both figures in an ambiguous figure and can switch sorting dimensions on the DCCS task (Diamond 2002).

Not until 7 to 9 years of age, however, can children switch flexibly on a trial-by-trial basis as all standard task-switching paradigms require (Davidson et al. 2006, Gupta et al. 2009). For adults, it is trivially easy to execute a block of one task and a block of the other. Even when one of the tasks asks you to do something counter to your prepotent tendency it is not that hard for adults to get in the groove of doing that over a block of trials. Indeed, adults show no cost at all of always responding across a block of trials on the side opposite to where a stimulus appears (Davidson et al. 2006, Lu & Proctor 1995). It's not that demanding for adults to keep doing what they've been doing, even if it is counter-intuitive or counter to their initial inclination; after a while it requires little top-down control. What's far more difficult is switching back and forth between mental sets. Simply put, it is easier to inhibit a dominant response all the time than only some of the time. Cognitive flexibility, overcoming inertial tendencies so you can switch back and forth between mental sets or ways of thinking about the stimuli, is one of the most demanding of the EFs.

A Flanker effect 6 to 10 times larger than what all labs report is obtained simply by having subjects switch between focusing on the center stimulus and focusing on the Flankers, assessing the Flanker effect only on trials where subjects are to focus on the same place they focused on the previous trial (i.e., nonswitch trials). Moreover, in the mixed block the Flanker effect (on nonswitch trials) is robust in the face of variations in stimulus parameters (such as size), unlike the Flanker effect in the standard single-task block (Munro et al. 2006).

Development of Cognitive Flexibility

A very easy type of switching involves continuing to focus on the same dimension (on the same aspect of the stimuli) but reversing the stimulus-response mappings. This is called reversal, within-dimension switching, or intradimensional shifting (e.g., Kendler & Kendler 1959, Kendler et al. 1972, Roberts et al. 1988). For example, in Task 1 you might press left for circle and right for triangle, while in Task 2 that would be reversed, so you'd press right for circle and left for triangle. Children only $2^1/_2$ years of age can succeed at such tasks (Brooks et al. 2003, Perner & Lang 2002). The ability to change where you respond (switch stimulus-response mappings, as on reversal tasks) develops earlier than the ability to change how you think about the stimuli or change what aspect of the stimuli you attend to. Although children cannot usually succeed at the DCCS task until $4^1/_2$ to 5 years of age (see above), if color is a property of the background of the card rather than of the shape pictured on the card (so a truck

is always a truck and the background is always red, instead of the shape itself being colored so that from one perspective a truck is a truck but from another perspective it is a red thing), children can succeed by 3 to $3^1/_2$ years of age (Diamond et al. 2005, Kloo & Perner 2005).

Task switching improves during child development and declines during aging (Cepeda et al. 2001, Kray 2006). Older adults slow down on a mixed block (where on any trial it might be Task 1 or Task 2), hence the difference in their speed on mixed blocks versus single-task blocks is much greater than that of young adults, but unlike young adults they are almost as slow on repeat trials in a mixed block as on switch trials (Kray & Lindenberger 2000, Mayr & Liebscher 2001, Meiran & Gotler 2001). Children show much larger differences in their speed (like older adults) and accuracy (unlike older adults) on mixed blocks versus single-task blocks than do young adults (Cepeda et al. 2001, Cohen et al. 2001).

Young children and older adults tend to exercise EFs in response to environmental demands (reactively), whereas older children and young adults tend to be more planful and anticipatory (recruiting EFs proactively; Czernochowski et al. 2010, Karayanidis et al. 2011, Munakata et al. 2012).

A HIGHER-ORDER EXECUTIVE FUNCTION: RELATIONAL REASONING/LOGICAL REASONING/FLUID INTELLIGENCE

Fluid intelligence is the ability to reason, problem solve, and to see patterns or relations among items (Ferrer et al. 2009). It includes both inductive and deductive logical reasoning. It involves being able to figure out the abstract relations underlying analogies. It is synonymous with the reasoning and problem-solving subcomponents of EFs (see **Figure 4**). No surprise then that measures of fluid intelligence [e.g., Raven's Matrices (Raven 2000)] are highly correlated with independent measures of EFs

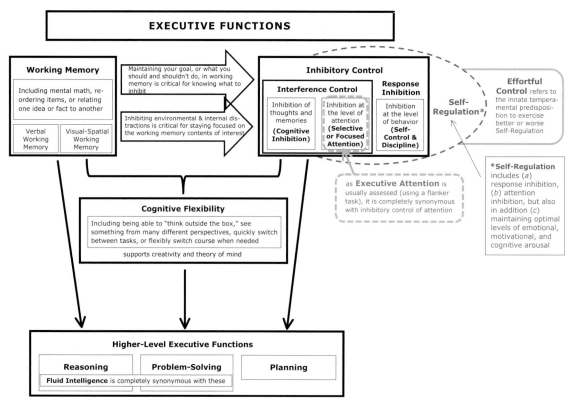

Figure 4

Executive functions and related terms.

(Conway et al. 2003, Duncan et al. 2008, Kane & Engle 2002, Roca et al. 2010).

DIFFERENCES AND SIMILARITIES BETWEEN EXECUTIVE FUNCTIONS AND RELATED TERMS

Self-regulation refers to processes that enable us to maintain optimal levels of emotional, motivational, and cognitive arousal (Eisenberg et al. 2007, Liew 2011). It refers primarily to control and regulation of one's emotions (Eisenberg et al. 2010, Mischel & Ayduk 2002) and overlaps substantially with inhibitory control (see **Figure 4**). EF researchers have historically focused more on thoughts, attention, and actions [and hence more on lateral prefrontal cortex (dorso- and ventrolateral prefrontal)]; self-regulation researchers have focused more on emotions [and hence more on medial prefrontal cortex (especially orbitofrontal) and on the parasympathetic nervous system]. EF researchers have addressed emotions primarily as problems to be inhibited; self-regulation researchers also embrace the importance of motivation and interest as helpful emotional responses for achieving one's goals (Blair & Diamond 2008). Historically, self-regulation has been assessed through (*a*) adult ratings of children's behavior observed in real-world settings such as home or school, and (*b*) observation of children's behavior when they have to delay gratification in an emotionally laden "hot" situation (Mischel et al. 1989) or in a frustrating situation (Kochanska et al. 2009). Historically, EFs have been assessed directly from children's behavior, but on arbitrary laboratory-based tests far removed from the real world in fairly emotionally neutral "cool" situations.

Effortful control (Rothbart & Bates 2006) refers to an aspect of temperament. It is an innate predisposition to exercise self-regulation with ease (e.g., easily able to slow down or lower one's voice), perhaps even being too regulated (lacking in spontaneity) versus finding self-regulation difficult or less natural. It is usually assessed by parental report (Goldsmith 1996, Rothbart et al. 2001).

Executive attention (Posner & DiGirolamo 1998) refers to the top-down regulation of attention. It is usually assessed using measures of selective attention such as the Flanker task (Fan et al. 2002, Rueda et al. 2005). Much confusion has been engendered by the overly broad use of the term executive attention to apply to such skills as WM capacity (Engle 2002) and response inhibition or the resolution of response conflict (as in a Simon-type task; Jones et al. 2003).

IT IS *NOT* ALWAYS BENEFICIAL TO EXERT EXECUTIVE FUNCTIONS OR TOP-DOWN CONTROL

We need lateral prefrontal cortex (EFs) when learning something new. When something is new, those who recruit lateral prefrontal cortex most often perform best (Duncan & Owen 2000, Poldrack et al. 2005). However, after something is no longer new, those who perform best often recruit lateral prefrontal cortex least (Chein & Schneider 2005, Garavan et al. 2000, Landau et al. 2007, Milham et al. 2003). When you are really good at something, you are using top-down control very little if at all (as in *Zen in the Art of Archery*; Herrigel 1999). Indeed, when you are truly good at something, thinking about what you are doing often gets in the way of performing well. Thus, early in training, disrupting lateral prefrontal cortex function impairs task performance, but disrupting lateral prefrontal function after a task is familiar can improve performance (Miller et al. 2003).

Phylogenetically older brain regions have had far longer to perfect their functioning; they can subserve task performance ever so much more efficiently than can prefrontal cortex. You might say that your goal in trying to master something is to have it become so well learned that prefrontal cortex and EFs are no longer needed for it. Instead, performance is handed off to older regions that have had thousands of more years of evolutionary time to perfect their functioning and can subserve task performance ever so much more efficiently than can prefrontal. A child may know intellectually (at the level of prefrontal cortex) that s/he should not hit another, but in the heat of the moment if that knowledge has not become automatic (passed on from prefrontal to subcortical regions), the child will hit another (though if asked, s/he knows not to do that). It's the difference between knowing what you should do at an intellectual level and having it become second nature. The way something becomes second nature or automatic is through repeated practice. This is consistent with what Ericsson has repeatedly found to be key for being truly excellent at anything (e.g., Ericsson et al. 2009), i.e., hours and hours of practice.

CANARY IN THE COAL MINE: EXECUTIVE FUNCTIONS AS AN EARLY WARNING SYSTEM

EFs and prefrontal cortex are the first to suffer, and suffer disproportionately, if something is not right in your life. They suffer first, and most, if you are stressed (Arnsten 1998, Liston et al. 2009, Oaten & Cheng 2005), sad (Hirt et al. 2008, von Hecker & Meiser 2005), lonely (Baumeister et al. 2002, Cacioppo & Patrick 2008, Campbell et al. 2006, Tun et al. 2012), sleep deprived (Barnes et al. 2012, Huang et al. 2007), or not physically fit (Best 2010, Chaddock et al. 2011, Hillman et al. 2008). Any of these can cause you to appear to have a disorder of EFs, such as ADHD, when you do not. You can see the deleterious effects of stress, sadness, loneliness, and lack of physical health or fitness at the physiological and neuroanatomical level in prefrontal cortex and at the behavioral level in worse EFs (poorer reasoning and problem

PATHS: Promoting Alternative Thinking Strategies

CSRP: Chicago School Readiness Project

solving, forgetting things, and impaired ability to exercise discipline and self-control).

If we want schoolchildren, workers, or business executives to have better attention and concentration, be better able to reason and problem solve, we cannot ignore stresses in their lives. Each schoolchild and each employee will do better if that individual's passionate interests can be engaged, energizing the person. They will perform better and show better EFs if they feel they are in a supportive community they can count on. They will perform better and show better EFs if their bodies are strong and healthy. A school or corporation that ignores students' or employees' emotional, social, or physical needs is likely to find that those unmet needs will work against achieving performance goals.

TRAINING AND PRACTICE IMPROVE EXECUTIVE FUNCTIONS

EFs can be improved (Diamond & Lee 2011, Klingberg 2010). The strongest evidence for an activity improving children's EFs exists for CogMed© computerized training (Bergman Nutley et al. 2011, Holmes et al. 2009, Klingberg et al. 2005, Thorell et al. 2009), a combination of computerized and interactive games (Mackey et al. 2011), task-switching computerized training (Karbach & Kray 2009), Taekwondo traditional martial arts (Lakes & Hoyt 2004), and two add-ons to school curricula, Promoting Alternative Thinking Strategies (PATHS; Riggs et al. 2006) and the Chicago School Readiness Project (CSRP; Raver et al. 2008, 2011). The above-referenced studies used random assignment and included an active control group and pre- and post-intervention measures; they found convincing transfer to more than one objective measure of EFs on which the children had not been trained. Studies that have thus far looked at the benefits to children's EFs from aerobics (Davis et al. 2011, Kamijo et al. 2011), mindfulness (Flook et al. 2010), yoga (Manjunath & Telles 2001), Tools of the Mind early childhood curriculum

(Diamond et al. 2007), and Montessori curriculum (Lillard & Else-Quest 2006) have found positive results but lacked one or more of the above design features. With adults, the focus has most often been on computerized training, especially of WM. Recent reviews of such computerized EF training with adults are cautiously optimistic but note important design flaws (Morrison & Chein 2011, Shipstead et al. 2012).

A few principles hold regardless of the EF program or intervention:

1. The children most behind on EFs (including disadvantaged children) benefit the most from any EF intervention or program (Flook et al. 2010, Karbach & Kray 2009, Lakes & Hoyt 2004). Hence, early EF training might level the playing field by reducing social disparities in EFs, thus heading off social disparities in academic achievement and health (O'Shaughnessy et al. 2003).

2. EF training appears to transfer, but transfer from computerized WM or reasoning training has been narrow (e.g., computer training on spatial WM transfers to other measures of spatial WM but not to visual WM or other EF subcomponents; Bergman Nutley et al. 2011). EF gains from training in task switching (Karbach & Kray 2009), traditional martial arts (Lakes & Hoyt 2004) and school curricula (Raver et al. 2011, Riggs et al. 2006) have been wider, perhaps because the programs address EFs more globally. For example, training task switching (which arguably requires all three core EFs) transferred not only to an untrained task-switching task, but also to inhibition (Stroop interference), verbal and nonverbal WM, and reasoning (Karbach & Kray 2009).

3. EF demands need to be continually incrementally increased or few gains are seen (Bergman Nutley et al. 2011, Holmes et al. 2009, Klingberg et al. 2005). There may be two reasons for that. (*a*) If difficulty doesn't increase, the activity becomes boring and people lose interest.

(Which raises a general question about the appropriateness of a control group where difficulty does not increase, if that means the groups also differ in their sustained interest.) (*b*) You need to keep pushing yourself to do better or you stop improving. Similarly, Ericsson et al. (2009) emphasize that the practice that leads to expertise at anything consists of trying to master what is just beyond your current level of competence and comfort.

4. Repeated practice is key. Whether EF gains are seen depends on the amount of time spent doggedly working on those skills, pushing oneself to improve (Klingberg et al. 2005). School curricula shown to improve EFs train and challenge EFs throughout the day, embedding that in all activities, not only in a module (which may also have the benefit of varying the content and kind of EF practice; Diamond et al. 2007, Lillard & Else-Quest 2006, Riggs et al. 2006).

5. The largest differences between intervention groups and controls are consistently found on the most demanding EF tasks and task conditions. It is often only in pushing the limits of children's EF skills that group differences emerge (Davis et al. 2011, Diamond et al. 2007, Manjunath & Telles 2001). For example, in their first year of data collection, Farran & Wilson (2011) found no EF benefits from Tools of the Mind, but their assessment tasks were plagued by ceiling and floor effects.

At any age across the life cycle EFs can be improved, including in the elderly and in infants. There has been much work with excellent results on improving EFs in the elderly by improving physical fitness (Erickson & Kramer 2009, Voss et al. 2011). Increasingly, research is also showing promising results from computerized EF training with older adults (Lövdén et al. 2010, Richmond et al. 2011). Much but not all of the work on improving EFs in young adults has focused on computerized training (Morrison & Chein 2011, Muraven 2010,

Shipstead et al. 2012). Exposure to bilingual input has been one of the foci, though not the only focus, of work on accelerating the development of EFs in infants (Kovács & Mehler 2009, Wass et al. 2011). [Bilingualism appears to accelerate EF development during childhood and preserve EFs longer during aging (e.g., Bialystok & Viswanathan 2009), but its chief benefit appears to be in improving speed of processing. For example, bilingual older adults do not show a smaller Simon effect (i.e., do not show better inhibitory control on the task) but rather are faster on all trials (Bialystok et al. 2004).]

No one has yet looked at what distinguishes those who benefit from EF training from those who don't, other than the amount of practice and baseline EFs. We know little about whether benefits last or how long they might last, or about what dose or frequency is best. What factors affect how long benefits last? Are refresher or booster sessions needed, and if so at what intervals and for how long? Are different programs more beneficial at different ages? Who might benefit most from which activity? Does the optimal dose or frequency vary by age? These questions are particularly pressing because "interventions that achieve even small improvements in [inhibitory control] for individuals could shift the entire distribution of outcomes in a salutary direction and yield large improvements in health, wealth, and crime rate for a nation" (Moffitt et al. 2011, p. 2694).

In conclusion, EFs are critical for many of the skills that most people would agree will be important for success in the twenty-first century—such as creativity, flexibility, self-control, and discipline. EFs make it possible for us to mentally play with ideas, quickly and flexibly adapt to changed circumstances, take time to consider what to do next, resist temptations, stay focused, and meet novel, unanticipated challenges.

We share with even simple organisms the ability to be conditioned (to be affected by our experience), and we, like them, come into the world with certain biological predispositions. However, we are able to hold in mind things we cannot see and to inhibit our predispositions and conditioned responses, however fragile and incomplete those abilities may be. We have the possibility to exercise choice and control over what we do. Now is an exciting time because we have the tools to answer many of the unresolved questions about EFs. Finding the answers to these questions is critical because the ability of our generation and succeeding ones to meet the world's challenges may depend on that.

SUMMARY POINTS

1. EFs and prefrontal cortex are the first to suffer and suffer disproportionately if you are stressed, sad, lonely, or not physically fit. Because EFs are critical for academic achievement, a society that wants its students to excel needs to take seriously that the different parts of the human being are fundamentally interrelated. If emotional, social, or physical needs are ignored, those unmet needs will work against good EFs and hence against academic excellence. A person may be incorrectly diagnosed with an EF disorder when what is really wrong is that stress, sadness, loneliness, lack of sleep, or lack of physical exercise in that person's life are impairing his ability to display the EFs of which he is capable.

2. It's extremely important to help young children have good executive functioning because EFs early in life have been found to predict lifelong achievement, health, wealth, and quality of life.

3. EFs are trainable and can be improved at any age—probably by many different approaches.

4. Repeated practice is key; exercising and challenging executive functions improves them and thus is beneficial for our mental health, much as physical exercise improves our physical fitness and is beneficial for our bodily health.

5. It is *not* always beneficial to exert EFs; sometimes thinking about what you are doing and trying to exercise top-down control gets in the way of optimal performance.

6. What is commonly called "fluid intelligence" is the reasoning and problem-solving component of EFs; like other EFs, it can be improved through training and practice.

7. Not all tasks measure what their name implies (e.g., "working memory span" tasks often measure EFs more generally and not just WM). Two widely used measures of response inhibition—the go/no-go and stop-signal tasks—differ from many real-world instances of inhibitory control and appear to be unusual cases of when inhibitory control is needed rather than paradigmatic examples.

8. Although "interference control" (selective attention and cognitive inhibition) is usually grouped under inhibitory control, it may more properly belong with WM. Focusing on information held in working memory might as easily be called keeping your attention focused on those mental contents. Empirically, selective attention and WM could hardly be more tightly linked. Cognitive inhibition is inhibition in the service of protecting WM's mental workspace (keeping irrelevant information out and deleting no-longer-relevant information from WM). It coheres more strongly with working memory measures than with measures of other aspects of inhibition.

FUTURE ISSUES

1. What can parents do to aid the development of EFs in their children?

2. For programs and interventions that appear to improve EFs—which are best; what are the best doses, durations, and frequency; how long do benefits last; and does this differ by age, gender, cultural group, or type of program?

3. Given that EF training disproportionately benefits those with poorer EFs and disadvantaged children have poorer EFs, might early EF training reduce social disparities in achievement and health by reducing the EF gap before school entry?

4. Which activities not yet studied might improve EFs? Excellent candidates include the arts (such as theater, orchestra, dance, choir, and filmmaking), caring for an animal, service activities to improve the local or global community, and athletic activities (such as rock climbing, basketball, soccer, capoeira, and rowing crew). Will the type of program end up mattering more, or will the way it is done be more significant?

5. There are so many diverse forms of inhibitory control. What are the commonalities and differences among them? And how do they relate to working memory—can working memory account for all, some, or none of them?

6. Much more in-depth and detailed study is needed of the roles of subcortical regions in EFs.

7. What roles do neurotransmitters other than dopamine and norepinephrine, and interactions among neurotransmitters, play in EFs?

8. Given that sex hormones affect neurotransmitter levels, what sex differences might be found, and how might those impact proper dosages of medications that affect EFs?

DISCLOSURE STATEMENT

The author is not aware of any affiliations, memberships, funding, or financial holdings that might be perceived as affecting the objectivity of this review.

ACKNOWLEDGMENTS

I would like to express my gratitude to Silvia Bunge, Patti Reuter-Lorenz, Yuko Munakata, and Daphne Ling for extremely helpful comments on an earlier version of this manuscript. I would also like to express my gratitude for financial support from NIDA R01 #DA019685 during the writing of this article.

LITERATURE CITED

Alain C, Woods DL. 1999. Age-related changes in processing auditory stimuli during visual attention: evidence for deficits in inhibitory control and sensory memory. *Psychol. Aging* 14:507–19

Alloway TP. 2007. Working memory, reading and mathematical skills in children with developmental coordination disorder. *J. Exp. Child Psychol.* 96:20–36

Alloway TP, Gathercole SE, Kirkwood H, Elliott J. 2009. The cognitive and behavioral characteristics of children with low working memory. *Child Dev.* 80:606–21

Alloway TP, Gathercole SE, Willis C, Adams A-M. 2004. A structural analysis of working memory and related cognitive skills in young children. *J. Exp. Child Psychol.* 87:85–106

Allport A, Wylie G. 2000. Task switching, stimulus-response bindings, and negative priming. In *Control of Cognitive Processes: Attention and Performance XVII*, ed. S Monsell, J Driver, pp. 35–70. Cambridge, MA: MIT Press

Anderson MC, Levy B. 2009. Suppressing unwanted memories. *Curr. Dir. Psychol. Sci.* 18:189–94

Arnsten AFT. 1998. The biology of being frazzled. *Science* 280:1711–12

Aron AR. 2011. From reactive to proactive and selective control: developing a richer model for stopping inappropriate responses. *Biol. Psychiatry* 69:e55–68

Awh E, Anllo-Vento L, Hillyard SA. 2000. The role of spatial selective attention in working memory for locations: evidence from event-related potentials. *J. Cogn. Neurosci.* 12:840–47

Awh E, Jonides J. 2001. Overlapping mechanisms of attention and spatial working memory. *Trends Cogn. Sci.* 5:119–26

Baddeley AD, Hitch GJ. 1994. Developments in the concept of working memory. *Neuropsychology* 8:485–93

Bailey CE. 2007. Cognitive accuracy and intelligent executive function in the brain and in business. *Ann. N. Y. Acad. Sci.* 1118:122–41

Baldo JV, Shimamura AP. 1997. Letter and category fluency in patients with frontal lobe lesions. *Neuropsychology* 12:259–67

Baldo JV, Shimamura AP, Delis DC, Kramer J, Kaplan E. 2001. Verbal and design fluency in patients with frontal lobe lesions. *J. Int. Neuropsychol. Soc.* 7:586–96

Baler RD, Volkow ND. 2006. Drug addiction: the neurobiology of disrupted self-control. *Trends Mol. Med.* 12:559–66

Band GP, van der Molen MW, Logan GD. 2003. Horse-race model simulations of the stop-signal procedure. *Acta Psychol. (Amsterdam)* 112:105–42

Barch DM. 2005. The cognitive neuroscience of schizophrenia. *Annu. Rev. Psychol.* 1:321–53

Barnes ME, Gozal D, Molfese DL. 2012. Attention in children with obstructive sleep apnoea: an event-related potentials study. *Sleep Med.* 13:368–77

Barr RA, Giambra LM. 1990. Age-related decrement in auditory selective attention. *Psychol. Aging* 5:597–99

Barrouillet P, Gavens N, Vergauwe E, Gaillard V, Camos V. 2009. Working memory span development: a time-based resource-sharing model account. *Dev. Psychol.* 45:477–90

Baumeister RF, Twenge JM, Nuss CK. 2002. Effects of social exclusion on cognitive processes: anticipated aloneness reduces intelligent thought. *J. Pers. Soc. Psychol.* 83:817–27

Bell MA, Cuevas K. 2012. Psychobiology of executive function in early development. In *Executive Function in Preschool Age Children: Integrating Measurement, Neurodevelopment and Translational Research*, ed. P McCardle, L Freund, JA Griffin. Washington, DC: Am. Psychol. Assoc. In press

Bergman Nutley S, Söderqvist S, Bryde S, Thorell LB, Humphreys K, Klingberg T. 2011. Gains in fluid intelligence after training non-verbal reasoning in 4-year-old children: a controlled, randomized study. *Dev. Sci.* 14:591–601

Best JR. 2010. Effects of physical activity on children's executive function: contributions of experimental research on aerobic exercise. *Dev. Rev.* 30:331–551

Bialystok E, Craik FIM, Klein R, Mythili V. 2004. Bilingualism, aging, and cognitive control: evidence from the Simon task. *Psychol. Aging* 19:290–303

Bialystok E, Viswanathan M. 2009. Components of executive control with advantages for bilingual children in two cultures. *Cognition* 112:494–500

Blair C, Diamond A. 2008. Biological processes in prevention and intervention: the promotion of self-regulation as a means of preventing school failure. *Dev. Psychopathol.* 20:899–911

Blair C, Razza RP. 2007. Relating effortful control, executive function, and false-belief understanding to emerging math and literacy ability in kindergarten. *Child Dev.* 78:647–63

Bodrova E, Leong DJ. 2007. *Tools of the Mind: The Vygotskian Approach to Early Childhood education.* New York: Merrill/Prentice Hall

Borella E, Carretti B, Pelgrina S. 2010. The specific role of inhibition in reading comprehension in good and poor comprehenders. *J. Learn. Disabil.* 43:541–52

Broidy LM, Nagin DS, Tremblay RE, Brame B, Dodge KA, Fergusson DE. 2003. Developmental trajectories of childhood disruptive behaviors and adolescent delinquency: a six-site cross-national study. *Dev. Psychol.* 30:222–45

Brooks P, Hanauer JB, Padowska B, Rosman H. 2003. The role of selective attention in preschoolers' rule use in a novel dimensional card sort. *Cogn. Dev.* 117:1–21

Brown TE, Landgraf JM. 2010. Improvements in executive function correlate with enhanced performance and functioning and health-related quality of life: evidence from 2 large, double-blind, randomized, placebo-controlled trials in ADHD. *Postgrad. Med.* 122:42–51

Bruner JS, Olver RR, Greenfield PM. 1966. *Studies in Cognitive Growth: A Collaboration at the Center for Cognitive Studies.* New York: Wiley

Bunge SA, Dudukovic NM, Thomason ME, Vaidya CJ, Gabrieli JDE. 2002. Immature frontal lobe contributions to cognitive control in children: evidence from fMRI. *Neuron* 33:301–11

Burgess PW, Simons JS. 2005. Theories of frontal lobe executive function: clinical applications. In *Effectiveness of Rehabilitation for Cognitive Deficits,* ed. PW Halligan, DT Wade, pp. 211–31. New York: Oxford Univ. Press

Cacioppo J, Patrick W. 2008. *Loneliness: Human Nature and the Need for Social Connection.* New York: Norton

Campbell WK, Krusemark EA, Dyckman KA, Brunell AB, McDowell JE, et al. 2006. A magnetoencephalography investigation of neural correlates for social exclusion and self-control. *Soc. Neurosci.* 1:124–34

Carr LA, Nigg JT, Henderson JM. 2006. Attentional versus motor inhibition in adults with attention-deficit/hyperactivity disorder. *Neuropsychology* 20:430–41

Case R. 1995. Capacity-based explanations of working memory growth: a brief history and reevaluation. In *Memory Performance and Competencies: Issues in Growth and Development,* ed. FE Weinert, W Schneider, pp. 23–44. Mahwah, NJ: Erlbaum

Case R, Kurland DM, Goldberg J. 1982. Operational efficiency and the growth of short-term memory span. *J. Exp. Child Psychol.* 33:386–404

Casey BJ. 2001. Development and disruption of inhibitory mechanisms of attention. In *Mechanisms of Cognitive Development: The Carnegie Symposium on Cognition,* ed. RS Siegler, JL McClelland, Vol. 28, pp. 327–49. Hillsdale, NJ: Erlbaum

Cepeda NJ, Kramer AF, Gonzalez de Sather JC. 2001. Changes in executive control across the life span: examination of task-switching performance. *Dev. Psychol.* 37:715–30

Cepeda NJ, Munakata Y. 2007. Why do children perseverate when they seem to know better: graded working memory, or directed inhibition? *Psychon. Bull. Rev.* 14:1058–65

Chaddock L, Hillman CH, Buck SM, Cohen NJ. 2011. Aerobic fitness and executive control of relational memory in preadolescent children. *Med. Sci. Sports Exerc.* 43:344–49

Chatham CH, Yerys BE, Munakata Y. 2012. Why won't you do what I want? The informative failures of children and models. *Cogn. Dev.* In press

Chein JM, Schneider W. 2005. Neuroimaging studies of practice-related change: fMRI and meta-analytic evidence of a domain-general control network for learning. *Cogn. Brain Res.* 25:607–23

Chi YK, Kim TH, Han JW, Lee SB, Park JH, et al. 2012. Impaired design fluency is a marker of pathological cognitive aging: results from the Korean longitudinal study on health and aging. *Psychiatry Invest.* 9:59–64

Cohen JR, Berkman ET, Lieberman MD. 2012. Ventrolateral PFC as a self-control muscle and how to use it without trying. *Oxford Handb. Frontal Lobe Funct.* In press

Cohen S, Bixenman M, Meiran N, Diamond A. 2001. Task switching in children. Presented at *S. Carolina Bicentenn. Symp. Attention,* Univ. S. Carolina, Columbia

Collins A, Koechlin E. 2012. Reasoning, learning, and creativity: frontal lobe function and human decision-making. *PLoS Biol.* 10:e1001293

Collins P, Roberts AC, Dias R, Everitt BJ, Robbins TW. 1998. Perseveration and strategy in a novel spatial self-ordered task for nonhuman primates: effect of excitotoxic lesions and dopamine depletions of the prefrontal cortex. *J. Cogn. Neurosci.* 10:332–54

Conway ARA, Engle RW. 1994. Working memory and retrieval: a resource-dependent inhibition model. *J. Exp. Psychol.: Gen.* 123:354–73

Conway ARA, Kane MJ, Bunting MF, Hambrick DZ, Wilhelm O, Engle RW. 2005. Working memory span tasks: a methodological review and user's guide. *Psychon. Bull. Rev.* 12:769–86

Conway ARA, Kane MJ, Engle RW. 2003. Working memory capacity and its relation to general intelligence. *Trends Cogn. Sci.* 7:547–52

Summarizes pioneering research on startling and profound effects of loneliness.

Cowan N, AuBuchon AM, Gilchrist AL, Ricker TJ, Saults JS. 2011. Age differences in visual working memory capacity: not based on encoding limitations. *Dev. Sci.* 14:1066–74

Cowan N, Saults JS, Elliot EM. 2002. The search for what is fundamental in the development of working memory. *Adv. Child Dev. Behav.* 29:1–49

Cragg L, Nation K. 2008. Go or no-go? Developmental improvements in the efficiency of response inhibition in mid-childhood. *Dev. Sci.* 11:819–27

Crescioni AW, Ehrlinger J, Alquist JL, Conlon KE, Baumeister RF, et al. 2011. High trait self-control predicts positive health behaviors and success in weight loss. *J. Health Psychol.* 16:750–59

Crone EA, Wendelken C, Donohue SE, van Leijenhorst L, Bunge SA. 2006. Neurocognitive development of the ability to manipulate information in working memory. *Proc. Natl. Acad. Sci. USA* 103:9315–20

Czernochowski D, Nessler D, Friedman D. 2010. On why not to rush older adults—relying on reactive cognitive control can effectively reduce errors at the expense of slowed responses. *Psychophysiology* 47:637–46

Daneman M, Carpenter P. 1980. Individual differences in working memory and reading. *J. Verbal Learn. Verbal Behav.* 19:450–66

Darowski ES, Helder E, Zacks RT, Hasher L, Hambrick DZ. 2008. Age-related differences in cognition: the role of distraction control. *Neuropsychology* 22:638–44

Davidson MC, Amso D, Anderson LC, Diamond A. 2006. Development of cognitive control and executive functions from 4–13 years: evidence from manipulations of memory, inhibition, and task switching. *Neuropsychologia* 44:2037–78

Davis CL, Tomporowski PD, McDowell JE, Austin BP, Miller PH, et al. 2011. Exercise improves executive function and achievement and alters brain activation in overweight children: a randomized, controlled trial. *Health Psychol.* 30:91–98

Davis JC, Marra CA, Najafzadeh M, Lui-Ambrose T. 2010. The independent contribution of executive functions to health related quality of life in older women. *BMC Geriatr.* 10:16–23

de Jong R, Coles MGH, Logan GD. 1995. Strategies and mechanisms in nonselective and selective inhibitory motor control. *J. Exp. Psychol.: Hum. Percept. Perform.* 21:498–511

Denson TF, Pederson WC, Friese M, Hahm A, Roberts L. 2011. Understanding impulsive aggression: Angry rumination and reduced self-control capacity are mechanisms underlying the provocation-aggression relationship. *Pers. Soc. Psychol. Bull.* 37:850–62

D'Esposito M, Postle BR, Ballard D, Lease J. 1999. Maintenance versus manipulation of information held in working memory: an event-related fMRI study. *Brain Cogn.* 41:66–86

Diamond A. 1985. Development of the ability to use recall to guide action, as indicated by infants' performance on A-not-B. *Child Dev.* 56:868–83

Diamond A. 1990. Developmental time course in human infants and infant monkeys, and the neural bases, of inhibitory control in reaching. *Ann. N. Y. Acad. Sci.* 608:637–76

Diamond A. 1991. Neuropsychological insights into the meaning of object concept development. In *The Epigenesis of Mind: Essays on Biology and Cognition*, ed. S Carey, R Gelman, pp. 67–110. Hillsdale, NJ: Erlbaum

Diamond A. 1995. Evidence of robust recognition memory early in life even when assessed by reaching behavior. *J. Exp. Child Psychol.* 59:419–56

Diamond A. 2002. Normal development of prefrontal cortex from birth to young adulthood: cognitive functions, anatomy, and biochemistry. In *Principles of Frontal Lobe Function*, ed. DT Stuss, RT Knight, pp. 466–503. London: Oxford Univ. Press

Diamond A. 2005. Attention-deficit disorder (attention-deficit/hyperactivity disorder without hyperactivity): a neurobiologically and behaviorally distinct disorder from attention-deficit/hyperactivity disorder (with hyperactivity). *Dev. Psychopathol.* 17:807–25

Diamond A. 2009. All or none hypothesis: a global-default mode that characterizes the brain and mind. *Dev. Psychol.* 45:130–38

Diamond A, Barnett WS, Thomas J, Munro S. 2007. Preschool program improves cognitive control. *Science* 318:1387–88

Diamond A, Briand L, Fossella J, Gehlbach L. 2004. Genetic and neurochemical modulation of prefrontal cognitive functions in children. *Am. J. Psychiatry* 16:125–32

Diamond A, Carlson SM, Beck DM. 2005. Preschool children's performance in task switching on the dimensional change card sort task: Separating the dimensions aids the ability to switch. *Dev. Neuropsychol.* 28:689–729

Diamond A, Kirkham NZ. 2005. Not quite as grown-up as we like to think: parallels between cognition in childhood and adulthood. *Psychol. Sci.* 16:291–97

Diamond A, Kirkham NZ, Amso D. 2002. Conditions under which young children can hold two rules in mind and inhibit a prepotent response. *Dev. Psychol.* 38:352–62

Diamond A, Lee K. 2011. Interventions and programs demonstrated to aid executive function development in children 4–12 years of age. *Science* 333:959–64

Diamond A, Prevor M, Callender G, Druin DP. 1997. Prefrontal cortex cognitive deficits in children treated early and continuously for PKU. *Monogr. Soc. Res. Child Dev.* 62(Ser. No. 252):1–7

Duncan GJ, Dowsett CJ, Claessens A, Magnuson K, Huston AC, et al. 2007. School readiness and later achievement. *Dev. Psychol.* 43:1428–46

Duncan J, Owen AM. 2000. Common regions of the human frontal lobe recruited by diverse cognitive demands. *Trends Neurosci.* 23:475–83

Duncan J, Parr A, Woolgar A, Thompson R, Bright P, et al. 2008. Goal neglect and Spearman's g: competing parts of a complex task. *J. Exp. Psychol.: Gen.* 137:131–48

Eakin L, Minde K, Hechtman L, Ochs E, Krane E, et al. 2004. The marital and family functioning of adults with ADHD and their spouses. *J. Attention Disord.* 8:1–10

Egner T, Hirsch J. 2005. Cognitive control mechanisms resolve conflict through cortical amplification of task-relevant information. *Nat. Neurosci.* 8:1784–90

Eigsti I, Zayas V, Mischel W, Shoda Y, Ayduk O, et al. 2006. Predicting cognitive control from preschool to late adolescence and young adulthood. *Psychol. Sci.* 17:478–84

Eisenberg N, Hofer J, Vaughan C. 2007. Effortful control and its socioemotional consequences. In *Handbook of Emotion Regulation*, ed. JJ Gross, pp. 287–306. New York: Guilford

Eisenberg N, Spinrad TL, Eggum ND. 2010. Emotion-related self-regulation and its relation to children's maladjustment. *Annu. Rev. Clin. Psychol.* 6:495–525

Eldreth DA, Patterson MD, Porcelli AJ, Biswal BB, Rebbechi D, Rypma B. 2006. Evidence for multiple manipulation processes in prefrontal cortex. *Brain Res.* 1123:145–56

Engelhardt PE, Nigg JT, Carr LA, Ferreira F. 2008. Cognitive inhibition and working memory in attention-deficit/hyperactivity disorder. *J. Abnorm. Psychol.* 117:591–605

Engle RW. 2002. Working memory capacity as executive attention. *Curr. Dir. Psychol. Sci.* 11:19–23

Engle RW, Kane MJ. 2004. Executive attention, working memory capacity, and a two-factor theory of cognitive control. In *The Psychology of Learning and Motivation*, ed. B Ross, pp. 145–99. New York: Elsevier

Erickson KL, Kramer AF. 2009. Aerobic exercise effects on cognitive and neural plasticity in older adults. *Br. J. Sports Med.* 43:22–24

Ericsson KA, Nandagopal K, Roring RW. 2009. Toward a science of exceptional achievement: attaining superior performance through deliberate practice. *Ann. N. Y. Acad. Sci.* 1172:199–217

Eriksen BA, Eriksen CW. 1974. Effects of noise letters upon the identification of a target letter in a nonsearch task. *Percept. Psychophys.* 16:143–49

Espy KA. 2004. Using developmental, cognitive, and neuroscience approaches to understand executive control in young children. *Dev. Neuropsychol.* 26:379–84

Fairchild G, van Goozen SH, Stollery SJ, Aitken MR, Savage J, et al. 2009. Decision making and executive function in male adolescents with early-onset or adolescence-onset conduct disorder and control subjects. *Biol. Psychiatry* 66:162–68

Fan J, Flombaum JI, McCandliss BD, Thomas KM, Posner MI. 2002. Cognitive and brain consequences of conflict. *Neuroimage* 18:42–57

Farran DC, Wilson SJ. 2011. Is self-regulation malleable? Results from an evaluation of the Tools of the Mind curriculum. Paper presented at *Peabody Res. Inst. Colloquium Ser.*, Nashville, TN

Feng X, Bialystok E, Diamond A. 2007. Manipulating information in working memory: an advantage for bilinguals. *Bienn. Meet. Soc. Res. Child Dev.*, Boston, MA

Ferrer E, Shaywitz BA, Holahan JM, Marchione KE, Shaywitz SE. 2009. Uncoupling of reading and IQ over time: empirical evidence for a definition of dyslexia. *Psychol. Sci.* 21:93–101

The only review of EF interventions with children thus far; reviews diverse approaches.

Fiore F, Borella E, Mammarella IC, De Beni R. 2012. Age differences in verbal and visuo-spatial working memory updating: evidence from analysis of serial position curves. *Memory* 20:14–27

Flook L, Smalley SL, Kitil JM, Galla BM, Kaiser-Greenland S, et al. 2010. Effects of mindful awareness practices on executive functions in elementary school children. *J. Appl. School Psychol.* 26:70–95

Fournet N, Roulin JL, Vallet F, Beaudoin M, Agrigoroaei S, et al. 2012. Evaluating short-term and working memory in older adults: French normative data. *Aging Ment. Health.* 16:922–30

Frank MJ. 2006. Hold your horses: a dynamic computational role for the subthalamic nucleus in decision making. *Neural Netw.* 19:1120–36

Friedman NP, Miyake A. 2004. The relations among inhibition and interference control functions: a latent-variable analysis. *J. Exp. Psychol.: Gen.* 133:101–35

Fry AF, Hale S. 2000. Relationships among processing speed, working memory, and fluid intelligence in children. *Biol. Psychol.* 54:1–34

Gamboz N, Russo R, Fox E. 2002. Age differences and the identity negative priming effect: an updated meta-analysis. *Psychol. Aging* 17:525–31

Garavan H, Kelley D, Rosen A, Rao SM, Stein EA. 2000. Practice-related functional activation changes in a working memory task. *Microsc. Res. Tech.* 51:54–63

Garon N, Bryson SE, Smith IM. 2008. Executive function in preschoolers: a review using an integrative framework. *Psychol. Bull.* 134:31–60

Gathercole SE, Pickering SJ, Knight C, Stegmann Z. 2004. Working memory skills and educational attainment: evidence from National Curriculum assessments at 7 and 14 years of age. *Appl. Cogn. Psychol.* 18:1–16

Gazzaley A, Cooney JW, McEvoy K, Knight RT, D'Esposito M. 2005. Top-down enhancement and suppression of the magnitude and speed of neural activity. *J. Cogn. Neurosci.* 17:507–17

Gazzaley A, Nobre AC. 2012. Top-down modulation: bridging selective attention and working memory. *Trends Cogn. Sci.* 16:129–35

Gernsbacher MA, Faust ME. 1991. The mechanism of suppression: a component of general comprehension skill. *J. Exp. Psychol.* 17:245–62

Georgopoulos AP, Lurito JT, Petrides M, Schwartz AB, Massey JT. 1989. Mental rotation of the neuronal population vector. *Science* 243:234–36

Goldsmith HH. 1996. Studying temperament via construction of the Toddler Behavior Assessment Questionnaire. *Child Dev.* 67:218–35

Gopnik A, Rosati A. 2001. Duck or rabbit? Reversing ambiguous figures and understanding ambiguous representations. *Dev. Sci.* 4:175–83

Gupta R, Kar BR, Srinivasan N. 2009. Development of task switching and post-error-slowing in children. *Behav. Brain Funct.* 5:38

Hale S, Bronik MD, Fry AF. 1997. Verbal and spatial working memory in school-age children: developmental differences in susceptibility to interference. *Dev. Psychol.* 33:364–71

Hall P, Crossley M, D'Arcy C. 2010. Executive function and survival in the context of chronic illness. *Ann. Behav. Med.* 39:119–27

Hanania R, Smith LB. 2010. Selective attention and attention switching: towards a unified developmental approach. *Dev. Sci.* 13:622–35

Hasher L, Stoltzfus ER, Zacks RT, Rypma B. 1991. Age and inhibition. *J. Exp. Psychol.* 17:163–69

Hasher L, Zacks RT. 1988. Working memory, comprehension, and aging: a review and a new view. In *The Psychology of Learning and Motivation: Advances in Research and Theory*, ed. GH Bower, pp. 193–225. San Diego, CA: Academic

Heberle J, Clune M, Kelly K. 1999. Development of young children's understanding of the appearance–reality distinction. *Bienn. Meet. Soc. Res. Child Dev.*, Albuquerque, NM

Hedden T, Park D. 2001. Aging and interference in verbal working memory. *Psychology and Aging* 16: 666–81

Herrigel E. 1999. *Zen in the Art of Archery*. New York: Vintage

Hillman CH, Erickson KI, Kramer AF. 2008. Be smart, exercise your heart: exercise effects on brain and cognition. *Nat. Rev. Neurosci.* 9:58–65

Hirt ER, Devers EE, McCrea SM. 2008. I want to be creative: exploring the role of hedonic contingency theory in the positive mood–cognitive flexibility link. *J. Pers. Soc. Psychol.* 94:214–30

Hofmann W, Friese M, Strack F. 2009. Impulse and self-control from a dual-systems perspective. *Perspect. Psychol. Sci.* 4:162–76

Holmes J, Gathercole SE, Dunning DL. 2009. Adaptive training leads to sustained enhancement of poor working memory in children. *Dev. Sci.* 12:F9–15

Hölzel BK, Lazar SW, Gard T, Schuman-Olivier Z, Vago DR, Ott U. 2011. How does mindfulness meditation work? Proposing mechanisms of action from a conceptual and neural perspective. *Persp. Psychol. Sci.* 6:537–59

Huang YS, Guilleminault C, Li HY, Yang CM, Wu YY, Chen NH. 2007. Attention-deficit/hyperactivity disorder with obstructive sleep apnea: a treatment outcome study. *Sleep Med.* 8:18–30

Ikkai A, Curtis CE. 2011. Common neural mechanisms supporting spatial working memory, attention and motor intention. *Neuropsychologia* 49:1428–34

Jones LB, Rothbart MK, Posner MI. 2003. Development of executive attention in preschool children. *Dev. Sci.* 6:498–504

Kamijo K, Pontifex MB, O'Leary KC, Scudder MR, Wu C-T, et al. 2011. The effects of an afterschool physical activity program on working memory in preadolescent children. *Dev. Sci.* 14:1046–58

Kane MJ, Brown LH, McVay JC, Silvia PJ, Myin-Germeys I, Kwapil TR. 2007. For whom the mind wanders, and when: an experience-sampling study of working memory and executive control in daily life. *Psychol. Sci.* 18:614–21

Kane MJ, Engle RW. 2000. Working-memory capacity, proactive interference, and divided attention: limits on long-term memory retrieval. *J. Exp. Psychol.* 26:336–58

Kane MJ, Engle RW. 2002. The role of prefrontal cortex in working-memory capacity, executive attention, and general fluid intelligence: an individual-differences perspective. *Psychon. Bull. Rev.* 9:637–71

Karayanidis F, Whitson LR, Heathcote A, Michie PT. 2011. Variability in proactive and reactive cognitive control processes across the adult lifespan. *Front. Psychol.* 2:318

Karbach J, Kray J. 2009. How useful is executive control training? Age differences in near and far transfer of task-switching training. *Dev. Sci.* 12:978–90

Kendler HH, Kendler TS, Ward JW. 1972. An ontogenetic analysis of optional intradimensional and extradimensional shifts. *J. Exp. Psychol.* 95:102–9

Kendler TS, Kendler HH. 1959. Reversal and nonreversal shifts in kindergarten children. *J. Exp. Psychol.* 58:56–60

Kirkham NZ, Cruess L, Diamond A. 2003. Helping children apply their knowledge to their behavior on a dimension-switching task. *Dev. Sci.* 6:449–67

Klingberg T. 2010. Training and plasticity of working memory. *Trends Cogn. Sci.* 14:317–24

Klingberg T, Fernell E, Olesen P, Johnson M, Gustafsson P, et al. 2005. Computerized training of working memory in children with ADHD—a randomized, controlled trial. *J. Am. Acad. Child Adolesc. Psychiatry* 44:177–86

Kloo D, Perner J. 2005. Disentangling dimensions in the dimensional change card sorting task. *Dev. Sci.* 8:44–56

Kochanska G, Coy KC, Murray KT. 2001. The development of self-regulation in the first four years of life. *Child Dev.* 72:1091–111

Kochanska G, Philibert RA, Barry RA. 2009. Interplay of genes and early mother-child relationship in the development of self-regulation from toddler to preschool age. *J. Child Psychol. Psychiatry* 50:1331–38

Kovács AM, Mehler J. 2009. Cognitive gains in 7-month-old bilingual infants. *Proc. Natl. Acad. Sci. USA* 106:6556–60

Kray J. 2006. Task-set switching under cue-based versus memory-based switching conditions in younger and older adults. *Brain Res.* 1105:83–92

Kray J, Lindenberger U. 2000. Adult age differences in task switching. *Psychol. Aging* 15:126–47

Kuo BC, Stokes MG, Nobre AC. 2012. Attention modulates maintenance of representations in visual short-term memory. *J. Cogn. Neurosci.* 24:51–60

LaBar KS, Gitelman DR, Parrish TB, Mesulam M. 1999. Neuroanatomic overlap of working memory and spatial attention networks: a functional MRI comparison within subjects. *Neuroimage* 10:695–704

Lakes KD, Hoyt WT. 2004. Promoting self-regulation through school-based martial arts training. *Appl. Dev. Psychol.* 25:283–302

This pioneering research demonstrated effects of bilingualism from just listening to two languages without yet speaking.

Landau SM, Garavan H, Schumacher EH, D'Esposito M. 2007. Regional specificity and practice: dynamic changes in object and spatial working memory. *Brain Res.* 1180:78–89

Lehto JE, Juujärvi P, Kooistra L, Pulkkinen L. 2003. Dimensions of executive functioning: evidence from children. *Br. J. Dev. Psychol.* 21:59–80

Lezak M. 1983. *Neuropsychological Assessment.* New York: Oxford Univ. Press

Liew J. 2011. Effortful control, executive functions, and education: bringing self-regulatory and social-emotional competencies to the table. *Child Dev. Perspect.* 6:105–11

Lillard A, Else-Quest N. 2006. The early years: evaluating Montessori education. *Science* 313:1893–94

Liston C, McEwen BS, Casey BJ. 2009. Psychosocial stress reversibly disrupts prefrontal processing and attentional control. *Proc. Natl. Acad. Sci. USA* 106:912–17

Louie K, Glimcher PW. 2010. Separating value from choice: delay discounting activity in the lateral intra-parietal area. *J. Neurosci.* 30:5498–507

Lövdén M, Bodammer NC, Kühn S, Kaufmann J, Schütze H, et al. 2010. Experience-dependent plasticity of white-matter microstructure extends into old age. *Neuropsychologia* 48:3878–83

Lu CH, Proctor RW. 1995. The influence of irrelevant location information on performance: a review of the Simon and spatial Stroop effects. *Psychon. Bull. Rev.* 2:174–207

Luciana M, Conklin HM, Hooper CJ, Yarger RS. 2005. The development of nonverbal working memory and executive control processes in adolescents. *Child Dev.* 76:697–712

Luciana M, Nelson CA. 2002. Assessment of neuropsychological function in children using the Cambridge Neuropsychological Testing Automated Battery (CANTAB): performance in 4- to 12-year-olds. *Dev. Neuropsychol.* 22:595–623

Lui M, Tannock R. 2007. Working memory and inattentive behaviour in a community sample of children. *Behav. Brain Funct.* 3:12

Luna B. 2009. Developmental changes in cognitive control through adolescence. *Adv. Child Dev. Behav.* 37:233–78

Luna B, Garver KE, Urban TA, Lazar NA, Sweeney JA. 2004. Maturation of cognitive processes from late childhood to adulthood. *Child Dev.* 75:1357–72

Luna B, Merriam EP, Minshew NJ, Keshavan MS, Genovese CR, et al. 1999. Response inhibition improves from late childhood to adulthood: eye movement and fMRI studies. *Proc. 6th Annu. Meet. Cogn. Neurosci. Meet., Washington, DC*

Lunt L, Bramham J, Morris RG, Bullock PR, Selway RP, et al. 2012. Prefrontal cortex dysfunction and "jumping to conclusions": bias or deficit? *J. Neuropsychol.* 6:65–78

Mackey AP, Hill SS, Stone SI, Bunge SA. 2011. Differential effects of reasoning and speed training in children. *Dev. Sci.* 14:582–90

MacLeod CM. 1991. Half a century of research on the Stroop effect: an integrative review. *Psychol. Bull.* 109:163–203

MacLeod CM, Dodd MD, Sheard ED, Wilson DE, Bibi U. 2003. In opposition to inhibition. *Psychol. Learn. Motiv.* 43:163–214

Manjunath NK, Telles S. 2001. Improved performance in the Tower of London test following yoga. *Indian J. Physiol. Pharmacol.* 45:351–54

Mason M, Norton M, Van Horn JD, Wegner DW, Grafton ST, Macrae CN. 2007. Wandering minds: the default network and stimulus-independent thought. *Science* 315:393–95

Mayr U, Liebscher T. 2001. Is there an age deficit in the selection of mental sets? *Eur. J. Cogn. Psychol.* 13:47–69

Meiran N. 1996. Reconfiguration of processing mode prior to task performance. *J. Exp. Psychol.: Learn. Mem. Cogn.* 22:1423–42

Meiran N, Gotler A. 2001. Modeling cognitive control in task switching and aging. *Eur. J. Cogn. Psychol.* 13:165–86

Melby-Lervåg, M, Hulme C. 2012. Is working memory training effective? A meta-analytic review. *Dev. Psychol.* In press

Milham MP, Banich MT, Claus ED, Cohen NJ. 2003. Practice-related effects demonstrate complementary roles of anterior cingulate and prefrontal cortices in attentional control. *Neuroimage* 18:483–93

Miller EK, Cohen JD. 2001. An integrative theory of prefrontal cortex function. *Annu. Rev. Neurosci.* 24:167–202

Miller HV, Barnes JC, Beaver KM. 2011. Self-control and health outcomes in a nationally representative sample. *Am. J. Health Behav.* 35:15–27

Miller P, Brody CD, Romo R, Wang XJ. 2003. A recurrent network model of somatosensory parametric working memory in the prefrontal cortex. *Cereb. Cortex* 13:1208–18

Milner B. 1964. Some effects of frontal lobectomy in man. In *The Frontal Granular Cortex and Behavior*, ed. JM Warren, K Akert, pp. 313–34. New York: McGraw-Hill

Mischel W, Ayduk O. 2002. Self-regulation in a cognitive-affective personality system: attentional control in the service of the self. *Self Identity* 1:113–20

Mischel W, Shoda Y, Rodriguez ML. 1989. Delay of gratification in children. *Science* 244:933–38

Miyake A, Friedman NP, Emerson MJ, Witzki AH, Howerter A, Wager TD. 2000. The unity and diversity of executive functions and their contributions to complex "frontal lobe" tasks: a latent variable analysis. *Cogn. Psychol.* 41:49–100

Moffitt TE. 2012. Childhood self-control predicts adult health, wealth, and crime. *Multi-Discipl. Symp. Improv. Well-Being Children Youth*, Copenhagen

Moffitt TE, Arseneault L, Belsky D, Dickson N, Hancox RJ, et al. 2011. A gradient of childhood self-control predicts health, wealth, and public safety. *Proc. Natl. Acad. Sci. USA* 108:2693–98

Monsell S. 2003. Task switching. *Trends Cogn. Sci.* 7:134–40

Monsell S, Driver J, eds. 2000. *Control of Cognitive Processes: Attention and Performance XVIII*. Cambridge, MA: MIT Press

Morrison AB, Chein JM. 2011. Does working memory training work? The promise and challenges of enhancing cognition by training working memory. *Psychon. Bull. Rev.* 18:46–60

Morrison FJ, Ponitz CC, McClelland MM. 2010. Self-regulation and academic achievement in the transition to school. In *Child Development at the Intersection of Emotion and Cognition*, ed. SD Calkins, M Bell, pp. 203–24. Washington, DC: Am. Psychol. Assoc.

Mullane JC, Corkum PV, Klein RM, McLaughlin E. 2009. Interference control in children with and without ADHD: a systematic review of Flanker and Simon task performance. *Child Neuropsychol.* 15:321–42

Munakata Y, Herd SA, Chatham CH, Depue BE, Banich MT, O'Reilly RC. 2011. A unified framework for inhibitory control. *Trends Cogn. Sci.* 15:453–59

Munakata Y, Snyder HR, Chatham CH. 2012. Developing cognitive control. *Curr. Dir. Psychol. Sci.* 21:71–77

Munoz DP, Everling S. 2004. Look away: the anti-saccade task and the voluntary control of eye movement. *Nat. Rev. Neurosci.* 5:218–28

Munro S, Chau C, Gazarian K, Diamond A. 2006. Dramatically larger flanker effects (6-fold elevation). Poster presented at *Cogn. Neurosci. Soc. Annu. Meet.*, San Francisco, CA

Muraven M. 2010. Building self-control strength: practicing self-control leads to improved self-control performance. *J. Exp. Soc. Psychol.* 46:465–68

Muraven M, Baumeister RF. 2000. Self-regulation and depletion of limited resources: Does self-control resemble a muscle? *Psychol. Bull.* 126:247–59

Nelson JM, Sheffield TD, Chevalier N, Clark CAC, Espy KA. 2012. Psychobiology of executive function in early development. In *Executive Function in Preschool Age Children: Integrating Measurement, Neurodevelopment and Translational Research*, ed. P McCardle, L Freund, JA Griffin. Washington, DC: Am. Psychol. Assoc. In press

Nieuwenhuis S, Yeung N. 2005. Neural mechanisms of attention and control: losing our inhibitions? *Nat. Neurosci.* 8:1631–33

Nigg JT. 2000. On inhibition/disinhibition in developmental psychopathology: views from cognitive and personality psychology and a working inhibition taxonomy. *Psychol. Bull.* 126:220–46

Nigg JT, Butler KM, Huang-Pollock CL, Henderson JM. 2002. Inhibitory processes in adults with persistent childhood onset ADHD. *J. Consult. Clin. Psychol.* 70:153–57

Nobre AC, Stokes MG. 2011. Attention and short-term memory: crossroads. *Neuropsychologia* 49:1391–92

Oaten M, Cheng K. 2005. Academic examination stress impairs self-control. *J. Soc. Clin. Psychol.* 24:254–79

Best and longest prospective study of EFs, showing they affect health, wealth, and public safety.

The best single source for theory and research on task switching (set shifting).

Insightful review of EF computerized training that considers methodological problems and what's needed next.

Thoughtful articulation of view that there's no need to postulate a separate inhibitory control function.

This special issue explores diverse findings on interrelations between selective attention and short-term memory.

O'Shaughnessy T, Lane KL, Gresham FM, Beebe-Frankenberger M. 2003. Children placed at risk for learning and behavioral difficulties: implementing a school-wide system of early identification and prevention. *Remedial Spec. Educ.* 24:27–35

Owen AM, McMillan KM, Laird AR, Bullmore E. 2005. N-back working memory paradigm: a meta-analysis of normative functional neuroimaging studies. *Hum. Brain Mapp.* 25:46–59

Owen AM, Morris RG, Sahakian BJ, Polkey CE, Robbins TW. 1996. Double dissociations of memory and executive functions in a self-ordered working memory task following frontal lobe excision, temporal lobe excisions or amygdalo-hippocampectomy in man. *Brain* 119:1597–615

Peltsch A, Hemraj A, Garcia A, Munoz DP. 2011. Age-related trends in saccade characteristics among the elderly. *Neurobiol. Aging* 32:669–79

Penadés R, Catalán R, Rubia K, Andrés S, Salamero M, Gastó C. 2007. Impaired response inhibition in obsessive compulsive disorder. *Eur. Psychiatry* 22:404–10

Perner J, Lang B. 2002. What causes 3-year-olds' difficulty on the dimensional change card sorting task? *Infant Child Dev.* 11:93–105

Petrides M. 1986. The effect of periarcuate lesions in the monkey on the performance of symmetrically and asymmetrically reinforced visual and auditory go, no-go tasks. *J. Neurosci.* 6:2054–63

Petrides M. 1995. Impairments on nonspatial self-ordered and externally ordered working memory tasks after lesions of the mid-dorsal part of the lateral frontal cortex in the monkey. *J. Neurosci.* 15:359–75

Petrides M, Alivisatos B, Evans AC, Meyer E. 1993. Dissociation of human mid-dorsolateral from posterior dorsolateral frontal cortex in memory processing. *Proc. Natl. Acad. Sci. USA* 90:873–77

Petrides M, Milner B. 1982. Deficits on subject-ordered tasks after frontal- and temporal-lobe lesions in man. *Neuropsychologia* 20:249–62

Piaget J. 1952/1941. *The Child's Conception of Number* (transl. by C Gattegno, FM Hodgson). London: Routledge & Kegan Paul

Poldrack RA, Sabb FW, Foerde K, Tom SM, Asarnow RF, et al. 2005. The neural correlates of motor skill automaticity. *J. Neurosci.* 25:5356–64

Posner MI, DiGirolamo GJ. 1998. Executive attention: conflict, target detection, and cognitive control. In *The Attentive Brain*, ed. R Parasuraman, pp. 401–23. Cambridge, MA: MIT Press

Postle BR, Brush LN, Nick AM. 2004. Prefrontal cortex and the mediation of proactive interference in working memory. *Cogn. Affect. Behav. Neurosci.* 4:600–8

Rachlin H, Ranieri A, Cross D. 1991. Subjective probability and delay. *J. Exp. Anal. Behav.* 55:233–44

Raven J. 2000. The Raven's Progressive Matrices: change and stability over culture and time. *Cogn. Psychol.* 41:1–48

Raver CC, Jones SM, Li-Grining CP, Metzger M, Champion KM, Sardin L. 2008. Improving preschool classroom processes: preliminary findings from a randomized trial implemented in Head Start settings. *Early Child. Res. Q.* 23:10–26

Raver CC, Jones SM, Li-Grining C, Zhai F, Bub K, Pressler E. 2011. CSRP's impact on low-income preschoolers' preacademic skills: self-regulation as a mediating mechanism. *Child Dev.* 82:362–78

Reason J, Mycielska K. 1982. *Absent-Minded? The Psychology of Mental Lapses and Everyday Errors.* Englewood Cliffs, NJ: Prentice-Hall

Richmond LL, Morrison AB, Chein JM, Olson IR. 2011. Working memory training and transfer in older adults. *Psychol. Aging* 26:813–22

Riggs NR, Greenberg MT, Kusché CA, Pentz MA. 2006. The mediational role of neurocognition in the behavioral outcomes of a social-emotional prevention program in elementary school students: effects of the PATHS curriculum. *Prev. Sci.* 7:91–102

Riggs NR, Spruijt-Metz D, Sakuma KK, Chou CP, Pentz MA. 2010. Executive cognitive function and food intake in children. *J. Nutr. Educ. Behav.* 42:398–403

Riviere J, Lecuyer R. 2003. The C-not-B error: a comparative study. *Cogn. Dev.* 18:285–97

Robbins TW, James M, Owen AM, Sahakian BJ, Lawrence AD, et al. 1998. A study of performance on tests from the CANTAB battery sensitive to frontal lobe dysfunction in a large sample of normal volunteers: implications for theories of executive functioning and cognitive aging. *J. Int. Neuropsychol. Soc.* 4:474–90

Roberts AC, Robbins TW, Everitt BJ. 1988. The effects of intradimensional and extradimensional shifts on visual discrimination learning in humans and non-human primates. *Q. J. Exp. Psychol.* 40B:321–41

Roberts RJ, Pennington BF. 1996. An interactive framework for examining prefrontal cognitive processes. *Dev. Neuropsychol.* 12:105–26

Roca M, Parr A, Thompson R, Woolgar A, Torralva T, et al. 2010. Executive function and fluid intelligence after frontal lobe lesions. *Brain* 133:234–47

Rogers RD, Monsell S. 1995. Costs of a predictable switch between simple cognitive tasks. *J. Exp. Psychol.: Gen.* 124:207–31

Rothbart MK, Ahadi SA, Hershey KL, Fisher P. 2001. Investigations of temperament at 3–7 years: the Children's Behavior Questionnaire. *Child Dev.* 72:1394–408

Rothbart MK, Bates JE. 2006. Temperament. In *Handbook of Child Psychology. Vol. 3: Social Emotional and Personality Development*, ed. W Damon, N Eisenberg, pp. 105–76. New York: Wiley

Rozas AX, Juncos-Rabadán O, González MS. 2008. Processing speed, inhibitory control, and working memory: three important factors to account for age-related cognitive decline. *Int. J. Aging Hum. Dev.* 66:115–30

Rueda MR, Posner MI, Rothbart MK. 2005. The development of executive attention: contributions to the emergence of self-regulation. *Dev. Neuropsychol.* 28:573–94

Rutman AM, Clapp WC, Chadick JZ, Gazzaley A. 2010. Early top-down control of visual processing predicts working memory performance. *J. Cogn. Neurosci.* 22:1224–34

Sahakian BJ, Morris RG, Evenden JL, Heald A, Levy R, et al. 1988. A comparative study of visuospatial memory and learning in Alzheimer-type dementia and Parkinson's disease. *Brain* 111:695–718

Salthouse TA. 1992. Influence of processing speed on adult age differences in working memory. *Acta Psychol.* 79:155–70

Sethi A, Mischel W, Aber J, Shoda Y, Rodriguez M. 2000. The role of strategic attention deployment in development of self-regulation: predicting preschoolers' delay of gratification from mother-toddler interactions. *Dev. Psychol.* 36:767–77

Shipstead Z, Redick TS, Engle RW. 2012. Is working memory training effective? *Psychol. Bull.* 138:628–54

Simpson A, Riggs KJ. 2007. Under what conditions do young children have difficulty inhibiting manual actions? *Dev. Psychol.* 43:417–28

Simpson A, Riggs KJ, Beck SR, Gorniak SL, Wu Y, et al. 2012. Refining the understanding of inhibitory control: how response prepotency is created and overcome. *Dev. Sci.* 15:62–73

Smallwood J, Schooler JW. 2009. Mind-wandering. In *The Oxford Companion to Consciousness*, ed. T Bayne, A Cleermans, P Wilken, pp. 443–45. Oxford, UK: Oxford Univ. Press

Smith EE, Jonides J. 1999. Storage and executive processes in the frontal lobes. *Science* 283:1657–61

Solesio-Jofre E, Lorenzo-López L, Gutiérrez R, Lópezv-Frutos JM, Ruiz-Vargas JM, Maestú F. 2012. Age-related effects in working memory recognition modulated by retroactive interference. *J. Gerontol. Ser. A Biol. Sci.* 67:565–72

Stedron JM, Sahni SD, Munakata Y. 2005. Common mechanisms for working memory and attention: the case of perseveration with visible solutions. *J. Cogn. Neurosci.* 17:623–31

Stuss DT, Levine B, Alexander MP, Hong J, Palumbo C, et al. 2000. Wisconsin Card Sorting Test performance in patients with focal frontal and posterior brain damage: effects of lesion location and test structure on separable cognitive processes. *Neuropsychologia* 38:388–402

Sweeney JA, Rosano C, Berman RA, Luna B. 2001. Inhibitory control of attention declines more than working memory during normal aging. *Neurobiol. Aging* 22:39–47

Taylor Tavares JV, Clark L, Cannon DM, Erickson K, Drevets WC, Sahakian BJ. 2007. Distinct profiles of neurocognitive function in unmedicated unipolar depression and bipolar II depression. *Biol. Psychiatry* 62:917–24

Theeuwes J. 1991. Exogenous and endogenous control of attention: the effect of visual onsets and offsets. *Percept. Psychophys.* 49:83–90

Theeuwes J. 2010. Top-down and bottom-up control of visual selection. *Acta Psychol.* 315:77–99

Thorell LB, Lindqvist S, Bergman N, Bohlin G, Klingberg T. 2009. Training and transfer effects of executive functions in preschool children. *Dev. Sci.* 12:106–13

Tun PA, Miller-Martinez D, Lachman ME, Seeman T. 2012. Social strain and executive function across the lifespan: the dark (and light) sides of social engagement. *Neuropsychol. Dev. Cogn.* In press

Insightful review of computerized EF training that raises important methodological considerations.

Valle-Inclán F. 1996. The locus of interference in the Simon effect: an ERP study. *Biol. Psychol.* 43:147–62

Van der Elst W, Hurks P, Wassenberg R, Meijs C, Jolles J. 2011. Animal verbal fluency and design fluency in school-aged children: effects of age, sex, and mean level of parental education, and regression-based normative data. *J. Exp. Neuropsychol.* 33:1005–15

Verbruggen F, Logan GD. 2008. Automatic and controlled response inhibition: associative learning in the go/no-go and stop-signal paradigms. *J. Exp. Psychol.: Gen.* 137:649–72

Verhaeghen P, Basak C. 2005. Ageing and switching of the focus of attention in working memory: results from a modified N-back task. *Q. J. Exp. Psychol.* 58:134–54

von Hecker U, Meiser T. 2005. Defocused attention in depressed mood: evidence from source monitoring. *Emotion* 5:456–63

Voss MW, Nagamatsu LS, Liu-Ambrose T, Kramer AF. 2011. Exercise, brain, and cognition across the lifespan. *J. Appl. Physiol.* 111:1505–13

Wais P, Gazzaley A. 2011. The impact of auditory distraction on retrieval of visual memories. *Psychon. Bull. Rev.* 18:1090–97

Wais P, Rubens M, Boccanfuso J, Gazzaley A. 2010. Neural mechanisms underlying the impact of visual distraction on retrieval of long-term memory. *J. Neurosci.* 30:8541–50

Wass S, Porayska-Pomsta K, Johnson MH. 2011. Training attentional control in infancy. *Curr. Biol.* 21:1–5

Wendelken C, Munakata Y, Baym C, Souza M, Bunge S. 2012. Flexible rule use: common neural substrates in children and adults. *Dev. Cogn. Neurosci.* 2:329–39

Wiebe SA, Lukowski AF, Bauer PJ. 2010. Sequence imitation and reaching measures of executive control: a longitudinal examination in the second year of life. *Dev. Neuropsychol.* 35:522–38

Wright A, Diamond A. 2012. Dissociating working memory and inhibition: an effect of inhibitory load while keeping working memory load constant. Manuscript submitted

Zacks RT, Hasher L. 2006. Aging and long-term memory: Deficits are not inevitable. In *Lifespan Cognition: Mechanisms of Change*, ed. E Bialystock, FIM Craik, pp. 162–77. New York: Oxford Univ. Press

Zanto TP, Gazzaley A. 2009. Neural suppression of irrelevant information underlies optimal working memory performance. *J. Neurosci.* 29:3059–66

Zanto TP, Hennigan K, Östberg M, Clapp WC, Gazzaley A. 2010. Predictive knowledge of stimulus relevance does not influence top-down suppression of irrelevant information in older adults. *Cortex* 46:564–74

Zanto TP, Rubens MT, Thangavel A, Gazzaley A. 2011. Causal role of the prefrontal cortex in top-down modulation of visual processing and working memory. *Nat. Neurosci.* 14:656–61

Zeidan F, Johnson SK, Diamond BJ, David Z, Goolkasian P. 2010. Mindfulness meditation improves cognition: evidence of brief mental training. *Conscious. Cogn.* 19:597–605

Zelazo PD, Frye D, Rapus T. 1996. An age-related dissociation between knowing rules and using them. *Cogn. Dev.* 11:37–63

Zelazo PD, Mueller U, Frye D, Marcovitch S. 2003. The development of executive function in early childhood. *Monogr. Soc. Res. Child Dev.* 68:1–137

Zimprich D, Kurtz T. 14 2012. Individual differences and predictors of forgetting in old age: the role of processing speed and working memory. *Neuropsychol. Dev. Cogn.:* In press

The Neuroscience of Learning: Beyond the Hebbian Synapse

C.R. Gallistel[1] and Louis D. Matzel[2]

[1]Rutgers Center for Cognitive Science and [2]Department of Psychology, Rutgers University, Piscataway, New Jersey 08854-8020; email: galliste@ruccs.rutgers.edu

Annu. Rev. Psychol. 2013. 64:169–200

First published online as a Review in Advance on July 12, 2012

The *Annual Review of Psychology* is online at psych.annualreviews.org

This article's doi:
10.1146/annurev-psych-113011-143807

Keywords

LTP, spatial learning, Bayesian inference, information theory, cognitive map, geometric module

Abstract

From the traditional perspective of associative learning theory, the hypothesis linking modifications of synaptic transmission to learning and memory is plausible. It is less so from an information-processing perspective, in which learning is mediated by computations that make implicit commitments to physical and mathematical principles governing the domains where domain-specific cognitive mechanisms operate. We compare the properties of associative learning and memory to the properties of long-term potentiation, concluding that the properties of the latter do not explain the fundamental properties of the former. We briefly review the neuroscience of reinforcement learning, emphasizing the representational implications of the neuroscientific findings. We then review more extensively findings that confirm the existence of complex computations in three information-processing domains: probabilistic inference, the representation of uncertainty, and the representation of space. We argue for a change in the conceptual framework within which neuroscientists approach the study of learning mechanisms in the brain.

Contents

INTRODUCTION

The theoretical frameworks with which we describe learning and memory have traditionally taken one of two forms. In the associative conceptual framework, the mechanism of learning cannot be separated from the mechanism of memory expression. At the psychological level of analysis, learning is the formation of associations, and memory is the translation of that association into a behavioral change. At the neuroscientific level of analysis, learning is the rewiring of a plastic nervous system by experience, and memory resides in the changed wiring.

When approached from the second perspective, the information-processing perspective, learning and memory are distinct mechanisms with different functions: Learning mechanisms extract potentially useful information from experience, while memory carries the acquired information forward in time in a computationally accessible form that is acted upon by the animal at the time of retrieval (Gallistel & King 2009). We review portions of the recent behavioral neuroscience literature, briefly from the first perspective, and more extensively from the latter perspective, focusing on neurobio-logical systems that extract different kinds of information from different kinds of experience.

The distinction between the associative and information-processing frameworks is of critical importance: By the first view, what is learned is a mapping from inputs to outputs. Thus, the learned behavior (of the animal or the network, as the case may be) is always recapitulative of the input-output conditions during learning: An input that is part of the training input, or similar to it, evokes the trained output, or an output similar to it. By the second view, what is learned is a representation of important aspects of the experienced world. This representation supports input-output mappings that are in no way recapitulations of the mappings (if any) that occurred during the learning.

Before focusing on domain-specific learning, and most extensively on spatial learning, we briefly review some of the vast neuroscience literature on the two commonly proposed general-purpose associative learning mechanisms, Pavlovian conditioning (a.k.a. classical conditioning) and reinforcement learning (a.k.a. instrumental conditioning, a.k.a. operant conditioning). Historically, these theories are non- (or anti-) representational. They propose that the brain adapts behavior (its input-output mappings) to environmental circumstances without representing those aspects of the environment that make the behavior adaptive. Most contemporary cognitive science is, by contrast, representational; it assumes that brains construct a behaviorally useful representation of the experienced world through extensive computation.

ASSOCIATIVE LEARNING AND SYNAPTIC PLASTICITY

The hypothesis that the modification of synaptic transmission by experience mediates associative learning dates back to the elaboration of the concept of the synapse itself (Cajal 1894, Tanzi 1893). Hebb's (1949) influential statement of the hypothesis was that if a presynaptic neuron repeatedly played a role in firing a postsynaptic neuron, there ensued an enduring modification of synaptic structure, such that activity in the presynaptic neuron became more likely to excite activity in the postsynaptic neuron. A snappier statement of this idea is that neurons that fire together wire together. Synapses that exhibit these properties are commonly called Hebbian synapses. Martin and colleagues (2000, 2002) review the arguments in favor of this hypothesis, which is widely accepted by psychologists, cognitive scientists, and neuroscientists.

The neurobiological process or phenomenon now most often identified with the Hebbian synapse is long-term potentiation (LTP). Recently, interest has focused on a form of LTP called spike timing–dependent plasticity (STDP; for a recent review, see Caporale & Dan 2008). In a variety of neural circuits, an enduring modification of synaptic transmission is produced by varying the timing of weak and strong synaptic inputs over a range of a few tens of milliseconds. The sign of the modification depends critically on the relative strength of stimulation and the timing of the two inputs. For some parameter values, transmission increases; that is, a presynaptic spike now produces a "potentiated" (i.e., larger amplitude or shorter latency) postsynaptic response. For other combinations, transmission decreases; that is, a presynaptic spike now produces a reduced postsynaptic response.

Most of the neurobiological literature on LTP focuses on its cellular and molecular mechanism. The relevance of this research to the neuroscience of learning depends on the hypothesis that links LTP to associative learning and to memory. The evidence for this link would be strong if the properties of LTP aligned closely with those of the associative learning process as revealed by behavioral experimentation. Here we review those properties and conclude that the alignment is poor.

Effects of Interstimulus Interval and Intertrial Interval

Behaviorally measured association formation depends on time parameters in a fundamen-

tally different way than does LTP. In LTP, differences of a few milliseconds to at most a few tens of milliseconds in the timing of the pre- and postsynaptic inputs are critical. This dependence is often cited in support of the linkage hypothesis (Quinn 2005, Thompson & Mattison 2009, Usherwood 1993). There is, however, nothing in the associative learning literature showing a dependence of association formation on event-timing differences measured in tens of milliseconds. The interstimulus intervals in behavioral experiments are orders of magnitude longer (seconds, minutes, and hours rather than milliseconds).

More fundamentally, there is no independent effect of the interstimulus interval [ISI, also known as the conditioned stimulus-unconditioned stimulus (CS-US) interval] in behavioral association formation: The number of trials to acquisition of a conditioned response in Pavlovian conditioning depends on the ratio of the CS-US interval to the US-US interval. The shorter the CS-US interval is relative to the US-US interval, the fewer the trials to acquisition (Gallistel & Gibbon 2000, Gibbon & Balsam 1981, Gottlieb 2008, Lattal 1999, Ward et al. 2012). The critical role of the CS-US/US-US ratio is dramatically shown by holding the CS-US interval constant and progressively shortening the US-US interval; there comes a point at which the association that forms is inhibitory rather than excitatory (Kaplan 1984). In short, there is no critical interstimulus interval for the behavioral phenomenon. Moreover, the more widely separated the instances of pairing, the more rapidly the association develops. The opposites are true for LTP: There is a critical interstimulus interval, which is orders of magnitude smaller than any interval relevant at the behavioral level. And, the more widely separated the instances of pairing, the weaker their cumulative effect (de Jonge & Racine 1985).

In defense of the linkage hypothesis, it may be argued that "This [disconnect] is only paradoxical, however, if [it is assumed that] CS-US associations occur online at the level of individual synapses. It is less problematic if the time-scale for information representation in a given brain region is different from that pertaining to events as they happen" (Martin & Morris 2002, p. 610). This argument stipulates that the temporal properties of LTP do not explain the temporal properties of behaviorally measured association formation.

Persistence

Behaviorally measured associations can last indefinitely, whereas LTP always decays and usually does so rapidly. Its rate of decay is measured in hours or days (for review, see Abraham 2003). Even with extended "training," a decay to baseline levels is observed within days to a week (e.g., Castro et al. 1989). An experiment by Power et al. (1997) highlights the lack of correspondence: They recorded changes in CA1-evoked responses in brain slices obtained from animals trained on a trace eyeblink conditioning task, which is dependent on the hippocampus for its behavioral expression. Potentiated post-synaptic responses were observed at 1 hour, but not at 24 hours after training. By contrast, the learned eye-blink response remains intact for weeks or months. Again, it may be argued that "it would be premature to reject synaptic plasticity as a memory mechanism merely for this reason [lack of sufficient persistence]. Hippocampal LTP may need only last long enough (a few weeks perhaps) to permit completion of a slower neocortical consolidation process" (Martin & Morris 2002, p. 610). This argument stipulates that the persistence of LTP does not explain the persistence of associative learning.

Reacquisition

Although behavioral evidence for the presence of an association can generally be obtained months and even years after its establishment, the strength of the conditioned response does commonly decline somewhat with time. And, of course, the learned response may be weakened by extinction and/or counter-conditioning. Both forgotten and extinguished conditioned responses exhibit facilitated reacquisition; that is, they are relearned more efficiently than

when they were initially acquired (e.g., Napier et al. 1992; for review, see Miller et al. 1986). Following its decay to baseline, LTP is neither more easily induced nor more persistent than it was after previous inductions (de Jonge & Racine 1985).

Coding

Perhaps most importantly, the hypothesis that a change in synaptic transmission is the mechanism of memory does not address the coding problem. The encoding of the temporal intervals in conditioning protocols routinely occurs (Arcediano et al. 2003, Barnet et al. 1996, Blaisdell et al. 1998, Burger et al. 2001, Cole et al. 1995), probably before the emergence of the conditioned response (Balsam et al. 2006, 2010; Balsam & Gallistel 2009). More tellingly, the sign (excitatory or inhibitory) and rate of association formation depend on the ratio between the expectations of two intervals in the protocol (the CS-US and the US-US intervals; see Gallistel & Gibbon 2000, Ward et al. 2012), which suggests that the encoding of temporal intervals may be a precondition for the appearance of conditioned responses. Thus, the mechanism that mediates associative learning and memory must be able to encode the intervals between events in a computationally accessible form. There is no hypothesis as to how this could be accomplished through the modification of synaptic transmission.

The lack of suggestions in the literature about how Hebbian synapses might encode the durations of intervals reflects a more general failing of the associative conceptual framework when viewed from the perspective of cognitive science: It may explain reflex modification phenomena, but it does not explain the learning of behaviorally important facts and the formation of data structures. It fails to address the question of how facts about the experienced spatio-temporal environment may be carried forward for indefinite periods of time to inform subsequent behavior in ways not foreseeable when the facts were learned. The neuroscientific literature on the representation of space, to which we soon turn, shows that the brain carries in memory the learned geometry of the experienced environment in a way that makes this acquired information accessible to computation in small fractions of a second.

The failure to address the coding problem would not count against the hypothesis that links LTP to memory if "what gets encoded and how is an emergent property of the network in which this plasticity is embedded, rather than of the mechanisms operating at the synapse in isolation" (Martin et al. 2000, p. 650). This appeal to emergent properties stipulates that the properties of LTP do not explain the essential property of a memory mechanism, the ability to store information in a computationally accessible form (Gallistel & King 2009). That most basic property is said to reside in "the network." One naturally asks where it resides and how that storage is implemented. Does the claim that the storage of information is an emergent property imply that we are never to have answers to these questions?

In summary, if synaptic LTP is the mechanism of associative learning—and more generally, of memory—then it is disappointing that its properties explain neither the basic properties of associative learning nor the essential property of a memory mechanism. This dual failure contrasts instructively with the success of the hypothesis that DNA is the physical realization of the gene. This linkage hypothesis asserts that DNA is the molecule that stores hereditary information and makes it accessible to orchestrate ontogeny and much else. The structure of the molecule explains not only its ability to store information but also how copies of it may be made. There is no need to appeal to elusive (and possibly illusive) emergent properties in support of this linkage hypothesis. This explanatory power is a major reason why the hypothesis that links the gene to DNA is so much more compelling than the hypothesis that links LTP to associative learning and to memory.

In **Table 1**, we catalog the discrepancies between the properties of LTP and the properties of associative learning.

REINFORCEMENT LEARNING

Historically, two different association-forming processes have often been posited, one dependent only on temporal contiguity, the other on response-contingent reinforcement (and temporal contiguity). The latter process is often called instrumental conditioning, to distinguish it from the former, which is called Pavlovian or classical conditioning. In the traditional conception of the effects of reinforcement, there was no representation of the reinforcement. The reinforcement "stamped in" an association between a stimulus and the response that produced the reinforcement (Hull 1952), but neither the reinforcement nor its being a consequence of the response was represented. In the quite different contemporary formulation, which has been strongly influenced by theoretical work on reinforcement learning in computer science (Sutton & Barto 1998), reinforcement history is explicitly represented by a value variable associated with the response: A temporal-difference learning algorithm computes the value of an action in a given situation (Dayan & Daw 2008, Redish et al. 2007). The estimated value is updated after each performance of the response in proportion to an error term, which is the difference between the obtained reinforcement and the predicted reinforcement.

Neurobiological support for these models is found in the similarity between the value prediction error term and the signals observed in dopamine neurons following reinforcement and nonreinforcement. There are several recent, theoretically oriented reviews of the relevant literature (Berridge 2012, Dayan & Daw 2008, Flagel et al. 2011, Schultz 2006, Zhang et al. 2009). The general finding is that dopaminergic neurons in the basolateral diencephalon fire in response to events that occur at unpredictable times. If the time of reinforcement (the US) may be predicted by reference to an earlier temporal "landmark," then dopaminergic neurons do not fire. Rather, they fire in response to the occurrence of the landmark (the CS), whose time of occurrence is

Table 1 Disparate properties of LTP and associative learning

Property	Hebbian LTP	Associative learning
Coding	Not implemented by LTP itself: an "emergent property" of circuits	Depends on encoding of temporal intervals, stimulus properties, and stimulus relationships
Necessary CS-US relation	Close temporal contiguity	Contingency
Form of learned output	Recapitulative: When stimulus recurs, output recurs	Anticipatory: Learned behavior usually differs from behavior during learning
Critical ISI	1–100 ms	None: Rate of conditioning is inversely proportional to ISI/ITI
Effect of ITI	The longer the ITI, the weaker the LTP	The longer the ITI relative to ISI, the faster and stronger the learning
Induction kinetics	Expression requires tens of seconds to minutes	Behavioral expression is immediate, <1 s after induction
Acquisition function	Requires repetition	Often complete within single trial
Persistence	Hours–weeks	Months–years (up to a lifetime)
Reacquisition	Not facilitated by previous acquisition	Facilitated by previous acquisition
Context learning	Not consistent with ISI requirement	Ubiquitous and fundamental
Long delay and trace conditioning	Seemingly incompatible with ISI requirement	Easily attained
Cue competition (blocking, overshadowing, etc.)	Not explained by properties of LTP	Ubiquitous and fundamental

Note: Some of these properties are not discussed in text; see Matzel & Shors (2001) and Gallistel & King (2009) for full discussion. For temporal pairing versus contingency, dependence of associative learning on ISI/ITI, and cue competition, see Gallistel & Gibbon (2000), Balsam & Gallistel (2009), Balsam et al. (2010), and Ward et al. (2012). Abbreviations: CS-US, conditioned stimulus-unconditioned stimulus; ISI, interstimulus interval; ITI, intertrial interval; LTP, long-term potentiation.

itself unpredictable. If the US fails to occur at the predicted time, the neuron fires. The neuron also fires if the US occurs at an unexpected time in relation to the CS. Thus, contemporary reinforcement learning theory assumes that the duration of the previously experienced CS-US interval resides in memory, where it forms the expectation against which a currently experienced CS-US interval is compared. The comparison between present experience of the CS-US interval and the information about past intervals stored in memory is on the causal pathway from a reinforcing event to the firing of dopaminergic neurons elicited by that event.

The enduring appeal of antirepresentational associative theory has been its neurobiological transparency: It is easy to imagine that the formation of an associative bond is physically realized by a change in synaptic transmission. Conceptually, both are simple conductive connections. In associative learning theory, the associative bond does not represent an aspect of the experienced world, so our inability to specify how changes in synaptic transmission encode facts is not a problem. The convergence of behavioral and neuroscientific evidence on the conclusion that the coding of temporal facts (interval durations) is an essential feature of both Pavlovian and reinforcement learning suggests that the antirepresentational form of associative theorizing may need to be abandoned. If so, we must now face squarely the unanswered question as to the physical realization of the neural memory mechanism that stores simple abstract experiential facts, such as durations, distances, directions, and probabilities, in a structured form and makes them accessible to computation on a millisecond time scale.

INFORMATION-PROCESSING DOMAINS

In associative learning theory, the brain rewires itself so as to perform better in the experienced world, but it does not represent what it is about the world that makes the new performance better suited to it. When so conceived, the association-forming process may be mathematically modeled, but it is not the physical realization of a computation (or a memory). The information-processing framework, by contrast, is closely allied to the computational theory of mind, which holds that a necessary level of analysis in connecting neuroscience to behavioral phenomena is an analysis of the computations that the brain performs in extracting behaviorally useful information from raw experience (Marr 1982). On this theory, to understand the operations of the mind/brain, we must understand what aspects of the experienced world the brain represents (the representational question), how it represents them (the encoding question), how it computes that representation from the relevant aspects of its experience (the computational question), and how it translates its representations into behavior (the performance question).

Framing learning problems as computational problems leads to the postulation of domain-specific learning mechanisms (Chomsky 1975, Gallistel 1999) because no general-purpose computation could serve the demands of all types of learning. Some computations are broadly useful whereas others are only useful in a single context. However, they all apply the primitive operations of arithmetic and logic to different combinations of inputs to achieve different results.

Framing learning as the problem of how the brain computes a behaviorally useful representation of the experienced world more or less eliminates any distinction between perception and learning. In the study of perception, it is understood that an understanding of the physical and mathematical principles operative in a domain is a precondition for psychological and neuroscientific understanding of how the brain functions in that domain. You cannot understand vision without understanding the rudiments of geometric optics. Similarly, the information-processing approach to learning mechanisms requires an understanding of the rudiments of the different domains in which different learning mechanisms operate. In the balance of this review, we consider three domains: probabilistic inference, the representation of uncertainty, and the representation of space. In each domain, we review the rudiments before focusing on neuroscientific findings relevant to the first two of Marr's questions: What is represented, and how is it represented?

When it is assumed that the neuroscience of learning is the neuroscience of synapse modification, then the study of processes that modify synaptic transmission is naturally conceived of as the study of the cellular and molecular mechanism of learning. But if learning is the result of domain-specific computations, then studying the mechanism of learning is indistinguishable from studying the neural mechanisms that implement computations. Although there is a large body of theoretical work in computational neuroscience, there is as yet no consensus about foundational questions, such as:

1. How is information encoded in spike trains?
2. What are the primitive computational operations in neural tissue?
3. Are they implemented at the network level, the molecular level (intracellularly), or both?
4. What cellular and/or molecular mechanisms implement the arithmetic operations?
5. What mechanism implements memory (the storage of information in a computationally accessible form; see Gallistel & King 2009)?
6. What mechanism implements variable binding in memory? (For an explanation of variable binding and its importance in computation, see Gallistel & King 2009.)
7. What mechanism implements data structures in memory?

Thus, at this stage of our science, neuroscientific findings bear strongly on representational questions in learning—on what is learned—but they do not yet give us a cellular and molecular understanding of underlying computational mechanisms.

Our review of the neuroscience of domain-specific learning mechanisms begins with the neural mechanism of Bayesian inference because it is an example of a broadly applicable complex computation. Its relevance to perception is now well understood, but it also applies to learning, because learning the state of the world is an inferential process. Gallistel (2012) models extinction as Bayesian change detection. This treatment of a basic issue in traditional learning theory explains quantitatively the partial reinforcement extinction effect,[1] which has resisted principled explanation for more than half a century. A second reason for beginning with the neuroscience of probabilistic inference is that there is interesting recent work on the neural mechanism of marginalization, which is an essential component of Bayesian inference.

Probabilistic Inference

Rudiments: Bayes rule. The Bayesian computation mediates probabilistic inference about the state, w, of some aspect of the world by taking the product of a likelihood function and a prior probability distribution:

$$L(w|\mathbf{D}, \pi(w)) = L(w|\mathbf{D})\pi(w).$$

The prior distribution, $\pi(w)$, represents the probability of the different possible states in the light of previous or extraneous evidence. The likelihood function, $L(w|\mathbf{D})$, represents the likelihood of those states in the light of some new data (or event or signal), symbolized by $\mathbf{D}$, that carries information about that state of the world. The product of the two functions weights each prior probability by the corresponding likelihood, giving the relative likelihoods of the different possibilities "all considered." When normalized so that it integrates to one, the product is called the posterior probability distribution.

Rudiments: Likelihood. From a neurobiological perspective, a likelihood function is a neuronal firing pattern viewed backwards, viewed, that is, from the brain's perspective rather than from the perspective of the experimenter (cf. Rieke et al. 1997), which is why likelihood is sometimes called reverse probability. The experimenter, who knows the experimentally given stimulus (the relevant state of the world), determines by experiment the probabilities of the different possible neuronal responses (different numbers of spikes) and plots them as a neuronal tuning curve, a staple of experimental systems neuroscience. The tuning curves for an array of neurons of the same class, for example, the simple cells in the primary visual cortex (V1), determine the firing pattern across an array of neurons of that class. However, from the brain's perspective, this firing pattern is the given; what it must infer are the relative likelihoods of the different plausible stimuli, i.e., what it was out there in the world that produced this pattern of firing.

Rudiments: Marginalization. To assess the risks attendant on different possible decisions, the brain needs to represent the entire likelihood function, not just the most likely value of w. The problem it almost always faces is that several different aspects of the world affect the firing pattern. For example, the firing of the so-called simple neurons in the primary visual cortex (V1) is jointly determined by (among several other factors) the location, orientation, and contrast of the image on the retina. Put more formally, tuning curves, hence also the likelihood functions, are almost always

---

[1] Partial reinforcement during training increases the number of unreinforced trials or responses required to extinguish the learned response. This is paradoxical in associative learning theory because the unreinforced trials during training should weaken net excitatory associative strength at the end of training. Fewer nonreinforced trials should then be required to reduce this weak association to insignificance, whereas in fact the number of unreinforced trials required for extinction increases in proportion as the pre-extinction probability of reinforcement decreases.

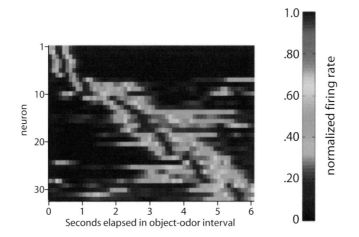

Figure 3

The firing of cells in the hippocampus is tuned to location in time as well as location in space. Each row gives the normalized firing pattern from one of more than 30 neurons whose activity was simultaneously recorded on repeated trials during the 10 s delay between object sampling and odor presentation (peak firing indicated by red). The neurons have been ordered from top to bottom in accord with where in the interval their firing peaked. For similar results from neurons in posterior parietal cortex in mice, see Harvey et al. (2012). (Reproduced from figure 2, panel B in MacDonald et al. 2011 by permission of the authors and publisher.)

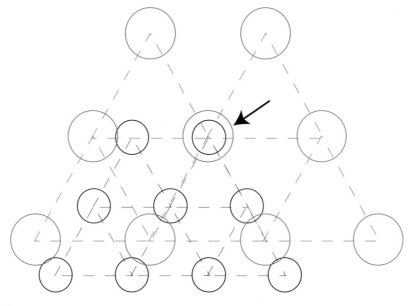

Figure 4

Schematic rendering of the firing fields of two different grid cells (black and red). The regions where a cell fires are represented by the circles. They are connected by dashed lines to emphasize the triangular structure of the grid. The scale factor for the two grids differs by a factor of 1.5. The arrow points to the unique region where both cells would fire. This shows how the firing field of a place cell could be constructed by thresholding the summed input from these two grid cells (cf. Cheng & Frank 2011, Giocomo et al. 2011). The firing of grid cells represents spatial location in a basis function format.

multidimensional. For any one decision, the brain commonly needs a one-dimensional likelihood function, a function, for example, that gives the likelihoods of different possible orientations, regardless of contrast and location. To obtain a one-dimensional likelihood function, it must marginalize the multidimensional likelihood function; that is, it must "integrate out" the effects of the "nuisance" parameters. (In this example, they are the location and contrast in the light pattern.) Metaphorically, marginalization is a bulldozer that moves along one dimension of a multidimensional likelihood function, piling up the likelihood against an orthogonal wall.

Neural implementation. Beck and colleagues (2011) show that combining two widely observed properties of neuronal stimulus-response functions—divisive normalization and quadratic nonlinearities—gives a neurobiologically plausible implementation of marginalization. Divisive normalization is a form of lateral inhibition in which the response of one neuron in a class of neurons (e.g., the simple cells in V1) is suppressed in proportion to the inverse of the sum of the responses of the other neurons in its class (see, e.g., Heeger 1992, Olsen et al. 2010, Simoncelli & Heeger 1998). Quadratic nonlinearities occur when the inputs to a neuron combine multiplicatively rather than additively (see, e.g., Andersen et al. 1985, Galletti & Battaglini 1989, Groh et al. 2001, Werner-Reiss et al. 2003).

Beck et al. (2011) emphasize the broad range of applications of marginalization, from coordinate transformations to causal inference. As they stress, it is a key operation in Bayesian inference. According to much contemporary thinking in cognitive science, Bayesian inference is everywhere in cognition, from perception to learning and causal reasoning (Chater et al. 2006, Griffiths et al. 2010).

Representation of Uncertainty

Probabilistic inference plays a central role in the construction of useful representations of the experienced world because there is a complex, noisy, and ambiguous relation between the behaviorally important properties of the world and the first-order neural signals from which the brain must infer the states of the world. The inferences to be drawn from sensory input are for that reason uncertain to varying degrees. The quantification of this uncertainty through information-theoretic computations complements Bayesian inference.

Rudiments: Uncertainty = entropy = available information. A counterintuitive aspect of information theory is that information and uncertainty are two words for the same quantity. The objective amount of uncertainty about some aspect of the world, that is, the range of possibilities and their probabilities, is the source information, also called the available information. It puts an upper limit on the amount of information that a neural signal (or correlated event, or variable, or memory) can convey about that aspect of the world. Intuitively, the more uncertainty there is about something, the more there is to learn, that is, the more information to be gained. If there is no uncertainty, then there is nothing to learn, that is, no information to be gained.

A probability distribution specifies the probabilities of a set of mutually exclusive and exhaustive possibilities. The possibilities are the support for the distribution. Signals, signs, and events carry information insofar as they may be used to narrow the range of plausible possibilities. A probability distribution is an example of structured information: It links the symbols for the possibilities to the symbols for their relative frequencies.

The entropy of a probability distribution measures the amount of uncertainty. If the probability distribution is in the brain's representation of an empirical variable, then its entropy measures the brain's uncertainty about the value of that variable. A signal or predictor event is informative about that value to the extent that it reduces the entropy of this distribution, because information is defined as the reduction of uncertainty (Shannon 1948).

The formula for computing the entropy of a distribution is a probability-weighted sum, as are the formulae for mean, variance, and the still higher moments:

$$H = \sum_{i=1}^{i=n} p_i \log(1/p_i) \text{ entropy of}$$

the distribution

$$\mu = \sum_{i=1}^{i=n} p_i w_i \text{ the mean (1st moment)}$$

$$\sigma^2 = \sum_{i=1}^{i=n} p_i (w_i - \mu)^2 \text{ the variance}$$

(2nd moment about the mean)

$$\gamma = \sum_{i=1}^{i=n} p_i (w_i - \mu)^3 \text{ the skew}$$

(3rd moment about the mean)

where i indexes the possibilities that constitute the support for the distribution. The log of $1/p_i$ measures the information attendant on the occurrence of w_i, the ith possibility. The summation weights each such amount by the relative frequency of its occurrence, that is, by p_i.

Rudiments: Contingency. An important advance in our understanding of associative learning came from experiments demonstrating that the emergence of a conditioned response depends not on the temporal pairing of two events but rather on the contingency between them. Eliminating the contingency while preserving the temporal pairing prevents the emergence of a conditioned response (Rescorla 1967, 1968). Thus the simple contiguity of events is insufficient to support learning. This is another case in which the Hebbian properties of LTP fail to explain the properties of associative learning: LTP is driven by temporal pairing; association formation is driven by contingency.

Neuroscientific evidence. The importance of this insight to our understanding of the neurobiology of associative learning is shown by the finding that signals in the mesolimbic dopaminergic neurons encode the probability and uncertainty of reinforcement (Fiorillo et al. 2003) and by the more recent discovery

that the response of neurons in the amygdala to reward-predicting stimuli depends on the contingency between the stimulus and the reward rather than on their temporal pairing (Bermudez & Schultz 2010). Thus, to understand the neurobiology of associative learning, a measure of contingency is needed.

Information theory provides a generally applicable measure:

$$C_{YX} = I_{YX}/H(p(X)) \neq C_{XY} = I_{YX}/H(p(Y)),$$

where I_{YX} is the mutual information between variables Y and X, C_{YX} measures the extent to which Y is contingent on X, and $H(p(X))$ is the entropy of the distribution of X, which distribution is symbolized by p(X). The mutual information is the sum of the entropies of the individual distributions minus the entropy of their joint distribution:

$$I_{YX} = H(p(X)) + H(p(Y)) - H(p(X \times Y)),$$

where $p(X \times Y)$ symbolizes the joint distribution. Intuitively, the information-theoretic measure of contingency quantifies the extent to which knowledge of a putative predictor (Y, the CS or a response) reduces the uncertainty about when reinforcement (X) will occur.

Given the evidence from both behavior and neuroscience that contingency is fundamental, an important challenge for further neuroscientific investigation is to discover the mechanisms that represent distributions, compute their entropies, and measure the contingencies between events.

Spatial Learning

For decades, psychologists, cognitive scientists, and neuroscientists with an empiricist bent resisted the assumption that the mind/brain explicitly represents anything (Brooks 1991, Chemero 2011, Edelman 1989, Elman & Zipser 1988, Hull 1930, Markman & Dietrich 2000, Rumelhart & McClelland 1986, Shastri & Ajjanagadde 1993, Skinner 1938, Smolensky 1986), let alone aspects of experience as far removed from sense data as probability, uncertainty, time, and space.

There is, however, a large behavioral literature implying that learned representations of spatial locations and directions underlie animal navigation, including the navigation of many insects (for reviews, see Cheng 2008, Cheng et al. 2007, Collett & Collett 2004, Collett & Graham 2004, Gallistel 1990, Legge et al. 2010, Menzel et al. 2005, Merkle & Wehner 2008, Sommer et al. 2008, Wystrach et al. 2011). Another substantial literature implies the representation of time-of-day, time-of-month, time-of-year, and temporal duration and direction (Antle & Silver 2005, Bouton & Garcia-Gutierrez 2006, Budzynski & Bingman 1999, Buhusi & Meck 2005, Crystal 2001, Denniston et al. 2004, Gwinner 1996, Matzel et al. 1988, Meck 2003, Savastano & Miller 1998, Zhang et al. 2006), but there is not space to review that literature here.

Fundamentals of navigation and spatial representation. To assume that animals represent space is to assume that the brain has one or more spatial coordinate systems that encode locations in one or more frames of reference. It also assumes brain mechanisms for estimating distance and direction. Without a mechanism that implements a system of coordinates, there is no way to represent location. Without mechanisms for estimating direction and distance, there is no way to assign to a notable point in the environment a vector representing its location. In short, the postulation of spatial representations assumes the existence of nontrivial, genetically specified, purpose-specific representational machinery. This machinery does the spatial learning when it constructs a representation of the geometry of the experienced environment and tracks the animal's position and heading within that representation.

Frames of reference. A behaviorally useful coordinate system for representing location and/or direction must be anchored to a frame of reference. Coordinates are symbols that represent locations. Typically, they are vectors, ordered pairs (or triplets) of numbers that are subject, as ordered pairs, to some mathematical

operations such as addition and subtraction. A frame of reference is established when at least two of these vectors are assigned a referent in a physically instantiated space: this vector refers to that place or that direction. Assigning referents for at least two vectors establishes referents for all possible vectors (all the possible location symbols within a given framework). Changing the frame of reference changes which symbols refer to which locations. Symbols carry information forward in time (Gallistel & King 2009). Their physical realization in neural tissue is as yet unknown (unless one imagines that altered synaptic conductances can somehow function as symbols). Signals carry information from place to place. In the brain, information is carried over long distances by spikes (nerve impulses). As we will see, changes in the frame of reference are common in the neurons whose firing signals spatial locations and directions.

Frames of spatial reference fall into two broad classes, egocentric (self centered) and allocentric (other centered), depending on whether the system of coordinates is anchored to a part of the animal's body or to an aspect of the environment. Prominent among the egocentric frameworks are the eye-centered and head-centered frameworks. Prominent among the allocentric frameworks are the geocentric (earth-centered), enclosure-centered, object-centered, and array-centered frameworks.

A well-established behavioral result, to be borne in mind when assessing the neurobiological results, is that animals of widely diverse species maintain a geocentric orientation: a sense of their orientation (and location) in a framework anchored to an indefinitely extended surrounding environment (Baird et al. 2004, Douglas 1966, Dudchenko & Davidson 2002, Etienne et al. 1986). Mammals are compass-oriented even when they have no immediate sensory basis for this orientation. Their compass sense is based on inertial dead reckoning, not on the earth's magnetic field; that is, it is based on integrating the angular velocity signals from the semicircular canals in the ear. This integration rests on an implicit commitment to the principle that direction (angular position) is the integral of angular velocity.

An early and striking manifestation of rats' compass orientation came in experiments designed to determine the cues that a rat uses in navigating a familiar maze (Carr 1917). Rats were trained to run rapidly through a complex maze, inside a square enclosure of heavy black curtains, within a large laboratory room. Between trials, the rats were kept in home cages at the other end of the room, outside and some distance from the curtained enclosure. Running trials in complete darkness had little effect on performance, as did blinding the rats, deafening them, or rendering them anosmic. On the other hand, rotating the maze and the surrounding curtain enclosure by 90° produced a profound disruption of maze performance, even though the maze itself and its relation to the perceivable surroundings (the black curtains) were in no way altered.

One of the present authors observed a similar effect in a similar experiment, again with rats (Margules & Gallistel 1988). The rats were trained to find buried food at previously demonstrated locations in a rectangular box with high walls and prominent, multimodally distinctive landmarks in the corners. The landmarks were intended to distinguish one end of the box from the other. Between trials, the rats were kept in a cage elsewhere in the room. Rotating the experimental box between trials within a normally lighted room noticeably upset them, causing freezing and other signs of fear. Despite the high walls, which prevented their seeing anything but the ceiling of the room when in the box, they were aware of and greatly perturbed by the change in the geocentric orientation of the test box. On the other hand, under red light (complete darkness for the rat) and after slow rotation of their cage for a few minutes before they were transferred to the box, which destroyed their inertial orientation, they were no longer perturbed by rotation of the test box in the room, because they could no longer detect it.

Our intent in rotating the box within the room was to force the rats to rely on the prominent landmarks in the box to distinguish one end of the box from the other. In this, we failed. As in earlier experiments, when geocentrically disoriented, the rats ignored the corner landmarks when digging at what they took to be the location of the buried food, with the result that half the time they dug at the rotationally equivalent location (Cheng 1986, Gallistel 1990, Margules & Gallistel 1988). A rotationally correct location is correct except for a 180° rotation of the box; it is the location one digs at when one is misoriented within the rectangle. In other words, when the geometry of the test box limited the possible reorientations to two, rats consistently failed to use prominent landmarks in the corners to establish a unique (and correct) orientation.

The evidence for the maintenance of geocentric orientation does not imply that animals do not rely on more local frames of reference when navigating within enclosed spaces. Neurobiological results on place and head direction cells show clearly that they do use these local coordinate frameworks. However, unless the animal is geocentrically disoriented before placement in the enclosure, the geocentric orientation of the enclosure itself is also represented, even when this may not be apparent in the firing of head direction cells. This representation is a basis for the subjective polarization of symmetrical enclosures, such as rectangles and cylinders. Rotational confusions in symmetric enclosures (Cheng 1986) are observed only when the rats are geocentrically disoriented by slow rotation in the dark. When subjects enter an enclosure with their geocentric orientation intact, their geocentric orientation polarizes the enclosure, establishing for the animal which way is which within that enclosure. When an intrinsically polarized enclosure—one without rotational symmetries—has been rotated, then the animal's geocentric orientation enables it to detect and respond to that rotation.

The midbrain's capacity to integrate the angular velocity signal from the vestibular system so as to maintain the geocentric orientation by inertial means explains rats' remarkable sensitivity to changes in the geocentric orientation of experimental closures (Angelaki et al. 2010, Rochefort et al. 2011). This capacity enables rats to carry the directional parallel from their cage and the larger room into test enclosures that eliminate or greatly restrict sensory access to the larger space. To "carry a parallel" is to preserve a directional axis when going from one part of the world to another (or one part of a map to another). Doing so is essential to dead reckoning, which is an essential aspect of navigation, map construction, and landmark recognition.

Dead reckoning, also known as path integration, plays a fundamental role in animal navigation (Cheung et al. 2008, Collett & Graham 2004, Gallistel 1990, Loomis et al. 1998, Wehner & Srinivasan 2003, Wittlinger et al. 2006). It is the reckoning of a new position and heading from an old position by summing successive intervening displacements and changes in heading to obtain the net change in position and heading.

Dead reckoning provides the animal with a moment-to-moment representation of its location and orientation on its cognitive map. The mechanism that mediates dead reckoning is a learning mechanism, by means of which the animal learns where it is. Diverse species of animals rely strongly on this dynamic representation of their position and heading, as did marine navigators until the very recent advent of the global positioning system. When a rat has learned to run a complex maze rapidly and the experimenter then shortens the paths, the rat runs full tilt into the walls at the end (Carr 1917). If it is an elevated maze, the rat runs off the end of the shortened segments into thin air (Dennis 1932). These results are analogous to the many shipwrecks caused by faulty dead reckoning. The rat, like the mariner, only looks (or feels) for landmarks when its dead reckoned position on its map approaches a mapped boundary or waypoint.

Dead reckoning plays an important role in map construction (Biegler 2000; Clark & Taube 2009; Collett & Collett 2009a,b; Gallistel 1990; McNaughton et al. 2006; Tcheang et al. 2011). It provides the animal with its own approximate

coordinates in a frame that remains the same as the animal moves between widely separated parts of its environment. This makes it possible for the animal to represent in a common system of coordinates the location and orientation of the surfaces it encounters in locations far removed from one another. The mechanism that mediates map construction is the spatial learning mechanism.

Dead reckoning plays an important role in landmark recognition, that is, in the establishment of an identity between a currently perceived distinctive feature of the environment and a charted feature, which is a feature whose location and orientation has previously been recorded on the cognitive map. In natural environments, the readily perceptible features of most landmarks are rarely sufficient in and of themselves to uniquely identify them. The animal's dead-reckoning-based sense of its location and heading on its cognitive map establishes a prior probability distribution on the charted landmarks that might plausibly correspond to a terrain feature it currently perceives. Landmarks in improbable locations or with an improbable orientation are treated as "impostors" and ignored, no matter how much they may resemble the one that animal is looking to use (Gallistel 1990). Landmarks in the right location and orientation are accepted despite wide variation in their salient surface characteristics, such as color (Cartwright & Collett 1983). Thus, the learning of where you are by dead reckoning is intimately connected to your ability to recognize that what you are looking at now is a unique landmark that you have seen before and represented on your cognitive map.

A stable frame of reference is a sine qua non for functional dead reckoning. The summing of successive small displacements (in the limit, the integration of velocity with respect to time) only yields a useable representation of current location if the displacements are all computed within the same frame of reference. If the frame of reference varies during the summation/integration, the resulting vector does not correctly represent the animal's location in any frame of reference (**Figure 1**). Thus, dead

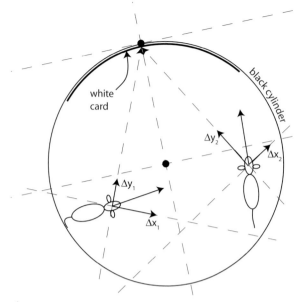

Figure 1

Dead reckoning requires using at every location a frame of reference whose axes are parallel to the frame at the other locations ("carrying the parallel"). It cannot be validly carried out in a changing frame of reference, such as a frame of reference in which the end of one axis is anchored to a prominent landmark. In this example, the landmark is a large white card set against the wall of a black cylinder. If the animal were to use the ever-changing direction from itself to the center of the white card as one axis in its dead-reckoning frame of reference, the vector that results from summing successive displacements, $\langle \sum \Delta x \quad \sum \Delta y \rangle$, would not represent its location in any frame of reference. For the resultant vector to be useful, the animal's displacements in different parts of the environment must be represented in the same coordinate framework and by reference to a single system of directional parallels. In this figure, one such framework has its origin at the center of the cylinder and one axis passing through the center of the white card. This is an array-centered framework whose origin is derived from the geometry of the cylinder. Another has its origin at the center of the white card, with one axis perpendicular to it and the other tangential. This is an object-centered framework, defined by reference to the geometry of the card. Direction for dead-reckoning purposes must be reckoned with respect to what for practical purposes is a point at infinity, a point so far away that its direction does not change as the animal moves. Perceptible terrestrial landmarks are rarely far enough away.

reckoning and map construction are intimately intertwined. Without dead reckoning, map construction is not possible. Without map construction, there is no world-anchored framework within which to represent one's current position and heading.

Piloting. Piloting is navigation by reference to charted landmarks. It presupposes an ability to identify currently perceived terrain features with features recorded on a cognitive map. Thus, it presupposes a cognitive map. The map is, of course, learned; the brain is not born with a representation of the geometry of the environment in which the animal happens to find itself. What the brain is born with is the machinery it needs to construct such a representation. This machinery is what enables the animal to learn from experience.

The first and most basic task in piloting is to establish geocentric orientation, orientation within the largest accessible frame of reference. Colloquially, this is called getting one's bearings. For most animals outdoors, the sun, if visible, is the preferred directional referent. For practical purposes, it is a point at infinity, which means that all lines of sight to it are functionally parallel. Its direction changes because of the earth's rotation, but animals of diverse species rapidly learn the solar ephemeris, the sun's direction as a function of the time of day at a given season and latitude, which enables them to compensate for the predictable changes in its azimuth (Dyer & Dickinson 1994, Foa et al. 2009, Gagliardo et al. 2005, Gallistel 1990, Heinze & Reppert 2011, Sauman et al. 2005, Wehner 1984, Wehner & Müller 1993).

Establishing a geocentric orientation without reference to a perceptible point at infinity or to the earth's magnetic field is an image-registration problem. By "image," we mean a representation in the brain of a set of perceptible surfaces with substantial relief. Getting oriented under these conditions presupposes two such representations: a cognitive map, constructed from earlier experience in the environment, and a current perception of a portion of the mapped environment, constructed from ongoing sensory input. The map is encoded in one framework. The current perception of the surroundings is encoded in another. The computational challenge is to discover the translation and rotation of the current perception that brings it into register with the corresponding portion of the cognitive map. This computation mediates an animal's learning which way it is headed when it emerges into a familiar environment after becoming disoriented with respect to that frame of reference.

There are two basic approaches to image registration: feature matching and computing shape parameters. Feature matching requires finding distinctive features in each image followed by the establishment of cross-image feature correspondences (landmark recognition). It requires that localized regions of an image contain information that makes them unique (hence unambiguously recognizable). Discovering which features in one image "match" which features in another is inherently a trial-and-error process; hence, it is computationally intensive. This contrasts with the closed-form computation of geometric parameters, such as the centroid, principal axes, and higher moments of a shape.

Registration by the computation of shape parameters operates purely on the sets of coordinates that represent the shape. The locations of the surfaces that form a shape, when represented by coordinates, are, from a mathematical perspective, highly structured scatter plots. Image parameters are the centroid, principal axes, medial axes, skews, and so on of these scatter plots; they characterize the spatial distribution of sensible points in the environment by measures computed from the coordinates representing the locations of those points. Image registration by means of shape parameters does not single out features, nor, a fortiori, does it establish between-image feature correspondences; that is, there is no landmark-recognition stage in this computation. The feature-matching approach focuses on local distinctive, easily sensed surface properties, whereas the shape-parameters approach focuses on the global shape of the experienced environment, that is, on its geometry.

The unexpected finding that disoriented(!) rats do not use easily sensed, highly salient corner landmarks to distinguish one end of a rectangular enclosure from the other (Cheng 1986, Margules & Gallistel 1988) led to the suggestion that the image-registration computation mediating the establishment of a geocentric orientation in a disoriented animal was mediated by the computation of shape parameters (Gallistel 1990). This would explain the rat's failure to use distinctive nonpositional features to determine which way was which within a rectangular enclosure. If getting reoriented depends on feature matching, the rat's failure to attend to the landmarks is hard to understand. They were exactly what a feature-matching algorithm most needs—highly distinctive in several sensory modalities and well localized, therefore easily recognized. The hypothesized brain mechanism for establishing orientation on the basis of shape parameters has come to be called the geometric module. There is now a large behavioral literature pro and con (for recent reviews, see Burgess 2008, Cheng 2008, Cheng & Newcombe 2005, Vallortigara 2009). This hypothesis about how a disoriented animal learns its orientation presupposes that the animal has a representation of the overall shape of the experienced environment—a metric cognitive map. On that score, there is now considerable consensus in the behavioral literature, a consensus strongly supported by the to-be-reviewed neuroscientific findings.

Should this hypothesis about the nature of the orientation computation prove correct, landmarks may nonetheless play a role in establishing an orientation. In some environments (e.g., rectangles, which are symmetrical about both principal axes), the principal axes together with the centroid and/or other shape parameters (medial axes, higher-order moments) do not suffice to uniquely orient the navigator. Shape-parameter computations yield two equally acceptable alignments (orientations). Absent other input, the orientation settled on will be wrong half the time. When it is wrong, it will fail to correctly predict salient features (landmarks). This failure may alert the brain to its image-alignment error. It may then try whether the other, equally probably alignment does correctly predict landmark location(s). On this hypothesis, correct alignment precedes and makes possible landmark recognition. On the hypothesis that alignment is achieved by feature matching, alignment follows from landmark recognition. Thus, the question is not fundamentally about which cues are used, shape parameters, or landmarks; rather, it is about the nature of the image-aligning computation by which an animal becomes oriented on its cognitive map. The nature of the computation determines how the cues are used and the order in which the alignment and recognition processes occur.

The sign-landmark distinction. An important distinction, which has not been clearly maintained in the behavioral literature, and which is rarely recognized in the neurobiological literature, is the distinction between landmarks and signs. A distinctive feature is a landmark when it is used to establish the navigator's bearings (orientation and location in an allocentric frame of reference). A sign, sometimes called a beacon, marks a region where something of motivational interest may be located, something to be approached or avoided. Landmarks cannot be duplicated, because a landmark is, by definition, a unique and recognizable location. In contrast, there can be many instances of a sign. An oak tree, if it is a particularly distinctive one, may function as a landmark, but it more typically functions as a sign that acorns may be found in its vicinity. A storm cloud is a sign that there is bad weather in that direction; it is not a landmark, no matter how salient. The farther away a landmark is, the more effective it is for establishing orientation, whereas the closer a sign is to a goal, the better it serves as a beacon.

There are two considerations of methodological importance for behavioral and neurobiological investigations in connection with the distinction between signs and landmarks: (*a*) A geocentric reorientation by reference to the shape of, and/or landmarks in, an experimental enclosure is only likely to occur when subjects have been disoriented by prolonged slow rotation in the dark. Absent this inertial disorientation, subjects probably carry a geocentric parallel into an experimental enclosure. In that case, the enclosure is subjectively polarized by its perceived orientation within the broader geocentric framework. Intuitively, the animal that is not geocentrically disoriented knows which way is which in any enclosure, no matter how symmetrical and how featureless. The violation of this sense of the enclosing maze's geocentric orientation was what confused the rats in the Carr (1917) experiments that first revealed the devastating effect on animal navigation of rotating a maze. (*b*) The essential test of geocentric reorientation by reference to a putative landmark is the effect of changing that landmark's location on the locus of a subject's search for goals at a substantial distance from the feature. When the goal is at or near or directly behind the distinctive feature and the rat is not disoriented, one is probably not testing properties of the hypothesized geometric module. One is probably testing sign learning (cf. Cheng 2008, Graham et al. 2006, Pearce et al. 2006).

Coordinate formats. Symbol systems for encoding locations differ in how they do it. The most familiar such difference is that between the Cartesian and polar coordinates. In the Cartesian system, the coordinates specify distances from two orthogonal axes. In the polar system, the two coordinates specify an angular deviation from a directional axis (a bearing) and a distance (range). The form of a geometric computation depends strongly on the coordinate format. For computational reasons, it is likely that path integration (dead reckoning, discussed above) is computed in a Cartesian format. In that format, the errors in the estimates of direction are not compounded in the ongoing integration, whereas these unavoidable errors are compounded when the computation is carried on in the polar format. This compounding leads to the rapid buildup of a large error (Cheung & Vickerstaff 2010, Gallistel 1990).

A less familiar means of spatial representation is by spatial basis functions. Spatial basis functions are distributions that may be combined in weighted sums to create a probability distribution that peaks at the subject's probable location. We say more about this less familiar way of representing location when we review the properties of grid cells.

An advantage of the basis-function format is that it naturally encodes spatial probability distributions rather than points. Thus it naturally represents positional uncertainty. Representing positional uncertainty is almost as important as representing position, as many amateur navigators learn to their cost. Also, transformation into a basis-function representation is frequently used in image-registration and image-stitching computations. As already mentioned, computing a geocentric orientation is an image-registration computation. Keeping track of how one local coordinate system relates to the next as one moves through a complex space is closely related to what are called image-stitching problems in image processing. Image registration and image stitching computations map between coordinate frameworks. The maintenance of mappings between different coordinate frameworks is the essence of navigation (cf. Worden 1992).

The place cell system. Neuroscientific evidence for an abstract representation of the geometry of experienced space and for the representation of the animal's location within that geometry (i.e., a cognitive map) comes from the extensive literature on place cells, grid cells, head direction cells, border cells, and boundary-vector cells. As their names suggest, these functionally specialized neurons signal abstract properties of the animal's relation to its spatial environment. These cells are present in rudimentary form as soon as rat pups leave the nest (Langston et al. 2010, Wills et al. 2010), suggesting important genetic control over their development, that is, a genetic basis for the mechanisms by which the brain represents experienced spatial geometry. These specialized neurons are compelling evidence for problem-specific learning mechanisms, that is, mechanisms specialized for learning in a mathematically and physically definable domain of experience. Their specialization for this function makes implicit commitments to domain-defining principles.

Place cells fire when the animal is in a particular place in a familiar environment. In the rat, where they have been most studied, they are found in the hippocampus, the adjacent subicular complex, and in the entorhinal cortex, which is the main interface between the hippocampus and the neocortex (Moser et al. 2008). Circuits within these three closely connected structures in the medial temporal lobe appear to be specialized for navigational computations.

The sizes of the firing fields for place cells increase as the recording electrode moves from dorsal to ventral within the hippocampus (Jung et al. 1994, Kjelstrup et al. 2008). Viewed from the brain's perspective, different place cells represent spatial location with different degrees of resolution, just as different simple cells in V1 represent local spatial frequencies on the retina with different degrees of resolution.

The striking feature of the firing of place cells is that it does not depend on concurrent sensory input. A place cell fires when a rat stands in or moves through a delimited region of a particular environment. The region is often well away from the walls and other distinctive features of the environment. Different place cells fire in different places. In some environments, a place cell fires regardless of what the rat is looking at, and it fires even if the rat is navigating in complete darkness. Neither immediate visual experience nor prior visual experience is necessary; place cells with normal properties develop in rats blinded soon after birth (Save et al. 1998).

It should be recalled that turning off the lights or blinding rats has little effect on their ability to navigate a familiar maze. The combination of these behavioral and neurobiological findings is not consistent with recurring suggestions in the behavioral literature that places are defined by views (Cheng 2008, Sheynikhovich et al. 2009). Place is defined by reference to coordinates stored in memory that represent the learned geometry of the experienced environment, that is, by reference to a cognitive map. Vision is only one of many different sensory modalities that convey information about the animal's coordinates in a frame of reference. The firing of a place cell represents the integration of and abstraction away from the more sensible aspects of experience to signal a highly abstract aspect of that experience, namely, its location.

A cognitive map is a repository for acquired information about the positions of sensible features of the animal's environment, as encoded in one or more frames of reference. The firing of place cells is fundamentally dependent on such a repository, which is why the study of such cells is central to the neuroscience of learning and memory.

A striking feature of the results from experiments that have sought to determine what stimuli control the firing of place cells is that removing from the environment a cue that has been shown to affect the place in the experimental environment at which a place cell fires, e.g., a distal landmark, does not terminate its effect on the cell's firing. In many experiments of this kind, rotating a cue by 90° or 180° rotates the cell's place field by a similar amount. However, the cell continues to fire when the animal returns to that place after the cue has been removed altogether (Muller & Kubie 1987, O'Keefe & Speakman 1987, Quirk et al. 1990, Shapiro et al. 1997). What matters is not the current sensory input from the cue, but rather the relation between the rat's current location and the remembered location of the cue.

In another environment, a given place cell will fire to a different place or may not have a field. Thus, the firing of a place cell does not signal that the rat is in a place unique in its experienced world, although the aggregate firing pattern across place cells may do so. In multichamber or multiarm environments, a place cell may fire in different places in different chambers or arms (Gothard et al. 1996a,b; Shapiro et al. 1997; Skaggs & McNaughton 1998).

The place where a given neuron fires when in one copy of a box does not predict the box-relative place (if any) where it fires in an exact copy of that box in another room (Leutgeb et al. 2004; O'Keefe & Conway 1978). This reinforces the conclusion drawn from behavioral work that a subject's behavior in one box may differ systematically from its behavior inside a copy of that box when the copies are in different locations in the macro environment, even when there is no sensory/perceptual access to the macroenvironment from inside the boxes. This re-emphasizes the important point that animals keep track of their own position and orientation in the macroenvironment as well as the position and orientation of the enclosed spaces they enter. They behave differently in different but seemingly identical experimental boxes because the information in memory about the different locations of the two boxes in the macroenvironment informs the brain that the two otherwise indistinguishable boxes are not one and the same (Collett et al. 1997, Collett & Kelber 1988). With enclosures, as with landmarks, location confers identity. No matter how much one enclosure looks and feels and smells like another, it is not that other enclosure if it is not where the animal has the other located on its large-scale map of its experienced environment (or if it has the wrong orientation on that large-scale map). The behavioral results and the neuroscientific results are in accord on this fundamentally important point: Location determines the subjective determination of identity, not vice versa.

Multiple frames of reference. The effects of moving landmarks on the location of place fields suggest conclusions about how the brain uses local landmarks to maintain a geocentric orientation. It does so by using sensed position in a framework established by one or more local landmarks to correct accumulating error in its dead-reckoned orientation. Geocentric orientations based solely on vestibular and optic-flow cues inevitably degrade over time because there is noise in the signals being integrated (Cheung & Vickerstaff 2010, Vickerstaff & Cheung 2010). Frames of reference anchored to perceptible landmarks in an enclosed space can prevent the accumulation of error while the animal is in that environment (**Figure 2**).

Only by keeping track of position in more than one framework can the animal make probable inferences about what is moving with respect to what. It has no way of knowing a priori which objects (potential landmarks) are movable and which are not. If the card moves with respect to the cylinder, then other points of interest on the circumference of the cylinder (a nest or escape hole, for example) change their coordinates in the card-based frame of reference but not in a cylinder-based frame. To distinguish rotation of the card within the cylinder from rotation of the cylinder itself, the brain must represent places and directions within the cylinder in more than one frame of reference.

When a white card is rotated within an otherwise featureless black cylinder, most place cells change their firing field correspondingly (Yoder et al. 2011). If subjects have been geocentrically disoriented before placement in the cylinder, the card is the only thing that permits the establishment of a stable direction. However, the same shift occurs even when the card is moved while the rat is in the cylinder. This manipulation places the card-centered framework in conflict with cylinder-centered and geocentric frameworks (Blair & Sharp 1996, Sharp et al. 1995). During the small interval over which rotation of the card within the cylinder takes place, there is little accumulation of error in the inertial geocentric framework. If the world (the cylinder, including its floor) were to rotate, there would be a signal from the semicircular canals. Absent a signal indicating rotation in an inertial frame, the probable inference is that the card moved, not the cylinder. Thus, for locating the nest or escape hole, a coordinate frame anchored to the cylinder is the one to use.

Thus, a fundamental question in these experiments is, when the card is rotated in the presence of a geocentrically oriented subject, does behaviorally measured orientation go with the card? In posing this question, one must not use a behavioral test that puts the goal at the card, because then the card may function as a sign. What is required is a behavioral test of a kind already reported in the literature on animal navigation (Mittelstaedt & Mittelstaedt 1980): A mother gerbil with a nest located behind a hole in a wall of the cylinder leaves the nest to retrieve a pup in the center of the cylinder. If the cylinder (with the nest) is rotated while she gets her pup from a stationary cup in the center, her return run is "correct" in the now erroneous

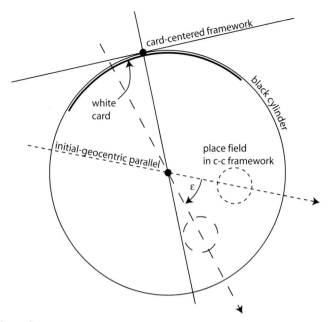

Figure 2

By maintaining its position concurrently in both local and global frameworks, a navigator can prevent the accumulation of directional error in the global framework. The finely dashed directed line is an initial geocentric parallel; it represents the animal's orientation in a large-scale geocentric framework on entering the enclosed, maximally symmetrical space. The finely dashed circle represents a place field in the framework established by the large white card, which is the only distinctive feature in a black cylinder, an enclosure with no principal axes. In such an enclosure, the only way to maintain a geocentric orientation is by angular dead reckoning, but exclusive reliance on this computation will bring with it unavoidable directional drift (coarsely dashed directed line). The directional drift, ε, will put the geocentric framework out of register with the local landmark framework; a position in global coordinates that initially superposed on the place in local coordinates will no longer superpose (coarsely dashed circle). The discrepancy between the referents of what should be corresponding coordinates can be used to correct the drift error in the geocentric direction. Intuitively, if the correct geocentric orientation were that indicated by the coarsely dashed line, then the animal should find itself close to the orientation axis of the card-centered framework. From the quite different gaze angle from the place where a neuron fires, the accumulated error in its geocentric orientation may be computed and corrected.

inertial frame of reference rather than in the cylinder-centered frame. She ignores the highly salient odor cues and pup cries coming from the nest. This is one of many demonstrations of the navigational importance of inertial (hence, geocentric) frames of reference. The question thus is, assuming that a large white card in such a cylinder would establish a frame of reference for place fields, would the rotation of the card that caused a relocation of the place fields also cause the rat to run 90° off the true direction of a nest located well away from the card? Or, as the hypothesis about the function of place fields in card-centered frames of reference implies, would the rat still return directly to its nest, despite the change in the place fields? To our knowledge, this question has not been put to the experimental test.

When individual landmarks, landmark arrays, or components of more complex environments are moved, the results resist easy summary (Gothard et al. 1996a,b; Shapiro et al. 1997; Tanila et al. 1997), but they are consistent with the hypothesis that the brain's navigation system tracks the animal's position and orientation in several different frameworks simultaneously.

Dependence on vestibular input. Vestibular input is essential to the computational mechanisms that generate the firing of place cells. Temporary inactivation of this signal eliminates the place-specific firing of hippocampal cells for the duration of the inactivation (Stackman et al. 2002). Lesioning the vestibular apparatus eliminates it permanently (Russell et al. 2003). Given the many demonstrations that the place fields depend strongly on local landmarks, the dependence on vestibular input may seem surprising. The explanation is probably that vestibular input is essential to the maintenance of orientation in an inertial (hence geocentric) frame of reference. The maintenance of this orientation is essential to the dead reckoning that plays a critical role in the construction of cognitive maps, landmark recognition, and inferences about what moves relative to what. Whatever disrupts dead reckoning can be expected to disrupt all of these processes.

The evidence that much of the basic machinery of navigation does not operate properly in the absence of appropriate vestibular signals is important for the methodology of behavioral studies of navigation. It suggests caution in interpreting the results from virtual reality experiments and functional magnetic resonance imaging (fMRI) experiments, in which

vestibular signals processed in the midbrain (Angelaki et al. 2010) indicate no translation or rotation in an inertial framework, whereas optic-flow signals processed in the forebrain (Britten 2008) indicate self-motion. Much of the brain's navigational machinery may not function properly under these conditions.

What else place cells signal. Many other aspects of the animal's experience affect the firing of hippocampal place cells. In more complex environments, firing varies strongly with the direction in which the animal moves through a place. Changing the color of the walls has a large effect (Leutgeb et al. 2005), as does changing the task that the animal is carrying out (Colgin et al. 2008, Komorowski et al. 2009, Leutgeb et al. 2005, Manns & Eichenbaum 2009, Markus et al. 1995). Many of these effects cause what is called rate remapping: The place field does not change but the firing rate and firing pattern in that field does. The effects of highly diverse nonspatial cues demonstrate the dependence of neural firing in the hippocampus on a vast repository of acquired information, much of it highly abstract. When we learn how to read the spike train code, the firing of a single hippocampal neuron may tell volumes about the animal's current experience in relation to its past experience in that environment.

It may seem puzzling that a neural structure that is a critical component of a complex system for navigating should also be strongly implicated in memory phenomena that, on their surface, have nothing to do with navigation and the representation of space. Gallistel (1990), in a chapter on "The Unity of Remembered Experience," adduced evidence that spatio-temporal indexing is the mechanism by which the brain knits together the diverse aspects of experience computed by the many different problem-specific modules that are implied by the neuroanatomy and electrophysiology of the cortex. On this hypothesis, the brain binds the remembered color of an object to its remembered shape on the basis that the physically separated (at the level of brain substrates) memories of the object's color and its shape have the same spatio-temporal index. They have the same spatio-temporal index because they were perceived in the same place at the same time. This hypothesis maintains that episodic memory, that is, the ability to reconstruct an experience in all of its diversity, depends fundamentally on the representation of the spatial and temporal location of the elements of the experience.

Consistent with this hypothesis about the key role in memory of the encoding of spatio-temporal location is the recent discovery that hippocampal place cells also signal position in time. MacDonald et al. (2011) taught rats to associate one of two objects with one of two odors presented 10 s after the rats had inspected the objects. On a given trial, one or the other odor was mixed into the sand in a flowerpot and presented to the rat 10 s after it inspected the object. If the odor was that associated with the recently inspected object, digging in the flowerpot yielded food. If it was the wrong odor, the one associated with the other object, the rat had to avoid digging in the pot and go to another location to obtain food. The experimenters recorded from multiple pyramidal cells in the hippocampus throughout each trial. They found that the firing rates of different cells peaked at different times during the 10 s delay between the inspection of the object and the presentation of the odiferous flowerpot (**Figure 3**, see color insert). Thus different cells signaled different locations within the interval. As expected from the scalar variability seen in behavioral work on interval timing (Gallistel & Gibbon 2000), the signals from cells whose firing peaked later in the interval were more spread out in time.

The grid cell system. Grid cells are multimodal place cells. A grid cell fires at multiple locations within a familiar environment (see Derdikman & Moser 2010, Moser et al. 2008, Yoder et al. 2011). The locations where it fires form a triangular grid (**Figure 4**, see color insert). The grids for different cells have different phases, different compass orientations, and different scales, as would be expected if they mediate a basis function representation of the

animal's probable location. The scale of the grids increases as one moves the recording electrode from dorsal to ventral in the entorhinal cortex (Brun et al. 2008). (Recall that a similar increase in the size of place fields occurs along the same dorsal-to-ventral axis in the hippocampus.) The effects of moving landmarks on grid cells are similar to their effects on place and head direction cells; the relevant experiments show that grid cells are anchored to multiple frames of reference and can change their frame of reference within less than 100 ms (Derdikman et al. 2009; Diba & Buzsáki 2008; Frank et al. 2000; Gothard et al. 1996a,b; McNaughton et al. 1996; Redish et al. 2000; Rivard et al. 2004).

An important difference between grid cells and place cells is that the entorhinal grid cell map (together with the head direction cells, border cells, and boundary-vector cells) appears to be a single map with different phase and alignment to the environment in different places or in different conditions (Fyhn et al. 2007, Solstad et al. 2008). The place cell system, by contrast, appears to reflect several different more local maps (Derdikman et al. 2009). An analogy to marine charts may help. Between ports, navigators use a large-scale map on which there are many ports. The navigator uses different parts of this map from different orientations under different circumstances, but it is all one map. Elsewhere in the chart book (or sometimes on the back of the large-scale chart) there are port maps, one for each port. This difference between the grid cell system and the place cell system is consistent with the behavioral evidence that animals maintain their sense of place within the large-scale environment (extramaze cues) while also being sensitive to their location relative to local features (intramaze cues).

Grid cells are found in the medial entorhinal cortex and in the subiculum and parasubiculum, the subset of the medial temporal lobe structures that contain a neural system specialized for the representation of the animal's position and heading on its cognitive map.

Head direction cells fire when the head is oriented within roughly +/– 45° of a

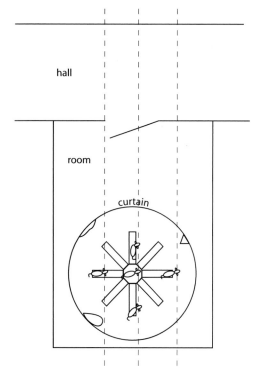

hall

room

curtain

Figure 5

A head direction cell fires whenever the rat's head is at a specific angle with respect to directional parallels (dashed lines), regardless of where the rat is in the environment and even in complete darkness. The experimental set-up portrayed schematizes common features of those actually used: A test arena (radial maze or cylinder or box) surrounded by curtains, often with some landmarks on them (the differently shaped lumps against the curtain), located in a laboratory room off a hall through which the rat is transported prior to testing. Behavioral and electrophysiological results imply that the entire space is represented on at least some of the maps that inform behavior and the firing of place and head direction cells.

They are not, however, components of a magnetic compass, as their directional tuning is not dependent on the earth's magnetic field.

Head direction cells are found in diverse and widely separated brain structures: the anterior dorsal thalamic nucleus, the lateral dorsal thalamus, and the lateral mammillary nuclei, which are widely separated loci in the diencephalon; also in the dorsal tegmental nucleus in the midbrain; the dorsal striatum in the subcortical telencephalon; and in diverse cortical areas, including entorhinal, retrosplenial, medial precentral, and medial prestriate cortex. They are most prevalent in the anterior dorsal nucleus of the thalamus (~60% of cells recorded there), but the population in the subiculum has also been intensively studied. The subiculum is intermediate between the hippocampus and the entorhinal cortex. Like the entorhinal cortex, it is a way station for signals going into and coming out of the hippocampus. Like place cells, head direction cells require a vestibular signal.

The firing of a head direction cell signals a highly abstract property of the relation between an animal and its surroundings. It does not signal that the head is directed toward a particular place or object in the local environment, because the place toward which the head is oriented differs depending on where the animal is (**Figure 5**). A head direction cell fires when the head has the cell's preferred orientation even in complete darkness. Direction, like location, is defined only by reference to the learned geometry of the experienced environment.

The effects of moving prominent landmarks on the tuning curves of head direction cells are similar to the effects on place cells: In complex environments, when proximal and distal landmarks are rotated in conflicting directions, the frame of reference usually goes with the distal landmarks (Yoganarasimha et al. 2006, Zugaro et al. 2001), as one would expect, given that for determining direction, the farther away a landmark is, the better it will function. This is another manifestation of the many ways in which the signaling of these specialized cells reveals implicit commitments to domain-specific mathematical principles. In a cylinder

directional parallel in some frame of reference (for a recent review, see Taube 2007). The more closely the head's orientation matches the center of a cell's directional tuning, the more rapidly the cell fires. At the optimal orientation, firing is typically brisk (20–100 spikes/s) and sustained. Different cells are tuned to different directions. In the population of head direction cells, there does not appear to be a favored direction. Their directional tuning in a given environment is stable across many days. Thus head direction cells could be described as compass cells. They provide the directional signal required for dead reckoning.

environment, where most such experiments have been done, rotating the card 90° or 180° on the wall of the cylinder rotates the frame of reference for all the head direction cells by the same amount. Notice in **Figure 5** that such a rotation (for example, of the triangle in the northeast quadrant) constitutes a much greater change in viewing angle for the rat when it is looking from the end of the east arm than when it is looking from the end of the south arm. This emphasizes the fact that what rotates coherently is the frame of reference within which directional parallels are defined, not landmark-viewing angles.

When a rat walks from a familiar chamber into an unfamiliar one, a head direction cell typically maintains the frame of reference established in the familiar room (Dudchenko & Zinyuk 2005, Golob & Taube 1999, Stackman et al. 2003, Taube & Burton 1995). This is an example of carrying the directional parallel into unexplored parts of an environment. As the new chamber becomes familiar, the frame of reference mediating the neuron's signaling often shifts to the landmarks in that chamber. However, as the subject gains familiarity with a multichambered environment, some head direction cells adopt a frame of reference that remains the same from chamber to chamber (Dudchenko & Zinyuk 2005).

The shifts in the frame of reference for the head direction signal in response to changes in enclosure shape and landmarks is often taken to indicate that this signal does not participate in the behaviorally well-documented process of maintaining a geocentric orientation with respect to the environment outside the enclosure. This is a mistake. The neuron is not the rat. Carrying a directional parallel depends on computations performed on the overall geometry of the so-far experienced space. Carrying the parallel further, as one enters unexplored regions, is essential to the construction of a coherent map of the large-scale environment. The construction of such a map makes it possible for the place- cum-head-direction-cum-boundary-cell system to signal direction and location in a large-scale framework. It enables

the animal to keep track of where it is in the world.

Border cells fire when the rat is near a compass-oriented boundary (Solstad et al. 2009). What drives the cell's firing is not concurrent sensory input (e.g., a view or feel or touch). What drives firing is a geometric abstraction, the existence of an extended boundary or obstacle to navigation with a particular orientation with respect to the large-scale environment. For example, a boundary cell may fire all along the east side of a north-south wall, whether the lights are on or not. If it is the wall of a square box and the box is elongated parallel to that wall, the firing field now extends all along the elongated wall. When the wall is removed so that the boundary becomes the limit of the navigable surface on which the rat is supported, the cell still fires all along this limit, even though its sensory properties are now radically different. When the rat is moved into other environments with north-south boundaries, the same cell fires all along the east side of those boundaries, too. If a north-south-oriented wall is inserted partway into one of these environments, the cell fires along the east side of that wall *and* along the east side of the enclosing environment. The moving of landmarks and the changing of environmental shape that cause remapping of place and head direction cell firing do not cause remapping of boundary cells; that is, they do not cause them to fire along boundaries with a different compass orientation. The existence of these cells is strong confirmation of the conclusion drawn from behavioral work that rats generally maintain a sense of their orientation in the large-scale environment. Border cells may be special cases of boundary-vector cells.

Boundary-vector cells fire when a limit to navigation lies at some remove in a particular compass direction from the rat, regardless of the color, material, or shape of the boundary and regardless of whether it is a material obstacle to navigation or an immaterial obstacle, that is, the void where the supporting platform ends (Lever et al. 2009). Like border cells, boundary-vector cells do not usually remap in response to the manipulation of landmarks, and they fire at the same remove and direction from a limit in different environments with different shapes in different locations within the macroenvironment. The longer a boundary cell's vector, that is, the farther from the boundary its firing field is located, the greater is the extent of the field. This suggests scalar uncertainty in the representation of distance as well as time, a result consistent with behavioral results (Durgin et al. 2009).

Border cells and boundary-vector cells are found intermingled with head direction cells and grid cells in what are by now "the usual suspects," that is, the medial entorhinal cortex and the subiculum, which are in the medial temporal lobe next to the hippocampus.

CONCLUSIONS

The mechanisms of synaptic plasticity (e.g., associative LTP or the Hebbian synapse) do not explain the properties of associative learning. The hypothesis that LTP is the mechanism of memory offers no account of how the highly structured, acquired information that mediates animal navigation and the firing of place, head direction, grid, and boundary-vector cells may be carried forward in time in a manner that makes it available to computation on a millisecond time scale. The stored information in the causal chain that informs the firing of cells in the navigation system can change radically in a fraction of a second, as, for example, when the frame of reference for a place or head direction cell changes (Jezek et al. 2011).

The shortcomings of the synaptic plasticity hypothesis highlight the necessity for a more behaviorally and cognitively sophisticated approach to the neuroscience of learning and memory. The literature on the functional properties of neurons in the medial temporal lobe that are sensitive to environmental geometry implies the existence in the brain of genetically specified, purpose-specific computational mechanisms that construct a metric representation of the geometry of the experienced spatial environment and continually signal the animal's location and orientation within that

representation. The neurobiological results testify to the neurophysiological reality of metric cognitive maps, whose existence has been a controversial hypothesis in psychology and cognitive science for decades. Similar conclusions may be drawn from fMRI results in humans (Epstein 2008, 2011; MacEvoy & Epstein 2011; Morgan et al. 2010), but space does not permit a review.

A common feature of space-representing neurons is the highly abstract nature of their tuning. Their tuning cannot be described in terms of the stimuli acting on sensory receptors when the neuron fires. It can only be described by reference to a map in memory and to entities, such as directional parallels and boundaries, which must be constructed by computations performed on that map. A place is not defined by anything acting on the rat's sensorium when it is at that place, and likewise for a head direction. Position and heading are defined only by reference to the learned geometry of the surrounding space. Most of that geometry is not directly sensible by the rat on any particular occasion when it happens to pass through that place on that heading. Under many circumstances, it is dead reckoning that mediates the brain's representation of the animal's location and heading, rather than the processing of contemporary sensory input unique to that place and heading. That is, the animal's representation of itself as being in a certain place with a certain heading depends on computations that took as inputs idiothetic signals generated while it was moving toward that place, rather than signals emanating from extracorporeal features of that place (its feel, its reflectance, the views from that place, the sounds heard there, the odors smelled there, and so on).

The neurobiological evidence confirms the conclusion drawn from studies of animal navigation that dead reckoning is foundational. Dead reckoning is a domain-specific computation that makes an implicit commitment to a domain-specific mathematical principle. It presupposes nontrivial genetically specified neural mechanisms that implement a system of coordinates anchored to a large-scale frame of reference. The representation of the geometrical relation between a place and the surrounding navigationally important surfaces comes from the cognitive map, which is the repository in memory of the spatial information acquired in past explorations of the environment. Geometric information enters the brain via many different sensory modalities (and, probably, from reafferent motor commands) and over extended periods of time.

The extended period of time required for the construction of a global map reminds us that the fundamental function of memory is to carry acquired information forward in time in a computationally accessible form (Gallistel & King 2009). Any hypothesis about the neurobiological mechanism of memory must make clear how the proposed memory mechanism stores structured information and makes it accessible to computation. The hypothesis that synaptic plasticity is the mechanism of memory has yet to meet (or even address) this challenge. In the words of Griffiths et al. (2010, p. 363), "...the single biggest challenge for theoretical neuroscience is not to understand how the brain implements probabilistic inference, but how it represents the structured knowledge over which such inference is defined." The representation of the geometry of the experienced environment is a prime example of structured knowledge. The firing of place- and direction-sensitive neurons gives direct neurobiological evidence that such a representation exists in

neural tissue and that it is every bit as abstract as the term "cognitive map" implies.

The aspects of experience that drive learning in other domains are similarly far removed from elementary sense experience. Associative learning—and the signaling of neurons that participate in it—is driven by contingency, not by the temporal pairing of events. Contingency is a property of the global distributions of events in time, just as shape is a property of the global distribution of surfaces in space. Contingency is comprehended through the computation of entropies, just as shape is comprehended through the computation of locations. The signaling of neurons that participate in reinforcement learning is driven by computations that refer to remembered temporal structure. In both the spatial and the temporal domain, these computations can only be performed on a symbolic representation of where events have occurred—where in space and where in time.

Seen from a broad historical perspective, these conclusions support a materialist form of Kantian rationalism: The brain has genetically specified machinery for the construction of a spatio-temporal probabilistic representation of the experienced world. This machinery is a precondition for what have traditionally been thought of as "elementary" sense experiences, because all remembered experience is localized in space and time, with an explicitly represented degree of uncertainty.

FUTURE ISSUES

1. Where and how is the acquired geometric information that informs the firing of place, grid, head-direction, and boundary-vector cells stored? In the synaptic conductances between neurons in the circuits in which the cells are embedded? In molecules within the cells (e.g., in micro RNAs selected on the basis of their base-pair sequences, or in the methylation patterns on stretches of junk DNA, or in switch-like molecules, of which rhodopsin is an example)? In the conformation of molecules embedded in the synaptic membranes?

2. Where and how is the acquired temporal information that informs the firing of hippocampal cells stored?

3. Is environmental shape encoded using the same code as object shape?

4. Complex computations reduce to sequences of the basic arithmetic operations. How are these operations implemented and at what level of neural structure (circuit, cellular, molecular)?

5. How is it possible for the frame of reference in which a cell signals place or head direction to change in less than 100 ms, given that this frame of reference depends on acquired information stored in memory?

DISCLOSURE STATEMENT

The authors are not aware of any affiliations, memberships, funding, or financial holdings that might be perceived as affecting the objectivity of this review.

ACKNOWLEDGMENTS

The final form of our review has benefitted greatly from comments and suggestions made by far-flung colleagues. For taking the time to make these comments, we offer heartfelt thanks to Ken Cheng, Howard Eichenbaum, Russell Epstein, Rochel Gelman, Edvard Moser, Robert Stackman, Jeffrey Taube, and Barbara Tversky. The views expressed are, of course, those of the authors and not necessarily those of these generous colleagues. C.R. Gallistel's research is supported by NIMH grant RO1MH077027. Louis Matzel's research is supported by grants from the NIA (R01AG029289) and the Office of Naval Research.

LITERATURE CITED

Abraham WC. 2003. How long will long-term potentiation last? *Philos. Trans. R. Soc. Lond. B Biol. Sci.* 358(1432):735–44

Andersen RA, Essick GK, Siegel RM. 1985. Encoding of spatial location by posterior parietal neurons. *Science* 230:456–58

Angelaki DE, Yakusheva TA, Green AM, Dickman JD, Blazquez PM. 2010. Computation of egomotion in the macaque cerebellar vermis. *Cerebellum* 9:174–82

Antle MC, Silver R. 2005. Orchestrating time: arrangements of the brain circadian clock. *Trends Neurosci.* 28:145–51

Arcediano F, Escobar M, Miller RR. 2003. Temporal integration and temporal backward associations in humans and nonhuman subjects. *Learn. Behav.* 31:242–56

Baird AL, Putter JE, Muir JL, Aggleton JP. 2004. On the transience of egocentric working memory: evidence from testing the contribution of limbic brain regions. *Behav. Neurosci.* 118:785–97

Balsam PD, Drew MR, Gallistel CR. 2010. Time and associative learning. *Comp. Cogn. Behav. Rev.* 5:1–22

Balsam PD, Fairhurst S, Gallistel CR. 2006. Pavlovian contingencies and temporal information. *J. Exp. Psychol.: Anim. Behav. Proc.* 32:284–94

Balsam PD, Gallistel CR. 2009. Temporal maps and informativeness in associative learning. *Trends Neurosci.* 32:73–78

Barnet RC, Grahame NJ, Miller RR. 1996. Temporal encoding as a determinant of inhibitory control. *Learn. Motiv.* 27:73–91

Beck JM, Latham P, Pouget A. 2011. Marginalization in neural circuits with divisive normalization. *J. Neurosci.* 31:15310–19

Bermudez MA, Schultz W. 2010. Responses of amygdala neurons to positive reward-predicting stimuli depend on background reward (contingency) rather than stimulus-reward pairing (contiguity). *J. Neurophysiol.* 103:1158–70

Berridge KC. 2012. From prediction error to incentive salience: mesolimbic computation of reward motivation. *Eur. J. Neurosci.* 35:1124–43

Biegler R. 2000. Possible uses of path integration in animal navigation. *Anim. Learn. Behav.* 25:257–77

Blair HT, Sharp PE. 1996. Visual and vestibular influences on head-direction cells in the anterior thalamus of the rat. *Behav. Neurosci.* 110:643–60

Blaisdell AP, Denniston JC, Miller RR. 1998. Temporal encoding as a determinant of overshadowing. *J. Exp. Psychol.: Anim. Behav. Proc.* 24:72–83

Bouton ME, Garcia-Gutierrez A. 2006. Intertrial interval as a contextual stimulus. *Behav. Proc.* 71:307–17

Britten KH. 2008. Mechanism of self-motion perception. *Annu. Rev. Neurosci.* 31:389–410

Brooks RA. 1991. Intelligence without representation. *Artif. Intell.* 47:139–59

Brun VH, Solstad T, Kjelstrup KB, Fyhn M, Witter MP, et al. 2008. Progressive increase in grid scale from dorsal to ventral medial entorhinal cortex. *Hippocampus* 18:1200–12

Budzynski CA, Bingman VP. 1999. Time-of-day discriminative learning in homing pigeons, *Columbia livia*. *Anim. Learn. Behav.* 27:295–301

Buhusi CV, Meck WH. 2005. What makes us tick? Functional and neural mechanisms of interval timing. *Nat. Rev. Neurosci.* 6:755–65

Burger DC, Denniston JC, Miller RR. 2001. Temporal coding in conditioned inhibition: retardation tests. *Anim. Learn. Behav.* 29:281–90

Burgess N. 2008. Spatial cognition and the brain. *Ann. N. Y. Acad. Sci.* 1124:77–97

Cajal SR. 1894. La fine structure des centres nerveux. *Proc. R. Soc. Lond.* 55:444–68

Caporale N, Dan Y. 2008. Spike timing-dependent plasticity: a Hebbian learning rule. *Annu. Rev. Neurosci.* 31:25–46

Carr H. 1917. Maze studies with the white rat. *J. Anim. Behav.* 7:259–306

Cartwright BA, Collett TS. 1983. Landmark learning in bees: experiments and models. *J. Comp. Physiol. A* 151:521–43

Castro CA, Silbert LH, McNaughton BL, Barnes CA. 1989. Recovery of spatial learning deficits following decay of electrically-induced synaptic enhancement in the hippocampus. *Nature* 342:545–58

Chater N, Tenenbaum JB, Yuille A. 2006. Probabilistic models of cognition: conceptual foundations. *Trends Cogn. Sci.* 10:287–91

Chemero A. 2011. *Radical Embodied Cognitive Science*. Cambridge, MA: MIT Press

Cheng K. 1986. A purely geometric module in the rat's spatial representation. *Cognition* 23:149–78

Cheng K. 2008. Whither geometry? Troubles of the geometric module. *Trends Cogn. Sci.* 12:355–61

Cheng K, Newcombe NS. 2005. Is there a geometric module for spatial orientation? Squaring theory and evidence. *Psychon. Bull. Rev.* 12:1–23

Cheng K, Shettleworth SJ, Huttenlocher J, Rieser JJ. 2007. Bayesian integration of spatial information. *Psychol. Bull. Rev.* 133:625–37

Cheng S, Frank LM. 2011. The structure of networks that produce the transformation from grid cells to place cells. *J. Neurosci.* 197:293–306

Cheung A, Vickerstaff R. 2010. Finding the way with a noisy brain. *PLoS Comput. Biol.* 6:e1000992

Cheung A, Zhang S, Stricker C. 2008. Animal navigation: general properties of directed walks. *Biol. Cybern.* 99:197–217

Chomsky N. 1975. *Reflections on Language*. New York: Pantheon

Clark B, Taube JS. 2009. Deficits in landmark navigation and path integration after lesions of the interpeduncular nucleus. *Behav. Neurosci.* 123:490–503

Cole RP, Barnet RC, Miller RR. 1995. Temporal encoding in trace conditioning. *Anim. Learn. Behav.* 23:144–53

Colgin LL, Moser EI, Moser M-B. 2008. Understanding memory through hippocampal remapping. *Trends Neurosci.* 31:469–77

Collett M, Collett TS. 2009a. The learning and maintenance of local vectors in desert ant navigation. *J. Exp. Biol.* 212:895–900

Collett M, Collett TS. 2009b. Local and global navigational coordinate systems in desert ants. *J. Exp. Biol.* 212:901–5

Collett TS, Collett M. 2004. How do insects represent familiar terrain? *J. Physiol. Paris* 98:259–64

Collett TS, Fauria K, Dale K, Baron J. 1997. Places and patterns—a study of context learning in honeybees. *J. Comp. Physiol. A* 181:343–53

Collett TS, Graham P. 2004. Animal navigation: path integration, visual landmarks and cognitive maps. *Curr. Biol.* 14:R475–77

Collett TS, Kelber A. 1988. The retrieval of visuo-spatial memories by honeybees. *J. Comp. Physiol. Ser. A* 163:145–50

Crystal JD. 2001. Circadian time perception. *J. Exp. Psychol.: Anim. Behav. Proc.* 27:68–78

Dayan P, Daw ND. 2008. Decision theory, reinforcement learning, and the brain. *Cogn. Affect. Behav. Neurosci.* 8:429–53

de Jonge M, Racine RJ. 1985. The effects of repeated induction of long-term potentiation in the dentate gyrus. *Brain Res.* 328:181–85

Dennis W. 1932. Multiple visual discrimination in the block elevated maze. *J. Comp. Physiol. Psychol.* 13:391–96

Denniston JC, Blaisdell AP, Miller RR. 2004. Temporal coding in conditioned inhibition: analysis of associative structure of inhibition. *J. Exp. Psychol.: Anim. Behav. Proc.* 30:190–202

Derdikman D, Moser EI. 2010. A manifold of spatial maps in the brain. *Trends Cogn. Sci.* 14:561–69

Derdikman D, Whitlock JR, Tsao A, Fyhn M, Hafting T, et al. 2009. Fragmentation of grid cell maps in a multicompartment environment. *Nat. Neurosci.* 12:1325–32

Diba K, Buzsáki G. 2008. Hippocampal network dynamics constrain the time lag between pyramidal cells across modified environments. *J. Neurosci.* 28:13448–56

Douglas RJ. 1966. Cues for spontaneous alternation. *J. Comp. Physiol. Psychol.* 62:171–83

Dudchenko PA, Davidson M. 2002. Rats use a sense of direction to alternate on T-mazes located in adjacent rooms. *Anim. Cogn.* 5:115–18

Dudchenko PA, Zinyuk LE. 2005. The formation of cognitive maps of adjacent environments: evidence from the head direction cell system. *Behav. Neurosci.* 119:1511–23

Durgin FH, Akagi M, Gallistel CR, Haiken W. 2009. The precision of human odometery. *Exp. Brain Res.* 193:429–36

Dyer FC, Dickinson JA. 1994. Development of sun compensation by honeybees: how partially experienced bees estimate the sun's course. *Proc. Natl. Acad. Sci. USA* 91:4471–74

Edelman GM. 1989. *Neural Darwinism*. New York: Oxford Univ. Press

Elman JL, Zipser D. 1988. Learning the hidden structure of speech. *J. Acoust. Soc. Am.* 83:1615–26

Epstein RA. 2008. Parahippocampal and retrosplenial contributions to human spatial navigation. *Trends Cogn. Sci.* 12:388–96

Epstein RA. 2011. Cognitive neuroscience: scene layout from vision and touch. *Curr. Biol.* 21:R437–38

Etienne A, Maurer R, Saucy F, Teroni E. 1986. Short-distance homing in the golden hamster after a passive outward journey. *Anim. Behav.* 34:696–715

Fiorillo CD, Tobler CD, Schultz W. 2003. Discrete coding of reward probability and uncertainty by dopamine neurons. *Science* 299:1898–902

Flagel SB, Clark JJ, Robinson TE, Mayo L, Czuj A, et al. 2011. A selective role for dopamine in stimulus-reward learning. *Nature* 469:53–57

Foa A, Basaglia F, Beltrami G, Carnacina M, Moretto E, Bertolucci C. 2009. Orientation of lizards in a Morris water-maze: roles of the sun compass and the parietal eye. *J. Exp. Biol.* 212:2918–24

Frank LM, Brown EN, Wilson M. 2000. Trajectory encoding in the hippocampus and entorhinal cortex. *Neuron* 27:169–78

Fyhn M, Hafting T, Treves A, Moser M-B, Moser EI. 2007. Hippocampal remapping and grid realignment in entorhinal cortex. *Nature* 446:190–94

Gagliardo A, Vallortigara G, Nardi D, Bingman VP. 2005. A lateralized avian hippocampus: preferential role of the left hippocampal formation in homing pigeon sun compass-based spatial learning. *Eur. J. Neurosci.* 22:2549–59

Galletti C, Battaglini PP. 1989. Gaze-dependent visual neurons in area V3A of monkey prestriate cortex. *J. Neurosci.* 9:1112–25

Gallistel CR. 1990. *The Organization of Learning*. Cambridge, MA: Bradford Books/MIT Press. 648 pp.

Gallistel CR. 1999. The replacement of general-purpose learning models with adaptively specialized learning modules. In *The Cognitive Neurosciences*, ed. MS Gazzaniga, pp. 1179–91. Cambridge, MA: MIT Press. 2nd ed.

Gallistel CR. 2012. Extinction from a rationalist perspective. *Behav. Proc.* 90:66–88

Gallistel CR, Gibbon J. 2000. Time, rate, and conditioning. *Psychol. Rev.* 107:289–344

Gallistel CR, King AP. 2009. *Memory and the Computational Brain: Why Cognitive Science Will Transform Neuroscience*. New York: Wiley/Blackwell

Gibbon J, Balsam P. 1981. Spreading associations in time. In *Autoshaping and Conditioning Theory*, ed. CM Locurto, HS Terrace, J Gibbon, pp. 219–53. New York: Academic

Giocomo LM, Moser M-B, Moser EI. 2011. Computational models of grid cells. *Neuron* 71:589–603

Golob EJ, Taube JS. 1999. Head direction cells in rats with hippocampal or overlying neocortical lesions: evidence for impaired angular path integration. *J. Neurosci.* 19:7198–211

Gothard KM, Skaggs WE, McNaughton BL. 1996a. Dynamics of mismatch correction in the hippocampal ensemble code for space: interaction between path integration and environmental cues. *J. Neurosci.* 16:8027–40

Gothard KM, Skaggs WE, Moore KM, McNaughton BL. 1996b. Binding of hippocampal CA1 neural activity to multiple reference frames in a landmark-based navigation task. *J. Neurosci.* 16:823–35

Gottlieb DA. 2008. Is the number of trials a primary determinant of conditioned responding? *J. Exp. Psychol.: Anim. Behav. Proc.* 34:185–201

Graham M, Good MA, McGregor A, Pearce JM. 2006. Spatial learning based on the shape of the environment is influenced by properties of the objects forming the shapes. *J. Exp. Psychol.: Anim. Behav. Proc.* 32:44–59

Griffiths TL, Chater N, Kemp C, Perfors A, Tenenbaum JB. 2010. Probabilistic models of cognition: exploring representations and inductive biases. *Trends Cogn. Sci.* 14:357–64

Groh JM, Trause AS, Underhill AM, Clark KR, Inati S. 2001. Eye position influences auditory responses in primate inferior colliculus. *Neuron* 29:509–18

Gwinner E. 1996. Circadian and cirannual programmes in avian migration. *J. Exp. Biol.* 199:39–48

Harvey CD, Coen P, Tank DW. 2012. Choice-specific sequences in parietal cortex during virtual-navigation decision task. *Nature* 484:62–68

Hebb DO. 1949. *The Organization of Behavior: A Neuropsychological Theory*. New York: Wiley

Heeger DJ. 1992. Normalization of cell responses in cat striate cortex. *Vis. Neurosci.* 9:181–97

Heinze S, Reppert SM. 2011. Sun compass integration of skylight cues in migratory monarch butterflies. *Neuron* 69:345–58

Hull CL. 1930. Knowledge and purpose as habit mechanisms. *Psychol. Rev.* 37:511–25

Hull CL. 1952. *A Behavior System*. New Haven, CT: Yale Univ. Press

Jezek K, Henriksen EJ, Treves A, Moser EI, Moser M-B. 2011. Theta-paced flickering between place-cell maps in the hippocampus. *Nature* 478:246–49

Jung MW, Wiener SI, McNaughton BL. 1994. Comparison of spatial firing characteristics of units in dorsal and ventral hippocampus of the rat. *J. Neurosci.* 14:7347–56

Kaplan P. 1984. Importance of relative temporal parameters in trace autoshaping: from excitation to inhibition. *J. Exp. Psychol.: Anim. Behav. Proc.* 10:113–26

Kjelstrup KB, Solstad T, Brun VH, Hafting1 T, Leutgeb S, et al. 2008. Finite scale of spatial representation in the hippocampus. *Science* 321:140–43

Komorowski RW, Manns JR, Eichenbaum H. 2009. Robust conjunctive item-place coding by hippocampal neurons parallels learning what happens where. *J. Neurosci.* 29:9918–29

Langston RF, Ainge JA, Couey JJ, Canto CB, Bjerknes TL, et al. 2010. Development of the spatial representation system in the rat. *Science* 328:1576–80

Lattal KM. 1999. Trial and intertrial durations in Pavlovian conditioning: issues of learning and performance. *J. Exp. Psychol.: Anim. Behav. Proc.* 25:433–50

Legge ELG, Spetch ML, Cheng K. 2010. Not using the obvious: Desert ants, *Melophorus bagoti*, learn local vectors but not beacons in an arena. *Anim. Cogn.* 13:849–60

Leutgeb S, Leutgeb JK, Barnes CA, Moser EI, McNaughton BL, Moser M-B. 2004. Distinct ensemble codes in hippocampal areas CA3 and CA1. *Science* 305:1295–98

Leutgeb S, Leutgeb JK, Barnes CA, Moser EI, McNaughton BL, Moser M-B. 2005. Independent codes for spatial and episodic memory in hippocampal neuronal ensembles. *Science* 309:619–23

Lever C, Burton S, Ali Jeewajee A, O'Keefe J, Burgess N. 2009. Boundary vector cells in the subiculum of the hippocampal formation. *J. Neurosci.* 29:9771–77

Loomis JM, Klatzky RL, Golledge RG, Philbeck JW. 1998. Human navigation by path integration. In *Wayfinding: Cognitive Mapping and Spatial Behavior*, ed. RG Golledge, pp. 121–51. Baltimore, MD: Johns Hopkins Univ. Press

MacDonald CJ, Lepage KQ, Eden UT, Eichenbaum H. 2011. Hippocampal "time cells" bridge the gap in memory for discontiguous events. *Neuron* 71:737–49

MacEvoy SP, Epstein RA. 2011. Constructing scenes from objects in human occipitotemporal cortex. *Nat. Neurosci.* 14:1323–29

Manns J, Eichenbaum H. 2009. A cognitive map for object memory in the hippocampus. *Learn. Mem.* 16:616–24

Margules J, Gallistel CR. 1988. Heading in the rat: determination by environmental shape. *Anim. Learn. Behav.* 16:404–10

Markman AB, Dietrich E. 2000. In defense of representation. *Cogn. Psychol.* 40:138–71

Markus EJ, Qin Y-L, Beonard B, Skaggs WE, McNaughton BL, Barnes CA. 1995. Interactions between location and task affect the spatial and directional firing of hippocampal neurons. *J. Neurosci.* 15:7079–94

Marr D. 1982. *Vision.* San Francisco, CA: Freeman

Martin SJ, Grimwood PD, Morris RGM. 2000. Synaptic plasticity and memory: an evaluation of the hypothesis. *Annu. Rev. Neurosci.* 23:649–711

Martin SJ, Morris RGM. 2002. New life in an old idea: the synaptic plasticity and memory hypothesis revisited. *Hippocampus* 12:609–36

Matzel LD, Held FP, Miller RR. 1988. Information and expression of simultaneous and backward associations: implications for contiguity theory. *Learn. Motiv.* 19:317–44

Matzel LD, Shors TJ. 2001. Long-term potentiation and associative learning: Can the mechanism subserve the process? In *Neuronal Mechanisms of Memory Formation: Concepts of Long-Term Potentiation and Beyond*, ed. C Holshcer, pp. 294–324. London: Cambridge Univ. Press

McNaughton BL, Barnes CA, Gerrard JL, Gothard K, Jung MW, et al. 1996. Deciphering the hippocamapal polyglot: the hippocampus as a path integration system. *J. Exp. Biol.* 199:173–85

McNaughton BL, Battaglia FP, Jensen O, Moser EI, Moser M-B. 2006. Path integration and the neural basis of the "cognitive map." *Nat. Rev. Neurosci.* 7:663–78

Meck WH, ed. 2003. *Functional and Neural Mechanisms of Interval Timing.* New York: CRC

Menzel R, Greggers U, Smith A, Berger S, Brandt R, et al. 2005. Honey bees navigate according to a map-like spatial memory. *Proc. Natl. Acad. Sci. USA* 102:3040–45

Merkle T, Wehner JM. 2008. Landmark guidance and vector navigation in outbound desert ants. *J. Exp. Biol.* 211:3370–77

Miller RR, Kasprow WJ, Schachtman TR. 1986. Retrieval variability: sources and consequences. *Am. J. Psychol.* 99:145–218

Mittelstaedt ML, Mittelstaedt H. 1980. Homing by path integration in a mammal. *Naturwissenschaften* 67:566–67

Morgan LK, MacEvoy SP, Aguirre GK, Epstein RA. 2010. Distances between real-world locations are represented in the human hippocampus. *J. Neurosci.* 31:1238–45

Moser EI, Kripff E, Moser M-B. 2008. Place cells, grid cells, and the brain's spatial representation system. *Annu. Rev. Neurosci.* 31:69–89

Muller RU, Kubie JL. 1987. The effects of changes in the environment on the spatial firing of hippocampal complex-spike cells. *J. Neurosci.* 7:1951–68

Napier RM, Macrae M, Kehoe EJ. 1992. Rapid reacquisition in conditioning of the rabbit's nictitating membrane response. *J. Exp. Psychol.: Anim. Behav. Proc.* 18:182–92

O'Keefe J, Speakman A. 1987. Single unit activity in the rat hippocampus during a spatial memory task. *Exp. Brain Res.* 68:1–27

O'Keefe JO, Conway DH. 1978. Hippocampal place units in the freely moving rat: why they fire where they fire. *Exp. Brain Res.* 31:573–90

Olsen SR, Bhandawat V, Wilson RI. 2010. Divisive normalization in olfactory population codes. *Neuron* 66:287–99

Pearce JM, Graham M, Good MA, Jones PM, McGregor A. 2006. Potentiation, overshadowing, and blocking of spatial learning based on the shape of the environment. *J. Exp. Psychol.: Anim. Behav. Proc.* 32:201–14

Power JM, Thompson LT, Moyer JR, Disterhoft JF. 1997. Enhanced synaptic transmission in CA1 hippocampus after eyeblink conditioning. *J. Neurophysiol.* 78:1184–87

Quinn WG. 2005. Nematodes learn: Now what? *Nat. Neurosci.* 8:1639–40

Quirk GJ, Muller RU, Kubie JL. 1990. The firing of hippocampal place cells in the dark depends on the rat's recent experience. *J. Neurosci.* 10:2008–17

Redish AD, Jensen S, Johnson A, Kurth-Nelson A. 2007. Reconciling reinforcement learning models with behavioral extinction and renewal: implications for addiction, relapse, and problem gambling. *Psychol. Rev.* 114:784–805

Redish AD, Rosenzweig ES, Bohanick JD, McNaughton BL, Barnes CA. 2000. Dynamics of hippocampal ensemble activity realignment: time versus space. *J. Neurosci.* 20:9298–309

Rescorla RA. 1967. Pavlovian conditioning and its proper control procedures. *Psychol. Rev.* 74:71–80

Rescorla RA. 1968. Probability of shock in the presence and absence of CS in fear conditioning. *J. Comp. Physiol. Psychol.* 66:1–5

Rieke F, Warland D, de Ruyter van Steveninck R, Bialek W. 1997. *Spikes: Exploring the Neural Code.* Cambridge, MA: MIT Press. 395 pp.

Rivard B, Lenck-Santini PP, Poucet B, Muller RU. 2004. Representation of objects in space by two classes of hippocampal pyramidal cells. *J. Gen. Physiol.* 124:9–25

Rochefort C, Arabo A, André M, Poucet B, Save E, Rondi L. 2011. Cerebellum shapes hippocampal spatial code. *Science* 334:385–89

Rumelhart DE, McClelland JL, eds. 1986. *Parallel Distributed Processing.* Cambridge, MA: MIT Press

Russell NA, Horii A, Smith PF, Darlington CL, Bilkey DK. 2003. Long-term effects of permanent vestibular lesions on hippocampal spatial firing. *J. Neurosci.* 23:6490–98

Sauman I, Briscoe AD, Zhu H, Shi D, Froy O, et al. 2005. Connecting the navigational clock to sun compass input in monarch butterfly brain. *Neuron* 46:457–67

Savastano HI, Miller RR. 1998. Time as content in Pavlovian conditioning. *Behav. Proc.* 44:147–62

Save E, Cressant A, Thinus-Blanc C, Poucet B. 1998. Spatial firing of hippocampal place cells in blind rats. *J. Neurosci.* 18:1818–26

Schultz W. 2006. Behavioral theories and the neurophysiology of reward. *Annu. Rev. Psychol.* 57:87–115

Shannon CE. 1948. A mathematical theory of communication. *Bell Syst. Tech. J.* 27:379–423, 623–56

Shapiro ML, Tanila H, Eichenbaum H. 1997. Cues that hippocampal place cells encode: dynamic and hierarchical representation of local and distal stimuli. *Hippocampus* 7:624–42

Sharp PE, Blair HT, Etkin D, Tzanetos DB. 1995. Influences of vestibular and visual motion information on the spatial firing patterns of hippocampal place cells. *J. Neurosci.* 15:173–89

Shastri L, Ajjanagadde V. 1993. From simple associations to systematic reasoning: a connectionist representation of rules, variables, and dynamic bindings using temporal synchrony. *Behav. Brain Sci.* 16:417–94

Sheynikhovich D, Chavarriaga R, Strösslin T, Arleo A, Gerstner W. 2009. Is there a geometric module for spatial orientation? Insights from a rodent navigation model. *Psychol. Rev.* 116:540–66

Simoncelli EP, Heeger DJ. 1998. A model of neuronal responses in visual area MT. *Vis. Res.* 38:743–61

Skaggs WE, McNaughton BL. 1998. Spatial firing properties of hippocampal CA1 populations in an environment containing two visually identical regions. *J. Neurosci.* 18:8455–66

Skinner BF. 1938. *The Behavior of Organisms.* New York: Appleton-Century-Crofts

Smolensky P. 1986. Information processing in dynamical systems: foundations of harmony theory. In *Parallel Distributed Processing: Foundations*, ed. DE Rumelhart, JL McClelland, pp. 194–281. Cambridge, MA: MIT Press

Solstad T, Boccara CN, Kropff E, Moser M-B, Moser EI. 2008. Representation of geometric borders in the entorhinal cortex. *Science* 322:1865–68

Sommer S, Beeren Cv, Wehner R. 2008. Multiroute memories in desert ants. *Proc. Natl. Acad. Sci. USA* 105:317–22

Stackman RW, Clark AS, Taube JS. 2002. Hippocampal spatial representations require vestibular input. *Hippocampus Online* 12:291–303

Stackman RW, Golob EJ, Bassett JP, Taube JS. 2003. Passive transport disrupts directional path integration by rat head direction cells. *J. Neurophysiol.* 90:2862–74

Sutton RS, Barto AG. 1998. *Reinforcement Learning: An Introduction.* Cambridge, MA: MIT Press

Tanila H, Shapiro ML, Eichenbaum H. 1997. Discordance of spatial representation in ensembles of hippocampal place cells. *Hippocampus* 7:613–23

Tanzi E. 1893. I fatti e le induzioni nell'odierna istologia del sistema nervoso. *Riv. Sper. Freniatr. Med. Legale* 19:419–72

Taube JS. 2007. The head direction signal: origins and sensory-motor integration. *Annu. Rev. Neurosci.* 30:259–88

Taube JS, Burton HL. 1995. Head direction cell activity monitored in a novel environment and during a cue conflict situation. *J. Neurophysiol.* 74:1953–71

Tcheang L, Bülthoff HH, Burgess N. 2011. Visual influence on path integration in darkness indicates a multimodal representation of large-scale space. *Proc. Natl. Acad. Sci. USA* 108:1152–57

Thompson SM, Mattison HA. 2009. Secret of synapse specificity. *Nature* 458:296–97

Usherwood PNR. 1993. Memories are made of this. *Trends Neurosci.* 16:427–29

Vallortigara G. 2009. Animals as natural geometers. In *Cognitive Biology: Evolutionary and Developmental Perspectives on Mind, Brain and Behavior*, ed. L Tommasi, L Nadel, M Peterson, pp. 83–104. Cambridge, MA: MIT Press

Vickerstaff RJ, Cheung A. 2010. Which coordinate system for modelling path integration? *J. Theor. Biol.* 263:242–61

Ward RD, Gallistel CR, Jensen G, Richards VL, Fairhurst S, Balsam PD. 2012. Conditioned stimulus informativeness governs conditioned stimulus-unconditioned stimulus associability. *J. Exp. Psychol.: Anim. Behav. Proc.* 38:217–32

Wehner R, Srinivasan MV. 2003. Path integration in insects. In *The Neurobiology of Spatial Behaviour*, ed. KJ Jeffery, pp. 9–30. London: Oxford Univ. Press

Wehner R. 1984. Astronavigation in insects. *Annu. Rev. Entomol.* 29:277–98

Wehner R, Müller M. 1993. How do ants acquire their celestial ephemeris function? *Naturwissenschaften* 80:331–33

Werner-Reiss U, Kelly KA, Trause AS, Underhill AM, Groh JM. 2003. Eye position affects activity in primary auditory cortex of primates. *Curr. Biol.* 13:554–62

Wills TJ, Cacucci F, Burgess N, O'Keefe J. 2010. Development of the hippocampal cognitive map in preweanling rats. *Science* 328:1573–76

Wittlinger M, Wehner R, Wolf H. 2006. The ant odometer: stepping on stilts and stumps. *Science* 312:1965–67

Worden R. 1992. Navigation by fragment fitting: a theory of hippocampal function. *Hippocampus* 2:165–87

Wystrach A, Cheng K, Sosa S, Beugnon G. 2011. Geometry, features, and panoramic views: ants in rectangular arenas. *J. Exp. Psychol.: Anim. Behav. Proc.* 37:420–35

Yoder RM, Clark BJ, Taube JS. 2011. Origins of landmark encoding in the brain. *Trends Neurosci.* 34:561–71

Yoganarasimha D, Yu X, Knierim JJ. 2006. Head direction cell representations maintain internal coherence during conflicting proximal and distal cue rotations: comparison with hippocampal place cells. *J. Neurosci.* 26:622–31

Zhang J, Berridge KC, Tindell AJ, Smith KS, Aldridge JW. 2009. A neural computational model of incentive salience. *PLoS Comput. Biol.* 5:1–14

Zhang S, Schwarz S, Pahl M, Shu M, Tautz J. 2006. Honeybee memory: A honeybee knows what to do and when. *J. Exp. Biol.* 209:4420–28

Zugaro MB, Berthoz A, Wiener SI. 2001. Background, but not foreground, spatial cues are taken as references for head direction responses by rat anterodorsal thalamus neurons. *J. Neurosci.* 21:RC154

Evolutionary Psychology: New Perspectives on Cognition and Motivation

Leda Cosmides[1] and John Tooby[2]

[1]Department of Psychological & Brain Sciences and Center for Evolutionary Psychology and [2]Department of Anthropology and Center for Evolutionary Psychology, University of California, Santa Barbara, California 93106; email: cosmides@psych.ucsb.edu, tooby@anth.ucsb.edu

Annu. Rev. Psychol. 2013. 64:201–29

The *Annual Review of Psychology* is online at psych.annualreviews.org

This article's doi:
10.1146/annurev.psych.121208.131628

Keywords

motivation, domain-specificity, evolutionary game theory, visual attention, concepts, reasoning

Abstract

Evolutionary psychology is the second wave of the cognitive revolution. The first wave focused on computational processes that generate knowledge about the world: perception, attention, categorization, reasoning, learning, and memory. The second wave views the brain as composed of evolved computational systems, engineered by natural selection to use information to adaptively regulate physiology and behavior. This shift in focus—from knowledge acquisition to the adaptive regulation of behavior—provides new ways of thinking about every topic in psychology. It suggests a mind populated by a large number of adaptive specializations, each equipped with content-rich representations, concepts, inference systems, and regulatory variables, which are functionally organized to solve the complex problems of survival and reproduction encountered by the ancestral hunter-gatherers from whom we are descended. We present recent empirical examples that illustrate how this approach has been used to discover new features of attention, categorization, reasoning, learning, emotion, and motivation.

Contents

INTRODUCTION

Both before and after Darwin, a common view among philosophers and scientists has been that the human mind resembles a blank slate, virtually free of content until written on by the hand of experience. Over the years, the technological metaphor used to describe the structure of the human mind has been consistently updated, from blank slate to switchboard to general-purpose computer, but the deeper assumption remained. The implications are wide ranging. According to this view, the mechanisms that produce learning operate in the same way, whether they are acquiring the grammar of a language, a fear of snakes, or an aversion to sex with siblings. The mechanisms that produce reasoning deploy the same procedures, whether they are making inferences about the trajectory of a billiard ball, the beliefs and desires of another person, or what counts as cheating in social exchange. The same goes for attention, categorization, memory, motivation, and decision making.

This perspective grants that evolution may have equipped the mind with a few primary reinforcers that have hedonic value (food, water, pain avoidance, sex). But it assumes that the neurocomputational systems that collect and process experiences are largely content free and domain general, designed to operate uniformly on information drawn from any stimulus class (cf. Herrnstein 1977, Gallistel 1995).

A very different picture of the human mind is emerging from evolutionary psychology, an approach to the cognitive sciences that integrates evolutionary biology, psychology, information theory, anthropology, cognitive neuroscience, and allied fields (for reviews, see Barkow et al. 1992, Buss 2005). In this view, human nature—the species-typical information-processing architecture of the human brain—is packed with content-rich adaptive problem-solving systems. Like expert systems (in artificial intelligence), each is designed to deploy different concepts, principles, inference procedures, regulatory variables, and decision rules when activated by cues of its proper domain. Why?

From this perspective, the cognitive and evolutionary sciences are connected as follows:

1. Each organ in the body evolved to serve a function: the intestines digest, the heart pumps blood, the liver detoxifies poisons. The brain is also an organ, and its evolved function is to extract information from the environment and use that information to generate behavior and regulate physiology. From this perspective, the brain is a computer, that is, a physical system that was designed to process information. Its programs were designed not by an engineer, but by natural selection, a causal process that retains and discards design features on the basis of how well they solved problems that affect reproduction (Williams 1966, Dawkins 1982).

    The fact that the brain processes information is not an accidental side effect of some metabolic process: The brain was designed by natural selection to be a computer. Therefore, if you want to describe its operation in a way that captures its evolved function, you need to think of it as composed of programs that process information. The question then becomes, what programs are to be found in the human brain? What are the reliably developing, species-typical programs that, taken together, constitute the human mind?

2. These programs were sculpted over evolutionary time by the ancestral environments and selection pressures experienced by the hunter-gatherers from whom we are descended. Each evolved program exists because it produced behavior that promoted the survival and reproduction of our ancestors better than alternative programs that arose during human evolutionary history. Evolutionary psychologists emphasize hunter-gatherer life because it takes a long time for natural selection to build a computational adaptation of any complexity. Simple, quantitative traits can change faster, but it takes thousands of years (i.e., many human generations) for natural selection to assemble a complex program composed of many different, functionally integrated parts (Tooby & Cosmides 1990a).

3. Although the behavior our evolved programs generate would, on average, have been adaptive (i.e., reproduction promoting) in the ancestral environments that selected for their design (their environment of evolutionary adaptedness), there is no guarantee that it will be so now (Tooby & Cosmides 1990b, Symons 1992). Modern environments differ importantly from ancestral ones, particularly when it comes to social behavior. We no longer live in small, face-to-face societies, in seminomadic bands of 25–200 men, women, and children, many of whom were close relatives. Yet our cognitive programs were designed for that social world.

4. Perhaps most importantly, the brain must be composed of many different programs, each specialized for solving a different adaptive problem our ancestors faced.

    Our hunter-gatherer ancestors were, in effect, on a camping trip that lasted a lifetime, and they had to solve many different kinds of problems well to survive and reproduce under those conditions: hunting, evaluating plant resources, cooperating with others, avoiding predators, dividing resources among kin, selecting fertile mates, deterring sexual rivals, avoiding infectious diseases, detecting alliances, avoiding incest, learning grammar, negotiating dominance hierarchies, and managing aggression, for example. When natural selection was reconceptualized as replicator dynamics and combined with game theory (Williams 1966, Dawkins 1982, Maynard Smith 1982), it became possible to derive powerful (and nonintuitive) inferences about what counts as adaptive behavior in these domains.

    Results from evolutionary game theory and data about ancestral environments

Computational adaptations: evolved systems designed (by natural selection) to monitor information and use it to functionally regulate behavior or physiology

Environment of Evolutionary Adaptedness: the series of ancestral environments/selection pressures that sculpted the design of an adaptation

Replicator dynamics: how genes change in frequency in a population

can be used to identify and dissect adaptive information-processing problems, to see what properties programs capable of solving them would need. This exercise often reveals that what counts as a solution differs radically and incommensurably for different adaptive problems. Consider, for example, food choice versus mate choice. The computational structure of programs that are well engineered for choosing nutritious foods will fail to produce adaptive behavior unless they generate different preferences and trade-offs than programs designed for choosing fertile sexual partners. Similarly, machinery that reliably and efficiently learns which local organisms are predators and the best way to respond to each (freeze? run? climb a tree?) lacks properties that will cause the reliable and efficient acquisition of grammar (and vice versa).

Evolutionary psychologists therefore expect (and find) that the human mind contains a large number of information-processing devices that are functionally specialized and therefore domain specific, with different devices activated by different kinds of content (snakes versus smiles, food versus mates, cues of social exchange versus cues of aggression). No one doubts that the mind contains some adaptive specializations that execute (relatively) domain-general computations (e.g., Brase et al. 1998, Rode et al. 1999, Gallistel & Gibbon 2000, Gigerenzer & Selten 2001). But these cannot produce adaptive behavior unless they interact with a large number of expert systems that are domain specialized and content rich (e.g., Pinker 1997, 2010; Cosmides & Tooby 2001; Cosmides et al. 2010). True blank slates—architectures that are content free except for a few hedonic reinforcers—lack the computational properties necessary to produce behavior that tracks fitness (Cosmides & Tooby 1987, Tooby et al. 2005). (For comprehensive introductions to the conceptual foundations of evolutionary psychology, which include detailed arguments for each point listed above, along with controversies and responses, see Tooby & Cosmides 1992, 2005.)

Knowing that natural selection produces computational systems that solve adaptive problems reliably, quickly, and efficiently allows evolutionary psychologists to approach the study of the mind like an engineer. One starts with a good specification of an adaptive information-processing problem and does a task analysis of that problem. This allows one to see what properties a program would have to have in order to solve that problem well. This approach generates testable hypotheses about the structure of the programs that compose the mind—a point we hope to illustrate in this review.

From the earliest days of the field, evolutionary psychologists have used sexual selection theory to explore the psychology of mating relationships in humans and other animals (Trivers 1972, Symons 1979, Daly & Wilson 1988, Buss 1989). They have already produced a massive literature on this topic, opening up an area of study that had been neglected by the psychological sciences (for recent reviews, see Buss 2005, part III, and Roney 2009).

It is less obvious how knowledge and principles from evolutionary biology can guide research in more traditional areas of the cognitive sciences. So we have chosen examples from visual attention, spatial cognition, categorization, reasoning, learning, and motivation. In each case, the theoretical framework provided by evolutionary psychology led to new questions and surprising results—ones suggesting the existence of content-specialized procedures. Through these cases, we hope to illustrate key features of evolutionary psychology: the importance of considering ancestral environments; how hunter-gatherer studies and models from behavioral ecology, such as optimal foraging theory, can lead research in strange new directions; the role of evolutionary game theory in generating specific hypotheses about cognitive design; how adaptationist hypotheses are tested against alternatives; the importance of content-specificity; and the need to be computational, even when researching motivation and emotion.

VISUAL ATTENTION

Visual attention is an umbrella term for a suite of operations that select some portions of a scene, rather than others, for more extensive processing. Most research in this area has explored how attention is deployed in response to either (*a*) low-level visual features (color, intensity, orientation, contrast) or (*b*) information that is personally or task relevant, given a volitionally chosen goal. This reflects a usually implicit assumption of the field: that the function of attention is to enhance the processing of features necessary for building accurate knowledge of what exists in the world and the performance of goals chosen by the individual.

Very few studies have considered the possibility that there are evolved systems designed to deploy attention in response to particular categories of information, in a way that is independent of volitional goals. Volitional attention is important for a tool-using species, but focusing too exclusively on a single task can be very costly. An evolutionary perspective suggests there should be systems that incidentally scan the environment for opportunities and dangers; when there are sufficient cues that a more pressing adaptive problem is at hand—an angry antagonist, a stalking predator, a mating opportunity—this should trigger an interrupt circuit on volitional attention and activate programs specialized for processing information about the new problem in an adaptive manner. According to this view, attention is a complex system with interacting components, some serving object perception, some deployed volitionally, and some monitoring the environment in an ongoing manner for adaptively important situations. These monitoring systems are likely to be category driven because their function is to detect the presence of situations defined over high-level objects (e.g., people, animals, antagonists,

cooperators), which can rarely be identified on the basis of low-level features alone.

Faces regulate social interaction, so initial attempts to look for category-specific attentional systems started with the human face. In short order, systems were found that preferentially attend to human faces (Ro et al. 2001) and that snap attention to the location at which a pair of eyes is gazing (Friesen & Kingstone 2003). But is this caused by an adaptive specialization that evolved for attending to faces—one with design features that were functionally organized by natural selection for that purpose? Because faces are important now, as well as ancestrally, a skeptic could argue that preferential attention to faces is caused by a domain-general expertise system—an evolved system to be sure, but one that will cause preferential attention to any perceptual cue that, if attended, would enhance performance on current tasks.

In principle, evidence from developmental disorders could rule out this expertise hypothesis, just as it did in the debate about face recognition (Duchaine et al. 2006). Autism, for example, may selectively disrupt attention to faces (Chawarska et al. 2010, Remington et al. 2012). But a different way of approaching the question is to compare attention to faces with attention to stimulus classes with which people have much less experience, but that were important ancestrally. Could there be a category-specific attentional system analogous to the appendix: there because it was adaptive in our evolutionary past, but relatively useless now?

Animal Monitoring: An Appendix in Visual Attention?

The survival of the typical undergraduate research subject might depend on how vigilantly she monitors cars and trucks as she drives or crosses the street, but not on her ability to spot edible turtles, avoid an ornery warthog, or judge whether the lion laying sated in the grass has just started attending to potential prey. The opposite is true of the hunter-gatherers from whom she is descended. For our foraging ancestors, nonhuman animals presented either dangers (e.g., predators) or opportunities for hunting (e.g., prey). Snakes and spiders—ancestral dangers of little consequence in modern cities and suburbs—do capture attention in what appears to be a parallel search process (Öhman et al. 2001). But what about other animals, including ones that may not be fear relevant? And what about attentional monitoring, as distinct from attentional capture? Because animals can change their behavior and location quickly, the lives and livelihoods of our ancestors turned on their ability to monitor them for changes in their state and location. Does our visual attention system harbor a mechanism that monitors animals in an ongoing fashion?

It does. New et al. (2007a) addressed this question using the change detection protocol, in which subjects are asked to spot the difference between two rapidly alternating photos that are almost identical, but include one difference. This paradigm is famous for eliciting change blindness—a condition in which observers are unaware that an element of the scene is changing (e.g., whole buildings can repeatedly appear and disappear without the subject noticing). In this protocol, the only task subjects are given is to detect changes, so they are free to follow their own inclinations in attending to different entities in photos of complex natural scenes. This allows one to see whether the attentional system monitors animals more than other objects.

It turns out that change blindness is limited largely to inanimate objects. Changes to nonhuman animals (and to people) are detected faster and more accurately than changes to plants, buildings, tools, and even vehicles. For example, changes to a small bird at the periphery of a complex natural scene were detected faster and more accurately than changes to a large building at a scene's center. The time course of responses revealed that animals not only capture attention, but they are monitored in an ongoing manner for changes in their state and location.

A series of control tasks showed that the attentional advantage found for animals was not due to lower-level visual features, expectation of motion, task demands, properties of the back-

ground scene, or how interesting the targets were judged to be. The monitoring system responsible appears to be category driven, that is, it is automatically activated by any target the visual recognition system has categorized as an animal.

What is the origin of this animal-monitoring system? It could have been built into visual attention because of its benefits over evolutionary time, regardless of its current utility. Another possibility is that the visual system does not start out biased to monitor some categories of information over others; but it might be designed to create category-specific monitoring systems as an expertise, for any class of stimuli that are frequently encountered and important to monitor. New et al. (2007a) tested between these phylogenetic and ontogenetic accounts by comparing change detection for nonhuman animals to that for vehicles and humans.

Vehicles versus animals. Ontogenetically, monitoring vehicles for sudden changes in their states and locations is a highly trained skill of life-and-death importance to car-driving, street-crossing research subjects, but it was of no importance phylogenetically. In contrast, monitoring animals was important phylogenetically, but having your attention drawn to pigeons and squirrels is merely a distraction in modern cities and suburbs. If the ontogenetic expertise hypothesis were true, one would expect people to develop a category-specialized system for monitoring vehicles, such that changes to vehicles are detected as well as—or, indeed, better than—changes to nonhuman animals. But the reverse was true: Speed and accuracy at noticing changes were far greater for nonhuman animals than for vehicles. This is what one would expect if animal monitoring arises from an animal-specific evolved system rather than content-free learning.

People are an interesting stimulus class because they were important and frequently encountered phylogenetically and ontogenetically. As such, they represent an upper boundary on the effects that expertise can create, over and above any evolved bias. How well are nonhuman animals monitored, compared to people?

People versus nonhuman animals. If preferential attention to a given category is acquired by domain-general learning processes alone, then category-driven differences in expertise would have to arise from differences in the frequency of experience with a stimulus class and differences in the current utility of monitoring it. This would predict that preferential attention to people should be much stronger than preferential attention to nonhuman animals.

From infancy, we are immersed in immense numbers of important transactions with other humans, which could have driven the acquisition of human-oriented attentional expertise without invoking any evolved bias toward humans. Moreover, the amount of experience subjects living in American cities and suburbs have with the human species is greater, by many orders of magnitude, than their experience with taxa such as birds, turtles, fish, insects, or African mammals. Do these vast differences in exposure rates and current utility translate into vast differences in the extent to which people are monitored compared to nonhuman animals?

No. New and his associates found that the differences between attention to humans and to other species were marginal at best; indeed, changes to nonhuman animals were detected just as well as changes to people in some of their experiments. Finding similar performance when exposure rates differ by orders of magnitude is inconsistent with any acquisition theory that invokes domain-general expertise with no evolved biases.

People are more important and more frequently seen than virtually any other category of stimuli, yet they recruit little more attention than nonhuman animals. This suggests that domain-general expertise systems, if they exist, do little more than fine tune an evolved system for monitoring people. At the same time, the fact that nonhuman animals were monitored about as well as people—and much better than vehicles and other objects—implies the existence of a content-specialized system that was shaped by ancestral selection pressures, not general learning processes.

Automatic Regulation of Attention by High-Level Social Cues

Paleoanthropology and studies of modern hunter-gatherers show that our ancestors evolved as a group-living species, in small, face-to-face bands consisting of 25–200 men, women, and children. Because most of one's interactions will be with ingroup members in this social ecology, a default setting that allocates more attention to ingroup than outgroup members would be functional. Not surprisingly, people find it easier to visually distinguish and recall individuating information about ingroup members than outgroup members. This phenomenon—ingroup heterogeneity paired with outgroup homogeneity—is well-established in social psychology (Anthony et al. 1992, Ostrom & Sedikides 1992). It is often mentioned in conjunction with the cross-race recognition deficit: For some perceivers, people of a different race "all look alike"—another case of outgroup homogeneity (for an interesting discussion, see Levin 2000). Are there circumstances that modulate attention in a way that reverses this bias?

It may be safe to ignore outgroup members in most circumstances, but not when there are cues that they might intend to harm you. This line of reasoning led Ackerman et al. (2006) to propose a system that automatically upregulates attention to outgroup faces in response to cues of aggressive intent. To test this hypothesis, the researchers used race as a proxy for group membership, and tested recognition memory for ingroup and outgroup faces when their expression was neutral versus angry. The faces of black and white men were briefly shown to white subjects, who were then given an old/new recognition test. When expressions on the faces were neutral, subjects were better at recognizing the faces of white than black men, replicating the well-known outgroup homogeneity effect. But when the faces were angry, subjects were just as good—and sometimes better—at recognizing the faces of black men. Not only did outgroup homogeneity disappear for angry faces, but it was reversed when subjects were operating under processing constraints. When exposure times were brief and distractor photos were present, the subjects were better at recognizing the faces of angry black men than angry white men, demonstrating outgroup heterogeneity.

This striking result reverses well-established effects from two large literatures: outgroup homogeneity and the cross-race recognition deficit. Yet it is precisely what one would expect on an evolutionary-functional account. The anger of an ingroup member is less likely to erupt into aggression because ingroup members participate in a network of cooperative relationships that afford other opportunities for resolving disagreements (see below). Because outgroup members are outside this network, aggression may be the only bargaining tool open to them, making their anger more dangerous. Importantly, angry expressions increased attention to the individuating features of outgroup members only; ingroup faces were recognized just as well when they were neutral as when they were angry.

Activating evolutionarily important goals, such as self-protection and mating, can modulate attention and other cognitive processes in functional ways (Maner et al. 2005, Becker et al. 2010, Kenrick et al. 2010). But the upregulation of attention to angry outgroup faces found by Ackerman et al. was not in response to any instruction or explicitly represented goal state. It occurred spontaneously in response to an ancestrally relevant threat cue: the species-typical facial expression associated with anger. More interestingly, attention was upregulated only when this species-typical threat expression was on the face of an outgroup member. Ingroup members elicited attention regardless of their emotional state; but when processing limitations forced a trade-off between angry ingroup and outgroup members, the system preferentially attended to angry outgroup members. This pattern suggests a system that is func-

tionally specialized for adaptively regulating attention in response to high-level social cues.

SPATIAL COGNITION AND NAVIGATION

Evolutionary psychology is concerned with the evolved architecture of the mind. Many computational mechanisms within this architecture will be the same in males and females (i.e., sexually monomorphic), and others will be different (i.e., sexually dimorphic). Sex differences in behavior can arise in either case. When boys and men encounter different social feedback, environments, and experiences than girls and women, sexually monomorphic mechanisms can generate sex differences in behavior. Sexually dimorphic mechanisms can also generate sex differences in behavior. The design of a computational system in women might differ from the design of the homologous system in men: different inferences, decision rules, signal detection thresholds, preferences, and motivational systems can cause women and men to make different decisions based on the same information. But a sexually dimorphic design could also lead men and women to seek out and remember different kinds of information, social feedback, environments, and experiences. For this reason, the mere discovery that men and women have different experiences is not sufficient to support the hypothesis that sex differences in their behavior were generated by a sexually monomorphic psychology.

Evolutionary psychology provides a framework for predicting the presence and absence of sex differences in the design of computational systems. No sex differences are expected in mechanisms that evolved to solve problems that were the same for ancestral men and women. The evolved architecture of mechanisms should differ between the sexes only when the adaptive problems faced by ancestral males and females were systematically different over long periods of evolutionary time. This principle can slice domains very finely indeed, as we illustrate using research on the presence—and absence—of sex differences in spatial cognition.

Spatial Specializations for Foraging

In cognitive tests tapping spatial cognition and navigation, men often outperform women (Voyer et al. 1995). Psychologists have long assumed that this male advantage is general, holding across spatial problems and domains. It is not. Evolutionary psychologists have discovered that women outperform men in certain spatial tasks. This female advantage was predicted in advance of any data, based on a careful analysis of how the spatial and navigational problems associated with foraging for plant foods differ from those associated with hunting.

There is a sexual division of labor in hunter-gatherer societies, with men specializing in hunting and women specializing in gathering sessile resources, such as plant foods (Marlowe 2007). These tasks place different demands on spatial cognition. Animals move from place to place, and they do their best to evade their predators. Tracking an animal can take a hunter into unknown territory, requiring a certain amount of dead reckoning to return to camp in an energy-efficient way (spatial tasks showing a male advantage, such as mental rotation, are thought to tap this navigational skill; Silverman et al. 2000). Plants, by contrast, stay in one place. But when a forager encounters a plant, the berries may need another week to ripen, the twining vine may be too young to have produced a mature tuber, and it may be a month before mature nuts appear on the mongongo tree. A hunter who is opportunistically harvesting plants as he tracks animals does not need to remember the location of plants that are of no immediate use. But being able to relocate a plant at a later time, when it has become harvestable, is important for a forager who specializes in gathering edible plant foods. And, although foraging women occasionally hunt small animals when the opportunity arises, they typically specialize in gathering plants and other sessile resources.

To return to these sessile resources when they are harvestable, a forager needs to remember their location at two scales. The first scale is within a patch: this requires encoding an edible plant's position relative to other plants and landmarks in a tangled bank of vegetation. Based on this adaptive problem, Silverman & Eals (1992) had looked for and found a female advantage in object-location memory, which was content-general—as it should be, given the need to encode the position of edible plants relative to rocks, trees, and other objects. The second scale is one that supports navigation back to the resource patch at a later time. Navigation at this scale requires encoding the resource's absolute location within a represented environment—a quite different task, more similar to dead reckoning. Reasoning that navigational specializations in women at this larger scale should be triggered by the presence of plant resources, New et al. (2007b) conducted their first study at a farmers' market.

After taking people around and having them taste and rate foods at different stands, the researchers brought subjects back to a place where they could not see any of the stands and asked them to point to where each of the foods had been—a task that taps both spatial memory and the kind of vector integration necessary for efficient navigation. Women outperformed men—an advantage that held even when the researchers controlled for a variety of experiential variables, including visits to the farmer's market and particular stalls, and how often each food is eaten and liked (none of which predicted any variance in pointing accuracy). This is not because the researchers happened to find a particularly gifted sample of women: Men scored higher than the women did on a general not-plant-related sense-of-direction test (one that also predicted unique variance in pointing accuracy across sexes). Consistent with the idea that pointing accuracy taps navigation between patches, women succeeded without the relational cues that Silverman & Eals (1992) identified as important for finding a resource within a tangled bank. Follow-up studies by Krasnow and colleagues (2011) showed that this female spatial advantage is not caused by differences in women's ability to remember the identity of food resources they have seen; it reflects better spatial memory for the absolute location of plant foods within a spatial frame. This female spatial memory advantage was highly domain specific: It was elicited only by fruiting trees. No spatial sex differences were found for other categories tested, including buildings, animals, tools, or gender-stereotyped objects, including jewelry and electronics.

An adaptationist approach to sex differences can slice a domain with remarkable precision, a point nicely illustrated by a second finding from the farmer's market study. Although the sexual division of labor among hunter-gatherers suggested the hypothesis that women will have an advantage in remembering the location of gatherable resources, other factors can affect spatial memory as well. Some of these—such as the nutritional quality of the resource—should be relevant to both sexes.

Optimal foraging theory was developed by behavioral ecologists to predict and explain which species foragers will harvest (Schoener 1971). Not surprisingly, its formal models have identified a food's caloric density as one important predictor of whether foragers will spend time searching for it. This led the farmer's market researchers to ask what would otherwise be a very strange question for a traditional cognitive psychologist: All else equal, are people more accurate at pointing to the location of foods of higher caloric density? Is their spatial/navigational performance better for, say, almonds and avocados than for cucumbers and lettuce?

The answer is yes: Calories count for both sexes. There was a robust correlation between a food's caloric density and accuracy at pointing to its location. This was not because people preferred the taste of high-calorie foods: Subjects had rated how much they liked each food during the initial tasting-and-rating phase of the experiment, but there was no correlation whatsoever between how much they liked each food and their pointing accuracy. Moreover, the extent to which calories improved spatial memory was independent of sex and had a similar effect size for women and men.

Content matters. A psychologist expecting to find spatial and navigational processes that operate independently of content would never think to look for any of these effects. Nor were they stumbled upon during more than 50 years of intuition-driven research in spatial cognition.

That calories count for navigation—that high-caloric-density foods activate better spatial memory and processes for returning to their location—is a result undreamt of in the philosophy of most cognitive scientists. So is the discovery that women have a spatial advantage that is not found for most objects, but emerges when the task involves gatherable plant resources. These surprising results imply that content matters deeply: Embedded within the computational systems that govern spatial memory and navigation are elements that respond differentially to plant resources and to the caloric density of foods.

EVOLUTIONARY GAME THEORY AND THE ANALYSIS OF SOCIAL BEHAVIOR

Game theory is a tool for analyzing strategic social behavior—how agents will behave when they are interacting with others who can anticipate and respond to their behavior. Economists use it to analyze how people will respond to incentives present in the immediate situation. Their models typically assume rational actors, who calculate the payoffs of alternative options (anticipating that other players will do likewise) and choose the one most likely to maximize their short-term profits (but see Hoffman et al. 1998).

Evolutionary biologists also adopted game theory as an analytic tool (Maynard Smith 1982), because the behavior of other people can be as relentless a selection pressure as predators and foraging. In contrast to economics, evolutionary game theory requires no assumptions about rationality; indeed, it can be usefully applied to cooperation among bacteria or fighting in spiders. It is used to model interactions among agents endowed with well-defined decision rules that produce situationally contingent behavior. Although these decision rules are sometimes called strategies by evolutionary biologists, no conscious deliberation by bacteria (or humans) is implied (or ruled out) by this term. Whether the decision rules being analyzed are designed to regulate foraging, fighting, or cooperating, the immediate payoffs of these decisions, in food or resources, are translated into the currency of offspring produced by the decision-making agent, and these offspring inherit their parents' decision rule. In evolutionary game theory, a decision rule or strategy that garners higher payoffs leaves more copies of itself in the next generation than alternatives that garner lower payoffs. By analyzing the reproductive consequences of alternative decision rules over generations, evolutionary biologists can determine which strategies natural selection is likely to favor and which are likely to be selected out.

The evolution of cooperation has been vigorously investigated using game theory. We illustrate the method below and then show how it has led to the discovery of domain-specialized concepts and reasoning procedures.

The Evolution of Two-Party Cooperation: Constraints from Game Theory

The evolution of adaptations for cooperation is tricky, even when only two individuals are involved and they can interact repeatedly. Two-party cooperation, also known as reciprocal altruism, reciprocation, or social exchange, is often modeled as a repeated Prisoner's dilemma game. In each round of the game, the player must decide whether to cooperate or defect—to provide a benefit of magnitude B to the other player (at cost C to oneself) or refrain from doing so. In these games, $B - C > 0$ for both players. In these environments, strategies that always cooperate—no matter how their partners respond—are outcompeted by strategies that always defect, and eventually disappear from the population (see sidebar Unconditional Cooperation Is Not Evolutionarily Stable).

UNCONDITIONAL COOPERATION IS NOT EVOLUTIONARILY STABLE

Imagine a population of agents participating in a series of prisoners' dilemma games. Each agent is equipped with one of two possible decision rules: "always cooperate" or "always defect." "Always cooperate" causes unconditional cooperation: agents with this design incur cost C to provide their partner with benefit B, regardless of how their partner behaves in return. The other decision rule, "always defect," accepts benefits from others but never provides them, so it never suffers cost C. When two unconditional cooperators interact, their payoff is positive, because $B - C > 0$. When two defectors interact, they get nothing—they are no better or worse off than if they had not interacted at all. But every time a cooperator interacts with a defector, the cooperator suffers a net loss (because it pays cost C with no compensating benefit) and the defector gets B (the benefit provided by the cooperator) while incurring no cost.

Now imagine that the agents are randomly sorted into pairs for each new round, there are n rounds during a generation, and the probability of being paired with a cooperator versus a defector is p versus $(1 - p)$, a function of their relative proportions in the population. The "always defect" rule never suffers a cost, but it earns B every time it is paired with an agent who always cooperates, which is $n*p$ times; thus $np*B$ is the total payoff earned by each defector that generation. In contrast, the "always cooperate" rule suffers cost C in every round, for a total cost of $n*C$. It earns B only from the $n*p$ rounds in which it meets another cooperator, for a total benefit of $np*B$. Hence, $n(pB - C)$ is the total payoff earned by each cooperator that generation. These payoffs determine the relative number of offspring each design produces. Because $npB > npB - nC$, the "always defect" design will leave more copies of itself in the next generation than the "always cooperate" design. As this continues over generations, unconditional cooperators will eventually disappear from the population, and only defectors will remain. "Always defect" is an evolutionarily stable strategy in an environment where the only alternative is a design that always cooperates. "Always cooperate" is not an evolutionarily stable strategy—a population of unconditional cooperators can be invaded and displaced by designs that always defect.

Although unconditional cooperation fails, agent-based simulations show that decision rules that cause cooperation can evolve and be maintained by natural selection if they implement a strategy for cooperation that is conditional—a strategy that not only recognizes and remembers its history of interaction with other agents, but also uses that information to cooperate with other cooperators and defect on defectors (Tit-for-Tat is an example; Axelrod & Hamilton 1981, Axelrod 1984). Conditional cooperators remember acts of cooperation and cooperate in response, so they provide benefits to one another, earning a payoff of $(B - C)$ every time they interact. Because the cooperation of one elicits future cooperation from the other, they cooperate repeatedly, and these positive payoffs accumulate over rounds. In this, they are like unconditional cooperators. The difference is that conditional cooperators limit their losses to defectors. The first time a conditional cooperator interacts with a particular defector, it suffers a one-time loss, C, and the defector earns a one-time benefit, B. But the next time these two individuals meet, the conditional cooperator defects, and it does not resume cooperation unless its partner responds by cooperating. As a result, designs that defect cannot continue to prosper at the expense of designs that cooperate conditionally. Nor can they harvest gains in trade from interacting with one another. Over generations, conditional cooperators outreproduce defectors because they harvest gains in trade from interacting repeatedly with one another.

Defectors are often referred to as "cheaters" in two-party reciprocation or social exchange. The results of evolutionary game theory tell us that cognitive adaptations for participating in social exchange can be favored and maintained by natural selection, but only if they implement some form of conditional cooperation. To do so, they require design features that detect and respond to cheaters (see Reasoning section, below).

Collective Action

A similar analysis applies to collective actions: situations in which three or more individuals cooperate to achieve a common goal and then share the resulting benefits. Defectors in

this form of group cooperation are called "free riders."

There are many situations, such as common defense, in which the benefits of group cooperation will be shared by everyone in the group, regardless of how much they contributed to producing them. When this is true, those who contribute to the common goal at high levels are at a selective disadvantage compared to those who contribute at low levels (or not at all). The benefits of collective action will be reaped by high and low contributors alike, but the costs of contribution fall disproportionately on the high contributors. Consequently, the low contributors—the free riders—experience higher net payoffs than the high contributors, and those who contribute nothing do best of all. Because net payoffs are translated into offspring produced, decision rules that cause free riding will leave more copies of themselves in the next generation than those that always contribute at high levels. This will continue over generations. Eventually the population will consist entirely of agents who free ride; as a result, no one in this population will contribute to collective actions. Indeed, the total population may end up smaller than it was originally, because it is now composed entirely of agents who do not benefit from resources that can be harvested only by cooperating with others and sharing the resulting benefits.

As in two-party cooperation, adaptations for participating in collective action can be selected for only if they cause contributors to cooperate conditionally. In social exchange, a cooperator can avoid cheaters by switching partners when alternatives are available. This is more difficult in collective actions, because withdrawing from free riders means withdrawing from the group. A better solution is to keep the group, and either exclude free riders from it or else punish them to incentivize higher contributions in the future (Boyd & Richerson 1992, Hauert et al. 2002, Panchanathan & Boyd 2004, Tooby et al. 2006, Tooby & Cosmides 2010).

With these selection pressures in mind, we turn to concepts, categorization, and reasoning.

CONCEPTS AND CATEGORIZATION

Are our brains designed to reliably develop concepts as specific as "cheater" or "free rider," which categorize people using criteria that satisfy constraints from evolutionary game theory? The idea seems eccentric. Indeed, the study of concepts and categorization started from the assumption that categorization is a unitary and general process, driven by perceptual similarity and shared features (e.g., Bruner et al. 1956, Rips et al. 1973). Some categorization processes do operate widely over many content domains (for review, see Ashby & Maddox 2005), but they coexist in the brain with a large number of content-rich, domain-specific inference systems (for reviews, see Pinker 1997, Boyer & Barrett 2005). These include the theory of mind system (e.g., Baron-Cohen 1995, Leslie et al. 2004, Onishi & Baillargeon 2005, Saxe & Powell 2006), intuitive physics (e.g., Spelke 1990, Leslie 1994), and folk biology (Medin & Atran 1999, Barrett 2005, Mahon & Caramazza 2009).

Each of these systems represents the world using specialized concepts and embodies inferences that, when applied to those concepts, are well designed for solving a different adaptive problem faced by the ancestral hunter-gatherers from whom we are descended. For example, the theory of mind system uses cues such as self-propelled motion and contingent reactivity to distinguish "agents" from other "objects"; proprietary concepts, such as "belief," "desire," and "intention," which are attributed only to entities classified as "agents"; and specialized reasoning circuits for inferring these mental states and using them to predict and explain behavior.

Broad concepts, such as "agents" whose actions reflect their "beliefs" and "desires," and physical "objects" that move only when acted upon by an outside "force," are necessary for interacting with the world. But as systems for regulating social interactions, they are blunt instruments.

Intricate rules of obligation, entitlement, and moral violation regulate social interactions, and these differ by domain—consider, for example, the differences between cooperating with a team, negotiating rank in a status hierarchy, courting a romantic partner, trading favors with a friend, and helping a sibling. Evolutionary biologists and behavioral ecologists have developed sophisticated, game-theoretic models of what counts as adaptive social behavior in each of these domains. Implementing these behavioral strategies requires a number of fine-grained social categories and nuanced moral concepts. As a first example, we consider evidence for a domain-specialized concept, "free rider," designed for regulating cooperation in collective actions.

Concepts for Collective Action: Free Riders Versus Cooperators

Humans are almost unique in the extent to which they participate in collective actions. It is fundamental to the human propensity to work in teams and form coalitions, so understanding the psychological mechanisms that make this zoologically unusual form of cooperation possible is fundamental to understanding organizational behavior, social systems, economics, and even politics (Olson 1965, Brewer & Kramer 1986, Ostrom 1990, Price et al. 2002).

As discussed above, adaptations for contributing to collective actions cannot evolve unless they are accompanied by a desire to exclude or punish free riders: those with motivational systems inclining them to avoid the costs of contributing to a collective action while benefiting from the contributions of others. Economists argue similarly, that rational actors will withdraw from collective actions when free riders are present; indeed, while noting that rational choice theory cannot explain it, behavioral economists and social psychologists have repeatedly shown that people are willing to punish free riders, even when they incur a personal cost to do so (Yamagishi 1986, Fehr & Gächter 2000, Masclet et al. 2003). But what criteria does the mind use to categorize someone as a free rider?

Economists assume that individuals assess incentives in the immediate situation and make decisions that will maximize their short-term profit. This view suggests that participants in a collective action will classify anyone who has contributed less than themselves (or others) as a free rider (e.g., Masclet et al. 2003). Evolutionary game theory asks a different question: given the structure of ancestral environments, which decision rule for categorizing free riders will best promote its own reproduction over generations? Given the ecological conditions faced by ancestral hunter-gatherers, a concept that classifies everyone who undercontributes as a free rider—to be excluded or punished—is a losing strategy.

Error management. Two categorization errors threaten the evolutionary stability of conditional cooperation: mistakenly treating a free rider as a cooperator (a miss) and mistakenly treating a cooperator as a free rider (a false alarm). In foraging societies, false alarms are more costly than misses. Based on estimates of injury rates and variance in foraging success among existing hunter-gatherers, our ancestors experienced frequent reversals of fortune (Kaplan & Hill 1985, Gurven 2004, Sugiyama 2004). As a result, every individual endowed with neurocognitive mechanisms that cause conditional cooperation will sometimes fail to contribute to a collective action due to errors, accidents, bad luck, or injury. Categorizing these conditional cooperators as free riders will trigger cycles of mutual defection (you defect on the supposed free rider, who defects on you in return. . .). These cycles prevent both parties from harvesting the benefits of repeated mutual cooperation that occur when conditional cooperators correctly recognize one another. Without these benefits, decision rules that cause cooperation are eventually outcompeted by those that cause free riding, and collective action disappears from the population.

This means false alarms were very costly fitness errors for strategies that cooperate con-ditionally. Misses were less costly: Mistakenly cooperating with a free rider results in a one-time loss, because strategies that cooperate conditionally defect on partners who have defected on them (see above; for agent-based simulations demonstrating this point in the context of two-person cooperation, see Delton et al. 2011).

When false alarms are more costly than misses, natural selection should equip categorization systems with criteria that minimize them, even if that increases the frequency of misses (on error management theory, see Haselton & Buss 2000, Haselton & Nettle 2006). A categorization system that uses level of contribution as its sole criterion for classifying someone as a free rider does exactly the wrong thing: It minimizes misses (the less costly error) at the expense of generating many false alarms (the more costly error). An evolutionarily stable strategy for collective action requires a "free rider" concept that distinguishes between undercontributors, sorting them on the basis of whether they show cues of cooperative versus exploitive intent.

Exploitive designs. Using an unobtrusive measure of social categorization based on recall errors (a "who did what?" protocol, analogous to the "who said what?" protocol developed by Taylor et al. 1978), Delton et al. (2012) showed that people who try to contribute to a collective action but fail are not categorized as free riders—even when they contribute less than others. To be categorized as a free rider, the target must undercontribute in a way suggesting exploitive intent—that is, a motivation to benefit from the collective action without incurring the costs of contributing to it (e.g., by consuming the resource they had promised to contribute or by making no effort to procure the promised resource). These individuals were subsequently judged to be less trustworthy, more selfish, more deserving of punishment, and less desirable as future cooperative partners.

The discovery that targets with exploitive intent are sorted into a distinct mental category—and evaluated more negatively than targets who try to contribute but fail due to accident or bad luck—is robust. Moreover, it cannot be accounted for by a domain-general process that sifts for any behavioral difference between targets and uses it to categorize them. In a control condition using the same cooperative targets that had previously been categorized (when the other targets were free riders), Delton and colleagues showed that targets who try to contribute, but fail in one of two distinct ways, are not sorted into separate categories.

Moral psychology and free riders. Although these results suggest a domain-specialized system for categorizing free riders, they could also be accounted for if the mind has criteria for distinguishing those who violate moral rules from those who do not. To test this "moral violator" counter-hypothesis, Delton et al. (2012) used the same unobtrusive method to show that the mind distinguishes free riders from other kinds of moral violators. As in the other "who did what?" experiments, subjects saw that everyone who had agreed to participate in the collective action contributed resources on three of five days. But on the other two days, subjects saw that some targets consumed a resource they had promised to contribute to the group (free riders), and others stole a resource owned by the group. Every one of these targets was intentionally violating a moral rule—and illicitly taking a benefit for themselves that was obligated to the group. Nevertheless, subjects sharply distinguished them, as revealed by the categorization measure and the response and character ratings gathered subsequently.

That the mind slices the moral domain so thinly is remarkable: stealing a resource from the group and consuming a resource promised to the group are so similar that most approaches to moral psychology would not distinguish them. These experiments suggest that our minds really are prepared to notice and remember which individuals are free riders on collective actions, making very subtle distinctions between free riders and people who commit other, very similar kinds of moral violations.

REASONING

We take for granted that two parties can make themselves better off than they were before by exchanging things each values less for things each values more (help, favors, goods, services). This form of cooperation for mutual benefit—social exchange—does not exist in many species, but it is as characteristic of human life as language and tool use. From evolutionary game theory, we saw that adaptations for two-party cooperation can be favored and maintained by selection only if they implement a strategy that cooperates conditionally.

Conditional cooperation requires cognitive systems that not only recognize different individuals, but also remember whether they had cooperated or defected in the past. Memory research shows that faces of cooperators and cheaters are remembered better than faces of individuals who did neither (Bell et al. 2010), and faces of cooperators activate reward centers in the brain (Singer et al. 2004). Indeed, participating in social exchange activates reward centers more than nonsocial activities that provide the same payoffs (Elliott et al. 2006). It also triggers a very specialized form of conditional reasoning (reviewed in Cosmides & Tooby 2005, 2008a,b).

Conditional Reasoning and Social Exchange

The study of conditional reasoning was pioneered by Peter Wason, who began his inquiries with a simple question: Does the brain contain a reasoning system that implements first-order logic? (Wason & Johnson-Laird 1972). First-order logic is very useful: It has rules of inference that generate true conclusions from true premises—a very specialized function. But its procedures are blank—free of content—so they can operate uniformly on information from any domain. Logic's domain generality is a good feature if your goal is to acquire valid knowledge about the world, no matter what subject you are studying. But this design feature is a bug for a system designed to reason adaptively about social exchange.

Conditional reasoning: reasoning about conditionals—rules with the format "If *P* then *Q*"

When participating in social exchange, you agree to deliver a benefit conditionally (conditional on the other person doing what you required in return). This contingency can be expressed as a "social contract", a conditional rule that fits the following template: "If you accept benefit *B* from me, then you must satisfy my requirement *R*." The social contract is offered because the individual providing the benefit expects to be better off if its conditions are satisfied [e.g., if the theater owner receives the price of a ticket ("requirement *R*") in return for access to the symphony ("benefit *B*")]. The target accepts these terms only if the benefit provided more than compensates for any losses he incurs by satisfying the requirement (e.g., if hearing the symphony is worth the cost of the ticket to him). This mutual provisioning of benefits, each conditional on the others' compliance, is what is meant by social exchange or reciprocation (Cosmides 1985, 1989; Tooby & Cosmides 1996). Understanding it requires a form of conditional reasoning. But the inferential rules required do not conform to the inferential rules of truth-preserving logics (Cosmides & Tooby 1989, 2008a).

For example, there is no logical inference by which "If *P* then *Q*" implies "If *Q* then *P*" (e.g., "If a person is a biologist, then he enjoys camping," does not imply "If a person enjoys camping, then he is a biologist"). But what if *P* and *Q* refer to benefits and requirements, and the conditional rule expresses a social exchange between two parties?

Because conditional cooperation makes entitlement to benefits contingent on satisfying obligations, it is natural to infer that "If you accept benefit *B* from me, then you must satisfy my requirement *R*" also implies "If you satisfy my requirement *R* then you are entitled to receive benefit *B* from me" (e.g., when I say, "If you borrow my car, then you have to fill my tank with gas," I also mean "If you fill my tank with gas, then you may borrow my car"). Logic forbids this inference, but reasoning procedures designed for social exchange require it. An evolutionarily stable strategy for reasoning about conditional rules involving

social exchange requires functionally specialized inference rules like these, which operate on abstract yet content-specific conceptual elements, such as "agent," "benefit," "requirement," "obligation," and "entitlement"—what Cosmides & Tooby (1989, 1992, 2008a) call social contract algorithms.

To implement decision rules for conditional cooperation, social contract algorithms also require an information search function, designed to look for cheaters. "Cheaters" are individuals with a disposition to violate social contracts by taking the benefit offered without satisfying the requirement on which it was made contingent.

Investigations with the Wason Selection Task

The hypothesis that the brain contains social contract algorithms, which include a subroutine for detecting cheaters, predicts a dissociation in reasoning performance by content: a sharply enhanced ability to reason adaptively about conditional rules when those rules specify a social exchange.

Peter Wason's four-card selection task is a standard tool for investigating conditional reasoning (see **Supplemental Figure 1**; follow the **Supplemental Material link** from the Annual Reviews home page at **http://www.annualreviews.org**). Subjects are given a conditional rule of the form "If *P* then *Q*" and asked to identify possible violations of it—a format that easily allows one to see how performance varies as a function of the rule's content. Wason developed this task to see if we humans are natural falsificationists: if we spontaneously apply first-order logic to look for cases that might violate a conditional rule. It turns out that people perform poorly on this task: For most conditional rules, only 5% to 30% of normal subjects respond with the logically correct answer, even when the rule describes familiar content drawn from everyday life—such as a disease causing a particular symptom or a rule describing people's preferences or habits (Wason 1983, Cosmides & Tooby 2008a).

Content matters, however. When the conditional rule involves social exchange and detecting a violation corresponds to looking for cheaters, 65% to 80% of subjects correctly detect violations on the Wason selection task (see **Supplemental Figure 2**; follow the **Supplemental Material link** from the Annual Reviews home page at **http://www.annualreviews.org**). They succeed even when the rule specifies a wildly unfamiliar social contract (e.g., "If you get a tattoo on your face, then I'll give you cassava root"). The ability to detect cheaters on social contracts is already present by age 3–4 (Núñez & Harris 1998, Harris et al. 2001), and it is found cross-culturally—not just in industrialized market economies, but also among Shiwiar hunter-horticulturalists of the Ecuadorian Amazon (Sugiyama et al. 2002).

This is not because social contracts activate the inferences of first-order logic. Looking for cheaters requires one to investigate two classes of individuals: those who have accepted the benefit offered in the social contract rule (to see if they failed to satisfy the requirement) and those who have not satisfied the requirement (to see if they took the benefit anyway). In many Wason selection tasks, these choices are (by coincidence) logically correct. But it is simple to create a social contract problem where investigating the same individuals is logically incorrect (see **Supplemental Figure 3**; follow the **Supplemental Material link** from the Annual Reviews home page at **http://www.annualreviews.org**). When this is done, people do not respect the rules of logic; they look for cheaters instead (Cosmides 1989, Gigerenzer & Hug 1992).

The claim that the mind contains reasoning procedures specialized for detecting cheaters was (and is) very controversial (Cosmides & Tooby 2005, 2008a,b; Fodor 2008). A common response is that people are good at detecting violations of any conditional rule that is deontic (i.e., that expresses permission, obligation, entitlement, or prohibition), whether it is a social contract or not (e.g., Cheng & Holyoak 1985, Manktelow & Over 1991, Sperber et al. 1995, Fodor 2000). In support of this, they note—correctly—that people are good at detecting violations of (deontic) precautionary rules, such as "if you work with toxic gases, then you must wear a gas mask" (Cheng & Holyoak 1989, Fiddick et al. 2000). But two separate systems regulate reasoning about these two domains: Brain damage can selectively impair a person's ability to detect cheaters on social contracts while leaving intact their ability to detect violations of precautionary rules (Stone et al. 2002)—a neural dissociation that is supported by brain imaging studies (Fiddick et al. 2005, Ermer et al. 2006, Reis et al. 2007).

Most tellingly, however, good violation detection is not found for deontic rules that are neither precautions nor social contracts (Cosmides & Tooby 2008a,b). Indeed, social contracts themselves do not elicit violation detection unless this can reveal potential cheaters—individuals with a disposition to illicitly benefit by violating the rule (for explanation, see section Concepts for Collective Action: Free Riders Versus Cooperators). Using the same social contract rule—which was given the same deontic interpretation in all problems—Cosmides et al. (2010) parametrically varied three cues relevant to detecting cheaters. Violation detection was high when potential violators were acting intentionally, would get the benefit regulated by the rule, and the situation allowed violations. But removing any one of these cues independently (and additively) down-regulated detection of social contract violations (see **Supplemental Figure 4**; follow the **Supplemental Material link** from the Annual Reviews home page at **http://www.annualreviews.org**). Performance was lower (*a*) when violations reflected innocent mistakes (rather than intentional actions), (*b*) when the violators would not get the benefit regulated by the rule, and (*c*) when the situation made cheating difficult (when violations are unlikely, the search for them is unlikely to reveal those with a disposition to cheat). These results indicate that the reasoning mechanism involved is not designed to look for general rule violators, or deontic rule violators, or violators of social contracts, or even cases in which someone has been cheated; it does not deign to look for people who violated a social exchange by mistake—not even when they have accidentally benefited by doing so. Instead, this reasoning system is monomaniacally focused on looking for social contract rule violations when this is likely to lead to detecting "cheaters"—defined as agents who obtain a rationed benefit while intentionally not meeting the requirement.

MOTIVATION: THE ROLE OF EVOLVED REGULATORY VARIABLES

During the first wave of the cognitive revolution, researchers focused on the design of systems that evolved for knowledge acquisition, not motivation. Some areas, such as vision science, made progress despite the use of intuitive and informal ideas about their adaptive function. Not all biological functions correspond so transparently to our intuitions, however. Notable among these are adaptive problems relevant to value and motivation.

The adaptive regulation of behavior requires systems that value alternative behavioral choices in ways that tracked their fitness consequences. But what counts? For example, in making choices, how much weight should an organism place on the welfare of a sibling compared to its own? How intimidated should one individual be by the threat posed by another? When does the value of forging relationships with strangers offset the risk of exposure to new pathogens? Computational systems that make trade-offs like these should exist, and their study can benefit from systematic analyses of the biological problems that selected for their design.

Biologically speaking, computing value requires more than a general system for maximizing "utility," as some economists (and psychologists) conceive it. What constitutes biologically successful valuation (i.e., values enabling choices that promote fitness) differs from one domain to the next. In many cases, the criteria for computing value are fundamentally incommensurable across domains (Cosmides & Tooby 1987, Tooby et al. 2005). There is no general set of cross-domain choice criteria whose uniform application can adaptively guide food choice, mate choice, group affiliation, response to mate infidelity, incest avoidance, predator avoidance, friend-directed altruism, free rider punishment, cheater avoidance, infant nursing, sexual arousal, food sharing, aggression titrating, contagion avoidance, and so on. When valuation systems require distinct and incommensurable criteria to solve motivational problems (e.g., food choice versus mate choice versus predator avoidance), each incommensurable domain will require (at least) one functionally distinct, domain-specialized component.

Internal Regulatory Variables

By starting with models of specific adaptive problems drawn from evolutionary biology and evolutionary anthropology, evolutionary psychologists have identified candidate problems for which there should be evolved motivational specializations. When this is done, it becomes clear that computational strategies capable of solving these problems require elements that have no counterpart in traditional models of motivation. For example, what drive is reduced by helping family members? By sexual jealousy? By avoiding incest? By punishing free riders? By favoring the ingroup? By expressing anger? From what general goal could they be backward derived?

The kind of programs necessary to solve motivational problems require computational elements that are not exactly concepts, beliefs, representations of goal states, desires, preferences, or drives, but something else: internal regulatory variables (along with evolved specializations that compute them and deliver them to evolved decision-making systems) (Lieberman et al. 2007, Ermer et al. 2008, Tooby et al. 2008, Sell et al. 2009a). Each regulatory variable evolved to track a narrow, targeted property of the body, the social environment, or the physical environment—such as aggressive formidability, relative status, reliability as a cooperator, or kinship—whose computation provided the necessary inputs to evolved decision rules. These regulatory variables store magnitudes (or parameters), which either express value or provide input to mechanisms that compute value.

Below we illustrate with research exploring the architecture of the kin detection system. Evidence so far indicates that this system produces kinship indexes—variables that regulate motivational systems governing altruism and sexual attraction/aversion.

Genetic Relatedness and Motivation: Siblings, Incest, and Altruism

One family of adaptive problems involving valuation arises from asking how genetic relatedness should affect social behavior. Prior to the integration of the evolutionary sciences with psychology, questions like this were rarely considered. Yet adaptive problems posed by relatedness are nonintuitive, biologically real, and have large fitness consequences.

Kin-directed altruism. The theory of kin selection (Hamilton 1964) was a fundamental advance in the theory of natural selection, which follows from replicator dynamics. A gene can cause its own spread not only by increasing the reproduction of the individual it is in, but also by increasing the reproduction of others who are more likely to carry the same gene than a random member of the population—that is, close genetic relatives. This means that natural selection can favor the evolution of motivational designs that, under the right envelope of conditions, cause the individual to sacrifice his or her own welfare to increase the welfare of a genetic relative. There is evidence supporting the predictions of kin selection theory in species in which close genetic relatives frequently interact, including amoebas, plants, shrimp, social insects, rodents, and primates (reviewed in Lieberman et al. 2007). Given that our ancestors lived in small bands with close genetic relatives, kin selection theory predicts that human motivational systems governing welfare trade-offs (including altruism) should take kinship into account.

Inbreeding avoidance. A second adaptive problem that arises from proximity to close genetic relatives is inbreeding depression. Recessive alleles that are harmless when matched with a healthy allele can be injurious when matched with duplicates of themselves. Because all people carry many unexpressed deleterious recessives they received from their parents, zygotes produced when two close relatives mate are far more likely to carry defective alleles that match than zygotes produced by individuals who are not related to one another. This leads to a sharp increase in the number of genetic diseases expressed in children produced by incestuous matings—costs that may be further aggravated by parasites differentially exploiting more genetically homogeneous hosts (Charlesworth & Charlesworth 1999, Lieberman et al. 2007). This makes incest a major fitness error, like approaching predators, eating gravel, or killing your children. Consequently, computational designs that cost-effectively reduce inbreeding depression by avoiding mating with close genetic relatives outcompete variants in which mating decisions are unaffected by relatedness. Hence, the human psychological architecture should contain evolved systems designed to inhibit incest.

A Kin Detection System

These two adaptive problems—inbreeding avoidance and kin-directed altruism—both require a kin detection system: a neurocomputational system that is well engineered (given the structure of ancestral environments) for computing which individuals in one's social environment are close genetic relatives. By analyzing the adaptive problem, Lieberman et al. (2007) derived a model of this architecture (see **Figure 1**) and conducted a series of tests of predictions drawn from the model.

According to this theory, the kin detection system uses ancestrally reliable cues to compute and update a continuous variable, a kinship

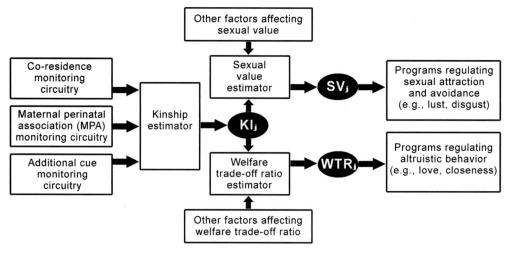

Figure 1

Architecture of a kin detection system, and its relationship to motivational systems regulating altruism (welfare trade-offs) and sexual attraction. The system includes several internal regulatory variables. A high kinship index (KI_j) between self and individual j should lower the sexual value of j to self (SV_j), and increase how much weight one places on j's welfare when making choices (WTR_j).

index, KI_{ij}, for each familiar other, j. The magnitude of KI_{ij} embodies the system's pairwise estimate of genetic relatedness between self (i) and other (j). Kinship indexes are evolved regulatory variables that should serve as input to neural programs regulating altruism by i toward j and, separately, to programs regulating i's sexual attraction to j. When KI_{ij} is high, it should up-regulate motivations to provide aid to j, and it should down-regulate sexual attraction by activating disgust at the possibility of sex with j.

Ancestrally reliable cues to genetic relatedness. The adaptive problem of detecting relatedness is hard to solve because genetic relatedness cannot be directly observed. Instead, the system must infer it, based on cues that predict genetic relatedness. A domain-general learning system cannot, by itself, identify and then use whatever transient cues best predict relatedness in the local environment. Discovering which novel cues are best would require the system to already know the genetic relatedness of others—the exact problem the kin detection system needs to solve. Instead, the kin detection system must contain within its evolved design a specification of the core cues that it will use

to determine relatedness—cues picked out over evolutionary time by natural selection because they reliably tracked genetic relatedness in the ancestral social world.

For our hunter-gatherer ancestors, a reliable cue to relatedness is provided by the close association between mother and infant that begins with birth and is maintained by maternal attachment. Maternal perinatal association (MPA) provides an effective psychophysical foundation for the mutual kin detection of mother and child. It also provides a foundation for sibling detection. Among our ancestors, when an individual observed an infant in an enduring caretaking association with the observer's mother, that infant was likely to be the observer's sibling. To use this high-quality information, the kin detection system would need a monitoring subsystem specialized for registering MPA.

Although MPA allows older offspring to detect their younger siblings, it cannot be used by younger siblings because they did not exist when their older siblings were born and nursed. This implies that the kin detection system's psychophysical front end must monitor at least one additional cue to relatedness. The cumulative duration of coresidence between two children, summed over the full period of parental care until late adolescence, is a cue that could be used to predict genetic relatedness—an expansion and modification of the early ethological proposal about imprinting during early childhood.

Hunter-gatherer bands fission and fuse over time, as their members forage and visit other bands; this means individuals frequently spent short periods of time with unrelated or distantly related persons. However, hunter-gatherer parents (especially mothers) maintained close association with their dependent children in order to care for them. Siblings, therefore, maintained a higher-than-average cumulative association with each other within the band structure. As association is summed over longer periods of time, it monotonically becomes an increasingly good cue to genetic relatedness. This invites the hypothesis that the kin detection system has a system for monitoring duration of coresidence between i and j during i's childhood, and that its output allows younger offspring to detect their older siblings.

Does a kin detection system regulate sibling altruism and sexual aversion? To compute the kinship index, the kin detection system requires (*a*) monitoring circuitry designed to register cues to relatedness (MPA, coresidence during childhood, possibly others) and (*b*) a computational device, the kinship estimator, whose procedures have been tuned by a history of selection to take these registered inputs and transform them into a kinship index—the regulatory variable that evolved to track genetic relatedness.

If these cues are integrated into a single kinship index—that is, if the kinship index for each familiar individual is a real computational element of human psychology—then two distinct motivational systems should be regulated by the same pattern of input cues. For example, when i is younger than j, i's kinship index toward j should be higher the longer they coresided during i's childhood. As a result, i's levels of altruism and sexual aversion toward j will be predicted by their duration of childhood coresidence.

Lieberman et al. (2007) tested these hypotheses about the computational architecture of human kin detection by quantitatively matching naturally generated individual variation in two predicted cues of genetic relatedness—maternal perinatal association and duration of coresidence during childhood—to individual variation in altruism directed toward a given sibling and opposition to incest with that sibling. When the MPA cue was absent (as it always is for youngers detecting older siblings), duration of childhood coresidence with a specific sibling predicted measures of altruism and sexual aversion toward that sibling, with similar effect sizes. When the MPA cue was present (which is possible only for olders detecting younger siblings), measures of altruism and sexual aversion toward the younger sibling were high, regardless of childhood coresidence.

These results support the model in **Figure 1**. At least two cue-monitoring systems must be present, because motivational outcomes were regulated by both MPA and coresidence duration. Moreover, these two inputs regulated two different motivational outputs, altruism and sexual aversion, representing two entirely independent adaptive problems (titrating kin-directed altruism and avoiding incest). The fact that two different motivational systems are regulated in parallel by the same cues to genetic relatedness implicates a single underlying computational variable—a kinship index—that is accessed by both motivational systems. Finally, the kinship estimator must be a part of the architecture because, where both cues are available, the more reliable cue—maternal perinatal association—trumps coresidence duration. The two cues interact in a noncompensatory way, rather than being additive, meaning there is unlikely to be a direct path from the input variables (cues) to the motivational systems they regulate.

This entire computational system appears to operate nonconsciously and independently of conscious beliefs. When beliefs about genetic relatedness conflict with the cues this system uses (as they do when people have coresided with step-siblings), the motivational outputs (caring, sexual disgust) are shaped by the cues, not the beliefs. It is worth noting that this system influences moral sentiments as well: Those who have opposite-sex siblings associated with a high kinship index are more morally opposed to incestuous relationships, even between third parties (Lieberman et al. 2003, 2007; Fessler & Navarete 2004).

Finally, it is important to recognize that the kin detection system constitutes a learning system: It is designed to learn the genetic relatedness of familiar others. What makes it especially interesting is that it does not resemble the general-purpose learning systems psychologists are used to positing as explanations for behavior. Instead, it is a proprietary learning system, with a dedicated function, whose complex architecture incorporates content-inflected computational elements (e.g., mother, neonate, coresidence). The computational problem-solving strategy evolved to exploit the particular relationships of the ancestral world (foraging patterns, mother-infant association) in order to successfully acquire information it was designed to learn. It is an open question how much of human learning is carried out by domain-specific or content-sensitive devices, and how much by more general-purpose systems.

The case of kin detection (including incest avoidance and kin-directed altruism) is instructive in that it provides an example of what the computational architectures of evolved motivational adaptations are likely to look like. It suggests that the architecture of human motivation is full of registers for evolved variables: kinship indexes, sexual value indexes, coresidence measures, welfare trade-off ratios, and others. These variables acquire their properties and meaning by the evolved behavior-controlling and motivation-generating procedures that compute and access them (Tooby et al. 2008). That is, each has a location embedded in the input–output relations of our evolved programs, and their function inheres in the role they play in the control architecture of these programs. The kinship index is located downstream of input cues, it tracks relatedness, and it is accessed by downstream sexual valuation and welfare trade-off motivations.

On this view, there is a hidden, previously unmapped layer of neurocomputational procedures and representations, consisting of (*a*) internal regulatory variables (e.g., a kinship index), (*b*) procedures that compute them (e.g., the kinship estimator), (*c*) psychophysical front ends that monitor cues that serve as inputs to the procedures that compute these variables (e.g., maternal perinatal association monitoring), and (*d*) the entities that these variables feed, such as decision rules, motivational intensities, emotion programs, and conscious feelings (e.g., disgust at the idea of sexual contact with a sibling). These systems embody an evolved functional logic that reflects the adaptive problems they evolved to solve, and they cause us to experience specific motivations, value specific outcomes, and express specific behaviors given certain inputs. Given the complexity of these systems, one would never discover them using blind empiricism. However, models of adaptive problems give strong guidance in how to construct experimental programs to detect these systems and to map their computational structure.

EMOTION AND THE RECALIBRATION OF REGULATORY VARIABLES

In **Figure 1**, the kinship index feeds systems that compute at least two other regulatory variables: (*a*) the sexual value index ($SV_{i,j}$), a regulatory variable whose magnitude represents i's assessment of j's value as a sexual partner, and (*b*) a welfare trade-off ratio ($WTR_{i,j}$), a variable whose magnitude represents the weight i puts on j's welfare when making decisions that impact them both. Ample literature supports the view that many ancestrally reliable cues of a potential sexual partner's health and fertility are integrated to form a sexual value index, whose magnitude is experienced as the person's sexual attractiveness (for review, see Sugiyama 2005). But why posit the existence of welfare trade-off ratios?

Welfare Trade-Offs

In social species, actions undertaken by one individual sometimes impact the welfare of others. Although biologists had previously assumed that selection favored choices that were completely selfish, over the past five decades, evolutionary biologists have identified a series of selection pressures that favor taking the welfare of others into account. That is, there are classes of situations in which the most fitness-promoting choice is not simply to maximize one's own welfare. Instead, under various conditions selection favors placing weight on the welfare of another as well, so that decisions reflect a trade-off between the welfare of self and other. Adaptive problems that favor calibrating such trade-offs include kin selection (Hamilton 1964), reciprocation or exchange (Trivers 1971, Axelrod & Hamilton 1981), aggression and the asymmetric war of attrition (Hammerstein & Parker 1982), and externalities (Tooby & Cosmides 1996).

Most evolutionary models tend to dissect strategic games involving kinship, aggressive formidability, reciprocity, and so on as independent, isolated problems. However, real organisms facing real choices cannot. Humans are often playing a number of games at once with the same individuals. Each act or choice is an expression of the weight the actor places on the target's welfare, and so a single act cannot express inconsistent weights at the same time. Yet different games will rarely converge on the same weighting function for a specific target: A target may be a sibling, for example, yet have cheated recently in a dyadic reciprocation. A person cannot simultaneously give aid (e.g., if the other is indexed as close kin) and withhold aid (e.g., if the other is indexed as someone who has cheated in their reciprocity relationship).

For the neural architecture to be able to decide which self-favoring or other-favoring acts to choose at any given moment, the brain needs a motivational architecture that registers the factors that, taken individually, might call for different weightings, and integrates them (at any given time) into a single welfare trade-off ratio (Tooby et al. 2008). Multiple converging lines of evidence support the hypothesis that WTRs are not just post hoc theoretical constructs, but exist as real neurocognitive elements within the human motivational architecture—elements that play a role in decision making. A number of empirical studies now support the view that WTRs are person-specific stored values that display remarkable consistency across large numbers of benefit allocations between self and other (Delton 2010).

Anger and the Recalibration of Welfare Trade-Off Ratios

If WTRs actually exist in human brains, then selection can design adaptations whose function is to recalibrate their magnitude in oneself and in others. Gratitude, guilt, and anger may be social emotions that evolved to recalibrate WTRs (Tooby & Cosmides 2008). Evidence supports the view that the gratitude emotion program is activated when someone puts an unexpectedly high weight on your welfare. The gratitude program then recalibrates your WTR toward the generous person upward—serving the function of consolidating cooperative relationships (Lim 2012). Guilt is hypothesized to be activated when a person discovers they have placed too low a weight on someone else's welfare. It also triggers an upward recalibration of the transgressor's WTR toward the victim, so that future treatment is less exploitive (Sznycer 2010).

Within this framework, the greatest amount of research has been done on the recalibrational theory of anger (Sell 2005, Tooby et al. 2008, Sell et al. 2009a). In this view, anger is the expression of a neurocomputational system that evolved to adaptively regulate behavior in the context of resolving conflicts of interest in favor of the angry individual. The anger system is triggered by actions indicating that the other party is placing too little weight on the welfare of the actor (i.e., when their actions express a WTR that is too low). For example, an action by j that imposes a given cost on self is more likely to activate one's anger program when *j* did it to gain a small benefit than a large one, because this indicates *j*'s WTR toward oneself is low (Sell 2005, Lim 2012).

Once triggered, the anger system deploys bargaining tactics designed to incentivize the target of the anger to place greater weight on the welfare of the angry individual in the future. It does this by activating one of two social negotiating tactics: threatening to inflict costs (aggression) or threatening to withdraw expected benefits (i.e., lowering one's own WTR toward the target of the anger). Acts or signals of anger (such as the anger face) communicate that, unless the target starts to place more weight on the angry individual's welfare, the angry individual will inflict costs on the target (in noncooperative relationships) or withdraw benefits from the target (in cooperative relationships)—that is, the angry individual will lower her WTR toward the target unless the target raises his WTR toward her. Experiments show that choices revealing a low WTR trigger anger in cooperative relationships, which in turn leads the angry individuals to lower their own WTR toward their partner (the predicted bargaining response). The magnitude of the subject's anger predicts the magnitude of the subject's WTR recalibration (Lim 2012).

Because interpersonal bargaining power arises from the relative ability to inflict costs or to confer/withhold benefits, the recalibrational model of anger predicts that individuals with enhanced abilities to deploy these tactics will anger more easily, will feel entitled to better treatment (to a higher WTR from others), and will prevail more in conflicts of interest. Their greater ability to inflict costs or withdraw benefits translates into greater leverage in bargaining—meaning that anger is more likely to be successful for them than for others with less leverage. This suggests that there should be two regulatory variables that summarize these dimensions of social power and feed into the anger system: a formidability index that encodes the individual's self-assessment of his ability to inflict costs (fighting ability) and a conferral index that encodes the individual's self-assessment of his ability to confer/withhold benefits. For our male ancestors, upper-body strength was a major component of the ability to inflict costs on others (by injuring or killing them). Hence, greater strength should set a man's formidability index higher. Even now, people can accurately assess men's strength from sparse visual or vocal cues, and they spontaneously base their assessment of others' fighting ability on it (Sell et al. 2009b, 2010; Fessler et al. 2012). The ability to confer/withhold benefits has many sources, but one factor that is easy to operationalize is sexual attractiveness in women. As predicted by the recalibrational theory of anger, Sell et al. (2009a) found that men with greater upper-body strength were more prone to anger, felt more entitled to better treatment, and prevailed more in conflicts of interest than men with less upper-body strength. In women, attractiveness produced these same effects.

CONCLUSION

Evolutionary psychology is an organizing framework that can be applied to any topic in the psychological sciences. Discovering the design of the mind is easier when evolutionary biology tells us what we might find.

DISCLOSURE STATEMENT

The authors are not aware of any affiliations, memberships, funding, or financial holdings that might be perceived as affecting the objectivity of this review.

LITERATURE CITED

Ackerman JM, Shapiro JR, Neuberg SL, Kenrick DT, Becker DV, et al. 2006. They all look the same to me (unless they're angry): from out-group homogeneity to out-group heterogeneity. *Psychol. Sci.* 17:836–40

Anthony T, Copper C, Mullen B. 1992. Cross-racial facial identification: a social cognitive integration. *Pers. Soc. Psychol. Bull.* 18:296–301

Ashby FG, Maddox WT. 2005. Human category learning. *Annu. Rev. Psychol.* 56:149–78

Axelrod R. 1984. *The Evolution of Cooperation*. New York: Basic Books

Axelrod R, Hamilton W. 1981. The evolution of cooperation. *Science* 211:1390–96

Barkow JH, Cosmides L, Tooby J, eds. 1992. *The Adapted Mind: Evolutionary Psychology and the Generation of Culture*. **New York: Oxford Univ. Press**

Introduces the field of evolutionary psychology; provides many empirical examples.

Baron-Cohen S. 1995. *Mind Blindness: An Essay on Autism and Theory of Mind*. Cambridge, MA: MIT Press

Barrett HC. 2005. Adaptations to predators and prey. See Buss 2005, pp. 200–23

Becker DV, Anderson US, Neuberg SL, Maner JK, Shapiro JR, et al. 2010. More memory bang for the attentional buck: Self-protection goals enhance encoding efficiency for potentially threatening males. *Soc. Psychol. Pers. Sci.* 1:182–89

Bell R, Buchner A, Musch J. 2010. Enhanced old–new recognition and source memory for faces of cooperators and defectors in a social-dilemma game. *Cognition* 117:261–75

Boyd R, Richerson PJ. 1992. Punishment allows the evolution of cooperation (or anything else) in sizable groups. *Ethol. Sociobiol.* 13:171–95

Boyer P, Barrett HC. 2005. Domain specificity and intuitive ontology. See Buss 2005, pp. 96–188

Brase GL, Cosmides L, Tooby J. 1998. Individuation, counting, and statistical inference: the role of frequency and whole-object representations in judgment under uncertainty. *J. Exp. Psychol. Gen.* 127:3–21

Brewer MB, Kramer RM. 1986. Choice behavior in social dilemmas: effects of social identity, group size, and decision framing. *J. Pers. Soc. Psychol.* 50:543–49

Bruner JS, Goodnow JJ, Austin GA. 1956. *A Study of Thinking*. New York: Wiley

Buss DM. 1989. Sex differences in human mate preferences: evolutionary hypotheses tested in 37 cultures. *Behav. Brain Sci.* 12:1–14

Buss DM, ed. 2005. *The Handbook of Evolutionary Psychology*. Hoboken, NJ: Wiley

Charlesworth B, Charlesworth D. 1999. The genetic basis of inbreeding depression. *Genet. Res.* 74:329–40

Chawarska K, Volkmar F, Klin A. 2010. Limited attentional bias for faces in toddlers with autism spectrum disorders. *Arch. Gen. Psychiatry* 67:178–85

Cheng PW, Holyoak KJ. 1985. Pragmatic reasoning schemas. *Cogn. Psychol.* 17:391–416

Cheng PW, Holyoak KJ. 1989. On the natural selection of reasoning theories. *Cognition* 33:285–313

Cosmides L. 1985. *Deduction or Darwinian algorithms? An explanation of the "elusive" content effect on the Wason selection task*. PhD thesis. Harvard Univ.

Cosmides L. 1989. The logic of social exchange: Has natural selection shaped how humans reason? Studies with the Wason selection task. *Cognition* 31:187–276

Cosmides L, Barrett HC, Tooby J. 2010. Adaptive specializations, social exchange, and the evolution of human intelligence. *Proc. Natl. Acad. Sci. USA* 107:9007–14

Cosmides L, Tooby J. 1987. From evolution to behavior: evolutionary psychology as the missing link. In *The Latest on the Best: Essays on Evolution and Optimality*, ed. J Dupré, pp. 277–306. Cambridge, MA: MIT Press

Cosmides L, Tooby J. 1989. Evolutionary psychology and the generation of culture, part II. Case study: a computational theory of social exchange. *Ethol. Sociobiol.* 10:51–97

Cosmides L, Tooby J. 1992. Cognitive adaptations for social exchange. See Barkow et al. 1992, pp. 163–228

Cosmides L, Tooby J. 2001. Unraveling the enigma of human intelligence: evolutionary psychology and the multimodular mind. In *The Evolution of Intelligence*, ed. RJ Sternberg, JC Kaufman, pp. 145–98. Hillsdale, NJ: Erlbaum

Cosmides L, Tooby J. 2005. Neurocognitive adaptations designed for social exchange. See Buss 2005, pp. 584–627

Cosmides L, Tooby J. 2008a. Can a general deontic logic capture the facts of human moral reasoning? How the mind interprets social exchange rules and detects cheaters. See Sinnott-Armstrong 2008, pp. 53–119

Discusses replicator dynamics; complex functional design is a downstream consequence of natural selection.

Cosmides L, Tooby J. 2008b. When falsification strikes: a reply to Fodor. See Sinnott-Armstrong 2008, pp. 143–64

Daly M, Wilson M. 1988. *Homicide*. New York: Aldine de Gruyter

Dawkins R. 1982. *The Extended Phenotype*. **Oxford, UK: Oxford Univ. Press**

Delton AW. 2010. *A psychological calculus for welfare tradeoffs*. PhD thesis, Univ. Calif., Santa Barbara

Delton AW, Cosmides L, Guemo M, Robertson TE, Tooby J. 2012. The psychosemantics of free riding: dissecting the architecture of a moral concept. *J. Pers. Soc. Psychol.* 102:1252–70

Delton AW, Krasnow MM, Cosmides L, Tooby J. 2011. The evolution of direct reciprocity under uncertainty can explain human generosity in one-shot encounters. *Proc. Natl. Acad. Sci. USA* 108:13335–40

Duchaine BC, Yovel G, Butterworth EJ, Nakayama K. 2006. Prosopagnosia as an impairment to face-specific mechanisms: elimination of the alternative hypotheses in a developmental case. *Cogn. Neuropsychol.* 23:714–47

Elliott R, Völlm B, Drury A, McKie S, Richardson P, Deakin JF. 2006. Co-operation with another player in a financially rewarded guessing game activates regions implicated in theory of mind. *Soc. Neurosci.* 1:385–95

Ermer E, Cosmides L, Tooby J. 2008. Relative status regulates risky decision making about resources in men: evidence for the co-evolution of motivation and cognition. *Evol. Hum. Behav.* 29:106–18

Ermer E, Guerin SA, Cosmides L, Tooby J, Miller MB. 2006. Theory of mind broad and narrow: Reasoning about social exchange engages ToM areas, precautionary reasoning does not. *Soc. Neurosci.* 1:196–219

Fehr E, Gächter S. 2000. Cooperation and punishment in public goods experiments. *Am. Econ. Rev.* 90:980–94

Fessler DMT, Holbrook C, Snyder JK. 2012. Weapons make the man (larger): Formidability is represented as size and strength in humans. *PLoS ONE* 7:e32751

Fessler DMT, Navarrete CD. 2004. Third-party attitudes toward sibling incest: evidence for Westermarck's hypotheses. *Evol. Hum. Behav.* 25:277–94

Fiddick L, Cosmides L, Tooby J. 2000. No interpretation without representation: the role of domain-specific representations and inferences in the Wason selection task. *Cognition* 77:1–79

Fiddick L, Spampinato MV, Grafman J. 2005. Social contracts and precautions activate different neurological systems: an fMRI investigation of deontic reasoning. *Neuroimage* 28:778–86

Fodor J. 2000. Why we are so good at catching cheaters. *Cognition* 75:29–32

Fodor J. 2008. Comment on Cosmides and Tooby. See Sinnott-Armstrong 2008, pp. 137–42

Friesen CK, Kingstone A. 2003. Abrupt onsets and gaze direction cues trigger independent reflexive attentional effects. *Cognition* 87:B1–10

Gallistel CR. 1995. The replacement of general purpose theories with adaptive specializations. In *The Cognitive Neurosciences*, ed. MS Gazzaniga, pp. 1255–67. Cambridge, MA: MIT Press

Gallistel CR, Gibbon J. 2000. Time, rate, and conditioning. *Psychol. Rev.* 107:289–344

Gigerenzer G, Hug K. 1992. Domain-specific reasoning: social contracts, cheating, and perspective change. *Cognition* 43:127–71

Gigerenzer G, Selten R, eds. 2001. *Bounded Rationality: The Adaptive Toolbox*. Cambridge, MA: MIT Press

Gurven M. 2004. To give and to give not: the behavioral ecology of human food transfers. *Behav. Brain Sci.* 27:543–83

Hamilton WD. 1964. The genetical evolution of social behaviour, I and II. *J. Theor. Biol.* 7:1–52

Hammerstein P, Parker GA. 1982. The asymmetric war of attrition. *J. Theor. Biol.* 96:647–82

Harris P, Núñez M, Brett C. 2001. Let's swap: early understanding of social exchange by British and Nepali children. *Mem. Cogn.* 29:757–64

Haselton MG, Buss DM. 2000. Error management theory: a new perspective on biases in cross-sex mind reading. *J. Pers. Soc. Psychol.* 78:81–91

Haselton MG, Nettle D. 2006. The paranoid optimist: an integrative evolutionary model of cognitive biases. *Pers. Soc. Psychol. Rev.* 10:47–66

Hauert C, De Monte S, Hofbauer J, Sigmund K. 2002. Replicator dynamics for optional public good games. *J. Theor. Biol.* 218:187–94

Herrnstein RJ. 1977. The evolution of behaviorism. *Am. Psychol.* 32:593–603

Hoffman E, McCabe KA, Smith VL. 1998. Behavioral foundations of reciprocity: experimental economics and evolutionary psychology. *Econ. Inq.* 36:335–52

Kaplan H, Hill K. 1985. Food sharing among Ache foragers: tests of explanatory hypotheses. *Curr. Anthropol.* 26:223–46

Kenrick DT, Neuberg SL, Griskevicius V, Becker DV, Schaller M. 2010. Goal-driven cognition and functional behavior: the fundamental motives framework. *Curr. Dir. Psychol. Sci.* 19:63–67

Krasnow MM, Truxaw D, Gaulin SJC, New J, Ozono H, et al. 2011. Cognitive adaptations for gathering-related navigation in humans. *Evol. Hum. Behav.* 32:1–12

Leslie AM. 1994. ToMM, ToBy, and agency: core architecture and domain specificity. In *Mapping the Mind: Domain Specificity in Cognition and Culture*, ed. LA Hirschfeld, SA Gelman, pp. 119–48. New York: Cambridge Univ. Press

Leslie AM, Friedman O, German TP. 2004. Core mechanisms in "theory of mind." *Trends Cogn. Sci.* 8:528–33

Levin DT. 2000. Race as a visual feature: using visual search and perceptual discrimination tasks to understand face categories and the cross-race recognition deficit. *J. Exp. Psychol.: Gen.* 129:559–74

Lieberman D, Tooby J, Cosmides L. 2003. Does morality have a biological basis? An empirical test of the factors governing moral sentiments relating to incest. *Proc. R. Soc. Lond. B Biol. Sci.* 270:819–26

Lieberman D, Tooby J, Cosmides L. 2007. The architecture of human kin detection. *Nature* 445:727–31

Lim J. 2012. *Welfare tradeoff ratios and emotions: psychological foundations of human reciprocity*. PhD thesis. Univ. Calif., Santa Barbara

Mahon BZ, Caramazza A. 2009. Concepts and categories: a cognitive neuropsychological perspective. *Annu. Rev. Psychol.* 60:27–51

Maner JK, Kenrick DT, Becker DV, Robertson TE, Hofer B, et al. 2005. Functional projection: how fundamental social motives can bias interpersonal perception. *J. Pers. Soc. Psychol.* 88:63–78

Manktelow KI, Over DE. 1991. Social roles and utilities in reasoning with deontic conditionals. *Cognition* 39:85–105

Marlowe FW. 2007. Hunting and gathering: the human sexual division of foraging labor. *Cross-Cult. Res.* 41:170–95

Masclet D, Noussair C, Tucker S, Villeval MC. 2003. Monetary and nonmonetary punishment in the voluntary contributions mechanism. *Am. Econ. Rev.* 93:366–80

Maynard Smith J. 1982. *Evolution and the Theory of Games*. Cambridge, UK: Cambridge Univ. Press

Medin D, Atran S, eds. 1999. *Folkbiology*. Cambridge, MA: MIT Press

New J, Cosmides L, Tooby J. 2007a. Category-specific attention for animals reflects ancestral priorities, not expertise. *Proc. Natl. Acad. Sci. USA* 104:16598–603

New J, Krasnow MM, Truxaw D, Gaulin SJC. 2007b. Spatial adaptations for plant foraging: Women excel and calories count. *Proc. R. Soc. Lond. B Biol. Sci.* 274:2679–84

Núñez M, Harris PL. 1998. Psychological and deontic concepts: separate domains or intimate connection? *Mind Lang.* 13:153–70

Öhman A, Flykt A, Esteves F. 2001. Emotion drives attention: detecting the snake in the grass. *J. Exp. Psychol.: Gen.* 130:466–78

Olson M. 1965. *The Logic of Collective Action: Public Goods and the Theory of Groups*. Cambridge, MA: Harvard Univ. Press

Onishi KH, Baillargeon R. 2005. Do 15-month-old infants understand false beliefs? *Science* 308:255–58

Ostrom E. 1990. *Governing the Commons: The Evolution of Institutions for Collective Action*. Cambridge, UK: Cambridge Univ. Press

Ostrom TM, Sedikides C. 1992. Out-group homogeneity effects in natural and minimal groups. *Psychol. Bull.* 112:536–52

Panchanathan K, Boyd R. 2004. Indirect reciprocity can stabilize cooperation without the second-order free rider problem. *Nature* 432:499–502

Pinker S. 1997. *How the Mind Works*. New York: Norton

Pinker S. 2010. The cognitive niche: coevolution of intelligence, sociality, and language. *Proc. Natl. Acad. Sci. USA* 107:8993–99

Price ME, Cosmides L, Tooby J. 2002. Punitive sentiment as an anti-free rider psychological device. *Evol. Hum. Behav.* 23:203–31

Reis DL, Brackett MA, Shamosh NA, Kiehl KA, Salovey P, Gray JR. 2007. Emotional intelligence predicts individual differences in social exchange reasoning. *Neuroimage* 35:1385–91

Remington A, Campbell R, Swettenham J. 2012. Attentional status of faces for people with autism spectrum disorder. *Autism* 16:59–73

Rips LJ, Shoben EJ, Smith EE. 1973. Semantic distance and the verification of semantic relations. *J. Verbal Learn. Verbal Behav.* 12:1–20

Ro T, Russell C, Lavie N. 2001. Changing faces: a detection advantage in the flicker paradigm. *Psychol. Sci.* 12:94–99

Uses game theory to model evolution of social behavior.

Rode C, Cosmides L, Hell W, Tooby J. 1999. When and why do people avoid unknown probabilities in decisions under uncertainty? Testing some predictions from optimal foraging theory. *Cognition* 72:269–304

Roney JR. 2009. The role of sex hormones in the initiation of human mating relationships. In *Endocrinology of Social Relationships*, ed. PT Ellison, PB Gray, pp. 246–69. Cambridge, MA: Harvard Univ. Press

Saxe R, Powell LJ. 2006. It's the thought that counts. *Psychol. Sci.* 17:692–99

Schoener TW. 1971. Theory of feeding strategies. *Annu. Rev. Ecol. Syst.* 2:369–404

Sell A. 2005. *Regulating Welfare-Tradeoff Ratios: Three Tests of an Evolutionary-Computational Model of Human Anger*. PhD thesis. Univ. Calif., Santa Barbara

Sell A, Bryant GA, Cosmides L, Tooby J, Sznycer D, et al. 2010. Adaptations in humans for assessing physical strength from the voice. *Proc. R. Soc. Lond. B Biol. Sci.* 277:3509–18

Sell A, Cosmides L, Tooby J, Sznycer D, von Rueden C, Gurven M. 2009b. Human adaptations for the visual assessment of strength and fighting ability from the body and face. *Proc. R. Soc. Lond. B Biol. Sci.* 276:575–84

Sell A, Tooby J, Cosmides L. 2009a. Formidability and the logic of human anger. *Proc. Natl. Acad. Sci. USA* 106:15073–78

Silverman I, Choi J, Mackewn A, Fisher M, Moro J, Olshansky E. 2000. Evolved mechanisms underlying wayfinding: further studies on the hunter-gatherer theory of spatial sex differences. *Evol. Hum. Behav.* 21:201–13

Silverman I, Eals M. 1992. Sex differences in spatial abilities: evolutionary theory and data. See Barkow et al. 1992, pp. 533–49

Singer T, Kiebel SJ, Winston JS, Dolan RJ, Frith CD. 2004. Brain responses to the acquired moral status of faces. *Neuron* 41:653–62

Sinnott-Armstrong W, ed. 2008. *Moral Psychology. The Evolution of Morality: Adaptations and Innateness.* Cambridge, MA: MIT Press

Spelke ES. 1990. Principles of object perception. *Cogn. Sci.* 14:29–56

Sperber D, Cara F, Girotto V. 1995. Relevance theory explains the selection task. *Cognition* 57:31–95

Stone VE, Cosmides L, Tooby J, Kroll N, Knight RT. 2002. Selective impairment of reasoning about social exchange in a patient with bilateral limbic system damage. *Proc. Natl. Acad. Sci. USA* 99:11531–36

Sugiyama LS. 2004. Illness, injury, and disability among Shiwiar forager-horticulturists: implications of health-risk buffering for the evolution of human life history. *Am. J. Phys. Anthropol.* 123:371–89

Sugiyama LS. 2005. Physical attractiveness in adaptationist perspective. See Buss 2005, pp. 292–343

Sugiyama LS, Tooby J, Cosmides L. 2002. Cross-cultural evidence of cognitive adaptations for social exchange among the Shiwiar of Ecuadorian Amazonia. *Proc. Natl. Acad. Sci. USA* 99:11537–42

Symons D. 1979. *The Evolution of Human Sexuality*. New York: Oxford Univ. Press

Symons D. 1992. On the use and misuse of Darwinism in the study of human behavior. See Barkow et al. 1992, pp. 137–59

Sznycer D. 2010. Cognitive adaptations for calibrating welfare tradeoff motivations, with special reference to the emotion of shame. PhD thesis. Univ. Calif., Santa Barbara

Taylor SE, Fiske ST, Etcoff NL, Ruderman AJ. 1978. Categorical and contextual bases of person memory and stereotyping. *J. Pers. Soc. Psychol.* 36:778–93

Tooby J, Cosmides L. 1990a. On the universality of human nature and the uniqueness of the individual: the role of genetics and adaptation. *J. Pers.* 58:17–67

Tooby J, Cosmides L. 1990b. The past explains the present: emotional adaptations and the structure of ancestral environments. *Ethol. Sociobiol.* 11:375–424

Tooby J, Cosmides L. 1992. The psychological foundations of culture. See Barkow et al. 1992, pp. 19–136

Tooby J, Cosmides L. 1996. Friendship and the banker's paradox: other pathways to the evolution of adaptations for altruism. In *Evolution of Social Behaviour Patterns in Primates and Man*, ed. WG Runciman, J Maynard Smith, RIM Dunbar, pp. 119–43. New York: Oxford Univ. Press

Tooby J, Cosmides L. 2005. Conceptual foundations of evolutionary psychology. See Buss 2005, pp. 5–67

Argues that organisms do not have motives to "maximize fitness"; behavior is generated by mechanisms that promoted fitness in the past.

Discusses why the genetic basis of complex adaptations must be universal (quantitative traits freer to vary).

Describes defects of blank-slate psychology and the standard social science model; argues for domain-specificity of many evolved mechanisms.

Tooby J, Cosmides L. 2008. The evolutionary psychology of the emotions and their relationship to internal regulatory variables. In *Handbook of Emotions*, ed. M Lewis, JM Haviland-Jones, LF Barrett, pp. 114–37. New York: Guilford. 3rd ed.

Tooby J, Cosmides L. 2010. Groups in mind: the coalitional roots of war and morality. In *Human Morality and Sociality: Evolutionary and Comparative Perspectives*, ed. H Høgh-Olesen, pp. 191–234. New York: Palgrave MacMillan

Tooby J, Cosmides L, Barrett HC. 2005. Resolving the debate on innate ideas: learnability constraints and the evolved interpenetration of motivational and conceptual functions. In *The Innate Mind: Structure and Content*, ed. P Carruthers, S Laurence, S Stich, pp. 305–37. New York: Oxford Univ. Press

Tooby J, Cosmides L, Price ME. 2006. Cognitive adaptations for *n*-person exchange: the evolutionary roots of organizational behavior. *Manag. Decis. Econ.* 27:103–29

Tooby J, Cosmides L, Sell A, Lieberman D, Sznycer D. 2008. Internal regulatory variables and the design of human motivation: a computational and evolutionary approach. In *Handbook of Approach and Avoidance Motivation*, ed. AJ Elliot, pp. 251–71. Mahwah, NJ: Erlbaum

Trivers RL. 1971. Evolution of reciprocal altruism. *Q. Rev. Biol.* 46:35–57

Trivers RL. 1972. Parental investment and sexual selection. In *Sexual Selection and the Descent of Man, 1871–1971*, ed. B Campbell, pp. 136–79. Chicago: Aldine-Atherton

Voyer D, Voyer S, Bryden MP. 1995. Magnitude of sex differences in spatial abilities: a meta-analysis and consideration of critical variables. *Psychol. Bull.* 117:250–70

Wason PC. 1983. Realism and rationality in the selection task. In *Thinking and Reasoning: Psychological Approaches*, ed. J St BT Evans, pp. 44–75. London: Routledge & Kegan Paul

Wason PC, Johnson-Laird P. 1972. *Psychology of Reasoning: Structure and Content*. Cambridge, MA: Harvard Univ. Press

Williams GC. 1966. *Adaptation and Natural Selection*. Princeton, NJ: Princeton Univ. Press

Yamagishi T. 1986. The provision of a sanctioning system as a public good. *J. Pers. Soc. Psychol.* 51:110–16

Discusses gene as unit of selection; stresses importance of design evidence for recognizing adaptations.

Origins of Human Cooperation and Morality

Michael Tomasello and Amrisha Vaish

Department of Developmental Psychology, Max Planck Institute for Evolutionary Anthropology, 04103 Leipzig, Germany; email: tomas@eva.mpg.de, vaish@eva.mpg.de

Annu. Rev. Psychol. 2013. 64:231–55

First published online as a Review in Advance on July 12, 2012

The *Annual Review of Psychology* is online at psych.annualreviews.org

This article's doi:
10.1146/annurev-psych-113011-143812

Keywords

altrusim, fairness, justice, evolution

Abstract

From an evolutionary perspective, morality is a form of cooperation. Cooperation requires individuals either to suppress their own self-interest or to equate it with that of others. We review recent research on the origins of human morality, both phylogenetic (research with apes) and ontogenetic (research with children). For both time frames we propose a two-step sequence: first a second-personal morality in which individuals are sympathetic or fair to particular others, and second an agent-neutral morality in which individuals follow and enforce group-wide social norms. Human morality arose evolutionarily as a set of skills and motives for cooperating with others, and the ontogeny of these skills and motives unfolds in part naturally and in part as a result of sociocultural contexts and interactions.

Contents

INTRODUCTION

After centuries of philosophical speculation about human morality, in the past half-century psychologists have begun to empirically investigate human moral behavior and judgment. In social psychology, researchers have sought to determine the factors that influence humans' prosocial behavior, cooperative interactions, and moral judgments. In the relatively new field of moral psychology, researchers have begun to probe the mechanisms of moral judgment more deeply, including cognitive and emotional factors as well as underlying neurophysiological processes.

During this same half-century, developmental psychologists have asked the question of origins: How do seemingly amoral human infants turn into actively moral children and adults? Recently, several novel lines of research have established that young children are much more moral—by at least some definitions—at a much younger age than previously thought. This research focuses on actual moral behavior as opposed to the more studied topic of moral judgment. In addition, recent comparative research has addressed the related question of the phylogenetic origins of human morality: How did presumably amoral prehumans turn into moral beings? Research with humans' closest living relatives, the great apes, has revealed both similarities and striking differences in how individuals interact with others socially,

with particular regard to cooperation and something like moral behavior.

In this article, our goal is to review these new data from young children and great apes—primarily from the past decade or two—in an attempt to provide an up-to-date account of the question of the origins of human morality, both phylogenetic and ontogenetic. Without attempting a complete definition, in our evolutionary perspective, moral interactions are a subset of cooperative interactions. Arguably, the main function of morality is to regulate an individual's social interactions with others in the general direction of cooperation, given that all individuals are at least somewhat selfish. And so we may stipulate that at the very least moral actions must involve individuals either suppressing their own self-interest in favor of that of others (e.g., helping, sharing) or else equating their own self-interest with that of others (e.g., reciprocity, justice, equity, and norm following and enforcement).

We proceed as follows. We first look at great ape cooperation and contrast it with the cooperation of modern humans. In making this comparison we attempt to outline two steps in the evolution of human cooperation that together constitute something like the evolutionary emergence of human morality. We then look at cooperation in human children, again in two developmental steps that, together, constitute something like the ontogenetic emergence of human morality. In both cases, the first step in the sequence is mutualistic collaboration and prosocially motivated interactions with specific other individuals, and the second step is the more abstract, agent-neutral, norm-based morality of individuals who live in more large-scale cultural worlds full of impersonal and mutually known conventions, norms, and institutions.

EVOLUTIONARY ORIGINS OF HUMAN MORALITY

Humans are great apes, along with orangutans, gorillas, chimpanzees, and bonobos. The social life of the great apes is highly complex.

Individuals not only form relatively long-term social relationships with others, they also understand the social relationships among third parties, for example, who is dominant to whom and who is friends with whom in the social group. Moreover, they recognize that the actions of individuals are driven both by their goals and by their perception of the situation (a kind of perception-goal psychology; Call & Tomasello 2008). This means that great ape individuals make virtually all of their behavioral decisions in a complex social field comprising all the other individuals in the vicinity with their individual goals and perceptions, as well as the social relationships of those individuals both to the self and to one another.

Cooperation in Great Ape Societies

Nonhuman great ape social life is mainly about competition. Although there are differences among the four species, competitive disputes generally are resolved via one or another form of dominance (based, ultimately, on fighting ability). Most obvious is individual dominance, such as when an alpha male chimpanzee takes whatever food he wants while others take what is left. But great apes also cooperate with allies in order to compete with others over valued resources. This cooperating in order to compete requires individuals to simultaneously monitor two or more ongoing social relationships (and the social relationships among the third parties involved as well), requiring complex skills of social cognition. But despite some skills and tendencies of cooperation, which we now document, it is important to remember that among all species of nonhuman great apes, even the "peaceful" bonobos, the individuals who get what they want will almost always be the ones who bring the most force.

With this clear recognition of the dominance of dominance in the social lives of nonhuman great apes, we may now look more closely at their cooperation, especially that of chimpanzees because they have been by far the most studied. Proceeding with a bottom-up strategy, let us look at two sets of behaviors in nonhuman great apes that almost everyone would agree are morally relevant: (*a*) helping and sharing with others (sometimes based on reciprocity) and (*b*) collaborating with others for mutual benefit.

Helping, sharing, and reciprocity. A number of well-controlled experiments have demonstrated that chimpanzees will help both humans and other chimpanzees. First, Warneken & Tomasello (2006) found that three human-raised chimpanzees fetched out-of-reach objects for humans visibly trying to reach them. Warneken et al. (2007) found further that chimpanzees will also go to some effort to help humans, for example, climbing a few meters high to fetch something for them. In this same study, chimpanzees also helped conspecifics. Specifically, when one individual was trying to get through a door, subjects pulled open a latch for her—which they did not do if the first chimpanzee was not trying to get through the door. Moreover, Melis and colleagues (2011) found that chimpanzees will also release a hook to send food down a ramp to a desirous conspecific, if it is clear that they cannot get the food themselves and if the recipient actively signals his need. Finally, Yamamoto and colleagues (2009) observed chimpanzees giving tools to others that needed to rake in food for themselves, and more recently showed that chimpanzees demonstrate flexible "targeted" helping, i.e., giving the specific tool that the conspecific needs from an array of possible tools (Yamamoto et al. 2012).

Helping others reach their goals in these ways is fairly low cost, basically requiring only a few extra ergs of energy. Sharing food is another story, as it requires relinquishing a valued resource. Nevertheless, chimpanzees and other great apes do share food with others under some circumstances. First and most obviously, mothers share food with their offspring (although mostly they engage in passive sharing in which they allow the offspring to take food from them, and then mostly the shells, husks, and peelings; Ueno & Matsuzawa 2004). Second, if the food is not very highly valued and not easily monopolizable (e.g., a branch full of leaves), then a group of apes may peaceably feed on it together, and occasionally there may be some more active sharing among friends (de Waal 1989). And third, if the food is very highly valued and somewhat monopolizable (e.g., meat), then typically subordinates and nonpossessors beg and harass dominants and possessors until they get some, again with some instances of more active sharing (Gilby 2006). But all of this food sharing is more active and reliable in situations involving some form of reciprocity.

Indeed, a variety of lines of evidence suggest that chimpanzees help and share most readily in the context of reciprocity. Thus, although there is no reciprocity in short-term grooming bouts, over time, individuals who have been groomed by one partner later groom that partner (as opposed to others) in return more often (Gomes et al. 2009). In an experimental setting, Melis and colleagues (2008) found that individuals tended to help those who had helped them previously (by opening a door for them, allowing access to food). Furthermore, de Waal & Luttrell (1988) found that captive chimpanzees support one another in fights reciprocally, and reciprocity can seemingly also involve different currencies. For example, the most active meat sharing in the wild occurs between individuals who are coalition partners and therefore reliably help one another in fights in other contexts (Muller & Mitani 2005). Further, male chimpanzees sometimes share food with reproductively cycling females, presumably in hopes of sex (Hockings et al. 2007).

On the negative side—sometimes called negative reciprocity or retaliation or revenge—if a chimpanzee in the wild attacks or steals food from another, he will often be attacked by that victim in return [what de Waal & Lutrell (1988) call a revenge system]. Importantly, the goal in these retaliations is not material reward for the retaliator. In an experimental setting, when one chimpanzee intentionally took the other's food, the victim overtly expressed anger and acted to trash the stolen food before the thief could eat it—even though this did not result in any food for the victim (Jensen et al. 2007). Importantly as well, victims did not do this if the other chimpanzee came into possession of the food accidentally (i.e., through the human experimenter's efforts). The goal here thus seems to be truly to punish the other.

There is no reason to believe that these acts of helping and sharing and retaliation are anything other than the genuine article. When costs are negligible and the recipient's need is clear, great apes help others. When costs are greater, as with food sharing, great ape altruism is most active and reliable in the context of something like reciprocity. But, as de Waal (2005) has argued, this is very likely not a "calculated reciprocity" in which individuals keep quantitative track of favors given and received. More likely it is a kind of "attitudinal reciprocity" in which individuals have more positive affect toward those who have helped them or shared with them in the past. If you help me in fights regularly, then I should invest in your well-being by, for example, helping you in fights, and maybe even sharing food with you. In general, if I depend on you for doing X, then I should do whatever I can to ensure that you are available and capable of doing X—and you should do the same for me. Attitudinal reciprocity (I feel more affiliative toward those on whom I depend) can generate reciprocal patterns of helping and sharing—and without the threat of defection. On the negative side, great apes get angry at and punish those who caused them distress. This presumably has the effect that the punished individual will be less likely to repeat his harmful actions in the future, which benefits the punisher directly.

Collaboration. Chimpanzees and other great apes collaborate with conspecifics in several different contexts. First, as in many mammalian species, individuals form alliances and support one another in fights (Harcourt & de Waal 1992). Whereas in many monkey species it is typically kin that support one another, among chimpanzees it is mostly nonkin (Langergraber et al. 2011). Again as in many mammalian species, great ape combatants often actively reconcile with one another after fights, presumably in an attempt to repair the long-term relationship on which they both depend for various reasons (de Waal 1997).

Second, like many mammalian species, great apes engage in various forms of group defense. Most interestingly, small groups of male chimpanzees actively patrol their border, engaging agonistically with any individuals from neighboring groups that they encounter (Goodall 1986). Presumably, acts of group defense are a reflection of individuals' interdependence with one another as well, at the very least as a need to maintain a certain group size but more urgently in protecting and facilitating the lives of those on whom they depend for everything from sex to grooming.

Third, and especially important in the current context, is collaboration in the acquisition of food. Although all four great ape species forage for food almost exclusively individually—traveling in small social parties but then procuring food on their own—there is one major exception. In some but not all groups of chimpanzees, males hunt in small social parties for monkeys (although less frequently, bonobos hunt in small parties for monkeys as well; Surbeck & Hohmann 2008). In some cases the hunt resembles a kind of helter-skelter chase in which multiple individuals attempt to capture the monkey with little if any coordination. In the Taï Forest, however, the canopy is continuous and the monkeys are quite agile, so such uncoordinated chasing typically will not succeed. Here the chimpanzees must, in effect, surround a monkey in order to capture him, requiring individuals to in some sense coordinate with others (Boesch & Boesch 1989). Typically all participants get at least some meat, but many bystanders do too (Boesch 1994).

Note that although chimpanzees are interdependent with one another in the hunt itself—and indeed experiments have shown that chimpanzees understand when they need the other participants for success (Melis et al. 2006)—individuals do not depend on the group hunting of monkeys to survive. In fact, and perhaps surprisingly, chimpanzees hunt most often for monkeys not in the dry season when fruit and vegetation are more scarce, but rather in the rainy season when fruit and vegetation are much more abundant (Muller & Mitani 2005), presumably because spending energy in a monkey hunt for an uncertain return makes most sense when there are plenty of backup alternatives if the hunt fails. This absence of an overarching interdependent "attitude" is reflected in a further aspect of chimpanzee collaborative behavior: In experiments, although chimpanzees do coordinate their actions with a partner to achieve individual goals, they do not seem interested in achieving joint, social goals, and if their partner becomes passive and unengaged during a joint activity, they make no effort to re-engage their partner in order to continue that activity (Warneken et al. 2006).

The degree to which chimpanzees in the wild may actively choose collaborative partners for monkey hunting—a key dimension of human collaborative foraging—is unclear. Melis et al. (2006) found that after a fairly small amount of experience with one another, captive chimpanzees know which individuals are good partners for them—in the sense of leading to collaborative success and the consumption of a good quantity of food—and they subsequently choose those partners in preference to others. They are almost certainly not attempting to actively punish bad partners by not choosing them, but the effect is that bad partners have fewer opportunities for collaboration. If indeed partner choice of this type happens in the wild—which is not clear, as hunting is mostly instigated opportunistically with little choice of partners—then poor collaborative partners would suffer the loss of some opportunities.

Chimpanzees and other great apes thus collaborate with conspecifics in various contexts for their mutual benefit. In coalitions and alliances and group defense, it is typically in the interest of all individuals to participate to defeat the opponent. As always, there are situations in which it might pay for individuals to lag and let others do the work, but normally there is a direct benefit for all participants, with more participants increasing the probability of success. In the case of group hunting, individuals clearly are responsive to the actions of others and know that they need them for success; moreover, they seem to avoid bad partners, who suffer by not being chosen to participate in the collaboration, and typically everyone gets at least some meat at the end.

Great ape sociality and "morality." The individuals of many social species simply stay in proximity to one another, with little active social interaction beyond mating and/or fighting. Let us call this zero-order morality, as individuals are rarely if ever inhibiting or otherwise controlling their self-serving motivations in deference to others. Chimpanzees and other great apes—despite the importance of dominance in their everyday interactions—are much more social, and so in a sense more moral, than this.

On the evolutionary level, it is viable that in some contexts, great apes control their self-serving motivations in deference to others because they are somehow compensated for the loss. Sometimes the act is immediately mutually beneficial, and sometimes there is later reciprocity, but these may be conceptualized as individuals investing in others on whom they are dependent or with whom they are interdependent. The social situations that generate these opportunities for reciprocally mutualistic actions derive from complex social lives in which many different activities—from group defense to foraging to intragroup conflicts over mating to grooming—are important if an individual is to survive and thrive in the group.

On the proximate level, the empirical evidence would seem to suggest that great ape individuals do have some proximate mechanisms that are genuinely moral, in the sense that the individual acts to benefit the other without any direct anticipation or planning for any kind of payback. In the case of helping, and to a lesser degree with more costly food sharing, the proximate mechanism may be some kind of sympathetic concern for those for whom one has a positive affect based on their helping and/or sharing in the past (attitudinal reciprocity).

Great apes collaborate for mutual benefit, and it is not clear to what degree they might control their own self-serving motivations in these collaborations. It would seem very little, except perhaps for sharing the food at the end of a group hunt (and then only to avoid fights). Certainly allies in a fight either within the group or against an external stranger do not attend to the needs of those allies. And since chimpanzees' group hunting of monkeys is not necessary for their survival, collaboration is not an obligatory part of their lives. In these collaborative interactions (to presage our comparison to humans), chimpanzees coordinate, but they show no commitment to their partner; they share food, but they have no sense of equality in doing so; they do their part, but they do not help their partner with its role in the collaboration; and they avoid bad partners, but they do not seem to resent them or punish them actively for being a bad partner alone—all of which means that individuals do not regulate their behavior in deference to the attitudes of their potential partners (there is no concern for self-reputation). One way to characterize chimpanzee collaboration is thus that individuals use their partner as a kind of social tool—which they know is necessary in the context—in order to get what they want. Neither partner is worried about what the other is getting out of it or how they are being judged as a partner by either their collaborator or any onlookers.

Overall, it is clear that great apes have genuine social relationships with others based on patterns of social interactions over time. A key pattern, perhaps *the* key pattern, is dominance: Disputes are settled by the dominant doing just what he wants to do, and the subordinate must simply defer. The morality of apes' social interactions—individuals inhibiting their immediate self-interest in favor of others—is governed mostly by their personal relationships; that is to say, individuals form prosocial relationships with others based on a kind of attitudinal reciprocity that develops as each individual helps those toward whom they have formed a positive attitude (precisely because they have helped them in the past). Individuals' actions thus reward those with whom they have a positive relationship and fail to reward, or even punish, those with whom they have a negative relationship. Much human morality is based on this kind of attitudinal reciprocity as well, especially with family. It is just that humans have developed some other moral motivations and mechanisms in addition.

The Evolution of Human Cooperation and Morality

Even the smallest and seemingly simplest of human societies are cooperatively structured and organized in a way that the societies of other great apes are not. This can be clearly seen by looking at six key dimensions of social organization, with humans in each case doing things much more cooperatively than other apes (for a fuller account, see Tomasello 2011).

The cooperative organization of human societies.

Subsistence. All four species of nonhuman great apes forage basically individually. They may travel in small groups, but they procure and consume food on their own. The one exception to this pattern is the group hunting of chimpanzees, in which individuals surround a monkey and capture it in basically the same manner as social carnivores like lions and wolves. But even this is not really a collaborative activity in the human sense, as evidenced by the fact that the captor of the monkey only shares with others under duress (Gilby 2006), and no one shares more with those who participated in the hunt than with those who did not (Boesch 1994).

In contrast, humans procure the vast majority of their food through collaborative efforts of one type or another. Clear evidence is the fact that during their foraging, contemporary foragers help one another by doing such things as cutting a trail for others to follow; making a bridge for others to cross a river; carrying another's child; climbing a tree to flush a monkey for another hunter; calling the location of a resource for another to exploit while he himself continues searching for something else; carrying game shot by another hunter;

climbing a tree to knock down fruit for others to gather; helping look for others' lost arrows; and helping repair others' broken arrows. Hill (2002) documents that the Ache foragers of South America spend from about 10% to 50% of their foraging time engaged in such altruistic activities—pretty much all of which would be unthinkable for nonhuman primates. At the end of their foraging, humans, unlike other apes, share the spoils of their collaboration fairly, even bringing it back to some central location to do so (Hill & Hurtado 1996).

Property. Great apes often respect the fact that another individual physically possesses some object or piece of food, and they do not start a fight for it (Kummer & Cords 1991). But the human institution of property is a cooperative regime through and through. Individuals may claim objects for themselves by virtue of mutually agreed-upon norms and institutions. For example, moviegoers may simply leave a sweater on their seat to claim at least temporary ownership. Not only do others mostly respect this signal, but if they do not respect it others will often intervene to enforce the absent individual's property rights. Similarly, in terms of food, Gurven (2004) documents how widespread the sharing and trading of food among humans in small-scale societies is. In assessing possible hypotheses to explain this pattern of widespread food sharing, Gurven concludes that it is probably multiply determined, and the big picture is not tit-for-tat reciprocity but rather "more complicated social arrangements, including those whereby important social support is provided only if one adheres to socially negotiated sharing norms" (p. 559). And of course in many small-scale societies a large role is played by a special kind of property exchange, the gift (Mauss 1954), which not only transfers property but also serves to establish and cement cooperative bonds as well as create obligations of reciprocation.

Childcare and prosocial behavior. In all four species of nonhuman great apes, mothers provide almost 100% of the childcare for their child. In contrast, human mothers—both those in traditional societies and those in more modern industrialized societies—typically provide about 50% of the childcare for their child. Human fathers, grandparents, and other females all pitch in to help. Hrdy (2009) has in fact proposed that this so-called cooperative breeding may very well have been the instigating factor leading to humans' hypercooperativeness. In any case, humans do seem to sacrifice themselves for others—everything from donating blood to donating to charity to going to war for the group—in ways that other apes do not (Richerson & Boyd 2005; for experimental evidence, see Warneken & Tomasello 2006).

Communication and teaching. Great apes communicate basically to tell others what to do. In contrast, humans often communicate helpfully in order to inform others of things that are of interest to them, the recipients of the information (Tomasello 2008). Even in their very earliest nonverbal gestures, human infants use the pointing gesture to inform others of the location of objects they are seeking and to point out some interesting object to others only in order to share their excitement with another person (Liszkowski et al. 2004, 2006).

Deriving from this, human adults also inform young children of things they need to know, for their benefit. Although great ape juveniles learn much from the behavior of their parents and others, adults do not actively teach youngsters things in the way that humans do (Hoppit et al. 2008). Csibra & Gergely (2009) speculate that human teaching is absolutely critical to the human way of life, as children discern general principles of how things work and how one behaves in their society.

Politics. Politics is about social power, and the lines of social power are relatively clear for all four great ape species, with dominance and physical strength (including greater numbers on one side) ruling the day. In contrast, human forager societies are notoriously egalitarian. Dominance plays a much less powerful role than in other great ape societies, as the group exercises a kind of cooperative power in making sure that no individual becomes too powerful (Boehm 1999). Indeed, in human small-scale societies the most powerful individuals often obtain and retain their power not by dominating resources directly in the manner of other great apes, but rather by demonstrating both their ability to control resources and their cooperative propensities by distributing resources generously to others (Mauss 1954).

In terms of enforcement, in human small-scale societies peace is kept not only by retaliation for harms done and reconciliation after fights, as in great apes, but also by third-party enforcement. That is, human observers punish perpetrators who victimize others, sometimes at a cost to themselves, whereas there is no solid evidence of such third-party punishment in other great apes (Fehr & Fischbacher 2003, 2004; Riedl et al. 2011). Third-party punishment may be thought of as a kind of cooperative enforcement of peace and well-being in the group and plays a critical role in the creation and maintenance of social norms in general.

Norms and institutions. In many ways, the most distinctive feature of human social organization is its normative structure. Human beings not only have statistical expectations about what others *will* do—which all apes have—they also have normative expectations about what others *should* do. These vary across different cultures and form a continuum from moral norms (typically concerning harm to others) to social conventions. Thus, we all know and expect that people in our society should dress sedately for a funeral, and so anyone who wears a red shirt cannot plead ignorance and thus may be thought of as flaunting our norm without regard for our group. We may reasonably respond to this flaunting with disapproval, gossip, and, in egregious cases, by social ostracism—which means that all of us must be ever vigilant about our reputations as norm followers (leading to various impression-management strategies; Goffman 1959). If the glue of primate societies is social relationships, the superglue of human societies is social norms.

The ultimate outcome of social norms in human groups is the creation of social institutions whose existence is constituted by the collective agreement of all group members that things should be done in a particular way. Institutions create both joint goals and individual social roles (for both persons and objects). Searle (1995) refers to the creation of these roles as the creation of status functions because as individual people and objects assume these roles, they acquire deontic powers. For example, in the process of trade, some objects (e.g., pieces of gold, special pieces of paper) have acquired in some societies the status of money and so play a special role in the trading process. And although nonhuman primates have some understanding of familial relatedness, humans assign special status to social roles such as "spouse" and "parent"—which everyone recognizes and which create certain entitlements and obligations. In the case of morality, the institutions of law and organized religion obviously interact in important ways with humans' natural proclivities for cooperation and norm following to produce an institutional dimension to much of human morality.

Summary. The ineluctable conclusion is thus that human social interaction and organization are fundamentally cooperative in ways that the social interaction and organization of other great apes simply are not.

Two evolutionary steps: the interdependence hypothesis. Tomasello and colleagues (2012) argue and present evidence that humans became ultracooperative in all of these many ways in two main evolutionary steps. They call their theory the interdependence hypothesis.

In a first step, something in the ecology changed, which forced humans to become collaborative foragers: Individuals had to be good collaborators or else starve. In collaborative interactions of this type, individuals developed new skills of joint intentionality and new forms of second-personal social engagement. Individuals became interdependent with one another, such that each individual had a direct interest in the well-being of others as partners. Thus, during a mutualistic collaboration, if my partner is having trouble, it is in my interest to help her, since performance of her role is vital to our joint success. Moreover, if I have some sense of the future, if one of my regular partners is having trouble at any time, I will help her so that I will have a good partner for tomorrow. Interdependence thus breeds helping. And the fact of partner choice helps to keep everyone cooperating and helps control cheating, as all individuals (who have the requisite cognitive abilities) know that others are judging them for their cooperativeness and that their survival depends on others choosing them as a partner. The result is that if I monopolize all the food at the end of the foraging instead of sharing it equitably, or if I slack off on my work during the foraging, others will simply exclude me the next time. This social selection of partners in interdependent contexts thus advantages good cooperators. The result was what one may call a joint morality, in which individuals helped others with whom they were interdependent, considered those others to be equally deserving of their share of the collaborative spoils, and felt answerable to others (as others were answerable to them) for being a good partner.

In a second step, as modern humans faced competition from other groups, they scaled up these new collaborative skills and motivations to group life in general. With a constant threat from other groups, group life in general became one big interdependent collaboration for maintaining group survival, in which each individual had to play his or her role. In these larger cultural groups—typically with a tribal structure comprising smaller bands—many interactions were not based on personal histories of individuals with one another but rather on group membership alone. It was thus crucial for each individual to do things the way that "we" as a group do them, that is, to actively conform to the ways of the group in order to coordinate with others and display one's group membership. This kind of group-mindedness, underlain by skills of collective intentionality, engendered truly impersonal, agent-neutral, objective social norms.

Humans not only assiduously follow such norms themselves, but they also enforce them in an impersonal manner on all in the group, including even on themselves through feelings of guilt and shame. The result was what one may call a collective morality, in which individuals regulated their actions via the morally legitimate expectations of others and the group—morally legitimate by their own assessment—engendering what some have called normative self-governance (Korsgaard 1996).

An argument could be made that contemporary humans are less cooperative than were their forebears at either of these two previous periods. But contemporary humans are in the process of adapting their cooperative skills and motivations to novel conditions, namely, the mixing together of people from different ethnic groups into modern cities, along with the emergence of important institutions such as law and organized religion. Our assumption is that the two key steps in the evolution of human cooperation, and thus morality, took place before the advent of agriculture and cities, and law and organized religion, as humans first became obligate collaborative foragers and second created cultural groups that competed with one another.

ONTOGENETIC ORIGINS OF HUMAN MORALITY

The classic theoretical perspectives on the ontogeny of human cooperation and morality were laid out centuries ago by Hobbes and Rousseau. Hobbes believed that humans were naturally selfish and that society, including the force of a central government, was necessary for people to become cooperative. Rousseau, on the other hand, believed that humans were more naturally cooperative and that as they entered society as children, they were corrupted.

The reality of course is that young children are both selfish and cooperative. The interesting question here is how they become moral beings that have concerns for the well-being of others in the group and at the same time look out for their own individual interests. The difference between ontogeny and phylogeny in this context is that young children are born into a cultural world already full of all kinds of moral norms and institutions. In Piaget's (1997/1932) classic account, children's earliest premorality is basically respect for and conformity to the norms and rules of adults, based on a respect for authority. They only later come to understand how these norms and rules essentially work as agreements among peers of equal status in a community.

Our contention here is that young children before about 3 years of age may not really understand social norms as such. Instead, they may be responding only to adult imperatives and not to the force of any agreements among members of their group. And so our ontogenetic account parallels our phylogenetic account. In their first step toward human morality, young children collaborate with and act prosocially toward other specific individuals. In their second step, they begin to participate in the social norms and institutions of their culture. These two steps—an initial second-personal morality followed by a more norm-based morality—take infants into a full-fledged human morality.

Toddlers' Second-Personal Morality

Human infants begin forming social relationships with others during the first year of life. They also presumably have some sense of their dependence on, if not interdependence with, other people. Although young children are of course selfish in many situations, in many other situations they subordinate their self-interests in order to do such things as collaborate with others, sympathize with and help others, and share resources with others. They also evaluate others in terms of such cooperative behaviors and begin to help and share with others more selectively as a result.

Collaboration and commitment. Young children are surprisingly skilled collaborative and cooperative partners. Already early in the second year of life, toddlers can take turns to achieve social coordination with others (e.g.,

Eckerman et al. 1989, Eckerman & Didow 1989). More relevant for our purposes, young children are motivated to participate jointly in joint activities: When a cooperative activity breaks down (such as when the partner suddenly stops participating), 18-month-olds and 2-year-olds, and to some degree even 14-month-olds, actively try to re-engage the partner in order to continue the joint activity rather than attempt to continue the activity by themselves (Warneken et al. 2006, Warneken & Tomasello 2007). Strikingly, this is true even when the partner is not needed for the child to complete the activity (Warneken et al. 2012).

Thus, children do not view their collaborative partner as a social tool to achieve their own goal but rather in a truly collaborative light. This is in contrast to chimpanzees, which do not show this motivation for jointness in their collaborative behavior, as discussed above (Warneken et al. 2006). Indeed, when given a free choice of how to obtain food, chimpanzees choose a solo option over a collaborative one, whereas 3-year-old children more often choose the collaborative option (Rekers et al. 2011). These findings together point to a fundamental human drive to collaborate with others to achieve joint and shared goals.

Furthermore, once people have formed a joint goal, they feel committed to it: They know that opting out will harm or disappoint the others, and they act in ways that prevent this. Recent work has revealed that even toddlers show an understanding of such commitments. For instance, when working jointly with a partner on a task that should result in both actors receiving a reward, 3.5-year-olds continue to work until the partner has received his reward even if they have already received their own reward earlier in the process (Hamann et al. 2012). Moreover, when 3-year-olds need to break away from a joint commitment with a partner, they do not simply walk away but "take leave" from the other as a way of acknowledging and asking to be excused for breaking the commitment (Gräfenhain et al. 2009).

Thus, even very young children are social, collaborative, and cooperative beings who view their collaborative and cooperative efforts as inherently joint. Such jointness makes children interdependent; they need the other to achieve their (social) goals, and they know that the other needs them. They thus experience collaboration and cooperation as committed activities. Certainly by 3 years of age, children feel responsible for their joint commitments and either make an effort to honor them or "apologize" for breaking them. From early on, then, children show strong signs of interdependence.

Sympathy and helping. Young children and even infants demonstrate remarkable prosocial tendencies. By 14 to 18 months of age, they readily engage in instrumental helping such as picking up an object that an adult has accidentally dropped or opening a cabinet door when an adult cannot do so because his hands are full. They do not do these things in control situations that are similar but in which the adult does not need help; for instance, they do not pick up an object the adult has thrown down intentionally or open a door he approaches with no intention of opening it (Warneken & Tomasello 2006, 2007). Toddlers even help others at some cost to themselves (Svetlova et al. 2010). Importantly, infants' helping is not limited to completing others' action goals. Thus, when 12-month-old infants see an adult searching for an object that they know the location of, they point to direct the adult's attention to it (Liszkowski et al. 2006, 2008). Given that infants themselves do not gain anything by providing this information, their informative pointing may be considered a prosocial act.

A common belief is that young children become prosocial as a result of encouragement and rewards from adults. However, in a recent study, when 20-month-old children were materially rewarded for their helpful behavior, their helpfulness actually decreased over time once the reward was taken away; children who were not rewarded at all or received only verbal praise maintained a high level of helpfulness throughout (Warneken & Tomasello 2008). Following the logic of overjustification, this finding suggests that young children's motivation to help is intrinsic and not dependent on concrete extrinsic rewards, and indeed it is undermined by such rewards (Lepper et al. 1973). Reinforcing this finding, Hepach and colleagues (2012b) found, using a physiological measure of children's arousal, that 2-year-olds are not motivated primarily by a need to help a person themselves (and thus to benefit themselves via reciprocity or an improved reputation) but rather by a need just to see the person helped.

During this same early period, young children also begin to provide comfort and assistance to those in emotional distress, such as a person who is in pain after bumping her knee or is upset about her broken teddy bear (e.g., Bischof-Köhler 1991, Eisenberg & Fabes 1998, Zahn-Waxler et al. 1992). The concern children show for a distressed individual correlates with and is thought to motivate their prosocial acts toward that individual (Eisenberg & Miller 1987). Strikingly, young children's concern is not an automatic response to distress cues but rather a flexible and sophisticated response. This has recently been shown in two ways. First, 1.5- and 2-year-old children show concern and subsequent prosocial behavior toward a victim of harm even if the victim expresses no overt distress cues while being harmed (Vaish et al. 2009). Second, 3-year-old children show reduced concern and prosocial behavior toward a crybaby, i.e., a person who is considerably distressed after being very mildly inconvenienced, than toward a person who is similarly distressed after being more seriously harmed (Hepach et al. 2012a; see also Leslie et al. 2006). Thus, children's sympathetic responses take into account not only the presence or absence of distress cues from a person but also the contextual cues surrounding the distress. From early in ontogeny, then, sympathy is a multidetermined and thus reliable response (see Hoffman 2000, Vaish & Warneken 2012).

Around the same time that young children demonstrate these remarkable prosocial behaviors themselves, they also show a preference for prosocial over antisocial others. Indeed, even early in the very first year, infants distinguish prosocial from antisocial characters and prefer to touch prosocial characters (Hamlin & Wynn 2011, Hamlin et al. 2007, Kuhlmeier et al. 2003). These preferences soon become evident in children's prosocial behaviors. By age 2 years, for instance, toddlers help those who were helpful to them in previous interactions more than those who were not helpful, demonstrating direct reciprocity (Dunfield & Kuhlmeier 2010). Just a year later, children also demonstrate indirect reciprocity: For instance, 3- to 4-year-old children reduce their prosocial behavior toward an individual who caused or intended to cause harm to another individual (Kenward & Dahl 2011, Vaish et al. 2010). Through such selective helping, young children demonstrate their recognition of and preference to interact and cooperate with those who are prosocial and their avoidance of those who are harmful or noncooperative, both toward them and toward others.

Moreover, and in line with our evolutionary analysis, there is evidence that children help an individual more in a collaborative context than a noncollaborative context. In a recent study, Hamann et al. (2012) showed that 3.5-year-olds are more likely to help a peer attain a reward when they previously attained a reward by participating in a collaborative task with the peer than when they previously attained a reward without participating in a collaborative task. On the other hand, although chimpanzees do show some prosocial behaviors toward humans and conspecifics (e.g., Melis et al. 2011, Warneken & Tomasello 2006), this behavior is not affected by whether the context is a collaborative or a noncollaborative one (Greenberg et al. 2010). This is consistent with the idea that human prosocial behavior evolved in interdependent, collaborative contexts.

Together, these findings on infants' and toddlers' instrumental helping, informative pointing, concern, comforting, and selective helping of harmed and/or cooperative others demonstrate that from early on, children are tuned to others' needs and emotional states and are motivated to act prosocially toward them. Moreover, the research shows that children's early prosociality is the real thing in that it is intrinsically motivated, based in concern for others, grounded in an interpretation of the situation, flexible depending on interactions and evaluations of others, and facilitated by collaboration.

Equality and sharing. Young children's prosocial proclivities are apparent not only in their helping and sympathizing but also in their sharing behaviors. Naturalistic observations suggest that as early as 8 months of age, infants may show or give toys to parents, other infants, siblings, and strangers, even when resources are low (e.g., Hay 1979, Rheingold et al. 1976). With development, sharing becomes increasingly selective: Even 12-month-old infants make some distinctions between recipients of their prosocial actions, being more likely to share objects with their peers and with their own mothers than with the peers' mothers (Young & Lewis 1979).

Some experimental work on early sharing suggests, however, that toddlers are not so willing to share. For instance, spontaneous sharing of food was not found among 18- or 25-month-old children in an experimental setting (Brownell et al. 2009). Furthermore, 3- to 4-year-olds are generally found to be selfish in their distributions, whereas at 5 to 6 years of age, children show a greater sense of equality and fairness (Fehr et al. 2008, Lane & Coon 1972, Rochat et al. 2009). However, these experimental studies involved windfall situations in which a child is given some resources by a third party without having to work for them and must relinquish some resources to demonstrate fairness. Such situations are removed from the evolutionary mechanisms that we believe likely shape these phenomena in early ontogeny. Our hypothesis is that from early in ontogeny, children's sharing and fairness-related behaviors should reflect the effects of the collaborative foraging context of early humans, in which one shares the spoils equally among those who took part in the collaborative effort. We thus argue that prior work has underestimated children's sensitivity to equality because it has not provided the relevant context.

Accordingly, recent work shows that 3-year-old children who have obtained rewards by working collaboratively with each other divide up their spoils equitably rather than monopolizing them, even when the resources could easily be monopolized (Warneken et al. 2011). This is in stark contrast to chimpanzees, whose strong tendency to compete over the spoils of collaborative efforts severely limits their collaboration (Melis et al. 2006). Most strikingly, 3-year-old children are also more likely to divide up their rewards equally if they obtained the rewards by working collaboratively than by working individually or receiving a windfall (Hamann et al. 2011).

Young children not only distribute resources equally themselves but also distinguish equal from unequal distributions and prefer equal distributors and distributions. For instance, Schmidt & Sommerville (2011) showed that 15-month-old infants expect resources to be distributed equally among recipients. Geraci & Surian (2011) further showed that when 16-month-olds see one distributor being fair toward a recipient (by distributing resources equally between the recipient and a second individual) and another distributor being unfair toward the same recipient, they expect the recipient to approach the equal distributor, and in a manual choice task, they themselves show a preference for the equal distributor. These preferences also play out in the distribution behavior of somewhat older children: 3.5-year-olds distribute more resources to individuals who have previously shared with others than to individuals who have not shared (Olson & Spelke 2008), although to our knowledge, whether children would give more resources to equal than to unequal distributors remains an unexplored question.

Over the course of development, children's resource distribution moves beyond only equality and becomes more sensitive to reciprocity norms, relationships, and the behaviors of others. Thus, around 3 years of age, children's sharing of toys with a peer increases if that peer had previously shared toys with them, suggesting a sensitivity to direct reciprocity by this age

(Levitt et al. 1985). Moreover, 3-year-olds display negative emotional responses to distributions in which they receive less, and indeed, even occasionally when they receive more than another child (LoBue et al. 2011). By about 4 years of age, children share (even at a cost to themselves) with their friends more than with nonfriends or strangers (Birch & Billman 1986, Moore 2009), and by 8 years of age, children share more with their in-group than their out-group members (Fehr et al. 2008).

A full-blown concept of fairness, i.e., an understanding of distributive justice or the proper way to divide up resources among people taking into account multiple factors (Nisan 1984), begins to emerge only in the school years. In the traditional work on the development of fairness, children are presented with hypothetical fair or unfair scenarios and are interviewed about their responses to the scenarios. This work has revealed a developmental trend such that young children progress from considering largely irrelevant characteristics of recipients such as desire, age, or height, to a preference for equal division of resources at about 5 or 6 years of age, to a preference for reward in proportion to the input (i.e., equity) among children older than 6 years of age (e.g., Damon 1975, Hook & Cook 1979). Eventually, children move beyond the equity rule to integrate both need and merit information (see Damon 1977). By 8 years of age, children can vary their allocation decisions appropriately depending on context. For instance, they rely on the principle of equity in a reward-for-work context, of equality in a voting context, and of need in a charity context (Sigelman & Waitzman 1991; see also Enright et al. 1984).

Interestingly, however, a recent study showed that the context of collaboration facilitates even young children's understanding of equity (Ng et al. 2011). In this study, children were presented with scenarios in which one giver gave an equal proportion of his resources to himself and a receiver, whereas another giver gave himself a greater proportion than the receiver. The scenarios differed in whether the givers had obtained the resources by working collaboratively with the receiver or by working individually. Even 3-year-olds judged the fair giver—the one who gave an equal proportion—to be nicer than the unfair giver, but only in the collaborative context; children did not distinguish the proportional distributions in the individual context. Thus, in a collaborative context, which we argue is highly relevant for resource distribution, even preschoolers demonstrate sophisticated intuitions about proportional distribution, which is central to the full-fledged concept of fairness.

In sum, recent work has provided evidence for a surprisingly early ontogenetic emergence of sharing and the foundations of fairness, at least in the sense of equality. Toddlers, and to some degree even infants, show a sense of equality in resource distributions, in particular when examined in collaboration situations. Moreover, when faced with the choice of interacting with or distributing resources to others, even very young children show a preference for individuals who distribute to others equally. In collaborative situations, they also show sensitivity to a critical aspect of fairness—equity. Thus, sharing and some foundational aspects of fairness appear early in moral development, especially in early collaborative and cooperative contexts. They are an important aspect of toddlers' second-personal morality and are, we argue, the seeds of the full-fledged norm-based sense of fairness that emerges later in development.

Summary. Evidence is mounting for a remarkably rich and multifaceted morality, in the sense of prosociality, very early in human ontogeny. Toddlers and even infants readily engage in collaborative activities with others and recognize the jointness, or interdependence, therein. They also help others in a variety of ways, even when it does not benefit them to do so, and they show a sense of equality in dividing up resources in some situations. Importantly, toddlers help others more and are more likely to share equally with them when they are collaborating with them, providing support for our hypothesis that it was within the context of collaboration or interdependence that prosocial behavior likely emerged. Toddlers also evaluate others in terms of their prosocial and cooperative behaviors and withdraw their helping and sharing from noncooperative individuals.

Still, all of these behaviors and evaluations are, we argue, based less in a normative, agent-neutral understanding of morality that applies to everyone equally and more in a second-personal morality based on personal relationships and social emotions (Darwall 2006). Thus, toddlers view others primarily from their own individual standpoint based on their own evaluation of whether the others' behavior is deserving of sympathy or blame. This is the first stage of morality, but it is not a fully adult-like morality; the critical second stage of norm-based, agent-neutral morality is still to come.

Preschoolers' Norm-Based Morality

Toddlers certainly respond when adults enforce norms, for example, when adults tell them things such as, "We don't hit other children." They thus seem to follow all kinds of social norms. It is not clear, though, whether they are responding to the norm per se. They could equally be responding simply to the adult's individual imperative utterance that they do or do not do something at that moment. But responding to the norm itself means responding to something more general and timeless than that.

In adult society, social norms are mutual expectations, indeed mutual agreements or commitments, about the way that individuals ought to behave in certain situations. Norms go beyond the particular—they are general and agent neutral—in at least three ways. First, social norms articulate an objective standard of behavior that is mutually known by all in the group: In situations like this, one ought to behave like that—and we all, including you, know this. Second, the force of the norm is not individual opinion but rather group opinion (or perhaps some other larger entity such as the group's gods), based ultimately in an agreement or commitment into which each

individual enters. It is not just that I don't like you doing that, but rather that it is wrong, and we (including you) have agreed that we don't behave like that. Third, the norm applies to everyone in the group (or perhaps subgroup) equally, including the self. "One" does not behave like that in this group, and that applies to me as well. Social norms are thus mutually known group expectations and commitments, with respect to group-known standards, which all group members are expected to respect.

Until there is more research, we may remain agnostic about precisely how toddlers understand social norms as adults enforce them, and in particular whether they understand their generality and agent neutrality. However, starting at approximately 3 years of age, children begin enforcing social norms on others, and the way they do this provides strong evidence that they have begun to understand social norms as something that goes beyond individuals and, importantly, beyond themselves.

Enforcement of social norms. As documented above, toddlers socially evaluate other persons in selectively helping and sharing with them depending on, essentially, whether they view them as nice or mean. In addition, toddlers are building up knowledge of what the norm is, statistically speaking, in many situations. They thus learn and apply words such as broken, dirty, and bad to situations that violate standards and are thus not "normal" (Kagan 1981). But beyond avoiding mean people and noticing statistical irregularities, children approximately 3 years of age also begin to actively intervene in situations—either physically or in acts of verbal protest—to try to set right deviations and violations of the norm. Crucially, they do this from a third-party stance, when they themselves are not directly involved or affected by the norm violation, and they often do this with normative language, using generic terms that explicitly mark the generality and agent neutrality of the judgment.

For example, in a recent study (Vaish et al. 2011b) children and two puppets each created a drawing or a sculpture, after which one puppet (the recipient) left the room. When the remaining puppet (the actor) then began to destroy the recipient's creation, 3-year-olds protested verbally against the actor's actions. Impressively, approximately one-quarter of the children protested using normative language such as "You can't do that," versus, for instance, imperatives or desire-dependent language such as "I don't want you to do that" (Searle 2001). Pilot work with 2-year-olds showed almost no protest in such situations. Rossano et al. (2011) found something very similar: 3-year-olds protested, again sometimes normatively, when one puppet threatened to take home or throw away another puppet's possession, whereas 2-year-olds only protested in an agent-specific manner (when the actor acted on the children's possessions and thus directly caused harm to them) but not in an agent-neutral manner. In both of these studies, 3-year-olds went beyond objecting to harm done to them and applied the moral norm against causing harm in an agent-neutral way: on behalf of someone else, as a disinterested enforcer, with the judgment marked as applying generally to all in the group.

Beyond protesting verbally, children demonstrate several other enforcement-like behaviors during third-party moral transgressions. For instance, 3-year-olds who witness an actor destroying an absent recipient's artwork later tattle to the recipient about the actor's actions, perhaps as a way to have the transgressor punished (Vaish et al. 2011b). Children of this age also carry out restorative justice by returning to a victim what a thief had stolen (Riedl et al. 2011). They thus intervene and respond to third-party moral transgressions in multiple ways that provide converging evidence for their emerging agent-neutral morality.

Interestingly, and perhaps even more tellingly, 3-year-old children also intervene and protest when someone violates a conventional norm, in which there is no harm involved. Thus, Rakoczy and colleagues (2008) had children watch as a puppet announced that he would now "dax," but he then performed a different action than the one the child had previously seen an adult doing and calling "daxing." Most children objected in some way, even though the game was a solitary activity so that playing it incorrectly did not harm, or even inconvenience, anyone. Again, as with moral norms, children often used normative, generic language such as "No, it does not go like that!" Two-year-olds protested to some extent in this study, but almost always imperatively rather than normatively. Importantly, children were not just objecting to the fact that the puppet did not perform the action he said he would, as a subsequent study obtained the same results with a nonverbal indication of the game context: A particular action was acceptable when carried out in a particular location that marked the appropriate context for the action, but not when it was carried out in a different location that marked a different, inappropriate context for the action (Wyman et al. 2009).

Three-year-olds' emerging understanding of social norms as agreements among people is especially clear in studies involving joint pretense. In studies by Rakoczy (2008) and Wyman et al. (2009), 3-year-old children again objected—in much the same way as in the other studies of moral norms and game rules—when a puppet used a wooden block as a pretend sandwich if the child and an adult had previously designated that block as pretend soap ("No, one can't eat that. It's soap!"). When the same block was later designated as a sandwich in a different game, then children objected if it was used as soap. This flexible behavior clearly demonstrates that young children can, at least in pretense contexts, understand that the norms constituting the game are, in a sense, agreements that can be changed.

Finally, even further evidence for young children's understanding of the basic workings of social norms is provided by their selective enforcement of different types of social norms depending on group membership. Thus, children not only distinguish moral from conventional norms on multiple levels (see, e.g., Turiel 2006), but they also enforce the two distinctly. In particular, when 3-year-old children see a moral norm being broken by an in-group member and an out-group member (as determined by their accents), they protest equivalently. But when they see a conventional norm being broken by these same agents, they protest more against an in-group member than an out-group member (Schmidt et al. 2011). In this way as well, then, 3-year-olds have a sense of the conventional nature of conventional norms, that is, that these norms have been decided on by, and thus apply only to, one's own group but that members of other groups may not be aware of or need not follow the same conventions. The same is not true of moral norms involving harm, toward which they take a more universalist approach.

Together, these recent findings suggest that, at least by 3 years of age, children do not view social norms solely in terms of authority, as Piaget assumed. Rather, they recognize them as general, agent-neutral, mutual expectations that represent some kind of implicit agreement of how we ought to behave—with the "we" conceptualized differently in the case of moral versus conventional norms. Because children's emerging understanding of social norms involves such things as agent neutrality, generic language, and reference to the group, it may be seen as reflecting their emerging skills and motivations for collective intentionality (Tomasello et al. 2012).

Reputation, guilt, and shame. In their everyday worlds, young children are less often judging and enforcing norms on others, and more often being judged and having norms enforced on them. Once more, the degree to which toddlers do or do not understand this fact is not totally clear, but children certainly seem to know that their behavior is being normatively assessed, and they sometimes alter their behavior accordingly (self-presentational behavior). Moreover, when they transgress, they may even judge and punish themselves via internalized social norms in acts of guilt and shame.

Research using verbal tasks has suggested that it is only around 8 years of age that children start to engage in self-presentational behavior

(e.g., Banerjee 2002). However, two recent studies have found evidence of such behaviors even in preschoolers. In one recent study by Piazza and colleagues (2011), 5- to 6-year-olds were faced with a challenging rule-based task while they were either "watched by an invisible person," watched by an adult, or were unobserved. Children cheated significantly less on the task when they were observed, either by the invisible person or by the adult, than when they were unobserved. Engelmann et al. (2012) found similar results with peer observers and extended the findings to a prosocial condition. Specifically, they found that children stole less from an imaginary child recipient, and tended to help that recipient more, if a peer was observing them. Relatedly, in a different experimental paradigm, Haun & Tomasello (2012) found that 4-year-olds conformed to their peers' perceptual judgments (even when they knew better themselves) if they had to express their judgment publicly, in front of the peers, but not if they expressed it alone. Thus, not only do young children judge and form reputations about others' behavior, but they also know that they are being judged and actively try to manage those judgments.

Children in these studies anticipate being judged and then behave so as to increase positive and decrease negative evaluations of themselves. They manage to avoid having norms applied to them by, in effect, preemptively applying the norms to themselves. But when children do transgress, even if no one sees them and so no one applies the norm, they still quite often apply the norm to themselves through guilt or shame. Thus, if they break a toy that belongs to someone else, many preschoolers show signs of feeling guilty or ashamed (e.g., Barrett et al. 1993, Kochanska et al. 2002, Zahn-Waxler & Kochanska 1990). These feelings may be seen as a kind of self-punishment that function to prevent individuals from repeating the transgression, lessening the chances of actual punishment from others in the future. Under special conditions individuals may also reward themselves by feeling pride at having lived up to a social norm when they could have gotten away with ignoring it (e.g., they helped others at great cost to themselves), and this self-praise presumably leads to more norm following in the future (Tangney et al. 2007).

Guilt, shame, and pride are thus internalized versions of the kind of moral judgments that humans mete out to others who violate or follow social norms. These norm-related, self-conscious emotions thus demonstrate with special clarity that the judgment being made is not my personal feeling about things, but rather the group's. I am sanctioning myself or praising myself on behalf of the group, as it were. I pushed the child off the swing because I wanted to play on the swing, and I still like playing on it, but I also feel guilty about harming the other child. As a particularly strong demonstration of group-mindedness, school-age children even show collective guilt, shame, and pride; that is, they feel guilt, shame, or pride if a member of the group with which they identify does something blameworthy or praiseworthy, as if they themselves had transgressed (Bennett & Sani 2008).

Interestingly and importantly, another function of social emotions such as guilt and shame comes from their display for others. For instance, displaying guilt to others serves important appeasement functions, showing others that I am already suffering, which I hope will evoke concern and forgiveness from the victim and from bystanders, thus reducing the likelihood of punishment (Keltner & Anderson 2000). Guilt displays also indicate that the transgressor did not mean to cause harm and, more generally, that he is not the kind of person that means harm. They signal that he intends to make amends and to behave more appropriately in the future and that he is aware of and committed to the norms of the group (Castelfranchi & Poggi 1990). A remorseful transgressor should thus be seen as self-policing, dependable, and cooperative, eliciting forgiveness, affiliation, and cooperation from the victim and other group members (Darby & Schlenker 1982, 1989; Goffman 1967).

Indeed, there is evidence that 6-year-old children blame apologetic actors less, punish them less, forgive them more, and like them better than unapologetic actors (Darby & Schlenker 1982, 1989). Children 4 to 5 years of age also regard situations in which an actor apologizes as better and more just than ones in which the actor is unapologetic (Irwin & Moore 1971, Wellman et al. 1979). Even in the absence of explicit apologies, 5-year-olds show a preference for transgressors who display guilt, and they prefer to distribute more resources to guilt-displaying transgressors than to unremorseful ones (Vaish et al. 2011a). Thus, preschoolers are tuned in to the social functions that displaying an emotion such as guilt serves.

Interestingly, not only do preschoolers prefer those who follow norms, but they also prefer those who enforce them. In a recent study (Vaish et al. 2012), 4.5- to 6-year-old children watched videos of an observer responding to a transgression she witnessed by either enforcing the norm that the transgressor had broken (e.g., she said in a mildly angry tone, "Hey, you've broken [the victim's] doll! You shouldn't do that. It's not good") or by not enforcing the violated norm (e.g., she said in a neutral tone, "Oh, you've broken [the victim's] ball. Oh well, it doesn't matter"). Children judged that the enforcer had done the right thing, they evaluated the nonenforcer as less good, and they preferred the enforcer. This was despite the fact that the enforcer was actually more negative and unpleasant in her behavior (since she showed some anger) than was the nonenforcer.

We may thus see a continuous line from toddlers' social evaluations of others as either helpful or harmful individuals to their enforcement of social norms. From very early on, they are judging others and even being selective about the target of their own cooperative behaviors based on those judgments (see previous section). But it is only during later preschool years that children understand this process of judgment such that they know they are being judged and so can do things to manage those judgments (impression management or self-presentational behaviors). One hypothesis is that this is made possible by some kind of second-order mental reasoning of the form, "I am thinking about what you are thinking about me" (Banerjee 2002). Perhaps such second-order reasoning is also involved as they judge the judgers and find good those who find moral transgressions bad.

Summary. During the later preschool years, then, children become truly moral agents—though of course there are still many further developments to come. The key is that they no longer consider and act toward individuals based only on their own individual judgments of them (although they certainly continue to do that). Rather, they have in addition begun to understand and even internalize the agent-neutral social norms of the group and to consider individuals as group members who both apply social norms to others and have social norms applied to them. And, crucially, they come to consider themselves as just one individual among others—nothing special in the eyes of social norms—and even, in an astounding testament to their bifurcated sense of self, to apply the norms and accompanying punishment equally to themselves.

Four- and 5-year-old children thus operate with an agent-neutral, norm-based morality in which all individuals, including themselves, are equal players. Moreover, they come to self-regulate their behavior in accordance with these norms, so much so that older preschoolers typically enter new situations not just following norms, but actively seeking out what those norms are: "What am I supposed to do here? How do I do it?" (Kalish 1998). Their sense of self is bound up with behaving in accordance with norms.

CONCLUSION

There is no doubt that humans are a prosocial and cooperative species, but it is becoming increasingly clear that humans are not unique in this regard. Our closest living relatives, the nonhuman great apes, are also prosocial and cooperative in several ways: Under some circumstances, they help others instrumentally, share food with others, reciprocate favors, coordinate efforts with others, and choose partners selectively based on their prior experiences with them. The evolutionary origins of human morality and cooperation are thus undoubtedly to be found in our primate cousins. Yet humans are vastly more, and distinctly, cooperative as compared to other primates. In contrast to great apes, human societies are much more egalitarian in nature, as evident, for instance, in our childcare practices, in which many individuals help mothers raise children. Moreover, human societies are universally marked by the cooperative endeavors of norms and institutions that have been mutually agreed upon by the members of the group and that govern the behavior of those in the group.

We have argued that these unique aspects of human cooperation have resulted from changes in human feeding ecology that caused humans, in a first step, to become obligate collaborative foragers, which created an interdependence among individuals unprecedented in the primate order. At this point in humans' evolutionary history, prosocial and cooperative behaviors were based on interpersonal interactions with specific individuals, as they seem to be with apes. What was different was that humans began to take a mutualistic rather than a purely individualistic approach to cooperative activity such that they became deeply invested in not only their own but also their partners' welfare—they began to care about the joint nature of their cooperative activities—and they began to care about how they were perceived by others as partners.

In a second step, the rise of intergroup competition gave way to a group-mindedness that is, we argue, totally unique to humans among primates. At this stage, humans began to care not only about their personal interactions and histories with others but also about the more general functioning of the group, which meant keeping track of how individuals (including the self) contributed to or detracted from the group's well-being. This was the beginning of the agent-neutral, group-level, norm-based psychology that marks so much of human cooperation and morality today. We may thus propose that although great apes are certainly prosocial and cooperative in some ways, and early humans extended this considerably, later humans cooperated in a special, agent-neutral way that is fully "moral."

Interestingly, these two evolutionary steps are, at least to some degree, paralleled in ontogeny. From very early on, children and perhaps even infants seem to cooperate at the interpersonal, or second-personal, level wherein they collaborate with others, sympathize with those in need, have a basic sense of equality, evaluate others' behaviors, and engage in reciprocity. Moreover, even children's early cooperative tendencies are marked by the mutualistic or joint attitude that we argue emerged in the first step of our evolutionary history. Thus, already in the early toddler years, the nature of children's prosocial and cooperative behaviors is distinct from that of apes.

By 3 to 4 years of age, children begin to demonstrate the norm-based group-mindedness that also represents the second evolutionary step in our story. Children now function not only at the second-personal but also at the agent-neutral level, and they now view individuals (including themselves) as group members who ought to follow the group's social norms. Moreover, they begin to enforce these norms on others and on themselves. With these developments, children begin to demonstrate the special, agent-neutral, and norm-based sort of cooperation that is considered to be fully moral. Thus, in both the evolutionary and the ontogenetic stories, the first step in the sequence is mutualistic collaboration and prosocially motivated interactions with specific other individuals, and the second step is the more abstract, agent-neutral, norm-based morality of individuals who live in more large-scale cultural worlds full of impersonal and mutually known conventions, norms, and institutions.

One question that arises is what contributes to the ontogenetic shift from a second-personal to a norm-based morality. A part of the answer certainly lies in social-cognitive development:

In order to engage in a norm-based morality, children must move from seeing individuals and social interactions purely in interpersonal terms to additionally seeing all individuals from an agent-neutral or bird's-eye perspective (the "view from nowhere"; Nagel 1986). They must also develop the capacity to see themselves as individuals just like all other individuals, to evaluate their own behavior, and to understand that others evaluate them in the same way that they evaluate others. These are all quite challenging developmental feats that are likely accomplished gradually over time rather than all at once. The transition from a second-personal to a norm-based morality is thus not an abrupt one, and so it is plausible that some norm-based morality is evident even at age 2 years, whereas in many circumstances, even adults may not demonstrate a full-fledged norm-based morality or else the two forms may conflict in a moral dilemma (e.g., should I break the law to help my friend or relative?).

Furthermore, there are certainly enormous influences of culture and socialization on the emergence and development of morality in childhood. There is, for example, evidence of cultural and experiential influences on children's prosocial behavior (see Eisenberg 1989, 1992). For instance, although similar levels of instrumental helping were recently found among 18-month-olds in Canada, India, and Peru (Callaghan et al. 2011), a study of 5-year-olds' prosocial behavior revealed that German and Israeli children displayed more prosocial behavior toward a distressed adult as compared to Indonesian and Malaysian children (Trommsdorff et al. 2007). Trommsdorff et al. (2007) propose that in cultures that promote face-saving values and respect for hierarchical relations (such as Indonesia and Malaysia), ignoring the mishap of another person (especially an authority figure) can be more valued than attempting to help and thereby risking that the other person lose face. The learning and internalization of such society-specific norms likely takes some time, meaning that cross-cultural differences in prosocial behavior and in morality more generally may often become apparent only in the late preschool years. Such findings of variation across contexts are provocative because they highlight the ways in which culture and experience fundamentally shape prosocial responding, and they demonstrate vividly that prosocial responding is not a unitary process but rather is open to a diverse set of influences. Still, we would argue that these influences do not create the basic prosocial and cooperative tendencies seen in children but rather modify and shape them.

In conclusion, from an evolutionary perspective, cooperation (and therefore morality) is always problematic, as it requires individuals to suppress their own interests in favor of those of others or equate their own interests with those of others. Cooperation can thus evolve only in certain specific circumstances. Humans have managed to evolve highly cooperative lifeways through participating in a variety of collaborative activities in which they are interdependent. These collaborative activities are the origins of human morality.

DISCLOSURE STATEMENT

The authors are not aware of any affiliations, memberships, funding, or financial holdings that might be perceived as affecting the objectivity of this review.

LITERATURE CITED

Banerjee R. 2002. Children's understanding of self-presentational behavior: links with mental-state reasoning and the attribution of embarrassment. *Merrill-Palmer Q.* 48(4):378–404

Barrett KC, Zahn-Waxler C, Cole PM. 1993. Avoiders versus amenders: implications for the investigation of guilt and shame during toddlerhood? *Cogn. Emot.* 7(6):481–505

Bennett M, Sani F. 2008. Children's identification with social groups. In *Intergroup Attitudes and Relations in Childhood Through Adulthood*, ed. SR Levy, M Killen, pp. 19–31. New York: Oxford Univ. Press

Birch LL, Billman J. 1986. Preschool children's food sharing with friends and acquaintances. *Child Dev.* 57(2):387–95

Bischof-Köhler D. 1991. The development of empathy in infants. In *Infant Development: Perspectives from German Speaking Countries*, ed. ME Lamb, H Keller, pp. 245–73. Hillsdale, NJ: Erlbaum

Boehm C. 1999. *Hierarchy in the Forest: The Evolution of Egalitarian Behavior*. Cambridge, MA: Harvard Univ. Press

Boesch C. 1994. Cooperative hunting in wild chimpanzees. *Anim. Behav.* 48(3):653–67

Boesch C, Boesch H. 1989. Hunting behavior of wild chimpanzees in the Taï National Park. *Am. J. Phys. Anthropol.* 78:547–73

Brownell CA, Svetlova M, Nichols SR. 2009. To share or not to share: When do toddlers respond to another's needs? *Infancy* 14(1):117–30

Call J, Tomasello M. 2008. Does the chimpanzee have a theory of mind? 30 years later. *Trends Cogn. Sci.* 12(5):187–92

Callaghan T, Moll H, Rakoczy H, Warneken F, Liszkowski U, et al. 2011. Early social cognition in three cultural contexts. *Monogr. Soc. Res. Child Dev.* 76(2):1–142

Castelfranchi C, Poggi I. 1990. Blushing as discourse: Was Darwin wrong? In *Shyness and Embarrassment: Perspectives from Social Psychology*, ed. WR Crozier, pp. 230–54. London: Cambridge Univ. Press

Csibra G, Gergely G. 2009. Natural pedagogy. *Trends Cogn. Sci.* 13:148–53

Damon W. 1975. Early conceptions of positive justice as related to the development of logical operations. *Child Dev.* 46:301–12

Damon W. 1977. *The Social World of the Child*. San Francisco: Jossey-Bass

Darby BW, Schlenker BR. 1982. Children's reactions to apologies. *J. Personal. Soc. Psychol.* 43(4):742–53

Darby BW, Schlenker BR. 1989. Children's reactions to transgressions: effects of the actor's apology, reputation and remorse. *Br. J. Soc. Psychol.* 28:353–64

Darwall S. 2006. *The Second-Person Standpoint: Morality, Respect and Accountability*. Cambridge, MA: Harvard Univ. Press

de Waal FBM. 1989. Food sharing and reciprocal obligations among chimpanzees. *J. Hum. Evol.* 18:433–59

de Waal FBM. 1997. The chimpanzee's service economy: food for grooming. *Evol. Hum. Behav.* 18:375–86

de Waal FBM. 2005. How animals do business. *Sci. Am.* 292(4):72–79

de Waal FBM, Luttrell S. 1988. Mechanisms of social reciprocity in three primate species: symmetrical relationship characteristics or cognition? *Ethol. Sociobiol.* 9:101–18

Dunfield KA, Kuhlmeier VA. 2010. Intention-mediated selective helping in infancy. *Psychol. Sci.* 21(4):523–27

Eckerman CO, Davis CC, Didow SM. 1989. Toddlers' emerging ways of achieving social coordinations with a peer. *Child Dev.* 60:440–53

Eckerman CO, Didow SM. 1989. Toddlers' social coordinations: changing responses to another's invitation to play. *Dev. Psychol.* 25:794–804

Eisenberg N. 1989. *The Roots of Prosocial Behavior in Children*. London: Cambridge Univ. Press

Eisenberg N. 1992. *The Caring Child*. Cambridge, MA: Harvard Univ. Press

Eisenberg N, Fabes RA. 1998. Prosocial development. In *Handbook of Child Psychology, Vol. 3: Social, Emotional, and Personality Development*, ed. N Eisenberg, pp. 701–78. New York: Wiley. 5th ed.

Eisenberg N, Miller PA. 1987. The relation of empathy to prosocial and related behaviors. *Psychol. Bull.* 101:91–119

Engelmann J, Herrmann E, Tomasello M. 2012. Five-year-olds, but not chimpanzees, attempt to manage their reputations. Manuscript submitted

Enright RD, Bjerstedt Ö, Enright WF, Levy VM Jr, Lapsley DK, et al. 1984. Distributive justice development: cross-cultural, contextual, and longitudinal evaluations. *Child Dev.* 55(5):1737–51

Fehr E, Bernhard H, Rockenbach B. 2008. Egalitarianism in young children. *Nature* 454(28):1079–84

Fehr E, Fischbacher U. 2003. The nature of human altruism. *Nature* 425:785–91

Fehr E, Fischbacher U. 2004. Third-party punishment and social norms. *Evol. Hum. Behav.* 25:63–87

Geraci A, Surian L. 2011. The developmental roots of fairness: infants' reactions to equal and unequal distributions of resources. *Dev. Sci.* 14(5):1012–20

Gilby IC. 2006. Meat sharing among the Gombe chimpanzees: harassment and reciprocal exchange. *Anim. Behav.* 71(4):953–63

Goffman E. 1959. *The Presentation of Self in Everyday Life*. New York: Doubleday

Goffman E. 1967. *Interaction Ritual: Essays on Face-to-Face Behavior*. Garden City, NY: Anchor

Gomes CM, Mundry R, Boesch C. 2009. Long-term reciprocation of grooming in wild West African chimpanzees. *Proc. Biol. Sci.* 276(1657):699–706

Goodall J. 1986. *The Chimpanzees of Gombe: Patterns of Behavior*. Cambridge, MA: Harvard Univ. Press

Gräfenhain M, Behne T, Carpenter M, Tomasello M. 2009. Young children's understanding of joint commitments. *Dev. Psychol.* 45(5):1430–43

Greenberg JR, Hamann K, Warneken F, Tomasello M. 2010. Chimpanzee helping in collaborative and noncollaborative contexts. *Anim. Behav.* 80(5):873–80

Gurven M. 2004. To give and to give not: the behavioral ecology of human food transfers. *Behav. Brain Sci.* 27:543–83

Hamann K, Warneken F, Greenberg J, Tomasello M. 2011. Collaboration encourages equal sharing in children but not chimpanzees. *Nature* 476:328–31

Hamann K, Warneken F, Tomasello M. 2012. Children's developing commitments to joint goals. *Child Dev.* 83(1):137–45

Hamlin JK, Wynn K. 2011. Young infants prefer prosocial to antisocial others. *Cogn. Dev.* 26:30–39

Hamlin JK, Wynn K, Bloom P. 2007. Social evaluation by preverbal infants. *Nature* 450(22):557–60

Harcourt AH, de Waal FBM. 1992. *Coalitions and Alliances in Humans and Other Animals*. New York: Oxford Univ. Press

Haun DBM, Tomasello M. 2012. Conformity to peer pressure in preschool children. *Child Dev.* 82(60):1759–67

Hay DF. 1979. Cooperative interactions and sharing between very young children and their parents. *Dev. Psychol.* 15(6):647–53

Hepach R, Vaish A, Tomasello M. 2012a. Young children's responses to justified versus unjustified emotional distress. *Dev. Psychol.* In press

Hepach R, Vaish A, Tomasello M. 2012b. Young children are intrinsically motivated to see others helped. *Psychol. Sci.* In press

Hill K. 2002. Altruistic cooperation during foraging by the Ache, and the evolved human predisposition to cooperation. *Hum. Nat.* 13:105–28

Hill K, Hurtado AM. 1996. *Ache Life History: The Ecology and Demography of a Foraging People.* New York: Aldine

Hockings KJ, Humle T, Anderson JR, Biro D, Sousa C, et al. 2007. Chimpanzees share forbidden fruit. *PLoS One* 2(9):e886

Hoffman ML. 2000. *Empathy and Moral Development: Implications for Caring and Justice.* London: Cambridge Univ. Press

Hook JG, Cook TD. 1979. Equity theory and the cognitive ability of children. *Psychol. Bull.* 86:429–45

Hoppit WJE, Brown GR, Kendal R, Thornton A, Webster MM, Laland KN. 2008. Lessons from animal teaching. *Trends Ecol. Evol.* 23:486–93

Hrdy S. 2009. *Mothers and Others.* Cambridge, MA: Harvard Univ. Press

Irwin DM, Moore SG. 1971. The young child's understanding of justice. *Dev. Psychol.* 5(3):406–10

Jensen K, Call J, Tomasello M. 2007. Chimpanzees are vengeful but not spiteful. *Proc. Natl. Acad. Sci.* 104:13046–50

Kagan J. 1981. *The Second Year: The Emergence of Self-Awareness.* Cambridge, MA: Harvard Univ. Press

Kalish C. 1998. Reasons and causes: children's understanding of conformity to social rules and physical laws. *Child Dev.* 69(3):706–20

Keltner D, Anderson C. 2000. Saving face for Darwin: the functions and uses of embarrassment. *Curr. Dir. Psychol. Sci.* 9(6):187–92

Kenward B, Dahl M. 2011. Preschoolers distribute scarce resources according to the moral valence of recipients' previous actions. *Dev. Psychol.* 47(4):1054–64

Kochanska G, Gross JN, Lin M-H, Nichols KE. 2002. Guilt in young children: development, determinants, and relations with a broader system of standards. *Child Dev.* 73(2):461–82

Korsgaard CM. 1996. *The Sources of Normativity.* London: Cambridge Univ. Press

Kuhlmeier VA, Wynn K, Bloom P. 2003. Attribution of dispositional states by 12-month-olds. *Psychol. Sci.* 14(5):402–8

Kummer H, Cords M. 1991. Cues of ownership in *Macaca fascicularis.* *Anim. Behav.* 42:529–49

Lane IM, Coon RC. 1972. Reward allocation in preschool children. *Child Dev.* 43:1382–89

Langergraber KE, Schubert G, Rowney C, Wrangham R, Zommers Z, Vigilant L. 2011. Genetic differentiation and the evolution of cooperation in chimpanzees and humans. *Proc. Biol. Sci.* 278:2546–52

Lepper MR, Greene D, Nisbett RE. 1973. Undermining children's intrinsic interest with extrinsic rewards: a test of the "overjustification" hypothesis. *J. Personal. Soc. Psychol.* 28:129–37

Leslie AM, Mallon R, Dicorcia JA. 2006. Transgressors, victims, and cry babies: Is basic moral judgment spared in autism? *Soc. Neurosci.* 1(3–4):270–83

Levitt MJ, Weber RA, Clark MC, McDonnell P. 1985. Reciprocity of exchange in toddler sharing behavior. *Dev. Psychol.* 21:122–23

Liszkowski U, Carpenter M, Henning A, Striano T, Tomasello M. 2004. Twelve-month-olds point to share attention and interest. *Dev. Sci.* 7(3):297–307

Liszkowski U, Carpenter M, Striano T, Tomasello M. 2006. Twelve- and 18-month-olds point to provide information for others. *J. Cogn. Dev.* 7:173–87

Liszkowski U, Carpenter M, Tomasello M. 2008. Twelve-month-olds communicate helpfully and appropriately for knowledgeable and ignorant partners. *Cognition* 108(3):732–39

LoBue V, Nishida T, Chiong C, DeLoache JS, Haidt J. 2011. When getting something good is bad: Even 3-year-olds react to inequity. *Soc. Dev.* 20:154–70

Mauss M. 1954. *Forms and Functions of Exchange in Archaic Societies.* New York: Routledge & Keegan Paul

Melis AP, Hare B, Tomasello M. 2006. Engineering cooperation in chimpanzees: tolerance constraints on cooperation. *Anim. Behav.* 72:275–86

Melis AP, Hare B, Tomasello M. 2008. Do chimpanzees reciprocate received favors? *Anim. Behav.* 76:951–62

Melis AP, Warneken F, Jensen K, Schneider A-C, Call J, Tomasello M. 2011. Chimpanzees help conspecifics obtain food and non-food items. *Proc. Biol. Sci.* 278(1710):1405–13

Moore C. 2009. Fairness in children's resource allocation depends on the recipient. *Psychol. Sci.* 20(8):944–48

Muller M, Mitani JC. 2005. Conflict and cooperation in wild chimpanzees. In *Advances in the Study of Behavior*, ed. PJB Slater, J Rosenblatt, C Snowdon, T Roper, M Naguib, 35:275–331. New York: Elsevier

Nagel T. 1986. *The View from Nowhere*. New York: Oxford Univ. Press

Ng R, Heyman GD, Barner D. 2011. Collaboration promotes proportional reasoning about resource distribution in young children. *Dev. Psychol.* 47(5):1230–38

Nichols S. 2004. *Sentimental Rules: On the Natural Foundations of Moral Judgment*. New York: Oxford Univ. Press

Nisan M. 1984. Distributive justice and social norms. *Child Dev.* 55(3):1020–29

Olson KR, Spelke ES. 2008. Foundations of cooperation in young children. *Cognition* 108:222–31

Piaget J. 1997/1932. *The Moral Judgment of the Child*. New York: Free Press

Piazza J, Bering JM, Ingram G. 2011. "Princess Alice is watching you": Children's belief in an invisible person inhibits cheating. *J. Exp. Child Psychol.* 109(3):311–20

Rakoczy H. 2008. Taking fiction seriously: Young children understand the normative structure of joint pretence games. *Dev. Psychol.* 44(4):1195–201

Rakoczy H, Warneken F, Tomasello M. 2008. The sources of normativity: young children's awareness of the normative structure of games. *Dev. Psychol.* 44(3):875–81

Rekers Y, Haun DBM, Tomasello M. 2011. Children, but not chimpanzees, prefer to collaborate. *Curr. Biol.* 21(20):1756–58

Rheingold HL, Hay DF, West MJ. 1976. Sharing in the second year of life. *Child Dev.* 47:1148–58

Richerson PJ, Boyd R. 2005. *Not By Genes Alone: How Culture Transformed Human Evolution*. Chicago: Univ. Chicago Press

Riedl K, Jensen K, Call J, Tomasello M. 2012. No third party punishment in chimpanzees. Manuscript submitted

Rochat P, Dias MDG, Liping G, Broesch T, Passos-Ferreira C, et al. 2009. Fairness in distributive justice by 3- and 5-year-olds across seven cultures. *J. Cross-Cult. Psychol.* 40(3):416–42

Rossano F, Rakoczy H, Tomasello M. 2011. Young children's understanding of violations of property rights. *Cognition* 121:219–27

Schmidt MFH, Rakoczy H, Tomasello M. 2012. Young children enforce social norms selectively. Manuscript submitted

Schmidt MFH, Sommerville JA. 2011. Fairness expectations and altruistic sharing in 15-month-old human infants. *PLoS ONE* 6(10):e23223

Searle JR. 1995. *The Construction of Social Reality*. New York: Free Press

Searle JR. 2001. *Rationality in Action*. Cambridge, MA: MIT Press

Sigelman CK, Waitzman KA. 1991. The development of distributive justice orientations: contextual influences on children's resource allocation. *Child Dev.* 62:1367–78

Surbeck M, Hohmann G. 2008. Primate hunting by bonobos at LuiKotale, Salonga National Park. *Curr. Biol.* 18(19):R906–7

Svetlova M, Nichols S, Brownell C. 2010. Toddlers' prosocial behavior: from instrumental to empathetic to altruistic helping. *Child Dev.* 81(6):1814–27

Tangney JP, Stuewig J, Mashek DJ. 2007. Moral emotions and moral behavior. *Annu. Rev. Psychol.* 58:345–72

Tomasello M. 2008. *Origins of Human Communication*. Cambridge, MA: MIT Press

Tomasello M. 2011. Human culture in evolutionary perspective. In *Advances in Culture and Psychology*, ed. M Gelfand, pp. 5–52. New York: Oxford Univ. Press

Tomasello M, Melis A, Tennie C, Wyman E, Herrmann E. 2012. Two key steps in the evolution of human cooperation: the interdependence hypothesis. *Curr. Anthropol.* In press

Trommsdorff G, Friedlmeier W, Mayer B. 2007. Sympathy, distress, and prosocial behavior of preschool children in four cultures. *Int. J. Behav. Dev.* 31(3):284–93

Turiel E. 2006. Thought, emotions, and social interactional processes in moral development. In *Handbook of Moral Development*, ed. M Killen, J Smetana, pp. 7–35. Mahwah, NJ: Erlbaum

Ueno A, Matsuzawa T. 2004. Food transfer between chimpanzee mothers and their infants. *Primates* 45(4):231–39

Vaish A, Carpenter M, Tomasello M. 2009. Sympathy through affective perspective-taking and its relation to prosocial behavior in toddlers. *Dev. Psychol.* 45(2):534–43

Vaish A, Carpenter M, Tomasello M. 2010. Young children selectively avoid helping people with harmful intentions. *Child Dev.* 81(6):1661–69

Vaish A, Carpenter M, Tomasello M. 2011a. Young children's responses to guilt displays. *Dev. Psychol.* 47(5):1248–62

Vaish A, Herrmann E, Markmann C, Tomasello M. 2012. Preschoolers value and prefer norm-enforcers. Manuscript in preparation

Vaish A, Missana M, Tomasello M. 2011b. Three-year-old children intervene in third-party moral transgressions. *Br. J. Dev. Psychol.* 29:124–30

Vaish A, Warneken F. 2012. Social-cognitive contributors to young children's empathic and prosocial behavior. In *Empathy: From Bench to Bedside*, ed. J Decety, pp. 131–46. Cambridge, MA: MIT Press

Warneken F, Chen F, Tomasello M. 2006. Cooperative activities in young children and chimpanzees. *Child Dev.* 77(3):640–63

Warneken F, Gräfenhain M, Tomasello M. 2012. Collaborative partner or social tool? New evidence for young children's understanding of joint intentions in collaborative activities. *Dev. Sci.* 15(1):54–61

Warneken F, Hare B, Melis A, Hanus D, Tomasello M. 2007. Spontaneous altruism by chimpanzees and young children. *PLoS Biol.* 5(7):1414–20

Warneken F, Lohse K, Melis AP, Tomasello M. 2011. Young children share the spoils after collaboration. *Psychol. Sci.* 22(2):267–73

Warneken F, Tomasello M. 2006. Altruistic helping in human infants and young chimpanzees. *Science* 311:1301–3

Warneken F, Tomasello M. 2007. Helping and cooperation at 14 months of age. *Infancy* 11(3):271–94

Warneken F, Tomasello M. 2008. Extrinsic rewards undermine altruistic tendencies in 20-month-olds. *Dev. Psychol.* 44(6):1785–88

Wellman HM, Larkey C, Somerville SC. 1979. The early development of moral criteria. *Child Dev.* 50:869–73

Wyman E, Rakoczy H, Tomasello M. 2009. Normativity and context in young children's pretend play. *Cogn. Dev.* 24:149–55

Yamamoto S, Humle T, Tanaka M. 2009. Chimpanzees help each other upon request. *PLoS ONE* 4(10):e7416

Yamamoto S, Humle T, Tanaka M. 2012. Chimpanzees' flexible targeted helping based on an understanding of conspecifics' goals. *Proc. Natl. Acad. Sci.* 109(9):3588–92

Young G, Lewis M. 1979. Effects of familiarity and maternal attention on infant peer relations. *Merrill-Palmer Q.* 25:105–19

Zahn-Waxler C, Kochanska G. 1990. The origins of guilt. In *The Nebraska Symposium on Motivation 1988: Socioemotional Development*, ed. RA Thompson, 36:183–258. Lincoln: Univ. Nebraska Press

Zahn-Waxler C, Radke-Yarrow M, Wagner E, Chapman M. 1992. Development of concern for others. *Dev. Psychol.* 28(1):126–36

Gesture's Role in Speaking, Learning, and Creating Language

Susan Goldin-Meadow[1] and Martha Wagner Alibali[2]

[1]Department of Psychology, University of Chicago, Chicago, Illinois 60637;
email: sgm@uchicago.edu

[2]Department of Psychology, University of Wisconsin, Madison, Wisconsin 53706

Annu. Rev. Psychol. 2013. 64:257–83

First published online as a Review in Advance on
July 25, 2012

The *Annual Review of Psychology* is online at
psych.annualreviews.org

This article's doi:
10.1146/annurev-psych-113011-143802

Keywords

gesture-speech mismatch, homesign, emergent sign languages,
cognitive development

Abstract

When speakers talk, they gesture. The goal of this review is to investigate the contribution that these gestures make to how we communicate and think. Gesture can play a role in communication and thought at many timespans. We explore, in turn, gesture's contribution to how language is produced and understood in the moment; its contribution to how we learn language and other cognitive skills; and its contribution to how language is created over generations, over childhood, and on the spot. We find that the gestures speakers produce when they talk are integral to communication and can be harnessed in a number of ways. (*a*) Gesture reflects speakers' thoughts, often their unspoken thoughts, and thus can serve as a window onto cognition. Encouraging speakers to gesture can thus provide another route for teachers, clinicians, interviewers, etc., to better understand their communication partners. (*b*) Gesture can change speakers' thoughts. Encouraging gesture thus has the potential to change how students, patients, witnesses, etc., think about a problem and, as a result, alter the course of learning, therapy, or an interchange. (*c*) Gesture provides building blocks that can be used to construct a language. By watching how children and adults who do not already have a language put those blocks together, we can observe the process of language creation. Our hands are with us at all times and thus provide researchers and learners with an ever-present tool for understanding how we talk and think.

Contents

WHY STUDY GESTURE?

The goal of this review is to explore the role that our hands play in communication and cognition. We focus on the hands for a number of reasons. First, hand movements during talk—better known as gestures—are ubiquitous. Speakers in all cultures gesture when they talk, and the topics that elicit gesture can be as simple as a child's board game (Evans & Rubin 1979) or as complex as kinship relations (Enfield 2005). Even congenitally blind individuals, who have never seen anyone gesture, move their hands when they talk (Iverson & Goldin-Meadow 1998), which highlights the robustness of gesture in communication.

Equally important, the gestures that speakers produce when they talk do not go unnoticed by their listeners. For example, an interviewee is just as likely to be led astray by the interviewer's misleading gestures as by his misleading words. Asking the listener the open-ended question, "What else was the man wearing?" accompanied by a hat gesture (moving the hand as though donning a hat) elicits just as many hat responses as the pointed question, "What color was the hat that the man was wearing?"—in both cases, the man was not wearing a hat (Broaders & Goldin-Meadow 2010). Gesture is part of our conversations and, as such, requires our research attention.

Gesture plays a role in communication at a variety of timespans—in speaking at the moment, in learning language over developmental time, and in creating language over shorter and longer periods of time. We use this structure in organizing our review. We begin by exploring gesture's role in how language is processed in the moment—how it is produced and how it is understood. We then explore the role that gesture plays over development, initially in learning language and later, once language has been mastered, in learning other concepts and skills. Finally, we explore the role that gesture plays in creating language over generations (in deaf individuals who share a communication system and transmit that system to the next generation), over developmental time (in deaf children who do not have access to a usable model for language, spoken or signed), and on the spot (in adults who are asked to communicate without using speech).

Having shown that gesture is an integral part of communication, we end with a discussion of how gesture can be put to good use—how it can be harnessed for diagnosis and intervention in the clinic and for assessment and instruction in the classroom.

GESTURE'S ROLE IN LANGUAGE PROCESSING

Gesture Production and Its Role in Producing Language

The gestures that speakers produce along with their speech may actually help them to produce that speech. In this section, we consider a number of accounts of this process.

Speakers' gestures convey meaning but, importantly, they do so using a different representational format from speech. Gesture conveys meaning globally, relying on visual and mimetic imagery, whereas speech conveys meaning discretely, relying on codified words and grammatical devices (McNeill 1992). According to McNeill's (1992, 2005; McNeill & Duncan 2000) growth point theory, the internal core or growth point of an utterance contains both the global-synthetic image carried by gesture and the linear-segmented hierarchical linguistic structure carried by speech. Moreover, the visuo-spatial and linguistic aspects of an utterance cannot be separated—gesture and speech form a single integrated system.

Building on these ideas, the information-packaging hypothesis (Kita 2000) holds that producing gestures helps speakers organize and package visuo-spatial information into units that are compatible with the linear, sequential format of speech. The visuo-spatial representations that underlie gestures offer possibilities for organizing information that differ from the more analytic representations that underlie speech. When describing complex spatial information (such as a set of actions or an array of objects), there are many possible ways in which the information can be broken down into units and sequenced. According to the information-packaging hypothesis, gestures, which are individual actions in space, help speakers to select and organize the visuo-spatial information into units that are appropriate for verbalization. For example, in describing the layout of furniture in a room, a speaker might produce a gesture in which her two hands represent a couch and a chair as they are positioned in the room,

and this might help in formulating the utterance, "The couch and the chair are facing one another."

The most straightforward way to test the information-packaging hypothesis would be to manipulate gesture and observe the impact of that manipulation on how speech is packaged. At the moment, the evidence for the theory is more indirect—studies have manipulated the demands of packaging visuo-spatial information and shown that this manipulation has an effect on gesture production. In tasks where it is more challenging to package information into linguistic form, speakers produce more gestures, even when other factors are controlled. For example, Hostetter et al. (2007) asked participants to describe arrays of dots in terms of the geometric shapes that connected those dots (e.g., "The top three dots form a triangle, and the base of that triangle is the top of a square with dots at each corner"). For some participants, the shapes were drawn in the dot arrays, so packaging the information into units was easy; for other participants, the shapes were not provided, so participants had to decide on their own how to group the dots into shapes. In the second case, packaging the information into units for speaking was more challenging. As predicted by the information-packaging hypothesis, participants in this latter group produced more gestures when describing the arrays.

Whether or not we gesture is also influenced by the ease with which we can access words, as proposed in Krauss's (1998, Krauss et al. 2000) lexical gesture process model. According to this theory, gestures cross-modally prime lexical items, increasing their activation and making them easier to access. For example, if a speaker produces a circular gesture as he starts to say, "The ball rolled down the hill," the gesture will increase activation of the lexical item "roll," making it easier for the speaker to access that word. As evidence, when lexical access is made more difficult, speakers gesture at higher rates (Chawla & Krauss 1994, Morsella & Krauss 2004). Conversely, when

Global-synthetic: a representation that is not divided into parts but rather captures the whole of the referent

Linear-segmented: a representation that is composed of discrete parts produced in a sequence

gesture is prohibited, speakers become more dysfluent (Rauscher et al. 1996).

The interface model proposed by Kita & Özyürek (2003) extends these theories, arguing that gestures are planned by an action generator and verbal utterances by a message generator. According to this view, although speech and gesture are generated by separate systems, those systems communicate bidirectionally and interact as utterances are conceptualized and formulated. Gestures are thus shaped by the linguistic possibilities and constraints provided by the language they accompany. Evidence for this view comes from cross-linguistic findings showing that the gestures that speakers produce are shaped by the syntactic structures that underlie their language. For example, in English, the manner and path of a motion event are expressed in the same clause (run down), with manner in the verb and path in a satellite to the verb, as in "The child runs (manner) down (path) the street." In contrast, in Turkish, manner and path are expressed in separate clauses (run and descend), with path in one verb and manner in another, as in "*Cocuk kosarak tepeden asagi indi*" = child as running (manner) descended (path) the hill. When English speakers produce gestures for manner and path, they typically conflate the two into a single gesture (an inverted V with wiggling fingers produced while moving the hand in a downward trajectory = run + down), paralleling the single-clause structure of their speech. Turkish speakers, in contrast, typically produce separate gestures for manner and path (a palm moved downward = down, followed by an inverted V with wiggling fingers in place = run), paralleling the two-clause structure of their speech (Özyürek et al. 2008). The particular gestures we produce are shaped by the words we speak.

An alternative view of the mechanism underlying gesture production is the gesture-as-simulated-action framework (Hostetter & Alibali 2008, 2010), which holds that speakers naturally activate simulations of actions and perceptual states when they produce speech. These simulations activate areas of motor and premotor cortex responsible for producing movements. If the level of motor activation exceeds a preset threshold (which is influenced by individual, social, and contextual factors), then the speaker produces overt motor movements, which we recognize as gestures. For example, according to this view, in speaking about a child running down a hill, a speaker forms a mental simulation of the scene that includes action and perceptual components. This simulation will activate corresponding motor and premotor areas, and if activation in those areas exceeds the speaker's gesture threshold, the speaker will produce a gesture. In support of this view, a number of studies have found that gesture rates increase when action and perceptual simulations are activated (Hostetter & Alibali 2010, Sassenberg & Van Der Meer 2010). Within this framework, linguistic factors may also influence the form of the gestures, as long as they influence the nature of speakers' simulations. For example, if linguistic factors affect the way the speaker simulates a child running down a hill, they will also shape the form of the gestures that the speaker uses to describe that event because gesture and speech are expressions of the same simulation. Thus, according to the gesture-as-simulated-action framework, speaking involves simulations of perception and action, and gestures arise as a natural consequence of these simulations.

Gesture Comprehension and Its Role in Understanding Language

Although some argue that gesture plays little role in language comprehension (Krauss et al. 1995, 1996), there is a great deal of evidence that gesture can have an impact on language comprehension. Consider a speaker who says, "The man was wearing a hat," while moving her hand as though grasping the bill of a baseball cap. This gesture could help listeners understand that the man was wearing a hat, and it might even encourage them to infer that the hat was a baseball cap. Both observational and experimental studies support these claims.

A recent quantitative meta-analysis that included 63 separate samples found that gestures foster comprehension in listeners (Hostetter 2011). The overall effect size was moderate, and the size of the beneficial effect depended on several factors, including the topic of the gestures, their semantic overlap with speech, and the age of the listeners. Across studies, gestures about topics involving movement (e.g., how to make pottery; Sueyoshi & Hardison 2005) yielded greater benefits for listeners' comprehension than gestures about abstract topics (e.g., the taste of tea; Krauss et al. 1995). In addition, gestures that conveyed task-relevant information not expressed in speech (e.g., a gesture depicting width while saying "this cup is bigger") played a greater role in comprehension than gestures that conveyed information that was also expressed in speech (e.g., a gesture depicting width while saying "this cup is wider"). Finally, children showed greater benefits from gesture than did older listeners.

In this section, we review two types of evidence arguing that gesture has an effect on language comprehension: (*a*) evidence that speakers' gestures affect listeners' comprehension of speech and (*b*) evidence that speakers' gestures communicate information that is not expressed in speech. We conclude by considering whether there is evidence that speakers intend their gestures to be communicative.

Do speakers' gestures affect listeners' comprehension of speech? Under ordinary circumstances, listeners comprehend speech with ease. However, if speech is difficult to comprehend because it is unclear, ambiguous, or difficult relative to the listeners' skills, gesture can provide a second channel that makes successful comprehension more likely.

Many studies have investigated whether gestures influence listeners' comprehension of speech. These include studies using video clips as stimuli (e.g., Kelly & Church 1997) and studies in which listeners view or participate in "live" interactions (e.g., Goldin-Meadow et al. 1999, Goldin-Meadow & Sandhofer 1999, Holler et al. 2009). Across studies, researchers have used a variety of outcome measures to evaluate comprehension. In some studies, par-

ticipants are asked to answer questions about the speech they heard (e.g., Kelly & Church 1998); in others, they are asked to restate or reiterate that speech (e.g., Alibali et al. 1997). In still other studies, participants' spontaneous uptake of information from others' speech was assessed, either in their next speaking turn (Goldin-Meadow et al. 1999) or in their behavioral responses (McNeil et al. 2000).

Across studies, there is strong evidence that gestures affect listeners' comprehension of speech. When gestures express information that is redundant with speech, they contribute to successful comprehension (Goldin-Meadow et al. 1999, McNeil et al. 2000). When gestures express information that is not expressed in speech, they can detract from listeners' direct uptake of the information in speech (e.g., Goldin-Meadow & Sandhofer 1999), but they often communicate important information in their own right, an issue we address in the next section.

Does gesture communicate information on its own? When gesture conveys the same information as speech, it appears to help listeners pick up that information. But what happens when gesture conveys different information from speech? In the earlier hypothetical example in which the speaker said, "The man was wearing a hat," while moving her hand as if grasping the bill of a baseball cap, the speaker expressed information about the type of hat (a baseball cap—not a cowboy hat, a stocking cap, or a sombrero) uniquely in gesture. Do listeners detect information that speakers express uniquely in gesture? They do. For example, Kelly & Church (1998) presented video clips of children explaining their judgments of Piagetian conservation tasks and asked participants to respond to yes/no questions about the reasoning that the children expressed. A child in one video clip mentioned the height of a container in speech, but indicated the width of the container in gesture. When probed, observers often credited this child with reasoning about both the height and the width of the container. Other studies have also shown that listeners often incorporate the information conveyed uniquely in gesture into their own speech (Goldin-Meadow et al. 1992, McNeill et al. 1994). Thus, observers credit speakers with saying things that they express uniquely in gesture.

Are gestures intended to be communicative? It is clear that gestures contribute to listeners' comprehension. But do speakers intend for their gestures to communicate or are gestures' communicative effects merely an epiphenomenon of the gestures that speakers produce in the effort of speech production?

Several lines of evidence suggest that speakers do intend at least some of their gestures to be communicative. First, speakers gesture more when their listeners can see those gestures than when visibility between speaker and listener is blocked (Alibali et al. 2001, Mol et al. 2011). Second, when speakers repeat a message to different listeners, their gesture rates do not decline as they might if gestures were produced solely to help with speech production (Jacobs & Garnham 2007). Third, when speakers are explicitly asked to communicate specific information to their listeners, they sometimes express some of that information uniquely in gesture and not in speech. For example, Melinger & Levelt (2004) explicitly directed speakers to communicate specific spatial information about a task to their addressees. Speakers frequently expressed this requested information in gesture and not in speech, suggesting that at least these gestures were intended to be communicative.

To summarize thus far, gesture plays a role in both language production and comprehension. One area that has received very little attention is individual differences (but see Bergmann & Kopp 2010, Hostetter & Alibali 2007)—are there differences in the rate at which people gesture when they speak or in the reliance people put on gesture when they listen to the speech of others? We know little about what accounts for individual differences in gesture, or even how consistent those differences are across tasks and conversational partners. This is an area of re-

search in gesture studies that is ripe for future examination.

GESTURE'S ROLE IN LANGUAGE LEARNING AND BEYOND

Mature speakers of a language routinely use gesture when they talk, but so do young children just learning to talk. In fact, most children use gesture prior to speaking, and these gestures not only precede linguistic progress, but they also play a role in bringing that progress about.

Gesture's Role in the Early Stages of Language Learning

Gesture precedes and predicts changes in language. Children typically begin to gesture between 8 and 12 months (Bates 1976, Bates et al. 1979). They first use deictic gestures, whose meaning is given entirely by context and not by their form. For example, a child can hold up or point at an object to draw an adult's attention to it months before the child produces her first word (Iverson & Goldin-Meadow 2005). Pointing gestures function like context-sensitive pronouns ("this" or "that") in that an adult has to follow the gesture's trajectory to its target in order to figure out which object the child is indicating. In addition to deictic gestures, children produce conventional gestures common to their cultures (Guidetti 2002). For example, in the United States, children may produce a side-to-side headshake to mean "no" or a finger held over the lips to mean "shush." Children also produce iconic gestures, although initially the number tends to be quite small and varies across children (Acredolo & Goodwyn 1988). For example, a child might open and close her mouth to represent a fish or flap her hands at her sides to represent a bird (Iverson et al. 1994). Unlike pointing gestures, the form of an iconic gesture captures aspects of its intended referent—its meaning is consequently less dependent on context. These gestures therefore have the potential to function like words; according to Goodwyn & Acredolo

(1998, p. 70), they do just that and can be used to express an idea that the child cannot yet express in speech.[1]

Even though they treat their early gestures like words in some respects, children rarely combine gestures with other gestures, and if they do, the phase is short lived (Goldin-Meadow & Morford 1985). But children do frequently combine their gestures with words, and they produce these combinations well before they combine words with words. Because gesture and speech convey meaning differently, it is rare for the two modalities to contribute identical information to a message. Even simple pointing gestures are not completely redundant with speech. For example, when a child says "bottle" while pointing at the bottle, the word labels and thus classifies, but does not locate, the object. The point, in contrast, indicates where the object is, but not what it is. When produced together, point and word work together to more richly specify the same object. Children's earliest gesture-speech combinations are of this type—gesture conveys information that further specifies the information conveyed in speech; for example, pointing at a box while saying "box" (Capirci et al. 1996, de Laguna 1927, Greenfield & Smith 1976, Guillaume 1927, Leopold 1949).

But gesture can also convey information that overlaps very little, if at all, with the information conveyed in the word it accompanies. A point, for example, can indicate an object that is not referred to in speech—the child says "bottle" while pointing at the baby. In this case, word and gesture together convey a simple proposition—"the bottle is the baby's"—that neither modality conveys on its own (Goldin-Meadow & Morford 1985; Greenfield & Smith 1976; Masur 1982, 1983; Morford & Goldin-Meadow 1992; Zinober & Martlew 1985).

The types of semantic relations conveyed in these gesture-speech combinations change over time and presage changes in children's speech (Özçalişkan & Goldin-Meadow 2005). For example, children produce constructions containing an argument and a predicate in gesture + speech ("you" + HIT gesture) at 18 months but do not produce these constructions in speech alone ("me touch") until 22 months.

Children thus use gesture to communicate before they use words. But do these gestures merely precede language development or are they fundamentally tied to it? If gesture is integral to language learning, changes in gesture should not only predate, but also predict, changes in language. And they do. With respect to words, we can predict which lexical items will enter a child's verbal vocabulary by looking at the objects that child indicated in gesture several months earlier (Iverson & Goldin-Meadow 2005). With respect to sentences, we can predict when a child will produce her first two-word utterance by looking at the age at which she first produced combinations in which gesture conveys one idea and speech another (e.g., point at bird + "nap"; Goldin-Meadow & Butcher 2003, Iverson et al. 2008, Iverson & Goldin-Meadow 2005).

Gesture can cause linguistic change. There are (at least) two ways in which children's own gestures can change what they know about language. First, as we discussed above, gesture gives young children the opportunity to express ideas that they are not yet able to express in speech. Parents and other listeners may attend to those gestures and translate them into speech, thus providing children with timely input about how to express particular ideas in their language. Under this scenario, gesture plays a role in the process of change by shaping children's learning environments. Mothers do, in fact, respond to the gestures their children produce (Golinkoff 1986, Masur 1982), often translating gestures that children produce without speech into words (Goldin-Meadow et al. 2007a). These mother translations have been found to have an effect on language learning.

---

[1]Two other types of gestures found in adult repertoires—the simple rhythmic beat gesture that patterns with discourse and does not convey semantic content, and the metaphoric gesture that represents abstract ideas rather than concrete ones—are not produced by children until much later in development (McNeill 1992).

With respect to word learning, when mothers translate the gestures that their children produce into words, those words are more likely to quickly become part of the child's vocabulary than are words for gestures that mothers do not translate. With respect to sentence learning, children whose mothers frequently translate their child's gestures into speech tend to be first to produce two-word utterances (Goldin-Meadow et al. 2007a).

Second, gesture could play a causal role in language learning by providing children with the opportunity to practice ideas and communicative devices that underlie the words and constructions that they are not yet able to express in speech. Repeated practice could then pave the way for later acquisition. Under this scenario, gesture plays a role in the process of change by affecting the learners themselves. Evidence for this hypothesis comes from the fact that child gesture at 14 months is an excellent predictor of child vocabulary at 42 months, often better than other predictors (e.g., family income, parent speech, and even child speech at 14 months; Rowe & Goldin-Meadow 2009, Rowe et al. 2008). However, to convincingly demonstrate that child gesture plays a causal role in word learning, we would need to randomly select children and manipulate their gestures, encouraging some to gesture and discouraging others. If the act of gesturing itself contributes to progress in language development (as it does in other domains; see Gesture Can Cause Knowledge Change section below), children who are encouraged to gesture should have larger vocabularies than children who are discouraged from gesturing.

The gestures that others produce may also play a causal role in language learning. By 12 months, children can understand the gestures that other people produce. For example, they can follow an adult's pointing gesture to a target object (Butterworth & Grover 1988, Carpenter et al. 1998, Murphy & Messer 1977). Moreover, parents gesture frequently when they interact with their children, and the majority of these gestures co-occur with speech (Acredolo & Goodwyn 1988, Greenfield &

Smith 1976, Shatz 1982). Parent gesture could facilitate the child's comprehension, and eventual acquisition, of new words simply by providing nonverbal support for understanding speech (see Zukow-Goldring 1996).

However, it is often hard to tell whether parent gesture has an impact on child language learning above and beyond parent speech. For example, Iverson et al. (1999) and Pan et al. (2005) both found a relation between parent gesture and later child language, but the relation disappeared when parent speech was taken into account. The best way to convincingly test this hypothesis is to manipulate parent gesture and observe the effects on child language. Acredolo & Goodwyn (1988) instructed parents to use symbolic gestures (now called baby signs; Acredolo & Goodwyn 2002) in addition to words when talking to their children. They found that these children showed greater gains in vocabulary than children whose parents were encouraged to use only words or were not trained at all. But the children whose parents used gesture also used more of their own gestures. The vocabulary gains may thus have been mediated by child gesture.

Previous work has, in fact, found a link between parent gesture and child gesture—parents who gesture a great deal have children who gesture a great deal (Iverson et al. 1999, Namy et al. 2000, Rowe 2000). Moreover, parent gesture at 14 months predicts child gesture at 14 months, which, in turn, predicts child receptive vocabulary at 42 months (Rowe & Goldin-Meadow 2009). Importantly, parent gesture at 14 months does not directly predict child vocabulary at 42 months (Rowe et al. 2008), suggesting that parent gesture affects later child vocabulary through child gesture—parents who gesture more have children who gesture more who, in turn, go on to develop relatively large receptive vocabularies in speech.

To summarize thus far, gesture appears to play a role in learning when the task to be learned is language itself. When gesture is produced by children who are learning language, it often substitutes for a word that the child has not yet acquired. As we will discuss in the next section, gesture continues throughout development to convey ideas that are not expressed in speech, but often those ideas cannot easily be translated into a single word (McNeill 1992). Thus, once children have become proficient language users, we should see a change in the kinds of ideas that gesture conveys. Future studies are needed to determine when this transition takes place.

Once Language Has Been Mastered: Gesture's Role in Learning Other Domains

Gesture thus seems to offer children a helping hand as they learn language. Does gesture play a comparable role in other domains? We turn next to this question.

Gesture reveals understanding not found in speech. When children explain their understanding of concepts and problem-solving procedures, they often express some aspects of their knowledge in gestures and not in speech. Consider a six-year-old child explaining a Piagetian conservation of matter task, in which two rows of checkers contain the same number; the checkers in one row are spread out and the child is asked whether the two rows continue to have the same number of checkers. Children who do not yet understand number conservation believe that the number of checkers in the transformed row has changed. **Figure 1a** displays a nonconserving child who says the number is different "because you spreaded them out" and conveys the same information in her gestures (she produces a spreading-out motion over the transformed row). In contrast, **Figure 1b,c** displays another nonconserving child who also focuses on the movements of the experimenter in his speech—he says the number is different "because you moved them." However, in his gestures, he indicates that the checkers in one row can be paired with the checkers in the second row; that is, he has focused on the one-to-one correspondence between the rows. This child has expressed information about the task in gestures that he

did not express at all in his speech. Responses of this sort have been called gesture-speech mismatches (Church & Goldin-Meadow 1986).

People express aspects of their knowledge in gesture on a wide range of cognitive tasks, including mathematical equations (e.g., Perry et al. 1988), balance tasks (e.g., Pine et al. 2004), logical puzzles (e.g., the Tower of Hanoi; Garber & Goldin-Meadow 2002), science explanations (Roth 2002), and even moral reasoning (Church et al. 1995). In all of these domains, people sometimes express information in gesture that they do not express in the accompanying speech. Thus, across a wide range of cognitive domains, gesture reveals information about people's reasoning and problem solving that is not found in their speech.

Gesture-speech mismatches may occur when children explore aspects of the task stimuli in gesture but do not ultimately express all of those aspects in speech. In the example presented in **Figure 1b,c**, the child uses gesture to explore the one-to-one-correspondence between the checkers in the two rows, but he does not ultimately express this aspect of the task in his speech.

The mismatch between gesture and speech presages knowledge change. Gesture-speech mismatches are of interest because they provide insight into aspects of learners' knowledge that they do not express in speech. But even more important, mismatches are a good index of the stability of a learner's knowledge. Several studies across a variety of domains have shown that children who produce gesture-speech mismatches when explaining a concept are in a state of transitional knowledge with respect to that concept. For example, in the domain of Piagetian conservation, Church & Goldin-Meadow (1986) found that, among partial conservers (i.e., children who conserved on some tasks and not on others), those who produced a majority of mismatches in their conservation explanations prior to instruction were more likely to profit from instruction about conservation than were those who produced few mismatches. Thus, frequent

Conservation of matter: understanding that quantity does not change when it is merely rearranged

Gesture-speech mismatch: an utterance in which the information conveyed in gesture is different from the information conveyed in the speech that it accompanies

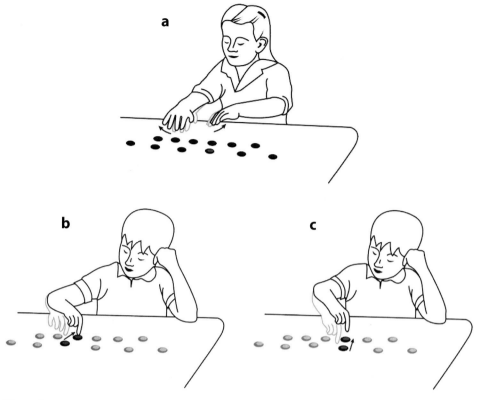

Figure 1

Examples of children gesturing while giving explanations for their nonconserving judgments on a number conservation task. In the top picture (*a*), the child says, "you spreaded them out," while producing a spreading motion with her hands, thus producing a gesture-speech match. In the bottom pictures (*b,c*), the child says, "you moved them," again focusing on the experimenter's movements in speech, but he produces pointing gestures that align the checkers in one row with the checkers in the other row (one-to-one correspondence), thus producing a gesture-speech mismatch.

mismatches between speech and gesture in children's task explanations at pretest indexed their readiness to benefit from instruction. Similar findings have been documented in children learning about mathematical equations such as $3 + 4 + 5 = 3 + \_\_$ (Perry et al. 1988), in children solving balance problems (Pine et al. 2004), and in adults learning about stereoisomers in organic chemistry (Ping et al. 2012).

Gesture-speech mismatch thus reflects readiness to learn—and does so better than other possible indices of learning that rely on the verbal channel alone. Church (1999) compared three indices that can be used to predict children's readiness to learn from a conservation lesson: number of pretest responses containing a gesture-speech mismatch (i.e., two different strategies, one in speech and one in gesture), number of pretest responses containing more than one strategy in speech (i.e., two different strategies, both in speech), and total number of different strategies conveyed in speech across the entire pretest. Each of these indices individually predicted learning from the lesson, but when all three were included in the same model, the only significant predictor was gesture-speech mismatch.

Gesture-speech mismatches also index knowledge transition in another sense: The state in which children frequently produce mismatches is both preceded and followed by a state in which they seldom produce mismatches. In a microlongitudinal study, Alibali & Goldin-Meadow (1993) tracked the relationship between gesture and speech in children's explanations over a series of problems as the children learned to solve mathematical equations, such as $3 + 4 + 5 = 3 + \_\_$. Among children who produced gestures on the task, the large majority of children traversed all or part of the following path: (*a*) Children began in a state in which they predominantly produced gesture-speech match responses, expressing a single, incorrect strategy for solving the problems conveyed in both gesture and speech. (*b*) They then progressed to a state in which they produced gesture-speech mismatches, expressing more than one strategy, one in gesture and the other in speech. (*c*) Finally, they reached a state in which they produced gesture-speech match responses, now expressing a single, correct strategy conveyed in both gesture and speech. Thus, the state in which children frequently produce gesture-speech mismatches is also transitional in the sense that it is both preceded and followed by a more stable state.

Gesture can cause knowledge change. Gesture can provide information about the content and stability of children's knowledge. But can gesture do more? As in language learning, gesture might play a causal role in the process of knowledge change. There are (at least) two classes of mechanisms by which gestures could play a causal role in bringing about knowledge change: social mechanisms by which learners' gestures convey information about their knowledge states to listeners who, in turn, alter the input they provide to the learners, and cognitive mechanisms by which learners' own gestures alter the state of their knowledge. We consider each class of mechanisms in turn.

Social mechanisms by which gesture can cause change. Gesture is implicated in social mechanisms of knowledge change. According to these mechanisms, learners' gestures convey information about their cognitive states to listeners (teachers, parents, or peers), and those listeners then use this information to guide their ongoing interactions with the learners. Learners' gestures can provide information about the leading edge of their knowledge, information that could be used to scaffold their developing understanding. Learners thus have the potential to influence the input they receive just by moving their hands. For the social construction of knowledge to occur in this way, listeners must grasp the information that learners express in their gestures, and they must also change their responses to those learners as a function of the information. Evidence supports both of these steps.

As reviewed in the section on gesture's role in language comprehension, there is evidence that listeners detect and interpret the information that speakers express solely in their gestures on a variety of tasks, for example, on Piagetian conservation problems (Goldin-Meadow et al. 1992; Kelly & Church 1997, 1998) and mathematical equations (Alibali et al. 1997). Moreover, there is evidence that listeners can detect gestured information not only when viewing speakers on video, but also when interacting with live speakers in real time (Goldin-Meadow & Sandhofer 1999).

As one example, Alibali and colleagues (1997) presented clips of children explaining mathematics problems to two groups of adults—teachers and college students—and asked the adults to describe each child's reasoning about the problems. Both teachers and college students detected the information that children expressed in their gestures. In some of the clips, the child expressed a strategy for solving the problems solely in gesture. For example, one boy explained his incorrect solution (he put 18 in the blank) to the problem $5 + 6 + 7 = \_\_ + 7$ by saying that he added the numbers on the left side of the equation. In gesture; however, he pointed to the 5 and the 6—the two numbers that should be added to yield the correct solution of 11. In reacting to this clip, one teacher said, "What I'm picking up now is [the child's] inability to realize that these (5 and

6) are meant to represent the same number.... There isn't a connection being made by the fact that the 7 on this (left) side of the equal sign is supposed to also be the same as this 7 on this (right) side of the equal sign, which would, you know, once you made that connection it should be fairly clear that the 5 and 6 belong in the box." It seems likely that the teacher's reaction was prompted by the child's gestures. Indeed, the teachers were more likely to mention a strategy when the target child expressed that strategy solely in gesture than when the target child did not express the strategy in either gesture or speech.

Communication partners can thus glean information from a learner's gestures. But do they use this information to guide their interactions with the learner? If the teacher in the preceding example were asked to instruct the child she viewed in the video, she might point out the two 7's and suggest that the child cancel the like addends and then group and add the remaining numbers. In this way, the teacher would be tailoring her instruction to the child's knowledge state, and instruction that is targeted to a child's knowledge state might be particularly helpful in promoting learning in the child.

Teachers have been found to alter their input to children on the basis of the children's gestures. Goldin-Meadow & Singer (2003) asked teachers to instruct children in one-on-one tutorials on mathematical equations; they asked whether the teachers' instruction varied as a function of their pupils' gestures. They found that the teachers offered more different types of problem-solving strategies to children who produced gesture-speech mismatches, and also produced more mismatches of their own (i.e., typically a correct strategy in speech and a different correct strategy in gesture), when instructing children who produced mismatches than when instructing children who produced matches. Importantly, including mismatches of this sort in instruction greatly increases the likelihood that children will profit from that instruction (Singer & Goldin-Meadow 2005). Children can thus have an active hand in shaping their own instruction.

Cognitive mechanisms by which gesture can cause change. There is growing evidence that producing gestures can alter the gesturer's cognitive state. If this is the case, then a learner's gestures will not only reflect the process of cognitive change but also cause that change. A number of specific claims regarding how gesturing might cause cognitive change have been made.

First, gestures may manifest implicit knowledge that a learner has about a concept or problem. When learners express this implicit knowledge and express other more explicit knowledge at the same time, the simultaneous activation of these ideas may destabilize their knowledge, making them more receptive to instructional input and more likely to alter their problem-solving strategies. In support of this view, Broaders and colleagues (2007) told some children to gesture and others not to gesture as they solved a series of mathematical equations. When required to gesture, many children expressed problem-solving strategies in gesture that they had not previously expressed in either speech or gesture. When later given instruction in the problems, it was the children who had been told to gesture and expressed novel information in those gestures who were particularly likely to learn mathematical equivalence.

Second, gesturing could help learners manage how much cognitive effort they expend. Goldin-Meadow et al. (2001; see also Ping & Goldin-Meadow 2010, Wagner et al. 2004) found that speakers who gestured when explaining how they solved a series of math problems while at the same time trying to remember an unrelated list of items had better recall than speakers who did not gesture. This effect holds even when speakers are told when to gesture and told when not to gesture (Cook et al. 2012). If gesturing does serve to reduce a learner's effort, that saved effort could be put toward other facets of the problem and thus facilitate learning.

Third, gesturing could serve to highlight perceptual or motor information in a learner's representations of a problem, making that information more likely to be engaged when solving the problem. In line with this view, Alibali & Kita (2010) found that children asked to solve a series of Piagetian conservation tasks were more likely to express information about the perceptual state of the task objects when they were allowed to gesture than when they were not allowed to gesture. Similarly, in a study of adult learners asked to predict how a gear in an array of gears would move if the first gear were rotated in a particular direction, Alibali et al. (2011) found that learners who were allowed to gesture were more likely to persist in using a perceptual-motor strategy to solve the problems (i.e., modeling the movements of each individual gear) and less likely to shift to a more abstract strategy (i.e., predicting the movement of the gear based on whether the total number of gears was even or odd).

As another example, Beilock & Goldin-Meadow (2010) demonstrated that gesturing can introduce motor information into a speaker's mental representations of a problem. They used two versions of the Tower of Hanoi task, a puzzle in which four disks must be moved from one of three pegs to another peg; only one disk can be moved at a time and a bigger disk can never be placed on top of a smaller disk. In one version, the heaviest disk was also the largest disk; in the other, the heaviest disk was the smallest disk. Importantly, the heaviest disk could not be lifted with one hand. Participants solved the problem twice. Some participants used the largest = heaviest version for both trials (the No Switch group); others used the largest = heaviest version on the first trial and the smallest = heaviest version on the second trial (the Switch group). In between the two trials, participants were asked to explain how they solved the problem and to gesture during their explanation. Participants who used one-handed gestures when describing the smallest disk during their explanation of the first trial performed worse on the second trial than participants who used two-handed gestures to describe the smallest disk—but only in the Switch group (recall that the smallest disk could no longer be lifted with one hand after the disks were switched). Participants in the No Switch group improved on the task no matter which gestures they produced, as did participants who were not asked to explain their reasoning and thus produced no gestures at all. The participants never mentioned weight in their talk. But weight information is an inherent part of gesturing on this task—one has to use either one hand (light disk) or two (heavy disk) when gesturing. When the participants' gestures highlighted weight information that did not align with the actual movement needed to solve the problem, subsequent performance suffered. Gesturing thus introduced action information into the participants' problem representations, and this information affected their later problem solving.

It is likely that both cognitive and social mechanisms operate when gesture is involved in bringing about change (Goldin-Meadow 2003a). For example, Streeck (2009) argues that gesturing does not just reflect thought, but it is part of the cognitive process that accomplishes a task, and in this sense, is itself thought. Moreover, because gesture is an observable and external aspect of the cognitive process, it puts thought in the public domain and thus opens the learner to social mechanisms (see also Alac & Hutchins 2004, Goodwin 2007).

GESTURE'S ROLE IN CREATING LANGUAGE

We have seen that when gesture is produced along with speech, it provides a second window onto the speaker's thoughts, offering insight into those thoughts that cannot be found in speech and predicting (perhaps even contributing to) cognitive change. The form that gesture assumes when it accompanies speech is imagistic and continuous, complementing the segmented and combinatorial form that characterizes speech. But what happens when the manual modality is called upon to fulfill, on its own, all of the functions of language? Interestingly, when the manual modality takes over the functions of language, as in sign languages of the deaf, it also takes over its segmented and combinatorial form.

Sign Language: Codified Manual Language Systems Transmitted Across Generations

Sign languages of the deaf are autonomous languages that do not depend on the spoken language of the surrounding hearing community. For example, American Sign Language (ASL) is structured very differently from British Sign Language, despite the fact that English is the spoken language that surrounds both sign communities.

Even though sign languages are processed by the hand and eye rather than the mouth and ear, they have the defining properties of segmentation and combination that characterize all spoken language systems (Klima & Bellugi 1979, Sandler & Lillo-Martin 2006). Sign languages are structured at the sentence level (syntactic structure), at the sign level (morphological structure), and at the subsign level and thus have meaningless elements akin to phonemes (phonological structure). Just like words in spoken languages (but unlike the gestures that accompany speech; Goldin-Meadow et al. 1996), signs combine to create larger wholes (sentences) that are typically characterized by a basic order, for example, SVO (Subject-Verb-Object) in ASL (Chen Pichler 2008) and SOV in Sign Language of the Netherlands (Coerts 2000). Moreover, the signs that comprise the sentences are themselves composed of meaningful components (morphemes; Klima & Bellugi 1979).

Although many of the signs in a language like ASL are iconic (i.e., the form of the sign is transparently related to its referent), iconicity characterizes only a small portion of the signs and structures in any conventional sign language. Moreover, sign languages do not always take advantage of the iconic potential that the manual modality offers. For example, although it would be physically easy to indicate the manner by which a skateboarder moves in a circle within the sign that conveys the path, to be grammatically correct the ASL signer must produce separate, serially linked signs, one for the manner and a separate one for the path (Supalla 1990). As another example, the sign for "slow" in ASL is made by moving one hand across the back of the other hand. When the sign is modified to be "very slow," it is made more rapidly since this is the particular modification of movement associated with an intensification meaning in ASL (Klima & Bellugi 1979). Thus, modifying the meaning of a sign can reduce its iconicity.

Moreover, the iconicity found in a sign language does not appear to play a significant role in the way the language is processed or learned. For example, young children are just as likely to learn a sign whose form does not resemble its referent as a sign whose form is an iconic depiction of the referent (Bonvillian et al. 1983). Similarly, young sign learners find morphologically complex constructions difficult to learn even if they are iconic. Moving the sign "give" from the chest toward the listener would seem to be an iconically transparent way of expressing "I give to you" and thus ought to be an early acquisition if children are paying attention to iconicity. However, the sign turns out to be a relatively late acquisition, presumably because the sign is marked for both the agent (I) and the recipient (you) and is thus morphologically complex (Meier 1987).

Interestingly, the segmentation and combination that characterizes established languages, signed or spoken, is also found in newly emerging sign languages, as we discuss in the next section.

Emerging Sign Systems

Deaf children born to deaf parents who are exposed to a conventional sign language learn that language as naturally, and following the same major milestones, as hearing children learning a spoken language from their hearing parents (Lillo-Martin 1999, Newport & Meier 1985). But 90% of deaf children are born to hearing parents who are not likely to know a conventional sign language (Hoffmeister & Wilbur 1980). These hearing parents very often prefer that their deaf child learn a spoken rather than a signed language. They thus choose to educate the child using an oral method of instruction, instruction that focuses on lip-reading and discourages the use of sign language and gesture. Unfortunately, it is extremely difficult for a profoundly deaf child to learn a spoken language, even when that child is given intensive oral education (Mayberry 1992). Under these circumstances, one might expect that a child would not communicate at all. But that is not what happens—deaf children who are unable to use the spoken language input that surrounds them and have not been exposed to sign language do communicate with the hearing individuals in their households, and they use gesture to do so.

The gestures that deaf children in these circumstances develop are called homesigns. Interestingly, homesigns are characterized by segmentation and combination, as well as many other properties found in natural languages (Goldin-Meadow 2003b). For example, homesigners' gestures form a lexicon, and these lexical items are composed of morphemes and thus form a system at the word level (Goldin-Meadow et al. 2007b). Moreover, the lexical items combine to form syntactically structured strings and thus form a system at the sentence level (Feldman et al. 1978, Goldin-Meadow & Mylander 1998), with negative and question sentence modulators (Franklin et al. 2011), grammatical categories (Goldin-Meadow et al. 1994), and hierarchical structure built around the noun (Hunsicker & Goldin-Meadow 2012). Importantly, homesigners use their gestures not only to make requests of others, but also to comment on the present and nonpresent (Morford & Goldin-Meadow 1997), to make generic statements about classes of objects (Goldin-Meadow et al. 2005), to tell stories about real and imagined events (Morford 1995, Phillips et al. 2001), to talk to themselves, and to talk about language (Goldin-Meadow 2003b)—that is, to serve typical functions that all languages serve, signed or spoken.

But homesign does not exhibit all of the properties found in natural language. We can explore the conditions under which homesign takes on more and more linguistic properties to get a handle on factors that may have shaped human language. For example, deaf children rarely remain homesigners in countries such as the United States; they either learn a conventional sign language or receive cochlear implants and focus on spoken language. However, in Nicaragua, not only do some homesigners continue to use their gesture systems into adulthood, but in the late 1970s and early 1980s, rapidly expanding programs in special education brought together in great numbers deaf children and adolescents who were, at the time, homesigners (Kegl et al. 1999, Senghas 1995). As these children interacted on school buses and in the schoolyard, they converged on a common vocabulary of signs and ways to combine those signs into sentences, and a new language—Nicaraguan Sign Language (NSL)—was born.

NSL has continued to develop as new waves of children enter the community and learn to sign from older peers. NSL is not unique—other sign languages have originated in communal contexts and been passed from generation to generation. The Nicaraguan case is special because the originators of the language are still alive. We thus have in this first generation, taken together with subsequent generations and current-day homesigners (child and adult), a living historical record of a language as it develops through its earliest stages.

Analyses of adult homesign in Nicaragua have, in fact, uncovered linguistic structures that may turn out to go beyond the structures found in child homesign: the grammatical category subject (Coppola & Newport 2005), pointing devices representing locations versus nominals (Coppola & Senghas 2010), morphophonological finger complexity patterns (Brentari et al. 2012), and morphological devices that mark number (Coppola et al. 2012). By contrasting the linguistic systems constructed by child and adult homesigners, we can see the impact that growing older has on language creation.

In addition, by contrasting the linguistic systems constructed by adult homesigners in Nicaragua with the structures used by the first cohort of NSL signers, we can see the impact that a community of users has on language. Having a group with whom they could communicate meant that the first cohort of signers were both producers and receivers of their linguistic system, a circumstance that could lead to a system with greater systematicity, but perhaps less complexity, as the group may need to adjust to the lowest common denominator (i.e., to the homesigner with the least complex system).

Finally, by contrasting the linguistic systems developed by the first and second cohorts of NSL signers (e.g., Senghas 2003), we can see the impact that passing a language through a new generation of learners has on language. Once learners are exposed to a system that has linguistic structure, the processes of language change may be identical to the processes studied in historical linguistics. One interesting question is whether the changes seen in NSL in its earliest stages are of the same type and magnitude as the changes that occur in mature languages over historical time.

Gestures Used by Hearing Adults When They Are Not Permitted to Speak

A defining feature of homesign is that it is not shared in the way that conventional communication systems are. Deaf homesigners produce gestures to communicate with the hearing individuals in their homes. But the hearing individuals, particularly hearing parents who are committed to teaching their children to talk and thus to oral education, use speech back. Although this speech is often accompanied by gesture (Flaherty & Goldin-Meadow 2010), as we discussed previously, the gestures that co-occur with speech form an integrated system with that speech and, in this sense, are not free to take on the properties of the deaf child's gestures. As a result, although hearing parents respond to their deaf child's gestures, they do not adopt the gestures themselves (nor do they typically acknowledge that the child even uses gesture to communicate). The parents produce cospeech gestures, not homesigns.

Not surprisingly, then, the structures found in child homesign cannot be traced back to the spontaneous gestures that hearing parents produce while talking to their children (Goldin-Meadow et al. 1994, Goldin-Meadow & Mylander 1983). Homesigners see the global and unsegmented gestures that their parents produce. But when gesturing themselves, they use gestures that are characterized by segmentation and combination. The gestures that hearing individuals produce when they talk therefore do not provide a model for the linguistic structures found in homesign.

Nevertheless, cospeech gestures could provide the raw materials (e.g., hand shapes, motions) for the linguistic constructions that homesigners build (see, for example, Goldin-Meadow et al. 2007b) and, as such, could contribute to the initial stages of an emerging sign language (see Senghas et al. 2004). Moreover, the disparity between cospeech gesture and homesign has important implications for language learning. To the extent that the properties of homesign differ from the properties of cospeech gesture, the deaf children themselves are likely to be imposing these particular structural properties on their communication systems. It is an intriguing, but as yet unanswered, question as to where the tendency to impose structure on homesign comes from.

We have seen that cospeech gestures do not assume the linguistic properties found in homesign. But what would happen if we were to ask hearing speakers to abandon speech and create a manual communication system on the spot? Would that system contain the linguistic properties found in homesign? Examining the gestures that hearing speakers produce when requested to communicate without speech allows us to explore the robustness of linguistic constructions created on-line in the manual modality.

Hearing gesturers asked to gesture without speaking are able to construct some properties of language with their hands. For example, the order of the gestures they construct on the spot indicates who does what to whom (Gershkoff-Stowe & Goldin-Meadow 2002,

Goldin-Meadow et al. 1996). However, hearing gesturers do not display other linguistic properties found in established sign languages and even in homesign. For example, they do not use consistent form-meaning pairings akin to morphemes (Singleton et al. 1993), nor do they use the same finger complexity patterns that established sign languages and homesign display (Brentari et al. 2012).

Interestingly, the gestures that hearing speakers construct on the spot without speech do not appear to be derived from their spoken language. When hearing speakers of different languages (English, Spanish, Chinese, Turkish) are asked to describe animated events using their hands and no speech, they abandon the order typical of their respective spoken languages and produce gestures that all conform to the same order—SOV (e.g., captain-pail-swings; Goldin-Meadow et al. 2008). This order has been found in some emerging sign languages (e.g., Al-Sayyid Bedouin Sign Language; Sandler et al. 2005). Moreover, the SOV order is also found when hearing speakers of the same four languages perform a noncommunicative, nongestural task (Goldin-Meadow et al. 2008). Recent work on English-, Turkish-, and Italian-language speakers has replicated the SOV order in hearing gesturers but finds that gesturers move away from this order when given a lexicon (either spoken or manual; Hall et al. 2010), when asked to describe reversible events involving two animates (girl pulled man; Meir et al. 2010), and when asked to describe more complex events (man tells child that girl catches fish; Langus & Nespor 2010). Studies of hearing gesturers give us the opportunity to manipulate conditions that have the potential to affect communication, and to then observe the effect of those conditions on the structure of the emerging language.

Do Signers Gesture?

We have seen that hearing speakers produce analog, imagistic signals in the manual modality (i.e., gesture) along with the segmented, discrete signals they produce in the oral modality (i.e., speech), and that these gestures serve a number of communicative and cognitive functions. The question we now ask is whether signers also produce gestures and, if so, whether those gestures serve the same functions as cospeech gesture.

Deaf signers have been found to gesture when they sign (Emmorey 1999). But do they produce mismatches, and do those mismatches predict learning? ASL-signing deaf children were asked to explain their solutions to the same math problems studied in hearing children (Perry et al. 1988) and were then given instruction in those problems in ASL. The deaf children produced gestures as often as the hearing children. Moreover, the deaf children who produced many gestures conveying different information from their signs (i.e., gesture-sign mismatches) were more likely to succeed after instruction than the deaf children who produced few (Goldin-Meadow et al. 2012).

These findings suggest not only that mismatch can occur within a single modality (hand alone), but also that within-modality mismatch can predict learning just as well as cross-modality mismatch (hand and mouth). Juxtaposing different ideas across two modalities is thus not essential for mismatch to predict learning. Rather, it appears to be the juxtaposition of different ideas across two distinct representational formats—an analog format underlying gesture versus a discrete segmented format underlying words or signs—that is responsible for mismatch predicting learning.

GESTURE'S ROLE IN THE CLINIC AND THE CLASSROOM

The gestures learners spontaneously produce when they talk provide insight into their thoughts—often their cutting-edge thoughts. This fact opens up the possibility that gesture can be used to assess children's knowledge in the clinic and the classroom. Moreover, the fact that encouraging learners to gesture on a task can lead to better understanding of the task opens up the possibility that gesture can also

Aphasia:
an impairment in
language ability caused
by trauma, stroke,
tumor, infection, or
dementia

be used to change what children know in the clinic or the classroom.

Clinical Situations

Gesture can provide unique information about the nature and extent of underlying deficits in children and adults with a variety of language and communication disorders (Capone & McGregor 2004, Goldin-Meadow & Iverson 2010). Studies of a range of disordered populations across the lifespan have identified subgroups on the basis of gesture use and then examined future language in relation to subgroup membership. For example, spontaneous gesture production at 18 months in children with early focal brain injury can be used to distinguish children who are likely to recover from initial language delay from children who are not likely to recover (Sauer et al. 2010).

As another example, infants subsequently diagnosed with autism produce fewer gestures overall and almost no instances of pointing at 12 months, compared to typically developing infants at the same age (Osterling & Dawson 1994; see also Bernabei et al. 1998). This finding has been replicated in prospective studies of younger infant siblings of older children already diagnosed with autism. Infant siblings who later turn out to be diagnosed with autism have significantly smaller gesture repertoires at 12 and 18 months than infant siblings who do not receive such a diagnosis, and than a comparison group of infants with no family history of autism. Importantly, at early ages, gesture seems to be more informative about future diagnostic status than word comprehension or production—differences between infant siblings later diagnosed with autism and the two comparison groups do not emerge in speech until 18 months of age (Mitchell et al. 2006). Future work is needed to determine whether gesture use (or its lack) is a specific marker of autism or a general marker of language and communication delay independent of etiology.

Early gesture thus appears to be a sign of resilience in children with language difficulties and an indicator that they may not be delayed in the future. In contrast, adults with aphasia who gesture within the first months after the onset of their illness appear to do less well in terms of recovery than aphasic adults who do not gesture (Braddock 2007). An initial pattern of compensation via gesture thus appears to be a positive prognostic indicator for language recovery in children but not in adults. These findings suggest that encouraging gesture might be more helpful to children with language disabilities than to adults.

Educational Situations

Because children's gestures often display information about their thinking that they do not express in speech, gesture can provide teachers with important information about their pupils' knowledge. As reviewed previously, there is evidence that teachers not only detect information that children express in gesture (e.g., Alibali et al. 1997) but also alter their input to children as a function of those gestures (Goldin-Meadow & Singer 2003).

It is also becoming increasingly clear that the gestures teachers produce during their lessons matter for students' learning. Many studies have shown that lessons with gestures promote deeper learning (i.e., new forms of reasoning, generalization to new problem types, retention of knowledge) better than lessons without gestures. For example, Church et al. (2004) examined first-grade students learning about Piagetian conservation from videotaped lessons and found that, for native English speakers, 91% showed deep learning (i.e., added new same judgments) from a speech-plus-gesture lesson, compared to 53% from a speech-only lesson. For Spanish speakers with little English proficiency, 50% showed deep learning from the speech-plus-gesture lesson, compared to 20% from the speech-only lesson. As a second example, Valenzeno et al. (2003) studied preschoolers learning about symmetry from a videotaped lesson and found that children who viewed a speech-plus-gesture lesson succeeded on more than twice as many posttest problems as children who viewed a speech-only lesson

(2.08 versus 0.85 out of 6). Clearly, teachers' gestures can have a substantial impact on student learning. A teacher's inclination to support difficult material with gesture may be precisely what their students need to grasp challenging material.

Building on growing evidence that teachers' gestures matter for student learning, recent studies have sought to characterize how teachers use gesture in naturalistic instructional settings (e.g., Alibali & Nathan 2012, Richland et al. 2007). Other research has sought to instruct teachers about how to effectively use gesture (Hostetter et al. 2006). Given that teachers' gestures affect the information that students take up from a lesson, and given that teachers can alter their gestures if they wish to do so, it may be worthwhile for teachers to use gesture intentionally, in a planned and purposeful fashion, to reinforce the messages they intend to convey.

In light of evidence that the act of gesturing can itself promote learning, teachers and clinicians may also wish to encourage children and patients to produce gestures themselves. Encouraging children to gesture may serve to activate their implicit knowledge, making them particularly receptive to instruction (Broaders et al. 2007). Teachers may also encourage their students to gesture by producing gestures of their own. Cook & Goldin-Meadow (2006) found that children imitated their instructor's gestures in a lesson about a mathematics task and, in turn, children's gestures predicted their success on the math problems after instruction. Thus, teacher gesture promoted student gesture, which in turn fostered cognitive change.

CONCLUSIONS

We have seen that gesture is a robust part of human communication and can be harnessed in a variety of ways. First, gesture reflects what speakers know and can therefore serve as a window onto their thoughts. Importantly, this window often reveals thoughts that speakers do not even know they have. Encouraging speakers (e.g., students, patients, witnesses) to gesture thus has the potential to uncover thoughts that would be useful for individuals who interact with these speakers (teachers, clinicians, interviewers) to know. Second, gesture can change what speakers know. The act of producing gesture can bring out previously unexpressed thoughts and may even introduce new thoughts into a speaker's repertoire, altering the course of a conversation or developmental trajectory as a result. Encouraging gesture thus also has the potential to change cognition. Finally, gesture provides building blocks that can be used to construct a language. By watching how children and adults who do not already have a language put those blocks together, we can observe the process of language creation first hand. Our hands are with us at all times, and we routinely use them for communication. They thus provide both researchers and learners with an ever-present tool for understanding how we talk and think.

SUMMARY POINTS

1. The gestures that speakers produce along with their speech not only help speakers produce, and listeners understand, that speech, but they can also convey information on their own (i.e., listeners can glean information from gesture that is not conveyed in the accompanying speech).

2. The gestures children produce at the earliest stages of language learning precede speech and predict which nouns a child is likely to acquire and when the child will begin to produce two-word utterances.

3. The gestures children produce can play a causal role in language learning by eliciting timely input from parents and other adults and by providing an early medium in which to practice expressing ideas symbolically.

4. After language has been mastered, gesture continues to predict learning in both children and adults. Learners who convey information in gesture that differs from the information in speech on a particular task are likely to learn when given instruction in that task.

5. The gestures that children and adults produce can play a causal role in learning through social mechanisms, that is, by conveying information about learners' knowledge states to listeners who, in turn, alter the input they provide to the learners.

6. The gestures that children and adults produce can also alter the state of their own knowledge, thus playing a more direct role in learning through cognitive mechanisms (e.g., by activating implicit knowledge, by lightening their cognitive load, by highlighting perceptual or motor information).

7. When the manual modality is called upon to fulfill the communicative functions of language, as in sign languages of the deaf, it also assumes language's segmented and combinatorial form.

8. The segmentation and combination that characterize established languages, signed or spoken, is also found in newly emerging sign languages, for example, in deaf children whose hearing losses prevent them from learning the speech that surrounds them and whose hearing parents have not exposed them to sign, and in hearing speakers asked to communicate using their hands and not their mouths.

FUTURE ISSUES

1. We know very little about individual differences with respect to gesturing. Are some individuals particularly likely to produce gestures not just on one task but on all tasks? Are some particularly likely to rely on gestures when listening to speech? Are some particularly likely to rely on gesture in a learning task, and, if so, are these the same individuals (that is, does reliance on gesture in one area predict reliance on gesture in another)?

2. When gesture is produced at the earliest stage of language learning, it often substitutes for a word that the child has not yet acquired. Gesture continues throughout development to convey ideas that are not expressed in speech, but often those ideas cannot easily be translated into a single word. As a result, once children have become proficient language users, we might expect to see a change in the kinds of ideas that gesture conveys. Future work is needed to determine when this transition takes place.

3. Encouraging school-aged children to gesture on a task makes those children ready to profit from instruction on that task, suggesting that gesture can play a causal role in learning. A question for future work is whether gesture plays the same instrumental role in all learners (e.g., young learners who are at the earliest stages of language learning; old learners who may be losing their capacities) and on all tasks (e.g., spatial tasks whose properties are particularly easy to capture in gesture; nonspatial tasks, such as moral reasoning, whose properties are less easily conveyed through gesture).

4. The absence of gesturing has been found to be a characteristic of young children who are later diagnosed as autistic. A question for future research is whether gesture use (or its absence) is a specific marker of autism or a general marker of language and communication delay independent of etiology.

5. Early gesture has been found to be a sign of resilience in children with language difficulties and an indicator that children who gesture may not be delayed in the future. In contrast, adults with aphasia who gesture within the first months after the onset of their illness often do less well in terms of recovery than aphasic adults who do not gesture. Future work is needed to determine how robust this contrast is.

6. Growing evidence indicates that teachers' gestures matter for students' learning. However, future work is needed to establish a set of empirically based recommendations for teachers about how to most effectively use gesture in classrooms and other instructional settings.

7. Homesigns, the gesture systems profoundly deaf children born to hearing parents use to communicate if they are not exposed to sign language, exhibit many—but not all—of the properties found in natural language. Exploring the conditions under which homesign takes on more and more linguistic properties would provide insight into factors that may have shaped human language in the past and that may influence current-day language learning.

DISCLOSURE STATEMENT

The authors are not aware of any affiliations, memberships, funding, or financial holdings that might be perceived as affecting the objectivity of this review.

ACKNOWLEDGMENTS

Preparation of this review was supported by NIDCD R01-DC00491, NICHD P01-HD40605 and R01-HD47450, NSF BCS-0925595 and NSF Science of Learning Center funding SBE-0541957 to S.G.M. and by NSF DRL-0909699 and 0816406 to M.W.A.

LITERATURE CITED

Acredolo LP, Goodwyn SW. 1988. Symbolic gesturing in normal infants. *Child Dev.* 59:450–56

Acredolo LP, Goodwyn SW. 2002. *Baby Signs: How to Talk with Your Baby Before Your Baby Can Talk*. New York: McGraw-Hill

Alac M, Hutchins E. 2004. I see what you are saying: action as cognition in fMRI brain mapping practice. *J. Cogn. Cult.* 4:629–61

Alibali MW, Flevares L, Goldin-Meadow S. 1997. Assessing knowledge conveyed in gesture: Do teachers have the upper hand? *J. Educ. Psychol.* 89:183–93

Alibali MW, Goldin-Meadow S. 1993. Gesture-speech mismatch and mechanisms of learning: what the hands reveal about a child's state of mind. *Cogn. Psychol.* 25:468–523

Alibali MW, Heath DC, Myers HJ. 2001. Effects of visibility between speaker and listener on gesture production: Some gestures are meant to be seen. *J. Mem. Lang.* 44:169–88

Alibali MW, Kita S. 2010. Gesture highlights perceptually present information for speakers. *Gesture* 10:3–28

Alibali MW, Nathan MJ. 2012. Embodiment in mathematics teaching and learning: Evidence from students' and teachers' gestures. *J. Learn. Sci.* 21:207–15

Alibali MW, Spencer RC, Knox L, Kita S. 2011. Spontaneous gestures influence strategy choices in problem solving. *Psychol. Sci.* 22:1138–44

Bates E. 1976. *Language and Context: The Acquisition of Pragmatics.* New York: Academic

Bates E, Benigni L, Bretherton I, Camaioni L, Volterra V. 1979. *The Emergence of Symbols: Cognition and Communication in Infancy.* New York: Academic

Beilock SL, Goldin-Meadow S. 2010. Gesture changes thought by grounding it in action. *Psychol. Sci.* 21:1605–10

Bergmann K, Kopp S. 2010. Systematicity and idiosyncrasy in iconic gesture use: empirical analysis and computational modeling. In *Gesture in Embodied Communication and Human-Computer Interaction*, ed. S Kopp, I Wachsmuth, pp. 182–94. Berlin/Heidelberg, Germany: Springer

Bernabei P, Camaoini L, Levi G. 1998. An evaluation of early development in children with autism and pervasive developmental disorders from home movies: preliminary findings. *Autism* 2:243–58

Bonvillian JD, Orlansky MO, Novack LL. 1983. Developmental milestones: sign language acquisition and motor development. *Child Dev.* 54:1435–45

Braddock BA. 2007. *Links between language, gesture, and motor skill: a longitudinal study of communication recovery in Broca's aphasia.* PhD thesis, Univ. Missouri-Columbia

Brentari D, Coppola M, Mazzoni L, Goldin-Meadow S. 2012. When does a system become phonological? Handshape production in gesturers, signers, and homesigners. *Nat. Lang. Linguistic Theory* 30(1):1–31

Broaders SC, Cook SW, Mitchell Z, Goldin-Meadow S. 2007. Making children gesture brings out implicit knowledge and leads to learning. *J. Exp. Psychol.: Gen.* 136:539–50

Broaders SC, Goldin-Meadow S. 2010. Truth is at hand: how gesture adds information during investigative interviews. *Psychol. Sci.* 21:623–28

Butterworth G, Grover L. 1988. The origins of referential communication in human infancy. In *Thought Without Language*, ed. L Weiskrantz, pp. 5–24. Oxford: Oxford Univ. Press

Capirci O, Iverson JM, Pizzuto E, Volterra V. 1996. Communicative gestures during the transition to two-word speech. *J. Child Lang.* 23:645–73

Capone N, McGregor K. 2004. Gesture development: a review for clinical and research practices. *J. Speech Lang. Hear. Res.* 47:173–86

Carpenter M, Nagell K, Tomasello M. 1998. Social cognition, joint attention, and communicative competence from 9 to 15 months of age. *Monogr. Soc. Res. Child Dev.* 63:i–vi, 1–143

Chawla P, Krauss RM. 1994. Gesture and speech in spontaneous and rehearsed narratives. *J. Exp. Soc. Psychol.* 30:580–601

Chen Pichler D. 2008. Acquisition of word order: then and now. In *Selected Papers from the 8th Congress on Theoretical Issues in Sign Language Research*, ed. J Quer, pp. 293–315. Seedorf, Germany: Signum-Verlag

Church RB. 1999. Using gesture and speech to capture transitions in learning. *Cogn. Dev.* 14:313–42

Church RB, Ayman-Nolley S, Mahootian S. 2004. The role of gesture in bilingual education: Does gesture enhance learning? *Int. J. Bilingual Educ. Bilingualism* 7:303–19

Church RB, Goldin-Meadow S. 1986. The mismatch between gesture and speech as an index of transitional knowledge. *Cognition* 23:43–71

Church RB, Schonert-Reichl K, Goodman N, Kelly S, Ayman-Nolley S. 1995. The role of gesture and speech communication as a reflection of cognitive understanding. *J. Contemp. Legal Issues* 6:237–80

Coerts JA. 2000. Early sign combinations in the acquisition of Sign Language of the Netherlands: evidence for language-specific features. In *Language Acquisition By Eye*, ed. C Chamberlain, JP Morford, R Mayberry, pp. 91–109. Mahwah, NJ: Erlbaum

Cook SW, Goldin-Meadow S. 2006. The role of gesture in learning: Do children use their hands to change their minds? *J. Cogn. Dev.* 7:211–32

Cook SW, Yip T, Goldin-Meadow S. 2012. Gestures, but not meaningless movements, lighten working memory load when explaining math. *Lang. Cogn. Proc.* 27:594–610

Coppola M, Newport EL. 2005. Grammatical subjects in homesign: abstract linguistic structure in adult primary gesture systems without linguistic input. *Proc. Natl. Acad. Sci. USA* 102:19249–53

Coppola M, Senghas A. 2010. The emergence of deixis in Nicaraguan signing. In *Sign Languages: A Cambridge Language Survey*, ed. D Brentari, pp. 543–69. Cambridge, UK: Cambridge Univ. Press

Coppola M, Spaepen E, Goldin-Meadow S. 2012. Communicating about number without a language model: Linguistic devices for number are robust. Under review

de Laguna G. 1927. *Speech: Its Function and Development*. Bloomington: Indiana Univ. Press

Emmorey K. 1999. Do signers gesture? In *Gesture, Speech, and Sign*, ed. LS Messing, R Campbell, pp. 133–59. Oxford: Oxford Univ. Press

Enfield NJ. 2005. The body as a cognitive artifact in kinship representations. Hand gesture diagrams by speakers of Lao. *Curr. Anthropol.* 46(1):51–81

Evans MA, Rubin KH. 1979. Hand gestures as a communicative mode in school-aged children. *J. Genet. Psychol.* 135:189–96

Feldman H, Goldin-Meadow S, Gleitman L. 1978. Beyond Herodotus: the creation of language by linguistically deprived deaf children. In *Action, Symbol, and Gesture: The Emergence of Language*, ed. A Lock, pp. 351–414. New York: Academic

Flaherty M, Goldin-Meadow S. 2010. Does input matter? Gesture and homesign in Nicaragua, China, Turkey, and the USA. In *Proceedings of the Eighth Evolution of Language Conference*, ed. ADM Smith, M Schouwstra, BD Boer, K Smith, pp. 403–4. Singapore: World Sci. Publ.

Franklin A, Giannakidou A, Goldin-Meadow S. 2011. Negation, questions, and structure building in a home-sign system. *Cognition* 118:398–416

Garber P, Goldin-Meadow S. 2002. Gesture offers insight into problem solving in adults and children. *Cogn. Sci.* 26:817–31

Gershkoff-Stowe L, Goldin-Meadow S. 2002. Is there a natural order for expressing semantic relations? *Cogn. Psychol.* 45:375–412

Goldin-Meadow S. 2003a. *Hearing Gesture: How Our Hands Help Us Think*. Cambridge, MA: Harvard Univ. Press

Goldin-Meadow S. 2003b. *The Resilience of Language: What Gesture Creation in Deaf Children Can Tell Us About How All Children Learn Language*. New York: Psychol. Press

Goldin-Meadow S, Butcher C. 2003. Pointing toward two-word speech in young children. In *Pointing: Where Language, Culture, and Cognition Meet*, ed. S Kita, pp. 85–107. Mahwah, NJ: Erlbaum

Goldin-Meadow S, Butcher C, Mylander C, Dodge M. 1994. Nouns and verbs in a self-styled gesture system: What's in a name? *Cogn. Psychol.* 27:259–319

Goldin-Meadow S, Gelman S, Mylander C. 2005. Expressing generic concepts with and without a language model. *Cognition* 96:109–26

Goldin-Meadow S, Goodrich W, Sauer E, Iverson JM. 2007a. Young children use their hands to tell their mothers what to say. *Dev. Sci.* 10:778–85

Goldin-Meadow S, Iverson JM. 2010. Gesturing across the lifespan. In *Cognition, Biology, and Methods Across the Lifespan*, ed. WF Overton, pp. 36–55. Hoboken, NJ: Wiley

Goldin-Meadow S, Kim S, Singer M. 1999. What the teachers' hands tell the students' minds about math. *J. Educ. Psychol.* 91:720–30

Goldin-Meadow S, McNeill D, Singleton J. 1996. Silence is liberating: removing the handcuffs on grammatical expression in the manual modality. *Psychol. Rev.* 103:34–55

Goldin-Meadow S, Morford M. 1985. Gesture in early child language: studies of deaf and hearing children. *Merrill-Palmer Q.* 31:145–76

Goldin-Meadow S, Mylander C. 1983. Gestural communication in deaf children: the non-effects of parental input on language development. *Science* 221:372–74

Goldin-Meadow S, Mylander C. 1998. Spontaneous sign systems created by deaf children in two cultures. *Nature* 91:279–81

Goldin-Meadow S, Mylander C, Franklin A. 2007b. How children make language out of gesture: morphological structure in gesture systems developed by American and Chinese deaf children. *Cogn. Psychol.* 55:87–135

Goldin-Meadow S, Nusbaum H, Kelly SD, Wagner SM. 2001. Explaining math: gesturing lightens the load. *Psychol. Sci.* 12:516–22

Goldin-Meadow S, Sandhofer CM. 1999. Gesture conveys substantive information about a child's thoughts to ordinary listeners. *Dev. Sci.* 2:67–74

Goldin-Meadow S, Shield A, Lenzen D, Herzig M, Padden C. 2012. The gestures ASL signers use tell us when they are ready to learn math. *Cognition* 123:448–53

Goldin-Meadow S, Singer MA. 2003. From children's hands to adults' ears: gesture's role in the learning process. *Dev. Psychol.* 39:509–20

Goldin-Meadow S, So W-C, Özyürek A, Mylander C. 2008. The natural order of events: how speakers of different languages represent events nonverbally. *Proc. Natl. Acad. Sci. USA* 105:9163–68

Goldin-Meadow S, Wein D, Chang C. 1992. Assessing knowledge through gesture: using children's hands to read their minds. *Cogn. Instr.* 9:201–19

Golinkoff RM. 1986. "I beg your pardon?": the preverbal negotiation of failed messages. *J. Child Lang.* 13:455–76

Goodwin C. 2007. Environmentally coupled gestures. In *Gesture and the Dynamic Dimensions of Language*, ed. S Duncan, J Cassell, E Levy, pp. 195–212. Amsterdam/Philadelphia: Benjamins

Goodwyn S, Acredolo L. 1998. Encouraging symbolic gestures: a new perspective on the relationship between gesture and speech. In *The Nature and Functions of Gesture in Children's Communication*, ed. JM Iverson, S Goldin-Meadow, pp. 61–73. San Francisco: Jossey-Bass

Greenfield P, Smith J. 1976. *The Structure of Communication in Early Language Development*. New York: Academic

Guidetti M. 2002. The emergence of pragmatics: forms and functions of conventional gestures in young French children. *First Lang.* 22:265–85

Guillaume P. 1927. Les debuts de la phrase dans le langage de l'enfant. *J. Psychol.* 24:1–25

Hall M, Mayberry R, Ferreira V. 2010. Communication systems shape the natural order of events: competing biases from grammar and pantomime. In *Abstr. 4th Conf. Intl. Soc. Gesture Stud.*, Frankfurt an der Oder, Germany

Hoffmeister R, Wilbur R. 1980. Developmental: the acquisition of sign language. In *Recent Perspectives on American Sign Language*, ed. H Lane, F Grosjean, pp. 64–78. Hillsdale, NJ: Erlbaum

Holler J, Shovelton H, Beattie G. 2009. Do iconic hand gestures really contribute to the communication of semantic information in a face-to-face context? *J. Nonverbal Behav.* 33:73–88

Hostetter AB. 2011. When do gestures communicate? A meta-analysis. *Psychol. Bull.* 137:297–315

Hostetter AB, Alibali MW. 2007. Raise your hand if you're spatial: relations between verbal and spatial skills and gesture production. *Gesture* 7:73–95

Hostetter AB, Alibali MW. 2008. Visible embodiment: gestures as simulated action. *Psychon. Bull. Rev.* 15:495–514

Hostetter AB, Alibali MW. 2010. Language, gesture, action! A test of the Gesture as Simulated Action framework. *J. Mem. Lang.* 63:245–57

Hostetter AB, Alibali MW, Kita S. 2007. I see it in my hands' eye: Representational gestures reflect conceptual demands. *Lang. Cogn. Proc.* 22:313–36

Hostetter AB, Bieda K, Alibali MW, Nathan MJ, Knuth EJ. 2006. Don't just tell them, show them! Teachers can intentionally alter their instructional gestures. In *Proceedings of the 28th Annual Conference of the Cognitive Science Society*, ed. R Sun, pp. 1523–28. Mahwah, NJ: Erlbaum

Hunsicker D, Goldin-Meadow S. 2012. Hierarchical structure in a self-created communication system: building nominal constituents in homesign. *Language*. In press

Iverson JM, Capirci O, Caselli MS. 1994. From communication to language in two modalities. *Cogn. Dev.* 9:23–43

Iverson JM, Capirci O, Longobardi E, Caselli MC. 1999. Gesturing in mother-child interactions. *Cogn. Dev.* 14:57–75

Iverson JM, Capirci O, Volterra V, Goldin-Meadow S. 2008. Learning to talk in a gesture-rich world: early communication of Italian versus American children. *First Lang.* 28:164–81

Iverson JM, Goldin-Meadow S. 1998. Why people gesture when they speak. *Nature* 396:228

Iverson JM, Goldin-Meadow S. 2005. Gesture paves the way for language development. *Psychol. Sci.* 16:368–71

Jacobs N, Garnham A. 2007. The role of conversational hand gestures in a narrative task. *J. Mem. Lang.* 56:291–303

Kegl J, Senghas A, Coppola M. 1999. Creation through contact: sign language emergence and sign language change in Nicaragua. In *Language Creation and Language Change: Creolization, Diachrony, and Development*, ed. M DeGraff, pp. 179–237. Cambridge, MA: MIT Press

Kelly SD, Church RB. 1997. Can children detect conceptual information conveyed through other children's nonverbal behaviors? *Cogn. Instr.* 15:107–34

Kelly SD, Church RB. 1998. A comparison between children's and adults' ability to detect conceptual information conveyed through representational gestures. *Child Dev.* 69:85–93

Kita S. 2000. How representational gestures help speaking. In *Language and Gesture*, ed. D McNeill, pp. 162–85. Cambridge, UK: Cambridge Univ. Press

Kita S, Özyürek A. 2003. What does cross-linguistic variation in semantic coordination of speech and gesture reveal? Evidence for an interface representation of spatial thinking and speaking. *J. Mem. Lang.* 48:16–32

Klima E, Bellugi U. 1979. *The Signs of Language*. Cambridge, MA: Harvard Univ. Press

Krauss RM. 1998. Why do we gesture when we speak? *Curr. Dir. Psychol. Sci.* 7:54–60

Krauss RM, Chen Y, Chawla P. 1996. Nonverbal behavior and nonverbal communication: What do conversational hand gestures tell us? *Adv. Exp. Soc. Psychol.* 28:389–450

Krauss RM, Chen Y, Gottesman R. 2000. Lexical gestures and lexical access: a process model. In *Language and Gesture*, ed. D McNeill, pp. 261–83. Cambridge, UK: Cambridge Univ. Press

Krauss RM, Dushay R, Chen Y, Rauscher F. 1995. The communicative value of conversational hand gestures. *J. Exp. Soc. Psychol.* 31:533–52

Langus A, Nespor M. 2010. Cognitive systems struggling for word order. *Cogn. Psychol.* 60:291–318

Leopold W. 1949. *Speech Development of a Bilingual Child: A Linguist's Record, Vol. 3*. Evanston, IL: Northwestern Univ. Press

Lillo-Martin D. 1999. Modality effects and modularity in language acquisition: the acquisition of American Sign Language. In *Handbook of Child Language Acquisition*, ed. WC Ritchie, TK Bhatia, pp. 531–67. New York: Academic

Masur EF. 1982. Mothers' responses to infants' object-related gestures: influences on lexical development. *J. Child Lang.* 9:23–30

Masur EF. 1983. Gestural development, dual-directional signaling, and the transition to words. *J. Psycholinguist. Res.* 12:93–109

Mayberry RI. 1992. The cognitive development of deaf children: recent insights. In *Child Neuropsychology*, ed. S Segalowitz, I Rapin, pp. 51–68. Amsterdam: Elsevier

McNeil NM, Alibali MW, Evans JL. 2000. The role of gesture in children's comprehension of spoken language: Now they need it, now they don't. *J. Nonverbal Behav.* 24:131–50

McNeill D. 1992. *Hand and Mind: What Gestures Reveal About Thought*. Chicago: Univ. Chicago Press

McNeill D. 2005. *Gesture and Thought*. Chicago: Univ. Chicago Press

McNeill D, Cassell J, McCullough K-E. 1994. Communicative effects of speech-mismatched gestures. *Res. Lang. Soc. Interact.* 27:223–37

McNeill D, Duncan S. 2000. Growth points in thinking-for-speaking. In *Language and Gesture*, ed. D McNeill, pp. 141–61. Cambridge, UK: Cambridge Univ. Press

Meier RP. 1987. Elicited imitation of verb agreement in American Sign Language: iconically or morphologically determined? *J. Mem. Lang.* 26:362–76

Meir I, Lifshitz A, Ilkbasaran D, Padden C. 2010. The interaction of animacy and word order in human languages: a study of strategies in a novel communication task. In *Proceedings of the Eighth Evolution of Language Conference*, ed. ADM Smith, M Schouwstra, B de Boer, K Smith, pp. 455–56. Singapore: World Sci. Publ.

Melinger A, Levelt WJM. 2004. Gesture and the communicative intention of the speaker. *Gesture* 4:119–41

Mitchell S, Brian J, Zwaigenbaum L, Roberts W, Szatmari P, et al. 2006. Early language and communication development of infants later diagnosed with autism spectrum disorder. *Dev. Behav. Pediatr.* 27:S69–78

Mol L, Krahmer E, Maes A, Swerts M. 2011. Seeing and being seen: the effects on gesture production. *J. Comput. Med. Commun.* 17:77–100

Morford JP. 1995. How to hunt an iguana: the gestured narratives of non-signing deaf children. In *Sign Language Research 1994: Proceedings of the Fourth European Congress on Sign Language Research*, ed. H Bos, T Schermer, pp. 99–115. Hamburg: Signum

Morford M, Goldin-Meadow S. 1992. Comprehension and production of gesture in combination with speech in one-word speakers. *J. Child Lang.* 19:559–80

Morford JP, Goldin-Meadow S. 1997. From here and now to there and then: the development of displaced reference in homesign and English. *Child Dev.* 68:420–35

Morsella E, Krauss RM. 2004. The role of gestures in spatial working memory and speech. *Am. J. Psychol.* 117:411–24

Murphy CM, Messer DJ. 1977. Mothers, infants and pointing: a study of a gesture. In *Studies in Mother-Infant Interaction*, ed. HR Schaffer, pp. 325–54. London: Academic

Namy LL, Acredolo LP, Goodwyn SW. 2000. Verbal labels and gestural routines in parental communication with young children. *J. Nonverbal Behav.* 24:63–79

Newport EL, Meier RP. 1985. The acquisition of American Sign Language. In *The Cross-Linguistic Study of Language Acquisition*, Vol. 1: *The Data*, ed. DI Slobin, pp. 881–938. Hillsdale, NJ: Erlbaum

Osterling J, Dawson G. 1994. Early recognition of children with autism: a study of first birthday home videotapes. *J. Autism Dev. Disord.* 24:247–57

Özçaliskan S, Goldin-Meadow S. 2005. Gesture is at the cutting edge of early language development. *Cognition* 96:B101–13

Özyürek A, Kita S, Allen S, Brown A, Furman R, Ishizuka T. 2008. Development of cross-linguistic variation in speech and gesture: motion events in English and Turkish. *Dev. Psychol.* 44:1040–54

Pan BA, Rowe ML, Singer JD, Snow CE. 2005. Maternal correlates of growth in toddler vocabulary production in low-income families. *Child Dev.* 76:763–82

Perry M, Church RB, Goldin-Meadow S. 1988. Transitional knowledge in the acquisition of concepts. *Cogn. Dev.* 3:359–400

Phillips SBVD, Goldin-Meadow S, Miller PJ. 2001. Enacting stories, seeing worlds: similarities and differences in the cross-cultural narrative development of linguistically isolated deaf children. *Hum. Dev.* 44:311–36

Pine KJ, Lufkin N, Messer D. 2004. More gestures than answers: children learning about balance. *Dev. Psychol.* 40:1059–67

Ping R, Goldin-Meadow S. 2010. Gesturing saves cognitive resources when talking about nonpresent objects. *Cogn. Sci.* 34:602–19

Ping R, Decatur MA, Larson SW, Zinchenko E, Goldin-Meadow S. 2012. *Gesture-speech mismatch predicts who will learn to solve an organic chemistry problem.* Presented at annu. meet. Am. Educ. Res. Assoc., New Orleans

Rauscher FH, Krauss RM, Chen Y. 1996. Gesture, speech, and lexical access: the role of lexical movements in speech production. *Psychol. Sci.* 7:226–31

Richland LE, Zur O, Holyoak KJ. 2007. Cognitive supports for analogies in the mathematics classroom. *Science* 316:1128–29

Roth W-M. 2002. Gestures: their role in teaching and learning. *Rev. Educ. Res.* 71:365–92

Rowe ML. 2000. Pointing and talk by low-income mothers and their 14-month-old children. *First Lang.* 20:305–30

Rowe ML, Goldin-Meadow S. 2009. Differences in early gesture explain SES disparities in child vocabulary size at school entry. *Science* 323:951–53

Rowe ML, Özçalıskan S, Goldin-Meadow S. 2008. Learning words by hand: gesture's role in predicting vocabulary development. *First Lang.* 28:185–203

Sandler W, Lillo-Martin D. 2006. *Sign Language and Linguistic Universals.* Cambridge, UK: Cambridge Univ. Press

Sandler W, Meir I, Padden C, Aronoff M. 2005. The emergence of grammar: systematic structure in a new language. *Proc. Natl. Acad. Sci. Am.* 102:2661–65

Sassenberg U, Van Der Meer E. 2010. Do we really gesture more when it is more difficult? *Cogn. Sci.* 34:643–64

Sauer E, Levine SC, Goldin-Meadow S. 2010. Early gesture predicts language delay in children with pre- and perinatal brain lesions. *Child Dev.* 81:528–39

Senghas A. 1995. The development of Nicaraguan Sign Language via the language acquisition process. *Proc. Boston Univ. Child Lang. Dev.* 19:543–52

Senghas A. 2003. Intergenerational influence and ontogenetic development in the emergence of spatial grammar in Nicaraguan Sign Language. *Cogn. Dev.* 18:511–31

Senghas A, Kita S, Ozyurek A. 2004. Children creating core properties of language: evidence from an emerging sign language in Nicaragua. *Science* 305:1779–82

Shatz M. 1982. On mechanisms of language acquisition: Can features of the communicative environment account for development? In *Language Acquisition: The State of the Art*, ed. E Wanner, L Gleitman, pp. 102–27. New York: Cambridge Univ. Press

Singer MA, Goldin-Meadow S. 2005. Children learn when their teacher's gestures and speech differ. *Psychol. Sci.* 16:85–89

Singleton JL, Morford JP, Goldin-Meadow S. 1993. Once is not enough: standards of well-formedness in manual communication created over three different timespans. *Language* 69:683–715

Streeck J. 2009. *Gesturecraft: The Manu-facture of Meaning*. Amsterdam: Benjamins

Sueyoshi A, Hardison DM. 2005. The role of gestures and facial cues in second language listening comprehension. *Lang. Learn.* 55:661–99

Supalla T. 1990. Serial verbs of motion in American Sign Language. In *Issues in Sign Language Research*, ed. S Fischer, P Siple, pp. 127–52. Chicago: Univ. Chicago Press

Valenzeno L, Alibali MW, Klatzky RL. 2003. Teachers' gestures facilitate students' learning: a lesson in symmetry. *Contemp. Educ. Psychol.* 28:187–204

Wagner SM, Nusbaum H, Goldin-Meadow S. 2004. Probing the mental representation of gesture: Is hand-waving spatial? *J. Mem. Lang.* 50:395–407

Zinober B, Martlew M. 1985. Developmental changes in four types of gesture in relation to acts and vocalizations from 10 to 21 months. *Br. J. Dev. Psychol.* 3:293–306

Zukow-Goldring P. 1996. Sensitive caregivers foster the comprehension of speech: when gestures speak louder than words. *Early Dev. Parenting* 5:195–211

The Antecedents and Consequences of Human Behavioral Mimicry

Tanya L. Chartrand[1] and Jessica L. Lakin[2]

[1] Fuqua School of Business, Duke University, Durham, North Carolina 27708, [2] Department of Psychology, Drew University, Madison, New Jersey 07940; email: TLC10@duke.edu, JLakin@drew.edu

Annu. Rev. Psychol. 2013. 64:285–308

First published online as a Review in Advance on September 27, 2012

The *Annual Review of Psychology* is online at psych.annualreviews.org

This article's doi: 10.1146/annurev-psych-113011-143754

Keywords

imitation, automaticity, nonconscious processes, nonverbal behavior

Abstract

Behavioral mimicry—the automatic imitation of gestures, postures, mannerisms, and other motor movements—is pervasive in human interactions. The current review focuses on two recent themes in the mimicry literature. First, an analysis of the moderators of mimicry uncovers the various motivational, social, emotional, and personality factors that lead to more or less mimicry of an interaction partner in a given situation. Second, a significant amount of recent research has identified important downstream consequences of mimicking or being mimicked by another person. These include not only increased prosociality between interactants, but also unexpected effects on the individual, such as cognitive processing style, attitudes, consumer preferences, self-regulatory ability, and academic performance. Behavioral mimicry is also placed in its broader context: a form of interpersonal coordination. It is compared to interactional synchrony and other social contagion effects, including verbal, goal, and emotional contagion and attitudinal convergence.

Contents

INTRODUCTION

The ubiquity of human mimicry has long been of interest to researchers in fields such as social psychology, communication, clinical psychology, neuroscience, developmental psychology, and consumer behavior. People mimic virtually everything they observe in others, including their motor movements and behaviors (e.g., gestures, mannerisms, postures). This behavioral mimicry can occur automatically, without conscious awareness or intent to imitate. Due to the proliferation of studies on behavioral mimicry in recent years, an exhaustive review is beyond the scope of this article. Instead, we highlight the key findings in the field and focus on two major questions. (*a*) What causes more or less mimicry to occur in a given social interaction? (*b*) What are the downstream consequences of such mimicry occurring, both for the individual and for the dyad? The review is organized as follows. First, we define behavioral mimicry and describe the various types that have been identified. Next, we give a brief historical survey of behavioral mimicry research, describing the initial demonstrations and findings, followed by an in-depth discussion of the moderators and downstream consequences of mimicry. Finally, we place this literature in the broader context of interpersonal coordination, comparing the behavioral mimicry findings to what has been found thus far in the interactional synchrony literature and other literatures related to social contagion.

DEFINITION AND TYPES OF BEHAVIORAL MIMICRY

We first define the terms we will be using. Behavioral mimicry occurs when two or more people engage in the same behavior at the same time. This includes mimicry of mannerisms, gestures, postures, and other motor movements. It is commonly assessed by verifying that people are engaging in the same (or a similar) action at a certain time, or that a particular behavior is repeated by an interaction partner within a short window of time, typically no longer than three to five seconds. Research on behavioral mimicry has examined a variety of motor movements, including yawning (Helt et al. 2010, Provine 1986), body posture (La France 1982, Tia et al. 2011, Tiedens & Fragale 2003), face touching (Chartrand & Bargh 1999, Lakin & Chartrand 2003, Stel et al. 2010b, Yabar et al. 2006), foot shaking (Chartrand & Bargh 1999, Lakin et al. 2008), food consumption (Herrmann et al. 2011, Johnston 2002, Tanner et al. 2008), pen playing (Stel et al. 2010b, van Baaren et al. 2006), coloring (van Leeuwen et al. 2009b), handshake angle and speed (Bailenson & Yee 2007), cospeech gestures (Goldin-Meadow & Alibali 2013, Holler & Wilkin 2011), and a variety of health-related behaviors (e.g., smoking, Harakeh et al. 2007; taking the stairs rather than an escalator, Webb et al. 2011; eating, Hermans et al. 2012). Other research has looked at micro movements, such as finger tapping (van Leeuwen et al. 2009a), and has even tested impossible movements, like a finger movement that appears to cross a physical barrier (Liepelt & Brass 2010).

Recently, Heyes (2011) has argued that stimulus compatibility effects (e.g., quicker response times when opening a hand when someone else opens her hand, as opposed to when she closes her hand; Brass et al. 2001, Leighton et al. 2010) should also be classified as automatic imitation. She suggests that behavioral mimicry is simply a temporal facilitation of a congruent behavioral response compared to an incongruent behavioral response. Stimulus compatibility measures are quite different from other measures of imitation; time is the dependent variable instead of behavior and, unlike other measures of behavioral mimicry, there is a correct response to be given after a stimulus is presented. Will stimulus compatibility measures share the same precursors and consequences as other behavioral mimicry measures? Though there is some evidence to suggest this will be the case (Leighton et al. 2010), it is still quite early.

Mimicry can manifest in other ways as well. People mimic facial expressions (Bavelas et al. 1986, Dimberg et al. 2000, Lundqvist & Dimberg 1995) and emotional reactions (Hatfield et al. 1994, 2009; Hawk et al. 2011; Huntsinger et al. 2009; Neumann & Strack 2000) of interaction partners, often beginning at an extremely young age (Meltzoff & Moore 1983, Termine & Izard 1988). In addition, people mimic verbal characteristics of interaction partners, including accents (Giles et al. 1991), linguistic style (Ireland & Pennebaker 2010, Niederhoffer & Pennebaker 2002), speech rate (Webb 1969), and syntax (Levelt & Kelter 1982). It could be argued that these are, to some extent, behavioral phenomena, but the current review largely focuses on mimicry of gross motor movements. We return to the relationship between behavioral mimicry and other types of social contagion at the end of this review.

Finally, one may ask whether this type of interpersonal coordination is deliberately and consciously engaged in or not (Lakin 2006). Although people intentionally imitate each other all the time, and this is an important component of social learning (Bandura 1977), the mimicry of gross and fine motor movements (e.g., gestures, mannerisms, finger movements), facial expressions, and vocalizations is often nonconscious, unintentional, and effortless. In fact, people often feel it is uncontrollable and are embarrassed when it is pointed out to them (Chartrand et al. 2005, White & Argo 2011). It is this automatic mimicry that we focus on in this review.

EARLY WORK ON BEHAVIORAL MIMICRY

There are several detailed and relatively recent literature reviews focusing on behavioral mimicry (Chartrand & Dalton 2009, Chartrand & van Baaren 2009, van Baaren et al. 2009), but in this article we will offer a brief historical survey in order to provide a context for the most recent discoveries. The early studies of behavioral mimicry chiefly focused on interactions between people who knew one another, such as children and parents (Bernieri et al. 1988), clients and therapists (Charney 1966, Maurer & Tindall 1983, Scheflen 1964), and students and teachers (Bernieri 1988, La France 1979, La France & Broadbent 1976). Behavioral matching was exhibited among all of these groups, often increasing as the duration of contact increased (e.g., Charney 1966).

Though some recent research has continued to explore behavioral mimicry between familiar interactants (e.g., Jones 2007), most has focused upon that which occurs between strangers. Chartrand & Bargh (1999) demonstrated that participants engaged in more foot shaking when with a foot-shaking than face-touching confederate, and more face touching when with a face-touching than foot-shaking confederate. Behavioral mimicry occurred despite the fact that (*a*) the participant and confederates did not know one another, (*b*) welcoming or affiliative behaviors were not performed by the confederates, and (*c*) participants were later unable to recall the confederates' behaviors and the change in their own behaviors. This phenomenon was coined "the chameleon effect" because, much like chameleons change their color to blend into the surrounding environment, humans alter their behavior to blend into social environments (see also Chartrand et al. 2005 and Lakin et al. 2003). Following this initial laboratory demonstration, research turned to uncovering the moderators and consequences of this chameleon-like behavior.

THE MODERATORS: WHO, WHEN, WHERE, AND HOW MUCH DO PEOPLE MIMIC?

Though behavioral mimicry is ubiquitous and engaged in automatically, various features of the social environment and the individuals involved render a person even more susceptible to chameleon-like behaviors.

Facilitators

Pre-existing rapport. When considering the connection between behavioral mimicry and rapport (Tickle-Degnen 2006), it is not surprising that behavioral mimicry increases when one has pre-existing rapport with an interaction partner. Participants mimic friends more than strangers and likeable confederates more than unlikeable confederates (McIntosh 2006; see also Likowski et al. 2008). Stel et al. (2010b) manipulated participants' prior opinions of a confederate by presenting him as either honest and open or dishonest and detached, and effectively replicated the results of McIntosh's earlier study: Participants were more likely to mimic face touching or pen playing with a likeable confederate than with a dislikable confederate. Similarly, Yabar et al. (2006) and Bourgeois & Hess (2008) found evidence that members of an ingroup are mimicked more than people who belong to an outgroup. Even

incidental similarities such as sharing the same first name leads to more mimicry (Guéguen & Martin 2009).

Goal to affiliate. The mere desire to affiliate or create rapport also leads to more behavioral mimicry. Lakin & Chartrand (2003) gave participants either a conscious or unconscious affiliation goal (or no goal) and recorded their behavior while watching a videotaped confederate touch her face subtly and consistently. For the conscious affiliation goal condition, participants were told that they would be interacting with another person in order to complete a task, and it would be beneficial for the task if they got along well; in the unconscious goal condition, participants were subliminally primed using affiliative words (e.g., affiliate, friend, together). Both groups—regardless of the source of the goal—engaged in more face-touching behaviors than did participants in a control no-goal condition. Those with a conscious goal and an unconscious goal showed the same amount of behavioral mimicry.

Leighton et al. (2010) recently generalized this finding to a stimulus compatibility measure of behavioral mimicry by priming participants with prosocial words (similar to those used by Lakin & Chartrand 2003) or antisocial words (e.g., rebel, alone, single) and then asking them to complete a stimulus compatibility task. Participants performed a particular hand-opening or hand-closing action while observing a hand open or close on a computer screen, and reaction times for movement initiation were recorded. The authors posited that automatic behavioral mimicry occurs to the extent that participants move faster when watching a congruent movement than an incongruent one (Heyes 2011). Automatic imitation was greater when participants were primed with prosocial, affiliative words than with antisocial words (for an exception, see Cook & Bird 2011).

There is also evidence that features of the environment that should trigger an affiliation goal in daily life also lead to more mimicry. For instance, Lakin & Chartrand (2003) demonstrated that an unfulfilled affiliation goal—for example, a primed affiliation goal that could not be pursued initially due to the unfriendliness of a confederate—led to increased levels of behavioral mimicry with a new interaction partner. In another set of studies, Cheng & Chartrand (2003) found that high self-monitors—who alter their behavior as a result of affiliative social clues—mimic peers more than nonpeers and the powerful more than the powerless (and mimic more than low self-monitors in either situation; see also Estow et al. 2007). Lakin et al. (2008; see also Lakin & Chartrand 2005, 2012; Over & Carpenter 2009) identified exclusion as a trigger of an affiliative motivation and found that those who had recently experienced social exclusion were especially motivated to affiliate through behavioral mimicry of a subsequent interaction partner. People were selective in whom they mimicked after an exclusion experience; their mimicry of a confederate increased when (*a*) the participant had been excluded by ingroup members and (*b*) the confederate was a member of that ingroup (representing an opportunity to "regain status" within that ingroup). Collectively, these results support a positive correlation between the desire to affiliate—even if it is more acute in certain individuals or groups than others—and an increase in behavioral mimicry.

Individual differences in prosocial orientation. There are also individual differences that impact the amount of behavioral mimicry in which people engage. Some of these variables are loosely related to prosociality (i.e., an increased interest in understanding and relating to others). One example of such a variable is dispositional empathy. Specifically, individuals high in perspective taking mimic an interaction partner more than those who are low in perspective taking (Chartrand & Bargh 1999). Later research extended this to mimicry of facial muscles, with high-empathy participants more likely to mimic both happy and angry expressions, even if exposure to those expressions was short (Sonnby-Borgström 2002; see also Sonnby-Borgström et al. 2003).

People possessing an interdependent self-construal focus on the self as it relates to others relative to those who have a more independent self-construal (Markus & Kitayama 1991). As such, van Baaren et al. (2003b) proposed that those with an interdependent self-construal (either temporarily active through priming or chronically active through cultural transmission) would exhibit more mimicry. Their results supported the hypothesis, as participants were more likely to mimic a confederate's pen-playing behaviors when primed with an interdependent self. Japanese participants were also more likely to mimic the face touching of a confederate than were American participants, regardless of that confederate's ethnicity. A field-dependent cognitive processing style (i.e., where objects are perceived within their context) yielded similar results; both chronic and primed field dependence both resulted in more mimicry than dispositional or situational field independence (van Baaren et al. 2004b).

Similarity. Van Swol & Drury (2006) have examined whether people mimic others more if those others have similar opinions to their own. They found that shared opinions in fact moderate mimicry, such that people engage in more mimicry of a confederate who expresses agreement with them on various viewpoints relative to a confederate who expresses disagreement. Another form of similarity is shared knowledge, and stereotypes can be conceptualized as one form of shared knowledge. As a result, Clark & Kashima (2007) argued that we should mimic another person more if that person expresses stereotypes (thus signaling similarity). Supporting this, Castelli et al. (2009) found that people mimic others who are stereotyping more than those who are not currently stereotyping.

In addition, the amount of mimicry observed also varies as a function of the number of actors who are both observing and producing the behavior. Tsai et al. (2011) predicted that groups would tend to mimic the behaviors of groups more than the behaviors of individuals, presumably due to greater similarity and perceived "appropriateness." They employed a stimulus compatibility measure similar to that used in Leighton et al. (2010), also adding a numerical compatibility manipulation. Participants performed two types of tasks with a confederate: numerically compatible (participants watched two actors perform a behavior in which both participant and confederate then had to engage) or numerically incompatible (participants watched two actors perform a behavior, and the participant alone engaged in said behavior). The results confirmed the hypothesis; groups responded faster with mimicry behavior of other groups, and individuals responded faster with mimicry behavior of single individuals. In short, groups tend to mimic other groups, whereas individuals mimic other individuals.

Mood and emotion. One's current mood and emotional state have also been found to affect behavioral mimicry. van Baaren et al. (2006) induced either a positive or a negative mood in participants with media clips. Afterward, participants watched two experimenters: one who played with a pen and one who did not. The participants in a positive mood mimicked the pen playing more than those in a negative mood. Recently, Likowski et al. (2011) replicated these findings: Happy participants mimicked happy, sad, neutral, and angry facial expressions more than unhappy participants. Although social anxiety is a more chronic form of negative affect, it relates to behavioral mimicry in a similar way; women with high social anxiety are less likely to mimic the head movements of a computerized avatar delivering a speech than are women with lower levels of social anxiety (Vrijsen et al. 2010a).

There is, however, one negative emotion that can actually lead to more mimicry: guilt. Martin et al. (2010) instructed a confederate carrying a stack of papers and other items to exit her office and bump into participants, who were walking down a long narrow hallway. To induce guilt, the confederate blamed the collision on the participant; in conditions inducing no guilt, the confederate took the blame herself. Later, the participants were unobtrusively filmed while watching a recording of a young woman touching her face. The guilty participants exhibited more mimicry, and this was moderated by the degree of guilt felt, with the participants who were not able to make amends (i.e., the confederate left immediately after laying blame) displaying the highest levels of mimicry, presumably in order to forge affiliation in light of their earlier "transgression."

Executive functioning. Research continues to support the notion that behavioral mimicry is the default in most social interactions, occurring even when people are cognitively occupied with other tasks. Van Leeuwen et al. (2009a) had participants perform a finger movement when prompted with either a movement or a spatial cue (i.e., "X") on a screen, half while under working memory load and the other half not. Participants were quicker to respond to the finger movement than the spatial cue, but only when they were under cognitive load; that is, behavioral mimicry increased under cognitive load.

Inhibitors

Less work has focused on inhibitors of mimicry, but some attenuating factors have been found. These are reviewed next.

Goal to disaffiliate. Johnston (2002) found that people mimic less when they do not want to affiliate with another person. Specifically, participants mimicked the ice cream consumption of a confederate less if that confederate was stigmatized in some way (e.g., obese, facial scar). Another variable leading to less mimicry is outgroup status. Yabar et al. (2006) found that non-Christian female participants mimicked the face-touching behavior of openly Christian confederates less than confederates not identified as being from any particular religion. Subsequent studies revealed the underlying mechanism to be a lack of liking. Similarly, Stel et al. (2008) found that when a target is disliked, facial mimicry is attenuated. They also found that the more negative a participant's implicit attitude was toward a racial outgroup, the less someone of that outgroup was mimicked. Thus, when people want to disaffiliate with others, they automatically mimic those others less.

Another variable that may reduce the amount of mimicry in which people engage is one's relationship status. Given the connections between mimicry, rapport, and affiliation, people tend to mimic the behaviors of attractive people—regardless of gender (van Leeuwen et al. 2009b)—to a greater extent. In other words, behavioral mimicry is one potential method of communicating romantic interest (Guéguen 2009, van Straaten et al. 2008). As demonstrated by Karremans & Verwijmeren (2008), however, relationship status moderates these tendencies. Male and female participants who were either in a relationship or not interacted with attractive confederates of the opposite sex for four minutes, during which the confederates rubbed their faces. Participants in a relationship showed lower levels of mimicry than did single participants, and for participants in close committed relationships, levels were lower still. By avoiding mimicry of the attractive, alternative partner, participants appeared to be protecting or shielding their current relationships. In another intriguing use of mimicry inhibition to shield and maintain relationships, people do not mimic the angry facial expressions of their partners (particularly if they are in communal relationships with them), but rather respond spontaneously with a smile. This doesn't hold true for strangers, however; people do mimic their angry expressions (Häfner & IJzerman 2011).

THE CONSEQUENCES: WHAT IMPACT DOES MIMICRY HAVE ON INDIVIDUALS AND THEIR RELATIONSHIPS WITH OTHERS?

The previous section focused on the moderators of mimicry: What individual or situational factors lead one to mimic more or less in a given social interaction? Once mimicry occurs, there are both individual and social consequences. People who are mimicked by others become more prosocial, and this is expressed in many

ways, both toward the mimicker and beyond the dyad. People who are mimicked also experience outcomes unrelated to prosociality, and it is to these individual consequences that we turn first.

Consequences for the Individual

Cognitive processing. Being mimicked has the power to change the way that people think in a number of ways. As van Baaren et al. (2004b) demonstrated, mimicry is more likely to occur when one is field dependent, but the reverse is also true: When participants are mimicked (compared to when they are not) they become more field dependent and thus are able to better recall object positions in a complex memory task. This phenomenon has been replicated conceptually with a more assimilative mindset; participants who are mimicked notice more similarities when shown two loosely related images (van Baaren et al. 2009).

Leander et al. (2011a) hypothesized that the assimilative mindset resulting from mimicry might have another consequence. Specifically, they theorized that mimicked individuals might be more likely to conform to stereotypic expectancies. They found that women and African American men who were mimicked (versus not mimicked) performed worse on a math test than did members of groups not stereotypically associated with poor math performance. When participants believed that others held stereotypic expectancies of them, this effect was more pronounced.

Mimicry (or the lack thereof) also serves as a cue for different types of creative thinking. Being mimicked stimulates convergent thinking, whereas not being mimicked leads to an increase in divergent thinking (Ashton-James & Chartrand 2009). Finally, behavioral mimicry affects self-focus; both private and public self-consciousness increase after one is mimicked (Guéguen 2011).

Persuasion and consumer behavior. Another consequence of behavioral mimicry is an increase in persuasion and subsequent changes in consumer behavior and product preferences.

Van Swol (2003) had a confederate, while trying to change the participant's opinion on a topic, imitate his or her behaviors (or not). Later, participants reported that they perceived the mimicking confederate as more knowledgeable and persuasive, even though they did not ultimately change their opinion on the topics. In a twist on this, Bailenson & Yee (2005) found that participants liked a computer avatar that mimicked their head movements more than one that didn't, and were more persuaded by its arguments.

If mimicry affects persuasiveness, it should also affect subsequent consumer preferences and behavior. When introducing a new sports drink to participants, Tanner et al. (2008) had confederates mimic their behaviors (or not); those who were mimicked enjoyed the product more and stated a higher likelihood of purchasing it than did those who were not mimicked. In a later study, this effect proved to be stronger when the facilitator expressed open investment in the product. Recently, this phenomenon was replicated in an applied context by Jacob et al. (2011; see also Herrmann et al. 2011). Salespeople mimicked both verbal and nonverbal behaviors of their patrons; customers were then more likely to buy a product, especially those recommended by the sales clerk, and clerk and store both received better evaluations. In fact, these effects were not limited to the person being mimicked. Participants expressed opinions that were more favorable after mimicking the behaviors of a model displaying a product on a television commercial, and showed stronger intent to purchase (Stel et al. 2011a; see also Tanner et al. 2008).

Self-regulatory ability. Given how much mimicry we encounter in our daily lives, it would be adaptive to develop "expectations" or schemas for how much mimicry there typically is in a given type of social interaction. Dalton et al. (2010) argued that just as people organize relevant information about interacting with others into schemas, they might also incorporate (implicitly) learned information and rules concerning mimicry into schemas that can

be (unconsciously) deployed when necessary. They posited implicit mimicry schemas, which essentially are unconsciously held expectations for levels of mimicry. Moreover, when those expectations are violated, they suggested that self-regulatory ability and self-control should be diminished (i.e., people should be "depleted"). Finkel et al. (2006) found that people who were mimicked did better on a fine-motor control task than did people who were not mimicked. Dalton et al. (2010) replicated this difference for a very different self-control task: eating junk food. Specifically, those who were mimicked ate less junk food than did people who were not mimicked. Dalton et al. (2010) further found that it was the conditions in which there was no mimicry that were driving these effects. Compared to participants who had been mimicked or who interacted with another person through a divider, participants who had not been mimicked at all procrastinated more on an upcoming math task. This suggests that it is not the case that being mimicked repletes resources; rather, not being mimicked depletes resources (when there is an expectation of some default amount of mimicry).

The previous studies are consistent with two different explanations: a lack of mimicry in itself being depleting, and a violation of implicit expectations for mimicry being depleting. To test these competing accounts, Dalton et al. examined a situation in which there is typically not a lot of mimicry: cross-race interactions (J.D. Heider and J.J. Skowronski, unpublished manuscript., Dep. Psychol., Stephen F. Austin State Univ., Nacogdoches, Texas).

If it is simply not being mimicked that leads to self-regulatory depletion, then not being mimicked by someone of a different race should lead to more depletion. If, however, it is the violation of implicit expectations that leads to the depletion, then the presence of a lot of mimicry in a cross-race interaction should lead to more depletion. The results supported the latter account. The authors also found a similar pattern with power differences; people who were mimicked by someone who had power over them (which presumably violated implicit expectations) showed worse performance on a Stroop task than did those who were not mimicked, while the reverse was true for those who were mimicked by someone over whom they had power.

Extension to embodied cognition. Leander and colleagues (2012) recently extended the notion of implicit schemas for mimicry into the embodiment domain. Previous research has found that mimicry can elicit feelings of disliking and threat if applied to the wrong person or situation (Liu et al. 2011, Stel et al. 2010a). Thus, Leander et al. (2012) argued that an inappropriate amount of behavioral mimicry (either too much or too little) might serve as a basic cue to suspicion; it might signal social coldness or that something is "off," which could lead to physical feelings of chill or coldness (Bargh & Shalev 2012, Zhong & Leonardelli 2008). Across several studies, the authors found that being mimicked either more or less than implicitly anticipated led people to feel colder and guess the current temperature of a room to be colder.

Social Consequences

The previous review suggests that mimicry has many important consequences for the individual, including cognitive processing style, performance on tests of ability, creativity, preferences in consumer products, self-control and self-regulatory ability, and physical feelings of coldness. However, there are also consequences of mimicry that go beyond the individual; these are the prosocial consequences. Mimicry creates liking, empathy, and affiliation between interactants. It has been called the "social glue" that brings people together and bonds them (Lakin et al. 2003).

Liking and empathy. As evidenced earlier in the review, many of the factors that increase behavioral mimicry are related in some way to affiliation and rapport. It is perhaps not surprising then that one of the most robust and early findings in the mimicry literature was the

impact it has on prosociality. Most of the early work was correlational, revealing a strong positive association between shared postures and self-reported rapport. For example, an increase in rapport between a patient and therapist corresponded with increased postural mimicry on behalf of the patient (Charney 1966; see also Scheflen 1964); similarly, classrooms in which teachers and students shared behaviors, like posture or arm positioning, also expressed higher levels of rapport (Bernieri 1988, La France & Broadbent 1976). In fact, Bavelas et al. (1986) have argued that mimicry serves a communicative function because mimicry of pained expressions is more likely when eye contact is made; this suggests that feelings are being shared and understood between interaction partners, which is characteristic of empathy (for recent replications of how eye contact affects mimicry, see also Holler & Wilkin 2011, Ramanathan & McGill 2008, and Wang et al. 2010).

Chartrand & Bargh (1999) investigated one causal direction between mimicry and liking by directing a confederate to either mimic or not mimic participants' behaviors. The mimicked participants reported that they liked the confederate more and expressed that the interaction went more smoothly (see also Lakin & Chartrand 2003). Given that bonding between people is important and mimicry increases these bonds, mimicry can be an important tool for people to use when feeling excluded (Lakin et al. 2008). In fact, Kouzakova et al. (2010b) recently demonstrated that low levels of mimicry during an encounter increase cortisol levels, as the body reacts with stress to the implication of rejection. Research has also found that people evaluate their close relationship partners more favorably if they have just had a mimicry-free interaction with a stranger, in theory because that lack of mimicry is akin to mild social exclusion (Kouzakova et al. 2010a).

Behavioral mimicry also leads to feelings of empathy. Maurer & Tindall (1983) established that adolescents found their counselors to be more empathic when mimicked by them, and Stel & Vonk (2010) found that mimicry triggers both affective and cognitive empathetic reactions. It also attenuates typical "belief in a just world" findings and reduces the blaming of innocent victims (Stel et al. 2012). However, the extent to which mimicry leads to empathy depends on how genuine one deems the mimicked emotions. Stel & Vonk (2009) instructed participants to mimic angry and sad expressions as modeled by a popular television character, and although all participants reported feeling the same emotions while mimicking, only the participants who felt the emotions were "real" reported that they were able to assume that character's perspective.

The effects of mimicry on liking were recently replicated in an applied context by Sanchez-Burks et al. (2009). Confederates interviewed Latino and Anglo managers and professionals while either mimicking or not mimicking their behaviors; measures of anxiety and interview performance were collected afterward. Objective analysis of measures including variables such as body language and interpersonal skills revealed that interview performance was better and anxiety lower when participants were mimicked. However, this effect was strongest among the Latino participants, presumably because they were more culturally sensitive to interpersonal cues.

Liking and empathy are not only affected by being mimicked; the mimicker often reports affective benefits from the experience as well. Participants who were instructed to mimic their interaction partner's behaviors reported feeling closer to the mimickee and in general experienced a smoother interaction than did the participants told not to mimic (Stel & Vonk 2010).

When mimicry does not lead to liking. However, increasing amounts of behavioral mimicry do not always lead to more liking between interaction partners. Specifically, mimicking a disliked person or member of a disliked group does not engender rapport. For instance, Stel et al. (2010a) instructed people to mimic the behaviors of a disliked interaction partner and found that mimicry did not lead to increased liking. Similarly, mimicking outgroup

members does not lead to more liking (van der Schalk et al. 2011). Mimicry also does not increase liking when one has to mimic a nonaffiliative expression (i.e., anger; van der Velde et al. 2010). Furthermore, mimicry is not as directly associated with liking when people possess a proself mindset (as opposed to a prosocial mindset; Stel et al. 2011b), have dispositionally high levels of social anxiety (Vrijsen et al. 2010b), or are reminded of money (Liu et al. 2011).

It turns out that one does need to mimic the "right" people to enjoy the positive consequences of mimicry. Recent research has found that mimicking may backfire (in terms of public opinion about one's social competence) if someone mimics an unfriendly person. After watching someone mimicking unfriendly behaviors, people thought the mimicker was less socially competent than someone who mimicked a friendly partner or someone who mimicked no one (Kavanagh et al. 2011).

Helping behavior. Prosociality can manifest in several ways. One is a positive emotional response to the mimicker. Another is a behavioral response: helping the mimicker. In fact, mimicry often leads to displays of helpful behaviors directed both toward the person who did the mimicking and toward others more generally. Customers with servers who verbally mimicked their orders left bigger tips than those whose orders were not repeated verbatim (van Baaren et al. 2003a). In another study, participants were more likely to pick up pens dropped by an experimenter (the mimicker) or by a fellow participant (unrelated to the mimicking) when their nonverbal behaviors had been mimicked (van Baaren et al. 2004a). This latter finding suggests that mimicry leads to a more general prosocial orientation, as the helping behavior extends beyond the mimicry dyad. Supporting this, subsequent findings suggest that mimicry also makes people more likely to donate money to charitable causes (Stel et al. 2008, van Baaren et al. 2004a), help a stranded person (Fischer-Lokou et al. 2011), volunteer to fill out a tedious survey (Ashton-James et al. 2007), and complete a long, critical essay (Guéguen et al. 2011). These effects seem to be influenced by feelings of empathetic concern and extend to the mimickers as well (Stel et al. 2008).

Interdependence and feelings of closeness. A general prosocial orientation should not only entail increased liking and helping, but also a change in the way one sees oneself, or self-construal. Supporting this, mimicry has been found to increase interdependent self-construals (van Baaren et al. 2003b). In another study, after being mimicked participants expressed more interdependent self-descriptors when completing the Twenty Statements Test, reported feeling closer to others, and chose to sit closer to another hypothetical participant whose belongings were left on a chair (Ashton-James et al. 2007). Mimickers have also reported feelings of increased interdependence (Redeker et al. 2011). This change in self-construal and prosocial orientation can have significant consequences: Participants who are mimicked show more support for liberal political ideas and groups (an effect mediated by prosocial feelings toward others; Stel & Harinck 2011).

Trust between interaction partners is another way of operationalizing feelings of closeness. Trusting behaviors tend to increase after a person has been mimicked. For example, mimicked participants seem more willing than those who were not mimicked to divulge personal information to strangers, even when that information could be embarrassing (Guéguen et al. 2012). According to Maddux et al. (2008), mimicry also smoothes the progress of negotiations. They instructed negotiators to either mimic or not mimic partners' behavior and later assessed mimicry's impact on negotiation outcomes. Mimickers experienced higher individual and dyadic gains and were more willing to come to an agreement with others regarding a difficult decision, and the relationship was mediated by interpersonal trust (see also Swaab et al. 2011).

Accuracy in emotion perception. Due to the link between mimicry and empathy, it is not surprising that behavioral mimicry can lead to more accuracy in understanding the emotions of others. Compared to participants who were told to keep their shoulders still, those told to avoid making any facial movements while viewing photographs capturing certain emotions were slower to identify those emotions (Stel & van Knippenberg 2008; see also Oberman et al. 2007). Moreover, affective judgments are influenced by affective cues only if those cues can be mimicked (Foroni & Semin 2011). Recent research has found that when participants are unable to mimic the facial expressions of others (e.g., through getting Botox injections that paralyze facial muscles), they are less accurate at identifying the emotions other people are experiencing (Neal & Chartrand 2011). However, Stel et al. (2009) uncovered a negative consequence of the mimicry-empathy connection from the mimicker's perspective. Compared to people who don't mimic, mimickers have more trouble discerning when an interaction partner is lying, likely because mimicry interferes with objectivity, making it difficult to identify genuine emotions (for more on this, see Maringer et al. 2011).

Reducing prejudice. Another consequence resulting from the link between behavioral mimicry and empathy is a reduction in prejudiced thinking. Inzlicht et al. (2012) had participants watch a video in which a member of an ingroup or outgroup reached for a glass and drank water repeatedly; they were then asked to either mimic the behaviors of the confederate or not before completing measures of both implicit and explicit prejudice. The results showed that levels of both implicit and explicit prejudice went down when the participant mimicked an outgroup member compared to an ingroup member. Thus, although people may be generally less likely to mimic outgroup behaviors (Dalton et al. 2010; J.D. Heider and J.J. Skowronski, unpublished manuscript., Dep. Psychol., Stephen F. Austin State Univ., Nacogdoches, Texas), when they do, it can lead to a reduction in bias.

RELATIONSHIP BETWEEN BEHAVIORAL MIMICRY AND INTERACTIONAL SYNCHRONY

Research on behavioral mimicry is best understood within the larger context of research on interpersonal coordination. Interpersonal coordination refers to the fact that behaviors in social interactions are often patterned and synchronized; they are similar or identical in form, or they occur at roughly or exactly the same time (Bernieri & Rosenthal 1991, Lakin 2012). These two facets of interpersonal coordination loosely reflect the differences between behavioral mimicry and interactional synchrony. Whereas behavioral mimicry always yields behaviors that are similar in form and close in timing, interactional synchrony may or may not yield behaviors that are similar in form. And although the behaviors of interaction partners occur close in time when observing behavioral mimicry, timing of behaviors is critical to determining whether one person is in sync with others. The complexity of the issue of timing in interactional synchrony cannot be underestimated; because interactional synchrony involves more than one person, it requires anticipation of another person's behaviors so that movement can be coordinated (Knoblich et al. 2011, Marsh et al. 2009, Schmidt & Richardson 2008, Sebanz & Knoblich 2009). However, the evidence to date demonstrates that both the precursors and the consequences of behavioral mimicry and interactional synchrony are often similar (see below), suggesting that both reliably serve the goal of interpersonal coordination more broadly, which is to facilitate and regulate the numerous and complex social interactions people navigate daily (Chartrand & van Baaren 2009, Knoblich & Sebanz 2006, Lakin et al. 2003, Marsh et al. 2009).

A short review of the developing literature on interactional synchrony can illustrate some of the similarities with and differences from the behavioral mimicry literature. Bernieri and his colleagues were the first to experimentally demonstrate that interactional synchrony can be reliably observed in social interactions; compared to unknown interaction partners, mothers were judged to be more in sync with their own children (Bernieri et al. 1988) and teachers were judged to be more in sync with their own students (Bernieri 1988). Since these initial demonstrations, researchers have explored many phenomena that can be synchronized, such as leg movements when walking (van Ulzen et al. 2008) or sitting (Schmidt et al. 1990), body posture sway when conversing (Shockley et al. 2003, Varlet et al. 2010), eye movements (Richardson & Dale 2005), clapping (Neda et al. 2000), pendulum swinging (Richardson et al. 2005, Schmidt & O'Brien 1997), rocking chair movement (Richardson et al. 2007), waving (Lakens 2010), finger tapping (Oullier et al. 2008), music making (e.g., piano playing; Keller et al. 2007), and dancing (Kirschner & Tomasello 2010).

Subsequent research has also demonstrated, consistent with the earlier work of Bernieri and colleagues, that true therapist-client interactions are more synchronous than pseudointeractions (Ramseyer & Tschacher 2011). Other moderators of interactional synchrony effects are remarkably similar to the moderators of behavioral mimicry effects reviewed earlier; people synchronize more with others with whom they have positive relationships (Julien et al. 2000, Miles et al. 2010a), those with whom they might want to develop positive relationships (Miles et al. 2011), and those with whom they have self-disclosed (Vacharkulksemsuk & Fredrickson 2012). Additionally, people who either dispositionally or temporarily have a prosocial orientation synchronize their behaviors with interaction partners more than people who have a proself orientation (Lumsden et al. 2012).

Not surprisingly, the prosocial consequences of being in sync with an interaction partner are also quite similar to the prosocial consequences of being behaviorally mimicked by an interaction partner. Interpersonal synchrony increases liking: Compared to conditions where participants tapped alone or asynchronously with an experimenter, those who tapped synchronously reported more liking for the experimenter (Hove & Risen 2009). Conceptual replications have shown that synchronous behavior increases perceptions of similarity, feelings of closeness, and rapport with partners as well (Mazzurega et al. 2011; Paladino et al. 2010; Vacharkulksemsuk & Fredrickson 2012; Valdesolo et al. 2010; Wiltermuth 2012a,b), and can even positively impact the therapeutic process (Ramseyer & Tschacher 2011). Behaving synchronously also promotes cooperation and helping behavior (Kirschner & Tomasello 2010, Valdesolo & DeSteno 2011, Wiltermuth & Heath 2009); increases conformity (Paladino et al. 2010), compliance with a request to aggress (Wiltermuth 2012a), and obedience (Wiltermuth 2012b); improves memory for information provided by and about an interaction partner (Macrae et al. 2008, Miles et al. 2010b); increases pain thresholds (Cohen et al. 2010); and engenders judgments of entitativity (Lakens 2010, Lakens & Stel 2011, Miles et al. 2009). With few exceptions, then, a strong case can be made for the prosociality of interactional synchrony. It remains to be seen if the same consequences for the individual arise from synchrony as well.

There are other similarities between the behavioral mimicry and interactional synchrony literatures. Interpersonal coordination is a skill that would have been important in our evolutionary history, as getting along with others and creating and maintaining social bonds would have been critical for both social and physical survival (Lakin et al. 2003, Rizzolatti & Craighero 2004). Thus, it is not surprising that there may be common neurological underpinnings to behavioral mimicry and interactional synchrony (Hogeveen & Obhi 2011, Obhi et al. 2011). A review of this work is beyond the scope of this article, but suffice it to say, the recent exciting work on mirror neurons has begun to outline the nature of this common biological foundation (interested readers can consult a number of recent reviews for more detailed information: Heyes 2011, Hurley 2008, Iacoboni 2009, Knoblich et al. 2011).

On the other hand, there are some differences between the mimicry and synchrony literatures, and it is not clear yet the degree to which these differences will be important moving forward. One of the largest differences between work on behavioral mimicry and interactional synchrony has been the focus on timing. The timing of behavior is inherently important when thinking about interactional synchrony, but researchers have focused on this issue much less when thinking about behavioral mimicry (depending on the methodology utilized, some have largely ignored this issue). It is also fair to say that past research on behavioral mimicry has taken a broader view of the phenomenon, focusing heavily on moderators and consequences of our chameleon-like tendencies. The different levels of analysis in each literature have led to correspondingly different levels of information about the specifics of each phenomenon, although to some degree this is changing as interest in the correlates and consequences of interactional synchrony increases.

RELATIONSHIP BETWEEN BEHAVIORAL MIMICRY AND OTHER TYPES OF SOCIAL CONTAGION

In addition to understanding behavioral mimicry in the context of interpersonal coordination, one can also think about behavioral mimicry as an example of a much broader phenomenon known as social contagion. In other words, mimicry does not occur solely for gross motor behavior: Individuals mimic many different aspects of their social experiences, including other people's verbal behaviors, emotions, goals, and attitudes. Despite the fact that these other types of contagion are often less direct than simply observing a behavior in one's environment and then ultimately producing the same or very similar output, social contagion occurs frequently and unconsciously.

Verbal Mimicry

Beyond observable behaviors, people also imitate their interaction partners' vocal behaviors, including syntax (Levelt & Kelter 1982), speech rates (Webb 1969), and accents (Giles et al. 1991). Recent research extended these findings to demonstrate that people also mimic the general linguistic style of others, including number of spoken words and the degree to which different types of words are utilized (e.g., prepositions, past tense verbs, function words; Ireland & Pennebaker 2010, Niederhoffer & Pennebaker 2002).

Emotional Contagion

Humans often spontaneously read and take on the emotional and affective states of others, a phenomenon known as emotional contagion (Hatfield et al. 1994, 2009). For example, in one demonstration, Neumann & Strack (2000) presented participants with a clip of a neutral speech that was read in either a slightly happy or slightly sad tone. Participants who heard the happy speech reported being in a better mood than participants who heard the sad speech. Additionally, when participants in a separate study repeated the speech that they had heard, objective raters indicated that they mimicked the affective tone of the original speech (i.e., participants who heard the slightly happy speech repeated the speech in a happier tone than participants who heard the slightly sad speech). An actual interaction with others is not even necessary to catch their moods; when people are motivated to affiliate with others, they will match their moods to others in anticipation of those interactions (Huntsinger et al. 2009).

In another set of studies, Lundqvist & Dimberg (1995) exposed participants to visual images of faces expressing several different emotions (e.g., sadness, anger, happiness). In addition to demonstrating that participants mimicked the specific patterns of muscular activity associated with the different emotional expressions (see also Dimberg et al. 2000), participants reported experiencing the related emotion (see also McIntosh 2006). There are moderators to this effect [e.g., people who interpret self-produced emotional cues are more likely to experience emotional contagion from facial expressions (Laird et al. 1994);

women may experience emotional contagion more than men (Sonnby-Borgström et al. 2008)], but it seems reasonable to assume that emotional contagion effects are at least sometimes grounded in people's automatic mimicry of others' facial expressions (although there is debate about this issue; e.g., Hess & Blairy 2001).

Goal Contagion

People also automatically pursue goals associated with important significant others. That is, goals can be "caught" from others in the same way that verbal characteristics and emotions can be (Fitzsimons & Finkel 2010). In one of several studies, Fitzsimons & Bargh (2003) showed that participants who had a goal to understand their best friend's behaviors made situational attributions for another's behavior when subliminally primed with their best friend's name more than did participants who did not have this goal. Similarly, participants who had a goal to make their mother proud worked harder on a difficult task when primed with their mothers than did participants who did not have this goal associated with their mother. Whereas the Fitzsimons & Bargh (2003) findings suggest that significant others activate goals we often have when we are with those significant others, Shah (2003) found that significant others can also activate goals that they chronically have for us. He also found that these effects are moderated by closeness to the other individual.

These effects are not limited to those with whom we have a close relationship; just witnessing another person's behavior causes people to automatically infer the underlying goal (Hassin et al. 2005) and then adopt and pursue that goal themselves (Aarts et al. 2004). Aarts et al. (2004) coined this "goal contagion" and have found that we even "catch" goals of strangers. Subsequent work on goal contagion has found that it is moderated by consistency with chronic motives, perception of effort, group membership, and goal strength (Aarts et al. 2005, Dik & Aarts 2007, Leander et al. 2011b, Loersch et al. 2008).

Attitudinal Mimicry

More general attitudes can be caught and shared as well, even when those attitudes are self-relevant. One particularly striking example has been supplied by Sinclair and colleagues. In their studies, participants adopted attitudes similar to those of another person with whom they were interacting, especially if they were motivated to affiliate with that person (Sinclair et al. 2005b). Self-evaluations (i.e., attitudes about the self) and behavior also shifted to be more in accord with the attitudes of others when affiliative motivation was high (Sinclair et al. 2005a). It has been argued that adopting the attitudes of others, even when those attitudes might be personally detrimental or constraining, contributes to the development of a shared reality, which establishes and maintains social bonds (Hardin & Higgins 1996).

FUTURE DIRECTIONS

This review only begins to explore a few of the questions that still need to be addressed as we move forward in our understanding of these phenomena, as behavioral mimicry, interactional synchrony, and social contagion more generally continue to garner the attention of scholars. There are other questions, however, worthy of future attention beyond those that have already been raised.

First, as evidenced by this review, one issue that will be important to explore in future research is the relationship between interpersonal coordination, as demonstrated by both behavioral mimicry and interactional synchrony, and social contagion more generally. Both behavioral mimicry and interactional synchrony create rapport and smooth social interactions; some social contagion effects accomplish this goal as well. Additionally, all three phenomena seem to occur mostly outside of conscious awareness and without intent. On the other hand, each phenomenon is unique in some ways; behavioral mimicry and interactional synchrony involve fairly direct coordination of visible behavioral output, whereas social contagion rarely deals with output that is physically observable. Timing plays a critical role in interactional synchrony, whereas it is somewhat less of an issue in behavioral mimicry, and even less of an issue in certain types of social contagion. What is the nature of the relationship between these three phenomena? Are they all examples of the same basic underlying process? Looking at the relationships between these literatures will be complicated by the fact that scholars in many different areas research these topics, and approaches to studying these phenomena vary greatly.

For the behavioral mimicry literature specifically, there are several avenues of investigation that should be particularly fruitful in the next decade or so. For example, the behaviors that have been explored thus far have been reasonably neutral, such as leg crossing and face touching; it remains to be seen if people will mimic valenced behaviors to the same degree. It might be especially important to explore negative behaviors and the consequences of coordination—typically positive—in this negative context. Another question is when mimicry versus complementarity should be observed in the nonverbal behaviors of interaction partners. A difference in status between interactants seems to be one variable that can lead to complementarity rather than mimicry (Tiedens & Fragale 2003), as can relationship status (Häfner & IJzerman 2011). Are there other variables that have similar effects? What is the exact relationship between mimicry and complementarity?

Behavioral mimicry has thus far almost exclusively been examined within the dyad (for an exception, see Tsai et al. 2011). However, future research can explore how mimicry plays out when there are more than two interactants. Examining who tends to be more mimicked within a group might have implications for understanding leadership development or popularity. What mannerisms or gestures tend to be most mimicked? Are there certain personality traits that lead some people to be more mimicked than others? There also has been limited research thus far focusing on the observation of mimicry (or lack thereof) between others.

What kinds of inferences are made about the dynamics of the relationship and about the individuals mimicking more or less than expected?

Finally, antimimicry represents an important direction for future research. Despite sporadic usage of this term, it is not clear exactly how this term should be defined. Consistent with the idea of complementarity, antimimicry might be characterized as performing opposite behaviors (as opposed to just not mimicking), but not all behaviors have clear conceptual opposites; it is also not clear whether engaging in an opposite behavior has consequences that are different from simply not engaging in the behavior. A conceptually related question is whether there can ever be "too much" mimicry (and if so, what the consequences might be). These are rich questions that future research can explore as work on behavioral mimicry continues to deepen.

CONCLUSION

In sum, behavioral mimicry is a ubiquitous phenomenon that often occurs outside of conscious awareness and intent. People mimic frequently in most situations, although certain features of the environment or the individuals involved (including their goals, emotions, attitudes, and certain traits) can increase the amount of mimicry in a given interaction. In fact, people seem to "use" mimicry as a (nonconscious) strategy to get others to like them, increasing the frequency of mimicry in a selective manner when they want to affiliate with another person. This turns out to be an effective and adaptive automatic tendency, because as long as it remains unnoticed, mimicry can lead to prosociality between interaction partners, including increased liking, empathy, smoother interactions, and helping behavior. Being mimicked also has consequences for the individual, influencing outcomes as wide-ranging as cognitive style, attitudes and preferences, and self-regulatory ability. Hopefully future generations of researchers will continue to explore behavioral mimicry and illuminate the functions it serves, the mechanisms underlying it, and the role it plays in building and fostering relationships.

SUMMARY POINTS

1. Behavioral mimicry occurs when two or more people engage in the same behavior at the same time. This includes mimicry of mannerisms, gestures, postures, and other motor movements.

2. Automatic behavioral mimicry has been called the chameleon effect because, much like chameleons change their color to blend into the surrounding environment, humans alter their behavior to blend into social environments.

3. More automatic behavioral mimicry is observed when there is preexisting rapport or a goal to attain such rapport between interactants, when the interactants feel similar to each other, or when one of the interactants is high in prosocial orientation or in a positive mood.

4. Less behavioral mimicry is observed when there is a goal to disaffiliate among interaction partners.

5. There are consequences of behavioral mimicry for individuals being mimicked. Specifically, it impacts the information-processing style they adopt as well as their performance on achievement tasks, creativity, self-control, and consumer preferences and behavior.

6. There are also consequences of behavioral mimicry for social interactions. Individuals who are mimicked manifest greater liking, empathy, helping behavior, closeness and interdependence with others, accuracy in understanding emotions, and reduction in prejudice.

7. Individuals mimic many different aspects of their social experiences as well, including other people's verbal behaviors, emotions, goals, and attitudes. Despite the fact that these other types of social contagion are less direct than behavioral mimicry, they also occur frequently and unconsciously.

FUTURE ISSUES

1. One issue that will be important to explore in future research is the relationship between behavioral mimicry, interactional synchrony, and social contagion more generally. Are they all examples of the same basic underlying process?

2. Behavioral mimicry has thus far focused on neutral behaviors, such as leg crossing and face touching; it remains to be seen if people will mimic valenced behaviors to the same degree.

3. It might be especially important to explore negative behaviors and the consequences of coordination—typically positive—in this negative context.

4. Another question is when mimicry versus complementarity should be observed in the nonverbal behaviors of interaction partners. What is the relationship between mimicry and complementarity?

5. Future research can explore how mimicry plays out when there are more than two interactants. Examining who tends to be more mimicked within a group might have implications for understanding leadership development or popularity.

6. What mannerisms or gestures tend to be most mimicked? Are there certain personality traits that lead some people to be more mimicked than others?

7. What happens when people witness mimicry or a lack of mimicry between other people? What kinds of inferences are made about the dynamics of the relationship and about the individuals mimicking more or less than expected?

DISCLOSURE STATEMENT

The authors are not aware of any affiliations, memberships, funding, or financial holdings that might be perceived as affecting the objectivity of this review.

LITERATURE CITED

Aarts H, Chartrand T, Custers R, Danner U, Dik G, et al. 2005. Social stereotypes and automatic goal pursuit. *Soc. Cogn.* 23:465–90

Aarts H, Gollwitzer PM, Hassin RR. 2004. Goal contagion: Perceiving is for pursuing. *J. Pers. Soc. Psychol.* 87:23–37

Ashton-James C, Chartrand TL. 2009. Social cues for creativity: the impact of behavioral mimicry on convergent and divergent thinking. *J. Exp. Soc. Psychol.* 45:1036–40

Ashton-James C, van Baaren RB, Chartrand TL, Decety J, Karremans J. 2007. Mimicry and me: the impact of mimicry on self-construal. *Soc. Cogn.* 25:518–35

Bailenson JN, Yee N. 2005. Digital chameleons: automatic assimilation of nonverbal gestures in immersive virtual environments. *Psychol. Sci.* 16:814–19

Bailenson JN, Yee N. 2007. Virtual interpersonal touch and digital chameleons. *J. Nonverbal Behav.* 31:225–42

Bandura A. 1977. Self-efficacy: toward a unifying theory of behavioral change. *Psychol. Rev.* 84(2):191–215

Bargh JA, Shalev I. 2012. The substitutability of physical and social warmth in daily life. *Emotion* 12(1):154–62

Bavelas JB, Black A, Lemery CR, Mullett J. 1986. "I show how you feel": motor mimicry as a communicative act. *J. Pers. Soc. Psychol.* 50:322–29

Bernieri FJ. 1988. Coordinated movement and rapport in teacher-student interactions. *J. Nonverbal Behav.* 12:120–38

Bernieri FJ, Reznick JS, Rosenthal R. 1988. Synchrony, pseudosynchrony, and dissynchrony: measuring the entertainment process in mother-infant interactions. *J. Pers. Soc. Psychol.* 54:243–53

Bernieri FJ, Rosenthal R. 1991. Interpersonal coordination: behavior matching and interactional synchrony. In *Fundamentals of Nonverbal Behavior*, ed. RS Feldman, B Rimé, pp. 401–32. New York: Cambridge Univ. Press

Bourgeois P, Hess U. 2008. The impact of social context on mimicry. *Biol. Psychol.* 77:343–52

Brass M, Bekkering H, Prinz W. 2001. Movement observation affects movement execution in a simple response task. *Acta Psychol.* 106:3–22

Castelli L, Pavan G, Ferrari E, Kashima Y. 2009. The stereotyper and the chameleon: the effects of stereotype use on perceivers' mimicry. *J. Exp. Soc. Psychol.* 45:835–39

Charney EJ. 1966. Psychosomatic manifestations of rapport in psychotherapy. *Psychosom. Med.* 28:305–15

Chartrand TL, Bargh JA. 1999. The chameleon effect: the perception-behavior link and social interaction. *J. Pers. Soc. Psycho.* 76:893–910

Chartrand TL, Dalton AN. 2009. Mimicry: its ubiquity, importance, and functionality. In *Oxford Handbook of Human Action*, ed. E Morsella, JA Bargh, PM Gollwitzer, pp. 458–83. New York: Oxford Univ. Press

Chartrand TL, Maddux WW, Lakin JL. 2005. Beyond the perception-behavior link: the ubiquitous utility and motivational moderators of nonconscious mimicry. In *The New Unconscious*, ed. RR Hassin, JS Uleman, JA Bargh, pp. 334–61. New York: Oxford Univ. Press

Chartrand TL, van Baaren RB. 2009. Human mimicry. In *Advances in Experimental Social Psychology*, ed. MP Zanna, pp. 219–74. San Diego, CA: Academic

Cheng CM, Chartrand TL. 2003. Self-monitoring without awareness: using mimicry as a nonconscious affiliation strategy. *J. Pers. Soc. Psychol.* 85:1170–79

Clark AE, Kashima Y. 2007. Stereotypes help people connect with others in the community: a situated functional analysis of the stereotype consistency bias in communication. *J. Pers. Soc. Psychol.* 93:1028–39

Cohen EEA, Ejsmond-Frey R, Knight N, Dunbar RIM. 2010. Rowers' high: behavioural synchrony is correlated with elevated pain thresholds. *Biol. Lett.* 6:106–8

Cook J, Bird G. 2011. Social attitudes differentially modulate imitation in adolescents and adults. *Exp. Brain Res.* 211:601–12

Dalton AN, Chartrand TL, Finkel EJ. 2010. The schema-driven chameleon: how mimicry affects executive and self-regulatory resources. *J. Pers. Soc. Psychol.* 98:605–17

Dik G, Aarts H. 2007. Behavioral cues to others' motivation and goal pursuits: the perception of effort facilitates goal inference and contagion. *J. Exp. Soc. Psychol.* 43:727–37

Dimberg U, Thunberg M, Elmehed K. 2000. Unconscious facial reactions to emotional facial expressions. *Psychol. Sci.* 11:86–89

Estow S, Jamieson JP, Yates JR. 2007. Self-monitoring and mimicry of positive and negative social behaviors. *J. Res. Pers.* 41:425–33

Finkel EJ, Campbell WK, Brunell AB, Dalton AN, Scarbeck SJ, Chartrand TL. 2006. High-maintenance interaction: Inefficient social coordination impairs self-regulation. *J. Pers. Soc. Psychol.* 91:456–75

Fischer-Lokou J, Martin A, Guéguen N. 2011. Mimicry and propagation of prosocial behavior in a natural setting. *Psychol. Rep.* 108:599–605

Fitzsimons GM, Bargh JA. 2003. Thinking of you: nonconscious pursuit of interpersonal goals associated with relationship partners. *J. Pers. Soc. Psychol.* 84:148–63

Fitzsimons GM, Finkel EJ. 2010. Interpersonal influences on self-regulation. *Curr. Dir. Psychol. Sci.* 19:101–5

Foroni F, Semin GR. 2011. When does mimicry affect evaluative judgment? *Emotion* 11:687–90

Giles H, Coupland J, Coupland N. 1991. *Contexts of Accommodation: Developments in Applied Sociolinguistics.* New York: Cambridge Univ. Press

Goldin-Meadow S, Alibali MW. 2013. Gesture's role in speaking, learning, and creating language. *Annu. Rev. Psychol.* 64:257–84

Guéguen N. 2009. Mimicry and seduction: an evaluation in a courtship context. *Soc. Influence* 4:249–55

Guéguen N. 2011. The mimicker is a mirror of myself: impact of mimicking on self-consciousness and social anxiety. *Soc. Behav. Personal.* 39:725–28

Guéguen N, Martin A. 2009. Incidental similarity facilitates behavioral mimicry. *Soc. Psychol.* 40:88–92

Guéguen N, Martin A, Meineri S. 2011. Mimicry and helping behavior: an evaluation of mimicry on explicit helping request. *J. Soc. Psychol.* 151:1–4

Guéguen N, Martin A, Simon J, Meineri S. 2012. Mimicry, sensitive topics, and surveys: when mimickers obtain more intimate revelations through mimicry. *Field Methods.* In press

Häfner M, IJzerman H. 2011. The face of love: spontaneous accommodation as social emotional regulation. *Pers. Soc. Psychol. Bull.* 37:1551–63

Harakeh Z, Engels RC, van Baaren RB, Scholte RH. 2007. Imitation of cigarette smoking: an experimental study in smoking in a naturalistic setting. *Drug Alcohol Depend.* 86:199–206

Hardin CD, Higgins ET. 1996. Shared reality: how social verification makes the subjective objective. In *Handbook of Motivation and Cognition: The Interpersonal Context*, ed. ET Higgins, RM Sorrentino, 3:28–77. New York: Guilford

Hassin RR, Aarts H, Ferguson MJ. 2005. Automatic goal inferences. *J. Exp. Soc. Psychol.* 41:129–40

Hatfield E, Cacioppo JT, Rapson RL. 1994. *Emotional Contagion*. New York: Cambridge Univ. Press

Hatfield E, Rapson RL, Le YL. 2009. Primitive emotional contagion: recent research. In *The Social Neuroscience of Empathy*, ed. J Decety, W Ickes, pp. 19–30. Cambridge, MA: MIT Press

Hawk ST, Fischer AH, Van Kleef GA. 2011. Taking your place or matching your face: two paths to empathic embarrassment. *Emotion* 11:502–13

Helt MS, Eigsti IM, Snyder PJ, Fein DA. 2010. Contagious yawning in autistic and typical development. *Child Dev.* 81:1620–31

Hermans RCJ, Lichtwarck-Aschoff A, Bevelander KE, Herman CP, Larsen JK, Engels RC. 2012. Mimicry of food intake: the dynamic interplay between eating companions. *PLoS ONE* 7(2):e31027

Herrmann A, Rossberg N, Huber F, Landwehr JR, Henkel S. 2011. The impact of mimicry on sales—evidence from field and lab experiments. *J. Econ. Psychol.* 32:502–14

Hess U, Blairy S. 2001. Facial mimicry and emotional contagion to dynamic emotional facial expressions and their influence on decoding accuracy. *Int. J. Psychophysiol.* 40:129–41

Heyes C. 2011. Automatic imitation. *Psychol. Bull.* 137:463–83

Hogeveen J, Obhi SS. 2011. Altogether now: Activating interdependent self-construal induces hypermotor resonance. *Cogn. Neurosci.* 2:74–82

Holler J, Wilkin K. 2011. Co-speech gesture mimicry in the process of collaborative referring during face-to-face dialogue. *J. Nonverbal Behav.* 35:133–53

Hove MJ, Risen JL. 2009. It's all in the timing: Interpersonal synchrony increases affiliation. *Soc. Cogn.* 27:949–61

Huntsinger JR, Lun J, Sinclair S, Clore GL. 2009. Contagion without contact: Anticipatory mood matching in response to affiliative motivation. *Pers. Soc. Psychol. Bull.* 35:909–22

Hurley S. 2008. The shared circuits model (SCM): how control, mirroring, and simulation can enable imitation, deliberation, and mindreading. *Behav. Brain Sci.* 31:1–22

Iacoboni M. 2009. Imitation, empathy, and mirror neurons. *Annu. Rev. Psychol.* 60:653–70

Ireland ME, Pennebaker JW. 2010. Language style matching in writing: synchrony in essays, correspondence, and poetry. *J. Pers. Soc. Psychol.* 99:549–71

Inzlicht M, Gutsell JN, Legault L. 2012. Mimicry reduces racial prejudice. *J. Exp. Soc. Psychol.* 48(1):361–65

Jacob C, Guéguen N, Martin A, Boulbry G. 2011. Retail salespeople's mimicry of customers: effects on consumer behavior. *J. Retailing Consum. Serv.* 18:381–88

Johnston L. 2002. Behavioral mimicry and stigmatization. *Soc. Cogn.* 20:18–35

Jones SS. 2007. Imitation in infancy: the development of mimicry. *Psychol. Sci.* 18:593–99

Julien D, Brault M, Chartrand E, Bégin J. 2000. Immediacy behaviours and synchrony in satisfied and dissatisfied couples. *Can. J. Behav. Sci.* 32:84–90

Karremans JC, Verwijmeren T. 2008. Mimicking attractive opposite-sex others: the role of romantic relationship status. *Pers. Soc. Psychol. Bull.* 34:939–50

Kavanagh L, Suhler C, Churchland P, Winkielman P. 2011. When it's an error to mirror: the surprising reputational costs of mimicry. *Psychol. Sci.* 22:1274–76

Keller PE, Knoblich G, Repp BH. 2007. Pianists duet better when they play with themselves: on the possible role of action simulation in synchronization. *Conscious. Cogn. Int. J.* 16:102–11

Kirschner S, Tomasello M. 2010. Joint music making promotes prosocial behavior in 4-year-old children. *Evol. Hum. Behav.* 31:354–64

Knoblich G, Butterfill S, Sebanz N. 2011. Psychological research on joint action: theory and data. In *The Psychology of Learning and Motivation*, ed. B Ross, pp. 59–101. Waltham, MA: Academic

Knoblich G, Sebanz N. 2006. The social nature of perception and action. *Curr. Dir. Psychol. Sci.* 15:99–104

Kouzakova M, Karremans JC, van Baaren RB, van Knippenberg A. 2010a. A stranger's cold shoulder makes the heart grow fonder: why not being mimicked by a stranger enhances longstanding relationship evaluations. *Soc. Psychol. Personal. Sci.* 1:87–93

Kouzakova M, van Baaren R, van Knippenberg A. 2010b. Lack of behavioral imitation in human interactions enhances salivary cortisol levels. *Horm. Behav.* 57:421–26

La France M. 1979. Nonverbal synchrony and rapport: analysis by the cross-lag panel technique. *Soc. Psychol. Q.* 42:66–70

La France M. 1982. Posture mirroring and rapport. In *Interaction Rhythms: Periodicity in Communicative Behavior*, ed. M Davis, pp. 279–98. New York: Human Sci. Press

La France M, Broadbent M. 1976. Group rapport: posture sharing as a nonverbal indicator. *Group Organ. Manage.* 1:328–33

Laird JD, Alibozak T, Davainis D, Deignan K, Fontanella K, et al. 1994. Individual differences in the effects of spontaneous mimicry on emotional contagion. *Motiv. Emot.* 18:231–47

Lakens D. 2010. Movement synchrony and perceived entitativity. *J. Exp. Soc. Psychol.* 46:701–8

Lakens D, Stel M. 2011. If they move in sync, they must feel in sync: Movement synchrony leads to attributions of rapport and entitativity. *Soc. Cogn.* 29:1–14

Lakin JL. 2006. Automatic cognitive processes and nonverbal communication. See Manusov & Patterson 2006, pp. 59–77

Lakin JL. 2012. Behavioral mimicry and interactional synchrony. In *Handbook of Communication Science*, ed. JL Hall, ML Knapp. Berlin: Mouton de Gruyter. In press

Lakin JL, Chartrand TL. 2003. Using nonconscious behavioral mimicry to create affiliation and rapport. *Psychol. Sci.* 14:334–39

Lakin JL, Chartrand TL. 2005. Exclusion and nonconscious behavioral mimicry. In *The Social Outcast: Ostracism, Social Exclusion, Rejection, and Bullying*, ed. KD Williams, JP Forgas, W von Hippel, pp. 279–95. New York: Psychol. Press

Lakin JL, Chartrand TL. 2012. Behavioral mimicry as an affiliative response to social exclusion. In *The Oxford Handbook of Social Exclusion*, ed. CN DeWall. New York: Oxford Univ. Press. In press

Lakin JL, Chartrand TL, Arkin RM. 2008. I am too just like you: nonconscious behavioral mimicry as an automatic behavioral response to social exclusion. *Psychol. Sci.* 19:816–22

Lakin JL, Jefferis VE, Cheng CM, Chartrand TL. 2003. The chameleon effect as social glue: evidence for the evolutionary significance of nonconscious mimicry. *J. Nonverbal Behav.* 27:145–62

Leander NP, Chartrand TL, Bargh JA. 2012. You give me the chills: embodied reactions to inappropriate amounts of behavioral mimicry. *Psychol. Sci.* 23:772–79

Leander NP, Chartrand TL, Wood W. 2011a. Mind your mannerisms: behavioral mimicry elicits stereotype conformity. *J. Exp. Soc. Psychol.* 47:195–201

Leander NP, Shah JY, Chartrand TL. 2011b. The object of my protection: shielding fundamental motives from the implicit motivational influence of others. *J. Exp. Soc. Psychol.* 47:1078–87

Leighton J, Bird G, Orsini C, Heyes C. 2010. Social attitudes modulate automatic imitation. *J. Exp. Soc. Psychol.* 46:905–10

Levelt WJM, Kelter S. 1982. Surface form and memory in question answering. *Cogn. Psychol.* 14:78–106

Lumsden J, Miles L, Richardson MJ, Smith C, Macrae N. 2012. Who syncs? Social motives and interpersonal coordination. *J. Exp. Soc. Psychol.* 48:746–51

Lundqvist LO, Dimberg U. 1995. Facial expressions are contagious. *J. Psychophysiol.* 9:203–11

Liepelt R, Brass M. 2010. Automatic imitation of physically impossible movements. *Soc. Cognit.* 28:59–73

Likowski KU, Muhlberger A, Seibt B, Pauli P, Weyers P. 2008. Modulation of facial mimicry by attitudes. *J. Exp. Soc. Psychol.* 44:1065–72

Likowski KU, Weyers P, Seibt B, Stohr C, Pauli P, Muhlberger A. 2011. Sad and lonely? Sad mood suppresses facial mimicry. *J. Nonverbal Behav.* 35:101–17

Liu J, Vohs KD, Smeesters D. 2011. Money and mimicry: when being mimicked makes people feel threatened. *Psychol. Sci.* 22:1150–51

Loersch C, Aarts H, Payne BK, Jefferis VE. 2008. The influence of social groups on goal contagion. *J. Exp. Soc. Psychol.* 44:1555–58

Macrae CN, Duffy OK, Miles LK, Lawrence J. 2008. A case of hand waving: action synchrony and person perception. *Cognition* 109:152–56

Maddux WW, Mullen E, Galinsky AD. 2008. Chameleons bake bigger pies and take bigger pieces: Strategic behavioral mimicry facilitates negotiation outcomes. *J. Exp. Soc. Psychol.* 44:461–68

Manusov V, Patterson ML, eds. 2006. *The SAGE Handbook of Nonverbal Communication.* Thousand Oaks, CA: Sage

Maringer M, Krumhuber EG, Fischer AH, Niedenthal PM. 2011. Beyond smile dynamics: mimicry and beliefs in judgments of smiles. *Emotion* 11:181–87

Markus HR, Kitayama S. 1991. Culture and the self: implications for cognition, emotion, and motivation. *Psychol. Rev.* 98:224–53

Marsh KL, Richardson MJ, Schmidt RC. 2009. Social connection through joint action and interpersonal coordination. *Top. Cogn. Sci.* 1:320–39

Martin A, Guéguen N, Fischer-Lokou J. 2010. The impact of guilt on mimicry behavior. *Soc. Behav. Personal.* 38:987–92

Maurer RE, Tindall JH. 1983. Effect of postural congruence on client's perception of counselor empathy. *J. Couns. Psychol.* 30:158–63

Mazzurega M, Pavani F, Paladino MP, Schubert TW. 2011. It is a matter of time: self-other bodily merging in the context of synchronous but arbitrary related multisensory inputs. *Exp. Brain Res.* 213:213–21

McIntosh DN. 2006. Spontaneous facial mimicry, liking, and emotional contagion. *Polish Psychol. Bull.* 37:31–42

Meltzoff AN, Moore MK. 1983. Newborn infants imitate adult facial gestures. *Child Dev.* 54:702–9

Miles LK, Griffiths JL, Richardson MJ, Macrae CN. 2010a. Too late to coordinate: contextual influences on behavioral synchrony. *Eur. J. Soc. Psychol.* 40:52–60

Miles LK, Lumsden J, Richardson MJ, Macrae CN. 2011. Do birds of a feather move together? Group membership and behavioral synchrony. *Exp. Brain Res.* 211:495–503

Miles LK, Nind LK, Henderson Z, Macrae CN. 2010b. Moving memories: behavioral synchrony and memory for self and others. *J. Exp. Soc. Psychol.* 46:457–60

Miles LK, Nind LK, Macrae CN. 2009. The rhythm of rapport: interpersonal synchrony and social perception. *J. Exp. Soc. Psychol.* 45:585–89

Neal DT, Chartrand TL. 2011. Embodied emotion perception: amplifying and dampening facial feedback modulates emotion perception accuracy. *Soc. Psychol. Pers. Sci.* 2:673–78

Neda Z, Ravasz E, Brechte Y, Vicsek T, Barabasi AL. 2000. The sound of many hands clapping. *Nature* 403:849–50

Neumann R, Strack F. 2000. "Mood contagion": the automatic transfer of mood between persons. *J. Pers. Soc. Psychol.* 79:211–23

Niederhoffer KG, Pennebaker JW. 2002. Linguistic style matching in social interaction. *J. Lang. Soc. Psychol.* 21:337–60

Oberman LM, Winkielman P, Ramachandran VS. 2007. Face to face: Blocking facial mimicry can selectively impair recognition of emotional expressions. *Soc. Neurosci.* 2:167–78

Obhi SS, Hogeveen J, Pascual-Leone A. 2011. Resonating with others: the effects of self-construal type on motor cortical output. *J. Neurosci.* 31:14531–35

Oullier O, de Guzman GC, Jantzman KJ, Lagarde J, Scott Kelso JA. 2008. Social coordination dynamics: measuring human bonding. *Soc. Neurosci.* 3:178–92

Over H, Carpenter M. 2009. Priming third-party ostracism increases affiliative imitation. *Dev. Sci.* 12:F1–8

Paladino MP, Mazzurega M, Pavani F, Schubert TW. 2010. Synchronous multisensory stimulation blurs self-other boundaries. *Psychol. Sci.* 21:1202–7

Provine RR. 1986. Yawning as a stereotyped action pattern and releasing stimulus. *Ethology* 72:109–22

Ramanathan S, McGill AL. 2008. Consuming with others: social influences on moment-to-moment and retrospective evaluations of an experience. *J. Consum. Res.* 34:506–24

Ramseyer F, Tschacher W. 2011. Nonverbal synchrony in psychotherapy: Coordinated body movement reflects relationship quality and outcome. *J. Consult. Clin. Psychol.* 79:284–95

Redeker M, Stel M, Mastop J. 2011. Does mimicking others change your self-view? *J. Soc. Psychol.* 151:387–90

Richardson DC, Dale R. 2005. Looking to understand: the coupling between speakers' and listeners' eye movements and its relationship to discourse comprehension. *Cogn. Sci.* 29:1046–60

Richardson MJ, Marsh KL, Isenhower RW, Goodman JR, Schmidt RC. 2007. Rocking together: dynamics of intentional and unintentional interpersonal coordination. *Hum. Mov. Sci.* 26:867–91

Richardson MJ, Marsh KL, Schmidt RC. 2005. Effects of visual and verbal interaction on unintentional interpersonal coordination. *J. Exp. Psychol.: Hum. Percept. Perform.* 31:62–79

Rizzolatti G, Craighero L. 2004. The mirror-neuron system. *Annu. Rev. Neurosci.* 27:169–92

Sanchez-Burks J, Bartel CA, Blount S. 2009. Performance in intercultural interactions at work: cross-cultural differences in response to behavioral mirroring. *J. Appl. Psychol.* 94:216–23

Scheflen AE. 1964. The significance of posture in communication systems. *Psychiatry* 27:316–31

Schmidt RC, Carello C, Turvey MT. 1990. Phase transitions and critical fluctuations in the visual coordination of rhythmic movements between people. *J. Exp. Psychol.: Hum. Percept. Perform.* 16:227–47

Schmidt RC, O'Brien B. 1997. Evaluating the dynamics of unintended interpersonal coordination. *Ecol. Psychol.* 9:189–206

Schmidt RC, Richardson MJ. 2008. Dynamics of interpersonal coordination. In *Coordination: Neural, Behavioral and Social Dynamics*, ed. A Fuchs, VK Jirsa, pp. 281–307. Berlin: Springer-Verlag

Sebanz N, Knoblich G. 2009. Prediction in joint action: what, when, and where. *Top. Cogn. Sci.* 1:353–67

Shah JY. 2003. The motivational looking glass: how significant others implicitly affect goal appraisals. *J. Pers. Soc. Psychol.* 85:424–39

Shockley K, Santana MV, Fowler CA. 2003. Mutual interpersonal postural constraints are involved in cooperative conversation. *J. Exp. Psychol.: Hum. Percept. Perform.* 29:326–32

Sinclair S, Huntsinger J, Skorinko J, Hardin CD. 2005a. Social tuning of the self: consequences for the self-evaluations of stereotype targets. *J. Pers. Soc. Psychol.* 89:160–75

Sinclair S, Lowery BS, Hardin CD, Colangelo A. 2005b. Social tuning of automatic racial attitudes: the role of affiliative motivation. *J. Pers. Soc. Psychol.* 89:583–92

Sonnby-Borgström M. 2002. Automatic mimicry reactions as related to differences in emotional empathy. *Scand. J. Psychol.* 43:433–43

Sonnby-Borgström M, Jönsson P, Svensson O. 2003. Emotional empathy as related to mimicry reactions at different levels of information processing. *J. Nonverbal Behav.* 27:3–23

Sonnby-Borgström M, Jönsson P, Svensson O. 2008. Gender differences in facial imitation and verbally reported emotional contagion from spontaneous to emotionally regulated processing levels. *Scand. J. Psychol.* 49:111–22

Stel M, Blascovich J, McCall C, Mastop J, van Baaren RB, Vonk R. 2010a. Mimicking disliked others: effects of a priori liking on the mimicry-liking link. *Eur. J. Soc. Psychol.* 40:867–80

Stel M, Harinck F. 2011. Being mimicked makes you a prosocial voter. *Exp. Psychol.* 58:79–84

Stel M, Mastop J, Strick M. 2011a. The impact of mimicking on attitudes toward products presented in TV commercials. *Soc. Influence* 6:142–52

Stel M, Rispens S, Leliveld M, Lokhorst AM. 2011b. The consequences of mimicry for prosocials and proselfs: effects of social value orientation on the mimicry-liking link. *Eur. J. Soc. Psychol.* 41:269–74

Stel M, van Baaren RB, Blascovich J, van Dijk E, McCall C, et al. 2010b. Effects of a priori liking on the elicitation of mimicry. *Exp. Psychol.* 57:412–18

Stel M, van Baaren RB, Vonk R. 2008. Effects of mimicking: acting prosocially by being emotionally moved. *Eur. J. Soc. Psychol.* 38:965–76

Stel M, van den Bos K, Bal M. 2012. On mimicry and the psychology of the belief in a just world: Imitating the behaviors of others reduces the blaming of innocent victims. *Soc. Justice Res.* 25:14–24

Stel M, van Dijk, E, Olivier E. 2009. You want to know the truth? Then don't mimic! *Psychol. Sci.* 20:693–99

Stel M, van Knippenberg A. 2008. The role of facial mimicry in the recognition of affect. *Psychol. Sci.* 19:984–85

Stel M, Vonk R. 2009. Empathizing via mimicry depends on whether emotional expressions are seen as real. *Eur. Psychol.* 14:342–50

Stel M, Vonk R. 2010. Mimicry in social interaction: benefits for mimickers, mimickees, and their interaction. *Br. J. Psychol.* 101:311–23

Swaab RI, Maddux WW, Sinaceur M. 2011. Early words that work: when and how virtual linguistic mimicry facilitates negotiation outcomes. *J. Exp. Soc. Psychol.* 47:616–21

Tanner RJ, Ferraro R, Chartrand TL, Bettman JR, van Baaren R. 2008. Of chameleons and consumption: the impact of mimicry on choice and preferences. *J. Consum. Res.* 34:754–66

Termine NT, Izard CE. 1988. Infants' responses to their mothers' expressions of joy and sadness. *Dev. Psychol.* 24:223–29

Tia B, Saimpont A, Paizis C, Mourey F, Fadiga L, Pozzo T. 2011. Does observation of postural imbalance induce a postural reaction? *PLoS ONE* 6(3):e17799

Tickle-Degnen L. 2006. Nonverbal behavior and its functions in the ecosystem of rapport. See Manusov & Patterson 2006, pp. 381–99

Tiedens LZ, Fragale AR. 2003. Power moves: complementarity in dominant and submissive nonverbal behavior. *J. Pers. Soc. Psychol.* 84:558–68

Tsai JC, Sebanz N, Knoblich G. 2011. The GROOP effect: Groups mimic group actions. *Cognition* 118:135–40

Vacharkulksemsuk T, Fredrickson BL. 2012. Strangers in sync: achieving embodied rapport through shared movements. *J. Exp. Soc. Psychol.* 48:399–402

Valdesolo P, DeSteno D. 2011. Synchrony and the social tuning of compassion. *Emotion* 11:262–66

Valdesolo P, Ouyang J, DeSteno D. 2010. The rhythm of joint action: Synchrony promotes cooperative ability. *J. Exp. Soc. Psychol.* 46:693–95

van Baaren RB, Fockenberg DA, Holland RW, Janssen L, van Knippenberg A. 2006. The moody chameleon: the effect of mood on non-conscious mimicry. *Soc. Cogn.* 24:426–37

van Baaren RB, Holland RW, Kawakami K, van Knippenberg A. 2004a. Mimicry and prosocial behavior. *Psychol. Sci.* 15:71–74

van Baaren RB, Holland RW, Steenaert B, van Knippenberg A. 2003a. Mimicry for money: behavioral consequences of imitation. *J. Exp. Soc. Psychol.* 39:393–98

van Baaren RB, Horgan TG, Chartrand TL, Dijkmans M. 2004b. The forest, the trees, and the chameleon: context dependence and mimicry. *J. Pers. Soc. Psychol.* 86:453–59

van Baaren R, Janssen L, Chartrand TL, Dijksterhuis A. 2009. Where is the love? The social aspect of mimicry. *Philos. Trans. R. Soc. B* 364:2381–89

van Baaren RB, Maddux WW, Chartrand TL, de Bouter C, van Knippenberg A. 2003b. It takes two to mimic: behavioral consequences of self-construals. *J. Pers. Soc. Psychol.* 84:1093–102

van der Schalk J, Fischer A, Doosje B, Wigboldus D, Hawk S, et al. 2011. Convergent and discriminant responses to emotional displays of ingroups and outgroups. *Emotion* 11:286–98

van der Velde SW, Stapel DA, Gordijn EH. 2010. Imitation of emotion: when meaning leads to aversion. *Eur. J. Soc. Psychol.* 40:536–42

van Leeuwen ML, van Baaren RB, Martin D, Dijksterhuis A, Bekkering H. 2009a. Executive functioning and imitation: Increasing working memory load facilitates behavioural imitation. *Neuropsychologia* 47:3265–70

van Leeuwen ML, Veling H, van Baaren RB, Dijksterhuis A. 2009b. The influence of facial attractiveness on imitation. *J. Exp. Soc. Psychol.* 45:1295–98

van Straaten I, Engels RC, Finkenauer C, Holland RW. 2008. Sex differences in short-term mate preferences and behavioral mimicry: a semi-naturalistic experiment. *Arch. Sex. Behav.* 37:902–11

Van Swol LM. 2003. The effects of nonverbal mirroring on perceived persuasiveness, agreement with an imitator, and reciprocity in a group discussion. *Commun. Res.* 30:461–80

Van Swol LM, Drury M. 2006. *The effects of shared opinions on nonverbal mimicry*. Paper presented at Annu. Int. Communic. Assoc. Conf., Dresden, Germany van Ulzen NR, Lamoth CJ, Daffertshofer A, Semin GR, Beek PJ. 2008. Characteristics of instructed and uninstructed interpersonal coordination while walking in pairs. *Neurosci. Lett.* 432:88–93

Varlet M, Marin L, Lagarde J, Bardy BG. 2010. Social postural coordination. *J. Exp. Psychol.: Hum. Percept. Perform.* 37:473–83

Vrijsen JN, Lange WG, Becker ES, Rick M. 2010a. Socially anxious individuals lack unintentional mimicry. *Behav. Res. Ther.* 48:561–64

Vrijsen JN, Lange WG, Dotsch R, Wigboldus DHJ, Rinck M. 2010b. How do socially anxious women evaluate mimicry? A virtual reality study. *Cogn. Emot.* 24:840–47

Wang Y, Newport R, Hamilton AFC. 2010. Eye contact enhances mimicry of intransitive hand movements. *Biol. Lett.* 7:7–10

Webb JT. 1969. Subject speech rates as a function of interviewer behaviour. *Lang. Speech* 12:54–67

Webb OJ, Eves FF, Smith L. 2011. Investigating behavioural mimicry in the context of stair/escalator choice. *Br. J. Health Psychol.* 16:373–85

White K, Argo J. 2011. When imitation doesn't flatter: the role of consumer distinctiveness in response to mimicry. *J. Consum. Res.* 38(4):667–80

Wiltermuth SS. 2012a. Synchronous activity boosts compliance with requests to aggress. *J. Exp. Soc. Psychol.* 48:453–56

Wiltermuth SS. 2012b. Synchrony and destructive obedience. *Soc. Influence* 7(2):78–89

Wiltermuth SS, Heath C. 2009. Synchrony and cooperation. *Psychol. Sci.* 20:1–5

Yabar Y, Johnston L, Miles L, Peace V. 2006. Implicit behavioral mimicry: investigating the impact of group membership. *J. Nonverbal Behav.* 30:97–113

Zhong CB, Leonardelli GJ. 2008. Cold and lonely: Does social exclusion literally feel cold? *Psychol. Sci.* 19:838–42

Sexual Prejudice

Gregory M. Herek and Kevin A. McLemore

Department of Psychology, University of California, Davis, California 95616-8686;
email: AR2013@herek.net, KAMcLemore@ucdavis.edu

Annu. Rev. Psychol. 2013. 64:309–33

First published online as a Review in Advance on
September 17, 2012

The *Annual Review of Psychology* is online at
psych.annualreviews.org

This article's doi:
10.1146/annurev-psych-113011-143826

Keywords

sexual stigma, attitudes, prejudice, sexual minorities, lesbians, gay
men, bisexuals, homophobia

Abstract

Despite shifts toward greater acceptance in U.S. public opinion and
policy, lesbian, gay, and bisexual people remain widely stigmatized.
This article reviews empirical research on sexual prejudice, that is, heterosexuals' internalization of cultural stigma, manifested in the form of
negative attitudes toward sexual minorities and same-sex desires and behaviors. After briefly reviewing measurement issues, we discuss linkages
between sexual prejudice and religion, gender, sexuality, and related
variables, and consider how the cultural institutions encompassing these
domains create a social context within which individual expressions of
prejudice can meet important psychological needs. These include needs
for securing social acceptance, affirming values that are central to one's
self-concept, and avoiding anxiety and other negative emotions associated with threats to self-esteem. We conclude by discussing factors
that may motivate heterosexuals to reduce their own sexual prejudice,
including intergroup contact, as well as avenues for future empirical
inquiry.

Contents

INTRODUCTION

An observer of recent cultural trends in the United States might be inclined to ask whether societal and individual hostility toward lesbian, gay, and bisexual people—phenomena that often are subsumed collectively under the rubric of homophobia—are nearing extinction. Several institutional barriers to equality for sexual minorities have fallen in the new millennium, including state sodomy laws and the ban on military service by openly gay and lesbian individuals. A growing number of states provide some degree of legal recognition to same-sex couples and their children, and a majority of the U.S. population now resides in a jurisdiction where sexual minorities are afforded statutory protection against employment discrimination (Herek 2007, Natl. Gay Lesbian Task Force 2012). At the level of individual attitudes, U.S. adults are less condemning of same-sex sexual relations and more supportive of basic civil liberties than at any time since public opinion about these issues began to be measured (Andersen & Fetner 2008, Herek 2009c, Wilcox & Norrander 2002).

Despite these signs of reduced discrimination and greater acceptance, it would be premature to herald the imminent demise of societal stigma and individual prejudice against sexual minorities. A variety of structural factors perpetuate differential treatment based on sexual orientation. For example, many religious institutions still condemn homosexuality and have actively endeavored to prevent or overturn legal protections for sexual minorities (e.g., Herek et al. 2007). Institutional policies create disparities in health care between heterosexuals and lesbian, gay, and bisexual people (Inst. Med. 2011). Gay men have lower annual incomes than comparable heterosexual men (Carpenter 2007, Herek et al. 2007). More than 80% of the states have statutes or constitutional provisions that bar legal recognition of marriages between two adults of the same sex (Natl. Gay Lesbian Task Force 2012), and even in states that recognize their marriage, same-sex couples are denied federal rights and economic benefits under the Defense of Marriage Act, or DOMA (Herek 2006).[1]

Even if all institutional barriers to equality are eventually eliminated, the experiences of racial, ethnic, and religious minorities suggest that individual prejudice and antipathy toward lesbian, gay, and bisexual people will endure. Consistent with this observation, national opinion surveys reveal that substantial numbers of Americans still harbor negative feelings toward sexual minorities (Herek 2002a, Norton & Herek 2012, Wilcox & Norrander 2002). In 2010, the Federal Bureau of Investigation (FBI) recorded more than 1,200 hate crimes based on the victim's sexual orientation (FBI 2011). Because most such crimes are never reported to police authorities (Langton & Planty 2011), the actual incidence is probably much higher. Approximately 20% of sexual minority adults report having experienced crime against their person or property based on their sexual orientation, about half have experienced verbal harassment, and more than one in ten report having experienced employment or

---

Homophobia: originally defined as heterosexuals' dread of close contact with homosexuals, and self-loathing in homosexual individuals; also used to refer to societal hostility toward and discrimination against nonheterosexuals

Sexual minorities: individuals who self-identify as lesbian, gay, or bisexual; experience significant levels of same-sex attractions; or engage in significant amounts of homosexual behavior

Prejudice: a negative attitude (i.e., evaluative response) to a group or to an individual based on her or his group membership

---

[1]As this article goes to press, DOMA has been ruled unconstitutional in several federal cases and appears likely to be reviewed by the U.S. Supreme Court.

housing discrimination (Herek 2009a). Harassment and bullying of children and adolescents because of their perceived nonheterosexual orientation or gender nonconformity are widespread (U.S. Commiss. Civil Rights 2011).

Thus, despite an overall shift toward less hostility and discrimination, prejudice against sexual minorities persists. In this article, we review current knowledge about such prejudice and highlight some ways in which it is often psychologically and socially functional for heterosexuals. Recognizing that the social foundation for individual prejudice varies across cultures, we focus on empirical studies conducted in North America, primarily the United States.[2] We first present a conceptual framework that situates individual prejudice against sexual minorities within the broader context of sexual stigma in society. Then, after briefly reviewing measurement issues, we discuss the associations between sexual prejudice and religion, gender, and related variables, and how the cultural institutions encompassing these domains create a social context within which individual expressions of such prejudice can meet important psychological needs. We conclude by discussing how sexual prejudice can be reduced and identifying topics for empirical inquiry in that area.

HOMOPHOBIA VERSUS SEXUAL PREJUDICE AND STIGMA: A CONCEPTUAL FRAMEWORK

In 1972, psychologist George Weinberg introduced the American public to "homophobia," a word he defined as "the dread of being in close quarters with homosexuals—and in the case of homosexuals themselves, self-loathing" (Weinberg 1972, p. 4). Rejecting the prevailing cultural assumption that homosexuality was

an individual pathology and societal problem, Weinberg instead shifted the focus of attention to Americans' "unwarranted distress" over homosexuality (p. 4). At a time when views of sexuality and gender were rapidly changing and sexual minorities were increasingly challenging their stigmatized status, his analysis received widespread attention. Today homophobia is used around the world to describe hostility toward homosexuality and people who are not heterosexual (Herek 2004).

Although Weinberg's introduction of homophobia marked a watershed in popular thinking about homosexuality and sexual minorities, the term has significant limitations for scientific inquiry (Herek 2004). Perhaps most importantly, it presumes that hostility toward homosexuality is a phobia, which clinicians understand to be an intense fear response associated with unpleasant physiological symptoms that interfere with the individual's life and that the individual recognizes as irrational. Conceptualizing antigay attitudes as a phobia makes two unnecessarily limiting assumptions. First, it focuses on fear as the basis for heterosexuals' negative attitudes toward nonheterosexuals. Fear may indeed play a role for some individuals, but empirical research has not documented it at levels comparable to those observed in other phobias (e.g., Shields & Harriman 1984). Other emotions, including anger and disgust, are probably more prevalent (Giner-Sorolla et al. 2012, Herek 2002a, Parrott et al. 2008).

A second problem is that the phobia construction frames these attitudes as inherently irrational. The multiple meanings of rationality and irrationality (e.g., Kruglanski & Orehek 2009) can be especially confusing in the domain of sexual attitudes. Phobias are considered irrational because their characteristic fear is unwarranted; objectively, the target poses no danger to the individual. In this sense, homophobia is irrational because the gay, lesbian, and bisexual population does not physically endanger homophobic heterosexuals. This fact, however, does not mean that "homophobic" heterosexuals cannot furnish what they consider to be rational

Sexual orientation: an enduring pattern of or disposition to experience sexual, affectional, or romantic desires for and attractions to men, women, or both sexes. Also refers to an individual's sense of personal and social identity based on those desires and attractions, behaviors expressing them, and membership in a community of others who share them

Sexual prejudice: a negative attitude toward an individual based on her or his membership in a group defined by its members' sexual attractions, behaviors, or orientation

Sexual stigma: a culture's shared knowledge about the negative regard, inferior status, and relative powerlessness that society collectively accords to nonheterosexual behaviors, identity, relationships, and communities

[2]For information about attitudes and policies in other countries, see, e.g., United Nations High Commissioner for Human Rights (2011) and the Web sites of the International Lesbian, Gay, Bisexual, Trans, and Intersex Association (**http://www.ilga.org**) and Human Rights Watch (**http://www.hrw.org/topic/lgbt-rights**).

justifications for their negative attitudes, just as many individuals harboring other forms of prejudice provide reasons for it that are at least superficially plausible (e.g., Billig 1988). And, as discussed below, prejudice can be highly rational in a utilitarian or functional sense.

To avoid these limitations, the present article conceives of heterosexuals' negative reactions to sexual minorities not as an individual pathology but rather as the internalization of cultural stigma (e.g., Herek 2009c). We use "sexual stigma" to refer to "the negative regard, inferior status, and relative powerlessness that society collectively accords to nonheterosexual behaviors, identity, relationships, or communities" (Herek 2009c, p. 66). It is a cultural phenomenon rather than a psychological one, comprising knowledge that is shared by the members of society about the devalued status of homosexuality and sexual minorities relative to heterosexuality and heterosexuals.

Although most people know that sexual minorities are devalued, any individual may or may not internalize sexual stigma, that is, endorse it as a part of her or his own value system. For sexual minorities, internalizing sexual stigma involves directing negative feelings inward toward oneself and one's own same-sex attractions, referred to here as "self-stigma." It has also been labeled internalized homophobia, internalized heterosexism, and internalized homonegativity (Herek et al. 2009). By contrast, when heterosexuals internalize sexual stigma, their feelings are directed outward at sexual minorities in the form of negative attitudes, which are referred to here as "sexual prejudice" (Herek 2004, 2009c).

Like homophobia, the term sexual prejudice can spark arguments about the rationality of heterosexuals' attitudes. In popular discussion, "prejudice" often has been defined as an irrational rejection of groups and their members based solely on an emotional reaction or mere personal preference (e.g., Duckitt 1992), a pejorative connotation that can be traced back to the Enlightenment (Billig 1988). Contemporary social psychologists, however, have found that value judgments about whether a prejudice

is rational or irrational, justified or unjustified, are unnecessary and even a hindrance to its scientific study. Consequently, prejudice today is often defined simply as a negative evaluative response (i.e., an attitude) to a group or to an individual based on her or his group membership (e.g., Dovidio & Gaertner 2010, Duckitt 1992, Fiske 2009). Whether or not a person can cite reasons for such an attitude is immaterial to its status as a prejudice. Accordingly, sexual prejudice is used here to refer to a negative attitude toward an individual based on her or his membership in a group defined by sexual attractions, behaviors, or orientation.

Sexual minorities and heterosexuals can each harbor negative attitudes toward the other, and both types of attitudes can be labeled sexual prejudice. However, the two groups' attitudes are not mirror images of each other. Because heterosexuals' prejudice against sexual minorities is founded on cultural stigma, it reinforces—and is reinforced by—power and status differences between the groups. It legitimizes and fosters socially sanctioned enactments of stigma by other majority group members, such as ostracism, discrimination, and even violence. By contrast, a lesbian, gay, or bisexual person's prejudice against heterosexuals is not backed by the devaluing and disempowering effects of stigma (Herek 2007, 2009c). Given the role it plays in perpetuating the vulnerability and inferior status of sexual minorities, we limit our focus to sexual prejudice among heterosexuals.

As an attitude, sexual prejudice—like other forms of prejudice—is based on information that individuals derive from their affective responses, beliefs, and past behaviors (Herek 2009b). It shares many demographic, psychological, and social correlates with other forms of prejudice (Duckitt 1992, Herek 2009c). For example, it tends to be more common among heterosexuals who have a low educational level, are older, reside in rural areas, and manifest high levels of psychological authoritarianism (Herek 2009b). And, as with other forms of prejudice (Pettigrew & Tropp 2006), it is negatively correlated with intergroup contact experiences: Heterosexuals tend to be less prejudiced toward sexual minorities as a group if they have personal relationships with lesbians and gay men.

Despite these similarities, sexual prejudice differs in important ways from many other forms of antiminority prejudice in the contemporary United States (Herek 2009c). Because an individual's sexual orientation is usually not apparent during social interactions, anyone can potentially be perceived as nonheterosexual and consequently face social rejection, loss of status, discrimination, and violence. Understandably, most people wish to avoid such outcomes, and many modify their behavior accordingly. This knowledge about the likelihood that stigma enactments will occur under certain circumstances and the accompanying motivation to avoid them is referred to here as "felt sexual stigma" (Herek 2009c, Herek et al. 2013). It has also been labeled perceived stigma, stereotype awareness, and anticipated stigma (e.g., Corrigan et al. 2006, Quinn & Chaudoir 2009). Whereas some approaches limit consideration of felt stigma to individuals who belong to a stigmatized group, we conceptualize it as including the experiences of majority group members who could potentially be misperceived as part of the minority. As elaborated below, felt stigma often motivates heterosexuals to engage in behaviors whose primary purpose is to avoid being labeled homosexual by others.

Another consequence of sexual orientation's concealability is that heterosexuals often develop close personal relationships with sexual minority individuals before becoming aware of the latter's group membership. Sometimes such relationships even predate the minority individual's own recognition of her or his nonheterosexual orientation. As discussed below, this fact has important implications for the effects of intergroup contact on sexual prejudice.

Sexual prejudice also differs from many other types of prejudice in that it remains acceptable in segments of American society. By contrast, although religious, ethnic, and racial prejudices persist, they are widely condemned

and their expression is typically discouraged by social norms. Moreover, institutional discrimination based on race, ethnicity, and religion has been outlawed and largely eliminated, at least in its obvious manifestations. By contrast, social norms still support sexual prejudice in many settings, and overt sexual stigma remains embedded in many cultural institutions, including the law. The persistence of structural sexual stigma and the widespread social acceptability of sexual prejudice have methodological implications for how it is operationally defined and measured.

MEASURING SEXUAL PREJUDICE

Sexual prejudice can be operationalized in multiple ways. As with other attitude domains, self-report measures have been used most often for this purpose and have included both single-item (e.g., Haddock et al. 1993, Herek 2002b, Wilcox & Norrander 2002, Yang 1997) and multi-item scales. The latter usually require respondents to indicate their level of agreement with a series of evaluative statements about homosexuality or bisexuality, or about sexual minority individuals (e.g., Herek 1994, 2002a; Herek & McLemore 2011; Kite & Deaux 1986; Larsen et al. 1980; Mohr & Rochlen 1999; Morrison et al. 1999; Wright et al. 1999), or report their levels of comfort at the prospect of encountering a gay or lesbian individual in various social settings (e.g., Herek 2009c, Ricketts & Hudson 1998). The results yielded by single- and multi-item approaches are highly correlated. For example, in a 2005 national telephone survey, zero-order correlations between the two types of measures approached $r = 0.60$ (Herek 2009c).

Because prejudices based on race, ethnicity, and many other characteristics are no longer widely acceptable, individuals with such prejudices often are unwilling to express them openly. The measurement challenge created by this reluctance has spurred researchers to develop "modern" prejudice scales whose items are intended to be less blatantly negative than those used in so-called "old-fashioned" measures of racism, sexism, and other prejudices

Felt stigma: knowledge of the existence of stigma and the conditions under which it is likely to be enacted, accompanied by the motivation to avoid being the target of stigma enactments; often manifested in purposeful modification of behavior (e.g., McConahay 1986, Swim et al. 1995). Self-report measures of modern sexual prejudice have also been developed (Cowan et al. 2005, Morrison & Morrison 2002, Raja & Stokes 1998), but they tend to be highly correlated with old-fashioned measures. In a Canadian sample, for example, zero-order correlations between modern and traditional sexual prejudice scales were in excess of $r = 0.70$, indicating an extremely close correspondence between the two types of measures (Morrison & Morrison 2011).[3]

This high level of shared variance is perhaps not surprising. As noted above, much of the public is still willing to express negative attitudes toward sexual minorities. If social trends continue on their present trajectory, however, the acceptability of overt expressions of sexual prejudice may decline to a point where greater divergence is observed between the two types of measures. At present, researchers may find that modern sexual prejudice scales are advantageous mainly in settings where respondents are strongly motivated to present themselves as nonprejudiced, as on college campuses (e.g., Morrison & Morrison 2002, Rye & Meaney 2010; but see Lottes & Grollman 2010).

Traditional and modern operationalizations of sexual prejudice both rely on self-report measures. By contrast, implicit assessment methods have been developed to detect attitudes that a respondent may intentionally distort (e.g., because of social desirability concerns) or that may not be consciously accessible to the respondent (Teige-Mocigemba et al. 2010). They include measures of physiological reactions such as enhanced startle response (Mahaffey et al. 2005) and accelerated heart rate (Shields & Harriman 1984), as well as the Implicit Association Test (IAT; Dasgupta & Rivera 2006, Jellison et al. 2004, Steffens 2005) and other assessments based on differential reaction times to various pairings of stimuli (e.g., Meier

et al. 2006). In the domain of sexual prejudice, the patterns of correlations between these measures and other theoretically relevant variables are similar to those obtained with self-report measures (Jonathan 2008, Lemm 2006, Rowatt et al. 2006). Duplicating a pattern observed with comparable measures of other domains of attitudes, however, may better predict nonverbal and spontaneous behaviors than do explicit measures (Dasgupta & Rivera 2006). As discussed below, they may be especially useful for assessing the underlying motivations for sexual prejudice.

Measuring sexual prejudice inevitably involves referencing sexual orientation, a multidimensional phenomenon that encompasses many components of intimate relationships, including erotic desire, romantic attraction, and sexual behavior. Sexual orientation is also a basis for personal and collective identity, and laws and policies related to it are often a focus of conflicting political, religious, and moral beliefs (e.g., Herek 2006, Inst. Med. 2011). Because of this complexity, operational definitions of sexual prejudice can focus on many different phenomena, including attitudes toward same-sex attractions or sexual behaviors; attitudes toward "homosexuality" or "bisexuality" in general; attitudes toward lesbians, gay men, bisexual women, or bisexual men; and attitudes toward institutional aspects of sexual stigma, such as laws concerning marriage rights or employment discrimination.

Heterosexuals' attitudes across these different aspects of sexual orientation tend to be intercorrelated, but not identical. For example, self-reported affective reactions to sexual minorities are highly correlated with attitudes toward laws and social policy affecting them, but the latter are also independently predicted by political ideology, moral values, and other variables (Brewer 2003, Herek 2009c, Wilcox & Norrander 2002). Heterosexuals' attitudes toward lesbians often differ from their attitudes toward gay men, and their attitudes toward bisexuals differ from their attitudes toward homosexuals (Herek 2002a,b; Norton & Herek 2012). Sexual prejudice researchers, however,

---

[3]These coefficients were uncorrected for attenuation due to the imperfect reliability of the instruments. By our calculations, correcting for attenuation increased these correlations to $r \geq 0.80$.

have not always specified which domains of sexual attitudes they were measuring. For example, some self-report measures refer collectively to "homosexuals" or "LGB people," obscuring variations in attitudes toward sexual minority men versus women, and bisexuals versus homosexuals. Studies examining implicit sexual prejudice have operationalized attitude targets using photographs of same-sex and different-sex couples displaying (e.g., Lemm 2006) or not displaying (e.g., Dasgupta & Rivera 2006, 2008; Jellison et al. 2004) physical contact, same-sex and different-sex name pairs (e.g., Steffens & Buchner 2003), and abstract images such as wedding cake toppers and stick figures (e.g., Jonathan 2008, Weinstein et al. 2012). These stimuli may evoke reactions to, variously, sexual behavior, couples, sexual minority groups, or policy issues. It is important that researchers identify the specific facet of sexual prejudice that is most germane to their research question and ensure that their measures assess it.

PSYCHOLOGICAL FUNCTIONS OF CONTEMPORARY SEXUAL PREJUDICE

Whether sexual prejudice is "rational" can be judged not only by the extent to which an individual is able to supply logically coherent reasons or justifications for it, but also by whether it has utility for meeting personal goals (e.g., Kruglanski & Orehek 2009). In the latter, instrumental sense, attitudes can be considered rational if they benefit the actor, that is, if they facilitate achievement of a desired end by helping to meet one or more important psychological needs. This is the fundamental premise of the functional approach to attitudes: People generally form and maintain attitudes because they are psychologically functional.

For example, sexual prejudice can help individuals to meet affiliative needs by mediating their interpersonal relations and strengthening their bonds with valued groups, a "social adjustment" or "social expressive" function. Alternatively, by providing a vehicle for heterosexuals to assert allegiance to moral, ethical, or political principles that are central to their self-concept, it can serve a "value-expressive" function. Sexual prejudice can also constitute a strategy for coping with anxiety and other negative emotions that result from perceived threats to one's self-esteem, a "defensive" function (Herek 1987a; see generally Katz 1960, Maio & Olson 2000, Smith et al. 1956).

Whether an attitude can meet these and other needs is determined by characteristics of the actor as well as by situational and cultural factors that define the relationship between the attitude object and the actor's social groups, values, and criteria for self-esteem. Thus, the functional perspective highlights the importance of understanding the confluence of dispositional, contextual, and cultural factors that make attitudes toward sexual minorities—whether positive or negative—functional in different ways for different heterosexuals. In the following section, we use this perspective as an organizing framework for explicating and integrating empirical findings about sexual prejudice. We focus on two key cultural institutions that have a variety of robust linkages with sexual prejudice: religion and gender.

Sexual Prejudice and Religion

Questions about the rationality of sexual prejudice and the assumptions underlying the construct of homophobia have particular relevance to the domain of religion. At the aggregate level, sexual prejudice is positively correlated with religiosity, operationally defined in a variety of ways (Herek 1994, Herek & Capitanio 1996, Lewis 2003, Scott 1998, Whitley 2009). Despite this pattern, objections have been raised to the very notion that heterosexuals' negative reactions to sexual minorities can be appropriately considered a prejudice if they are based on religious beliefs. O'Donohue & Caselles (1993), for example, rejected the characterization of such attitudes as "homophobic" and, implicitly, as a prejudice,[4] asserting "it

---

[4]Although religion-based critiques such as that of O'Donohue & Caselles (1993) are often framed in terms of

is not irrational for an individual who believes that an act is immoral to want to avoid people who act in such a manner and to become anxious in the presence of such people or such acts" (p. 190). They proposed instead that "fear and avoidance [of homosexuals and homosexuality] in the presence of intellectual reactions which include negative moral arguments might be... simply called a reaction based on a moral stance and, hence... rational" (O'Donohue & Caselles 1993, p. 192). Similarly, Rosik (2007) argued for differentiating "between prejudice and a formed moral judgment, whereby individuals conduct a rational assessment of relevant concerns and make moral evaluations, while allowing for a legitimate diversity of belief" (p. 142). For reasons already discussed, we do not label negative reactions to sexual minorities homophobic whether they stem from religious or other sources. However, the mere fact that intergroup attitudes are grounded in moral beliefs or religion does not exempt them from being considered a prejudice. As Allport (1954) noted, history is filled with examples of prejudices based on prevailing religious beliefs. These include individuals' support for such instances of structural stigma as the institution of slavery, the Holy Inquisition's stance toward Jews and other non-Christians, and the Indian caste system. Support for racial segregation in the twentieth-century United States can also be added to this list of attitudes that, in their time, could each be characterized as "based on a moral stance," using O'Donohue & Caselles's (1993) phrasing, and thus "rational." Despite the religious support they once enjoyed, they are now recognized as instances of prejudice.

In theory, simply holding a faith-based belief that same-sex sexual behavior is sinful need not in itself constitute sexual prejudice, any more than rejecting beliefs promulgated

by faiths other than one's own is necessarily religious prejudice. In practice, however, moral rejection of same-sex sexual behavior is often part of a general negative evaluation of sexual minorities (e.g., Bassett et al. 2005, Batson et al. 1999, Fulton et al. 1999). Highly religious people are more likely than others to express negative affect toward gay and bisexual people, to oppose policies and laws prohibiting employment discrimination against them, and to oppose laws providing same-sex couples with entirely secular protections such as the ability to make medical decisions for an incapacitated partner and access to health insurance coverage through a partner's workplace benefits (Brint & Abrutyn 2010, Haider-Markel & Joslyn 2008, Herek 2002b, Lewis 2003, Olson et al. 2006). These patterns go beyond moral rejection of same-sex sexual behavior and instead indicate a more generalized antipathy. Thus, whereas homophobia is arguably inappropriate for describing the attitudes discussed by O'Donohue & Caselles (1993), Rosik (2007), and others, sexual prejudice is an apt label.

Explaining the relationship between religiosity and sexual prejudice requires addressing two important questions. First, why do highly religious individuals tend to express more hostile and vociferous reactions to homosexuality than to many other behaviors they consider sinful? For example, divorce is condemned by many religions, and religious Americans tend to support tightening of divorce laws (Stokes & Ellison 2010). In contrast to extensive religiously based efforts to ban legal recognition of same-sex unions, however, no comparable large-scale social movement has arisen to outlaw divorce, deny divorced people equal opportunities in employment, or bar them from civil marriage. Similarly, although many religious people have strong convictions that the teachings of other faiths are theologically false and contrary to the deity's will, most do not try to deprive other denominations of their tax-exempt status or legally bar their members from worshipping or marrying within their chosen faith. Homosexuality and sexual minority individuals seem to evoke

---

"homophobia," their broader question is whether religiously based negative attitudes toward a group can be considered a prejudice. Rosik (2007), for example, explicitly acknowledged that he "appropriate[d] the language of homophobia" for his discussion of sexual prejudice and heterosexuals' attitudes toward lesbians and gay men (p. 135).

a disproportionately strong response from religious groups and individuals.

Second, why is sexual prejudice observed in some religious heterosexuals but not others? Although aggregate data reveal a consistent correlation between religiosity and sexual prejudice, it is far from perfect. Some highly religious individuals appear to differentiate their moral condemnation of homosexual behavior from their attitudes toward lesbian and gay individuals (e.g., Bassett et al. 2005, Mak & Tsang 2008). Many religious heterosexuals have supported sexual minorities, sometimes in open defiance of their denomination's teachings (e.g., Smith 2012). The notion that religiosity is inherently antithetical to homosexuality is further discredited by the fact that many sexual minority individuals are highly religious and belong to welcoming congregations (e.g., Rodriguez 2010).

One approach to answering these questions borrows from earlier research on the consistently observed correlation between religiosity and racial prejudice. To explain this pattern, Allport proposed that whites whose religion served mainly as a means for obtaining social status and personal security (an extrinsic religious orientation) were likely to be racially prejudiced to the extent that social norms favored it. By contrast, those for whom religion serves as an end in itself (an intrinsic orientation) were likely to be unprejudiced because for them "there is no place for rejection, contempt, or condescension" toward other human beings (Allport & Ross 1967, p. 441). Consistent with Allport's hypothesis, research among U.S. Christians generally documented more racial and ethnic prejudice among those with an extrinsic religious orientation and less among those with an intrinsic orientation (Hall et al. 2010).

Comparable studies of sexual prejudice, however, found it is positively correlated with intrinsic religiosity but uncorrelated with an extrinsic orientation (Whitley 2009). Thus, contrary to Allport's conceptualization, the outgroup attitudes of intrinsically religious people are not always accepting but instead appear to follow the dictates of their religion—they are negative toward groups condemned by their denomination but positive toward groups against whom prejudice is proscribed (Duck & Hunsberger 1999, Herek 1987b). Moreover, the correlation between sexual prejudice and intrinsic religiosity appears to be explained by the relationship of both variables to religious fundamentalism (e.g., Herek 1987b, Kirkpatrick 1993, McFarland 1989). Thus, understanding the link between sexual prejudice and religiosity requires an examination of fundamentalism.

Fundamentalism can be defined variously as an historical movement in American Protestantism (Hood et al. 2005, Woodberry & Smith 1998); a particular set of orthodox Christian beliefs, especially belief in the literal truth of the Bible (Kellstedt & Smidt 1991); or, more broadly, as a religious reaction against modernism that conceives of the world in dualistic terms, with one's own religious ingroup allied with an all-powerful deity against the secular forces of evil (Herriot 2007). The last sense also includes the beliefs that only one's own religion comprises "the fundamental, basic, intrinsic, essential, inerrant truth about humanity and deity" (Altemeyer & Hunsberger 1992, p. 118) and that this truth is to be found entirely within an inerrant sacred text (Hood et al. 2005).

However it is operationally defined, fundamentalism is strongly correlated with sexual prejudice (Whitley 2009). One explanation for this pattern is straightforward belief consistency: The sacred texts of Judaism, Christianity, and Islam—each considered by its respective fundamentalist followers to be inerrant—have long been understood to condemn homosexual behavior as inherently sinful (Boswell 1980). Consequently, fundamentalists who reject homosexuality might be understood as simply behaving in a manner consistent with the tenets of their faith. But this account does not explain why many fundamentalists reject sexual minority people as well as same-sex sexual behavior, and why their reactions to homosexuality are often so much more vigorous and hostile than their reactions to other behaviors they also consider sinful. To address these questions, it is helpful to consider the correlation between sexual prejudice and fundamentalism in functional terms. Consistent with the current article's focus, we mainly examine U.S. fundamentalism, which is predominantly Christian.

Condemnation of homosexuality and the demonization of lesbians and gay men became defining features of conservative Christianity historically recently, concurrent with the emergence of gay people as a widely recognized minority group in the United States. Rhetorical themes in the evangelical Christian movement shifted during the latter twentieth century, from goals in the 1950s of ministering to homosexuals and trying to win them to Christianity through love and compassion, to a view in the 1990s of gay men and lesbians as "an anti-Christian force, promoting a heresy increasingly sanctioned by the state in the form of decriminalization and the extension of civil rights" (Herman 1997, p. 50). During this period, many conservative Christians came to see themselves as a persecuted minority and defined their own identities in opposition to the gay community and other societal forces they perceived to be antithetical to their values concerning family, sexuality, and gender. These perceptions made it possible for sexual prejudice to assume a central role in contemporary fundamentalist identity (Herriot 2007), providing a vehicle for affirming deeply felt values and solidifying social ties with like-minded others. This account explains how sexual prejudice can serve value-expressive and social adjustment functions among many people of faith, especially among those who define themselves as fundamentalist.

A competing hypothesis has also been proposed: that religiously based sexual prejudice serves a defensive function. This view posits that fundamentalism—which it characterizes as being focused on unequivocal obedience to religious authority, strict conformity to religious teachings, feelings of moral superiority over outgroups, and self-righteousness—disproportionately attracts highly authoritarian individuals, who also tend to have high

levels of sexual prejudice (e.g., Altemeyer 2003, Altemeyer & Hunsberger 1992, Duck & Hunsberger 1999, Hunsberger 1995). Authoritarianism has historically been linked with psychological defensiveness (Adorno et al. 1950, Smith 1997). Stenner (2005), for example, described themes that are common to authoritarianism (defined as a psychological predisposition to intolerance that is exacerbated by increases in social threat) and the ego-defensive function of prejudice. In her model, various forms of intolerance (including sexual prejudice) are "functionally related elements of a kind of defensive stance, concerned with minimizing difference and promoting uniformity, with instituting and preserving some collective normative order" (Stenner 2005, p. 25). Noting the correlation between religious fundamentalism and authoritarianism, she distinguished religious disapproval of certain behaviors from authoritarian demands for their regulation. The latter, she argued, reflect "a need to regulate other people's behavior" (p. 272). To the extent that an individual's fundamentalist religious beliefs are rooted in his or her psychological authoritarianism, religiously based expressions of sexual prejudice can be understood as serving a defensive function.

Several studies have indeed found that controlling for authoritarianism (operationally defined as scores on a measure of right-wing authoritarianism, or RWA) entirely eliminates or even reverses the relationship between fundamentalism and sexual prejudice (e.g., Ford et al. 2009, Jonathan 2008, Laythe et al. 2001, Stefurak et al. 2010). However, many RWA scale items also tap orthodox religious beliefs, which artificially inflates correlations between the two variables (Mavor et al. 2009). When those overlapping items are dropped from analyses, authoritarianism still accounts for a significant portion of variance in sexual prejudice, but fundamentalism also remains significantly correlated with sexual prejudice, controlling for RWA (Johnson et al. 2011). Thus, in the aggregate, authoritarianism and fundamentalism are each independently associated with sexual prejudice. High levels of authoritarianism account for the sexual prejudice of some fundamentalists, but not all of them.

As this discussion illustrates, rather than assuming that negative attitudes toward sexual minorities are pathological or irrational, a functional perspective prompts consideration of how those attitudes are related to factors such as a heterosexual's self-defining values, ties to important social groups, and desires to avoid negative emotions and threats to self-esteem. Religiously based sexual prejudice may assist an individual in meeting needs in all of these domains. For some heterosexuals, expressing sexual prejudice solidifies social ties with their faith community. For others, it affirms their self-concept as a person of faith. These functions may both be concurrently salient for many religious heterosexuals and, in both cases, the individual's social and personal identities are likely to be closely tied to her or his attitudes toward sexual minorities. For some heterosexuals, sexual prejudice represents an attempt to deal with personal insecurities and anxieties by preserving order and promoting uniformity.

Sexual prejudice can serve these functions in the contemporary United States because of cultural constructions of sexual orientation and religious identity that have emerged since the mid-twentieth century. As noted above, these constructions have provided a foundation for many Christians to define themselves as members of an oppressed minority and to perceive sexual minorities as a social outgroup that threatens their core values, violates important moral rules, and is regarded negatively by religious authorities and most other members of their faith. **Table 1** illustrates how cultural,

Table 1 How do religiously based attitudes toward sexual minorities serve psychological functions?

Function	Person characteristics: Religion is important to the person, and...	Cultural context	Situational catalysts	Outcome of expressing attitudes
Social-adjustment or social-expressive function	The person has strong needs for affiliation, social acceptance, group membership	Religious groups (e.g., denominations, congregations, social clubs, prayer groups) strongly endorse specific attitudes concerning sexual orientation and sexual minorities	The group's position is made salient, e.g., at religious services a clergy member articulates the denomination's official position relevant to sexual orientation and sexual minorities	The person's ties to other members of the religious group are strengthened
Value-expressive function	The person's identity is closely tied to religious values	Religious teachings articulate specific beliefs concerning sexual orientation and sexual minorities, and adherence to these beliefs is considered to be a central tenet of faith	Religious values relevant to sexual minorities are made salient, e.g., by media framing of debates about marriage equality in terms of religious beliefs	The person experiences an increased or renewed sense of identity as a virtuous or good person
Defensive function	The person has fragile self-esteem or experiences negative emotions (e.g., anxiety) related to gender, sexuality, or perceived threats to collective normative order	Religious teachings place negative sanctions on being nonheterosexual, violating cultural standards for masculinity or femininity, or failing to maintain clear boundaries between genders	Situational factors create self-doubts about the person's own heterosexuality or ability to meet gender standards, or they blur established boundaries between genders	The person experiences anxiety reduction, a restoration of self-esteem, and a sense of alignment with authority figures (including the deity)

individual, and situational factors can converge to make sexual prejudice (as well as positive attitudes toward sexual minorities) functional for highly religious individuals.

Sexual Prejudice, Gender, and Sexuality

The construction of sexual prejudice as an irrational phobia also raises important questions in domains other than religion. For example, it resonates with the popular belief that sexual prejudice, especially in its more extreme manifestations, is a disguise for an individual's own deep-seated, unconscious homosexual attractions. This folk wisdom derives from psychodynamic theories of personality, which regard strong feelings of aversion, hostility, and disgust toward homosexuality as a defense against the overwhelming anxiety that would result if inadequately repressed homosexual urges were to become conscious (Adorno et al. 1950, Ferenczi 1950). From this perspective, "homophobia" truly is a fear: of oneself or, more specifically, one's own homoerotic desires. As embodied in the "homosexual panic" legal defense (e.g., Wall 2000), this model has even been used in courtroom proceedings to justify antigay violence and murder. Despite its popularity, the psychodynamic explanation of sexual prejudice has not received extensive empirical testing, probably because of the difficulties inherent in objectively measuring unconscious phenomena.

Some researchers have attempted to surmount this obstacle by using physiological and reaction time measures, with mixed results. Adams et al. (1996) recorded penile tumescence and self-reported sexual arousal among heterosexual male undergraduates while they watched sexually explicit video clips. Although a male-male video elicited the smallest overall physiological response of all the stimuli, participants scoring high on a self-report measure of sexual prejudice exhibited significantly greater tumescence while viewing it than did low-prejudice males, consistent with the psychodynamic account (Adams et al. 1996). More recently, Weinstein et al. (2012) also reported findings in line with the psychodynamic model. Using a complex methodology with several predominantly female and heterosexual undergraduate samples, they concluded that participants who perceived their parents as not supporting their autonomy exhibited higher levels of concealed same-sex attraction and sexual prejudice than students who reported that their parents supported their autonomy. They characterized the former group's sexual prejudice as a form of psychological defense (Weinstein et al. 2012).

While provocative, the conclusions of both studies have important qualifications. Weinstein et al.'s (2012) interpretation of their findings assumes that their newly developed reaction-time task measured hidden same-sex attraction, a claim not validated by other researchers at the time of this writing. Adams and his colleagues (1996) acknowledged that the modest increase in tumescence among highly prejudiced men in their study during the male-male video could have resulted from heightened anxiety rather than unconscious sexual attractions.

Other studies have failed to find evidence of homosexual attraction associated with heterosexuals' negative attitudes toward sexual minorities. Mahaffey and her colleagues detected increases in the magnitude of startle eye blink responses among highly prejudiced men viewing nude or seminude images of male couples, indicating a negative emotional reaction to the images rather than an unconscious positive response (Mahaffey et al. 2005, 2011). Meier et al. (2006) found that self-report and implicit measures of sexual prejudice were consistent (i.e., positively correlated) among male undergraduates high in ego-defensiveness (operationally defined as scores on a measure of self-deception). In addition, compared to other participants who viewed images of clothed and semiclothed male-male and heterosexual couples, highly prejudiced high-defensive males opted to view the male couples for relatively shorter durations than the heterosexual couples (Meier et al. 2006). The researchers interpreted these patterns as indicating true aversion or loathing among the defensive men.

Thus in contrast to the conclusions of Adams et al. (1996) and Weinstein et al. (2012), these findings do not indicate a secret same-sex attraction among highly prejudiced heterosexual males. Rather, they are consistent with the conclusion that most highly prejudiced men harbor strong antipathy toward gay men and try to minimize their exposure to them.

With the exception of the Weinstein et al. (2012) study, the investigations described above focused on heterosexual males rather than females. This emphasis on men reflects a recognition of gender differences in sexual prejudice. On average, heterosexual men express more negative attitudes toward sexual minorities than heterosexual women, and their reactions tend to be more hostile to gay men than to lesbians (e.g., Ahrold & Meston 2010; Herek 2000; Herek & Gonzalez-Rivera 2006; Kite 1994; Kite & Whitley 1996, 1998). Although heterosexual women and men alike tend to feel less comfortable being around a sexual minority individual of their own sex than of the other sex, men express less comfort with sexual minorities overall (Herek 2002a).

Gender differences have also been observed in the cognitive dynamics underlying these attitudes. Heterosexual men tend to respond to sexual minorities in terms of gender, expressing more negative attitudes toward gay and bisexual men than toward lesbian and bisexual women. By contrast, heterosexual women appear to respond more in terms of sexual orientation group. They express more negative attitudes toward bisexuals (regardless of gender) than toward homosexuals (Herek 2000, 2002b, 2009b; Steffens & Wagner 2004), perhaps reflecting acceptance of popular stereotypes that bisexuals are nonmonogamous and likely to spread HIV and other sexually transmitted diseases (Herek & Capitanio 1999a, Spalding & Peplau 1997). Highly prejudiced heterosexual men display longer response latencies to attitude questions about lesbians than to similar questions about gay men, suggesting that their attitudes toward gay men are more readily accessible than their attitudes toward lesbians (Herek 2002a). Consistent with this observation, heterosexual

men's attitudes toward lesbians (but generally not their attitudes toward gay men) are sensitive to influence by contextual variables: They tend to be significantly more negative when they are measured immediately after the respondent has answered similar questions about gay men than when thoughts about gay males have not been primed (Herek 2002a, Herek & Capitanio 1999b, Steffens 2005).

Why do heterosexual men manifest greater sexual prejudice than heterosexual women, and why does it focus especially strongly on male sexual minorities? Whereas the psychodynamic account of unconscious homosexual attraction does not appear to fit the sexual prejudice of most men, another explanation may be more widely applicable. According to this account, gender differences in sexual prejudice reflect cultural constructions of masculinity and femininity, which create different expectations for men and women. Masculinity is often conceptualized as a status that must be achieved, one that can be easily lost unless men repeatedly prove themselves to others (e.g., Gilmore 1990). Because the male role can be particularly precarious, men are more likely than women to feel compelled to affirm or bolster their gendered (masculine) identity and thereby avoid losing the acceptance of their same-sex heterosexual peers (Franklin 2000, Glick et al. 2007, Herek 1986, Kimmel 1997, Theodore & Basow 2000). Males who do not conform to gender role expectations risk a variety of negative consequences (e.g., Waldo et al. 1998, Martin & Ruble 2010), including being labeled homosexual (Bosson et al. 2005, 2006; Bosson & Vandello 2011) and being punished with antigay anger and aggression (Parrott 2009, Parrott et al. 2011). Thus, sexual prejudice is expressed by men both to establish their own masculinity and to punish other men who fail to meet gender role requirements.

Whereas endorsing antigay attitudes can reaffirm heterosexual men's masculinity, preserve their social status, and maintain clear gender boundaries, heterosexual women do not face parallel social pressures associated with their feminine identity. To be sure, women encounter social pressures to conform to cultural gender norms and thereby preserve male dominance (Glick & Fiske 2001), but women's gender roles allow for greater flexibility than do male roles (Basow & Johnson 2000, Eagly et al. 2004). As a result, endorsing negative attitudes toward sexual minorities is not highly relevant to most heterosexual women's self-image as women (Herek 2000).

In this context, Kimmel (1997) suggested that the construct of "homophobia" is applicable mainly to men, proposing that it should be understood as men's fear of being labeled homosexual by other men. A desire to avoid such labeling and its attendant loss of status and belongingness, he argued, leads men to shun anything that can be perceived as nonmasculine, to endorse antigay attitudes, and to attack gay men. In this conceptualization, homophobia corresponds to the previously discussed construct of felt stigma: It helps men to demonstrate their heterosexuality and their distinctiveness from gay men, maintain their social status associated with masculinity, and avoid being the target of antigay behaviors.

Kimmel's approach suggests an alternative interpretation of the previously described findings of Adams et al. (1996). Rather than unconscious homosexual attraction, the increased penile tumescence they documented in some high-prejudice men while viewing sexually explicit male videos may have resulted from anxiety about being believed by others to be homosexual. Knowing that their levels of sexual arousal were being monitored, the men may have worried they would be mistakenly perceived as homosexual by the (male) experimenters. Insofar as anxiety can increase penile tumescence (e.g., Barlow et al. 1983), the Adams et al. results might be explained by felt stigma rather than unconscious sexual attraction. Consistent with this argument, Adams and his colleagues found in a separate study that highly prejudiced heterosexual men reported significantly more anxiety when viewing the same male-male video clip used in the penile plethysmography study, compared to men who scored low in sexual prejudice (Bernat et al. 2001).

Empirical data generally support the argument that sexual prejudice is often a strategy for men to demonstrate—both to others and themselves—their ability to meet cultural expectations about masculinity. Endorsing traits and beliefs that are consistent with cultural norms for masculinity—e.g., toughness, status, and antifemininity—is correlated with expressing prejudice against gay men (Barron et al. 2008, Baunach et al. 2010, Keiller 2010, Kilianski 2003, Meaney & Rye 2010, Parrott et al. 2002, Sinn 1997). Endorsing a strong masculine ideology has also been demonstrated to motivate antigay anger and aggression (Franklin 2000; Parrott 2009; Vincent et al. 2011a,b).

In situations in which heterosexual men's masculinity may be called into question, they often respond by expressing sexual prejudice or engaging in antigay behavior. Induction of masculinity threat in experimental studies (by leading heterosexual men to believe that some aspect of their behavior, such as test performance, was more feminine or less masculine than that of other men) has been shown to result in aggressive behavior toward other research participants believed to be gay (Talley & Bettencourt 2008) and expressions of negative affect toward effeminate (but not stereotypically masculine) gay men (Glick et al. 2007). Vandello et al. (2008) found that when heterosexual men's masculinity was threatened, they showed increased cognitive accessibility to physically aggressive thoughts. Heterosexual women did not demonstrate a comparable pattern (Vandello et al. 2008). Bosson et al. (2009) found that heterosexual men whose masculinity was publicly challenged reacted with more aggressive tendencies (e.g., preferring to hit a punching bag over playing basketball) compared to other men. These tendencies mitigated anxious reactions to masculinity threat (Bosson et al. 2009).

The connection between sexual prejudice and endorsement of gender role norms is also grounded in more abstract ideologies about gender and sexuality. Empirical research has consistently revealed significant correlations between sexual prejudice and traditional beliefs about the proper roles for men and women (Goodman & Moradi 2008, Kilianski 2003, Nagoshi et al. 2008, Parrott et al. 2002, Whitley 2001) as well as traditional values concerning sexual behavior and family structure (Callahan & Vescio 2011, Herek 1988, Kite & Whitley 1998, Vescio & Biernat 2003). Valuing traditional male and female roles is tied to sexual prejudice even more strongly for heterosexual women than men (Basow & Johnson 2000, Baunach et al. 2010, Keiller 2010, Kilianski 2003), and religiosity tends to be more strongly predictive of sexual prejudice among women than men (e.g., Ahrold & Meston 2010, Brown & Henriquez 2008, Herek 2002b, Stefurak et al. 2010).

Thus, as with religion, the relationship between sexual prejudice and variables related to gender is multifaceted and probably reflects the operation of different psychological functions for different people. For some heterosexuals, especially men, sexual prejudice may be primarily a defense against anxiety or other negative emotions that would result if one's unconscious same-sex attractions were to be acknowledged. For others, again mainly for men, it may be a defense not against repressed same-sex desires, but rather against anxiety and loss of self-esteem resulting from perceptions that one has not lived up to cultural standards for one's gender. Sexual prejudice also may serve a social-expressive function for men by maintaining their public image as appropriately masculine and thus solidifying their membership in the male ingroup. For still other heterosexuals, perhaps especially women, sexual prejudice may signify endorsement of a broader value system that supports traditionalist values concerning sexuality, gender roles, and family structure.

REDUCING PREJUDICE

The aggregate shift in public attitudes toward homosexuality and sexual minorities in recent decades reflects at least two processes at work. First, older generations of heterosexuals, among whom attitudes toward sexual minorities are predominantly negative, are gradually being replaced by younger generations with more positive attitudes. Second, within generational cohorts, many individual heterosexuals' attitudes are becoming more positive over time (Andersen & Fetner 2008, Scott 1998, Wilcox & Norrander 2002). Our conceptual framework suggests that understanding why these changes are occurring requires consideration both of the cultural processes underlying reductions in societal sexual stigma as well as the social psychological processes through which that stigma is internalized by individuals. A discussion of the former is beyond the scope of the present article (see, e.g., Chauncey 2004; Epstein 1999; Herek 2007, 2009c, 2010). In the following section, we discuss factors that help to explain why sexual prejudice has lessened among so many heterosexuals.

Because sexual stigma is pervasive, most people internalize it to at least some extent in the course of normal socialization, regardless of their sexual orientation. Consequently, the negative affect, stereotypes, and behavioral responses that comprise sexual prejudice are likely to be automatically activated whenever homosexuality or sexual minorities become salient. Replacing this automatic association with nonprejudiced or accepting feelings, beliefs, and behaviors involves extended cognitive effort (Devine 1989, 2005), which an individual is unlikely to undertake without adequate motivation (Monteith 1993, 1996).

What might be the source of such motivation in heterosexuals? To answer this question, it is instructive first to consider the case of sexual minority individuals, most of whom also internalize sexual stigma to some extent before they become aware of their own sexual orientation. When they initially recognize their same-sex attractions, they often direct their internalized sexual stigma at themselves, resulting in reduced self-esteem and heightened psychological distress (e.g., Herek et al. 2009). To achieve a positive and integrated sense of self, they must critically question and change many longstanding attitudes, emotions, beliefs, and behavioral patterns (Bieschke et al. 2007, Herek & Garnets 2007).

Because internalized sexual stigma does not produce the same kinds of conflicts in heterosexuals, undertaking the effortful and lengthy process of rejecting their own sexual prejudice is not a matter of psychological survival, as it often is for sexual minorities. What, then, motivates them to do it? Our discussion of the utilitarian rationality of sexual prejudice suggests that heterosexuals are most likely to undertake this task when their negative attitudes toward sexual minorities stop being functional and instead prevent them from meeting important psychological needs.

Sexual prejudice that is motivated mainly by a need for social acceptance, for example, is likely to become dysfunctional if community and peer group norms change such that expressions of antigay attitudes evoke social rejection rather than support. Normative pressures to refrain from expressions of prejudice or to avow positive feelings toward sexual minorities are probably most likely to prevail among younger age cohorts and in settings such as college campuses (e.g., Monteith et al. 1996, Morrison et al. 2009). Because behavior that is elicited through external reinforcement or coercion may not be lasting (Kelman 1958), however, a need for social acceptance may not provide an enduring foundation for positive attitudes toward sexual minorities. Unless the individual internalizes those attitudes, he or she may revert to sexual prejudice in settings where group norms favor it.

Sexual prejudice can also become dysfunctional if it is perceived as sharply conflicting with deep-seated core values—including a commitment to equality, social justice, and the humane treatment of others—as well as one's self-concept as a nonprejudiced person (Borgman 2009). Individuals who perceive such conflicts may experience their prejudice as hypocritical and inconsistent with their personal standards of conduct, a conflict that is likely to induce negative affect (Devine et al. 1991) and may motivate them to eradicate their own sexual prejudice and work on behalf of sexual minorities in political and other arenas (Duhigg et al. 2010, Russell 2011).

Probably the most powerful instigator for a heterosexual person to undertake the work of reducing sexual prejudice is having a close personal relationship with a sexual minority friend, relative, or associate. Heterosexuals who personally know at least one gay or lesbian person tend to express more favorable attitudes toward sexual minorities than those lacking such contact (Herek 2009c, Herek & Capitanio 1996, Lewis 2011, Pettigrew & Tropp 2006, Vonofakou et al. 2007) and are more likely to engage in political or social action opposing sexual stigma (Duhigg et al. 2010, Fingerhut 2011). Among heterosexuals reporting such contact, those who say they have spoken directly with a gay or lesbian friend or relative about the latter's experiences express significantly more positive attitudes than those who have not (Herek 2009c).

DIRECTIONS FOR FUTURE RESEARCH

As a relatively new area of scientific inquiry, sexual prejudice poses many unanswered questions. In this final section, we consider a small sampling of promising issues for future study. First, more research is needed on the varied motivations underlying sexual prejudice and their sources in dispositional characteristics, social contexts, and individuals' perceptions of the cultural meanings attached to sexual orientation and related phenomena. A functional approach suggests that prejudice should not be assumed to have a single source for all heterosexuals. Psychological defense probably drives sexual prejudice in some individuals, whereas needs to affirm values or maintain social support likely play key roles for others. Still other psychological needs may be met by sexual prejudice beyond those discussed here. We believe that sexual prejudice researchers will gain more insights to the extent that they employ a perspective that is sensitive to such variation among individuals. Insofar as indirect assessment techniques such as the IAT can detect the influence of processes occurring outside of conscious awareness, they are likely to be especially valuable tools for illuminating these variations.

A second, related area for further research is the study of prejudice reduction (see generally Wood 2000). This can encompass naturalistic study of the events in heterosexuals' lives that have led them to hold less prejudiced attitudes as well as experimental studies of antiprejudice interventions. Here again, understanding individuals' motivations for sexual prejudice may yield important insights into how it can be reduced. The functional approach is usually interpreted as predicting that the success of an intervention will depend on how well it resonates with the psychological needs served by prejudice in the target audience. For example, interventions that reduce sexual prejudice in a person with value-expressive attitudes will probably not be as effective for someone with attitudes serving a defensive function. Research that specifies the parameters of the interaction between the intervention, characteristics of the receiver, and the context in which it is presented is a longstanding need in this area.

A third promising research focus is the process whereby heterosexuals not only reduce their own prejudice but also become advocates or "allies" for sexual minority individuals, acting as agents for changing the attitudes of other heterosexuals and opposing institutionalized sexual stigma. Data are needed that explain how and why some heterosexual people become allies and how their attitudes and actions influence their heterosexual friends and family. Studying gender patterns may be especially interesting in this area insofar as women appear more likely than men to take on this role, and they may be highly effective at influencing the heterosexual men in their life by communicating norms and values that oppose sexual prejudice.

A fourth area follows from past findings related to interpersonal contact and attitude change. One likely motivation for heterosexuals to become allies is through their personal relationships with lesbian, gay, and bisexual individuals. Although these relationships appear to be especially likely to reduce prejudice when they include discussions about the lives and concerns of sexual minorities, most lesbian, gay, and bisexual adults do not routinely engage in such conversations with the heterosexuals in their life (Herek et al. 2010). This pattern highlights the need for research on the factors that facilitate such disclosure and discussion and also make it a positive experience for the participants.

Finally, although the focus of this article has been sexual prejudice among heterosexuals, more empirical research is also needed on self-stigma among sexual minorities. Because both can be conceptualized as the internalization of societal stigma, understanding how the process operates in lesbian, gay, and bisexual people may yield insights that are applicable to heterosexuals, and vice-versa. A similar dual focus may also shed light on the psychological dynamics underlying the internalization by majority and minority groups of other forms of concealable stigma. More research is especially needed on the development of both sexual prejudice and self-stigma during adolescence (e.g., Espelage et al. 2008, Poteat 2007, Poteat et al. 2007), a time of sexual awakening and identity development. Despite clear indications that newer generations of heterosexuals have more favorable attitudes toward sexual minorities than their older counterparts, many young people nevertheless encounter enactments of sexual prejudice in the form of ostracism, harassment, bullying, and violence (e.g., Russell et al. 2010, U.S. Commiss. Civil Rights 2011). Shedding light on how to prevent such attacks and undo the psychological damage they cause is an important goal of psychological research.

SUMMARY POINTS

1. Despite shifts toward greater acceptance in U.S. public opinion and policy, prejudice against sexual minorities persists, and lesbian, gay, and bisexual people remain widely stigmatized.

2. Heterosexuals' negative attitudes toward sexual minorities are better understood as sexual prejudice than as homophobia; the latter term's limitations include its implicit assumption that such attitudes are based on irrational fears and are an individual pathology rather than a manifestation of cultural stigma.

3. Although sexual prejudice shares many characteristics with other forms of prejudice, it differs in that (*a*) it remains acceptable in many sectors of society and (*b*) sexual orientation is often concealable, which means that anyone can potentially be perceived as a sexual minority and that heterosexuals often establish relationships with nonheterosexuals without knowing about their sexual orientation.

4. Cultural institutions and ideologies—including those related to religion and gender—create a social context within which individual expressions of sexual prejudice can help heterosexuals to meet important psychological needs, including needs for securing social acceptance, affirming values that are central to one's self-concept, and avoiding anxiety and other negative emotions associated with threats to self-esteem.

5. High levels of religiosity are consistently associated with sexual prejudice for multiple reasons, including condemnation of homosexuality by many religious denominations, historically recent social constructions of sexual prejudice as a defining feature of some forms of religious identity, and high levels of psychological authoritarianism in some religious individuals.

6. Heterosexual men tend to express higher levels of sexual prejudice than heterosexual women, especially toward sexual minority males. Although this pattern may partly reflect the ambivalence or insecurity that some heterosexual males have about their own sexual orientation, it occurs largely because expressing sexual prejudice allows men to demonstrate—both to others and themselves—their ability to meet cultural expectations about masculinity.

7. Recent shifts in public attitudes toward greater acceptance of sexual minorities reflect the replacement of older, more prejudiced generations of heterosexuals in the population with more accepting younger generations, as well as reductions in prejudice in many individual heterosexuals.

8. Heterosexuals are likely to develop more positive attitudes toward sexual minorities when their prejudice is no longer psychologically functional for them. One of the most powerful catalysts for such a change is having a close personal relationship with a sexual minority friend, relative, or associate, especially when that relationship includes open discussion of the latter's experiences.

DISCLOSURE STATEMENT

The authors are not aware of any affiliations, memberships, funding, or financial holdings that might be perceived as affecting the objectivity of this review.

ACKNOWLEDGMENTS

We thank Clinton Anderson and Susan Fiske for their helpful comments on an earlier draft of this article.

LITERATURE CITED

Adams HE, Wright LW Jr, Lohr BA. 1996. Is homophobia associated with homosexual arousal? *J. Abnorm. Psychol.* 105:440–45

Adorno TW, Frenkel-Brunswik E, Levinson DJ, Sanford RN. 1950. *The Authoritarian Personality*. New York: Harper

Ahrold TK, Meston CM. 2010. Ethnic differences in sexual attitudes of US college students: gender, acculturation, and religiosity factors. *Arch. Sex. Behav.* 39:190–202

Allport GW. 1954. *The Nature of Prejudice*. Garden City, NY: Doubleday

Allport GW, Ross JM. 1967. Personal religious orientation and prejudice. *J. Pers. Soc. Psychol.* 5:432–43

Altemeyer B. 2003. Why do religious fundamentalists tend to be prejudiced? *Int. J. Psychol. Relig.* 13:17–28

Altemeyer B, Hunsberger BE. 1992. Authoritarianism, religious fundamentalism, quest, and prejudice. *Int. J. Psychol. Relig.* 2:113–33

Andersen R, Fetner T. 2008. Cohort differences in tolerance of homosexuality: attitudinal change in Canada and the United States, 1981–2000. *Public Opin. Q.* 72:311–30

Barlow DH, Sakheim DK, Beck JG. 1983. Anxiety increases sexual arousal. *J. Abnorm. Psychol.* 92:49–54

Barron JM, Struckman-Johnson C, Quevillon R, Banka SR. 2008. Heterosexual men's attitudes toward gay men: a hierarchical model including masculinity, openness, and theoretical explanations. *Psychol. Men Masc.* 9:154–66

Basow SA, Johnson K. 2000. Predictors of homophobia in female college students. *Sex Roles* 42:391–404

Bassett RL, Kirnan R, Hill M, Schultz A. 2005. SOAP: validating the Sexual Orientation and Practices Scale. *J. Psychol. Christianity* 24(2):165–75

Batson CD, Floyd RB, Meyer JM, Winner AL. 1999. "And who is my neighbor?" Intrinsic religion as a source of universal compassion. *J. Sci. Study Relig.* 38:445–57

Baunach DM, Burgess EO, Muse CS. 2010. Southern (dis)comfort: sexual prejudice and contact with gay men and lesbians in the South. *Sociol. Spect.* 30(1):30–64

Bernat JA, Calhoun KS, Adams HE, Zeichner A. 2001. Homophobia and physical aggression toward homosexual and heterosexual individuals. *J. Abnorm. Psychol.* 110:179–87

Bieschke KJ, Perez RM, DeBord KA. 2007. *Handbook of Counseling and Psychotherapy with Lesbian, Gay, Bisexual, and Transgender Clients*. Washington, DC: Am. Psychol. Assoc. 2nd ed.

Billig M. 1988. The notion of "prejudice": some rhetorical and ideological aspects. *Text* 8:91–110

Borgman AL. 2009. LGB allies and Christian identity: a qualitative exploration of resolving conflicts and integrating identities. *J. Couns. Psychol.* 56:508–20

Bosson JK, Prewitt-Freilino JL, Taylor JN. 2005. Role rigidity: a problem of identity misclassification? *J. Pers. Soc. Psychol.* 89:552–65

Bosson JK, Taylor JN, Prewitt-Freilino JL. 2006. Gender role violations and identity misclassification: the roles of audience and actor variables. *Sex Roles* 55:13–24

Bosson JK, Vandello JA. 2011. Precarious manhood and its links to action and aggression. *Curr. Dir. Psychol. Sci.* 20:82–86

Bosson JK, Vandello JA, Burnaford RM, Weaver JR, Wasti SA. 2009. Precarious manhood and displays of physical aggression. *Pers. Soc. Psychol. Bull.* 35:623–34

Boswell J. 1980. *Christianity, Social Tolerance, and Homosexuality: Gay People in Western Europe from the Beginning of the Christian Era to the Fourteenth Century*. Chicago: Univ. Chicago Press

Brewer PR. 2003. Values, political knowledge, and public opinion about gay rights: a framing-based account. *Public Opin. Q.* 67:173–201

Brint S, Abrutyn S. 2010. Who's right about the right? Comparing competing explanations of the link between white evangelicals and conservative politics in the United States. *J. Sci. Study Relig.* 49:328–50

Brown MJ, Henriquez E. 2008. Socio-demographic predictors of attitudes towards gays and lesbians. *Indiv. Differ. Res.* 6:193–202

Callahan MP, Vescio TK. 2011. Core American values and the structure of antigay prejudice. *J. Homosex.* 58:248–62

Carpenter CS. 2007. Revisiting the income penalty for behaviorally gay men: evidence from NHANES III. *Labour Econ.* 14:25–34

Chauncey G Jr. 2004. *Why Marriage? The History Shaping Today's Debate Over Gay Equality*. New York: Basic Books

Corrigan PW, Watson AC, Barr L. 2006. The self-stigma of mental illness: implications for self-esteem and self-efficacy. *J. Soc. Clin. Psychol.* 25:875–84

Cowan G, Heiple B, Marquez C, Khatchadourian D, McNevin M. 2005. Heterosexuals' attitudes toward hate crimes and hate speech against gays and lesbians: old-fashioned and modern heterosexism. *J. Homosex.* 49(2):67–82

Dasgupta N, Rivera LM. 2006. From automatic antigay prejudice to behavior: the moderating role of conscious beliefs about gender and behavioral control. *J. Pers. Soc. Psychol.* 91:268–80

Dasgupta N, Rivera LM. 2008. When social context matters: the influence of long-term contact and short-term exposure to admired outgroup members on implicit attitudes and behavioral intentions. *Soc. Cogn.* 26:112–23

Devine PG. 1989. Stereotypes and prejudice: their automatic and controlled components. *J. Pers. Soc. Psychol.* 56:5–18

Devine PG. 2005. Breaking the prejudice habit: Allport's "inner conflict" revisited. In *On the Nature of Prejudice: Fifty Years After Allport*, ed. J Dovidio, P Glick, L Rudman, pp. 327–42. Malden, MA: Blackwell

Devine PG, Monteith MJ, Zuwerink JR, Elliot AJ. 1991. Prejudice with and without compunction. *J. Pers. Soc. Psychol.* 60:817–30

Dovidio JF, Gaertner SL. 2010. Intergroup bias. In *Handbook of Social Psychology*, ed. ST Fiske, DT Gilbert, G Lindzey, pp. 1084–121. Hoboken, NJ: Wiley

Duck RJ, Hunsberger B. 1999. Religious orientation and prejudice: the role of religious proscription, right-wing authoritarianism and social desirability. *Int. J. Psychol. Relig.* 9:157–79

Duckitt JH. 1992. *The Social Psychology of Prejudice*. New York: Praeger

Duhigg JM, Rostosky SS, Gray BE, Wimsatt MK. 2010. Development of heterosexuals into sexual-minority allies: a qualitative exploration. *Sex. Res. Soc. Policy* 7(1):2–14

Eagly AH, Diekman AB, Johannesen-Schmidt MC, Koenig AM. 2004. Gender gaps in sociopolitical attitudes: a social psychological analysis. *J. Pers. Soc. Psychol.* 87:796–816

Epstein S. 1999. Gay and lesbian movements in the United States: dilemmas of identity, diversity, and political strategy. In *The Global Emergence of Gay and Lesbian Politics: National Imprints of a Worldwide Movement*, ed. BD Adam, JW Duyvendak, A Krouwel, pp. 30–90. Philadelphia, PA: Temple Univ. Press

Espelage DL, Aragon SR, Birkett M, Koenig BW. 2008. Homophobic teasing, psychological outcomes, and sexual orientation among high school students: What influence do parents and schools have? *School Psychol. Rev.* 37:202–16

Fed. Bur. Investig. (FBI). 2011. *Hate Crime Statistics 2010*. Washington, DC: U.S. Dep. Justice. **http://www. fbi.gov/ucr/ucr.htm**

Ferenczi S. 1950. The nosology of male homosexuality (homo-erotism). In *Sex in Psychoanalysis*, ed. E Jones, pp. 250–68. New York: Basic Books

Fingerhut AW. 2011. Straight allies: What predicts heterosexuals' alliance with the LGBT community? *J. Appl. Soc. Psychol.* 41:2230–48

Fiske ST. 2009. *Social Beings: Core Motives in Social Psychology*. New York: Wiley. 2nd ed.

Ford TE, Brignall T, Vanvaley TL, Macaluso MJ. 2009. The unmaking of prejudice: how Christian beliefs relate to attitudes toward homosexuals. *J. Sci. Study Relig.* 48:146–60

Franklin K. 2000. Antigay behaviors among young adults: prevalence, patterns and motivators in a noncriminal population. *J. Interpers. Viol.* 15:339–62

Fulton AS, Gorsuch RL, Maynard EA. 1999. Religious orientation, antihomosexual sentiment, and fundamentalism among Christians. *J. Sci. Study Relig.* 38:14–22

Gilmore DD. 1990. *Manhood in the Making: Cultural Concepts of Masculinity*. New Haven, CT: Yale Univ. Press

Giner-Sorolla R, Bosson JK, Caswell TA, Hettinger VE. 2012. Emotions in sexual morality: testing the separate elicitors of anger and disgust. *Cogn. Emot.* 26:1208–22

Glick P, Fiske ST. 2001. An ambivalent alliance: hostile and benevolent sexism as complementary justifications for gender inequality. *Am. Psychol.* 56(2):109–18

Glick P, Gangl C, Gibb S, Klumpner S, Weinberg E. 2007. Defensive reactions to masculinity threat: more negative affect toward effeminate (but not masculine) gay men. *Sex Roles* 57:55–59

Goodman MB, Moradi B. 2008. Attitudes and behaviors toward lesbian and gay persons: critical correlates and mediated relations. *J. Counsel. Psychol.* 55:371–84

Haddock G, Zanna MP, Esses VM. 1993. Assessing the structure of prejudicial attitudes: the case of attitudes toward homosexuals. *J. Pers. Soc. Psychol.* 65:1105–18

Haider-Markel DP, Joslyn MR. 2008. Beliefs about the origins of homosexuality and support for gay rights: an empirical test of attribution theory. *Public Opin. Q.* 72:291–310

Hall DL, Matz DC, Wood W. 2010. Why don't we practice what we preach? A meta-analytic review of religious racism. *Pers. Soc. Psychol. Rev.* 14:126–39

Herek GM. 1986. On heterosexual masculinity: some psychical consequences of the social construction of gender and sexuality. *Am. Behav. Sci.* 29:563–77

Herek GM. 1987a. Can functions be measured? A new perspective on the functional approach to attitudes. *Soc. Psychol. Q.* 50:285–303

Herek GM. 1987b. Religious orientation and prejudice: a comparison of racial and sexual attitudes. *Pers. Soc. Psychol. Bull.* 13:34–44

Herek GM. 1988. Heterosexuals' attitudes toward lesbians and gay men: correlates and gender differences. *J. Sex Res.* 25:451–77

Herek GM. 1994. Assessing heterosexuals' attitudes toward lesbians and gay men: a review of empirical research with the ATLG scale. In *Lesbian and Gay Psychology: Theory, Research, and Clinical Applications*, ed. B Greene, GM Herek, pp. 206–28. Thousand Oaks, CA: Sage

Herek GM. 2000. Sexual prejudice and gender: Do heterosexuals' attitudes toward lesbians and gay men differ? *J. Soc. Issues* 56:251–66

Herek GM. 2002a. Gender gaps in public opinion about lesbians and gay men. *Public Opin. Q.* 66:40–66

Herek GM. 2002b. Heterosexuals' attitudes toward bisexual men and women in the United States. *J. Sex Res.* 39:264–74

Herek GM. 2004. Beyond "homophobia": thinking about sexual stigma and prejudice in the twenty-first century. *Sex. Res. Soc. Policy* 1(2):6–24

Herek GM. 2006. Legal recognition of same-sex relationships in the United States: a social science perspective. *Am. Psychol.* 61:607–21

Herek GM. 2007. Confronting sexual stigma and prejudice: theory and practice. *J. Soc. Issues* 63:905–25

Herek GM. 2009a. Hate crimes and stigma-related experiences among sexual minority adults in the United States: prevalence estimates from a national probability sample. *J. Interpers. Viol.* 24:54–74

Herek GM. 2009b. Sexual prejudice. In *Handbook of Prejudice, Stereotyping, and Discrimination*, ed. T Nelson, pp. 439–65. New York: Psychol. Press

Herek GM. 2009c. Sexual stigma and sexual prejudice in the United States: a conceptual framework. In *Contemporary Perspectives on Lesbian, Gay and Bisexual Identities: The 54th Nebraska Symposium on Motivation*, ed. DA Hope, pp. 65–111. New York: Springer

Herek GM. 2010. Sexual orientation differences as deficits: Science and stigma in the history of American psychology. *Perspect. Psychol. Sci.* 5:693–99

Herek GM, Capitanio JP. 1996. "Some of my best friends": intergroup contact, concealable stigma, and heterosexuals' attitudes toward gay men and lesbians. *Pers. Soc. Psychol. Bull.* 22:412–24

Herek GM, Capitanio JP. 1999a. AIDS stigma and sexual prejudice. *Am. Behav. Sci.* 42:1130–47

Herek GM, Capitanio JP. 1999b. Sex differences in how heterosexuals think about lesbians and gay men: evidence from survey context effects. *J. Sex Res.* 36:348–60

Herek GM, Chopp R, Strohl D. 2007. Sexual stigma: putting sexual minority health issues in context. In *The Health of Sexual Minorities: Public Health Perspectives on Lesbian, Gay, Bisexual, and Transgender Populations*, ed. I Meyer, M Northridge, pp. 171–208. New York: Springer

Herek GM, Garnets LD. 2007. Sexual orientation and mental health. *Annu. Rev. Clin. Psychol.* 3:353–75

Herek GM, Gillis JR, Cogan JC. 2009. Internalized stigma among sexual minority adults: insights from a social psychological perspective. *J. Counsel. Psychol.* 56:32–43

Herek GM, Gonzalez-Rivera M. 2006. Attitudes toward homosexuality among U.S. residents of Mexican descent. *J. Sex Res.* 43:122–35

Herek GM, McLemore KA. 2011. The Attitudes Toward Lesbians and Gay Men (ATLG) scale. In *Handbook of Sexuality-Related Measures*, ed. T Fisher, CM Davis, WL Yarber, SL Davis, pp. 415–17. Oxford, U.K.: Taylor & Francis

Herek GM, Norton AT, Allen TJ, Sims CL. 2010. Demographic, psychological, and social characteristics of self-identified lesbian, gay, and bisexual adults in a U.S. probability sample. *Sex. Res. Soc. Policy* 7:176–200

Herek GM, Saha S, Burack J. 2013. Stigma and psychological distress in people with HIV/AIDS. Manuscript submitted

Herman D. 1997. *The Antigay Agenda: Orthodox Vision and the Christian Right*. Chicago: Univ. Chicago Press

Herriot P. 2007. *Religious Fundamentalism and Social Identity*. New York: Routledge

Hood RW Jr, Hill PC, Williamson WP. 2005. *The Psychology of Religious Fundamentalism*. New York: Guilford

Hunsberger B. 1995. Religion and prejudice: the role of religious fundamentalism, quest, and right-wing authoritarianism. *J. Soc. Iss.* 51:113–29

Inst. Med. 2011. *The Health of Lesbian, Gay, Bisexual, and Transgender People: Building a Foundation for Better Understanding*. Washington, DC: Natl. Acad. Press. **http://www.nap.edu/catalog.php?record_id=13128**

Jellison WA, McConnell AR, Gabriel S. 2004. Implicit and explicit measures of sexual orientation attitudes: ingroup preferences and related behaviors and beliefs among gay and straight men. *Pers. Soc. Psychol. Bull.* 30:629–42

Johnson MK, Rowatt WC, Barnard-Brak LM, Patock-Peckham JA, LaBouff JP, Carlisle RD. 2011. A mediational analysis of the role of right-wing authoritarianism and religious fundamentalism in the religiosity-prejudice link. *Pers. Indiv. Differ.* 50:851–56

Jonathan E. 2008. The influence of religious fundamentalism, right-wing authoritarianism, and Christian orthodoxy on explicit and implicit measures of attitudes toward homosexuals. *Int. J. Psychol. Relig.* 18:316–29

Katz D. 1960. The functional approach to the study of attitudes. *Public Opin. Q.* 24:163–204

Keiller SW. 2010. Masculine norms as correlates of heterosexual men's attitudes toward gay men and lesbian women. *Psychol. Men Masc.* 11:38–52

Kellstedt LA, Smidt C. 1991. Measuring fundamentalism: an analysis of different operational strategies. *J. Sci. Study Relig.* 30:259–78

Kelman HC. 1958. Compliance, identification, and internalization: three processes of attitude change. *J. Confl. Resolut.* 2(1):51–60

Kilianski SE. 2003. Explaining heterosexual men's attitudes toward women and gay men: the theory of exclusively masculine identity. *Psychol. Men Masc.* 4:37–56

Kimmel MS. 1997. Masculinity as homophobia: Fear, shame and silence in the construction of gender identity. In *Toward a New Psychology of Gender*, ed. MM Gergen, SN Davis, pp. 223–42. New York: Routledge

Kirkpatrick LA. 1993. Fundamentalism, Christian orthodoxy, and intrinsic religious orientation as predictors of discriminatory attitudes. *J. Sci. Study Relig.* 32:256–68

Kite ME. 1994. When perceptions meet reality: individual differences in reactions to lesbians and gay men. In *Lesbian and Gay Psychology: Theory, Research, and Clinical Applications*, ed. B Greene, GM Herek, pp. 25–53. Thousand Oaks, CA: Sage

Kite ME, Deaux K. 1986. Attitudes toward homosexuality: assessment and behavioral consequences. *Basic Appl. Soc. Psychol.* 7:137–62

Kite ME, Whitley BE Jr. 1996. Sex differences in attitudes toward homosexual persons, behaviors, and civil rights: a meta-analysis. *Pers. Soc. Psychol. Bull.* 22:336–53

Kite ME, Whitley BE Jr. 1998. Do heterosexual women and men differ in their attitudes toward homosexuality? A conceptual and methodological analysis. In *Stigma and Sexual Orientation: Understanding Prejudice Against Lesbians, Gay Men, and Bisexuals*, ed. GM Herek, pp. 39–61. Thousand Oaks, CA: Sage

Kruglanski AW, Orehek E. 2009. Toward a relativity theory of rationality. *Soc. Cogn.* 27:639–60

Langton L, Planty M. 2011. *Hate Crime, 2003–2009*. Washington, DC: U.S. Dep. Justice. **http://bjs.ojp.usdoj.gov/index.cfm?ty=pbdetail&iid=1760**

Larsen KS, Reed M, Hoffman S. 1980. Attitudes of heterosexuals toward homosexuality: a Likert-type scale and construct validity. *J. Sex Res.* 16:245–57

Laythe B, Finkel D, Kirkpatrick LA. 2001. Predicting prejudice from religious fundamentalism and right-wing authoritarianism: a multiple-regression approach. *J. Sci. Study Relig.* 40:1–10

Lemm KM. 2006. Positive associations among interpersonal contact, motivation, and implicit and explicit attitudes toward gay men. *J. Homosex.* 51(2):79–99

Lewis GB. 2003. Black-white differences in attitudes toward homosexuality and gay rights. *Public Opin. Q.* 67:59–78

Lewis GB. 2011. The friends and family plan: contact with gays and support for gay rights. *Pol. Stud. J.* 39:217–38

Lottes IL, Grollman EA. 2010. Conceptualization and assessment of homonegativity. *Int. J. Sex. Health* 22:219–33

Mahaffey AL, Bryan A, Hutchison KE. 2005. Using startle eye blink to measure the affective component of antigay bias. *Basic Appl. Soc. Psychol.* 27:37–45

Mahaffey AL, Bryan AD, Ito TA, Hutchison KE. 2011. In search of the defensive function of sexual prejudice: exploring antigay bias through shorter and longer lead startle eye blink. *J. Appl. Soc. Psychol.* 41:27–44

Maio GR, Olson JM. 2000. *Why We Evaluate: Functions of Attitudes.* Mahwah, NJ: Erlbaum

Mak HK, Tsang J-A. 2008. Separating the "sinner" from the "sin": religious orientation and prejudiced behavior toward sexual orientation and promiscuous sex. *J. Sci. Study Relig.* 47:379–92

Martin CL, Ruble DN. 2010. Patterns of gender development. *Annu. Rev. Psychol.* 61:353–81

Mavor KI, Macleod CJ, Boal MJ, Louis WR. 2009. Right-wing authoritarianism, fundamentalism and prejudice revisited: removing suppression and statistical artefact. *Pers. Indiv. Differ.* 46:592–97

McConahay JB. 1986. Modern racism, ambivalence, and the Modern Racism Scale. In *Prejudice, Discrimination, and Racism*, ed. JF Dovidio, SL Gaertner, pp. 91–125. Orlando, FL: Academic

McFarland SG. 1989. Religious orientations and the targets of discrimination. *J. Sci. Study Relig.* 28:324–36

Meaney GJ, Rye BJ. 2010. Gendered egos: attitude functions and gender as predictors of homonegativity. *J. Homosex.* 57:1274–302

Meier BP, Robinson MD, Gaither GA, Heinert NJ. 2006. A secret attraction or defensive loathing? Homophobia, defense, and implicit cognition. *J. Res. Pers.* 40:377–94

Mohr JJ, Rochlen AB. 1999. Measuring attitudes regarding bisexuality in lesbian, gay male, and heterosexual populations. *J. Counsel. Psychol.* 46:353–69

Monteith MJ. 1993. Self-regulation of prejudiced responses: implication for progress in prejudice-reduction efforts. *J. Pers. Soc. Psychol.* 65:469–84

Monteith MJ. 1996. Affective reactions to prejudice-related discrepant responses: the impact of standard salience. *Pers. Soc. Psychol. Bull.* 22:48–59

Monteith MJ, Deneen NE, Tooman GD. 1996. The effect of social norm activation on the expression of opinions concerning gay men and blacks. *Basic Appl. Soc. Psychol.* 18:267–88

Morrison MA, Morrison TG. 2002. Development and validation of a scale measuring modern prejudice toward gay men and lesbian women. *J. Homosex.* 43(2):15–37

Morrison MA, Morrison TG. 2011. Sexual orientation bias toward gay men and lesbian women: modern homonegative attitudes and their association with discriminatory behavioral intentions. *J. Appl. Soc. Psychol.* 41:2573–99

Morrison MA, Morrison TG, Franklin R. 2009. Modern and old-fashioned homonegativity among samples of Canadian and American university students. *J. Cross-Cult. Psychol.* 40:523–42

Morrison TG, Parriag AV, Morrison MA. 1999. The psychometric properties of the homonegativity scale. *J. Homosex.* 37(4):111–26

Nagoshi JL, Adams KA, Terrell HK, Hill ED, Brzuzy S, Nagoshi CT. 2008. Gender differences in correlates of homophobia and transphobia. *Sex Roles* 59:521–31

Natl. Gay Lesbian Task Force. 2012. *Reports and Research: Issue Maps.* **http://ngltf.org/reports_and_research/issue_maps**

Norton AT, Herek GM. 2012. Heterosexuals' attitudes toward transgender people: findings from a national probability sample of U.S. adults. *Sex Roles.* DOI: 10.1007/s11199-011-0110-6. In press

O'Donohue WT, Caselles CE. 1993. Homophobia: conceptual, definitional, and value issues. *J. Psychopath. Behav. Assess.* 15:177–95

Olson LR, Cadge W, Harrison JT. 2006. Religion and public opinion about same-sex marriage. *Soc. Sci. Q.* 87:340–60

Parrott DJ. 2009. Aggression toward gay men as gender role enforcement: effects of male role norms, sexual prejudice, and masculine gender role stress. *J. Pers.* 77:1137–66

Parrott DJ, Adams HE, Zeichner A. 2002. Homophobia: personality and attitudinal correlates. *Pers. Indiv. Differ.* 32:1269–78

Parrott DJ, Peterson JL, Bakeman R. 2011. Determinants of aggression toward sexual minorities in a community sample. *Psychol. Viol.* 1:41–52

Parrott DJ, Peterson JL, Vincent W, Bakeman R. 2008. Correlates of anger in response to gay men: effects of male gender role beliefs, sexual prejudice, and masculine gender role stress. *Psychol. Men Masc.* 9:167–78

Pettigrew TF, Tropp LR. 2006. A meta-analytic test of intergroup contact theory. *J. Pers. Soc. Psychol.* 90:751–83

Poteat VP. 2007. Peer group socialization of homophobic attitudes and behavior during adolescence. *Child Dev.* 78:1830–42

Poteat VP, Espelage DL, Green HD Jr. 2007. The socialization of dominance: peer group contextual effects on homophobic and dominance attitudes. *J. Pers. Soc. Psychol.* 92:1040–50

Quinn DM, Chaudoir SR. 2009. Living with a concealable stigmatized identity: the impact of anticipated stigma, centrality, salience, and cultural stigma on psychological distress and health. *J. Pers. Soc. Psychol.* 97:634–51

Raja S, Stokes JP. 1998. Assessing attitudes toward lesbians and gay men: the modern homophobia scale. *J. Gay Lesbian Bisex. Identity* 3(2):113–34

Ricketts WA, Hudson WW. 1998. Index of homophobia (Index of Attitudes Toward Homosexuals). In *Handbook of Sexuality-Related Measures*, ed. CM Davis, WL Yarber, R Bauserman, G Schreer, SL Davis, pp. 367–68. Thousand Oaks, CA: Sage

Rodriguez EM. 2010. At the intersection of church and gay: a review of the psychological research on gay and lesbian Christians. *J. Homosex.* 57(1):5–38

Rosik CH. 2007. Ideological concerns in the operationalization of homophobia, part I: an analysis of Herek's ATLG-R scale. *J. Psychol. Theol.* 35:132–44

Rowatt WC, Tsang J-A, Kelly J, LaMartina B, McCullers M, McKinley A. 2006. Associations between religious personality dimensions and implicit homosexual prejudice. *J. Sci. Study Relig.* 45:397–406

Russell GM. 2011. Motives of heterosexual allies in collective action for equality. *J. Soc. Issues* 67:376–93

Russell ST, Kosciw J, Horn S, Saewyc E. 2010. Safe schools policy for LGBTQ students. *Soc. Policy Rep.* 24(4):3–17

Rye BJ, Meaney GJ. 2010. Measuring homonegativity: a psychometric analysis. *Can. J. Behav. Sci.* 42(3):158–67

Scott J. 1998. Changing attitudes to sexual morality: a cross-national comparison. *Sociology* 32:815–45

Shields SA, Harriman RE. 1984. Fear of male homosexuality: cardiac responses of low and high homonegative males. *J. Homosex.* 10(1–2):53–67

Sinn JS. 1997. The predictive and discriminant validity of masculinity ideology. *J. Res. Pers.* 31:117–35

Smith MB. 1997. *The Authoritarian Personality*: a re-review 46 years later. *Pol. Psychol.* 18:159–63

Smith MB, Bruner JS, White RW. 1956. *Opinions and Personality*. New York: Wiley

Smith M. 2012. A quiet struggle within the gay marriage fight. *N.Y. Times*, Feb. 19, p. A25 **http://www.nytimes.com/2012/02/19/us/within-gay-marriage-battle-a-quiet-struggle-in-churches.html**

Spalding LR, Peplau LA. 1997. The unfaithful lover: heterosexuals' perceptions of bisexuals and their relationships. *Psychol. Women Quart.* 21:611–25

Steffens MC. 2005. Implicit and explicit attitudes towards lesbians and gay men. *J. Homosex.* 49(2):39–66

Steffens MC, Buchner A. 2003. Implicit Association Test: separating transsituationally stable and variable components of attitudes toward gay men. *Exp. Psychol.* 50:33–48

Steffens MC, Wagner C. 2004. Attitudes toward lesbians, gay men, bisexual women, and bisexual men in Germany. *J. Sex Res.* 41:137–49

Stefurak T, Taylor C, Mehta S. 2010. Gender-specific models of homosexual prejudice: religiosity, authoritarianism, and gender roles. *Psychol. Relig. Spirit.* 2:247–61

Stenner K. 2005. *The Authoritarian Dynamic*. Cambridge, UK: Cambridge Univ. Press

Stokes CE, Ellison CG. 2010. Religion and attitudes toward divorce laws among U.S. adults. *J. Fam. Iss.* 31:1279–304

Swim JK, Aikin KJ, Hall WS, Hunter BA. 1995. Sexism and racism: old-fashioned and modern prejudices. *J. Pers. Soc. Psychol.* 68:199–214

Talley AE, Bettencourt BA. 2008. Evaluations and aggression directed at a gay male target: the role of threat and antigay prejudice. *J. Appl. Soc. Psychol.* 38:647–83

Teige-Mocigemba S, Klauer KC, Sherman JW. 2010. A practical guide to implicit association tests and related tasks. In *Handbook of Implicit Social Cognition: Measurement, Theory, and Applications*, ed. B Gawronski, BK Payne, pp. 117–39. New York: Guilford

Theodore PS, Basow SA. 2000. Heterosexual masculinity and homophobia: a reaction to the self? *J. Homosex.* 40(2):31–48

U.S. Commiss. Civil Rights. 2011. *Peer-to-Peer Violence and Bullying: Examining the Federal Response.* Washington, DC: U.S. Commiss. Civil Rights. **http://www.usccr.gov/pubs/2011statutory.pdf**

U.N. High Commiss. Human Rights. 2011. *Discriminatory laws and practices and acts of violence against individuals based on their sexual orientation and gender identity.* New York: U.N. High Commiss. Human Rights. **http://www2.ohchr.org/english/bodies/hrcouncil/docs/19session/A.HRC.19.41_English.pdf**

Vandello JA, Bosson JK, Cohen D, Burnaford RM, Weaver JR. 2008. Precarious manhood. *J. Pers. Soc. Psychol.* 95:1325–39

Vescio TK, Biernat M. 2003. Family values and antipathy toward gay men. *J. Appl. Soc. Psychol.* 33:833–47

Vincent W, Parrott DJ, Peterson JL. 2011a. Combined effects of masculine gender-role stress and sexual prejudice on anger and aggression toward gay men. *J. Appl. Soc. Psychol.* 41:1237–57

Vincent W, Parrott DJ, Peterson JL. 2011b. Effects of traditional gender role norms and religious fundamentalism on self-identified heterosexual men's attitudes, anger, and aggression toward gay men and lesbians. *Psychol. Men Masc.* 12:383–400

Vonofakou C, Hewstone M, Voci A. 2007. Contact with out-group friends as a predictor of meta-attitudinal strength and accessibility of attitudes toward gay men. *J. Pers. Soc. Psychol.* 92:804–20

Waldo CR, Berdahl JL, Fitzgerald LF. 1998. Are men sexually harassed? If so, by whom? *Law Hum. Behav.* 22(1):59–79

Wall BW. 2000. Criminal responsibility, diminished capacity, and the gay panic defense. *J. Am. Acad. Psychiatry Law* 28:454–59

Weinberg G. 1972. *Society and the Healthy Homosexual.* New York: St. Martin's

Weinstein N, Ryan WS, DeHaan CR, Przybylski AK, Legate N, et al. 2012. Parental autonomy support and discrepancies between implicit and explicit sexual identities: dynamics of self-acceptance and defense. *J. Pers. Soc. Psychol.* 102:815–32

Whitley BE Jr. 2001. Gender-role variables and attitudes toward homosexuality. *Sex Roles* 45:691–721

Whitley BE Jr. 2009. Religiosity and attitudes toward lesbians and gay men: a meta-analysis. *Int. J. Psychol. Relig.* 19:21–38

Wilcox C, Norrander B. 2002. Of moods and morals: the dynamics of opinion on abortion and gay rights. In *Understanding Public Opinion*, ed. B Norrander, C Wilcox, pp. 121–47. Washington, DC: CQ Press

Wood W. 2000. Attitude change: persuasion and social influence. *Annu. Rev. Psychol.* 51:539–70

Woodberry RD, Smith CS. 1998. Fundamentalism et al: conservative Protestants in America. *Annu. Rev. Sociol.* 24:25–56

Wright LW Jr, Adams HE, Bernat J. 1999. Development and validation of the homophobia scale. *J. Psychopath. Behav. Assess.* 21:337–47

Yang AS. 1997. Trends: attitudes toward homosexuality. *Public Opin. Quart.* 61:477–507

A Cultural Neuroscience Approach to the Biosocial Nature of the Human Brain

Shihui Han,[1] Georg Northoff,[2] Kai Vogeley,[3,4] Bruce E. Wexler,[5] Shinobu Kitayama,[6] and Michael E.W. Varnum[1]

[1] Department of Psychology, Peking University, Beijing, 100871, People's Republic of China; email: shan@pku.edu.cn

[2] Mind, Brain Imaging and Neuroethics, Institute of Mental Health Research University of Ottawa, Ottawa ON K1Z 7K4, Canada

[3] Department of Psychiatry, University of Cologne, Cologne 50924, Germany

[4] Institute of Neuroscience and Medicine, Cognitive Neuroscience (INM3), Research Center Juelich, Juelich 52425, Germany

[5] Department of Psychiatry, Yale University, New Haven, Connecticut 06519

[6] Department of Psychology, University of Michigan, Ann Arbor, Michigan 48109-1109

Annu. Rev. Psychol. 2013. 64:335–59

First published online as a Review in Advance on September 17, 2012

The *Annual Review of Psychology* is online at psych.annualreviews.org

This article's doi: 10.1146/annurev-psych-071112-054629

Keywords

cultural neuroscience, culture, brain imaging, human brain, race

Abstract

Cultural neuroscience (CN) is an interdisciplinary field that investigates the relationship between culture (e.g., value and belief systems and practices shared by groups) and human brain functions. In this review we describe the origin, aims, and methods of CN as well as its conceptual framework and major findings. We also clarify several misunderstandings of CN research. Finally, we discuss the implications of CN findings for understanding human brain function in sociocultural contexts and novel questions that future CN research should address. By doing so, we hope to provide a clear picture of the CN approach to the human brain and culture and to elucidate the intrinsically biosocial nature of the functional organization of the human brain.

Contents

INTRODUCTION

During the past few years, brain imaging studies have uncovered variations in the neural substrates of human cognition in different cultural groups. The integration of theory and methods from social and cultural psychology, cognitive neuroscience, and other related disciplines gave birth to a new field—cultural neuroscience (CN). This new field investigates how human brain functions are shaped by interactions between culture, the brain, and genes. CN has developed specific methods for uncovering cultural influences on human brain functions, and it has provided a new perspective on the functional organization of the human brain in sociocultural environments. The growth of this new field can be seen in the increasing number of research articles and several special issues dedicated to CN (e.g., *Progress in Brain Research* in 2009; *Social Cognitive and Affective Neuroscience* in 2010) in addition to edited books (e.g., Han & Pöppel 2011) and its coverage in textbooks (e.g., Ward 2012).

CN is receiving more and more attention from researchers in different fields because CN touches upon concepts such as humans, culture, and race that are often used in a wider context beyond and outside CN. Thus it is important to take stock of the progress so far by providing a comprehensive overview of the field as well as addressing some questions and concerns that have been voiced about this endeavor. The goals of the current review are (*a*) to elucidate the origin, aims and concepts, empirical methods, and findings of CN studies; (*b*) to clarify misunderstanding of CN findings; (*c*) to discuss the implications of CN findings for understanding the biosocial nature of the human brain; and (*d*) to address key questions for future CN studies.

WHAT IS CULTURAL NEUROSCIENCE?

The term cultural neuroscience was initially introduced by Chiao & Ambady (2007, p. 238), who defined CN as "a theoretical and empirical approach to investigate and characterize the mechanisms by which [the] hypothesized bidirectional, mutual constitution of culture, brain, and genes occurs." This definition was further refined by Chiao (2010, p. 109), who described CN as an "interdisciplinary field bridging cultural psychology, neurosciences and neurogenetics that explains how the neurobiological processes, such as genetic expression and brain function, give rise to cultural values, practices and beliefs as well as how culture shapes neurobiological processes across macro- and microtime scales." These concepts resonate with recent efforts to integrate research findings from neuroscience, genetics, developmental psychology, and sociology by highlighting the role of postnatal neuroplasticity in human development (e.g., Li 2003, Wexler 2006). In the remainder of this section we seek to provide a description of CN, starting with its origin and aims. Next we define key theoretical concepts in CN. This is followed by an overview of common CN methodology. Finally, we end the section by reviewing the empirical findings of CN studies using different methods.

Origin

CN emerges from the integration of different branches of social sciences and natural sciences and arises mainly from two disciplines, i.e., cultural psychology, which has provided the insight that cognitive, emotional, and motivational tendencies and habits are shaped by culture, and neuroscience, which has demonstrated that the brain is shaped by experience. We here show that CN is based on four key approaches, i.e., cultural psychology, social cognitive neuroscience, the study of neuroplasticity, and the study of culture × gene interactions.

Cultural psychology. Although there is a long history of the debate about the concept of culture (Kroeber & Kluckhohn 1952), it is commonly acknowledged that cultural groups have differentiated over thousands of years to create what has been called cultural speciation (Goodall & Berman 1999). The resulting cultural differences still exist in our globalized world and are associated with certain differences in the ways people think and behave. These differences exist side by side with many cross-cultural commonalities. Cultural differences in human behaviors are very well documented in anthropology (e.g., Haviland et al. 2008), and human development has been viewed as a process of acquiring and embodying culture's belief systems (Rogoff 2003). Cultural differences in human mental processes and underlying cognitive mechanisms have been investigated extensively in cultural psychology during the past two decades. From this line of research, theoretical frameworks such as individualistic versus collectivistic values, independent self-construals versus interdependent self-construals, and holistic versus analytic cognitive tendencies have emerged to guide empirical studies of cultural discrepancy in human cognition and emotion (Kitayama & Cohen 2007, Nisbett et al. 2001, Varnum et al. 2010). Cultural psychology takes the view that human cognitive and affective processes vary as a function of cultural environments that provide unique social contexts in which psychological

processes develop and are shaped (Kitayama & Uskul 2011). The findings of cultural psychological research stimulate researchers to investigate neural substrates of cultural diversity of human cognition and emotion.

Social cognitive neuroscience. Social cognitive neuroscience research investigates brain mechanisms that allow human beings to understand the self and others and to efficiently navigate social environments (Ochsner & Lieberman 2001). Early social cognitive neuroscience research focused on the neural substrates underpinning social cognition by combining brain imaging and social psychological paradigms. Most of these studies aimed to uncover the neural mechanisms of social cognition and behavior without considering potential cultural differences. However, an important feature of social cognition and behavior is context dependence. We are always situationally embedded in a certain environment, the "context," which substantially influences our perception of others and our understanding of the behavior of others. This context dependency itself underlies substantial influences exerted by culture. In other words, what social information is processed and how it is processed rely heavily on one's interaction partners (in the case of dyadic interactions) and, more broadly, on the social context in which the interactions occur. For example, cultural psychological studies have documented numerous variations in social cognitive processes across different cultural contexts, such as construal of the self (Markus & Kitayama 1991, 2010), causal attribution of physical and social events (Choi et al. 1999), analytic versus holistic attention (Masuda & Nisbett 2001), affective states that people ideally like to feel (Tsai et al. 2006), and choice-induced dissonance (Kitayama et al. 2004), among many others. Due to the considerable evidence for cultural divergence of human subjective experiences and psychological processes, recently neuroscientists have shown increasing interest in whether parallel differences in neural mechanisms might also be present

Independent self-construal: a tendency to view the self as autonomous and bounded; an emphasis on affirming the independence and uniqueness of the self

Interdependent self-construal: a tendency to view the self as interconnected and overlapping with close others; an emphasis on affirming close relationships and maintaining harmony within them

among people who were raised in different sociocultural contexts (Ambady & Bharucha 2009; Ames & Fiske 2010; Chiao & Bebko 2011; Han & Northoff 2008, 2009; Kitayama & Uskul 2011; Park & Gutchess 2006; Park & Huang 2010; Rule et al. 2012). On the theoretical basis alone, cultural influences on the neural substrates underlying human cognitive and affective processes would seem highly plausible given that it takes almost 20 years for a large portion of the brain to mature (Gogtay et al. 2004). During this period the brain is influenced by personal experiences in a specific cultural context. Thus in the beginning of the twenty-first century, researchers started to examine potential cultural differences in human brain mechanisms involved in multiple cognitive and affective processes by comparing brain imaging results obtained from different cultural groups. There is now substantial evidence that individuals from different sociocultural contexts show distinct patterns of brain activity involved in cognition and behavior.

Neuroplasticity. Biological research has shown ample evidence for the intrinsic plasticity of the human brain; that is, the brain changes both structurally and functionally in response to the environment and experience (Shaw & McEachern 2001). For example, the occipital cortex, which is commonly involved in visual processing in sighted humans, can be engaged in auditory processing in blind individuals (Burton et al. 2002, Gougoux et al. 2009). Auditory deprivation results in the recruitment of the primary auditory cortex in the processing of vibrotactile stimuli (Levanen et al. 1998) and sign language (Nishimura et al. 1999) in deaf humans. The medial prefrontal cortex is engaged during self-reflection on visually but not aurally presented trait words in sighted humans, while the region is recruited during self-reflection on aurally presented trait words in congenitally blind individuals (Ma & Han 2011). These findings demonstrate an intrinsic property of the brain, plasticity, which enables the nervous system to respond to environmental pressures, physiological changes,

and personal experiences (Pascual-Leone et al. 2005) and to adapt to social contexts during development (Blakemore 2008). Given that human thoughts and behaviors differ substantially across a variety of sociocultural contexts, it is not surprising that the human brain, the source of human behaviors and the carrier of human thoughts, is modulated by sociocultural environments and develops unique neural mechanisms that help an individual to adapt to culturally specific changes and pressures. Thus an intrinsic feature of the brain is its sociocultural context dependence.

Gene × environment interactions. The basic assumption of CN is that culture provides a framework for social behavior, communication, and interaction that generates social values and norms, assigns meaning to social events, interacts with biological variables (e.g., genes), and codetermines the functional organization of the brain. The CN approach investigates mutual interactions between culture, the brain, and genome, consistent with culture-gene coevolution theory (Boyd & Richerson 1985, Lumsden & Wilson 1981). This theory guides research that explores how two complementary and interacting evolutionary processes, i.e., genetic evolution and cultural evolution, influence human behavior. The CN approach aims to understand how sociocultural contexts influence human behavior by examining cultural influences on underlying neural mechanisms. CN views cultural differences in the neural mechanisms underlying cognition as the product of the interaction between genes and cultural environment, an idea that researchers in this field are beginning to test empirically.

Key Concepts

Next we review some key concepts related to CN. We provide definitions and also highlight conceptual distinctions between terms such as culture, nationality, and race, which some may mistakenly use interchangeably.

Culture is obviously the most important concept in the field of CN. From anthropologists' perspective, culture refers to a system of meanings used to make sense of life (i.e., Kuper 1999). Although there are myriad definitions of culture [indeed, Kroeber & Kluckhohn (1952) listed 164 definitions of culture], culture is often used in three basic senses in social psychology (Chiu & Hong 2006). Material culture consists of all material artifacts produced by human beings. Social culture consists of social rules and social institutions. Subjective culture refers to shared ideas, values, beliefs, and behavioral scripts. These aspects of culture, however, are dynamically related within a given cultural tradition, locale, and/or community and together form a unique social environment for the group of individuals. From the very beginning of their life, people engage in the complex composed of materials and social rules or practices as well as folk beliefs of their respective local communities, and by doing so, they have their brains changed in such a way that the resulting brain functions are attuned closely to the surrounding sociocultural environment.

Culture is different from nationality, which is defined by social group membership based on a shared nation state of origin. Although the term culture emphasizes shared ideas, values, beliefs, and practices, people of the same nationality do not necessarily share the same beliefs, values, or practices. Similar to social psychology studies, most CN studies use the term culture in the sense of a social group whose members share social values, knowledge, and practices. Some CN studies have recruited participants from two different cultural groups (e.g., Westerners and East Asians) based on cultural psychology findings that suggest that the two groups differ in specific cultural values or specific cognitive processes. In some cases race and language are concomitants that also differentiate two cultural groups. Other CN studies have investigated two cultural groups who are from the same nation but are defined by religious or political beliefs. In such cases two groups of participants share the same nationality, race, and language but differ only in a set of shared beliefs/values and practices that are

hypothesized to be relevant to a particular pattern of neural activity.

Recent CN studies have directly measured cultural values from different groups and have assessed the relationship between these values and neural responses. For example, the Self-Construal Scale (Singelis 1994) has been used in several recent CN studies to evaluate individuals' independent versus interdependent self-construals (e.g., Chiao et al. 2009a, de Greck et al. 2012, Na & Kitayama 2011, Sul et al. 2012). This approach seeks to simultaneously capture both within- and between-group variations instead of assuming, a priori, that people from two sociocultural contexts must have different cultural values. It therefore acknowledges individual differences in cultural values among those who grow up in the same sociocultural context. Moreover, measuring cultural values allows researchers to examine whether a group difference in brain activity is associated with a specific cultural value, whether cultural group differences in brain activity are mediated by a specific cultural value, and how individual differences in brain activity are associated with variations in cultural values within a given cultural group.

Cultural psychology views culture as a dynamic knowledge system rather than a rigid set of stereotypes about a social group (Markus & Hamedani 2007). Culture represents a dynamic concept of the social environment that is not part of the innate biological condition of humans. Humans are not born with propensities for any particular culture but rather with the potential and the capacity to acquire and to create culture (Harris 1999). Thus an individual may change his/her cultural values and beliefs as a result of experience (such as emigrating from his/her native country). People from the same cultural groups can be quite heterogeneous in terms of the values and beliefs they acquire. This is particularly true in contemporary societies where cultural exchanges occur often and rapidly. People in modern societies are rarely monocultural because they are almost always exposed, often deeply, to other cultures' practices and beliefs in multiple sociocultural contexts. Thus multiple cultural systems may become part of any single individual, and as a consequence, it is often required to switch to and fro between different cultural systems during social interactions depending on specific contexts of social encounters (Hong et al. 2000). This dynamic model of culture allows us to test whether brain activity underlying human cognition can vary on a short temporal scale as a function of recent use of one cultural system or another (e.g., cultural priming, as is discussed in more detail when we turn to the methodology of CN research). Taken together, CN studies view culture as a complex and dynamic external social environment in which the human brain is fostered and shaped. Rather than considering the brain and its neuronal states by themselves, CN emphasizes the sociocultural nature of the human brain and places great weight on the influence of cultural values, beliefs, and practices shared by a social group on functional organization of the human brain.

Race is a way of categorizing human beings on the basis of external attributes, such as skin tone and facial and body shapes, that differentiate human populations. In many racial theories, and in lay theories, racial groups also possess different fixed and biologically determined psychological traits and tendencies. Race is viewed as fixed both over the course of the lifespan and across cultural contexts. People from the same racial group are thought to be homogenous in terms of heritage and physical appearance. However, in reality individuals classified as belonging to the same race do not necessarily share the same cultural values and experiences. For example, Native Chinese and Chinese Americans may be thought to belong to the same racial group but may have distinct cultural values and beliefs and experiences. There has long been a debate over whether racial differences in psychological tendencies and behavior exist and if so whether such differences are biologically determined. As a starting point, there is the question of whether contemporary racial categories can be genetically differentiated. Although some have noted a great deal of genetic similarities across races (humans are 99.9%

alike) and argued that it is very difficult to ascertain the racial identity of individuals through their genes (Littlefield et al. 1982), recent large-scale studies using genetic cluster analysis have found correlations between self-reported racial group membership and the genetic cluster of racial groups (e.g., Paschou et al. 2010, Tang et al. 2005). However, these data do not speak to the question of whether racial groups are psychologically different, nor do they address whether such differences (if they exist) are solely or partially genetically driven.

Regardless of whether race has a biological component, race does have a number of complex sociopolitical implications and may be analyzed as a sociocultural construction. Moya & Markus (2011, p. 21) recently defined race as "a dynamic set of historically derived and institutionalized ideas and practices that (1) sorts people into ethnic groups according to perceived physical and behavioral human characteristics; (2) associates differential value, power, and privilege with these characteristics and establishes a social status ranking among the different groups; and (3) emerges when groups are perceived (a) to pose a threat (political, economic, or cultural) to each other's world view or way of life; and/or (b) to justify the denigration and exploitation (past, current, or future) of, and prejudice toward, other groups." In addition, race has a strong evaluative component that has been often used to qualify individuals from different races as superior or inferior on the basis of untested or discredited assumptions related to genetics.

Aims

The goal of CN studies is to investigate human brain function and structure in diverse sociocultural contexts. Like cultural psychologists (Markus & Hamedani 2007), CN researchers have little interest in using brain activity as a way to classify people into groups. Instead, CN research investigates whether and how the functional organization of the human brain is shaped by culture and by the interaction between culture and genes on different time scales (Chiao & Ambady 2007, Han & Northoff 2008). In addition, CN research aims to investigate how neurobiological processes in the human brain contribute to the rise of divergent cultures in the world. Theories built on CN findings will eventually help to explain how cultural differences in human brain function mediate divergent social behaviors across cultures while at the same time pointing out the neural predispositions of psychosocial commonalities across different cultures. CN considers culture as a highly dynamic system of continuous interaction and exchange among individuals. This system of social interaction feeds back into social practices, values, and belief systems, thereby establishing circular, recursive, and reciprocal influences between interacting individuals and culture (Hacking 1999, Vogeley & Roepstorff 2009).

Most current CN studies focus on cross-cultural differences in the neural substrates of human psychological processes including cognition, emotion, and motivation (Ambady & Bharucha 2009; Han & Northoff 2008, 2009; Kitayama & Uskul 2011). This line of research has mainly been stimulated by findings in cultural psychology that show cross-cultural variation in multiple levels of psychological processes (Kitayama & Cohen 2007, Nisbett et al. 2001). By comparing behavioral performances among individuals from Western (e.g., European and American) and East Asian (e.g., Chinese, Japanese, Korean) contexts, cultural psychologists have shown evidence for distinct, culture-dependent cognitive processing styles in perception (Ji et al. 2000), attention (Kitayama et al. 2003, Masuda & Nisbett 2001), memory (Wang & Conway 2004), perspective taking (Wu & Keysar 2007), causal attribution of events (Morris & Peng 1994, Peng & Knowles 2003), object categorization (Ji et al. 2004), recognition of one's own face (Liew et al. 2011b; Ma & Han 2009, 2010; Sui et al. 2009), self-construal (Markus & Kitayama 1991), and affect valuation (Tsai et al. 2006), among many others.

Based on the fundamental hypothesis that human psychological processes are mediated by specific neural substrates in the brain, CN studies have initially focused on whether different neural substrates may be engaged in a variety of cognitive processes among individuals in East Asian and Western cultural contexts. As a part of this line of research, CN researchers have found evidence for cultural differences in the neural mechanisms involved in visual perception (Goh et al. 2007, 2010; Gutchess et al. 2006; Jenkins et al. 2010), attention (Hedden et al. 2008, Lewis et al. 2008), causal attribution of physical events (Han et al. 2011), semantic relationship processing (Gutchess et al. 2010), musical processing (Nan et al. 2006, 2009), mental calculation (Tang et al. 2006), recognition of one's own face (Sui et al. 2009), self-reflection on personality traits (Chiao et al. 2009a,b; Wang et al. 2012; Zhu et al. 2007), perception of bodily expression (Freeman et al. 2009), mental state reasoning (Adams et al. 2009, Kobayashi et al. 2006), empathy (de Greck et al. 2012), and in other domains. These CN findings indicate that a fundamental aspect of the functional organization of the human brain is its sensitivity to the sociocultural contexts in which individuals are brought up. However, the final goal of CN research is not simply to show differences in brain activity across cultural groups. Rather, CN studies aim to provide a neuroscientific account of cross-cultural variation in human psychological functions and behaviors by discovering socioculturally patterned neural mechanisms and their development. Thus CN studies aim to reveal both culturally universal and culturally unique neural processes by which human brains predispose us to perceive self and others, communicate and interact with conspecifics, and guide actions.

Recently, there has been an increasing interest in how brain function is shaped by culture-gene interaction, based on culture-gene coevolution theory (Boyd & Richerson 1985, Lumsden & Wilson 1981). However, although recent studies have shown that psychological tendencies and behavioral outcomes associated with specific genotypes are moderated by culture (e.g., Kim et al. 2010a,b), direct evidence that culture moderates the effect of genotype on

Functional magnetic resonance imaging (fMRI): a noninvasive method for recording blood-oxygenation-level-dependent signals that have high spatial resolution and are used to examine brain activations associated with specific stimuli or tasks

Event-related potential (ERP): synchronous activities of neuronal populations engaged in specific psychological processing, which are time locked to stimulus events, can be recorded from electrodes over the scalp, and have high temporal resolution

the functional organization of the brain is still lacking. Another line of research has focused on how the allelic frequencies of a genotype within a population may relate to cultural differences in values. Chiao & Blizinsky (2010) examined the relationship between the cultural phenotypes of individualism-collectivism and allelic frequency of the serotonin transporter functional polymorphism (5-HTTLPR) by assessing the prevalence of the short allele of 5-HTTLPR among different populations. In a comparison of 29 countries, they found that cultures that were high in collectivism contained a significantly greater proportion of short allele carriers and that increased frequency of short allele carriers predicted decreased anxiety and mood disorder prevalence. Further, the relationships between the prevalence of short allele carriers within a population and the prevalence of anxiety and mood disorders were mediated by collectivism. Similarly, Way & Lieberman (2010) suggested that collectivism may have developed and persisted in populations with a high proportion of a functional polymorphism (A118G) in the μ-opioid receptor gene—a putative social sensitivity genotype that is compatible with collectivistic cultural groups. Caution is due because this body of evidence is entirely correlational. Nevertheless, given that cultures may interact with the 5-HTTLPR genotypes to influence the prevalence of affective disorders such as anxiety and depression (Chiao & Blizinsky 2010), it would be interesting to study how the culture-gene interaction codetermines the intermediate endophenotype (i.e., neurobiological responsiveness) associated with culture-sensitive cognitive processes.

Methods

Although CN is a young field, CN researchers have developed quite sophisticated methodologies by drawing on prior brain imaging and social and cultural psychology research. Methodological challenges include both the design of psychological experiments and brain imaging techniques. Early CN studies focused

on whether and how two cultural groups differ in neural substrates of specific cognitive and affective processes. A typical way to address this issue is to compare functional magnetic resonance imaging (fMRI) or event-related potential (ERP) brain data obtained from individuals who were raised in two different sociocultural contexts.

One assumption of this approach is that, because participants from two cultural groups differ in cultural knowledge, values, and/or cognitive and affective processes, the underlying neural activity should be different between the groups in a specific way. To address this assumption, CN research has taken cultural psychological research as a guide for its hypotheses about neural differences between specific cultural groups. For example, behavioral research first showed that individuals in Western cultures are more sensitive to salient foreground objects compared to people in East Asian cultures, whereas individuals in East Asian cultures are more inclined to focus their attention broadly on backgrounds relative to people in Western cultures (Ji et al. 2000, Kitayama et al. 2003, Masuda & Nisbett 2001). Such findings lead to a reasonable hypothesis that neural substrates underlying visual perception of and attention to salient objects and contexts may show different patterns between individuals in the Western and East Asian cultures (Goh et al. 2007, Gutchess et al. 2006, Hedden et al. 2008). Similarly, evidence from cultural psychology that the self is viewed as independent in Western cultures and interdependent in East Asian cultures (Markus & Kitayama 1991, Singelis 1994) leads to the hypothesis that neural representation of the self and close others may overlap to a greater degree among East Asians than among Westerners (Zhu et al. 2007).

However, selection of participants from two different nations or sociocultural contexts does not necessarily imply that the participants have distinct cultural values (Oyserman et al. 2002). CN seeks to address this question by measuring the value or self-construal dimensions that are hypothesized to drive the relevant cultural differences in the neural process being studied. Often, CN researchers directly assess the cultural values or self-construals of interest; this can be done using well-established questionnaires developed by social and cultural psychologists. For example, the Self-Construal Scale (Singelis 1994) is widely used to evaluate how people view themselves (either as independent or interdependent) and has been shown to differentiate cultural groups. Current CN studies usually compare participants from two countries, usually a Western culture and an East Asian culture (e.g., British versus Chinese, American versus Japanese). Although previous studies have demonstrated differences between these cultures in terms of values and cognitive and affective processes, it is important to demonstrate that the participants recruited in CN studies actually differ in these dimensions. Measurements of cultural values are also helpful in situating CN studies as dealing with cultural differences rather than racial or national differences. Equally important, measuring cultural values allows for stronger inferences. By examining whether individual differences in cultural values can predict individual differences in brain activity, researchers can probe the association between these values and patterns of brain activity. In addition, measuring cultural values in individual subjects makes it possible to assess whether cultural values mediate differences in brain activity associated with specific tasks, which may be performed in different ways according to the respective degree of the cultural value, between two cultural groups.

Of course, when comparing participants from different sociocultural contexts, it is important to control for potentially confounding variables such as gender, age, and education as well as socioeconomic status. Language is another potential confound in cultural comparisons if stimuli used in brain imaging studies are based on verbal materials. This, however, can be controlled by using the native language for each cultural group so that the same language is used in an experimental condition and a control condition. Such designs allow us to compare the experimental and control conditions so as

to reduce the effect of language processing to a minimum degree.

Another elegant psychological paradigm used by CN researchers is to prime cultural identity or values before recording brain activity during a specific task. Such studies are based on the assumption that individuals can acquire more than one set of cultural knowledge and can use different sets of cultural knowledge depending on contextual cues (Hong et al. 2000). According to this dynamic constructivist model of culture, people who have been exposed to multiple cultures may acquire multiple sets of cultural knowledge, and exposing individuals to cultural symbols may activate specific cultural knowledge and result in mindsets and behaviors that are consistent with that culture. For instance, after cultural priming, bicultural individuals may switch between Western and East Asian mindsets that are consistent with the most accessible cultural knowledge tradition (e.g., Hong et al. 2003). A number of studies have also shown that priming independence and interdependence of self-construals influences patterns of cognitive processes that tend to differ between cultural groups (e.g., Kühnen & Oyserman 2002, Lin & Han 2009; for a review, see Oyserman & Lee 2008). Similarly, CN studies take culture as a dynamic knowledge and meaning system, and they manipulate cultural values as variables (Chiao et al. 2009b, Lin et al. 2008, Ng et al. 2010, Sui & Han 2007, Sui et al. 2012). CN studies using cultural priming test for dynamic changes in brain activity as a function of cultural values and provide information that allows for causal inference regarding the relationship between cultural values and specific brain activity.

CN studies often compare brain-imaging results from multiple cultural groups, and thus several technical issues have to be considered when designing CN research. It is ideal to scan multiple cultural groups at the same experimental site in cross-cultural fMRI studies. This can certainly avoid systematic, site-dependent effects in fMRI sensitivity between the scanner facilities, although between-subject differences can account for nearly ten times more variance than site effects when participants are scanned using the same type of scanner at two sites (Sutton et al. 2008). For those CN studies that scan multiple cultural groups at different sites, Chiao et al. (2010) has suggested several ways to reduce the probability of systematic, site-dependent effects in fMRI sensitivity. First, both functional and anatomical MRI data should be collected using scanners from the same vendor with identical protocols. Second, an interscanner reliability test can be conducted by scanning a separate cohort of participants or phantom data at each scanner facility, thus enabling one to quantify and statistically compare signal-to-noise ratio across scanner sites. Third, the presentation software and hardware should be identical, calibrated and tested at each session, and scripts should be written and implemented across the sites in a culturally appropriate manner.

Relative to fMRI, electroencephalogram (EEG) is a simpler method for cross-cultural comparisons of brain activity. Similar EEG recording systems can be found easily at different recording sites. Portable EEG amplifiers are available and can be easily transferred between different recording sites so that EEG data from different cultural groups can be recorded using the same system. Analyzing ERPs that are time locked to a stimulus or a response is particularly helpful for uncovering the time course of neural responses to multiple cognitive processes such as recognition of one's own face (Sui et al. 2009, 2012), inference of one's own and others' personality traits (Mu & Han 2010, Na & Kitayama 2011), implicit processing of vocal tone (Ishii et al. 2010), emotion regulation (Murata et al. 2012), and musical processing (Nan et al. 2006, 2009).

Findings

Several recent review articles have summarized major findings from CN research (e.g., Ambady & Bharucha 2009; Ames & Fiske 2010; Chiao & Bebko 2011; Han & Northoff 2008, 2009; Kitayama & Uskul 2011; Park & Huang 2010; Rule et al. 2012). Thus this section is not intended to give an extensive review of current CN findings. Instead, we highlight a select set of recent CN studies in terms of their methodology in order to illustrate the intellectual development of CN research.

Distinct neural activity to cultural familiar/unfamiliar stimuli. One question that CN researchers are interested in is how human brain activity is tuned by culturally familiar/unfamiliar information. To address this, CN researchers simply recorded neural activity to culturally familiar/unfamiliar stimuli from one cultural group. For example, to investigate the neural basis of musical phrase boundary processing during the perception of music from native and nonnative cultures, Nan et al. (2008) used fMRI to record brain activity in German musicians while they categorized phrased Western and Chinese musical excerpts. They found that culturally familiar musical excerpts more strongly activated multiple brain regions including the superior frontal gyrus, the posterior precentral gyrus, and the superior temporal gyrus, possibly reflecting enhanced sensorimotor integration. Culturally unfamiliar musical excerpts, however, more strongly activated the posterior insula as well as the middle frontal and angular gyri, possibly due to higher demands on attention systems and higher loads on basic auditory processing. Similarly, Demorest & Osterhout (2012) recorded ERPs while American participants listened to melodies based in the Western folk tradition or North Indian classical music. ERPs showed that a long latency positive activity was sensitive to the original and deviation form of the melodies, and this effect was more salient in the Western than in the Indian context. The results suggest that people may generate specific expectancies when listening to culturally familiar music, whereas they may remain unable to develop such expectancies when hearing culturally unfamiliar music.

Another example of this line of research examined whether observations of culturally familiar/unfamiliar symbolic gestures engage distinct neural subsystems. Liew and colleagues (2011a) scanned Chinese participants while they perceived video clips in which a model showed culturally familiar/unfamiliar symbolic gestures. They found that culturally familiar gestures increased activity in the posterior cingulate cortex, the dorsal portion of the medial prefrontal cortex and the bilateral temporoparietal junction. These brain regions constitute the neural circuit engaged in inference of others' intentions and beliefs (Frith & Frith 2006). In contrast, unfamiliar gestures generated activity in the left inferior parietal lobule, the left superior frontal gyrus, and the bilateral superior parietal lobule. These brain regions make up the neural network involved in automatic motor simulations of observed actions (Rizzolatti & Sinigaglia 2010). Apparently, the mentalizing system is engaged during observation of culturally familiar gestures in order to understand others' intentions or beliefs, whereas the mirror neuron system may be activated during perception of culturally unfamiliar gestures so as to capture others' mind through automatic motor simulations of observed actions. Taken together, these findings indicate that long-term cultural experiences may result in specific neural mechanisms in the human brain that deal with culturally familiar information. This may allow the individual to quickly comprehend the meaning of social information in one's own culture, predict others' behavior, and take appropriate actions in a specific cultural context.

Cultural group differences in neural activity. The mainstream of CN studies focuses on whether differences in cognitive processes between two cultural groups revealed by cultural psychology are associated with distinct patterns of brain activity. There is now increasing evidence that two cultural groups may employ distinct neural mechanisms while performing seemingly identical cognitive and emotional tasks. This is of fundamental importance to understanding brain-behavior relationships in general as well as to CN. There are two patterns of cultural group difference in the neural activity involved in cognitive and affective processes.

One type of cultural modulation of brain activity is that a specific neural activity is significantly modulated by a particular task in one cultural group but not in another cultural group. Based on the assumption that Westerners tend to attend to salient objects whereas East Asians are inclined to attend to a broad perceptual and conceptual field (Nisbett et al. 2001, Nisbett & Masuda 2003), Jenkins et al. (2010) tested whether the neural activity in the lateral occipital cortex to a target stimulus was more sensitive to background scenes in East Asians than in Westerners. They scanned American and Chinese participants during perception of pictures consisting of a focal object superimposed upon a background scene that was congruent (e.g., a deer in the woods) or incongruent (e.g., a television in the desert) with the target object. The target object was presented on different novel scenes or on a single repeated scene on four successive trials. Adaptation magnitude was calculated by subtracting the neural activity to objects on a repeated scene from that to objects on different novel scenes. Jenkins et al. found that the neural activity in both the right and left lateral occipital cortex showed significantly greater adaptation to incongruent scenes than to congruent scenes, suggesting sensitivity of the occipital activity to the background scenes. However, this effect was evident in Chinese participants but not in American participants. Similar results were observed in another study that recorded ERPs to target objects that were presented on semantic congruent or incongruent background scenes (Goto et al. 2010). It was found that a negative ERP component peaking at about 400 ms after stimulus onset (N400), which has been shown to be sensitive to processing semantic relationships (Kutas & Hillyard 1984), was enlarged by target objects presented on semantically incongruent versus congruent background scenes; however, this effect was observed in Asian Americans but not in European Americans.

This pattern of cultural differences was also observed in neural activity involved in high-level social cognition. To investigate cultural differences in the neural mechanisms

Temporoparietal junction: the cortical junction zone at the border of the posterior parts of the temporal lobe and the inferior parts of the parietal lobe, which has been shown to be involved in belief reasoning and perspective taking

N400: a negative potential that peaks around 400 ms after stimulus onset with the maximum amplitude over the parietal scale site and is sensitive to semantic incongruity between stimuli

underlying causal attribution of physical events, Han and colleagues (2011) first scanned Chinese participants during causality versus motion direction judgments on animations of object collisions. Causality judgments asked participants to infer causes of physical events (i.e., changes of motion direction of a target object after colliding with another object), and motion direction judgments required identification of the motion direction of a target object after colliding with another object. They showed that, relative to motion direction judgments, causality judgments activated the medial prefrontal cortex (MPFC) and the left parietal cortex (LPC). Moreover, they found that MPFC activity was sensitive to the demand to infer causes of events, whereas LPC activity was modulated by the contextual complexity of physical events. In a subsequent experiment, Han et al. (2011) scanned American and Chinese participants during causality versus motion direction judgments on animations of object collisions. They found that American and Chinese participants showed similar MPFC activity involved in causality judgments. However, LPC activity elicited by causality judgments of physical events was evident in Chinese but not in Americans. Thus it can be concluded that LPC activity associated with the contextual processing is more sensitive to cultural differences in causality perception than is MPFC activity engaged in inference of causal relationships.

Zhu et al. (2007) tested cultural differences in the neural activity underlying representation of personality traits of oneself and a close other. According to Markus & Kitayama (1991, 2010), Western cultures encourage self-identity that is independent of social contexts and others, whereas East Asian cultures emphasize fundamental social connections, leading to an interdependent view of the self and partial overlap in representation of the self and close others. This proposition may predict shared neural mechanisms of representation of the self and a close other in East Asian cultures but not in Western cultures. To test this, Zhu and colleagues (2007) scanned Chinese

and Westerners using fMRI during trait judgments of oneself, a close other (i.e., one's mother), and a celebrity. They found that, relative to trait judgments of a celebrity, trait judgments of oneself significantly activated the ventral region of the MPFC in both Chinese and Westerners, suggesting a similar neural substrate of representation of oneself in the two cultural groups. However, trait judgments of one's mother versus a celebrity activated the same brain region in Chinese but not in Westerners, suggesting shared neural representation of the self and a close other in Chinese but not in Westerners. This finding reveals a neural model of cross-cultural variations in representations of a close other in relation to the self.

It is not always true that individuals from East Asian cultures show additional modulations of neural activity in comparison with individuals from Western cultures. In a recent fMRI study, de Greck et al. (2012) examined cultural differences in brain activity during empathy with anger. They scanned Chinese and German participants during an intentional empathy task and found empathy-related neural activity that was specific for each cultural group. Specifically, empathy for angry faces activated the left dorsolateral prefrontal cortex in Chinese participants, but it activated the right temporoparietal junction, the right inferior and superior temporal gyrus, and the left middle insula in Germany participants. These results implicate enhanced emotion regulation during empathy with anger in Chinese culture, in which the attitude toward harmony is more valued (Kim & Markus 1999, Markus & Kitayama 1991). However, in Germans, empathy with anger may be characterized by enhanced inference of others' mind, given the key role of the temporoparietal junction in mental state reasoning (Frith & Frith 2006).

The aforementioned neuroimaging findings are consistent with the idea that cultural practices may produce specific psychological processes that are significant in one culture but not in another culture. One may consequently associate culturally specific psychological process with particular underlying neural mechanisms that are observed in one culture but not in others.

Another type of cultural modulation of brain activity is that a specific neural activity is modulated by a particular task in two cultural groups but in opposite ways. These opposite patterns of neural activity may have nothing to do with the cultural familiarity of the stimuli, but may instead reflect culturally specific cognitive styles. Hedden et al. (2008) assessed cultural differences in the neural activity underlying attentional control by scanning East Asians and Americans in context-dependent or context-independent judgment tasks. Participants were presented with a series of stimuli, each consisting of a vertical line inside a box. The context-dependent task required judgments of whether the box and line combination of each stimulus matched the proportional scaling of the preceding combination. The context-independent judgment task required judgments of whether the current line matched the previous line, regardless of the size of the accompanying box. It was found that the neural activity in the prefrontal and parietal cortices involved in the tasks showed an opposite pattern of activations in the two cultural groups; that is, Americans showed greater prefrontal and parietal activity during the context-dependent than context-independent tasks, whereas East Asians exhibited stronger activity in the prefrontal and parietal cortices during the context-independent than context-dependent tasks. The opposite pattern of neural activity was interpreted as reflecting enhanced sustained attentional control during culturally nonpreferred in comparison with preferred tasks.

Opposite patterns of neural activity in two cultural groups may also arise from distinct cultural values. To examine why American culture tends to reinforce dominant behavior whereas Japanese culture tends to reinforce subordinate behavior, Freeman et al. (2009) scanned American and Japanese individuals during perception of body displays related to dominance and subordination. The neural activity in the bilateral caudate nucleus and MPFC showed an opposite pattern of

modulation by the stimuli in the two cultural groups. Americans showed greater activity in these brain regions when perceiving dominant stimuli than when perceiving subordinate stimuli, whereas the reverse pattern of neural activity in the same brain regions was evident among Japanese. Consistent with the fMRI results, Americans self-reported a tendency toward more dominant behavior, whereas Japanese self-reported a tendency toward more subordinate behavior. Moreover, activity in the right caudate and MPFC correlated with behavioral tendencies toward dominance versus subordination. The findings suggest that functional activity in the mesolimbic reward system is modulated in different (and opposite) ways in order to coordinate with cultural preferences for dominant or subordinate behavior.

Taken together, these brain-imaging findings indicate that the same neural substrates are tuned to a particular task in opposite patterns in different cultures. This may reflect the effects of culturally specific cognitive styles or values. These findings are in concordance with contemporary social psychological models of cultural differences in cognition and provide possible neural accounts of previously observed cultural differences in psychological tendencies and behavior. As discussed below, in many of these studies explicit effort has been made to link the cultural difference to underlying values, self-construals, and/or acculturation levels. Hence, it is neither race nor nationality per se, but rather pertinent psycho-cultural dimensions such as independence/interdependence, individualism/collectivism, or hierarchical/egalitarian orientations that modulate the brain activities that are observed. Thus the concept of race may be regarded as irrelevant on the empirical level. Moreover, none of the aforementioned CN findings can be simply attributed to differences in physical appearance, if any, between different cultural groups.

Other CN studies have investigated cultural influences on neural activity by comparing subcultural groups within a single national culture. For example, Han et al. (2008, 2010) examined whether and how religious beliefs as cultural practice modulate the neural mechanisms underlying self-reflection. They scanned Christian and nonreligious Chinese participants during personal trait judgments of the self and a celebrity and found that in nonreligious Chinese, self-judgments activated the ventral MPFC, a region that is associated with coding the self-relevance of stimuli (Han & Northoff 2009, Northoff et al. 2006). In contrast, in Christian Chinese, self-judgments activated the dorsal MPFC, a brain region that is engaged in inference of others' mental states (Grèzes et al. 2004). The results suggest that religious beliefs produce significant effects on the functional organization of the MPFC in self-reflection independently of race (and also language and nationality). Similarly, using an ERP paradigm, Varnum et al. (2012) found differences in neural responses indicating spontaneous trait inference when comparing European Americans from working-class and middle-class backgrounds that are parallel to differences between those observed between European Americans and East Asians using the same paradigm (Na & Kitayama 2011).

Association between cultural value and brain activity. Increasingly, CN researchers have noticed that it is not enough to show cultural group differences in brain activity involved in a specific task. It is also important to test whether neural activity varies across individuals with different cultural values and whether an observed cultural group difference in brain activity is mediated by a specific cultural value. This line of research helps to further uncover the mechanisms of cultural modulation of human brain activity.

Even individuals from the same cultural groups may differ in many culture-related values and behaviors. Thus it is a novel issue whether observed brain activity in a specific task is associated with a cultural value across individuals. For example, given the difference in self-construals between Western and East Asian cultures (Markus & Kitayama 1991), recent CN studies have investigated whether the variation

of brain activity across individuals is associated with one's self-construal. Self-construal styles can be estimated using the Self-Construal Scale (Singelis 1994), which assesses individual differences in independent/interdependent self-construals. Goto et al. (2010) found that the modulation of the N400 amplitude to target objects by semantically incongruent versus congruent background scenes was stronger in Asian Americans than in European Americans. They also showed evidence that smaller-magnitude N400 incongruity effects were associated with higher independent self-construal scores across the whole subject sample.

Other CN studies found an association between self-construal measurements and brain activity that is directly related to the processing of self-related information. Chiao et al. (2009a) studied Japanese and Caucasian Americans using a general self-referential task (i.e., to judge whether a sentence can describe oneself in general) and a contextual self-referential task (i.e., to judge whether a sentence can describe oneself in a specific context). They found that MPFC activity during contextual versus general self-judgments was positively correlated with self-reported collectivism/ individualism. Similarly, Sul et al. (2012) examined the neural substrates underlying self-reflection in Koreans with different cultural orientations and showed that interdependent self-construals predicted stronger activation in the left superior temporal gyrus related to personality trait judgments. These findings provide evidence that individual differences in brain activity can be associated with a specific cultural value.

While some CN studies have shown cultural group differences in both brain activity and a specific cultural value (e.g., de Greck et al. 2012, Goto et al. 2010), other CN studies have tried to address whether cultural values mediate differences in neural activities that differentiate between two cultural groups. This has been tested using mediation analysis (MacKinnon et al. 2007), which can assess whether a mediating variable transmits the effect of an independent variable on a dependent variable.

To examine cultural effects on neural responses to target objects and stimulus context, Lewis et al. (2008) recorded ERPs from European and East Asian Americans while they responded to a target stimulus (the number 6) and ignored frequent nontarget stimuli (three-character words or numbers) and an infrequent nontarget stimulus (the number 8). A cultural value was measured using the Individualism and Collectivism Attitude Scale (Triandis 1995). Independent self-construal was measured by calculating the average response on the Individualism subscale, and interdependent self-construal was measured by calculating the average response on the Collectivism subscale. They first showed that European Americans displayed relatively greater P3 amplitudes to target events, whereas East Asian Americans displayed relatively greater P3 amplitudes to the infrequent nontarget stimulus (novelty P3). They further found that culture predicted self-construal (the East Asian Americans were significantly more interdependent than the European Americans) and the P3 novelty amplitudes. Most importantly, the effects of culture on the novelty P3 amplitudes were significantly reduced after including the measurement of interdependent self-construal as a mediator. These results indicate that the relationship between culture and novelty P3 was mediated by self-construal.

Similarly, Na & Kitayama (2011) found that the N400 to a trait adjective during a lexical decision task was enlarged when preceded by a facial photo with trait-implying behavior that was semantically incongruent versus congruent with the target trait adjective. This effect was evident in European Americans but not in Asian Americans. Moreover, the N400 incongruity effect was significantly enhanced with increasing independent self-construal, and the cultural difference in the N400 incongruity effect was mediated by independent self-construal. Ma and colleagues (2012) recently investigated whether the brain activity engaged during self-reflection is different between individuals who grow up in Western and East Asian cultural contexts. They scanned Chinese and Danish participants during judgments of social, mental, and physical attributes of themselves and public figures to assess cultural influences on self-referential processing of personal attributes in different dimensions. Self-construal scale measure first confirmed greater endorsement of the cultural value of interdependence in Chinese than in Danes. fMRI results showed that judgments of self versus a public figure elicited greater activation in the MPFC in Danes than in Chinese regardless of attribute dimensions for judgments. In contrast, self-judgments of social attributes induced greater activity in the temporoparietal junction in Chinese than in Danes. Moreover, the temporoparietal junction activity was correlated with interdependence of self-construal across all participants, being stronger in those with greater endorsement of the cultural value of interdependence. Finally, the group difference in the temporoparietal junction activity was mediated by the measure of interdependence of self-construal. Thus the findings of differences in the brain activity are consistent at both the cultural group level and at the individual level. These CN studies not only demonstrated group differences in brain activity but also suggest that the variation in brain activity across cultural groups is mediated by specific cultural values.

Modulations of neural activity by cultural priming. CN researchers have also used priming in order to enable causal inference and to assess the degree to which culturally influenced patterns of neural function are stable or malleable. This more proximal approach to the exploration of the relationship between culture and brain allows researchers to examine cultural influences on neural activity as dynamic processes operating on a short time scale. One approach is to apply iconic cultural primes to bicultural participants. For example, in a study with bicultural participants living in Hong Kong, Ng et al. (2010) used images of Chinese or Western cultural icons

P3: a positive potential that peaks around 300–400 ms after stimulus onset with the maximum amplitude over the parietal or frontal scale sites and is sensitive to stimulus probability and task relevance

as cultural primes. Chinese cultural priming decreased MPFC activity that differentiated between trait judgments of the self and mother, whereas Western cultural priming produced the opposite effect. Such dynamic variation of the neural correlates of the self is consistent with previously observed differences in the neural representations of the self between Chinese and Westerners that reflects the chronic influences of cultural values and practices.

Another line of priming research has focused on manipulating cultural values that are hypothesized to underlie group differences in neural function. For example, Sui & Han (2007) used self-construal priming (Gardner et al. 1999) with a group of Chinese participants, asking them to search for independent or interdependent pronouns (e.g., "I" or "we") in essays. They showed that the right frontal activity related to recognition of one's own face was significantly reduced after the interdependent versus independent self-construal priming. This finding indicates that the neural process involved in recognition of one's own face is shaped by dynamic variation of self-construals. Self-construal priming has also been shown to modulate neural activity related to early perceptual processing (Lin et al. 2008). In this study, Chinese participants were primed with independent or interdependent self-construals before discriminating global or local features of hierarchical stimuli. The ERP results showed that independent self-construal priming resulted in larger occipital P1 amplitudes to local targets than to global targets, whereas a reverse pattern was observed after the interdependent self-construal priming. Similarly, Chiao et al. (2009a) primed Asian Americans using the Sumerian Warrior Story Task and the Similarities and Differences with Family and Friends Task (Trafimow et al. 1991), which have been shown to influence self-construal. They found that priming individualistic values increased activation in the ventral MPFC and posterior cingulate cortex during general self-judgments relative to contextual self-judgments. Priming collectivism led to the opposite pattern.

Thus the findings from priming studies indicate that cultural values dynamically shape neural representations of the self and close others.

How does temporary access to other cultural frameworks interact with long-term cultural experiences to shape human brain activity? In an initial attempt to answer this question, Sui and colleagues (2012) recorded ERPs from British and Chinese adults during judgments of orientations of one's own and a friend's faces after they were primed with independent and interdependent self-construals. They found that priming an interdependent self-construal reduced the default anterior N2 in response to their own faces for British participants. By contrast, priming an independent self-construal suppressed the default anterior N2 in response to their friend's face for Chinese participants. These findings illustrate how temporary and chronic cultural orientation may interact to shape neural responses. Chronic cultural orientation may constrain the effect of cultural priming on brain activity, reflecting a complex pattern of interactions between short-term and long-term cultural experiences.

In sum, CN findings are obtained using three distinct sets of methods. Initial demonstrations of cultural differences in brain activity focus on comparisons between individuals from two cultural groups (e.g., East Asians and Westerners). This type of work suggests that sociocultural contexts may result in different patterns of brain activity related to human cognition. These initial demonstrations are often followed by further analyses on underlying value or self-construal dimensions, providing further evidence that the observed cultural group differences in brain activity are associated with specific cultural values (e.g., self-construals). A similar extension has also been attempted with priming (manipulating the salience of either culture or important cultural values) to test whether there are causal relationships between culture and the neurocognitive processes involved in human cognition. In addition to showing a causal role of cultural values and self-construals, the priming studies have demonstrated that culturally typical patterns of brain activity are sometimes quite malleable.

WHAT IS CULTURAL NEUROSCIENCE NOT?

The rapid development of CN has induced several misunderstandings of CN research. These misunderstandings relate to the origin of CN research, the biological versus social nature of the human brain, and the relationship between culture and race (e.g., Mateo et al. 2012).

One misunderstanding of CN research is to connect CN studies with anthropological approaches to explain the nature of culture, which produces the misimpression that the goal of CN studies is simply to find biological markers in the brain that differentiate cultural groups and to demonstrate that any cultural differences in brain activity are determined biologically and are immutable. Such misunderstanding also arises from an ontologically dualistic opposition of the biological and cultural nature of the human brain. Such a false dichotomy leads to a view of biology and culture as two opposite accounts of the nature of the human brain. CN actually has a nonreductionist view of the relationships between formative biological and cultural properties of the human brain. As previously noted, CN studies aim to elucidate neuroplastic and culturally generated processes. This is fundamentally at odds with cultural essentialism and hard-wired biological determinism. CN researchers generate specific hypotheses about neurocognitive processes grounded in both behavioral findings from cultural psychology and brain imaging findings from cognitive neuroscience. These hypotheses limit the brain regions under investigation and predict specific patterns of cultural group differences and individual differences in brain activity. Thus CN research does not study culture as a set of biologically determined predispositions/constraints that can be used to rigidly categorize collections of people. Instead, the CN approach emphasizes the flexibility of the human brain that enables humans to adapt to sociocultural environments.

Another misunderstanding of CN arises from the confusion between culture and race. While some CN studies have compared participants from cultural groups that are also purported to be racial groups, other CN studies have examined cultural effects such as differences in brain activity between religious groups and between social classes of the same race. CN assumes that any difference between these groups is primarily the result of socialization and chronic cultural experiences. None of the aforementioned CN findings can be simply explained by group differences in physical attributes (e.g., skin tone). CN studies have shown evidence that differences in brain activity between Westerners and East Asians can be mediated by specific cultural values (e.g., independent versus interdependent self-construals). Cultural priming research has demonstrated causal effects of culture on brain activity. These findings indicate the importance of neuroplasticity in the study of culture and demonstrate that culture is not viewed as an analog for race in CN research.

The confusion between culture and race may lead to allegations of racism against CN research (e.g., CN findings "exert a tremendous impact on the reproduction of stereotypes and racism"; Mateo et al. 2012, p. 158). Racist accounts of human difference hold that human traits are biologically determined, fixed, and that members of racial groups are homogenous in these traits. In stark contrast to these beliefs, CN researchers view a cultural group as a dynamic collection of individuals who share a similar sociocultural context and whose members are affected by that context in divergent ways (a view shared by cultural psychologists; Heine 2012). CN research regards human neurocognitive processes as being flexible and being continuously shaped by sociocultural environments. CN findings demonstrate that an individual's brain is not doomed by biology to work in a specific way, but rather that the brain is strongly shaped by long-term and short-term cultural experiences. It is sociocultural context rather than race that matters. Knowing about cultural differences in neurocognitive processes may discourage people from believing biologically essentialist accounts of race and thus may facilitate cross-cultural communication. In this sense, CN studies should help to reduce rather than facilitate the reproduction of stereotypes and racism.

IMPLICATIONS OF CULTURAL NEUROSCIENCE FINDINGS

CN findings have a host of both theoretical and practical implications. Here we list a few of them. First, CN studies reveal the culturally sensitive nature of the human brain and help us to understand how the human brain as a biological organ is shaped by man-made sociocultural contexts. Human beings are different from other animals in that humans create the most complicated and varied social environments. We are also unique in our capacity for culture. Although there are cultural universals, the specific contents of culture are greatly important. In comparison with other species, this is an important advantage for the development of culture in a generalized sense as social communities of conspecifics. Every person is fostered in a unique artificial environment, speaks his/her mother language, behaves in accordance with specific social rules, acts as a member of social institutions, and interacts with people who share specific cultural values with each other. Thus the human brain develops in a specific sociocultural context during interactions with others. Because there are large variations across cultures, how to fit into one's specific society and how to cooperate with others efficiently is a challenge for each person. CN studies indicate that the human brain has the capacity to develop culture-specific neurocognitive processes that help an individual to function in a specific sociocultural environment.

Second, the context-dependent nature of the human brain can be understood in two different senses. One possibility is that the culturally different stimuli merely modulate already preexisting neural activity that, as such, remains independent of any contextual effects. This amounts to what has been called modulatory context dependence (Han & Northoff 2008, Northoff 2012). Alternatively, the constitution of any neural activity is dependent upon the context; this amounts to what can be described as constitutive context dependence (Han & Northoff 2008, Northoff 2012). The distinction between these two conceptions of context dependence has far reaching implications for the relationship between biological and social domains. In the case of modulatory context dependence, neuronal and social activities interact with each other while remaining independent from each other in their respective constitution. The brain is then purely neuronal and thus biological, whereas culture is social. This differs from the model of constitutive context dependence, which posits that, if the constitution of the brain's neuronal activity depends on the respective social context, a clear-cut distinction between the biological domain of the brain and the social domain of culture is impossible. Rather than being exclusively and completely biological, the brain and its neuronal activity must then be considered to be a hybrid of both biological and social influences. In other words, our brains are biosocial. The brain is then a relational organ that bridges the gap between the biological world of the organism and the social world of the environment and its culture (Northoff 2012).

Third, CN findings help us to understand cultural differences in human behaviors. Traditionally, there was usually a dominant culture in a given society, and contact with out-groups was limited. Cognition and behavior adhere to the cultural environment, and this may result in cultural imprinting effects on the brain. In current societies, however, it is much easier for people to meet members of many different cultures. One issue raised by CN studies is what kind of experiences during development may facilitate the ability of individuals' brains to fit into their specific culture and to interact with individuals from other cultures. This is particularly important for those who emigrate to another culture. Does the brain adapt to a new culture, and if so, how quickly? CN studies, particularly those using cultural priming, suggest that even an adult's brain is quite flexibly attuned to sociocultural environments. Thus cultural education and experience may shape the brain in order to fit into new cultural contexts.

Fourth, because CN studies help us to understand cultural differences in behavior, practices, and psychological tendencies from a neuroscience perspective, CN findings may help to develop constructive ways to deal with misunderstandings and conflicts between different cultural groups. In fact, CN studies not only show differences in brain activity mediating behavioral discrepancy in distinct sociocultural contexts, but also highlight commonalities of the human species across cultures. Understanding both cultural distinctiveness and cultural universality in the neural mechanisms underlying human cognition and behavior may help to reduce intergroup conflict and prejudice and may provide insight in how best to facilitate intergroup cooperation.

Finally, CN findings lead us to rethink the nature of culture. If the brain shows constitutive context dependence and can no longer be regarded as purely biological but rather as biosocial, it means conversely that the environment and thus culture also are not as purely social as is often assumed. Instead, culture is ingrained by the neuronal structures and organization of the brain's neural activity via the latter's constitutive context dependence. Hence rather than being completely and exclusively social, culture must then be considered to be sociobiological. The empirical results from CN clearly call into question any simplified characterization of the brain as merely biological and suggest that a more sophisticated account of the brain as biosocial better fits the evidence. This in turn entails the need to redefine our concept of culture and to reject any simplifications of culture as an exclusively social construction.

FUTURE QUESTIONS FOR CULTURAL NEUROSCIENCE

CN research provides a new approach to the understanding of the human brain from a cultural perspective, and it offers at the same time a new way to enrich concepts of culture from a neuroscience perspective. CN research has already provided many important insights into the mutual constitution of culture and the brain, and it has raised intriguing questions for future researchers to address, some of which are discussed below.

Brain and cultural value. Although there has been increasing evidence for cultural differences in brain activity underlying multiple cognitive and affective processes, future research should further explore the association between cultural values and cultural group differences in brain activity. This may help to ascribe observed culture-specific neurocognitive processes to the effect of specific cultural values or practices, and it may provide a more complete account of variation in neurocognitive processes as a function of cultural values. CN studies have shown culturally specific patterns of brain activity. But it remains unclear why some neural processes are sensitive to cultural influences whereas others are not. A more conceptual issue concerns how much the structure and organization of human culture in general, and the extent to which specific cultures in particular, mirror the structure and organization of the brain.

Culture, genes, and biochemistry. CN research has so far demonstrated cultural influences on the brain in terms of activity changes in brain regions or networks. However, CN has yet to explore how culture may affect or interact with biochemical substances of the brain. Cultural effects should be traced to the neuronal and biochemical levels in order to understand the relationship between culture and micro-level neural processes. For instance, an important question for future researchers will be to determine whether and how certain biochemical substances or neurotransmitters are sensitive to cultural experiences. Exploring this question may help us to understand the extent to which cultural influences on the brain operate not only on the functional neural level but also on the biochemical level.

CN research also needs to be integrated with genetic imaging. Although imaging studies have shown both cultural and genetic effects on brain function, there has been little research that examines whether and how culture and genes interact to affect neural processes. One possible approach to this issue is to examine genotype and culture simultaneously using brain imaging. Studies along this line will offer a comprehensive description of how culture and genes interact to shape the human brain and may further challenge purely biological accounts of the brain.

Brain and acculturation. The increasing number of immigrants in the current society raises another important issue for CN research: Is there a sensitive period during development for acculturation of the brain? Recent behavioral research suggests that, for individuals who immigrated before approximately age 14.5, identification with a new culture increased with time living in the new culture (Cheung et al. 2011). However, for older immigrants, identification with a new culture seemed not to change with the time in the new culture. Such findings imply that there may be a sensitive period for acculturation of the human brain. Among individuals of different ages, this can be examined by investigating the variation of brain activity as a function of the time spent in a new culture.

Culture and abnormal brain function. CN studies also raise issues concerning cross-cultural differences in the prevalence (and neural correlates) of psychiatric disorders such as schizophrenia and depression. Although these mental disorders appear to occur with similar lifetime prevalence in different cultures, it remains unclear whether their symptomatic expression is influenced by cultural predispositions (e.g., collectivism versus individualism) and whether their symptomatology is mediated by similar patterns of abnormal neural activity. Do the same neurocognitive mechanisms mediate these psychiatric disorders across cultures?

Further, is the association between genotype and mental illness similar across cultures, or is it moderated by cultural context? Answering these questions may help to determine whether the same treatments are appropriate for mental disorders in different cultures.

Brain and the creation of culture. Finally, one of the main goals of CN research is to address how the brain is involved in the creation and maintenance of the cultures that exist today. This may seem like a research question that is beyond the grasp of CN. However, CN studies may create new paradigms to distribute values and practices in a small group of participants and examine whether and how such manipulations may result in corresponding changes in brain activity. Such an approach may provide the ability to directly test neuroscience accounts of cultural differences. Further, such an approach may provide insights into how culturally influenced ways of thinking and feeling are acquired and represented in the human brain.

CONCLUSION

This review presents a refined account of CN in terms of origin, concept, method, findings, and theory, and clarifies several misunderstandings of the field. In sum, CN investigates the biosocial nature of the human brain by examining whether and how implicit and explicit patterns of beliefs, values, meanings, and practices in specific sociocultural contexts shape the neural mechanisms underlying human cognition, emotion, and behavior. CN research has helped to provide a nuanced understanding of culture by integrating methods from social and cultural psychology and neuroscience. The accumulating findings in the field show strong evidence for cultural influences on the human brain and raise exciting new questions about the biosocial nature of human beings. We believe that the continued growth and development of CN will promote cross-cultural understanding and provide strong evidence against racist accounts of human difference.

DISCLOSURE STATEMENT

The authors are not aware of any affiliations, memberships, funding, or financial holdings that might be perceived as affecting the objectivity of this review.

ACKNOWLEDGMENTS

S.H. and M.V. were supported by the National Basic Research Program of China (973 Program 2010CB833903) and the National Natural Science Foundation of China (Project 30910103901, 91024032, 81161120539). G.N. was supported by the HDRF/ISAN, the CIHR, and the CIHR-EJLB, as well as the Michael Smith Foundation. K.V. was supported by the German Volkswagen Foundation.

LITERATURE CITED

Adams RB Jr, Rule NO, Franklin RG Jr, Wang E, Stevenson MT, et al. 2009. Cross-cultural reading the mind in the eyes: an fMRI investigation. *J. Cogn. Neurosci.* 22:97–108

Ambady N, Bharucha J. 2009. Culture and the brain. *Curr. Dir. Psychol. Sci.* 18:342–45

Ames DL, Fiske ST. 2010. Cultural neuroscience. *Asian J. Soc. Psychol.* 13:72–82

Blakemore SJ. 2008. The social brain in adolescence. *Nat. Rev. Neurosci.* 9:267–77

Boyd R, Richerson PJ. 1985. *Culture and the Evolutionary Process*. Chicago: Univ. Chicago Press

Burton H, Snyder AZ, Diamond JB, Raichle ME. 2002. Adaptive changes in early and late blind: a fMRI study of verb generation to heard nouns. *J. Neurophysiol.* 88:3359–71

Cheung BY, Chudek M, Heine SJ. 2011. Evidence for a sensitive period for acculturation: Younger immigrants report acculturating at a faster rate. *Psychol. Sci.* 22:147–52

Chiao JY. 2010. At the frontier of cultural neuroscience: introduction to the special issue. *Soc. Cogn. Affect. Neurosci.* 5:109–10

Chiao JY, Ambady N. 2007. Cultural neuroscience: parsing universality and diversity across levels of analysis. In *Handbook of Cultural Psychology*, ed. S Kitayama, D Cohen, pp. 237–54. New York: Guilford

Chiao JY, Blizinsky KD. 2010. Culture-gene coevolution of individualism-collectivism and the serotonin transporter gene. *Proc. Biol. Sci.* 277:529–37

Chiao JY, Bebko GM. 2011. Cultural neuroscience of social cognition. See Han & Pöppel 2011, pp. 19–40

Chiao JY, Harada T, Komeda H, Li Z, Mano Y, et al. 2009a. Neural basis of individualistic and collectivistic views of self. *Hum. Brain Mapp.* 30:2813–20

Chiao JY, Harada T, Komeda H, Li Z, Mano Y, et al. 2009b. Dynamic cultural influences on neural representations of the self. *J. Cogn. Neurosci.* 22:1–11

Chiao JY, Hariri AR, Harada T, Mano Y, Sadato N, et al. 2010. Theory and methods in cultural neuroscience. *Soc. Cogn. Affect. Neurosci.* 5:356–61

Chiu CY, Hong YY. 2006. *Social Psychology of Culture*. New York: Psychol. Press

Choi I, Nisbett RE, Norenzayan A. 1999. Causal attribution across cultures: variation and universality. *Psychol. Bull.* 125:47–63

de Greck M, Shi Z, Wang G, Zuo X, Yang X, et al. 2012. Culture modulates brain activity during empathy with anger. *Neuroimage* 59:2871–82

Demorest SM, Osterhout L. 2012. ERP responses to cross-cultural melodic expectancy violations. *Ann. N. Y. Acad. Sci.* 1252:152–57

Freeman JB, Rule NO, Adams RB Jr, Ambady N. 2009. Culture shapes a mesolimbic response to signals of dominance and subordination that associates with behavior. *Neuroimage* 47:353–59

Frith C, Frith U. 2006. The neural basis of mentalizing. *Neuron* 50:531–34

Gardner WL, Gabriel S, Lee AY. 1999. "I" value freedom, but "we" value relationships: Self-construal priming mirrors cultural differences in judgment. *Psychol. Sci.* 10:321–26

Gogtay N, Giedd JN, Lusk L, Hayashi KM, Greenstein D, et al. 2004. Dynamic mapping of human cortical development during childhood through early adulthood. *Proc. Natl. Acad. Sci. USA* 101:8174–79

Goh JO, Chee MW, Tan JC, Venkatraman V, Hebrank A, et al. 2007. Age and culture modulate object processing and object-scene binding in the ventral visual area. *Cogn. Affect. Behav. Neurosci.* 7:44–52

Goh JO, Leshikar ED, Sutton BP, Tan JC, Sim SK, et al. 2010. Culture differences in neural processing of faces and houses in the ventral visual cortex. *Soc. Cogn. Affect. Neurosci.* 5:227–35

Goodall J, Berman P. 1999. *Reason for Hope: A Spiritual Journey.* New York: Warner

Goto SG, Ando Y, Huang C, Yee A, Lewis RS. 2010. Cultural differences in the visual processing of meaning: detecting incongruities between background and foreground objects using the N400. *Soc. Cogn. Affect. Neurosci.* 5:242–53

Gougoux F, Belinb P, Vossa P, Leporea F, Lassondea M, Zatorre RJ. 2009. Voice perception in blind persons: a functional magnetic resonance imaging study. *Neuropsychologia* 47:2967–74

Grèzes J, Frith CD, Passingham RE. 2004. Inferring false beliefs from the actions of oneself and others: an fMRI study. *Neuroimage* 21:744–50

Gutchess AH, Hedden T, Ketay S, Aron A, Gabrieli JD. 2010. Neural differences in the processing of semantic relationships across cultures. *Soc. Cogn. Affect. Neurosci.* 5:254–63

Gutchess AH, Welsh RC, Boduroglu A, Park DC. 2006. Cultural differences in neural function associated with object processing. *Cogn. Affect. Behav. Neurosci.* 6:102–9

Hacking I. 1999. *The Social Construction of What?* Cambridge, MA: Harvard Univ. Press

Han S, Gu X, Mao L, Ge J, Wang G, Ma Y. 2010. Neural substrates of self-referential processing in Chinese Buddhists. *Soc. Cogn. Affect. Neurosci.* 5:332–39

Han S, Mao L, Gu X, Zhu Y, Ge J, Ma Y. 2008. Neural consequences of religious belief on self-referential processing. *Soc. Neurosci.* 3:1–15

Han S, Mao L, Qin J, Friederici AD, Ge J. 2011. Functional roles and cultural modulations of the medial prefrontal and parietal activity associated with causal attribution. *Neuropsychologia* 49:83–91

Han S, Northoff G. 2008. Culture-sensitive neural substrates of human cognition: a transcultural neuroimaging approach. *Nat. Rev. Neurosci.* 9:646–54

Han S, Northoff G. 2009. Understanding the self: a cultural neuroscience approach. *Prog. Brain Res.* 178:203–12

Han S, Pöppel E, eds. 2011. *Culture and Neural Frames of Cognition and Communication (On Thinking).* Berlin: Springer

Harris M. 1999. *Theories of Culture in Postmodern Times.* Walnut Creek, CA: AltaMira

Haviland WA, Prins HEL, Walrath D, McBride B. 2008. *Cultural Anthropology.* Belmont, CA: Thomson Wadsworth

Hedden T, Ketay S, Aron A, Markus HR, Gabrieli DE. 2008. Cultural influences on neural substrates of attentional control. *Psychol. Sci.* 19:12–17

Heine SJ. 2012. *Cultural Psychology.* New York: Norton. 2nd ed.

Hong Y, Benet-Martinez V, Chiu C, Morris MW. 2003. Boundaries of cultural influence: construct activation as a mechanism for cultural differences in social perception. *J. Cross-Cult. Psychol.* 34:453–64

Hong Y, Morris M, Chiu C, Benet-Martinez V. 2000. Multicultural minds: a dynamic constructivist approach to culture and cognition. *Am. Psychol.* 55:709–20

Ishii K, Kobayashi Y, Kitayama S. 2010. Interdependence modulates the brain response to word-voice incongruity. *Soc. Cogn. Affect. Neurosci.* 5:307–17

Jenkins LJ, Yang YJ, Goh J, Hong YY, Park DC. 2010. Cultural differences in the lateral occipital complex while viewing incongruent scenes. *Soc. Cogn. Affect. Neurosci.* 5:236–41

Ji L, Peng K, Nisbett RE. 2000. Culture, control, and perception of relationships in the environment. *J. Pers. Soc. Psychol.* 78:943–55

Ji L, Zhang Z, Nisbett RE. 2004. Is it culture or is it language? Examination of language effects in cross-cultural research on categorization. *J. Pers. Soc. Psychol.* 87:57–65

Kim H, Markus HR. 1999. Deviance or uniqueness, harmony or conformity? A cultural analysis. *J. Pers. Soc. Psychol.* 77:785–800

Kim HS, Sherman DK, Sasaki JY, Xu J, Chu TQ, et al. 2010a. Culture, distress, and oxytocin receptor polymorphism (OXTR) interact to influence emotional support seeking. *Proc. Natl. Acad. Sci. USA* 107:15717–21

Kim HS, Sherman DK, Taylor SE, Sasaki JY, Chu TQ, et al. 2010b. Culture, serotonin receptor polymorphism and locus of attention. *Soc. Cogn. Affect. Neurosci.* 5:212–18

Kitayama S, Cohen D, eds. 2007. *Handbook of Cultural Psychology*. New York: Guilford

Kitayama S, Duffy S, Kawamura T, Larsen JT. 2003. Perceiving an object and its context in different cultures: a cultural look at new look. *Psychol. Sci.* 14:201–6

Kitayama S, Snibbe AC, Markus HR, Suzuki T. 2004. Is there any "free" choice? Self and dissonance in two cultures. *Psychol. Sci.* 15:527–33

Kitayama S, Uskul AK. 2011. Culture, mind, and the brain: current evidence and future directions. *Annu. Rev. Psychol.* 62:419–49

Kobayashi C, Glover GH, Temple E. 2006. Cultural and linguistic influence on neural bases of "theory of mind": an fMRI study with Japanese bilinguals. *Brain Lang.* 98:210–20

Kroeber A, Kluckhohn C. 1952. *Culture. A Critical Review of Concepts and Definitions*. New York: Random House

Kühnen U, Oyserman D. 2002. Thinking about the self influences thinking in general: cognitive consequences of salient self-concept. *J. Exp. Soc. Psychol.* 38:492–99

Kuper A. 1999. *Culture: The Anthropologists' Account*. Cambridge, MA: Harvard Univ. Press

Kutas M, Hillyard SA. 1984. Brain potentials during reading reflect word expectancy and semantic association. *Nature* 307:161–63

Levanen S, Jousmaki V, Hari R. 1998. Vibration-induced auditory-cortex activation in a congenitally deaf adult. *Curr. Biol.* 8:869–72

Lewis RS, Goto SG, Kong LL. 2008. Culture and context: East Asian American and European American differences in P3 event-related potentials and self-construal. *Pers. Soc. Psychol. Bull.* 34:623–34

Li SC. 2003. Biocultural orchestration of developmental plasticity across levels: the interplay of biology and culture in shaping the mind and behavior across the life span. *Psychol. Bull.* 129:171–94

Liew S, Han S, Aziz-Zadeh L. 2011a. Familiarity modulates mirror neuron and mentalizing regions during intention understanding. *Hum. Brain Mapp.* 32:1986–97

Liew SL, Ma Y, Han S, Aziz-Zadeh L. 2011b. Who's afraid of the boss: Cultural differences in social hierarchies modulate self-face recognition in Chinese and Americans. *PLoS ONE* 6:e16901

Lin Z, Han S. 2009. Self-construal priming modulates the scope of visual attention. *Q. J. Exp. Psychol. (Hove)* 62:802–13

Lin Z, Lin Y, Han S. 2008. Self-construal priming modulates visual activity underlying global/local perception. *Biol. Psychol.* 77:93–97

Littlefield A, Lieberman L, Reynolds L. 1982. Redefining race: the potential demise of a concept in physical anthropology. *Curr. Anthropol.* 23:641–56

Lumsden CJ, Wilson EO. 1981 *Genes, Mind and Culture: The Coevolutionary Process*. Cambridge, MA: Harvard Univ. Press

Ma Y, Han S. 2009. Self-face advantage is modulated by social threat—boss effect on self-face recognition. *J. Exp. Soc. Psychol.* 45:1048–51

Ma Y, Han S. 2010. Why respond faster to the self than others? An implicit positive association theory of self advantage during implicit face recognition. *J. Exp. Psychol.: Hum. Percept. Perform.* 36:619–33

Ma Y, Han S. 2011. Neural representation of self-concept in sighted and congenitally blind adults. *Brain* 134:235–46

Ma Y, Bang D, Wang C, Allen M, Frith C, et al. 2012. Sociocultural patterning of neural activity during self-reflection. *Soc. Cogn. Affect. Neurosci.* In press

MacKinnon DP, Fairchild AJ, Fritz MS. 2007. Mediation analysis. *Annu. Rev. Psychol.* 58:593–614

Markus HR, Hamedani MG. 2007. Sociocultural psychology: the dynamic interdependence among self systems and social systems. In *Handbook of Cultural Psychology*, ed. S Kitayama, D Cohen, pp. 3–39. New York: Guilford

Markus HR, Kitayama S. 1991. Culture and the self: implication for cognition, emotion and motivation. *Psychol. Rev.* 98:224–53

Markus HR, Kitayama S. 2010. Cultures and selves: a cycle of mutual constitution. *Perspect. Psychol. Sci.* 5:420–30

Masuda T, Nisbett RE. 2001. Attending holistically versus analytically: comparing the context sensitivity of Japanese and Americans. *J. Pers. Soc. Psychol.* 81:922–34

Mateo MM, Cabanis M, Loebell NC, Krach S. 2012. Concerns about cultural neurosciences: a critical analysis. *Neurosci. Biobehav. Rev.* 36:152–61

Morris M, Peng K. 1994. Culture and cause: American and Chinese attributions for social and physical events. *J. Pers. Soc. Psychol.* 67:949–71

Moya P, Markus HR. 2011. Doing race: a conceptual overview. In *Doing Race: 21 Essays for the 21st Century*, ed. HR Markus, P Moya, pp. 1–102. New York: Norton

Mu Y, Han S. 2010. Neural oscillations involved in self-referential processing. *Neuroimage* 53:757–68

Murata A, Moser JS, Kitayama S. 2012. Culture shapes electrocortical responses during emotion suppression. *Soc. Cogn. Affect. Neurosci.* In press

Na J, Kitayama S. 2011. Spontaneous trait inference is culture-specific: behavioral and neural evidence. *Psychol. Sci.* 22:1025–32

Nan Y, Knösche TR, Friederici AD. 2006. The perception of musical phrase structure: a cross-cultural ERP study. *Brain Res.* 1094:179–91

Nan Y, Knösche TR, Friederici AD. 2009. Non-musicians' perception of phrase boundaries in music: a cross-cultural ERP study. *Biol. Psychol.* 82:70–81

Nan Y, Knösche TR, Zysset S, Friederici AD. 2008. Cross-cultural music phrase processing: an fMRI study. *Hum. Brain Mapp.* 29:312–28

Ng SH, Han S, Mao L, Lai JCL. 2010. Dynamic bicultural brains: a fMRI study of their flexible neural representation of self and significant others in response to culture priming. *Asian J. Soc. Psychol.* 13:83–91

Nisbett RE, Masuda T. 2003. Culture and point of view. *Proc. Natl. Acad. Sci. USA* 100:11164–70

Nisbett RE, Peng K, Choi I, Norenzayan A. 2001. Culture and systems of thought: holistic versus analytic cognition. *Psychol. Rev.* 108:291–310

Nishimura H, Hashikawa K, Doi K, Iwaki T, Watanabe Y, Kusuoka H. 1999. Sign language "heard" in the auditory cortex. *Nature* 397:116

Northoff G. 2012. *Unlocking the Brain. Volume I: Neural Code. Volume II: Consciousness.* Oxford, UK/New York: Oxford Univ. Press

Northoff G, Heinzel A, de Greck M, Bermpohl F, Dobrowolny H, Panksepp J. 2006. Self-referential processing in our brain—a meta-analysis of imaging studies on the self. *Neuroimage* 31:440–57

Ochsner KN, Lieberman MD. 2001. The emergence of social cognitive neuroscience. *Am. Psychol.* 56:717–34

Oyserman D, Coon H, Kemmelmeie M. 2002. Rethinking individualism and collectivism: evaluation of theoretical assumptions and meta analyses. *Psychol. Bull.* 128:3–73

Oyserman D, Lee SW. 2008. Does culture influence what and how we think? Effects of priming individualism and collectivism. *Psychol. Bull.* 134:311–42

Park DC, Gutchess A. 2006. The cognitive neuroscience of aging and culture. *Curr. Direct. Psychol. Sci.* 15:105–8

Park DC, Huang CM. 2010. Culture wires the brain: a cognitive neuroscience perspective. *Perspect. Psychol. Sci.* 5:391–400

Paschou P, Lewis J, Javed A, Drineis P. 2010. Ancestry informative markers for fine-scale individual assignment to worldwide populations. *J. Med. Genet.* 47:835–47

Pascual-Leone A, Amedi A, Fregni F, Merabet LB. 2005. The plastic human brain cortex. *Annu. Rev. Neurosci.* 28:377–401

Peng K, Knowles E. 2003. Culture, education, and the attribution of physical causality. *Pers. Soc. Psychol. Bull.* 29:1272–84

Rizzolatti G, Sinigaglia C. 2010. The functional role of the parieto-frontal mirror circuit: interpretations and misinterpretations. *Nat. Rev. Neurosci.* 11:264–74

Rogoff B. 2003. *The Cultural Nature of Human Development.* Oxford, UK: Oxford Univ. Press

Rule NO, Freeman JB, Ambady N. 2012. Culture in social neuroscience: a review. *Soc. Neurosci.* In press

Shaw C, McEachern J, eds. 2001. *Toward a Theory of Neuroplasticity.* London: Psychol. Press

Singelis TM. 1994. The measurement of independent and interdependent self-construals. *Pers. Soc. Psychol. Bull.* 20:580–91

Sui J, Han S. 2007. Self-construal priming modulates neural substrates of self-awareness. *Psychol. Sci.* 18:861–66

Sui J, Hong YY, Liu C, Humphreys GW, Han S. 2012. Dynamic cultural modulation of neural responses to one's own and friend's faces. *Soc. Cogn. Affect. Neurosci.* In press

Sui J, Liu CH, Han S. 2009. Cultural difference in neural mechanisms of self-recognition. *Soc. Neurosci.* 4:402–11

Sul S, Choi I, Kang P. 2012. Cultural modulation of self-referential brain activity for personality traits and social identities. *Soc. Neurosci.* 7:280–91

Sutton BP, Go HJ, Hebrank A, Welsh RC, Chee MWL, Park DC. 2008. Investigation and validation of intersite fMRI studies using the same imaging hardware. *J. Magn. Reson. Imaging* 28:21–28

Tang H, Quertermous T, Rodriguez B, Kardia SL, Zhu X, et al. 2005. Genetic structure, self-identified race/ethnicity, and confounding in case-control association studies. *Am. J. Hum. Genet.* 76:268–75

Tang Y, Zhang W, Chen K, Feng S, Ji Y, et al. 2006. Arithmetic processing in the brain shaped by cultures. *Proc. Natl. Acad. Sci. USA* 103:10775–80

Trafimow D, Triandis HC, Goto SG. 1991. Some tests of the distinction between the private self and the collective self. *J. Pers. Soc. Psychol.* 60:649–55

Triandis HC. 1995. *Individualism and Collectivism*. Boulder, CO: Westview

Tsai JL, Knutson B, Fung HH. 2006. Cultural variation in affect valuation. *J. Pers. Soc. Psychol.* 90:288–307

Varnum MEW, Grossmann I, Kitayama S, Nisbett RE. 2010. The origin of cultural differences in cognition: the social orientation hypothesis. *Curr. Direct. Psychol. Sci.* 19:9–13

Varnum MEW, Na J, Murata A, Kitayama S. 2012. Social class differences in N400 indicate differences in spontaneous trait inference. *J. Exp. Psychol. Gen.* 141:518–26

Vogeley K, Roepstorff A. 2009. Contextualising culture and social cognition. *Trends Cogn. Sci.* 13:511–16

Wang G, Mao L, Ma Y, Yang X, Cao J, et al. 2012. Neural representations of close others in collectivistic brains. *Soc. Cogn. Affect. Neurosci.* 7:222–29

Wang Q, Conway MA. 2004. The stories we keep: autobiographical memory in American and Chinese middle-aged adults. *J. Pers.* 72:911–38

Ward J. 2012. *The Student's Guide to Social Neuroscience*. New York: Psychol. Press

Way BM, Lieberman MD. 2010. Is there a genetic contribution to cultural differences? Collectivism, individualism and genetic markers of social sensitivity. *Soc. Cogn. Affect. Neurosci.* 5:203–11

Wexler BE. 2006. *Brain and Culture: Neurobiology, Ideology and Social Change*. Cambridge, MA: MIT Press

Wu S, Keysar B. 2007. The effect of culture on perspective taking. *Psychol. Sci.* 18:600–6

Zhu Y, Zhang L, Fan J, Han S. 2007. Neural basis of cultural influence on self representation. *Neuroimage* 34:1310–17

Organizational Climate and Culture

Benjamin Schneider,[1] Mark G. Ehrhart,[2] and William H. Macey[1]

[1] CEB Valtera, Rolling Meadows, Illinois 60008, [2] Department of Psychology, San Diego State University, San Diego, California 92182; email: bschneider@executiveboard.com, mehrhart@mail.sdsu.edu, wmacey@executiveboard.com

Annu. Rev. Psychol. 2013. 64:361–88

First published online as a Review in Advance on July 30, 2012

The *Annual Review of Psychology* is online at psych.annualreviews.org

This article's doi: 10.1146/annurev-psych-113011-143809

Keywords

organizational behavior, organizational effectiveness, data aggregation, linkage research, organizational values, levels of analysis

Abstract

Organizational climate and organizational culture theory and research are reviewed. The article is first framed with definitions of the constructs, and preliminary thoughts on their interrelationships are noted. Organizational climate is briefly defined as the meanings people attach to interrelated bundles of experiences they have at work. Organizational culture is briefly defined as the basic assumptions about the world and the values that guide life in organizations. A brief history of climate research is presented, followed by the major accomplishments in research on the topic with regard to levels issues, the foci of climate research, and studies of climate strength. A brief overview of the more recent study of organizational culture is then introduced, followed by samples of important thinking and research on the roles of leadership and national culture in understanding organizational culture and performance and culture as a moderator variable in research in organizational behavior. The final section of the article proposes an integration of climate and culture thinking and research and concludes with practical implications for the management of effective contemporary organizations. Throughout, recommendations are made for additional thinking and research.

Contents

FRAMING THE REVIEW

Organizational climate and organizational culture are two alternative constructs for conceptualizing the way people experience and describe their work settings (including not only businesses but also schools and governments). These topics, representing a subset of research in organizational behavior and organizational psychology, have never been reviewed in the *Annual Review of Psychology*, although they received some mention as early as 1985 (Schneider 1985). Given this void, we provide a brief historical overview of thinking and research on each topic, update the central issues identified as characterizing these literatures, and provide preliminary thoughts on integrating them.

Organizational climate may be defined as the shared perceptions of and the meaning attached to the policies, practices, and procedures employees experience and the behaviors they observe getting rewarded and that are supported and expected (Ostroff et al. 2003, Schneider & Reichers 1983, Schneider et al. 2011). On the other hand, organizational culture may be defined as the shared basic assumptions, values, and beliefs that characterize a setting and are taught to newcomers as the proper way to think and feel, communicated by the myths and stories people tell about how the organization came to be the way it is as it solved problems associated with external adaptation and internal integration (Schein 2010, Trice & Beyer 1993, Zohar & Hofmann 2012). Until the past two decades or so there have also been significant differences in the methods used to study climate and culture, with the former having been characterized by employee surveys and the latter by qualitative case studies. A historical review of the climate and culture literatures, however, reveals that culture recently has been much more often studied using surveys, and the issues addressed can both overlap and be considerably different from the issues addressed via climate surveys (Schneider et al. 2011, Zohar & Hofmann 2012).

The relative research interest in the two constructs has also varied over the decades. The topic of organizational climate dominated the early research on the human organizational environment in the 1960s and 1970s, but it moved to the background as interest in organizational culture dominated the 1980s. However, through the 1990s another transition took place, and interest in organizational climate appears to have eclipsed the focus on organizational culture in more recent years. To illustrate this shift, we reviewed articles in three of the top empirical journals in industrial/organizational psychology (*Journal of Applied Psychology*, *Academy of Management Journal*, and *Personnel Psychology*) since the turn of the century (2000–2012). We counted articles that had as one of their primary variables organizational climate or organizational culture, focusing on those that studied them as aggregate constructs (as opposed to individual perceptions, preferences, or beliefs). Our review revealed over 50 articles that studied organizational climate and fewer than 10 on organizational culture. Although our review was limited to three journals and there are certainly other outlets that do publish more on organizational culture, we think it is an accurate conclusion that there is currently more of a focus on organizational climate than organizational culture in the industrial/organizational psychology research literature.

In this review we describe climate and culture theory and research with a primary focus on the recent literature, albeit framed within the historical developments of both fields. In addition, we present ways in which organizational climate and culture complement each other and can be mutually useful in practice. The review unfolds as follows. We begin with some early thinking and research on organizational climate. Then we introduce the three major accomplishments over the recent past for climate research: (a) resolution of what has come to be called the levels-of-analysis issue; (b) the creation of various foci for climate research that has yielded increased understanding for what climate is, how to study it, and its potential practical usefulness; and (c) the recent research on climate strength. In the second major section of the review, we provide a brief overview of the construct of organizational culture before focusing on the four major themes we see in recent organizational culture research: (a) leadership, (b) national culture, (c) organizational effectiveness, and (d) organizational culture as a moderator variable. In the final section, we explore ways in which climate and culture thinking and research can complement each other both conceptually and practically.

ORGANIZATIONAL CLIMATE

Serious quantitative research on organizational climate began around 1970 (see the historical overview in Schneider et al. 2011). Early research on organizational climate was characterized by little agreement on the definition of it, almost no conceptual orientation to the early measures designed to assess it, and paradoxically an almost complete ignoring of the term "organizational." Thus, early climate research (say through the early 1980s) followed a more traditional individual differences methodology that was characteristic of the industrial psychology of the time. As the field of organizational culture began to explode in the early 1980s (following Pettigrew's introduction of it to organizational studies in 1979), organizational climate faded to the background (at least for a time) as it struggled with the levels-of-analysis issue. To some degree, the rise in interest in organizational culture in the 1980s could be attributed to the fact that it seemed to capture the richness of the organizational environment in ways that climate research had not. As Pettigrew (1990, p. 416) observed, "[There is] the impression that climate studies have been boxed in by the appearance in the nest of this rather overnourished, noisy, and enigmatic cuckoo called organizational culture. This pressure from an interloper may, however, be energizing climate researchers to rethink the role of climate studies." Pettigrew was prescient in his depiction of climate research, given that the renewed interest in the topic yielded significant progress in conceptual thinking and research methodologies (Kuenzi & Schminke 2009).

The Levels-of-Analysis Issue

Although early organizational and management writings about climate and climate-like constructs (e.g., Argyris 1957, Lewin et al. 1939) focused on aggregates and not individuals, the early quantitative research on climate that proliferated in the late 1960s and early 1970s was done by individual-differences-oriented industrial psychologists (e.g., Schneider & Bartlett 1968) and thus tended to focus on the individual level of analysis. Grappling with this issue was a major focus of researchers throughout the 1970s, with some resolution emerging in the 1980s. In brief, the issue was whether climate is an individual experience construct and/or a unit/organizational attribute. In other words, there was confusion between the level of the theory and the level of data and analysis. Glick (1985) succinctly argued that unless (*a*) climate survey items assessed organizational functioning, (*b*) the data were aggregated to the organizational level of analysis, and (*c*) the climate measurement was focused on important organizational outcomes (more on this later), then climate research was not different from other individual-level attitudinal research. The clarification of climate as an attribute of the group or organization was an important step for climate research, although some researchers do continue to study climate at the individual level. However, such research on psychological climate (e.g., James et al. 2008) is not relevant for the present review, which is concerned with organizational climate.

Recent writings by Bliese (2000), Chan (1998), Klein & Kozlowski (2000), and LeBreton & Senter (2008) indicate that research on climate is best characterized as a referent-shift consensus model (Chan 1998). The referent-shift model uses survey items that refer to attributes of the unit/organization rather than individuals' own perspectives. Referent-shift consensus items are conceptually appropriate because they refer to the level to which individual responses will be aggregated, and they tend to yield improved consensus when aggregated (LeBreton & Senter 2008).

Consensus implies that perceptions are shared. Assessments of "sharedness" have focused on interrater agreement and/or interrater reliability. Interrater agreement addresses the extent to which raters provide similar absolute ratings of climate such that their ratings are interchangeable. The most common measure of this form of agreement in climate research is $r_{WG(J)}$ (James et al. 1984), although other alternatives such as the average deviation index (Burke et al. 1999) and a_{WG} (Brown & Hauenstein 2005), have been proposed. Commonly accepted standards for legitimizing aggregation based on agreement are typically 0.70 or higher, although the usefulness of a broadly applied cutoff has been recently questioned (see LeBreton & Senter 2008).

Interrater reliability addresses the extent to which the rank ordering of the ratings is consistent across people within units. Climate researchers typically report ICC(1), a ratio of between-unit variance to total variance (like analysis of variance, or ANOVA; Bliese 2000), and as such technically a measure of both interrater reliability and interrater agreement (LeBreton & Senter 2008). Although no firm cutoffs exist for ICC(1), James (1982) reported a median value of 0.12 among the studies in his early review, and LeBreton & Senter (2008) suggested that values of 0.01, 0.10, and 0.25 might be considered small, medium, and large effects, respectively. It is also common for researchers to report ICC(2) [sometimes also referred to as ICC(K); LeBreton & Senter 2008]. ICC(2) is an index of the reliability of group means and is related to ICC(1) as a function of group size (Bliese 2000), and ICC(2) values are commonly interpreted in line with other measures of reliability, with 0.70 or higher deemed adequate (Bliese 2000, LeBreton & Senter 2008). Values that high are obviously quite challenging to achieve with smaller group sizes (e.g., 5–6 individuals per group).

In sum, it is common practice for climate researchers to include a measure of interrater agreement as well as both within- and between-group interrater reliability to support aggregation of individual perceptions to unit and/or organizational levels of analysis. Furthermore, we emphasize that a key to such agreement and reliability evidence is the appropriate wording of climate survey items such that they represent the level of analysis to which individual perception data will be aggregated.

A very recent levels issue that has emerged in climate research concerns the study of climate across multiple levels of analysis. Over the years, studies of "organizational" climate have most frequently been studies of organizational subunits and rarely if ever of organizations themselves, much less of multiple levels of analysis. In their recent research on safety climate, Zohar & Luria (2005) demonstrated a significant main effect on safety behavior both for organizations and for subunits (groups) nested within organizations. In addition, they showed that subunit safety climate mediated the effects of organizational safety climate on employee safety behavior. As Zohar & Hofmann (2012) note, this means that employees in organizations are able to distinguish what happens in their subunits from the larger organizational focus on safety, but that subunits within a company have more agreement in their safety climate perceptions than they have with people in the subunits of other companies. In short, levels issues are somewhat complex to conceptualize because they exist simultaneously within and between organizations, but it appears that the main effects at both levels have meaning for the people in them and their behavior.

The Focus of Organizational Climate Theory, Research, and Practice

A second major accomplishment of research on organizational climate is the development of research on focused climates. By focus we mean that early climate research might be characterized as having little focus on anything besides what might be called a climate for well-being, with a strong focus on leadership and supervisory style (Schneider et al. 2011). Industrial psychologists developed early measures of climate that had between 6 and 10 dimensions, but the dimensions chosen for study seemed to cover a variety of territories that emerged from a variety of researchers. Given this molar conceptual and measurement approach to climate, validity studies using such measures produced highly variable results at best because the generic nature of the climate measured was not useful for the prediction of specific outcomes.

Schneider (1975) recognized this issue and proposed that the bandwidth and focus of climate measures should match the bandwidth and focus of the outcome to be predicted. Adopting the personnel selection tactic of first identifying the outcome of interest, he suggested that climate measures follow suit. To clarify the distinction between molar climate and focused climate, here is what might have been a typical generic climate item followed by

the strategically focused version of the item: "My supervisor says a good word whenever he sees a job well done" versus "My supervisor says a good word whenever he sees a job done according to the safety rules" (Zohar 2000).

The two most prevalent examples of research on climates with a specific strategic focus are in the literatures on climate for customer service and climate for safety. One of the strongest tests of the outcomes of service climate was conducted by Schneider et al. (2009), who used longitudinal data at the organization level of analysis to show that companies with higher levels of service climate had higher customer satisfaction and subsequently superior financial performance. That study replicated many similar studies on the relationship between service climate and customer satisfaction. Indeed, the service climate literature now includes studies of both antecedents and consequences of it as well as studies of potential moderators. For example, Schneider et al. (2005) found that unit-level customer-oriented citizenship behavior was a mediator of service climate's effects on department-level customer satisfaction and sales. That study also showed that service leadership was an important antecedent of service climate. Indeed, our review showed that leadership has become an important antecedent theme in the service climate literature. For instance, research reveals that both transformational leadership (Liao & Chuang 2007) and servant leadership (Walumbwa et al. 2010) are significant predictors of service climate. Other research has shown that the leader's personal characteristics are also important to consider, such that a manager's service orientation was shown to fully mediate the relationship between their core-self-evaluations and the service climate of their department (Salvaggio et al. 2007). In addition to leadership, other antecedents that have been shown to predict service climate include organizational resources and unit-level engagement (Salanova et al. 2005) as well as high performance work practices (Chuang & Liao 2010). Finally, in terms of moderators of the climate-outcome relationship, Dietz et al. (2004) showed that service climate had stronger effects when customer contact was higher, and Mayer et al. (2009a) replicated that finding, also showing that the effects of service climate were stronger when the product was more intangible and when service employee interdependence was higher.

The literature on safety climate has touched on many of the same general themes as the service climate literature, including consistent validation of the construct. Thus, meta-analytic evidence supports the consistent relationship between safety climate and accidents (Christian et al. 2009, Clarke 2006), although Beus et al. (2010b) suggested that there may be reciprocal effects between safety climate and accidents, such that increased levels of accidents influence the shared perceptions of the unit's (poor) climate for safety. A safety climate is not only related to accidents but also the reporting of those accidents, such that underreporting is significantly higher in organizations with poor safety climates (Probst et al. 2008). The antecedents of safety climate have included general transformational leadership (Zohar & Tenne-Gazit 2008), safety-specific transformational leadership (Barling et al. 2002), the safety climate of higher organizational levels (Zohar & Luria 2005), and both management-employee relations and organizational support (Wallace et al. 2006). In terms of outcomes of safety climate, recent research by Neal & Griffin (2006) used longitudinal data to demonstrate how safety climate influences individual-level safety motivation and safety behavior, which in the aggregate predicts accident rates in the work unit. Finally, there is also evidence for moderators of the outcomes of safety climate. For instance, Hofmann & Mark (2006) showed in a sample of nurses that safety climate had a stronger influence on decreasing back injuries and medication errors when complexity of the patient's condition was high.

In addition to studying specific focused climates for tangible outcomes, scholars have studied climates for various organizational processes. In this research, the measurement of climate targets the organizational process of

interest rather than the strategic outcome of interest. Some of the earliest work on process climates focused on procedural justice climate (e.g., Naumann & Bennett 2000). Recent research in that area has demonstrated that procedural justice climate could be predicted by team size and team collectivism (Colquitt et al. 2002), servant leadership (Ehrhart 2004, Walumbwa et al. 2010), and leader personality (Mayer et al. 2007). In addition, procedural justice climate is related to unit-level outcomes such as turnover and customer satisfaction (Simons & Roberson 2003), team performance and absenteeism (Colquitt et al. 2002), and unit-level citizenship behavior (Ehrhart 2004), as well as individual-level attitudes and citizenship behavior (Liao & Rupp 2005, Naumann & Bennett 2000, Walumbwa et al. 2010). Moreover, the cross-level effects of justice climate are moderated by both individual (justice orientation; Liao & Rupp 2005) and structural attributes (group power distance; Yang et al. 2007).

Interest has recently increased in another process climate: diversity climate. Several recent examples are notable. For instance, McKay et al. (2008) showed that gaps in performance between racial/ethnic groups were significantly smaller when the organization was more supportive of diversity. Pugh et al. (2008) found that workforce racial diversity was more strongly related to diversity climate when the community in which the organizational unit is based is less diverse. McKay et al. (2009) found that unit sales improvements were most positive when managers and subordinates both reported that their organization had a supportive diversity climate. Finally, Gonzalez & DeNisi (2009) showed that racial/ethnic diversity was positively related to organizational performance when diversity climate was positive.

Other examples of process climates that have been the focus of recent research include ethical climate (Martin & Cullen 2006, Mayer et al. 2009b, Schminke et al. 2005), empowerment climate (Chen et al. 2007, Seibert et al. 2004), voice climate (Morrison et al. 2011), and climate for initiative (Baer & Frese 2003, Michaelis et al. 2010). Indeed, it is reasonable to suggest that any and all organizational processes might be usefully studied and understood through a climate lens. For example, one might conceptualize in climate terms such diverse organizational processes as organizational change (Weick & Quinn 1999), performance appraisal (Rynes et al. 2005), work motivation (Latham & Pinder 2005), and trust in organizations (Kramer 1999). The study of these from a climate perspective could yield new insights into the sets of contextual process variables that are their correlates and perhaps their antecedents.

In sum, the change to a strategic outcome and process focus for climate research has significantly improved not only the validity of climate research but also the understanding of the contexts that likely yield these focused climates. As such, the development of this more focused approach has resulted in the climate construct being more available to practitioners because it literally has focused on important organizational processes and outcomes and has indicated specific practices and behaviors that might serve as interventions in organizations to enhance performance in those areas (Burke 2011).

One topic that has yet to receive much research attention, however, is the issue of the link between process and outcome climates. Schneider et al. (2011) have proposed that process climates might be conceptualized as a foundation for outcome climates. That is, when workers perceive that their organization is concerned about their well-being through its emphasis on fairness, diversity, ethics, trust, and so forth, they are more amenable to the efforts of management to focus on strategic outcomes of value to the organization. Schneider et al. (1998) and Wallace et al. (2006) have provided empirical support for the idea that climates focused on specific outcomes require that the foundations on which they are built (foundational climates) be in place for the strategic climates to have an opportunity to emerge. Recent research by Schulte et al. (2009) supports this general premise by showing that it is the configuration of employee-supportive elements and strategy-focused elements (in their case, the focus on service) that matters most for

relevant strategic outcomes (such as financial performance and customer satisfaction). Furthermore, their results suggest that there may be a threshold of climate for well-being that is needed to build a strategic climate and that a moderate climate for well-being may suffice. Along similar lines, McKay et al. (2011) found support in a sample of retail stores for a three-way interaction between diversity climate, service climate, and minority representation in the stores to predict customer satisfaction; the graphs of this interaction indicated that customer satisfaction was generally highest when both diversity climate and service climate levels were high. More research along these lines that conceptually integrates focused climates and molar climates and that simultaneously studies multiple focused climates is needed.

On Climate Strength

In a prior section on levels issues we addressed the variety of techniques researchers employ to defend aggregation of individual perceptions to yield a score representative of the larger unit of analysis of interest. Researchers have more recently raised the following interesting question: What are the implications of observing variability in consensus within the units or organizations being studied? This is a question about the relative strength of the climate across settings and the impact that differences in climate strength may have. The fundamental idea behind climate strength is not new, being related to the concept of situational strength (Mischel 1976), a construct that has received renewed interest in recent years by Meyer, Dalal, and colleagues (Meyer & Dalal 2009; Meyer et al. 2009, 2010). As Zohar (2000; Zohar & Luria 2005) has noted, a weak climate can result when policies and procedures are inconsistent and/or when the practices that emerge from policies and procedures reveal inconsistencies.

Research on climate strength has focused on molar/generic climate (e.g., González-Romá et al. 2002, Lindell & Brandt 2000) as well as a number of focused climates, including procedural justice climate (e.g., Colquitt et al. 2002), service climate (e.g., Schneider et al. 2002), and safety climate (e.g., Zohar & Luria 2004, 2005). The usual model guiding such work is that climate strength will moderate the relationship between the climate and outcomes of interest such that the relationship will be stronger when climate strength is high. On a conceptual level, this interaction is expected because the more consistent the experiences of employees, the more likely employees are to behave consistently as a collective such that there should be more positive outcomes on the positive end and more negative outcomes on the low end. On a measurement level, high consensus (low variability within units) provides for a more reliable mean, and with a more reliable mean there should be greater validity in conceptually relevant relationship with outcomes. Recent research has provided some promising evidence in support of the moderating effect of strength on the relationship between climate level and outcomes (Colquitt et al. 2002, González-Romá et al. 2002, Schneider et al. 2002). An interesting corollary finding from the Schneider et al. (2002) article was that the less consensus there was among employees in bank branches (the weaker the service climate was), the higher was the variance in branch customer perceptions of the service quality they received.

But not all studies reveal a significant moderator effect for climate strength in predicting outcomes (Dawson et al. 2008, Lindell & Brandt 2000, Rafferty & Jimmieson 2010, Schneider et al. 2002, Sowinski et al. 2008, Zohar & Luria 2004). We must be tentative in offering an explanation for this inconsistency in findings, but we propose that a likely crucial issue presents an interesting paradox as follows: Climate researchers spent decades attempting to write items for climate surveys such that the consensus indicators discussed earlier would be high, legitimating aggregation. But in order to have a moderator there must be significant variability across units in consensus; if consensus is uniformly high, then climate strength will not serve as a moderator. Indeed, several of the studies that did not find support for strength as a moderator seem to have had quite low variability in the level of agreement across units (e.g.,

Dawson et al. 2008, Sowinski et al. 2008, Zohar & Luria 2004).

More research on the conditions under which climate strength will function as hypothesized is clearly required, but there is beginning to be some evidence on the conditions most likely to elicit strong versus weak climates. For example, climates have been found to be stronger when units are smaller and less diverse (Colquitt et al. 2002), when within-unit social interaction is high (González-Romá et al. 2002), when the unit's communication network is more dense (Zohar & Tenne-Gazit 2008), when units are more interdependent and have higher group identification (Roberson 2006), when units are more cohesive (Luria 2008), and when average unit tenure is higher (Beus et al. 2010a). The most commonly studied antecedent of climate strength has been leadership, with research showing that units have stronger climates when leaders are described as providing more information (González-Romá et al. 2002), being more straightforward and having less variable behavior patterns (Zohar & Luria 2004), and being more transformational (Luria 2008, Zohar & Luria 2004, Zohar & Tenne-Gazit 2008). In sum, when work units interact more, communicate more, and are more interdependent, and when leaders communicate more and share a clear strategic vision for the work, then the climate in those units will be stronger.

Although progress has been made in research on climate strength, there are still questions that need to be answered. Nevertheless, from a practical vantage point, what we can conclude is that a positive and strong climate is usually superior to a weak climate and for sure is superior to a negative climate, so the implications for practice are clear: In order to maximize the likelihood of achieving the organization's process and outcome performance goals, it is essential to consistently and forcefully promote a positive focused climate.

Climate Summary

A half century of thinking and research has produced a significant literature on organizational climate. Perhaps the major outcome of this area of research for psychology has been the acceptance of a level of theory and data other than the individual as relevant and important in organizational psychological research and practice. Thus, the resolution of the level-of-analysis issue has been central to positioning organizational climate as an integral and integrating conceptual force in the larger world of organizational psychology and organizational behavior. Testament to this enlarged role for the construct is *The Oxford Handbook of Organizational Climate and Culture* (Schneider & Barbera 2013), in which the research and practice related to the major topics in organizational psychology are approached from climate (and culture) perspectives. More specifically, the handbook chapters reveal ways in which climate and culture are both influenced by and have influence on more fundamental organizational psychology issues, from personnel selection to organizational change.

Particularly for the world of practice, the emphasis on focused climates (e.g., climates for service, safety, justice, ethics) that currently exists has revealed insight into organizational processes and the various climates they produce for people as well as robust evidence for the validity of climate perceptions for understanding and predicting important specific organizational outcomes such as accidents and customer satisfaction. Although this specific focus for climate research has improved the prediction and understanding of specific outcomes, issues about the variability in the prediction of more global measures of organizational effectiveness based on climate measures have not received much attention. In an exception, Kuenzi (2008) showed that molar climate can in fact be useful in understanding global performance when conceptualized and studied through the competing values framework (Quinn & Rohrbaugh 1983, Weick & Quinn 1999). More research of this sort, utilizing a common framework and measure across various global performance outcomes, is needed.

We emphasize that organizations do not have a singular climate but rather multiple simultaneous climates of both the process and strategic outcome sort. Although this may be obvious, it is also true that there has been very little theory and research on the issue of multiple climates (Zohar & Hofmann 2012). Theory and research on such possible additive and interactive effects from multiple climates would be useful, especially when such multiple climates include both process and outcome foci for climate as well as molar climates.

ORGANIZATIONAL CULTURE

The review of the organizational culture construct and research on it traces a different path from that for organizational climate. This is true basically because there were few level-of-analysis issues to deal with in the organizational culture world. Emerging from a conceptual and methodological base in anthropology, the collective was the natural unit of theory and analysis, with individual differences an irrelevant idea. Instead, while the climate literature in the 1980s struggled with the levels issues, the culture literature of the same era somewhat paradoxically struggled with success in the world of management consulting. That is, culture very quickly became the darling of the management consulting world, with books such as *In Search of Excellence* (Peters & Waterman 1982) and *Corporate Culture: The Rites and Rituals of Organizational Life* (Deal & Kennedy 1982) attracting headlines. From an academic standpoint, this presented some issues because academics were not quite sure about what culture was and what it represented—and even whether it was appropriate to try to link organizational culture with the financial success of corporations (Siehl & Martin 1990).

A Brief Overview of the Organizational Culture Construct and Research Methods

Although the construct of culture itself has a long history in anthropology, and the term had been used in earlier writings on organizations (Alvesson & Berg 1992, Trice & Beyer 1993), what Pettigrew (1979) did in introducing the topic to organizational studies was to legitimize the concept in all of its potential richness. He did this by showing how the concepts of beliefs, ideology, language, ritual, and myth could be applied to the study of organizations (Alvesson & Berg 1992), as complex as that obviously would be. This complexity scared neither culture scholars nor practitioners, the former group feeling liberated by the ambiguity the definition(s) presented, permitting them to explore culture as they saw fit, and the latter group identifying with the ambiguity as a realistic picture of the world in which they functioned.

At a more macro conceptual level, the best way to distinguish definitional (and methodological) approaches to culture is by a focus on culture as something an organization has versus something an organization is (Smircich 1983). From the "organizations have cultures" perspective, researchers are concerned with the ways in which organizations differ and are usually pragmatic in terms of their focus on organizational effectiveness and organizational change (Alvesson 2002, Weick & Quinn 1999). The research approach from this perspective is typically comparative—to explore those attributes of organizations that differentiate the more effective from the less effective (e.g., Sackmann 2011)—which explains why survey approaches have dominated research on culture from this perspective. In contrast, from the "organizations are cultures" perspective, the researcher's goal is description and understanding, including how organizational members develop meaning and come to share the very basic assumptions—the root metaphors (Smircich 1983)—that guide the way they as the organization function. The research approach here tends to be inductive (Ashkanasy et al. 2000a), using a native-view paradigm (Gregory 1983, Louis 1990) to report how insiders experience their organizations (e.g., an emic perspective). From a methodological standpoint, researchers from this perspective almost exclusively use qualitative methods in their research, as those permit the identification of the unique manifestations of culture in settings

and permit the identification of ambiguity in "the" culture as an attribute of a setting.

Simply stated, there is not agreement on what culture is nor how it should be studied, but the issues have been somewhat clarified. For every definition of what culture is, there is an important contrary view. For example, in most definitions of culture the idea that it is shared is present. Yet one of the most widely influential perspectives on culture, by Martin (1992, 2002), indicates that this integrationist idea about culture is but one of three perspectives, the other two being a fragmented view and a differentiated view. The integrationist view is that organizations are or have one culture shared by all; conflict and ambiguity and differences are ignored and, if mentioned, are seen as something to fix or an aberration. The fragmented perspective focuses on ambiguity; it forcefully denies the necessity for sharedness, arguing that it is unlikely that people in an organization at different levels and in different positions/occupations—and with different personalities—would have the same experiences and attach the same meaning to the organization and what it values. The differentiation perspective is a compromise position. It notes that people occupy subcultures in organizations (by function, by occupation, by gender, and so forth) and thus may have different experiences and may even attach different meaning to the same events. Martin (2002) has recently advocated for a three-perspective theory of culture, in which all three perspectives are applied simultaneously. Building on our discussions of both climate and culture thus far, it may be useful to think of the three perspectives as addressing the general culture (integration), subcultures (differentiation), and culture strength (fragmentation) in organizations at the same time. Along these lines, Yammarino & Dansereau (2011) identify a series of climate and culture studies in which levels-of-analysis issues, especially multilevel issues, are present and discuss the ways in which these issues may be simultaneously studied.

In organizational culture research, the issue of levels has typically concerned the extent to

Spin
- Metaphysics on a grand scale

- pure reason
- logic alone sufficient to reveal the fabric of reality

not only "what is" but "what ought to be"
add ethics

the faculty of reason rallies us to Salvation

subjective fit perceptions, or their
s for an organization's culture (for
see Ostroff & Judge 2007). Given
on aggregate perceptions of organi-
lture, we do not review these studies
we do note there are exceptions that
e aggregate indicators of organization
uch as recent research by Anderson
8).

hip and organizational culture. The
mmonly discussed source for the or-
on's assumptions and values is the
of the organization and his/her leader-
ein's (2010, p. 236) culture-embedding
isms describe what leaders do to articu-
r values (primary mechanisms) and re-
them (secondary mechanisms):

ary embedding mechanisms

What leaders pay attention to, measure,
nd control on a regular basis
How leaders react to critical incidents and
rganizational crises
How leaders allocate resources
Deliberate role modeling, teaching, and
coaching
How leaders allocate rewards and status
How leaders recruit, select, promote, and
excommunicate

Secondary embedding mechanisms

Organizational design and structure
Organizational systems and procedures
Rites and rituals of the organization
Design of physical space, facades, and
buildings
Stories about important events and
people
Formal statements of organizational phi-
losophy, creeds, and charters

Schein argues that these cultural embedding
mechanisms have an impact on culture to the
extent that they are found to be useful by the
organization in coping with the world in which
it functions. In other words, what determines
whether certain behaviors and values espoused
by management ultimately become assumptions is whether those behaviors and values
lead to success.

illuminate them.

Recent Themes in Organizational Culture Research

In this section, we attempt to summarize the recent empirical literature on organizational culture. We do not provide an exhaustive review,
but instead identify key themes and exemplars
in the literature of each. The themes we focus on are (a) leadership, (b) national culture,
(c) organizational effectiveness, and (d) organizational culture as a moderator variable.

One theme we do not include is research
on person-organization fit. The main idea of
person-organization fit involves the extent to
which there is an alignment between an individual's values and the values (or culture)
of their current or potential organization. Although culture is central to this literature, the
focus is on the consequences of fit for individ-

Although the theoretical literature on organizational culture is replete with discussions of the influence the founder and upper management have on an organization's culture, empirical studies of that relationship are hard to find. Nevertheless, we highlight three recent studies here that provide some insight into the role of leaders in organizational culture. Berson et al. (2008) examined the relationship between CEO values, organizational culture, and firm performance in a sample of 26 Israeli companies. Supporting their three primary hypotheses, they found that the CEO value of self-direction was positively associated with an innovative culture, security value was positively related to a bureaucratic culture, and benevolence value was positively associated with a supportive culture. In addition, these culture dimensions were subsequently related to several indices of organizational performance (including sales growth and efficiency).

The other two studies we highlight focused on leader behavior (not leader values). Ogbonna & Harris (2000) examined the extent to which the effects of three styles of leadership (supportive, participative, and instrumental) on organizational performance were mediated by organizational culture. They found partial support for culture as a mediator, with some leader behaviors having direct effects on performance. Finally, Tsui et al. (2006b) focused on the extent to which strength (consistency) of leadership was associated with the strength of the culture. Although they generally found that strength of leadership and strength of culture were related, they also identified exceptions to that relationship and clarified the reasons for the exceptions in follow-up interviews. Those interviews revealed that some leaders are able to build a strong culture through institution-building behaviors (working in the background to build strong organizational systems) rather than performance-building behaviors (showing energy and articulating a vision). More research clarifying how leaders influence culture is needed, especially research focusing on the effects of Schein's (2010) culture-embedding behaviors.

National culture and organizational culture. Multiple recent studies focus on the relationship between organizational culture and organizational effectiveness in different countries (e.g., Fey & Denison 2003, Lee & Yu 2004, Xenikou & Simosi 2006) or the measurement of organizational culture in countries outside the United States (e.g., Lamond 2003, Tsui et al. 2006a), but the primary theoretical issue of interest when it comes to national culture is the extent to which it shapes the cultures of the organizations within it. This issue has been of interest to researchers since the influential work of Hofstede (1980). In general, the results show that when national culture is correlated with the organizational culture of companies within them, a significant main effect invariably is found (Gelfand et al. 2007). The most thorough test of this relationship in recent years has been provided by the Global Leadership and Organizational Behavior Effectiveness (GLOBE) project (House et al. 2004), which collected data on societal culture, organizational culture, and leadership from over 17,000 people representing 62 societal cultures and 951 organizations. Brodbeck et al. (2004) used a subsample of that database with adequate representation within organizations and across countries and industries and showed that culture explained between 21% and 47% of the variance (with an average of 32.7%) across their nine organizational culture practice dimensions. In addition, they found that societal culture had much stronger effects than either industry or the society-by-industry interaction.

Two important points should be made in the light of this finding. First, national culture has an impact on organizational culture. Second, the impact leaves considerable variability in the organizational culture profiles possible; national culture is influential but not determinant. Indeed, Sagiv et al. (2011) report that within organizations and nations there is also significant variability in individual values. From this review, it is possible to provide some potential resolution of the theoretical issue with regard to the integrationist versus the differentiated culture, and it is in agreement with

Martin's (2002, p. 151) proposal that these can exist simultaneously as a function of the lens through which culture is viewed. Thus, through a macro lens, one might reveal whole nations as distinctive cultures but also differences between nations; a macromicro lens would reveal distinctive cultures for organizations as well as differences between organizations within a nation; a micro lens would reveal within-organization subcultures; and yet an even more refined view would reveal within-organization individual differences. More such multilevel research on organizational culture is obviously needed.

Culture and organizational performance. The idea that organizations have cultures yields a focus on the relationship between organizational culture and organizational effectiveness. A recent review of the work on this possible relationship makes it clear that such research will necessarily be based on survey measures of organizational culture (Sackmann 2011). Sackmann notes that such research is fraught with difficulties with regard to (*a*) what levels of culture should be the focus of assessments (e.g., myths, stories, values, behavior), (*b*) the unit of analysis for assessment (subcultures within organizations versus whole organizations), and (*c*) the content dimensions along which assessments might best be made (e.g., employee experiences, socialization tactics, leadership actions). Because of these difficulties, a relationship with organizational performance outcomes has been difficult to consistently establish (Wilderom et al. 2000). Nevertheless, a comparison of the Wilderom et al. (2000) review with the Sackmann (2011) review indicates that not only is there much interest in this relationship, but also that support for that relationship is growing.

Our review of recent (2000–2012) studies examining the relationship between organizational culture and performance revealed a variety of approaches to the issue, with consistent significant findings. Studies relied on a variety of fairly traditional outcomes, including objective financial measures of performance (e.g., Gregory et al. 2009, Kotrba et al. 2012,

Lee & Yu 2004), customer satisfaction (e.g., Gillespie et al. 2008), goal achievement (e.g., Xenikou & Simosi 2006), and top management reports (e.g., Chan et al. 2004, Glisson et al. 2008). Other less traditional indices of effectiveness were also studied, for example, the percentage of women in management (Bajdo & Dickson 2001) or the odds of children receiving mental health care (Glisson & Green 2006). Some studies included mediators of the culture-performance relationship (e.g., attitudes in Gregory et al. 2009), whereas others included interactive effects among dimensions of culture (Kotrba et al. 2012), with organizational practices (Chan et al. 2004), or with industry characteristics (Sørensen 2002). Researchers also used a variety of measures of culture: The Organizational Culture Inventory (Cooke & Lafferty 1989), the Denison Organizational Culture Survey (Denison 1990), and the Organizational Culture Profile (OCP; O'Reilly et al. 1991) seemed particularly common.

Using the competing values framework (CVF; Quinn & Rohrbaugh 1983) as a foundation, Hartnell et al. (2011) provided perhaps the most comprehensive test of the relationship between organizational culture and organizational performance. The CVF is characterized by two sets of competing values with bipolar dimensions defining four cells. The bipolar dimensions are flexibility versus stability in structure and an internal versus an external focus. Although more complex than we can report in detail here, the 2 × 2 framework yields four cells with conceptually competing values about what is important in organizations, the ways those values are manifest in organizations, and the likelihood of success in different domains of organizational performance. The four cells are named Clan (internal and flexible with a focus on people), Adhocracy (external and flexible with a focus on growth), Market (external and stable with a focus on competition), and Hierarchy (internal and stable with a focus on organizational structure). **Table 1** shows in detail the ways the four organizational culture cells hypothetically get played out with regard to basic assumptions, beliefs, values, and

Table 1 The competing values framework

Culture type	Assumptions	Beliefs	Values	Artifacts (behaviors)	Effectiveness criteria
Clan	Human affiliation	People behave appropriately when they have trust in, loyalty to, and membership in the organization	Attachment, affiliation, collaboration, trust, and support	Teamwork, participation, employee involvement, and open communication	Employee satisfaction and commitment
Adhocracy	Change	People behave appropriately when they understand the importance and impact of the task	Growth, stimulation, variety, autonomy, and attention to detail	Risk taking, creativity, and adaptability	Innovation
Market	Achievement	People behave appropriately when they have clear objectives and are rewarded based on their achievements	Communication, competition, competence, and achievement	Gathering customer and competitor information, goal setting, planning task focus, competitiveness, and aggressiveness	Increased market share profit, product quality, and productivity
Hierarchy	Stability	People behave appropriately when they have clear roles and procedures are formally defined by rules and regulations	Communication, routinization, formalization	Conformity and predictability	Efficiency, timeliness, and smooth functioning

behaviors (from Hartnell et al. 2011, p. 679, and based on Quinn & Kimberly 1984). Thus, the CVF takes the complex notion of different levels at which culture exists in companies and with different foci and proposes that the different levels of cultural variables do not exist randomly but tend to be associated with conceptually similar variables and that the likelihood of success for an organization is a function of the focus (e.g., employee well-being versus increased market share) of the assumptions, beliefs, values, and behavior that accrue in organizations.

In their meta-analysis, Hartnell et al. (2011) explored the structure of the CVF as well as the relationship between CVF dimensions and three indicators of organizational effectiveness (employee attitudes, operational performance, and financial performance). They found that for the most part, the CVF behaved as predicted, with organizations that were more Clan-like having employees who were more satisfied and committed, whereas those with a more market orientation had superior operational and financial performance. Perhaps most interestingly, the Hartnell et al. (2011) findings suggest that although some foci are superior for some criteria (as just reviewed), organizations scoring higher on the four cells generated in the framework also were more successful across all three effectiveness criteria. This finding is explained by Hartnell et al. (2011, p. 687) as follows: "...[T]he culture types in opposite quadrants are not competing or paradoxical. Instead they coexist and work together... [C]ompeting values may be more complementary than contradictory." In short, organizations that do many things well are more generally more effective, and organizations that in addition have a focus on different kinds of outcome criteria will be even more effective on those outcomes.

There are at least three avenues for future research that would deepen our understanding of the relationship between culture and performance. One would be to more clearly articulate (and measure) the role of the multiple levels of culture in this relationship. Thus, what most quantitative measures of culture capture are the espoused values and/or behavioral norms in organizations and not the full richness of the construct—including myths, stories, and socialization tactics. Such a narrow view of culture is one reason why researchers from the "organizations are culture" tradition strongly discourage quantitative culture measures. Second, most research on culture focuses on the direct relationship between culture and performance, but almost all theory related to how culture impacts performance would conceptualize it in a more moderated/mediated fashion (as we will shortly review). By this we mean it explores simultaneously the cultural levels and the various foci with an addition of more specific process and content dimensions of behavior a la the climate research we recommended earlier. More research capturing this complexity would be beneficial. Finally, there are many contextual social, economic, and political reasons why organizational culture will not have an impact (or at least as much of an impact) on organizational performance. More clarification of how context (e.g., national culture, industry, economic perturbations, product/service characteristics) moderates the culture-performance relationship would help identify when culture has its strongest (and weakest) effects.

Organizational culture as a moderator variable. The final theme we highlight in recent literature on organizational culture is research that focuses on organizational culture as a contextual variable that moderates relationships

between and among other constructs. Below, we highlight three studies that take this approach.

Erdogan et al. (2006) investigated whether specific dimensions of organizational culture (as measured by the OCP) would weaken or strengthen the relationship between organizational justice and leader-member exchange (LMX). Their logic was that the culture of the organization influences aspects of social relationships more or less salient to organizational members. In line with their hypotheses, they found that in cultures with high respect for people, the relationship between interpersonal justice and LMX was stronger, and in cultures high in aggressiveness, the relationship between distributive justice and LMX was stronger. In contrast, in cultures high in team orientation, the relationships between both types of justice and LMX were weaker, mainly because employees in those cultures tended to have higher-quality LMX relationships across the board.

Another example of the "culture as moderator" approach comes from Chatman & Spataro (2005). Their focus was on the relationship between being demographically different and cooperative behavior. Based on social categorization theory, they hypothesized that those who are demographically different will tend to show less cooperative behavior because they are more likely to be categorized as part of the out-group. However, using sex, race, and nationality as their demographics and the OCP as their measure of culture, they were able to show that a collectivistic culture counteracted these effects and resulted in significantly higher levels of cooperation among those who were demographically different. Thus, they concluded that the work environment in terms of its culture resulted in people looking beyond individual demographic differences and focusing on the group and the achievement of the group's goals.

Finally, Bezrukova et al. (2012) studied culture as a moderator of the relationship between group fault lines and performance. Specifically, they examined group fault lines from an informational diversity perspective, including educational, tenure, and functional background, and found that stronger fault lines were negatively related to performance as measured by group stock options and bonuses. However, they found that a results-focused culture moderated that relationship, but more importantly, that it was the alignment of the group's results-focused culture and the department's results-focused culture that was critical. Thus, this research takes the relatively rare step of examining culture at multiple levels simultaneously, similar to Zohar & Luria's (2005) approach with safety climate that we highlighted in the section on climate.

Culture Summary

Pettigrew (1979) added new dimensions to the study of organizational behavior when he promoted a culture focus for organizational research. His emphasis on the relevance of myths, values, and history for understanding what organizations are was instructive to both researchers and practitioners. Although there were debates for decades about how to study organizational culture, including on what facets of organizations one might focus and whether culture should be expected to be related to organizational performance, since the turn of the millennium survey approaches have become more common, and increasingly there is an emphasis on the organizational performance consequences of organizational culture.

The work of Schein (1985, 2010) indicates that it is agreed by most that a major building block for organizational culture is attributable to the early decisions founders make about structures and organizing principles and to what ends valuable resources will be expended. In addition, based largely on Schein's writings, the idea that culture manifests itself at different levels (artifacts, values, assumptions) of organizations also has been accepted. Martin's (2002) conceptualization of cultures being simultaneously macro and micro in form also seems to have been accepted but with less universality. We have found Martin's perspective useful here for understanding how national, organizational, and subcultural perspectives may

be simultaneously relevant, but the explication of each depends on the lens through which organizational culture is viewed.

In particular, we spent considerable time outlining the CVF of Quinn & Rohrbaugh (1983), especially via the recent meta-analysis of research within that framework (Hartnell et al. 2011). CVF is an elegant way to summarize the wide range of issues that have been studied under the culture rubric, revealing how they combine to produce particular foci for organizations on outcomes. The finding that the cells in the framework are positively related suggests that organizations that do some things appropriately also are likely doing many other things appropriately. The challenge, of course, is to make that happen (Burke 2011, Weick & Quinn 1999).

TOWARD INTEGRATING CLIMATE AND CULTURE—WITH PRACTICE IMPLICATIONS

Molloy et al. (2011) have written convincingly about the difficulties in crossing levels of analysis when more than one discipline is involved, and Reichers & Schneider (1990) decried the fact that climate and culture research of that era was characterized by parallel but not overlapping tracks of scholarship. Fortunately, both within the study of climate and within the study of culture, progress has been made in overcoming the difficulties identified by Molloy et al. and bridging the parallel tracks identified by Reichers and Schneider.

Climate and Culture Rapprochement

For example, as reviewed above, psychologists have moved from a study of climate that was at the individual level of analysis to a unit and organizational focus, and culture researchers (e.g., Martin 2002) have promoted the idea that cultures can manifest themselves simultaneously such that there are common experiences, clusters of people with different experiences, and unique experiences as well. Climate researchers have realized that a focus for their efforts (e.g., service, safety) might yield superior results in validity research against specific outcomes, and the recent Hartnell et al. (2011) meta-analysis of the CVF reveals a similar result for culture researchers: A focus on the Clan quadrant values and behavior yields superior employee satisfaction, whereas a focus on the Market quadrant values and behavior yields superior operational and financial performance. Perhaps most notably, Schein, who in the earlier editions of his book (1985, 1992) barely mentioned climate (simply lumping climate in with "artifacts"), has more recently (2004, 2010) characterized climate as providing the behavioral evidence for the culture of a setting, such that those behaviors form the bases for employees' conclusions about the values and beliefs that characterize their organization. In line with this view, he stated in his introductory chapter to the 2000 *Handbook of Culture and Climate* that "to understand what goes on in organizations and *why it happens in the way it does*, one needs *several* concepts. Climate and culture, if each is carefully defined, then become two crucial building blocks for organizational description and analysis" (Schein 2000, pp. xxiv–xxv; italics in original). We agree with this interpretation of the relationship between climate and culture and of their mutually reinforcing properties.

The CVF (Hartnell et al. 2011, Quinn & Rohrbaugh 1983) as represented in **Table 1** provides a possible framework for more such integration across climate and culture perspectives. Climate researchers have studiously avoided the assessment of values and basic assumptions, viewing them perhaps as "soft" and therefore not immediately under management control. Certainly climate researchers could assess, in addition to policies, practices, and procedures, the values these might imply to organizational members—values for customer satisfaction, for example. And culture researchers have avoided a focus on specific criteria, whether it be strategic issues such as customer satisfaction on the one hand or process issues such as trust on the other hand. One exception can be found in recent work by Denison, who markets a well-researched culture

inventory (**http://www.denisonconsulting. com/advantage/researchModel/model.aspx**) and who has developed a module focusing on trust—he could also of course have more focused modules on other outcomes or processes as well, for example, on customer satisfaction.

An especially attractive feature of **Table 1** is that it reveals the variety of values and behaviors that might be appropriate to create a culture of well-being or a culture of innovation, and this notion of a culture *for* something might help make the culture concept less complex both in research and practice. Recall that in early climate research it seems that the focus for such work was implicitly a climate for well-being. Recall also that in our review of climate we suggested that this climate for well-being might serve as a foundation on which more specifically focused climates might be built. The CVF, following the work of Kuenzi (2008), indicates that such a focus on well-being (a Clan culture) might serve as a foundation for more molar achievement, market, and operational/technical foci, and that these, in turn, might serve as foundations for more specifically focused strategic climates.

Needed Further Integration

But while the CVF offers the potential for increased integration of climate and culture research and the two approaches have become more like each other, we believe there are more ways in which they can learn from each other—and indeed from themselves. For example, in regard to the latter, a central variable in early writings on organizational culture—socialization experiences (Louis 1990, Trice & Beyer 1993)—paradoxically has gone missing in action. In the 2000 edition of the *Handbook of Organizational Culture and Climate* (Ashkanasy et al. 2000b), there was a chapter by Major (2000) on socialization, but the word is not even indexed in the 2011 edition. It is not that research on socialization has not been occurring. The issue is that the research has focused primarily on the tactics individuals report experiencing during socialization (see the meta-analysis by Bauer et al. 2007) or perhaps the effects of individuals' proactivity during socialization (for a review, see Bindl & Parker 2010), but less so the role the socialization plays in the perpetuation of organizational culture to new members. In short, both culture and climate measures should focus on the socialization experiences of newcomers to settings precisely because they are newcomers, and everything that happens to them is new and likely to enter awareness—and have a long-term impact (Louis 1990, Scandura 2002, Van Maanen 1975).

The mention of newcomers also raises the issue of the development of organizations over time and the resultant changes in climate and culture that might be expected. Schein (1985, 1992, 2004, 2010) has consistently explored the issue of organizational life cycle and the implications of such for (a) the leadership demands on managers and (b) the resultant cultures to be expected as organizations enter and pass through various stages of life. The issues of development and organizational life cycles are noticeably absent from the literature on organizational climate. Perhaps this is because of the more quantitative orientation of climate researchers and the difficulty of accessing data across multiple time points over enough time to meaningfully study such issues, particularly when the focus is on entire organizations and not just subunits. Nevertheless, research along these lines is needed. Presumably, organizations have a clearly identified and communicated strategy early in their life cycle (Flamholtz & Randle 2011), but as the organization grows in terms of numbers and sales, and perhaps spreads out geographically, it would be useful to know how organizations continue to maintain a strong strategic climate. Another example of potentially beneficial research along these lines would be on how major organizational changes such as mergers, acquisitions, or restructuring affect the climate of the organization and its strength.

One useful lens for exploring the interrelationships between organizational climate and culture is that of organizational change. The question is this: If someone wanted to change an organization and improve its performance, should they change the culture? The climate? Both? If there are assumptions and values in the organization that are preventing the organization from achieving its potential, then those need to be addressed. But just having the "right" culture will be unlikely to result in high performance unless management has created a strategic climate that communicates exactly what the goals of the organization are and that organizes the various processes and procedures in the organization around their achievement. On the flip side, management's efforts to build a strategic climate will struggle if they contradict deeply held assumptions in the organization (Schein 2000). Another way to think about this issue and to demonstrate the linkages between climate and culture would be to ask how change is viewed by the executives who would be responsible for making such change happen. We explore the issue from the executive vantage point next.

Practice Implications

Executives have little concern for the distinctions we have made between culture and climate. Indeed, culture is their commonly used term. As an example, in the wake of the 2005 BP Texas City catastrophe, the independent panel widely known as the Baker Committee conducted a review of BP's "safety culture." The ensuing report (Baker et al. 2007) includes the item content of a "safety culture survey" prepared by an independent consulting firm. This survey is a clear example of a safety climate survey with its focus on policies, practices and procedures, and behaviors that (fail to) get rewarded, supported, and expected. The panel calls this a culture survey because they implicitly understand that (a) executive interest in "corporate culture" is in creating processes that are reinforcing of the core values underlying existing strategy, (b) a focused strategy requires processes that are focused on valued outcomes (such as safety), and (c) only by the creation of such processes do values actually get embedded and become self-sustaining within the organization to serve as guideposts for organization members. Thus, contemporary popular business writers consider corporate culture to have the potential to "outlast any one charismatic leader" (Heskett et al. 2008).

In short, executives use corporate culture in a more expansive way than we have articulated in terms of the scholarly views we presented. Conversationally, the extended corporate vocabulary embraced by the term culture includes a broad range of intangible assets (or liabilities) such as image, brand, and the like. Such idiosyncratic frameworks may not have a foundation in scholarship, but they nonetheless serve as working frames of reference for culture as interpreted by executives.

Issues of importance to executives are (a) knowing the corporate culture, (b) changing the corporate culture, and/or (c) leveraging the corporate culture to create competitive advantage. Questions of "knowing" are relevant because the value of culture, like all intangible assets, is unknown. Both efforts to change and to leverage the culture are in fact dependent on the understanding of what that culture is, and perhaps the direction in which it is moving, an observation we return to shortly.

Knowing the culture. Of course, executives are agnostic with respect to how best to measure culture. They do care about the ability to make comparisons, though, leading to a natural inclination to hire consultants who can provide comparisons to benchmarks (e.g., industry comparisons, comparisons to the Best Companies to Work For or Most Admired Companies lists) that most interest them. Essential here is a quantitative measure that can be characterized by some finite number of (universal?) dimensions that are common across different organizations, with the measured constructs varying considerably. It is interesting to speculate that executives choose measures of their culture most in keeping with the values they wish to endorse and their strategic outcomes of interest a la the Quinn & Rohrbaugh (1983) CVF, and that best fit a felt need for knowledge

about a specific facet of culture/climate (such as safety or service). Executives who believe that culture is important purchase such measures and take action on results because of their beliefs in the importance of the intangible they confront in all of their activities.

From a practical standpoint, as from an academic standpoint, the emphasis on intangibles makes a complete reliance on quantitative approaches unsatisfactory to executives. This is true because the very vocabulary that is imposed by such measures on the description of the culture may be quite different from that used by those who experience it (Denison & Spreitzer 1991). Indeed, it seems reasonable to predict that the relatively near-term future of culture measurement may drift toward the ad hoc, textual-based reflections of verbal and written explanations captured through the natural language-processing mechanics now in vogue for measuring political and consumer sentiment (e.g., Pang & Lee 2008).

Changing the culture. Knowing the culture is almost always considered in the context of a felt need for cultural change or to ensure preservation of what is held as core to how the organization creates value. Indeed, interventions focused on cultural change often focus on closing the gap between existing and desired cultures, and these are typically captured in measures by asking respondents for both kinds of data. The underlying assumption (hope?) is that, with knowledge, culture can be changed through the right action. Executives implicitly understand that they have somewhat limited direct influence on effecting change because so many issues must be addressed simultaneously throughout the firm. Their job is to establish the mission and support the interventions necessary to embed the processes necessary to begin redirection—always understanding that larger social and economic forces play a significant role in who they are and what they can become (Burke 2011).

By itself, change is elusive to measure, and as such, models of corporate culture include dimensions that reflect constructs such as adaptability; indeed, Kotter & Heskett (1992) make adaptability a central feature of organizational effectiveness, arguing that today's change necessarily precedes the necessity to change tomorrow. It is worth adding that the practical interest is not just in the direction of change, but also in the pace of that change (Flamholtz & Randle 2011).

Leveraging culture for competitive advantage. The underlying theme of many conversations about culture is how it can be leveraged as an asset. Culture is a focus for competitive advantage when it is different from other cultures and the elements that constitute it are difficult to imitate (Ployhart 2012). "The elements that constitute it" are based on the processes that get embedded through knowledge and change with the resultant climates they create for the behaviors required for success. Culture, then, yields competitive advantage as the result of a cycle beginning with the development of a unique mission statement enacted by support for the unique processes necessary to embed the mission's values and to create the focused strategic and process climates that serve as guidelines for behavior. In short, doing better than what others are doing is not the key to competitive advantage.

In sum, the most successful executives implicitly understand how climate and culture are necessarily linked and the complex steps required for achieving competitive advantage. When the culture sought is unique, when the climates created are unique in their complex simultaneous focus on important internal organizational processes (e.g., fairness, ethics, inclusion) and strategic outcomes (e.g., service, safety, innovation), then competitive advantage is possible. A silver bullet still does not exist, and the best executives know and understand this truth.

CONCLUSION

Organizational climate and culture offer overlapping perspectives for understanding the kinds of integrative experiences people have in work settings—or in any organizational settings. The constructs address the meaning people attach to their experiences of how the organization works (process climates), the strategic foci the organization has (strategic climates), and the values they attribute to the setting (culture), all in attempts to make sense of their experiences (Weick & Quinn 1999). The climate literature has focused on what Schein (2010) calls the culture-embedding mechanisms of organizations, the tangibles enacted by leaders by which they express their values and basic assumptions (Quinn & Rohrbaugh 1983) and by which they attempt to focus the energies and competencies of the people in the setting. These processes and activities are designed to yield behaviors that pursue organizational goals and objectives, and it is these behaviors that come to characterize whole organizations and subcultures within them (Martin 2002).

Climate scholars have for the past 25 years been dealing with more tangible policies, practices, and procedures as the causes of the experiences people have, focusing their efforts on understanding how workers experience the strategic initiatives of management (e.g., service, safety, innovation) and the internal processes accompanying them (e.g., fairness, ethics, inclusion). Progress has now been made in understanding when people do not agree on those climates (i.e., climate strength), but there is not much work at all on conceptualizing and understanding how multiple climates in organizations interact and/or even conflict with each other (Kuenzi & Schminke 2009).

Culture scholars have taken two directions in their efforts to conceptualize and understand organizational culture. When culture is studied as something organizations *are*, the focus is on their uniqueness and what the specific peculiarities of their "artifacts" (i.e., myths, stories, and socialization tactics) tell us about the values and basic assumptions of the people there. Alternatively, when culture is studied as something organizations *have*, comparative organizational culture research yields quantitative assessments of the ways organizations display their values for and basic assumptions about people, achievement, formalization, and growth (a la the competing values framework shown in **Table 1**). Surveys designed to assess these inclinations share much in common with climate surveys, with the CVF providing more focus for such assessments than has been true of culture research in the past.

We obviously see these two perspectives as being useful ways to conceptualize and understand people's experiences at work. Climate offers an approach to the tangibles on which managers can focus to generate the behaviors they require for effectiveness, and culture offers the intangibles that likely accrue to produce the deeper psychology of people in a setting. The psychology of how people experience their work environment is difficult to assess but is likely what implicitly directs them in their daily lives, so it is important to understand. When a change in what directs people and their daily lives is required, then a focus on tangibles is the way to achieve it. As such, the conceptual connection between climate and culture is clear—and deserving of future research.

SUMMARY POINTS

1. Organizational climate emerges in organizations through a social information process that concerns the meaning employees attach to the policies, practices, and procedures they experience and the behaviors they observe being rewarded, supported, and expected.

2. Organizational climate research that has a focus on a strategically relevant outcome (safety, service) and/or process (fairness, ethics) is superior in understanding specific relevant outcomes to research on climate that is generic with no specific focus.

3. The aggregation of individual perceptions of climate into higher levels of analysis is accomplished both through the survey items that are written to capture climate (they are written to describe the level to which the data will be aggregated) and through the statistical procedures used to defend such aggregation.

4. Research on climate strength (the degree to which people in a unit agree in their perceptions) reveals that strength frequently moderates the relationship between climate aggregate means and outcomes of interest.

5. Organizational culture concerns the implicit values, beliefs, and assumptions that employees infer guide behavior, and they base these inferences on the stories, myths, and socialization experiences they have and the behaviors they observe (especially on the part of leaders) that prove to be useful and promote success.

6. Organizational culture may exist as an inclusive organizational construct for a whole organization but also simultaneously in the form of subcultures (e.g., based on level in the organization or occupation) and also in ways that suggest a lack of integration (the culture is fragmented).

7. Early research on organizational culture was predominantly via the qualitative case-method (emic), but more recently survey procedures have become predominant due to the comparative opportunities they present as well as the potential they offer for links to organizational performance outcomes across settings.

8. An integration of climate and culture theory and research has useful implications for practice, especially vis-à-vis practice that yields data suggestive of organizational changes that might yield improvements in organizational behavior and performance.

FUTURE ISSUES

1. Research that simultaneously studies macro generic climate, multiple strategically focused outcome, and process climates to more fully capture the reality of organizational life.

2. Research linking the fundamental beliefs, values, and assumptions that characterize culture research with the policies, practices, and procedures and accompanying behaviors that are typical of climate research.

3. Research on boundary conditions surrounding the outcome and process-focused climate studies in which links with important unit/organizational performance indicators are studied.

4. Research on the contributions human resource management practices make to the emergence and strength of climate and culture in organizations.

5. Research on the contributions of operations management, finance, legal, marketing, and other departments/functions to the experienced climate and couture of an organization.

6. Longitudinal research on the likely feedback loops in climate and culture research, especially feedback loops between outcomes and climate/culture.

7. Research on climate and culture as brand image extending beyond the boundaries of the organization with regard to image as a potential employer, service or product provider, and object of investment.

8. Research on the life cycles of organizations and the ways in which climate and culture change over time as a function of the stages of the life cycle.

DISCLOSURE STATEMENT

The authors are not aware of any affiliations, memberships, funding, or financial holdings that might be perceived as affecting the objectivity of this review.

LITERATURE CITED

Alvesson M. 2002. *Understanding Organizational Culture*. London: Sage

Alvesson M, Berg PO. 1992. *Corporate Culture and Organizational Symbolism*. New York/Berlin: de Gruyter

Anderson C, Spataro SE, Flynn FJ. 2008. Personality and organizational culture as determinants of influence. *J. Appl. Psychol.* 93:702–10

Argyris C. 1957. *Personality and Organization*. New York: Harper

Ashkanasy NM, Wilderom CPM, Peterson MF. 2000a. Introduction. See Ashkanasy et al. 2000b, pp. 1–18

Ashkanasy NM, Wilderom CPM, Peterson MF, eds. 2000b. *Handbook of Organizational Culture and Climate*. Thousand Oaks, CA: Sage

Ashkanasy NM, Wilderom CPM, Peterson MF, eds. 2011. *The Handbook of Organizational Culture and Climate*. Thousand Oaks, CA: Sage. 2nd ed.

Baer M, Frese M. 2003. Innovation is not enough: climates for initiative and psychological safety, process innovations, and firm performance. *J. Organ. Behav.* 24:45–68

Bajdo L, Dickson MW. 2001. Perceptions of organizational culture and women's advancement in organizations: a cross-cultural examination. *Sex Roles* 45:399–414

Baker J, Bowman FL, Erwin G, Gorton S, Hendershot D, et al. 2007. *The report of the BP U.S. refineries independent safety review panel*. **http://www.bp.com/liveassets/bp_internet/globalbp/globalbp_uk_english/SP/STAGING/local_assets/assets/pdfs/Baker_panel_report.pdf**

Barling J, Loughlin C, Kelloway EK. 2002. Development and test of a model linking safety-specific transformational leadership and occupational safety. *J. Appl. Psychol.* 87:488–96

Bauer TN, Bodner T, Erdogan B, Truxillo DM, Tucker JS. 2007. Newcomer adjustment during organizational socialization: a meta-analytic review of antecedents, outcomes, and methods. *J. Appl. Psychol.* 92:707–21

Berson Y, Oreg S, Dvir T. 2008. CEO values, organizational culture and firm outcomes. *J. Organ. Behav.* 29:615–33

Beus JM, Bergman ME, Payne SC. 2010a. The influence of organizational tenure on safety climate strength: a first look. *Accid. Anal. Prev.* 42:1431–7

Beus JM, Payne SC, Bergman ME, Arthur W Jr. 2010b. Safety climate and injuries: an examination of theoretical and empirical relationships. *J. Appl. Psychol.* 95:713–27

Bezrukova K, Thatcher SMB, Jehn KA, Spell CS. 2012. The effects of alignments: examining group faultlines, organizational cultures, and performance. *J. Appl. Psychol.* 97:77–92

Bindl UK, Parker SK. 2010. Proactive work behavior: forward-thinking and change-oriented action in organizations. In *APA Handbook of Industrial and Organizational Psychology*, Vol. 2: *Selecting and Developing Members for the Organization*, ed. S Zedeck, pp. 567–98. Washington, DC: Am. Psychol. Assoc.

Bliese PD. 2000. Within-group agreement, non-independence, and reliability: implications for data aggregation and analyses. In *Multilevel Theory, Research and Methods in Organizations: Foundations, Extensions, and New Directions*, ed. KJ Klein, SWJ Kozlowski, pp. 349–81. San Francisco: Jossey-Bass

Brodbeck FC, Hanges PJ, Dickson M, Gupta V, Dorfman P. 2004. Societal culture and industrial sector influences on organizational culture. See House et al. 2004, pp. 654–68

Brown RD, Hauenstein NMA. 2005. Interrater agreement reconsidered: an alternative to the r_{WG} indices. *Organ. Res. Methods* 8:165–84

Burke MJ, Finkelstein LM, Dusig MS. 1999. On average deviation indices for estimating interrater agreement. *Organ. Res. Methods* 2:49–68

Burke WW. 2011. *Organization Change: Theory and Practice*. Thousand Oaks, CA: Sage. 3rd ed.

Campbell JP, Dunnette MD, Lawler EE III, Weick KE. 1970. *Managerial Behavior, Performance, and Effectiveness*. New York: McGraw-Hill

Chan D. 1998. Functional relations among constructs in the same content domain at different levels of analysis: a typology of composition models. *J. Appl. Psychol.* 83:234–46

Chan LLM, Shaffer MA, Snape E. 2004. In search of sustained competitive advantage: the impact of organizational culture, competitive strategy and human resource management practices on firm performance. *Int. J. Hum. Resour. Manag.* 15:17–35

Chatman JA, Spataro SE. 2005. Using self-categorization theory to understand relationship demography-based variations in people's responsiveness to organizational culture. *Acad. Manag. J.* 48:321–31

Chen Z, Lam W, Zhong JA. 2007. Leader-member exchange and member performance: a new look at individual-level negative feedback-seeking behavior and team-level empowerment climate. *J. Appl. Psychol.* 92:202–12

Christian MS, Bradley JC, Wallace JC, Burke MJ. 2009. Workplace safety: a meta-analysis of the roles of person and situation factors. *J. Appl. Psychol.* 94:1103–27

Chuang C-H, Liao H. 2010. Strategic human resource management in service context: taking care of business by taking care of employees and customers. *Pers. Psychol.* 63:153–96

Clarke S. 2006. The relationship between safety climate and safety performance: a meta-analytic review. *J. Occup. Health Psychol.* 11:315–27

Colquitt JA, Noe RA, Jackson CL. 2002. Justice in teams: antecedents and consequences of procedural justice climate. *Pers. Psychol.* 58:83–109

Cooke RA, Lafferty JC. 1989. *Organizational Culture Inventory*. Plymouth, MI: Hum. Synerg.

Dawson JF, Gonzalez-Roma V, Davis A, West MA. 2008. Organizational climate and climate strength in UK hospitals. *Eur. J. Work Organ. Psychol.* 17:89–111

Deal TE, Kennedy AA. 1982. *Corporate Cultures: The Rites and Rituals of Organizational Life*. Reading, MA: Addison-Wesley

Denison DR. 1990. *Corporate Culture and Organizational Effectiveness*. New York: Wiley

Early inclusive review of climate theory and research.

Denison DR, Spreitzer GM. 1991. Organizational culture and organizational development. In *Research in Organizational Change and Development*, ed. RW Woodman, WA Pasmore, vol. 5, pp. 1–21. Greenwich, CT: JAI

Dietz J, Pugh SD, Wiley JW. 2004. Service climate effects on customer attitudes: an examination of boundary conditions. *Acad. Manag. J.* 47:81–92

Ehrhart MG. 2004. Leadership and procedural justice climate as antecedents of unit-level organizational citizenship behavior. *Pers. Psychol.* 57:61–94

Erdogan B, Liden RC, Kraimer ML. 2006. Justice and leader-member exchange: the moderating role of organizational culture. *Pers. Psychol.* 49:395–406

Fey CF, Denison DR. 2003. Organizational culture and effectiveness: Can American theory be applied in Russia? *Organ. Sci.* 14:686–706

Flamholtz WG, Randle Y. 2011. *Corporate Culture: The Ultimate Strategic Asset*. Stanford, CA: Stanford Univ. Press

Gelfand MJ, Erez M, Aycan Z. 2007. Cross-cultural organizational behavior. *Annu. Rev. Psychol.* 58:479–514

Gillespie MA, Denison DR, Haaland S, Smerek R, Neale WS. 2008. Linking organizational culture and customer satisfaction: results from two companies in different industries. *Eur. J. Work Organ. Psychol.* 17:112–32

Glick WH. 1985. Conceptualizing and measuring organizational and psychological climate: pitfalls of multi-level research. *Acad. Manag. Rev.* 10:601–10

Glisson C, Green P. 2006. The effects of organizational culture and climate on the access to mental health care in child welfare and juvenile justice systems. *Adm. Policy Ment. Health Ment. Health Serv. Res.* 33:433–48

Glisson C, Schoenwald SK, Kelleher K, Landsverk J, Hoagwood KE, et al. 2008. Therapist turnover and new program sustainability in mental health clinics as a function of organizational culture, climate, and service structure. *Adm. Policy Ment. Health Ment. Health Serv. Res.* 35:124–33

Gonzalez JA, DeNisi AS. 2009. Cross-level effects of demography and diversity climate on organizational attachment and firm effectiveness. *J. Organ. Behav.* 30:21–40

González-Romá V, Peiro JM, Tordera N. 2002. An examination of the antecedents and moderator influences of climate strength. *J. Appl. Psychol.* 87:465–73

Gregory BT, Harris SG, Armenakis AA, Shook CL. 2009. Organizational culture and effectiveness: a study of values, attitudes, and organizational outcomes. *J. Bus. Res.* 62:673–79

Gregory K. 1983. Native-view paradigms: multiple culture and culture conflicts in organizations. *Adm. Sci. Q.* 28:359–76

Hartnell CA, Ou AY, Kinicki A. 2011. Organizational culture and organizational effectiveness: a meta-analytic investigation of the competing values framework's theoretical suppositions. *J. Appl. Psychol.* 96:677–94

Heskett J, Sasser WE, Wheeler J. 2008. *10 Reasons to Design a Better Corporate Culture*. **http://hbswk.hbs.edu/item/5917.html**

Hofmann DA, Mark B. 2006. An investigation of the relationship between safety climate and medication errors as well as other nurse and patient outcomes. *Pers. Psychol.* 59:847–69

Hofstede G. 1980. *Culture's Consequences: International Differences in Work-Related Values*. Beverly Hills, CA: Sage

House RJ, Hanges PJ, Javidan M, Dorfman PW, Gupta V. 2004. *Culture, Leadership and Organizations: The GLOBE Study of 62 Societies*. Thousand Oaks, CA: Sage

James LR. 1982. Aggregation bias in estimates of perceptual agreement. *J. Appl. Psychol.* 67:219–29

James LR, Choi CC, Ko CHE, McNeil PK, Minton MK, et al. 2008. Organizational and psychological climate: a review of theory and research. *Eur. J. Work Organ. Psychol.* 17:5–32

James LR, Demaree RG, Wolf G. 1984. Estimating within-group interrater reliability with and without response bias. *J. Appl. Psychol.* 69:85–98

Klein KJ, Kozlowski SWJ, eds. 2000. *Multilevel Theory, Research and Methods in Organizations: Foundations, Extensions, and New Directions*. San Francisco: Jossey-Bass

Kotrba LM, Gillespie MA, Schmidt AM, Smerek RE, Ritchie SA, Denison DR. 2012. Do consistent corporate cultures have better business performance? Exploring the interaction effects. *Hum. Relat.* 65: 241–62

Important summary of the quantitative research on organizational culture, with conceptual implications for linking climate and culture.

Kramer RM. 1999. Trust and distrust in organizations: emerging perspectives, enduring questions. *Annu. Rev. Psychol.* 50:569–98

Kotter JP, Heskett JL. 1992. *Corporate Culture and Performance*. New York: Free Press

Kuenzi M. 2008. *An integrated model of work climate*. Ph.D. thesis, Univ. Central Florida, Orlando

Kuenzi M, Schminke M. 2009. Assembling fragments into a lens: a review, critique, and proposed research agenda for the organizational work climate literature. *J. Manag.* 35:634–717

Lamond D. 2003. The value of Quinn's competing values model in an Australian context. *J. Manag. Psychol.* 18:46–59

Latham GP, Pinder CC. 2005. Work motivation theory and research at the dawn of the twenty-first century. *Annu. Rev. Psychol.* 56:485–516

LeBreton JM, Senter JL. 2008. Answers to twenty questions about interrater reliability and interrater agreement. *Organ. Res. Methods* 11:815–52

Lee SKJ, Yu K. 2004. Corporate culture and organizational performance. *J. Manag. Psychol.* 19:340–59

Lewin K, Lippitt R, White RK. 1939. Patterns of aggressive behavior in experimentally created "social climates." *J. Soc. Psychol.* 10:271–99

Liao H, Chuang A. 2007. Transforming service employees and climate: a multilevel multi-source examination of transformational leadership in building long-term service relationships. *J. Appl. Psychol.* 92:1006–19

Liao H, Rupp DE. 2005. The impact of justice climate and justice orientation on work outcomes: a cross-level multifoci framework. *J. Appl. Psychol.* 90:242–56

Lindell MK, Brandt CJ. 2000. Climate quality and climate consensus as mediators of the relationship between organizational antecedents and outcomes. *J. Appl. Psychol.* 85:331–45

Louis M. 1990. Acculturation in the work place: newcomers as lay ethnographers. See Schneider 1990, pp. 85–129

Luria G. 2008. Climate strength—how leaders form consensus. *Leadersh. Q.* 19:42–53

Major DA. 2000. Effective newcomer socialization into high performance organizational cultures. See Ashkanasy et al. 2000b, pp. 355–68

Martin J. 1992. *Cultures in Organizations: Three Perspectives*. New York: Oxford Univ. Press

Martin J. 2002. *Organizational Culture: Mapping the Terrain*. Thousand Oaks, CA: Sage

Martin KD, Cullen JB. 2006. Continuities and extensions of ethical climate theory: a meta-analytic review. *J. Bus. Ethics* 69:175–94

Mayer DM, Ehrhart MG, Schneider B. 2009a. Service attribute boundary conditions of the service climate–customer satisfaction link. *Acad. Manag. J.* 52:1034–50

Mayer DM, Kuenzi M, Greenbaum RL. 2009b. Making ethical climate a mainstream management topic: a review, critique, and prescription for the empirical research on ethical climate. In *Psychological Perspectives on Ethical Behavior and Decision Making*, ed. D De Cremer, pp. 181–213. Greenwich, CT: Information Age

Mayer DM, Nishii LH, Schneider B, Goldstein HW. 2007. The precursors and products of fair climates: group leader antecedents and employee attitudinal consequences. *Pers. Psychol.* 60:929–63

McKay PF, Avery DR, Morris MA. 2008. Mean racial-ethnic differences in employee sales performance: the moderating role of diversity climate. *Pers. Psychol.* 61:349–74

McKay PF, Avery DR, Morris MA. 2009. A tale of two climates: diversity climate from subordinates' and managers' perspectives and their role in store unit sales performance. *Pers. Psychol.* 62:767–91

McKay PF, Avery DR, Liao H, Morris MA. 2011. Does diversity climate lead to customer satisfaction? It depends on the service climate and business unit demography. *Organ. Sci.* 22:788–803

Meyer RD, Dalal RS. 2009. Situational strength as a means of conceptualizing context. *Ind. Organ. Psychol.: Perspect. Sci. Pract.* 2:99–102

Meyer RD, Dalal RS, Bonaccio S. 2009. A meta-analytic investigation into situational strength as a moderator of the conscientiousness-performance relationship. *J. Organ. Behav.* 30:1077–102

Meyer RD, Dalal RS, Hermida R. 2010. A review and synthesis of situational strength in the organizational sciences. *J. Manag.* 36:121–40

Michaelis B, Stegmaier R, Sonntag K. 2010. Shedding light on followers' innovation implementation behavior: the role of transformational leadership, commitment to change, and climate for initiative. *J. Manag. Psychol.* 25:408–29

Comprehensive discussion of issues related to levels of analysis and data aggregation.

Clear explication of culture as a phenomenon that exists in organizations in numerous ways.

Mischel W. 1976. Towards a cognitive social model learning reconceptualization of personality. In *Interactional Psychology and Personality*, ed. NS Endler, D Magnusson, pp. 166–207. New York: Wiley

Molloy JC, Ployhart RE, Wright PM. 2011. The myth of "the" macro-micro divide: bridging systems level and disciplinary divides. *J. Manag.* 37:587–609

Morrison EW, Wheeler-Smith SL, Kamdar D. 2011. Speaking up in groups: a cross-level study of group voice climate and voice. *J. Appl. Psychol.* 96:183–91

Naumann SE, Bennett N. 2000. A case for procedural justice climate: development and test of a multilevel model. *Acad. Manag. J.* 43:881–89

Neal A, Griffin MA. 2006. A study of the lagged relationships among safety climate, safety motivation, safety behavior, and accidents at the individual and group levels. *J. Appl. Psychol.* 91:946–53

Ogbonna E, Harris LC. 2000. Leadership style, organizational culture and performance: empirical evidence from UK companies. *Int. J. Hum. Resour. Manag.* 11:766–88

O'Reilly C, Chatman J, Caldwell D. 1991. People and organizational culture: a profile comparison approach to assessing person-organization fit. *Acad. Manag. J.* 34:487–516

Ostroff C, Judge TA, eds. 2007. *Perspectives on Organizational Fit.* Mahwah, NJ: Erlbaum

Ostroff C, Kinicki AJ, Tamkins MM. 2003. Organizational culture and climate. In *Handbook of Psychology: Industrial and Organizational Psychology*, ed. WC Borman, DR Ilgen, RJ Klimoski, vol. 12, pp. 565–93. New York: Wiley

Pang B, Lee L. 2008. Opinion mining and sentiment analysis. *Found. Trends Inf. Retrieval* 2(1-2):1–135.

Peters TJ, Waterman RH Jr. 1982. *In Search of Excellence*. New York: Harper & Row

Pettigrew AM. 1979. On studying organizational cultures. *Adm. Sci. Q.* 24:570–81

Pettigrew AM. 1990. Organizational climate and culture: two constructs in search of a role. See Schneider 1990, pp. 413–34

Ployhart R. 2012. The psychology of competitive advantage: an adjacent possibility. *Ind. Organ. Psychol.* 5:62–81

Probst TM, Brubaker TL, Barsotti A. 2008. Organizational under-reporting of injury rates: an examination of the moderating effect of organizational safety climate. *J. Appl. Psychol.* 93:1147–54

Pugh SD, Dietz J, Brief AP, Wiley JW. 2008. Looking inside and out: the impact of employee and community demographic composition on organizational diversity climate. *J. Appl. Psychol.* 93:1422–28

Quinn RE, Kimberly JR. 1984. Paradox, planning, and perseverance: guidelines for managerial practice. In *Managing Organizational Transitions*, ed. JR Kimberly, RE Quinn, pp. 295–313. Homewood, IL: Dow Jones-Irwin

Quinn RE, Rohrbaugh J. 1983. A special model of effectiveness criteria: toward a competing values approach to organizational analysis. *Manag. Sci.* 29:363–77

Rafferty AE, Jimmieson NL. 2010. Team change climate: a group-level analysis of the relationships among change information and change participation, role stressors, and well-being. *Eur. J. Work Organ. Psychol.* 19:551–86

Reichers AE, Schneider B. 1990. Climate and culture: an evolution of constructs. See Schneider 1990, pp. 5–39

Roberson QM. 2006. Justice in teams: the activation and role of sensemaking in the emergence of justice climates. *Organ. Behav. Hum. Decis. Process.* 100:177–92

Rynes SL, Gerhart B, Parks L. 2005. Personnel psychology: performance evaluation and pay for performance. *Annu. Rev. Psychol.* 56:571–600

Sackmann SA. 2011. Culture and performance. See Ashkanasy et al. 2011, pp. 188–224

Sagiv L, Schwartz SH, Arieli S. 2011. Personal values, national, culture, and organizations: insights applying the Schwartz value framework. See Ashkanasy et al. 2011, pp. 515–37

Salanova M, Agut S, Peiró JM. 2005. Linking organizational resources and work engagement to employee performance and customer loyalty: the mediation of service climate. *J. Appl. Psychol.* 90:1217–27

Salvaggio AN, Schneider B, Nishii LH, Mayer DM, Ramesh A, Lyon J S. 2007. Manager personality, manager service quality orientation, and service climate: test of a model. *J. Appl. Psychol.* 92:1741–50

Scandura TA. 2002. The establishment years: the dependence perspective. In *Work Careers: A Developmental Perspective*, ed. DC Feldman, pp. 159–85. San Francisco: Jossey-Bass

Schein EH. 1985. *Organizational Culture and Leadership*. San Francisco: Jossey-Bass

The article that introduced the study of culture to organizational scholars.

Comprehensive summary of research on the organizational culture–organizational performance link.

Schein EH. 1992. *Organizational Culture and Leadership*. San Francisco: Jossey-Bass. 2nd ed.

Schein EH. 2000. Sense and nonsense about culture and climate. See Ashkanasy et al. 2000b, pp. xxiii–xxx

Schein EH. 2004. *Organizational Culture and Leadership*. San Francisco: Jossey-Bass. 3rd ed.

Schein EH. 2010. *Organizational Culture and Leadership*. San Francisco: Jossey-Bass. 4th ed.

Schminke M, Ambrose ML, Neubaum DO. 2005. The effects of leader moral development on ethical climate and employee attitudes. *Organ. Behav. Hum. Decis. Process.* 97:135–51

Schneider B. 1975. Organizational climates: an essay. *Pers. Psychol.* 28:447–79

Schneider B. 1985. Organizational behavior. *Annu. Rev. Psychol.* 36:573–611

Schneider B, ed. 1990. *Organizational Climate and Culture*. San Francisco: Jossey-Bass

Schneider B, Barbera KM, eds. 2013. *The Oxford Handbook of Organizational Climate and Culture*. Cheltenham, UK: Oxford Univ. Press. In press

Schneider B, Bartlett CJ. 1968. Individual differences and organizational climate: I. The research plan and questionnaire development. *Pers. Psychol.* 21:323–33

Schneider B, Ehrhart MG, Macey WH. 2011. Perspectives on organizational climate and culture. In *APA Handbook of Industrial and Organizational Psychology*: Vol. 1. *Building and Developing the Organization*, ed. S Zedeck, pp. 373–414. Washington, DC: Am. Psychol. Assoc.

Schneider B, Ehrhart MG, Mayer DM, Saltz JL, Niles-Jolly K. 2005. Understanding organization–customer links in service settings. *Acad. Manag. J.* 48:1017–32

Schneider B, Macey WH, Lee W, Young SA. 2009. Organizational service climate drivers of the American Customer Satisfaction Index (ACSI) and financial and market performance. *J. Serv. Res.* 12:3–14

Schneider B, Reichers AE. 1983. On the etiology of climates. *Pers. Psychol.* 36:19–39

Schneider B, Salvaggio AN, Subirats M. 2002. Climate strength: a new direction for climate research. *J. Appl. Psychol.* 87:220–29

Schneider B, White SS, Paul MC. 1998. Linking service climate and customer perceptions of service quality: test of a causal model. *J. Appl. Psychol.* 83:150–63

Schulte M, Ostroff C, Shmulyian S, Kinicki A. 2009. Organizational climate configurations: relationships to collective attitudes, customer satisfaction, and financial performance. *J. Appl. Psychol.* 94:618–34

Seibert SE, Silver SR, Randolph WA. 2004. Taking empowerment to the next level: a multiple-level model of empowerment, performance and satisfaction. *Acad. Manag. J.* 47:332–49

Siehl C, Martin J. 1990. Organizational culture: a key to financial performance? See Schneider 1990, pp. 241–81

Simons T, Roberson Q. 2003. Why managers should care about fairness: the effects of aggregate justice perceptions on organizational outcomes. *J. Appl. Psychol.* 88:432–43

Smircich L. 1983. Concepts of culture and organizational analysis. *Adm. Sci. Q.* 28:339–58

Sørensen JB. 2002. The strength of corporate culture and the reliability of firm performance. *Adm. Sci. Q.* 47:70–91

Sowinski DR, Fortmann KA, Lezotte DV. 2008. Climate for service and the moderating effects of climate strength on customer satisfaction, voluntary turnover, and profitability. *Eur. J. Work Organ. Psychol.* 17:73–88

Trice HM, Beyer JM. 1993. *The Cultures of Work Organizations*. Englewood Cliffs, NJ: Prentice-Hall

Tsui AS, Wang H, Xin KR. 2006a. Organizational culture in China: an analysis of culture dimensions and culture types. *Manag. Organ. Rev.* 2:345–76

Tsui AS, Zhang Z-X, Wang H, Xin KR, Wu JB. 2006b. Unpacking the relationship between CEO leadership behavior and organizational culture. *Leadersh. Q.* 17:113–37

Van Maanen J. 1975. Police socialization: a longitudinal examination of job attitudes in an urban police department. *Adm. Sci. Q.* 20:207–28

Wallace JC, Popp E, Mondore S. 2006. Safety climate as a mediator between foundation climates and occupational accidents: a group-level investigation. *J. Appl. Psychol.* 91:681–88

Walumbwa FO, Hartnell CA, Oke A. 2010. Servant leadership, procedural justice climate, service climate, employee attitudes, and organizational citizenship behavior: a cross-level investigation. *J. Appl. Psychol.* 95:517–29

Weick KE, Quinn RE. 1999. Organizational change and development. *Annu. Rev. Psychol.* 50:361–86

Very clear statement, with examples, of what culture is and how it emerges in organizations.

The article that first suggested that climate research should have specific foci.

A detailed examination of the historical roots of contemporary climate and culture thinking and research.

Wilderom CPM, Glunk U, Mazlowski R. 2000. Organizational culture as a predictor of organizational performance. See Ashkanasy et al. 2000b, pp. 193–209

Xenikou A, Simosi M. 2006. Organizational culture and transformational leadership as predictors of business unit performance. *J. Manag. Psychol.* 21:566–79

Yammarino FJ, Dansereau F. 2011. Multilevel issues in organizational culture and climate research. See Ashkanasy et al. 2011, pp. 50–76

Yang J, Mossholder KW, Peng TK. 2007. Procedural justice climate and group power distance: an examination of cross-level interaction effects. *J. Appl. Psychol.* 92:681–92

Zohar D. 2000. A group level model of safety climate: testing the effect of group climate on microaccidents in manufacturing jobs. *J. Appl. Psychol.* 85:587–96

Zohar D, Hofmann DH. 2012. Organizational culture and climate. In *The Oxford Handbook of Industrial and Organizational Psychology*, ed. SWJ Kozlowski. Oxford, UK: Oxford Univ. Press. In press

Zohar D, Luria G. 2004. Climate as social-cognitive construction of supervisory safety practices: scripts as proxy of behavior patterns. *J. Appl. Psychol.* 89:322–33

Zohar D, Luria G. 2005. A multi-level model of safety climate: cross-level relationships between organization and group-level climates. *J. Appl. Psychol.* 90:616–28

Zohar D, Tenne-Gazit O. 2008. Transformational leadership and group interaction as climate antecedents: a social network analysis. *J. Appl. Psychol.* 93:744–57

The importance of conceptualizing and studying climate at multiple levels of analysis.

Employee Recruitment

James A. Breaugh

College of Business Administration, University of Missouri-St. Louis, St. Louis,
Missouri 63121; email: jbreaugh@umsl.edu

Annu. Rev. Psychol. 2013. 64:389–416

First published online as a Review in Advance on
October 25, 2012

The *Annual Review of Psychology* is online at
psych.annualreviews.org

This article's doi:
10.1146/annurev-psych-113011-143757

Keywords

recruitment methods, recruitment message, recruiters, applicant
attraction, employee referral

Abstract

The way an organization recruits can influence the type of employees it hires, how they perform, and their retention rate. This article
provides a selective review of research that has addressed recruitment
targeting, recruitment methods, the recruitment message, recruiters,
the organizational site visit, the job offer, and the timing of recruitment
actions. These and other topics (e.g., the job applicant's perspective)
are discussed in terms of their potential influence on prehire (e.g., the
quality of job applicants) and posthire (e.g., new employee retention)
recruitment outcomes. In reviewing research, attention is given to the
current state of scientific knowledge, limitations of previous research,
and important issues meriting future investigation.

Contents

INTRODUCTION

Regardless of the type of organization, it is generally accepted that an employer's success is closely tied to the type of individuals it employs (Dineen & Soltis 2011). Given that the way an employer recruits affects the type of individuals who are hired, it is not surprising that the topic of employee recruitment has attracted considerable attention. The goals of this review are to provide a sense of the current state of scientific knowledge on major recruitment topics, point out limitations of previous research, and highlight important issues meriting future investigation.

This is the first article on employee recruitment to appear in the *Annual Review of*

Psychology. Therefore, for most topics, this article provides an overview of early research that has been conducted (arbitrarily defined as studies published prior to 2000) before more recent research is addressed (for some topics such as Web-based recruiting, there is no pre-2000 research to discuss). The first recruitment topic examined is the most fundamental issue an employer faces—the type of individuals to target for recruitment. Having decided on the type of individuals to recruit, an organization needs to determine the method to use to reach these individuals, the recruitment message to convey, and the type of recruiters to use. Following a review of studies on these three topics, this article examines research on a job

Recruitment method: an approach (e.g., job advertisements, job fair) used by an employer to publicize a job opening

applicant's organizational site visit, the job offer, and the timing of recruitment actions. Finally, this article reviews studies that have focused on the recruitment of members of underrepresented groups. This research is addressed in a separate section at the end of this article so that the multitude of issues involved can be more easily integrated. Prior to reviewing research on these recruitment topics, a number of basic issues (e.g., boundaries for this review) are addressed.

Employee Recruitment: A Definition and the Scope of This Review

The breadth of recruitment research necessitated that choices be made concerning the topics covered in this review. In this regard, given that Ryan & Delaney (2010) recently examined research relevant to recruiting in an international context, this article does not address this topic. Because little research on internal recruitment (i.e., an employer recruiting its own workers for new positions) exists, this review focuses on research concerning external recruitment, which is defined as "an employer's actions that are intended to (1) bring a job opening to the attention of potential job candidates who do not currently work for the organization, (2) influence whether these individuals apply for the opening, (3) affect whether they maintain interest in the position until a job offer is extended, and (4) influence whether a job offer is accepted" (Breaugh 2008, pp. 103–104).

Recruitment Criterion Measures

Several criteria have been utilized in recruitment studies (Carlson et al. 2002).[1] Prehire outcomes (e.g., number of applicants, job offer acceptance rate) involve information concerning job applicants. Posthire outcomes (e.g., job performance, employee turnover) involve

behaviors and attitudes of new employees. To date, posthire outcomes have been the primary focus in most areas of recruitment research. In contrast, little attention has been given to prehire variables such as attracting the attention of the type of individuals targeted for recruitment.

As will become apparent from this review of the recruitment literature, it is important for researchers to expand the range of criterion measures they include in future studies. In particular, more attention needs to be given to job applicant perceptions of and reactions to specific recruitment actions (e.g., timely job offers) given that they likely mediate the relationships between an organization's recruitment actions and outcomes in many situations. Several aspects of the job applicant's perspective are discussed after the topic of theory development in the context of recruitment research is addressed.

THEORY DEVELOPMENT IN THE CONTEXT OF RECRUITMENT RESEARCH

Despite the sizable amount of research that has been conducted, no general theory of employment recruitment (i.e., a theory that addresses the relationships among various recruitment variables and how these variables interact with job applicant attributes and organizational attributes in affecting recruitment outcomes) has been offered. Instead, some researchers (e.g., Dineen & Soltis 2011, Saks 2005) have provided incomplete models of the recruitment process (e.g., relationships between key variables are not fully explicated, important variables are not included), and other researchers (e.g., Allen et al. 2004, Breaugh 2010) have offered theoretical models that focused on a specific aspect of the recruitment process (e.g., communication media, the recruitment message) in isolation from other recruitment variables. These more micro-oriented theories are discussed in the relevant sections later in this review.

The failure of researchers to develop a general theory of recruitment that integrates various aspects of the recruitment process has

---

[1]In this article, causal terms such as "influences" and "outcomes" are used to reflect hypothesized relationships and to simplify the presentation of results even though in many cases the study being discussed did not use a research design that allows for the drawing of causal inferences.

resulted in a research literature that offers a fragmented treatment of topics. For example, separate theoretical treatments (i.e., Breaugh 2008, Earnest et al. 2011, Zottoli & Wanous 2000) of using current employees to recruit (a recruitment method), providing a realistic job preview (a recruitment message), and recruiting individuals who have held jobs similar to those being filled (recruitment targeting) all hypothesize an effect on the accuracy of recruits' job expectations. Yet, these three topics have been treated individually in studies rather than examined in combination as ways to influence job expectations.

Applicable Psychological Theory

As an initial step in developing a general theory of employee recruitment, it is useful to conceptualize much of what occurs during the recruitment process as reflecting an attitude formation/change process that involves individuals forming an impression of what working for an organization would be like. Viewing the recruitment process in this manner allows one to draw upon principles derived from psychological research on persuasion.[2] A useful starting point for introducing relevant research on attitude formation and change is a brief review of three models (i.e., Hovland et al. 1953, McGuire 1968, Petty & Cacioppo, 1986) followed by a discussion of several principles derived from these and other theories. The material presented in this section is largely drawn from Albarracin & Vargas (2010), Bohner & Dickel (2011), Kruglanski & Sleeth-Keppler (2007), and Maio & Haddock (2007). Readers interested in a more nuanced treatment of the persuasion process are referred to these sources.

Hovland et al.'s (1953) model of persuasion emphasizes the importance of the source of a

message (e.g., credible?), the audience for the message (e.g., personality?), the message itself (e.g., perceived as threatening?), and the sequence in which the persuasion process unfolds (i.e., a message is attended to, comprehended, and accepted). McGuire's (1968) information processing model highlights six stages, which occur in the following sequence: "presentation of the message, attention to the message, comprehension of the message, yielding to the argument, retention of the changed attitude in memory, and behavior relevant to the attitude" (Maio & Haddock 2007, p. 570). One implication of this information-processing sequence is that behavior relevant to an attitude will only occur if the prior stages occur. McGuire did not solely focus on the persuasion process from the perspective of an agent who is trying to influence attitudes. He also addressed the target of the persuasion effort. For example, he suggested intelligent message recipients are more likely to comprehend a message but less likely to be persuaded by it.

The third theory of persuasion addressed is Petty & Cacioppo's (1986) elaboration likelihood model (ELM), which describes when message processing is likely to be deliberative and when more superficial processing is likely. These authors suggested that a peripheral route to processing information is likely to be used when message recipients lack the motivation or the ability to carefully process (i.e., scrutinize and think about) a message. According to ELM, when an individual reflects carefully on message content (i.e., central route processing), the strength of the argument made is likely to be determinative of attitude change. In contrast to central route processing, Petty & Cacioppo posited that such factors as perceived communicator trustworthiness, message length, and the number of arguments presented are likely to be influential if peripheral processing occurs. The issue of information processing has been addressed in similar yet distinct ways by others (e.g., Kruglanski & Thompson 1999). For example, Chaiken (1987) discussed such processing as being either systematic or heuristic. Heuristic processing, which is similar to ELM's

---

[2]The relevance of research on persuasion for employee recruitment is reflected in the following statement by Allen et al. (2004, p. 144): "a core activity of recruitment, particularly in the early stage of the recruitment process, is communicating information about jobs, working conditions, expectations, values, and climate in order to persuade prospective employees to consider joining the organization."

peripheral processing, is thought to be based on the use of cognitive shortcuts such as the consensus heuristic—"if other people believe the message, it is likely to be true."

In terms of generalizing from basic research on persuasion to an employee recruitment context, of central importance is the fact that how carefully a message is scrutinized depends on factors related to a message recipient's attention, motivation, and ability. Having introduced three theories of persuasion (admittedly in a cursory fashion), the relevance of principles derived from these and other theories of persuasion to recruitment is addressed.

Examples of the Application of Psychological Principles to the Recruitment Process

A key issue in the recruitment process is bringing a job opening to the attention of individuals an employer would like to recruit. In this regard, the concept of goal-directed attention merits consideration. As discussed by Bohner & Dickel (2011), individuals have limited cognitive resources. Therefore, selective attention to environmental stimuli is needed for a person to function effectively (i.e., not be overwhelmed with information). One factor that has been shown to influence what stimuli a person attends to is his or her goals (Dijksterhuis & Aarts 2010). This selective attention effect suggests that although active job seekers are likely to attend to messages publicizing job openings, individuals who are not actively looking for a job may not be so attentive. As discussed later in this review, such selective attention has implications for recruiting individuals who are not searching for a job.

In terms of attitude formation, direct experience with an attitude object has been shown to have a great effect (Albarracin & Vargas 2010). Generalizing to a recruitment context, this direct experience effect suggests that such things as having had an internship with an employer is likely to have considerable influence on a person's initial attitude about the employer. A person's initial attitude also can be affected by

experiences that are not firsthand. For example, a prospective applicant may receive information about an employer as a result of his or her efforts (e.g., Web-based research). The effect of such secondhand information has been found to depend on its perceived credibility, which research has shown to be related to communicator expertise and trustworthiness (O'Keefe 2002). In turn, trustworthiness has been linked to whether a message is two-sided (e.g., presents positive and negative attributes of a job opening) rather than presenting information that only supports the sender's position (Chaiken & Stagnor 1987).[3] Research also has shown that receiving a consistent message from multiple sources results in an attribution of credibility (Harkins & Petty 1981).

In terms of information processing, most researchers have viewed job applicants as being quite deliberative given the consequences of the job search and the job choice processes. Thus, in going through the recruitment process, an applicant is generally viewed as using the central processing route. Given the importance of the job choice decision, it seems likely that most individuals do carefully consider the attributes of a job offer. However, the possibility of peripheral processing, especially in earlier stages of the recruitment process (e.g., forming an initial impression of an employer), also merits consideration. In this regard, research (e.g., Zajonc 1968, 2001) has demonstrated that attitudes can become more favorable with increasing exposure to an attitude object (e.g., an employer) even if a person is not consciously focusing on the stimulus. Research suggests this mere exposure effect occurs due to a twofold process: Repeated exposure facilitates ease of processing, and "any mental process that is fast and effortless engenders a positive affective response" (Albarracin & Vargas 2010, p. 404). One implication of the mere exposure effect for recruiting is that advertisements geared toward presenting

---

[3]In terms of attitude change, in contrast to increasing credibility, a two-sided message that includes a refutation of opposing arguments has been shown to be more persuasive than a two-sided message without refutation (O'Keefe 1999).

a positive image of an organization (i.e., image advertising) may prove beneficial for making an employer more attractive to potential job applicants even if the individuals are not consciously attending to the ads and even if the individuals are not actively looking for a job.

Once an initial attitude is formed, research has shown that this attitude can be hard to change. Three explanations for this phenomenon are particularly relevant for the recruitment process: selective exposure, confirmation bias, and initial impressions resulting in information-processing bias. With regard to selective exposure, the results of several studies suggest that, having formed an initial opinion, individuals are motivated to defend the attitude (Albarracin & Vargas 2010). One way for an individual to do so is to avoid information that is discrepant with the initial attitude. The tendency to avoid attitude-incongruent information has been shown to be more pronounced when a person's attitude is stronger (Brannon et al. 2007). The concept of confirmation bias is based on the assumption that people seek to avoid internal psychological conflict. To avoid such conflict, there is an inclination to "seek information that confirms our preexisting beliefs, feelings, and behaviors" (Maio & Haddock 2007, p. 566). In addition to initial attitudes being difficult to change due to the tendencies of individuals to avoid contradictory information and to seek out information that is supportive of them, the way information is processed contributes to attitude stability. Specifically, research suggests that an individual's initial attitude leads the person to process new information in a biased manner so as to alleviate cognitive inconsistency. Such bias may occur because "early information may increase the accessibility of certain inferences that then serve as a basis for interpreting subsequent information" (Bohner & Dickel 2011, p. 404). In the context of employee recruitment, one implication of the tendencies of selective exposure, confirmation bias, and biased information processing is that an organization may benefit from targeting individuals for recruitment who either have yet to form a strong opinion concerning the organization as a place of employment or who are favorably disposed toward working there.

Although other principles concerning persuasion could have been discussed [e.g., Cialdini's (2008) concept of social proof], it suffices to state that research on the persuasion process has direct relevance for the employee recruitment process and merits more attention than it has received. Before discussing research on specific recruitment topics, it is beneficial to address the job applicant's perspective, given that how an applicant reacts to various recruitment actions can moderate their effectiveness.

THE JOB APPLICANT'S PERSPECTIVE

Attracting the attention of potential job applicants is the first step in the recruitment process. It is useful to distinguish two aspects of this variable: persons becoming aware of a job opening and their actively processing the information presented. With regard to whether individuals targeted for recruitment are made aware of a job opening, researchers largely have ignored this variable. This is surprising given that for 50 years research dealing with persuasion (e.g., Hovland et al. 1953) has highlighted the importance of attracting the attention of intended information recipients. In terms of information that is noticed being actively processed, interviews with applicants suggest that job advertisements are often "skimmed" as opposed to being systematically processed (Jones et al. 2006). To generate deeper processing, recruitment research (Allen et al. 2004) suggests that job-related information that is unexpected, of personal relevance to the recipient, and is delivered in person is more likely to be carefully considered.

Considerable research has established that whether an individual applies for a job opening is strongly related to its perceived attractiveness (Ehrhart & Ziegert 2005). Not surprisingly, job and organizational attributes are key factors in determining a position's attractiveness (Chapman et al. 2005). In this regard, a key attribute is an employer's reputation. Studies have shown reputation to be important both because individuals want to impress others with their affiliation with a respected organization (e.g., Highhouse et al. 2007, Turban & Cable 2003) and because an organization's reputation is interpreted as a signal of positive job attributes (Cable & Turban 2003). In terms of a position's attractiveness, two other important factors are a person's expectancy of receiving a job offer and his or her having alternative opportunities such as another job offer (Chapman et al. 2005, Chapman & Webster 2006). That is, research has found that individuals tend to downgrade positions they are not likely to get, and they tend to have a higher threshold for what is an acceptable position if they have other opportunities.

In considering the perspective of a job applicant, researchers (e.g., Dineen & Noe 2009) frequently have assumed that an applicant possesses self-insight concerning his or her abilities, needs, etc. Based on this assumption, it has been suggested (e.g., Breaugh 2010, Earnest et al. 2011) that by providing accurate information about a job to an applicant, an employer enables the person to make an informed job choice decision (e.g., to withdraw as an applicant if a job is not perceived as a good fit). However, psychological research suggests that assuming self-insight may not always be reasonable. For example, studies have shown that individuals often have an inflated view of their abilities (see Dunning 2007). If this is true for recruits, and interviews with new employees suggest it is (e.g., Billsberry 2007, Louis 1980), then despite recruits possessing accurate information about a position, they may think they are capable of handling job duties they actually lack the ability to master. This issue of self-insight (or the lack thereof) has relevance for targeting individuals for recruitment and drafting a recruitment message, two topics discussed later in this review.

It is generally accepted that most individuals make decisions about a prospective job (e.g., whether to apply, whether to accept a job offer) using a noncompensatory decision-making approach initially followed by a compensatory approach (Highhouse & Hoffman 2001). That is, certain attributes must be present (e.g., a job is located in a certain city) for a position to be considered as a viable option [e.g., Osborn (1990) found that approximately 90% of the participants in his study reported that some minimum or special requirement was necessary in order for them to consider a job opening]. Once these threshold factors have been met, researchers generally assume that an applicant will consider other job attributes in a compensatory fashion. Although Gigerenzer & Gaissmaier (2011) did not address the topic of job applicant decision making, their discussion of the use of heuristics applies to a recruitment context. For example, research on the recognition heuristic suggests that in forming a consideration set (i.e., a subset of job openings that are carefully evaluated) from several advertised positions, job seekers would place a higher value on easily recognized alternatives. A key factor with regard to applicant decision making is the timing of recruitment activities, a topic discussed later in this review. For example, reflecting a desire for uncertainty reduction, there is evidence that a recruit is likely to accept the first job offer that exceeds his or her threshold for job and organizational attributes (Becker et al. 2010).

Given the importance of job applicant variables, it is surprising that they have not played a central role in most recruitment studies (e.g., an applicant's expectancy of receiving a job offer being tested as a mediating variable). One reason for this lack of attention may be that researchers have not given sufficient consideration to the type of individuals targeted for recruitment (e.g., whether they are likely to have self-insight), the next topic addressed.

TARGETING INDIVIDUALS FOR RECRUITMENT

In beginning the recruitment process, an organization needs to decide what type(s) of individuals to recruit (e.g., retirees, military veterans). In addressing the issue of whom

Noncompensatory decision making: a process in which the absence of a particular attribute (e.g., employer health insurance) eliminates the decision alternative from further consideration

Targeted
recruitment:
recruitment actions
that are designed to
generate a particular
type of job applicant
(e.g., seniors, veterans,
former employees)

to target, authors (e.g., Billsberry 2007) have highlighted such factors as (*a*) what type of individuals will be attracted to a job with an organization, (*b*) whether they will possess the personal attributes (e.g., job experience) needed to be hired, (*c*) whether job offers are likely to be accepted, and (*d*) if hired, whether targeted individuals will remain with the employer for a reasonable length of time. Although these factors have been highlighted by authors, little empirical research directly relevant to the topic of recruitment targeting exists (Dineen & Soltis 2011). For example, researchers have not compared different groups of recruits in terms of their receptivity to job offers. However, a few studies have been published that are tangentially related to the issue of targeted recruitment.

In terms of a group to target, former employees have traditionally been thought to be a beneficial group based on the assumption that they would have more accurate job expectations, and thus if hired would be more satisfied with their jobs and therefore less likely to leave them. To test such conventional wisdom, Taylor & Schmidt (1983) used data from personnel files to compare employees who found their jobs by means of newspaper ads or employment agencies against individuals who previously had worked for the employer. As hypothesized, Taylor & Schmidt found rehires were less likely to quit their jobs. This study shares three limitations with many of the studies that have focused on former employees as a group to target for recruitment. First, it failed to examine assumed job applicant mediator variables (e.g., did former employees have more accurate job expectations?). Second, the sample used was composed of new employees rather than applicants. This focus on new employees may mask applicant differences (e.g., an employer's selection system may reduce differences in applicant quality). Third, Taylor & Schmidt confounded the types of individuals recruited (i.e., former employees) with how they heard about a job opening (i.e., a newspaper ad is a recruitment method that may bring an opening to the attention of several different

types of individuals, including former employees). In a study that involved nurses who applied for jobs at several hospitals, Williams et al. (1993) gathered data on job applicants and those applicants who were hired. With regard to applicants, in comparison to persons recruited from colleges and newspaper ads, former employees had a higher level of education, greater prehire knowledge of the hospital to which they applied, and were more likely to accept job offers. No group differences were found for employee performance or turnover (the lack of posthire outcome differences could be due to differences linked to hospitals not being considered in data analysis). Taken as a whole, earlier research on recruiting former employees suggests that doing so may be beneficial. However, conclusions should be viewed as tentative due to methodological limitations in the studies conducted.

Recent studies suggest that certain types of individuals are more likely to be interested in a job opening and thus are relevant to the issue of targeted recruitment. In a study conducted with students, Devendorf & Highhouse (2008) investigated whether individuals would be more attracted to places of employment in which coworkers were seen as similar to themselves in terms of personality characteristics. They found support for a similarity-attraction relationship. In explaining their results, Devendorf & Highhouse noted that this relationship could be due to individuals feeling more comfortable working with people who are similar to themselves and/or the fact that individuals believe they are more likely to receive a job offer if an employer has hired people who are similar to themselves. In a study by Becker et al. (2010) that involved job applicants, individuals who had to relocate for a new job were found to be less likely to accept job offers. The results of these studies suggest that employers may benefit from targeting individuals for recruitment who are similar to current employees and/or will not need to relocate.

Although authors have noted the importance of an employer's decision with regard to the type of individuals to target for recruitment (e.g., unless an applicant pool is generated that possesses the personal attributes sought by an organization, the ability of its selection system to choose individuals who possess such attributes is limited), there is a lack of research comparing different groups. In terms of future research, studies are needed that examine whether some of the hypothesized advantages of certain groups really exist. For example, it has been suggested (Ryan et al. 2005) that individuals who have a family member who works for an organization should have a better understanding of what a job opening involves and thus be less likely to submit an application unless they perceive good person/job-organization fit. However, the merits of targeting family members have yet to be investigated. Similarly, Breaugh (2008) presented a theoretical rationale for why recruiting individuals who have worked in jobs similar to an advertised position should result in applicants who possess more realistic job expectations and greater self-insight. However, these ideas have not been formally tested.

Particularly valuable would be future studies that consider some of the theoretical principles derived from research on attention and persuasion. For example, research on goal-directed attention suggests it would be beneficial for an organization that is interested in recruiting individuals who are not actively looking for a job to go beyond relying on such commonly used recruitment methods as job advertisements and its Web site. If noticed at all, job openings publicized by such methods are likely to be processed in a peripheral manner (Jones et al. 2006, Rafaeli 2006). Research on selective exposure and confirmation bias also merits future study. For example, generalizing from psychological research on these topics, it seems likely that an employer would benefit from targeting individuals who have an initially positive view of working there or who have yet to form an initial attitude. Recruiting such individuals eliminates the challenge of having to overcome an established negative attitude toward the employer. The relevance of these basic psychological principles for future research is

further discussed in subsequent sections concerning recruitment methods and the recruitment message.

RECRUITMENT METHODS

Having decided on the type of individuals to target for recruitment, an employer needs to select one or more recruitment methods to use to bring a job opening to their attention. In this section, two explanations for why recruitment methods are thought to be important are presented, an overview of two representative studies that compared recruitment methods is provided, research on four popular recruitment methods (i.e., current employees, college placement offices, an employer's Web site, and job boards) is reviewed, and future directions for research are noted.

Although several explanations (see Zottoli & Wanous 2000) have been offered for why recruitment methods should affect certain prehire and posthire outcomes, two explanations (i.e., the realism hypothesis and the individual difference hypothesis) have attracted the most attention. The realism hypothesis suggests that persons recruited by certain methods (especially individuals referred by current employees) are likely to possess a more accurate understanding of what a job with an organization involves. Having such an understanding allows individuals to make an informed decision about whether a job is a good fit. The individual difference hypothesis assumes that different recruitment methods bring a job opening to the attention of individuals who systematically vary on personal attributes that are linked to recruitment outcomes. For example, it has been suggested that, in comparison to respondents to newspaper ads, direct applicants (i.e., persons who applied to an organization without knowing a job opening existed) would have greater motivation to work for an employer because they had put forward the effort to drive to a place of business to apply for a job with no assurance there was a job opening (this logic does not hold if applications are submitted online).

Job board: a third-party Web site that enables employers to list job openings

Two Examples of Past Research Comparing Several Recruitment Methods

Over the years, there has been considerable research on recruitment methods. Some studies have examined recruitment outcomes across a variety of recruitment methods. Two of these studies (Breaugh et al. 2003, Kirnan et al. 1989) are reviewed in order to provide a sense of this type of research. Kirnan et al. utilized data on job applicants and new employees and focused on prehire recruitment outcomes (i.e., applicant quality, receiving a job offer, and accepting a job offer) and posthire recruitment outcomes (i.e., retention and job performance). Based on the assumptions that employee referrals (i.e., individuals who were referred for jobs by current employees of the organization) would be better able to self-select out of consideration for a job that was not a good fit (given they would have received accurate job information from the employee who referred them) and would be prescreened by the current employee (i.e., only individuals who were seen as qualified for a position would be referred), Kirnan et al. (1989) hypothesized that employee referrals would be superior in terms of prehire outcomes in comparison to individuals recruited by means of newspaper ads, college placement offices, or employment agencies. Their hypotheses were confirmed. In looking at recruitment method effects on posthire outcomes, Kirnan et al. created two composite groups. The informal group included referrals and direct applicants. The formal group included individuals who were recruited by other methods. Results showed a small employee retention effect favoring those in the informal group; no difference was reported for job performance. Utilizing archival data on job applicants, Breaugh et al. (2003) examined the relationships between five recruitment methods (i.e., current employees making referrals, direct applicants, college recruitment, job fairs, and newspaper ads) and six prehire outcomes. No group differences were found for education, test score, and interview score. Compared to the other groups, college

recruits had less work experience. Unexpectedly, given the overall lack of applicant quality differences reported, employee referrals and direct applicants were more likely to receive job offers. Apparently, the organization had a positive view of employee referrals and direct applicants even if the objective selection data did not favor members of these groups. Employee referrals and direct applicants also were found to be more likely to accept job offers.

Employee Referrals

The use of current employees is generally viewed by employers as the best method for reaching individuals who possess desirable personal attributes (Breaugh 2009). Several studies have shown there is validity to this perspective and have increased our understanding of why using current employees to recruit can be advantageous. In the studies discussed, individuals recruited by current employees were compared against individuals recruited from all other recruitment methods combined.

Fernandez & Weinberg (1997) tested whether referred applicants for call center jobs had advantages at the interview and job offer stages of the recruitment process because they had been screened by the employees who referred them. Supporting their hypotheses, employee referrals were found to be superior to nonreferrals in terms of computer skills, language skills, education, and work experience. Given these advantages, it is not surprising that referrals were more likely to receive job offers. Castilla (2005) examined whether referrals were more likely to be hired and complete a training program than nonreferrals. As predicted, they were. Castilla also found the initial job performance of referrals exceeded that of nonreferrals, which he hypothesized was due to their receiving coaching and pressure to perform from the employees who referred them.

Based on their belief that researchers needed to be more nuanced in studying employee referral effects, Yakubovich & Lup (2006) investigated prehire differences for three groups of call center applicants (i.e., individuals who became aware of job opening by means of the Internet, persons who were referred by employees who had been rated as high performers by the organization, and individuals who were referred by employees who had been rated as performing at a lower level). For several reasons (e.g., high performers should be more aware of what personal attributes are needed to perform a job well and thus be better able to refer individuals who are qualified for the job; high performers should value their reputations more and thus be less likely to refer poor prospects), Yakubovich & Lup hypothesized that individuals referred by high-performing employees should have higher scores on selection measures than individuals referred by lower-performing employees, who should have higher scores than individuals recruited via the Internet. These authors found support for their hypotheses.

In summary, there is substantial evidence that the use of current employees for generating job applicants is beneficial for employers. Specifically, studies have shown that, in comparison to nonreferrals, persons referred by current employees were superior in terms of application credentials, were more likely to be hired, and performed at a higher level.

College Campus Recruiting

The coverage of research on college campus recruiting in this section is abbreviated given a good deal of the research discussed in other sections of this review was conducted with college students and thus applies to college recruiting. However, a series of studies by Collins and his colleagues merits attention. These researchers were particularly interested in the influence of early recruitment actions by an employer on job applicants.

Collins & Stevens (2002) investigated the impact of three recruitment-related actions: sponsorship (e.g., an employer funds campus scholarships), advertising (e.g., students reported seeing job ads on campus), and word-of-mouth (WOM) endorsements (e.g., faculty had said an employer is a good place to work) on three prehire outcomes (i.e., student opinions

of an employer, intent to apply for a job with the employer, and submission of an application). They found that advertising and WOM endorsements were related to all three outcomes, and sponsorship was linked to application intention. Collins & Han (2004) examined the effects of general recruitment advertisements, sponsorship, detailed recruitment ads, and employee endorsements on several prehire outcomes. They reported that the use of these recruitment practices was positively related to applicant grade point average and the percentage of positions filled. All of the practices except endorsements were related to the number of applicants. All of the practices except the use of detailed advertisements were predictive of the rated quality of applicants. Collins (2007) studied whether the same four recruitment practices examined in his research with Han predicted student intentions to apply for jobs and whether they subsequently did. All four practices predicted both outcomes. In summary, the studies by Collins and his associates suggest that, by taking a number of recruitment-related actions prior to visiting a college, an organization may influence the number of job applicants, applicant quality, and their interest in an employer.

Several variables (e.g., products, lawsuits) can affect an organization's general reputation (Highhouse et al. 2009). Therefore, research on this topic is not addressed in detail in this review. However, given that an organization's reputation and visibility have been shown to be important in terms of college recruitment, a couple of research results merit mention. One finding of interest was reported by Collins & Stevens (2002). In addition to studying recruitment variables, they examined the effects of general publicity concerning an organization (e.g., being familiar with a news story about an employer's products). They not only found general publicity to be related to individuals' attitudes and application intentions, but such publicity also predisposed students to more carefully process recruitment information. Turban & Cable (2003) looked at organizational reputation effects in two studies (reputation ratings were based on external sources such as *Fortune* magazine). In study 1, which was conducted with undergraduate students who applied for interviews through a college placement office, employer reputation was found to be related to the number of applications submitted and the quality of the applicants (rated in terms of academic performance, work experience, and extracurricular activities). In study 2, which was conducted with MBA students, employer reputation was shown to predict the number of students who attended on-campus information sessions held by an employer. Such sessions are important because they allow for an in-person two-way exchange of information, which research by other researchers has shown to be linked to central route processing of information and greater message credibility.

The Use of an Employer's Web Site

Because the use of employer Web sites for recruiting is a relatively new phenomenon, there is no pre-2000 research to review. More recently, there has been considerable research on this topic in an effort to understand whether Web site characteristics have a meaningful influence on job applicants. Most of this research has involved studies that either analyzed existing employer Web sites or manipulated Web site characteristics of hypothetical employers in experimental simulations in which students played the role of a job applicant.

In terms of the first type of study, research conducted by Cober et al. (2004) is representative. These researchers analyzed the ease with which a Web site could be navigated, aesthetic features of its design, and the positivity of the information provided. Each of these factors was shown to be important to potential recruits. Braddy et al. (2006) had students visit Web sites of large corporations. In addition to replicating the results of prior studies concerning the importance of Web site design, they found that providing information about awards an employer had won had a positive impact on student impressions. This impact likely resulted from awards being perceived as reflecting an objective judgment of an

employer by a third party and thus their having greater credibility than employer-generated information. Research also has documented that employer Web sites that provided more information concerning a job opening were viewed more positively by students and resulted in their expressing a greater likelihood of applying for a job (Allen et al. 2007).

Because past research (e.g., Cable & Yu 2006) has shown that employer Web sites are sometimes viewed as lacking in terms of providing useful and credible information, researchers have investigated ways that Web site effectiveness might be increased. For example, Walker et al. (2009) used a simulation study to manipulate the presence/absence of employee testimonials and the richness of the media used to present a testimonial (i.e., a video with audio versus a picture with text). The inclusion of a testimonial was found to be positively related to the amount of time a student spent on a Web site, employer attractiveness, and information credibility. Presenting a testimonial via a richer medium was linked to greater employer attractiveness and information credibility. Braddy et al. (2009) had students view fictitious Web sites in order to determine whether four Web site attributes (i.e., employee testimonials, awards received, pictures of employees, and stated organizational policies) would influence perceptions of organizational culture. They concluded that all four attributes were useful in communicating information about culture. Thus, the findings of this study parallel those reported by Walker et al. (2009) with regard to the value of including employee testimonials in a Web site and the results reported by Braddy et al. (2006) in terms of including information concerning awards received.

A concern with using a Web site for recruiting is that an employer will be inundated with applications, many from individuals who are not qualified for an advertised position. As a way to deal with this issue, Dineen et al. (2002, 2007) investigated the utility of providing information to applicants concerning person-organization fit (i.e., a score was provided that reflected the similarity between what a person sought in an employer and what the employer was like) in simulation studies with students. Their results suggest that providing individualized feedback concerning fit has beneficial outcomes. For example, students receiving feedback that they were a good fit were more attracted to an organization, spent more time viewing a Web site, and were better able to recall Web site information. Although the interactive capability of using a Web site to provide information concerning person-organization fit is intriguing, it remains an open question whether real job applicants will provide accurate information about themselves (e.g., their values and skills) so that valid fit information can be provided by an organization.

To date, most studies have involved students who evaluated the Web sites of actual employers or took part in simulation studies in which Web site characteristics were manipulated. Therefore, a study by Selden & Orenstein (2011) that examined the use of Web sites by state government agencies for recruiting provides a novel perspective. The results of this study support the findings of many of the studies conducted with students. For example, Selden & Orenstein found that Web sites that were rated as being easier to navigate generated more applicants. They also reported that sites with higher-quality content (e.g., more detailed job information) received fewer applications, which they interpreted to mean that such content allowed individuals to screen themselves out if they did not perceive a good fit with the job and/or the employer.

In terms of research on Web sites, one final issue deserves attention. Although most researchers have focused on main effects, two recent studies have reported interesting interaction effects. Assuming that individuals with greater work experience and job search experience would have a higher level of ability to process recruitment information, based on Petty & Cacioppo's (1986) ELM, Walker et al. (2008) hypothesized that information concerning a job opening (e.g., training provided) would have a greater impact on the organizational

attractiveness ratings of more experienced individuals than on the ratings of those with less work and job-hunting experience. Alternatively, given their lower level of ability in terms of a job search, Walker et al. hypothesized that individuals with less experience would be more affected by peripheral Web site characteristics (e.g., the physical attractiveness of the individuals portrayed). Both hypotheses were supported. In a latter study, Walker et al. (2011) examined whether the effects of Web site characteristics on ratings of organizational attractiveness varied depending upon how familiar a site visitor was with the organization. Specifically, they investigated whether the technological sophistication of a Web site (e.g., including video testimonials from employees) had a greater effect if individuals lacked familiarity with an employer. They found it did. It appears that being unfamiliar with an employer made it more likely for individuals to draw inferences about unknown job-related characteristics from the Web site.

Job Boards and Other Nonemployer Web Sites

Given their inherent advantages (e.g., low cost compared to college recruitment), many employers use their Web sites to recruit. However, for an organization that does not have great visibility, sole reliance on its Web site could result in a small pool of job applicants. Therefore, many employers use job boards to publicize job openings. To date, only a few studies have examined their use.

Jattuso & Sinar (2003) investigated differences in the type of applicants generated by general job boards (e.g., Hotjobs.com) and industry/profession-specific job boards (e.g., SalesJobs.com). They found that applicants from more focused job boards were rated as having better educational credentials and a higher level of skill but less work experience. A concern with using job boards is that they often result in an overwhelming influx of applications. A study by Backhaus (2004) of job advertisements placed on Monster.com may explain why this can occur. He discovered that the great majority of ads presented very favorable information and failed to provide information that would help a job seeker to differentiate one organization from another. As a way to affect both the number of applications received and the quality of the applicants, Dineen & Noe (2009) used a simulation study involving students in which customized person-job fit information was provided by a fictional job board. Their findings suggest that providing fit information can result in a smaller applicant pool and one that is of higher quality.

In addition to using employer Web sites and job boards in a job search, individuals may use other Web sites. Two recent studies have addressed such sites. Cable & Yu (2006) randomly assigned MBA students who were on the job market to one of three conditions: spend five minutes talking to an assigned company's representative at a career fair, spend five minutes on an assigned company's Web site, or spend five minutes studying postings about an assigned company on Vault.com (an electronic bulletin board on which company employees can share their perceptions). Cable & Yu predicted that information provided by a company representative or a company Web site would be rated as less credible than information presented by a bulletin board, given that the company controls the information provided by the first two sources. Surprisingly, they found just the opposite. Cable & Yu speculated that a bulletin board being rated as a less credible source of information may be due to individuals discounting negative comments as coming from disgruntled employees and positive comments as being testimonials that may be company initiated (data that might support this speculation were not gathered). Utilizing similar logic to that of Cable & Yu (2006), Van Hoye & Lievens (2007) hypothesized that information provided on an employer's Web site would be rated as less credible than information provided via a company-independent Web site and therefore have less impact on organizational attractiveness. The results of their simulation study supported their hypothesis.

Future Research Directions

In terms of future research on recruitment methods, three issues merit particular attention. First, it is important that more field research be conducted with actual job applicants. In this regard, researchers might be able to cooperate with organizations in conducting studies that involved manipulating characteristics of their Web sites and examining whether recruitment outcomes are affected. Second, more attention needs to be given to mediating variables that explain why recruitment methods may matter. For example, although it has been assumed that current employees making referrals provide realistic job information to individuals they refer and do preliminary screening (i.e., only refer good candidates), data have yet to be gathered from those making referrals on whether this occurred. In this regard, researchers also might examine whether the advantages linked to the use of current employees is at least partially due to their ability to bring job openings to the attention of talented individuals who are not actively looking for a job. A third issue for future research is to broaden the range of the recruitment methods examined. In recent years, employee referrals, college recruiting, and the use of an employer's Web site have drawn the majority of the attention. Given the increasing use of social networking sites and job boards, these and other methods of generating applicants merit attention.

RECRUITMENT MESSAGE

The way a recruitment message is worded has long been thought to be important both in terms of attracting job applicants and in subsequently filling job openings (Wanous 1992). Therefore, it is not surprising that the effects of conveying different types of recruitment messages have been extensively studied by researchers. Much of this research has focused on the wording of job advertisements. As will become apparent from the review of the research conducted, several findings from research on the persuasion process are applicable to the recruitment message.

The Amount and the Specificity of the Information Conveyed

One aspect of a recruitment message that has received attention is the amount of information communicated. In this regard, it has been well documented that recruits often lack information about a position being considered, and that this lack of information makes them less likely to accept job offers (e.g., Barber & Roehling 1993). Researchers have offered two explanations for negative reactions to a lack of information. One explanation is that individuals may perceive the failure of an employer to provide sufficient information as a signal of its lack of interest in them. A second explanation is that a lack of information creates a state of uncertainty for individuals, which they would prefer to avoid in making a job choice decision. In two studies that manipulated the amount of information provided, Allen et al. (2007) replicated the finding that providing a greater amount of job-related information is linked to position attractiveness, and Allen et al. (2004) showed that a recruitment message that provided more information was viewed as more credible.

A number of researchers have examined the effects of the specificity of a recruitment message in studies with college students. For example, research (Mason & Belt 1986) has shown that a job advertisement that provided specific information about the type of personal attributes (e.g., work experience) sought in an applicant reduced the percentage of unqualified individuals who applied. Providing more specific information also has been found to create a higher level of interest in a job opening and result in more attention being paid to the recruitment message (Barber & Roehling 1993). Providing a more detailed recruitment message also can result in individuals perceiving better person-organization fit (Roberson et al. 2005). In this regard, the results of a study by Stevens & Szmerekovsky (2010) are of interest. These researchers provided students with job advertisements that differed in terms of the personality characteristics sought in applicants. They reported that students expressed greater interest in job openings that included personality-related wording that matched their personality as assessed by a personality test (e.g., outgoing students were more attracted to a job opening that required outgoing applicants).

The Realism of the Information Provided

An aspect of a recruitment message that has received substantial attention is the realism of the information communicated. Most of this research has involved the use of a realistic job preview (RJP), which involves "the presentation by an organization of both favorable and unfavorable job-related information to job candidates" (Phillips 1998, p. 673). Theory (Breaugh 2010) suggests that providing realistic information about a job during the recruitment process should result in new employees being more likely to have their job expectations met based on the assumption that an RJP allows individuals who do not perceive good person-job/organization fit to withdraw as job candidates. In turn, met expectations have been shown to be related to lower employee turnover and higher job satisfaction (Wanous et al. 1992). It also has been hypothesized that providing an RJP can result in greater role clarity (which should affect job performance), an enhanced ability to cope with job demands (e.g., being forewarned of unpleasant interactions with customers allows a person to rehearse how to respond), and perceptions that an organization is honest. From this abbreviated description of why RJPs should "work," it should be apparent that several moderating and mediating variables may influence the relationship between receiving an RJP and outcomes such as voluntary turnover. In terms of moderators, Breaugh (2010) noted that RJPs should have larger effects when provided prior to hiring, when recruits have inaccurate information about a job, and when applicants have other job opportunities. In terms of mediators, variables such as job performance and employee turnover should be influenced through an RJP's impact on met

Realistic job preview (RJP): communication by an employer during the recruitment process of accurate information concerning a job opening

expectations, role clarity, coping ability, and perceptions of employer honesty.

In the 1970s and 1980s, several RJP field experiments (e.g., Ilgen & Seely 1974, Suszko & Breaugh 1986) were conducted. Most of these studies reported positive RJP effects. The results of Phillips's (1998) meta-analysis support many of the hypothesized relationships between RJPs and prehire (e.g., accurate initial job expectations) and posthire (e.g., job performance) outcomes. Although many of the overall RJP effect sizes Phillips reported were modest, her moderator analyses showed stronger effects. For example, as one would expect from the theory underlying their use, Phillips found RJPs to have greater impact on such variables as voluntary turnover and job satisfaction if they were provided prior to hiring rather than posthiring. Recently, Earnest et al. (2011) conducted a meta-analysis that incorporated several RJP studies published since Phillips's meta-analysis into her data set. They found similar results to those reported by Phillips. For example, RJPs were associated with higher ratings of role clarity and organizational honesty and with less voluntary turnover.

Other Areas of Research on the Recruitment Message

In addition to examining the effects of the amount of information, its specificity, and its realism, research on the recruitment message has investigated a number of other factors. For example, Highhouse et al. (1998) examined whether describing job openings as being scarce (i.e., few in number) would affect ratings of job and organizational attributes. They reported a number of scarcity effects. For example, their position scarcity manipulation resulted in pay being estimated as being $1.70 higher than in the nonscarcity condition, suggesting that individuals may infer certain information from the wording of an ad (e.g., if an employer has several openings, it must not pay well). Thorsteinson & Highhouse (2003) examined the framing of a job advertisement. They found that, in comparison to an ad that was phrased in terms of

what was lost by not applying, an ad phrased in terms of what is gained by applying resulted in higher ratings of organizational attractiveness.

Buckley et al. (1998) experimented with an expectation-lowering procedure (ELP) that reminded individuals that they "typically develop unrealistic expectations, which may result in mismatches of individual expectations and what an organization may realistically provide" (p. 453). They randomly assigned newly hired workers during a company orientation program to either an ELP group or a group that received a traditional orientation message. The ELP was effective in lowering job expectations and employee turnover. In a follow-up study with applicants for telemarketing jobs, Buckley et al. (2002) reported similar results.

Van Hoye & Lievens (2005, 2007, 2009) conducted a series of studies that examined the impact of WOM information (i.e., information about an employer that is independent of its recruitment efforts). Their first two studies involved simulations with students acting as recruits. The results of these studies suggest that compared to employer-provided information (e.g., Web-based testimonials), WOM information had a stronger effect on perceptions of organizational attractiveness. These WOM effects seem to be largely due to nonemployer sources having greater credibility, especially if the WOM source was a friend. Van Hoye & Lievens (2009) conducted a field study that involved potential applicants targeted by the Belgian Defense (i.e., persons who had visited its Web site). Among their findings were that the submission of a job application was predicted by organizational attractiveness and the amount of time spent receiving positive WOM information. The amount of time spent receiving negative WOM information was unrelated to the submission of an application. This finding may be explained by two factors. First, individuals reported they spent less time receiving negative WOM information compared to positive WOM information. Second, the positive WOM information was frequently received from friends or relatives (rather than acquaintances) and from individuals who were perceived as having greater expertise (e.g., persons who worked for Belgian Defense). The final WOM study reviewed was carried out by Jaidi et al. (2011). For their sample, receiving positive WOM information from alumni was positively related to the job pursuit of graduating master's students, and negative WOM information from alumni was inversely related to job pursuit behavior.

Future Research Directions

In terms of future research on the recruitment message, an issue that merits attention is how to effectively convey to job applicants information concerning how they are likely to react to various attributes of a position. In this regard, RJPs are deficient because they provide descriptive information. Although sharing factual information (e.g., a job requires working rotating shifts) is beneficial, it may not convey a complete picture of a job because many applicants "do not have the ability to interpret the meaning of purely descriptive information" (Wanous 1992, p. 129). To address this issue, Wanous recommended that, in addition to descriptive information, evaluative information should be communicated in order to provide a more visceral understanding of what a new position involves. Such evaluative information could address how new employees typically react to job attributes. Conveying evaluative information is likely to result in job applicants viewing an employer as being honest with them and should result in better person-job/organization fit.

RECRUITERS

The effects of using different types of recruiters have drawn considerable attention from researchers (e.g., Carless & Wintle 2007, Connerley 1997). Many of the early studies looked at recruiter demographic characteristics and tested whether recruiters who were similar in race or gender to an applicant would be viewed more favorably. For the most part, such recruiter/applicant similarity effects have not been found (for a review of this research, see

Breaugh 2008). More recently, researchers have focused on the influence of recruiter behavior. A meta-analysis by Chapman et al. (2005) provides a good summary of the results of these studies, most of which were conducted with college students. They reported that individuals who rated recruiters as being personable, competent, informative, and trustworthy also rated a job opening as being more attractive and expressed a higher probability of accepting a job offer.

Taken as a whole, research suggests the type of recruiter used may matter (a) because recruiters vary in the amount of job-related information they possess and thus can share (e.g., in comparison to a corporate recruiter, an employee in a department with a position to fill likely will be more informative concerning job duties), (b) because they differ in terms of their credibility (e.g., a corporate recruiter may be viewed as more interested in selling a position than in conveying a realistic job preview), and (c) because of inferences drawn by a recruit (in the next section, research is reviewed that shows that interacting with a higher-level employee may signal that the position is of greater significance to the organization).

The preceding three factors suggest that future research on recruiters needs to be more nuanced. For example, with regard to Chapman et al.'s (2005) finding that a recruiter's being viewed as competent has beneficial effects, an open question is—what factors result in being viewed as more competent? As another example of the need for more fine-grained research, it has been commonly assumed that current employees will screen individuals before referring them and that they will also provide realistic job information. However, if an employee receives a sizable bonus for making a referral, screening and providing a realistic job preview may not occur.

RECRUITMENT MEDIA

Media richness theory (Daft & Lengyl 1984) suggests that in conveying information, especially complex information, not all communication media are equally effective. Rather, face-to-face communication is seen as superior, followed by video, audio, and text. This rank-ordering is based on the following properties of in-person communication: A two-way interaction attracts greater attention from an information recipient, and it allows for questions to be answered, facial cues and tone of voice can be considered, information can be personalized, etc. The basic tenets of media richness theory clearly apply to recruitment research. For example, in considering recruitment methods, a current employee contacting a potential referral may involve an in-person two-way communication, whereas the use of a job advertisement would typically involve either audio (e.g., a radio ad) or text (e.g., a job board listing). However, it is difficult to compare recruitment methods in terms of media richness theory because the recruitment message is not standardized. Allen and his associates (e.g., Allen et al. 2004, Otondo et al. 2008) are among the few researchers who have investigated the effects of utilizing different media to convey the same recruitment message. Although results are not entirely consistent, initial findings suggest potential benefits of utilizing face-to-face communication as a recruitment media. In future studies, the psychological factors (e.g., physical presence attracting greater attention) comprising media richness theory need to be examined in order to better understand both recruitment method and recruiter effects.

THE JOB APPLICANT SITE VISIT

A job applicant's visit to an organization's headquarters has received relatively little attention from researchers. This is surprising when one considers that, in comparison to other recruitment activities (e.g., an interaction with a recruiter at a job fair), a site visit generally provides a "longer and more intense applicant-company interaction" (Taylor & Bergmann 1987, p. 273) and therefore should have a significant influence on a recruit. For example, during a site visit, a job candidate should get a firsthand view of an employer's work force (e.g.,

diversity) and location (e.g., safety of the neighborhood). Likely of greater importance, during a site visit an applicant generally has the opportunity to interact for the first time (or more intensively) with prospective coworkers and his or her potential supervisor and view the immediate work environment (e.g., spaciousness of cubicles). In summary, a site visit affords an employer the opportunity to provide more information about a job, more specific information, more realistic information, and more credible information (e.g., firsthand knowledge typically has more credibility than being informed by others). Acquiring such information has the potential to considerably modify an applicant's initial view of a job with an organization. In addition, being invited for a site visit often is viewed by an applicant as a signal that he or she has a good likelihood of receiving a job offer.

In one of the first studies to focus on the applicant site visit, Rynes et al. (1991) found it to have a sizable impact. For example, approximately 30% of their interviewees (i.e., college students seeking jobs) said they rejected job offers from organizations to which they had originally been attracted after their site visits (this suggests that initial attitudes can be changed by the firsthand experience of a company visit). Three factors were cited as being important by these interviewees: whether the employer was flexible in scheduling a visit, whether the applicant was treated in a professional manner, and whether the applicant met high-status individuals. In another early study, Turban et al. (1995) reported that applicants' ratings of site host likability were associated with their decision to accept a job offer. This finding may be due to the fact that the person hosting the visit would be a coworker of the recruit if the person were to be hired. In a more recent study, Boswell et al. (2003) found that applicants were positively influenced by having the opportunity to talk with current employees who held the same job for which they applied, to meet employees who had similar backgrounds to theirs, and to interact with high-level managers. They also reported that site arrangements (e.g., a well-organized schedule, an impressive hotel room) made a favorable impression on applicants. A simulation study conducted with college students by Saks & Uggerslev (2010) found effects similar to those of Boswell et al. (2003) with regard to being able to interact with prospective coworkers as well as higher-level managers.

In terms of future research, three issues are highlighted. First, more attention needs to be given to exactly what occurred during a visit and the effect it had. Second, more attention needs to be given to the effect of an employer providing information concerning the local community. In terms of a community, the following characteristics could be important to an applicant: (*a*) ethnicity (e.g., will an applicant's children be able to be raised in a diverse environment?), (*b*) religion (e.g., will an applicant be able to locate an acceptable religious community?), (*c*) employment opportunities (e.g., will a spouse or a significant other be able to find suitable employment?), and (*d*) community values (e.g., are dominant political beliefs compatible with those of the applicant?). The inferences that an applicant may draw about unknown job and/or organizational attributes based on a site visit is another topic in need of more research. For example, a poorly organized visit might be seen as an indicator of how other aspects of the business are run or how interested the employer is in the recruit.

THE JOB OFFER

Three types of research have been conducted concerning the job offer. Some researchers have focused on attributes of a position (e.g., location) that are predictive of job offer acceptance. Because this type of research was discussed previously in the context of job applicant decision making, it is not addressed here. The relationship between the timeliness of a job offer and its being accepted also has drawn research attention. This research is addressed in the next section. In terms of research on the effects of specific aspects of the job offer, very little research has been conducted. Two studies that are representative of this research are briefly reviewed.

Utilizing a sample of college students drawn from two universities, Barber et al. (1999) found that job offers that allowed applicants a degree of flexibility with regard to the start date for beginning employment were more likely to be accepted than offers with a fixed start date. Boswell et al. (2003) reported that, for a sample of college students, an employer's including a deadline for job offer acceptance did not result in negative reactions (these authors reported that several individuals in their sample asked for and received extensions to their deadline).

Given that the primary purpose of recruiting is to fill job openings, it is remarkable that so little research has focused on job offer acceptance as an outcome variable. In terms of future research, studies of all types are needed. However, research that addresses how the nature of a job offer may affect inferences drawn by applicants about a job with an organization seems particularly important. For example, what inferences might job applicants draw if required to sign an employment-at-will contract? Do recruits view having to sign a noncompete agreement or receiving a lowball salary offer as a signal of undesirable organizational attributes?

THE TIMING OF RECRUITMENT ACTIVITIES

Several studies have documented the importance of when recruitment activities occur. A key issue with regard to scheduling is when to begin recruiting. For jobs with a distinct hiring season, beginning to recruit late in the season can result in a job applicant pool that is lacking, as was demonstrated by Turban & Cable (2003), who found that employers that began interviewing college students later in the year received fewer job applications. Of potentially greater importance, the applications received were of lower quality. One explanation for why it can be advantageous for an employer to begin the recruitment process in a timely fashion is that individuals want to reduce the uncertainty involved in finding a job (Becker et al. 2010). If this explanation is accurate, one would expect that when an employer begins recruiting may be less important if it is trying to recruit persons who are already employed.

A number of studies have investigated the importance of an employer acting in a timely manner after applications have been submitted. For example, Rynes et al. (1991) documented that delays in replying to job applicants resulted in their viewing potential employers as being less attractive and sometimes in applicants eliminating them from consideration as a place of employment. Interestingly, these effects were stronger for higher-quality job applicants. Boswell et al. (2003) also found that recruits were positively disposed toward employers who responded to their inquiries promptly. More recent studies also have shown the importance of prompt recruitment actions. For example, Schreurs et al. (2009) measured the time lag between a person's date of application and the date the person was scheduled to take an employment test. They found that the longer the delay, the less likely an applicant was to show up for testing. Becker et al. (2010) investigated the influence of a time delay on the likelihood of a job offer being accepted. For samples of new college graduates and more experienced individuals, the longer the time lag between a job candidate's final interview and a job offer being extended, the less likely an offer was to be accepted (statistical analyses showed that differences in applicant quality did not explain this time lag). Carless & Hetherington (2011) focused on recruitment timeliness both in terms of an objective and a subjective indicator. Using a sample of applicants for jobs at a university, they measured the actual time that elapsed between the submission of a job application and an invitation for an interview, and they measured an applicant's perception of the timeliness of this invitation. In terms of perceptions of organizational attractiveness, the number of days that had elapsed was not a valid predictor. However, an applicant's perception of timeliness was a good predictor of attractiveness. Carless & Hetherington's findings suggest that objective timeliness should not be the sole focus of attention in future studies.

In summary, there is persuasive evidence that delays at various stages of the recruitment process can have an adverse effect on several recruitment outcomes, including the number of applicants and the quality of applicants. In terms of future research, investigations of the explanations that have been offered by researchers for why delays matter are needed. For example, although it has been hypothesized that recruits make attributions about what a delay signals (e.g., no job offer is likely to be forthcoming, a recruit was not the organization's first choice for filling a job opening), data to verify the accuracy of such attributions are lacking.

RECRUITING MEMBERS OF UNDERREPRESENTED GROUPS

In the past decade, considerable research has addressed the recruitment of members of underrepresented groups (e.g., racial minorities, women). Much of this research has focused on the effects of communicating information about the diversity of an employer's workforce or its affirmative action/diversity policy. In addition to addressing research on these two topics, in this section two recent studies that have significance for the recruitment of minorities and women are reviewed. Before addressing these topics, two common findings from pre-2000 research merit mention. First, as previously discussed, researchers (e.g., Chapman et al. 2005) have found a recruiter's race or gender to have little impact on job applicants. Second, studies conducted in the 1980s and 1990s often reported that minorities were less likely to be made aware of job openings if current employees were used as a recruitment method (for a review of this research, see Peterson et al. 2000).

With regard to recruitment communications that convey information about the diversity of an employer's workforce, several studies have been conducted, most with college students. For example, Avery et al. (2004) found that including pictures of minorities in a recruitment brochure increased the ratings of organizational attractiveness made by blacks and had no impact on the ratings of whites.

Avery (2003) showed that including pictures in a recruitment brochure had a greater impact on minorities if some of the minorities portrayed were in supervisory positions (whites were unaffected by the different portrayals of blacks). In their study 1 (study 2 is discussed shortly), Walker et al. (2012) examined whether diversity cues affected the way individuals processed information. They found that in the diversity cue condition (i.e., two of the four individuals pictured were black), more time was spent viewing a Web site and there was better recall of the information viewed than in the no-diversity cue condition (none of the four employees pictured were black). These effects were significant for black and white students but stronger for blacks.

In recent years, several researchers (e.g., McKay & Avery 2006) have investigated the effects of communicating variations in the strength of an organization's diversity/affirmative action policy. For example, for members of the Society of Black Engineers, Slaughter et al. (2005) found that, compared to an affirmative action program geared toward bringing job openings to the attention of minorities, a program involving preferential treatment was viewed as less fair and more likely to result in the stigmatization of new hires. Williamson et al. (2008) documented the complexity that can be involved in designing a diversity-oriented message. They reported that individuals' responses to identity-conscious diversity policies were influenced by their race and the explanation provided for the diversity policy (e.g., a moral obligation versus to improve business results). Specifically, blacks viewed the ideological explanation as signaling they would be less likely to face discrimination, whereas whites and Asians viewed the business explanation as less threatening to their careers.

Walker et al.'s (2012) study 2 addressed both the communication of information about the diversity of an organization's workforce and its diversity policy. In this study, students were randomly assigned to visit the Web site of one of two actual organizations. One Web site included pictures of a diverse workforce and information on diversity goals and initiatives; the other did not. In addition to being selected because of their difference on diversity cue information, these organizations were chosen because they were equivalent on other important dimensions (e.g., organizational attractiveness). Approximately two weeks after viewing the assigned Web site, student recall of Web site information was assessed. Walker et al. (2012) reported that recall was better for the Web site that provided diversity-related information, and this effect was stronger for blacks.

In terms of the recruitment of minorities and women, two recent studies merit attention. Newman & Lyon (2009) investigated whether the way an organization recruits can reduce the conflict that employers frequently face in trying to meet the dual goals of hiring individuals who will be most productive and hiring a diverse group of individuals. The first study they conducted, a simulation with college students, examined the effects of targeting groups for recruitment based on demographic characteristics. Newman & Lyon found that such targeting can increase adverse impact (i.e., members of minority groups being hired at a lower rate than nonminorities) because it can result in job applications from minorities who are not qualified for advertised positions. In a second study, Newman & Lyon (2009) examined the influence of how a job advertisement was worded. Specifically, they assessed whether emphasizing the importance of an applicant being smart or conscientious resulted in self-selection and/or adverse impact. These authors found that students who were higher on the attribute sought were more likely to apply for a position seeking that attribute and that no adverse impact resulted. They also found that minority students had a higher application rate across jobs, which may reflect the fact that they perceived they would have a harder time finding a job than would nonminority students.

The results of a series of studies by Gaucher et al. (2011) that focused on the wording of job advertisements raise a number of important issues for recruitment. In their study 1, Gaucher et al. analyzed actual job advertisements using an established list of masculine and feminine words. Results showed that masculine words were more common in ads for male-dominated jobs (e.g., engineer), but feminine words were equally likely to appear in ads for male-dominated and female-dominated (e.g., nurse) jobs. Similar results were found for Gaucher et al.'s study 2, which involved job postings at a university. In their study 3, these authors had students read several job ads that were constructed to be masculinely or femininely worded. For male-dominated, female-dominated, and gender-neutral jobs, both male and female students perceived there were fewer women within the occupations advertised with more masculine wording. In their study 4, Gaucher and her colleagues examined whether masculine wording resulted in women having less interest in a job because such wording suggested they do not belong. Masculine wording was found to result in both less interest and perceptions of not belonging in the job. Gaucher et al.'s study 5 replicated these results and extended them by showing that masculine wording in ads did not affect women's perceptions of their having the skill needed to perform the job. Taken as a whole, Gaucher et al.'s results suggest that gendered wording is common in job ads and that this wording can result in women believing they do not belong in an occupation, but not because of a lack of skill.

From the research reviewed, it is apparent that the wording of a recruitment message can influence the interest of minorities and nonminorities in a job opening. It also is apparent that effectively disseminating a diversity-oriented message is a delicate issue. In concluding this review of research on the recruitment of members of underrepresented groups, two additional findings should be noted. First, McKay & Avery (2005) have discussed how many minorities report that the information they received during the recruitment process concerning diversity initiatives did not correspond to the reality they experienced once hired. Second, in terms of the impact of a diversity-oriented recruitment message, an employer's reputation vis-à-vis diversity is likely to be more important (Avery & McKay 2006).

In terms of future research, two areas seem particularly important. The first area concerns ways for an organization to persuade individuals of its commitment to diversity. Generalizing from the results reported concerning awards received by an employer, it is likely that publicizing awards received from reputable sources for diversity-related outcomes should be beneficial, but this has yet to be demonstrated. Research is also needed on subtle ways by which an employer may discourage members of underrepresented groups from applying for jobs. In this regard, Gaucher et al.'s (2011) research on the gendering of job advertisements provides a starting point.

CONCLUDING REMARKS

This article provides a selective review of research that has been conducted on employee recruitment, especially studies that have been published since 2000. This research demonstrates the importance of the recruitment actions taken by employers. In particular, recruitment methods (e.g., using current employees), the recruitment message (e.g., its specificity), recruiters (e.g., their being informative), the organizational site visit (e.g., meeting with high-level employees), and the timing of recruitment activities (e.g., timely job offers) have been shown to be linked to important prehire (e.g., quality of job applicants) and posthire (e.g., employee retention) outcomes. In discussing recruitment studies, this article noted a number of methodological limitations (e.g., failure to test for mediator variables) in hopes of stimulating and improving future research. In addition, this review highlighted several topics (e.g., attracting the attention of potential job applicants) that have received insufficient attention from researchers. A theme that ran throughout this review was the applicability of basic psychological research (e.g., findings concerning selective exposure) to recruitment topics. Drawing more heavily on such research is likely to improve future empirical investigations of recruitment topics and future theory development.

SUMMARY POINTS

1. An employer's recruitment actions can influence the interest of prospective job applicants in a job opening and the ability of the individuals it hires, their diversity, their job performance, and their retention.

2. Deciding whom to recruit is the most important question an organization needs to address, given that the target population should influence the recruitment method an employer uses to reach these individuals, the recruitment message it conveys, and when it begins recruiting.

3. Insufficient research attention has been given to the topics of targeted recruitment and attracting the attention of prospective job applicants.

4. Research supports the use of current employees as being an effective recruitment method.

5. The wording of a recruitment message (e.g., its specificity, realism) has been linked to several prehire and posthire recruitment outcomes.

6. In investigating recruitment issues, researchers have relied heavily on the use of college students.

7. The findings of basic psychological research (e.g., selective exposure, confirmation bias) apply to many recruitment topics and should be considered in designing future studies.

FUTURE ISSUES

1. In making decisions about job openings, applicants often lack information about important job and organizational attributes. Several researchers have suggested that applicants use information acquired during the recruitment process as an indicator of unknown attributes. What information received about a job or organization is likely to be used as a signal of unknown aspects of a job opening? Under what conditions are such inferences likely to be made?

2. At present, no general model of the recruitment process (one that addresses interactions among recruitment variables and their relationships with job and organizational attributes and recruitment outcomes) exists. Can such a model be developed?

3. Most researchers seem willing to assume that the results of studies using college students will generalize to individuals with more job search and work experience. Do they?

4. Theory suggests that targeting certain types of individuals for recruitment (e.g., those with family members working for the organization, those who have previously worked in jobs similar to the job opening) should be beneficial for an employer. Do empirical studies support such hypothesized relationships?

5. It has been hypothesized that employee referrals tend to be more qualified applicants and make better employees because they have received realistic job information from the employee who referred them and because they have been prescreened by the current employee of the organization. However, data have not been gathered from current employees concerning whether such events occurred. Do future studies support the realism and prescreening hypotheses?

6. Very little attention has been given to the recruitment of so-called passive job seekers (i.e., individuals who would consider taking a new job but are not actively looking for one). What issues should be considered in recruiting such individuals?

DISCLOSURE STATEMENT

The author is not aware of any affiliations, funding, or financial holdings that might be perceived as affecting the objectivity of this review.

LITERATURE CITED

Albarracin D, Vargas P. 2010. Attitudes and persuasion. In *Handbook of Social Psychology*, ed. ST Fiske, DT Gilbert, G. Lindzey, pp. 394–427. Hoboken, NJ: Wiley

Allen DG, Mahto RV, Otondo RF. 2007. Web-based recruitment: effects of information, organizational brand, and attitudes toward a web site on applicant attraction. *J. Appl. Psychol.* 92:1696–708

Allen DG, Van Scotter JR, Otondo RF. 2004. Recruitment communication media: impact on prehire outcomes. *Pers. Psychol.* 57:143–71

Avery DR. 2003. Reactions to diversity in recruitment advertising—are differences black and white? *J. Appl. Psychol.* 88:672–79

Avery DR, Hernandez M, Hebl MR. 2004. Who's watching the race? Racial salience in recruitment advertising. *J. Appl. Soc. Psychol.* 34:146–61

Avery DR, McKay PF. 2006. Target practice: an organizational impression management approach to attracting minority and female job applicants. *Pers. Psychol.* 59:157–87

Backhaus KB. 2004. An exploration of corporate recruitment descriptions on Monster.com. *J. Bus. Commun.* 41:115–36

Barber AE, Roehling MV. 1993. Job postings and the decision to interview: a verbal protocol analysis. *J. Appl. Psychol.* 78:845–56

Barber AE, Wesson MJ, Roberson QM, Taylor MS. 1999. A tale of two job markets: organizational size and its effects on hiring practices and job search behavior. *Pers. Psychol.* 52:841–68

Becker WJ, Connolly T, Slaughter J E. 2010. The effect of job offer timing on offer acceptance, performance, and turnover. *Pers. Psychol.* 63:223–41

Billsberry J. 2007. *Experiencing Recruitment and Selection*. Hoboken, NJ: Wiley

Bohner G, Dickel N. 2011. Attitudes and attitude change. *Annu. Rev. Psychol.* 62:391–417

Boswell WR, Roehling MV, LePine MA, Moynihan LM. 2003. Individual job-choice decisions and the impact of job attributes and recruitment practices: a longitudinal field study. *Hum. Resour. Manage.* 42:23–37

Braddy PW, Meade AW, Kroustalis CM. 2006. Organizational recruitment website effects on viewers' perceptions of organizational culture. *J. Bus. Psychol.* 20:525–43

Braddy PW, Meade AW, Michael JJ, Fleenor JW. 2009. Internet recruiting: effects of website content features on viewers' perceptions of organizational culture. *Int. J. Select. Assess.* 17:19–34

Brannon LA, Tagler MJ, Eagly AH. 2007. The moderating role of attitude strength in selective exposure to information. *J. Exp. Soc. Psychol.* 43:611–17

Breaugh JA. 2008. Employee recruitment: current knowledge and important areas for future research. *Hum. Resour. Manage. Rev.* 18:103–18

Breaugh JA. 2009. Recruiting and attracting talent: a guide to understanding and managing the recruitment process. *SHRM Foundation's Effective Practice Guidelines Series*. Alexandria, VA: Soc. Hum. Resour. Manage.

Breaugh JA. 2010. Realistic job previews. In *Handbook of Improving Performance in the Workplace*, ed. R Watkins, D Leigh, pp. 203–18. San Francisco: Pfeiffer

Breaugh JA, Greising LA, Taggart JW, Chen H. 2003. The relationship of recruiting sources and pre-hire outcomes: examination of yield ratios and applicant quality. *J. Appl. Soc. Psychol.* 33:2267–87

Buckley MR, Fedor DB, Veres JG, Wiese DS, Carraher SM. 1998. Investigating newcomer expectations and job-related outcomes. *J. Appl. Psychol.* 83:452–61

Buckley MR, Mobbs TA, Mendoza JL, Novicevic MM, Carraher SM, Beu DS. 2002. Implementing realistic job previews and expectation-lowering procedures: a field experiment. *J. Vocat. Behav.* 61:263–78

Cable DM, Turban DB. 2003. The value of organizational reputation in the recruitment context: a brand-equity perspective. *J. Appl. Soc. Psychol.* 33:2244–66

Cable DM, Yu YT. 2006. Managing job seekers' organizational image beliefs: the role of media richness and media credibility. *J. Appl. Psychol.* 91:828–40

Carless SA, Hetherington K. 2011. Understanding the applicant recruitment experience: Does timeliness matter? *Int. J. Select. Assess.* 19:105–8

Carless SA, Wintle J. 2007. Applicant attraction: the role of recruiter function, work-life balance policies, and career salience. *Int. J. Select. Assess.* 15:394–404

Carlson KD, Connerley ML, Mecham RL. 2002. Recruitment evaluation: the case for assessing the quality of applicants attracted. *Pers. Psychol.* 55:461–90

Castilla EJ. 2005. Social networks and employee performance in a call center. *Am. J. Sociol.* 10:1243–83

Chaiken S. 1987. The heuristic model of persuasion. In *Social Influence: The Ontario Symposium*, ed. MP Zanna, JM Olson, CP Herman, Vol. 5, pp. 3–39. Hillsdale, NJ: Erlbaum

Chaiken S, Stangor C. 1987. Attitudes and attitude change. *Annu. Rev. Psychol.* 38:575–630

Chapman DS, Uggerslev KL, Carroll SA, Piasentin KA, Jones DA. 2005. Applicant attraction to organizations and job choice: a meta-analytic review of the correlates of recruiting outcomes. *J. Appl. Psychol.* 90:928–44

Chapman DS, Webster J. 2006. Toward an integrated model of applicant reactions and job choice. *Int. J. Hum. Resour. Manage.* 17:1032–57

Cialdini RB. 2008. *Influence: Science and Practice.* Boston: Allyn & Bacon

Cober RT, Brown DJ, Levy PE. 2004. Form, content, and function: an evaluative methodology for corporate employment web sites. *Hum. Resour. Manage.* 43:201–18

Collins CJ. 2007. The interactive effects of recruitment practices and product awareness on job seekers' employer knowledge and applicant behaviors. *J. Appl. Psychol.* 92:180–90

Collins CJ, Han J. 2004. Exploring applicant pool quantity and quality: the effects of early recruitment practices, corporate advertising, and firm reputation. *Pers. Psychol.* 57:685–717

Collins CJ, Stevens CK. 2002. The relationship between early recruitment-related activities and the application decisions of new labor-market entrants: a brand equity approach to recruitment. *J. Appl. Psychol.* 87:1121–33

Connerley ML. 1997. The influence of training on perceptions of recruiters' interpersonal skills and effectiveness. *J. Occup. Organ. Psychol.* 70:259–72

Daft RL, Lengel RH. 1984. Information richness: a new approach to managerial behavior and organizational design. *Res. Organ. Behav.* 6:191–233

Devendorf SA, Highhouse S. 2008. Applicant-employee similarity and attraction to an employer. *J. Occup. Organ. Psychol.* 81:607–17

Dijksterhuis A, Aarts H. 2010. Goals, attention, and (un)consciousness. *Annu. Rev. Psychol.* 61:467–90

Dineen BR, Ash SR, Noe RA. 2002. A web of applicant attraction: person-organization fit in the context of web-based recruitment. *J. Appl. Psychol.* 87:723–34

Dineen BR, Ling J, Ash SR, DelVecchio D. 2007. Aesthetic properties and message customization: navigating the dark side of web recruitment. *J. Appl. Psychol.* 9:356–72

Dineen BR, Noe RA. 2009. Effects of customization on application decisions and applicant pool characteristics in a web-based recruitment context. *J. Appl. Psychol.* 94:224–34

Dineen BR, Soltis SM. 2011. Recruitment: a review of research and emerging directions. In *APA Handbook of Industrial and Organizational Psychology*, ed. S Zedeck, Vol. 2, pp. 43–66. Washington, DC: Am. Psychol. Assoc.

Dunning D. 2007. Prediction: the inside view. In *Social Psychology: A Handbook*, ed. AW Kruglanski, ET Higgins, pp. 69–90. New York: Guildford

Earnest DR, Allen DG, Landis RS. 2011. Mechanisms linking realistic job previews with turnover. *Pers. Psychol.* 64:865–97

Ehrhart KH, Ziegert JC. 2005. Why are individuals attracted to organizations? *J. Manage.* 31:901–19

Fernandez RM, Weinberg N. 1997. Sifting and sorting: personal contacts and hiring in a retail bank. *Am. Sociol. Rev.* 62:883–903

Gaucher D, Friesen J, Kay AC. 2011. Evidence that gendered wording in job advertisements exists and sustains gender inequality. *J. Personal. Soc. Psychol.* 101:109–28

Gigerenzer G, Gaissmaier W. 2011. Heuristic decision making. *Annu. Rev. Psychol.* 62:451–82

Harkins SG, Petty RE. 1981. The multiple source effect in persuasion. *Personal. Soc. Psychol. Bull.* 7:627–35

Highhouse S, Beadle D, Gallo A, Miller L. 1998. Get 'em while they last: effects of scarcity information in job advertisements. *J. Appl. Soc. Psychol.* 28:779–95

Highhouse S, Brooks ME, Greguras G. 2009. An organizational impression management perspective on the formation of corporate reputations. *J. Manage.* 35:1481–93

Highhouse S, Hoffman JR. 2001. Organizational attraction and job choice. In *International Review of Industrial and Organizational Psychology*, ed. CL Cooper, IT Robertson, pp. 37–64. New York: Wiley

Highhouse S, Thornbury E, Little IS. 2007. Social-identity functions of attraction to organizations. *Organ. Behav. Hum. Decis. Process.* 103:134–46

Hovland CI, Janis IL, Kelley HH. 1953. *Communication and Persuasion: Psychological Studies of Opinion Change.* New Haven, CT: Yale Univ. Press

Ilgen DR, Seely W. 1974. Realistic expectations as an aid in reducing involuntary resignations. *J. Appl. Psychol.* 59:452–55

Jaidi Y, Van Hooft EA, Arends LR. 2011. Recruiting highly educated graduates: a study on the relationships between recruitment information sources, the theory of planned behavior, and actual job pursuit. *Hum. Perform.* 24:135–57

Jattuso ML, Sinar EF. 2003. Source effects in internet-based screening procedures. *Int. J. Select. Assess.* 11:137–40

Jones DA, Shultz JW, Chapman DS. 2006. Recruiting through job advertisements: the effects of cognitive elaborations on decision making. *Int. J. Select. Assess.* 14:167–79

Kirnan JP, Farley JA, Geisinger KF. 1989. The relationship between recruiting source, applicant quality, and hire performance: an analysis by sex, ethnicity, and age. *Pers. Psychol.* 42:293–308

Kruglanski AW, Sleeth-Keppler D. 2007. The principles of social judgment. In *Social Psychology: Handbook of Basic Principles*, ed. AW Kruglanski, ET Higgins, pp. 116–37. New York: Guildford

Kruglanski AW, Thompson EP. 1999. Persuasion by a single route: a view from the unimodel. *Psychol. Inq.* 10:83–109

Louis MR. 1980. Surprise and sensemaking: what newcomers experience in entering unfamiliar organizational environments. *Admin. Sci. Q.* 25:226–51

Maio GR, Haddock G. 2007. Attitude change. In *Social Psychology: Handbook of Basic Principles*, ed. AW Kruglanski, ET Higgins, pp. 565–86. New York: Guilford

Mason NA, Belt JA. 1986. The effectiveness of specificity in recruitment advertising. *J. Manage.* 12:425–32

McGuire WJ. 1968. Personality and attitude change: an information-processing theory. In *Psychological Foundations of Attitudes*, ed. AG Greenwald, TC Brock, TA Ostrom, pp. 171–96, San Diego, CA: Academic

McKay PF, Avery DR. 2005. Warning! Diversity recruitment could backfire. *J. Manage. Inq.* 14:330–36

McKay PF, Avery DR. 2006. What has race got to do with it? Unraveling the role of racioethnicity in job seekers' reactions to site visits. *Pers. Psychol.* 59:395–429

Newman DA, Lyon JS. 2009. Recruitment efforts to reduce adverse impact: targeted recruiting for personality, cognitive ability, and diversity. *J. Appl. Psychol.* 94:298–317

O'Keefe DJ. 1999. How to handle opposing arguments in persuasive messages: a meta-analytic review of the effects of one-sided and two-sided messages. *Commun. Yearb.* 22:209–49

O'Keefe DJ. 2002. *Persuasion: Theory and Research.* Thousand Oaks, CA: Sage

Otondo RF, Van Scotter JR, Allen DG, Palvia P. 2008. The complexity of richness: media, message, and communication outcomes. *Inform. Manage.* 45:21–30

Osborn DP. 1990. A reexamination of the organizational choice process. *J. Vocat. Behav.* 36:45–60

Peterson T, Saporta I, Seidel JL. 2000. Offering a job: meritocracy and social networks. *Am. J. Sociol.* 106:763–816

Petty RE, Cacioppo JT 1986. The elaboration likelihood model of persuasion. *Adv. Exp. Soc. Psychol.* 19:123–205

Phillips JM. 1998. Effects of realistic job previews on multiple organizational outcomes: a meta-analysis. *Acad. Manage. J.* 41:673–90

Rafaeli A. 2006. Sense-making of employment: on whether and why people read employment advertising. *J. Organ. Behav.* 27:747–70

Roberson QM, Collins CJ, Oreg S. 2005. The effects of recruitment message specificity on applicant attraction to organizations. *J. Bus. Psychol.* 19:319–39

Ryan AM, Delaney T. 2010. Attracting job candidates to organizations. In *Handbook of Employee Selection*, ed. JL Farr, NT Tippins, pp. 127–46. New York: Routledge

Ryan AM, Horvath M, Kriska D. 2005. The role of recruiting informativeness and organizational perceptions in decisions to apply. *Int. J. Select. Assess.* 4:235–49

Rynes SL, Bretz RD, Gerhart B. 1991. The importance of recruitment in job choice: a different way of looking. *Pers. Psychol.* 44:487–521

Saks AM. 2005. The impracticality of recruitment research. In *Handbook of Personnel Selection*, ed. A Evers, N Anderson, O Voskuijl, pp. 47–72. Malden, MA: Blackwell

Saks AM, Uggerslev KL. 2010. Sequential and combined effects of recruitment information on applicant reactions. *J. Bus. Psychol.* 25:381–96

Schreurs B, Derous E, Van Hooft EA, Proost K, De Witte K. 2009. Predicting applicants' job pursuit behavior from their selection expectations: the mediating role of the theory of planned behavior. *J. Organ. Behav.* 30:761–83

Selden S, Orenstein J. 2011. Government e-recruiting web sites: the influence of e-recruitment content and usability on recruiting and hiring outcomes in US state governments. *Int. J. Select. Assess.* 19:31–40

Slaughter JE, Bulger CA, Bachiochi PD. 2005. Black applicants' reactions to affirmative action plans: influence of perceived procedural fairness, anticipated stigmatization, and anticipated remediation of previous injustice. *J. Appl. Soc. Psychol.* 35:2437–76

Stevens CD, Szmerekovsky JG. 2010. Attraction to employment advertisements: advertisement wording and personality characteristics. *J. Manage. Iss.* 22:107–26

Suszko MK, Breaugh JA. 1986. The effects of realistic job previews on applicant self-selection and employee turnover, satisfaction, and coping ability. *J. Manage.* 12:513–23

Taylor M, Bergmann T. 1987. Organizational recruitment activities and applicants' reactions at different stages of the recruitment process. *Pers. Psychol.* 40:261–85

Taylor MS, Schmidt DW. 1983. A process source investigation of recruitment source effectiveness. *Pers. Psychol.* 36:343–54

Thorsteinson TJ, Highhouse S. 2003. Effects of goal framing in job advertisements on organizational attractiveness. *J. Appl. Soc. Psychol.* 33:2393–412

Turban DB, Cable DM. 2003. Firm reputation and applicant pool characteristics. *J. Organ. Behav.* 24:733–51

Turban DB, Campion JE, Eyring AR. 1995. Factors related to job acceptance decisions of college recruits. *J. Vocat. Behav.* 47:193–213

Van Hoye G, Lievens F. 2005. Recruitment-related information sources and organizational attractiveness: Can something be done about negative publicity? *Int. J. Select. Assess.* 13:179–87

Van Hoye G, Lievens F. 2007. Investigating web-based recruitment sources: employee testimonials vs. word-of-mouse. *Int. J. Select. Assess.* 15:372–82

Van Hoye G, Lievens F. 2009. Tapping the grapevine: a closer look at word-of-mouth as a recruiting source. *J. Appl. Psychol.* 94:341–52

Walker HJ, Feild HS, Bernerth JB, Becton JB. 2012. Diversity cues on recruitment websites: investigating the effects on job seekers' information processing. *J. Appl. Psychol.* 97:214–24

Walker HJ, Feild HS, Giles WF, Armenakis AA, Bernerth JB. 2009. Displaying employee testimonials on recruitment web sites: effects of communication media, employee race, and job seeker race on organizational attraction and information credibility. *J. Appl. Psychol.* 94:1354–64

Walker HJ, Feild HS, Giles WF, Bernerth JB. 2008. The interactive effects of job advertisement characteristics and applicant experience on reactions to recruitment messages. *J. Occup. Organ. Psychol.* 81:619–38

Walker HJ, Feild HS, Giles WF, Bernerth JB, Short JC. 2011. So what do you think of the organization? A contextual priming explanation for recruitment web site characteristics as antecedents of job seekers' organizational image perceptions. *Organ. Behav. Hum. Decis. Process.* 114:165–78

Wanous JP. 1992. *Organizational Entry: Recruitment, Selection, and Socialization of Newcomers.* Reading, MA: Addison-Wesley

Wanous JP, Polland TD, Premack SL, Davis KS. 1992. The effects of met expectations on newcomer attitudes and behaviors: a review and a synthesis. *J. Appl. Psychol.* 77:288–97

Williams CR, Labig CE, Stone TH. 1993. Recruitment sources and posthire outcomes for job applicants and new hires: a test of two hypotheses. *J. Appl. Psychol.* 42:163–72

Williamson IO, Slay HS, Shapiro DL, Shivers-Blackwell SL. 2008. The effect of explanations on prospective applicants' reactions to firm diversity practices. *Hum. Resour. Manage.* 47:311–30

Yakubovich V, Lup D. 2006. Stages of the recruitment process and the referrer's performance effect. *Organ. Sci.* 17:710–23

Zajonc RB. 1968. Attitudinal effects of mere exposure. *J. Personal. Soc. Psychol.* 9:1–27

Zajonc RB. 2001. Mere exposure: a gateway to the subliminal. *Curr. Dir. Psychol. Sci.* 10:224–28

Zottoli MA, Wanous JP. 2000. Recruitment source research: current status and future directions. *Hum. Resour. Manag. Rev.* 10:353–83

Self-Regulated Learning: Beliefs, Techniques, and Illusions

Robert A. Bjork,[1] John Dunlosky,[2] and Nate Kornell[3]

[1]Department of Psychology, University of California, Los Angeles, California 90095,
[2]Department of Psychology, Kent State University, Kent, Ohio 44242, [3]Department of
Psychology, Williams College, Williamstown, Massachusetts 01267;
email: rabjork@psych.ucla.edu, jdunlosk@kent.edu, nkornell@gmail.com

Annu. Rev. Psychol. 2013. 64:417–44

First published online as a Review in Advance on
September 27, 2012

The *Annual Review of Psychology* is online at
psych.annualreviews.org

This article's doi:
10.1146/annurev-psych-113011-143823

Keywords

illusions of comprehension, judgments of learning, learning versus
performance, learning from errors, metacognition, studying

Abstract

Knowing how to manage one's own learning has become increasingly
important in recent years, as both the need and the opportunities for
individuals to learn on their own outside of formal classroom settings
have grown. During that same period, however, research on learning,
memory, and metacognitive processes has provided evidence that people often have a faulty mental model of how they learn and remember,
making them prone to both misassessing and mismanaging their own
learning. After a discussion of what learners need to understand in order to become effective stewards of their own learning, we first review
research on what people believe about how they learn and then review
research on how people's ongoing assessments of their own learning are
influenced by current performance and the subjective sense of fluency.
We conclude with a discussion of societal assumptions and attitudes that
can be counterproductive in terms of individuals becoming maximally
effective learners.

Contents

INTRODUCTION

Increasingly, learning is happening outside of formal educational settings and in unsupervised environments. Our complex and rapidly changing world creates a need for self-initiated and self-managed learning—not only during the years typically associated with formal education, but also across the lifespan—and technological advances provide new opportunities for such learning. Knowing how to manage one's own learning activities has become, in short, an important survival tool. In this review we summarize recent research on what people do and do not understand about the learning activities and processes that promote comprehension, retention, and transfer.

Importantly, recent research has revealed that there is in fact much that we, as learners, do not tend to know about how best to assess and manage our own learning. For reasons that are not entirely clear, our intuitions and introspections appear to be unreliable as a guide to how we should manage our own learning activities. One might expect that our intuitions and practices would be informed by what Bjork (2011) has called the "trials and errors of everyday living and learning," but that appears not to be the case. Nor do customs and standard practices in training and education seem to be informed, at least reliably, by any such understanding.

Certain societal attitudes and assumptions also seem to play a role in our not learning how to become maximally effective learners. One such assumption seems to be that children and adults do not need to be taught how to manage their learning activities. In surveys of college students by Kornell & Bjork (2007) and Hartwig & Dunlosky (2012), for example, about 65% to 80% of students answered "no" to the question "Do you study the way you do because somebody taught you to study that way?" (Whether the 20% to 35% who said "yes" had been taught in a way that is consistent with research findings is, of course, another important question.) Institutions, such as colleges, tend to be concerned about whether incoming students possess background knowledge in certain important domains, such as English or mathematics, and tests are often administered to assess whether such knowledge has been acquired. Only rarely, though, are students tested for whether they have the learning skills and practices in place to take on the upcoming years of learning in an efficient, effective way.

It seems likely that the absence of instruction on how to learn does indeed reflect an assumption that people will gradually acquire learning skills on their own—because their experiences across years of learning in schools, the home, and elsewhere will teach them how to manage their own learning—but the prevailing societal emphasis on innate individual differences in learning ability or style may also play a role. The notion that individuals have their own styles of learning, for example, may lead, implicitly or explicitly, to the idea that it is not possible to come up with training on how to learn that is applicable to all individuals (for a review of the learning-styles concept and evidence, see Pashler et al. 2009). The research we review in this article suggests, in contrast, that there are indeed general principles and practices that can be applied to everybody's learning.

BECOMING SOPHISTICATED AS A LEARNER

Before proceeding to reviews of what learners tend to believe about how to learn and what influences learners' ongoing judgments of whether learning has been achieved, it seems useful to consider what someone would need to know in order to become truly sophisticated as a learner. In our view, as we sketch below, becoming truly effective as a learner entails (a) understanding key aspects of the functional architecture that characterizes human learning and memory, (b) knowing activities and techniques that enhance the storage and subsequent retrieval of to-be-learned information and procedures, (c) knowing how to monitor the state of one's learning and to control one's learning activities in response to such monitoring, and (d) understanding certain biases that can impair judgments of whether learning that will support later recall and transfer has been achieved.

Understanding Relevant Peculiarities of Human Memory

To become maximally effective as a learner requires, in part, understanding what Bjork & Bjork (1992) labeled "important peculiarities" of the storage and retrieval processes that characterize human learning and memory. Doing so involves understanding some key ways that humans differ from man-made recording devices. It is important to understand, for example, that we do not store information in our long-term memories by making any kind of literal recording of that information, but, instead, we do so by relating new information to what we already know. We store new information in terms of its meaning to us, as defined by its relationships and semantic associations to information that already exists in our memories. What that means, among other things, is that we have to be an active participant in the learning process—by interpreting, connecting, interrelating, and elaborating, not simply recording. Basically, information will not write itself on our memories. Conscientiously taking verbatim notes or reading to-be-learned content over, if it is done in a passive way, is not an efficient way to learn.

We need to understand, too, that our capacity for storing to-be-learned information or procedures is essentially unlimited. In fact, storing information in human memory appears to create capacity—that is, opportunities for additional linkages and storage—rather than use it up. It is also important to understand that information, once stored by virtue of having been interrelated with existing knowledge in long-term memory, tends to remain stored, if not necessarily accessible. Such knowledge is readily made accessible again and becomes a resource for new learning.

To be sophisticated as a learner also requires understanding that accessing information stored in our memories, given certain cues, does not correspond to the "playback" of a typical recording device. The retrieval of stored information or procedures from human memory is a fallible process that is inferential and reconstructive—not literal. Research dating back to a classic study by Bartlett (1932) has demonstrated repeatedly that what we recall of some prior episode, often confidently, can actually be features of the episode combined with, or replaced by, features that derive from our assumptions, goals, or prior experience, rather than from the episode itself. When we remember the past, we are driven, if not consciously, to make our recollections fit our background knowledge, our expectations, and the current context.

Importantly, retrieval is also cue dependent. The fact that some to-be-learned information is readily recallable during the learning process—owing, perhaps, to recency and/or cues that are present during learning but will not be present later—does not necessarily mean it will be recallable in another time and place, after the learning process has ended.

It is critical, too, for a learner to understand that retrieving information from our memories has consequences. In contrast to the playback of information from some man-made device, such as a compact disk, retrieving information from human memory is a "memory modifier" (Bjork 1975): The retrieved information, rather than being left in the same state, becomes more recallable in the future than it would have been without having been accessed. In fact, as a learning event, the act of retrieving information is considerably more potent than is an additional study opportunity, particularly in terms of facilitating long-term recall (for reviews of research on retrieval as a learning event, see Roediger & Butler 2011, Roediger & Karpicke 2006). Under some circumstances, it may also be important for a learner to understand that such positive effects of retrieval on the later recall of the retrieved information can be accompanied by impaired retrieval of competing information, that is, recall of other information associated to the same cues, an effect labeled retrieval-induced forgetting by Anderson et al. (1994) (see sidebar Retrieval-Induced Learning and Forgetting).

Broadly, then, to be a sophisticated learner requires understanding that creating durable and flexible access to to-be-learned information is partly a matter of achieving a meaningful encoding of that information and partly a matter of exercising the retrieval process. On the encoding side, the goal is to achieve an encoding that is part of a broader framework of interrelated concepts and ideas. On the retrieval side, practicing the retrieval process is crucial. To repeat an example provided by Bjork (1994), one chance to actually put on, fasten, and inflate an inflatable life vest would be of more value—in terms of the likelihood that one could actually perform that procedure correctly in an emergency—than the multitude of times any frequent flier has sat on an airplane and been shown the process by a flight attendant.

Knowing Activities and Techniques that Enhance Storage and Retrieval

Beyond achieving a general understanding of the storage and retrieval processes that characterize human learning and memory, a truly effective learner needs to engage in activities that foster storage of new information and subsequent access to that information. Doing so involves focusing on meaning, making connections between new concepts and concepts that are already understood, organizing to-be-learned knowledge, and so forth. It also involves taking advantage of technologies that have the potential to enhance such activities, as well as taking advantage of the power of collaborative interactions to enrich the encoding of information and concepts and exercise the retrieval of such information and concepts.

Becoming sophisticated as a learner also involves learning to manage the conditions of one's own learning. Aside from acquiring any conceptual understanding of why certain learning activities enhance later recall and transfer of to-be-learned knowledge and procedures, simply knowing that one should incorporate such activities into how one manages one's own learning can be a major asset. Thus, for example, knowing that one should space, rather than mass, one's study sessions on some to-be-learned topic can increase one's effectiveness as a learner, as can knowing that one should interleave, rather than block, successive study or practice sessions on separate to-be-learned tasks or topics (see, e.g., Cepeda et al. 2006). Similarly, knowing that one should vary the conditions of one's own learning, even, perhaps, the environmental context of studying (Smith et al 1978, Smith & Rothkopf 1984), versus keeping those conditions constant and predictable, can make one a more effective learner, as can knowing that one should test one's self and attempt to generate information or procedures rather than looking them up (e.g., Jacoby 1978). Some of the evidence that such manipulations of the conditions of learning enhance later recall is presented later in this review, but for now the point is that becoming sophisticated

RETRIEVAL-INDUCED LEARNING AND FORGETTING

In general, the fact that retrieving information from our memories not only makes the retrieved information more recallable in the future, but also renders competing information—that is, information associated with the same cues—less accessible, is adaptive. Making competing information less accessible, however, can be undesirable under some circumstances, such as when items subjected to such retrieval-induced forgetting are then needed later. Might practice tests, for example, which typically consist of items that differ from those on the later criterion text, actually impair access to information selected against on the practice test, but later needed on the criterion test? It is important to know what conditions and types of testing enhance retrieval-induced forgetting when it is adaptive and eliminate it when it is nonadaptive. Recent findings (see Little et al. 2012), for example, suggest that multiple-choice practice tests may have the virtue that items presented as incorrect alternatives become more, rather than less, accessible when they are later the correct answer to different questions.

as a learner requires knowing how to manage one's own learning activities. In that respect, we are both teacher and student.

What makes acquiring such sophistication difficult is that the short-term consequences of introducing manipulations such as spacing, variation, interleaving, and generating can seem far from beneficial. Such manipulations introduce difficulties and challenges for learners and can appear to slow the rate of learning, as measured by current performance. Because they often enhance long-term retention and transfer of to-be-learned information and procedures, they have been labeled desirable difficulties (Bjork 1994), but they nonetheless can create a sense of difficulty and slow progress for the learner.

Monitoring One's Learning and Controlling One's Learning Activities Effectively

Finally, learning effectively requires not only making accurate assessments of the degree to

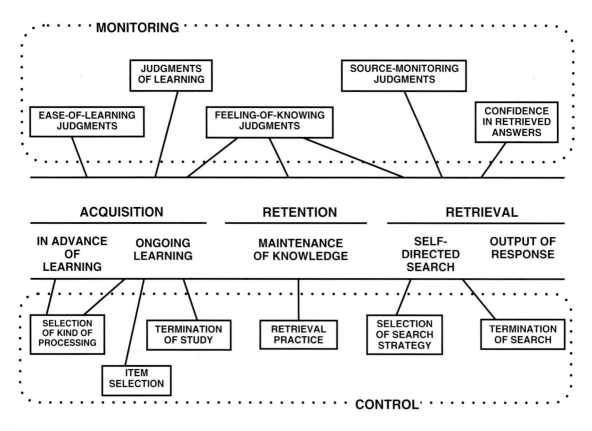

Figure 1

Adapted from Nelson & Narens's (1990) framework for metamemory. From Dunlosky et al. (2007).

which one's learning goals have been achieved, but also responding in effective ways to such assessments. As Nelson & Narens (1990) argued in an influential paper, metacognitive monitoring and metacognitive control play important roles—and interact in important ways—during the acquisition, the retention, and the retrieval of to-be-learned information. Their framework, shown with two additions in **Figure 1**, served as an early guide for research on metacognition and remains a useful framework. Dunlosky et al. (2007) added "source-monitoring judgments" to Nelson & Narens's (1990) framework, and we have added "retrieval practice" during the retention phase in order to reflect that a sophisticated learner may know that information and procedures, to remain accessible until some criterion test, must be reinstated/retrieved prior to that test.

Basically, the learning process involves making continual assessments and decisions, such as what should be studied next and how it should be studied, whether the learning that will support later access to some information, concept, or procedure has been achieved, whether what one has recalled is correct, and on and on. As captured in **Figure 1**, there is an important back and forth between monitoring and control. To become sophisticated and effective as a learner requires not only being able to assess, accurately, the state of one's learning (as illustrated by the monitoring judgments listed in the top of the figure), but also being able to control one's learning processes and activities in response to such monitoring (as illustrated by the control decisions).

Becoming sophisticated in monitoring and controlling one's learning and learning

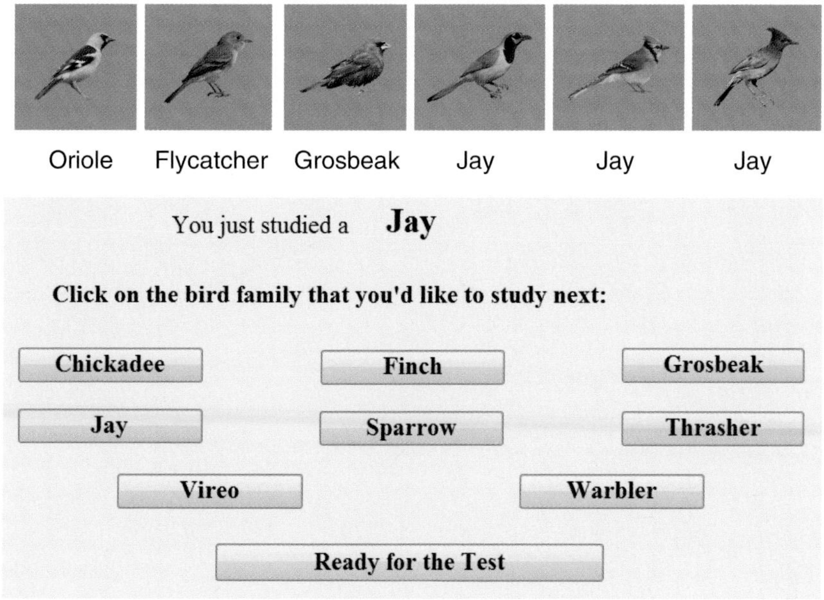

Figure 2

(*Top panel*) Exemplars from four bird families (materials from Wahlheim et al. 2011), with three exemplars (out of six studied) from the Jay family (from left to right: Green Jay, Blue Jay, Stellar Jay). (*Bottom panel*) Interface for choosing the next family. When a button for a given family is pressed, a bird (from the six presented in the familiarity phase) from the chosen family is presented for study along with the family name.

activities turns out to be no small challenge. As demonstrated by the research reviewed below, (*a*) learners can easily be misled as to whether learning has been achieved, typically resulting in overconfidence, and (*b*) what people tend to believe about activities that are and are not effective for learning is often at odds with reality. Assessing the state of one's learning is difficult because the objective and subjective indices on which one might base such assessments, such as current performance or the sense of familiarity or fluency in encoding or retrieving to-be-learned information, can reflect factors unrelated to whether learning has been achieved. Current performance—and the subjective sense of retrieval fluency, that is how readily information and procedures come to mind—can be heavily influenced by factors such as recency, predictability, and cues that are present during learning but will not be present later, and the subjective sense of familiarity or perceptual fluency can reflect factors such as priming rather than being a valid measure of learning.

Finally, to be effective in assessing one's own learning requires being aware that we are subject to both hindsight and foresight biases in judging whether we will be able to produce to-be-learned information at some later time. Hindsight bias (Fischhoff 1975) refers to the tendency we have, once information is made available to us, to think that we knew it all along. Thus, a student preparing for an examination and trying to decide what to study in the time remaining before the exam may try to base such judgments on scanning sections of a textbook chapter, but such judgments will tend to be unreliable because the information is at hand, so to speak. Foresight bias (Koriat & Bjork 2005), on the other hand, rather than reflecting a knew-it-all-along tendency, reflects a will-know-it-in-the-future tendency. It derives from an inherent difference between study and test situations—namely, that the answer is present during study, but will be absent and required at test—and it is most likely to occur when an answer that is solicited during testing is judged to be natural or obvious when presented along with the question, but is less likely to come forward, owing to the elicitation of other possible answers, when the question is presented alone.

WHAT DO STUDENTS BELIEVE ABOUT HOW TO LEARN?

What kinds of strategies do students believe work best? Which ones do they use, and does using them relate to their achievement? To answer such questions, researchers have generally used two methods—administering questionnaires about strategy use and examining how students use strategies to manage their learning in the laboratory. We review evidence from both methods below, and, to foreshadow, the evidence converges on a sobering conclusion: Although individual differences occur in effective strategy use, with some students using effective strategies that contribute to their achievement, many students not only use relatively ineffective strategies (e.g., rereading), but believe that they are relatively effective.

Surveys of Students' Strategy Use and Beliefs About Studying

One of the most frequently used assessments of student self-regulation is the Motivated Strategies for Learning Questionnaire (MSLQ; Pintrich et al. 1993). The MSLQ includes 81 items that measure 15 subscales that pertain to student motivation and strategy use. Of most relevance here, four subscales tap students' use of general learning strategies. These subscales are each measured by multiple items and include elaboration (e.g., pulling information together from multiple sources when studying), rehearsal (e.g., repeating materials over to oneself), organization (e.g., outlining the material to organize it), and critical thinking (e.g., questioning what one reads while studying). In a recent meta-analysis, Credé & Phillips (2011) examined the relationship among these subscales and student grades from 67 independent samples that included responses from over 19,000 college students. The relationships between these subscales and student grades were low and sometimes nonsignificant. As noted by Credé & Phillips (2011), however, these low relationships may arise for multiple reasons. The relationships may not be linear, with some strategies being used largely by average students. For instance, high performers may not need to use repetition and low performers may not be motivated to use repetition. Moreover, these general strategies will not be effective for all kinds of exams; thus, those endorsing the use of critical thinking during study may not outperform others when exams merely tap memory for the materials. Other limitations are that the general wording of the scale items may not be interpreted the same way by all students (Credé & Phillips 2011), that some of these strategies are just not that effective (e.g., rehearsal or repetition), and that others are effective only if used properly.

One way to sidestep some of these limitations—such as differences in scale interpretation—is simply to ask students to identify the specific strategies that they use while studying. For instance, self-testing is an effective strategy that may boost student performance because it can promote both elaboration and organization (e.g., Carpenter 2011; Pyc & Rawson 2010, 2012; Zaromb & Roediger 2010), but the single question about this effective strategy on the MSLQ is treated more generically as a learning strategy that contributes to only one subscale. To assess more directly the use of specific strategies, Kornell & Bjork (2007) had 472 college students at the University of California, Los Angeles fill out a study-habit survey that focused on their use of rereading and testing. Seventy-six percent indicated that they reread either whole chapters or what they had underlined, and around 90% indicated that they used self-testing in some fashion. In a follow-up to this survey study, Hartwig & Dunlosky (2012) reported nearly identical usage for 324 college students at Kent State University, and, importantly, they related frequency of use of these strategies to the students' grade point average (GPA). Both testing and rereading were significantly correlated with GPA (see also Gurung et al. 2010).

These survey results at first seem at odds with outcomes from students' free reports of study strategies. When simply asked, for example, "What kind of strategies do you use when you are studying," only 11% of college students from Washington University reported practicing retrieval (Karpicke et al. 2009). One possible resolution of the discrepancy is that college students may not believe testing is a strategy to enhance learning, so they may not include it in free reports of their strategy use. Consistent with that possibility, when Kornell & Bjork (2007) asked students why they used self-testing, only 18% indicated that they used it because they learn more when they self-test than when they reread; by contrast, about 70% indicated that they used self-testing to figure out how well they have learned the information.

Such beliefs may explain in part why few students reported the use of self-testing when asked about their strategy use on the open-ended survey administered by Karpicke et al. (2009). In fact, when the same students were given a forced-choice question about testing, many more (about 42%) endorsed its use. Thus, many students do use this effective learning strategy, but the prevalent belief is that self-testing is largely for self-evaluation, and most students believe that rereading is a more effective strategy than is self-testing (McCabe 2011). Both of these inaccurate beliefs about self-testing may curtail its use.

Self-testing is intrinsic to the use of flashcards that many students report using (Hartwig & Dunlosky 2012, Karpicke et al. 2009), but do students use them effectively? To address this question, Wissman et al. (2012) had college students complete a survey designed to reveal, among other things, how and when students use self-testing with flashcards. The students surveyed reported using flashcards mainly to learn vocabulary. Moreover, when using flashcards, they reported that they would continue until they had correctly recalled a response three or more times, which does, in fact, yield much better retention of vocabulary compared to recalling a response only once (Pyc & Rawson 2009, Vaughn & Rawson 2011). Almost all the students reported that they would use flash-cards more than once to learn materials for an exam, but they also reported that such use was largely limited to just a day or two before the exam. This kind of cramming is popular (Taraban et al. 1999) and certainly does not optimize retention, although students believe it is an effective way to learn (Kornell 2009).

Students' Beliefs as Indexed by Decisions They Make in Managing Their Learning

Another way researchers have investigated students' beliefs about how to learn is to have them complete a task and observe how they approach it. One straightforward method that has provided compelling results is to have students self-pace the study of to-be-learned materials and then examine how they allocate study time to each item (for a historical review, see Son & Kornell 2008). In a typical experiment, the students first study all the items at an experimenter-paced rate (e.g., study 60 paired associates for 3 seconds each), which familiarizes the students with the items; after this familiarity phase, the students then either choose which items they want to restudy (e.g., all items are presented in an array, and the students select which ones to restudy) and/or pace their restudy of each item. Several dependent measures have been widely used, such as how long each item is studied, whether an item is selected for restudy, and in what order items are selected for restudy.

The literature on these aspects of self-regulated study is massive (for a comprehensive overview, see both Dunlosky & Ariel 2011a and Son & Metcalfe 2000), but the evidence is largely consistent with a few basic conclusions. First, if students have a chance to practice retrieval prior to restudying items, they almost exclusively choose to restudy unrecalled items and drop the previously recalled items from restudy (Metcalfe & Kornell 2005). Second, when pacing their study of individual items that have been selected for restudy, students typically spend more time studying items that

are more, rather than less, difficult to learn. Such a strategy is consistent with a discrepancy-reduction model of self-paced study (which states that people continue to study an item until they reach mastery), although some key revisions to this model are needed to account for all the data. For instance, students may not continue to study until they reach some static criterion of mastery, but instead, they may continue to study until they perceive that they are no longer making progress (for details, see Dunlosky & Thiede 1998, Metcalfe & Kornell 2005).

Third, students develop agendas—that is, plans—for the allocation of their study time, and sometimes these agendas, in contrast to the discrepancy-reduction model, do not prioritize the most difficult items for study (Ariel et al. 2009). Thiede & Dunlosky (1999), for example, told students that their goal was merely to learn 6 out of the 30 items that were being presented for study. In this case, students presumably developed an agenda to complete the task efficiently and selected to restudy only a few of the easiest items to restudy. Similarly, Metcalfe (2009, Kornell & Metcalfe 2006) reported that under some conditions students choose the easiest items first for study and spend more time studying the easiest items. Focusing on the easier items first (which Metcalfe calls studying within the region of proximal learning) is one of many agendas that students can develop to allocate their study time, and doing so can even boost their learning (Atkinson 1972, Kornell & Metcalfe 2006).

Finally, developing agendas to allocate study time effectively is a mindful way to approach a new learning task, but students do not always mindfully regulate their study. Instead, their study choices are sometimes biased by habitual or prepotent responses. One habitual bias that can disrupt effective allocation of study time arises from reading. When students are given an array of items to study (e.g., a list of vocabulary items in a textbook), native English speakers choose items for study in a left-to-right (or top-down) manner (Dunlosky & Ariel 2011b) instead of first focusing on either the most difficult items (as per discrepancy reduction) or easiest items (as per the region of proximal learning). The idea here is simply that habitual biases can undermine the development of effective agendas for study time allocation. Thus, for example, a student preparing for a test might simply open a textbook and read through the assigned pages versus having any kind of plan of attack that might guide their studying. Such passive reading—and even rereading—is much less effective than active processing, such as self-explanation or self-testing.

Recent studies have used a modified version of the self-paced study method to investigate when and how students allocate their learning. As described above, participants typically receive a familiarity phase with the items (e.g., a brief experimenter-paced presentation of each item) and then make a control decision about what to do next. These studies explore the kinds of practice schedule that students use while studying, such as whether they prefer spacing or massing their study (e.g., Benjamin & Bird 2006; Pyc & Dunlosky 2010; Son 2004, 2010; Toppino & Cohen 2010; Toppino et al. 2009) and whether they prefer to reschedule practice-test trials or restudy trials (Karpicke 2009, Kornell & Son 2009). Researchers are only beginning to investigate these topics, but some intriguing issues have emerged, and we consider three of them next.

The first issue concerns students' decision to use (or not to use) an effective spacing strategy. Consider a commonly reported outcome: When students study an item and are asked either to study it again (i.e., massed study) or to study it later after other items have been studied (i.e., spaced study), they tend to space their study more than they mass it. Even though students prefer to space study in these laboratory experiments, it does not mean that they believe spacing is a more effective strategy. Much evidence suggests otherwise. When students are given the option to space study either after a short lag or after a long lag, they prefer the shorter lag (Cohen et al. 2011, Wissman et al. 2012), which typically yields

inferior performance and indicates that students do not understand the power of spacing. Moreover, McCabe (2011) had participants read a scenario where students were either spacing or massing their study of paintings from famous artists, with the goal of later being able to identify which of the studied artists painted each of a series of new paintings. Most participants said that massing would be better than spacing!

Given that students do not understand the power of spacing, it may not be surprising that they fail to incorporate spacing into their study routines. Consider results from Tauber et al. (2012, experiment 3), who had college students attempt to learn to categorize birds into their families. During a familiarity phase, six different birds from eight families (e.g., Jay, Grosbeak, Warbler) were presented individually for 6 seconds. Participants had 30 minutes to restudy the same birds, and they could choose the order in which they studied birds from the families. For this self-paced phase, they were first presented a randomly chosen bird from one family (e.g., a Green Jay, from the Jay family), and when they finished studying this bird, the interface depicted in **Figure 2** (see color insert) was presented.

During the self-paced phase, the participants were instructed to study the birds in an order that would best help them to classify new birds on the final test. On average, participants chose to restudy 57 birds, and a sizable majority of participants (75%) preferred to block (or mass) instead of interleave (or space). In fact, when massing their study, the students tended to study most of the birds within a family (about 5 out of 6) before moving to another one. These data are in line with Simon & Bjork's (2001) findings that contrary to the facts, participants predict higher future performance when getting blocked practice than they do when getting interleaved practice, as discussed in the next session. To summarize, despite the fact that students do choose spacing over massing in some contexts, this choice is unlikely a symptom of effective regulation because students appear not, based on other findings, to understand the power of spacing or use it consistently across different tasks.

The second issue concerns students' decision to stop studying. When given the option to drop items from study, they tend to do so prematurely: They drop them once they believe they have learned them (Metcalfe & Kornell 2005), even though another study attempt or retrieval attempt (e.g., practice test) would further enhance their learning (Karpicke 2009, Kornell & Bjork 2008b). Although this latter outcome suggests that students do not make effective control decisions with regard to the use of practice tests, note that outside of the laboratory, students report testing themselves on items many times after those items can already be successfully retrieved (Wissman et al. 2012). One difficulty here is that some laboratory tasks include constraints (e.g., allowing strategy selection only after all items have already been recalled) that may stifle students' natural use of strategies like self-testing.

Third, and finally, when given the choice to restudy a list of words or to be tested on those words, students tend to request practice tests, especially when these tests involve feedback (Kornell & Son 2009). Consistent with the survey data described above, however, most students report wanting to use a practice test to evaluate their learning and not to enhance it (Kornell & Son 2009). Although speculative, students' use of testing as a tool to monitor memory may ultimately lead them to underuse it as a learning tool.

In summary, students do endorse using some effective strategies for learning, such as self-testing, and they sometimes make good decisions about how to manage their time in laboratory experiments. Nevertheless, other outcomes suggest that students do not fully reap the benefits of these effective strategies. With respect to testing, many students believe that rereading is a superior strategy to testing (McCabe 2010), even though the benefits of rereading are modest at best (Dunloskey et al. 2012, Fritz et al. 2000, Rawson & Kintsch 2005). Moreover, most students use testing to evaluate their learning and hence may not use it more broadly as a strategy to enhance their learning. With respect to spaced practice, even though students sometimes prefer to space study in laboratory experiments, such spacing occurs within a single session. Unfortunately, given that students endorse cramming and believe doing so is effective, they will not obtain the long-term benefits that arise when spacing practice occurs across multiple sessions (e.g., Bahrick 1979, Rawson & Dunlosky 2011).

Why might students underuse effective strategies and believe that ineffective ones are actually effective? One reason why they may underuse effective strategies is that many students are not formally trained (or even told) about how to use effective strategies, perhaps because societal attitudes and assumptions indicate that children and adults do not need to be taught them. As noted by McNamara (2010), "there is an overwhelming assumption in our educational system that the most important thing to *deliver* to students is content" (p. 341, italics in original). Indeed, most college students report that how they study is not a consequence of having been taught how to study by teachers or others (Kornell & Bjork 2007).

Perhaps even worse, students' experience in using strategies may sometimes lead them to believe that ineffective techniques are actually the more effective ones (e.g., Kornell & Bjork 2008a, Simon & Bjork 2001). For instance, across multiple experiments, Kornell (2009) reported that 90% of the college student participants had better performance after spacing than massing practice. When the study sessions were over, however, 72% of the participants reported that massing was more effective than spacing. This metacognitive illusion may arise because processing during study is easier (or more fluent) for massing than spacing, and people in general tend to believe that easier processing means better processing (Alter & Oppenheimer 2009). Unfortunately, as the next section explains in more detail, these metacognitive illusions can trick students into believing that a bad strategy is rather good, which itself may lead to poor self-regulation and lower levels of achievement.

WHAT INFLUENCES LEARNERS' JUDGMENTS OF LEARNING AND PREDICTIONS OF FUTURE PERFORMANCE?

Making sound study decisions is a precondition of being a successful learner. These decisions depend on students' judgments of how well they know the material they are studying. Students often study until they have reached what they deem to be an acceptable level of knowledge (Ariel et al. 2009, Kornell & Metcalfe 2006, Thiede & Dunlosky 1999)—for example, they study chapter 3 until they judge that they will remember what it covers on an upcoming test, then turn to chapter 4, and so forth.

The term judgment of learning (JOL) is used to describe such predictions of future memory performance. In a typical JOL task, participants judge the probability that they will remember the information they are studying on an upcoming test. The accuracy of JOLs can play a large role in determining how adaptive (or maladaptive) study decisions end up being (Kornell & Metcalfe 2006, Nelson & Narens 1990).

What factors influence JOLs? Early metacognition researchers (e.g., Hart 1965) assumed that people judged a memory by making a direct, internal measurement of its strength. According to this direct-access view, a metacognitive judgment is similar to a thermometer, which measures temperature directly, without need for inference. The thermometer is a flawed analogy, however. Metacognition is more like a speedometer, which measures the rotation of a car's tires. A "judgment" of speed is inferred based on the rotation rate. Metacognitive judgments are also inferential (Schwartz et al. 1997). Support for this inferential view comes from studies reviewed in the next section, studies that reveal systematic biases and errors in the inferences people draw. These errors, which are not predicted by the direct-access view, are the clues researchers have used to uncover the mechanisms underlying metacognitive judgments. They are also a cause for concern for learners because faulty monitoring can lead to maladaptive study decisions.

Belief-Based Versus Experience-Based Judgments and Predictions

Judgments of learning are inferences based on cues, but what cues? There appear to be two broad categories of cues—beliefs and experiences (Jacoby & Kelley 1987, Koriat 1997). Belief-based cues (which are also known as theory-based or knowledge-based cues) refer to what one consciously believes about memory, such as "I learn by studying." Experience-based cues include anything learners can directly experience, including how familiar an answer seems, how loud a speaker is talking, how pronounceable a word is, and so forth.

Competition and interactions between experience-based and belief-based cues. A deep psychological difference appears to divide beliefs from experience. Although people clearly hold beliefs about their memories, they frequently fail to apply those beliefs when making JOLs—that is, they are insensitive to belief-based cues even (and perhaps especially) when they are, at the same time, highly sensitive to experience-based cues (see, e.g., Kelley & Jacoby 1996). A study by Kornell et al. (2011b) provides compelling evidence of this phenomenon. Participants were asked to study a list of single words. Two variables were manipulated: Items were presented in a font size that was either large or small, and participants were informed that a given word either would or would not be presented a second time. Font size is an experience-based cue, whereas a future study opportunity cannot be experienced, at least not in the present. Participants' JOLs were consistently affected by font size but were largely unaffected by the number of future study trials. Ironically, the number of study trials had a large effect on learning, whereas font size had no effect.

In addition to providing evidence for the inferential view of metacognition—in which judgments do not necessarily correspond to memory strength—Kornell et al.'s (2011b) findings highlight the fact that people can be sensitive to experience-based cues and not belief-based cues, even in a situation where the opposite should be true.

Evidence of a stability bias. Failing to predict that future studying will affect one's knowledge is an example of what Kornell & Bjork (2009) labeled a stability bias in memory—that is, a bias to act as though one's memory will not change in the future (see also Kornell 2011, 2012). Kornell and Bjork found that participants, when asked to study a list of word pairs once and then to predict their final test performance after 0–3 additional study trials, were underconfident in their ability to learn in the future, demonstrating a stability bias, but were also, at the same time, overconfident in their current level of knowledge. This pattern is troubling because it appears to provide dual reasons not to study as much as would be optimal.

Similarly, a study by Koriat et al. (2004) demonstrated a surprising stability bias with respect to forgetting: Participants' predictions of their later test performance were not affected by whether the participants were told they would

be tested immediately, after a week, or even after a year (but see Rawson et al. 2002). The participants did, in fact, have a theory of forgetting at the belief level, and when the idea of forgetting was made salient, the participants became sensitive to retention interval—but without such prompting their judgments were insensitive to forgetting and highly inaccurate.

The stability bias has troubling implications. One reason students do not give up on studying, even in the face of difficulty, is the knowledge that eventually they will improve. Students who underestimate how much they can improve by studying may give up hope when they should not. Ignoring forgetting is also dangerous. Students may unconsciously assume that if they know something today, they will know it next week or next month—which is not necessarily true—and stop studying prematurely. (Teachers are vulnerable to the same error when judging their students' knowledge.) Indeed, failing to account for forgetting can produce extreme amounts of long-term overconfidence (Kornell 2011). The effects of the stability bias on over- and underconfidence are illustrated in **Figure 3**.

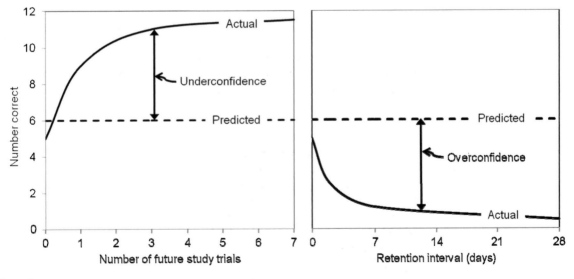

Figure 3

Hypothetical curves depicting changes in predicted and actual learning over time. Predicted recall remains constant due to the stability bias, whereas actual recall increases due to future study trials (*left panel*) or decreases due to forgetting (*right panel*). These dynamics produce an increasing gap between predicted and actual knowledge.

Thus, it appears that people can ignore even the most obvious of metacognitive beliefs, such as the beliefs that studying produces learning and forgetting happens over time. The reason belief-based cues are ignored appears to be that, in general, they fall into the category of cues that do not impact one's current experience. The foresight bias—that is, the failure to take into account how one's memory will be tested, which was discussed previously—falls into this category as well. The form taken by a future test does not affect current experience.

Interpreting Objective Indices of Current Performance: Heuristics and Illusions

It is experience-based cues that guide metacognitive judgments and, by extension, study decisions. One of the most important, salient, and reliable experience-based cues is whether one can presently recall some information or procedure.

Response accuracy. A pair of influential studies by Nelson & Dunlosky (1991) and Dunlosky & Nelson (1992) demonstrated the metacognitive value of testing long-term memory. In these studies, participants were asked to make JOLs about a series of word pairs and later took a test on the pairs. Metacognitive accuracy was operationalized as the gamma correlation—a nonparametric measure of association—between JOLs and subsequent recall. The JOLs were made either immediately after studying or after a delay; they were also made either based on both words in the pair or based on the cue only. Only the delayed cue-only condition allowed participants to make a meaningful test of their memories. This condition produced levels of metacognitive accuracy that were very high (gamma >0.9) and also much higher than in the other three conditions (gamma <0.6), a finding dubbed the delayed JOL effect.

These findings suggest that the best way to distinguish between what one does and does not know may be to test oneself. Doing so appears to benefit learning in two ways. First,

accurate monitoring can lead to study choices that enhance learning (Dunlosky & Rawson 2012, Kornell & Metcalfe 2006, Metcalfe & Finn 2008, Thiede 1999). Second, as mentioned previously, tests produce more learning than does similar time spent studying without being tested (e.g., Roediger & Butler 2011). [As Spellman & Bjork (1992) have argued (also see Kimball & Metcalfe 2003, Rhodes & Tauber 2011), it may be that the memory benefits of testing act to make participants' judgments of learning appear more accurate than they really are, but this is an issue that the authors of this article, much less the field, have not settled.]

It is clear that whether one can recall an answer has a powerful influence on JOLs. It seems possible, given the evidence presented thus far, that current experience has exclusive control over JOLs. That is, past events can influence current experience, but only current experience influences JOLs. As Finn & Metcalfe (2007, 2008) have shown (also see King et al. 1980), however, people tend to base their JOLs on their most recent test, even if the test occurred in the past and additional study trials have occurred in the meantime. This judgment strategy is referred to as the memory for past test heuristic. Thus, it appears that experiences, not necessarily current experiences, control JOLs.

Response time. Like the ability to answer a question, the speed with which an answer comes to mind has an important experience-based influence on JOLs. Benjamin et al. (1998) uncovered striking evidence for this claim. They asked participants to answer trivia questions. The participants were told that they would be tested later, and the nature of the test was made very clear: They would be given a blank sheet of paper and, without being asked the questions again, they would be asked to free-recall the answers. During the question-answering phase, after each correct answer, the participants were asked to predict the probability that they would be able to recall the answer again on the final test. The results were surprising: The more confident participants were that they would recall an answer, the less likely they were to recall it. This outcome occurred because participants gave higher JOLs to questions that they answered quickly, but they were most likely to free-recall answers that they had thought about for a long time (see **Figure 4**).

These findings can be interpreted as suggesting that participants have incomplete mental models of their own memories. In particular, answering trivia questions involves semantic memory but free-recalling answers provided earlier involves episodic memory, and one interpretation of the findings is that people do not understand the difference between semantic and episodic memory. Another interpretation of the findings, however, based on the foresight bias, is that the participants' mental models may have been irrelevant. That is, perhaps the participants never took the nature of the final test into account (in which case an accurate mental model would not have affected their judgments). In any event, what is clear is that these participants relied on current experience to make their judgments.

The speed with which an answer comes to mind is often a sensible basis for study decisions—stronger memories do tend to come to mind quickly (Benjamin et al. 1998). For instance, when the final criterion test is cued recall of paired associates, students' use of retrieval speed during prior cued recall is a diagnostic cue that improves the accuracy of students' judgments (Serra & Dunlosky 2005). Nevertheless, studies that dissociate knowledge and response speed are valuable because they make it clear that response time is a more powerful metacognitive cue than is memory strength.

Interpreting Subjective Indices of Performance: Heuristics and Illusions

Response time and retrieval success are objectively measurable cues, but they are closely related to a more subjective basis for judgments: fluency. Fluency during the perceptual processing of information is the sense of ease or speed of processing; fluency during the retrieval of information is the sense of how readily

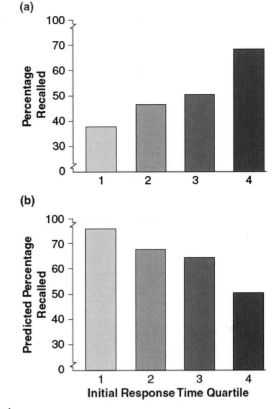

Figure 4

Percentage recalled (*a*) and mean judgment of learning (*b*) as a function of the latency of cued recall. Latency (response time in quartiles) is presented from fastest (*1*) to slowest (*4*). From Benjamin et al. (1998).

information "comes to mind." Because the subjective sense of fluency, either in processing information or in retrieving information, falls squarely in the category of experience-based cues, fluency has powerful effects on metacognitive judgments (e.g., Koriat 1993), as we describe next. (Fluency also influences a wide variety of other types of judgment; see Alter & Oppenheimer 2009, Kelley & Jacoby 1996, Kelley & Rhodes 2002, Oppenheimer 2008, Schwarz 2004.)

Retrieval fluency. Retrieval fluency, as mentioned above, is the ease and speed with which information is retrieved from memory (e.g., Benjamin & Bjork 1996, Matvey et al. 2001, Reder 1996). In general, retrieval fluency is a useful heuristic in terms of judging how well something is known, but it can be misleading and create illusions of knowing when it is the product of factors unrelated to degree of learning, such as priming. Kelley & Lindsay (1993), for example, demonstrated that participants' confidence in their answers to general-knowledge questions (e.g., "What was Buffalo Bill's last name?"), whether correct or incorrect, was increased when those answers (e.g., "Cody" or "Hickok") had been pre-exposed in an earlier phase of the experiment. It appears that people are susceptible to using (i.e., misattributing) the sense of familiarity or ease of perception as an index of knowing, even when such fluency does not reflect actual understanding or learning (see also Jacoby et al. 1989).

Confidence judgments like those manipulated by Kelley & Lindsay (1993) are retrospective judgments about an answer that has just been given. Troublingly, it is possible to manipulate confidence in eyewitness testimony by artificially boosting fluency (Shaw 1996). But confidence judgments probably influence study decisions less than JOLs do. The more fluently information comes to mind, the more likely students are to decide they know it, and therefore put it aside and stop studying.

Encoding fluency. Encoding fluency—that is, the subjective feeling that it is easy or difficult to learn a piece of information—is another important influence on decisions about studying (e.g., Miele et al. 2011). For example, Hertzog et al. (2003) asked participants to study unrelated pairs of concrete words. They were also asked to form a mental image of each pair and then make a JOL. Faster encoding (i.e., higher fluency) was associated with higher JOLs. Yet, encoding fluency was misleading (see also Castel et al. 2007) because recall was not correlated with fluency. Thus, like retrieval fluency, encoding fluency can be misleading, but high encoding fluency may decrease the chance that a student will restudy the item.

Perceptual fluency. Metacognitive judgments tend to be higher for items with greater perceptual fluency—that is, items that are subjectively easier to process at a perceptual level. Reder (1987), for example, found that simply pre-exposing key words in a question (such as the words "golf" and "par" in the question "What is the term in golf for scoring one under par?") increased subjects' confidence that they would be able to produce the answer to a given question. Also, as mentioned previously, words presented in larger fonts have been incorrectly judged to be more memorable (Kornell et al. 2011, Rhodes & Castel 2008). Words presented at a louder volume were also incorrectly rated as more memorable (Rhodes & Castel 2009). A recent study even suggested that perceptual fluency can decrease learning: Students learned more when in-class PowerPoint presentations and handouts were converted to fonts that decreased fluency (Diemand-Yauman et al. 2011). This is a worrying outcome given that students judge that they have learned more when information seems more fluent. Such misperceptions may lead to undesirable study decisions. Teachers are affected by fluency as well: The teachers involved in the Diemand-Yauman studies initially objected to using the disfluent fonts that ended up enhancing learning.

Fluency of induction. Self-regulated learning is not limited to one type of learning. Most of the research on the topic involves materials that can be memorized, but such materials do not capture inductive learning—learning a concept or category by observing examples. For example, learning to differentiate elm trees from oaks and maples requires seeing examples of each kind of tree.

Judging the progress of inductive learning is similar to judgments based on encoding fluency. In many cases it relates to perceptual fluency as well. For example, Kornell & Bjork (2008a) investigated inductive learning by presenting paintings by 12 different artists (also see Kornell et al. 2010). Some artists' paintings were presented on consecutive trials while other artists' paintings were presented interleaved with other paintings. As a test, participants were asked which artist painted each of a set of previously unpresented paintings. They were more accurate following interleaved (i.e., spaced) learning than following blocked (i.e., massed) learning.

Blocking may have made it easier to notice similarities within a given artist's paintings, whereas the value of interleaving appears to lie, at least in part, in highlighting differences between categories (Kang & Pashler 2012, Wahlheim et al. 2011). The benefit of interleaving is consistent with a large literature on the benefits of spaced practice in noninductive learning (e.g., Cepeda et al. 2006, Dempster 1996) (see sidebar Why Does Interleaving Enhance Learning?).

As **Figure 5** shows, the majority of Kornell & Bjork's (2008a) participants incorrectly believed that blocking had been more effective than interleaving (for similar results, see Kornell et al. 2010, Wahlheim et al. 2011, Zulkiply et al. 2012). Massing appears to increase the fluency of induction by increasing the retrieval fluency of prior exemplars of a category (also see Wahlheim et al. 2012). In a blocked schedule, the previous example of a category, which was just presented, is highly fluent, whereas it is not in an interleaved schedule. Thus blocked studying is rated as more effective than interleaving. This metacognitive error occurs in noninductive learning as well (Dunlosky & Nelson 1994, Kornell 2009, Simon & Bjork 2001, Zechmeister & Shaughnessy 1980), although, as mentioned previously, students do tend to space their studying at least to some degree (see Son & Kornell 2009 and section What Do Students Believe About How to Learn?).

When subjective experience is the best basis for predictions. We have stressed those instances when subjective experience can be misleading, but it is important to emphasize that there are situations in which subjective experience can be the best basis for judgments and predictions. Related to hindsight biases, for

example, being exposed to answers and solutions can deny us the type of subjective experience that might otherwise provide a valuable basis for judging our competence, and our subjective experience can be an especially valuable guide in situations where we lack other bases for making judgments and predictions. Jacoby & Kelley (1987), for example, demonstrated that subjects' judgments of the relative difficulty of anagrams (such as "FSCAR-?????"), as measured by the solution performance of other subjects, were much less accurate if made with the solution present (e.g., "FSCAR-SCARF") than if made after having the subjective experience of solving the anagram. Basically, when subjective experience is denied in situations where we do not have another valid basis for judgments and predictions—such as in solving anagrams, where people do not, apparently, have an adequate theory as to what makes anagrams difficult—judgments and predictions can be impaired.

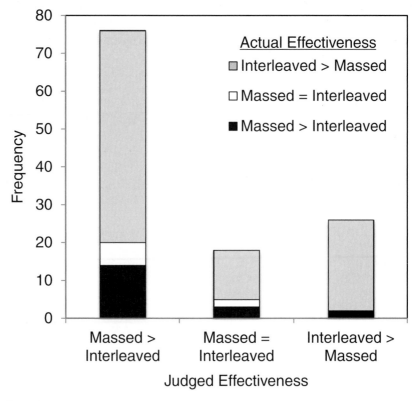

Figure 5

Number of participants (out of 120) who judged massing as more effective than, equally effective as, or less effective than interleaving in Kornell & Bjork (2008a). For each judgment, participants are divided into groups on the basis of their actual performance.

Learning Versus Performance and the Unintuitive Benefits of Desirable Difficulties

Because people make study decisions while they are studying, they tend to be drawn to techniques that lead to the best performance during study. Making study activities easier—by, for example, massing practice—tends to increase judgments of learning, which is problematic because conditions that make learning seem easier can actually decrease long-term learning. Activities such as spacing and interleaving, generating answers, testing oneself, and varying the conditions of learning are known as desirable difficulties (Bjork 1994, Bjork & Bjork 2011). They impair performance—and, hence, apparent learning—during acquisition, but enhance long-term learning. The

fundamental problem with using fluency as a basis for study decisions is that learners often interpret high fluency as signaling a high rate of improvement when it can actually, under some circumstances, signal just the opposite. Educators fall victim to this error when they design textbooks that mass studying on one topic at a time instead of periodically returning to prior topics in an effort to promote spaced learning (e.g., Rohrer & Taylor 2006, 2007). Students are prone to the same illusions when regulating their own study activities.

ATTITUDES AND ASSUMPTIONS THAT CAN IMPAIR SELF-REGULATED LEARNING

As we stated in the beginning of this review, it has become increasingly important that one be able to manage one's own learning effectively. We also stressed, though, that becoming truly effective in managing one's own learning is not easy: Doing so requires not only gaining a general understanding of the unique storage and retrieval processes that characterize human memory, but also overcoming certain intuitions, knowing what activities are and are not productive for learning, and avoiding being fooled by current performance and feelings of fluency that reflect factors other than the kind of encoding and understanding that supports long-term retention and transfer. Becoming sophisticated as a learner is also difficult, in our opinion, because doing so requires overcoming societal attitudes and assumptions that are often counterproductive for learning, which we discuss below.

Misunderstanding the Meaning and Role of Errors and Mistakes

Errors and mistakes are typically viewed as something to avoid during the learning process, in part out of fear that they will be interpreted—by ourselves or others—as documenting our inadequacies as a learner, but also out of a concern that such errors or mistakes, by virtue of being produced, will be learned. A variety of research findings suggest, by contrast, that making errors is often an essential component of efficient learning. Introducing desirable difficulties into learning procedures, for example, such as variation or interleaving, tends to result in more errors being made during the acquisition process, but it also tends to enhance long-term retention and transfer (e.g., Lee 2012, Simon & Bjork 2001, Taylor & Rohrer 2010). Conversely, manipulations that eliminate errors can often eliminate learning. Thus, for example, when retrieval of to-be-learned information is made so easy as to insure success, by virtue of recency, strong cue support, or some other factor, the benefits of such retrieval as a learning event tend to be mostly or entirely eliminated (e.g., Landauer & Bjork 1978, Rawson & Kintsch 2005, Whitten & Bjork 1977).

Kornell et al. (2009; also see Grimaldi & Karpicke 2012, Hays et al. 2012, Huelser & Metcalfe 2012, Knight et al. 2012, Vaughn & Rawson 2012) have also demonstrated that anticipating, unsuccessfully, a to-be-learned response can enhance learning. If participants are asked to predict what associate of a given cue word (e.g., Whale) is to be learned before they are shown the actual to-be-learned target (e.g., Mammal), their later cued recall (e.g., Whale: __?__) of the target word is enhanced, versus a pure study condition (e.g., Whale: Mammal), even when the predicted associate differs from the target associate and the total time is equated in the test and the study conditions. More specifically, using 8 seconds to generate a response that turns out to be wrong ("Dolphin," say, in response to the cue Whale), followed by 5 seconds studying the correct response, produces better recall than does studying the correct response for 13 seconds. Significantly, when Huelser & Metcalfe (2012) asked participants, after the final test, which condition, the study or test condition, helped them most to learn the pairs, they said the study condition, even after their own recall performance went in the other direction. Using a somewhat different procedure, Richland et al. (2009) found that long-term learning benefited when participants were asked questions that they could not answer prior to studying text materials.

Making errors appears to create opportunities for learning and, surprisingly, that seems particularly true when errors are made with high confidence. Butterfield & Metcalfe (2001) found that feedback was especially effective when it followed errors made with high confidence versus errors made with low confidence, a finding they labeled a hypercorrection effect. It is an effect that has now been replicated many times (e.g., Butler et al. 2011, Metcalfe & Finn 2011), including at retention intervals long enough to be educationally realistic.

From the standpoint of becoming sophisticated as a learner, the basic message is that making errors and struggling, rather than being simply discouraging, should also be viewed as important opportunities for learning.

Overattributing Differences in Performance to Innate Differences in Ability

There is, in our view, an overappreciation in our society of the role played by innate differences among individuals in determining what can be learned and how much can be learned, and that overappreciation is coupled with an underappreciation of the power of training, practice, and experience. This combination of overappreciating innate differences and underappreciating the roles of effort and practice can lead individuals to assume that there are certain limits on what they can learn, resulting in an underestimation of their own capacity to learn. Basically, to use Dweck's (2006) terms, learners need to have a growth mindset, not a fixed mindset. Differences between individuals do matter, but mostly because new learning builds on old learning, so the level of old learning an individual brings to new learning really matters, and because our personal family and cultural histories have a profound effect on our aspirations and expectations with respect to learning.

Assuming That Learning Should Be Easy

Finally, another common assumption that can be counterproductive is that learning can be, and should be, easy. Such an assumption is fueled by various "made-easy" self-help books, by the common assumption that it important to increase performance in classrooms (when doing so can actually damage long-term learning), and by the idea that we each have our own style of learning. The very influential styles-of-learning idea involves what Pashler et al. (2009) labeled a meshing hypothesis—namely, that learning will be effective and easy if material is presented to the learner in a way that meshes with his or her learning style. In their review of the existing evidence, Pashler et al. could find no support for the meshing hypothesis and even found some evidence that suggests the opposite—that, for example, someone with high visual/spatial ability scores may profit most from verbal instruction, whereas the converse may be true for individuals testing high for verbal abilities.

Our review suggests that effective learning can be fun, it can be rewarding, and it can save time, but it is seldom easy. The most effective cognitive processes involve some effort by the learner—to notice connections and linkages, to come up with examples and counterexamples, to generate and retrieve, and so forth. In short, effective learning requires the active participation of the learner.

CONCLUDING COMMENTS ON SOME FREQUENTLY ASKED HOW-TO-STUDY QUESTIONS

As teachers and researchers interested in improving student learning, we have compiled a list of frequently asked questions. We have tried to select questions that are on students' minds, which means the questions do not mesh perfectly with the principles discussed in this article. To conclude this review, we consider some of these questions and how we might answer them given current research on students' metacognitive and self-regulated learning.

"What Is the Format of the Upcoming Test?"

This may be the most common question students ask. It can annoy teachers because it is not about content, similar to the question "Will that be on the test?" It is, however, an insightful question from the standpoint of self-regulated learning because it implies that the student wants to regulate his or her own learning—and will presumably study differently depending on whether the test will have, say, a multiple-choice versus an essay format. For the former, they may decide to simply skim the relevant materials, whereas for the latter, they may attempt practice testing because doing so reflects essay writing. Unfortunately, the question posed in this manner further highlights misconceptions students have about learning, because regardless of whether the test is multiple choice or essay, the students will retain the sought-after information better if they actively participate in learning, such as by elaborating on the to-be-learned material and by using self-testing (although knowing what type of test to expect can increase students' grades; Lundeberg & Fox 1991). Thus, the answer we often give is that you will do best if you assume the exam will require that you truly understand, and can produce from memory, the sought-after information, whether doing so involves recalling facts, answering comprehension questions, or solving problems.

"I Study by Copying My Notes. Is That a Good Idea?"

The answer to this question depends on what is meant by copying. Because verbatim copying is a passive process, it is also not very effective. Rewriting one's notes, however, or reorganizing them, exercises active organizational and elaborative processing, which all introductory psychology students should know from their textbook is valuable (e.g., Schacter et al. 2011). Studying one's notes and then trying to reproduce them without the notes being visible is another active process and takes advantage of the learning benefits of retrieval practice. The answer to this question, therefore, requires finding out exactly what the students in question do when they copy their notes.

"Does Cramming Work?"

A reflexive "no" seems the right answer to this question, but even in this case the answer is not so straightforward. For one thing, if the student doesn't know the material the day before the exam, cramming will produce a better outcome than will not cramming. The best answer to this question is probably "Work for what?" If the student's goal is merely to obtain enough information to pass (or even do well on) an upcoming test, then cramming may work fine. There is even a subset of students who do well in school who frequently cram for tests (e.g., Hartwig & Dunlosky 2012). Massing study sessions, though bad in the long-term, can yield good recall at a short retention interval, even better than spacing study sessions under some circumstances (e.g., Rawson & Kintsch 2005). If, however, a student's goal is to retain what they learn for a longer period of time (e.g., until they take a more advanced course on the same topic), cramming is very ineffective compared to other techniques. If good performance on an upcoming test and good long-term retention is the goal, then students should study ahead of time and space their learning sessions across days, and then study the night before the exam (e.g., Kornell 2009, Rawson & Dunlosky 2011). Teachers, of course, can use homework assignments, weekly exams, and comprehensive finals to encourage such spaced studying.

"I Did So Much Worse Than I Expected. What Happened?"

As summarized in our review, there are many ways to overestimate one's learning, and some of us consistently overestimate our preparedness for exams. Two routes to such overestimation, as discussed previously in this review, are hindsight bias, looking at to-be-tested material and thinking that it was known all along, and foresight bias, not being aware that when the answer is not present and required on the test other possible answers will come to mind. Perhaps the best answer to this question is a simple one: Take a meaningful self-test without checking the answers until you are done. Only then can you be confident that you know the information (and even then, forgetting can still occur).

"How Much Time Should I Spend Studying?"

This is actually a question students never ask, but perhaps should. Simply spending a lot of time studying is not enough, because that time can be spent very unproductively, but students cannot excel without both (a) studying effectively and (b) spending enough time doing so. Compounding the problem, it is difficult to monitor one's own study time—because study sessions, even attending class, can include email, online shopping, social networks, YouTube, and so on.

"How Should I Study To Get Good Grades and Succeed in School?"

This question is truly basic and there is much to say in response, though not any single answer. Some strategies, such as self-testing and spacing of practice, do seem generally effective across a broad set of materials and contexts, but many strategies are not so broadly effective and will not always be useful. It makes sense to summarize what one is reading, for example, yet writing summaries does not always benefit learning and comprehension and is less effective for students who have difficulty writing summaries (Dunlosky et al. 2012). Moreover, summarizing a physics problem set may not be appropriate. Studying with other students may be effective if done well (e.g., if students take turns testing one another and providing feedback), but certainly will not work well if such a session turns into a social event or one group member takes the lead and everyone else becomes a passive observer.

As we hope this final section emphasizes, the answers to the questions students tend to ask are seldom simple, and for a good reason: There is much to learn about learning.

SUMMARY POINTS

1. Our complex and rapidly changing world increasingly requires self-initiated and self-managed learning, not simply during the years associated with formal schooling, but across the lifespan.

2. Learning how to learn is, therefore, a critical survival tool, but research on learning, memory, and metacognitive processes has demonstrated that learners are prone to intuitions and beliefs about learning that can impair, rather than enhance, their effectiveness as learners.

3. Becoming sophisticated as a learner requires not only acquiring a basic understanding of the encoding and retrieval processes that characterize the storage and subsequent access to the to-be-learned knowledge and procedures, but also knowing what learning activities and techniques support long-term retention and transfer.

4. Managing one's ongoing learning effectively requires accurate monitoring of the degree to which learning has been achieved, coupled with appropriate selection and control of one's learning activities in response to that monitoring.

5. Assessing whether learning has been achieved is difficult because conditions that enhance performance during learning can fail to support long-term retention and transfer, whereas other conditions that appear to create difficulties and slow the acquisition process can enhance long-term retention and transfer.

6. Learners' judgments of their own degree of learning are also influenced by subjective indices, such as the sense of fluency in perceiving or recalling to-be-learned information, but such fluency can be a product of low-level priming and other factors that are unrelated to whether learning has been achieved.

7. Becoming maximally effective as a learner requires interpreting errors and mistakes as an essential component of effective learning rather than as a reflection of one's inadequacies as a learner.

8. To be maximally effective also requires an appreciation of the incredible capacity humans have to learn and avoiding the mindset that one's learning abilities are fixed.

FUTURE ISSUES

With respect to how learners should optimize the self-regulation of their learning, there remain key issues, both theoretical and applied. We touched on some theoretical issues in sidebars, and we list some applied issues below.

1. What mixture of formal instruction and educational experiences is maximally effective in getting learners to understand how to learn? (For starters, see Morisano et al. 2010.)

2. Why does the retrieval practice triggered by testing have such significant effects on learning and how might those effects be maximized by teachers in classrooms and by learners on their own? (For starters, see Halamish & Bjork 2011, Kornell et al. 2011a, Pyc & Rawson 2010.)

3. How can teachers become better at monitoring their students' long-term learning or lack thereof? (For starters, see Duffy et al. 2009.)

4. Does the act of making metacognitive judgments, such as predicting future performance, enhance later test performance and, possibly, the effectiveness of subsequent study opportunities? If so, what judgments should students make to maximize such effects? (For starters, see McCabe & Soderstrom 2011.)

5. Accurate monitoring of learning is a crucial component of effective self-regulation of learning, but students have difficulties in monitoring their learning and comprehension of complex materials. What scaffolds can students use to ensure high levels of monitoring accuracy for complex materials? (For starters, see Dunlosky & Lipko 2007, Thiede et al. 2009.)

6. Why and when does making errors potentiate subsequent learning? Recent findings suggest that errors can facilitate the effectiveness of subsequent learning opportunities, but other findings suggest that there are circumstances in which producing errors propagates those errors. (For starters, see Grimaldi & Karpicke 2012, Kornell et al. 2009.)

DISCLOSURE STATEMENT

The authors are not aware of any affiliations, memberships, funding, or financial holdings that might be perceived as affecting the objectivity of this review.

LITERATURE CITED

Alter AL, Oppenheimer DM. 2009. Uniting the tribes of fluency to form a metacognitive nation. *Pers. Soc. Psychol. Rev.* 13:219–35

Anderson MC, Bjork RA, Bjork EL. 1994. Remembering can cause forgetting: retrieval dynamics in long-term memory. *J. Exp. Psychol.: Learn. Mem. Cogn.* 20:1063–87

Ariel R, Dunlosky J, Bailey H. 2009. Agenda-based regulation of study-time allocation: when agendas override item-based monitoring. *J. Exp. Psychol.: Gen.* 138:432–47

Atkinson RC. 1972. Optimizing the learning of a second-language vocabulary. *J. Exp. Psychol.* 96:124–29

Bahrick HP. 1979. Maintenance of knowledge: questions about memory we forgot to ask. *J. Exp. Psychol.: Gen.* 108:296–308

Bartlett FC. 1932. *Remembering: A Study in Experimental and Social Psychology.* New York: Cambridge Univ. Press

Benjamin AS, Bird RD. 2006. Metacognitive control of the spacing of study repetitions. *J. Mem. Lang.* 55:126–37

Benjamin AS, Bjork RA. 1996. Retrieval fluency as a metacognitive index. In *Implicit Memory and Metacognition*, ed. LM Reder, pp. 309–38. Mahwah, NJ: Erlbaum

Benjamin AS, Bjork RA, Schwartz BL. 1998. The mismeasure of memory: when retrieval fluency is misleading as a metamnemonic index. *J. Exp. Psychol.: Gen.* 127:55–68

Bjork EL, Bjork RA. 2011. Making things hard on yourself, but in a good way: creating desirable difficulties to enhance learning. In *Psychology and the Real World: Essays Illustrating Fundamental Contributions to Society*, ed. MA Gernsbacher, RW Pew, LM Hough, JR Pomerantz, pp. 56–64. New York: Worth

Bjork RA. 1975. Retrieval as a memory modifier. In *Information Processing and Cognition: The Loyola Symposium*, ed. R Solso, pp. 123–44. Hillsdale, NJ: Erlbaum

Bjork RA. 1994. Memory and metamemory considerations in the training of human beings. In *Metacognition: Knowing About Knowing*, ed. J Metcalfe, A Shimamura, pp. 185–205. Cambridge, MA: MIT Press

Bjork RA. 2011. On the symbiosis of remembering, forgetting and learning. In *Successful Remembering and Successful Forgetting: A Festschrift in Honor of Robert A. Bjork*, ed. AS Benjamin, pp. 1–22. London: Psychol. Press

Bjork RA, Bjork EL. 1992. A new theory of disuse and an old theory of stimulus fluctuation. In *From Learning Processes to Cognitive Processes: Essays in Honor of William K. Estes*, ed. A Healy, S Kosslyn, R Shiffrin, vol. 2, pp. 35–67. Hillsdale, NJ: Erlbaum

Butler AC, Fazio LK, Marsh EJ. 2011. The hypercorrection effect persists over a week, but high-confidence errors return. *Psychon. Bull. Rev.* 18:1238–44

Butterfield B, Metcalfe J. 2001. Errors committed with high confidence are hypercorrected. *J. Exp. Psychol.: Learn. Mem. Cogn.* 27:1491–94

Carpenter SK. 2011. Semantic information activated during retrieval contributes to later retention: support for the mediator effectiveness hypothesis of the testing effect. *J. Exp. Psychol.: Learn. Mem. Cogn.* 37:1547–52

Castel AD, McCabe DP, Roediger H. 2007. Illusions of competence and overestimation of associative memory for identical items: evidence from judgments of learning. *Psychon. Bull. Rev.* 14:107–11

Cepeda NJ, Pashler H, Vul E, Wixted JT, Rohrer D. 2006. Distributed practice in verbal recall tasks: a review and quantitative synthesis. *Psychol. Bull.* 132:354–80

Cohen MS, Halamish V, Bjork RA. 2011. *Learners fail to appreciate benefits of longer spacings over shorter spacings in repeated practice.* Poster presented at Annu. Meet. Psychon. Soc., 52nd, Seattle, Wash.

Credé M, Phillips L. 2011. A meta-analytic review of the motivated strategies for learning questionnaire. *Learn. Individ. Differ.* 21:337–46

Dempster FN. 1996. Distributing and managing the conditions of encoding and practice. In *Memory*, ed. R Bjork, E Bjork, pp. 317–44. San Diego, CA: Academic

Diemand-Yauman C, Oppenheimer DM, Vaughan EB. 2011. Fortune favors the bold (and the italicized): effects of disfluency on educational outcomes. *Cognition* 118:114–18

Duffy GG, Miller S, Parsons S, Meloth M. 2009. Teachers as metacogntive professionals. In *Handbook of Metacognition in Education*, ed. DJ Hacker, J Dunlosky, AC Graesser, pp. 240–56. New York: Taylor & Francis

Dunlosky J, Ariel R. 2011a. Self-regulated learning and the allocation of study time. In *The Psychology of Learning and Motivation: Advances in Research and Theory*, vol. 54, ed. BH Ross, pp. 103–40. San Diego, CA: Elsevier

Dunlosky J, Ariel R. 2011b. The influence of agenda-based and habitual processes on item selection during study. *J. Exp. Psychol.: Learn. Mem. Cogn.* 37:899–912

Dunlosky J, Lipko A. 2007. Metacomprehension: a brief history and how to improve its accuracy. *Curr. Dir. Psychol. Sci.* 16:228–32

Dunlosky J, Nelson TO. 1992. Importance of the kind of cue for judgments of learning (JOL) and the delayed JOL effect. *Mem. Cogn.* 20:374–80

Dunlosky J, Nelson TO. 1994. Does the sensitivity of judgments of learning (JOLs) to the effects of various study activities depend on when the JOLs occur? *J. Mem. Lang.* 33:545–65

Dunlosky J, Rawson KA. 2012. Overconfidence produces underachievement: inaccurate self evaluations undermine students' learning and retention. *Learn. Instr.* 22:271–80

Dunlosky J, Rawson KA, Marsh EJ, Nathan MJ, Willingham DT. 2012. Improving students' learning with effective learning techniques: promising directions from cognitive and educational psychology. *Psychol. Sci. Public Interest.* In press

Dunlosky J, Serra M, Baker JMC. 2007. Metamemory applied. In *Handbook of Applied Cognition*, ed. FT Durso, RS Nickerson, ST Dumais, S Lewandowsky, TJ Perfect, pp. 137–59. New York: Wiley. 2nd ed.

Dunlosky J, Thiede KW. 1998. What makes people study more? An evaluation of factors that affect people's self-paced study and yield "labor-and-gain" effects. *Acta Psychol.* 98:37–56

Dweck CS. 2006. *Mindset.* New York: Random House

Finn B, Metcalfe J. 2007. The role of memory for past test in the underconfidence with practice effect. *J. Exp. Psychol.: Learn. Mem. Cogn.* 33:238–44

Finn B, Metcalfe J. 2008. Judgments of learning are influenced by memory for past test. *J. Mem. Lang.* 58:19–34

Fischhoff B. 1975. Hindsight is not equal to foresight: the effects of outcome knowledge on judgment under uncertainty. *J. Exp. Psychol.: Hum. Percept. Perform.* 1:288–99

Fritz CO, Morris PE, Bjork RA, Gelman R, Wickens TD. 2000. When further learning fails: stability and change following repeated presentation of text. *Br. J. Psychol.* 91:493–511

Grimaldi PJ, Karpicke JD. 2012. When and why do retrieval attempts enhance subsequent encoding? *Mem. Cogn.* 40:505–13

Gurung RAR, Weidert J, Jeske A. 2010. Focusing on how students study. *J. Scholars. Teach. Learn.* 10:28–35

Halamish V, Bjork RA. 2011. When does testing enhance retention? A distribution-based interpretation of retrieval as a memory modifier. *J. Exp. Psychol.: Learn. Mem. Cogn.* 37:801–12

Hart JT. 1965. Memory and the feeling-of-knowing experience. *J. Educ. Psychol.* 56:208–16

Hartwig MK, Dunlosky J. 2012. Study strategies of college students: Are self-testing and scheduling related to achievement? *Psychon. Bull. Rev.* 19:126–34

Hays M, Kornell N, Bjork RA. 2012. When and why a failed test potentiates the effectiveness of subsequent study. *J. Exp. Psychol: Learn. Mem. Cogn.* In press

Hertzog C, Dunlosky J, Robinson AE, Kidder DP. 2003. Encoding fluency is a cue used for judgments about learning. *J. Exp. Psychol: Learn. Mem. Cogn.* 29:22–34

Huelser BJ, Metcalfe J. 2012. Making related errors facilitates learning, but learners do not know it. *Mem. Cogn.* 40:514–27

Jacoby LL. 1978. On interpreting the effects of repetition: solving a problem versus remembering a solution. *J. Verbal Learn. Verbal Behav.* 17:649–67

Jacoby LL, Kelley CM. 1987. Unconscious influences of memory for a prior event. *Pers. Soc. Psychol. Bull.* 13:314–36

Jacoby LL, Kelley CM, Dywan J. 1989. Memory attributions. In *Varieties of Memory and Consciousness: Essays in Honour of Endel Tulving*, ed. H Roediger, FM Craik, pp. 391–422. Hillsdale, NJ: Erlbaum

Kang SK, Pashler H. 2012. Learning painting styles: spacing is advantageous when it promotes discriminative contrast. *Appl. Cogn. Psychol.* 26:97–103

Karpicke JD. 2009. Metacognitive control and strategy selection: deciding to practice retrieval during learning. *J. Exp. Psychol.: Gen.* 138:469–86

Karpicke JD, Butler AC, Roediger H. 2009. Metacognitive strategies in student learning: Do students practise retrieval when they study on their own? *Memory* 17:471–79

Kelley CM, Jacoby LL. 1996. Adult egocentrism: subjective experience versus analytic bases for judgment. *J. Mem. Lang.* 35:157–75

Kelley CM, Lindsay DS. 1993. Remembering mistaken for knowing: ease of retrieval as a basis for confidence in answers to general knowledge questions. *J. Mem. Lang.* 32:1–24

Kelley CM, Rhodes MG. 2002. Making sense and nonsense of experience: attributions in memory and judgment. In *The Psychology of Learning and Motivation: Advances in Research and Theory*, vol. 41, ed. H Ross, pp. 293–320. San Diego, CA: Academic

Kimball DR, Metcalfe J. 2003. Delaying judgments of learning affects memory, not metamemory. *Mem. Cogn.* 31:918–29

King JF, Zechmeister EB, Shaughnessy JJ. 1980. Judgments of knowing: the influence of retrieval practice. *Am. J. Psychol.* 93:329–43

Knight JB, Hunter Ball B, Brewer GA, DeWitt MR, March RL. 2012. Testing unsuccessfully: a specification of the underlying mechanisms supporting its influence on retention. *J. Mem. Lang.* 66:731–46

Koriat A. 1993. How do we know that we know? The accessibility model of the feeling of knowing. *Psychol. Rev.* 100:609–39

Koriat A. 1997. Monitoring one's own knowledge during study: a cue-utilization approach to judgments of learning. *J. Exp. Psychol.: Gen.* 126:349–70

Koriat A, Bjork RA. 2005. Illusions of competence in monitoring one's knowledge during study. *J. Exp. Psychol.: Learn. Mem. Cogn.* 31:187–94

Koriat A, Bjork RA, Sheffer L, Bar SK. 2004. Predicting one's own forgetting: the role of experience-based and theory-based processes. *J. Exp. Psychol.: Gen.* 133:643–56

Kornell N. 2009. Optimizing learning using flashcards: Spacing is more effective than cramming. *Appl. Cogn. Psychol.* 23:1297–317

Kornell N. 2011. Failing to predict future changes in memory: A stability bias yields long-term overconfidence. In *Successful Remembering and Successful Forgetting: A Festschrift in Honor of Robert A. Bjork*, ed. AS Benjamin, pp. 365–86. New York: Psychol. Press

Kornell N. 2012. A stability bias in human memory. In *Encyclopedia of the Sciences of Learning*, ed. N Seel, pp. 4–7. New York: Springer

Kornell N, Bjork RA. 2007. The promise and perils of self-regulated study. *Psychon. Bull. Rev.* 6:219–24

Kornell N, Bjork RA. 2008a. Learning concepts and categories: Is spacing the "enemy of induction"? *Psychol. Sci.* 19:585–92

Kornell N, Bjork RA. 2008b. Optimising self-regulated study: the benefits—and costs—of dropping flashcards. *Memory* 16:125–36

Kornell N, Bjork RA. 2009. A stability bias in human memory: overestimating remembering and underestimating learning. *J. Exp. Psychol.: Gen.* 138:449–68

Kornell N, Bjork RA, Garcia MA. 2011a. Why tests appear to prevent forgetting: a distribution-based bifurcation model. *J. Mem. Lang.* 65:85–97

Kornell N, Castel AD, Eich TS, Bjork RA. 2010. Spacing as the friend of both memory and induction in young and older adults. *Psychol. Aging* 25:498–503

Kornell N, Hays MJ, Bjork RA. 2009. Unsuccessful retrieval attempts enhance subsequent learning. *J. Exp. Psychol.: Learn. Mem. Cogn.* 35:989–98

Kornell N, Metcalfe J. 2006. Study efficacy and the region of proximal learning framework. *J. Exp. Psychol.: Learn. Mem. Cogn.* 32:609–22

Kornell N, Rhodes MG, Castel AD, Tauber SK. 2011b. The ease of processing heuristic and the stability bias: dissociating memory, memory beliefs, and memory judgments. *Psychol. Sci.* 22:787–94

Kornell N, Son LK. 2009. Learners' choices and beliefs about self-testing. *Memory* 17:493–501

Landauer TK, Bjork RA. 1978. Optimum rehearsal patterns and name learning. In *Practical Aspects of Memory*, ed. MM Gruneberg, PE Morris, RN Sykes, pp. 625–32. London: Academic

Lee TD. 2012. Contextual interference: generalizability and limitations. In *Skill Acquisition in Sport: Research, Theory, and Practice II*, ed. NJ Hodges, AM Williams, pp. 79–93. London: Routledge

Little JL, Bjork EL, Bjork RA, Angello G. 2012. Multiple-choice tests exonerated, at least of some charges: fostering test-induced learning and avoiding test-induced forgetting. *Psychol. Sci.* In press

Lundeberg MA, Fox PW. 1991. Do laboratory findings on test expectancy generalize to classroom outcomes? *Rev. Educ. Res.* 61:94–106

Matvey G, Dunlosky J, Guttentag R. 2001. Fluency of retrieval at study affects judgments of learning (JOLs): an analytic or nonanalytic basis for JOLs? *Mem. Cogn.* 29:222–33

McCabe DP, Soderstrom NC. 2011. Recollection-based prospective metamemory judgments are more accurate than those based on confidence: judgments of remembering and knowing (JORKs). *J. Exp. Psychol.: Gen.* 140:605–21

McCabe JA. 2011. Metacognitive awareness of learning strategies in undergraduates. *Mem. Cogn.* 39:462–76

McNamara DS. 2010. Strategies to read and learn: overcoming learning by consumption. *Med. Educ.* 44:340–46

Metcalfe J. 2009. Metacognitive judgments and control of study. *Curr. Dir. Psychol. Sci.* 18:159–63

Metcalfe J, Finn B. 2008. Evidence that judgments of learning are causally related to study choice. *Psychon. Bull. Rev.* 15:174–79

Metcalfe J, Finn B. 2011. People's hypercorrection of high-confidence errors: Did they know it all along? *J. Exp. Psychol.: Learn. Mem. Cogn.* 37:437–48

Metcalfe J, Kornell N. 2005. A region of proximal learning model of study time allocation. *J. Mem. Lang.* 52:463–77

Miele DB, Finn B, Molden DC. 2011. Does easily learned mean easily remembered? It depends on your beliefs about intelligence. *Psychol. Sci.* 22:320–24

Morisano D, Hirsh JB, Peterson JB, Pihl RO, Shore BM. 2010. Setting, elaborating, and reflecting on personal goals improves academic performance. *J. Appl. Psychol.* 95:255–64

Nelson TO, Dunlosky J. 1991. When people's judgments of learning (JOLs) are extremely accurate at predicting subsequent recall: the "delayed-JOL effect." *Psychol. Sci.* 2:267–70

Nelson TO, Narens L. 1990. Metamemory: a theoretical framework and new findings. In *The Psychology of Learning and Motivation*, vol. 26, ed. GH Bower, pp. 125–73. New York: Academic

Oppenheimer DM. 2008. The secret life of fluency. *Trends Cogn. Sci.* 12:237–41

Pashler H, McDaniel M, Rohrer D, Bjork RA. 2009. Learning styles: concepts and evidence. *Psychol. Sci. Public Interest* 3:105–19

Pintrich PR, Smith DAF, Garcia T, McKeachie WJ. 1993. Reliability and predictive validity of the motivated strategies for learning questionnaire (MSLQ). *Educ. Psychol. Meas.* 53:801–3

Pyc MA, Dunlosky J. 2010. Toward an understanding of students' allocation of study time: Why do they decide to mass or space their practice? *Mem. Cogn.* 38:431–40

Pyc MA, Rawson KA. 2009. Testing the retrieval effort hypothesis: Does greater difficulty correctly recalling information lead to higher levels of memory? *J. Mem. Lang.* 60:437–47

Pyc MA, Rawson KA. 2010. Why testing improves memory: mediator effectiveness hypothesis. *Science* 330:335

Pyc MA, Rawson KA. 2012. Why is test–restudy practice beneficial for memory? An evaluation of the mediator shift hypothesis. *J. Exp. Psychol.: Learn. Mem. Cogn.* 38:737–46

Rawson KA, Dunlosky J. 2011. Optimizing schedules of retrieval practice for durable and efficient learning: How much is enough? *J. Exp. Psychol.: Gen.* 140:283–302

Rawson KA, Dunlosky J, McDonald SL. 2002. Influences of metamemory on performance predictions for text. *Q. J. Exp. Psychol.* 55A:505–24

Rawson KA, Kintsch W. 2005. Rereading effects depend on time of test. *J. Educ. Psychol.* 97:70–80

Reder LM. 1987. Strategy selection in question answering. *Cogn. Psychol.* 19:90–138

Reder LM. 1996. Different research programs on metacognition: Are the boundaries imaginary? *Learn. Individ. Differ.* 8:383–90

Rhodes MG, Castel AD. 2008. Memory predictions are influenced by perceptual information: evidence for metacognitive illusions. *J. Exp. Psychol.: Gen.* 137:615–25

Rhodes MG, Castel AD. 2009. Metacognitive illusions for auditory information: effects on monitoring and control. *Psychon. Bull. Rev.* 16:550–54

Rhodes MG, Tauber SK. 2011. The influence of delaying judgments of learning on metacognitive accuracy: a meta-analytic review. *Psychol. Bull.* 137:131–48

Richland LE, Kornell N, Kao LS. 2009. The pretesting effect: Do unsuccessful retrieval attempts enhance learning? *J. Exp. Psychol: Appl.* 15:243–57

Roediger HL, Butler AC. 2011. The critical role of retrieval practice in long-term retention. *Trends Cogn. Sci.* 15:20–27

Roediger HL, Karpicke JD. 2006. The power of testing memory: basic research and implications for educational practice. *Perspect. Psychol. Sci.* 1:181–210

Rohrer D, Taylor K. 2006. The effects of overlearning and distributed practice on the retention of mathematics knowledge. *Appl. Cogn. Psychol.* 20:1209–24

Rohrer D, Taylor K. 2007. The shuffling of mathematics problems improves learning. *Instr. Sci.* 35:481–98

Schacter DL, Gilbert DT, Wegner DM. 2011. *Psychology*. New York: Worth. 2nd ed.

Schwartz BL, Benjamin AS, Bjork RA. 1997. The inferential and experiential basis of metamemory. *Curr. Dir. Psychol. Sci.* 6:132–37

Schwarz N. 2004. Metacognitive experiences in consumer judgment and decision making. *J. Consumer Psychol.* 14:332–48

Serra MJ, Dunlosky J. 2005. Does retrieval fluency contribute to the underconfidence-with-practice effect? *J. Exp. Psychol.: Learn. Mem. Cogn.* 31:1258–66

Shaw J. 1996. Increases in eyewitness confidence resulting from postevent questioning. *J. Exp. Psychol.: Appl.* 2:126–46

Simon DA, Bjork RA. 2001. Metacognition in motor learning. *J. Exp. Psychol.: Learn. Mem. Cogn.* 27:907–12

Smith SM, Glenberg AM, Bjork RA. 1978. Environmental context and human memory. *Mem. Cogn.* 6:342–53

Smith SM, Rothkopf EZ. 1984. Contextual enrichment and distribution of practice in the classroom. *Cogn. Instr.* 1:341–58

Son LK. 2004. Spacing one's study: evidence for a metacognitive control strategy. *J. Exp. Psychol.: Learn. Mem. Cogn.* 30:601–4

Son LK. 2010. Metacognitive control and the spacing effect. *J. Exp. Psychol.: Learn. Mem. Cogn.* 36:255–62

Son LK, Kornell N. 2008. Research on the allocation of study time: key studies from 1890 to the present (and beyond). In *A Handbook of Memory and Metamemory*, ed. J Dunlosky, RA Bjork, pp. 333–51. Hillsdale, NJ: Psychol. Press

Son LK, Kornell N. 2009. Simultaneous decisions at study: time allocation, ordering, and spacing. *Metacogn. Learn.* 4:237–48

Son LK, Metcalfe J. 2000. Metacognitive and control strategies in study-time allocation. *J. Exp. Psychol.: Learn. Mem. Cogn.* 26:204–21

Spellman BA, Bjork RA. 1992. When predictions create reality: Judgments of learning may alter what they are intended to assess. *Psychol. Sci.* 3:315–16

Taraban R, Maki WS, Rynearson K. 1999. Measuring study time distributions: implications for designing computer-based courses. *Behav. Res. Methods Instrum. Comput.* 31:263–69

Tauber SK, Dunlosky J, Rawson KA, Wahlheim CN, Jacoby LJ. 2012. Self-regulated learning of a natural category: Do people interleave or block exemplars during study? In press

Taylor K, Rohrer D. 2010. The effects of interleaved practice. *Appl. Cogn. Psychol.* 24:837–48

Thiede KW. 1999. The importance of accurate monitoring and effective self-regulation during multitrial learning. *Psychon. Bull. Rev.* 6:662–67

Thiede KW, Dunlosky J. 1999. Toward a general model of self-regulated study: an analysis of selection of items for study and self-paced study time. *J. Exp. Psychol.: Learn. Mem. Cogn.* 25:1024–37

Thiede KW, Griffin TD, Wiley J, Redford JS. 2009. Metacognitive monitoring during and after reading. In *Handbook of Metacognition in Education*, ed. DJ Hacker, J Dunlosky, AC Graesser, pp. 85–106. New York: Taylor & Francis

Toppino TC, Cohen MS. 2010. Metacognitive control and spaced practice: clarifying what people do and why. *J. Exp. Psychol.: Learn. Mem. Cogn.* 36:1480–91

Toppino TC, Cohen MS, Davis M, Moors AC. 2009. Metacognitive control over distribution of practice: When is spacing preferred? *J. Exp. Psychol.: Learn. Mem. Cogn.* 35:1352–58

Vaughn KE, Rawson KA. 2011. Diagnosing criterion-level effects on memory: What aspects of memory are enhanced by repeated retrieval? *Psychol. Sci.* 22:1127–31

Vaughn KE, Rawson KA. 2012. When is guessing incorrectly better than studying for enhancing memory? *Psychon. Bull. Rev.* In press

Wahlheim CN, Dunlosky J, Jacoby LL. 2011. Spacing enhances the learning of natural concepts: an investigation of mechanisms, metacognition, and aging. *Mem. Cogn.* 39:750–63

Wahlheim CN, Finn B, Jacoby LL. 2012. Metacognitive judgments of repetition and variability effects in natural concept learning: evidence for variability neglect. *Mem. Cogn.* 40:703–16

Whitten WB, Bjork RA. 1977. Learning from tests: effects of spacing. *J. Verbal Learn. Verbal Behav.* 16:465–78

Wissman KT, Rawson KA, Pyc MA. 2012. How and when do students use flashcards? *Memory* 6:568–79

Zaromb FM, Roediger H. 2010. The testing effect in free recall is associated with enhanced organizational processes. *Mem. Cogn.* 38:995–1008

Zechmeister EB, Shaughnessy JJ. 1980. When you know that you know and when you think that you know but you don't. *Bull. Psychon. Soc.* 15:41–44

Zulkiply N, McLean J, Burt JS, Bath D. 2012. Spacing and induction: application to exemplars presented as auditory and visual text. *Learn. Instr.* 22:215–21

Student Learning: What Has Instruction Got to Do With It?

Hee Seung Lee and John R. Anderson

Department of Psychology, Carnegie Mellon University, Pittsburgh, Pennsylvania 15213;
email: heeseung@andrew.cmu.edu, ja@cmu.edu

Annu. Rev. Psychol. 2013. 64:445–69

First published online as a Review in Advance on
July 12, 2012

The *Annual Review of Psychology* is online at
psych.annualreviews.org

This article's doi:
10.1146/annurev-psych-113011-143833

Keywords

discovery learning, direct instruction, instructional guidance,
explanation, worked-examples

Abstract

A seemingly unending controversy in the field of instruction science
concerns how much instructional guidance needs to be provided in
a learning environment. At the one extreme lies the claim that it is
important for students to explore and construct knowledge for themselves, which is often called discovery learning, and at the other extreme
lies the claim that providing direct instruction is more beneficial than
withholding it. In this article, evidence and arguments that support
either of the approaches are reviewed. Also, we review how different
instructional approaches interact with other instructional factors that
have been known to be important, such as individual difference, self-
explanation, and comparison. The efforts to combine different instructional approaches suggest alternative ways to conceive of learning and
to test it.

Contents

INTRODUCTION

Learning results from what the student does and thinks, and only from what the student does and thinks. The teacher can advance learning only by influencing what the student does to learn.

Herbert A. Simon (1916–2001)

In the field of learning science, many efforts have been made to find optimal instructional conditions to promote student learning. As suggested by Herbert Simon, one of the founders of cognitive science, educators must understand how students learn and then translate this understanding into practice when designing a learning environment.

THE DEBATE OVER DISCOVERY LEARNING

A seemingly unending controversy in the field of instruction science concerns how much instructional guidance needs to be provided in a learning environment (Kirschner et al. 2006, Kuhn 2007, Tobias & Duffy 2009). Is it better to try to tell students what they need to know, or is it better to give students an opportunity to discover the knowledge for themselves? Conceiving of this problem as deciding whether to give or withhold assistance, Koedinger & Aleven (2007) called this issue the "assistance dilemma." The contrast between the two positions is best understood as a continuum, and both ends appear to have their own strengths and weaknesses. As a result, it is very difficult to find the right balance between the two extremes. The assistance dilemma is also related to the notion of "desirable difficulty" (Bjork 1994, Schmidt & Bjork 1992). Learning conditions that introduce certain difficulties during instruction appear to slow the rate of learning but often lead to better long-term retention and transfer than learning conditions with less difficulty (e.g., mixed- or spaced-practice effect).

In this article, we briefly review older evidence and then focus on the more recent studies on this issue. At one end of the continuum, it is argued that minimizing instruction encourages students to discover or construct knowledge for themselves by allowing students to freely explore learning materials (Bruner 1961, Papert 1980, Steffe & Gale 1995). This approach is based on a constructivist theory of learning, and Jean Piaget (1970, 1973, 1980) has been often referenced as a basis for constructivism. For instance, according to Piaget (1973), "To understand is to discover, or reconstruct by rediscovery, and such conditions must be complied with if in the future individuals are to be formed who are capable of production and creativity and not simply repetition" (p. 20). In a discovery learning environment, students are regarded as active learners and are given opportunities to digest materials for themselves rather than as passive learners who simply follow directions. Discovery-based approaches have been widely accepted as major teaching methods by teachers and educators with constructivist views of learning. In truth, however, most discovery learning environments actually involve some amount of guidance, so this approach might better be referred to as "minimal guidance."

Why has a discovery learning approach been widely advocated by many teachers and researchers? Reiser et al. (1994) summarized possible cognitive and motivational benefits of discovery learning. First, learning through discovery is believed to have several cognitive benefits such as the development of inquiry skills and the utility of learning from errors. Students are thought to have more meaningful understanding over rote learning due to great amounts of self-generating processes and from attempting to explain and understand their mistakes. Generating activity has been known to help long-term retention (Bobrow & Bower 1969, Lovett 1992, Slamecka & Graf 1978). However, these potential cognitive benefits can also be lost when trying to discover the knowledge. For instance, students may not be able to remember how they solved a problem after excessive floundering (Lewis & Anderson 1985). Also, this floundering tends to increase learning time, and students may never be able to discover the important principles that they are expected to learn (Ausubel 1964).

It has been also argued that discovery methods produce benefits for retention and transfer (Bruner 1961, Suchman 1961). To test this proposition, Gutherie (1967) trained students to decipher cryptograms with different forms of instructional methods. Gutherie compared students who were given explicit rules followed by problem practice with students who just tried to solve the problems and had to discover the rules. The discovery students did better on the transfer problems that required new rules. Similarly, McDaniel & Schlager (1990) found that the discovery method provided benefits when students had to generate a new strategy to solve a transfer problem but not when they could apply the learned strategy.

Second, discovery learning is believed to increase students' positive attitudes toward the learning domain (Bruner 1961, Suchman 1961). Learning through exploration allows students to have more control in a task, and this in turn fosters more intrinsic motivation. Intrinsically motivated students are known to find a learning task more rewarding and tend to do more productive cognitive processing in comparison with extrinsically motivated students (Lepper 1988). In addition, it is argued that discovery learning enables students to learn additional facts about the target domain. For instance, when preschool children were given an adult's pedagogical instruction without interruption, they tended to focus on only the target function of a toy that was shown by the adult (Bonawitz et al. 2011). In contrast, when the pedagogical demonstration was experimentally interrupted, children explored the function of the toy more broadly and were more likely to discover novel information.

Despite all the arguments for the benefits of discovery learning, the empirical evidence has been mixed at best. There now have been decades of efforts to dissuade educators of the benefits of discovery learning. For instance, in a 1968 summary of 25 years of research, Ausubel (1968, pp. 497–498) wrote:

> [A]ctual examination of the research literature allegedly supportive of learning by discovery reveals that valid evidence of this nature is virtually nonexistent. It appears that the various enthusiasts of the discovery method have been supporting each other research-wise by taking in each other's laundry, so to speak, that is, by citing each other's opinions and assertions as evidence and by generalizing wildly from equivocal and even negative findings.

Reviewing the more recent research in a paper provocatively titled "Should there be a three-strikes rule against pure discovery?", Mayer (2004, p. 17) concludes:

> Like some zombie that keeps returning from its grave, pure discovery continues to have its advocates. However, anyone who takes an evidence-based approach to educational practice must ask the same question: Where is the evidence that it works? In spite of calls for free discovery in every decade, the supporting evidence is hard to find.

Kirschner et al. (2006), in their similarly provocatively titled paper "Why minimal guidance during instruction does not work: an analysis of the failure of constructivist, discovery, problem-based, experiential, and inquiry-based teaching," come to a similar conclusion. However, as a sign that we do not have an all-or-none decision to make between pure discovery and direct instruction, Mayer (2004) concludes that it is important for students to construct their own knowledge and advocates "guided discovery" as the best way to achieve this. Also, Kirschner et al. acknowledge what they call the "expertise reversal effect" (Kalyuga 2007, Kalyuga et al. 2003), where experienced learners benefit more with low levels of guidance than with high levels of guidance. In this article, we review some of the previous studies that compare many different forms of direct instruction and discovery learning approaches to investigate the effect of different amounts of instructional guidance.

Instructional Design Based on a Constructivist Theory of Learning

Discovery learning is often aligned with what are called constructivist theories of learning, although as Anderson et al. (1998) note, there is a wide variety of constructivist positions, some of which are mutually contradictory. These various positions often suffer from a lack of clear operational definitions and replicable instructional procedures (Klahr & Li 2005).

That qualification being noted, there have been several reports of successful constructivist designs in studies conducted in a school environment (e.g., Carpenter et al. 1998, Cobb et al. 1991, Hiebert & Wearne 1996, Kamii & Dominick 1998, Schwartz et al. 2011).

Cobb and his colleagues (1991) developed a set of instructional activities based on a constructivist view of learning and investigated the effect of the design to help children's mathematical learning. In project classrooms, children used a variety of physical manipulatives and worked in pairs to solve mathematical problems. After working in pairs, a teacher led a whole-class discussion, and the children talked about their interpretations and solutions. At the end of the project, students were given a standardized achievement test and another arithmetic test developed by the project group. The results showed that students in project and nonproject classrooms were not different in terms of the level of computational performance. However, the students in the project classrooms demonstrated higher levels of conceptual understanding than those in the nonproject classrooms. Although the ability to perform computational tasks seemed similar between the groups, closer analysis showed that nonproject students heavily depended on the use of standard algorithms. This dependency was consistent with the beliefs nonproject students demonstrated on the questionnaire asking about reasons for success in mathematics. The nonproject students believed it was important to conform to the solution procedures of others. The project students, however, believed collaborating (explaining their thinking to others) and understanding were important for success in mathematics.

In another study, Hiebert & Wearne (1996) traced children's development of understanding of mathematical concepts and computational skills over the first three years of school in two different instructional environments. To teach place value and multidigit addition and subtraction, they provided students with either conventional instruction or alternative instruction. In the alternative instruction classrooms, students were presented with contextualized problem situations and encouraged to represent problem quantities with physical materials (base-ten blocks) and written numbers. Using both representations, students had to develop solution strategies and were encouraged to discuss their strategies with the class. The standard algorithms for addition and subtraction were not formally taught; instead, students discussed how and why invented procedures did or did not work. On the other hand, in the conventional instruction classroom, the instruction was mainly guided by the textbook. Teachers taught students how to find the answer, and students worked individually. The use of physical manipulatives was not required, so they were not used much. Assessments of mathematical understanding supported superiority of the alternative instruction at the end of the third grade. Also, when the relations between conceptual understanding and computational skill were analyzed, different patterns of development were identified between the two groups. The majority of students who received alternative instruction seemed to show good understanding prior to or concurrent with good computational skill. On the other hand, conventionally instructed students tended to show correct computation skills before they developed good understanding.

As shown in these studies, discovering one's own procedures can lead to better understanding and transfer. Carpenter and his colleagues (1998) investigated how inventing strategies was related to the understanding of mathematical concepts and procedures. In this study, children were traced for three years to assess understanding of concepts and procedures on multidigit addition and subtraction. The study compared students who used an invented strategy with students who used a standard algorithm. Students who invented a strategy were able to use not only their own invented strategy (if asked to do so), but also the standard algorithm after they learned that. Invention students also showed better understanding of base-ten number concepts and better performance in a transfer task. On the other hand,

the algorithm group showed significantly more buggy algorithms in their problem solving than did the invented-strategy group.

Kamii & Dominick (1998) also argued that teaching algorithms could harm understanding of multidigit computation. These investigators compared students who had been taught standard algorithms for multidigit computation with those who had not. The students who did not receive the algorithm instruction outperformed those who were taught algorithms. The algorithm-taught students also tended to produce more unreasonable answers, implying that they depended on the use of learned procedures and lacked a deep conceptual understanding about the computation procedures.

Practice Facilitates Successful Discovery Learning

The studies discussed above were conducted in the classroom, and in this setting it is difficult to control all the factors at play (nor would one want to). Some more-focused laboratory studies suggest that students learn better in a discovery learning environment. Interestingly, these studies are related to high levels of practice. When combined with high levels of practice or longer acquisition time, students appear to learn better in a discovery learning environment than in a direct instruction environment.

Brunstein et al. (2009) investigated how learning improves as students become more experienced through a series of learning sessions under different instructional conditions. Algebra-like problems were constructed in a novel graphical representation, and this novel format allowed studying of solving equations anew in college populations. Participants received different types of instructions according to experimental conditions; students were given verbal direction on general characterization of actions, direct demonstration on what to do, both, or none (discovery condition). Thus, in the discovery condition, participants were provided with none of the guidance, and they had to learn from the consequences of their actions. The results showed that although discovery students showed the worst performance in the early problems by making more errors, they performed best on the later problems by making fewer errors and taking shorter problem-solving time in comparison with the other-instructed students. Also, in the later phase of learning, students in the discovery learning condition showed the best performance, regardless of the position of the problems.

In their second study, Brunstein and her colleagues (2009) obtained quite different results when students only had one-quarter of the problems to practice on. About 50% of the participants in the discovery condition felt lost and wanted to quit the study, whereas none had quit in the first study. The remaining discovery participants did worse than those who received direct instruction. Comparing findings from the first and second study, the discovery learning approach appeared to be effective only with high levels of practice. Without this practice to consolidate their understanding, students in the discovery condition had an especially hard time in understanding problems.

Similar results were obtained by Dean & Kuhn (2006), who investigated the effects of direct instruction and discovery learning on teaching control-of-variable strategy (CVS) in the science domain. This study followed students' progress (acquisition and maintenance) over approximately six months. Fourth-grade students learned to design unconfounded experiments through computer-based inquiry tasks under one of the three conditions: direct instruction only (DI), practice only (PR), or a combination of instruction and practice (DI+PR). To design an unconfounded experiment, students were required to make a comparison by manipulating only one factor while setting all other conditions the same. In the DI condition, students received a single session of instruction without long engagement. In the PR condition, students freely practiced CVS with a computer program over 12 sessions without direct instruction. After general initial instruction, only direct instruction conditions (both DI and DI+PR) received a series of comparisons between two different experimental conditions and comments about whether the comparison was good or bad and an explanation as to why.

In a replication of the results of Klahr & Nigam (2004), direct instruction proved to be effective in an immediate assessment. However, in the tests given after the eleventh week, the advantage of direct instruction did not remain without further practice. In contrast, the practice group showed continually improving performance over time. Dean & Kuhn (2006, p. 394) conclude, "...direct instruction appears to be neither a necessary nor sufficient condition for robust acquisition or for maintenance over time." These results are consistent with the findings of Brunstein et al. (2009) in that although minimal guidance may not be effective in the earlier stage of learning, with high levels of practice, performance improves over time. However, Klahr and his colleagues (e.g., Klahr & Nigam 2004, Matlen & Klahr 2010) repeatedly found positive learning gains from direct instruction on teaching CVS; some of these studies are reviewed in detail in a later section.

The finding that discovery learning can be effective when accompanied with high levels of practice also suggests a new interpretation of a previous study (Charney et al. 1990) that investigated three different instructional approaches to teach college students to use a spreadsheet program with a command line interface. The three experimental conditions were tutorials, problem solving, and learner exploration. The tutorial condition was given the highest level of instruction and the exploration condition was given the lowest level of instruction, with the problem-solving condition in between. The results showed that the tutorial condition was worst and the problem-solving condition was best, with exploration coming in between. However, Tuovinen & Sweller (1999) criticized this study because time-on-task was not controlled. Alternatively, the longer training may have enabled minimal guidance to be effective, and the condition might have been superior to direct instruction even if direct instruction were given more time.

PROVISION OF DIRECT INSTRUCTION

Empirical Evidence on Superiority of Direct Instruction

Although the studies reviewed above might be seen as support for discovery learning, there is no lack of studies showing the superiority of direct instruction in many different domains, such as problem-solving rules (Craig 1956, Gagne & Brown 1961, Kittel 1957), programming (Fay & Mayer 1994, Lee & Thompson 1997), science (Chen & Klahr 1999, Klahr & Nigam 2004, Matlen & Klahr 2010, Strand-Cary & Klahr 2008), mathematics (Carroll 1994, Cooper & Sweller 1987, Sweller & Cooper 1985), and procedure learning (Rittle-Johnson et al. 2001). The success reported by tutoring programs in mathematics (such as the Cognitive Tutor) also supports the importance of providing instructional guidance in response to students' needs (Anderson et al. 1995, Koedinger et al. 1997).

Another good example showing the advantages of direct instruction is the series of studies Klahr and his colleagues have done on CVS. The original study (Chen & Klahr 1999) demonstrated that direct instruction was more effective than discovery learning in improving children's ability to design unconfounded experiments. However, this study has been criticized with respect to its epistemology because high CVS scores do not mean high level of authentic scientific inquiry (Chinn & Malhotra 2001). Following this criticism, Klahr & Nigam (2004) investigated effects of direct instruction and discovery learning on CVS in a more authentic context with third- and fourth-grade children. They found that, as in earlier studies, direct instruction was more effective than discovery learning. Moreover, they found that on the "far transfer" science fair assessment, the many children who mastered CVS in the direct condition performed just as well as the few children who mastered it in the discovery condition. Thus, contrary to one of the common claims for the superiority of discovery learning,

their study demonstrated that far transfer did not depend on how children learned something, only that they learned it. Further investigations by Strand-Cary & Klahr (2008) have also bolstered the effectiveness of direct instruction compared with the discovery learning approach. These studies are particularly noteworthy because they show the superiority of direct instruction in a more complex domain and on transfer tasks, which differs from commonly held beliefs that direct instruction is only effective for rote skills and direct tests of knowledge.

Matlen & Klahr (2010) examined the effect of different sequences of high versus low levels of instructional guidance on teaching CVS to find an optimal temporal sequence of guidance. By crossing the amount of instruction with two separate training sessions, four different orderings of instructional guidance were tested. The four conditions were high+high, high+low, low+high, and low+low, depending on whether early and late practice provided high or low instructional guidance. High guidance provided direct instruction and inquiry questions, whereas low guidance provided only inquiry questions. The study found best learning and transfer when high levels of guidance were repeated in the early and late training sessions (i.e., high+high condition).

Example-Based Learning: Worked Examples

A particularly interesting class of studies compares example-based learning with problem-based learning conditions. In example-based learning (often referred to as the worked-example condition), learners are provided with a worked example to study. Worked examples are instructional tools to provide an expert's solution that students can emulate. They typically involve a problem statement, step-by-step solution steps, and a final answer to the problem (Atkinson et al. 2000, Renkl et al. 1998). Worked examples are usually alternated with problems. In contrast, in problem-based learning, learners simply practice solving problems after initial instruction. In this kind of manipulation, the worked examples are often characterized as providing a form of direct instruction (Kirschner et al. 2006), but one could reasonably argue that the examples only provide scaffolding for a discovery process. In any case, as reviewed below, example-based instruction is often effective.

Carroll (1994) examined the effect of worked examples as an instructional support in the algebra classroom. High school students learned to translate words describing mathematical situations into formal equations (e.g., writing "five less than a number" as "$x-5$") in either a worked-example condition or conventional practice condition. Initial instruction included three examples and three practice problems in both conditions. In the worked-example condition, students were given a worksheet with 12 pairs of problems, one example followed by one problem. In the conventional practice condition, students had to solve 24 problems in the same order but without any examples. Students from the worked-example condition outperformed those from the practice condition by showing fewer errors on both immediate and delayed posttest (both learned and transfer problems), decreased need for assistance from the teacher, and less time taken to complete the work. It had been reported earlier in several other studies that the traditional practice of problem solving was not as effective as example-problem pairs (e.g., Cooper & Sweller 1987, Paas & Van Merriënboer 1994b, Sweller & Cooper 1985, Trafton & Reiser 1993).

Tuovinen & Sweller (1999) also compared the exploration-learning condition with the worked-example condition in college students learning to use a database program. The superiority of worked examples was again reported, consistent with findings by Carroll (1994), but this time the advantage occurred only for inexperienced learners. Tuovinen & Sweller had participants rate the cognitive load they experienced (ratings of mental effort required to complete the task using a Likert scale). Cognitive load is considered a multidimensional construct that represents the load imposed on the cognitive system while performing a particular task and is often conceptualized with mental load, mental effort, and performance (Paas & Van Merriënboer 1994a,b). The exploration group reported experiencing higher cognitive load than the worked-example group, but again the difference was reliable only for students who had less experience. This suggests that providing examples is effective in part because it lowers cognitive load for challenged learners.

Zhu & Simon (1987) claimed that students could learn from worked examples and problem solving equally successfully and efficiently without lectures or other forms of direct instruction as long as examples and/or problems are appropriately arranged in a way that students do not make too much trial-and-error search. When learning from examples, students use the worked examples to induce the relevant procedures and principles and then apply these to new problems. On the other hand, when learning by doing (i.e., problem solving), students have to first generate appropriate worked examples for themselves. When a problem solver correctly solves a problem, the solution path becomes a worked-out example.

In Zhu & Simon's (1987) study, students learned to factor quadratic algebraic expressions and showed learning in the problem-solving condition comparable to the learning-from-examples condition without lectures. Three possible explanations were suggested for this successful learning in both conditions. First, students had already studied the meaning of factoring and factoring of integers, thus all students had the background knowledge that was prerequisite for learning current materials. Second, students were provided with procedures for checking the correctness of their answers. This reduced the probability of students making errors of induction from incorrect solutions. Third, all examples and problems were carefully arranged so that students had to attend to only certain aspects of problems. This could reduce inefficient trial-and-error search and in turn reduce working memory load.

Besides studies on worked examples, there is a great abundance of studies showing that providing an example is an effective instructional method. Some studies have compared providing an example with providing procedures or rules. For example, Fong et al. (1986) reported that students who were trained with examples performed as well as students who were trained with explicit rules in learning statistical concepts. Both training methods were equally effective at improving the quality of statistical reasoning. Training on both methods had an additional positive effect. Reed & Bolstad (1991) also found that it was more effective to provide both examples and written procedures than to provide either examples or procedures alone when teaching to construct equations for work situation word problems. However, in this study, providing examples was more effective than providing written procedures only.

INTERACTION WITH OTHER INSTRUCTIONAL FACTORS

Individual Difference (Expertise Reversal Effect)

As Tuovinen & Sweller (1999) demonstrated, the effectiveness of instructional method might differ based on a learner's previous experience or prior knowledge level. One instructional approach might be ideal for experienced learners but might not be effective, or might even be detrimental, for inexperienced learners or novices. The expertise reversal effect (Kalyuga 2007, Kalyuga et al. 2003) is an example showing the interaction between the level of the learner and level of instruction. This occurs when instructional guidance helps inexperienced learners, but it is not beneficial for experienced learners. The idea of aptitude-treatment interaction (Cronbach & Snow 1977) has a long history and has been tested by many researchers. For example, Campbell (1964) found that the high-aptitude group benefited from a self-direction learning method, whereas the low-aptitude group benefited from a programmed instruction method. Cronbach & Snow (1977) also reported that when learners were given an opportunity to

process the information in their own way, only high-ability learners benefited; low-ability learners appeared to be handicapped by this. Aptitude-treatment interactions have been found in many domains including multimedia learning (Mayer & Sims 1994, Seufert et al. 2007), probability calculation (Renkl 1997), and logic programming (Kalyuga et al. 2001). This idea easily expands into the implementation of an adaptive instructional support found in intelligent tutoring systems, where instruction is adapted in response to the learner's progress (Anderson et al. 1995, Salden et al. 2010).

Shute (1992) argued that some studies perhaps failed to produce successful effects of instructional manipulations simply because their manipulations were having different effects on different ability groups. To test this idea, Shute (1992) investigated effects of two learning environments on mastering the basic principles of electricity and examined how effects differed depending on the learner's ability. In the rule-application environment, participants were given feedback that explicitly stated the variables and the relationships among those variables that were used to describe a principle for a given problem. In the rule-induction environment, the relevant variables were identified by feedback, but participants had to induce the relationships and generate their own interpretation. While there was no main effect of the learning environment on learning outcomes, there was a significant interaction between cognitive ability (an associative learning measure) and the learning environment. Also, the interaction pattern was different for different learning outcome measures. For declarative knowledge acquisition, rule-induction was more effective for high-ability learners, but rule-application was more effective for low-ability learners. In contrast, for procedural skill acquisition, high-ability learners benefited more from the rule-application environment, and low-ability learners showed poor learning outcome regardless of the type of learning environment.

A possible explanation for this intriguing interaction is that learning is enhanced when there is a good match among learning environment, outcome measure, and cognitive ability. For example, one will acquire more robust declarative representations if one induces the rules than if one just applies rules. Because the high-ability learners possessed relevant cognitive skills, they were able to understand concepts and formulate a rule in the rule-induction condition. However, the low-ability learners lacked these cognitive skills to induce the rules and were able to acquire more declarative knowledge when the rules were explicitly provided in the rule-application condition. In contrast, the rule-application environment supports acquisition of procedural skills. In the rule-application condition, the high-ability learners promptly applied rules and procedures without a demanding induction process. This allows more opportunity to practice procedural skills than in the rule-induction condition. However, the low-ability learners never proceduralized necessary skills within the training time because of their deficient skills, and they performed poorly regardless of the type of learning environment.

Kalyuga et al. (2001) examined the interaction between instructional guidance and learners' knowledge level. In their study, trade apprentices from manufacturing companies were given general instruction on programmable logic controller programs for relay circuits and then given experimental training sessions. Participants had either pure problem-solving practice or a mixed worked-example and problem-solving practice. They found that students benefited less from worked examples as they mastered more material. The worked-example group showed performance superior to that of the problem-solving group in the early phase of the learning, but the difference was reversed in the end of the learning.

The findings indicate that levels of learner knowledge interact with levels of instructional guidance and suggest that students may learn better if different instructional methods are used, depending on the learner's experience through the acquisition/learning phase. According to this rationale, Renkl et al. (2000) proposed the combination of two instructional methods (worked example and problem solving) by presenting examples in the early stage of learning and then presenting problems in the later stage of learning. Renkl and his colleagues (2002) tested this proposal and tested a fading procedure against traditional example-problem pairs. In the fading procedure, a complete example is presented first, and then increasingly more incomplete examples are presented by omitting solution steps. Finally, a complete problem is presented. The study found positive effects of the fading procedure on near-transfer items. Atkinson et al. (2003) replicated this fading-out example effect by comparing example-problem pair learning with the backward fading procedure (where the last solution steps are omitted first). Schwonke et al. (2007) also found that tutored problem solving combined with gradually faded examples led to a better transfer performance than did tutored problem solving alone. However, all of these studies employed a fixed fading scheme, and the fading schedule was not adapted to the student's learning. Schwonke et al. (2007) suggested the fading example would be more beneficial if worked-out steps were to fade adaptively for each individual learner.

Following this suggestion, Salden et al. (2010) examined the effects of the fading of worked-out examples that occurred either fixedly or adaptively within the Geometry Cognitive Tutor. In the fixed fading condition, students were initially provided with complete worked examples, the problems with example steps gradually faded, and at the end they received pure problems according to the fixed schedule. In the adaptive fading condition, an individual student's mastery of geometry theorems estimated by a Bayesian knowledge-tracing algorithm (Corbett & Anderson 1995) was used to decide when a worked-out step should be faded. The results showed that the adaptive fading of worked-examples led to a better performance on delayed posttests than did the fixed fading of worked-examples or the standard tutored problem-solving practice.

Self-Explanation

Researchers have also been interested in how the discovery versus instruction dichotomy interacts with other instructional factors. For instance, the effect of self-explanation has been investigated along with the amount of instructional guidance in several studies (e.g., Atkinson et al. 2003, Rittle-Johnson 2006). The self-explanation effect occurs when students try to explain the example solutions to themselves and then learn more than those who do not. The original study on self-explanation was performed by Chi et al. (1989) and has been followed up in many laboratory experiments (e.g., Renkl et al. 1998, Siegler 2002) and classroom studies (e.g., Aleven & Koedinger 2002, Hausmann & VanLehn 2007). Self-explanation activity is thought to help learning by causing the generation effect when students generate their own explanations. For example, Hausmann & VanLehn (2007) showed that students who were prompted to generate their own explanations for examples showed greater learning gains than those who were prompted to paraphrase provided explanations for the same examples. A follow-up study by Hausmann et al. (2009) examined effects of different types of self-explanation prompts and found that justification and step-focused prompts benefited more from studying examples than did the meta-cognitive prompts. It appears that the first two prompts facilitate the acquisition of problem schema when students generate justification for each solution step.

Chi and her colleagues (1989) divided students into "good" and "poor" categories based on their problem-solving scores and analyzed the quality of their self-generated explanations collected using the think-aloud method. The analysis revealed that good and poor students differed not only in the amount of verbal protocols they provided, but also with respect to the quality of their explanations. Good students produced more explanations, more idea statements, and more statements that identified their own misunderstandings. While solving problems, good students tended to make more specific inquiries to examples they studied earlier when they had difficulty. However, in this study, studying time was not controlled. Good students actually spent more time to study the worked-out examples than did the poor students. Therefore, it was not clear whether more time-on-task or better self-explanation achieved the successful learning.

This kind of different characterization of self-explanation from good versus poor students was also reported by Renkl (1997), who controlled time-on-task. With verbal protocol analysis, four groups of participants were identified with respect to self-explanation styles, independently from achievement data. The four styles were passive, superficial, principle based, and anticipative. Passive explainers generated a poor quality of self-explanations and did not inspect many examples. Superficial explainers inspected many examples, but they spent relatively little time when studying each example. These two groups showed worse performance on the posttest in comparison with principle-based and anticipative reasoners. Principle-based explainers attempted to emphasize the meaning and goal of operators and elaborate on the underlying principles of examples. Anticipative reasoners appeared to use an example to test their problem solving. This group of people anticipated the next step of the example solution and moved on to the next page to check whether their anticipated solution step was actually correct or not. Pretest score differences suggest that different levels of prior knowledge affected the preference of explanation style. Anticipative reasoners had a relatively high level of prior knowledge, whereas principle-based explainers had a low level of prior knowledge.

Aleven & Koedinger (2002) showed that prompting for self-explanation was beneficial for learning in a class environment by implementing it as part of the Cognitive Tutor Geometry course. Students practiced problem solving in an intelligent tutor program either with or without a prompt to explain solution steps. In the self-explanation condition, students had to type the name of the problem-solving principle that justified the solution step, and the tutor then provided feedback on the correctness of the typed principle. Students who were prompted to explain their solution steps showed greater understanding and better transfer performance than those who were not asked to explain steps. Students trained without self-explanation prompts appeared to show shallow procedural knowledge.

Rittle-Johnson (2006) investigated whether promoting self-explanation is effective in combination with either direct instruction or discovery learning conditions. Third- through fifth-grade children learned to solve mathematical equivalence problems. Children often understand the equal sign ($=$) as an operator signal that gets the answer rather than understanding it as a relational symbol meaning that two sides of the equations are the same (Baroody & Ginsburgh 1983, Rittle-Johnson & Alibali 1999). The four conditions were constructed by crossing two factors, instruction type (instruction versus invention) and self-explanation prompt (self-explanation versus no explanation). For the instruction groups, a teacher taught a correct add-subtract procedure for solving problems. For the invention groups, no instruction was provided, and instead children were simply told to think of a new way to solve the problem. For self-explanation groups, children were given an additional screen showing two different answers from two children at another school: one correct and one incorrect answer. The children were asked to explain how the answers were obtained by the other children and why each answer was correct or incorrect. For the no-explanation group, the additional screen was not provided. The results showed that self-explanation and instructional type did not interact; rather, they simply had an additive effect on learning in that both self-explanation and direct instruction helped children learn a correct procedure.

Cognitive Load Theory and Designing an Effective Worked Example

As we have reviewed, it is often found that conventional problem-solving practice is not an ideal instructional method (e.g., Cooper & Sweller 1987, Sweller & Cooper 1985), and worked examples have been suggested as a better instructional approach (e.g., Carroll 1994, Paas 1992, Renkl 2002, Tuovinen & Sweller 1999; for review, see Atkinson et al. 2000). Also, worked examples are especially effective for inexperienced learners. Because levels of knowledge tend to interact with levels of instructional guidance, some variants of this instructional method, such as the fading procedure, were suggested to maximize its effect. What makes the worked-example approach effective for inexperienced learners but not for experienced learners? One of the most discussed explanations is the cognitive load theory (Sweller 1988). Humans have limited working memory capacity (Baddeley 1992, Miller 1956), and problem solving requires using this limited working memory. Therefore, solving a problem involves high working memory demands (e.g., to keep track of where one is in a search space), and most of the working memory resources are consumed for this activity rather than for supporting learning.

Sweller (1988) elaborates this idea in terms of learning domain schemas. Problem solving and schema acquisition are both demanding of the mechanisms of selective attention and limited working memory capacity. Problem solvers tend to focus on reducing the difference between the current state and the goal problem state and try to find the right operators to reduce this difference. This focus on specific differences does not help construct the general schemas for a domain. Moreover, learners often flounder as they search for the right operators and lose touch with the important information. However, when direct instruction or a worked example is given, learners do not need to use their working memory resources for an inefficient search and instead can use them to learn the essential relations between problem-solving moves. If a means-ends strategy prevents learners from acquiring schemas, reducing or eliminating goal specificity helps enhance schema acquisition by eliminating the possibility of using a means-ends strategy to solve a problem.

In some studies, when a conventional specific goal was replaced by a nonspecific goal, learning was actually enhanced (Miller et al. 1999, Sweller & Levine 1982, Sweller et al. 1983).

Sweller and his colleagues (1998) further discuss three types of cognitive load: intrinsic, extraneous, and germane. Intrinsic cognitive load cannot be altered by instructional design because it is intrinsic to the learning material, whereas extraneous and germane cognitive load can be reduced or induced by instructional design. Intrinsic load is the inherent level of difficulty that is directly associated with the material. When learning material involves more elements to consider (e.g., learning to multiply out the denominator in an equation), it has a more intrinsic load than when it does not (e.g., memorizing Fe is the symbol for iron). Extraneous load is often a result of poor instructional design and consumes one's working memory capacity with irrelevant activity, whereas germane load is a result of mental efforts that contribute to schema construction. Thus, an appropriate instructional design should reduce the extraneous cognitive load while inducing the germane cognitive load within working memory capacity. For example, Paas & Van Merriënboer (1994b) demonstrated that providing worked examples (in comparison to problem solving) enhanced learning by reducing the extraneous load, and that introducing variability in examples had positive effects only when the extraneous cognitive load was reduced.

According to cognitive load theory, the expertise reversal effect (Kalyuga et al. 2003) is an example of this phenomenon. Novices do not have sufficient prior knowledge to organize key information provided in the problem. Therefore, they have to do unproductive problem-solving searches. However, as learners become more experienced, the knowledge is stored in long-term memory, and the well-organized knowledge structures help overcome working memory limitations. This difference in working memory capacity between experienced and inexperienced learners results in different beneficial effects from worked examples.

Can direct instruction or worked examples harm learning by increasing working memory load? Several studies have shown that this is actually possible and suggest that instruction needs to be designed to reduce extraneous working memory load so that learners can focus on essential learning activities. Learning materials often are presented in various modalities such as text and diagram. When multiple sources of information are presented together, learners need to integrate corresponding representations. Difficulty in integrating separate sources of information causes split attention (Tarmizi & Sweller 1988) and prevents learners from constructing a relevant schema by increasing working memory load. Chandler & Sweller (1991) demonstrated that in the design of instruction, a diagram alone was more effective than a diagram with text. Also, presenting text in both visual and auditory format was less effective than in auditory format only (Craig et al. 2002, Kalyuga et al. 2000, Mayer et al. 2001). However, a dual-mode presentation is not always worse than a single-mode representation. If integration of different formats of information does not create a working memory burden, it can be effectively used. One of the major reasons that a word-plus-diagram presentation is not superior to a stand-alone diagram is the extensive visual search it requires. In essence, people need to find which part of the text corresponds to which part of the diagram. Based on this idea, Jeung et al. (1997) tried to reduce the visual search by using visual flashes to identify the part of a diagram to which the auditory text was referring. This technique proved to enhance learning. The importance of visual cueing also has been reported in the domain of animations by several researchers (Boucheix & Lowe 2010, de Koning et al. 2010).

Koedinger and his colleagues (2010) provide an alternative account for the worked-example effect and the expertise reversal effect. They argue that problem-solving practice is not effective for novice learners, not because of exhausted working memory capacity (as argued by cognitive load theory), but rather because of lack of environmental support for filling in their knowledge gaps. Worked examples provide more input than problem solving and therefore offer beginning learners a better opportunity for the induction and sense-making process. In contrast, advanced learners need refinement and fluency building, and these skills are better provided by problem-solving practice than worked examples.

Effects of Comparison in Learning by Worked Examples

Many researchers have emphasized the importance of comparison for learning and transfer (e.g., Gentner et al. 2003, Gick & Holyoak 1983). The National Council of Teachers of Mathematics standards also emphasize the importance of comparing solution methods as an instructional practice (Natl. Counc. Teach. Math. 1989, 2000). Students are encouraged to share and compare their solution methods with their classmates. This comparing method has been used as one of the instructional changes in many constructivism-based classrooms (e.g., Cobb et al. 1991, Hiebert & Wearne 1996).

Rittle-Johnson and her colleagues investigated when and how comparison helped learning in mathematics with school-age children in a series of studies. Rittle-Johnson & Star (2007) had seventh-grade children learn to solve multistep linear equations [e.g., $3(x + 1) = 15$] under one of the two different conditions, either the comparison or sequential condition. In the comparison condition, students were provided with sets of two worked examples illustrating different solutions for the same problem and were encouraged to compare and contrast the two examples. The solution steps of the two worked examples were mutually aligned together on the same page, and each step of the solutions was labeled (e.g., distribute, combine) as well. In the sequential condition, students studied the identical worked examples, but each worked example was presented on a separate page. Also, students were prompted to reflect on the solution of each example. After two days of intervention, students were tested on conceptual knowledge, procedural knowledge,

and procedural flexibility. The results showed that students from the comparison condition gained more procedural knowledge and flexibility than those from the sequential condition, but there was no difference in conceptual knowledge between the two groups. Students who compared alternative solution methods were more likely to use the more efficient nonconventional methods and were better able to transfer their methods to novel problems.

Although the comparison proved to facilitate learning for multiple solution methods in mathematics, it is also important to know when and how comparison facilitates learning. Rittle-Johnson & Star (2009) showed that the effectiveness of comparison actually depended on what types of things were compared. Eighth-grade children learned to solve equations using worked examples in one of three different comparison conditions: comparing solution methods, comparing problem types, and comparing equivalent problems. The first condition was identical to the comparison condition used in the previous study by Rittle-Johnson & Star (2007) and involved learning multiple solution methods for one problem (i.e., one problem with two solution methods). In the comparing problem types condition, students learned to solve different problems with the same solution method (i.e., two different problems with one solution method). In the comparing equivalent problems condition, students learned to solve equivalent problems with the same solution method (i.e., two equivalent problems with one solution method). The posttest results showed that comparing solution methods was more effective for both conceptual knowledge and procedural flexibility than comparing problem types or comparing equivalent problems. Therefore, the benefits of comparison appear to depend on how worked examples differ.

Rittle-Johnson and her colleagues (2009) further examined the importance of prior knowledge in learning from comparison. Students were divided into two groups based on whether or not they attempted algebraic methods in a pretest. The results showed that students who attempted algebraic methods at pretest (high prior knowledge group) benefited most from comparing solution methods, but students who did not attempt algebraic methods at pretest (low prior knowledge group) were harmed by comparing solution methods. Students appeared to need sufficient prior knowledge in order to benefit from comparing alternative solution methods. When students do not have enough prior knowledge, two simultaneously presented worked examples are simply two unfamiliar examples, and the comparison activity just adds to the working memory load. In contrast, when students have enough prior knowledge, they can make an analogy from a familiar example to an unfamiliar example, and the comparison activity can be appropriately handled by their working memory resources.

Effects of Instructional Explanations in Learning by Worked Examples

In the studies reviewed, there was considerable variation in how much explicit (verbal) instruction accompanied the examples. Will students learn better from worked examples with instructional explanations or will they learn better if they are given only worked examples without instructional explanations? A large number of studies compared learning by worked examples with instructional explanation and without instructional explanation. In some studies, effects of receiving versus generating explanations have been compared when students learn with worked examples. There are both positive (e.g., Atkinson 2002, Lovett 1992, Renkl 2002) and negative (e.g., Ward & Sweller 1990) effects of the provision of instruction. Some studies showed neutral effects as well (e.g., Gerjets et al. 2006).

Lovett (1992) investigated the benefits of generating and receiving information when learning by problem solving versus when learning by example. Students learned to solve probability calculation problems in one of four experimental conditions. By crossing instruction type (worked example versus problem solving) with explanation type (instructional explanation versus self-explanation), four

conditions were constructed. All groups of students demonstrated comparably good performance on the near-transfer test. A far-transfer test, however, showed a significant interaction between the instruction type and explanation type. When students learned by worked examples, students who received instructional explanation outperformed those who did self-explanation. On the other hand, when students learned by problem-solving practice, the pattern of results was reversed. Students who did not receive instructional explanation (i.e., self-explanation) showed better performance than those who did receive instructional explanation. These results were explained by the consistency of source information. In the example-based learning, the source of the solution is the experimenter, whereas in problem-based learning, the source of the solution is the subject. Likewise, the source of elaboration is experimenter for instructional explanation and the subject for self-explanation. When there are inconsistent information sources, subjects have to integrate their own information with the experimenter's, and this might have increased cognitive load and weakened their problem memories. Whether this is the correct explanation or not, the benefits of providing instructional explanations were found only when students learned in worked-example conditions.

Renkl (2002) also demonstrated that instructional explanations had a positive effect on learning by worked-out examples. In this study, he first compared favorable features of self-explanation and instructional explanation and then created a learning environment by combining and maximizing their respective advantages. Relative to self-explaining activities, instructional explanations are not usually adapted to the prior knowledge of individual learners and are more likely to be provided without consideration of students' ongoing cognitive activity[1] (Renkl 2002). Also, students lose an

---

[1]Intelligent tutoring systems such as Cognitive Tutor often provide instructional explanations that are adapted to an individual learner's knowledge level (Corbett & Anderson 1995).

opportunity to benefit from the generation effect (Hausmann & VanLehn 2007, Lovett 1992). However, instructional explanations have the important benefit of correctness. Students are known to generate incorrect self-explanations and then suffer from the illusion of understanding (Chi et al. 1989). Also, instructional explanations help students overcome comprehension problems that they cannot solve for themselves. Renkl developed a learning environment based on this analysis. By including or excluding an instructional explanation button, student teachers learned to solve probability calculation problems under one of two different conditions. Instructional explanations had a positive effect in far transfer but not near transfer. He also found that the explanations were used mostly by participants with low levels of prior knowledge.

Catrambone (1998) found that the provision of a simple label for worked examples helps learning. When a label is provided for a group of solution steps that go together, students attempt to self-explain the purpose of the grouped solution steps and organize them with subgoals. This is consistent with the finding that students can understand the general rationale of problems better when problem solutions are broken down into smaller meaningful solution units (i.e., modular examples) rather than when examples focus on problem categories and their associated overall procedures (Catrambone 1994, Gerjets et al. 2004).

CONCLUSIONS

Although several studies support the critical role of instructional explanations in example-based learning, this effectiveness does not seem to be guaranteed. For instance, Gerjets et al. (2006) reported no effect of providing instruction on learning probability calculation problems. Although the amount of instruction had no effect on test performance, students who received high levels of instruction erroneously felt more successful at learning than those who received low levels of instruction. As a matter of fact, more instructional explanations increased studying time; thus, less-elaborated example-based instruction was more efficient than more-elaborated example-based instruction.

Provision of instructional explanation sometimes even produces negative effects when added in an inappropriate way. Through a series of experiments, Ward & Sweller (1990) demonstrated that when the instructional explanation failed to direct attention appropriately, it failed to reduce cognitive load and thus was not effective. In one experiment, tenth-grade students learned geometric optics problems in one of three different experimental learning conditions: conventional worked example, split-attention worked example, and conventional problem. In the split-attention worked-example condition, extra textual explanation was added, but not in an integrated format. This group was no better than the conventional problem-solving group, and both were worse than the conventional example group.

Negative effects of providing instructional explanations also seem to occur by reducing self-explanation activities. Schworm & Renkl (2006) investigated how generating explanations interacts with receiving explanation in a domain of instructional design. Student teachers learned to design effective worked-out examples for high school students in several domains including geometry and physics. By crossing presence of self-explanation (self-explanation versus no self-explanation) with presence of instruction (instructional explanation versus no instruction), four different learning conditions were constructed. Participants were given initial instructions on basic principles of worked-out example design, and they studied solved example problems. Schworm & Renkl (2006) found that instructional explanations hurt learning when participants generated self-explanations but helped learning when they did not. There was reduced self-explanation activity in the presence of instructions.

Given contradictory evidence, it is hard to draw a conclusion on the role of instructional explanations added on worked examples. To address this issue, Wittwer & Renkl (2010) conducted a meta analysis (see also

Wittwer & Renkl 2008). In order to investigate whether instructional explanations support example-based learning, 21 experimental studies were reviewed and analyzed with various moderating factors, and four major conclusions were reached. First, the overall effect of instructional explanation for example-based learning appears to be minimal. Although the provision of instructional explanation led to significantly better learning outcome than no instructional explanation, the effect size was small ($d = 0.16$). The benefit of instructional explanations was greater when the control condition was not supported by self-explanation. Second, instructional explanations were more effective for acquiring conceptual knowledge rather than procedural knowledge ($d = 0.36$). Third, the effectiveness of instructional explanations differed based on the learning domain. In mathematics, it had significantly positive effects ($d = 0.22$), but the effects were not clear in other domains including science and instructional design. Fourth, instructional explanations were not necessarily more helpful than the other supporting methods such as self-explanation. This analysis showed that prompting for self-explanation was as effective as adding instructional explanations for example-based learning.

COMBINING DISCOVERY LEARNING AND DIRECT INSTRUCTION APPROACHES

Invention Activity Followed by Direct Instruction

Both discovery learning and direct instruction approaches are known to have unique advantages (Koedinger & Aleven 2007), and there have been several attempts to combine discovery learning approaches with direct instruction approaches. For example, worked examples and problem-solving practice were successfully combined using a fading procedure (e.g., Atkinson et al. 2003, Renkl et al. 2002, Salden et al. 2010). When transitioning from worked examples to problem-solving practice depending on the stage of learning, it led to success-

ful learning. There have been other attempts to combine invention activity with a follow-up direct instruction (e.g., feedback, lecture, and text), and several studies have shown that this combined method is more beneficial than administering only direct instruction and practice without invention activities (e.g., Kapur 2011, Kapur & Bielaczye 2011, Schwartz & Martin 2004, Schwartz et al. 2011).

For example, Schwartz & Martin (2004) demonstrated that a student's invention activities appeared inefficient because they failed to generate canonical solutions, but when a subsequent instruction was embedded in a test, these students actually did better than those who were directly taught and had to practice without invention activities. In this study, ninth-grade algebra students studied statistical concepts under one of two instructional conditions (invention versus tell-and-practice) and then were tested under one of two test conditions (presence versus absence of a worked example embedded into the test). Students in the tell-and-practice condition performed on par, regardless of whether there was a worked example embedded in the test. In contrast, students in the invention group outperformed these two groups, but only when there was a worked example embedded in the test. This study shows that while one instructional approach may look ineffective, the efficacy of the approach may actually be hidden in what Bransford & Schwartz (1999) call a sequestered problem-solving paradigm. This is when participants are sequestered for tests of their learning to prevent them from possible exposure to other sources that may positively or negatively affect their performance in experiments. In contrast, in a preparation for future learning paradigm (Schwartz & Bransford 1998), learners are tested not based on whether they can generate a finished product, but rather based on whether they are prepared to learn to generate a new product.

Schwartz and his colleagues (2011) also reported similar findings with adolescent students. Students learned a concept of density under either a tell-and-practice condition or an invent-with-contrasting-cases condition. In the tell-and-practice condition, students were told the relevant concepts and formulas on density and then practiced with contrasting cases. In the invent-with-contrasting-cases condition, students had to invent formulas with the same contrasting cases first, and then formulas were provided only after they completed all the inventing tasks. Both groups of students showed a similar level of proficiency at applying a density formula on a word problem; however, the invention students showed better performance on the transfer tests that also required an understanding of ratio concepts but had semantically unrelated topics. Schwartz et al. (2011) argued that the tell-and-practice students did not have a chance to find the deep structure because they simply focused on what they had been told and practiced applying the learned formulas. Similar to the findings of Schwartz & Martin (2004), the inventing activity appeared to serve as preparation for future learning, and thus when the expert solutions were provided later, these students could appreciate the expert solutions better than those who were not prepared.

Kapur (2011, Kapur & Bielaczye 2011) also tested the effects of combining invention activities with follow-up instruction in multiple classroom studies and showed that it was indeed more effective than just providing direct instruction without invention activities. Kapur (2008) explains this with what he calls productive failure. Even though most students fail to generate valid methods on their own during the invention phase, this failure experience actually helps students become prepared to learn better in the following learning phase by activating students' prior knowledge and having students attend to critical features of the concept.

Based on the idea that invention activity can bolster learning when combined with a follow-up instruction, Roll and his colleagues (2010) integrated the strengths of exploration/invention with strengths of direct instruction in a computer-based tutor called the Invention Lab. In the Invention Lab, students are given invention tasks where they have to invent novel methods for computing certain properties of data. Roll et al. (2011) found that students who both designed and evaluated their own methods performed better than those who only evaluated methods without design activity on conceptual knowledge and debugging tests.

SUMMARY

We have reviewed several decades of debates and empirical evidence on discovery learning approaches and direct instructional approaches. Both positive and negative effects have been reported. Positive effects of discovery learning have been reported in alternative classroom projects where students were encouraged to invent their own procedure to solve a problem and discuss their solutions with their classmates. High levels of practice also facilitate successful discovery learning. Minimal guidance is known to have several cognitive benefits such as better memory and transfer as a result of the generation effect and to develop better attitudes toward a learning domain. However, it can be disadvantageous when, as a result of unnecessary excessive floundering, students fail to discover principles they are expected to learn.

On the other hand, a number of empirical studies suggest positive effects of providing direct instruction. Strong empirical evidence is especially found in example-based learning, although one can question whether this should be characterized as direct instruction. When students are given step-by-step solutions, they are known to learn better than when they simply practice problem solving. According to the cognitive load theory, worked examples help students focus on relevant problem solution steps by reducing irrelevant search activity such as means-ends analysis that is mostly found when solving unfamiliar problems. In contrast to the strong empirical support for worked examples, it is not still clear whether adding explanations to worked examples helps learning or not. It appears that extra explanation is only helpful when it is appropriately embedded into a worked example in a way that allows learners to integrate multiple sources of information without burdening their working memory. When multiple sources of information fail to be integrated, it causes a split-attention effect and thus hinders learning.

We have also reviewed other instructional factors that might influence the effectiveness of instructional methods. Learner characteristics, such as prior knowledge, interact with levels of instruction. The provision of guidance is sometimes not beneficial for advanced learners (i.e., expertise reversal effect), whereas it helps inexperienced learners. There is strong support to suggest that self-explanation helps learning through the generation process. Comparing multiple solutions also increases the effectiveness of worked examples, especially when learners have sufficient prior knowledge to make an analogy from one to the other.

Several attempts have been made to combine strengths of both discovery learning and direct instruction approaches. Worked examples and problem-solving practice were successfully combined using a fading procedure (e.g., Atkinson et al. 2003, Renkl et al. 2002, Salden et al. 2010). When transitioning from worked examples to problem-solving practice depending on the stage of learning, it led to better learning outcome than administering just one instructional method. Following suggestions from the preparation for future learning method, having students experience an exploration phase followed by an instruction phase also led to better learning. Productive failure can take advantage of the strengths of both the discovery learning and direct instruction approaches.

Although there are islands of clarity in this field, it is apparent that there is not a comprehensive understanding that would predict the outcome of different amounts of guidance across different learning situations. We think the fundamental reason for this is that despite all the pronouncements, there is not a detailed understanding of the mechanisms by which students turn their learning experiences into knowledge.

We have mainly focused on domains where the target competence is the ability to solve problems. In such domains it rarely (if ever) happens that students can simply take the words they hear from a teacher or find on a page and convert these into the sort of knowledge that they can transfer. In some way students must construct the knowledge by understanding how it applies to their problem solving. It is also a rare case that the best way for students to achieve such an understanding is by being left to figure it out entirely for themselves. Acquiring knowledge the first time this way took centuries. The key question is how students can be guided to construct this knowledge efficiently in a form that will transfer across the desired range of situations.

Looking back on this review, we are struck by two things. First, there is relatively little evidence (but not none) that verbal instruction helps. Second, there seems to be a great abundance of evidence that providing an example of a problem solution does help. We are tempted to believe that pure discovery learning succeeds only because successful discovery can provide the student with examples to learn from, which they have come to understand through the discovery process. We are equally tempted to believe that pure verbal instruction is effective only to the extent that it helps students understand real or imagined examples. That is, we suspect that learning in problem-solving domains is fundamentally example based and that both instruction and discovery have their effects in helping students understand the examples.

While the acquisition of problem-solving competence may be example based, we have also reviewed ample evidence that not all examples are equally effective and that what accompanies these examples can be critical. The most important role of verbal instruction may be to draw attention to the critical aspects of the examples. It is also important to do this in a way that is efficient and does not burden the student with unnecessary processing. It is often possible to achieve the same effect by nonverbal highlighting mechanisms. The sequencing and juxtaposition of examples can serve a role similar to highlighting critical features. If students can solve the problem on

Table 1 Advantages and disadvantages of providing instruction

Advantages	Disadvantages
• Provides correct solutions and explanations	• Solution methods may be rotely learned and poorly remembered
• Guides students to material to be learned	• Discourages learning that goes beyond the instruction
• Identifies critical features in the examples	• Prevents students from testing the adequacy of their understanding
• Makes time efficient by reducing floundering and irrelevant search	• Processing verbal instruction can pose a comprehension burden
• Reduces working memory demands created by managing problem solving	• Splits attention when multiple sources of information are not integrated

their own without guidance, this can be an effective way to identify what is critical about the example solution that is generated.

With this perspective in mind, we have put together **Table 1**, which summarizes some of the possible advantages and disadvantages from providing instructional guidance to the learner.[2] The biggest advantage of instruction is that it provides learners with correct information that may never be found by learners on their own. On the other hand, this information may be only rotely memorized and poorly remembered. Instruction will focus the student on critical material and pull their focusing away from the irrelevant, but it will also discourage types of learning that may be more useful. When studying an example, the instruction can highlight the critical features but can also prevent students from testing whether they really understand what is critical in the example. Typically, instruction will prevent floundering, but processing the instruction itself can be a time sink. Finally, problem solving on one's own can take resources away from learning, but so can trying to integrate the multiple sources of information that are frequently part of instruction.

DISCLOSURE STATEMENT

The authors are not aware of any affiliations, memberships, funding, or financial holdings that might be perceived as affecting the objectivity of this review.

ACKNOWLEDGMENTS

Preparation of this review was supported by IES grant R305A100109. We thank Abe Anderson, Jennifer Ferris, Keith Holyoak, David Klahr, Ken Koedinger, Marsha Lovett, and Daniel Schacter for valuable comments on the paper.

LITERATURE CITED

Aleven V, Koedinger KR. 2002. An effective meta-cognitive strategy: learning by doing and explaining with a computer-based cognitive tutor. *Cogn. Sci.* 26:147–79

Anderson JR, Corbett AT, Koedinger KR, Pelletier R. 1995. Cognitive tutors: lessons learned. *J. Learn. Sci.* 4:167–20

---

[2]A similar table on the benefits and cost of assistance giving and withholding is found in Koedinger & Aleven (2007).

Anderson JR, Reder LM, Simon H. 1998. Radical constructivism and cognitive psychology. In *Brookings Papers on Education Policy 1998*, ed. D Ravitch, pp. 227–78. Washington, DC: Brookings Inst. Press

Atkinson RK. 2002. Optimizing learning from examples using animated pedagogical agents. *J. Educ. Psychol.* 94:416–27

Atkinson RK, Derry SJ, Renkl A, Wortham DW. 2000. Learning from examples: instructional principles from the worked examples research. *Rev. Educ. Res.* 70:181–214

Atkinson RK, Renkl A, Merrill MM. 2003. Transitioning from studying examples to solving problems: effects of self-explanation prompts and fading worked-out steps. *J. Educ. Psychol.* 95:774–83

Ausubel DP. 1964. Some psychological and educational limitations of learning by discovery. *Arith. Teach.* 11:290–302

Ausubel DP. 1968. *Educational Psychology: A Cognitive View*. New York: Holt, Rinehart & Winston

Baddeley A. 1992. Working memory. *Science* 255:556–59

Baroody AJ, Ginsburgh HP. 1983. The effects of instruction on children's understanding of the "equals" sign. *Elem. Sch. J.* 84:199–212

Bjork RA. 1994. Memory and metamemory considerations in the training of human beings. In *Metacognition: Knowing About Knowing*, ed. J Metcalfe, A Shimamura, pp. 185–205. Cambridge, MA: MIT Press

Bobrow SA, Bower GH. 1969. Comprehension and recall of sentences. *J. Exp. Psychol.* 80:455–61

Bonawitz E, Shafto P, Gweon H, Goodman ND, Spelke E, Schulz L. 2011. The double-edged sword of pedagogy: Instruction limits spontaneous exploration and discovery. *Cognition* 120:322–30

Boucheix JM, Lowe RK. 2010. An eye tracking comparison of external pointing cues and internal continuous cues in learning with complex animations. *Learn. Instr.* 20:123–35

Bransford JD, Schwartz DL. 1999. Rethinking transfer: a simple proposal with multiple implications. In *Review of Research in Education*, ed. A Iran-Nejad, PD Pearson, 24:61–101. Washington, DC: Am. Educ. Res. Assoc.

Bruner JS. 1961. The act of discovery. *Harv. Educ. Rev.* 31:21–32

Brunstein A, Betts S, Anderson JR. 2009. Practice enables successful learning under minimal guidance. *J. Educ. Psychol.* 101:790–802

Campbell VN. 1964. Self-direction and programmed instruction for five different types of learning objectives. *Psychol. Sch.* 1:348–59

Carpenter TP, Franke ML, Jacobs VR, Fennema E, Empson SB. 1998. A longitudinal study of invention and understanding in children's multidigit addition and subtraction. *J. Res. Math. Educ.* 29:3–20

Carroll WM. 1994. Using worked examples as an instructional support in the algebra classroom. *J. Educ. Psychol.* 86:360–67

Catrambone R. 1994. Improving examples to improve transfer to novel problems. *Mem. Cogn.* 22:606–15

Catrambone R. 1998. The subgoal learning model: creating better examples so that students can solve novel problems. *J. Exp. Psychol.: Gen.* 127:355–76

Chandler P, Sweller J. 1991. Cognitive load theory and the format of instruction. *Cogn. Instr.* 8:293–332

Charney DH, Reder LM, Kusbit GW. 1990. Goal setting and procedure selection in acquiring computer skills: a comparison of tutorials, problem-solving, and learner exploration. *Cogn. Instr.* 7:323–42

Chen Z, Klahr D. 1999. All other things being equal: children's acquisition of the control of variables strategy. *Child Dev.* 70:1098–120

Chi MTH, Bassok M, Lewis MW, Reimann P, Glaser R. 1989. Self-explanations: How students study and use examples in learning to solve problems. *Cogn. Sci.* 13:145–82

Chinn CA, Malhotra BA. 2001. Epistemologically authentic scientific reasoning. In *Designing for Science: Implications from Everyday, Classroom, and Professional Settings*, ed. K Crowley, CD Schunn, T Okada, pp. 351–92. Mahwah, NJ: Erlbaum

Cobb P, Wood T, Yackel E, Nicholls J, Wheatley G, et al. 1991. Assessment of a problem-centered second-grade mathematics project. *J. Res. Math. Educ.* 22:3–29

Cooper G, Sweller J. 1987. The effects of schema acquisition and rule automation on mathematical problem-solving transfer. *J. Educ. Psychol.* 79:347–62

Corbett AT, Anderson JR. 1995. Knowledge tracing: modeling the acquisition of procedural knowledge. *User Model. User-Adapt. Interact.* 4:253–78

Craig R. 1956. Directed versus independent discovery of established relations. *J. Educ. Psychol.* 47:223–35

Craig S, Gholson B, Driscoll D. 2002. Animated pedagogical agents in multimedia educational environments: effects of agent properties, picture features, and redundancy. *J. Educ. Psychol.* 94:428–34

Cronbach LJ, Snow RE. 1977. *Aptitudes and Instructional Methods: A Handbook for Research on Interactions.* New York: Irvington

Dean D, Kuhn D. 2006. Direct instruction versus discovery: the long view. *Sci. Educ.* 91:384–97

De Koning BB, Tabbers HK, Rikers RMJP, Paas F. 2010. Learning by generating versus receiving instructional explanations: two approaches to enhance attention cueing in animations. *Comp. Educ.* 55:681–91

Fay AL, Mayer RE. 1994. Benefits of teaching design skills before teaching LOGO computer programming: evidence for syntax-independent learning. *J. Educ. Comp. Res.* 11:187–210

Fong GT, Krantz DH, Nisbett RE. 1986. The effects of statistical training on thinking about everyday problems. *Cogn. Psychol.* 18:253–92

Gagne RM, Brown LT. 1961. Some factors in the programming of conceptual learning. *J. Exp. Psychol.* 62:313–21

Gentner D, Loewenstein J, Thompson L. 2003. Learning and transfer: a general role for analogical encoding. *J. Educ. Psychol.* 95:393–405

Gerjets P, Scheiter K, Catrambone R. 2004. Designing instructional examples to reduce intrinsic cognitive load: molar versus modular presentation of solution procedures. *Instr. Sci.* 32:33–58

Gerjets P, Scheiter K, Catrambone R. 2006. Can learning from molar and modular worked examples be enhanced by providing instructional explanations and prompting self-explanations? *Learn. Instr.* 16:104–21

Gick ML, Holyoak KJ. 1983. Schema induction and analogical transfer. *Cogn. Psychol.* 15:1–38

Gutherie JT. 1967. Expository instruction versus a discovery method. *J. Educ. Psychol.* 1:45–49

Hausmann RGM, Nokes TJ, VanLehn K, Gershman S. 2009. The design of self-explanation prompts: the fit hypothesis. In *Proc. 31st Annu. Conf. Cogn. Sci. Soc.*, pp. 2626–31. Amsterdam: Cogn. Sci. Soc.

Hausmann RGM, VanLehn K. 2007. Explaining self-explaining: a contrast between content and generation. In *Proc. Artificial Intelligence in Educ.*, ed. R Luckin, KR Koedinger, J Greer, pp. 417–24. Amsterdam: IOS Press

Hiebert J, Wearne D. 1996. Instruction, understanding, and skill in multidigit addition and subtraction. *Cogn. Instr.* 14:251–83

Jeung H, Chandler P, Sweller J. 1997. The role of visual indicators in dual sensory mode instruction. *Educ. Psychol.* 17:329–43

Kalyuga S. 2007. Expertise reversal effect and its implications for learner-tailored instruction. *Educ. Psychol. Rev.* 19:509–39

Kalyuga S, Ayres P, Chandler P, Sweller J. 2003. The expertise reversal effect. *Educ. Psychol.* 38:23–31

Kalyuga S, Chandler P, Sweller J. 2000. Incorporating learner experience into the design of multimedia instruction. *J. Educ. Psychol.* 92:126–36

Kalyuga S, Chandler P, Tuovinen J, Sweller J. 2001. When problem solving is superior to studying worked examples. *J. Educ. Psychol.* 93:579–88

Kamii C, Dominick A. 1998. The harmful effects of algorithms in grades 1–4. In *The Teaching and Learning of Algorithms in School Mathematics: 1998 Yearbook*, ed. LJ Morrow, MJ Kenney, pp. 130–40. Reston, VA: Natl. Counc. Teach. Math.

Kapur M. 2008. Productive failure. *Cogn. Instr.* 26:379–425

Kapur M. 2011. A further study of productive failure in mathematical problem solving: unpacking the design components. *Instr. Sci.* 39:561–79

Kapur M, Bielaczye K. 2011. Classroom-based experiments in productive failure. In *Proc. 33rd Annu. Conf. Cogn. Sci. Soc.*, ed. L Carlson, C Hoelscher, TF Shipley, pp. 2812–17. Austin, TX: Cogn. Sci. Soc.

Kirschner PA, Sweller J, Clark RE. 2006. Why minimal guidance during instruction does not work: an analysis of the failure of constructivist, discovery, problem-based, experiential, and inquiry-based teaching. *Educ. Psychol.* 41:75–86

Kittel JE. 1957. An experimental study of the effect of external direction during learning on transfer and retention of principles. *J. Educ. Psychol.* 48:391–405

Klahr D, Li J. 2005. Cognitive research and elementary science instruction: from the laboratory, to the classroom, and back. *J. Sci. Educ. Technol.* 4:217–38

Klahr D, Nigam M. 2004. The equivalence of learning paths in early science instruction: effects of direct instruction and discovery learning. *Psychol. Sci.* 15:661–67

Koedinger KR, Aleven V. 2007. Exploring the assistance dilemma in experiments with cognitive tutors. *Educ. Psychol. Rev.* 19:239–64

Koedinger KR, Anderson JR, Hadley WH, Mark M. 1997. Intelligent tutoring goes to school in the big city. *Int. J. Artif. Intell. Educ.* 8:30–43

Koedinger KR, Corbett AT, Perfetti C. 2010. The knowledge-learning-instruction (KLI) framework: toward bridging the science-practice chasm to enhance robust student learning. Carnegie Mellon Univ. Tech. Rep. **http://pact.cs.cmu.edu/pubs/PSLC-Theory-Framework-Tech-Rep.pdf**

Kuhn D. 2007. Is direct instruction an answer to the right question? *Educ. Psychol.* 42:109–13

Lee M, Thompson A. 1997. Guided instruction in LOGO programming and the development of cognitive monitoring strategies among college students. *J. Educ. Comp. Res.* 16:125–44

Lepper MR. 1988. Motivational considerations in the study of instruction. *Cogn. Instr.* 5:289–309

Lewis MW, Anderson JR. 1985. Discrimination of operator schemata in problem solving: procedural learning from examples. *Cogn. Psychol.* 17:26–65

Lovett MC. 1992. Learning by problem solving versus by examples: the benefits of generating and receiving information. In *Proc. 14th Annu. Conf. Cogn. Sci. Soc.*, pp. 956–61. Hillsdale, NJ: Erlbaum

Matlen BJ, Klahr D. 2010. Sequential effects of high and low guidance on children's early science learning. In *Proc. 9th Int. Conf. Learn. Sci.*, ed. K Gomez, L Lyons, J Radinsky, pp. 1016–23. Chicago: Int. Soc. Learn. Sci.

Mayer RE. 2004. Should there be a three-strikes rule against pure discovery learning? The case for guided methods of instruction. *Am. Psychol.* 59:14–19

Mayer RE, Heiser J, Lonn S. 2001. Cognitive constraints on multimedia learning: when presenting more material results in less understanding. *J. Educ. Psychol.* 93:187–98

Mayer RE, Sims VK. 1994. For whom is a picture worth a thousand words? Extensions of a dual-coding theory of multimedia learning. *J. Educ. Psychol.* 84:389–460

McDaniel MA, Schlager MS. 1990. Discovery learning and transfer of problem-solving skills. *Cogn. Instr.* 7:129–59

Miller C, Lehman J, Koedinger K. 1999. Goals and learning in microworlds. *Cogn. Sci.* 23:305–36

Miller GA. 1956. The magical number seven, plus or minus two: some limits on our capacity for processing information. *Psychol. Rev.* 63:81–97

Natl. Counc. Teach. Math. 1989. *Curriculum and Evaluation Standards for School Mathematics.* Reston, VA: Natl. Counc. Teach. Math.

Natl. Counc. Teach. Math. 2000. *Principles and Standards for School Mathematics.* Reston, VA: Natl. Counc. Teach. Math.

Paas F. 1992. Training strategies for attaining transfer of problem-solving skill in statistics: a cognitive-load approach. *J. Educ. Psychol.* 84:429–34

Paas F, Van Merriënboer J. 1994a. Instructional control of cognitive load in the training of complex cognitive tasks. *Educ. Psychol. Rev.* 6:351–71

Paas F, Van Merriënboer J. 1994b. Variability of worked examples and transfer of geometrical problem solving skills: a cognitive-load approach. *J. Educ. Psychol.* 86:122–33

Papert S. 1980. *Mindstorms: Children, Computers, and Powerful Ideas.* New York: Basic Books

Piaget J. 1970. *Genetic Epistemology.* New York: Columbia Univ. Press

Piaget J. 1973. *To Understand Is to Invent.* New York: Grossman

Piaget J. 1980. *Adaptation and Intelligence: Organic Selection and Phenocopy.* Chicago: Univ. Chicago Press

Reed SK, Bolstad CA. 1991. Use of examples and procedures in problem solving. *J. Exp. Psychol.: Learn. Mem. Cogn.* 17:753–66

Reiser BJ, Copen WA, Ranney M, Hamid A, Kimberg DY. 1994. *Cognitive and Motivational Consequences of Tutoring and Discovery Learning.* Tech. Rep., Inst. Learn. Sci., Northwestern Univ.

Renkl A. 1997. Learning from worked-out examples: a study on individual differences. *Cogn. Sci.* 21:1–29

Renkl A. 2002. Worked-out examples: Instructional explanations support learning by self-explanations. *Learn. Instr.* 12:529–56

Renkl A, Atkinson RK, Maier UH. 2000. From studying examples to solving problems: Fading worked-out solution steps helps learning. In *Proc. 22nd Annu. Conf. Cogn. Sci. Soc.*, ed. L Gleitman, AK Joshi, pp. 393–98. Mahwah, NJ: Erlbaum

Renkl A, Atkinson RK, Maier UH, Staley R. 2002. From example study to problem solving: smooth transitions help learning. *J. Exp. Educ.* 70:293–315

Renkl A, Stark R, Gruber H, Mandl H. 1998. Learning from worked-out examples: the effects of example variability and elicited self-explanations. *Contemp. Educ. Psychol.* 23:90–108

Rittle-Johnson B. 2006. Promoting transfer: the effects of direct instruction and self-explanation. *Child Dev.* 77:1–15

Rittle-Johnson B, Alibali MW. 1999. Conceptual and procedural knowledge of mathematics: Does one lead to the other? *J. Educ. Psychol.* 91:175–89

Rittle-Johnson B, Siegler RS, Alibali MW. 2001. Developing conceptual understanding and procedural skill in mathematics: an iterative process. *J. Educ. Psychol.* 93:346–62

Rittle-Johnson B, Star JR. 2007. Does comparing solution methods facilitate conceptual and procedural knowledge? An experimental study on learning to solve equations. *J. Educ. Psychol.* 99:561–74

Rittle-Johnson B, Star JR. 2009. Compared with what? The effects of different comparisons on conceptual knowledge and procedural flexibility for equation solving. *J. Educ. Psychol.* 101:529–44

Rittle-Johnson B, Star JR, Durkin K. 2009. The importance of prior knowledge when comparing examples: influences on conceptual and procedural knowledge of equation solving. *J. Educ. Psychol.* 101:836–52

Roll I, Aleven V, Koedinger KR. 2010. The invention lab: using a hybrid of model tracing and constraint-based modeling to offer intelligent support in inquiry environments. In *Proc. Int. Conf. Intelligent Tutor. Syst.*, ed. V Aleven, J Kay, J Mostow, pp. 115–24. Berlin: Springer Verlag

Roll I, Aleven V, Koedinger KR. 2011. Outcomes and mechanisms of transfer in invention activities. In *Proc. 33rd Annu. Conf. Cogn. Sci. Soc.*, ed. L Carlson, C Hoelscher, TF Shipley, pp. 2824–29. Austin, TX: Cogn. Sci. Soc

Salden R, Aleven V, Schwonke R, Renkl A. 2010. The expertise reversal effect and worked examples in tutored problem solving. *Instr. Sci.* 38:289–307

Schmidt RA, Bjork RA. 1992. New conceptualization of practice: Common principles in three paradigms suggest new concepts for training. *Psychol. Sci.* 3:207–17

Schwonke R, Wittwer J, Alven V, Salden R, Krieg C, Renkl A. 2007. Can tutored problem solving benefit from faded worked-out examples? In *Proc. European Cogn. Sci. Conf. 2007*, ed. S Vosniadou, D Kayser, A Protopapas, pp. 59–64. New York: Erlbaum

Schworm S, Renkl A. 2006. Computer-supported example-based learning: when instructional explanations reduce self-explanations. *Comp. Educ.* 46:426–45

Schwartz DL, Bransford JD. 1998. A time for telling. *Cogn. Instr.* 16:475–522

Schwartz DL, Chase CC, Oppezzo MA, Chin DB. 2011. Practicing versus inventing with contrasting cases: the effects of telling first on learning and transfer. *J. Educ. Psychol.* 103:759–75

Schwartz DL, Martin T. 2004. Inventing to prepare for future learning: the hidden efficiency of encouraging original student production in statistics instruction. *Cogn. Instr.* 22:129–84

Seufert T, Jänen I, Brünken R. 2007. The impact of intrinsic cognitive load on the effectiveness of graphical help for coherence formation. *Comp. Hum. Behav.* 23:1055–71

Shute VJ. 1992. Aptitude-treatment interactions and cognitive skill diagnosis. In *Cognitive Approaches to Automated Instruction*, ed. JW Regian, VJ Shute, pp. 15–47. Hillsdale, NJ: Erlbaum

Siegler RS. 2002. Microgenetic studies of self-explanations. In *Microdevelopment: Transition Processes in Development and Learning*, ed. N Granott, J Parziale, pp. 31–58. New York: Cambridge Univ. Press

Slamecka NJ, Graf P. 1978. The generation effect: delineation of a phenomenon. *J. Exp. Psychol.: Hum. Learn. Mem.* 4:592–604

Steffe LP, Gale J. 1995. *Constructivism in Education*. Hillsdale, NJ: Erlbaum

Strand-Cary M, Klahr D. 2008. Developing elementary science skills: instructional effectiveness and path independence. *Cogn. Dev.* 23:488–511

Suchman JR. 1961. Inquiry training: building skills for autonomous discovery. *Merrill-Palmer Q. Behav. Dev.* 7:147–69

Sweller J. 1988. Cognitive load during problem solving: effects on learning. *Cogn. Sci.* 12:257–85

Sweller J, Cooper GA. 1985. The use of worked examples as a substitute for problem solving in learning algebra. *Cogn. Instr.* 2:59–89

Sweller J, Levine M. 1982. Effects of goal specificity on means-ends analysis and learning. *J. Exp. Psychol.: Learn. Mem. Cogn.* 8:463–74

Sweller J, Mawer R, Ward M. 1983. Development of expertise in mathematical problem solving. *J. Exp. Psychol.: Gen.* 112:639–61

Sweller J, Van Merriënboer J, Paas F. 1998. Cognitive architecture and instructional design. *Educ. Psychol. Rev.* 10:251–96

Tarmizi R, Sweller J. 1988. Guidance during mathematical problem solving. *J. Educ. Psychol.* 80:424–36

Tobias S, Duffy TM, eds. 2009. *Constructivist Instruction: Success or Failure*. New York: Routledge

Trafton JG, Reiser RJ. 1993. The contribution of studying examples and solving problems to skill acquisition. In *Proc. 15th Annu. Conf. Cogn. Sci. Soc.*, ed. M Polson, pp. 1017–22. Hillsdale, NJ: Erlbaum

Tuovinen JE, Sweller J. 1999. Comparison of cognitive load associated with discovery learning and worked examples. *J. Educ. Psychol.* 91:334–41

Ward M, Sweller J. 1990. Structuring effective worked examples. *Cogn. Instr.* 7:1–39

Wittwer J, Renkl A. 2008. Why instructional explanations often do not work: a framework for understanding the effectiveness of instructional explanations. *Educ. Psychol.* 43:49–64

Wittwer J, Renkl A. 2010. How effective are instructional explanations in example-based learning? A meta-analytic review. *Educ. Psychol. Rev.* 22:393–409

Zhu X, Simon HA. 1987. Learning mathematics from examples and by doing. *Cogn. Instr.* 4:137–66

Bringing the Laboratory and Clinic to the Community: Mobile Technologies for Health Promotion and Disease Prevention[a]

Robert M. Kaplan[1,b] and Arthur A. Stone[2]

[1] Office of Behavioral and Social Sciences Research, National Institutes of Health, Bethesda, Maryland 20892-2027; email: robert.kaplan@nih.gov

[2] Psychiatry and Behavioral Sciences Department, Stony Brook University, Stony Brook, New York 11794-8790

Annu. Rev. Psychol. 2013. 64:471–98

First published online as a Review in Advance on September 17, 2012

The *Annual Review of Psychology* is online at psych.annualreviews.org

This article's doi: 10.1146/annurev-psych-113011-143736

[a] Opinions expressed in this article are solely those of the authors and do not necessarily represent those of the National Institutes of Health.

[b] Corresponding author

Keywords

mHealth, ambulatory assessment, short message service (SMS), ecological momentary assessment (EMA), representative design

Abstract

Health-related information collected in psychological laboratories may not be representative of people's everyday health. For at least 70 years, there has been a call for methods that sample experiences from everyday environments and circumstances. New technologies, including cell phones, sensors, and monitors, now make it possible to collect information outside of the laboratory in environments representative of everyday life. We review the role of mobile technologies in the assessment of health-related behaviors, physiological responses, and self-reports. Ecological momentary assessment offers a wide range of new opportunities for ambulatory assessment and evaluation. The value of mobile technologies for interventions to improve health is less well established. Among 21 randomized clinical trials evaluating interventions that used mobile technologies, more than half failed to document significant improvements on health outcomes or health risk factors. Theoretical and practical issues for future research are discussed.

Contents

THE ROLE OF THE LABORATORY IN ASSESSING HEALTH OUTCOMES

The laboratory has an important role in the history of psychology (Boring 1950). The earliest roots of psychological science were founded in philosophy and in physiology. Psychology's transition to an independent scientific discipline was marked by the establishment of the first psychological laboratory in about 1879. This is typically attributed to Wilhelm Wundt, a physician from Leipzig who studied sensation, perception, and a variety of other phenomena (Schultz & Schultz 2011). At approximately the same time, William James developed a psychological laboratory at Harvard University (Boring 1950). During the 130 years following the establishment of the Wundt laboratory, psychological laboratories thrived because they allowed observations of behavior under controlled circumstances. Through experimentation in these environments, it was possible to manipulate independent variables and to observe their impact on behaviors. Because both Wundt and James were physicians, the laboratory incorporated elements of the hospital and clinic.

The Laboratory and Clinic as Nonrepresentative Environments

Science and the practice of health care typically involve bringing patients to the controlled environment of a laboratory or clinic. Despite the advantages of the psychological laboratory, early experimental psychologists also identified scientific limitations of the emerging laboratory science (Brunswik 1952, Brunswik et al. 2001a). The attractiveness of the laboratory is that systematic observations can be made in a controlled environment and variables can be manipulated to establish cause–effect associations within that environment. However, most outcomes of interest are determined by or modified by a wide variety of environmental or contextual factors, so what happens in the laboratory may not be representative of what happens in more complex nonlaboratory environments.

Studies of human perception provide numerous examples of the effects of context on judgment. The term constructive perception is used to describe the use of sensory information, and a variety of different cues are used to make judgments and identify objects (Sterzer et al. 2009). Identifying objects in laboratory settings may be quite artificial in contrast to identifying them within the more complex context of natural environments. Similarly, studying some physiological processes in laboratory or clinical settings may be misleading, particularly when the physiological process is affected by environmental context.

Brunswik and Representative Design

Taking the laboratory and clinic to people is not a new idea. Although it was suggested more than 70 years ago, collecting data in situations sampled from representative episodes in people's lives has only recently gained momentum. The ideas that underlie representative design result from Egon Brunswik's criticism of experimental psychology beginning in the early 1940s (Brunswik 1944). Brunswik argued that laboratories were artificial environments, and most experimental procedures that manipulated one variable at a time condemned the science to results that might not be replicated outside the laboratory. This line of reasoning had a strong connection to evolutionary biology (Petrinovich 1979). Brunswik recognized that humans and other animals evolved to adapt to a wide range of circumstances. Further, much like advocates for Bayesian statistics (McGrayne 2011), Brunswik emphasized that the world is probabilistic rather than deterministic. He argued for the use of procedures that study behavior in the wide range of natural situations that individuals encounter. While studying visual perception, Brunswik was reported to have followed his research assistant, asking her for judgments of objects while he photographed them, so as to compare the objective with the subjective (Brunswik 1941).

As an exceptionally clever methodologist, Brunswik argued against many of the basic principles of statistical inference. For example, he felt that acquiring large samples of individuals was less important than collecting observations of a few individuals in large representative samples of situations (Brunswik et al.

2001b). Brunswik emphasized that traditional laboratory-based experimental designs were limited in helping us understand how individuals are influenced by the major determinants of behavior. Systematic design was viewed as too narrow because it lacked connection to what happens outside the laboratory. Brunswik believed that representative design, which draws from observations in natural settings, must replace systematic designs that emphasize what happens in a very restricted set of circumstances; he suggested "representative design is based on sampling a large number of everyday situations drawn from a person's ecology" (Brunswik 1956, p. 489). It is notable that the term ecological validity has in contemporary usage taken on the meaning of representative design; for Brunswik, ecological validity was a different concept.

Although Brunswik's work eventually received positive critical acclaim, it was largely unappreciated during his lifetime, and there has been remarkably little attention to ecological approaches. One of the few early programs was the work of Roger Barker nearly 65 years ago (Barker & Wright 1949). Barker made the study of behavioral settings his life's work. For many years, he and colleagues described the publicly available behavioral settings in two small towns: Oskaloosa, Kansas and Leyburn, England. Barker documented each setting by describing how long the observed interactions lasted, who participated, the gender of the people in the setting, and so on (Barker 1965, Barker & Schoggen 1973). The study of behavioral settings reveals a great deal about the social rules of the environment. For example, in both Oskaloosa and Leyburn, women spent less time in public behavioral settings than did men (Barker & Schoggen 1973).

Progress in understanding the impact of behavioral settings has been slow because it is very difficult to observe individuals in the wide range of circumstances that they encounter. Such research is extremely demanding, expensive, and rarely feasible. However, new technologies and methodologies now enable the collection of data in a wide range of natural environments. Cell phones, sensors, and other electronic devices have stimulated an explosion of new approaches for capturing data and monitoring people in a wide range of circumstances. With informed consent, we are now capable of capturing information in the natural physical and social environment. This review focuses on the use of new electronic technologies to enhance health research and interventions in natural settings.

REPRESENTATIVE DESIGN IN SELF-REPORTS

Many people feel that diagnoses in medicine can be derived exclusively from biological tests, and, for many years, physicians simply ignored most of the information that was provided by their patients during clinic visits. However, it has become increasingly clear that patient reports provide the key to understanding many important illnesses and risk factors. In fact, in most cases, patients consult physicians because they experience symptoms and problems, and in this way they profoundly influence the delivery of health care.

Patient-reported outcomes (PROs) are defined as patients' reports about their health and the circumstances surrounding their heath. These measures are now recognized as a central part of health care and health care research. This is for a good reason: Patients' experience of illness drives utilization of the health care system, informs the use of medication, and greatly influences diagnostic decisions. The World Health Organization defines health as "a state of complete physical, mental and social well-being and not merely the absence of disease or infirmity" (World Health Org. 1946). A substantial portion of what we call health is phenomenological and comprises some of the most important and common symptoms in medicine, for example, pain, fatigue, malaise, and dozens of individual symptoms (coughs, aches, physical dysfunction, etc.). Individual interpretations of sensations are crucial in the experience of wellness and illness. The US Food and Drug Administration (FDA) now

recognizes patient-reported outcome (PRO) in clinical trials (Patrick et al. 2007), and these are becoming critical indicators for the approval of new drugs and devices.[1]

PROs are self-reports made by patients about health-related information. As such, they are susceptible to many types of bias, distortion, and error, which have been well documented by research in cognitive science and autobiographical memory. For example, when PROs ask individuals to report their symptoms over long periods of time (say, a month), many processes come into play that impact the validity and reliability of the resulting information (Stone et al. 2007). First, fundamental limitations of memory capacity preclude the veridical recall of some symptom information from a lengthy period. Second, after information has been encoded into memory, there are processes that enable the recall of selected information based on the individual's immediate context (e.g., when in a bad mood, relatively more negative memories are accessible; Bradburn et al. 1987, Sudman et al. 1996). Third, recall is influenced by a number of cognitive heuristics or rules of thumb used to reconstruct past experience. One heuristic is known as the peak-end rule because it results in a greater likelihood of people reporting high-intensity experiences (e.g., severe pain) than low-intensity experiences and because the experiences are more proximal to the time of assessment (Kahneman et al. 1999, Redelmeier et al. 2003). These factors are especially relevant when experiences are difficult to remember, such as over long periods or when experiences are rapidly fluctuating (pain and fatigue have these qualities, as is evident when to you try to report pain levels for a day that is a week or two removed). For all of these reasons, many researchers have recommended the collection of PRO data using short recall periods in order to

---

[1]These are summarized in a 2009 report, *Guidance for Industry. Patient-Reported Outcome Measures: Use in Medical Product Development to Support Labeling Claims.* (From **http:// www.fda.gov/downloads/Drugs/GuidanceCompliance RegulatoryInformation/Guidances/UCM193282.pdf**)

minimize bias and distortion (Dockray et al. 2010, Shiffman et al. 2008, Stone et al. 2007).

The development of assessments with brief recall periods (or even no recall period when the respondent is asked about immediate experience) has gone hand-in-hand with moving assessments out of the laboratory or clinic and into everyday life. Experience sampling method (ESM) and ecological momentary assessment (EMA) are techniques that use immediate reporting of experience in respondents' typical environments, thereby achieving a high level of data accuracy and representative design (Csikszentmihalyi & Hunter 2004, Stone et al. 2007).

Early versions of momentary assessment (ESM and EMA) were based on signaling respondents via electronic pagers or wristwatch alarms, wherein a pocket-size paper-and-pencil questionnaire would be completed. Typically, a series of questions about the time and date, where the person was, what they were doing, and who they were with were answered first. These questions were followed by the specific content meeting the needs of a study; typically, these questions were about affect, symptoms, or behaviors. For example, an EMA investigation of chronic pain would be likely to include questions about the severity of pain at the moment, if medications were recently taken for the pain, how the pain was impacting functioning, and, perhaps, coping methods currently employed to deal with the pain.

Newer versions of momentary assessment protocol have been greatly enhanced with the advent of handheld computers and smart cell phones (Byrom & Tiplady 2010). These devices allow sophisticated programs that greatly enhance the user's experience of the device and enable complex protocols to be implemented. An important component of momentary assessment is the scheduling of assessments. The early wristwatch methods were limited to whatever schedule of "beeps" was initially programmed into the device; beeps generated by pager systems were more flexible, but it was still difficult to implement more complex data collection routines. Handheld devices can be programmed to function as autonomous data collection devices that are preprogrammed to handle a variety of circumstances that respondents may face in the real world (Shiffman 2007). One aspect of this autonomy is that the scheduling of assessments can be set by an algorithm that randomly selects moments for assessment (within preset parameters) or samples moments at set times, depending upon the needs of the study design. But much more complex samplings are possible and are in the spirit of moving the laboratory into the real world because assessments can be made contingent upon information other than the time of day. For example, an investigator interested in how mood changes after an environmental event (e.g., marital dispute) might ask participants to self-initiate an assessment right after the event (a so-called event-driven assessment) and have the electronic diary systematically assess mood at 30-minute intervals thereafter for the next four hours. In this case, the environmental context is conditioning the assessment schedule, allowing a unique set of snapshots about outcomes in the real world (event-context-sensitive EMA; Intille 2007, Stone et al. 2007).

Readers seeking a deeper appreciation of real-time data collection can consult many excellent review articles and volumes that provide comprehensive and detailed information about the techniques, methods, and applications of these methods (Bolger et al. 2003, Hektner et al. 2006, Mehl & Conner 2011, Shiffman et al. 2008, Stone et al. 2007).

REPRESENTATIVE DESIGN IN PHYSIOLOGICAL ASSESSMENT

Information about physiological states is clearly critical for preventing, identifying, and treating medical conditions. Collection of physiological measures, with some exceptions, has been confined to laboratory and clinic settings, and a question arises that is parallel to the one just discussed for self-reports: Are physiological measures collected in restricted settings truly representative of physiological functioning in patients' everyday lives? Unlike the field of

PROs and, more generally, self-report, which has a long and rich history of research, representative design in physiological measurements is a younger field without a large body of empirical results supporting it. Therefore, there is no literature directly on the topic of representative design with physiological measures for us to summarize here; instead, we provide an example to make the point that representative design should be a concept of interest for this domain of research and practice.

The assessment of blood pressure provides an interesting example. A substantial number of studies suggest that 24-hour blood pressure assessment provides a significant amount of information beyond what is known from assessment of blood pressure in an office or a laboratory setting (Ishikawa et al. 2010, 2011; Palmas et al. 2009; Pickering & White 2008; Pickering et al. 2010; Shimbo et al. 2009). The study of blood pressure is important because hypertension is one of the best-known risk factors for premature death due to heart attack or stroke (Arima et al. 2011, Cohn 2011, Foocharoen et al. 2011, Goldenberg et al. 2011, Gray et al. 2011, Losito et al. 2011, Robitaille et al. 2012).

Many clinical decisions about the management of blood pressure are made on the basis of readings taken in an office setting. Although it has long been recommended that physicians capture blood pressure using multiple readings on multiple days (Mi et al. 2010), in practice it is common to prescribe medication on the basis of a few readings or, in some cases, only a single reading. Yet, blood pressure varies substantially over the course of time (Mi et al. 2010). There is a circadian pattern in which blood pressure surges during the morning hours, dips later in the day, and tends to be lower at night (de la Sierra et al. 2009). Considerable speculation exists about whether patterns of blood pressure variations throughout the circadian cycle are predictive of adverse health outcomes. For example, individuals whose blood pressure does not dip during the night might be at higher risk for heart attacks or strokes (Eguchi et al. 2008). Yet few epidemiologic studies have systematically evaluated the impact of these patterns. In

fact, most of what we know about the risks of high blood pressure is based on epidemiologic studies that characterize blood pressure at a few defined points in time and then follow participants prospectively to determine whether elevated blood pressure early in life results in poor health outcomes many years later (Egan et al. 2010). Many studies show that clinic-based blood pressure assessment misses much of the important variability that occurs outside the clinic. We return to the issue of blood pressure measurement when we discuss new assessment methodologies.

MOBILE AND WIRELESS HEALTH

Whereas ESM/EMA methods and technology are typically (although not exclusively) used to monitor patient experience, mobile health (mHealth) is about using mobile computing technologies to enhance all aspects of health care, including our focus, behavioral intervention strategies. Certainly an important advance in bringing the laboratory and clinic into natural environments is the rapid development of new portable communications technologies. The revolution in technology enables studies with representative designs and ESM/EMA to provide the scientific underpinnings of these developments. In fact, a direct outgrowth of EMA is an area known as ecological momentary interventions (EMI; for a review, see Heron & Smyth 2010). The characteristics of EMI are that they are methods intended to take interventions (usually behavioral) into the everyday lives of patients. These interventions are administered via mobile devices and are momentary in that they happen immediately in the natural environment (hence the analogy with EMA). A recent review examined 27 EMI interventions in the areas of smoking cessation, weight loss, anxiety, diabetes management, eating disorders, alcohol use, healthy eating, and physical activity (Heron & Smyth 2010), areas that partially overlap with the material summarized below.

mHealth, which includes a range of technologies from cell phones to wireless sensors, has developed at an exponential pace in recent years. The International Telecommunications Union (2011) estimated that about 5.6 billion cell phones are now in use around the world and that this number will at least double (far exceeding the number of people in the world) within the next decade. China, for example, has nearly one billion wireless accounts, and the United Arab Emirates has nearly two active wireless accounts for each person in the population. Wireless communication devices have leapfrogged wired systems. **Figure 1** shows the growth of wireless phones in relation to standard wired telephones between 2001 and 2011. About 91% of US adults use a mobile phone regularly. Financial resources have not hindered widespread dissemination of these technologies: The fast-growing markets include African American and Hispanic users and low-income families (Zickuhr & Smith 2012). Growing evidence indicates that electronic technologies may be the best way to help low-income people change behavior (Bennett et al. 2012). The almost universal availability of cell phones means that most people are connected to a data collection and intervention apparatus, allowing the implementation of a representative design as discussed above. Technologies are also available to collect real-time psycho-physiological responses.

Research using these new technologies is only now beginning to catch hold. For example, rapid advances in computer technology have yielded remarkably attractive low-cost, real-time devices to assess disease, movement, images, behavior, social interactions, environmental toxins, hormones, and other physiological variables (Schatz & Berlin 2011a). Miniaturized mobile electronic devices require little energy to operate and may provide the potential to advance research, prevent disease, enhance diagnostics, improve treatment, increase access to health services, and lower health care costs in ways previously unimaginable (Schatz & Berlin 2011b). There is now a Society for Ambulatory Assessment dedicated to research and applications using ambulatory monitoring

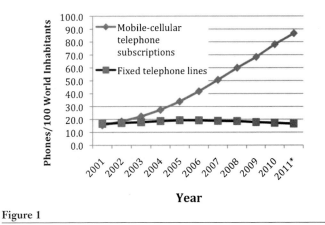

Figure 1

Mobile wireless telephone accounts versus fixed-line telephone subscriptions per 100 world inhabitants, 2001–2011. Data from International Telecommunications Union (**http://www.itu.int/ITU-D/ict/**). *2011 data are estimates.

(**http://www.ambulatory-assessment.org**), *Psychosomatic Medicine* recently devoted an entire journal issue to these methods (Kubiak & Stone 2012), and several review articles and books were mentioned previously. mHealth technologies have the potential to revolutionize behavioral research by advancing health measurement and treatment, areas discussed in the following sections.

mHEALTH: MEASUREMENT ADVANCES

mHealth measurement has the potential to advance health care by bringing measurements that would formerly have been made in the laboratory or clinic into the everyday lives of patients. ESM and EMA have demonstrated the potential of assessments in the real-life environment of study subjects. The explosion of new electronic devices has made available new real-time, continuous biological, behavioral, and environmental data collection by wireless and mobile technologies. The premise of mHealth is that this can improve our understanding of the etiology of health and disease, particularly when integrated with data from areas such as genomics, biomarkers, and electronic medical records. These data have the potential to contribute to our understanding of health behavior change and to inform the development of treatments and prevention programs that are preemptive, personalized, and adaptive over time. The remainder of this review provides many examples that demonstrate this potential.

Mobile technologies can be used to capture, store, analyze, manage, and present population-level data, including geographic information system (GIS) data, and potentially to deliver these data more efficiently. Research using these technologies could lead to the development of early detection and warning systems to address possible disease outbreaks. Further, these tools are now being used in clinical trials to capture outcomes in natural environments and reduce burden on participants. Remote monitoring and sensing can allow researchers to recruit and follow patients without the need and associated costs of transporting them to a research or health care setting. As a result, the trials may get higher-quality data at lower costs.

The techniques of ESM and EMA can be used to collect data for all manner of self-report information pertaining to health. The frequency of data collection depends upon the nature of the data to be collected, but in practice this has usually meant an end-of-day diary strategy or a momentary, within-the-day strategy. The principles discussed in the prior section provide the rationale for determining the data collection frequency as well as the precise reason for collecting the data. For example, if the goal of an mHealth assessment program is to monitor whether people were experiencing severe pain during the day, it is likely that a diary administered at the end of the day over several days would be an effective strategy. On the other hand, if the goal of the project was to monitor the number of micturitions during the waking day, a momentary data collection strategy might be more appropriate, given the difficulty of accurately recalling a large number of daily events. In both cases, the data could be collected with mobile devices that transmit data to central servers for timely data reduction and, if necessary, generation of reports to researchers or providers. An alternative method

of transmitting data could be via text messages wherein patients are signaled with an outbound message and respond to specific questions with a return text message (Berkman et al. 2011).

Measurements of physiological functions are open to the same mHealth opportunities for data collection in the real world and immediate transmittal of information to interested parties. A good example of this concerns the measurement of physical activity, which has traditionally relied on self-report. Recently, accelerometers have improved activity measurement, but it was clear that more data would better inform research and consumer applications (Atienza & Patrick 2011). Work such as the PALMS (Physical Activity Location Measurement System) combines heart rate with motion, GPS, and environmental sensors to develop a more complete profile of the user's actions, exposure, and responses (Patrick et al. 2011). This type of system allows for better activity and environmental assessment for research and clinical applications.

More generally, measuring biomarkers has traditionally required a blood draw or other invasive procedure. Recent advances in mHealth indicate that assessment of glucose and sodium can be achieved using nanosensor "tattoos." These tattoos are based on a gel solution (the same material that is used in children's washable tattoos), which is embedded with an array of tiny sensors that are read through a smartphone's camera system (Dubach & Caversaccio 2011, St. Martin 2010). A recent book by Eric Topol (2012), a renowned cardiologist, summarizes several other applications of new technology to medical monitoring. The book, entitled *The Creative Destruction of Medicine: How the Digital Revolution Will Create Better Health Care*, suggests that nanotech sensors will be able to recognize cells in the bloodstream for patients at imminent risk of a heart attack. These sensors would send messages to the patient's cell phone, suggesting immediate medical attention—much like the "check engine" light on a car. Applications already exist that allow continuous monitoring of vital signs and can transmit the information to health care providers anywhere in the world. In contrast to expensive sleep laboratories that can cost thousands of dollars for an assessment, there is now a much less invasive $100 iPhone application that can monitor sleep at home. The application calculates rapid eye movement cycles and produces estimates of apnea and sleep quality. Topol (2012) also describes sensor-based methods that can provide noninvasive continuous monitoring of blood glucose for people with diabetes and that can offer advice on disease management.

Environmental monitoring using mHealth devices has shown that environmental variables such as chemicals and airborne carbon can be efficiently collected in real time using mobile devices. For example, new mobile sensor systems enable researchers to understand the relationship between environmental factors and health at specific locales versus a predefined region, as well as allow individuals to better monitor the quality of their environment to protect their own health (Lein 2012).

In the following sections we detail two promising mHealth measurement developments that have yielded or seem likely to yield important insights into health: blood pressure monitoring and portable laboratories.

Blood Pressure

New technologies allow the assessment of blood pressure over an extended period of time. For example, we now have 24-hour blood pressure monitoring capability, and it is easier for people to monitor their own blood pressure in their homes using inexpensive, accurate technologies. Yet, there are no official guidelines on the application of ambulatory blood pressure monitoring (Pickering 1992, 1996; Pickering et al. 2010).

Out-of-office assessment of blood pressure has led to important discoveries. One of the best examples is the problem of white coat hypertension and masked hypertension. White coat hypertension is false positive high blood pressure. It occurs when people have high blood pressure readings when assessed in clinic and normal blood pressure readings when assessed

in other circumstances. Essentially, the clinical environment symbolized by the physician's white coat can produce enough anxiety to stimulate short-term reactive elevations in blood pressure, resulting in false positive readings (Pickering 1991). Pickering noted that, in addition to white coat hypertension, there is also a problem of false negative blood pressure readings. For some people, being in a quiet exam room may be stress relieving. Masked hypertension occurs when an individual has normal blood pressure in a clinic or laboratory assessment but is shown to have elevated blood pressure when assessed using 24-hour ambulatory monitoring (Pickering 2005).

A variety of studies suggest that individuals with masked hypertension are at increased risk. For example, Ishikawa and colleagues (2010) studied 129 participants whose blood pressure was normal (less than 140/90 mm Hg) when assessed in an office setting. None of the participants were taking hypertensive medication. When assessed using 24-hour ambulatory monitoring, the median blood pressure was greater than 130/80 mm Hg for 13 of the individuals. Those with masked hypertension had higher levels of serum glucose and urinary albumin-creatinine ratios. Masked hypertension may contribute to poor health outcomes in several ways (Franklin et al. 2012). For example, it is related to left ventricular remodeling and to exaggerated blood pressure responses to treadmill exercise (Schultz et al. 2011, Sharman et al. 2011).

Other reviews of existing studies confirm the risk for masked hypertension but not for white coat hypertension (Pierdomenico & Cuccurullo 2011). Some evidence suggests that ambulatory blood pressure monitoring is a better predictor of adverse cardiovascular events than is blood pressure monitored in an office (Ishikawa et al. 2011). A meta-analysis demonstrated that masked hypertension might be a more common problem than white coat hypertension (Pierdomenico & Cuccurullo 2010). Furthermore, white coat hypertension becomes more common with age, particularly for individuals older than age 50 for systolic pressure and over age 45 for diastolic pressure. For younger individuals, the masked hypertension problem is more common (Mancia et al. 2011).

Blood pressure is just one of many variables that is likely to be affected by context. Convenience sampling of blood pressure during medical office visits has led to the successful treatment of many individuals. However, new technologies allow the monitoring of blood pressure to go to the next level of precision. These studies help establish that traditional lab-based or clinic-based evaluation can yield misleading results. In order to better understand these processes, sampling at different times and different places is required. Blood pressure, like many other physiologic phenomena, is not static. Environmental circumstances have an important impact as blood pressure fluctuates over the course of the usual day.

Portable Laboratories

Assessing symptoms, risk factors, and biomarkers for disease in real time and without lab facilities has been an important new research direction in the United States and in the developing world. Research has made possible the smartphone-enabled detection of a variety of geological indicators using a chip-based micro-nuclear magnetic resonance unit. Early work on the unit shows that it is more accurate for cancer detection than is conventional biopsy and that the time to return test results is close to 30 minutes rather than the standard two- to three-day time frame (Issadore et al. 2011). LUCAS (Lensless Ultra-wide-field Cell monitoring Array platform based on Shadow imaging technology) (Isikman et al. 2012), a lens-free mobile microscope that uses a mobile phone camera as its base, is now being used to train health care providers in low- and middle-income countries (Mudanyali et al. 2011). Early results suggest that LUCAS can deliver laboratory-quality, low-cost visual images in the field. Devices such as these should allow for better disease surveillance at much lower cost in both research and practice.

mHEALTH: INTERVENTION ADVANCES IN RANDOMIZED TRIALS

In addition to the potential of new electronic technologies to improve measurement, they may also have the potential to alter the way behavioral interventions are delivered in nonclinic settings. mHealth tools have been promoted as having great potential for treating disease and providing support for people living with chronic disease. In the following sections we review the evidence for the effectiveness of these tools for interventions to address obesity, smoking cessation, diabetes management, HIV treatment and prevention, and adherence and aging. Our review focuses on randomized clinical trials because they provide the strongest evidence for treatment efficacy. Using Google Scholar, we searched under the terms mHealth, mobile devices, text messaging, SMS, and mobile health. All searches included the term randomized. Because of the newness of the mobile health field of investigation, we found few publications prior to 2008, and the majority were published since 2010.

Obesity

Programs are being tested that utilize youth-friendly sensors and feedback to youth, parents, and providers to help overweight minority youth lose weight and eat healthier diets (Eder et al. 2010). Some evidence suggests that self-monitoring increases weight loss in overweight adults and helps sustain these losses (Burke et al. 2011). Activity measures and sensors can accurately measure energy expenditure (Albinali et al. 2010) and diet (Sun et al. 2010). These tools will enable both research and consumer devices to better measure diet and activity to prevent or treat obesity and enhance healthy lifestyles.

Patrick and colleagues (2009) used an intervention based on text messaging for adults attempting to lose weight. Sixty-five overweight men and women were randomly assigned either to receive monthly printed materials about weight control or to a condition that sent personalized text messages two to five times a day in addition to receiving printed materials and monthly phone calls from a health counselor. At the end of 16 weeks, those receiving the electronic messages lost more weight (3.60 kg) in comparison with the control group (0.34 kg). However, the trial confounded text messaging with interpersonal counseling.

Cole-Lewis & Kershaw (2010) reviewed all of the randomized and quasi-experimental trials of text-messaging interventions published through June 2009. They concentrated on nine studies they considered to have adequate statistical power. Among these nine studies, eight found evidence that text messaging was an effective tool for behavior change. However, when we concentrated on recent randomized trials, we found the results of mHealth interventions for weight loss to be more mixed. One trial recruited 96 adults with body mass indexes greater than 32.6 kg/m^2 and randomly assigned them to one of two groups: podcasts about weight loss or podcasts plus mobile phone applications. Both groups received podcasts about weight loss two times per week for three months and then received two mini podcasts per week for an additional three months. The second group was given a diet- and physical-activity-monitoring application for a mobile device in addition to the podcasts. The results showed no incremental effect of the mobile application (p = 0.98) (Turner-McGrievy & Tate 2011).

In a trial conducted in the Netherlands, 539 overweight adults were randomly assigned to a tailored intervention or to generic information that was given over a Web site. Using a variety of anthropometric measures, the investigators were unable to find significant differences between the tailored intervention and generic groups. They concluded that the tailored intervention was no more effective than a generic approach for preventing weight gain or modifying dietary and physical activity (van Genugten et al. 2012).

Hurling and colleagues (2007) in Bedford, England randomly assigned 77 adults to one of two conditions. The intervention group

received tailored solutions for overcoming barriers to physical activity. They were also offered email reminders and mobile phone–delivered schedules for exercise, and had access to a message board. The control group did not receive these electronic assets, but both groups were given wrist accelerometers. After nine weeks, differences in METs were nonsignificant, although there was a trend toward more activity in the intervention group. Self-reported physical activity was higher in the intervention group. The accelerometer data were consistent with the self-report data, except for activity ranges above six METs (Hurling et al. 2007).

A randomized clinical trial by Spring and colleagues (2012) aimed at lifestyle change considered the management of multiple behaviors, a strategy that is typically required to achieve change. Spring and colleagues focused on 204 adults who had elevated rates of consumption of saturated fat and low rates of consumption of fruits and vegetables. In addition, the group members were sedentary in their leisure time and generally inactive. Using mobile decision-support technology and some financial incentives, participants were randomly assigned to one of four treatments: (*a*) increased fruit/vegetable consumption and increased physical activity, (*b*) decreased fat consumption and sedentary leisure and increased physical activity, (*c*) increased fruits and vegetables and decreased sedentary leisure activity, and (*d*) decreased sedentary leisure activity and decreased fat consumption. Among the four groups, the group that was coached to increase fruits and vegetables and decrease sedentary leisure improved more than the other three groups, and these differences were maintained through the five-month follow-up. Among alternatives, the focus on increasing fruits and vegetables and decreasing sedentary time during leisure activities appears to hold the most promise. Although the Spring study is an important achievement and is seen as support for mobile health technologies, it does not actually test the value of mobile devices. All four groups used the mobile technologies, and the group differences reflect different achievements in behavior change relevant to the content of the interventions.

Summary. Despite the promise of mHealth-based interventions for weight management, the current literature is at best mixed. Studies on weight loss are particularly challenging. It is not enough to show that a wireless reminder technology results in some dietary changes. We need to know whether those dietary changes translate into sustained weight loss. A substantial literature shows that most dietary interventions work in the short run, but few result in sustained weight loss (Mann et al. 2007). Weight loss alone is not clearly linked to improvements in obesity-related diseases such as diabetes, heart disease, and some cancers (Shea et al. 2010, 2011). Long-term studies are necessary to demonstrate that sustained changes in health behaviors result in reductions in the burden of these chronic conditions.

Diabetes Management

Large prospective clinical trials have established the long-term benefits of intensive blood glucose control in people with type 1 diabetes (Knowler et al. 2009). However, the application of intensive blood glucose control has been limited by a lack of technologies that would enable people with diabetes to easily and appropriately adjust delivery of insulin in response to minute-to-minute changes in circulating glucose. There is a need for more accurate and rapid detection in real time of glucose levels throughout the day and improved methods for rapidly translating real-time glucose measurements into adjustments in insulin delivery. Research has been crucial in the development of continuous glucose monitors, which are now being used clinically to give people with diabetes the ability to view real-time glucose levels, review trends and fluctuations in recent blood glucose levels, and receive alerts when blood glucose levels become too high or too low. Work in continuous glucose monitors has shown that mobile monitoring improves outcomes and provides a significant cost savings over traditional self-monitoring (Huang et al. 2010). The ability to provide patients and providers with real-time information on physiology may be especially critical for those in rural areas in which access to health providers may be challenging. Further, the widespread adoption of mHealth technologies may offer an excellent opportunity for research to improve the delivery of diabetes care and lower treatment costs by improving communication between patients, health care providers, and health care systems.

The value of text-messaging technologies to improve adherence in diabetes has been advocated by many diabetes providers. One trial evaluated cell phone–based software designed to help adults with type 2 diabetes. Thirty patients in the practices of three community physicians were randomly assigned to receive a cell phone–based software application that provided feedback on blood glucose levels, the medical regimen, and plans for dealing with hypo- or hyperglycemia. A control group did not receive the application. After three months, HbA1c (a measure of diabetes control over the past 90 days) declined by 2.03% in the treatment group in comparison with 0.68% in the control group (p < 0.02). It is noteworthy that several of the authors were employees of the software manufacturer (Quinn et al. 2008).

A small study from Bahrain randomized 34 patients with type 2 diabetes to a condition that offered SMS support for diabetes care or to a control group that did not get the support. Although there were no differences in weight loss, HbA1c declined more in the SMS group than in the control group (Hussein et al. 2011).

Despite the positive findings of a few studies, several randomized trials have failed to confirm the value of mHealth interventions for enhancing diabetes outcomes. In one trial, a text-messaging support system, Sweet Talk, was evaluated in children and adolescents with type 1 diabetes. Ninety-two participants were randomly assigned to one of three groups: conventional insulin therapy, conventional therapy plus Sweet Talk, or intensive insulin therapy plus Sweet Talk. Outcomes as measured by HbA1c did not differ between those in conventional therapy and those in conventional therapy plus Sweet Talk. HbA1c did improve in the patients in intensive therapy plus Sweet Talk, but the design of the study did not allow an assessment of the independent contribution of the text-message Sweet Talk intervention. Overall, the study provided no evidence that text messaging improved diabetes control (Franklin et al. 2006).

In the United Kingdom, Istepanian and colleagues (2009) randomly assigned 137 adults with complicated diabetes to one of two conditions. In the experimental arm, 72 patients learned to use a sensor that could measure their blood glucose and transmit the data to a mobile phone using Bluetooth technology. The data were reviewed by clinicians who were able to respond with feedback through an Internet site. This is a sophisticated application because it allowed feedback in real time. The 65 patients in the control arm did not transmit information about their blood glucose and experienced usual care. After nine months, there were no differences between the groups in HbA1c. The authors concluded that the absence of human contact might have spoiled the benefits of providing better information through the electronic devices (Istepanian et al. 2009).

Another trial randomly assigned 78 adolescents with type 1 diabetes to one of two conditions. The intervention group wore a pedometer and received regular text messages with motivational content. The control group received usual diabetes care. Both groups were followed for 12 weeks. Neither the number of steps taken (measured by the pedometer) nor self-reported physical activity was significantly affected by the text-messaging intervention (Newton et al. 2009).

It would seem that electronic reminders by cell phones might increase response rates in clinical trials. However, in one study, 125 participants were randomly assigned to get electronic text-message reminders to return questionnaires or to a no-reminder control group. Electronic reminders had no effect on either response rates for turning in questionnaires or for time to complete the questionnaire (Man et al. 2011).

Summary. The best evidence supporting the use of mHealth technologies in diabetes care comes from an industry-sponsored trial and from another very small study. Larger and more systematic trials tend to raise questions about the efficacy and effectiveness of the interventions. At present, text-messaging interventions to enhance adherence in diabetes care are not clearly supported by the evidence. More studies that offer real-time support for patients and for providers are needed. ●

Smoking Cessation

Smoking was an early target of mHealth research, with studies looking at short text messaging as an enhancement to smoking cessation programs. Research indicates that SMS and mobile Web programs are effective in increasing quit attempts, but we need additional work in this area to define the optimal timing, content, and methods for using mHealth to prevent and decrease smoking in the United States and globally (Berkman et al. 2011).

An example of a positive clinical trial is Happy Ending, an intensive smoking cessation program delivered through both cell phones and the Internet. The program requires more than 400 contacts via email, interactive voice messages, and SMS. Subjects were recruited over the Internet and then randomly assigned to the Happy Ending program or to a control group that received a 44-page self-help booklet. Self-reported abstinence was obtained via the Internet or through telephone interviews at one, three, six, and twelve months after planned cessation. Self-reported abstinence rates favored the Happy Ending program through six months. At the 12-month follow-up, 38% of those in the Happy Ending group were abstinent in comparison with 24% in the control group (p = 0.07) (Brendryen & Kraft 2008).

In another trial, adult smokers in the United Kingdom who were considering quitting were randomly assigned to either an intervention that involved text messaging for smoking cessation or to a control group that received text messages unrelated to smoking cessation. The study involved 5,800 participants and demonstrated that self-reported continuous abstinence was significantly higher in the SMS group than in the control group. Further, these reports were biochemically validated six months following the treatment (Free et al. 2011).

Not all mHealth interventions have produced the expected results. For example, Whittaker and colleagues (2011) tested a social-learning-theory-based video-messaging application designed for a mobile phone with the intent of reducing tobacco use. The study was a well-designed, randomized controlled clinical trial with a six-month follow-up. Current smokers were randomly assigned to receive automated video and text messages for a six-month period or to a control group that received a general health video message every other week. The study found continuous abstinence at six months to be 26.4% in the intervention group and 27.7% in the control group. The tailored high-tech intervention worked no better than the control group. However, the intervention group received generic messages rather than real-time feedback on their own behaviors.

Another randomized controlled trial allocated 207 pregnant smokers to receive 11 weeks of text messages about smoking cessation tailored to their own baseline behaviors along with a tailored leaflet or to a control group that received a nontailored self-help leaflet. Although those receiving the text messages were more likely to set a quit date and have a higher self-efficacy and determination to quit, differences in actual quit rates were nonsignificant (22.9% for intervention versus 19.6% for control group) (Naughton et al. 2012).

Riley and colleagues (2011) evaluated seven studies on smoking cessation published prior to 2010. Most of the studies found a benefit of SMS messages sent to smokers who were attempting to quit. However, not all of the studies had adequate control groups, and the effects varied considerably across studies. A Cochrane review of randomized studies also found inconsistency across studies. Although overall there was a significant decrease in the self-reported smoking rate (relative risk 2.18; CI 1.80–2.65), there was very little evidence of the maintenance of the effect over longer-term follow-up (Whittaker et al. 2009). The authors concluded, "the current evidence shows no effect of mobile phone-based smoking cessation interventions on long-term outcome."

Summary. There is some evidence that SMS is helpful for those attempting to quit smoking. However, most randomized clinical trials have failed to show the benefit of these interventions on long-term tobacco abstinence.

HIV Treatment and Prevention

In some areas, mobile phone reminders do appear to have an important impact. This may be particularly true in studies for patients with HIV. For example, an abstract from Pop-Eleches et al. (2011) describes a study in which 431 adults who had started antiretroviral therapy were randomly assigned to a control group or to one of four intervention groups. In all the intervention groups, participants received SMS reminders, on either a daily or a weekly interval, to take their antiretroviral therapy. The control group did not receive SMS messages. An event-monitoring system was used to assess adherence to the medications. All participants were followed for 48 weeks. About 53% of those receiving regular SMS messages achieved an adherence rate of 90% or more during the 48 weeks of this study in comparison with 40% in the control group (difference significance p = 0.003) (Pop-Eleches et al. 2011).

A much smaller industry-supported trial compared 19 AIDS patients who had been randomly assigned to a cell phone text-messaging reminder system or to use a beeper to prompt medication taking. Over six weeks, those receiving the text message were significantly more likely to comply with antiretroviral therapy if evaluated using a medication event monitoring system that electronically records when a pill bottle is opened. Benefits of text messaging were nonsignificant at both three- and six-week follow-ups if the measure was either pill counts or self-report. However, the data were not analyzed by intention to treat, and a significant number of participants were not included in the final analysis (Hardy et al. 2011).

In a study from Kenya (Lester et al. 2010), HIV-infected adults were randomly assigned to an intervention that involved SMS or standard care. The intervention was quite simple and typically sent the word *mambo*, which is Kiswahili for "How are you?" Participants were instructed to report back within 48 hours. If they reported that they were not doing well, a health care worker contacted them. The study demonstrated that the simple text-messaging intervention significantly increased self-reported adherence and also led to better viral suppression (Lester et al. 2010).

Another HIV trial used mixed methods in a randomized cluster trial to evaluate the impact of a mobile phone–supported intervention in Uganda. The unit of analysis was community peer-based health worker. Twenty-nine workers at 10 clinics were randomly assigned to an intervention that sent text messages and called workers to prompt them with patient-specific clinical information. A control group did not receive this intervention. Nested within the providers were 970 patients who were followed over the course of 26 months. Considering a wide number of virologic and nonvirologic outcomes, including patient adherence and death, there were no statistically significant differences between the conditions (Chang et al. 2011).

Summary. Our review identified several studies suggesting that text messaging may have value for improving the care of patients infected with HIV, particularly in the developing world. However, we found several methodological problems with the studies and some investigations with null results. A review by the Cochrane Collaboration considered randomized trials published between January 1980 and November 2011, evaluating text-messaging-related interventions to standard care. Among 243 references, only 17 appeared highly relevant. Among these, serious consideration was given to only two trials from Kenya. These two trials suggested that text messaging may improve adherence to antiretroviral therapy in Kenya. One trial suggested that weekly text messaging might result in better suppression of HIV load. However, it is remarkable that this comprehensive review found so few high-quality studies (Horvath et al. 2012, Petrie et al. 2012).

Telemonitoring, Adherence, and Aging

Poor adherence to prescription medications has been a persistent problem in the delivery of health care. Simple programs, such as SMS reminders for medications (Simoni et al. 2009), to complex systems for the elderly that support medication and activities of daily living will allow elders to avoid hospitalization (Cook & Holder 2011). Although the more complex programs are in early stages, simple reminders have been shown to enhance adherence to medications and vaccination schedules and attendance at medical appointments (Riley et al. 2011). Other trials have suggested that targeted text messaging may improve adherence among adults taking preventive medication for asthma (Kelly & Giordano 2011), although some studies have failed to show a benefit of text messaging for adherence to an asthma regimen (Prabhakaran et al. 2010).

As with other studies on text messaging, some careful studies fail to support the value of the interventions. For instance, one trial randomly assigned 108 adults to receive a text message about taking medication or to no text message activity (Cocosila et al. 2009). In this case the medicine was one vitamin C pill per day. The outcome was self-reported adherence and the number of times the participants acknowledged taking their vitamin. Although those in the text-messaging group were initially more adherent, differences were nonsignificant by the end of the study. However, power for the study was relatively low (0.54).

Another approach to mobile health technologies involves telemonitoring, generally using landline telephone systems. These methods have been particularly attractive because they allow the assessment and transmission of patient data from remote sites directly to a health care provider. There has been particular enthusiasm for telemonitoring for the care of older adults with chronic illnesses. Electronic systems can be used to monitor indicators such as blood pressure, pulse, blood oxygen, or peak expiratory flow. In addition, the equipment allows for real-time consultation. In one randomized controlled trial (Takahashi et al. 2012), older adults who had multiple health problems were randomly assigned to use telemonitoring or to usual care. The outcome was the number of hospitalizations or visits to the emergency room within the 12 months following enrollment ($N = 205$). The study was unable to document a benefit of telemonitoring. However, unexpectedly and inexplicably, mortality was significantly higher among those in the telemonitoring group.

Summary of mHealth Intervention Effectiveness

Table 1 summarizes the 21 trials that we were able to locate in the published literature. One trial used mHealth intervention in all conditions and only varied content. Among the remaining 20 trials, 11 (55%) failed to document a clear benefit of mHealth interventions, and another 3 (15%) had mixed results. About half of the trials on smoking cessation achieved a benefit of text-message-based intervention, whereas the record was less clear for weight loss. Most trials failed to show that text messaging improved diabetes outcomes. To date, the most consistent positive results are for improving adherence to antiretroviral therapy among adults with HIV in the developing world. Overall, most of the trials we evaluated failed to show a significant benefit of the mHealth interventions, and only 6 of 20 trials (30%) demonstrated a clear and unambiguous benefit across multiple measures and assessment periods.

NEXT STEPS: WHERE DO WE GO FROM HERE?

The examples we have provided suggest that new electronic technologies combined with thoughtful behaviorally based principles of data capture and interventions may advance medical science and the practice of health care. They will allow us to monitor people continuously and will permit capture of data in a representative sample of environments. These advantages have led many to conclude that electronic technologies will have a profound impact on human health.

If the promise is real, it should be demonstrable in systematic studies (Collins 2012). Yet surprisingly few studies have evaluated the effect of wireless technologies on health outcomes. There will be abundant research opportunities in this field, but we need to consider several challenges as the field moves forward.

Consistency with Previous Reviews

In addition to our review, several others have reviewed portions of the literature on the effects of electronic technologies on health behaviors. Our analysis appears to be at odds with the report from Fjeldsoe and colleagues (2009). These authors conducted an evidence synthesis of papers published between January 1990 and March 2008. That analysis included 14 studies evaluating an intervention delivered primarily via SMS and that assessed change in health behavior using a prepost test assessment. The analysis found that positive behavior change occurred in 13 of 14 studies. However, the analysis was based largely on pretest/posttest studies as opposed to randomized experimental trials. On the other hand and consistent with our review, Gurman and colleagues (2012) considered evaluations of electronic behavior-change strategies applied in the developing world. They found support for the use of these methods to be inconsistent at best.

The most similar review was reported by Lau and associates (2011) from Hong Kong. They included studies relevant to the use of

Table 1 Summary of 19 randomized clinical trials evaluating mHealth technologies

Reference	Topic	Intervention	N	Outcome measure	Outcome
Whittaker et al. 2011	Smoking cessation	Video plus SMS versus general video	226 daily smokers age 16 or older	Continuous abstinence at 6 months	Null
Naughton et al. 2012	Smoking cessation	11 Weeks of SMS messages with a tailored leaflet versus a nontailored leaflet	207 pregnant smokers	Quit rate	Null
Brendryen & Kraft 2008	Smoking cessation	Intensive 54-week smoking cessation program using more than 400 contacts delivered both by text messages and Internet versus 44-page self-help booklet	396 adult smokers	Self-reported abstinence at 1, 3, 6, and 12 months	Abstinence higher in treatment group at all follow-ups
Free et al. 2011	Smoking cessation	Text messages related to smoking cessation versus text messages unrelated to smoking	5,800 smokers in the U.K.	Self-reported abstinence at 6 months	Abstinence higher in relevant text-messaging group
Patrick et al. 2009	Weight loss	Personalized text messages 2 to 5 times a day versus monthly printed materials	65 overweight men and women	Weight loss at 16 weeks	More weight loss in mHealth condition
Turner-McGrievy & Tate 2011	Weight loss	Podcasts about weight loss versus podcasts plus mobile phone app	96 adults with BMIs greater than 32.6 kg/m^2	Weight loss at 12 weeks	Null
Van Genugten et al. 2012	Weight maintenance	Tailored mHealth intervention versus generic information from Web site	539 overweight adults	Prevention of weight gain, waist circumference, skinfold thickness	Null
Hurling et al. 2007	Physical activity	Tailored text messages and email reminders versus no messages	77 healthy adults	METs of activity and self-reported activity at 9 weeks	Null for overall METs. More self-reported activity in intervention group in leisure time. Test group lost more body fat

(Continued)

Table 1 (*Continued*)

Reference	Topic	Intervention	N	Outcome measure	Outcome
Spring et al. 2012	Diet and activity	Handheld device used to record diet and activity and to offer real-time decision support	204 sedentary adults with diets high in saturated fat and low in fruits and vegetables	Composite Diet-Activity Improvement Score composed of four health behaviors: saturated fat intake, fruit and vegetable consumption, physical activity, and sedentary behavior	An intervention targeting increased fruit and vegetable consumption and reduced sedentary activity achieved more change on the composite index than did more traditional diet and activity interventions
Quinn et al. 2008	Diabetes control	Cell phone feedback on blood glucose and planning for hyper- and hypoglycemia versus usual care	30 patients with type 2 diabetes mellitus	Glycated hemoglobin (HbA1c) at 3 months	Benefit favoring intervention
Hussein et al. 2011	Diabetes control	Text-message support for diabetes care versus no text-message support	34 patients with type 2 diabetes mellitus in Bahrain	Weight loss and HbA1c	Null for weight loss; benefit of text messages for HbA1c
Franklin et al. 2006	Diabetes control	Intensive insulin therapy plus text messages versus intensive therapy without text messages versus conventional therapy without text messages	92 children and adolescents with type 1 diabetes mellitus	HbA1C	Null. Nonsignificant differences between intensive therapy groups, but those in intensive therapy did better than those in conventional treatment
Istepanian et al. 2009	Diabetes control	Treatment: Sensor measures blood glucose and relays information to clinician who gives feedback via Internet site Control: Did not use sensor system	137 adults with complicated diabetes mellitus in the U.K.	HbA1C at 9 months	Null
Newton et al. 2009	Diabetes control/physical activity	Text messages with motivational content versus no messages	78 adolescents with type 1 diabetes mellitus	Physical activity at 12 weeks	Null

Man et al. 2011	Response rates in clinical trials	Electronic reminders to return questionnaires versus no reminders	125 participants in clinical trials	Response rating for returning questionnaires	Null
Pop-Eleches et al. 2011	Adherence in HIV	Text-message reminders versus no reminders	431 adults taking antiretroviral therapy for HIV	Adherence assessed using event-monitoring system	Greater adherence in text-messaging condition
Hardy et al. 2011	Adherence in HIV	Text-messaging adherence prompts versus beeper prompts	19 HIV-infected adults in Kenya	Medication adherence measured with MEMS caps at 3 and 6 weeks	Greater adherence in text-messaging condition measured by MEMS. Nonsignificant trend for pill count and self-report at both 3 and 6 weeks
Lester et al. 2010	Adherence in HIV	Text messages requesting wellness reports versus no messages	538 adults in Kenya initiating ART for HIV	Self-reported adherence and viral suppression	Greater adherence and reduced viral load in text-messaging group
Chang et al. 2011	Adherence in HIV treatment	Text messages and connection with health worker	Nested trial; unit of randomization 29 health workers caring for 970 patients in Uganda	Viral load and patient adherence over 26 months	Null
Cocosila et al. 2009	Adherence with vitamin C	Text message reminder versus no message	102 adults	Self-reported adherence	Null
Takahashi et al. 2012	Telemonitoring for older patients with chronic illness	Telemonitoring to oversee blood pressure, pulse, and O2 with availability of remote consultation versus usual care	205 adults, mean age >80 years	Hospitalizations, emergency department visits, and deaths over 12 months	Null. No differences in hospitalizations or emergency department visits; more deaths in telemonitored group

Abbreviations: ART, antiretroviral therapy; BMI, body mass index; HIV, human immunodeficiency virus; MEMS, medication event monitoring system; MET, metabolic equivalent of task; SMS, short message service.

communication technologies for improving physical activity in children and adolescents published between January 1997 and December 2009. Their review considered both Internet-based technologies and some communications technologies (our review focused on smartphones and related devices), and most of the studies they considered predated smartphone technologies. They identified nine studies, and among these, positive results were obtained in seven. However, looking at their analysis, it appears that significant between-group differences existed on the major outcome variables in only two of the nine studies. For most of the studies, both treatment and control groups improved, and it was common to find that the rate of improvement was comparable between these groups. Although some reviewers (Krishna et al. 2009) interpret most studies as supporting the value of text messaging, most reviews interpret the literature in a manner similar to ours. For example, Norman et al. (2007) reviewed electronic health interventions in studies for both adults and children. Their review differs from ours in that it includes a wide variety of electronic technologies focused on behavior change relevant to physical activity and healthy eating. They focused on 47 studies and found that eHealth interventions achieved better changes in health behaviors than did comparison groups in about half of the evaluations. Overall, they noted that interactive technologies had strengths and weaknesses and that further development was necessary.

Does the Literature Overestimate the Potential Benefit?

The literature on mHealth has emerged only in the past few years. Many of the studies are relatively small, and they typically include multiple outcome measures. The issue of publication bias has received substantial attention in recent reviews (Francis 2012a,b,c), and it may be relevant to these studies. Since there is a publication bias against null or negative studies, particularly in an emerging field, it is possible that the

published literature strays on the positive side, suggesting that mobile health interventions may be even less effective than our review reveals.

Repeated calls have been made for clearer prespecification of outcomes for experimental studies and for greater transparency in the research process (Schooler 2011, Simmons et al. 2011). Many of the studies on mHealth use multiple outcome measures, thus increasing the probability that finding at least one significant effect would occur by chance alone. Not only do we need more studies evaluating mHealth, but we also need more studies that are registered in resources such as the National Institutes of Health's Web site ClinicalTrials.gov. This will assure that we know in advance which variables were prospectively chosen as primary outcomes.

Ignoring the Basic Science?

Why would mHealth interventions that have so much promise offer such disappointing results in clinical trials? One explanation is that we have failed to connect the dots between mobile intervention technologies and sound evidence-based interventions. Some application inventors, for example, have not attended to the literature on evidence-based interventions. It is noteworthy that many mobile health applications are not based on the best evidence-based principles of behavioral intervention (Breton et al. 2011). Several reviews illustrate this point. Abroms and colleagues (2011) examined the content of 47 iPhone applications designed to help people stop smoking. Each app was coded as to whether or not it adhered to the U.S. Public Health Service's 2008 Clinical Practice Guideline for treating tobacco use and dependence. The investigators also obtained data on how often each app was downloaded. They found that most popular apps did not apply the key guidelines recommended for control of tobacco use and nicotine dependence. Further, few if any of the apps guided their users to proven treatments including counseling, medical therapy, or the use of an established quit line (Abroms et al. 2011).

Breton and colleagues (2011) reviewed the weight loss applications available on iTunes through September 2009. They found 204 applications. They then used a template listing 13 evidence-based practices for weight control and found that only about 15% of the available applications had five or more of the 13 evidence-based components. They concluded that evidence-based content is lacking in many of the commercial applications. Having sophisticated technology allowing mobile data capture and feedback is not enough; considerable expertise in developing mobile applications and behaviorally sound interventions is also necessary for a successful study.

Many application developers seem unaware that there is a basic science of behavior change. Not unlike the basic science of molecule development for pharmaceutical trials, applied interventions should build upon principles that have been demonstrated in systematic studies of behavior change. Many application developers rely on intuitive models of behavior change. Czajkowski (2011) argues that treatment development for behavioral interventions is very similar to the development of new pharmaceutical products. In the drug development literature, products go through a variety of stages. During Phase I, new molecules are tested on small numbers of subjects under very controlled conditions. If they are successful, they go on to Phase II of preliminary testing, and only when these tests are successful are they tried out on larger populations. In contrast, behavioral interventions are sometimes subjected to Phase III or efficacy evaluations without completion of the development (Phase I) and preliminary testing (Phase II) stages.

In many cases, mHealth application developers create products based on their intuition or clinical experience but without systematic developmental or preliminary evaluations. Typically, the developmental and preliminary testing phase identifies problems with the efficacy of the intervention and iterations that are needed to refine it. We believe interventions will be most successful if they are based on systematic observations from careful experimental studies.

Collaboration between behavioral scientists, software engineers, and the electronics community is needed to address this problem. Although there are a few good examples of collaboration, many application developers have failed to attend to basic principles of psychological and behavioral theory.

More and better randomized trials. In order to develop a credible evidence base for mHealth interventions, we need more high-quality randomized clinical trials to evaluate emerging mobile health technologies. Most importantly, we must develop a truly interdisciplinary science in which the development of new applications is informed by the best evidence-based behavioral science. The challenge will be the substantial funding necessary to support these efforts.

The moving target. Research on mHealth technologies will encounter many problems. One of the most challenging issues is that electronic technologies are themselves a moving target. New methods are rarely on the market more than a year or two before they are replaced with more advanced approaches. A cell phone that is two years old is almost certainly out of date. As a result, virtually all of the technologies being evaluated are obsolete by the time the evaluation is completed.

Several methods have been proposed to address this problem. For instance, some investigators have considered a revolving experimental design (Collins et al. 2007). The study may begin by assigning participants to the new technology or to a control condition. When the next-generation technology becomes available, new participants can be randomly assigned to the latest technology or to a control group that uses the previous technology. This continues over the course of time: Each time a new technology becomes available, the previous technology becomes the control group, and participants are randomly assigned to the latest technology versus the next-to-latest.

Privacy protection. Some of the other challenges involve the protection of information captured by the new electronic technologies. Privacy protection, particularly around health information, is likely to be a major challenge. A 2009 survey found that breaches are common. For example, about one-third of health information technology companies acknowledge that their data had been compromised at least once during the previous year. Although technologies to protect privacy are improving, so is the expertise of those breaking through privacy protection barriers.

Poor implementation and overuse. Another challenge is that electronic health technologies are likely to be misused. For example, beginning in 2014, the Affordable Care Act will reimburse providers for remote monitoring. In reaction, the FDA proposed guidance for the use of some mobile medical applications in July 2011. The FDA had a variety of concerns. First, there may be applications that simply don't do what they are supposed to do. Promoters of many applications claim to provide accurate diagnosis, for example, of heart rhythms, skin lesions, anxiety, or depression. Yet these applications have not been systematically evaluated and could lead to incorrect and inappropriate diagnosis. Many fear that use of these applications will result in overdiagnosis and excessive treatment for medical conditions that might have better been left alone. Systematic studies are necessary in order to validate the value of electronic remote diagnosis and to assess the impacts on cost and on health outcomes.

Big data. Perhaps the biggest challenge concerns the volume of information that electronic technologies will produce. Simply stated, we don't know what to do with it all. Instead of studying hundreds of data points, investigators will now have millions or perhaps billions of data points to analyze. Potentially they could have continuous flows of data from thousands of study participants. We do not currently have the technologies to store, retrieve, or analyze these masses of data. Most psychologists were trained to use statistical inference techniques designed for the study of agronomy in the 1930s. Although these methods have become much more sophisticated, inferential statistics can be meaningless for data sets composed of hundreds of millions of data points. Newer approaches involving data mining, machine learning, and other modern analytic methods may be required to confront the mountains of information that will soon be available.

Where Is the Field Going Next?

It is difficult to speculate about future directions. The entire field of mHealth has developed over the past few years. Since smartphones are one of the most successful consumer products worldwide, the potential for investment and rapid evolution is enormous. Many people believe that smartphone technologies will make major contributions to the health of populations. Yet the number of applications is growing exponentially, and few have been systematically evaluated. Unlike pharmaceutical products, which must undergo extensive testing before they receive a product license from the FDA, mHealth technologies are completely unregulated. They can be marketed without evidence that they improved human health outcomes. Greater attention to developing an evidence base for the value of these interventions is necessary.

In addition to the issues mentioned above, new measurement methodologies may require substantial changes in the graduate school curriculum. Issues such as privacy protection, large-scale data management, and next-generation analytic technologies will need to find their way into the classroom. Although current research methods will continue to need attention, the availability of new data collection technologies could have a transformative effect on the way the next generation of students is trained. Institutions offering graduate programs will need to reconsider their curricula in order to prepare for these likely changes.

CONCLUSION

The availability of the new mobile laboratory is likely to have a profound effect on clinical practice and on research. Our review suggests that mobile electronic technologies have already had a profound effect on measurement. Developments in ambulatory assessment and ecological momentary assessment have ushered in important advances in our ability to study behavior outside of the laboratory. They have made the notion of representative design and representative sampling a practical reality.

In contrast to our positive assessment of the role of new wireless technologies for assessment, we remain open-minded yet skeptical about the value of mobile technologies for changing health behavior and for improving the health of human populations. Although there is clearly great promise, most systematic trials fail to support the value of mHealth interventions. Additional trials are needed, and we most strongly encourage evaluations of applications that are based on evidence-based principles of behavior change.

DISCLOSURE

A.A.S. is a senior scientist with the Gallup Organization and a senior consultant with invivodata, Inc.

LITERATURE CITED

2011. *The World Telecommunication/ICT Indicators Database*. Geneva: Int. Telecomm. Union

Abroms LC, Padmanabhan N, Thaweethai L, Phillips T. 2011. iPhone apps for smoking cessation: a content analysis. *Am. J. Prev. Med.* 40:279–85

Albinali F, Intille S, Haskell W, Rosenberger M. 2010. Using wearable activity type detection to improve physical activity energy expenditure estimation. In *Proc. 12th ACM Int. Conf. Ubiquitous Computing*, pp. 311–20. New York: ACM

Arima H, Barzi F, Chalmers J. 2011. Mortality patterns in hypertension. *J. Hypertens.* 29(Suppl. 1):S3–7

Atienza AA, Patrick K. 2011. Mobile health: the killer app for cyberinfrastructure and consumer health. *Am. J. Prev. Med.* 40:S151–53

Barker RG, Schoggen P. 1973. *Qualities of Community Life. Methods of Measuring Environment and Behavior Applied to an American and an English Town*. San Francisco, CA: Jossey-Bass

Barker RG. 1965. Explorations in ecological psychology. *Am. Psychol.* 20:1–14

Barker RG, Wright HF. 1949. Psychological ecology and the problem of psychosocial development. *Child Dev.* 20:131–43

Bennett GG, Warner ET, Glasgow RE, Askew S, Goldman J, et al. 2012. Obesity treatment for socioeconomically disadvantaged patients in primary care practice. *Arch. Intern. Med.* 172:565–74

Berkman ET, Dickenson J, Falk EB, Lieberman MD. 2011. Using SMS text messaging to assess moderators of smoking reduction: validating a new tool for ecological measurement of health behaviors. *Health Psychol.* 30:186–94

Bolger N, Davis A, Rafaeli E. 2003. Diary methods: capturing life as it is lived. *Annu. Rev. Psychol.* 54:579–616

Boring EG. 1950. *A History of Experimental Psychology*. New York: Appleton-Century-Crofts. 777 pp.

Bradburn NM, Rips LJ, Shevell SK. 1987. Answering autobiographical questions: the impact of memory and inference on surveys. *Science* 236:157–61

Brendryen H, Kraft P. 2008. Happy Ending: a randomized controlled trial of a digital multimedia smoking cessation intervention. *Addiction* 103:478–84

Breton ER, Fuemmeler BF, Abroms LC. 2011. Weight loss—there is an app for that! But does it adhere to evidence-informed practices? *Transl. Behav. Med.* 1:523–29

Brunswik E. 1941. Systematic and representative design of psychological experiments. In *Proc. Berkeley Symp. Math. Stat. Probab.*, ed. J Neyman, pp. 143–202. Berkeley/Los Angeles: Univ. Calif. Press

Brunswik E. 1944. Distal focussing of perception: size-constancy in a representative sample of situations. *Psychol. Monogr.* 56:1–49

Brunswik E. 1952. The conceptual framework of psychology. *Int. Encycl. Unified Sci.* 1(10):4–102

Brunswik E. 1956. *Perception and the Representative Design of Psychological Experiments.* Berkeley: Univ. Calif. Press. xii, 154 pp.

Burke LE, Wang J, Sevick MA. 2011. Self-monitoring in weight loss: a systematic review of the literature. *J. Am. Diet. Assoc.* 111:92–102

Byrom B, Tiplady B. 2010. *ePRO: Electronic Solutions for Patient-Reported Data.* Farnham, Surrey, UK: Gower

Chang LW, Kagaayi J, Arem H, Nakigozi G, Ssempijja V, et al. 2011. Impact of a mHealth intervention for peer health workers on AIDS care in rural Uganda: a mixed methods evaluation of a cluster-randomized trial. *AIDS Behav.* 15:1776–84

Cocosila M, Archer N, Brian Haynes R, Yuan Y. 2009. Can wireless text messaging improve adherence to preventive activities? Results of a randomised controlled trial. *Int. J. Med. Inform.* 78:230–38

Cohn JN. 2011. ACP Journal Club. Review: antihypertensive treatment prevents cardiovascular events and mortality in cardiovascular disease without hypertension. *Ann. Intern. Med.* 154:JC6–6

Cole-Lewis H, Kershaw T. 2010. Text messaging as a tool for behavior change in disease prevention and management. *Epidemiol. Rev.* 32:56–69

Collins F. 2012. Technology and measurement. *Sci. Am.* In press

Collins LM, Murphy SA, Strecher V. 2007. The multiphase optimization strategy (MOST) and the sequential multiple assignment randomized trial (SMART): new methods for more potent eHealth interventions. *Am. J. Prev. Med.* 32:S112–18

Cook DJ, Holder LB. 2011. Sensor selection to support practical use of health-monitoring smart environments. *Data Min. Knowl. Discov.* 1:339–51

Csikszentmihalyi M, Hunter J. 2004. Happiness in everyday life: the uses of experience sampling. *J. Happiness Stud.* 4:185–99

Czajkowski SM. 2011. News from NIH: using basic behavioral science to develop better behavioral interventions. *Transl. Behav. Med.* 1:507–8

de la Sierra A, Redon J, Banegas JR, Segura J, Parati G, et al. 2009. Prevalence and factors associated with circadian blood pressure patterns in hypertensive patients. *Hypertension* 53:466–72

Dockray S, Grant N, Stone AA, Kahneman D, Wardle J, Steptoe A. 2010. A comparison of affect ratings obtained with ecological momentary assessment and the day reconstruction method. *Soc. Indic. Res.* 99:269–83

Dubach P, Caversaccio M. 2011. Images in clinical medicine. Amalgam tattoo. *N. Engl. J. Med.* 364:e29

Eder B, Kang D, Rao ST, Mathur R, Yu S, et al. 2010. Using National Air Quality Forecast Guidance to develop local air quality index forecasts. *Bull. Am. Meteorol. Soc.* 91:313–26

Egan BM, Zhao Y, Axon RN. 2010. US trends in prevalence, awareness, treatment, and control of hypertension, 1988–2008. *JAMA* 303:2043–50

Eguchi K, Ishikawa J, Hoshide S, Pickering TG, Schwartz JE, et al. 2008. Night time blood pressure variability is a strong predictor for cardiovascular events in patients with type 2 diabetes. *Am. J. Hypertens.* 22:46–51

Fjeldsoe BS, Marshall AL, Miller YD. 2009. Behavior change interventions delivered by mobile telephone short-message service. *Am. J. Prev. Med.* 36:165–73

Foocharoen C, Nanagara R, Kiatchoosakun S, Suwannaroj S, Mahakkanukrauh A. 2011. Prognostic factors of mortality and 2-year survival analysis of systemic sclerosis with pulmonary arterial hypertension in Thailand. *Int. J. Rheum. Dis.* 14:282–89

Francis G. 2012a. Evidence that publication bias contaminated studies relating social class and unethical behavior. *Proc. Natl. Acad. Sci. USA* 109:E1587

Francis G. 2012b. Replication initiative: beware misinterpretation. *Science* 336:802

Francis G. 2012c. Too good to be true: publication bias in two prominent studies from experimental psychology. *Psychon. Bull. Rev.* 19:151–56

Franklin SS, Thijs L, Hansen TW, Li Y, Boggia J, et al. 2012. Significance of white-coat hypertension in older persons with isolated systolic hypertension. *Hypertension* 59:564–71

Franklin VL, Waller A, Pagliari C, Greene SA. 2006. A randomized controlled trial of Sweet Talk, a text-messaging system to support young people with diabetes. *Diabet. Med.* 23:1332–38

Free C, Knight R, Robertson S, Whittaker R, Edwards P, et al. 2011. Smoking cessation support delivered via mobile phone text messaging (txt2stop): a single-blind, randomised trial. *Lancet* 378:49–55

Goldenberg RL, McClure EM, Macguire ER, Kamath BD, Jobe AH. 2011. Lessons for low-income regions following the reduction in hypertension-related maternal mortality in high-income countries. *Int. J. Gynaecol. Obstet.* 113:91–95

Gray L, Lee IM, Sesso HD, Batty GD. 2011. Blood pressure in early adulthood, hypertension in middle age, and future cardiovascular disease mortality: HAHS (Harvard Alumni Health Study). *J. Am. Coll. Cardiol.* 58:2396–403

Gurman TA, Rubin SE, Roess AA. 2012. Effectiveness of mHealth behavior change communication interventions in developing countries: a systematic review of the literature. *J. Health Commun.* 17(Suppl. 1):82–104

Hammond KR, Stewart TR, eds. 2001. *The Essential Brunswik: Beginnings, Explications, Applications.* Oxford/ New York: Oxford Univ. Press. 540 pp.

Hardy H, Kumar V, Doros G, Farmer E, Drainoni ML, et al. 2011. Randomized controlled trial of a personalized cellular phone reminder system to enhance adherence to antiretroviral therapy. *AIDS Patient Care STDs* 25:153–61

Hektner JM, Schmidt JM, Csikszentmihalyi M. 2006. *Experience Sampling Method: Measuring the Quality of Everyday Life.* London: Sage

Heron KE, Smyth JM. 2010. Ecological momentary interventions: incorporating mobile technology into psychosocial and health behaviour treatments. *Br. J. Health Psychol.* 15:1–39

Horvath T, Azman H, Kennedy GE, Rutherford GW. 2012. Mobile phone text messaging for promoting adherence to antiretroviral therapy in patients with HIV infection. *Cochrane Database Syst. Rev.* 3:CD009756

Huang ES, O'Grady M, Basu A, Winn A, John P, et al. 2010. The cost-effectiveness of continuous glucose monitoring in type 1 diabetes. *Diabetes Care* 33:1269–74

Hurling R, Catt M, Boni MD, Fairley BW, Hurst T, et al. 2007. Using internet and mobile phone technology to deliver an automated physical activity program: randomized controlled trial. *J. Med. Internet Res.* 9:e7

Hussein WI, Hasan K, Jaradat AA. 2011. Effectiveness of mobile phone short message service on diabetes mellitus management: the SMS-DM study. *Diabetes Res. Clin. Pract.* 94:e24–26

Intille SS. 2007. Technological innovations enabling automatic, context-sensitive ecological momentary assessment. See Stone et al. 2007, pp. 308–37

Ishikawa J, Hoshide S, Eguchi K, Schwartz JE, Pickering TG, et al. 2010. Masked hypertension defined by ambulatory blood pressure monitoring is associated with an increased serum glucose level and urinary albumin-creatinine ratio. *J. Clin. Hypertens.* 12:578–87

Ishikawa J, Ishikawa Y, Edmondson D, Pickering TG, Schwartz JE. 2011. Age and the difference between awake ambulatory blood pressure and office blood pressure: a meta-analysis. *Blood Press. Monit.* 16:159–67

Isikman SO, Bishara W, Mudanyali O, Su T, Tseng D, et al. 2012. Lensfree on-chip microscopy and tomography for bio-medical applications. *Sel. Top. Quantum Electron. IEEE J.* 18:1059–72

Issadore D, Min C, Liong M, Chung J, Weissleder R, Lee H. 2011. Miniature magnetic resonance system for point-of-care diagnostics. *Lab. Chip.* 11:2282–87

Istepanian RSH, Zitouni K, Harry D, Moutosammy N, Sungoor A, et al. 2009. Evaluation of a mobile phone telemonitoring system for glycaemic control in patients with diabetes. *J. Telemed. Telecare* 15:125–28

Kahneman D, Diener E, Schwarz N, eds. 1999. *Well-Being: The Foundations of Hedonic Psychology.* New York: Russell Sage Found.

Kelly JD, Giordano TP. 2011. Mobile phone technologies improve adherence to antiretroviral treatment in a resource-limited setting: a randomized controlled trial of text message reminders. *AIDS* 25:1137

Knowler WC, Fowler SE, Hamman RF, Christophi CA, Hoffman HJ, et al. 2009. 10-year follow-up of diabetes incidence and weight loss in the Diabetes Prevention Program Outcomes Study. *Lancet* 374:1677–86

Krishna S, Boren SA, Balas EA. 2009. Healthcare via cell phones: a systematic review. *Telemed. J. E Health* 15:231–40

Kubiak T, Stone AA. 2012. Ambulatory monitoring of biobehavioral processes in health and disease: introduction to a special issue of *Psychosomatic Medicine. Psychosom. Med.* 74:325–26

Lau PW, Lau EY, Wong DP, Ransdell L. 2011. A systematic review of information and communication technology-based interventions for promoting physical activity behavior change in children and adolescents. *J. Med. Internet Res.* 13:e48

Lein JK. 2012. Environmental monitoring and change detection. In *Environmental Sensing. Analytical Techniques for Earth Observation*, pp. 169–91. New York/Dordrecht: Springer

Lester RT, Ritvo P, Mills EJ, Kariri A, Karanja S, et al. 2010. Effects of a mobile phone short message service on antiretroviral treatment adherence in Kenya (WelTel Kenya1): a randomised trial. *Lancet* 376:1838–45

Losito A, Pittavini L, Ferri C, De Angelis L. 2011. Kidney function and mortality in different cardiovascular diseases: relationship with age, sex, diabetes and hypertension. *J. Nephrol.* 24:322–28

Man MS, Tilbrook HE, Jayakody S, Hewitt CE, Cox H, et al. 2011. Electronic reminders did not improve postal questionnaire response rates or response times: a randomized controlled trial. *J. Clin. Epidemiol.* 64:1001–4

Mancia G, Bombelli M, Seravalle G, Grassi G. 2011. Diagnosis and management of patients with white-coat and masked hypertension. *Nat. Rev. Cardiol.* 8:686–93

Mann T, Tomiyama AJ, Westling E, Lew AM, Samuels B, Chatman J. 2007. Medicare's search for effective obesity treatments: Diets are not the answer. *Am. Psychol.* 62:220–33

McGrayne SB. 2011. *The Theory That Would Not Die.* New Haven, CT: Yale Univ. Press

Mehl MR, Conner TS, eds. 2011. *Handbook of Research Methods for Studying Daily Life.* New York: Guilford

Mi J, Wang T, Meng L, Zhu G, Han S, et al. 2010. Development of blood pressure reference standards for Chinese children. *Chin. J. Evidence-Based Pediatr.* 5:4–14

Mudanyali O, Tseng D, Oh C, Isikman SO, Sencan I, et al. 2010. Compact, light-weight and cost-effective microscope based on lensless incoherent holography for telemedicine applications. *Lab Chip* 10:1417–28

Naughton F, Prevost AT, Gilbert H, Sutton S. 2012. Randomized controlled trial evaluation of a tailored leaflet and SMS text message self-help intervention for pregnant smokers (MiQuit). *Nicotine Tob. Res.* 14:569–77

Newton KH, Wiltshire EJ, Elley CR. 2009. Pedometers and text messaging to increase physical activity. *Diabetes Care* 32:813–15

Norman GJ, Zabinski MF, Adams MA, Rosenberg DE, Yaroch AL, Atienza AA. 2007. A review of eHealth interventions for physical activity and dietary behavior change. *Am. J. Prev. Med.* 33:336–45

Palmas W, Pickering TG, Teresi J, Schwartz JE, Moran A, et al. 2009. Ambulatory blood pressure monitoring and all-cause mortality in elderly people with diabetes mellitus. *Hypertension* 53:120–27

Patrick DL, Burke LB, Powers JH, Scott JA, Rock EP, et al. 2007. Patient reported outcomes to support medical product labeling claims: FDA perspective. *Value Health* 10:S125–37

Patrick K, Raab F, Adams MA, Dillon L, Zabinski M, et al. 2009. A text message–based intervention for weight loss: randomized controlled trial. *J. Med. Internet Res.* 11:e1

Patrick K, Wolszon L, Basen-Engquist KM, Demark-Wahnefried W, Prokhorov AV, et al. 2011. CYberin-frastructure for COmparative effectiveness REsearch (CYCORE): improving data from cancer clinical trials. *Transl. Behav. Med.* 1:83–88

Petrie KJ, Perry K, Broadbent E, Weinman J. 2012. A text message programme designed to modify patients illness and treatment beliefs improves self-reported adherence to asthma preventer medication. *Br. J. Health Psychol.* 17:74–84

Petrinovich L. 1979. Probabilistic functionalism: a conception of research method. *Am. Psychol.* 34:373–90

Pickering TG. 1991. Clinical applications of ambulatory blood pressure monitoring: the white coat syndrome. *Clin. Invest. Med.* 14:212–17

Pickering TG. 1992. Ambulatory blood pressure monitoring: an historical perspective. *Clin. Cardiol.* 15:II3–5

Pickering TG. 1996. Recommendations for the use of home (self) and ambulatory blood pressure monitoring. American Society of Hypertension Ad Hoc Panel. *Am. J. Hypertens.* 9:1–11

Pickering TG. 2005. Extending the reach of ambulatory blood pressure monitoring: masked and resistant hypertension. *Am. J. Hypertens.* 18:1385–87

Pickering TG, White WB. 2008. ASH Position Paper: home and ambulatory blood pressure monitoring. When and how to use self (home) and ambulatory blood pressure monitoring. *J. Clin. Hypertens.* 10:850–55

Pickering TG, White WB, Giles TD, Black HR, Izzo JL, et al. 2010. When and how to use self (home) and ambulatory blood pressure monitoring. *J. Am. Soc. Hypertens.* 4:56–61

Pierdomenico SD, Cuccurullo F. 2010. Prognostic value of white-coat and masked hypertension diagnosed by ambulatory monitoring in initially untreated subjects: an updated meta analysis. *Am. J. Hypertens.* 24:52–58

Pop-Eleches C, Thirumurthy H, Habyarimana JP, Zivin JG, Goldstein MP, et al. 2011. Mobile phone technologies improve adherence to antiretroviral treatment in a resource-limited setting: a randomized controlled trial of text message reminders. *AIDS* 25:825–34

Prabhakaran L, Chee WY, Chua KC, Abisheganaden J, Wong WM. 2010. The use of text messaging to improve asthma control: a pilot study using the mobile phone short messaging service (SMS). *J. Telemed. Telecare* 16:286–90

Quinn CC, Clough SS, Minor JM, Lender D, Okafor MC, Gruber-Baldini A. 2008. WellDoc mobile diabetes management randomized controlled trial: change in clinical and behavioral outcomes and patient and physician satisfaction. *Diabetes Technol. Ther.* 10:160–68

Redelmeier DA, Katz J, Kahneman D. 2003. Memories of colonoscopy: a randomized trial. *Pain* 104:187–94

Riley WT, Rivera DE, Atienza AA, Nilsen W, Allison SM, Mermelstein R. 2011. Health behavior models in the age of mobile interventions: Are our theories up to the task? *Transl. Behav. Med.* 1:53–71

Robitaille C, Dai S, Waters C, Loukine L, Bancej C, et al. 2012. Diagnosed hypertension in Canada: incidence, prevalence and associated mortality. *CMAJ* 184:E49–56

Schatz BR, Berlin RB Jr. 2011a. *Healthcare Infrastructure: Health Systems for Individuals and Populations*. London: Springer Verlag

Schatz BR, Berlin RB Jr. 2011b. Mobile monitors for health systems. See Schatz & Berlin 2011a, pp. 229–46

Schooler J. 2011. Unpublished results hide the decline effect. *Nature* 470:437

Schultz DP, Schultz SE. 2011. *A History of Modern Psychology*. Belmont, CA: Wadsworth

Schultz MG, Hare JL, Marwick TH, Stowasser M, Sharman JE. 2011. Masked hypertension is "unmasked" by low-intensity exercise blood pressure. *Blood Press* 20:284–89

Sharman JE, Hare JL, Thomas S, Davies JE, Leano R, et al. 2011. Association of masked hypertension and left ventricular remodeling with the hypertensive response to exercise. *Am. J. Hypertens.* 24:898–903

Shea M, Houston DK, Nicklas BJ, Messier SP, Davis CC, et al. 2010. The effect of randomization to weight loss on total mortality in older overweight and obese adults: the ADAPT study. *J. Gerontol. Ser. A* 65:519–25

Shea M, Nicklas BJ, Houston DK, Miller ME, Davis CC, et al. 2011. The effect of intentional weight loss on all-cause mortality in older adults: results of a randomized controlled weight-loss trial. *Am. J. Clin. Nutr.* 94:839–46

Shiffman S. 2007. Designing protocols for ecological momentary assessment. See Stone et al. 2007, pp. 27–53

Shiffman S, Stone AA, Hufford MR. 2008. Ecological momentary assessment. *Annu. Rev. Clin. Psychol.* 4:1–32

Shimbo D, Kuruvilla S, Haas D, Pickering TG, Schwartz JE, Gerin W. 2009. Preventing misdiagnosis of ambulatory hypertension: algorithm using office and home blood pressures. *J. Hypertens.* 27:1775–83

Simmons JP, Nelson LD, Simonsohn U. 2011. False-positive psychology: Undisclosed flexibility in data collection and analysis allows presenting anything as significant. *Psychol. Sci.* 22:1359–66

Simoni JM, Huh D, Frick PA, Pearson CR, Andrasik MP, et al. 2009. Peer support and pager messaging to promote antiretroviral modifying therapy in Seattle: a randomized controlled trial. *J. Acquir. Immune Defic. Syndr.* 52:465–73

Spring B, Schneider K, McFadden HG, Vaughn J, Kozak AT, et al. 2012. Multiple behavior changes in diet and activity: a randomized controlled trial using mobile technology. *Arch. Internal Med.* 172:789–96

St. Martin G. 2010. Tattoos that improve health. *News@Northeastern* Pap. 745

Sterzer P, Kleinschmidt A, Rees G. 2009. The neural bases of multistable perception. *Trends Cogn. Sci.* 13:310–18

Stone AA, Shiffman S, Atienza A, Nebling L, eds. 2007. *The Science of Real-Time Data Capture: Self-Reports in Health Research*. New York: Oxford Univ. Press

Sudman S, Bradburn NM, Schwarz N. 1996. *Thinking About Answers: The Application of Cognitive Processes to Survey Methodology*. San Francisco, CA: Jossey-Bass

Sun M, Fernstrom JD, Jia W, Hackworth SA, Yao N, et al. 2010. A wearable electronic system for objective dietary assessment. *J. Am. Diet. Assoc.* 110:45–47

Takahashi PY, Pecina JL, Upatising B, Chaudhry R, Shah ND, et al. 2012. A randomized controlled trial of telemonitoring in older adults with multiple health issues to prevent hospitalizations and emergency department visits. *Arch. Intern. Med.* 172:773–79

Topol E. 2012. *The Creative Destruction of Medicine: How the Digital Revolution Will Create Better Health Care*. New York: Basic Books

Turner-McGrievy G, Tate D. 2011. Tweets, apps, and pods: results of the 6-month Mobile Pounds Off Digitally (Mobile POD) randomized weight-loss intervention among adults. *J. Med. Internet Res.* 13:e120

van Genugten L, van Empelen P, Boon B, Borsboom G, Visscher T, Oenema A. 2012. Results from an online computer-tailored weight management intervention for overweight adults: randomized controlled trial. *J. Med. Internet Res.* 14:e44

Whittaker R, Borland R, Bullen C, Lin RB, McRobbie H, Rodgers A. 2009. Mobile phone-based interventions for smoking cessation. *Cochrane Database Syst. Rev.* (4):CD006611

Whittaker R, Dorey E, Bramley D, Bullen C, Denny S, et al. 2011. A theory-based video messaging mobile phone intervention for smoking cessation: randomized controlled trial. *J. Med. Internet Res.* 13:e10

World Health Org. 1946. *Preamble to the Constitution of the World Health Organization as adopted by the International Health Conference, New York, 19–22 June.* New York: Off. Rec. WHO, no. 2, p. 100

Zickuhr K, Smith A. 2012. *Digital Differences.* Washington, DC: Pew Charitable Trust

Multivariate Statistical Analyses for Neuroimaging Data

Anthony R. McIntosh and Bratislav Mišić

Rotman Research Institute, Baycrest, Toronto, Ontario, Canada, M6A 2E1;
email: rmcintosh@rotman-baycrest.on.ca

Annu. Rev. Psychol. 2013. 64:499–525

First published online as a Review in Advance on
July 12, 2012

The *Annual Review of Psychology* is online at
psych.annualreviews.org

This article's doi:
10.1146/annurev-psych-113011-143804

Keywords

multivariate, functional connectivity, effective connectivity, network

Abstract

As the focus of neuroscience shifts from studying individual brain regions to entire networks of regions, methods for statistical inference have also become geared toward network analysis. The purpose of the present review is to survey the multivariate statistical techniques that have been used to study neural interactions. We have selected the most common techniques and developed a taxonomy that instructively reflects their assumptions and practical use. For each family of analyses, we describe their application and the types of experimental questions they can address, as well as how they relate to other analyses both conceptually and mathematically. We intend to show that despite their diversity, all of these techniques offer complementary information about the functional architecture of the brain.

Contents

INTRODUCTION

The complex anatomical connectivity of the central nervous system suggests that interregional communication is a primary function. The notion that activity in individual regions is influenced by activity in other regions via direct or indirect projections has made the network organization of the brain a fundamental theme in neuroscience. A general systems theory has emerged that simultaneously emphasizes specialized local computation (functional specialization) and computation arising from interactions between regions (functional integration). Functional integration implies that the response properties of any one region must be studied with respect to the status of other regions in the network (neural context) (Bressler & McIntosh 2007; McIntosh 1998, 2000).

Univariate Versus Multivariate

Neuroimaging data mirror the complexity of the brain in the sense that signals can be recorded from a large number of spatially distributed sensors (e.g., voxels, electrodes) and often at multiple time points. Unsurprisingly, methods for statistical analysis of neuroimaging data have developed along distinct lines that focus either on functional specialization or integration.

The conventional "mass univariate" approach is optimal for identifying reliable task-dependent signal changes at the level of individual image elements (Friston et al. 1991). The general linear model (GLM) of the activity in each voxel ($\mathbf{Y}_{n \times 1}$) in n scans is a linear sum ($\boldsymbol{\beta}_{p \times 1}$) of p predictors ($\mathbf{X}_{n \times p}$) plus a residual error term, where each predictor is the time course of some effect

$$\mathbf{Y} = \mathbf{X}\boldsymbol{\beta} + \boldsymbol{\epsilon}. \qquad (1)$$

For instance, the predictor for the effect of a task on voxel activity is a vector of 1's at the time points when the task is on and 0's everywhere else. Ordinary least squares regression is used to estimate the β weights for each predictor. The weights indicate the contribution of the predictor to the variance of the voxel response. Depending on whether one or more contrasts are tested, either a t or F statistic is computed for each β weight. Critically, this type of analysis is performed separately for every image element, explicitly precluding the possibility that responses arise from coordinated dynamics among other elements. Conversely, multivariate statistical analyses take advantage of the spatial and temporal dependencies among image elements, enabling inference across space and/or time (Petersson et al. 1999). In the most general case, multivariate analyses enable one to capture spatiotemporal patterns of activity (e.g., time-varying networks) that have some functional significance (e.g., relate to a task contrast or behavior).

Exploratory Versus Confirmatory

Multivariate analyses can be broadly divided into those that are exploratory and those that are confirmatory. Exploratory techniques are primarily used to identify robust patterns of covarying neural activity [principal component analysis (PCA) and independent component

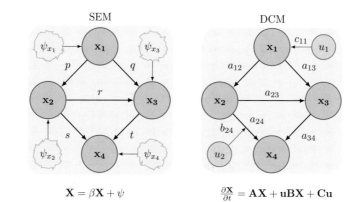

$$\mathbf{X} = \beta\mathbf{X} + \psi \qquad\qquad \frac{\partial\mathbf{X}}{\partial t} = \mathbf{AX} + \mathbf{uBX} + \mathbf{Cu}$$

SEM
$$\begin{pmatrix} x_1 \\ x_2 \\ x_3 \\ x_4 \end{pmatrix} = \begin{pmatrix} 0 & 0 & 0 & 0 \\ p & 0 & 0 & 0 \\ q & r & 0 & 0 \\ 0 & s & t & 0 \end{pmatrix} \begin{pmatrix} x_1 \\ x_2 \\ x_3 \\ x_4 \end{pmatrix} + \begin{pmatrix} \psi_{x_1} \\ \psi_{x_2} \\ \psi_{x_3} \\ \psi_{x_4} \end{pmatrix}$$

DCM
$$\begin{pmatrix} \dot{x}_1 \\ \dot{x}_2 \\ \dot{x}_3 \\ \dot{x}_4 \end{pmatrix} = \left(\begin{pmatrix} 0 & a_{12} & a_{13} & 0 \\ 0 & 0 & a_{23} & 0 \\ 0 & 0 & 0 & a_{34} \\ 0 & 0 & 0 & 0 \end{pmatrix} + u_2 \begin{pmatrix} 0 & 0 & 0 & 0 \\ 0 & 0 & 0 & b_{24} \\ 0 & 0 & 0 & 0 \\ 0 & 0 & 0 & 0 \end{pmatrix} \right) \begin{pmatrix} x_1 \\ x_2 \\ x_3 \\ x_4 \end{pmatrix} + \begin{pmatrix} c_{11} & 0 \\ 0 & 0 \\ 0 & 0 \\ 0 & 0 \end{pmatrix} \begin{pmatrix} u_1 \\ u_2 \end{pmatrix}$$

Figure 1

An example of typical structural equation modeling (SEM) (*left*) and dynamic causal modeling (DCM) (*right*). In SEM, causal order is specified by a system of linear regression equations with one set of path coefficients (β) and error terms (ψ). In DCM, causal order is specified by a system of differential equations parameterized in terms of synaptic couplings ($\mathbf{A}$) as well as exogenous inputs ($\mathbf{u}$) that may influence either the synaptic couplings between regions ($\mathbf{B}$) or intrinsic activity in individual regions ($\mathbf{C}$).

analysis (ICA)] and possibly relating these patterns to design variables and/or behavior [canonical correlation analysis (CCA), canonical variate analysis (CVA), partial least squares (PLS)]. They are usually data driven, and no explicit hypothesis needs to be specified about the contribution of individual brain regions or about the differentiation of conditions or groups. However, this does not imply that exploratory techniques are noninferential, and in most cases statistical inference is possible. In confirmatory analyses, an explicit model of regional interactions is formulated and tested to see whether it fits the data and/or whether it fits the observed data better than alternative models [structural equation modeling (SEM) and dynamic causal modeling (DCM)]. Thus, confirmatory techniques are used to test specific hypotheses.

The distinction between exploratory and confirmatory techniques parallels the distinction between functional and effective connectivity. Functional connectivity refers to statistical interdependencies between two remote regions (Friston et al. 1993). A functional connection between two regions does not imply that they are communicating directly, as their covariation could be due to common inputs from another source. Effective connectivity is defined as a directed causal influence of one region on another (Aertsen et al. 1989, Friston et al. 1993). Exploratory analyses extract distinct components of the covariance structure of the data. The networks of regions that they identify strongly covary with each other and possibly with some task effect and are interpreted as functional networks. Confirmatory analyses specify a model of interactions among units that takes into account external inputs and the anatomical substrate, and they are interpreted in terms of effective connectivity.

Multivariate Granger causality and the graph model are two techniques that do not perfectly fit in either category because they have both exploratory and confirmatory characteristics. For instance, Granger causality is a measure of causal influence, but it can be applied in an exploratory fashion to any number of pairs of regions. Likewise, the use of graph theoretic metrics is exploratory in the sense that they are usually calculated for all regions with no specific model, yet the measures used to estimate the connectivity of the graph may be measures of effective connectivity.

In the present article we give an overview of the most common strategies for multivariate analysis of neuroimaging data. By developing a simple taxonomy we hope to illustrate the potential applications of various methods and how they relate to each other. These techniques can be applied to most neuroimaging modalities, such as positron emission tomography (PET), near-infrared spectroscopy, functional magnetic resonance imaging (fMRI), local field potentials, electroencephalography (EEG), and magnetoencephalography (MEG).

EXPLORATORY TECHNIQUES

Principal Component Analysis

The goal of PCA is to factorize a data matrix with many variables by creating a set of new variables, termed principal components (Pearson 1901). Each component is a linear combination of the original variables, and the weights are chosen such that the first component has the greatest possible variance, while each successive component also has the highest possible variance, under the condition that all components are mutually uncorrelated. This constraint ensures that the components capture unique, nonoverlapping portions of variance and that together they can perfectly reproduce the variance-covariance structure of the original data set. In the context of neuroimaging, PCA can be used to summarize a data set of several thousand voxels into a smaller number of principal components that may be interpreted as functional networks (Friston et al. 1993, Moeller & Strother 1991, Strother et al. 1995).

PCA is performed by subjecting a data matrix $\mathbf{X}_{n \times p}$ (n observations in the rows, p variables in the columns) to singular value decomposition (SVD) (Eckart & Young 1936). Although SVD is not a statistical analysis per

PCA: principal component analysis

ICA: independent component analysis

CCA: canonical correlation analysis

PLS: partial least squares

SEM: structural equation modeling

DCM: dynamic causal modeling

Effective connectivity: a directed interaction between two regions

Functional connectivity: a systematic deviation from statistical independence between neural activity in two regions, which can be computed using any measure of association, such as correlation, phase locking, or mutual information

SVD: singular value decomposition

se, it is the engine behind PCA-, PLS-, and CCA-based techniques. The main difference between these techniques is what the matrix $\mathbf{X}$ represents (Worsley et al. 1997). SVD is an algebraic tool to deconstruct any given matrix $\mathbf{X}$ into its basic structure

$$\mathbf{X} = \mathbf{USV'}, \tag{2}$$

where $\mathbf{U}_{n \times n}$ and $\mathbf{V}_{p \times n}$ are orthonormal matrices with rank equal to the original matrix $\mathbf{X}$, and $\mathbf{S}_{n \times n}$ is a diagonal matrix of positive singular values. The vectors of $\mathbf{U}$ and $\mathbf{V}$ are termed the left and right singular vectors, respectively. An alternative way to perform PCA is to apply a spectral or eigen-decomposition to the covariance matrices of $\mathbf{X}$. The eigen-decomposition of the voxel $\times$ voxel covariance matrix $\mathbf{X'X}_{p \times p}$ yields $\mathbf{V}$

$$\mathbf{X'X} = (\mathbf{VS'U'})(\mathbf{USV'}) = \mathbf{V(S'S)V'}, \tag{3}$$

while the spectral decomposition of the scan $\times$ scan covariance matrix $\mathbf{XX'}_{n \times n}$ yields $\mathbf{U}$

$$\mathbf{XX'} = (\mathbf{USV'})(\mathbf{VS'U'}) = \mathbf{U(SS')U'}. \tag{4}$$

Both cases are made simpler by the fact that $\mathbf{U'U} = \mathbf{I}$ and $\mathbf{V'V} = \mathbf{I}$ because $\mathbf{U}$ and $\mathbf{V}$ are orthonormal. The vectors of $\mathbf{V}$ can be referred to either as the right singular vectors of $\mathbf{X}$ or the eigenvectors of $\mathbf{X'X}$. The vectors of $\mathbf{U}$ can be referred to either as the left singular vectors of $\mathbf{X}$ or the eigenvectors of $\mathbf{XX'}$. The squared singular value elements on the diagonals of the matrix $\mathbf{S'S}$ are also referred to as eigenvalues.

The rank of $\mathbf{X}$ is the smaller of its row and column dimensions and will determine how many components are extracted. In the illustration above, where $\mathbf{X}$ is a scan $\times$ voxel matrix, the total number of components will typically be equal to the number of scans rather than the number of voxels. In the case for group analysis, where $\mathbf{X}$ is a subjects $\times$ voxels matrix, the number of components will most typically be equal to the number of subjects. The ith principal component consists of the ith column vector of $\mathbf{U}$, the ith column vector of $\mathbf{V}$, and the ith singular value element of $\mathbf{S}$. The vector $\mathbf{V}(i)$ contains weights that indicate the degree to which each voxel contributes to the compo-

nent. Thus, $\mathbf{V}(i)$ is a spatial image (eigenimage) of that principal component. The corresponding vector $\mathbf{U}(i)$ also contains weights, but these indicate the degree to which the component is expressed in each scan (eigentimeseries, when the rows of $\mathbf{X}$ are scans). The contribution of the original variables to the component is often assessed in terms of loadings, but this term is ambiguous. It may refer to either the eigenvector weights or to the correlation between the original variables and components across the observations. The squared singular value associated with each component is proportional to the portion of variance accounted for by the component. The components are ordered by the magnitude of their squared singular values, from largest to smallest. Component scores indicate the value that each of the original n observations would have on the new variables. They are calculated by postmultiplying the data matrix by the eigenimage weights ($\mathbf{XV}_{n \times n}$).

The ability to concentrate as much variance as possible in as few components as possible makes PCA widely applicable in neuroimaging. The initial decomposition reduces the dimensionality of the data set from p (e.g., thousands of voxels) to n (e.g., hundreds of scans). Dimensionality can be reduced further by selecting the first k components and subtracting the variance associated with the rest, although there is no single best criterion to determine k. One option is to select the number of components that account for some minimum amount of total variance. This is a useful method of reducing dimensionality for computationally expensive techniques such as ICA. Another possible criterion is to keep all components up to the first discontinuity in the Scree plot of eigenvalues. Still another approach is to choose the number of components with respect to the generalizability of the decomposition (Hansen et al. 1999).

PCA aggregates variance in components by appropriately weighing original variables that tend to covary. As a result, PCA isolates prominent patterns of regional covariation that represent functional interactions (Friston et al. 1993). Although PCA is usually performed only on the neuroimaging data matrix without any reference to the experimental design, functional networks extracted using PCA can be submitted to another analysis to test for task or group differences, such as CVA (Friston et al. 1996).

Scaled subprofile model. The scaled subprofile model (SSM) is an extension of PCA whereby the expression of dominant patterns of functional connectivity can be compared across groups or for individual subjects (Alexander & Moeller 1994, Moeller et al. 1987, Moeller & Strother 1991, Strother et al. 1995). In the SSM framework it is assumed that there exist meaningful patterns of regional interactions that are independent of the global mean activity and that their expression may differ across groups. To this end, SSM first attempts to remove the main effects of subject and region. The residual values in the data matrix, bereft of these main effects, should contain meaningful information about regional covariance patterns.

Data from multiple groups are combined in a single data matrix $\mathbf{X}_{n \times p}$ with n subjects in the rows and p voxels in the columns. The main difference between SSM and conventional PCA lies in the initial normalization. In PCA, $\mathbf{X}_{n \times p}$ is column centered by subtracting the mean of the column from each element in that column. In SSM, each element of $\mathbf{X}_{n \times p}$ is natural log transformed and then mean centered twice. First, the mean activity for each region across subjects is computed and subtracted (column centering). Second, the mean activity across all regions for each subject is computed and subtracted (row centering).

The twice-normalized data matrix is subjected to SVD and the results are interpreted in a manner identical to traditional PCA. The left singular vectors $\mathbf{V}(i)$ index the contribution of individual voxels to the topography of the component (group invariant subprofiles). As the analysis is blind to group membership, these profiles are group invariant, and the only way to differentiate groups is in terms of their expression. The degree to which a given pattern of regional covariation manifests in individual subjects is given by the subject-specific

weights contained in the right singular vectors $\mathbf{U}(i)$ [subject scaling factor (SSF)].

As in traditional PCA, SSM reduces a large multivariate data set with thousands of voxel variables to a smaller number of topographic patterns. To investigate group and subject differences, SSFs for a specific pattern can be entered into a univariate analysis such as an analysis of variance. SSFs for a patient group can also be entered into a multivariate regression to investigate whether there exists any combination of functional connectivity patterns that predicts some specific behavioral trait.

Applications. Alexander et al. (1994) used SSM to investigate PET functional networks affected by Alzheimer's disease. They analyzed patients and healthy controls in the same step and found four consistent spatial patterns. The mean SSFs differed for the two groups on two of the four patterns, indicating that the expression of these patterns was significantly affected by the disease process. The first pattern indicated lower regional cerebral metabolism in bilateral parietal cortex and right superior temporal cortex and lower metabolism in anterior cingulate and orbital frontal cortex. Moreover, the patient SSFs correlated negatively with measures of visuospatial and attentional skills, indicating that the expression of the parietotemporal deficit pattern is related to poorer attentional performance. The second group-sensitive pattern revealed lower metabolism in the prefrontal, premotor, inferior parietal, medial temporal, and insular regions, as well as high metabolism in occipital association and calcarine regions. This pattern was related to deficits in verbal memory, language comprehension, and verbal fluency. Altogether, the analysis identified two functional networks affected by the disease with distinct behavioral consequences.

Independent Component Analysis

ICA is similar to PCA in the sense that both techniques seek to represent a large number of variables (e.g., voxels) in terms of a smaller number of dimensions that can be interpreted as cohesive functional networks (Beckmann & Smith 2004; Calhoun et al. 2001a,b; McKeown et al. 1998a,b, 2003). Whereas principal components are assumed to be mutually uncorrelated both spatially and temporally, independent components are maximally statistically independent only in one domain.

In both PCA and ICA, the objective is to choose components that have minimal interdependencies among each other. In PCA, a new set of variables, which can be thought of as a set of axes, is created and oriented such that the projection of the data on the first axis has the greatest variance, the projection on the second axis has the second greatest variance, and so on. The key characteristics are that the axes are orthogonal and the components they represent are uncorrelated. The idea behind ICA is that the independent components were somehow mixed to give rise to the observed variables [e.g., blood oxygen–level dependent (BOLD) signal]. In other words, the neural activity measured in different voxels can be thought of as a linear combination of a smaller number of underlying independent component sources. By the central limit theorem, any linear mixture of independent variables (e.g., voxels) will be more "Gaussian" than the original variables themselves (e.g., independent components). Thus, ICA also seeks to create a new set of axes in which to represent the original data set, but the axes are oriented such that the projection of data points onto the axes is maximally non-Gaussian. Therefore, the new axes need not be orthogonal, and independent components can be said to be maximally statistically independent, but they are not necessarily uncorrelated like principal components.

In neuroimaging, independence can be imposed either in the spatial domain (spatial ICA) or in the temporal domain (temporal ICA). The choice between the two depends on the assumptions of the investigator and on the characteristics of the data set (McKeown et al. 2003). Spatial ICA is more commonly used for fMRI data because task-dependent activations are assumed to be relatively sparse in a volume of several thousand voxels. As a result, independent components isolate networks of coherent regions that overlap as little as possible. Conversely, temporal ICA is more commonly used for event-related potential (ERP) data because scalp measurements are assumed to be a mixture of several coactive sources (Makeig et al. 1997, 1999). Thus, the components may have overlapping topographies, but they should have distinct time courses, and so it is desirable for the components to be temporally independent.

The generative model for ICA can be written as

$$\mathbf{X}' = \mathbf{A}\mathbf{S}. \qquad (5)$$

Here $\mathbf{X}_{n \times p}$ is the observed data matrix with n scans in the rows and p voxels in the columns. $\mathbf{S}_{r \times n}$ is the source matrix with r sources and their activity in each of the n scans. Spatial ICA assumes the rows of $\mathbf{S}_{r \times n}$ are independent, whereas temporal ICA assumes the columns of $\mathbf{S}_{r \times n}$ are independent. The mixing matrix $\mathbf{A}_{p \times r}$ indicates how the sources were combined to produce the observed data. ICA is an iterative algorithm that simultaneously tries to estimate both $\mathbf{A}$ and $\mathbf{S}$ by maximizing the non-Gaussianity of either the rows or columns of $\mathbf{S}$. The final step of ICA is to project the original data to source space

$$\mathbf{A}^{-1}\mathbf{X} = \mathbf{S}, \qquad (6)$$

where the unmixing matrix $\mathbf{A}_{r \times n}^{-1}$ is the inverse of $\mathbf{A}_{n \times r}$. The elements of each row vector of the unmixing matrix index the participation of each brain region and are effectively spatial maps, analogous to eigenimages. The row vectors of $\mathbf{S}$ reflect the activation of each component, analogous to eigentimeseries.

Independent components can be interpreted as the dominant functional networks or modes of activity that contribute to the observed neuroimaging data. In addition to a spatial distribution and a time course, each component will have a specific power spectrum and may time-lock to certain stimuli or sensitively respond to some other experimental manipulation. Together, these attributes help to reveal the true character of the component. For instance, ICA can identify artefactual sources of variability in a data set and remove only those components (Jung et al. 2000, Thomas et al. 2002). In fMRI, components with spatial activation ringing around the brain through the entire volume as well as a sudden spike in the time course indicate motion artifact (McKeown et al. 1998a). In EEG, lateral eye movements are marked by a stereotyped spatial distribution with most of the weights concentrated toward the frontal lateral positions on the scalp and a polarity reversal from one side to the other (Jung et al. 2000). Likewise, ICA can identify signal-carrying components, such as task-sensitive functional networks in fMRI (Calhoun et al. 2001c, 2008; McKeown et al. 1998a,b) or task-sensitive ERPs (Makeig et al. 1997, 1999).

A major difference between PCA and ICA is that ICA cannot be used to estimate how many sources of variability there are in the data. ICA is an iterative algorithm that seeks to maximize the independence of the components, but the number of components must be specified prior to the analysis. Because these algorithms are computationally expensive, in practice ICA is usually performed following dimensionality estimation and reduction with PCA (McKeown et al. 2003). Thus, only the first k largest principal components that capture some portion of variance (e.g., 99%) are kept, and the rest are discarded. The k components are then rotated by the ICA algorithm to maximize independence.

Group ICA. Up to this point we have described the extraction of independent components from single subjects, but how can components be made comparable across subjects to allow statistical inference? One approach is to first run the decomposition separately for each subject. Independent components common to most subjects can then be identified either by inspection (Calhoun et al. 2001a) or by a clustering analysis (Jung et al. 2001; Makeig et al. 2002; Onton et al. 2005, 2006). For the latter, some characteristic of the component is first selected (e.g., the spatial map), and the components are clustered into groups based on this characteristic.

An alternative approach is to decompose data from all subjects into the same independent components space. Here, data from all subjects are first concatenated or stacked together such that each subject is implicitly treated as an observation of the same underlying system (Calhoun et al. 2001b, Kovacevic & McIntosh 2007, Schmithorst & Holland 2004). If data are concatenated along the temporal dimension, subjects will have unique time courses but a common spatial map. If the data are concatenated along the spatial dimension, subjects will have unique spatial maps but common time courses. The matrix containing data from all subjects is then decomposed into independent components, which means that all subjects are now in the same space and can be compared directly. Statistical inference on the independent components is possible using univariate (Calhoun et al. 2001b) or multivariate analyses (Diaconescu et al. 2008, Kovacevic & McIntosh 2007, Mišić et al. 2010).

However, if data from individual subjects are concatenated prior to the analysis, components will have either the same spatial map or the same time course for all subjects. Ideally, the decomposition itself should account for between-subject variability as well, with each component having a subject-specific mode in addition to the spatial and temporal modes. The tensor ICA approach is a generalization of the ICA methodology to multiple dimensions, whereby the data are simultaneously decomposed into more than two modes (Beckmann & Smith 2005). In a typical fMRI experiment, these modes would be space, time, and subject. In this way, between-subject variability is estimated directly and allows subsequent between- and within-group analysis.

Applications. Damoiseaux et al. (2006) used tensor ICA to investigate the consistency with which resting-state functional networks manifest across subjects and scans. Resting-state BOLD signal was recorded from one group of subjects in two different sessions. Tensor ICA was used to decompose the data along three domains: space, frequency, and subject. In the initial analysis, data from the two sessions were decomposed separately but yielded ten common spatial patterns with possible biological relevance. For example, they extracted networks composed of regions thought to be involved in executive processing, motor control and execution, memory, and the default mode. To assess the reliability of these networks, the authors created additional data sets with randomly chosen subjects and scans and then performed an ICA for each of these data sets. They found that all but one of the ten resting-state networks consistently appeared in the additional data. Moreover, regions that displayed the greatest signal change were also the least variable across the additional data sets.

Canonical Correlation Analysis

In a typical neuroimaging study, neural activity is not recorded in isolation but rather in the context of an experimental manipulation or together with some measure of behavior. Multivariate analyses are thus ideally suited to capture either the distributed patterns that respond to experimental manipulation or the patterns that optimally predict behavior. The goal of CCA is to relate two sets of data, $\mathbf{X}_{n \times p}$ and $\mathbf{Y}_{n \times q}$, with p and q variables in their respective columns and n observations in the rows (Hotelling 1936). For example, $\mathbf{X}_{n \times p}$ may represent activity in p voxels while $\mathbf{Y}_{n \times q}$ may represent either the experimental design (e.g., with dummy-coded vectors for membership in $q + 1$ categories) or q behavioral scales. CVA (Friston et al. 1996, Strother et al. 2002), linear discriminant analysis (LDA), and multivariate analysis of variance are special cases of CCA where the matrix $\mathbf{Y}$ codes for class membership (Kustra & Strother 2001). If either of the two sets contains data from only one variable, the analysis simplifies to a multiple regression.

The mathematical objective of CCA is to create pairs of new variables (canonical variates) that are linear combinations of the original variables in $\mathbf{X}$ ($\mathbf{XU}(i)_{n \times 1}$) and the variables in $\mathbf{Y}$ ($\mathbf{YV}(i)_{n \times 1}$) and that have the maximum correlation with each other. In addition, pairs of canonical variates are mutually orthogonal with all the other pairs. When $\mathbf{X}_{n \times p}$ and $\mathbf{Y}_{n \times q}$ are standardized, their between-set correlation matrix is given by $\mathbf{X'Y}_{p \times q}$. The between-set correlations are adjusted for within-set correlations ($\mathbf{X'X}_{p \times p}$ and $\mathbf{Y'Y}_{q \times q}$). The adjusted correlation matrix is then factorized using SVD

$$(\mathbf{X'X})^{-1/2} \mathbf{X'Y} (\mathbf{Y'Y})^{-1/2} = \mathbf{USV'}. \quad (7)$$

Similar to principal components, each canonical variate pair is composed of an eigenvector $\mathbf{U}(i)_{p \times 1}$, which represents a pattern of neural activity that is maximally correlated with some differentiation of classes, captured by the corresponding eigenvector $\mathbf{V}(i)_{q \times 1}$. The singular values from the main diagonal of $\mathbf{S}_{q \times q}$ are the correlations between the two canonical variates. The squared canonical correlations (eigenvalues) index the proportion of variance shared by the canonical variates. Because the procedure optimizes the relationship between the two data sets, the first canonical correlation coefficient is guaranteed to be at least as large as the largest between-set correlation. The number of canonical variate pairs is determined by the rank r of the between-set correlation matrix, which is the smallest dimension in the two original matrices ($r = min\{n, p, q\}$). Statistical inference on the whole multivariate pattern is possible using several multivariate tests, such as Bartlett's χ^2 assessment of Wilks's Λ. The contributions of the original variables to a canonical variate are usually gauged—but not tested outright—by correlating each of the original variables with the canonical variate. The correlations (canonical loadings) are considered nontrivial if they exceed ± 0.3.

However, a typical neuroimaging data set has more variables (e.g., voxels) than observations (e.g., scans), and the matrix inverse $\mathbf{X'X}^{-1}$ does not exist because $\mathbf{X'X}$ is rank deficient. This can be rectified by reducing the number of variables prior to the analysis, such as first applying PCA and treating the principal components as the new variables (Friston et al. 1995, 1996). Friston et al. (1996) used this approach to analyze a verbal fluency PET experiment. A letter was presented aurally every 2 seconds. In one condition, subjects had to simply repeat the letter (word shadowing), while in the other condition subjects had to respond with a word that began with that letter (word generation). The data were first reduced by PCA: Out of 60 components (5 subjects × 12 scans), the first 16 components were selected and entered into a CVA. The first canonical variate pair had a statistically significant canonical correlation and easily differentiated the word-shadowing and word-generation scans across all subjects. To obtain a statistical image depicting the total contributions of individual voxels to this effect, the authors multiplied the eigenvector weights from the PCA with the eigenvector weights from the CVA. The statistical image revealed substantial involvement of the anterior cingulate, Broca's area, and ventromedial prefrontal cortex in the differentiation of word shadowing and generation.

Partial Least Squares Analysis

The goal of PLS analysis is to relate two sets of data in a manner similar to CCA-based methods (Bookstein 1994, Krishnan et al. 2010, McIntosh et al. 1996, McIntosh & Lobaugh 2004, Wold 1982). For a neuroimaging experiment, the set with neural activity, $\mathbf{X}_{(n \times q) \times p}$, is organized as follows: the columns correspond to the p variables (e.g., voxels), while the rows correspond to the n participants nested within q experimental conditions. Depending on what the second set represents, PLS may be used to find spatiotemporal patterns that support a particular differentiation of conditions (task PLS) that optimally relate to behavior, or demographic measures (behavior PLS) that optimally relate to activity in a particular seed voxel (seed PLS), or some combination of these (multi-block PLS). In the following subsection we initially focus on task PLS but eventually describe the other variants as well.

Two approaches for computing PLS have been reported in the literature. In the contrast approach, the matrix $\mathbf{Y}_{(n \times q) \times (q-1)}$ contains or-

thonormal contrasts that code for the $q - 1$ degrees of freedom in the design. The covariance matrix $\mathbf{X'Y}_{p \times (q-1)}$ is then subjected to SVD. Here it is easy to see that PLS is conceptually and mechanically similar to CCA, with the important distinction that the covariance matrix is not corrected for within-set covariance prior to the decomposition. This characteristic makes PLS ideally suited for neuroimaging data because signal measured by various imaging modalities tends to have a high degree of spatial and/or temporal autocorrelation, leading to a rank-deficient matrix that cannot be inverted.

The alternative approach is to mean center the data matrix $\mathbf{X}_{(n \times q) \times p}$. This is the currently used approach, and it produces identical results save for scaling differences (McIntosh & Lobaugh 2004). Here, the within-task average is computed for each column to create a matrix $\mathbf{M}_{q \times p}$, which is then column-centered and subjected to SVD

$$\mathbf{M}'_{dev} = \mathbf{USV}'. \qquad (8)$$

The decomposition yields a set of latent variables, each of which consists of the ith column vectors of $\mathbf{U}_{p \times q}$ and $\mathbf{V}_{q \times q}$, as well as the ith diagonal element of the diagonal matrix $\mathbf{S}_{q \times q}$. The left singular vector $\mathbf{U}(i)$ contains the element saliences (weights) that identify the voxels that collectively make the greatest contribution to the effects captured by the latent variable. The right singular vector $\mathbf{V}(i)$ contains the design saliences, which index the contribution of each task to the spatiotemporal pattern identified by the latent variable. The element and design saliences can be interpreted as the functional network and task contrast with maximal covariance. The strength of the relationship extracted by each latent variable is reflected by the relative size of the singular value. Note that the singular value is a covariance rather than a correlation (cf. canonical correlation). The proportion of between-set covariance accounted for by each latent variable is given by the ratio of the squared singular value to the sum of all other squared singular values. The expression of each latent variable can be calculated by taking the dot product of the singular vector and the original data, analogous to principal component scores. The projection of the original voxel activations on the element saliences ($\mathbf{XU}_{n \times q}$, brain scores) indicates the degree to which each of the n observations expresses the task effects.

From a practical point of view, PLS and its application to neuroimaging use a framework for nonparametric statistical inference at the level of the entire multivariate pattern as well as at the level of the element saliences and their individual contributions. Specifically, permutation tests (Edgington 1995) are used to test the significance of the latent variables, and bootstrapping (Efron & Tibshirani 1986) is used to estimate the standard errors of the element saliences.

To assess the significance of a latent variable, the rows (i.e., observations) of $\mathbf{X}_{n \times p}$ are randomly reordered (permuted). The new data are mean centered and subjected to SVD as before in order to obtain a new set of singular values. These singular values are effectively generated under the null hypothesis that there is no association between neural activity and the task. The procedure is then repeated many times (e.g., 1,000) to generate an entire sampling distribution of singular values under the null hypothesis. Because the singular value is proportional to the magnitude of the effect, the p-value is estimated as the probability that singular values from the distribution of permuted samples exceed the singular value from the original, nonpermuted data. In other words, the p-value is the probability of obtaining a singular value of this size under the null hypothesis that there is no association between the task and brain activity.

The contribution of individual element saliences to the latent variable is operationalized in terms of reliability or stability. Many bootstrap samples (e.g., 1,000) are generated by sampling with replacement subjects within conditions and then computing PLS for each sample to generate a distribution of saliences. The bootstrap distribution is then used to estimate the standard errors and confidence intervals for the saliences. The idea is to see which saliences are stable irrespective of the sample

and which saliences are sensitive to which subjects in the sample. The ratio of the salience to its bootstrap-estimated standard error (bootstrap ratio) allows saliences that are both large and reliable to be selected. If the bootstrap distribution is normal, this ratio is approximately equivalent to a z-score. Stable saliences identify voxels that make a robust contribution to the latent variable.

So far we have described how data from a single time point are analyzed, but the analysis can easily be extended to the temporal domain by treating each data point (i.e., each voxel at each scan) as a separate variable. For example, if there are p voxels and t scans, the data matrix $\mathbf{X}_{(n \times q) \times (p \times t)}$ is constructed by nesting the scans within the voxels in the columns. Thus, the first column contains the amplitude of the first voxel in the first scan, the second column contains the amplitude of the first voxel in the second scan, and so on. The rest of the analysis is performed as described above. The only difference is that the left singular vectors contain saliences that describe a spatiotemporal pattern of neural activity. In each vector $\mathbf{U}(i)_{(p \times t) \times 1}$ the saliences are organized in the same way as in $\mathbf{X}_{(n \times q) \times (p \times t)}$, with the scans nested within the voxels. This simple innovation permits analysis of neuroimaging data with a time component, such as event-related fMRI (McIntosh et al. 2004) and ERPs (Lobaugh et al. 2001).

Behavior PLS. A notable variant of the analysis described above is one where the matrix $\mathbf{Y}_{(n \times q) \times b}$ contains b demographic and/or behavioral measures. In this case, the input matrix should be constructed such that it contains correlations between neural activity and behavior within each of the q experimental conditions. The condition-specific correlations between the submatrices $\mathbf{X}_{n \times p}$ and $\mathbf{Y}_{n \times b}$ are calculated first and then stacked to form the input matrix

$$\mathbf{Y}'\mathbf{X}_{behavior} = \begin{bmatrix} \mathbf{Y}'_1\mathbf{X}_1 \\ \mathbf{Y}'_2\mathbf{X}_2 \\ \vdots \\ \mathbf{Y}'_q\mathbf{X}_q \end{bmatrix}. \qquad (9)$$

Rather than finding patterns of neural activity that relate to some differentiation of conditions, the analysis now finds patterns of neural activity that relate similarly and differently across conditions (or groups) to behavior. Behavior saliences $V(i)$ indicate the degree to which brain-behavior correlations are expressed for each task. Element saliences $U(i)$ indicate the degree to which individual regions express these brain-behavior correlations.

Seed PLS. The machinery for behavior PLS can also be used to assess task-dependent changes in the correlation (i.e., functional connectivity) between one or more seed regions and the rest of the brain. The seeds may be selected either on theoretical grounds or using another statistical analysis, such as task PLS. The activity of each of the b seed voxels is entered into the matrix $Y_{(n \times q) \times b}$, with the data from different conditions stacked on top of each other. The input matrix is constructed in a manner analogous to behavior PLS. Seed PLS analysis of this matrix identifies brain-seed correlations that are interpreted in terms of element and seed saliences. Seed saliences $V(i)$ indicate the degree to which the seed regions—during different tasks—are functionally connected to the spatiotemporal patterns of neural activity depicted by element saliences $U(i)$.

Multiblock PLS. Task, behavior, and seed PLS relate patterns of neural activity to one other "block" of data. Multiblock PLS is a way to simultaneously relate neural activity to two or more blocks of data (Caplan et al. 2007). For example, multiblock PLS can identify functional networks that support some differentiation of tasks and at the same time display robust functional connectivity with a particular seed region. The input matrix is constructed by columnwise concatenating the matrix of task means M_{dev} and the task/group dependent correlation of behavior/seed with brain activity (e.g.,

$Y'X_{behavior}$ and/or $Y'X_{seed}$):

$$Y'X_{multi} = \begin{bmatrix} M_{dev} \\ Y'X_{behavior} \\ Y'X_{seed} \end{bmatrix}. \qquad (10)$$

The multiblock covariance matrix $Y'X_{multi}$ is then decomposed by SVD, and the singular vectors are interpreted as before. The left singular vectors U are a spatial pattern of voxels. The only difference from a standard analysis is that the right singular vectors V now contain saliences that capture both task and behavior/seed relationships. The weights in the columns of V identify LVs that reflect either a task effect, a behavior/seed effect, or the convergence of the two:

$$V = \begin{bmatrix} V_{task} \\ V_{behavior} \\ V_{seed} \end{bmatrix}. \qquad (11)$$

Applications. Grady et al. (2010) used both task and seed PLS to study the effect of aging on default mode and task-positive networks. During scanning, young and older adults performed four visual tasks. During the fifth "condition," participants were required to fixate on a centrally presented dot but did not have to respond. Both groups and all conditions were entered into a task PLS analysis, which revealed two statistically significant latent variables. The first latent variable separated the no-task fixation condition from the other four task conditions in both groups. The design saliences were negative for fixation and positive for the tasks. The regional pattern that showed consistently greater activity during the tasks (indexed by positive bootstrap ratios) resembled the task-positive network. The regional pattern that showed the opposite trend (greater activity during fixation, indexed by negative bootstrap ratios) resembled the default mode network. The authors concluded that the first latent variable isolated default mode and task-positive networks that were similar for young and older participants. The authors then used seed PLS to investigate how functional connectivity within the default mode and task-positive networks changes during aging. Connectivity in the default mode network was analyzed by choosing two prominent default mode regions from the task PLS analysis as seeds. Seed PLS analyses revealed high correlations with other default mode regions. Likewise, prominent task-positive regions were chosen as seeds to assess connectivity in the task-positive network. The seeds mainly correlated with other task-positive regions. To assess whether functional connectivity within either network differed between groups, brain scores were correlated with seed activity, separately for each group. This comparison showed that connectivity within the default mode network decreased with age, whereas connectivity within the task-positive network did not change.

Classification Techniques

Neuroimaging experiments are specifically designed to differentiate and isolate brain states. Neural activity collected during an experiment can be stratified into several classes according to the experimental design. Classes may represent different stimuli that were presented and tasks that were performed as well as responses or decisions made by subjects. Classes may also represent different groups of subjects. The goal of classification is to use imaging data to find brain states that can reliably predict class membership (O'Toole et al. 2007, Pereira et al. 2009). Multivariate classification techniques seek patterns of data features (e.g., voxel activations) that maximally separate the classes. If conventional analyses such as GLM can be thought of as an attempt to use the design variables to predict neural activity, then classifiers effectively do the opposite: They use patterns of neural activity to predict the experimental design (Pereira et al. 2009). In a typical analysis, data are divided into a training set and a test set. The classifier is calibrated using the training set and then used to predict class membership in the test set. Classification accuracy on the test set allows for statistical assessment of classifier performance. Predictive

learning (Strother et al. 2002) and multivoxel pattern analysis (Haynes & Rees 2005, Norman et al. 2006) are also forms of classification.

Types of classifiers. Multivariate classifiers are a family of techniques defined more by purpose and application than by mechanics. Geometrically, the original p features (e.g., voxels) define a p-dimensional space, and each example (e.g., brain volume) represents a point in that space. Most classifiers identify patterns by learning a function that will take values of the features as an input and generate a class label. For linear classifiers this function is a simple linear combination of features that can be thought of as a hyperplane that maximizes the separation between points that belong to different classes (Campbell & Atchley 1981).

The flexible associative multivariate models previously described, such as CVA and PLS, are both examples of techniques that look for linear patterns to differentiate classes. One of the most commonly used classifiers in neuroimaging—LDA—is a special case of CVA with only two classes, which in turn is equivalent to CCA when the matrix $\mathbf{Y}$ codes for class membership (Kustra & Strother 2001). LDA is often framed in terms of maximizing the between-class covariance $\mathbf{B}$ (computed as the covariance of the class means) relative to the within-class covariance $\mathbf{W}$. The linear combinations that satisfy this condition are given by the eigenvectors of $\mathbf{W}^{-1}\mathbf{B}$, which are equivalent to the eigenvectors of the adjusted between-set correlation matrix for CCA (Equation 7). In choosing the best linear combination, multivariate classifiers will take into account the relationships between voxels. For example, the voxels that constitute the dominant pattern extracted by LDA were chosen because together they covaried with the differentiation of classes. Thus, discriminant functions can often be thought of as functional networks. The linear kernel support vector machine (SVM) is another salient example of a linear classifier. SVM focuses only on those examples that lie close to other classes and uses these to construct a discriminant function that maximizes the margin between the classes.

Nonlinear classifiers learn a nonlinear function of the features and are more diverse. Some nonlinear classifiers do not seek a hyperplane but more generally a surface to separate classes. For example, quadratic discriminant analysis assumes the discriminant function is a quadratic polynomial and computes a quadratic surface. Other methods change the space in which the data are represented. For example, SVMs with nonlinear kernels transform the original feature space to a higher-dimensional space where it is theoretically easier to construct separating hyperplanes.

Cross-validation. An important notion in classification is that the patterns extracted should be able to predict class membership of a new sample that the classifier has not previously encountered. The focus on prediction rather than explanation means that cross-validation plays a prominent role in multivariate classification for neuroimaging (Strother et al. 2002). The simplest approach would be to split the available data into halves, then train the classifier on one half and test it on the other. However, neuroimaging samples (scans, subjects) are scarce, and with a reduced data set the discriminant function may be too variable and may not generalize well to other cases. Ideally, the classifier should be trained with as many samples as possible.

This is made possible by k-fold cross-validation. The sample is randomly split into k subsamples, with each subsample containing the same number of examples for each class. In each of the k iterations ("folds"), $k-1$ subsamples are used to train the classifier, and the single remaining subsample is used for validation. The classification accuracies obtained from individual folds are combined and have effectively made use of the entire sample. If the training sets do not contain equal numbers of examples for each class, a classifier may not be able to learn how to discriminate among classes that are underrepresented. This is usually not a problem for studies with counterbalanced designs.

To determine the success of a classifier, one must assess whether the neuroimaging data

significantly helped to predict class membership. The null hypothesis is that the same classification accuracy could have been achieved simply by chance. Imagine that the probability of successfully classifying a single example by chance is p, and the probability of incorrectly classifying it is $1-p$. For example, if there are q classes, $p = \frac{1}{q}$. This helps to construct the null probability for any situation where the classifier correctly classified k examples by chance, out of a total of n test examples. The probability of being successful k times ($Pr\{X = k\}$) is given by the binomial distribution

$$Pr\{X = k\} = \binom{n}{k} p^k (1-p)^{n-k}, \qquad (12)$$

where p^k is the probability of k successful classifications, $(1-p)^{n-k}$ the probability of $n-k$ unsuccessful classifications, and $\binom{n}{k}$ the number of possible ways this could occur. The corresponding p-value is $Pr\{X \geq k\}$ and can be calculated by integration.

Applications. Carlson et al. (2003) used fMRI to investigate whether the perception of different object categories is modular (i.e., performed by category-specific areas) or distributed among many areas. Subjects were presented with pictures of multiple object categories (e.g., faces, houses) in the context of a delayed-match-to-sample task, as well as passive viewing. The data were first reduced by PCA and only the first 40 components were retained, corresponding to 80% to 85% variance. An LDA classifier was trained and assessed using a variant of the k-fold cross-validation procedure described above. One set of exemplars was removed and a subset of the remaining data (randomly chosen by sampling with replacement) used as a training set. The classifier was then tested on the exemplars that had been held out. The authors found that the trained classifiers discriminated at levels significantly above chance. Moreover, patterns of activity that distinguished one category from others had little spatial overlap, in support of the modularity hypothesis.

CONFIRMATORY TECHNIQUES

Psychophysiological Interactions

If the correlation between two brain regions changes significantly under different experimental manipulations, this suggests an interaction between the psychological variable and the underlying physiology—a psychophysiological interaction (PPI) (Friston et al. 1997). In PPI, the activity of one brain region is regressed onto the activity of another brain region in different experimental conditions, and the change in slope is assessed. PPI seeks to explain the physiological response in one region in terms of an interaction between a task and physiological activity in another region by explicitly looking for regions whose correlation with the seed changes in response to the task. The idea is that activity in a seed region of interest may correlate with activity in other regions not due to the experimental manipulation, but rather simply by virtue of anatomical connections, common sensory inputs, or neuromodulatory influence. Thus, rather than looking for significant correlations, PPI looks for correlations that change significantly during a task.

The first step is to select a seed region and to extract its time course. As in seed PLS, the region may be chosen either on the basis of theory or by prior analysis such as task PLS. The PPI analysis is performed in the framework of a standard GLM. If the objective were to find regions whose activity correlates with the seed region, activity from the seed region could be entered as a predictor. Rather, the objective is to find regions whose activity depends on the interaction between the task and the seed region. To this end, an "interaction" predictor is created by taking the scalar product of the time course of the task (exactly as in a standard GLM) and the time course of activity in the seed region. GLM analysis with this interaction predictor would identify voxels whose correlation with the seed region is significantly higher in one task than in the other.

For every voxel in the brain Y, PPI is formulated as a regression equation that tries to predict Y from seed X, task A, and the interaction of the seed and the task (XA) (McIntosh & Gonzalez-Lima 1994):

$$Y = \beta_{y.z}X + \beta_{y.a}A + \beta_{y.xa}XA + \epsilon. \quad (13)$$

Notice that the interaction predictor is actually a product of two main effects: the seed time course and the experimental design. Voxels whose activity correlates only with the seed or only with the experimental design will still display some correlation with the interaction predictor. Therefore, the relationship between the interaction predictor and the target voxel is assessed as a semipartial correlation $\beta_{y.xa}$.

Applications. Stephan et al. (2003) investigated whether cognitive control and task execution show lateralization effects. During an fMRI experiment, participants were presented with four-letter nouns that had a red letter either in the second or third position. In the letter-decision task, they had to indicate whether the word contained the letter "A"; in the visuospatial-decision task, they had to indicate whether the red letter was on the left or the right. In a baseline task, the participants simply had to respond as quickly as possible to the appearance of the stimuli. In an initial GLM analysis, the authors contrasted the letter-decision and visuospatial-decision tasks with the baseline and found significant differences in the left and right anterior cingulate cortex (ACC), implicating these regions as the locus of cognitive control. The goal of the subsequent PPI analysis was to determine whether the coupling between the ACC and any other region in the brain significantly changed during task execution. The analysis revealed that the effective connectivity between left ACC and left inferior frontal gyrus significantly increased during letter decisions, whereas the connectivity between the right ACC and the left intraparietal sulcus increased during visuospatial decisions. The authors were able to conclude that cognitive control over regions involved in task execution is exerted within the same hemisphere.

Structural Equation Modeling

The goal of SEM is to construct a causal model and to test whether it is consistent with the data (Jöreskog et al. 1979, Loehlin 1987). In neuroimaging, SEM models are usually a subset of brain regions and the pattern of causal influence among them (McIntosh & Gonzalez-Lima 1991, 1994; McIntosh et al. 1994). The regions to be included in the model are either chosen a priori or from some exploratory analysis. The influences between regions are constrained anatomically, such that direct influence between two regions is possible only if there is a known white matter pathway between them. The models are then used to assess how interregional influence (i.e., effective connectivity) differs between experimental conditions or groups.

Each brain region is treated as a variable, and casual influences between regions are specified in terms of linear regression equations. As an example, consider the system identified by the path diagram in **Figure 1** (see color insert). Here, putative anatomical projections (depicted by arrows) engender effective connections. Structural equations are essentially regression equations that define the sources of variance for each variable. In the present example, x_i represents the variance of each region. Each regional variance can be partitioned into variance explained by other regions, as well as an error or residual term (ψ_{x_i}). The residual terms may be thought of as exogenous influences from other brain regions that could not be included in the model, or the influence of a brain region upon itself. The strength of each connection is given by the regression weights p, q, r, s and t, also known as path coefficients. The causal order of the network is described by a system of structural equations:

$$
\begin{aligned}
x_1 &= \psi_{x_1} \\
x_2 &= p x_1 + \psi_{x_2} \\
x_3 &= q x_1 + r x_2 + \psi_{x_3} \\
x_4 &= s x_2 + t x_3 + \psi_{x_4}.
\end{aligned} \tag{14}
$$

The key idea behind SEM is that this system of equations assumes a particular causal order

and can be used to generate an implied covariance matrix (McArdle & McDonald 1984). The implied covariance matrix is a prediction of the variances and covariances between regions, parameterized in terms of the path coefficients. Here we show the corresponding correlations for simplicity:

$$
\begin{aligned}
R_{x_1,x_2} &= p \\
R_{x_1,x_3} &= q + pr \\
R_{x_1,x_3} &= ps + prt + qt \\
R_{x_2,x_3} &= r + pq \\
R_{x_2,x_3} &= s + rt + pqt \\
R_{x_3,x_4} &= t + sr + qps.
\end{aligned} \tag{15}
$$

The covariance matrix is fitted to the empirical covariance matrix to estimate the path coefficients and residual variances. Typically, a method such as maximum likelihood estimation (MLE) or weighted least squares is used to establish a fit criterion that must be maximized. The model is initialized by guessing the values of the unknown parameters. At each iteration of the algorithm, the parameters are slightly altered and the fit of the implied covariance matrix to the empirical covariance matrix is reassessed. The procedure continues until there is no appreciable improvement in fit. Thus, known parameters (variances and covariances) are used to estimate unknown parameters (path coefficients and residual variances). SEM can be thought of as a method of using patterns of functional connectivity (covariances) to draw inferences about effective connectivity (path coefficients).

Notice that for any given connection (e.g., x_1 to x_3), the corresponding structural equation contains terms for the influence of other regions (e.g., the path coefficients for x_1 to x_2 and x_2 to x_3) in addition to the path coefficient for that connection. The resulting path coefficient has a meaning similar to a semipartial correlation in the sense that it reflects the influence of one region on another, with influences from all other regions on the sink region held constant. In practice, maximum likelihood estimates of path coefficients differ only slightly from least-squares estimates of semipartial regression coefficients mainly because the former are calculated simultaneously, whereas the latter are calculated separately (McIntosh & Gonzalez-Lima 1994).

Model inference. The simplest application of SEM is one where a model is formulated and tested against the data. The discrepancy between the covariance matrix implied by the model and the empirical covariance matrix can be assessed using some goodness-of-fit test, such as the χ^2 statistic. A large χ^2 value indicates a significant departure from the empirical covariance matrix and indicates that there is sufficient evidence to reject the null hypothesis that the implied and empirical covariance matrices do not differ (i.e., the model is not consistent with the data).

However, there is no guarantee that the tested model will be the best-fitting model, and SEM can also be used to compare competing models. For example, if regions x_1 and x_2 were known to be part of a direct feedback loop, one may wish to test whether the effective connections between them are equal (symmetric) or unequal (asymmetric). The null model would constrain the connections to be equal by parameterizing each direction with the same path coefficient. The alternative model would assign different path coefficient parameters to the connections, allowing them to freely vary. An implied covariance matrix is generated for each model and statistically compared with the empirical covariance matrix using a χ^2 goodness-of-fit statistic. The models are then compared using the χ^2 difference test. The difference is computed by subtracting $\chi^2_{alternative}$ from χ^2_{null} and then assessed with respect to the differences in degrees of freedom for the two models. The test helps to determine whether the modification (i.e., additional parameter) significantly improves the fit of the model. In the present example, a significant difference test would imply that the path coefficients were significantly different in the two directions. Notice that the two models could not be distinguished in terms of functional connectivity, which is symmetric by definition (McIntosh & Gonzalez-Lima 1994).

Under the hierarchical testing scheme described above, SEM can be used to examine whether one or more causal influences change due to experimental manipulation by comparing models for two different conditions or groups of subjects. The simplest strategy would be to employ separate model runs and then describe where the models differ, although in this case there is no opportunity for statistical inference. The more common approach is to combine the models in a single multigroup or stacked run. The null hypothesis is that effective connections do not differ between groups, whereas the alternative hypothesis is that effective connections are group specific. Here, a null model is first constructed such that path coefficients of interest are constrained to be equal for both groups. In the alternative model these path coefficients are free to vary separately for each group. The alternative hypothesis is tested by generating an implied covariance matrix for each model and statistically comparing them with the empirical covariance matrix. An alternative χ^2 that is significantly lower than the null χ^2 implies that the path coefficients were statistically different for the two groups. An interesting situation arises if the omnibus test indicates a poor overall fit, but the difference test indicates a significant change from one task to another. SEM has been shown to be resilient in these situations because it can detect changes in effective connectivity even if the absolute fit of the model is inadequate (Protzner & McIntosh 2006).

Bullmore et al. (2000) describe an alternative approach to model selection, where the nodes of the network are specified a priori, but the paths are traced out in a data-driven manner. The starting point for the procedure is the null model with all path coefficients equal to zero. At each iteration, the path coefficient with the largest modification index (the improvement in model fit if that parameter were freed) is unconstrained and incorporated into the model. The addition of any path will improve the χ^2 value, so the fit of the new model is evaluated in terms of a parsimonious fit index, which is high for models with a well-fitting covariance matrix and with the fewest paths (Bollen 1986). A path is added permanently only if it improves the fit index; otherwise, the path with the next highest modification index is unconstrained and evaluated. The algorithm continues until a model with the maximum fit index is identified that cannot be increased by adding any more paths. A confidence interval for the parsimonious fit index of the final model is formed by bootstrapping. Bootstrap samples are created by randomly sampling subjects with replacement, and the entire procedure is repeated to generate a null distribution for the fit index.

Applications. Nyberg et al. (1996) used SEM to study how effective connectivity changes during episodic memory retrieval relative to a baseline reading task. An initial univariate subtraction analysis revealed that activity in some regions increased relative to baseline, while activity in a number of regions actually decreased. One possible explanation for the decreased activity is that the baseline activity in those regions was higher than during the task. An alternative explanation is that activity in these regions was suppressed. The authors used SEM to test the hypothesis that the decrease in regional cerebral blood flow was the result of direct, active inhibition by regions with increased activity. They used a stacked-run SEM analysis to construct a null model in which path coefficients feeding back from activated to deactivated regions were constrained to be equal across tasks, as well as an alternative model in which the path coefficients were allowed to differ. The modification resulted in a significant χ^2 difference test, indicating significantly improved model fit. Moreover, the feedback paths were negative in both conditions but more negative in the episodic retrieval condition, suggesting increased inhibition. Thus, SEM was used to disambiguate the mechanism behind task-dependent changes in neural activity. Interestingly, the areas of decreased blood flow that were the targets of "inhibitory" effects were key constituents of the default mode network (Raichle et al. 2001), including medial frontal and retrosplenial cortices.

Dynamic Causal Modeling

DCM uses a Bayesian framework to estimate causal influences in a network of brain regions and how these influences change due to experimental manipulation (Friston et al. 2003). Neural activity in each region is modeled by differential equations that describe the local dynamics. The causal architecture of the network arises from interactions among regions. The interactions are specified by a set of coupling parameters that represent the efficacy of synaptic coupling and model effective connectivity. The biologically plausible causal model generates neural activity in real time. A forward model translates hidden neural dynamics at each region to measured responses (e.g., BOLD signal). Bayesian model inversion allows information from the experiment to be incorporated back into the causal model to get a better estimate of effective connections. Competing hypotheses about how experimental context modulates synaptic coupling are formulated as different models and compared to each other in terms of their relative likelihood given the data. The optimal model can further be characterized in terms of its coupling parameters. As we discuss below, DCM does not mandate any specific biophysical model of neural activity nor any specific forward model. Rather, DCM is a generic framework for inferring context-dependent changes in synaptic coupling at the neural level.

Causal model. The first stage is to define a model of causal order. Each region in the model consists of neuronal subpopulations that are intrinsically coupled to each other. Extrinsic coupling between different neuronal populations models a network of regions. The state or activity of each neuronal population is described by a set of stochastic or ordinary differential equations that relate the rate of change in activity (i.e., the future state) to the present state. The synaptic coupling among different populations allows terms for the current state of one population to be introduced in the equation describing the state of another population. The coupling parameters can be thought of as rate constants that determine the speed with which one population influences another. Causal order is embodied in the ability of dynamics in one region to influence dynamics in another region. Experimental manipulations are modeled as external perturbations of the system. External inputs may induce either a change in coupling or a change in activity in a specific neuronal population. Therefore, the underlying causal model is a system of coupled differential equations,

$$\frac{\partial x}{\partial t} = f(x, u, \theta^c),$$ (16)

that describe how the rate of change of states x is a function of states of other populations (x), external inputs (u) and coupling parameters (θ^c). The coupling parameters θ^c are unknown and the purpose of DCM is to infer them, much like path coefficients in SEM. Notice that causality is engendered at the level of neural activity rather than at the level of the observed signal.

DCMs do not impose any one particular biophysical model of neural activity. The only stipulation is that the model is biologically plausible and adequately captures interactions between populations as well as externally induced perturbations. There is a well-developed literature on dynamical models of neural activity (Breakspear & Jirsa 2007), and the incorporation of new models into the DCM framework is an active topic of research (Daunizeau et al. 2009, Friston & Dolan 2010). For the present, we merely note that the type of model employed will depend on the imaging modality used in the experiment. Due to the slow and regionally variable hemodynamic response, fMRI does not provide sufficient information to estimate time delays in coupling between regions. Thus, DCMs for fMRI usually do not model conduction delays, whereas DCMs for EEG/MEG do. Recently developed DCMs for fMRI explicitly model excitatory and inhibitory subpopulations for each source (Marreiros et al. 2008). DCMs for EEG/MEG use more detailed neural mass models composed of populations of pyramidal

cells as well as populations of excitatory and inhibitory interneurons (David et al. 2006).

Forward model. The spatiotemporal evolution of system dynamics at the neuronal level is described in real time. The second stage of DCM is to enable comparison with observed data by using a forward model to translate neuronal system states into measurements. The forward model is an explicit mapping (g) from neuronal activity (x) to some feature of the data (y)

$$y = g(\mathbf{x}, \theta^f).$$ (17)

The form of the forward model will depend on the imaging modality. For example, if the data are evoked responses, such as ERPs or event-related fields, the function g is the lead field matrix that models the propagation and subsequent volume conduction of electromagnetic fields through brain tissue, cerebrospinal fluid, skull, and skin. In this case, the additional unknown parameters θ^f introduced are the location and orientation of the source dipole (Kiebel et al. 2006). On the other hand, if the signal is BOLD contrast, the function g models how state changes at the neuronal level induce change in local blood flow, inflating blood volume and reducing deoxygenated hemoglobin (Buxton et al. 1998). In that case, the unknown parameters specify quantities such as the rate constants of vasodilatory signal decay and autoregulatory feedback by blood flow (Stephan et al. 2007).

Despite apparent differences, SEM and DCM have much in common. Both techniques seek to estimate context-dependent changes in effective connectivity. Through the prism of SEM, the intrinsic connectivity implemented in DCM can be thought of as the grand average effective connectivity across all conditions and the modulatory effects as the changes in the intrinsic connections due to experimental manipulation. From the perspective of DCM, SEM can be thought of as a special case in which the system is driven by noise rather than systematic exogenous inputs (**Figure 1**), while the interactions are linear and take place at the level of the observations rather than at the neural level.

Model inversion. DCMs use a Bayesian framework for estimating the unknown parameters, and here we briefly outline the logic behind the approach. The parameters of interest are assumed to be random variables with some probability density. Before an experiment is performed, the parameters have a prior distribution, which reflects a priori knowledge about their values. Thus, unknown parameters are constrained either to an interval or to a fixed value. For example, one may have prior empirical knowledge about the likely range of values of some hemodynamic parameters. Likewise, one may make an explicit assumption that some coupling parameters are zero. After the experiment is performed, new information is obtained from the data and used to update the prior distribution. The new distribution of each parameter, which takes into account both prior beliefs and the available data, is called the posterior distribution. Estimation of the posterior distribution is essentially an optimization problem, and the priors can be thought of as soft constraints because they bias the parameter estimates.

Bayesian model inversion is a procedure that uses the observed data to update the model (i.e., estimate the parameters) in a way that maximizes the model evidence. This quantity, also known as the marginal likelihood of the model, is defined as the probability of the data given the model m. Model evidence is highest for models that explain the data as accurately as possible and at the same time have the fewest parameters. The unknown parameters from the causal and the forward model are denoted by $\theta = \{\theta^c, \theta^f\}$. The posterior density $p(\theta|y, m)$ is estimated by combining the prior density on the parameters $p(\theta|m)$ with the likelihood function $p(y|\theta, m)$,

$$p(\theta|y, m) \propto p(y|\theta, m)p(\theta|m), \qquad (18)$$

which follows from Bayes' rule.

Inference. DCMs allow statistical inference on models and on parameters. For example,

alternative models correspond to alternative hypotheses about context-dependent changes in neural activity. Thus, model space should be constructed systematically and include only plausible models. Two models can be compared directly either by taking the ratio of their respective evidence (Kass & Raftery 1995) or the difference in their respective log evidence. A model with evidence more than 20 times greater than another model is considered stronger. This procedure (Bayesian model selection) can be used to make a wide variety of comparisons, such as DCMs with different inputs, different anatomical connections, or different priors. Models with different numbers of parameters can be compared directly because evidence takes into account model complexity. Once the optimal model is selected, specific parameters can be statistically assessed with respect to their posterior densities. For instance, the probability of exceeding some preset threshold can be evaluated directly from the posterior probability.

Because model inversion is done on a subject-by-subject basis, there is no guarantee that the same model will necessarily be optimal for all subjects. Therefore, for between-subjects (group-level) inference the investigator must decide whether or not to enforce the same model for all subjects (Stephan et al. 2010). If there is reason to believe that the process under study is homogeneous in the population (e.g., a sensory response in healthy subjects), one can multiply the evidence for a specific model (or add the log-evidence) for each subject to get group-level evidence for that model. This is effectively a fixed-effects assumption. Conversely, if there is reason to believe that the process under study is heterogeneous in the population (e.g., a cognitive process in a spectrum disorder), one can compute the ratio of the number of subjects who show positive evidence for a given model m_i relative to the number of subjects who show greater evidence for another model m_j (Stephan et al. 2007). This is a random-effects assumption.

Inference on model parameters will also depend on whether individual effects are assumed to be fixed or random. In the fixed-effects case, the model is the same for all participants and posterior densities can be estimated for all participants. Thus, one approach to estimating group-average parameters is to compute a joint density for the subject-specific posterior estimates (e.g., Garrido et al. 2007). The probability of exceeding a particular threshold can be computed directly from the joint density, exactly as in the case of single-subject analysis. In the random-effects case, the models may be different for different subjects and thus a joint posterior probability cannot be computed. The most common approach is to treat the mode of each subject-specific posterior distribution as a summary statistic. Known as maximum a posteriori estimates, these can then be submitted to a traditional random-effects analysis of variance or t-test.

Applications. A study by Garrido et al. (2009) demonstrates how DCM can be used to study the mismatch negativity (MMN). The MMN is a pronounced negative potential in response to oddball stimuli (deviants) embedded in a stream of repeated stimuli (standards). The authors investigated whether the MMN is caused by comparison between sensory input and a memory trace of previous input or by local adaptation in primary auditory cortex as a result of repeating stimuli, or both. Regions for the network were selected on the basis of previous studies. Local adaptation and memory comparison were operationalized as changes in intrinsic (within a population) and extrinsic (between populations) coupling, respectively. Several models were constructed, involving no changes in coupling, changes in local coupling only, changes in extrinsic coupling only, or changes in both intrinsic and extrinsic coupling. The DCMs were inverted separately for each subject and log evidence was summed across subjects for each model in order to select the best one. The model that allowed changes in both intrinsic and extrinsic coupling had the highest total log evidence. The free effective connections for each subject-specific model were computed separately for each condition and compared.

Separate t-tests for each connection showed that coupling increased for deviants relative to standards, indicating learning-related changes in coupling.

OTHER TECHNIQUES

Multivariate Granger Causality

A signal x can be said to cause another signal y if the past of x can predict the future of y (Granger 1969). If one is interested in such causal relationships in a whole network of brain regions, this framework can be extended to include multiple predictors, such that the present activity of all regions is being predicted by the past activity of all other regions. If causal effects are assumed to be linear, the problem can be formulated as a multivariate linear regression and is termed a multivariate vector autoregressive model (MVAR) (Goebel et al. 2003). By default, the model contains terms for every possible connection in the network, so each connection is tested to see which ones are nonzero. In this manner, a directed subnetwork depicting causal flow can be extracted without any a priori hypothesis about the connectivity between regions.

An MVAR model of order m seeks to predict the present (tth) values of p variables (e.g., brain regions) as a linear combination of their m previous values. The tth sample from the multivariate time series is represented by the p-dimensional vector $\mathbf{X}(t)$:

$$\mathbf{X}(t) = \sum_{i=1}^{m} \mathbf{A}(i)\mathbf{X}(t - i) + \mathbf{E}(t). \quad (19)$$

The ith matrix $\mathbf{A}(i)$ is a $p \times p$ matrix of autoregressive coefficients, and $\mathbf{E}(t)$ is a vector of residuals. The current value of the jth voxel $x_j(n)$ is a linear combination of m past values of all voxels, with the jth column of each matrix $\mathbf{A}(i)$. This is the key aspect of the multivariate version of Granger causality. For any given connection, the influence of other nodes in the network is accounted for and partialled out. Thus, multivariate Granger causality measures whether the past of x helps to predict y over and above other variables z. The coefficients $\mathbf{A}(i)$ can be estimated by ordinary least-squares, i.e., by minimizing the sum of squared errors between the predicted and observed values of $\mathbf{X}(t)$. The effective connections are construed as regression equations, and their significance can be assessed via the F test. An alternative approach would be to assess the autoregression coefficients with respect to an empirical null distribution created by bootstrapping (Roebroeck et al. 2005).

The concept of Granger causality has been modified and adapted to accommodate many types of data features and interregional relationships, and here we outline two such innovations. The first involves the application of Granger causality after the original time series data are transformed to the frequency domain (Kaminski et al. 2001). Spectral Granger causality [also known as the directed transfer function (DTF)] is then calculated for each frequency and can be interpreted as the proportion of total power in some signal y that can be attributed to signal x. This variant of Granger causality may be particularly useful for studying regional interdependencies in data with high temporal resolution, where many effects of interest are specific to a certain frequency band.

Statistical inference is more complicated in this case because the parametric distribution of spectral Granger causality is not fully understood. A common approach is to estimate an empirical null (surrogate) distribution instead. Surrogate data are generated by transforming the original time series into the frequency domain, randomizing the phase coefficients, and then transforming the signal back into the time domain (Theiler et al. 1992). The surrogate signal is identical to the original in all aspects save for the causal temporal dependencies, which are now destroyed. The surrogate data can now be subjected to the same spectral Granger causality analysis to generate an empirical null distribution for each DTF coefficient. A p value can be calculated for each connection by comparing the DTF obtained from the original data against the corresponding null distribution.

A second major innovation is to assess predictability in terms of conditional mutual information rather than regression. This approach develops the concept of Granger causality to include nonlinear causal interactions between regions and is known as transfer entropy (TE) (Schreiber 2000). Although TE was a bivariate measure in its initial formulation, it has been extended to the multivariate case such that confounding influences from intervening regions are accounted for (Vakorin et al. 2009). This approach does not assume any particular causal order (TE is computed for all pairwise connections) or any particular type of causal influence (TE is sensitive to linear and nonlinear effects).

Applications. Deshpande et al. (2009) used multivariate Granger causality to delineate a series of effective connectivity networks while participants performed a hand-grip experiment and subsequently became fatigued. They characterized the effect of fatigue in terms of topological changes. Specifically, for each region, they calculated the number of incoming and outgoing connections (in- and out-degree) as well as the average shortest path to all other nodes in the network (eccentricity). They found that the onset of fatigue was concomitant with a decreased out-degree and eccentricity for primary sensory-motor areas and an increased eccentricity of the cerebellum, suggesting that the latter became a major driving influence in the network.

Graph Model

The techniques described so far try to detect patterns and changes in connectivity. However, the results are interpreted either as an increase or a decrease in functional or effective connectivity but are seldom considered in terms of how such changes impact the broader capacity of the network to process information. For example, a reduction in the functional connectivity of a small number of regions may streamline information flow through alternate paths and increase the overall capacity of the brain to integrate information, yet this level of

Surrogate data: a constrained realization of the observed data in which one or more parameters are altered to reflect the null hypothesis. This can be used to assess the likelihood of observing the data under the null hypothesis

description is not possible with the methods we have described so far. The graph model is a way to describe and quantify the topology of brain networks as well as the topological role of specific nodes in the network (Bullmore & Sporns 2009, Rubinov & Sporns 2010, Sporns et al. 2000, Stam & Reijneveld 2007). In this framework, the whole brain is spatially discretized into a set of nodes that are interconnected by a set of edges. In structural brain networks the edges correspond to white matter projections, whereas in functional networks they represent some measure of pairwise association, such as a Pearson correlation coefficient, mutual information, or transfer entropy. The former can be delineated using chemical tracers (Kötter 2004, Stephan et al. 2001) or diffusion-weighted MRI (Gong et al. 2009, Hagmann et al. 2008, Iturria-Medina et al. 2007), whereas the latter can be derived using virtually any measure of neural activity, such as fMRI (Achard et al. 2006), EEG (Stam et al. 2007), or MEG (Bassett et al. 2006, Stam 2004).

Graph theoretic metrics may describe either the global topological properties of the whole network or the role of a specific node. Moreover, different measures explicitly index either integration or segregation. At the level of individual regions, one can measure their connectedness by counting the total number of connections they have (degree); their tendency to occupy positions along the shortest paths between regions (betweenness); or their redundancy, measured as the fraction of a node's neighbors that are also neighbors of each other (clustering). At the level of the whole network, one can measure the average shortest path length between all pairs of nodes (characteristic path length) or the average clustering in the network. At an intermediate level, one can also profile the community structure of the network by measuring whether the network can be subdivided (modularity) or the frequency with which certain combinations of nodes and edges occur (motifs). Global metrics produce a single value per graph, and in that case statistical assessment of task or group differences is possible using standard univariate tests. Inference on local measures is a bigger challenge because if a separate test is performed for every node one must control the probability of type I errors. Likewise, inference on edges necessitates some form of false discovery rate correction (Zalesky et al. 2010).

Applications. Hagmann et al. (2008) mapped the large-scale anatomical connectivity of the brain using diffusion spectrum imaging and profiled the topological properties of the network. They identified a set of regions in posterior medial and parietal cortex that constitutes a putative structural "core." These regions were hubs by virtue of the fact that they had high degree and betweenness centrality. A modularity analysis revealed that these regions were "'connector" hubs that primarily link multiple modules (as opposed to regions only within a single module). Using a technique called k-core decomposition, the authors iteratively removed nodes with degrees lower than k until none remained. They were able to strip away most of the cortex down to the core regions, which remained highly mutually interconnected. The analysis revealed a highly central and densely interconnected component along the posterior medial axis of the cortex, situated at the very top of the topological hierarchy.

CONCLUSION

Multivariate statistical analyses have had a tangible effect on theoretical developments in neuroscience. Univariate analyses allow us to ask which regions show changes in activity; exploratory and confirmatory multivariate analyses allow us to investigate which networks show changes in activity as well as how these networks show changes in activity. As a result, interactions among regions in the context of system-level dynamics are an active area of research in imaging neuroscience. The multivariate techniques we have described all represent specific but complementary models of how these interactions are instantiated in the brain.

SUMMARY POINTS

1. Multivariate statistical techniques facilitate network discovery by simultaneously taking into account activity from multiple regions. In this way, they allow inference about the activity of any given region in the context of the entire brain.

2. Two characteristics influence how neuroimaging data are analyzed. First, there are usually more variables (e.g., voxels) than observations (e.g., subjects). Two, there is often a high degree of spatial and/or temporal autocorrelation. As a result, many exploratory techniques (e.g., PCA, ICA, CCA, PLS) are geared toward simplifying or reducing the original data.

3. Most exploratory techniques are mathematically related and feature matrix factorization by SVD. They are used to extract patterns of covariation between all possible pairs of regions and are usually interpreted from the perspective of functional connectivity.

4. Confirmatory techniques involve the fitting and comparison of models that embody hypotheses about causal influences between regions. Thus, they are mainly used to make inferences about effective connectivity. Analyses such as SEM and DCM may be thought of as extreme versions of each other that differ mainly in how they model these influences.

5. Recent tools, such as graph theoretic metrics, characterize neural networks as systems and quantitatively describe the topological role of individual regions in the context of subnetworks and networks.

DISCLOSURE STATEMENT

The authors are not aware of any affiliations, memberships, funding, or financial holdings that might be perceived as affecting the objectivity of this review.

LITERATURE CITED

Achard S, Salvador R, Whitcher B, Suckling J, Bullmore E. 2006. A resilient, low-frequency, small-world human brain functional network with highly connected association cortical hubs. *J. Neurosci.* 26:63–72

Aertsen A, Gerstein G, Habib M, Palm G. 1989. Dynamics of neuronal firing correlation: modulation of "effective connectivity." *J. Neurophysiol.* 61:900–17

Alexander G, Moeller J. 1994. Application of the scaled subprofile model to functional imaging in neuropsychiatric disorders: a principal component approach to modeling brain function in disease. *Hum. Brain Mapp.* 2:79–94

Alexander G, Moeller J, Grady C, Pietrini P, Mentis M, Schapiro M. 1994. Association of cognitive functions with regional networks of brain metabolism in Alzheimer's disease. *Neurobiol. Aging* 15:S36

Bassett D, Meyer-Lindenberg A, Achard S, Duke T, Bullmore E. 2006. Adaptive reconfiguration of fractal small-world human brain functional networks. *Proc. Natl. Acad. Sci. USA* 103:19518–23

Beckmann C, Smith S. 2004. Probabilistic independent component analysis for functional magnetic resonance imaging. *IEEE Trans. Med. Image* 23:137–52

Beckmann C, Smith S. 2005. Tensorial extensions of independent component analysis for multisubject fMRI analysis. *NeuroImage* 25:294–311

Bollen K. 1986. Sample size and Bentler and Bonett's nonnormed fit index. *Psychometrika* 51:375–77

Bookstein F. 1994. Partial least squares: a dose-response model for measurement in the behavioral and brain sciences. *Psycoloquy* 5(23):1

In this survey, the authors describe SSM as an adaptation of PCA to neuroimaging experiments and include a series of illustrative examples of how SSM can be used to analyze a wide variety of data sets from clinical populations.

The first application of tensor ICA to neuroimaging data.

Breakspear M, Jirsa V. 2007. Neuronal dynamics and brain connectivity. See Jirsa & McIntosh 2007, pp. 3–64

Bressler S, McIntosh A. 2007. The role of neural context in large-scale neurocognitive network operations. See Jirsa & McIntosh 2007, pp. 403–19

Bullmore E, Horwitz B, Honey G, Brammer M, Williams S, Sharma T. 2000. How good is good enough in path analysis of fMRI data? *NeuroImage* 11:289–301

Bullmore E, Sporns O. 2009. Complex brain networks: graph theoretical analysis of structural and functional systems. *Nat. Rev. Neurosci.* 10:186–98

Buxton R, Wong E, Frank L. 1998. Dynamics of blood flow and oxygenation changes during brain activation: the balloon model. *Magn. Reson. Med.* 39:855–64

Calhoun V, Adali T, McGinty V, Pekar J, Watson T, Pearlson G. 2001a. fMRI activation in a visual-perception task: network of areas detected using the general linear model and independent components analysis. *NeuroImage* 14:1080–88

Calhoun V, Adali T, Pearlson G, Pekar J. 2001b. A method for making group inferences from functional MRI data using independent component analysis. *Hum. Brain Mapp.* 14:140–51

Calhoun V, Adali T, Pearlson G, Pekar J. 2001c. Spatial and temporal independent component analysis of functional MRI data containing a pair of task-related waveforms. *Hum. Brain Mapp.* 13:43–53

Calhoun V, Kiehl K, Pearlson G. 2008. Modulation of temporally coherent brain networks estimated using ICA at rest and during cognitive tasks. *Hum. Brain Mapp.* 29:828–38

Campbell N, Atchley W. 1981. The geometry of canonical variate analysis. *Syst. Zool.* 30:268–80

Caplan J, McIntosh A, De Rosa E. 2007. Two distinct functional networks for successful resolution of proactive interference. *Cereb. Cortex* 17:1650–63

Carlson T, Schrater P, He S. 2003. Patterns of activity in the categorical representations of objects. *J. Cogn. Neurosci.* 15:704–17

Damoiseaux J, Rombouts S, Barkhof F, Scheltens P, Stam C, et al. 2006. Consistent resting-state networks across healthy subjects. *Proc. Natl. Acad. Sci. USA* 103:13848–53

Daunizeau J, David O, Stephan K. 2009. Dynamic causal modelling: a critical review of the biophysical and statistical foundations. *NeuroImage* 58:312–22

David O, Kiebel S, Harrison L, Mattout J, Kilner J, Friston K. 2006. Dynamic causal modeling of evoked responses in EEG and MEG. *NeuroImage* 30:1255–72

Deshpande G, LaConte S, James G, Peltier S, Hu X. 2009. Multivariate Granger causality analysis of fMRI data. *Hum. Brain Mapp.* 30:1361–73

Diaconescu A, Kovacevic N, McIntosh A. 2008. Modality-independent processes in cued motor preparation revealed by cortical potentials. *NeuroImage* 42:1255–65

Eckart C, Young G. 1936. The approximation of one matrix by another of lower rank. *Psychometrika* 1:211–18

Edgington E. 1995. *Randomization Tests*. Boca Raton, FL: CRC Press

Efron B, Tibshirani R. 1986. Bootstrap methods for standard errors, confidence intervals, and other measures of statistical accuracy. *Stat. Sci.* 1:54–75

Friston K, Buechel C, Fink G, Morris J, Rolls E, Dolan R. 1997. Psychophysiological and modulatory interactions in neuroimaging. *NeuroImage* 6:218–29

Friston K, Dolan R. 2010. Computational and dynamic models in neuroimaging. *NeuroImage* 52:752–65

Friston K, Frith C, Fiddle P, Frackowiak R. 1993. Functional connectivity: the principal-component analysis of large (PET) data sets. *J. Cereb. Blood Flow Metab.* 3:5–14

Friston K, Frith C, Frackowiak R, Turner R. 1995. Characterizing dynamic brain responses with fMRI: a multivariate approach. *NeuroImage* 2:166–72

Friston K, Frith C, Liddle P, Frackowiak R. 1991. Comparing functional (PET) images: the assessment of significant change. *J. Cereb. Blood Flow Metab.* 11:690–99

Friston K, Harrison L, Penny W. 2003. Dynamic causal modelling. *NeuroImage* 19:1273–302

Friston K, Poline J, Holmes A, Frith C, Frackowiak R. 1996. A multivariate analysis of PET activation studies. *Hum. Brain Mapp.* 4:140–51

Garrido M, Kilner J, Kiebel S, Friston K. 2009. Dynamic causal modeling of the response to frequency deviants. *J. Neurophysiol.* 101:2620–31

Introduces the method of PPI. The authors show that effective connectivity may be thought of as an experimentally induced modulation in the functional connectivity between two regions.

Garrido M, Kilner J, Kiebel S, Stephan K, Friston K. 2007. Dynamic causal modelling of evoked potentials: a reproducibility study. *NeuroImage* 36:571–80

Goebel R, Roebroeck A, Kim D, Formisano E. 2003. Investigating directed cortical interactions in time-resolved fMRI data using vector autoregressive modeling and Granger causality mapping. *Magn. Reson. Imaging* 21:1251–61

Gong G, He Y, Concha L, Lebel C, Gross D, et al. 2009. Mapping anatomical connectivity patterns of human cerebral cortex using in vivo diffusion tensor imaging tractography. *Cereb. Cortex* 19:524–36

Grady C, Protzner A, Kovacevic N, Strother S, Afshin-Pour B, et al. 2010. A multivariate analysis of age-related differences in default mode and task-positive networks across multiple cognitive domains. *Cereb. Cortex* 20:1432–47

Granger C. 1969. Investigating causal relations by econometric models and cross-spectral methods. *Econometrica* 37:424–38

Hagmann P, Cammoun L, Gigandet X, Meuli R, Honey C, et al. 2008. Mapping the structural core of human cerebral cortex. *PLoS Biol.* 6:e159

Hansen L, Larsen J, Nielsen F, Strother S, Rostrup E, et al. 1999. Generalizable patterns in neuroimaging: how many principal components? *NeuroImage* 9:534–44

Haynes J, Rees G. 2005. Predicting the orientation of invisible stimuli from activity in human primary visual cortex. *Nat. Neurosci.* 8:686–91

Hotelling H. 1936. Relations between two sets of variates. *Biometrika* 28:321–77

Iturria-Medina Y, Canales-Rodríguez E, Melie-García L, Valdes-Hernandez P, Martinez-Montes E, et al. 2007. Characterizing brain anatomical connections using diffusion weighted MRI and graph theory. *NeuroImage* 36:645–60

Jirsa V, McIntosh A, eds. 2007. *Handbook of Brain Connectivity.* Berlin: Springer-Verlag

Jöreskog K, Sörbom D, Magidson J, Cooley W. 1979. *Advances in Factor Analysis and Structural Equation Models.* Cambridge, MA: Abt Books

Jung T, Makeig S, Humphries C, Lee T, Mckeown M, et al. 2000. Removing electroencephalographic artifacts by blind source separation. *Psychophysiology* 37:163–78

Jung T, Makeig S, Westerfield M, Townsend J, Courchesne E, Sejnowski T. 2001. Analysis and visualization of single-trial event-related potentials. *Hum. Brain Mapp.* 14:166–85

Kaminski M, Ding M, Truccolo W, Bressler S. 2001. Evaluating causal relations in neural systems: Granger causality, directed transfer function and statistical assessment of significance. *Biol. Cybern.* 85:145–57

Kass R, Raftery A. 1995. Bayes factors. *J. Am. Stat. Assoc.* 90:773–95

Kiebel S, David O, Friston K. 2006. Dynamic causal modelling of evoked responses in EEG/MEG with lead field parameterization. *NeuroImage* 30:1273–84

Kötter R. 2004. Online retrieval, processing, and visualization of primate connectivity data from the CoCoMac database. *Neuroinformatics* 2:127–44

Kovacevic N, McIntosh A. 2007. Groupwise independent component decomposition of EEG data and partial least square analysis. *NeuroImage* 35:1103–12

Krishnan A, Williams L, McIntosh A, Abdi H. 2010. Partial least squares (PLS) methods for neuroimaging: a tutorial and review. *NeuroImage* 56:455–75

Kustra R, Strother S. 2001. Penalized discriminant analysis of [15O]-water PET brain images with prediction error selection of smoothness and regularization hyperparameters. *IEEE Trans. Med. Imaging* 20:376–87

Lobaugh N, West R, McIntosh A. 2001. Spatiotemporal analysis of experimental differences in event-related potential data with partial least squares. *Psychophysiology* 38:517–30

Loehlin J. 1987. *Latent Variable Models: An Introduction to Factor, Path, and Structural Equation Analysis.* Mahwah, NJ: Erlbaum

Makeig S, Jung T, Bell A, Ghahremani D, Sejnowski T. 1997. Blind separation of auditory event-related brain responses into independent components. *Proc. Natl. Acad. Sci. USA* 94:10979–84

Makeig S, Westerfield M, Jung T, Covington J, Townsend J, et al. 1999. Functionally independent components of the late positive event-related potential during visual spatial attention. *J. Neurosci.* 19:2665–80

Makeig S, Westerfield M, Jung T, Enghoff S, Townsend J, et al. 2002. Dynamic brain sources of visual evoked responses. *Science* 295:690–94

Marreiros A, Kiebel S, Friston K. 2008. Dynamic causal modelling for fMRI: a two-state model. *NeuroImage* 39:269–78

McArdle J, McDonald R. 1984. Some algebraic properties of the reticular action model for moment structures. *Br. J. Math. Stat. Psychol.* 37:234–51

McIntosh A. 1998. Understanding neural interactions in learning and memory using functional neuroimaging. *Ann. N.Y. Acad. Sci.* 855:556–71

McIntosh A. 2000. Towards a network theory of cognition. *Neural Netw.* 13:861–70

McIntosh A, Bookstein F, Haxby J, Grady C. 1996. Spatial pattern analysis of functional brain images using partial least squares. *NeuroImage* 3:143–57

McIntosh A, Chau W, Protzner A. 2004. Spatiotemporal analysis of event-related fMRI data using partial least squares. *NeuroImage* 23:764–75

McIntosh A, Gonzalez-Lima F. 1991. Structural modeling of functional neural pathways mapped with 2-deoxyglucose: effects of acoustic startle habituation on the auditory system. *Brain Res.* 547:295–302

McIntosh A, Gonzalez-Lima F. 1994. Structural equation modeling and its application to network analysis in functional brain imaging. *Hum. Brain Mapp.* 2:2–22

McIntosh A, Grady C, Ungerleider L, Haxby J, Rapoport S, Horwitz B. 1994. Network analysis of cortical visual pathways mapped with PET. *J. Neurosci.* 14:655–66

McIntosh A, Lobaugh N. 2004. Partial least squares analysis of neuroimaging data: applications and advances. *NeuroImage* 23:S250–63

McKeown M, Hansen L, Sejnowski T. 2003. Independent component analysis of functional MRI: What is signal and what is noise? *Curr. Opin. Neurobiol.* 13:620–29

McKeown M, Jung T, Makeig S, Brown G, Kindermann S, et al. 1998a. Spatially independent activity patterns in functional MRI data during the Stroop color-naming task. *Proc. Natl. Acad. Sci. USA* 95:803–10

McKeown M, Makeig S, Brown G, Jung T, Kindermann S, et al. 1998b. Analysis of fMRI data by blind separation into independent spatial components. *Hum. Brain Mapp.* 6:160–88

Mišić B, Schneider B, McIntosh A. 2010. Knowledge-driven contrast gain control is characterized by two distinct electrocortical markers. *Front. Hum. Neurosci.* 3:78

Moeller J, Strother S. 1991. A regional covariance approach to the analysis of functional patterns in positron emission tomographic data. *J. Cerebr. Blood Flow Metab.* 11:A121–35

Moeller J, Strother S, Sidtis J, Rottenberg D. 1987. Scaled subprofile model: a statistical approach to the analysis of functional patterns in positron emission tomographic data. *J. Cerebr. Blood Flow Metab.* 7:649–58

Norman K, Polyn S, Detre G, Haxby J. 2006. Beyond mind-reading: multi-voxel pattern analysis of fMRI data. *Trends Cogn. Sci.* 10:424–30

Nyberg L, McIntosh A, Cabeza R, Nilsson L, Houle S, et al. 1996. Network analysis of positron emission tomography regional cerebral blood flow data: ensemble inhibition during episodic memory retrieval. *J. Neurosci.* 16:3753–59

Onton J, Delorme A, Makeig S. 2005. Frontal midline EEG dynamics during working memory. *NeuroImage* 27:341–56

Onton J, Westerfield M, Townsend J, Makeig S. 2006. Imaging human EEG dynamics using independent component analysis. *Neurosci. Biobehav. Rev.* 30:808–22

O'Toole A, Jiang F, Abdi H, Pénard N, Dunlop J, Parent M. 2007. Theoretical, statistical, and practical perspectives on pattern-based classification approaches to the analysis of functional neuroimaging data. *J. Cogn. Neurosci.* 19:1735–52

Pearson K. 1901. On lines and planes of closest fit to systems of points in space. *Philos. Mag.* 2:559–72

Pereira F, Mitchell T, Botvinick M. 2009. Machine learning classifiers and fMRI: a tutorial overview. *NeuroImage* 45:S199–209

Develops the notion of neural context and why it is important to study interactions between brain areas rather than individual brain areas in isolation.

A tutorial and review of SEM and its application to neuroscience.

An overview of the different types of PLS analysis. The authors also discuss the use of resampling techniques for significance testing and estimating reliability.

The first application of ICA to fMRI data.

Compelling review that argues for the need to adopt pattern-based (i.e., multivariate) approaches to the analysis of imaging data. The authors place classification techniques in the broader context of exploratory multivariate analyses.

A comprehensive introduction to the logic and mechanics of classification techniques and how they can be applied to neuroimaging experiments.

Petersson K, Nichols T, Poline J-P, Holmes A. 1999. Statistical methods in functional neuroimaging. I. Non-inferential methods and statistical models. *Philos. Trans. R. Soc. Lond. B Biol. Sci.* 354:1239–60

Protzner A, McIntosh A. 2006. Testing effective connectivity changes with structural equation modeling: What does a bad model tell us? *Hum. Brain Mapp.* 27:935–47

Raichle M, MacLeod A, Snyder A, Powers W, Gusnard D, Shulman G. 2001. A default mode of brain function. *Proc. Natl. Acad. Sci. USA* 98:676–82

Roebroeck A, Formisano E, Goebel R. 2005. Mapping directed influence over the brain using Granger causality and fMRI. *NeuroImage* 25:230–42

Rubinov M, Sporns O. 2010. Complex network measures of brain connectivity: uses and interpretations. *NeuroImage* 52:1059–69

Schmithorst V, Holland S. 2004. Comparison of three methods for generating group statistical inferences from independent component analysis of functional magnetic resonance imaging data. *J. Magn. Reson. Imaging* 19:365–68

Schreiber T. 2000. Measuring information transfer. *Phys. Rev. Lett.* 85:461–64

Sporns O, Tononi G, Edelman G. 2000. Theoretical neuroanatomy: relating anatomical and functional connectivity in graphs and cortical connection matrices. *Cereb. Cortex* 10:127–41

Stam C. 2004. Functional connectivity patterns of human magnetoencephalographic recordings: a "small-world" network? *Neurosci. Lett.* 355:25–28

Stam C, Jones B, Nolte G, Breakspear M, Scheltens P. 2007. Small-world networks and functional connectivity in Alzheimer's disease. *Cereb. Cortex* 17:92–99

Stam C, Reijneveld J. 2007. Graph theoretical analysis of complex networks in the brain. *Nonlinear Biomed. Phys.* 1:1–19

Stephan K, Kamper L, Bozkurt A, Burns G, Young M, Kötter R. 2001. Advanced database methodology for the Collation of Connectivity data on the Macaque brain (CoCoMac). *Philos. Trans. R. Soc. Lond. B Biol. Sci.* 356:1159–86

Stephan K, Marshall J, Friston K, Rowe J, Ritzl A, et al. 2003. Lateralized cognitive processes and lateralized task control in the human brain. *Science* 301:384–86

Stephan K, Penny W, Moran R, den Ouden H, Daunizeau J, Friston K. 2010. Ten simple rules for dynamic causal modeling. *NeuroImage* 49:3099–109

Stephan K, Weiskopf N, Drysdale P, Robinson P, Friston K. 2007. Comparing hemodynamic models with DCM. *NeuroImage* 38:387–401

Strother S, Anderson J, Hansen L, Kjems U, Kustra R, et al. 2002. The quantitative evaluation of functional neuroimaging experiments: the NPAIRS data analysis framework. *NeuroImage* 15:747–71

Strother S, Anderson J, Schaper K, Sidtis J, Liow J, et al. 1995. Principal component analysis and the scaled subprofile model compared to intersubject averaging and statistical parametric mapping: I. "Functional connectivity" of the human motor system studied with [15O] water PET. *J. Cerebr. Blood Flow Metab.* 15:738–53

Theiler J, Eubank S, Longtin A, Galdrikian B, Doyne Farmer J. 1992. Testing for nonlinearity in time series: the method of surrogate data. *Phys. D* 58:77–94

Thomas C, Harshman R, Menon R. 2002. Noise reduction in bold-based fMRI using component analysis. *NeuroImage* 17:1521–37

Vakorin V, Krakovska O, McIntosh A. 2009. Confounding effects of indirect connections on causality estimation. *J. Neurosci. Methods* 184:152–60

Wold H. 1982. Soft modelling: the basic design and some extensions. In *Systems Under Indirect Observation: Causality-Structure-Prediction*, ed. H Wold, K Joreskog, 2:1–54. Amsterdam: North Holland

Worsley K, Poline J, Friston K, Evans A. 1997. Characterizing the response of PET and fMRI data using multivariate linear models. *NeuroImage* 6:305–19

Zalesky A, Fornito A, Harding I, Cocchi L, Yücel M, et al. 2010. Whole-brain anatomical networks: Does the choice of nodes matter? *NeuroImage* 50:970–83

Discusses advantages and disadvantages of univariate and multivariate models specifically from the perspective of neuroimaging. The authors argue that there is no universally correct analytic framework; rather, the choice of analysis depends on the experimental question.

A tutorial on how imaging data can be represented as graphs as well as the most commonly used graph theoretic metrics for cognitive neuroscience.

Thoroughly reviews the logic behind DCM and the ways in which it can be used to model and draw inferences about effective connectivity.

Social Network Analysis: Foundations and Frontiers on Advantage

Ronald S. Burt,[1] Martin Kilduff,[2]
and Stefano Tasselli[3]

[1] Booth School of Business, University of Chicago, Chicago, Illinois 60637;
email: ron.burt@chicagobooth.edu

[2] Department of Management Science and Innovation, University College London,
London WC1E 6BT, United Kingdom; email: m.kilduff@ucl.ac.uk

[3] Judge Business School, University of Cambridge, Cambridge CB2 1AG,
United Kingdom; email: st482@cam.ac.uk

Annu. Rev. Psychol. 2013. 64:527–47

The *Annual Review of Psychology* is online at
psych.annualreviews.org

This article's doi:
10.1146/annurev-psych-113011-143828

Keywords

achievement, creativity, dynamics, embeddedness, personality,
structural hole

Abstract

We provide an overview of social network analysis focusing on network
advantage as a lens that touches on much of the area. For reasons of
good data and abundant research, we draw heavily on studies of people
in organizations. Advantage is traced to network structure as a proxy
for the distribution of variably sticky information in a population. The
network around a person indicates the person's access and control in
the distribution. Advantage is a function of information breadth, timing,
and arbitrage. Advantage is manifest in higher odds of proposing good
ideas, more positive evaluations and recognition, higher compensation,
and faster promotions. We discuss frontiers of advantage contingent on
personality, cognition, embeddedness, and dynamics.

Contents

INTRODUCTION

Through the past decade, social network analysis (SNA) has experienced a golden age of rapid growth in participants, significant developments, and productive expansion into new substantive areas. Another such age occurred in the 1970s, and still another in the 1950s, during the broader golden age of social psychology. In fact, much of contemporary SNA builds on foundations established in that golden age of social psychology. Recent academic growth in SNA can be attributed in part to expanded computing and communication technology that creates detailed network data and machines with which to process the data. Growth is also a function of contemporary participation in social networks, though conclusions vary on practical implications: People accumulate hundreds of friends and acquaintances through social media (Rainie et al. 2011), but social and community engagement seems to be declining outside the ranks of affluent young white people (Putnam 2000), and people report fewer friends in whom they can confide than was the case even a decade earlier (McPherson et al. 2006). Before the advent of social network media, people were able to connect with complete strangers through about five intermediaries (Travers & Milgram 1969, Watts 1999), but it seems that email users still require five to seven intermediaries to reach

target persons by forwarding messages through acquaintances (Dodds et al. 2003).

One review is insufficient to cover the many developments in SNA; in fact, we know of no textbook treatment that provides general coverage. We focus on an area of SNA in which there has been significant progress related to social psychology, bringing in (as we have space) related developments in argument, methodology, and evidence. We cover a wide diversity of topics, but our focus is network advantage.[1] We draw extensively from research on people in organizations because of the abundant data and results available. Our setting is a person, ego, surrounded by a network of contacts, typically within a broader market or organization (i.e., the "ego-network"; Wellman 1993). This structure was initially described by Jacob Moreno, the father of American network analysis, as the "social atom," the smallest unit of

---

[1]Even within our focus on network advantage, there is a burgeoning literature (see reviews by Burt 2005, 2010; Lin 2002; Podolny 2005; Smith-Doerr & Powell 2005; Stovel & Shaw 2012). Here are leads into SNA more generally: There are general and specialist introductions (Borgatti et al. 2009, Cross & Parker 2004, Kadushin 2012, Kilduff & Brass 2010, Prell 2012, Rainie & Wellman 2012), Freeman's (2004) history of SNA development through the twentieth century, introductions to network computations (Hanneman & Riddle 2005, Hansen et al. 2011, Scott 2000), data strategies (Marsden 2011), advanced introductions to computations (Carrington et al. 2005, de Nooy et al. 2005, Wasserman & Faust 1994), textbooks providing an integrative view for people at the rich interface between computer science and the social sciences (Easley & Kleinberg 2010, Jackson 2008, Newman 2010), and encyclopedic handbooks covering topics ranging from introductory through sophisticated reviews (Scott & Carrington 2011). Software is readily available. UCINET (Borgatti et al. 2002) and Pajek (de Nooy et al. 2005) are widely used, but many useful software options can be found at the INSNA Web site (**http://www.insna.org**). Social contagion is the most glaring omission from this review. The topic is substantively important and well established in research. Relative to the topics we cover, however, contagion is most distant from our focus on network advantage. Christakis & Fowler (2009, 2012) offer a thorough introduction, and Aral et al. (2009) provide a sophisticated search for evidence. It is worth noting that these contagion works focus on a "pipes" image of networks in which influence flows through communication channels. Neglected is the broader image of networks in which influence also flows between structurally equivalent peers who communicate by social comparison (for historical review and illustrative evidence, see Burt 2010, pp. 329–365).

social structure in a community (Moreno 1934, p. 141ff). Our focus in this review is how ego gains advantage from the network around her. Network forms associated with advantage constitute social capital (Burt 1992, 2005; Coleman 1988; Lin 2002; Portes 1998; Putnam 2000), but we put aside the social capital abstraction to speak simply in terms of advantage. The gist of our story is that network structure can be studied as a proxy for the distribution of variably sticky information in a population, the network around ego indicates her advantaged or disadvantaged access and control in the distribution, and ego acting on her advantage is rewarded with recognition, compensation, and promotion for her work moving otherwise unknown or misunderstood information to places where it has value. We begin with information foundations, then turn to argument and evidence on advantage, and close with research frontiers.

FOUNDATIONS

Network models of advantage use structure as an indicator of how information is distributed in a system of people. The models build on two facts established in social psychology during the 1940s and 1950s (e.g., Festinger et al. 1950, Katz & Lazarsfeld 1955): (*a*) People cluster into groups as a result of interaction opportunities defined by the places where people meet; and (*b*) communication is more frequent and influential within than between groups such that people in the same group develop similar views. People tire of repeating arguments and stories explaining why they believe and behave the way they do. Within a group, people create systems of phrasing, opinions, symbols, and behaviors defining what it means to be a member. Beneath the familiar arguments and experiences are new, emerging arguments and experiences awaiting labeling, the emerging items more understood than said within the group. What was once explicit knowledge interpretable by anyone becomes tacit knowledge meaningful only to insiders. With continued time together, information in the group becomes "sticky"— difficult to move to other groups (Von Hippel

1994). Much of what we know is not easily understood beyond the colleagues around us. Explicit knowledge converted into local, tacit knowledge makes information sticky such that holes tear open in the flow of information between groups. These holes in the social structure of communication, or more simply "structural holes" (Burt 1992), are missing relations that inhibit information flow between people.

Figure 1 illustrates the resulting network image as a "sociogram" (Moreno 1934) of individuals variably connected as a function of prior contact, exchange, and attendant emotions. Lines indicate where information flows more routinely, or more clearly, between people represented by the dots. Solid (dashed) lines indicate strong (weak) flow. **Figure 1** is adapted from Burt (2005, p. 14), where discussion of the figure can be found in more breadth and detail. The defining feature in **Figure 1** is clusters demarked by line density greater within clusters than between clusters. Within a cluster, people share certain explicit and implicit understandings, which constitute the knowledge sticky to their cluster. Empty space between clusters in **Figure 1** indicates a structural hole. The structural hole between two groups need not mean that people in the groups are unaware of one another. It means only that the people focus on their own activities over the activities of people in the other group. A structural hole is a buffer, like an insulator in an electric circuit. People on either side of the hole circulate in different flows of information. When significant differences in understanding occur, they are more likely between people in separate clusters than between people in the same cluster. The value-potential of the structural holes is that they define nonredundant sources of information, sources that are more additive than overlapping.

An attractive feature of the network-information link is that network models of advantage are easy to move across levels of analysis. The people in **Figure 1** cluster into groups, but the clusters themselves cluster into three macro clusters—one to the northwest, one to the northeast, and one to the southeast. The three macro clusters could be organizations,

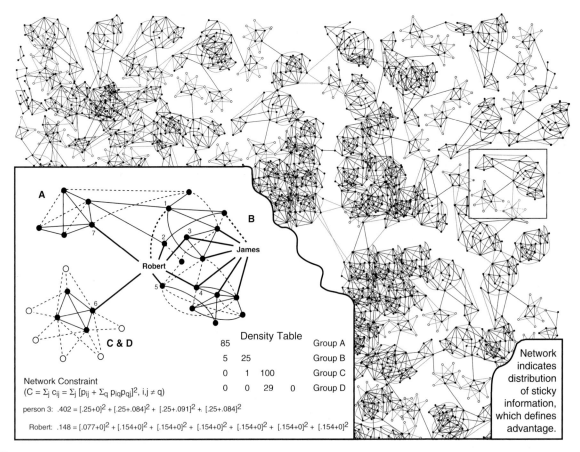

Network Constraint
$(C = \Sigma_j\, c_{ij} = \Sigma_j\, [p_{ij} + \Sigma_q\, p_{iq}p_{qj}]^2,\ i,j \neq q)$

person 3: $.402 = [.25+0]^2 + [.25+.084]^2 + [.25+.091]^2 + [.25+.084]^2$

Robert: $.148 = [.077+0]^2 + [.154+0]^2 + [.154+0]^2 + [.154+0]^2 + [.154+0]^2 + [.154+0]^2 + [.154+0]^2$

	Density Table			
85				Group A
5	25			Group B
0	1	100		Group C
0	0	29	0	Group D

Network indicates distribution of sticky information, which defines advantage.

Figure 1

Network bridge and cluster structure. Adapted from Burt (2005, p. 14).

each containing groups of people coordinated around a central cluster of senior people (indicated by dense areas toward the center of **Figure 1**). Or, the dots in **Figure 1** could be organizations. The three macro clusters then would be markets, or "institutional fields" in which individual organizations cluster in market niches around a central cluster of typical organizations (Powell et al. 2012). The dots in **Figure 1** could just as well be communities. The three broad clusters then would be geographic regions in which individual cities are variably linked as satellites around three hub cities (e.g., Eagle et al. 2010). Our focus is on individual people, but the network mechanisms to be described generalize across levels of analysis.

BROKERAGE, CREATIVITY, AND ACHIEVEMENT

People can play either of two roles in **Figure 1**: specialize within a cluster (closure) or build bridges between clusters (brokerage). Closure is about strengthening connections to gain advantage by getting better at what we already know. Brokerage is about connecting across clusters to engage diverse information. Several network concepts emerged in the 1970s on the advantages of bridges: Granovetter on weak ties (when they are bridges across clusters), Freeman on network centrality as a function of being the connection between otherwise disconnected people, Cook and Emerson on the advantage of having alternative exchange

partners, Burt on the advantage of disconnected contacts, later discussed as access to
structural holes, and Lin on the advantage of
distant, prestigious contacts, later elaborated
in terms of having contacts in statuses diverse
and prominent. Application of these models
to predict performance differences in representative cross-sections of managers began in
earnest in the 1980s and 1990s, encouraged by
earlier images of boundary-spanning personnel
(reviews are cited in Footnote 1).

Robert and James in **Figure 1** illustrate
the difference provided by connections across
clusters. The two men have the same number
of contacts, six strong ties and one weak tie,
but different structures surround them. James
is connected to people within group B, and
through them to friends of friends all within
group B. Like James, Robert is tied through
friends of friends to everyone within group B.
In addition, Robert's link with contact 7 is a network bridge connection for information from
group A, and his link with 6 is a bridge for information from group C.

Relative to James, Robert is advantaged
three ways by his network: information breadth,
timing, and arbitrage. With respect to breadth,
Robert's bridge relations give him access to
less redundant information. With respect to
timing, Robert is positioned at a crossroads in
the flow of information between groups, so he
will be early to learn about activities in the three
groups, and often be the person introducing
to one group information on another. Robert
is what early diffusion research identified as
an opinion leader, a person responsible for
the spread of new ideas and behaviors (Katz
& Lazarsfeld 1955 on opinion leaders; Burt
1999 on opinion leaders as network brokers).
Third, Robert is more likely to know when it
would be rewarding to bring together separate
groups, which gives him a disproportionate say
in whose interests are served when the contacts
come together. More, the structural holes
between his contacts mean that he can broker
communication while displaying different
beliefs and identities to each contact. Robert's
connections across social clusters give him an

advantage in translating opinion and behavior
familiar in one group into the dialect of a target
group. People who connect across structural
holes are presented with opportunities to
coordinate people otherwise disconnected,
which puts them in a position to derive ideas
or resources from exposure to contacts who
differ in opinion or practice. Thus, a structural
hole is a potentially valuable context for action,
brokerage is the action of coordinating across
the hole with bridge connections between people on opposite sides of the hole, and network
entrepreneurs, or more simply, brokers, are
the people who build the bridges. Network
brokers operate somewhere between the force
of corporate authority and the dexterity of
markets, building bridges between disconnected parts of markets and organizations
where it is valuable to do so. Relations with
contacts in otherwise disconnected groups
provide a competitive advantage in detecting
and developing rewarding opportunities.

Distinguishing Network Brokers

Figure 2 illustrates metrics that distinguish
the brokers in a network. The computations
are simple, typically described in introductory
works, and SNA software is readily available
(see Footnote 1). Ego's contacts are indicated
by gray circles in **Figure 2**. Lines indicate connections between contacts (here a simple 0,1
binary measure, but the measures all easily handle continuous measures of connection
strength). To keep the sociograms simple, ego's
relations with each contact are not presented.

A network is closed to the extent it is small
(providing few contacts that could be separated
by a structural hole) and the contacts in it are
interconnected (indicating that the contacts
are already coordinating with each other). In
Figure 2, network size (also discussed as
"degree" in graph theory) increases down the
figure, from networks of three contacts at the
top to networks of ten at the bottom. Connectivity between contacts increases from left to
right, from networks at the left in which none
of ego's contacts are connected (labeled Broker

	Broker Networks	Partner Networks	Clique Networks
Small Networks			
size (degree)	3	3	3
density x 100	0	67	100
hierarchy x 100	0	7	0
constraint x 100	33	84	93
from:			
A	11	44	31
B	11	20	31
C	11	20	31
nonredundant contacts	3.0	1.7	1.0
betweenness (holes)	3.0	0.5	0.0
Larger Networks			
size (degree)	5	5	5
density x 100	0	40	100
hierarchy x 100	0	25	0
constraint x 100	20	59	65
from:			
A	4	36	13
B	4	6	13
C	4	6	13
D	4	6	13
E	4	6	13
nonredundant contacts	5.0	3.4	1.0
betweenness (holes)	10.0	3.0	0.0
Still Larger Networks			
size (degree)	10	10	10
density x 100	0	20	100
hierarchy x 100	0	50	0
constraint x 100	10	41	36
nonredundant contacts	10.0	8.2	1.0
betweenness (holes)	45.0	18.0	0.0

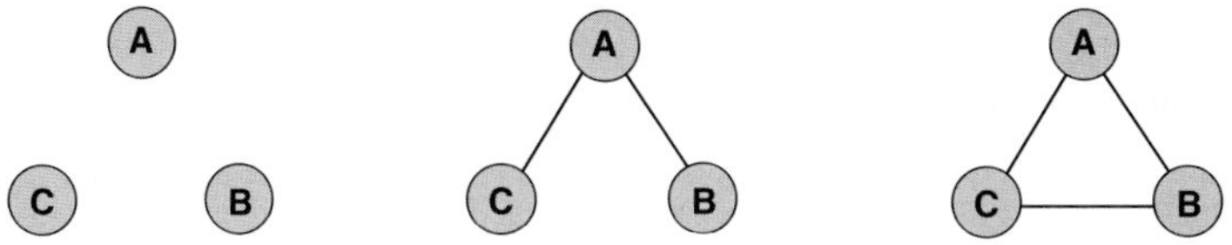

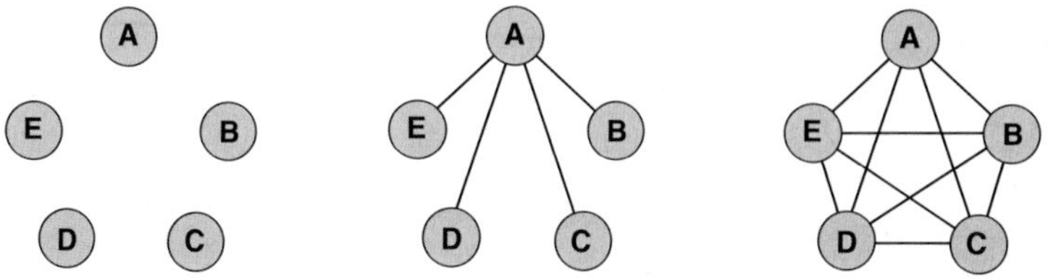

Figure 2

Network metrics. To keep the sociograms simple, relations with ego are not presented. Adapted from Burt (2010, p. 298).

Networks) to the networks on the right in which all of ego's contacts are connected (labeled Clique Networks). Network density is the average strength of connection between ego's contacts, which in **Figure 2** is the number of connections divided by the number possible. Density is zero for all networks in the left column, where no contact is connected with others, and 100 for all networks in the right column, where every contact is connected with every other.

A second way contacts can be connected so as to close the network around ego is by mutual connection with a central figure other than ego. This is illustrated by the partner networks in the middle column of **Figure 2**. Partner networks are a substantively significant kind of closure useful in detecting diversity problems in a population (discussed below). The middle-column networks in **Figure 2** are characterized by no connections between contacts except for all being connected with contact A. The networks are centralized around A, making contact A ego's "partner" in the network. This kind of network is detected with an inequality measure, such as the Coleman-Theil disorder measure in the third row of each panel in **Figure 2** (Burt 1992, pp. 70–71). Hierarchy varies with the extent to which connections among ego's contacts are all with one contact. There is zero hierarchy when contacts are all disconnected from one another (first column in **Figure 2**) or all connected with each other (third column). Hierarchy scores are only nonzero in the middle column. As ego's network gets larger, the partner's central role in the network becomes more obvious and hierarchy scores increase (from 7 for the three-person network, to 25 for the five-person network, and to 50 for the ten-person network).

The graph in **Figure 3** provides a sense of the population distributions from which manager networks are sampled. The graph plots hierarchy scores by density scores for 2,000 manager networks in six management populations. The populations, analyzed in detail elsewhere (Burt 2010), include stock analysts, investment bankers, and managers across functions in Asia, Europe, and North America. The large, open networks of brokers are in the lower left of the graph, low in density and low in hierarchy. Closure can involve simultaneous hierarchy and density, but the extremes of either exclude the other. To the lower right are clique networks, in which there is no hierarchy because all contacts are strongly

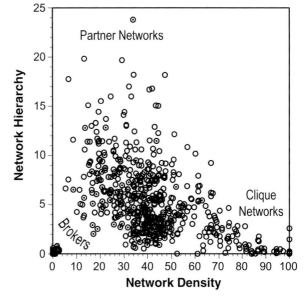

Figure 3

Plot of density and hierarchy for 1,989 networks observed in six populations (analysts, bankers, and managers in Asia, Europe, and North America; aggregated in **Figure 4** to illustrate returns to brokerage). Dotted circles are executives (managing director or more in finance, vice-president or more otherwise). Hollow circles are lower ranks. Executives have significantly larger, less dense, and less hierarchical networks.

connected with each other. To the upper left are partner networks, in which density is below 50% because there are no connections between contacts other than their mutual strong connection with ego's partner.

Network constraint is a summary index of closure around ego. Intuitively the percent of ego's network time and energy consumed by one group, constraint, decreases with the extent to which ego has many contacts (size), increases with the extent to which ego's network is closed by strong connections among ego's contacts (density), and increases with the extent to which ego's network is closed by a partner strongly connected with all of ego's contacts (hierarchy). The equation for network constraint is displayed and illustrated in the Robert-James insert box in **Figure 1**.[2] A maximum constraint

---

[2]More detailed discussion is available elsewhere (Burt 1992, p. 54ff.; Burt 2010, p. 293ff.). Caution: The index was

score of 100 indicates no access to structural holes (ego had no friends, or all of ego's friends were friends with one another). Across the networks in **Figure 2**, network constraint increases from left to right with closure by hierarchy or density (e.g., 20 points for the five-person disconnected network versus 65 points for the five-person clique network) and decreases from top to bottom with increasing network size (e.g., 93 points for the three-person clique network versus 10 points for the ten-person clique network).

Figure 2 includes two additional metrics often used to distinguish network brokers. "Nonredundant contacts" is a count of ego's contacts discounting contacts redundant with ego's other contacts—in essence a count of the clusters to which ego is attached (Burt 1992, p. 52). For the networks of disconnected contacts in the first column of **Figure 2**, nonredundant contacts equal network size. Every contact is nonredundant with the others. For the clique networks in the third column of **Figure 2**, ego has only one nonredundant contact regardless of increasing network size because every contact is redundant with the others. The final metric in **Figure 2** is Freeman's (1977) betweenness index that measures the structural holes to which ego has monopoly access. Two disconnected contacts give you one opportunity to broker a connection. Four contacts disconnected from one another gives you six opportunities to broker connections. For the networks of disconnected contacts in the first column of **Figure 2**, betweenness equals the number of possible connections between contacts because all are disconnected (e.g.,

betweenness is 10.0 for the broker network of five contacts because none of the 10 possible connections between ego's five contacts exist). For the clique networks in the third column of **Figure 2**, betweenness is zero because there are no holes between ego's contacts. In the middle column of **Figure 2**, ego shares access to structural holes with her partner. For example, ego has access to a disconnect between contacts B and C in the three-person network, but so does contact A, so ego's betweenness score is 0.5, half of one structural hole. Ego has access to six holes between contacts in the five-person partner network, but access is shared with the partner, so ego's betweenness score is 3.0, half the number of holes to which ego has access.[3]

Evidence of Broker Advantage

Figure 4 presents three graphical illustrations of broker advantage (network constraint measured on the horizontal axis). **Figure 4a** derives from an analysis of the social origins of good ideas in a supply-chain company (Burt 2004). Two senior executives evaluated each manager's idea for improving the value of the supply chain. Average evaluations vary up the vertical axis. There is a strong negative, nonlinear association in the graph. Brokers (relative to managers in closed networks) are likely to have their ideas evaluated as good and worth pursuing. These results are attractive for displaying a continuous quantitative association between a person's access to structural holes and the acknowledged value of their ideas, but more depth to the association is available from ethnographic network studies of creativity

---

designed to describe networks of connected managers. Scores can exceed one if ego has only two strongly connected contacts (Burt 1992, pp. 58–59). We convert constraint scores greater than one to equal one. Also, constraint is undefined for social isolates because proportional ties have no meaning (zero divided by zero). Some software outputs constraint scores of zero for isolates, which implies that isolates have unlimited access to structural holes when in fact they have no access (apparent from the low performance scores observed for managers who are social isolates). For social isolates, network constraint equals one.

[3] Two cautions: (a) If Freeman's betweenness index is used as a measure of access to structural holes, a control has to be added for network size. Freeman (1977) proposed dividing by the number of possible contacts that ego could broker, which is a function of network size. (b) Betweenness scores in **Figure 2** are computed from ego's direct access to structural holes, as Freeman (1977) initially proposed the index for small group research. When scores are computed across contacts beyond ego's network, as they often are, the index measures ego's direct and indirect access to structural holes, and the index is better interpreted as a measure of network centrality or status.

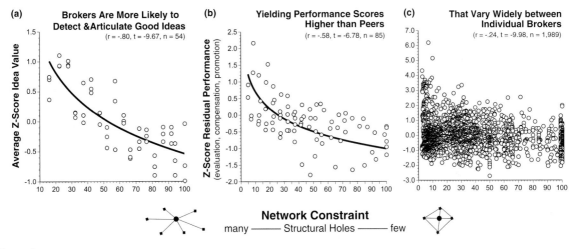

Figure 4

Brokerage for detecting and developing opportunities. (*a*) Idea quality increases with more access to structural holes. Circles are average scores on the vertical axis for a five-point interval of network constraint among supply-chain managers in a large electronics firm (Burt 2004, p. 382; Burt 2005, p. 92). Bold line is the vertical axis predicted by the natural logarithm of network constraint. (*b*) Performance increases with more access to structural holes. Circles are average scores on the vertical axis for a five-point interval of network constraint within each of six populations (analysts, bankers, and managers in Asia, Europe, and North America; heteroscedasticity is minor, chi-square = 2.97, 1 d.f., P ~ 0.08; Burt 2010, p. 26, cf. Burt 2005, p. 56). Graph *c* shows the raw data averaged in *b* (Burt 2012). Vertical axis is wider to accommodate wider range of performance scores. Heteroscedasticity is high because of wide performance differences between individual brokers (chi-square = 269.5, 1 d.f., P < 0.001).

(Leonardi & Bailey 2011, Lingo & O'Mahony 2010, Obstfeld 2005).

The data in **Figure 4b** illustrate the fact that network brokers are compensated for their work decoding and encoding information to move it between clusters. The performance association with networks in **Figure 4b** is similar to the association in **Figure 4a** with idea quality. **Figure 4b** contains stock analysts, investment bankers, and managers from diverse functions in Asia, Europe, and North America (Burt 2010, p. 26, provides more detail). The vertical axis is adjusted so that zero is the performance typical for a manager's peers, with respect to which an individual manager can be performing higher (positive z-scores) or lower (negative z-scores). Performance is measured for the investment bankers as bonus compensation, for the stock analysts as industry recognition (election to the Institutional Investor's All-America Research Team), and for the managers as compensation, annual evaluations, or early promotion to higher job rank. As in the first graph, the second shows a nonlinear,

downward sloping association in which network brokers (relative to their peers) are paid more, receive more positive evaluations and recognition, and get promoted more quickly to senior positions. The performance association in **Figure 4b** is replicated by numerous studies reporting performance metrics higher for network brokers (reviews in Burt 2005, 2010). More recently, analyses of email traffic between people in a small headhunter organization show that network brokers engage in diverse information exchanges, and headhunters in closed networks who exchange diverse information with contacts also have high performance (Aral & Van Alstyne 2011). Information diversity is the key factor predicting performance, not the network. Holes in ego's network are merely an indicator of ego's access to diverse information.

RESEARCH FRONTIERS

Social network analysis illustrates the general point that argument and debate drive theory and research forward (Lakatos 1970).

Currently, SNA is less a paradigmatic orthodoxy than it is a set of evolving ideas about behavioral and cognitive implications of network structure (Kilduff et al. 2006). With respect to network advantage, we note a few frontiers in the ongoing debate.

Agency and Personality

Our discussion of network advantage thus far could be read as though achievement springs directly from a network. But everyone knows that networks do not act—people act. Networks can facilitate or inhibit action, but people are the source of action. Thus the agency question in network analysis: How much does the psychology of the individual at the center of ego's network matter? Even controlling for relevant individual differences such as those held constant in **Figure 4** (rank, gender, age, etc.), we are likely to find that different kinds of people are better at bridging structural holes, and those kinds of people may be prone to high achievement. The lack of attention to human agency in network models has been noted from diverse perspectives (Baum & Rowley 2008; Emirbayer & Goodwin 1994; Kilduff & Brass 2010, pp. 335–336; Kilduff & Krackhardt 1994; Sasovova et al. 2010; Singh et al. 2010), but two recent discoveries bring the agency question back into focus.

The first is the lack of advantage spillover between adjacent networks. If the network advantage of brokers results from broader, earlier access to diverse information, then there should be an advantage to connections with other brokers. But across varied management populations, Burt (2010) shows that ego gains no increased benefit from contact with brokers versus contacts in closed networks. The advantage of access to structural holes is defined entirely by the diversity of ego's own contacts, not the diversity of her friends' contacts. The argued implication is that the advantage does not result from access to diverse information; rather, it is a by-product of processing diverse information. Advantage results from intellectual and emotional skills developed in the process of encoding and decoding information to communicate between diverse contacts. Even a little network training can produce substantial improvements in learning to see and benefit from structural holes (Burt & Ronchi 2007, Janicik & Larrick 2005).

And we know that performance differs widely between network brokers. This is the second empirical fact that demands attention to human agency—people often perform below their level of network advantage. The suspicion has long existed (Burt 1992, p. 37), but the fact is illustrated in **Figure 4c**, which plots the raw data averaged to define the data in **Figure 4b**. Vertical performance differences between network brokers (low constraint) are wider than the differences between people in closed networks (high constraint). This is evident from **Figure 4c**'s triangular data distribution and its statistically significant heteroscedasticity, both in the context of wider performance differences in the raw data (vertical axis goes from -3.0 to 7.0 in **Figure 4c**, from -2.0 to 2.5 in **Figure 4b**).

The two empirical facts have implications for research on network advantage. Work with formal models of network advantage often involves assuming agency away. Formal models have been used to explore theoretical questions such as what would happen if everyone focused on bridging structural holes (Buskens & van de Rijt 2008, Goyal & Vega-Redondo 2007, Ryall & Sorenson 2007) or if contacts exercised power to erode ego's returns to bridging structural holes (Reagans & Zuckerman 2008). In these models, the agency question is resolved by assuming that people act on all opportunities their network provides (subject to a budget constraint of limited time or resources). Agency can be ignored because it is coincident with opportunity. To know who acts on network advantage, you only need to know who has advantage.

Contrary to this agency-free depiction, the empirical research just summarized shows that performance differences among network brokers are substantial, with many brokers showing no higher performance than people in the most closed networks. The primary characteristic of the data displayed in **Figure 4c** is not the absence of low performers in broker networks; it is the absence of high performers in closed networks. A formal-model strategy more suited to the empirical facts would be to shift focus from the advantages of brokerage to the disadvantages of closed networks (e.g., Burt 2010, pp. 244–247, on network fear).

Second, the two empirical facts are a call for close study of broker behavior to distinguish high-performing brokers from low performers. Emerging work emphasizes the importance of behavior appropriate to the situation. Depending on the situation, it can be advantageous to play contacts against one another (Fernandez-Mateo 2007), facilitate exchange otherwise at risk of misunderstanding (Leonardi & Bailey 2011, Obstfeld 2005), connect contacts as a translation buffer to protect each side from the other's irritating specialist jargon (Kellogg 2012), or facilitate the development of broker skills in colleagues (Powell et al. 2012). Moreover, occupations have characteristic behaviors (it would be unseemly for a nun to behave like a salesman or a banker to behave like a construction worker), whereas organizational selection and socialization create company differences in characteristic employee personalities. For a large population of managers, Schneider et al. (1998) show similar Myers-Briggs personality scores for managers employed in the same organization. Burt et al. (2000) study network advantage among managers in a French engineering firm and an American engineering firm. The French networks are based on long-standing friendships that rarely span the boundary of the firm. The Americans build from work relations that often reach outside the firm. Differences notwithstanding, the French managers benefit from access to structural holes just as the Americans do. Xiao & Tsui (2007) argue that brokering connections across structural holes is inconsistent with Chinese social norms, and they show no network advantage in the job ranks on which they have data. On the other hand, Merluzzi (2011) finds higher performance evaluations for Chinese and other Asian managers with access to structural holes, so perhaps the key variable is not being Chinese but rather working in a Chinese company.

Third, the two empirical facts encourage a deeper recognition of personality in network analysis. What kinds of people are prone to brokerage, with higher odds of success? Despite the occasional voice lamenting the possible contamination of structural research through consideration of the attributes of individuals (e.g., Burt 1992, chapter 5; Mayhew 1980), there is a history of research relating personality to networks (for review, see Kilduff & Tsai 2003, chapter 4) and to interpersonal engagement more generally (for overview, see Snyder & Deaux 2012).

These exchanges notwithstanding, there is a sharp contradiction in the way sociologists and psychologists understand personality. A basic assumption of personality psychology is that there are stable individual traits that affect outcomes. The big five personality dimensions, for example, exhibit substantial heritability (Jang et al. 1996) as does the self-monitoring personality orientation (Snyder & Gangestad 1986). Thus, personality psychologists investigate the effects of personality on social relationships and report, for example, that extroverts tend to have numerous peer relations but that social relationships do not affect personality (Asendorpf & Wilpers 1998). Stable individual differences include distinctive patterns of behavioral variability across situations, that is, distinctive individual behavioral signatures (Mischel & Shoda 1995). In contrast, SNA derives much of its intellectual capital from sociology, where the prevailing assumption is that the dispositions of individuals reflect the structural positions that they occupy. In its early years, for example, the Social Science Research Council funded research that investigated the ways in which social settings affected personality formation and the ways in which individuals' personalities adapted to their cultural environments (Bryson 2009). Carrying the sociological perspective into network analysis, Burt (1992, pp. 251–264) analyzed personality as structure's "emotional residue."

The return of personality to the social network agenda has coincided with an interest in self-monitoring, a personality variable especially relevant to network advantage. In establishing theory, evidence, and measurement concerning individual differences in the control of self-presentations for situational appropriateness, self-monitoring research (for a review, see Gangestad & Snyder 2000) offers a personality analogue to the brokerage versus closure distinction in network research. Without implying causality one way or the other, network brokers should have higher scores on self-monitoring, and they do (Mehra et al. 2001). Further, a study of ethnic entrepreneurs shows that the effects of self-monitoring ripple across social structure. Entrepreneurs high in self-monitoring tend to have acquaintances who are unconnected with each other, and high self-monitors also tend to occupy positions such that the acquaintances of their acquaintances are unconnected with each other (Oh & Kilduff 2008). The above studies are cross-sectional. Panel analysis of personality and network connections in a Dutch hospital show that high self-monitors are more likely than low self-monitors to attract new friends and to occupy new bridging positions over time, and the new friends the high self-monitors attract tend to be unconnected with previous friends—thereby increasing the number of structural holes in the high self-monitors' networks (Sasovova et al. 2010).

Given the correlation between achievement and structural holes, and the correlation between self-monitoring and structural holes, achievement should be correlated with self-monitoring. It is. Kilduff & Day (1994) show for a cohort of MBA students that high self-monitors were more likely to receive promotions within and between companies in the five years after graduation. Holding constant network differences between employees in a small technology company, Mehra et al. (2001) show that employees with high self-monitoring scores received more positive evaluations from their supervisors, but the network association with performance remains: Self-monitoring neither moderates nor mediates the network

association with work performance. Virtual worlds provide more behavioral detail. In a network analysis of people playing multiple roles in a virtual world game, Burt (2012) shows that about one-third of the variance in network advantage is consistent across the roles a person plays. For example, people who build a closed network in one role tend to build closed networks in their other roles. However, the consistent variation in a person's networks contributes almost nothing to predicting achievement. Achievement in a role is predicted by role-specific factors: the experience a person accumulates in the role and the broker network built up in the role.

Empirical success with measures of self-monitoring should encourage research with related measures. A recent study with cross-sectional and panel data showed that leader charisma (a personality dimension evaluated by the reports of subordinates) did not predict leaders being central in team advice networks (Balkundi et al. 2011). Rather, formal leaders who were central in team advice networks tended to be seen as charismatic by subordinates. This suggests that a leadership-relevant aspect of personality—charisma—may derive from network centrality, compatible with a sociological approach to leadership emergence and compatible with the social network emphasis on the ways in which "a person's social environment elicits a specific personality" (Burt 1992, p. 262). Of course these results are also compatible with personality psychology's emphasis on the ways in which appropriate situations allow personality traits to be exhibited and channeled (Winter et al. 1998). Beyond charisma, people differ in the extent to which they believe their actions affect events, which is likely to explain why certain people act on their brokerage opportunities. To answer this question, example personality measures would include Rotter's locus of control in which high internal control refers to a belief that your actions have a causal effect on events (e.g., Hansemark 2003 on internal-control men more likely to be entrepreneurs, Rotter 1966 for the initial statement, Hodgkinson 1992 for a scale adapted to business settings), or Bandura's concept of self-efficacy in which stronger belief in one's capabilities is associated with greater and more persistent effort (for review, see Bandura 2001, Wood & Bandura 1989). People also differ in the extent to which they look for network advantages on which they can act. McClelland (1961) argues that early formation of a need to achieve is a personality factor significant for later entrepreneurial behavior. People raised insecure in their childhood should have a need to achieve that would predispose them to act on network advantage, resulting in them achieving more than peers. Anderson (2008) shows that managers with a high "need for cognition" (Cacioppo et al. 1996) are more likely to take advantage of the information advantages of the network around them.

In sum, research on network advantage is rapidly expanding to include individual differences associated with how people play the role of network broker and their psychological fit to the role. The practical note to take away from the work is that access to structural holes does not guarantee achievement, and it enhances the risk of productive accident—the risk of encountering a new opinion or practice not yet familiar to colleagues, the risk of envisioning a new synthesis of existing opinion or practice, the risk of finding a course of action through conflicting interests, the risk of discovering a new source for needed resources.

Cognition

Network structure is by no means obvious to the person at the center of the network. Individuals are often mistaken about patterns of relationships that include themselves and their colleagues. They tend to perceive themselves as more central in their friendship networks than they really are (Kumbasar et al. 1994). They forget casual attendees at meetings, tending to recall the meetings as attended by the habitual members of their social groups (Freeman et al. 1987). They are attentive to different qualities of their network depending on experience (Janicik & Larrick 2005) and situational stimuli (Smith et al. 2012).

SNA from its beginnings has shown a creative tension between approaches that treat networks as cognitions in the minds of perceivers (e.g., Heider 1958) and approaches that treat networks as concrete patterns of interpersonal interactions (e.g., Cartwright & Harary 1956). To the extent that the theoretical basis of research is psychological, it is the perceptions in the minds of social network participants that constitute the relevant phenomena (Krackhardt 1987). Perhaps the most firmly established body of work examining cognitive perceptions of social networks has flowed from De Soto's early experiments (e.g., De Soto 1960). Recent examples have examined how the experience of low power leads to more controlled cognition and therefore more accurate perceptions of social networks (Simpson et al. 2011a) and the paradox that more accurate knowledge about ties between others in the network can be collectively disadvantageous for low-power actors (Simpson et al. 2011b). Such results could result from powerless individuals processing more peripheral and detailed information, treating all information as equally important (Guinote 2007), or from socially peripheral, and therefore powerless, individuals focusing on information from people too similar to themselves (Singh et al. 2010). Relatedly, we know that people of low status who encounter a job threat (such as the likelihood of getting laid off) tend to call to mind smaller and tighter subsections of their networks. By contrast, people of high status activate larger and less constrained subsections of their networks (Smith et al. 2012). In sum, people's cognitive representations of their networks shift in response to situational pressures and threats.

Even if there are discrepancies, it would seem evident that patterns in the mind are derived from experience with real-world social networks. For example, people who have a network rich in structural holes find it easier to learn new network structures that contain structural holes (Janicik & Larrick 2005). A range of features that are present in actual networks (such as clustering, structural holes, and actors more central than others) are exhibited in perceptions—but in simplified and exaggerated fashion (Freeman 1992). People tend to economize on cognitive demands, and they also exhibit biased perceptions of social networks through their use of default expectations such as the expectation that friendship ties are likely to be reciprocated and the expectation that if two individuals have a mutual friend then the two individuals themselves will be friends (Krackhardt & Kilduff 1999). There is a range of more complex biases as well. For example, the small worlds described in cocitation analyses and elsewhere (Dorogovtsev & Mendes 2003) are more apparent in individuals' perceptions than in their actual social interactions (Kilduff et al. 2008).

The ongoing creative tension between networks as social interaction and networks as cognitive structures has been updated in terms of the distinction between networks as pipes versus prisms (Podolny 2001). Social networks are considered as pipes through which resources (such as affection or money) flow or as prisms through which individuals attempt to evaluate others. If social networks are considered as prisms, then there is the potential for such lenses to distort the true nature of the individuals being focused on. The old adage "we are known by the company we keep" is represented by the prisms view, although little work so far has addressed the ways in which perceived social network connections distort the evaluation of individuals (but see Kilduff & Krackhardt 1994 for preliminary work on this theme).

Future research on networks as prisms will depend on assumptions that are basic to the cognitive perspective: first that the monitoring and recall of relationships among even relatively small numbers of people (e.g., 20 people) pose cognitive challenges given that the number of potential relationships increases exponentially with the size of the network (Kilduff et al. 2008, Krackhardt & Kilduff 1999), and second that the accurate mapping of relationships is of importance to individuals trying to form project teams and build alliances (Janicik & Larrick 2005). Intriguingly, research on the actual group structures of interconnected individuals also suggests cognitive constraints on the size of social networks (Dunbar 2008). The argument with respect to actual interactions is not so much about the recall and learning of relationships, but more about the cognitive limitations on how many people the individual can be expected to know on a personal basis so that the individual can discern qualities such as trustworthiness and potential cooperation. Thus, the evidence suggests that individuals' social worlds are limited in size to about 150 people, and these people are cognitively structured around the individual so that those people with whom we have intense relationships are closer and those with whom we have less intense relationships are further away. The human brain, it is suggested, is limited in the number of people it can acquire knowledge about in order to predict others' behavior, and it is also limited in terms of the number of relationships that can be serviced at a given level of emotional intensity (Roberts & Dunbar 2011).

To summarize this section, we can say that the biggest avenue for further research on cognitive networks concerns outcomes such as performance in organizations. Although there has been impressive work detailing the various biases that afflict people's perceptions of social networks, there is much less attention to how these biases affect outcomes at the individual, team, or organizational level. There is speculation concerning how cognitions in the minds of leaders concerning the flow of social capital within and across organizational boundaries and the presence and meaning of social divides contribute to leader effectiveness (Balkundi & Kilduff 2005). But this speculation has not been matched as yet by empirical work detailing important outcomes. The pipes and prisms contrast is likely to feature prominently in future work on network cognition.

Embeddedness

It could seem as though nothing but disadvantage accrues to people like James in **Figure 1**, people who live inside one of a network's dense clusters. To the contrary, dense clusters produce trust and reputation, which constitute the governance mechanism in social networks. Network theory and research on this topic is voluminous (for review, see Burt 2005, chapters 3 and 4; Burt 2010, chapter 6). Within our focus for this review, we discuss the work as it bears on network advantage.

Work in this area was energized by Granovetter's (1985) argument for the importance of understanding economic relations in social context because context has implications for behavior in a relationship. "Relational" embedding refers to a relationship in which the two connected people have a deep history and investment with each other. "Structural" embedding refers to people who have many mutual contacts.

The more embedded a relationship, the more likely bad behavior by either party will become known, thereby creating a reputation cost for bad behavior, which facilitates trust and collaboration. With bad behavior likely to be detected, people are expected to be more careful about their behavior. Thus, trust is facilitated between people in a closed network, making collaborations possible that would otherwise be difficult or unwise. Examples abound on the Internet, such as the reputation system of eBay, oyster.com, or dontdatehimgirl.com. The same logic can be found in significant contemporaneous work, such as the argument of sociologist Coleman (1988) that closed networks are social capital and the argument of economist Greif (1989) that trust within closed networks facilitated medieval trade in the Mediterranean.

Empirical research has shown that closed networks increase trust and preserve reputations (for review and illustrative results, see Burt 2005, pp. 196–213; Burt 2010, pp. 161–179). For example, in a large population of investment bankers and analysts, bridge relations decay at a rate of 92% one year after formation, whereas relations embedded in closed networks decay at a 53% rate (Burt 2010, p. 182; cf. Rivera et al. 2010). The higher decay rates in bridge relations make sense in that bridge relations are more subject to short-term cost-benefit analysis because bridge relations are not protected by obligations ensured by mutual friends and so are more open to suspicions about the person on the other side (Stovel et al. 2011). Aggregating to banker reputations, reputation is autocorrelated from year to year about 0.73 for bankers evaluated by colleagues in closed networks. In contrast, the reputations of bankers evaluated by colleagues separated by structural holes show almost no stability. The year-to-year autocorrelation is a negligible 0.09 (Burt 2010, p. 164). As Coleman (1988, pp. 107–108) summarizes, "Reputation cannot arise in an open structure, and collective sanctions that would ensure trustworthiness cannot be applied."

To the point of this review, embedding is a critical contingency factor for returns to network brokerage. First, understanding, trust, and collaboration are more likely across strong bridges relative to weak bridges (relational embedding). Example studies are Uzzi (1996) on garment manufacturers less likely to go bankrupt if they concentrate their business in a small number of suppliers; Reagans & McEvily (2003) on strong bridges facilitating knowledge transfer; Centola & Macy (2007) on complex ideas more likely to diffuse through "wide" bridges; Tortoriello & Krackhardt (2010) on innovation associated with strong bridges, termed "Simmelian ties"; and Sosa (2011) on creativity associated with strong rather than weak bridges. Second, returns to brokerage depend on being known as trustworthy (structural embedding). Burt & Merluzzi (2013) describes high returns to brokerage for investment bankers, salesmen, and managers who have above-average social standing in their organizations. For people in the same populations with below-average social standing, returns to brokerage cannot be distinguished from random noise, even for a person rich in access to structural holes.

Dynamics

Network analysis developed in sociology against a backdrop of functional theory in which the imprimatur of "social structure" was reserved for the stable features of networks. Networks that persist in time have meaning, serve some purpose, and are real in their consequences. Much like human capital is anchored in enduring education credentials acquired as a person moves up through a stable stratification of grade levels, network advantage was studied and taught as a level to be developed and preserved. As Laumann & Pappi (1976, p. 213) expressed the sentiment during the 1970s resurgence of network images in sociology, "Despite differences in nuance associated with 'structure,' the root meaning refers to a persisting order or pattern of relations among units." And well after network images were again mainstream in sociology, Sewell (1992, p. 2) broadened the observation as criticism: "structural language lends itself readily to explanations of how social life is shaped into consistent patterns, but not to explanations of how these patterns change over time. In structural discourse, change is commonly located outside of structures."

The focus on stability was reinforced by empirical research. The most-replicated fact we know about network dynamics is that the more closed a network, the more stable the relations in it and the more stable the reputations emergent from it. And patterns of relations such as friendship seem to stabilize relatively quickly within a bounded social system (such as a student living group; Newcomb 1961). Under the surface one suspects movement in that some actors form stable relations whereas others "dance between friends throughout the observation period" (Moody et al. 2005, p. 1229). However, despite contemporary technology offering people many opportunities to expand their networks, to meet new people, and so to pursue new opportunities, it seems that people fail to take advantage of social occasions to forge new relationships (Ingram & Morris 2007).

Broker networks are less stable than closed, but they too exhibit surprising stability. In theory, they should not. Theoretical models describe how advantage should be distributed in stable "equilibrium" networks (Buskens & van de Rijt 2008, Dogan et al. 2009, Goyal &

Vega-Redondo 2007, Kleinberg et al. 2008, Reagans & Zuckerman 2008, Ryall & Sorenson 2007). The models imply pessimistic conclusions about the feasibility of stable access to structural holes, though people seem able to muddle through (Burger & Buskens 2009), and the people who have advantaged access to holes today are often the people who had network advantage yesterday. For example, among the bankers analyzed by Burt & Burrows (2011), relative access to structural holes is correlated 0.64 from year to year. Zaheer & Soda (2009) report that Italian television production teams rich in access to structural holes tend to be composed of people who were rich in access several years ago. Sasovova et al. (2010) report that continuing access to structural holes in their Dutch hospital includes access to many of the same structural holes along with expanding access to new ones.

More recently, network dynamics have become less a question of orthodoxy and more an empirical question—in part because of more available detailed network data and in part because of improved time-sensitive statistical models (Rivera et al. 2010, Snijders 2011). Quintane et al. (2012) is an exemplary study. Network data were collected on eight months of email traffic among employees in the U.S. and European offices of a digital advertising company. The network data were analyzed in continuous time using Butts's (2008) relational event model. Each message is predicted by the history of message events before it and becomes a defining element in the social context for the next message event. The analysis describes decay in structural holes. Brokers connect across certain holes, those holes close, then the brokers move to new places in the network. The Quintane et al. results are consistent with a less sophisticated analysis of a broader population. In a study of network advantage for bankers observed in four annual panels, Burt & Burrows (2011) show that advantage is enhanced by a certain amount of volatility. Too much volatility can erode advantage, but too little erases advantage. Banker bonus compensation is strongly associated with network advantage for bankers who have some churn in their network contacts but not at all associated with network advantage for bankers whose network metrics are stable over time.

CONCLUSION

Social network analysis (SNA) continues to develop many themes enunciated by pioneering social psychologists. At its best, SNA draws from traditions of research and theory in psychology, sociology, and other areas to describe how patterns of interpersonal relations are associated with diverse behavioral, cognitive, and emotional outcomes. Looking to the future, we see deepening interest in the psychological underpinnings of why some people more than others engage and benefit from the network of contacts within which they are embedded.

DISCLOSURE STATEMENT

The authors are not aware of any affiliations, memberships, funding, or financial holdings that might be perceived as affecting the objectivity of this review.

ACKNOWLEDGMENTS

Professor Burt is grateful to the Booth School of Business for financial support during work on the manuscript, which benefitted from discussion at the 2012 meeting of the Strategy Research Initiative at Columbia University.

LITERATURE CITED

Anderson MH. 2008. Social networks and the cognitive motivation to realize network opportunities: a study of managers' information gathering behaviors. *J. Org. Behav.* 29:51–78

Aral S, Muchnik L, Sundararajan A. 2009. Distinguishing influence-based contagion from homophily-driven diffusion in dynamic networks. *Proc. Natl. Acad. Sci. USA* 106:21544–49

Aral S, Van Alstyne M. 2011. Networks, information and brokerage: the diversity-bandwidth tradeoff. *Am. J. Sociol.* 117:90–171

Asendorpf JB, Wilpers S. 1998. Personality effects on social relationships. *J. Personal. Soc. Psychol.* 74:1531–44

Balkundi P, Kilduff M. 2005. The ties that lead: a social network approach to leadership. *Leadersh. Q.* 16:941–61

Balkundi P, Kilduff M, Harrison DA. 2011. Centrality and charisma: comparing how leader networks and attributions affect team performance. *J. Appl. Psychol.* 96:1209–22

Bandura A. 2001. Social cognitive theory: an agentic perspective. *Annu. Rev. Psychol.* 52:1–26

Baum JAC, Rowley TJ, eds. 2008. *Advances in Strategic Management*, Vol. 25. Oxford, UK: JAI/Elsevier

Borgatti SP, Everett MG, Freeman LC. 2002. *UCINET for Windows*. Harvard, MA: Anal. Technol.

Borgatti SP, Mehra A, Brass DJ, Labianca G. 2009. Network analysis in the social sciences. *Science* 323:892–95

Bryson D. 2009. Personality and culture, the Social Science Research Council, and liberal social engineering: the Advisory Committee on Personality and Culture, 1930–1934. *J. Hist. Behav. Sci.* 45:355–86

Burger MJ, Buskens V. 2009. Social context and network formation: an experimental study. *Soc. Netw.* 31:63–75

Burt RS. 1992. *Structural Holes*. Cambridge, MA: Harvard Univ. Press

Burt RS. 1999. The social capital of opinion leaders. *Ann. Am. Acad. Polit. Soc. Sci.* 566:37–54

Burt RS. 2004. Structural holes and good ideas. *Am. J. Sociol.* 110:349–99

Burt RS. 2005. *Brokerage and Closure*. Oxford, UK: Oxford Univ. Press

Burt RS. 2010. *Neighbor Networks*. Oxford, UK: Oxford Univ. Press

Burt RS. 2012. Network-related personality and the agency question: multi-role evidence from a virtual world. *Am. J. of Sociol.* 117:In press

Burt RS, Burrows JG. 2011. *Network volatility and advantage*. Presented at Annu. Meet. Acad. Manag., San Antonio, TX

Burt RS, Hogarth RM, Michaud C. 2000. The social capital of French and American managers. *Organ. Sci.* 11:123–47

Burt RS, Merluzzi J. 2013. Embedded brokerage. *Res. Sociol. Org.* 36:In press

Burt RS, Ronchi D. 2007. Teaching executives to see social capital: results from a field experiment. *Soc. Sci. Res.* 36:1156–83

Buskens V, van de Rijt A. 2008. Dynamics of networks if everyone strives for structural holes. *Am. J. Sociol.* 114:371–407

Butts CT. 2008. A relational event framework for social action. *Sociol. Methodol.* 38:155–200

Cacioppo JT, Petty RE, Feinstein JA, Jarvis WBG. 1996. Dispositional differences in cognitive motivation: the life and times of individuals varying in need for cognition. *Psychol. Bull.* 119:197–253

Carrington PJ, Scott JS, Wasserman S. 2005. *Models and Methods in Social Network Analysis.* New York: Cambridge Univ. Press

Cartwright D, Harary F. 1956. Structural balance: a generalization of Heider's theory. *Psychol. Rev.* 63:277–92

Centola D, Macy M. 2007. Complex contagions and the weakness of long ties. *Am. J. Sociol.* 113:702–34

Christakis NA, Fowler JH. 2009. *Connected.* New York: Little, Brown

Christakis NA, Fowler JH. 2012. Social contagion theory: examining dynamic social networks and human behavior. *Stat. Med.* In press

Coleman JS. 1988. Social capital in the creation of human capital. *Am. J. Sociol.* 94:95–120

Cross R, Parker A. 2004. *The Hidden Power of Social Networks.* Cambridge, MA: Harvard Bus. Sch. Press

De Nooy W, Mrva A, Batagelj V. 2005. *Exploratory Social Network Analysis with Pajek.* New York: Cambridge Univ. Press

De Soto CB. 1960. Learning a social structure. *J. Abnorm. Soc. Psychol.* 60:417–21

Dodds PS, Muhamad R, Watts DJ. 2003. An experimental study of search in global social networks. *Science* 301:827–29

Dogan G, van Assen MALM, van de Rijt A, Buskens V. 2009. The stability of exchange networks. *Soc. Netw.* 31:118–25

Dorogovtsev SN, Mendes JF. 2003. *Evolution of Networks.* Oxford, UK: Oxford Univ. Press

Dunbar RI. 2008. Cognitive constraints on the structure and dynamics of social networks. *Group Dyn. Theor. Res. Pract.* 12:7–16

Eagle N, Macy M, Claxton R. 2010. Network diversity and economic development. *Science* 138:1029–31

Easley D, Kleinberg J. 2010. *Networks, Crowds, and Markets.* New York: Cambridge Univ. Press

Emirbayer M, Goodwin J. 1994. Network analysis, culture, and the problem of agency. *Am. J. Sociol.* 99:1411–54

Fernandez-Mateo I. 2007. Who pays the price of brokerage? Transferring constraint through price-setting in the staffing sector. *Am. Sociol. Rev.* 72:291–317

Festinger L, Schachter S, Back KW. 1950. *Social Pressures in Informal Groups.* Stanford, CA: Stanford Univ. Press

Freeman LC. 1977. A set of measures of centrality based on betweenness. *Sociometry* 40:35–40

Freeman LC. 1992. Filling in the blanks: a theory of cognitive categories and the structure of social affiliation. *Soc. Psychol. Q.* 55:118–27

Freeman LC. 2004. *The Development of Social Network Analysis.* Vancouver, BC: Empir. Press

Freeman LC, Romney AK, Freeman SC. 1987. Cognitive structure and informant accuracy. *Am. Anthropol.* 89:310–25

Gangestad SW, Snyder M. 2000. Self-monitoring: appraisal and reappraisal. *Psychol. Bull.* 126:530–55

Goyal S, Vega-Redondo F. 2007. Structural holes in social networks. *J. Econ. Theory* 137:460–92

Granovetter M. 1985. Economic action and social structure: the problem of embeddedness. *Am. J. Sociol.* 91:481–510

Greif A. 1989. Reputation and coalitions in medieval trade: evidence on the Maghribi traders. *J. Econ. Hist.* 49:857–82

Guinote A. 2007. Behaviour variability and the situated focus theory of power. *Eur. Rev. Soc. Psychol.* 18:256–295

Hanneman RA, Riddle M. 2005. *Introduction to Social Network Methods.* Riverside: Univ. Calif. **http://faculty.ucr.edu/~hanneman/nettext**

Hansemark OC. 2003. Need for achievement, locus of control and the prediction of business start-ups: a longitudinal study. *J. Econ. Psychol.* 24:301–19

Hansen D, Shneiderman B, Smith MA. 2011. *Analyzing Social Media Networks with NodeXL*. Burlington, MA: Morgan Kaufmann

Heider F. 1958. *The Psychology of Interpersonal Relations*. New York: Wiley

Hodgkinson GP. 1992. Research notes and communications development and validation of the strategic locus of control scale. *Strat. Manag. J.* 13:311–17

Ingram P, Morris MW. 2007. Do people mix at mixers? Structure, homophily, and the "life of the party." *Admin. Sci. Quart.* 52:558–85

Jackson MO. 2008. *Social and Economic Networks*. Princeton, NJ: Princeton Univ. Press

Jang KL, Livesley WJ, Vernon PA. 1996. Heritability of the big five personality dimensions and their facets: a twin study. *J. Personal.* 64:577–91

Janicik GA, Larrick RP. 2005. Social network schemas and the learning of incomplete networks. *J. Personal. Soc. Psychol.* 88:348–64

Kadushin C. 2012. *Understanding Social Networks*. New York: Oxford Univ. Press

Katz E, Lazarsfeld PF. 1955. *Personal Influence*. New York: Free Press

Kellogg K. 2012. *Keeping it real: inter-occupational guardians and institutional change in two community health centers*. Work. pap., MIT Sloan, Cambridge, MA

Kilduff M, Brass DJ. 2010. Organizational social network research: core ideas and key debates. *Acad. Manag. Ann.* 4:317–57

Kilduff M, Crossland C, Tsai W, Krackhardt D. 2008. Network perceptions versus reality: a small world after all? *Organ. Behav. Hum. Decis. Process.* 107:15–28

Kilduff M, Day D. 1994. Do chameleons get ahead? The effects of self-monitoring on managerial careers. *Acad. Manag. J.* 37:1047–60

Kilduff M, Krackhardt D. 1994. Bringing the individual back in: a structural analysis of the internal market for reputation in organizations. *Acad. Manag. J.* 37:87–108

Kilduff M, Tsai W. 2003. *Social Networks and Organizations*. London: Sage

Kilduff M, Tsai W, Hanke R. 2006. A paradigm too far? A dynamic stability reconsideration of the social network research program. *Acad. Manag. Rev.* 31:1031–48

Kleinberg J, Suri S, Tardos É, Wexler T. 2008. Strategic network formation with structural holes. *Proc. 9th ACM Conf. Electron, Commer.*, Chicago, IL

Krackhardt D. 1987. Cognitive social structures. *Soc. Netw.* 9:109–34

Krackhardt D, Kilduff M. 1999. Whether close or far: social distance effects on perceived balance in friendship networks. *J. Personal. Soc. Psychol.* 76:770–82

Kumbasar EA, Romney K, Batchelder WH. 1994. Systematic biases in social perception. *Am. J. Sociol.* 100:477–505

Lakatos I. 1970. Falsification and the methodology of scientific research programs. In *Criticism and the Growth of Knowledge*, ed. I Lakatos, A Musgrave, pp. 91–132. New York: Cambridge Univ. Press

Laumann EO, Pappi FU. 1976. New directions in the study of community elites. *Am. Sociol. Rev.* 38:212–30

Leonardi P, Bailey D. 2011. *Sharing the work of brokerage: network articulation for idea generation and implementation*. Presented at Chicago-Northwest. Conf. Innov., Organ., Soc., Chicago, IL

Lin N. 2002. *Social Capital*. New York: Cambridge Univ. Press

Lingo EL, O'Mahony S. 2010. Nexus work: brokerage on creative projects. *Admin. Sci. Quart.* 55:47–81

Marsden PV. 2011. Survey methods for network data. In *The Sage Handbook of Social Network Analysis*, ed. JS Scott, PJ Carrington, pp. 370–86. Thousand Oaks, CA: Sage

Mayhew B. 1980. Structuralism versus individualism: part I. Shadowboxing in the dark. *Soc. Forces* 59:335–75

McClelland DC. 1961. *The Achieving Society*. Princeton, NJ: Van Nostrand

McPherson JM, Smith-Lovin L, Brashears M. 2006. Social isolation in America. *Am. Sociol. Rev.* 71:363–75

Mehra A, Kilduff M, Brass DJ. 2001. The social networks of high and low self-monitors: implications for workplace performance. *Admin. Sci. Quart.* 46:121–46

Merluzzi J. 2011. *Social capital in Asia: investigating returns to brokerage in collectivistic national cultures*. Work. pap., Freeman Sch. Bus., Tulane Univ., New Orleans, LA

Mischel W, Shoda Y. 1995. A cognitive-affective system theory of personality: reconceptualizing situations, dispositions, dynamics, and invariance in personality structure. *Psychol. Rev.* 102:246–68

Moody J, McFarland D, Bender-deMoll S. 2005. Dynamic network visualization. *Am. J. Sociol.* 110:1206–41

Moreno JL. 1934. *Who Shall Survive? A New Approach to the Problem of Human Interrelations. Nerv. Ment. Disease Monogr. Ser.*, No. 58, pp. 2–20. Washington, DC: Nerv. Ment. Disease

Newcomb TM. 1961. *The Acquaintance Process*. New York: Holt, Rinehart & Winston

Newman M. 2010. *Networks*. New York: Oxford Univ. Press

Obstfeld D. 2005. Social networks, the *tertius iungens* orientation, and involvement in innovation. *Admin. Sci. Quart.* 50:100–30

Oh H, Kilduff M. 2008. The ripple effect of personality on social structure: self-monitoring origins of network brokerage. *J. Appl. Psychol.* 93:1155–64

Podolny JM. 2001. Networks as the pipes and prisms of the market. *Am. J. Sociol.* 107:33–60

Podolny JM. 2005. *Status Signals*. Princeton, NJ: Princeton Univ. Press

Portes A. 1998. Social capital: its origins and applications in modern sociology. *Annu. Rev. Sociol.* 24:1–24

Powell WW, Packalen K, Whittington K. 2012. Organizational and institutional genesis: the emergence of high-tech clusters in the life sciences. In *The Emergence of Markets and Organizations*, ed. JF Padgett, WW Powell, pp. 434–65. Princeton, NJ: Princeton Univ. Press

Prell C. 2012. *Social Network Analysis*. Thousand Oaks, CA: Sage

Putnam R. 2000. *Bowling Alone*. New York: Simon & Schuster

Quintane E, Carnabuci G, Robins GL, Pattison PE. 2012. *How do brokers broker? An investigation of the temporality of structural holes*. Presented at Annu. Sunbelt Soc. Netw. Conf., Los Angeles, CA

Rainie L, Purcell K, Smith A. 2011. *The Social Side of the Internet*. Washington, DC: Pew Res. Cent.

Rainie L, Wellman B. 2012. *Networked*. Cambridge, MA: MIT Press

Reagans RE, McEvily B. 2003. Network structure and knowledge transfer: the effects of cohesion and range. *Admin. Sci. Quart.* 48:240–67

Reagans RE, Zuckerman EW. 2008. Why knowledge does not equal power: the network redundancy trade-off. *Ind. Corp. Change* 17:903–44

Rivera MT, Soderstrom SB, Uzzi B. 2010. Dynamics of dyads in social networks: assortative, relational, and proximity mechanisms. *Annu. Rev. Sociol.* 36:91–115

Roberts SG, Dunbar RI. 2011. Communication in social networks: effects of kinship, network size, and emotional closeness. *Personal. Relat.* 18:439–52

Rotter JB. 1966. Generalized expectancies for internal versus external control of reinforcement. *Psychol. Monogr.* 80:1–28

Ryall MD, Sorenson O. 2007. Brokers and competitive advantage. *Manag. Sci.* 53:566–83

Sasovova Z, Mehra A, Borgatti S, Schippers MC. 2010. Network churn: the effects of self-monitoring personality on brokerage dynamics. *Admin. Sci. Quart.* 55:639–70

Schneider B, Smith DB, Taylor S, Fleenor J. 1998. Personality and organizations: a test of the homogeneity of personality hypothesis. *J. Appl. Psychol.* 83:462–70

Scott JP. 2000. *Social Network Analysis*. Thousand Oaks, CA: Sage

Scott JP, Carrington PJ. 2011. *The SAGE Handbook of Social Network Analysis*. Thousand Oaks, CA: Sage

Sewell WH Jr. 1992. A theory of structure: duality, agency, and transformation. *Am. J. Sociol.* 98:1–29

Simpson B, Markovsky B, Steketee M. 2011a. Power and the perception of social networks. *Soc. Netw.* 33:166–71

Simpson B, Markovsky B, Steketee M. 2011b. Network knowledge and the use of power. *Soc. Netw.* 33:172–76

Singh J, Hansen MT, Podolny JM. 2010. The world is not small for everyone: inequality in searching for knowledge in organizations. *Manag. Sci.* 56:1415–38

Smith EB, Menon T, Thompson L. 2012. Status differences in the cognitive activation of social networks. *Organ. Sci.* 23:67–82

Smith-Doerr L, Powell WW. 2005. Networks and economic life. In *The Handbook Of Economic Sociology*, ed. N Smelser, R Swedberg, pp. 379–402. Princeton, NJ: Princeton Univ. Press

Snijders TAB. 2011. Statistical models for social networks. *Annu. Rev. Sociol.* 37:131–53

Snyder M, Deaux K. 2012. Personality and social psychology. In *The Oxford Handbook of Personality and Social Psychology*, ed. K Deaux, M Snyder, pp. 3–9. Oxford, UK: Oxford Univ. Press

Snyder M, Gangestad S. 1986. On the nature of self-monitoring: matters of assessment, matters of validity. *J. Personal. Soc. Psychol.* 51:125–39

Sosa ME. 2011. Where do creative interactions come from? The role of tie content and social networks. *Organ. Sci.* 22:1–21

Stovel K, Golub B, Milgrom EM. 2011. Stabilizing brokerage. *Proc. Natl. Acad. Sci. USA* 108(Suppl. 4):21326–32

Stovel K, Shaw L. 2012. Brokerage. *Annu. Rev. Sociol.* 38:139–58

Tortoriello M, Krackhardt D. 2010. Activating cross-boundary knowledge: the role of Simmelian ties in the generation of innovation. *Acad. Manag. J.* 53:167–81

Travers J, Milgram S. 1969. An experimental study of the small-world problem. *Sociometry* 32:425–43

Uzzi B. 1996. The sources and consequences of embeddedness for the economic performance of organizations: the network effect. *Am. Sociol. Rev.* 61:674–98

Von Hippel E. 1994. "Sticky information" and the locus of problem solving: implications for innovation. *Manag. Sci.* 40:429–39

Wasserman S, Faust K. 1994. *Social Network Analysis*. New York: Cambridge Univ. Press

Watts DJ. 1999. Networks, dynamics, and the small world phenomenon. *Am. J. Sociol.* 105:493–527

Wellman B. 1993. An egocentric network tale: comment on Bien et al. 1991. *Soc. Netw.* 15:423–36

Winter DG, Stewart OP, Klohnen ED, Duncan LE. 1998. Traits and motives: toward an integration of two traditions in personality research. *Psychol. Rev.* 105:230–50

Wood R, Bandura A. 1989. Social cognitive theory of organizational management. *Acad. Manag. Rev.* 14:361–84

Xiao Z, Tsui AS. 2007. When brokers may not work: the cultural contingency of social capital in Chinese high-tech firms. *Admin. Sci. Quart.* 52:1–31

Zaheer A, Soda G. 2009. Network evolution: the origins of structural holes. *Admin. Sci. Quart.* 54:1–31

RELATED RESOURCE

http://www.insna.org

Cumulative Indexes

Contributing Authors, Volumes 54–64

Correa-Chávez M, 54:175–203
Cosmides L, 64:201–29
Crano WD, 57:345–74
Crosby FJ, 57:585–611
Cudeck R, 58:615–37
Curran PJ, 62:583–619
Curry SJ, 60:229–55

D

Davis A, 54:579–616
Deary IJ, 63:453–82
Delicato LS, 55:181–205
Derrington AM, 55:181–205
de Waal FBM, 59:279–300
Diamond A, 64:135–68
Dickel N, 62:391–417
Diefendorff JM, 61:543–68
Diehl RL, 55:149–79
Diener E, 54:403–25
Dijksterhuis A, 61:467–90
Dishion TJ, 62:189–214
DiZio P, 56:115–47
Doctoroff GL, 54:517–45
Domjan M, 56:179–206
Donnellan MB, 58:175–99
Doss AJ, 56:337–63
Dovidio JF, 56:365–92
Dudai Y, 55:51–86
Dunkel Schetter C, 62:531–58
Dunlosky J, 64:417–44
Dunn EW, 55:493–518
Dupré KE, 60:671–92

E

Eby LT, 61:599–622
Echterhoff G, 63:55–79
Ehrhart MG, 64:361–88
Einarsson E, 61:141–67
Emery NJ, 60:87–113
Emmons RA, 54:377–402
Erez M, 58:479–514
Evans GW, 57:423–51
Evans JSBT, 59:255–78

F

Faigman DL, 56:631–59
Fairchild AJ, 58:593–614

Fanselow MS, 56:207–34
Farah MJ, 63:571–91
Fazio RH, 54:297–327
Federico CM, 60:307–37
Federmeier KD, 62:621–47
Fernández-Dols J-M, 54:329–49
Fingerhut AW, 58:405–24
Finniss DG, 59:565–90
Fivush R, 62:559–82
Folkman S, 55:745–74
Fouad NA, 58:543–64
Fox NA, 56:235–62
French DC, 59:591–616
Fried I, 63:511–37
Friston KJ, 56:57–87
Frith CD, 63:287–313
Frith U, 63:287–313
Fritz MS, 58:593–614
Fuligni A, 54:461–90
Furman W, 60:631–52

G

Gaissmaier W, 62:451–82
Gallistel CR, 64:169–200
Gallo LC, 62:501–30
Gazzaniga MS, 64:1–20
Geisler WS, 59:167–92
Gelfand MJ, 58:479–514
Gelman SA, 60:115–40
Gerhart B, 56:571–600
Gernsbacher MA, 54:91–114
Gervain J, 61:191–218
Ghera MA, 56:235–62
Gigerenzer G, 62:451–82
Glimcher PW, 56:25–56
Glück J, 62:215–41
Goethals GR, 56:545–70
Goldin-Meadow S, 64:257–83
Goldstein NJ, 55:591–621
Golomb JD, 62:73–101
Gonzalez CM, 59:329–60
Goodman GS, 61:325–51
Gorman-Smith D, 57:557–83
Gottesman II, 56:263–86
Gould E, 61:111–40
Graber D, 55:545–71
Graham JW, 60:549–76
Green DP, 60:339–67
Greenfield PM, 54:461–90
Gross JJ, 58:373–403
Grusec JE, 62:243–69

Gunia BC, 61:491–515
Gunnar M, 58:145–73

H

Hall RJ, 61:543–68
Hampson SE, 63:315–39
Han S, 64:335–59
Hanson DR, 56:263–86
Hardt O, 61:141–67
Harring JR, 58:615–37
Hauser M, 61:303–24
Hawkins EH, 60:197–227
Hawley KM, 56:337–63
Healey MP, 59:387–417
Heatherton TF, 62:363–90
Heil SH, 55:431–61
Heine SJ, 60:369–94
Hen R, 57:117–37
Henderson HA, 56:235–62
Hennessey BA, 61:569–98
Henry D, 57:557–83
Herek GM, 64:309–33
Higgins ET, 59:361–85
Higgins ST, 55:431–61
Hirst W, 63:55–79
Hochman KM, 55:401–30
Hodgkinson GP, 59:387–417
Hollenbeck JR, 56:517–43
Hollins M, 61:243–71
Hollon SD, 57:285–315
Holsboer F, 61:81–109
Holt LL, 55:149–79
Holyoak KJ, 62:135–63
Huston AC, 61:411–37
Hwang E, 61:169–90

I

Iacoboni M, 60:653–70
Ilgen DR, 56:517–43
Ising M, 61:81–109
Iyer A, 57:585–611
Izard CE, 60:1–25

J

Johnson EJ, 60:53–85
Johnson M, 56:517–43
Joiner TE Jr, 56:287–314
Jonides J, 59:193–224

Paluck EL 60:339–67
Paradise R, 54:175–203
Park DC, 60:173–96
Parke RD, 55:365–99
Parker LA, 64:21–47
Parks L, 56:571–600
Peissig JJ, 58:75–96
Penn DC, 58:97–118
Pennebaker JW, 54:547–77
Penner LA, 56:365–92
Pennington BF, 60:283–306
Peplau LA, 58:405–24
Peretz I, 56:89–114
Phelps EA, 57:27–53
Phillips DA, 62:483–500
Phillips LA, 59:477–505
Piliavin JA, 56:365–92
Pinder CC, 56:485–516
Pittman TS, 59:361–85
Plomin R, 54:205–28
Podsakoff NP, 63:539–69
Podsakoff PM, 63:539–69
Posner MI, 58:1–23
Poulos AM, 56:207–34
Povinelli DJ, 58:97–118
Pratte MS, 63:483–509
Price DD, 59:565–90
Prislin R, 57:345–74
Proctor RW, 61:623–51

Q

Quas JA, 61:325–51
Quevedo K, 58:145–73
Quirk GJ, 63:129–51

R

Rafaeli E, 54:579–616
Rausch JR, 59:537–63
Rauschecker AM, 63:31–53
Recanzone GH, 59:119–42
Reuter-Lorenz P, 60:173–96
Revenson TA, 58:565–92
Rhodes G, 57:199–226
Rick S, 59:647–72
Rilling JK, 62:23–48
Rissman J, 63:101–28
Robbins P, 63:81–99
Roberts BW, 56:453–84
Roberts RD, 59:507–36

Robinson TE, 54:25–53
Roediger HL III, 59:225–54
Rogoff B, 54:175–203
Rothbart MK, 58:1–23
Rubin KH, 60:141–71
Ruble DN, 61:353–81
Runco MA, 55:657–87
Rusbult CE, 54:351–75
Russell JA, 54:329–49
Rynes SL, 56:571–600

S

Sackett PR, 59:419–50
Salmon DP, 60:257–82
Salthouse T, 63:201–26
Sammartino J, 64:77–107
Samuel AG, 62:49–72
Sanchez JI, 63:397–425
Sandler IN, 62:299–329
Sanfey AG, 62:23–48
Sargis EG, 57:529–55
Saribay SA, 59:329–60
Sarkissian H, 63:81–99
Saxe R, 55:87–124
Schall JD, 55:23–50
Schaller M, 55:689–714
Schippers MC, 58:515–41
Schloss KB, 64:77–107
Schmidt AC, 61:543–68
Schneider B, 64:361–88
Schoenfelder EN, 62:299–329
Schroeder DA, 56:365–92
Schultz W, 57:87–115
Serbin LA, 55:333–63
Seyfarth RM, 54:145–73;
    63:153–77
Shadish WR, 60:607–29
Shanks DR, 61:273–301
Shaywitz BA, 59:451–75
Shaywitz SE, 59:451–75
Sherry DF, 57:167–97
Shevell SK, 59:143–66
Shiffrar M, 58:47–73
Shiner RL, 56:453–84
Shinn M, 54:427–59
Shors TJ, 57:55–85
Siegel JM, 55:125–48
Simonton DK, 54:617–40
Sincharoen S, 57:585–611
Skinner EA, 58:119–44
Skitka LJ, 57:529–55

Smetana JG, 57:255–84
Snyder DK, 57:317–44
Sobel N, 61:219–41
Sommers T, 63:81–99
Sporer AK, 60:229–55
Staddon JER, 54:115–44
Stanton AL, 58:565–92
Staudinger UM, 62:215–41
Stewart AJ, 55:519–44
Stewart MO, 57:285–315
Stickgold R, 57:139–66
Stone AA, 64:471–98
Strunk D, 57:285–315
Stuewig J, 58:345–72
Sue S, 60:525–48
Sutter ML, 59:119–42

T

Tangney JP, 58:345–72
Tarr MJ, 58:75–96
Tasselli S, 64:527–47
Tennen H, 58:565–92
Thau S, 60:717–41
Thompson LL, 61:491–515
Thompson RF, 56:1–23
Tindale RS, 55:623–55
Tipsord JM, 62:189–214
Tolan P, 57:557–83
Tomasello M, 64:231–55
Tong F, 63:483–509
Tooby J, 64:201–29
Toohey SM, 54:427–59
Tourangeau R, 55:775–801
Trickett EJ, 60:395–419
Turk-Browne NB, 62:73–101
Tyler TR, 57:375–400

U

Uleman JS, 59:329–60
Uskul AK, 62:419–49

V

Vaish A, 64:231–55
van Knippenberg D, 58:515–41
Van Lange PAM, 54:351–75
Varnum MEW, 64:335–59

Chapter Titles, Volumes 54–64

Marketing and Consumer Behavior

Organizational Psychology or Organizational Behavior

Cognition in Organizations

Groups and Teams

Leadership

Organizational Climate/Culture

Work Attitudes (Job Satisfaction, Commitment, Identification)

Work Motivation

Psycholinguistics

See COGNITIVE PROCESSES

Psychology and Culture

Psychopathology (See also CLINICAL AND COUNSELING PSYCHOLOGY)